Criminal Procedure in Scotland:
Cases & Materials

Criminal Procedure in Scotland: Cases & Materials

C.H.W. GANE,
LL.B.
Professor of Law,
University of Aberdeen

&

C.N. STODDART,
LL.B., LL.M.(McGill), Ph.D., S.S.C.
Sheriff of North Strathclyde
at Paisley

SECOND EDITION

W. GREEN/Sweet & Maxwell
EDINBURGH
1994

First published 1983
Second Edition 1994

ISBN 0 41401028 0

A catalogue record for this book is
available from the British Library

The moral rights of the authors have been asserted

Printed in Great Britain by
Butler & Tanner Ltd.,
Frome and London

PREFACE

Anyone who has practised criminal law in Scotland since the first edition of this book was published in 1983 knows that the intervening period has been one of great activity in the criminal courts. When we first approached the task of preparing a casebook, the most important recent event had been the enactment of the Criminal Justice (Scotland) Act 1980 following many of the reforms suggested by the Thomson Committee on Criminal Procedure. Like many commentators, we were curious to see how the new rules would be operated in practice; in the first edition we were fortunate enough to be able to include, along with some of the statutory material, the first few cases which by then had been decided on aspects of the new provisions. Now, 11 years later, we have carried out a comprehensive revisal of our earlier work in view of all the developments during that time.

The chapter titles in this edition, with one exception, correspond to those previously used. But the contents of those chapters in many cases bear little relation to the material we formerly utilised. A large number of cases have been excised and replaced by more modern decisions, particularly in the earlier chapters on procedure prior to the initiation of proceedings. Later chapters have not escaped the pruning exercise; but throughout the work the recurring problem has been what to leave out. Any casebook is, to a great extent, a matter of personal preference, but we have tried to make our selection with the current needs of the practitioner at the forefront of our minds.

It was to this end that we decided, regretfully, that we ought not to include a revised chapter on sentencing. Quite apart from the fact that a large number of sentencing cases have been decided and reported and reported since the appearance of our first edition, we felt that the publication in 1992 of the second edition of Nicholson, *Sentencing: Law and Practice in Scotland* had rendered superfluous any efforts we might make in this field, especially since that work is updated six times annually by its author in his regular column in *Greens Criminal Law Bulletin* wherein he notes current sentencing trends and cases of interest.

We have followed our usual practice of including what we consider are the leading cases in the various fields of procedure, with a commentary of a length appropriate to the points raised, with references to related cases and other materials. We are grateful to all those who have written or spoken to us over the years with helpful suggestions as to what might be covered in a future edition. We would also like to thank our respective wives for the forebearance each has shown as again we put pen to paper; and special thanks are due to Ms Lynn O'Meara of the Centre for Legal Studies at Sussex University for her assistance in connection with the preparation of the manuscript. As before, we accept art and part responsibility for the contents of this work, including its errors and omissions.

We have included cases reported up to December 31, 1993.

Glasgow, May 1994   C.H.W. GANE
C.N. STODDART

CONTENTS

TABLE OF CASES

TABLE OF EC CASES

TABLE OF STATUTES

TABLE OF STATUTORY INSTRUMENTS

INTERNATIONAL TREATIES AND CONVENTIONS

REPORTS OF COMMITTEES, ETC.

CHAPTER 1

GENERAL AIMS AND PRINCIPLES OF SCOTTISH CRIMINAL PROCEDURE

It has not been the practice of the standard works on criminal procedure to articulate or examine the general aims or guiding principles of Scottish criminal procedure. A similar reluctance to state explicitly any general philosophy seems to have been shared by the Thomson Committee (though one member of that Committee has since attempted to summarise the Committee's general aims: Gordon, *The Criminal Justice (Scotland) Act 1980*, p.xiii). This seems rather surprising. In the first place, criminal procedure has received considerably more attention from Parliament and the courts than has the substantive criminal law of Scotland, and one might have expected their activities to have provoked some general analysis of their efforts. Secondly, there now exists a substantial body of international and conventional guidelines for standards in criminal procedure, inviting comparison (critical or otherwise) with the present state of Scottish criminal procedure.

This chapter attempts to identify and illustrate some of these basic principles. However, certain issues which might be considered fundamental are not dealt with here, since they may be more aptly dealt with in the context of specific topics in later chapters. But it would perhaps be valuable to bear in mind these issues when considering the remainder of the topics in this book.

A. MINIMUM STANDARDS FOR CRIMINAL PROCEDURES

The system of criminal procedure should at least meet internationally agreed minimum standards for all stages of the criminal process. Such standards are to be found in a bewildering range of conventions, agreements and resolutions, but the most significant in practical terms (since departures from them may be made the subject of individual complaint to the European Commission on Human Rights) are the principles set out in the European Convention on Human Rights:

The European Convention on Human Rights

"Article 3
No one shall be subjected to torture or to inhuman or degrading treatment or punishment ...

Article 5
1.   Everyone has the right to liberty and security of person. No one shall be deprived of his liberty save in the following cases and in accordance with a procedure prescribed by law:
   (*a*) the lawful detention of a person after conviction by a competent court;
   (*b*) the lawful arrest or detention of a person for non-compliance with the lawful order of a court or in order to secure the fulfilment of any obligation prescribed by law;

1

(*c*) the lawful arrest or detention of a person effected for the purpose of bringing him before the competent legal authority on reasonable suspicion of having committed an offence or when it is reasonably considered necessary to prevent his committing an offence or fleeing after having done so;

(*d*) the detention of a minor by lawful order for the purpose of educational supervision or his lawful detention for the purpose of bringing him before the competent legal authority;

(*e*) the lawful detention of persons for the prevention of the spreading of infectious diseases, of persons of unsound mind, alcoholics or drug addicts or vagrants;

(*f*) the lawful arrest or detention of a person to prevent his effecting an unauthorised entry into the country or of a person against whom action is being taken with a view to deportation or extradition.

2.   Everyone who is arrested shall be informed promptly, in a language which he understands, of the reasons for his arrest and of any charge against him.

3.   Everyone arrested or detained in accordance with the provisions of paragraph 1(*c*) of this Article shall be brought promptly before a judge or other officer authorised by law to exercise judicial power and shall be entitled to trial within a reasonable time or to release pending trial. Release may be conditioned by guarantees to appear for trial.

4.   Everyone who is deprived of his liberty by arrest or detention shall be entitled to take proceedings by which the lawfulness of his detention shall be decided speedily by a court and his release ordered if the detention is not lawful.

5.   Everyone who has been the victim of arrest or detention in contravention of the provisions of this Article shall have an enforceable right to compensation.

Article 6

1.   In the determination of his civil rights and obligations or of any criminal charge against him, everyone is entitled to a fair and public hearing within a reasonable time by an independent and impartial tribunal established by law. Judgment shall be pronounced publicly but the press and public may be excluded from all or part of the trial in the interests of morals, public order or national security in a democratic society, where the interests of juveniles or the protection of the private life of the parties so require, or to the extent strictly necessary in the opinion of the court in special circumstances where publicity would prejudice the interests of justice.

2.   Everyone charged with a criminal offence shall be presumed innocent until proved guilty according to law.

3.   Everyone charged with a criminal offence has the following minimum rights:

(*a*) to be informed promptly, in a language which he understands and in detail, of the nature and cause of the accusation against him;

(*b*) to have adequate time and facilities for the preparation of his defence;

(*c*) to defend himself in person or through legal assistance of his own choosing or, if he has not sufficient means to pay for legal assistance, to be given it free when the interests of justice so require;

(*d*) to examine or have examined witnesses against him and to obtain the attendance and examination of witnesses on his behalf under the same conditions as witnesses against him;

(*e*) to have the free assistance of an interpreter if he cannot understand or speak the language used in court."

NOTES

1. The Convention does not form part of Scots law, nor can it be relied upon as an aid to the construction of a statute of the United Kingdom Parliament: *Surjit Kaur v. Lord Advocate*, 1981 S.L.T. 322; *Moore v. Secretary of State for Scotland*, 1985 S.L.T. 38. Indeed, it was suggested in *Montes and Others v. H.M. Advocate*, 1990 S.C.C.R. 645, *infra*, p.191, that it was not even *competent* for the court to consider, within the context of a criminal appeal, decisions of the European Court of Human Rights on the interpretation of the Convention. This seems to be an unnecessarily extreme view. Indeed, in those areas where United Kingdom law has given effect to a Convention obligation (for example, in the case of the Interception of Communications Act 1985, giving effect to the obligation to respect privacy under Article 8 in the context of telephone tapping and related practices: *Malone v. United Kingdom*, Series A No. 82, or the Contempt of Court Act 1981, giving effect to freedom of expression under article 10 in the context of media reports which run the risk of prejudicing a fair trial: *Sunday Times and Others v. UK* [1979] Yearbook of E.C.H.R. 402) it would seem to be quite wrong to ignore the Convention where there is some ambiguity in the domestic law. The courts in England are in no doubt about the status of the Convention. While it does not form part of English domestic law it may be relied upon as a guide to the interpretation of all statutes and, indeed, the common law, in cases of ambiguity. This seems to be an entirely reasonable approach, which combines respect for the legislative supremacy of Parliament while at the same time attempting, so far as possible, to ensure that English domestic law complies with our international obligations.

2. Although the Convention is foreign to our courts, the right of individual application under Article 25 of the Convention is recognised by the United Kingdom, and a failure to observe these minimum standards secured by the Convention can be made the subject of such an application. The procedures governing such applications are briefly outlined in Chap. 18, *infra*.

3. Similar rights are guaranteed by other international conventions. See, in particular, Part III of the International Covenant on Civil and Political Rights, adopted by the General Assembly of the United Nations in 1966, and its associated Protocols. The United Kingdom is a party to this Convention, although it has not adopted the First Optional Protocol which confers the right of individual application to the United Nations Human Rights Committee. Regard should also be had to the standards set by the United Nations, the Council of Europe and other international bodies for penal and criminal procedures in the following: *Convention against Torture and other Cruel, Inhuman or Degrading Treatment or Punishment* (UN, 1984, in force from 1987); *European Convention for the Prevention of Torture and Inhuman or Degrading Treatment or Punishment* (1987, in force from 1989); *Standard Minimum Rules for the Treatment of Prisoners* (UN); *European Prison Rules* (Recommendation No. (87)3 of the Committee of Ministers of the Council of Europe); *United Nations Standard Minimum Rules for the Administration of Juvenile Justice ("The Beijing Rules")*.

4. There is, of course, an extensive body of case law on the application of the European Convention on Human Rights which it is not possible to reproduce within the limits of this book. However, the following may be consulted as an indication of the views of the European Court of Human Rights in relation to the Articles set out above: The Council of Europe,

Stock-taking on the European Convention on Human Rights (periodic reports from 1954 onwards); Council of Europe, *Digest of Strasbourg case-law relating to the European Convention on Human Rights* (especially Vols. 1 and 2 and updates thereto); Council of Europe, *The Right to Liberty and the Rights of Persons Deprived of their Liberty as Guaranteed by Article 5 of the European Convention on Human Rights* (Human Rights Files, No. 4).

5.   It should also be recalled that other Articles in the Convention may be relevant to criminal procedure, even though they are not expressly so directed. So, for example, the right to respect for privacy set out in Article 8 has been invoked in relation to such diverse matters as police investigations by means of telephone tapping (*Malone* v. *United Kingdom*, Series A No. 82) and the right of a prisoner to unimpeded correspondence with his lawyer (*Golder* v. *United Kingdom*, Series A No. 18; *Campbell* v. *United Kingdom*, Series A No. 233).

B.   THE PRINCIPLE OF FAIRNESS

It has been said that the "central theme of Scots criminal procedure is the need for fairness" (Gordon, *The Criminal Justice (Scotland) Act 1980*, p.xii). But what does "fairness" mean in this context?

1.   Miln v. Cullen
1967 J.C. 21

An accused person challenged the admissibility in evidence of a reply which he was alleged to have made in response to a question put to him by a police officer after a road accident. The trial judge upheld his objection and he was acquitted. The prosecutor appealed:

> LORD WHEATLEY: "... The legal principles in this field of evidence were exhaustively canvassed in *Chalmers* v. *H. M. Advocate*, and it would appear from the arguments addressed to us by counsel for the respondent and other expressions of opinion voiced elsewhere that certain misconceptions have arisen from the decision and opinions in that case. If that be so, then the sooner these misconceptions are cleared, the better it is for all concerned. For instance, counsel for the respondent submitted that once a person came under suspicion, no questions by a police officer and *a fortiori* no answers by the suspect were admissible in evidence. In *Chalmers* the Lord Justice-General, supported by a Full Bench, reviewed the legal position at three different and progressive stages, namely, (1) where routine investigations are being carried out and the person ultimately accused has not fallen under suspicion, (2) where that person has fallen under suspicion but has not been cautioned and charged, and (3) where that person has been cautioned and charged. I need not rehearse all that was said by Lord Cooper in that context, but I deem it important to stress that in the variety of circumstances which might attend cases in each of these categories the basic and ultimate test is fairness. While the law of Scotland has always very properly regarded fairness to an accused person as being an integral part of the administration of justice, fairness is not a unilateral consideration. Fairness to the public is also a legitimate consideration, and in so far as police officers in the exercise of their duties are prosecuting and protecting the public interest, it is the function of the Court to seek to provide a proper balance to secure that the rights of individuals are properly preserved, while not hamstringing the police in their

investigations of crime with a series of academic vetoes which ignore the
realities and practicalities of the situation and discount completely the public
interest."

Appeal allowed.

NOTES

1. Lord Wheatley's remarks were made in the context of the
admissibility of statements made to the police. This has been the area in
which the "principle" has been most frequently invoked (see the cases on
police questioning discussed *infra*, Chap. 5), but it is not the only area in
which it has been referred to. See, for example, *Wilson* v. *Milne*, 1975 S.L.T.
(Notes) 26 (application for a warrant to take blood samples from a suspect);
Stirling v. *Herron*, 1976 S.L.T. (Notes) 2 (same judge sitting in consecutive
trials arising out of same offence).

2. If for "fairness" one reads "balance" then Scots law falls into line
with those systems which postulate a "fundamental balance" between the
interests of the accused and the interests of the community at large. This
notion of "balance" was considered in England by the Royal Commission
on Criminal Procedure (1979):

2.   Royal Commission on Criminal Procedure

"The concept of a fundamental balance

1.11. The terms of reference require us to examine the pre-trial criminal
process and in so doing have regard 'to the interests of the community in
bringing offenders to justice and to the rights and liberties of persons
suspected or accused of crime'. And in his statement in the House of Commons
the then Prime Minister expressed the view that there was 'a balance to be
struck here between the interest of the whole community and the rights and
liberties of the individual citizen ... The Government', he said, 'consider that
the time has come for the whole criminal process, from investigation to trial, to
be reviewed with the fundamental balance in mind'. This is the central
challenge which the Royal Commission faces.

1.12. At first sight the notion of a fundamental balance of the kind specified
may appear unarguable, almost axiomatic, a matter of common sense; but
further consideration of the matter raises a number of difficult, and perhaps, in
the last analysis, insoluble questions. Can there be in any strict sense an
equation drawn between the individual on one side and society on the other?
Is the balance some sort of social contract between the individual and society?
What are the rights and liberties of the individual which are assumed to
provide part of the balance? Who gives them and what justifies them? Are they
all of equal weight; all equally and totally negotiable or are some natural,
absolute, fundamental, above the law, part of the human being's birthright?
On the other side of this assumed balance, especially in an increasingly
heterogeneous and specialised society, how is the interest of the whole
community to be defined with any useful precision? And where does one see,
where do the police see, the role of the police being applied; in one or other of
the scales, or at the fulcrum, or both? What is clear is that in speaking of a
balance between the interests of the community and the rights of the
individual issues are being formulated which should be the concern not only
of lawyers or police officers but of every citizen."

C.   "EQUALITY OF ARMS"

In a sense, this might be regarded as an aspect of the principle of "fairness" as it is currently applied in the Scottish courts or, at least, as an aspect of the balance between prosecution and defence. "Equality of arms" suggests that neither party should have an advantage over the other in the preparation and presentation of their case. This is particularly important in an adversarial system such as operates in Scotland, where each side is responsible for gathering evidence to support their case, and where, in practice, the resources of the prosecution may significantly outweigh those of the defence. An important issue which arises here is the extent to which there is an obligation of disclosure on either side:

Higgins v. H.M. Advocate
1990 S.C.C.R. 268

The appellants were convicted on two charges of assault, which were alleged to have occurred in a public house. They appealed against conviction on the ground, *inter alia*, that the Crown did not supply to them a list of all of the persons present at the scene of the alleged crime.

> LORD COWIE: "In these two appeals the appellants are Kevin Michael Higgins and Graham Alexander Higgins. The appellant Kevin Michael Higgins was convicted at Glasgow Sheriff Court of two charges of assault, which were said to have occurred in a public house in Glasgow. The appellant Graham Alexander Higgins was convicted of the first of those charges, which was the more serious of the two charges on the indictment. They both appeal against their convictions for the same reasons. They explained that they had been refused legal aid for their appeals but that anything that they said to us today was on the advice of the solicitor who appeared for them at the trial but who is of course no longer acting for them. In the grounds of appeal which have obviously been framed by that solicitor it is said, in the first place, that the appellants did not have the opportunity of leading before the jury the evidence of all relevant and competent eyewitnesses because the Crown were unable to tell the defence who were present other than those people on the Crown list. It was said by the appellants today that, having regard to the exclusive powers given to the police and the procurator-fiscal service to investigate crime, it was the duty of the procurator fiscal to make known to the defence any information in their possession which would tend to exculpate the appellants and which the defence were not likely to discover in their own investigations. It is quite clear that not only the grounds of appeal themselves but also the reasons which were given today for quashing the convictions were framed by the same solicitor who, as I have just said, is no longer acting for the appellants. In our opinion it is just as well, because we regard this ground of appeal as wholly without foundation, not to say impertinent. There is no obligation on the Crown to provide any list of witnesses other than those which are attached to an indictment, and there is no obligation on the Crown to disclose any information in their possession which would tend to exculpate the accused. Very often the Crown of their own free will are prepared to give that information and it appears in this case that everything was done within the power of the Crown to do so but because the Crown could not get the necessary information from the other witnesses, obviously they could not pass it on to the defence. For that reason alone this particular ground of appeal must fail."

Appeal refused.

NOTES

1. In *Slater* v. *H.M. Advocate*, 1928 J.C. 94, the court made the following observations (at p.103);

> "An accused person has no right to demand that the prosecution should—in addition to supplying him with the names and addresses of all the witnesses who may be called—communicate to him all the results, material or immaterial, of the investigation made by the procurator-fiscal under direction of the Crown Office. No doubt a very different question would arise, if it could be shown that the prosecution had betrayed its duty by insisting in a charge in the knowledge of the existence of reliable evidence proving the innocence of the person accused which it concealed from him. Such a proceeding would constitute a violation of every tradition observed in the Scottish Crown Office. To assume, without evidence, that the responsible officers of the Crown concealed from an accused person anything known to them which it was material for him to know would be wholly unwarrantable."

For an attempt to rely on these dicta, see *McDonald* v. *H.M. Advocate*, 1987 S.C.C.R. 153.

2. In practice, it may be possible for the defence to obtain access to the Crown case. Procurators-fiscal have been instructed that it is part of their duty to meet with defence solicitors in order to discuss various matters, including the evidence available for the Crown. The purpose of such meetings is, however, largely to save time and expense (See 1980 S.L.T. (News) 42; 1983 S.L.T. (News) 47).

3. The proposition that the Crown is under no obligation to disclose information which would tend to exculpate the accused suggests that this aspect of Scottish criminal procedure is in violation of Article 6 of the European Convention on Human Rights. In *Edwards* v. *United Kingdom*, Series A, No. 247-B, the European Court of Human Rights held that "it is a requirement of fairness under paragraph 1 of article 6 ... that the prosecution authorities disclose to the defence all material evidence for or against the accused" (para. 36).

In the case of *H.M. Advocate* v. *Ward*, 1993 S.C.C.R. 595, the Crown expressly dissociated itself from the broad proposition that there is no obligation on the Crown to disclose any information in their possession which would tend to exculpate the accused.

4. Crown precognitions are treated as highly confidential. It may be that in exceptional cases the court may order their production (see *Donald* v. *Hart* (1844) 6 D. 1255), but in *H.M. Advocate* v. *Ward* (*supra*), Lord McCluskey refused to order the disclosure of precognitions, partly because they are confidential documents, partly because precognitions cannot be put in evidence even under the statutory rules that govern the admissibility of statements made on a previous occasion.

5. In Scottish criminal procedure, the defence is under a limited obligation of disclosure in respect of the so-called "special defences" (alibi, insanity at the time of the offence, incrimination of a named third party, self-defence and (possibly) non-insane automatism: See, generally, Renton and Brown, para. 7–21). In solemn proceedings, these defences cannot be pleaded at the trial unless intimation of an intention to do so has been lodged, not less than 10 clear days before the trial diet, with the clerk of the trial court and the Crown: 1975 Act, s. 82(1). It appears that, in summary

proceedings, advance notice is required only in the case of alibi and insanity: 1975 Act, ss. 339, 375(3) and *Adam* v. *MacNeill*, 1972 J.C. 1.

D. THE PRESUMPTION OF INNOCENCE AND THE BURDEN OF PROOF

1. Slater v. H.M. Advocate
1928 J.C. 94

The appellant was charged with the murder of an old woman by striking her on the head with a hammer. The alleged motive for the killing was theft, the old lady having in her home a large quantity of jewellery. Evidence was led that the appellant lived by gambling and dealing in jewels. There was also evidence that he was supported by the earnings of a prostitute. These circumstances were remarked upon by the Lord Advocate in his speech to the jury as indicating a character depraved enough to commit the crime in question. In his charge to the jury, the presiding judge (Lord Guthrie) made the following remarks (*inter alia*):

> "That is the kind of man, and you will see at once that his character is double-edged. The Lord Advocate takes it in his own favour, and he may quite fairly do so because, in the first place, a man of that kind has not the presumption of innocence in his favour which is not only a form in the case of every man but is a reality in the case of the ordinary man. Not only is every man presumed to be innocent, but the ordinary man has a strong presumption in his favour. Such a man may be capable of having committed this offence, and that man also may be capable from his previous character of exhibiting a callous behaviour after the offence. That was founded upon by Mr McClure. A man of such character does not exhibit the symptoms that a respectable man who has been goaded into some serious crime of violence does after the crime is over, and so you will consider that matter from both points of view, telling in favour of the prisoner and telling against him. [After dealing with the prisoner's financial circumstances his Lordship continued]—Gentlemen, all these circumstances are relevant to the case, but I think if you make up your minds to convict the prisoner you will be wise to be in this position; to be able to say to yourselves, 'we have disregarded his character, we have disregarded his financial circumstances, we have convicted him without regard to these.' Having reached that conclusion, it might very well strengthen the conclusion to reflect on the two elements that I have mentioned, but I do not think they should be factors in enabling you to reach a conclusion, although they might support it after the conclusion had been reached."

The jury returned a verdict of guilty of murder. The appellant appealed on the ground, *inter alia*, of misdirection by the trial judge:

> LORD JUSTICE-GENERAL (CLYDE): "It would be absurd to hold that a miscarriage of justice occurs whenever, in the report of a speech by counsel to the jury, anything is found which can be read as involving either a misstatement of some fact, or as presenting a wrong view of the relevancy of some piece of evidence; and there are many other passages in the prosecutor's speech which put the case against the appellant independently of any reference to any of the points in the evidence which were other than strictly relevant. But the specialty in this trial was that some of the aspects of the life which the appellant lived were relevant, while others were irrelevant, to the question of his guilt. Thus, the circumstances that the appellant never had a dentistry practice in Glasgow, but dealt in some way in articles of jewellery,

was relevant to the motive which, according to the prosecution, drew the appellant to Miss Gilchrist's house in search of the valuables she kept there. But that other aspect of his life, with its peculiarly heinous implications, in which he was shown to be partly dependent on the proceeds of prostitution, was as remote from any bearing on the question of his guilt as it was suggestive of prejudice against his case. Both the former aspects of the appellant's mode of life, and latter aspect, unavoidably came—together and immixed—to the knowledge of the jury; and this made the possibility of misunderstanding on the jury's part the more likely if the odious (and irrelevant) aspect was referred to in the prosecutor's address to the jury for any other purpose than to distinguish it from the others as one which was irrelevant, and which must be put entirely out of their consideration. So far from this, it was unfortunately made the point of the opening passage of the presentation of the case for the prosecution.

We have already indicated our view that the decision of the case—particularly with regard to the vital point of satisfactory proof of identity—presented an unusually difficult and narrow issue, upon which the balance of judgment might easily be influenced in one direction or the other. It follows that the danger of allowing the minds of the jury to be distracted by considerations which were at once so irrelevant and so prejudicial as those connected with the relations of the appellant to his female associates was real and great; and in these circumstances we are of opinion that the clearest and most unambiguous instruction by the presiding judge was imperatively demanded, to prevent the possibility of any misunderstanding on the part of the jury with regard to so important a matter. As appears from the shorthand report of the judge's charge, however, the matter in question was the only one on which the directions given to the jury were open to serious criticism. They did nothing to remove the erroneous impression which the opening passages of the speech for the prosecution might so easily have produced in the minds of the jury. On the contrary, they were calculated to confirm them. No distinction was made between those aspects of the appellant's life which were relevant to the charge of murdering Miss Gilchrist, and those which were not. It was pointed out—quite justly—that the considerations arising out of the appellant's mode of life, as exhibited at the trial, were double-edged, and were founded on (for different purposes) by the prosecution and the defence alike. But the jury were told that what is familiarly known as the presumption of innocence in criminal cases applied to the appellant (in the light of his ambiguous character) with less effect than it would have applied to a man whose character was not open to suspicion. This amounted, in our opinion, to a clear misdirection in law. The presumption of innocence applies to every person charged with a criminal offence in precisely the same way, and it can be overcome only by evidence relevant to prove the crime with the commission of which he is charged. The presumption of innocence is fundamental to the whole system of criminal prosecution, and it was a radical error to suggest that the appellant did not have the benefit of it to the same effect as any other accused person. It is true that an accused person of evil repute has not the advantage, enjoyed by an accused person of proved good character, of being able to urge on the jury in his defence the improbability that a person of good character would commit the crime charged. The passage in the charge at present under discussion is suggestive that this was what was in the judge's mind. But, however that may be, he put the appellant's bad character as a consideration upon which the prosecution was entitled to found as qualifying the ordinary presumption of innocence ... That a man should support himself on the proceeds of prostitution is regarded by all men as blackguardism, but by many people as a sign of almost inhuman depravity. It cannot be affirmed that any members of the jury were misled by feelings of this kind in weighing the question of the appellant's guilt, but neither can it be affirmed that none of them was. What is certain is that the judge's charge entirely failed to give the jury the essential warning against allowing themselves to be misled by any feelings of the kind referred to. It is manifestly possible that, but for the prejudicial effect of denying to the appellant the full benefit of the presumption of innocence, and of allowing the point of his dependence on the immoral earnings of his partner to go to the jury as a point not irrelevant to his guilt of Miss Gilchrist's murder, the proportion of nine to five, for 'guilty' and 'not proven' respectively, might have been reversed."

Appeal allowed: conviction quashed.

NOTES

1. It follows from the presumption of innocence that the burden of proof in criminal cases rests on the prosecution. Normally, there is no onus on the accused to establish his or her innocence. See the notes following *McKenzie* v. *H.M. Advocate, infra*.

2. The presumption of innocence is reinforced in a number of ways in the Scottish system. Thus, for example, it is not normally permissible for the prosecution to introduce evidence of the accused's previous convictions, if any, prior to the verdict being returned. See the 1975 Act, ss. 141(*f*), 346(*f*), 160(1) and (2) and 357(1)(*b*). The effect of wrongly introducing evidence of previous convictions is discussed *infra*, Chap. 15.

2. McKenzie v. H.M. Advocate
1959 J.C. 32

The appellant was charged, *inter alia*, with the culpable homicide of a police constable. He was alleged to have been the driver of a lorry which struck and killed the deceased. There was no dispute that he was travelling in the vehicle at the time of the accident, that he was drunk at that time, and that shortly before the accident he was driving the vehicle. The allegation that he was the driver of the vehicle at the material time was, however, disputed. The presiding judge omitted to give the jury any directions on the burden or standard of proof in a criminal case. On appeal on the ground of misdirection:

LORD JUSTICE-CLERK (THOMSON): "The presumption of innocence is a fundamental tenet of our criminal procedure. It follows that the burden of proof rests on the Crown to displace this presumption. It is further a fundamental tenet that the standard by which this burden falls to be discharged is the establishing of the guilt of the accused beyond reasonable doubt. As this is a fundamental matter, judges ought, as a matter of course, to tell the jury about it. The emphasis and elaboration called for will depend on the circumstances of the case and on whether the evidence is overwhelming or narrow. The bare minimum is to say that it is for the Crown to prove the guilt of the accused beyond reasonable doubt. It is better, however, to split the direction into its two stages, first, that the burden of proof is on the Crown and, second, that the standard of proof required of the Crown is the establishing of guilt beyond reasonable doubt. This tends to emphasise that the second is truly the more important element. Some judges like to tell the jury about the presumption of innocence as that helps to make the jury understand the reason behind the direction. Some like to underline that ordinarily no burden of proof rests on the accused. Most judges give some explanation of what is meant by a reasonable doubt generally by pointing out that a merely speculative or academic doubt is not enough. Others tell the jury that if they have a reasonable doubt on any matter of moment they must give the accused the benefit of the doubt. That is a popular way of putting it which most juries are able to understand and to apply. But as we have said the amount of elaboration and emphasis is dictated by the nature of the case and predilection of the individual judge. We add that in our view it is desirable to adhere so far as possible to the traditional formula and to avoid experiments in reformulation.

In charging the jury the presiding Judge began, as was natural, by explaining the indictment to them. . . . Having given the jury a lucid exposition of the problems which faced them, the Judge passed immediately to the facts which also raised complicated issues with which he dealt with his customary thoroughness and clarity. The natural point at which to say something to the jury about the burden of proof and the standard required would have been at the point of transition but his not having done so then or later meant that the jury had no guidance on what was a fundamental issue. There was therefore, to use the words of Lord Justice-Clerk Aitchison, 'Non-direction amounting to misdirection.' As the same Judge said in a later case, 'It is very easy in a serious case for the most experienced judge to omit to give some direction that ought to have been given.'

As the non-direction here was on a fundamental matter the conviction cannot be sustained unless the proviso to section 2(1) of the Criminal Appeal Act can be applied. The test for its application has been variously formulated and we do not attempt to do it again. It is usefully and succinctly stated by Viscount Simon in *Stirland* [[1944] A.C. 315] that 'the provision that the Court of Criminal Appeal may dismiss the appeal if they consider that no substantial miscarriage of justice has actually occurred in convicting the accused assumes a situation where a reasonable jury, after being properly directed, would, on the evidence properly admissible, without doubt convict.' It is a high and exacting test and we have come to be of the view, that it has not been passed in the present case."

Appeal allowed; conviction quashed;
conviction of contravention of section 15 of
the Road Traffic Act 1930 substituted.

NOTES

1. The burden of proof remains on the Crown even when the accused tables a special defence (other than insanity): *Lambie* v. *H.M. Advocate*, 1973 S.L.T. 219, *infra*, Chap. 10.

2. There are cases in which the accused incurs a burden of proof. Here it is appropriate to distinguish between a "legal" or "persuasive" burden and an "evidential" burden of proof. The former may only be discharged by the accused leading evidence which satisfies the court or the jury *on a balance of probabilities*. The latter may be discharged by the accused pointing to any evidence (whether introduced by the defence or the prosecution) which supports his case, or would give rise to a reasonable doubt as to guilt.

3. A "legal" burden is imposed on the accused when he tables a special defence of insanity, or a plea of diminished responsibility, to establish his mental abnormality. This is said to follow from a presumption of sanity: *Lambie* v. *H.M. Advocate, supra*; *H.M. Advocate* v. *Mitchell*, 1951 J.C. 53. But in relation to the doctrine of "recent possession," the approach of the courts is not so clear.

3. Fox v. Patterson
1948 J.C. 104

The appellant was convicted of reset of a quantity of phosphor bronze, on a complaint charging him with theft of the metal. The appellant apparently bought the metal from a stranger at a cattle market in Glasgow. He resold it, openly, to a third party. When he discovered that he was suspected of having stolen the metal, he offered to reimburse the purchaser. In convicting the appellant, the sheriff relied on the fact that the appellant had been in *de recenti* possession of stolen property without being able to give a satisfactory explanation of his possession. On appeal:

> LORD JUSTICE-GENERAL (COOPER): "When applied with due regard to its limitations, the rule of recent possession of stolen goods is salutory and sensible: but, if its limitations are not observed, the cardinal presumption of innocence may easily be transformed into a rash assumption of guilt. The rule and its limitations are stated in substantially the same sense by Hume (Commentaries, vol. i, p.111), Alison (Criminal Law, vol. i, pp.320 *et seq.*) and Dickson (Evidence, (Grierson's ed.) vol. i, secs. 73 and 157); and to these classical citations I add a quotation aptly given by Dickson (sec. 73) from Bentham; 'Nothing can be more persuasive,' he says, 'than the circumstance of possession commonly is, when corroborated by other criminative circumstances; nothing more inconclusive, supposing it to stand alone. ... Possession of the jewel, *actual* possession, may thus belong to half a dozen different persons at the same time; and as to *antecedent* possession, the number of possible successive possessors is manifestly beyond all limit.'
>
> If the rule is to have full effect in shifting the onus from the prosecution to the accused and raising a presumption of guilt which the accused must redargue or fail, three conditions must concur:—(*a*) that the stolen goods should be found in the possession of the accused; (*b*) that the interval between the theft of the goods and their discovery in the accused's possession should be short—how short I need not in this case inquire; and (*c*) that there should be 'other criminative circumstances' over and above the bare fact of possession. If all these conditions are not present—if, for instance, the interval between the theft and the discovery is prolonged, or if the accused has only had temporary possession of the goods and has parted with them normally and openly—the facts which can be proved may well constitute ingredients (*quantum valeant*) in the case, and may combine with other factors to enable the Crown to establish guilt. But, unless all three conditions concur, the accused cannot be required to accept the full onus of positively excluding every element of guilt. Even when they concur, the weight of the resulting presumption, and the evidence required to elide it, will vary from case to case."

Conviction quashed.

NOTES

1. In *McDonald (J. McF.)* v. *H.M. Advocate*, 1989 S.C.C.R. 559, the appellant was charged with reset. In his charge to the jury, the sheriff referred to the doctrine of recent possession and told them that if they found the conditions for the application of the doctrine to be made out, "then it is for the accused thereafter to prove his or her innocence ... In other words, the onus in that instance shifts on to the accused." The jury convicted the appellant of reset and he appealed on the ground of

misdirection. In allowing the appeal and quashing the conviction, the Lord Justice-General made the following observations (1989 S.C.C.R. 559 at p.562):

> "We were treated in argument to an interesting discussion about the matter of the shifting of the onus from the prosecutor to the accused in the context of the doctrine of recent possession. The discussion led us to the case of *Fox* v. *Patterson* (*supra*) and a number of subsequent authorities. We do not find it necessary to elaborate upon the effect and significance of the shifting of the onus because we are satisfied that the particular words the sheriff used in this case, in the context in which he used them, did amount to a misdirection. We stress that the phrase which we criticise is the phrase 'to prove his or her innocence', which goes further than any formulation of the effect of the shifting of onus in any of the authorities to which we were referred. In *Fox* v. *Patterson* at p.108 Lord Justice-General Cooper referred to the rule as having the effect of shifting the onus from the prosecution to the accused and raising a presumption of guilt which the accused must redargue or fail. In *Cameron* v. *H.M. Advocate* 1959 J.C. 59 at p.63 Lord Justice-General Clyde referred to Lord Justice-General Cooper's formulations as the standard definition of the doctrine of recent possession, of which he said:
>
> > 'The doctrine is, of course, an exception to the general rule, that throughout the onus of proof remains upon the Crown. But the nature of the offence is the justification for this exception.'
>
> It is clear, therefore, ... that the doctrine cannot be confined within the ordinary rule that the onus of proof remains throughout on the Crown. But it is another matter to assert, without further guidance or explanation, that [it] is for the accused to prove his or her innocence."

If the doctrine is an exception to the general rule regarding the onus of proof, and its effect is to shift the onus from the prosecution to the accused and raise a presumption of guilt, then in what sense was it a misdirection for the sheriff to tell the jury that it was for the accused to prove his innocence? Probably what the sheriff said was too broadly stated (it could, for example, have misled the jury regarding the onus of proving that the goods were stolen), and certainly it makes no mention of any standard of proof required. But suppose that the sheriff had told the jury that if the conditions for the doctrine were made out, it was for the accused to establish, on a balance of probabilities, that he did not know the goods were stolen, would that be inconsistent with the earlier formulations of the law?

2.   For further authorities on the doctrine of recent possession, see: *Christie* v. *H.M. Advocate*, 1939 J.C. 72; *Simpson* v. *H.M. Advocate*, 1952 J.C. 1; *Brannan* v. *H.M. Advocate*, 1954 J.C. 44; *Cryans* v. *Nixon*, 1955 J.C. 1; *Wightman* v. *H.M. Advocate*, 1959 J.C. 44; *McSorley* v. *H.M. Advocate*, 1975 S.L.T. (Notes) 43; *Cassidy* v. *McLeod*, 1981 S.C.C.R. 270. *Cf. McLeod* v. *Mason and Ors.*, 1981 S.L.T. (Notes) 109.

3.   The doctrine of recent possession is open to the fundamental objection that it converts a normal inference of fact into a rule of law. See, Gordon, "The Burden of Proof on the Accused," 1968 S.L.T. (News) 29, 37; Macphail, *Research Paper on the Law of Evidence of Scotland*, para. 22.13; Renton and Brown, para. 18–02. Indeed, it is even open to doubt if the "rule" exists at all, beyond imposing on the accused an "evidential"

burden. Certainly, it is difficult to see how "the weight of the resulting presumption, and the evidence required to elide it" could "vary from case to case" if a full "legal" burden is imposed upon the accused.

4.   Earnshaw v. H.M. Advocate
1982 S.L.T. 179; 1981 S.C.C.R. 279

LORD JUSTICE-GENERAL (EMSLIE): "After trial on indictment the appellant was found guilty of five charges arising from a road accident with tragic consequences which took place on the night of 22nd December 1979 when the appellant, who was driving a badly loaded articulated lorry downhill into Hurlford, lost control of it at a left-hand bend. The lorry then 'jack-knifed' and travelled, partly on its side, to collide with, and roll over on top of, a motor-car coming in the opposite direction. The most serious of these charges was charge 1 in its alternative form, namely, contravention of section 1 of the Road Traffic Act 1972—causing the death, by reckless driving, of the three occupants of the motor-car. Charges 2, 3 and 4 libelled contraventions of section 5(1), section 25(1) and (4) and section 25(2) and (4) of the Act respectively, and charge 5 was a charge of contravention of section 9(3) of the Act. In particular charge 5 libelled that having been the driver of the lorry involved in the accident described in charge 1 and having been arrested following a positive breath test required under section 8(2) of the Act, the appellant failed without reasonable excuse to provide the specimen for a laboratory test lawfully required of him in terms of section 9.

This appeal against conviction relates only to charge 5 and the amended ground is in these terms:

> 'That there has been a miscarriage of justice in that the learned trial judge misdirected the jury in law in that he directed the jury that there was a burden of proof on the defence to prove that there was a reasonable excuse for failure under section 9 of the Road Traffic Act 1972 to provide a specimen for a laboratory test.'

In course of his directions to the jury upon the issues for their decision under charge 5 the trial judge referred to certain evidence which had been given and left it to the jury to say whether the appellant's admitted failure to provide the required specimen for a laboratory test was a failure with or without reasonable excuse. He then went on to say this: 'It is for the accused to show that he had a reasonable excuse, not for the Crown to show that he hadn't, but as in every case, whether there is a burden of proof on the defence, that burden can be satisfied on a lower standard of proof than that lying upon the Crown to establish guilt. If an accused satisfies you on a balance of probability that he had a reasonable excuse, that is enough for you to acquit him on this charge, but I am bound to say that if you accept that the requirement was properly made, it is difficult to see how what he said could be a reasonable excuse. You have also to consider of course whether he was too dazed to apply his mind properly to the matter and if you think he was, then of course you could acquit him on that ground.'

In the submission of counsel for the appellant the quoted passage contains a material misdirection in law. The offence created by section 9(3) is committed only if the accused person fails to provide the specimen of blood or urine 'without reasonable excuse'. It is for the Crown to establish this. In particular there is no onus upon an accused person who has failed to supply such a specimen to prove that he had a reasonable excuse for that failure. This has for long been settled in England where the matter of onus has been explained in various ways. For example, in *Regina* v. *Clarke (Christopher)* [1969] 1 W.L.R. 1109 Geoffrey Lane J. (as he then was) giving the judgment of the court said this at p.1113 G-H: 'It is true, of course, that there must be some evidence of such an excuse [and here he is referring to what might amount to a reasonable excuse in law] before the necessity arises of leaving the matter to the jury at all: however, once such evidence does emerge it is for the prosecution to eliminate the existence of such a defence to the satisfaction of the jury.' Further, for example, the matter was disposed of thus by Lord Parker C.J. in *Rowland* v. *Thorpe* [1970] 3 All E.R. 192 at p.197c: 'Of course, once the defence is raised of reasonable excuse, it is for the prosecution in every case to negative it. . . .' The question of the onus of proof in a section 9(3) case has never been the subject of judicial decision in Scotland but, as counsel for the appellant very properly pointed out, there are sentences in opinions in two Scots cases which, although clearly obiter, might at first sight appear to contradict his submission. The cases are *Milne* v. *Elliot*, 1974 S.L.T. (Notes) 71 and *MacDonald* v. *McKenzie*, 1975 S.L.T. 190. In *Milne* the relevant passage which found its echo in *MacDonald* was this: 'If a conviction is not to follow a refusal to supply both blood and urine, it is for the accused to show that he had a reasonable excuse for not providing a sample of either blood or urine.' This passage was in the context of a case in which there was no suggestion in the evidence that there was any excuse at all for the accused's failure to supply a sample of urine and, properly understood, it means only that if a conviction is not to follow upon proof of *refusal* to supply a sample of either blood or urine it is for the accused to introduce the issue of alleged reasonable excuse. Upon the whole matter there was a misdirection by the trial judge in the present case and it was plainly a misdirection upon a fundamental matter. The verdict of guilt against the appellant on charge 5 was by a majority and that misdirection is fatal to the appellant's conviction on that charge.

For the Crown the learned advocate-depute accepted that it was for the Crown, in a charge laid under section 9(3), to establish that there has been a failure, without reasonable excuse, to supply the relevant specimens. It is no doubt for the accused to introduce the issue of reasonable excuse if he considers that there was such an excuse for an admitted failure, but the burden of proof of the commission of the offence, viz., failure to provide the required specimen 'without reasonable excuse', rests on the Crown throughout. In these circumstances it was accepted that the trial judge did misdirect the jury in the respect complained of. This, however, was not fatal to the conviction as the appellant has contended because there was no evidence of any circumstances capable in law of amounting to reasonable excuse. Whether any facts are capable of constituting a 'reasonable excuse' within the meaning of section 9(3) is a question of law and under reference to the case of *Glickman* v. *MacKinnon*, 1978 J.C. 81 and the English cases therein considered the trial judge ought to have directed the jury that there was no evidence before them which they were entitled to treat as evidence of 'reasonable excuse' for the appellant's admitted failure to comply with the requirement made under section 9. Following the course taken in the case of *Regina* v. *Clarke* it should be held that there was, accordingly, no miscarriage of justice in spite of the misdirection, and the conviction should be allowed to stand.

We have no difficulty at all in deciding that counsel for the appellant is well founded in his criticism of the charge of the trial judge. In section 9 Parliament did not make failure to provide the relevant laboratory specimen an offence subject to a statutory defence of reasonable excuse which it is for the accused to establish. The language of section 9(3) makes it clear that a person is guilty of the offence which it created only if, without reasonable excuse, he fails to provide the required specimen. In these circumstances, as the Crown accepts, no charge of contravention of section 9(3) will be relevant unless it libels failure to provide the specimen *without reasonable excuse* (the emphasis is ours). This is what must be established by the Crown in every such case and the burden of proof lies on the Crown throughout. In most or at least many cases there will be no suggestion that there was any excuse at all—far less any reasonable excuse—for a driver's failure or refusal to comply with his obligation under section 9(1) or (2). In those cases, however, in which there is some evidence of some fact or circumstance which could in law amount to 'reasonable excuse' the trial judge, where the charge is tried on indictment, should not only remind the jury that it is for the Crown to satisfy them beyond reasonable doubt that there was a failure without reasonable excuse, but should go on to direct them that if they accept that evidence, or if that evidence casts reasonable doubt on whether the alleged failure was without reasonable excuse they must acquit. In the result, upon this chapter of the appeal, we agree with the courts in England that it is not for the accused who has failed to provide a required specimen to prove that he had a reasonable excuse for that failure. We do not, however, with respect, adopt the language of Geoffrey Lane J. in *Clarke* or that of Lord Parker C.J. in *Rowland* to the effect that 'reasonable excuse' is a defence which it is for the Crown to negative or to eliminate."

> Conviction of contravention
> of section 9(3) quashed.

NOTES

1. A large number of statutes provide that the burden of proving certain matters (such as lawful authority or reasonable excuse for conduct otherwise unlawful) rests upon the accused. See, for example, the Prevention of Crime Act 1953, s. 1(1), the Misuse of Drugs Act 1971, s. 28(2), the Contempt of Court Act 1981, s. 3(3), the Civic Government (Scotland) Act 1982, ss. 58(1) and (4), and the Sexual Offences (Scotland) Act 1976, ss. 2A(1), 2B, 2C and 4(2). The terminology of such provisions varies. Some create an offence, and add to it a defence. In such cases the defence must be established by the accused. Others, as here, include the absence of exculpation as a factor in the definition of the offence. In such cases there is only an "evidential" burden on the accused.

2. Section 66 of the 1975 Act provides:

> "Any exception, exemption, proviso, excuse, or qualification, whether it does or does not accompany in the same section the description of the offence in the statute or order creating the offence, may be proved by the accused, but need not be specified or negatived in the indictment, and no proof in relation to such exception, exemption, proviso, excuse, or qualification shall be required on behalf of the prosecution."

Why did the Crown not rely on this provision? See *Kennedy* v. *Clark*, 1970 J.C. 53.

3. Notwithstanding the general principle that the burden of proof rests generally on the prosecution, it may happen in some cases that the Crown case is so strong that conviction is inevitable unless the accused provides some explanation consistent with innocence. (See *Hardy* v. *H.M. Advocate*, 1938 J.C. 144; *McLeod* v. *Mason and Ors., supra; Tallis* v. *H.M. Advocate*, 1982 S.C.C.R. 91.) In such a case, however, only an evidential burden is imposed on the accused. It is a misdirection for the court to suggest that there is any legal onus on the accused to prove his innocence: *Tallis* v. *H.M. Advocate*, *supra*.

4. Article 6(2) of the European Convention on Human Rights (*supra*) does not prohibit presumptions as elements in the proof of guilt, provided

that these are confined within reasonable limits "which take into account the importance of what is at stake and maintain the rights of the defence": *Pham Hoang* v. *France*, Series A No. 243. Thus, in cases of serious offences, such as drug trafficking, it appears that presumptions of fact which are subject to restricted grounds of rebuttal may be acceptable (*ibid.*). It would not, however, be acceptable to set up irrebuttable presumptions.

E. THE RIGHT TO A FAIR TRIAL

The rules of criminal procedure must guarantee the right to a fair trial. The right of an accused to a fair trial is widely acknowledged, both in domestic legal systems and as an element of international law. But what is included in the notion of a fair trial? A tribunal free from bias, or the appearance of bias may be axiomatic. But what about the freedom from prejudicial publicity, the right to call witnesses and to challenge evidence presented by the other side? And to what extent should the right to a fair trial be guaranteed to *both* the accused and the prosecutor? If Scottish criminal procedure is based on notions of "fairness" and "balance" then it is difficult to see why the right to a fair trial should be regarded in unilateral terms. Presumably the prosecution is as entitled as the defence to an impartial tribunal, to call witnesses and to examine witnesses called by the defence. And the provisions of the Contempt of Court Act 1981 which are directed towards preventing prejudicial pre-trial publicity are expressed in entirely neutral terms.

The following materials illustrate some of the issues raised by the right to a fair trial.

1. McDevitt v. McLeod
1982 S.C.C.R. 282

LORD JUSTICE-CLERK (WHEATLEY): "The appellant was charged with a breach of the peace which was said to have taken place on board the vessel plying between Larne in Northern Ireland and Stranraer in Wigtownshire. It is accepted, and it could not have been otherwise, that there was abundant evidence before the bench of justices to warrant a conviction in the case. In particular there was a statement made by the appellant in answer to a caution and charge which can only be interpreted as an admission that he had committed a breach of the peace. The only point raised in the appeal is to be found in question 3 which relates to the fact that certain remarks were made by the chairman of the bench of justices which indicated that the appellant could not have had a fair trial and that accordingly the conviction recorded against him should be quashed. What happened was this. The chairman after the accused had been found guilty and sentenced said, 'I personally was a passenger on the boat that night and was in the public bar area from time to time. There were many supporters on board who were well behaved and a tribute to Scottish football. I may say that, to my mind, the police carried out their most onerous duties during the period in question in exemplary fashion.' The reference to the police was to the conduct of the police as found in findings in fact in relation to their apprehension of the appellant and the circumstances antecedent thereto that led to the charge of breach of peace. Before turning to consider whether or not those remarks were in the context and the circumstances of the case sufficient to vitiate the conviction, I would like to stress that it was most unfortunate and indeed improper for the chairman of the bench of justices to have sat in this case at all, in that he admittedly was present when the incidents took place which gave rise to the offence that was charged. Since the charge was defended and there was liable to be a conflict of evidence, as indeed there was, between witnesses for the prosecution in the form of the police officers and the defence, including at least the appellant himself, the chairman was not in a position to give the appearance of impartiality in that he himself had witnessed at least some of the incidents. It would have been much better if he had never sat at all, and I trust that such a situation will not occur again. However, that having been said, one has got to consider whether the fact that he did sit was in the circumstances here present sufficient to warrant the quashing of the conviction. In this particular case I am satisfied that the evidence was so clear that the appellant had committed the offence libelled including, as I have indicated, an admission by himself that he had committed it that I cannot think that the interests of justice would be served by quashing this conviction. In each case it is a balance whether or not conduct can so affect the conviction as to warrant its quashing. The balance here, in my opinion, remains in favour of sustaining the conviction, and accordingly I move your Lordships to answer question 3 in the negative and refuse the appeal."

Appeal refused.

NOTES

1.   The interest of this case lies in the fact that there was no suggestion of malice or oppression on the part of the chairman of the justices. This was very much a case in which there was a risk of justice not being seen to be done.

What would have been required to tip the balance in favour of quashing the conviction? What would have been the outcome if the appellant had been acquitted at first instance? And what if he had been highly critical of the police action?

2.   For further discussion of declinature of jurisdiction and the need to maintain an impartial tribunal, see *McPherson* v. *Hamilton*, 1990 S.C.C.R. 270; *Robb* v. *Hillary*, 1992 S.C.C.R. 307; *Bradford* v. *McLeod*, 1985 S.C.C.R. 379 (*infra*, p.466); *Anderson* v. *Hillary*, 1990 S.C.C.R. 684; *Robertson* v. *MacPhail*, 1989 S.C.C.R. 693.

2.   Stewart v. Lowe
1991 S.C.C.R. 317

LORD JUSTICE-GENERAL: "The complainer is Jack Richard Stewart, also known as Stevens, who went to trial in the sheriff court at Edinburgh with a co-accused on summary complaint. The principal charge which he faced was one which was expressed in these terms: that he did on 3rd June 1989 with his co-accused, by means of attempting to remove a window grill, attempt to break into the shop premises at 16 Bank Street, Edinburgh, occupied by Castle Photographic, with intent to steal. There were certain related charges alleging contraventions of conditions of bail. The only charge on which evidence was led against the appellant was charge (1), and at the conclusion of the evidence there was a motion made by each accused who were represented by the same solicitor that there was no case to answer. The sheriff did not call on the procurator fiscal depute to respond to the submissions which [were] made to him and without further ado he rejected both of these submissions. At the conclusion of the evidence the procurator fiscal depute intimated that she was no longer insisting on the charge against the co-accused. Thereupon the sheriff, without calling on the complainer's solicitor to address him, proceeded to convict the complainer and to give his reasons for doing so. Having realised his error he then attempted to retrieve the situation by adjourning the matter overnight and, next morning, when the case had called again, he formally convicted the appellant.

The bill which we have before us today directs attention to two matters which had previously been mentioned in an application for a stated case which was abandoned for the reasons described in statement 2 of the bill. So we have had the benefit of considering the note which the sheriff appended to the stated case.

The first point which is raised relates to an alleged persistent and partial manner of questioning which the sheriff embarked [on] in the course of the trial. We have not been addressed on that point and, since there is a more significant and more fundamental issue which arises on the second point, nothing more need be said about it, except to note the sheriff's comment that nothing which he did by way of questioning was oppressive or improper in this particular case.

The point which we come to now, however, is the central issue, and we have had the benefit of submissions on it from the learned advocate-depute. First of all there is the fact that the sheriff did not call upon the procurator fiscal depute to address him on the defence submission that there was no case to answer. As the advocate-depute points out, that was a breach of the provisions of section 345A(2) and (3) which make it clear that the sheriff must hear both parties before sustaining or rejecting a submission on this ground. That error would not, however, of itself, persuade us that the trial had been conducted in a manner which was oppressive to the complainer.

The more serious error lies in the sheriff's conduct in proceeding to convict the complainer without having heard any submissions at all for the defence. In this case because of the sheriff's attitude to the only defence witness, Marie Cummings, whose evidence might be thought to have cast doubt on the reliability of the one witness who corroborated the evidence of a police officer in support of the principal charge, the sheriff dismissed her evidence as totally irrelevant. It is averred in the bill that he did so peremptorily, and we have confirmation of this by the sheriff's own note that the evidence of Miss Cummings was totally irrelevant to the guilt or innocence of either accused. In our opinion that is not self-evident and there was a point of substance to be made in the submissions on behalf of the defence. The advocate-depute points out that there may also have been a question as to whether the essential matter alleged in the complaint had been proved at all.

In our opinion this is a case where it can be said without hesitation that the sheriff's conduct was such that the complainer was not seen to have received a fair trial and that the conduct which is narrated in the bill is sufficiently serious to justify the remedy which is sought. For these reasons the course which we must take is to pass the bill and quash the conviction."

> The court passed the Bill
> and quashed the conviction.

NOTE

 Cf. Bassi v. *Normand*, 1992 S.C.C.R. 413. The appellant was convicted in the district court of a contravention of the Litter Act 1983. The justice imposed a fine of £100 on him without hearing a plea in mitigation. When this was pointed out to him by the assessor, the justice heard a plea in mitigation and reimposed the fine. On appeal, the High Court held that there was a clear failure by the justice to follow ordinary rules of fair conduct. Justice was clearly not seen to be done because the justice imposed a fine without giving any opportunity to the defence to address the court. (See also, *Martin* v. *Crowe*, 1992 S.C.C.R. 388 in which sentence was passed without hearing from either prosecution or defence. The accused presented a bill of suspension. The sentences were suspended and the case remitted to a different sheriff for sentencing.)

3.   **Atkins v. London Weekend Television Ltd.**
1978 J.C. 48

The respondents were responsible for the transmission throughout the United Kingdom of a programme called *Weekend World* which contained a feature entitled "The Living Dead". This feature discussed the issues surrounding the provision of life-support measures for seriously brain-damaged patients. Reference was made in the feature to certain well-known cases of this kind. The feature began, however, with detailed references to the petitioner who was due to stand trial the following day at Edinburgh sheriff court on charges of assault to the danger of life. The petitioner, a nurse in Edinburgh Royal Infirmary, was charged with having twice attempted to stop the air supply to a patient in the hospital's intensive care unit. As well as giving details of the charge against the petitioner, the respondents also transmitted pictures of her taken admittedly without her permission.

The petitioner presented a petition to the *nobile officium* of the High Court craving that the court prohibit the respondents and others from broadcasting or publishing any material calculated to prejudice, or giving rise to possible prejudice to, any future trial of the petitioner.

LORD JUSTICE-GENERAL (EMSLIE): "... We come now to the question of whether the complaint of contempt of court has been made out. The offence alleged by the petitioner consists, to quote the words of Lord President Clyde in *Johnson* v. *Grant* 1923 S.C. 789 at p.790, 'in interfering with the administration of the law, in impeding and perverting the course of justice'. It is the paramount duty of this Court to ensure that persons charged on indictment in Scotland shall receive a fair and impartial trial. Accordingly, where any person has been charged with crime and is awaiting trial 'the public dissemination of insinuations or suggestions capable of prejudicing the public mind and the minds of prospective jurors' with regard to the impending trial 'cannot be tolerated for it is in our view prejudicial to the interests of justice' [*vide* the opinion of the Lord Justice-General in *M'Alister*, p.16]. The essence of a charge of contempt of the kind with which this petition is concerned is, therefore, the allegation that what was said and done was likely to prejudice the fair and impartial trial of the accused person and, thus, to be prejudicial to the interests of justice itself.

In this case the question for us is whether the contents of the programme complained of were such as to give rise to a real risk of prejudice to the fair and impartial trial of the petitioner on the charges on which she stood indicted ... and we must approach this question as a jury would and examine the programme as it was likely to be understood by those who saw and heard it.

Mr Bruce with characteristic skill sought to persuade us that neither the feature as a whole nor any of its constituent parts created any such risk. Leaving aside the references to the petitioner the discussion was, he said, and we can readily accept this, quite unobjectionable in that it bore to be and was a serious debate upon a live question of immediate public concern. A reference to the impending trial of the petitioner and the nature of the charge against her could not by itself be an offence against the interests of justice for the charge and the fact that she was to be tried in Edinburgh on 14th November 1977 were public facts. We readily accept this also. The petitioner does not aver that the showing of her photograph was likely, by itself, to prejudice her in her defence and the feature as a whole involved no detailed discussion of the petitioner's case and it made no attempt to prejudge her guilt or innocence. Indeed express mention was made of her plea of not guilty. Even if there had been no reference made to the petitioner at all the feature might have had just the same effect upon the petitioner's trial.

The complaint is, however, that the showing of photographs of the petitioner and the particular references to her in sound made all the difference and converted a discussion of what was already a matter of public interest and comment into an act of contempt. So far as the photographs were concerned, said Mr Bruce, there is no hard and fast rule that the publication of a photograph of an accused person will always constitute contempt. We have no difficulty in accepting this proposition and we accept, too, the further proposition that the publication of a photograph of an accused person will only constitute contempt where a question of identification has arisen or may arise and where the publication is calculated to prejudice the prospects of a fair trial.

In our judgment there is not the slightest doubt that the references to the petitioner in the context of this particular feature as a whole were in the highest degree likely to prejudice the petitioner's prospects of a fair and impartial trial. We have seen and heard a videotape recording of the introduction to the programme and of the entire feature. For the purposes of considering the arguments of parties we have been supplied with, and we have had an opportunity of reading, the transcript of the sound track. The feature was specifically concerned, and no doubt properly concerned, to debate the serious issue on which medical opinion is divided, namely whether or not life support for certain patients who have suffered severe brain damage should, as matter of policy, be withdrawn. In course of that feature it was no doubt highly relevant and perfectly legitimate to refer to the two very recent cases, one in England and one in the United States, in which a decision to switch off the patient's breathing machine was deliberately taken. To introduce references to the case of Elizabeth Semple and to the petitioner's trial on the indictment the very next day was, however, utterly indefensible and irresponsible for the references were made in such a way as to imply that this was another case of the same kind as those of Caroline Wilkinson and Karen Quinlan and, it may be, the latest example of actings by a nurse towards a patient in implement of a view held by eminent medical men in Scotland that withdrawal of life support for certain victims of severe brain damage is desirable and morally justifiable. 'A jury at the Sheriff's (*sic*) Court in the city will be told that Nurse Atkins twice tried to block the air supply to a 13-year-old girl in her care,' said the commentator. Contrary to Mr Bruce's submission that this would be understood as no more than a reference to the allegations in the charges this sentence was, in our judgment, calculated to convey and likely to convey to the public mind in Scotland, and to the minds of prospective jurors in Scotland, that the evidence would be that the petitioner had committed the acts charged, and the sting is not removed by the bare mention of the fact that she 'will plead not guilty to the charges' because the commentator immediately added <u>but</u> (the underlining is ours) 'by the middle of the week the whole country will be talking about the issues raised in this case.' We accept from Mr Bruce that the references to the petitioner were included for the sole purpose of giving topicality to the programme and, in short, we hold that this gratuitous introduction of the references to the petitioner, in the context of the feature as a whole and, in particular, in close company with the references to the

Wilkinson and Quinlan cases, contained the clear insinuation that the real if not the only question which would arise out of the petitioner's trial would be whether she was medically and morally justified in committing the acts charged. In fact the petitioner's plea of not guilty necessarily raised the question of the identity of the person, if any, who attempted to block the child's air supply as well as the initial question whether any such acts as those charged were perpetrated at all by any person. It was therefore essential for the Crown to identify the petitioner as the perpetrator. In the whole circumstances the inclusion of the photographs but, more importantly, the verbal references to her in the context of the feature as a whole, were likely to be highly damaging to the prospects of a fair and impartial trial of the petitioner in Scotland. The Lord Advocate has informed us that in his opinion the conduct complained of on the part of those responsible for the feature 'The Living Dead' undoubtedly constituted a material interference with the due and proper administration of criminal justice in Scotland. We agree with him. Indeed, in our judgment, what was said and shown with reference to the petitioner in this feature was so prejudicial to the proper administration of justice in Scotland that we entertain the gravest doubt whether fair and impartial trial of the petitioner on the charges of assaulting Elizabeth Semple is now possible, however carefully the trial Judge may direct the jury. However that may be, and we are sure that the Lord Advocate will consider the question of further prosecution of the petitioner with anxious care, we say without hesitation that the complaint of contempt of court by those responsible for the feature 'The Living Dead' has been shown to be well founded."

Respondents held to be in contempt.

NOTES

1. The Contempt of Court Act 1981 now provides a statutory test for contempt by "publications" (which include "any speech, writing, broadcast or other communication which is addressed to the public at large or any section of the public": 1981 Act, s. 2(1)). The strict liability rule provided for by section 1 of the Act applies to any publication which "creates a substantial risk that the course of justice in the proceedings in question will be seriously impeded or prejudiced," provided that the "proceedings" are "active": s. 2(2), (3), and Schedule 1. The changed test does not, of course, affect the premises upon which this form of contempt is based.

In *H.M. Advocate* v. *News Group Newspapers*; *H.M. Advocate* v. *Scottish Express Newspapers Ltd.*, 1989 S.C.C.R. 156 (which involved proceedings for contempt under the 1981 Act) the Lord Justice-General made the following remarks:

"Publishers and responsible editors must not only try to avoid committing contempt of court. They must succeed in doing so. The reason for that is that our system of criminal justice in Scotland depends essentially upon the proposition that jurors called to try an accused person should arrive in the jury box without knowledge or impressions of facts, or alleged facts, relating to the crime charged in the indictment."

2. By section 5 of the 1981 Act a publication made as or as part of a discussion in good faith of public affairs or other matters of general public interest will not be treated as a contempt under the strict liability rule "if the risk of impediment or prejudice to particular legal proceedings is

merely incidental to the discussion." Although the test for contempt under
the Act is now rather different from that put forward in *Atkins*, it seems
likely that the respondents would still be held in contempt under the new
test.

3.   Prejudice arising from pre-trial publicity may be pleaded as a bar to
trial: *Stuurman* v. *H.M. Advocate*, 1980 J.C. 111, *infra*, Chap. 10. As yet, no
such plea has been successfully maintained (and see the comments of Lord
Avonside in *Stuurman* as to whether such a plea would have succeeded
had the petitioner in *Atkins* been tried: *ibid.*, p.117). The new test for
contempt requires a *substantial* risk that the course of justice will be
seriously impeded or prejudiced. Could the court consistently hold that
there had been contempt under that rule in a given case, and yet hold that it
was not oppressive to insist in prosecuting the accused? (The risk of
prejudice must, after all, mean a risk of prejudice which is in existence at
the time of the trial.)

4.   H.M. Advocate v. Waddell and Another
High Court, 1 December 1976, *unreported*

The accused were charged, *inter alia*, with the murder of an elderly woman.
During the course of his charge to the jury the presiding judge, Lord
Robertson, made the following remarks. The circumstances of the case are
fully set out in his Lordship's charge. For earlier proceedings in this case,
see *infra*, Chap. 2

LORD ROBERTSON: "Members of the jury, this has been described by both
counsel as a unique case, and it certainly has been a remarkable case, I think
unprecedented in the annals of Scottish justice. The bald fact is that a crime was
committed at 2 Blackburn Place, Ayr, on the night of 5, 6 July 1969,
seven-and-a-half years ago, a vicious robbery following upon which Mrs Ross
died. I shall deal later with the question of murder in law, but at the moment I
assume, for the purposes of what I have to say that that is what happened,
nobody in fact disputes it.

The remarkable thing about this is in the sequel. On 20 October 1969, at the
High Court in Edinburgh there was a trial at which Patrick Meehan was
charged with the robbery and, inter alia the murder of Mrs Ross, and after a
long trial in which a large number of witnesses gave evidence for the Crown
and also for the defence a jury returned a verdict of guilty upon the evidence
which appeared amply to justify the verdict. An appeal was taken and was
carefully considered by the Court of Criminal Appeal; the appeal failed.
Thereafter the convicted man went to prison and from time to time tried to
re-open the case in various ways, all of which attempts failed. But some public
support was whipped up over a period of years and a campaign developed,
from motives which are not entirely clear, but may be imagined, on behalf of
Meehan. I shall deal later with some of the aspects of that campaign, but it
appears that there have been undesirable consequences, most particularly in
the use of money and inducements which have encouraged lying and
fabricated stories, and also unscrupulous and biased questioning and the like,
no doubt by well-meaning persons, which has interfered with due processes of
law and the administration of justice in this country.

For a long time the Lord Advocate and the Crown authorities paid no
attention to this clamour, but in 1976 a decision was apparently taken to advise
the Queen to give a Free Pardon to Meehan. This was a quite unprecedented
step which has had far-reaching consequences. The reasons for this decision
have not become apparent in this trial. It is well to stress, ladies and gentlemen,

that this decision was a decision by the executive, not reached by due process of law. Such action, ladies and gentlemen, runs counter to the whole basis of justice in Scotland, which is trial by jury and by proper process of law in independent courts. If the executive are going to interfere in such a way with the administration of justice by due process of law, there is no end to it and one of the great bulwarks of liberty in this country is threatened, because of course it could be done in every case or any case. This decision was all the more strange because the due processes of law were not exhausted before the decision was taken.

In a somewhat similar case, the celebrated case of Oscar Slater in 1928, this was not the procedure adopted by the then Secretary of State. The trial of Oscar Slater for the murder of an old lady in Glasgow in 1909 resulted in his conviction, sentence to death and reprieve. The evidence in that case against the accused it is safe to say was weak and the verdict marginal. At that time there was no Court of Criminal Appeal in Scotland and it is possible that had there been such a court the conviction might well not have stood at the time. Over the years there was a continual rumbling of criticism of the verdict, and after the Court of Criminal Appeal had been set up in 1926 the Secretary of State for Scotland remitted the case back to the new court for a reappraisal and reconsideration, including the hearing of fresh evidence which had become available in the interval. The court, after a prolonged hearing of the fresh evidence and reconsideration of the whole case, finally, in 1928 quashed the conviction of Oscar Slater, as it happened upon a legal point relating to the judge's charge and not on the effect of the new evidence. That procedure, ladies and gentlemen, was open to the Secretary of State in the present case and one might have thought would have been an appropriate step to take; at least the court might have been enabled to examine critically any new evidence placed before it with regard to the first verdict of the jury. But without exhausting this obvious process of law the Crown in the present case has seen fit to advise a pardon for the convicted man without due process of law, in itself a rare step, and then have gone on to charge a different person with the same crime. In other words, the Crown who had asked one jury to hold it proved beyond reasonable doubt that Meehan was guilty, now ask another jury to hold that Waddell is guilty or was guilty beyond reasonable doubt of the same crime.

This has created a most unusual and, I think, unfortunate situation. In the first place it has put into question the legal meaning and effect of the Free Pardon granted to Meehan about which there was extensive legal debate at the outset of this trial. The Lord Advocate has stated that this question has never been resolved before. For my part I have always thought, in the ordinary use of language, that if you pardon someone, you pardon them for something that they have done, and not for something that they haven't done. This indeed is an interpretation supported by the actual terms of the Free Pardon itself which appear to free Meehan from the consequences of the conviction and not from the conviction itself. It certainly doesn't quash the conviction by due process of law. This is borne out by the fact that the conviction against Meehan has been duly extracted and lodged in process in the present trial, so the Crown is endeavouring to persuade you to convict a man for a crime for which another man has been convicted by a proper process of law and whose conviction has never been quashed by due process of law.

Ladies and gentlemen, when this question was raised at the outset of the trial I considered it very carefully and, as you know, convened a larger court in order that the whole matter should be more fully argued. The result was that, with the assistance of two other judges, I reached the conclusion that the decision whether to prosecute a second man for a crime for which another man had been properly convicted by due process of law and his conviction had never been quashed was one for the Lord Advocate, in the exercise of his discretion, and was not a legal bar, but the circumstances in which an unprecedented step should be taken should only, in my view, be very exceptional. I understood the Lord Advocate to say repeatedly that save in very exceptional circumstances it would be unconscionable for him to proceed against a second man and I had rather expected that he would have acted accordingly, but he has not done so, and now asks you to convict another man for the same crime. This is a decision, ladies and gentlemen, which I think has far-reaching consequences. The most important of these is upon the basic fairness of any trial of Waddell, the second man, in these circumstances. It is of the very essence of the administration of justice in Scotland that an accused man comes into court without any previous publicity or speculation upon the crime and his responsibility for it. Thus in Scotland, before a criminal trial there is no preliminary hearing and no advance publicity of any kind.

Furthermore, it is fundamental that no reference is made to any previous convictions or criminal record that he may have. All this is contained on the vital principle known as the presumption of innocence. Some people think we go too far in this and that a man's previous record should be before a jury, but that isn't the present law. It is, for instance, an interesting speculation in the present case, what would have been the reaction of the jury in Meehan's trial if his life-long record of crime of housebreaking and proud claim to be an expert safeblower had been before them. Not a whisper of this of course was before them when they convicted him, but in this trial of Waddell he has very properly, and understandably put in a special defence of impeachment against Meehan, saying in effect that the murder was committed by Meehan and Griffiths and the Crown have gone on record some months ago, having taken steps publicly to free Meehan from the consequences of his conviction and has repeatedly stated, or impliedly rather, stated that Meehan did not commit the crime. Indeed, there has been in addition some extensive publicity in the media over a period of months, very often referring to Meehan, in terms such as—a man wrongly convicted of the murder. Members of the jury, there is no legal justification whatever in saying that Meehan was wrongly convicted of the murder, and indeed having heard all the evidence in this case you may well have come to the clear conclusion, although I don't pre-judge it because I will be dealing with this in detail later, but you may well have come to the clear conclusion that he was in fact rightly convicted as another jury found seven-and-a-half years ago. I shall deal of course with this later in some more detail, but at the moment I am stressing the basic background unfairness to this trial so far as Waddell is concerned and my belief that for this reason alone the Lord Advocate in the exercise of his discretion might well have not proceeded in this prosecution or asked you to convict Waddell.

This consideration is perhaps emphasised by the tendency which I think has become apparent from time to time in the course of the trial, for the Lord Advocate to treat the case as if it were a public inquiry into the death of Mrs Ross. Members of the jury, this is not a public inquiry, no doubt had the Secretary of State wanted, he could have set up a public inquiry of some sort into the whole affair, but he has not done so. This is the criminal trial of Waddell and he is entitled to all the rights of any other citizen accused of a crime. The presumption of innocence, proper observance of the rules of evidence, the rights to fairness, etc.

I also cannot refrain in passing from commenting upon the way in which this case has been handled in some particulars, especially in regard to the very senior and experienced policemen who have, over a period of years, been maligned, defamed and accused by Meehan of very grave dereliction of duty, perjury, planting of evidence, and the like, without as it has turned out any shred of justification whatsoever. I should have thought that in the absence of any evidence to support these allegations the Crown would have at least led these witnesses and supported them in their denial, instead, as we saw on

Monday, forcing the defence to lead them as witnesses and then attempt to demean them by cross-examination.

Ladies and gentlemen, the discharge of its criminal duty by the Crown in Scotland has always been characterised by the highest standards of fairness and equity, and I can only hope that there will be no slipping from these standards.

Ladies and gentlemen, I should like you at the outset to remember that Waddell is entitled to be treated just like any other citizen, with complete fairness, bearing in mind the presumption of innocence, and I would invite you, if you think that all that has gone before has prevented him from receiving such treatment, to acquit him on that ground alone, without any further consideration, if you think he is prejudiced by what has gone before. If you do not take that step initially then I direct you to put out of your mind all considerations of the kind I have mentioned and, in particular, the decision of the Crown to proceed with the case after having apparently, with full publicity and without due process of law pre-judged it."

Verdict: not guilty.

NOTES

1.   It is impossible to tell, of course, whether the jury's verdict was returned in response to Lord Robertson's invitation or on the basis of the evidence presented to them.

2.   Just how far Lord Robertson's remarks could be developed is not clear. It should be remembered that the case was quite exceptional (as his Lordship pointed out), and many of his comments can be read as marks of censure on the conduct of the Crown as much as anything else. Certainly, the invitation to the jury to acquit if they thought Waddell had not been dealt with fairly seems a novel extension of the fairness principle, or of the right to a fair trial.

3.   The whole ghastly affair of the "Ayr Murder" and its sequel(s) was made the subject of a searching inquiry by Lord Hunter: *Report of Inquiry into the whole circumstances of the murder of Mrs Rachel Ross*, etc., House of Commons Paper 444, July 1982.

F.   The Right to a Speedy Trial

A guarantee of a speedy determination of the issue of guilt or innocence is generally regarded as a basic requirement of any system of criminal justice (*cf.* Gordon, *The Criminal Justice (Scotland) Act 1980*, p.xiii) and the right to a fair and public hearing "within a reasonable time" is set out in Article 6 of the European Convention. Various rules exist in Scots law, both in solemn and summary proceedings, to ensure that there is no undue delay in bringing an accused to trial. These rules are discussed at the relevant points in the examination of solemn and summary proceedings, *infra*, Chaps. 8 and 12. It is clear that the rules of Scottish criminal procedure more than fulfil the requirements of the Convention (as to which, see, *inter alia, Lawless* v. *Ireland (No. 3)*, Series A No. 3; *Ringeisen* v. *Austria (No. 1)*, Series A No. 13; *Neumeister* v. *Austria (No. 1)*, Series A No. 8 for statements of principle by the European Court of Human Rights. For examples of current practice, see, *inter alia, Kemmache* v. *France*, Series A

No. 218 and the sequence of cases against Italy, Series A Nos. 194-A to 197-D).

G.   THE RIGHT TO LEGAL REPRESENTATION

There are really two aspects to this issue. There is, first of all, the question of access to legal representation, and the extent to which such representation is available to those who cannot afford to pay for it. There is in Scotland a long tradition of the provision of free representation by the legal profession (the first statute in this area was passed in 1424). In *Thomson* v. *H.M. Advocate*, 1959 J.C. 15 the Lord Justice-Clerk suggested that the provision of free legal assistance for those unable to afford it was one aspect of ensuring a fair trial.

Legal assistance in criminal cases is today governed by Part IV of the Legal Aid (Scotland) Act 1986 and the Criminal Legal Aid (Scotland) Regulations 1987. In a work of this size it is not possible to do more than note the existence of such provision. For a full discussion of legal aid in criminal cases, see Stoddart, *The Law and Practice of Legal Aid in Scotland*, 3rd edition.

The second question arises in connection with the person who has secured legal assistance. What guarantees are there of access to that assistance, and what are the consequences of denying such access? In *Fraser* v. *Mackinnon*, 1981 S.C.C.R. 91, a sheriff insisted in proceeding with the trial of two accused persons in the absence of their legal adviser. The sheriff knew that he was in the building, acting as duty solicitor for that day, and that he would be released shortly from that duty. The solicitor arrived towards the close of the Crown case and moved for an adjournment. This was refused and the accused were convicted. In a suspension, the High Court held that in the circumstances of the case the sheriff's conduct amounted to oppression. What he had done was not necessary in the public interest, or to avoid prejudice to the prosecutor. It was, on the other hand, likely to prejudice the accused. (See also, *Kane* v. *Tudhope*, 1986 S.C.C.R. 161 and *Benson* v. *Tudhope*, 1986 S.C.C.R. 422.)

It is interesting to note, however, that the right to free legal assistance for those who cannot afford it is not generally regarded as an absolute right. Article 6(3)(*b*) of the European Convention on Human Rights provides only that such assistance should be provided "when the interests of justice so require." A similar restriction is imposed by section 24(1)(*b*) of the Legal Aid (Scotland) Act 1986 in relation to legal aid in summary criminal proceedings. In other words, it is assumed that in some circumstances it is not contrary to the interests of justice for a person who cannot afford to pay for legal representation to go without.

The European Court of Human Rights has held that in determining whether or not it is in the interests of justice that a person should receive free legal assistance, regard should be had to the following factors. (a) The seriousness of the offence, including the likely punishment if convicted. Where anything more than a short period of imprisonment is possible, that fact alone would require that legal assistance be granted. (b) The complexity of the case. This is not limited to the circumstances of the case itself, but would include such factors as the impact of a conviction on other legal measures to which the accused was subject. This would include, for example, the fact that he committed the offence while on bail or during the period of a deferral of a sentence or while on probation. (c) The personal circumstances of the accused, including his or her age, educational and social background, etc. See, generally, *Quaranta* v. *Switzerland*, Series A No. 205. See also *Granger* v. *United Kingdom* (1990) 12 E.H.R.R. 469.

The factors to be taken into account in determining whether it is in the interests of justice that criminal legal aid be made available in a summary case are set out in s. 24(3) of the Legal Aid (Scotland) Act 1986. No such test is applied in solemn proceedings. For observations on the refusal of legal aid in summary proceedings on the ground that the interests of justice do not require it, see *McLachlan, Petitioner*, 1987 S.C.C.R. 195.

For the rights of persons in custody to consult with a solicitor, see *infra*, Chap. 4.

CHAPTER 2

THE SYSTEM OF PROSECUTION

In keeping with most western legal systems, Scots law regards the prosecution of crime as primarily a public function performed on behalf of the public by an official appointed for that purpose. Consequently, much of the material in this chapter concerns the powers and duties of the public prosecutor. The latter does not, however, enjoy exclusive title to prosecute. Whilst public prosecution may be the norm, private prosecution is competent in both solemn and summary proceedings, and the rules governing such prosecutions may conveniently be considered in this chapter. Furthermore, Scottish criminal procedure appears to recognise a third "breed" of prosecutor, occupying a position midway between public and private prosecutor, known as the prosecutor in the public interest. The status of this prosecutor likewise deserves some examination.

A.   HISTORICAL DEVELOPMENT—FROM PRIVATE TO PUBLIC PROSECUTION

Lord Normand, The Public Prosecutor in Scotland
(1938) 54 L.Q.R. 345

"The prosecution of crime in Scotland is a public function exercised by the Lord Advocate with the assistance of the Solicitor-General, of other advocates depute nominated by the Lord Advocate and acting under deputations personally granted by him, and of procurators fiscal, who are local but permanent officials appointed as vacancies occur by the Lord Advocate.

This was not always the rule and there are still vestiges of an earlier system of private prosecution. It will be proper to trace briefly the history of criminal prosecution in Scotland before describing the practice of the present day.

Popular prosecution, by which *quivis e populo* might institute criminal proceedings, was unknown in Scotland. Scots law did not recognize at any time a general right of private individuals to prosecute for any offence that could be considered injurious to the public. Originally the person injured by the crime or certain of his relatives were entitled to prosecute the offender. That was a system of prosecution not unsuited to the primitive conditions of communication, the prevalence of sectional feuds, and the weakness of the central authority of the Crown in Scottish history down to the sixteenth century. But it was rude and partial in operation and directed more to private vengeance than to the securing of public order. The powerful criminal escaped justice; the wealthy purchased immunity from punishment; and the poor and weak suffered wrongs without daring to bring the perpetrator to justice. Private arrangements by which criminals were left at liberty to repeat their offences were common, and money which should have come to the royal treasury from forfeitures and fines remained in the pockets of the wrong-doers or was divided between them and the parties whom they had injured. There were besides certain crimes against the State for which no private person could prosecute, and in these cases the right of the Lord Advocate to prosecute as the King's Advocate was recognised before 1579. In an Act of the Scottish Parliament of that year dealing with malicious and unnecessary prosecutions, provision was made for the punishment of unjust pursuers and of unjust informers where the King's Majesty's Advocate was the only pursuer. The crimes in which the King's Advocate was the only pursuer were mainly those of a public nature committed against the Crown or the State. In 1579 also the Privy Council directed the King's Advocate and the Treasury to prosecute in certain cases though the private persons wronged declined to do so. The association of the Treasurer with the King's Advocate reveals the motive of the Privy Council's action. It was to prevent private arrangements by which the Treasury was deprived of fines and forfeitures. Eight years later the King's Advocate and the Treasurer are again associated in criminal prosecutions, this time by an Act of Parliament which marks an important step in the history of public prosecutions. The Act of 1587, cap. 77, provided that the Treasurer and Advocate pursue slaughters and other crimes although the parties be silent or would otherwise privily agree. Thus the Crown's right to prosecute, whether the private parties injured chose to prosecute or not, was clearly established, and immediately afterwards there are decisions by the Court affirming the Lord Advocate's title to prosecute in circumstances where it was formerly negatived. The position at the end of the sixteenth century is thus summed up in a judgment delivered in 1836 [*King's Advocate* v. *Lord Dunglas* (1836) 15 S. *per* Lord Medwyn at p.327]: 'The King's Advocate was authorised to act as public prosecutor of crimes in the time of James VI. This is implied in 1579, c. 78, and still more expressly by 1587, c. 77, which authorised the Treasurer and Advocate to pursue, although the private party did not. He may have had power previously from the Sovereign to prosecute in the pleas of the Crown; but in that large class of crimes, then prosecuted at the instance of the private party, his power was confirmed and firmly recognised by these statutes; so that, since the date of the latter Act, his right to prosecute all crimes has been unquestioned.' The Treasurer did not prosecute alone, and his association with the Lord Advocate as prosecutor ultimately ceased. Even after 1587 the Lord Advocate was frequently specially directed by the Privy Council to prosecute in certain cases. The explanation of this is probably to be found in the unruly condition of the country which made it unsafe for the Lord Advocate to act on his own initiative and caused him to seek such protection as a special order of Government might afford against the vindictiveness of powerful criminals and of their retainers or associates.

The Act of 1587 did not withdraw from the party injured his right to prosecute. But gradually the Lord Advocate assumed complete control of the administration of the criminal law. This change may have been favoured by decisions of the Court that the Lord Advocate could not be compelled to disclose the name of his informer [*James Connell*, 1599. Omond, *The Lord Advocates of Scotland*, 59; *Muirhead*, 1681. Fountainhall's *Decisions*, i, 136]. Under these decisions an injured party might well prefer that the Lord Advocate should act as prosecutor, for the private prosecutor, besides incurring the cost and trouble of conducting the prosecution, was exposed to a claim for expenses by the person accused if the trial resulted in an acquittal So in time the private prosecutor almost disappeared, and his right to institute proceedings became so far subordinate to that of the Lord Advocate that he was required to obtain the Lord Advocate's concurrence. 'Prosecution [by the private prosecutor] is attended with this peculiarity', says a great institutional authority [Hume, ii, 125], 'that the libel [*i.e.* charge] cannot be raised at the pleasure of the individual; and bears, by ancient and invariable style, to be raised with the concourse of his Majesty's Advocate, for his Majesty's interest; and truly receives his concourse, by the subscription of that officer, or some one authorised by him, at the bill for the criminal letters' [the writ instituting proceedings]. 'This practice seems to be grounded on two considerations. First, his Majesty's interest in the fines, forfeitures, and confiscations, that accrue on occasion of convictions; which interest is guarded in this way, against any collusive dealings between the private accuser and the pannel' [the accused person]. 'And, next, that far superior interest which his Majesty has in the execution of his laws, and especially, in the due and equal distribution of criminal justice to all his subjects.' "

NOTE

In common with many other commentators Lord Normand is critical of the haphazard enforcement of the criminal law in early times, and in particular of the way in which the guilty could purchase immunity from punishment. This could be achieved by informal arrangements made between the wrongdoer and his victim, but there was a recognised legal procedure whereby the wrongdoer offered compensation (known as *assythment*) to the victim (or in appropriate cases his relatives). In return for assythment the victim granted the offender forgiveness in a document known as a "letter of slaines" and thereby relinquished any interest in prosecuting the offender. (For a general account of the system, see R. B. Black, "A Historical Survey of Delictual Liability in Scotland for Personal Injuries and Death" (1975) 8 C.I.L.J.S.A. 46, at pp.52 *et seq.*, and *McKendrick v. Sinclair*, 1971 S.L.T. 17, 234, and 1972 S.L.T. 110.)

The increasing intervention of the Crown after 1587 did not lead to a reduction in the incidence of bought justice. Immunity from punishment at the hands of the Crown could be obtained by means of a pardon or remission. Such remissions were frequently obtained from the Crown in exchange for cash or favours, and the income from remissions figured prominently in the revenues of most of the Stuart monarchs.

B.   PUBLIC PROSECUTION

Responsibility for all public prosecutions in Scotland rests, ultimately, with the Lord Advocate who is the chief Law Officer of the Crown in Scotland. In the discharge of his functions as public prosecutor the Lord Advocate is assisted by the second Law Officer, the Solicitor-General for Scotland, and a permanent staff of civil servants in the Crown Office in Edinburgh headed by the Crown Agent.

All prosecutions on indictment, whether in the High Court or the sheriff court, are conducted in the name of the Lord Advocate (1975 Act, s. 41). While the Lord Advocate may appear personally to prosecute it is customary today for him to be represented. In the High Court this task is performed by Crown counsel appointed by the Lord Advocate and known as advocates-depute. Prosecutions on indictment in the sheriff court are conducted on behalf of the Lord Advocate by the procurator-fiscal of the court.

Summary prosecutions are conducted in the sheriff and district courts by the procurator-fiscal of the appropriate court. In such cases the fiscal does not prosecute in the name of the Lord Advocate, but he remains responsible to him and acts under his general supervision and guidance.

All public prosecutors in Scotland enjoy, at least in principle, a considerable degree of discretion in the discharge of their functions as prosecutors, and a consideration of the limits of this discretion is the key to the appreciation of the role of the public prosecutor in the criminal justice system in Scotland.

(i) The Basic Principle: The Public Prosecutor as Master of the Instance

Boyle v. H.M. Advocate
1976 J.C. 32

LORD CAMERON: "... In Scotland the master of the instance in all prosecutions for the public interest is the Lord Advocate. It is for him to decide when and against whom to launch prosecution and upon what charges. It is for him to decide in which court they shall be prosecuted. It is for him to decide what pleas of guilt he will accept and it is for him to decide when to withdraw or abandon proceedings. Not only so, even when a verdict of guilt has been returned and recorded it still lies with the Lord Advocate whether to move the court to pronounce sentence and without that motion no sentence can be pronounced or imposed."

NOTES

1. Lord Cameron's summary of the public prosecutor's powers is amplified in the following materials. It should be noted in particular that his Lordship gives no indications of the controls—judicial and extra-judicial—which may be brought to bear on the exercise of prosecutorial discretion. See also *Skeen* v. *Fullarton*, 1980 S.L.T. (Notes) 46 for the position of the procurator-fiscal as master of the instance of summary cases.

2. On the substantive issue raised by Boyle's appeal, that is, the conditions governing an appeal against conviction based on a plea of guilty, see: *McKnight* v. *H.M. Advocate*, 1991 S.C.C.R. 751; *Evans, Petitioner*, 1992 S.L.T. 401; 1991 S.C.C.R. 160; *Slater* v. *H.M. Advocate*, 1987 S.C.C.R. 745. On the related question of withdrawal of a guilty plea, see *Healy* v. *H.M. Advocate*, 1990 S.C.C.R. 110 and the authorities discussed in that case.

(ii) The Decision to Prosecute

The decision to prosecute rests, in theory at least, with the public prosecutor, and it is a commonly-held view that in Scotland the role of the police in bringing offenders to justice is restricted to the investigation of offences under the control or supervision of the prosecutor (see, *e.g.* Dickens, "The Control of Prosecutions in the United Kingdom" (1973) 22 N.I.L.Q. 1 at p.21). It is also assumed, generally, that the separation of investigative and prosecution functions is a desirable objective.

Smith v. H.M. Advocate
1952 J.C. 66

The appellant was convicted of assault and murder by stabbing a man at a dance hall. At the *locus* of the crime the police found, in addition to the murder weapon, a sheath knife. They did not disclose the discovery of the sheath knife to the procurator-fiscal, with the result that it was not included on the Crown list of productions, nor was the name of the finder placed on the Crown list of witnesses. In disposing of the appeal the Lord Justice-Clerk made the following observations on the respective functions of the police and the procurator-fiscal.

LORD JUSTICE-CLERK (THOMPSON): "... When a crime is committed it is the responsibility of the Procurator fiscal to investigate it. In actual practice much of the preliminary investigation is nowadays, especially in the larger centres of population with highly organised police forces, increasingly conducted by the police under the general supervision of the Fiscal. This is due to the remarkable development in recent years of the efficiency of the criminal investigation departments of the police forces, especially on the technical side of crime detection. However, the duty of the police is simply one of investigation under the supervision of the Procurator fiscal and the results of the investigation are communicated to the Procurator fiscal as the inquiries progress. It is for the Crown Office and not for the police to decide whether the results of the investigation justify prosecution. The two functions are quite distinct. In carrying out their initial investigation the police perform a public duty. Their investigation is entirely private and no one else is entitled to take part in it. As the police have a monopoly, two results follow. First, the manner in which they are allowed to carry out their investigation is regulated by certain rules. Second, as they are the sole investigators and no more than investigators, it is their duty to put before the Procurator fiscal everything which may be relevant and material to the issue of whether the suspected party is innocent or guilty. We repeat, it is not for the police to decide what is relevant and material but to give all the information which may be relevant and material.

Clearly, in reporting the results of their investigation, the police must exercise a power of selection. It would be absurd to suggest that all their results should be submitted. But a cautious officer will remember that he is not the judge of what is relevant and material and will tend to err on the safe side. If he is in doubt, he should consult the Procurator fiscal. He will also remember that, as he and he alone has the opportunity of the initial investigation in the public interest, he must put the result of his investigations fairly before the Fiscal in order that the Crown may have a fair basis on which to decide whether or not to prosecute.

On the basis of the information provided by the police the Crown prepare the precognition and carry out any necessary further investigation to enable them to decide whether to prosecute."

NOTES

1. Section 17(2) of the Police (Scotland) Act 1967 provides that in relation to the investigation of offences the chief constable of a police force shall comply with such lawful instructions as he may receive from the appropriate prosecutor. At a more general level, section 9 of the 1975 Act provides that the Lord Advocate may issue instructions to a chief constable with regard to the reporting of offences alleged to have been committed within this area "and it shall be the duty of a chief constable to whom such instruction is issued to secure compliance therewith." Compare, in this respect, the position of the Scottish chief constable with that of his English counterpart, as outlined by Lord Denning M.R. in *R. v. Metropolitan Police Commissioner, ex p. Blackburn* [1968] 1 All E.R. 763 at p.769.

2. The formal legal position of the prosecutor must be seen in the light of practice in relation to the exercise of prosecutorial discretion. In a study conducted in the early 1980s (S. R. Moody and J. Toombs, *Prosecution in the Public Interest* (Scottish Academic Press, 1982)) the authors observed:

"When a fiscal makes a decision relating to the prosecution of crime the wide discretion which he has in law is limited and shaped by a number of factors. These include both the general framework which structures the marking task and the particular organisational style adopted by different fiscal offices. In addition, boundaries to decision-making are set by external factors inherent in the criminal process itself, by internal restrictions derived from the nature of the fiscal service and by fiscals' own perceptions of their role as prosecutors" (at p.55).

The study also noted that the exercise of prosecutorial discretion tended, in most cases, to result in prosecution. Crown Office statistics for the 10 years preceding the study indicated that in only eight per cent. of cases did the exercise of discretion result in a decision not to proceed. (A census conducted by the authors reached similar conclusions: *op. cit.*, p.57.) The authors concluded:

"The fact that fiscals are not in law required to prosecute all alleged offences does not appear to influence decision-making at the marking stage in the vast majority of cases. Scottish prosecutors seem to regard the option not to prosecute which, in theory, is always available to them, as a marginal issue with little relevance to the processing of most criminal matters. Those cases where proceedings are not brought are regarded by fiscals as inappropriate for prosecution because they are defined as legally untenable or too trivial or because of unusual characteristics associated with the alleged offence or offender. Such cases often fall into identifiable categories ... Nevertheless, it is clear that fiscals vary considerably in their exercise of the no pro [*i.e.* no proceedings] option and do not necessarily deal with similar types of offences or accused persons in the same way. For all fiscals the emphasis is on prosecution. While this may be in part a reflection of the lack of alternatives available to prosecutors it is largely a product of the particular orientation of the criminal justice process in Scotland towards court proceedings" (at p.79).

More recently, however, figures produced by the Crown Office (see the first *Annual Report of the Crown Office and Procurator Fiscal Service for 1991/92* (Edinburgh, HMSO)) suggest that the number of cases reported to the fiscal which result in criminal proceedings is decreasing, and that the number of disposals by other means is on the increase due, in part, to the increased range of alternatives to prosecution now available to the public prosecutor. The number of cases disposed of by such alternative means now exceeds the number of cases which result in prosecution.

(iii)   Renouncing the Right to Prosecute

The discretion to prosecute may be exercised either way, and the bulk of this book is concerned with the procedures which follow on a decision to prosecute. In the vast majority of cases a decision not to proceed will put an end to matters in a given case, at least so far as a public prosecution is concerned. Particular problems may arise, however, where the prosecutor wishes to recall a decision not to proceed.

1.   Thom v. H.M. Advocate
1976 J.C. 49

On May 15, 1975 the applicant appeared on petition before the sheriff at Forfar, charged with embezzlement. Having been fully committed he was liberated on bail. On July 18, 1975 the applicant's solicitor received from the procurator-fiscal at Forfar a letter, dated July 17, 1975. The letter was in the following terms:

"Since we last met I have been making a thorough inquiry into the circumstances of this case which of course required obtaining statements from witnesses in other areas and which occasioned a certain delay.

Although I am left in the end of the day with a strong suspicion that Mr Thom is responsible for the defalcations in question, I have come to the conclusion, having considered the whole matter, that the case is not good enough to put before a jury, nor for that matter do I think that I could persuade my sheriff to convict on a summary prosecution—because of the number of loose ends that appear to exist in the evidence relating to what occurred in Mr Thom's former office.

As a result, therefore, I am taking no further steps in this matter and your client, accordingly, may uplift his bail."

The procurator-fiscal then made a statement to the press, which was published in the *Dundee Courier* and *The Scotsman* to the effect that no proceedings were to be taken against Mr Thom in respect of this charge.

On November 29, 1975 an indictment was served on the applicant containing the same charge which had been libelled in the petition. At the first diet the applicant submitted a plea in bar of trial on the ground that the prosecutor had "disclaimed the process" on July 17, 1975. This plea was repelled. The applicant was subsequently found guilty of the charge. He appealed to the High Court.

THE COURT (FULL BENCH): ". . . For the applicant the main submission was that where the Lord Advocate has publicly and unequivocally relinquished or discharged his right of prosecution of a particular individual upon a particular charge he may not thereafter serve upon that individual a competent indictment libelling that charge. A motion by a prosecutor, be he a Procurator-fiscal or an Advocate-depute, to desert the diet *simpliciter* is construed as a thorough relinquishment or discharge of the prosecutor's right of prosecution, with the result that no fresh proceedings may competently be brought against the accused on the same charge. (See Hume on Crimes, vol. ii, p.277.) The letter dated 17th July 1975 by itself, and the terms of the public announcement in the Press, can be construed only as just such a public relinquishment or discharge of the right to prosecute the applicant on the charge on which he appeared on petition. In the result the indictment served on 29th November 1975 was incompetent and the conviction should be quashed.

In his reply for the Crown, the Solicitor-General conceded that where the Lord Advocate has publicly relinquished or discharged his right of prosecution in the case of a particular charge against a particular individual—or has made a public announcement which falls to be construed as such a relinquishment or discharge—no prosecution on that charge may competently follow. This concession was made, however, subject to the proviso that the public relinquishment or discharge of the right to prosecute, or the public announcement of the kind to which we have referred, must be made in open court. In any event, so ran the argument for the Crown, the letter of 17th July 1975 and the public announcement ought to be construed as no more than a statement of present intention.

From the foregoing narrative of the competing arguments it will be seen that the gap between the applicant and the Crown is a narrow one. In particular these arguments leave only two questions to be resolved. The first is whether the terms of the letter of 17th July 1975 or the terms of the Press announcement, or both, fall to be construed as an unequivocal public declaration by the

Procurator-fiscal that the right to prosecute the applicant upon the charge on which he had appeared on petition had been relinquished or discharged. If they are, then it is accepted that this will bind the Lord Advocate. The second, which will arise if the first is answered in favour of the applicant, is whether the only public declaration by or on behalf of the Lord Advocate which will render subsequent proceedings on the same charge incompetent is one made in open court.

As to the first question, we have no doubt that the letter by itself cannot be read as a mere statement of the intention of the Crown for the time being. Properly construed it constitutes an unequivocal and unqualified announcement on behalf of the Lord Advocate that no further steps are to be taken in respect of the charge on which the applicant appeared on petition, or, putting the matter in another way, that the Lord Advocate has decided not to exercise his right of prosecution in the applicant's case. Such an announcement in our opinion can, like a motion to desert *simpliciter*, only be regarded as a declaration of relinquishment or discharge of the right to prosecute upon the relevant charge. The announcement to the Press thereafter merely reinforces the construction which we are compelled to put upon the letter.

There remains the second question. The Lord Advocate is undoubtedly a prosecutor in the public interest and, in general, his right to prosecute cannot be challenged in a particular case unless it has been surrendered by his own act, or by the act of a prosecutor on his behalf. In these circumstances it is right that the act of surrender should be a public act. Is it however necessary, before the public act shall fetter the Crown in the matter of future proceedings on the same charge, that it shall have taken place in open court? This is the question presented by the proviso to the concession of the learned Solicitor-General, and in moving us to answer it in his favour he was unable to cite any authority. Since we are not constrained by authority we ask ourselves whether there is any justification in principle or good sense for restricting the forum in which, or the means by which, an unequivocal relinquishment or discharge of the right to prosecute will be effective to render subsequent proceedings on the same charge incompetent. In our opinion there is none and in the result we hold that the indictment on which the applicant went to trial was incompetent, and that the conviction must be quashed. We have only to say that the letter was written and the Press announcement was made without reference to the Crown Office. It will no doubt be for consideration by the Lord Advocate whether authority to write such a letter or to make such an announcement, without reference to the Crown Office, should in future be confided to a Procurator-fiscal.

In light of our decision upon the principal submission for the applicant it is unnecessary for us to express any opinion upon his subsidiary submission that the right to prosecute the applicant had been exercised so oppressively, to his prejudice, that the court should have intervened to stop the proceedings."

The court allowed
the appeal and
quashed the conviction.

2. H.M. Advocate v. Waddell and Another
1976 S.L.T. (Notes) 61

In August 1976 the accused were charged, *inter alia*, with the murder of a woman. By way of a preliminary plea Waddell contended that the Crown had unequivocally renounced its right to prosecute him for this crime. The alleged renunciation was contained in a number of public statements by the Crown, and in particular in a statement by the Lord Advocate in a written answer to a parliamentary question in November 1975, to the effect that prosecution of Waddell for the crime in question would not be justified.

> LORD ROBERTSON: "... Of the preliminary pleas submitted on behalf of the panel, Waddell, only two were argued videlicet: (1) that the Lord Advocate or others on his behalf by various public statements had unequivocally discharged his right to prosecute Waddell. This argument was said to rest on the authority of *Thom* v. *H.M. Advocate*, 1976 S.L.T. 232. This argument in my opinion is ill-founded. In *Thom* the panel had appeared on petition in respect of a specific charge, and having been fully committed for trial on this charge was liberated on bail. Subsequently by an unequivocal public statement the Crown intimated that this charge was not to be proceeded with. This public statement was held to be equivalent to desertion of the charge simpliciter, the consequence of which has long been held to bar as incompetent further proceedings by the Crown on the same charge. The decision in *Thom* has no bearing on the present situation where the panel was not charged and committed on these charges at the time when the statements were made. This argument therefore fails."

The court repelled
the preliminary plea.

NOTE

For the background to this case see *H.M. Advocate* v. *Waddell*, *supra*, p.23. The second preliminary plea raised by Waddell is discussed *infra*, p.622.

3. H.M. Advocate v. Stewart
1980 J.C. 84

The panel, a former member of Dundee City Council, was charged, along with two other accused, with offences against the Public Bodies Corrupt Practices Act 1889, as amended by the Prevention of Corruption Act 1916. The indictment related to a large number of incidents alleged to have taken place over a period of 16 years, between June 1959 and May 1975, while the panel and one of the other accused were city councillors in Dundee. In respect of certain of these charges the panel entered a plea in bar of trial on two grounds: (1) that the Lord Advocate had renounced his right to prosecute the accused; and (2) that because of the long delay in bringing the accused to trial, the panel had, or might have, suffered prejudice in his defence, and that it was oppressive for the Lord Advocate to pursue the prosecution.

In support of the first ground the panel referred, *inter alia*, to: (1) correspondence in 1965 between the then Lord Advocate and two Members of Parliament concerning the progress of investigations in the case; (2) a statement made at or about that time by the procurator-fiscal to the panel's solicitor that no proceedings would be taken against the panel; (3) a statement by the then chief constable of Dundee to the town clerk of Dundee that after investigations no proceedings would be taken against the panel; (4) a statement by the town clerk of Dundee to the Lord Provost that there would be no proceedings against the panel; (5) a statement by a senior C.I.D. officer that papers sent to the Crown Office after investigation were returned marked "No proceedings"; (6) the return of documents seized by the procurator-fiscal; (7) widespread press and media reports, following on the above-mentioned statements, to the effect that as a result of investigations by the Crown there would be no criminal proceedings against the panel.

LORD KINCRAIG: "I shall deal with the first accused on the first charge.

The plea in bar of trial to charge 1, under exception of 1 (d) in relation to the contracts numbered 14, 19, 20, 21 and 23 in the Schedule, is taken on two grounds: (1) that the Lord Advocate has renounced his right to prosecute the accused on that charge and his right is thus extinguished; and (2) that the long, unexplained and unjustified delay in bringing him to trial has caused, or may have caused, gross prejudice to him in his defence, due to the death of potentially helpful witnesses, the destruction of important documents and the dimming of the recollection of witnesses, which delay is contrary to normal justice and a violation of the right to a fair trial within a reasonable time.

The first charge alleges, in short, that the accused corruptly solicited and received goods, and other benefits, over a period between March 1960 and February 1965, as inducements to show favour to Crudens in the awarding of specified contracts. As regards the first ground, the accused refers to certain correspondence in 1965 and 1966 between the then Lord Advocate, Mr G. G. Stott, Q.C., and two Members of Parliament, and in particular to a letter dated 10th October 1966 from the Lord Advocate to the Member for South Angus in the following terms—and here I quote from No. 16 of the defence productions as follows: 'I promised to write you as soon as a decision was reached on the allegations concerning the housing committee of Dundee Town Council. These allegations have, as you know, been inquired into, the inquiry being directed in particular into the question of whether there was evidence to justify a charge under the Prevention of Corruption Acts against two members of the Town Council. After investigation by the Procurator-fiscal I have come to the conclusion that the evidence does not warrant criminal proceedings.' This was in response to two letters from the Member of Parliament concerned, the latter of which was dated 7th June 1966, and ended thus: 'I appreciate that enquiries into a matter of this kind are bound to be protracted. But I wonder whether you can give me any indication yet as to how soon you may be in a position to decide whether or not any action is called for by your Department.' The accused also refers in the plea to item 2, which is in the following terms: 'At or about the said time the solicitor for the first-named panel, John M. Boath, was advised by the then Procurator-fiscal of Dundee that after investigations there would be no proceedings taken against the first-named accused.' The accused also refers to other circumstances itemised as 3 to 9 in the written plea.

The Advocate-Depute has submitted that all of the matters are irrelevant to the plea in bar. He argued that three features must be present before it can be affirmed that the Lord Advocate has renounced his right to prosecute, namely, (1) the accused has previously been charged with the same offences as appear in the charges in the indictment; (2) the Lord Advocate has intimated in unequivocal terms that he has renounced his right; and (3) such announcement has been made to the public. He found on the case of *Thom* v. *H.M. Advocate*, 1976 J.C. 48 in support of his submissions.

I agree that all of the items in the plea in bar are irrelevant except items 1 and 2. These items are to the effect that by the said letter dated 10th October 1966, after investigations into the activities of the accused in respect of a possible contravention of the Prevention of Corruption Acts 1889 and 1916, the Lord Advocate informed the Member of Parliament for South Angus that there was no evidence to justify proceedings. I have already quoted item 2. It appears that said letter was written by the Lord Advocate in response to a letter from the Member of Parliament concerned in relation to possible criminal proceedings against two members of Dundee Town Council in which the Lord

Advocate was asked to inform the Members of Parliament whether he had decided to take any action in relation to these matters.

I have come to the conclusion that, properly construed, this letter is an unequivocal announcement of the decision by the Lord Advocate not to prosecute the two persons referred to in the letter in respect of charges which formed the subject matter of the investigations which had been carried out on his behalf and the results of which he had considered. In my judgment his intimation that there was no evidence to warrant proceedings must be construed in the context of the whole correspondence as a decision not to prosecute, and an abandonment of his right to do so. The letter does not name the persons the right to prosecute whom had been renounced, nor the criminal charges upon which the right to prosecute existed and had been renounced. If, however, the accused can be identified as one of the two persons referred to, and charge 1 in the indictment identified as arising out of and directly relating to matters investigated in 1966 with a view to prosecution, the letter in my judgment constitutes a renunciation of the Lord Advocate's right to prosecute the accused, and a bar to proceeding with charge 1 as restricted. I do not consider it necessary that the accused should have been charged prior to October 1966, with the same offences, if he can be thus identified. I consider therefore that the accused should be allowed to lead evidence to prove such identification.

It was submitted that the decision not to prosecute, not having been made public, cannot amount to a renunciation of the right to prosecute. Support for this proposition was said to be found in the decision of the Court in *Thom*. The passage relied on is as follows: 'The Lord Advocate is undoubtedly a Prosecutor in the public interest and, in general, his right to prosecute cannot be challenged in a particular case unless it has been surrendered by his own act or by the act of a Prosecutor on his behalf. In these circumstances it is right that the act of surrender should be a public act.' In *Thom* the Lord Advocate's decision was in fact announced to the Press and published. It was not argued in that case that it had to be published to constitute a renunciation; it was conceded by the Crown to constitute an effective renunciation if the decision did not have to be announced in open Court. So long as the Lord Advocate's decision is communicated to the accused, to his agent or to one who could be reasonably expected to communicate it to the accused, it does not seem to me to be material that it is not published. It was so communicated, according to the accused, by the Procurator-fiscal to his solicitor."

The court sustained the
first ground of the plea
in bar of trial.

4.   Lockhart v. Deighan
1985 S.C.C.R. 204

The respondent was charged on summary complaint with driving with excess alcohol in his blood, contrary to section 6(1)(*a*) of the Road Traffic Act 1972, as amended by section 25 of, and Schedule 8 to the Transport Act 1981. A plea to the competency of this charge was lodged, based on a statement issued by the Crown agent which, the respondent argued, presented a bar to prosecution in his case. The sheriff upheld the plea, and the prosecutor appealed to the High Court:

LORD JUSTICE-GENERAL: "The respondent was charged on a summary complaint in the following terms—[His Lordship narrated the charge]. At the trial diet he sought leave to challenge the competency of the complaint and after sundry procedure, including an appeal to this court, he was allowed to do so. The respondent's proposition was that the terms of a letter from the Crown Agent dated 14th July 1983, which was published in the September issue of the *Journal of the Law Society of Scotland* shortly before the date of service of the complaint, constituted an unequivocal and unqualified public announcement by the Crown that it had surrendered the right to prosecute him on the particular charge libelled. The sheriff accepted that proposition and sustained the objection to the competency of the complaint. The procurator fiscal has appealed against that decision.

The statutory provisions which are relevant for the purposes of this appeal are these—

Section 6(1)(*a*) of the Road Traffic Act 1972, as amended by section 25 of and Schedule 8 to the Transport Act 1981, provides as follows—

'6(1) If a person—
(*a*) drives or attempts to drive a motor vehicle on a road or other public place ... after consuming so much alcohol that the proportion of it in his breath, blood or urine exceeds the prescribed limit he shall be guilty of an offence.'

Sections 8(1) and 8(6) of that Act as amended are in these terms—

'8(1) In the course of an investigation whether a person has committed an offence under section 5 or section 6 of this Act a constable may, subject to the following provisions of this section and section 9 below, require him—
(a) to provide two specimens of breath for analysis by means of a device of a type approved by the Secretary of State; or
(b) to provide a specimen of blood or urine for a laboratory test.'
'8(6) Of any two specimens of breath provided by any person in pursuance of this section that with the lower proportion of alcohol in the breath shall be used and the other shall be disregarded; but if the specimen with the lower proportion of alcohol contains no more than 50 microgrammes of alcohol in 100 millilitres of breath the person who provided it may claim that it should be replaced by such a specimen as may be required under subsection (4), and if he then provides such a specimen neither specimen of breath shall be used.'

The agreed history of events which led to the institution of these proceedings against the respondent began when he was lawfully arrested after being stopped by the police while he was driving his motor-car. At the police station he was duly required under section 8(1) to provide two specimens of breath for analysis by means of an approved device. The results of that analysis were readings of 39 and 37 microgrammes of alcohol in 100 millilitres of the respondent's breath. Since the lower of these readings was below 50 microgrammes the respondent was informed of the right conferred upon him by section 8(6). He elected to exercise it and there and then provided a specimen of blood for a laboratory test. The laboratory test disclosed the presence of 100 milligrammes of alcohol in 100 millilitres of blood—a proportion which exceeded the prescribed limit of 80 milligrammes. Under reference to the terms of section 8(6) it will be understood that in these events which happened the only basis upon which the institution of proceedings against the respondent for a contravention of section 6(1)(*a*) could thereafter be considered was the result of the analysis of the respondent's blood sample which had been lawfully obtained. To complete the agreed history all that requires to be said is that on 23rd September 1983 this complaint was served upon the respondent. Before that date the letter from the Crown Agent dated

14th July 1983, which formed the foundation of the respondent's objection to the complaint, had been published in the September issue of the *Journal*.

The terms of the letter of 14th July 1983 which was written in response to a query from the Law Society have been agreed by joint minute and were as follows—

> 'The position in Scotland is that no proceedings will be instituted for contravention of section 6 of the Road Traffic Act 1972, as amended by Schedule 8 to the Transport Act 1981, on the basis of a breath/alcohol reading of less than 40 microgrammes. It will, however, be a matter for individual procurators fiscal to decide whether proceedings are appropriate in such cases for a contravention of section 5 of the Road Traffic Act 1972 (driving, etc., when under the influence of drink or drugs).'

It is accepted by the Crown that this letter when published was capable of binding the Crown and thus disentitling the Crown to prosecute any person in the particular circumstances therein defined.

In sustaining the plea to competency the sheriff appears to have considered that the procedure described in section 8(6) is a 'two-tier' procedure. His conclusion was that since the blood sample had been provided after a breath/alcohol reading of less than 40 microgrammes had been disclosed by analysis of the breath samples under section 8(1) 'the critical phrase in the letter that no proceedings will be instituted *on the basis of* . . . a reading of less than 40 microgrammes applies to such a case as this in which the analysis of blood is derived from the original breath test and so cannot be other than based on it'.

Although counsel for the respondent sought valiantly to support the approach taken by the sheriff and the result at which he arrived, and argued that in any event there would be some unfairness in allowing the Crown to prosecute the respondent who had exercised his right to supply a blood sample before the Crown Agent's letter was written and published, and in ignorance of a policy shortly to be introduced under which no proceedings can be taken for a contravention of section 6(1)(a) on the basis of a breath/alcohol reading of less than 40 microgrammes, we have no hesitation in allowing this appeal, and giving effect to the submissions of the learned advocate-depute.

The single question in this case was and is, under reference to *Thom* v. *H.M. Advocate*, 1976 J.C. 48, whether the letter of 14th July 1983 falls to be construed as an unequivocal and unqualified announcement on behalf of the Lord Advocate that, as from the date of its publication, he relinquished or discharged his right to prosecute the respondent upon the particular charge libelled in this complaint. In our opinion the answer to that question is not in doubt and is in the negative. As has already been seen, an offence under section 6(1)(a) can be committed in three distinct sets of circumstances. A person who drives after consuming alcohol is guilty of an offence if (i) the proportion of it in his breath exceeds the prescribed limit, or (ii) the proportion of it in his blood exceeds the prescribed limit, or (iii) the proportion of it in his urine exceeds the prescribed limit. There are accordingly three alternative bases upon which proceedings for a contravention of section 6(1)(a) may be instituted. In the case of the respondent the only basis on which the institution of proceedings against him for such a contravention after 2nd July 1983 could be considered was the finding, upon a laboratory test of a blood sample lawfully obtained from him, that the amount of alcohol in his blood exceeded the prescribed limit. The charge in the complaint libels the commission of the statutory offence for that reason. It is not a charge that he drove a motor vehicle when the proportion of alcohol in his breath exceeded the prescribed limit. In our opinion the letter of 14th July 1983, properly construed, merely disabled the Crown from instituting proceedings against the respondent for a contravention of section 6(1)(a) upon the basis of a breath/alcohol reading of less than 40 microgrammes. There may be good reasons why the Crown has decided not to prosecute where the lower of the two readings of the proportion of alcohol in breath samples, analysed by an approved device, is not more than four microgrammes above the prescribed limit. The degree of accuracy to be expected on analysis of breath by such a device may well be one of them but there is no material before us to suggest that there are any sound reasons which would justify the Crown in relinquishing the right to prosecute a motorist where the proportion of alcohol in his blood is shown to have exceeded the prescribed limit, even by as little as one milligramme. It is well known that the right to prosecute upon such a basis has been regularly exercised. In any event, leaving aside all speculation as to the reasons which may lie behind the policy disclosed by the letter, it falls to be construed strictly according to its terms and in our opinion its terms bind the Crown only in the matter of proceedings for a contravention of section 6(1)(a) alleged to have been committed because the proportion of alcohol in the accused's breath exceeded the prescribed limit by fewer than five microgrammes. Where proceedings are instituted upon the basis of the allegation that the contravention of section 6(1)(a) consisted in driving when the proportion of alcohol in the accused's blood, established by the analysis of a blood sample lawfully obtained, exceeded the prescribed limit, it is of no moment that the blood sample may have been lawfully obtained following the results of analyses of breath which ceased to have any evidential effect in, or to be capable of founding, proceedings for contravention of section 6(1)(a) as soon as the suspect exercised the right conferred upon him by section 8(6). Such proceedings cannot conceivably be described as proceedings on the basis of a breath/alcohol reading, and these proceedings which have been instituted against the respondent are not proceedings 'instituted . . . on the basis of a breath/alcohol reading of less than 40 microgrammes' within the meaning of the Crown Agent's letter, even if it is accepted that a breath/alcohol reading of 'less than 40 microgrammes' provided the occasion for the lawful supply of a blood sample by the respondent. The sole basis of the proceedings against the respondent in this complaint is the proportion of alcohol in his blood at the relevant time and it is that proportion which is libelled as the contravention charged. The respondent may well feel that it was unfortunate that he was given the section 8(6) option before the date of publication of the Crown Agent's letter and, indeed, before the charge libelled can be described as unfair or oppressive.

In the whole matter we shall recall the interlocutor of the sheriff, repel the objection to the competency of the complaint, and remit to the sheriff with a direction to proceed as accords."

Appeal allowed.

NOTES

1. A number of important and difficult questions arise from *Thom*, *Waddell* and *Stewart*. There is, first of all, the question of the method of renunciation. *Stewart* rejects the necessity for a public renunciation, provided that it is communicated to the accused, his agent or to someone who could reasonably be expected to communicate it to the accused. What of a private communication to a third party who might not be expected to communicate it to the accused? Suppose, for example that A, a solicitor, believes that his client, B, has been wrongly convicted of an offence. C has several times publicly confessed to the crime. A writes to the Lord Advocate asking if he will prosecute C. In a private reply to A the Lord

Advocate states that he will not prosecute C. Is the Lord Advocate barred from subsequently proceeding against C?

There is also the question of the time of renunciation. At what stage in the proceedings will renunciation present an effective bar to future proceedings? In *Stewart* it was held that the Crown could find itself barred from proceeding against an accused by statements made even before that accused was charged—though it would seem to be difficult to reconcile this with the view expressed by Lord Robertson in *Waddell* where his Lordship distinguished *Waddell* from *Thom* on the ground that Waddell had not even been charged at the time when the Lord Advocate made his alleged renunciation. *Stewart* adopts a very strict line against the Crown, and it is certainly undesirable that the individual should be subjected to the strain of a prosecution which he thought had never really got off the ground. But is it necessarily in the public interest that the prosecutor should find himself irrevocably barred from proceeding against a suspect as a result of a statement made at a very early stage in the proceedings? The moral for prosecutors, no doubt, is "keep mum."

Finally, there is the question of the effect of renunciation. It is clear that an unequivocal renunciation presents a bar to future proceedings at the instance of the Crown. (As to the effect of a Crown renunciation on the rights of other prosecutors see *H.* v. *Sweeney, infra*, p.71.) Again the question arises as to whether the rule that renunciation is an absolute bar is justifiable or necessary in the public interest. Suppose, for example, that a suspect has so well covered his tracks (even to the extent of incapacitating a principal witness) that there seems to be no reasonable prospect of a successful prosecution being brought. A decision not to proceed is communicated to the suspect. At a later date circumstances change so as to permit proceedings to be taken. What interest is served by an absolute bar to those proceedings? It is doubtful if the public interest is served by such a bar. In some cases there would undoubtedly be a risk of serious prejudice to the accused in allowing a prosecution in such circumstances. It is submitted, however, that the appropriate way to deal with this problem is by application of the developing doctrine that the court will not permit a prosecution to proceed if it is considered to be oppressive (see *infra*, p.351) rather than by an absolute bar to proceedings.

2. The situation revealed in *Lockhart* v. *Deighan* is clearly distinguishable from that revealed in *Thom* and the cases which follow that decision. The rule in *Thom* relates to *ad hominem* decisions, taken entirely with regard to the facts of each case, and is based on some apparent principle of fairness to a suspect who has been informed, actually or constructively, that he or she will not be prosecuted. The Crown Agent's statement in *Lockhart* v. *Deighan*, in contrast, was not related to the facts of any particular case and was not based on any notion of fairness to any particular accused. This was not a case in which the prosecutor, having said that he would not prosecute an individual, attempted to go back on his word. Given that the principle in *Thom* can have undesirable consequences, it seems unfortunate that it has been extended in this way.

3. *Lockhart* v. *Deighan* raises an issue of constitutional importance. In effect, it holds that the Lord Advocate may unilaterally, and without reference to Parliament, amend an Act of Parliament, at least to the extent of restricting (rather than extending) the ambit of the criminal law. It is not clear what are the limits of this power, and whether it applies only to

statutory offences or also to the common law. Suppose, for example, that the Lord Advocate were to state that for the future no criminal proceedings would be brought in cases of theft where the value of the property was less than £5. Would such a statement effectively "de-criminalise" such thefts? Prior to the decriminalisation of certain homosexual acts by section 80 of the Criminal Justice (Scotland) Act 1980, it was the practice of the Lord Advocate to pursue a policy of non-prosecution in cases which would not be subject to the criminal law in England. It now appears that these were more than statements of policy, but effective bars to prosecution. It is not clear what, if any, judicial control exists in relation to this aspect of the Lord Advocate's powers.

4. What is needed to remove such a bar? Presumably, a public announcement that the policy has been changed. But this raises yet more problems. Perhaps the courts would not tolerate a retrospective change of policy, since this would arguably be oppressive.

5. In *Mowbray* v. *Crowe*, 1993 S.C.C.R. 730 the Crown were held to have acted oppressively in prosecuting a woman who had been charged by the police, but who had subsequently attended at the offices of the procurator-fiscal in response to his request to "discuss the matter"; the discussion was in fact an interview without any legal safeguards as a result of which the woman revealed her defence to the charge.

Warnings and fiscal fines

An alternative method of renouncing the right to prosecute is for the fiscal to give the alleged offender a warning either in writing, or orally. The giving of a warning is regarded by the Crown as a bar to the Crown (but presumably not a private prosecutor) raising criminal proceedings in respect of that case, as the following Crown Office direction makes clear.

C/O Circular No. 1685: Warnings to Accused Persons

"This subject has been much considered both in Parliament and elsewhere. In the light of that consideration the Lord Advocate considers that a warning is a valuable option available to the Crown and can in appropriate cases be more effective in promoting the aims of the law in a humane and merciful manner than raising proceedings in court.

In a case where the procurator fiscal considers that a warning is the appropriate method of dealing with the alleged offender, *i.e.* where there is in his opinion sufficient evidence that the person concerned has committed a crime known to the law of Scotland but the case is not so trivial as to merit no action, the procurator fiscal will require to give the warning either in writing or in exceptional cases personally. A warning should be an alternative to prosecution and should only be issued in cases in which if the procurator fiscal were not disposed to warn he would prosecute.

In considering whether or not to administer a warning procurators fiscal should have regard to the following:

1. In no circumstances should a warning be administered unless the procurator fiscal has in his possession sufficient evidence which would in his opinion justify him in taking proceedings in court.

2. A warning may be administered whether or not the accused person is alleged to have admitted or denied the offence or made no statement to the police.

3.   If the procurator fiscal gives a warning he will be regarded as having decided not to take court proceedings in respect of that case. Accordingly no warning will be administered on the understanding that if it is not accepted, the procurator fiscal will take proceedings in court.

4.   Any warnings should avoid giving the impression that the procurator fiscal is adjudicating on the guilt or innocence of the person concerned. Although the framing of warning letters is a matter for the discretion of procurators fiscal, the Lord Advocate suggests that it might be said that a report has been submitted to the procurator fiscal alleging a certain offence and that the procurator fiscal considers that there is evidence sufficient in his opinion to justify him in taking proceedings in court against the person concerned, that the procurator fiscal has, however, decided in this case not to take proceedings, but that in the circumstances the procurator fiscal thinks it right to say that should a similar report be submitted against the person in future, the procurator fiscal may well take proceedings in court.

If the procurator fiscal considers that the circumstances require him to deliver a personal warning he will arrange for the person concerned to attend at his office either by writing to him or by such special arrangements as may appear appropriate in the circumstances. For the reason given in 3 above, the invitation to attend at the procurator fiscal's office should be couched in neutral terms and should not in any way amount to a warning. If the person to whom the procurator fiscal desires to deliver a personal warning fails to attend at the procurator fiscal's office after having been given a sufficient opportunity to do so, the procurator fiscal should normally take court proceedings.

Similar considerations will apply to offences reported by public agencies other than the police such as the Investigation Branch of the Department of Health and Social Security and the consumer protection departments of local authorities.

Only the procurator fiscal or the person substituting for him may sign a warning letter. Where the accused's solicitor is known there is no objection to the warning letter being sent to him. Alternatively, the letter may be sent to the accused and a copy sent to the solicitor. A standard style of letter should not be used since each case must be reviewed in the light of its own circumstances although the style in each case may be similar.

It is not possible exhaustively to list the categories of offences which may be dealt with by a warning but examples are: speeding offences, careless driving where no injury has occurred, minor breaches of the peace, shoplifting offences and offences against section 12 of the Children and Young Persons (Scotland) Act 1937 where a normally caring parent has, due to some exceptional circumstances, become the subject of a report. Much will depend on the previous convictions of the accused and what is known of his character.

Once the police have reported a case to the procurator fiscal they are not subject to any directions from him to warn the person concerned in place of criminal proceedings.

Procurators fiscal should maintain a local register of persons whom they have warned. The procurator fiscal must ensure its security in order that its contents do not become known outside his office. Where a second report against a person is received containing evidence of another similar offence sufficient to justify court proceedings, the procurator fiscal should consider the full circumstances of the first report in respect of which the warning was given, including any representations made by or on behalf of the accused in response to the warning, before he decides upon his course of action in respect of the second report."

Conditional offer of fixed penalty

Another alternative to prosecution is the making by the procurator-fiscal of an offer of a fixed penalty. This procedure was introduced by section 56 of the Criminal Justice (Scotland) Act 1987 and relates to offences which can competently be tried in the district court. Briefly, where the fiscal receives a report of a relevant offence, he may notify the offender of the existence of any fixed penalty, the amount thereof and the amount of any instalments thereof payable, together with an offer that if the offender makes payment of the fixed penalty or the first instalment thereof within 28 days, any liability to conviction of the offence shall be discharged. Section 56 contains detailed provisions relating to recovery of the penalty and the effect of non-acceptance, which is generally that proceedings may be commenced in court for the offence.

(iv)   Determining the Mode of Trial

Dunbar v. Johnston
(1904) 7 F. (J.) 40

With the consent of the procurator-fiscal, Dunbar brought a summary complaint against Johnston in the sheriff court at Edinburgh, alleging a contravention of section 2 of the Merchandise Marks Act 1887. Section 2(6) of that Act contained the following proviso:

> "Provided that a person charged with an offence under this section before a Court of Summary Jurisdiction shall on appearing before the Court, and before the charge is gone into, be informed of his right to be tried on indictment, and if he requires be so tried accordingly."

The sheriff informed Johnston of his apparent rights under section 2(6), and the latter claimed the right to be tried by a jury. Dunbar then sought to bring a private prosecution on indictment (with the concurrence of the Lord Advocate) in the sheriff court. The sheriff held the indictment to be incompetent, and Dunbar appealed to the High Court by bill of advocation. The High Court held that it was not competent to bring a private prosecution by indictment in the sheriff court. The following observations were made on the alleged right to jury trial:

> LORD ADAM: "... We may be of the opinion that there is no right in an offender brought up on a summary charge in Scotland to require trial on an indictment. The statute assumes that a right exists, which may exist in England, but certainly does not in Scotland. We were informed that in England there is such a right to demand trial on indictment, when the trial would proceed before a jury, and not summarily before a Judge. I can see, therefore, how the section operates in England, but by no means am I to be held as being of the opinion that there is such a right in Scotland."

> LORD McLAREN: "... It may be said that the Merchandise Marks Act assumes

a right on the part of an accused person to be tried by indictment, and no doubt an offender can be tried on indictment in Scotland if the Crown thinks that such procedure is appropriate. But I should not wish it to be assumed as entering into my opinion that any such right exists in Scotland as a right to be tried on indictment.

A magistrate may try an offender summarily, or he may commit him for trial, but if he commits him it rests with the Lord Advocate or his depute to decide whether he shall be tried on indictment in the High Court or before the Sheriff and a jury. The question is not a question of form, at least it is a case where form may become substance, and I know of no right on the part of an accused person in Scotland to insist on being tried by indictment.

I do not think that in this view any violence is done to the language of the Merchandise Marks Act, for I have no difficulty in holding that it applies only to cases where the right to be tried on indictment exists, and I cannot help thinking that all this difficulty has arisen out of an attempt to apply to Scotland a provision which was meant to apply only to prosecutions in England."

LORD KINNEAR: "I agree that this indictment was incompetent in the Sheriff court, and as this is enough for the decision of the case, I do not desire to say anything on the other very interesting questions which were argued before us. But I desire, like your Lordships, that it should be understood that we are not deciding that persons prosecuted under the Merchandise Marks Act have a right to be tried on indictment if they demand it. The question is not before us for decision, but since it has been discussed at the bar, I may say that, as at present advised, it seems to me at least arguable that the proviso founded on in subsection (6) of section 2 of the Act does not confer any right, but assumes that there is or may be an existing right to be tried on indictment if the accused so requires. The magistrate is to inform the accused of his right to be tried on indictment. The section applies to both England and Scotland, and enacts that an offender may be prosecuted 'in manner provided by the Summary Jurisdiction Acts.' Now, there are Summary Jurisdiction Acts in England and also in Scotland. Trial in the manner provided by the Summary Jurisdiction Acts means trial in the manner provided by the Summary Jurisdiction Acts in force in either country, according as the trial takes place in the one or the other. Reading the clause therefore upon the ordinary principle of construction, *applicando singula singulis*, it appears to me that trials in England and Scotland are to be conducted according to the procedure prescribed by the Acts in force in each of these countries respectively. Now, it appears that there is a clause in the English Summary Jurisdiction Act which confers a right to trial on indictment if it is demanded. But it is admitted that no such right is given by any Summary Procedure Act in Scotland. All that the Merchandise Marks Act says is that the magistrate is to inform the accused of his right. The record in this case states that the sheriff informed the accused of his right to be tried on indictment, but we are not told what specific information the sheriff gave him on the subject. But whatever be the true meaning of section 2(6) of the Merchandise Marks Act, it does not affect the question whether this indictment was competent in the Sheriff Court, and I agree with your Lordships that it was not, and that on that ground alone the decision must be upheld."

The court refused
the bill.

NOTE

For a discussion of private prosecution, see *infra*, pp.56 to 77. Advocation is discussed *infra*, at pp.562 to 569.

The discretion of the prosecutor in selecting the mode of trial, though wide, is not absolute. It is limited in the first place by the rules which determine the jurisdiction of the High Court, the sheriff court and the district court. It will be seen from Chap. 3, for example, that the High Court has exclusive jurisdiction in respect of the "pleas of the Crown" and certain statutory offences. Technically this is a reservation of forum rather than a mode of trial (since trial on indictment is of course competent for many crimes in the sheriff court), but since the High Court has no summary trial jurisdiction in effect a right to jury trial is conferred in such cases.

Secondly, there are some suggestions that the High Court has the power to control this aspect of the prosecutor's discretion, at least *ex post facto*. In *Clark and Bendall* v. *Stuart* (1886) 1 White 191, Lord McLaren put forward the following proposition:

> "There is no rigorous classification of crimes which the Sheriff may try summarily, and crimes which he may not try without a Jury, and it is not necessary that there should be one, because under our system of public prosecutions, the discretion of determining whether the crimes reported to them should or should not be tried summarily is vested, in the first instance, in the Crown officers. Should a case arise of a crime manifestly unsuited for summary trial being tried by the Sheriff without a Jury, there can be no doubt that the Court of Justiciary has power to give redress by quashing the conviction."

Finally, the prosecutor's discretion may be limited by any specific or general statutory provision determining the mode of trial. See, *e.g.* section 457A of the 1975 Act (inserted by Criminal Justice Act 1982, s. 55).

For a discussion of the factors affecting the prosecutor's choice of court, see Moody and Tombs, *op. cit.*, Chap. IV.

(v)   The Prosecutor's Discretion to Accept or Reject Pleas

Strathern v. Sloan
1937 J.C. 76

The respondent was charged in the sheriff court along with another man with theft of a motor car. The respondent pleaded guilty. The other man pleaded not guilty. The procurator-fiscal refused to accept the plea of guilty and moved the court to record a plea of not guilty. The sheriff refused. The procurator-fiscal appealed to the High Court by bill of advocation.

> LORD JUSTICE-CLERK (AITCHISON): "... It is well settled that, in criminal causes triable under solemn procedure, the Crown is not bound to accept a plea of guilty, but may insist upon the indictment proceeding to trial. This was affirmed in the case of *H.M. Advocate* v. *Peter and Smith* [(1840) 2 Swinton 492]
> ...
> It has never been doubted that the rule of *Peter's* case applies equally to criminal causes triable upon indictment in the Sheriff Court. The question now to be decided for the first time is whether the rule applies to causes that are triable upon summary complaint. The case in which the question was most nearly raised is *Kirkwood* v. *Coalburn District Co-operative Society* [1930 J.C. 38], which was a summary prosecution at the instance of H.M. Inspector of Factories in which alternative charges were libelled in the complaint. The

panel tendered a plea of guilty to the minor of the alternative charges. The prosecutor objected to the plea being recorded, but the Sheriff recorded it. It was held on appeal that the prosecutor was entitled to proceed to trial with a view to proving the major charge, upon the ground that a prosecutor is never bound to accept a plea to the minor of two alternative charges so as to be compelled to give up the major alternative. In the course of his judgment the Lord Justice-General (Clyde) stated the wider proposition in these terms (at p.41): 'I do not think a prosecutor is ever bound to accept a plea, whether the charge be alternative or not, but is always entitled to insist on leading evidence before the jury and obtaining a verdict if he can—Macdonald on Criminal Law, (4th ed.), p.484, and authorities there collected.' I respectfully agree with this wider proposition, and, as the case Lord Clyde was dealing with arose upon a summary complaint, the observation must be taken as applying to summary complaints in the same way as to charges upon indictment.

This right of the public prosecutor may at first sight appear to be arbitrary, but consideration will point to many good grounds why the right should exist. In serious crime evidence may be necessary to bring out the full enormity of the crime, or perhaps to show mitigating circumstances; or again there may be concern as to whether the proper crime has been libelled, as, for example, where murder is charged, but where there is doubt whether the crime of the panel amounts to more than culpable homicide. Thus, the practice of our Courts in Scotland, and in England also, although not invariably in England, has been for the public prosecutor to refuse to accept a plea of guilty to a murder charge. Again, there may be a question, which can only be fully explored in evidence, as to the mental state of the panel. Or two or more persons may be charged, and the prosecutor may be unable, without injury, to assign the proper degree of guilt to each of the panels. There may be other reasons deemed sufficient by the public prosecutor for declining a plea of guilty. It is not necessary that he should assign any reason, the right being one which the law commits to his own judgment and discretion, and which he can exercise whether the proceedings are summary or on indictment.

That being the general law, I desire to add one or two qualifications. (1) The right to refuse a plea of guilty is a right which is vested in the Lord Advocate, or his Deputes, or the Procurator-fiscal, who derives his authority from the Lord Advocate. How far the right extends to other prosecutors, public or private, is a more difficult question, and it may be difficult to differentiate, at any rate as between public prosecutors. (2) Where a plea of guilty is tendered by the panel, and is not accepted by the prosecutor, the formal entry on the record should not be an entry of not guilty, which is contrary to the fact, but should be to the effect that the panel has tendered a plea of guilty, and that the prosecutor has intimated that he declines to accept the plea. The practice of entering a plea of not guilty, contrary to an express and unqualified plea of guilty, is, in my opinion, wrong and should not be continued. In the case of summary complaints the entry of the plea on the record is expressly directed by section 41 of the Summary Jurisdiction Act, 1908. (3) Wherever a plea of guilty is tendered and not accepted by the prosecutor, the plea of guilty must under no circumstances be used against the panel, and, where the trial is on indictment, must not be disclosed to the jury. In all cases, therefore, under solemn procedure, where a plea of guilty is declined at the first diet, the panel should not be called upon to plead at the second diet, unless in the interval the prosecutor has made up his mind to accept the plea if again tendered. If the panel, notwithstanding his plea of guilty, chooses to enter the witness-box, he must have entire freedom to give his evidence, contrary to his plea of guilty which the prosecutor has declined to accept. This does not involve any encouragement of false testimony, as it is not unfamiliar that a panel may offer a plea of guilty, not because he is guilty of the offence charged, but because a public trial might disclose facts more hurtful to his own reputation, or the reputation of others, than the recording of a plea on his own confession. (4) If the prosecutor elects to proceed to trial, and in the course of the trial decides to accept a plea of guilty, he cannot do so unless the panel of new pleads guilty to the offence charged. Whether the panel is willing to do so can always be ascertained by communication with his counsel or agent, and until the panel's mind is known the question should not be put to him in open Court. There may be cases in which, the evidence having disclosed facts prejudicial to the panel, the panel may desire that the trial should proceed notwithstanding his recorded plea, either on the chance of his obtaining an acquittal, or for the purpose of bringing out circumstances that may go to alleviate the offence, if proved against him.

It is unnecessary to add that the right of the public prosecutor to decline a plea of guilty is a right which should be sparingly exercised, and, in my judgment, it should not be exercised where it may result in prejudice to another panel charged under the same indictment or complaint. the governing consideration in every case should be the public interest."

The court passed
the bill.

NOTE

The procedure for the taking and recording of pleas is now largely governed by sections 124 and 336 *et seq.* of the 1975 Act.

Strictly speaking, a plea tendered by an accused person is tendered not to the Crown, but to the court: "The question … of calling to plead, and of replying to the call, lies between the Court and the panel. It is not a tender addressed to the Crown" (*per* Lord Mackay, *Strathern* v. *Sloan* at p.82). This has no practical significance, however, other than that the court is obliged to record accurately the accused's plea. In particular, the court has no power to dictate the Crown's reaction to any plea. If, notwithstanding a plea of guilty, the Crown elects to lead evidence against the accused, the court cannot prevent this. Equally, if the Crown elects to accept a plea of guilty to a lesser charge the court cannot insist on the original charge being tried.

The latter point is of particular importance when considering the practice of "plea negotiation." The practice exists in Scotland as in other systems. The important question is how to regulate it in the interests both of the public and the accused. A system which vests in the prosecutor an absolute discretion to accept or reject a plea tendered by the accused puts the practice beyond any external controls. Is it really satisfactory that such issues should be beyond the scrutiny even of the court?

(vi)   Control Over the Imposition of Sentence

Noon v. H.M. Advocate
1960 J.C. 52

The applicant was tried on indictment in the sheriff court on a charge of theft. At the end of the trial the jury returned a verdict of guilty. The prosecutor then informed the sheriff of the appellant's age, employment, family circumstances, and also tendered to the court a schedule of previous convictions. These were admitted by the accused, and his solicitor presented a plea in mitigation of sentence. The sheriff then passed sentence. No formal motion for sentence had been made by the prosecutor. Noon applied to the High Court for leave to appeal.

LORD JUSTICE-GENERAL (CLYDE): "The present application is made to this Court upon the ground that, since the prosecutor omitted formally to move for sentence, no sentence could competently be pronounced, and we should consequently quash the sentence leaving the conviction standing.

This objection is a purely procedural one, devoid of any true merits, for, in the circumstances, the sentence pronounced was amply justified. But that, of course, does not absolve us from considering carefully the procedural objection taken and so carefully argued to us by counsel.

It has always been an essential feature of our criminal procedure in Scotland that the prosecutor should remain in charge of the prosecution right up to the time when sentence is actually pronounced. Hence it has always been part of our procedure that, even after the guilt of an accused has been established, the prosecutor should have an opportunity, if he thinks fit, to withdraw the case and allow the accused to go free—see Macdonald on Criminal Law, (5th ed.) p.348. This, no doubt, dates from the time when, owing to the depth of partisan feelings, juries and even sometimes Judges, might be perverse or unfair, and the right to withdraw a case was thus preserved, to enable an impartial prosecutor to secure that justice was done. But today these partisan feelings in criminal matters at least have faded and perversity on the part of Judges and juries is much more rare. Yet the procedural rule that the prosecutor must still have the opportunity of withdrawing the case, even after a verdict of guilty has been pronounced, is still preserved in the form of his moving for sentence.

If, in the present case, the Sheriff-substitute had proceeded to sentence the applicant without affording an opportunity to the prosecutor to withdraw the case, I should have regarded the sentence as incompetent. But that is not the situation. An opportunity was afforded for this step to be taken. Indeed, the circumstances of the present case are even stronger than that, for the prosecutor proceeded to lay before the Court the previous convictions applicable to the appellant. In terms of section 39(1)(e) of the Criminal Justice (Scotland) Act, 1949, 'Previous convictions cannot be laid before the Court until the prosecutor moves for sentence.' In the present case, therefore, the prosecutor clearly did not take advantage of his inherent right to withdraw the prosecution after the verdict was pronounced, but, on the contrary, by referring to the previous convictions, he made it clear beyond doubt that he was doing the very reverse.

It is true that he did not formally move for sentence by using those precise words. It would have been much better had he done so and in future, to avoid any possibility of confusion, this course should always be explicitly taken. But, in my opinion, his failure to use these actual words is not fatal, and, provided he is given an opportunity to withdraw the case, and by his conduct he shows clearly that the Court is being asked to pronounce sentence, the law is satisfied. It is nowhere laid down that he must actually use the words: 'I move for sentence' in order to make the sentence competent—see Hume on Crime, vol. ii, p.471, Alison, Criminal Law, vol. ii, p.653. In the present case, by dealing with the previous convictions, the prosecutor was in effect asking the Court to deal with the sentence and giving up his right to withdraw the case. In a very real sense, therefore, he was inviting the Court to proceed to sentence the applicant, since it would have been illegal for him to have referred to the previous convictions upon any other basis.

We were referred to the case of *H.M. Advocate* v. *Fraser* [(1852) 1 Irvine 1] in support of the applicant's contention. But I do not regard that case as of assistance in the present connexion. In the case, the prosecutor had moved for sentence in terms, and the issue in the case turned upon the failure of the

Circuit Court to continue the case to a specified day and the competency of that Court's order continuing the cause in general terms. This issue does not arise in the present case. I am, therefore, of opinion that the present application fails. I am confirmed in this conclusion by the fact that the Sheriff-substitute obviously regarded the prosecutor as waiving his right to withdraw the case once the jury had reached their conclusion, and, so far from objecting to that course and to the reference to the previous convictions, the applicant's agent admitted them, and addressed the Court in mitigation of sentence. There was, therefore, no dubiety in the minds of parties, or of the Sheriff-substitute, that the Court was being invited to sentence the applicant for the crime of which the jury had found him guilty. I move your Lordships that we refuse the application."

LORD SORN: "In solemn procedure, the prosecutor is in control of the instance and may abandon the prosecution at any stage. Even after the verdict has been returned, he may decline to move for sentence, or may refrain from doing so. In such a situation, the Court cannot, against the will of the prosecutor, proceed to pronounce a sentence. In other words, under our practice, the Judge in solemn procedure only pronounces sentence upon the invitation of the prosecutor. That invitation should be given in formal terms, and a prosecutor should never omit to make a formal motion. But the invitation, in my opinion, does not absolutely require to be made expressly and in formal terms. It is enough if there is an invitation by clear implication.

Turning to the situation here, it seems to me that when, after the verdict, the prosecutor tabled the previous convictions recorded against the accused, and stated certain facts to the Sheriff, which were germane to the question of sentence, he gave an unequivocal invitation to the Court to proceed to the final step. I therefore agree that the application fails."

The court refused
the application.

NOTE

A particular danger in not moving for sentence was highlighted by the case of *Paterson* v. *H.M. Advocate*, 1974 J.C. 35. In that case the appellant, having been found guilty on a charge of murder, and one of attempted murder, appealed against his conviction on the charge of murder. The appeal was successful, and the conviction and sentence quashed. There remained the conviction for attempted murder, but the Crown, in accordance with the normal practice at that time, had not moved for sentence on the lesser charge. The appellant thus escaped without any penalty being imposed. Needless to say, Crown Office policy was appropriately amended.

It should be noted that the public prosecutor has no direct control over the nature of the sentence imposed. However, his control over the choice of court and form of procedure gives him a measure of indirect control in that the selection of the court will in most cases fix the sentencing parameters.

(vii) Controlling the Exercise of the Prosecutor's Discretion

Notwithstanding the extensive nature of the public prosecutor's discretion (*supra*, p.33), it is clear that in the exercise of that discretion the prosecutor is subject to a variety of controls, both judicial and extra-judicial. Thus, a decision not to prosecute in a particular case may be challenged by the victim applying to the High Court for permission to bring a private prosecution (*infra*, pp.56–77). Conversely, a decision to bring a prosecution may be open to challenge, for example, on the ground that the prosecutor has previously renounced the right to prosecute (*supra*, p.34).

In addition, the courts have an inherent power to disallow proceedings in the case of oppressive conduct by the prosecutor. In such cases it may be significant, but not crucial, that the allegedly oppressive nature of the prosecution stems from conduct within the control of the prosecutor such as delay or improper actings (see, *e.g. Mowbray* v. *Crowe*, 1993 S.C.C.R. 730). On the other hand, oppression may arise from matters outwith the control of the prosecutor, as, for example, in the case of prejudicial pre-trial publicity (see, for example, *Stuurman* v. *H.M. Advocate*, 1980 S.L.T. (Notes) 95, *infra*, p.359).

Although the prosecutor's power to initiate proceedings is not unfettered, and is subject to the power of the court to prevent oppression, it is clear that the courts are most reluctant to exercise this power to interfere with the discretion of the prosecutor. There must be a material risk of real prejudice to the accused: *H.M. Advocate* v. *O'Neill*, 1992 S.C.C.R. 130.

For a further discussion of "oppression" see *infra*, Chap. 10 and the cases of *Herron* v. *A, B, C and D*, 1977 S.L.T. (Sh.Ct.) 24; *Skeen* v. *Fullarton*, 1980 S.L.T. (Notes) 46; *Normand* v. *McQuillan*, 1987 S.C.C.R. 440 and the quite extraordinary case of *Boyle, Petitioner*, 1992 S.C.C.R. 824, 939 and 949, *infra*, p.615. The question of bringing civil proceedings against the public prosecutor for wrongful prosecution has also been raised, with little success.

Hester v. MacDonald
1961 S.C. 370

Hester brought an action of damages against (1) the procurator-fiscal for the Lower Ward of Lanarkshire, (2) the Lord Advocate, and (3) a procurator-fiscal depute for Glasgow. The action arose out of the respondent's prosecution and conviction on indictment on a charge of theft. It appeared that due to an administrative error the respondent had never had the indictment served upon him by the Crown and that, despite protests to this effect during the trial, no attempt was made to verify this fact, and the procurator-fiscal conducting the prosecution carried on to the point of conviction and sentence. The action was dismissed *quoad* the first and second defenders, but not the third. On appeal by the third defender:

> LORD PRESIDENT (CLYDE): "... The first issue raised is the competency of this action of damages by a person tried on indictment before a Sheriff and jury, who sues the Depute Procurator-fiscal who conducted the trial. This question raises a matter of quite fundamental importance in our unique Scottish system relating to indictable offences.
>
> To appreciate its significance, it is necessary, first of all, to consider the position of the Lord Advocate in this system. Under our constitution, the Lord Advocate has a universal and exclusive title to prosecute on indictment (Macdonald, Criminal Law, p.212). As Baron Hume says (Crimes, vol. ii, p.155): 'By custom, the process by indictment is the exclusive privilege of the Lord Advocate, or public prosecutor, who alone is possessed of that notorious

and public character, which entitles him summarily, and of his own authority, to state himself to the Court as accuser, and call on the Judges for trial of his charge, without any previous licence obtained.' In our system, the Lord Advocate alone possesses the function, in indictable offences, of deciding whether he will prosecute or whether he will withdraw a prosecution, and there is no appeal to any Court against his decision on these matters. No Court or magistrate can compel or direct or recommend to him what he should do. These are matters exclusively for him and exclusively within his province—Alison's Criminal Law, vol. ii, p.87. His responsibilities and privileges are quite unique, and they depend for their continuance on the confidence of the public in the utter impartiality with which he has always administered his onerous duties regarding crime. From time immemorial it has, therefore, been recognised, as Baron Hume puts it—Crimes, vol. ii, p.135—that 'a constitutional trust is reposed in that high officer, selected by His Majesty from among the most eminent at the Bar; and it will not be supposed of him, that he can be actuated by unworthy motives in commencing a prosecution, or fall into such irregularities or blunders in conducting his process, as ought properly to make him liable in ... amends.' As Alison says (vol. ii, p.93) he is absolutely exempt from penalties and expenses.

It is, therefore, an essential element in the very structure of our criminal administration in Scotland that the Lord Advocate is protected by an absolute privilege in respect of matters in connexion with proceedings brought before a Scottish Criminal Court by way of indictment. (Compare Renton and Brown, Criminal Procedure, (3rd ed.) p.450.) Never in our history has a Lord Advocate been sued for damages in connexion with such proceedings. On the contrary, our Courts have consistently affirmed the existence of such immunity on his part. For instance, in *Henderson* v. *Robertson* [(1853) 15 D.292], Lord Justice-Clerk Hope said (at p.295): 'It is impossible to disguise the great importance of this question, one of the most important that can be raised in reference to the office of public prosecutor. The public prosecutor has by law a great and most important protection. As against the Lord Advocate, I do not think that a case of liability to damages could be even stated.' (Compare Lord Young in *M'Murchy* v. *Campbell* [(1887) 14 R. 725], at p.728.)

It may be that in other departments of his duties and responsibilities a civil action for damages may lie against him, but in connexion with his administration of crime he is in this special position. He is subject, of course, in regard to criminal matters, to the constitutional safeguards of Parliamentary action, but there is no remedy against him by way of action at law.

The position of the Procurator-fiscal is not precisely the same. In the old days he could be liable in damages, if he acted maliciously and without probable cause (Alison's Criminal Law, vol. ii, p.93). But the position of the Procurator-fiscal has altered with the coming into operation of the Criminal Procedure (Scotland) Act, 1887. Many of the decisions on the rights and liabilities of Procurators-fiscal pronounced prior to that Act do not apply thereafter. For the Act resulted in a much closer and more substantial control by the Lord Advocate over the Procurator-fiscal so far as cases tried by jury are concerned. Prior to the Act, prosecution by indictment was confined to the High Court of Justiciary, where the control of the prosecution rested in the Lord Advocate, or was under his authority. The Sheriff's Procurator-fiscal had a certain measure of independence in connexion with the prosecution of crimes in the Sheriff Court, and criminal letters could be taken in his own name there for the purpose of prosecutions before the Sheriff. Under section 2 of the 1887 Act, however, the existing system was materially altered, and thereafter, all prosecutions for the public interest in the Sheriff Court where the Sheriff was sitting with a jury 'shall proceed on indictment in name of Her Majesty's Advocate ... and shall be signed by Her Majesty's Advocate or one of his deputes, or by a procurator fiscal, and the words "By authority of Her

Majesty's Advocate" shall be prefixed to the signature of such procurator fiscal.' By section 1, 'procurator fiscal' includes a 'depute procurator fiscal.'

This change involved a radical alteration. It left summary prosecutions to be conducted by the Procurator-fiscal on his own authority and in his own name. But it required prosecutions for crimes in the Sheriff Court appropriate for trial by jury to be conducted, not on the authority of the Procurator-fiscal, but on the instructions, and under the authority, and in name, of the Lord Advocate, just like indictments in the High Court. It, therefore, assimilated criminal trials by jury in the Sheriff Court on indictment to trials in the High Court of Justiciary. The Lord Advocate was in complete control in both cases.

The criminal trial with which the present case is concerned was a Sheriff and jury trial on indictment. It was approved and authorised by the Lord Advocate, who instructed its prosecution. The Lord Advocate was directly responsible for its conduct, and the immunity from a claim of damages which he enjoyed was, in my opinion, therefore enjoyed also by the Procurator-fiscal and the Depute, who were acting on his authority, and carrying out his instructions, in this criminal trial, as his direct representatives.

The contrast between the situation in a Sheriff and jury case such as that involved in the present instance and a summary case in the Sheriff Court is worth noting. In the latter, the prosecution is at the instance of the Procurator-fiscal (see Sheriff Courts and Legal Officers (Scotland) Act, 1927, sec. 12), and Parliament has expressly recognised the liability of a Procurator-fiscal in such cases to damages, provided, *inter alia*, the person suing for damages shall prove that such Procurator-fiscal did something in the course of the proceedings which was malicious and without probable cause. (Summary Jurisdiction (Scotland) Act, 1954, sec. 75(1)(c)). A similar provision is incorporated in the earlier Summary Procedure (Scotland) Act, 1864, and the Summary Jurisdiction (Scotland) Act, 1908. It has always been a feature of such summary proceedings in Scotland. But Parliament has never made any such provision in regard to solemn procedure by way of indictment where the Procurator-fiscal is not acting on his own authority, but expressly on the authority and instructions and in name of the Lord Advocate. The reason is that, in connexion with proceedings by indictment, our law does not recognise any right to damages against the Lord Advocate or against those acting on his instructions. Moreover, it would be astonishing indeed, if a Procurator-fiscal Depute, when conducting a summary case, should only be liable in damages if malice is proved, but (as the pursuer here claims) that he should be liable in damages, even without proof of malice in a prosecution on indictment where he is acting, not on his own, but on the express instructions of the Lord Advocate.

The result is, therefore, in my opinion, that the pursuer's claim against the third defender in this case is incompetent, and must fail; for, in the proceedings out of which the claim arises, the third defender was acting as the hand of the Lord Advocate. In condescendence 2 the pursuer avers that 'in conducting the prosecution the third-named defender was authorised and instructed by the first-named defender who was responsible for the third-named defender's actions.' This is true, and is fatal to the competency of the pursuer's claim.

It was argued to us that, although the action against the Lord Advocate was incompetent, owing to his immunity from civil claims under the constitution of his office, this did not apply to the third-named defender. But this argument appears to me to be unstateable. If the Lord Advocate, as the responsible criminal prosecutor, is immune, it necessarily must follow that his immunity covers those, such as the third-named defender, who are acting on the instructions and under the responsibility of the Procurator-fiscal who in turn was the hand of the Lord Advocate. It was argued that this result involves a great extension of the immunity from civil claims enjoyed by the Lord Advocate. But it relates to that class of prosecution (indictments in the Sheriff

Court) where Parliament has seen fit to put the Lord Advocate expressly in control. It is a tribute to the fairness and efficiency with which the Procurator fiscal service has performed its work in this class of prosecution that, since 1887, there has never been any suggestion that a Procurator-fiscal is liable in damages for actings in such prosecutions, and it would be a misfortune for our criminal administration if any doubt were to be cast on the immunity which he has hitherto always enjoyed in this regard. The standard of conduct in this service has in the eyes of the public well merited this protection, and the assertion of this protection involves no departure from our well settled practice, but, on the contrary, an affirmation and recognition of it. The Procurator-fiscal's immunity from the consequences of his actings is, of course, not absolute. He may be removed from his office by the Lord Advocate on a report by the Lord President of the Court of Session and the Lord Justice-Clerk (see Sheriff Courts and Legal Officers (Scotland) Act, 1927, section 1). In these circumstances, in my opinion, it is not open to the pursuer to claim damages in this case against the third-named defender. This is enough to dispose of this present case and would entitle us to hold the action incompetent."

> The court allowed the appeal
> and dismissed the action.

NOTE

The court also held that even if such an action was competent, it would have failed on the merits.

The liability of a prosecutor in summary proceedings, where he is not acting for or on behalf of the Lord Advocate is governed by section 456 of the 1975 Act. In order to succeed in an action against such a prosecutor the pursuer must have suffered imprisonment as a result of proceedings, sentence, etc., which has subsequently been quashed, and the person suing must aver and prove malice and want of probable cause on the part of the prosecutor; see also *Graham* v. *Strathern*, 1924 S.C. 699.

Article 13 of the European Convention on Human Rights provides that everyone whose rights and freedoms as set forth in the Convention are violated "shall have an effective remedy before a national authority, notwithstanding that the violation has been committed by persons acting in an official capacity." Does the absolute privilege accorded to the Lord Advocate and his deputies in *Hester* v. *MacDonald* violate article 13?

C.   PRIVATE PROSECUTION

Due to the dominant position of the public prosecutor in the initiation and conduct of criminal proceedings, private prosecution is very much the exception to the rule. In saying this, however, it is useful to distinguish solemn and summary proceedings. While private prosecution is extremely rare in solemn proceedings, summary private prosecutions are rather more frequent, at least where the title to prosecute is conferred by statute. The following materials discuss private prosecution on indictment.

1. J. & P. Coats Ltd. v. Brown
1909 S.C. (J.) 29

By a contract dated January 11, 1908 the respondent, a coal merchant, agreed to supply the complainers with a quantity of coal described as "Bent Splint Coal." To the respondent's knowledge, only a small proportion of the coal delivered to the complainers conformed to this description. He nevertheless requested, and obtained, payment as if delivery had been made as per the contract. The Lord Advocate refused to prosecute the respondent or to grant his concurrence to a private prosecution at the instance of the complainers. The latter presented to the High Court a bill for criminal letters to prosecute the respondent for fraud.

LORD JUSTICE-CLERK (MACDONALD): "The prosecution of crime in Scotland has for so long a period been practically in the hands of the King's Advocate, and of subordinate public prosecutors acting under his control, and this procedure has been attended with such satisfactory results to the administration of the criminal law, that private prosecution for serious crimes is practically unknown, the public being well satisfied that as a general rule the interests of justice are well guarded by the Lord Advocate's department. The question now arises for the first time for very many years whether a private prosecution shall be allowed to proceed, seeing that the Lord Advocate declines to take up the case or to give his concurrence to a prosecution at the instance of the party who alleges that a criminal wrong has been done to his injury.

A citizen desiring to institute a prosecution at common law for crime requires by law to be in the position—(1) that he has applied to the Lord Advocate to obtain his concurrence to the prosecution, and (2) that the crime alleged be a wrong towards himself. By these rules the accused citizen is safeguarded from malicious or vindictive prosecution by private individuals, the Lord Advocate, or those who represent the public interest under him in the inferior Courts, being responsible for the proper exercise of their office in any question relating to the granting of concurrence to a private prosecutor's action.

But there is not vested in the public prosecutor an absolute right of veto. It is the right of the citizen to complain to the High Court of Justiciary against a refusal by the public prosecutor to grant his concurrence to a private prosecutor where he has declined to take up the prosecution on behalf of the Crown. The Lord Advocate frankly conceded this at the discussion. He must, if called on, shew cause for his declinature, and the Court can consider the question whether the withholding of the concurrence in the circumstances may involve a wrong to the citizen complaining, and a failure of public justice. For the citizen desiring to prosecute is seeking to invoke the law not for reparation to himself, but *ad vindictam publicam*, and this is clearly expressed in the criminal letters granted to him. If he desires personal reparation he must seek that in a civil Court. It is only for the purpose of preventing the right to prosecute being used for vindictive or malicious ends that he must ask for the Lord Advocate's concurrence.

It is in that state of the law that in the present case the complainer presents to this Court a complaint and form of charge by criminal letters, and asks that a private prosecution shall be sanctioned by the Court, either without the concurrence of the Lord Advocate, or by the Court ordaining the Lord Advocate to grant his concurrence. At the debate the Lord Advocate said that if in the end either of these courses commended itself to the Court, he would act as the Court might order.

It seems to me not to be a question of serious importance which of these courses is to be adopted, if the ultimate decision of this case should be that a prosecution is to be allowed. In either case the prosecution would proceed in exactly the same manner. My suggestion to your Lordships would be that the more practical and least embarrassing course would be that the Court should authorise the private party to proceed, rather than that a prosecutor, unwilling in the exercise of his discretion to grant concurrence, should be directed to do so, for it seems to me to be not a good mode of correcting an unsatisfactory exercise of a vested discretion that an official should be forced into the position of saying in words that he concurs, when his non-concurrence is overruled as not being in the circumstances right. Therefore, if your Lordships should be of opinion that this case forms an exception to the rule and requires exceptional treatment, I would suggest that it be rather made an exception by allowing the prosecution without the usual condition of concurrence by the public prosecutor, than that the Lord Advocate should by an order of the Court be made to appear to concur in a prosecution, as to which he has formed an opinion, to which he adheres, that his concurrence ought not to be given … [His Lordship considered the charge and concluded that it was relevant.]

No doubt it may be said that there may be many cases in which such a thing is done where the criminality would be small and perhaps such that the public prosecutor might in his discretion not think it necessary that the act done should be followed by a criminal prosecution. Further, it might be said that explanations might be given which would give a complexion to the case that might justify holding back from public prosecution. But in this case I do not think that there is ground for giving weight to such considerations. The complainers have laid before the Court documents referred to in the proposed criminal letters which, if proved, would tend to shew that the accused endeavoured to support his fraud by the use of a certificate obtained from a colliery official to the effect that the coal shipped on board in fulfilment of the contract was 'Bent Splint Coal,' and he, knowing the certificate to be false, caused it to be delivered as a true certificate to the complainers. If this were to be proved at a trial, it could not but have a very strong bearing on the question what answer should be made to the charge stated in the criminal letters, unless the defence were able to overcome its weight by evidence which would alter the balance. As regards the magnitude of the fraud, if committed, there can be no doubt, seeing that it related to 500 tons of coal. And as regards possible explanations, these are properly matters of defence, and the Court has nothing before it bearing upon that matter. The Lord Advocate did not in any way suggest that there were such explanations before him as would make the charge untenable if proved. If there are such, they are quite open as matter of defence at the trial. But if it is not thought proper or necessary by the public prosecutor to put such forward as a ground for refusing his concurrence, the Court must deal with the case before it as if there were none, in considering whether a private prosecutor should be permitted to have criminal letters issued.

The Lord Advocate told the Court that if the complainers would proceed to endeavour to obtain reparation by a civil action, he would consider the proceedings in such a case, and if he saw ground for a criminal prosecution in them, would reconsider his determination. I confess I was not able to follow the line of thought indicated by such a statement. If the Lord Advocate has already had the case fully investigated in his department, one would expect that he would know now whether it was permissible to take criminal proceedings. If he has not had such an investigation made, then it is difficult to see how he can be held to be in a proper position to consider whether he should give his concurrence to a prosecution or not. But it seems to me that such a suggestion can hardly be one to influence the Court in the matter. It is quite contrary to the order of procedure in criminal law administration that the whole circumstances of a case should first be thrashed out in a civil Court, with possibly a succession of proceedings of review, ending, it may be, in the House of Lords after a litigation extending over years, and that then the question of criminal prosecution should be finally determined. The case of perjury in civil proceedings was suggested as analogous, but there is plainly no analogy. In such a case the crime does not consist in the past acts which form the subject of the litigation, but in false swearing in the conduct of the case. There is no crime committed before the civil suit, the crime is only committed when perjured evidence is given in that suit. Here it is the very subject-matter of the alleged crime which forms the essence of the civil claim itself. I do not think your Lordships can give any weight to such a suggestion as that it would be proper to postpone consideration of a question of criminal prosecution until civil proceedings had been concluded. Criminal prosecution should follow the crime with all due dispatch, and our law expressly forbids delay in prosecution unless the accused party is allowed to remain at large, which in many cases might be most injurious to the course of justice. And in addition to all this, civil proceedings might be seriously hampered by a defender being able to decline to give evidence which might incriminate him, if he was in the position of knowing that a future criminal prosecution was hanging over his head. Both sides might be hampered by such a course being taken.

My opinion is that in the circumstances as disclosed to us at this stage the private prosecutor has shewn grounds why he should not be shut out from his rights as a citizen to have an alleged crime investigated now, in regard to a matter in which he alleges relevantly that he has been wronged."

LORD McLAREN: "I understand that your Lordships propose to dispense with the Lord Advocate's concurrence to a private prosecution at the instance of the complainers. I take a different view as to the scope and exercise of the powers of the Court, and as the question is one of public importance, I feel bound to state my reasons for this difference of opinion.

The right of private prosecution in Scotland is very rarely exercised. The Lord Advocate in his address to the Court said that he did not think there had been a case during the last century. This is not strictly correct, because there has been at least one case, the trial of Colonel Charteris in 1823, to which I shall afterwards refer. Yet it is the case that the investigation of crime under the Lord Advocate's department has been so efficiently performed, and the confidence which the public has uniformly extended to the administrators of this department of state has been such, that the right of private prosecution has ceased to be of any practical importance in our criminal law.

It is one of the normal conditions of the right of private prosecution that the bill for criminal letters has to be subscribed by the Lord Advocate in token of his concurrence. This concurrence does not commit the Lord Advocate to an opinion on the case; it only means that the matter of the bill is fit for consideration by a Court of criminal jurisdiction. It is therefore, to say the least, extremely unlikely that this concurrence would be refused to a prosecution that had any substance in it.

It is plain enough that an unrestricted right of private prosecution would not be tolerated in any country. That any spiteful or irrational person should have the power to subject his adversary to the indignity of being placed at the bar of a criminal Court, without preliminary inquiry or check of any kind, is a notion too absurd to be seriously entertained.

In England, where we know it is usual to bind over the injured party to prosecute, the necessary check is provided by the preliminary inquiry before a magistrate, who, of course, will not commit the accused person for trial unless the depositions disclose a *prima facie* case of crime or misdemeanour. There is also the further protection of the grand jury, who may dismiss the bill ('ignore,' I think, is the legal word), and thus put a stop to an unconscientious or unsubstantial accusation. I say nothing as to the Attorney-General's right to stay a prosecution by his fiat, because I understand it is rarely, if ever, exercised.

In Scotland we have neither public inquiry before a magistrate nor consideration by a grand jury as a necessary preliminary to a private prosecution, but the object is attained in a different way, by the requirement of the Lord Advocate's concurrence, which will not be given without an inquiry through his department into the facts of the case.

It is, of course, recognised that the Lord Advocate has no arbitrary power, but must exercise the functions of his department impartially and in accordance with sound discretion. The control of the Court in this matter is considered by Hume in a well-known passage in the chapter on 'Prosecutors and their title,' and the author opens the subject by propounding the question, Whether the Lord Advocate, 'by refusing his concourse, may at his pleasure suppress the private instance, and protect the transgressor from the just consequences of his crime?'

To the question as thus put, there can be but one answer, and the author states his opinion that in such a case the Court may either direct the Lord Advocate to give his concurrence, or may dispense with his concurrence, and authorise the issue of criminal letters.

No case was cited by the complainers' counsel, and I know of no case, in which the Court has granted the prayer of a bill for criminal letters without the concurrence of His Majesty's Advocate. But the absence of direct authority does not in any way militate against the power of the Court, which is undoubted. It only proves that this is an extraordinary remedy for an extraordinary and unprecedented occurrence, viz., the undue and arbitrary exercise by an officer of the Crown of a power entrusted to him for public purposes. That I may not be supposed to suggest a doubt as to the powers of the Court, I note that the power has been very distinctly recognised in two modern cases, in one of which I was present as a Judge, but in neither case was the party complainer successful in challenging the Lord Advocate's decision to refuse his concurrence to the desired prosecution.

I will make one other general observation. Hume is a very high authority, but personally I should be disposed to go further than the dictum of Hume. If the Lord Advocate should state as his reason for not giving his concurrence to a bill that the statements contained in the bill did not in his judgment disclose a crime according to the law of Scotland, and if we were of opinion that the bill did disclose a *prima facie* relevant charge of crime, I think we might sustain the bill, leaving the relevancy of the charge to be further considered at the trial. I say this, because I think that in the case of a pure question of law the Supreme Court of criminal jurisdiction may act on its own judgment, and is not bound by the Lord Advocate's opinion. In such a case I do not doubt that the Lord Advocate would give his concurrence, if desired by the Court.

But in the present case the Lord Advocate has withheld his concurrence, because after investigation he came to be of opinion, on the facts of the case, that there was not reasonable ground for a criminal prosecution. In his address to the Court the Lord Advocate said—'The line between the domain of civil and criminal law was sometimes difficult to draw, but in this case the information laid before him disclosed a question which, in his judgment, lay well within the region of the civil law, and plainly outside the region of the criminal law.' On a second consideration of the case, his Lordship continued, 'he satisfied himself that he had information to enable him to form a judgment' and he came without any hesitation to think that there was no reason for altering the judgment at which he had formerly arrived, and that there were no sufficient grounds here for a criminal prosecution.' It is necessary for the purposes of the case that I should say that I am entirely satisfied that the Lord Advocate has made a sufficient inquiry into the facts of the case, and that I have no reason to doubt that the decision neither to prosecute nor to grant concurrence was the result of an attentive and impartial examination into the facts of the case.

In such circumstances I am confronted with the question, how am I to form an independent opinion on the facts as to whether there are or are not grounds for a criminal prosecution? It is one thing to say that we may give redress against an arbitrary refusal of the Lord Advocate's concurrence, or a refusal on legal grounds which are disclosed to us; and it is quite a different proposition that we are to review the Lord Advocate's decision that the facts do not warrant a prosecution. If it were intended by the constitution of the country that this Court should undertake such a review, we should either have the power of calling for the Crown precognitions, or of employing an agent to institute an independent inquiry and to report to us. Nothing of the kind has ever been done, and your Lordships are not proposing to make such an inquiry.

It was argued for the complainers that the charge of fraud depended on documentary evidence, which he said discloses a *prima facie* case.

In my opinion the documents prove nothing. I do not doubt that the defender made use of a colliery certificate that was untrue in fact, but we have only the complainers' statement in the bill for the all-important points that the document was uttered knowing it to be false, and with intent to defraud. Now, I may be altogether wrong, but I must frankly say that on the question whether there is a *prima facie* case for prosecution, I prefer the dispassionate opinion of the Lord Advocate who has studied the case, to the unsupported statements of Messrs Coats, who no doubt honestly believe that they have been defrauded, but who are not the best judges in their own case.

Nor am I much moved by the argument that if the respondent is innocent he will have an opportunity of proving his innocence at the trial of the case. This answer, as I think, entirely fails, because it is an answer that may be made in every case in which the Lord Advocate's decision to concur or not to concur is challenged. I have already observed that I do not find any reported case in which the Court has dispensed with the Lord Advocate's concurrence. The nearest approach to a precedent is in the two cases cited by Hume (*Crimes*, ii, 118) in the paragraph referred to. In the first case, the date of which is 1633, the Court directed the Lord Advocate to give his concurrence to an action of reduction-improbation; but this, as Hume points out, is not a genuine criminal process, and unless a caveat is lodged, I believe the practice has been to grant the concurrence as a matter of course. The second case, which occurred two centuries later, is that of Colonel Charteris, in 1823, where the Lord Advocate withdrew his concurrence at the trial, and the case was allowed to proceed. I may respectfully say that this decision seems to be sound in principle, because the concurrence is only required to the bill for criminal letters, and after the criminal letters are issued the case is out of the Lord Advocate's hands. I may add, with the utmost deference to the opinions of other members of the Court, that personally I should deprecate very strongly the notion that this Court is to be a Court of review of the work of the Lord Advocate's department, a task for which, by its constitution and means of informing itself, the Court is alike unfitted; and my opinion is that the bill should be refused."

LORD JUSTICE-GENERAL (DUNEDIN): "... But the chief reason which has influenced my brother Lord M'Laren in his dissent from the majority of your Lordships has been his extreme repugnance of the idea that this Court should sit as a Court of review of the discretion of the Lord Advocate. I do not think there is any difference of opinion upon this bench upon this matter. It is no light matter to interfere with the discretion of the Lord Advocate, and I can conceive very few cases in which we would so interfere.

But we are bound, none the less, to direct our minds to the particular case that has been brought before us, and I agree with the Lord Justice-Clerk in thinking that the actual written documents that are here brought before us go very far to establish the case. Of course I do not wish to say too much upon that matter, because I am not going to prejudice the defence which may be finally brought forward. But when my brother Lord M'Laren went on to say that he thought that the whole matter would turn upon whether it was shewn that the party charged here really knew or did not know that this certificate was false, I am compelled to observe, first of all, that the complainer says so most distinctly, and that, if the Lord Advocate in the exercise of his discretion chooses to maintain a more than usual reticence, I am afraid he must take the consequences of that reticence.

It seems to me nothing would have been easier than for the Lord Advocate to have said—if he could say it—that upon a consideration of the whole circumstances, he had come to the conclusion that the party charged here was under the belief that the certificate was true. If the Lord Advocate had said he was satisfied of that, or even if he had gone so far as this, that he had not had brought before him any evidence which would lead to the conclusion that the party charged knew that the certificate was false, I imagine—at least speaking for myself—that I would not have interfered with the discretion of the Lord Advocate. The Lord Advocate says none of those things, and he leaves us—and that is a matter for him to judge—completely in the dark as to what the form of defence is to be. Under these circumstances the disagreeable necessity—as I think I must call it—is laid upon us of affirming that this is a case where a subject has seemingly been wronged and no real reason has been laid before us why a prosecution should not be allowed."

[Lords Kinnear, Low and Pearson concurred with the Lord Justice-Clerk]

The court passed
the bill.

NOTE

The respondent was subsequently convicted and admonished (High Court, May 26, 1909).

Lord McLaren was the only member of the court to dissent. His dissent did not concern the complainer's title to prosecute, or the competency of the procedure adopted by the complainer, both of which appear to have been more or less taken for granted by the court. The disagreement related to the extent to which the court was entitled to act as a court of review of the Lord Advocate's discretion. In its narrowest construction the majority opinion seems to have been that if the Lord Advocate failed to provide reasons for his refusal to prosecute, and the complainer established a prima facie case, then the court was entitled to authorise a prosecution. A rather broader view is suggested by the Lord Justice-Clerk whose opinion appears to have been that the court could "consider the question whether the withholding of the concurrence in the circumstances may involve a wrong to the citizen complaining, and a failure of public justice."

Lord McLaren, however, took the view that the granting of criminal letters by the court was an "extraordinary remedy" only available in the event of "the undue and arbitrary exercise by an officer of the Crown of a power entrusted to him for public purposes."

2. McBain v. Crichton
1961 J.C. 26

LORD JUSTICE-GENERAL (CLYDE): "This bill for criminal letters has been presented to the High Court of Justiciary by Mr A. G. M'Bain, chartered accountant, Glasgow, asking for criminal letters to enable him to initiate a prosecution against a certain bookseller in Glasgow for exposing for sale and selling in his place of business a book called *Lady Chatterley's Lover*, by D. H. Lawrence, which he alleges is lewd, impure, gross and obscene, and contains passages contrived and intended to corrupt the morals of the lieges, and particularly of the youth of both sexes.

Since the Lord Advocate has refused his concurrence to the proposed prosecution, this Court ordered intimation of the bill to be made to the Lord Advocate, as is the custom, and appointed a day for the hearing of the bill. The Lord Advocate has appeared in person at this hearing and has informed the Court that he has fully investigated the matter more than once and, in the exercise of that wide discretion which is invested in the Lord Advocate, he has come to the conclusion that a prosecution would not be justified in connexion with this matter. He has therefore decided not to prosecute at his own instance and not to give his concurrence to the private prosecution which the present complainer desires to raise.

The Lord Advocate is quite entitled to take up this position. In this country he is the recognised prosecutor in the public interest. It is for him, in the exercise of his responsible office, to decide whether he will prosecute in the public interest and at the public expense, and under our constitutional practice this decision is a matter for him, and for him alone. No one can compel him to give his reasons, nor order him to concur in a private prosecution. The basic principle of our system of criminal administration in Scotland is to submit the question of whether there is to be a public prosecution to the impartial and skilled investigation of the Lord Advocate and his department, and the decision whether or not to prosecute is exclusively within his discretion. This system has operated in Scotland for centuries, and—see Alison on Criminal Law, vol. ii, p.88—the result has completely proved the justice of these principles, for such has become the public confidence in the decision of the Lord Advocate and his deputes on the grounds of prosecution, that private prosecutions have almost gone into disuse. It is utterly inconsistent with such a system that the Courts should examine, as it was suggested it would be proper or competent for us to do, the reasons which have affected the Lord Advocate in deciding how to exercise his discretion, and it would be still more absurd for this Court to proceed to review their soundness. Any *dicta* indicating that such a course is open to any Court are, in my view, quite unsound.

But the lack of the Lord Advocate's concurrence is not necessarily fatal to a private prosecution. Although we cannot review the exercise of the Lord Advocate's discretion nor his reasons for exercising it in the way he did, this Court can permit, and on rare occasions has permitted, a private prosecutor to proceed without the Lord Advocate's concurrence. But to entitle a private prosecutor to do so, he must be able to show some special personal interest in the matter which, notwithstanding the Lord Advocate's decision in the public interest, satisfies us that a private prosecution in respect of this special personal interest may proceed. Hume on Crimes, vol. ii, at p.119, puts it thus: 'To support his instance the individual complainer must be able therefore to show some substantial and peculiar interest in the issue of the trial; an interest arising out of some injury which he, beyond others, has suffered on the occasion libelled, and at which he is entitled to feel more than the ordinary indignation, with which his fellow citizens will regard it. It is not therefore sufficient, that he has some feeble and remote concern in the issue, or one of a general nature, in common with a whole neighbourhood, or with all of the same order or class of society.' A similar principle is laid down in Alison on Criminal Law, vol. ii, p.100, where the learned author expresses the matter thus:—'To support his instance or title to carry on such a process (that is to say, a private prosecution) the private party must be able to show some substantial and peculiar interest in the issue of the trial, an interest arising from what he, beyond all others, has suffered on the occasion libelled, and at which he is entitled to feel more than ordinary indignation.' (Compare also Macdonald on Criminal Law, (5th ed.) p.212; Renton and Brown, Criminal Procedure, (3rd ed.) p.27 and p.197.) The same principle is referred to in the opinion of Lord Justice-Clerk Macdonald (with whose opinion Lord Kinnear, Lord Low and Lord Pearson concurred), in the case of *J. & P. Coats, Limited* v. *Brown* [*supra*] at pp.33 and 34. This was a case where a private prosecution for fraud was allowed to be instituted without the concurrence of the Lord Advocate. In that case, however, the special personal interest was demonstrable since the complainers were themselves the persons alleged to have been defrauded in the sale of coal to them by a coal merchant. They were, therefore, able to show that, in the words of Alison and of Hume, which I have already quoted, they, 'beyond all others,' had 'suffered on the occasion libelled.'

But, in the present case, the wrong complained of, if it is a wrong (and on that matter, of course, it would be quite improper for us at this stage to express an opinion one way or the other), the wrong, if it exists, is of a quite general and public nature, committed against a whole neighbourhood or perhaps against the whole country, and, in its very nature, devoid of that personal and peculiar interest without which no private prosecution ever has been sustained in Scotland. In the terms of the complainer's bill itself the wrong is not a wrong alleged to have been done to a particular individual, but a wrong to the lieges in general, or, at any rate, to the younger members of the public in general. The wrong alleged is therefore a purely public one.

It was contended before us that there was an element of private interest as well, because of the official position which the complainer held as vice-president of the Glasgow Union of Boys' Clubs. But that interest, even if it had been averred in the bill, is just as much a public interest as the interest which is averred in the bill. It does not partake of that essential quality without which the prosecution could not proceed at the instance of a private party, because it does not show that the complainer personally and beyond all others has suffered owing to the wrong libelled. At the highest it would only invest him with an interest as protector of the morals of a class of persons in the community—namely the younger members of it. This is in its very nature a public and not a private or personal interest.

This distinction is no mere technicality. It involves a clear and definite principle embedded in our law, stated in the institutional writers and referred to again and again in the decisions of this Court. Mr Gow has said all that could be said in favour of this prosecution proceeding at the complainer's instance without the Lord Advocate's concurrence, but I am clearly satisfied that no interest sufficient for that purpose has been made out. In these circumstances, there is no case which would justify this Court in granting the present application.

My motion to your Lordships is that we should refuse it."

The court refused
the application.

NOTE

From the point of view of title to prosecute the complainer's case was doomed from the outset. A private prosecutor must satisfy the court that he has suffered a personal wrong through the commission of the alleged offence. On any view of this test the complainer could not establish such an interest—notwithstanding his interest in the moral welfare of the youth of Glasgow. Would it have made any difference if, for example, the complainer had found his own children reading the work in question?

The court's statements on the power to review the Lord Advocate's discretion are not supported by the other authorities. The statement that, "No one can compel him to give his reasons, nor order him to concur in a private prosecution" conflicts, for example, with what was said in *J. & P. Coats Ltd.* v. *Brown*. As regards the first proposition, the majority view was that the Lord Advocate must, if called on, show cause for his declinature. As regards the second, the court in *J. & P. Coats Ltd.* v. *Brown* was of the opinion that the court should not order the Lord Advocate to concur, not because this was incompetent, but because it was inexpedient.

3. Trapp v. M; Trapp v. Y
1971 S.L.T. (Notes) 30

The complainer was dismissed from his post as headmaster of an education authority school. A public inquiry was held into the reasons for his dismissal. The complainer alleged that the respondents, who were representatives of the education authority, committed perjury at the inquiry. A succession of Lord Advocates had refused to prosecute the respondents or to concur in a private prosecution. The complainer presented two bills for criminal letters to the High Court.

> LORD JUSTICE-GENERAL (CLYDE): "In the present case the crime which the complainer seeks to establish against the two respondents is the crime of perjury in the course of the evidence which each gave at the inquiry before referred to. In Hume, *Crime*, Vol. I, crimes are analysed as falling into two categories, firstly offences to the injury of individuals whether in person, fame or property, and secondly (see Vol. I, p.366) 'such offences as immediately concern the public as they are hostile to the course of public justice.' Of these the most important is the crime of perjury (see Hume, Vol. I, p.366). The present two cases are therefore concerned with allegations of a crime which in its nature essentially concerns the public as a whole, and the proper administration of even handed justice in the public interest. These considerations make it all the more difficult for the complainer to qualify a right to prosecute in the case of the crime of perjury. The mere fact that in his two Bills he claims damages against each of the respondents for the wrongs which he alleges were done to him does not advance the matter. Every crime involves in one way or another injury or damage to someone, and a criminal prosecution is not an appropriate process in which to claim damages. As the Lord Justice-Clerk said in *J. & P. Coats Ltd.* v. *Brown*, 1909 S.C.(J.) 29, at p.34 (1909, 1 S.L.T. 432), 'if he desires personal reparation he must seek that in a civil court.'
>
> Apart from these more general considerations, a scrutiny of the particular allegations in each of the Bills merely confirms how unwarranted the granting of the prayer in either would be. Where the concurrence of the Lord Advocate has been refused the relevancy of the charge made by the complainer must be considered and determined before this court could grant the prayer of a Bill for criminal letters." [His Lordship went on to hold that the averments in the Bills could not form a relevant basis for a prosecution for perjury. Reference was also made to *McBain* v. *C*, 1961 J.C. 25, 1961 S.L.T. 209.]

The court refused
the bill.

NOTE

Mr Trapp's contribution to the jurisprudence of private prosecution has been outstanding. He presented a third bill alleging perjury by a Mr G at the public inquiry. It too was unsuccessful, though the court which rejected the bill based its refusal to an unwillingness to interfere with the Lord Advocate's discretion, rather than the ground that perjury was a "public" and not a private wrong: *Trapp* v. *G*, 1972 S.L.T. (Notes) 46.

4. Meehan v. Inglis and Others
1974 S.L.T. (Notes) 61

The complainer was convicted of murder in October 1969. The respondents were police officers who had been Crown witnesses at his trial. The complainer alleged that they had committed perjury. Since the Lord Advocate refused to prosecute them, or to concur in a private prosecution at the complainer's instance, a bill was presented for criminal letters.

THE COURT: "Much of the complainer's argument was directed towards establishing that the Lord Advocate was not the *complete* master in deciding whether a prosecution for perjury should be initiated. He sought to persuade the court that in the case of *Trapp*, which is only reported in 1971 S.L.T. (Notes) 30, Lord Justice-General Clyde had implied that in a case of perjury (which was the allegation in *Trapp* (supra)) the Lord Advocate was the complete master of the decision to prosecute or not. This argument concentrated on one passage in Lord Clyde's judgment, where he was quoting from the case of *McBain* v. *C.*, 1961 J.C. 25, at p.29 (1961 S.L.T. 209), in relation to the exclusive discretion of the Lord Advocate in deciding whether or not there should be a public prosecution. When the judgment is read as a whole (and the court had the benefit of the full judgment in that case and not just the abbreviated version in 1971 S.L.T. (Notes)) it is quite clear that Lord Clyde recognised that the right to decide whether a prosecution should be sanctioned was not a matter for the absolute and sole decision of the Lord Advocate. What he did say was that, for the reasons he gave, private prosecutions in Scotland have steadily grown rarer as time has gone by, and in the last 50 years they have fallen into virtual disuse. The court has the ultimate say on whether a private prosecution should be granted, even when the Lord Advocate has refused his concurrence, but as Lord Clyde pointed out in *Trapp* it would require some very special circumstances indeed to induce the court to make an exception to what has now almost become a settled practice. What Lord Clyde said in *Trapp* was in effect a reiteration of the judicial view of the role of the Lord Advocate as public prosecutor and the stringent conditions which have to be satisfied before a private prosecution will be sanctioned by the court, as enunciated in an anthology of cases of which the most modern examples are *J. & P. Coats Limited* v. *Brown*, 1909 S.C. (J.) 29, 1909 1 S.L.T. 432, *McBain* v. *C.* (supra) and *Trapp* itself. The last reported case where the court granted a bill of criminal letters, and this was a case where the Lord Advocate had refused to give his concurrence to a private prosecution, was *J. & P. Coats Limited* (supra). That, however, was a very special case, and incidentally not a case of perjury, where the interest was much more private than public, and the prima facie case for a prosecution was available from undisputed documents, and was not dependent upon statements from witnesses furnished ex parte.

The complainer in this case seemed to rely on the establishment of three propositions, namely (1) that he, as a private individual, had a right to initiate a criminal prosecution, since the Lord Advocate had not the exclusive right to do so; (2) that he could qualify an interest by showing that he had suffered injury of a substantial, particular, special and peculiarly personal nature beyond all others as a result of the alleged criminal acts of the respondents; and (3) that ex facie of the bill he had made out a prima facie case of the commission of a crime or crimes by the respondents.

There is no doubt that the complainer has the right to initiate a private criminal prosecution, provided always that he receives the sanction of the court to do so. But that sanction will only be granted in very special circumstances. It is true that the complainer has suffered a substantial and personal injury as a result of being sentenced to imprisonment for life if he was wrongly convicted of murder as a result of perjured evidence and a conspiracy to pervert the course of justice. Whether he has stated a relevant charge of conspiracy to pervert the course of justice, and the stating of a relevant charge is a pre-requisite to the consideration of the matter at all, is open to doubt ... On the third point, he was given a latitude to refer to statements of witnesses whom he said he would adduce to support of his allegations. Whether the court was right in allowing that latitude may be doubted, but it was granted and we shall refer to the position of these statements later.

In the first place we have to consider whether the very special circumstances have been made out by the complainer. This involves the position of the Lord Advocate as public prosecutor, particularly in relation to matters affecting the public interest. The independence of his role in this capacity has long been recognised, and the extent of that independence and its impartiality have been amply demonstrated over the years. As the focal point of our system of public prosecutions, he is here to protect the public interest, to prosecute malefactors in the public interest, and to safeguard individuals against malicious, vindictive and unjustified prosecutions at the hands of interested private parties. Perjury and conspiracy to pervert the course of justice are crimes which strike at the very heart of the proper administration of justice. They are pre-eminently crimes which the Lord Advocate as public prosecutor should investigate and prosecute when the investigation produces evidence to merit such a course. The investigation should be impartial and not ex parte, and the Lord Advocate is the impartial investigator. He has to have regard to all the evidence available to him, and not just the evidence from one source, before arriving at his decision. While, therefore, an individual can say that he has suffered substantial personal injury as a result of perjury and/or conspiracy to pervert the course of justice, if these crimes are established, that is not in itself sufficient to justify the granting of criminal letters since other factors have to be taken into account. If it were sufficient, then any person convicted of a crime and particularly a serious crime such as murder, could allege perjury or conspiracy to pervert the course of justice by witnesses on whose evidence he was convicted and be entitled to criminal letters, despite the fact that the Lord Advocate had investigated the matter fully and had refused to prosecute. This could open the flood-gates of private prosecutions which our system of criminal administration has been devised and developed to prevent, both in the public interest generally and the interests of private citizens. Since such offences strike at the root of the proper and fair administration of justice, the decision whether or not to prosecute them must normally be left to the independent and impartial decision of the public prosecutor. It would require to be a very special case indeed to justify a departure from this general rule, and this broad consideration of public interest and public policy must normally outweigh the private interest which an individual may seek to qualify. This view is reinforced by the other consideration to which we have referred, namely the requirement to have all the evidence investigated before a decision to prosecute is reached and not just the evidence produced by an interested party. In the present case the Lord Advocate in the full sense of his responsibility has informed the court that he has carefully examined the evidence and decided that it neither warrants a public prosecution at his instance nor his concurrence to a private prosecution at the instance of the complainer.

For all these reasons we are of the opinion that the bill should be refused."

The court refused the bill.

NOTE

It seems from the *Trapp* and *Meehan* cases that it is not enough for the private prosecutor to satisfy the court that he or she has suffered a peculiar personal wrong as a result of the alleged offence. These cases suggest that, leaving aside wholly exceptional cases, a bill will be refused if the wrong in question falls into an (undefined) category of "public" offences—such as perjury or perverting the course of justice. In *Trapp* the court relied on Hume's classification of crimes into those which injure individuals and those which more immediately concern the public because of their interference with justice. It is clear, however, from the passages in which these views are expressed that Hume is not discussing title to prosecute, and indeed it is also clear from Hume's discussion of title to prosecute that private prosecutions for perjury and subornation of perjury had proceeded before the courts on more than one occasion.

5. McDonald v. Lord Advocate and Another
1988 S.C.C.R. 239

The complainer brought a bill for criminal letters against the Lord Advocate and a procurator-fiscal, alleging subornation of perjury and perjury in connection with criminal proceedings brought against the complainer and in his subsequent appeal against conviction in those proceedings. The Bill was in the following terms:

"THAT ALBEIT by the laws of this and every other well-ordered realm SUBORDINATION of PERJURY and PERJURY are crimes of a heinous nature and severely punishable. YET TRUE IT IS AND OF VERITY that the said (First) Lord Cameron of Lochbroom, (Second) Keith Valentine are guilty of the said crimes actor or act and part IN SO FAR AS the said (First) Lord Cameron, (Second) Keith Valentine, did on 27th January 1986 at the High Court, Saltmarket, Glasgow, interfear with the wittness, John Robert Alexander McLeod, during the coarse of his giving of evidence in the trial of H.M.A. v James McF. McDonald, by charging him with telling the truth, detaining said wittness at Police Headquarters, Randolphfeild, Stirling, attempted to coerse said wittness to change his evidence the next day 28th January 1986, J. R. A. McLeod maintained that his evidence of the previous day was the solem truth. AND IN SO FAR AS the said Lord Cameron and Keith Valentine caused the said John Robert Alexander McLeod to appear before the sheriff at Stirling after concluding his evidence on 28th January 1986, in custody, on petition containing the charge preferred against him on the evening of 27th January 1986, and further did conseal this crime from the trial judge, defence counsel, and the jury:

AND IN SO FAR AS the said Lord Cameron and Keith Valentine did at hearings of appeal by James McFarlane McDonald on the 10th October 1986, 5th December 1986, 22nd January 1987, and 19th February 1987 pretend to the Court of Appeal that (First) the actions against J. R. A. McLeod did not take place, (Second) the actions against J. R. A. McLeod were a blunder, (Third) mislead the Court of Appeal concerning the extended notes of J. R. A. McLeod's evidence, (Forth) mislead the Court of Appeal in relation to a statement by J. R. A. McLeod dated 10th October 1985, the said Lord Cameron and Keith Valentine did commit perjury.

Evidence as to the guilt on said crimes of the said Lord Cameron and Keith Valentine is available and particulars thereof are set forth in the inventory annexed hereto. Such of said evidence as is appropriate to be used at any trial of the said Lord Cameron and Keith Valentine in the form of productions will be lodged in due time in the hands of the Clerk of the High Court of Justiciary before which they are to be tried in order that they may have the opportunity of seeing the same:

All of which or part thereof being found proven by the verdict of an assize or admitted before Your Lordships in a Court of Justiciary to be holden by you or any one or more of your number within the Criminal Court House, Edinburgh, upon a date to be appointed by Your Lordships, the said Lord Cameron and Keith Valentine ought to be punished with the pains of law.

Therefore I beseech Your Lordships for
Criminal Letters at my instance in the
premises in common form."

LORD JUSTICE-CLERK: "In his opening address, the complainer, who appeared for himself and stated his submissions very clearly, explained that he was asking for criminal letters to enable him to initiate a prosecution against the respondents for subornation of perjury and perjury. The complainer submitted that he had a title to prosecute for perjury, and he founded upon the statement in Hume on Crimes, vol. i, p.379:

'The title to prosecute for perjury is common, as in the case of other crimes, to the Lord Advocate, and to the private party, showing a sufficient interest: As if he has been convicted of a crime.'

The complainer submitted that the crimes alleged against the respondents had resulted in his being wrongly convicted of charges (4), (5) and (6) on the indictment. The more modern view is that perjury and associated crimes are pre-eminently crimes which the Lord Advocate as public prosecutor should investigate and prosecute (*Meehan* v. *Inglis* at p.13). In that case the Lord Justice-Clerk said:

'It would require to be a very special case indeed to justify a departure from this general rule, and this broad consideration of public interest and public policy must normally outweigh the private interest which an individual may seek to qualify.'

In the present case, of course, there is the specialty that the alleged crimes of perjury and subornation of perjury are said to have been committed by the Lord Advocate and the procurator fiscal.

So far as private prosecutions under the law of Scotland are concerned, the rule is now well established:

'A citizen desiring to institute a prosecution at common law for crime requires by law to be in the position—(1) that he has applied to the Lord Advocate to obtain his concurrence to the prosecution, and (2) that the crime alleged be a wrong towards himself' [*J. & P. Coats Ltd.* v. *Brown*, Lord Justice-Clerk Macdonald at pp.33–34].

It is also recognised that if the Lord Advocate withholds his concurrence, the citizen has a right to complain to the High Court of Justiciary against the refusal by the public prosecutor to grant his concurrence to a private prosecution (*J. & P. Coats Ltd* v. *Brown*; *McBain* v. *Crichton*; and *Meehan* v. *Inglis*). So far as title is concerned, the Lord Justice-General in *Meehan* v. *Inglis* stated (p.15):

> 'The private citizen has no right or title to initiate a prosecution for perjury or any other crime without the Lord Advocate's concurrence or where that has been refused without the authority of this Court.'

In the present case, the complainer has lodged correspondence showing that he had formally requested the Lord Advocate's concurrence to this bill for criminal letters and that the Lord Advocate has intimated that he does not concur. In such a situation, the court requires to consider whether criminal letters should be granted enabling the complainer to bring the prosecution as a private citizen. The approach to be adopted in such circumstances was stated in *McBain* v. *Crichton* by Lord Guthrie [at p.31] to be as follows:

> 'In deciding whether or not such an application will be granted, the Court will consider the facts alleged in the bill in order to decide whether the circumstances therein set forth are such, that an exceptional remedy should be allowed to the complainer.'

[His Lordship considered the Bill, concluding that the allegation of perjury was 'wholly irrelevant and misconceived' (p.242). Having considered the allegations concerning perjury, he continued:]

At the end of the day, the complainer maintained that he had made public accusations accusing the respondents of serious crimes; natural justice required that they should be given the opportunity of confronting their accuser at a trial. He accordingly asked the court to pass the bill. He also maintained that it would in this case be inappropriate to ask the Lord Advocate why he had not concurred since the Lord Advocate was entitled to observe silence when a criminal charge was being directed against him.

On behalf of the respondents, the advocate-depute confirmed that the Lord Advocate did not concur in the bill. However, he intimated that he had come forward to explain the reasons why the Lord Advocate had taken up that position. The attitude of the Lord Advocate appears to be consistent with what was stated in *Meehan* v. *Inglis* at p.14:

> 'It is undoubtedly the law that where the Court is considering a Bill for Criminal Letters, the Lord Advocate is expected to state his reasons for refusing to give his concurrence.'

In the present case, where the complainer is seeking authority of the court to prosecute the Lord Advocate, I would not have thought it necessary for the Lord Advocate to state his reasons for refusing to concur, but in this case the Lord Advocate has chosen to do so.

[His Lordship reviewed the background to this Bill and concluded that the allegations made against the Crown were not supported. He then continued:]

That is sufficient for the disposal of this bill. The advocate-depute, however, also contended that although the Lord Advocate was politically responsible for the actings of Crown counsel, the Crown Office and procurators fiscal, if there was a failure on their part he was not criminally responsible to the court. In other words, he would be responsible only for his own actings and he would not be vicariously responsible for the actings of others. This submission would appear to me to accord with principle. Of course, the advocate-depute accepted that at the appeal hearing certain statements were made on the specific instructions of the Lord Advocate and expressly upon his responsibility. However, I am quite satisfied that nothing of that nature which was said could be regarded as designed to conceal the truth from the court or to mislead the court.

I am accordingly satisfied that the circumstances set forth in the bill are wholly insufficient to support the remedy which the complainer seeks in this bill. No good grounds have been put forward for the prosecution which the complainer seeks to direct against the Lord Advocate. So far as the procurator fiscal is concerned, it is plain that he all along was acting in good faith and on the instructions of the advocate-depute, and there is nothing in the bill which would justify the court in authorising a private prosecution against him at the instance of the complainer.

In all the circumstances I am entirely satisfied that this bill for criminal letters is wholly misconceived. When the averments in the bill are examined, it becomes quite clear that the complainer has failed to demonstrate any circumstances which would justify the court in authorising the private prosecution which he seeks to bring. I would accordingly move your Lordships that we should refuse the bill."

The court refused the Bill.

6. H. v. Sweeney and Others
1983 S.L.T. 48

LORD JUSTICE-GENERAL (EMSLIE): "This is a bill for criminal letters by the alleged victim of the crime of rape and of what appears to have been a gruesome and hideous assault in which she was grievously injured and disfigured by repeated slashing cuts of a razor. These events are said to have occurred during the late evening of 31 October 1980 in a disused yard at 10 Davaar Street, Glasgow. What she seeks to do is to bring to trial three youths, the respondents in this bill, upon the following charges: (i) that they did on 31 October or 1 November 1980, in London Road, near Davaar Street, Glasgow, assault the said C.H., strike her on the head with an unknown instrument whereby she became unconscious, drag or carry her to a structure situated in the disused premises at 10 Davaar Street, Glasgow, and there place her on the floor, forcibly remove her clothing, hold her down, lie on top of her and repeatedly rape her; (ii) that they did further at the same place and on the same date, assault the said C.H. by striking her repeatedly upon the head and body with a razor or similar instrument all to her severe injury, permanent disfigurement and to the danger of her life.

In answer to the bill the respondents plead that in the events which have happened the bill at the complainer's instance is incompetent, and that in any event prosecution of the respondents now would be oppressive.

The history of the matter is as follows. The Lord Advocate indicted the three respondents for trial at the May sitting of the High Court, Glasgow. All three pled not guilty to the two charges in that indictment which were in terms identical to those on which the complainer seeks leave to prosecute them now. For two reasons this indictment was not called. The first was that the complainer had moved to an unknown address in England. The second was that the sitting could not proceed anyway because of a strike by sheriff court staff in Glasgow, the result of which was that no jurors were cited for the sitting. The instance accordingly fell and the Lord Advocate then re-indicted the respondents for trial at the next sitting of the High Court, Glasgow, in June 1981. Once again pleas of not guilty to the same two charges were tendered by each respondent and all three were present and available for trial when the sitting began. This second indictment, however, was not called either. The reason for this was that when the complainer presented herself at Justiciary Buildings grave doubt was entertained as to her fitness to give evidence. Arrangements were made to have her examined by a distinguished psychiatrist who gave the following advice in a lengthy and detailed report:

'In my opinion, a court appearance at present would be detrimental to her health, and in fact would be hazardous, which may lead not only to pre-trial suicide attempt, but may disturb her even after the trial, whatever the outcome would be, to the same extent.

I would respectfully suggest to the court that evidence should be taken from her should the court decide to proceed with the case, without the public being present, and with the absolute minimum number of representatives from the legal system. A cross-examination at this stage is only likely to produce a severe block in her communication, which would lead to her retreating in silence.

Finally, it is difficult to foresee an improvement in her state in the next two to four months, as the history reveals that her general mental state and attitude towards the court case has not improved since the incident which occurred in September 1980.

One must never forget that this woman has been very severely physically and psychologically traumatised, and that any further pressure put upon her will only cause more unhappiness, despair and isolation.'

In light of that advice the very proper decision was that the indictment should be allowed to fall. The risk to the complainer's health was so serious as to be quite unacceptable. In September 1981 careful consideration was given to the question whether the proceedings against the three respondents should be kept alive. The decision was that they should not. The background against which this decision was taken was that two of the respondents were under 16 years of age at the time of the alleged crimes and the third was then a young person. They had already been called to answer to two indictments and had presented themselves twice for trials which did not take place. In the particular circumstances of this case there was sufficient evidence to justify prosecution of the respondents on the two charges only if the complainer was available to give evidence herself. The reason for the decision was, as the Lord Advocate has explained to us, that in light of the prognosis contained in the report obtained from the psychiatrist in June 1981 it was concluded that the prospect of material improvement in the complainer's health within the foreseeable future was slight; that accordingly there seemed to be no real likelihood of being able to proceed to the trial of the respondents at a reasonably early date; and that it was therefore thought not to be justifiable to keep the proceedings hanging over the heads of the respondents indefinitely. In these circumstances a letter was sent to each of the respondents dated 15 September 1981 informing them that the Lord Advocate intended to take no further proceedings against them. The effect of that letter was, as the case of *Thom* v. *H.M. Advocate* shows, to deprive the Lord Advocate of his right to prosecute the respondents at any time thereafter on the charges contained in the indictments which had fallen. After 15 September 1981, accordingly, public prosecution of the three respondents ceased to be competent.

In presenting this bill the complainer asserts that in the events which have happened she, as a private individual, has the right with leave of this court, to prosecute the respondents to trial. She qualifies the necessary interest in respect that she is able to show that she has suffered injury of a substantial, particular, special, and peculiarly personal nature beyond all others as the result of the alleged criminal acts of the respondents. Ex facie of the bill, and of the precognition of necessary witnesses and of the productions lodged in support of the bill, she has made out, she claims, a prima facie case of the commission of the two crimes libelled by the respondents.

Let us first of all test the bill by assuming that it may competently be passed and by ignoring for the moment a special plea by the respondents that to pass it now would be oppressive. There is no doubt that the complainer is well founded in saying that she has the necessary title, and has qualified the necessary interest, to prosecute privately. There is no doubt either that upon the precognitions and productions submitted in support of the bill a prima facie case, sufficient to justify bringing the respondents to trial upon the two charges, is disclosed. The evidential material, indeed, is in all essential respects that upon which the Lord Advocate thought it right to indict the respondents. The Lord Advocate has, however, declined to grant his concurrence and the question for the court thus comes to be whether there are to be found in this case very special circumstances which would justify us in taking the now exceptional step of issuing criminal letters at the request of a private individual. We have no doubt that in this case the circumstances are sufficiently special to require us to pass this bill (a) if it is competent, and (b) if it would not be oppressive to pass it now. The position is that the Lord Advocate, while finding himself disabled from granting his concurrence by reason of his decision in September 1981, has informed us that he does not oppose the passing of the bill on the assumption that the court is satisfied on the material now before it that circumstances have changed materially since September 1981, i.e. that the complainer is now likely to be able to give evidence at a trial of the respondents without exposing herself to the risk of serious injury to her health. As the Lord Advocate explained, the position of the Crown is and always has been since the case was first considered that on the assumption that the complainer was available as a witness there is a sufficient case against the three respondents to justify their prosecution on the two charges. In light of what the Lord Advocate has said to us we have considered the sufficiency of the evidential material available. In our opinion, in the particular circumstances of this case, sufficiency appears to depend essentially (a) upon the complainer herself giving evidence, and (b) depending on circumstances, perhaps also upon a young man who might fall to be regarded as a socius criminis, being willing to testify against the respondents. The learned Dean of Faculty accepted, at once, the correctness of this view upon the question of sufficiency of evidence and we therefore have to ask ourselves (first) whether we have been satisfied that the health of the complainer is now such that she can be expected to present herself as a crucial witness without serious risk and (second) whether the young man can reasonably be expected to testify without incriminating himself. As to the second question, there is, we think, no difficulty, for the complainer, through the Dean of Faculty, has declared an intention to grant him immunity from prosecution at her instance and the Lord Advocate for his interest has intimated to us that the young man will have immunity from suit at the instance of the Crown. As to the first question there is we think enough material before us to warrant the conclusion that the complainer is probably now fit to give evidence. That material is in the form of two recent reports by a consultant forensic psychiatrist and, subject only to the necessity for a last-minute precautionary check on the complainer's health very shortly before any trial, we are informed that her condition has now so much improved that she appears to be capable of giving evidence in court. It is clear, therefore, that in this case the necessary very special circumstances are present. They consist essentially of the marked change which has taken place in the complainer's health and, in light of that change, the Lord Advocate's indication to us that he does not oppose the passing of the bill.

From what I have said so far this is one of those very rare instances in which, unless the bill is incompetent for the reasons advanced by the respondents, or it is demonstrated that to require the respondents to stand trial now would be oppressive, this court would, in my opinion, be prepared to pass the bill and order the issue of criminal letters.

In these circumstances I come now to the important question of the competency of the bill. In support of the plea that it is now incompetent the respondents presented two submissions.

The first was that although the right of a private individual to seek leave to prosecute privately exists in circumstances in which the Lord Advocate declines to prosecute, that is to say refuses to take any steps towards the prosecution of an alleged offender, it is extinguished at once and for all time when the Lord Advocate has taken the step of raising an indictment against him. The mere raising of the indictment, regardless of its fate has, it was said, this dramatic effect. For this somewhat startling proposition the first respondent's counsel, who presented the argument on competency for all three respondents with clarity and skill, relied essentially upon short passages in the opinions of Lord Mackenzie and Lord Justice-Clerk Boyle in the bill of advocation in the case of *Wilson* v. *Hare* in 1829. The most reliable record of the opinions delivered in that case is, I believe, to be found in the supplement to the *Trial of William Burke and Helen McDougal* and from that report I quote the particular passages with which counsel's submission was concerned. Lord Mackenzie at p.107 said this: 'It is true, that by the law of Scotland, there is a right of private, as well as public prosecution for crimes, and that not for reparation only, but for punishment—a right of which I rather think the Information for Hare speaks too lightly. But then it is just equally true, that unless the private party, having title to prosecute, come forward in time to prevent it, the King's Advocate, raising an indictment in his own name alone, comes to have full power of accusation vested in him ... Accordingly, it seems that, in general, those ways by which a party obtains protection from punishment by the act of the Lord Advocate, do avail against the private prosecutor, who has not previously come forward.' At p.138 the Lord Justice-Clerk who had been discussing certain clear abridgements of the rights of private parties to prosecute certain persons criminally, said this: 'They are, however, made to bend, in other respects, to the same interests, as the public prosecutor has the undoubted right of restricting any indictment, at any stage of the proceedings, previous to pronouncing sentence—a privilege that has arisen from usage alone. If, again, he has taken the lead, and raised an indictment, in which he happens to fail from the most purely accidental mistake or blunder, no subsequent trial for the same offence or criminal act, though attempted to be shaped as a different charge, can ever be instituted by the private party.' These passages, said counsel for the first respondent, demonstrate conclusively that the true scope of the right of private prosecution is accurately defined by Alison where, at p.xi of the introduction to vol. 2 of his work on the *Criminal Law of Scotland*, he expressed the fourth of the four principles upon which the criminal institution of Scotland are founded, in these terms: 'That if the public authorities decline to prosecute at the public expense, an opportunity should still be afforded to the injured party, of himself conducting the prosecution on his own responsibility.' It is not at all surprising to find therefore that in the 153 years which have passed since 1829 the only recorded attempts to initiate private prosecution were in cases in which the Lord Advocate had declined to take any steps at all to prosecute alleged offenders.

I have no hesitation in rejecting this first submission on behalf of the respondents. The rights of a private prosecutor in our system of criminal jurisprudence have grown up alongside those of the Lord Advocate and indeed, historically, bulked larger in earlier times than those of the King's Advocate. These rights still exist and there seems to be no good reason in principle for saying that they should not be available in any case in which the Lord Advocate has, for any reason, declined to prosecute an offender to a conclusion. The passages relied upon by the first respondent's counsel in the opinions of Lord Mackenzie and the Lord Justice-Clerk in *Wilson* v. *Hare* were clearly obiter. The case before the court was concerned merely with the question as to the extent of the immunity from all prosecution of a socius criminis who had given evidence for the prosecution in a criminal trial, and the decision did not turn at all upon the issue which is now before us. In any event, when these passages are read in their context it is impossible to conclude that the judges intended to convey that the mere act of serving an indictment extinguishes for all time the right of a private individual to seek leave to prosecute privately. Lord Mackenzie, indeed, immediately after the two passages quoted from p.107, explains perfectly clearly that what he had in mind was the effect upon the right of private prosecution of the Act of 1701 and of the comparable effect of a public prosecution which has reached its conclusion in the verdict of a jury. This is what he says: 'Thus, if the King's Advocate is dilatory, or inaccurate in proceedings, after apprehension of the criminal, who thereby obtains final liberation on the act 1701, that criminal is as safe from private, as from public prosecution—though the private prosecutor may be absolutely blameless,—may be absent, abroad, on a sick-bed, *non compos*, or a pupil. The intimation ordered by that statute is, to—"His Majesty's Advocate, or procurator-fiscal, and party appearing by the warrant to be concerned, *if any be within the kingdom."* So that it is manifest, that in many cases prosecuted by the Lord Advocate, there can be no information to any private *party*, particularly in cases of murder. Yet, the act provides,—"that if the Lord Advocate failzie, the process shall be deserted *simpliciter*, the party imprisoned to be for ever free from all question or process for the foresaid crime or offence:" So, if the Lord Advocate draw the indictment erroneously, in respect of time, place, or circumstance,—or if he omit necessary witnesses (as, for instance, by not calling necessary *socii criminis*), or cite them erroneously, or examine them insufficiently, or allow them to be present in Court, or suffer them to be disqualified by improper communications, or in any other way fail in his prosecution, and the criminal is acquitted,—it cannot be denied that his acquittal is as valid against the private party, who might have prosecuted, as against the King's Advocate: So, if the Lord Advocate restrict the indictment to an arbitrary punishment, or depart from part of it, this avails the criminal equally against the private prosecutor: So, if the King's Advocate decline to move for judgment after conviction.' The quoted passage from the opinion of Lord Justice-Clerk Boyle at p.138 is, when it is properly understood, concerned with the same set of circumstances and, in particular, with the effect upon the right of private prosecution of a public prosecution which has proceeded to a conclusion and has failed. In the result, I am persuaded that the passages relied upon by the first respondent's counsel do not lend any support for a proposition which seems to accord ill with principle.

The second submission for the respondents on the alleged incompetency of the bill was that in any event the right of private prosecution which the complainer once had was forever extinguished when the Lord Advocate, on 15 September 1981, publicly relinquished his right to prosecute the respondents further on the charges contained in the two indictments which had been allowed to fall. The proposition was that whatever avails against the public prosecutor avails against all the world, and it took as its starting-point those passages from the opinions of Lord Mackenzie and the Lord Justice-Clerk which I have already quoted in their relevant context. In this case, said counsel for the first respondent, the effect of the letters of 15 September 1981 was the same as that of desertion simpliciter on the prosecutor's motion. It made all further proceedings at the Lord Advocate's instance incompetent and this was expressly decided in the case of *Thom* v. *H.M. Advocate.* In order to find out what effect the sending of these letters had upon the complainer's right to seek to prosecute the respondents privately, all that one has to do is to ask what is the effect upon the right of private prosecution of desertion simpliciter on the motion of the public prosecutor. The answer to that question is that it makes *all* further prosecution incompetent, and that includes prosecution at the instance of a private individual. In the *Commentaries* (3rd ed.), ii, 277 Brown Hume said this: 'But if the prosecutor, being present, shall himself move the Court to desert the diet *simpliciter,* and thus neither allude to any dilatory cause for dropping his present libel, nor intimate any purpose to raise a new one; such a measure cannot well be construed any otherwise than as a thorough relinquishment or discharge of his right to prosecution.' That this discharge of the public prosecutor's right of prosecution discharges all right of prosecution was made clear in the case of *H.M. Advocate* v. *Hall.* In that case, in an opinion in which Lord Justice-Clerk Moncreiff, and Lords Deas, Mure, Craighill and Adam concurred, the Lord Justice-General (Inglis), after quoting the same passage from Hume with approval, added: 'Now, it appears to me that that expounds the law on this matter quite consistently, and very clearly, to be that the desertion of a diet *simpliciter* on the motion of the prosecutor is an end of all proceedings against the panel for the offence libelled against him.' It cannot be supposed, so ran the argument, that the Lord Justice-General did not mean precisely what he said, and giving to his opinion all the force it commands, the respondents' plea to competency in this case must be sustained.

I have no hesitation, either, in rejecting this second submission on behalf of the respondents. In the case of *Hall,* which was concerned with the effect upon the Crown's right to prosecute further when there had been desertion of a diet simpliciter by the court, ex proprio motu, the court was considering only the right of the public prosecutor. No question as to private prosecution was in mind at all and I cannot accept that the Lord Justice-General's observation on which the first respondent's counsel relied was intended to do more than echo the words of Hume which he had just quoted. Properly understood in its context in the case of *Hall* the Lord Justice-General's reference to 'all proceedings' against the panel can only have been intended to relate to proceedings at the instance of the prosecutor concerned. The proposition for which the first respondent's counsel contended requires us to accept that desertion of a diet simpliciter on the motion of the public prosecutor is equivalent to acquittal or absolvitor of the accused on the charges upon which he answered at his trial. The opinions in *Hall* and in the earlier case of *Tabram,* which was concerned with a similar narrow question, lend no support for this, and it is of material significance to observe that although in the first edition of the *Commentaries,* ii, 30–31, Baron Hume concluded the passage quoted from the 3rd edition (ii, 277) with the words: 'and equal to a judicial consent on his part, to the passing of *absolvitor* in favour of the pannel,' these words were deliberately excised in all subsequent editions, including the second and third for which the author was himself responsible.

Why these words were deliberately struck out is not known with any certainty. What is important, however, is that they were deliberately struck out by that great authority upon our criminal law. In my opinion the passage which I have quoted from Hume's *Commentaries* (3rd ed., ii, 277) discloses that the only effect of desertion of a diet simpliciter on the prosecutor's motion is to disable that prosecutor from taking fresh proceedings against the accused upon the same charge or charges.

Upon the whole issue of competency of this bill, therefore, I am not persuaded that there are any good reasons, in principle or authority, for holding that in the events which have happened this bill must be rejected as incompetent. In so saying I am content to record that the Lord Advocate, in addressing us, said that he was satisfied that the bill was competent and that had he entertained any doubt upon the question he would have felt it his duty so to inform this court."

The court passed the bill.

NOTE

This was the first successful application for a bill for criminal letters since the case of *J. & P. Coats Ltd.* v. *Brown*. The first respondent was subsequently convicted of rape and assault; the other respondents were convicted of indecent asault (High Court, May 28, 1982). The terms of the criminal letters issued by the court may be found at 1982 S.C.C.R. at pp.178–180.

It is worth remembering that this case stems very largely from the rule in *Thom* v. *H.M. Advocate* (*supra*, p.34). The outcome of the application for criminal letters was hardly unexpected. There was a clear title to prosecute, there was a relevant charge (and this question seems to have been assumed as an appropriate question for the court considering the application) and the Lord Advocate did not oppose the application. And it is also clear that the court was concerned for the public's confidence in the administration of criminal justice in Scotland. The court could hardly be seen to be condoning a situation in which allegations of a serious crime could not be tested in court.

D. Prosecution in the Public Interest

Prior to this Summary Jurisdiction (Scotland) Act 1908 only two kinds of prosecutor were recognised—public and private. The definition of "prosecutor" in that Act (now contained in section 462(1) of the 1975 Act) appears to have created a third category, that of "prosecutor in the public interest." This is curious since the central premise of the system of prosecution in Scotland is that the public prosecutor prosecutes in the public interest.

Templeton v. King
1933 J.C. 58

The respondent was charged on a summary complaint with having failed, without reasonable excuse, to comply with a school attendance order pronounced in respect of his daughter. The complaint was at the instance of the county clerk of Dumbarton, and was signed by a solicitor as agent for the complainer. Objections to the competency of the complaint were upheld by the sheriff, who stated a case for appeal to the High Court. The grounds for the sheriff's decision appear from the opinion of the Lord Justice-General. The question for the opinion of the court was whether the sheriff was right in dismissing the complaint as incompetent.

LORD JUSTICE-GENERAL (CLYDE): "Objections were taken to the competency of this complaint; and the Sheriff-substitute before whom the complaint depended sustained these objections and dismissed the complaint as incompetent. His grounds were (1) that the complainer, not being the 'public prosecutor of a Court' was, within the meaning of section 18 of the Summary Jurisdiction (Scotland) Act, 1908, a 'private prosecutor'; (2) that, being a private prosecutor, he could not prosecute in Dumbarton Sheriff Court without the concurrence of the public prosecutor of that Court, the complaint being one in which imprisonment without the option of a fine was competent; (3) that, although, by section 4 of the Day Industrial Schools (Scotland) Act of 1893, and the Local Government (Scotland) Act, 1929, the County Council has power to institute such a complaint as the present, and is (by section 14 of the Education (Scotland) Act of 1883 and the Local Government (Scotland) Act of 1929) authorised to appoint any person 'to appear before the Court and conduct the prosecution,' yet—notwithstanding— the County Council has no power to delegate its power to institute such a complaint as the present.

Some explanation is necessary. There are two ways in which school attendance can be enforced. There is the method which was initiated by section 70 of the Act of 1872, according to which a school board, having ascertained the facts and done what it could by remonstrance and otherwise, hands over the papers to the procurator-fiscal 'or other person appointed by the school board,' and the procurator-fiscal or such other person then raises proceedings by way of prosecution. There is another method, originally introduced by section 9 of the Act of 1883 (subsequently repealed), and definitely established by section 8 of the Act of 1908, according to which the school board in the first place pronounces an attendance order of its own, and then prosecutes—if necessary—in order to enforce it. By section 14 of the Act of 1883 (which has not been repealed) it was enacted that, in any prosecution under the Education Acts (including the Act of 1870), 'any person appointed by the school board . . . may appear before the Court and conduct the prosecution.' The complaint is described in said section 14 as the complaint of the school board. But (as has been seen), in section 70 of the Act of 1872 the prosecutor is named as the procurator-fiscal 'or other person appointed by the school board'; and by section 14 of the Act of 1883, the 'person appointed by the school board' is authorised to 'appear before the Court and conduct the prosecution.' Accordingly, neither under the Act of 1872, nor under that of 1883, is there any *express* authority to appoint a person for any purpose connected with prosecution. The power to appoint is left to implication from the fact that a person so appointed is referred to; but there is no express authority to appoint. It would plainly be a mistake to confuse the functions of a 'person appointed'—that is, a person *appointed to prosecute*—with those of a person (who may, or may not, be the prosecutor himself) who is authorised to *appear in Court and conduct the prosecution*. If the procurator-fiscal is prosecutor, then, not only must the complaint run in his name, but he (or the procurator-fiscal-depute) must appear in Court and conduct the prosecution. He cannot employ a law agent to represent him. But 'a person appointed' to prosecute within the meaning of the Acts may have no legal qualifications; and, if—prior to the Act of 1883—he had no such qualifications, he necessarily employed a law agent to appear in Court on his behalf, and to conduct the prosecution raised in his name. All that the Act of 1883 did was to authorise 'a person appointed'— although without legal qualification—to appear in a Court and conduct the prosecution. If this is right, the third ground of the Sheriff-substitute's objections cannot be sustained. The power to delegate the capacity to prosecute is one thing, and the County Council plainly has it by implication. The power of the delegate to appear in Court and conduct the prosecution is another, and—while the delegate is authorised to do this—there is nothing in the statutes to prevent him from employing a law agent to appear in Court on his behalf and conduct the prosecution.

The only other statutory enactment which bears upon the question is the Summary Jurisdiction (Scotland) Act, 1908. Under section 18 of that statute all proceedings under the Act for the trial of offences and the recovery of penalties are to be instituted by complaint in the form contained in Schedule C. That itself is significant, because it is a form which bears to run in the name of the prosecutor but may be signed in the name of a solicitor acting for him. But, passing that by, the section goes on to enact that 'such complaint shall be signed by the prosecutor or by any law agent on behalf of a prosecutor other than the public prosecutor of a Court, and any law agent may appear for and conduct any prosecution on behalf of a prosecutor other than the public prosecutor of a Court.' Now, in the present case, the complaint is signed by a law agent on behalf of the prosecutor, that is, the person appointed to prosecute; and it is clear that the person so appointed is not the public prosecutor of the Dumbarton Sheriff Court. He is simply prosecutor appointed by the County Council for a particular purpose. If so, it would seem that any law agent may appear for him and conduct the prosecution.

This may be enough to remove the Sheriff-substitute's second ground of objection, but the matter cannot be disposed of without taking into account, at the same time, his first ground, namely, that the person appointed in the present case is a private prosecutor. Prior to the Act of 1908 a great many questions of this kind occurred (under various statutes) in which the prosecutor was not the procurator-fiscal. Not being the procurator-fiscal, could he be anything but a private prosecutor? How the matter might have stood in the present case if the Act of 1908 had not been passed I do not need to inquire. But when I turn to the Act of 1908 I find that section 2 introduces the following definitions:—'Prosecutor shall include procurator-fiscal, assistant procurator-fiscal, burgh prosecutor, and any other persons prosecuting in the public interest, private prosecutor, and complainer.' Here we have a classification of 'prosecutors.' To which class does the 'person appointed' in the present case belong? I think the answer must be that he belongs to the class of prosecutors 'prosecuting in the public interest.' Therefore he cannot be a 'private prosecutor', and, therefore, he does not require the concurrence of the Procurator-fiscal. As it is impossible to call him the public prosecutor of Dumbarton Sheriff Court, both the first and second grounds of the Sheriff-substitute's objection fail. If that is right, I think the question put to us should be answered in the negative."

> The court answered the
> question in the negative.

NOTE
So a "prosecutor in the public interest" appears to straddle the distinction between public and private prosecutor. Like a private prosecutor he need not appear personally, but may employ a solicitor or counsel to appear for him: 1975 Act, s. 311(3). On the other hand, unlike the private prosecutor, he does not require the concurrence of the public prosecutor of the court in which such complaint is brought: 1975 Act, s. 311(4). Given his "hybrid" quality, what rules should govern his liability for malicious prosecution? Section 456(1) of the 1975 Act (*supra*, p.56) refers to "prosecutor(s) in the public interest." This cannot be read literally as only referring to this intermediate category, since it would exclude "public prosecutors." But it clearly includes this intermediate category.

CHAPTER 3

JURISDICTION

There are two aspects to the question of jurisdiction which, in turn, give rise to the two questions addressed in this chapter. The first is generally regarded as an issue of international law, and relates to a state's competence to prosecute and punish crimes *vis-à-vis* other states. Can state A try and punish the offender, or is this a matter which falls within the competence of state B, or neither, or, indeed, both? Of course, Scotland is not a state in international law, but given the unusual constitutional arrangements of the United Kingdom, and the express preservation of the Scottish courts and legal system by the Act of Union, this is a question which needs to be addressed in relation to the powers of the Scottish courts. The first question is, therefore: Does *any* Scottish court have jurisdiction in this case?

The second issue arises only once the first has been determined: How, *within* the jurisdiction, is competence to try the offence in question determined? Very few states have one criminal court of universal jurisdiction, and Scotland is no exception. Apart from courts of special jurisdiction (such as courts-martial), three courts exercise criminal jurisdiction in Scotland: the High Court of Justiciary, the sheriff court and the district court. The second question is, therefore: *Which* court has jurisdiction in this case?

A.   JURISDICTIONAL COMPETENCE *VIS-À-VIS* OTHER STATES

An extensive examination of the grounds on which states claimed jurisdiction over crime, conducted in connection with the *Harvard Research Draft Convention on Jurisdiction with Respect to Crime* (1935), identified five general principles on which states claimed jurisdiction (29 Am.Jo.Int.Law, Supplement, 443 (1935)):

> "These five principles are: first, the territorial principle, determining jurisdiction by reference to the place where the offence is committed; second, the nationality principle, determining jurisdiction by reference to the nationality or national character of the person committing the offence; third, the protective principle, determining jurisdiction by reference to the national interest injured by the offence; fourth, the universality principle, determining jurisdiction by reference to the custody of the person committing the offence; and fifth, the passive personality principle, determining jurisdiction by reference to the nationality or national character of the person injured by the offence."

The study went on to conclude that of these, the territorial principle was universally recognised and applied as the primary ground of jurisdiction. The nationality principle received universal recognition, but it was not necessarily adopted and applied by all states. The three other grounds were accepted to varying degrees. While some were recognised in several states as a primary ground of jurisdiction, with the exception of universal jurisdiction in respect of piracy, none were generally recognised as justifying, by themselves, the exercise of jurisdiction. The first four principles were eventually incorporated into the *Draft Convention*, but the fifth, the so-called "passive personality" principle was omitted.

It should be noted that the study was carried out some time ago and during the second half of this century there has been a significant expansion in the exercise of jurisdiction on grounds other than territoriality or nationality. In particular, in response to both crimes against international law, and crimes of an international character such as offences against aircraft and drug-trafficking, there is today a much greater reliance on the principle of universality.

(i)   The Territorial Principle

1.   H.M. Advocate v. Hall
(1881) 4 Couper 438

LORD YOUNG: "... The general rule is that criminal law is strictly territorial—so that a man is subject only to the criminal law of the country where he is, and that his conduct there, whether acting, speaking, or writing, shall be judged of as criminal or not by that law and no other. The law of allegiance affords an exception in cases of treason; and there are also ... some other exceptions, as, for example, in the case of a British subject murdering another abroad; but the rule is as I have stated."

2.   Lewis v. Blair
(1858) 3 Irvine 16

The suspender, a citizen of the United States, was convicted of a serious assault committed on board a United States ship lying in the Clyde near Greenock. A bill of suspension was presented to the High Court in which it was objected:

"That the Sheriff had no jurisdiction to try him, in respect that as the offence charged was said to have been committed by him, a foreigner, on board a foreign vessel, and upon seamen engaged in that vessel, it must be held to have been committed within the territory of the country to which the vessel belonged; and that the mere circumstance of the vessel being within the Sheriff's jurisdiction (assuming it to have been so), did not render foreigners employed in that vessel subjects to her Majesty, and, as such, subject to the magistrate's jurisdiction.

The Court was unanimously of opinion that this ground of suspension was untenable."

NOTE

There are, then, two aspects to the rule that criminal law is territorial. The jurisdiction of the various courts will not normally extend beyond their territorial limits. At the same time, criminal jurisdiction will normally encompass everyone within those limits, irrespective of their origins. The exceptions to this rule are discussed *infra*, p.102. For a discussion of the factors behind the rule, see Williams, "Venue and the Ambit of Criminal Law" 1965 81 L.Q.R. 276, 395, 518; *Report on the Territorial and*

Extraterritorial Extent of the Criminal Law (Law Com. Rep. No. 91, 1978). See also Pt. I of the Criminal Justice Act 1993.

(ii)   The Territorial Principle in Scots Law

The primary basis for jurisdiction in Scots law is the territorial principle. The principle is most clearly applied when the offence is entirely committed within Scotland. But there will be instances where the offence was committed partly in Scotland, and partly elsewhere. Must all the material elements of the offence take place in Scotland before the Scottish courts have jurisdiction?

1.   H.M. Advocate v. Witherington
(1881) 4 Couper 475

Witherington sent letters from England to several traders in Scotland containing false representations, by means of which he induced them to send goods to him in England. He did not pay for these goods, and had no intention of doing so. He was arrested in England and brought to Scotland for trial on a charge of falsehood, fraud and wilful imposition. It was objected on his behalf, *inter alia*, that the High Court had no jurisdiction, the alleged offence having been committed in England.

LORD JUSTICE-GENERAL (INGLIS): "... The objection to the jurisdiction of this Court to try the panel for this crime raises a question of much greater interest and importance. But this question has, I apprehend, been settled in the sense adverse to the panel's contention by two decisions of this Court—the case of *Bradbury* in 1872, and the case of *Allan* in 1873, both to be found in the second volume of Couper's Reports.

Under ordinary circumstances I should have thought it enough to refer to these authorities as a sufficient ground for repelling the objection; but some doubts having been suggested as to the soundness of these judgments, and a full Court having been summoned to dispose of the objections to this indictment, it would hardly be satisfactory if the Judges now present did not expound the principle of law on which these prior judgments are founded.

The objection is rested on these considerations; that the panel is an Englishman; that the only fraud or criminal act alleged against him was committed in England; that he never was in Scotland, and is not subject to the criminal law or to the jurisdiction of the criminal Courts of Scotland; that criminal jurisdiction does not extend *extra territorium*, and that the true foundation of ordinary criminal jurisdiction is the *locus delicti*.

The argument is certainly plausible, and there is, at first sight, something startling and paradoxical in the proposition that a man may commit a crime in a place in which he was never personally present. The proposition is nevertheless not only technically or constructively, but actually true; and if this is so, then the Court of the territory where the crime was committed, and where the panel was never personally present, has jurisdiction *ratione loci delicti*, and the whole argument of the objector falls.

The best and most conclusive example, to my mind, in support of the truth of the above proposition, is the case of a murder by poisoning, which takes place in Edinburgh, while the murderer is domiciled and resident in London, and never was in Scotland. The manner in which the murderer accomplishes his purpose is to send by post, or otherwise, to his victim in Edinburgh, a packet of deadly poison, recommending it to him (knowingly and maliciously for the purpose of accomplishing the death) as a salutary medicine fitted to cure a disease under which he is labouring. If the victim acts on the suggestion and swallows the poison it is not doubtful that a murder has been committed in Edinburgh, and that the murderer was in London all the while. The *species facti* may be varied by supposing that the murderer employs an innocent agent to take the poison to the victim in Edinburgh, and persuade him to swallow it as a useful and potent medicine. The result is the same—the crime is committed in Edinburgh by a man who was never there. Baron Hume, in treating of criminal jurisdiction, after stating that this Court can never sustain its own jurisdiction against a Scotchman, *ratione domicilii*, for a murder or other crime committed beyond the limits of Scotland, proceeds to say—'It does not, however, follow that the law shall apply to those offences which have a continuance of time and succession of acts whereof part may happen here and part abroad. If one compose and print a libel in England and circulate it here, or if one forge a deed abroad and utter it here, certainly the proper Courts for the trial of such a case are those of this country, since it is here that the main act is done which completes the crime, ... nay, more, it may be plausibly argued that he shall be subjected to the same course of trial who shall write an incendiary letter in England, and put it into a course of conveyance, thence by means of which it is received by the person to whom it is addressed in Scotland.' In support of this latter statement the learned author cites a case which actually occurred in 1818.

Mr Alison, in his Practice of the Criminal Law, following the earlier authority, says—'The principle applies to one who writes an incendiary letter in England and sends it down, whether by post or otherwise, to this country. He stands in the same position with one, who standing on the English side of the border, discharges a gun at a man on the Scotch side, and no reasonable doubt can be entertained of the competence of trying him in this country, where his crime has taken its destined effect.

To shew that this doctrine is not peculiar to the law of Scotland it may be worth while to advert to a very good example in support of the general proposition which I have advanced, stated by Mr Justice Story (Conflict of Laws, sec. 625, *b*), as having occurred in the Supreme Court of New York. A citizen of Ohio had written what is called a fraudulent paper addressed to citizens of New York, which made him liable to punishment as for a criminal offence. He sent the paper to New York by an innocent agent, and it was there published and the offence there completed. 'The defendant being afterwards indicted in New York for the offence, pleaded that he was a natural-born citizen of Ohio, and owed allegiance to that state; that he had never been within the state of New York, and that the fraudulent paper was executed in Ohio. It was determined that this was no answer to the indictment.'

In all the examples which I have adduced the commencement of the criminal action is in one country and the completion of it in another. But in most of these cases the perpetrator's success in his criminal object is necessary to complete the crime. In the case of poisoners there would have been no murder if the victim had not swallowed the poison, and in the case of incendiary letters there would have been no completed crime if they had not been received by the persons to whom they were addressed. There might, no doubt, have been in either case an attempt to commit a crime, which might have been criminally punishable, but the crime intended would not have been effected.

There are crimes of a different description which may be fully committed without the criminal succeeding in the object for which he commits the crime. The most obvious of these are forging and uttering. If a man forges a bill of exchange or a bank cheque, and sends it by post or by messenger to a correspondent for the purpose of its being used and acted on as genuine, the crime is completed as soon as the document passes out of his own possession or control, although the forger may be immediately afterwards detected, and no one is injured. A good example of this occurs in the case of *Smith*, Couper, vol. ii., p.1.

Now, the question of jurisdiction here seems to me to depend on whether the offence charged in this indictment belongs to the former or the latter of these descriptions of crime. The false and fraudulent representations are contained in a letter written in Blackburn. But the writing of that letter was not in itself a criminal act. The sending of the letter to Muirhead and its receipt by him would still fall short of constituting the crime charged. It is the success of the scheme which is necessary to complete the crime, and without such success in imposing upon Muirhead and inducing him to send the goods ordered there would be no ground for this indictment. While, therefore, the initiatory act of writing and posting the letter takes place in Blackburn, every other step in the action which is necessary to the constitution of the crime takes place in Edinburgh. It is here that Muirhead is imposed on and induced to believe the false and fraudulent representations of the panel; it is here that he acts on the belief so fraudulently created and delivers the goods in Scotland to a public carrier, who is thereby constituted the innocent agent of the panel in carrying out the fraudulent scheme to its completion. When the goods were delivered to the carrier they passed beyond the control of Muirhead, and the imposition was successful and complete. The poison contained in the Blackburn letter had done its work. For these reasons, I am of opinion that Edinburgh is the *locus delicti* in the present case, just as much as if the panel had sent either an accomplice or an innocent agent to carry out his fraudulent scheme to completion in Edinburgh."

LORD JUSTICE-CLERK (MONCREIFF): "... As a question of international jurisprudence this point is ruled by the most elementary rules. Two elements are requisite to complete the jurisdiction of any criminal Court, and these must coincide. The crime must be committed within the territory; and the Court must have power over the person of the criminal. But if these do coincide, no further question remains.

As to the first, every State has the right to punish offences committed within its territory, whatever may be the nationality or residence of the offender. This is, of course, the fundamental principle of civil government, and is of universal application. On the second, it may, no doubt, be that the culprit resides beyond the territory, and so beyond the executive power of the Court; but if the executive authority of the country where he resides thinks fit, by treaty or by legislation, to come in aid of the authorities in the *locus delicti*, that difficulty disappears, and if so, no further question can arise.

Now, here, in my opinion, the crime is sufficiently alleged in the indictment to have been committed in Scotland. It is said that the trader who was defrauded was a Scottish trader; he resided in Scotland; his goods of which he was defrauded were in Scotland, and he parted with them in Scotland in consequence of the fraudulent representations of the accused. It can make no difference that the letters which led to the fraud were written in England. They were intended to take effect, and did take effect in Scotland, and I know of no privilege which an Englishman has to commit offences in Scotland which a Scotchman could not plead.

As to the power of this Court over the person of the accused there is no question. The accused sits at our bar. He is not said to be there illegally, but, on the contrary, he is there through the intervention of an Act of Parliament. Both elements of jurisdiction therefore in this case concur."

The court repelled the objection to jurisdiction.

NOTES

For a general discussion of this case and related issues see Gordon, *The Criminal Law of Scotland* (2nd ed.), pp.93 *et seq.*

In *Lipsey* v. *Mackintosh*, 1913 S.C. (J.) 104, the Lord Justice-General (Dunedin), with whom the other members of the court agreed, stated: "In all these cases, where something is going on by the medium of the post, the offence is really committed . . . at both ends of the transmission by the post office." His Lordship was relying on the so-called "Long-firm cases" of which *Witherington* is the leading example. This may be so in the case of "continuing" or "conduct" crimes. But the court in *Witherington* was clearly of the opinion that where the offence required proof of some particular result, there was no offence until that result was brought about, and that jurisdiction lay where the representations of the accused were intended to, and actually did, take effect.

The question of jurisdiction in the converse situation to *Witherington*, *i.e.* where acts done within the jurisdiction take effect elsewhere, is unsettled. Macdonald's view (*A Practical Treatise on the Criminal Law of Scotland*, p.191) was that the Scottish courts would have jurisdiction if the "main act" was committed in Scotland. Quite apart from the difficulties in deciding what the "main act" might be in any given offence, problems arise, for example, where that "main act" is not criminal in Scotland, but gives rise to a consequence which is criminal elsewhere. Gordon's view (*op. cit.*, p.97 is that "on principle the better view is . . . that the crime is committed where it takes effect, and only there."

In *Kirkcaldy District Council* v. *Household Manufacturing Ltd.*, 1987 S.L.T. 617 the Outer House of the Court of Session held that the principles governing jurisdiction in crime, as set out in *Witherington* were of no assistance when attempting to determine questions of jurisdiction in delict under the Law Reform (Jurisdiction in Delict) (Scotland) Act 1971.

2. Laird and Goddard v. H.M. Advocate
1984 S.C.C.R. 469

The appellants were convicted on an indictment which, *inter alia*, charged them with forming a fraudulent scheme to obtain money from a company in England, and in pursuance of that scheme doing certain acts, while acting as directors of a company which had its registered office in Glasgow. The acts in question (as amended) were: (a) at the Glasgow office, and elsewhere in Great Britain, pretending to the English company that they could supply steel which complied with a certain specification and entering into a contract for such supply; (b) at a *locus* in England, uttering as genuine false certificates relating to the quality of the steel and thereby inducing a representative of the English company to confirm that the steel was of the required standard; (c) at a *locus* in England, uttering as genuine the said certificates to a representative of the company, pretending to him that they related to the steel and inducing him to hand over to the accused a cheque for £81,713.72; and (d) delivering to the purchasers, at a *locus* in Scotland, a quantity of steel and copies of the forged certificates.

Objections to the competency of this charge, on the ground that it was committed outwith the jurisdiction of the High Court, were repelled and the accused convicted. On appeal:

LORD JUSTICE-CLERK: "[This] appeal is taken by both appellants against conviction only. The basic ground in each case was that since the substantial and effective part of the alleged fraud had, on the Crown case as libelled in the charge and presented in evidence, taken place in England, the charge was incompetently laid in a Scottish court. ...

The submissions on the proposition that the Scottish courts had no jurisdiction to try this case, having regard to its circumstances, were to the same effect, although independently presented by counsel for each of the appellants. It was succinctly stated by Mr Macdonald as follows. The crime of fraud is the bringing about of a practical result by means of false representations. The crime is committed where the practical result is brought about, and there is no fraud until the result has been achieved. In the instant case Conoco was defrauded in England and not in Scotland. Accordingly the Scottish court had no jurisdiction to try the case. In support of that submission counsel founded principally on the six-judge case of *H.M. Advocate* v. *Witherington* (1881) 4 Couper 475. The opinion of the judges in that case passim would prima facie appear to give support to the submission. As in every case, however, what is said in judicial opinions has to be looked at in the context of the circumstances of the case. While that case, like the present one, libelled the concoction of a fraudulent scheme and libelled certain occurrences said to have been carried out in prosecution thereof, the facts were, as Lord Justice-General Inglis pointed out at p.492, that while the initiatory act of writing and posting the letter took place in Blackburn, every other step in the action which was necessary to the constitution of the crime took place in Edinburgh. What was under consideration was whether in these circumstances the Scottish courts had jurisdiction. There was ample evidence that material acts in the perpetration of the crime were committed in Scotland. It seems to me important to note that five out of the six judges in that case gave unqualified approval to what was said in the cases of *H.M. Advocate* v. *Bradbury* (1872) 2 Couper 311 and *H.M. Advocate* v. *Allan* (1873) 2 Couper 402. *Allan* was a case of money being obtained from people in Scotland as a result of fraudulent misrepresentations in advertisements in newspapers published in England and Scotland, where the money had to be sent to an address in England and correspondence in connection with the transaction was sent from England, all in furtherance of a fraudulent scheme. In the course of his opinion Lord Justice-Clerk Moncreiff said:

> 'This is a continuous [sic] crime requiring some time for its perpetration. It begins in England and continues and takes effect in Scotland, and in such cases the panel is, in my opinion, amenable to either jurisdiction. The forming of the design, the fraudulent scheme, takes place in one country, and the panel is amenable there; and, on the other hand, the fruit of the defrauding takes its effect elsewhere, and he is answerable also there.'

The case of *Bradbury* was one where the accused in pursuance of a fraudulent scheme formed by him in England to obtain articles from other persons by false pretences without paying or intending to pay for them, wrote and posted letters in England to persons in Scotland which led them to believe that he was a bona fide purchaser, and induced them to send certain articles to him in England, which articles he appropriated to his own use. A view, similar to that expressed supra by the Lord Justice-Clerk later in the case of *Allan*, was voiced by Lord Neaves and concurred in by the Lord Justice-Clerk Moncreiff, and that view was approved of and accepted by Lord Ardmillan in the case of *Allan* at page 407. Whilst it might be said that the approval of five of the judges in *Witherington* of what was said in *Allan* and *Bradbury* did not necessarily extend to the passages therein dealing with dual jurisdiction, there was no exclusion of that point from the acceptance of the opinions in the earlier cases, and in my view the approval must be deemed to cover those passages. If I might presume to advance my own view, it seems to me that where a crime is of such a nature that it has to originate with the forming of a fraudulent plan, and that thereafter various steps have to be taken to bring that fraudulent plan to fruition, if some of these subsequent steps take place in one jurisdiction and some in another, then if the totality of the events in one country plays a material part in the operation and fulfilment of the fraudulent scheme as a whole there should be jurisdiction in that country. ... [His Lordship summarised the evidence and continued:]

Thus this fraudulent scheme, which was initiated in Scotland and which involved various follow-up activities of a material nature carried out in Scotland to bring it to fruition, was concluded by bringing to Scotland, in pursuance of the original arrangement, the requisite quantity, if not quality, of steel, without which delivery a fraud would have been instantly exposed. The fraudulent scheme accordingly ended where it began—in Scotland—and in between there were these other activities by the appellants in Scotland. These collective circumstances played such a material part, not only in the formation of the fraudulent scheme but in its execution, that in my view it is justifiable to hold that the Scottish court had jurisdiction to try the case. For these reasons I move your Lordships to repel the various grounds of appeal relative to jurisdiction."

NOTES

1. Lords Dunpark and Robertson agreed with the Lord Justice-Clerk. Lord Dunpark's summary of the law was as follows:

"When a fraudulent scheme is formulated in Scotland by two men who are resident there and purporting to act on behalf of a company registered in Scotland, and the initial step of offering to sell goods which they knew that they could not supply is made from Scotland, the stage is set for further fraudulent misrepresentations in order to implement that scheme. The fact that some of the further acts take place in England, including the exchange of the goods for the purchase price, cannot, in my opinion, deprive the High Court of Justiciary of jurisdiction."

2. The ground of jurisdiction put forward here by the Lord Justice-Clerk and Lord Dunpark might be described as the "material part" theory. As such, it is clearly related to the "main act" approach discussed above, and, it is submitted, subject to the same doubts and criticisms as that theory. Certainly the effect of the decision is to detract from the relatively clear and simple rule propounded in *Witherington*.

3. *Witherington* and *Laird and Goddard* are obviously different versions of the territorial principle. *Laird and Goddard* is an example of the so-called "subjective" territorial principle according to which jurisdiction may be established in the state in which the crime is commenced even if it is completed abroad. *Witherington* is an example of the so-called "objective" territorial principle, according to which jurisdiction may be established in the state in which the crime is completed, even if it was commenced outside that state. (See the discussion of the *Draft Convention*, above, at pp.484 *et seq.*)

4. Criticisms of this decision may, of course, be dependent on the fact that it is seen as a decision on jurisdiction in relation to fraud. Why was this not charged as a case of conspiracy to commit fraud? If it was a conspiracy

to commit fraud, entered into in Scotland, would that not have provided grounds for jurisdiction?

5. In all of the cases so far discussed, some conduct related to the offence took place in Scotland. But can the territorial principle be applied in the absence of any conduct within the jurisdiction? See the following cases:

3. **Liangsiriprasert v. United States Government and Another**
[1990] 2 All E.R. 866

The appellant was suspected by the United States Federal Drug Enforcement Administration of smuggling drugs from Thailand to the United States. A DEA agent, posing as the representative of a criminal organisation in New York went to Thailand and obtained an agreement from the appellant that he would supply the agent with a quantity of heroin for distribution in New York. Since the extradition treaty between the United States and Thailand did not apply to drug trafficking offences, the agent induced the appellant and an associate to go to Hong Kong to receive payment for the heroin, from which territory they could be extradited to the United States. The appellant and his associate went to Hong Kong, met the DEA agent and were arrested by the Hong Kong police. A warrant was issued in the United States for the arrest of the appellant and his associate on a charge of conspiracy to import a quantity of heroin into the United States.

An extradition warrant was granted in Hong Kong, on various charges, including conspiracy to traffic in a dangerous drug, contrary to the common law and section 39 of the (Hong Kong) Dangerous Drugs Ordinance, Cap. 134, and the appellant and his associate were committed to prison to await extradition. The appellant unsuccessfully applied for a writ of *habeas corpus*, arguing, *inter alia*, that since the alleged conspiracy was entered into outside Hong Kong, and nothing had been done in pursuance of the conspiracy within Hong Kong, no offence had been committed there. On appeal from the Court of Appeal of Hong Kong to the Privy Council:

LORD GRIFFITHS: "As a broad general statement it is true to say that English criminal law is local in its effect and that the common law does not concern itself with crimes committed abroad. The reason for this is obvious: the criminal law is developed to protect English society and not that of other nationals, who must be left to make and enforce such laws as they see fit to protect their own societies. To put the matter bluntly, it is no direct concern of English society if a crime is committed in another country. It was for this reason that the law of extradition was introduced between civilised nations so that fugitive offenders might be returned for trial in the country against whose laws they had offended.

There have, however, from medieval times been a number of exceptions to this general principle, such as treason, piracy and murder committed by a British subject abroad. In more recent times the English Parliament has legislated to make certain crimes committed abroad triable in England, particularly those crimes which have been the subject of international conventions. There has as yet, however, been no decision in which it has been held that a conspiracy entered into abroad to commit a crime in England is a common law crime triable in English courts in the absence of any overt act pursuant to the conspiracy taking place in England. There are however a number of dicta in judgments and academic commentaries suggesting that it should be so.

[His Lordship considered a number of English and Commonwealth authorities, including *Board of Trade* v. *Owen* [1957] A.C. 602; *R.* v. *Baxter* [1972] 1 Q.B. 1; *D.P.P.* v. *Stonehouse* [1978] A.C. 55; *D.P.P.* v. *Doot* [1973] A.C. 807; *Attorney-General* v. *Yeung Sun-Shun* [1987] H.K.L.R. 987 and *Libman* v. *R.* (1985) 21 D.L.R. (4th) 174 and continued:] Apart from the dictum of Lord Keith in *D.P.P.* v. *Stonehouse* [1977] 2 All E.R. 909 at 939–940, [1978] A.C. 55 at 93, there is no affirmative statement in the authorities that an inchoate crime is not justiciable in England unless its effect or some action pursuant to the crime takes place in England, and there are the dicta of the Court of Appeal, Lord Diplock and Lord Salmon to the contrary effect. As Lord Tucker pointed out in *Board of Trade* v. *Owen* [1957] 1 All E.R. 411 at 416, [1957] A.C. 602 at 626, the inchoate crimes of conspiracy, attempt and incitement developed with the principal object of frustrating the commission of a contemplated crime by arresting and punishing the offenders before they committed the crime. If the inchoate crime is aimed at England with the consequent injury to English society, why should the English courts not accept jurisdiction to try it if the authorities can lay hands on the offenders, either because they come within the jurisdiction or through extradition procedures? If evidence is obtained that a terrorist cell operating abroad is planning a bombing campaign in London what sense can there be in the authorities holding their hand and not acting until the cell comes to England to plant the bombs, with the risk that the terrorists may slip through the net? Extradition should be sought before they have a chance to put their plan into action and they should be tried for the conspiracy or the attempt as the case may be. Furthermore, if one of the conspirators should chance to come to England, for whatever purpose, he should be liable to arrest and trial for the criminal agreement he has entered into abroad.

The Law Commission in *Territorial and Extra-Territorial Extent of the Criminal Law* (Working Paper no. 29 (1970)) para. 96 said:

> 'As to conspiracies abroad to commit offences in England, we take the view that such conspiracies should not constitute offences in English Law unless overt acts pursuant thereto take place in England.'

But why should an overt act be necessary to found jurisdiction? In the case of conspiracy in England the crime is complete once the agreement is made and no further overt act need to be proved as an ingredient of the crime. The only purpose of looking for an overt act in England in the case of a conspiracy entered into abroad can be to establish the link between the conspiracy and England or possibly to show the conspiracy is continuing. But if this can be established by other evidence, for example the taping of conversations between the conspirators showing a firm agreement to commit the crime at some future date, it defeats the preventative purpose of the crime of conspiracy to have to wait until some overt act is performed in pursuance of the conspiracy.

Unfortunately in this century crime has ceased to be largely local in origin and effect. Crime is now established on an international scale and the common law must face this new reality. Their Lordships can find nothing in precedent, comity or good sense that should inhibit the common law from regarding as justiciable in England inchoate crimes committed abroad which are intended to result in the commission of criminal offences in England. Accordingly, a conspiracy entered into in Thailand with the intention of committing the criminal offence of trafficking in drugs in Hong Kong is justiciable in Hong Kong even if no overt act pursuant to the conspiracy has yet occurred in

Hong Kong. This then is a sufficient reason to justify the magistrate's order under crime 1.

There is a further ground on which the magistrate's order under crime 1 is justified and this applies also to crime 3 which alleges trafficking contrary to s. 4 of the Dangerous Drugs Ordinance on 23 September 1988. This was the date on which the DEA agents took the drugs into the United States in the diplomatic bag and thus imported them into the United States (or Hong Kong for the purposes of the extradition proceedings).

The drugs were imported into Hong Kong (the United States) in breach of s. 4 of the ordinance and in the manner intended by the appellant and SC. If the DEA agents had been co-conspirators or if they had been innocent couriers unaware of what they were carrying both the appellant and SC would have been criminally liable for the importation. The importation would have been an overt act carried out in pursuance of the conspiracy, thus bringing the case within the direct authority of *D.P.P.* v. *Doot* [1973] 1 All E.R. 940, [1973] A.C. 807 for the purpose of crime 1 and would have established trafficking by importation for the purpose of crime 3. The appellant, however, submits that the fact that the persons whom the appellant and SC believed were parties to their criminal plan to sell heroin in the United States were in truth law officers breaks the chain of causation and that the importation cannot be attributed to criminal activity on their part. Their Lordships cannot accept this submission. The heroin was imported illegally and as intended by the conspirators, the criminality of their intent never varied and they cannot be permitted to take advantage of the fact that those carrying out their plan intended to hand them over to justice. If the appellant's submission is accepted it will go far to frustrate the actions of undercover law officers who penetrate drug dealing rings and obtain evidence by appearing to co-operate in their plans."

Appeal allowed in part.

NOTES

1. The decision and reasoning in this case were subsequently approved and followed by the Court of Appeal in *R.* v. *Sansom* [1991] 2 All E.R. 145.

2. Although the appellants failed on the question of conspiracy, they succeeded in a further argument in respect of other charges in the extradition warrant which appeared to give extra-territorial effect to the Hong Kong Dangerous Drugs Ordinance. In holding that the Ordinance could not be construed as having extra-territorial effect, Lord Griffiths stated the following:

> "When approaching the construction of a statute, particularly a criminal statute, there is a strong presumption that it is not intended to have extra-territorial effect and clear and specific words are required to show the contrary ... This presumption arises from the assumption that the legislature does not intend to intrude on the affairs of other countries, which should be left to order affairs within their own boundaries by their own laws."

Why should this principle apply only to statute, and not to the common law?

3. This decision represents an extreme version of the territorial principle and appears to suggest that a state may punish conspirators for actions which they *intend* to have an effect on its territory. Can this doctrine be extended to cover attempted crime? It is clear from the above that if A and B were to conspire, in Scotland, to kill C in England, the English courts

would have jurisdiction to try A and B for conspiracy to murder. Now, suppose that in pursuance of the conspiracy A, in Scotland, points a gun at C, who is in England, pulls the trigger, but the gun misfires. Would the English courts have jurisdiction to try A with attempted murder?

4. Since many legal systems do not have a generalised crime of conspiracy, it is possible that the English courts would have jurisdiction to try conspirators for agreeing to commit an offence in England where the state in which the conspiracy is entered into could not.

4. Clements and Another v. H.M. Advocate
1991 S.C.C.R. 266

LORD JUSTICE-GENERAL: "The appellants are Keith Richard John Clements and Mehmet Gouner, who were found guilty in the High Court at Edinburgh on a charge of being concerned in the supplying of a controlled drug, contrary to section 4(3)(b) of the Misuse of Drugs Act 1971. Four other men went to trial on the same charge, which was charge (33) on a lengthy indictment, and one of them, named David Webster Wright, was also found guilty. His appeal against conviction, together with that of James Henderson, who was found guilty on other charges, was the subject of an opinion of this court dated 29th March 1990. The Crown withdrew the libel against the co-accused Robert Fyvie, and the other two, named James Henry Dunn and George Ronald Angus, pled guilty to the charge in the course of the trial.

These appeals have been heard separately from those of Wright and Henderson. This is because they raise a point about the jurisdiction of the High Court of Justiciary to convict them on charge (33), which was of no relevance to the case against their co-accused. The charge libelled that on 26th and 27th June 1988 at various addresses in Essex, Kent and London, on a train travelling between London and Edinburgh, and at various addresses in Edinburgh all six men were concerned in the supplying of the controlled drug, namely cannabis resin, to other persons, in contravention of section 4(1)(b) of the Act. The issue of jurisdiction was not raised at a preliminary diet, but even if it had been, the terms of the charge were such that the point would not have been capable of argument at that stage since the Crown would have been entitled to lead evidence of actings by the appellants in Scotland as well as in England. But in the event no evidence was led at the trial to show that the appellants travelled to Scotland on either of these dates or that they had ever been to Scotland prior to their arrest. So far as they were concerned, the evidence was confined to various movements and other activities in the London area on 26th June in the course of which they met Dunn, who had travelled from Edinburgh that day and who returned to Edinburgh on the same night and was arrested in Edinburgh on 27th June. There was no submission at the end of the Crown case that the court had no jurisdiction to convict the appellants, but the point has now been raised on appeal.

There are some differences in the facts as they affect each appellant, but the principal argument in the case is common to them both. The difference lies in the evidence as to their state of knowledge as to the place to which the drugs were to be supplied. It was submitted on behalf of both appellants that there was insufficient evidence from which the jury could infer that they were aware that the drugs were for supply to persons in Scotland. This point has ceased to be a live issue so far as the appellant Gouner is concerned because the learned Solicitor-General accepted that in the case of this appellant the evidence was not sufficient to justify the inference. I shall deal later with the question whether the evidence was sufficient to justify the inference that Clements was aware of the destination of the drugs. The principal argument, however, which is common to both appellants is that, in the absence of evidence that they had ever been in Scotland or done anything in Scotland on the dates specified in the charge in regard to the supplying of the controlled drugs, the High Court of Justiciary had no jurisdiction to convict them on that charge. [His Lordship summarised the facts and continued:]

I turn now to the question, which is common to both appellants, whether the fact that the only evidence against them was of things done by them in England was sufficient in itself to deprive the Scottish criminal courts of jurisdiction on this charge. At this stage the question of Clements's knowledge of the destination of the drugs can be left out of account. His argument is that, even if the jury were entitled to be satisfied that he was aware that the drugs were destined for Scotland to be supplied to other persons in this country, nevertheless the place where he conducted his activities is critical and that, since none of these activities took place in Scotland, the courts of this country have no jurisdiction to convict him of the offence. Mr Mackay submitted that, whatever might be the position at common law, this case was regulated by statute since his client had been charged with a statutory offence. The correct approach, he said, was that it was to be presumed that the Scottish courts did not have power under the Misuse of Drugs Act 1971 to try offences under that Act which had been committed outside Scotland. He submitted that there was a strong presumption that a criminal statute was not intended to have extraterritorial effect, and that there was nothing in the 1971 Act to overcome that presumption. We were referred, by way of contrast, to section 148(1) of the Customs and Excise Management Act 1979 which enables proceedings for an offence under the Customs and Excise Acts to be commenced in any court having jurisdiction in the place where the person charged with the offence resides or is found, or where anything was detained or seized in connection with the offence, as well as any court having jurisdiction in the part of the United Kingdom in which the place where the offence was committed is situated. It was said that in the absence of similar provisions in the 1971 Act, the Scottish courts had jurisdiction only where the actings which amounted to being concerned in the supply of the controlled drug took place within Scotland—although it was conceded that it was competent for the Crown to libel and lead evidence about actings furth of Scotland as part of the surrounding circumstances. Mr Mackay told us that he was unable to find any authority to support the proposition that where a statutory offence was committed in England, the Scottish courts also had jurisdiction based solely on the fact that the ultimate effect of the activities in England was to take place in this country.

This argument raises questions about the proper interpretation of section 4(3)(b) of the 1971 Act and in particular as to what is necessary to complete the offence. The general rule is that in the absence of any legislation to the contrary the jurisdiction of the Scottish criminal courts is limited to crimes committed in Scotland: Gordon on Criminal Law (2nd edn), paragraph 3–39. It is relatively easy to say that a crime has been committed in Scotland if something which has been done here was necessary to complete the offence. The argument also raises questions about the basis for the presumption which Mr Mackay invited us to apply.

Section 4(3)(b) of the 1971 Act must be read together with subsection (1)(b) of the same section which provides that, subject to any regulations to the contrary, it shall not be lawful for a person 'to supply or offer to supply a controlled drug to another'. Section 4(3)(b) then provides that it is an offence for a person 'to be concerned in the supplying of such a drug to another' in contravention of subsection (1). It is clear that, in the case of both of these subsections, the accused's conduct may occur in one place and its result may occur in another. In the case of section 4(1)(b), for example, the supply may be made by sending the drugs from one place to another by post, and that is equally true of an offer to supply. The actings in one place may have their result in another where the recipient of the supply or the offer to supply is to be found. The position is similar in the case of an offence under section 4(3)(b). In *Kerr* v. *H.M. Advocate* at p.87 Lord Hunter said:

> 'Judging from its terms and the context in which it occurs, I consider that section 4(3)(b) was purposely enacted in the widest terms and was intended to cover a great variety of activities both at the centre and also on the fringes of dealing in controlled drugs. It would, for example, in appropriate circumstances include the activities of financiers, couriers and other go-betweens, lookouts, advertisers, agents and many links in the chain of distribution.'

Here again, the actings of whatever nature in one place may have their result elsewhere according to what happens along the chain. The separation between the activity and its effect may cross the border, as is the situation in this case, so that one finds an act done in England which is part of a chain of activities extending over the border into Scotland. But I think that there is a difference between the two subsections as to whether the result is part of the offence—and must therefore be proved in order to complete it. In the case of section 4(1)(b) it is clear that the supply must be made, or the offer communicated, in order to complete the offence. But in the case of section 4(3)(b) there need not actually be a supply. The word used is 'supplying' which, I think, allows for the possibility, as in this case, of interception of the drugs before any supply takes place in contravention of section 4(1)(b). It seems to follow that each person who participates in the chain of distribution commits a self-subsisting statutory offence. He may not know, of course, where the drugs are bound for, and in the clandestine world of drug dealing it may not be possible to find out. But it is not a requirement of the subsection that knowledge of this, or any such intention, should be proved.

The fact remains, however, that each person who is found to have been concerned in the supplying of a controlled drug was involved in a single enterprise—that is, of obtaining the drug from source and transmitting it to the point of supply. There is an obvious territorial connection between the activities of each one of them and the point of supply, where the harmful act was to occur in contravention of section 4(1)(b). I do not see why, in these circumstances, jurisdiction should be confined to the place where each person conducted his activities unless there is some rule or principle which compels us to this view.

Mr Mackay's argument about the presumption relied heavily upon the following passage in the judgment delivered by Lord Griffiths in *Somchai Liangsiriprasert* v. *Government of the United States of America* at p.252D–E:

> 'When approaching the construction of a statute, particularly a criminal statute, there is a strong presumption that it is not intended to have extraterritorial effect and clear and specific words are required to show the contrary: see *Air-India* v. *Wiggins* [1980] 1 W.L.R. 815 and *Holmes* v. *Bangladesh Biman Corporation* [1989] A.C. 1112. This presumption arises from the assumption that the legislature does not intend to intrude upon the affairs of other countries which should be left to order affairs within their own boundaries by their own laws.'

In my opinion, however, the passage has no relevance to the circumstances of this case. I do not think that we are concerned here at all with the extraterritorial effect, if any, of the Misuse of Drugs Act 1971. All the activities in this case took place in the United Kingdom, within the jurisdiction of the United Kingdom Parliament. The problem in this case is one as to territorial limitation as between the different jurisdictions within the United Kingdom.

This depends on constitutional practice, not on international comity: see *R. v. Treacy*, per Lord Diplock at p.564D. I accept that questions of comity could arise if the physical activities of the appellants had taken place outside the United Kingdom, such as were envisaged by Lord Diplock in his discussion to this topic in that case at p.562. But for the purposes of the present case it is, I think, sufficient to look only to the situation within the United Kingdom and to ask why the courts of one part of it should be denied jurisdiction if the activities of persons elsewhere in the United Kingdom are seen to have their harmful effects in that part. The presumption for which Mr Mackay contended does not apply.

The Solicitor-General's response to this argument was that the supplying with which the appellants were concerned was the supplying of drugs to Scotland. The evidence showed that, whatever may have been their knowledge or intention, the supplying of the drugs did not stop at the point when Dunn reached the minicab office. The chain led on to Scotland where the other persons were to whom the drugs were to be supplied. On this approach he submitted that the problem of jurisdiction disappeared, the question then being one only as to the sufficiency of the evidence that the appellants were concerned in that supply. The emphasis was on the territorial connection with Scotland which was proved in this case, not on what was necessary to complete the offence as defined by the Act. As I understood him, the appellants' position was also to be seen as if they were guilty art and part in the offence which was being committed by others, including Dunn, who undeniably were within the jurisdiction of the Scottish courts.

It is, of course, implied in all Scottish indictments that the person accused is guilty actor or art and part in the crime charged: see section 46 of the Criminal Procedure (Scotland) Act 1975. But that provision does not seem to me to be helpful in the present case where the evidence was that the appellants were both actors in the contravention of section 4(3)(*b*). They both met Dunn on the day in question and they both participated in the collection and handing over of the drugs to him. They were, with Dunn, all principals in the commission of the offence. As Lord Hunter pointed out in *Kerr* v. *H.M. Advocate*, the wide terms of section 4(3)(*b*) are such that actings which, in a common law context, might be considered to be criminal on the principle of concert are treated here as being criminal acts in themselves contrary to the statute. So far as the appellants were concerned, all that was necessary to complete the commission of the statutory offence by them had occurred by the time Dunn reached the minicab office and went on his way.

On the other hand the nature of the offence which is created by section 4(3)(*b*) suggests strongly that all those who participated in the chain should be subject to the jurisdiction of the courts of the place in the United Kingdom where the chain comes to an end. For the criminal enterprise with which they were concerned was the whole network or chain of supply, right up to the end of the chain. It is at the end of the chain that the harmful effects will be felt, and the single purpose, with which all those involved were in their own way concerned, was to bring this about. There seems to me therefore to be much force in the Solicitor-General's argument that in this case an offence under section 4(3)(*b*) was committed here by them all.

I think that it is worth noting also that the interests of justice are best served by trying all those who participated in the chain together in the same courts, rather than separating them out according to the parts of the United Kingdom where their activities occurred. It seems to me that this is in the public interest because of the complication and expense which would inevitably result if two or perhaps three separate trials were to be necessary, in England, Scotland and Northern Ireland, involving for the most part the same witnesses and the same productions, in order to establish the necessary basis for inferences of guilt to be drawn. It is also in the interest of the accused, should they ultimately be convicted, because comparative justice is best achieved if they are all tried and all sentenced by the same court. In my opinion, therefore, the critical question in the case is whether there is anything in the language of the statute, in the absence of any relevant presumption, to prevent this from being done.

I am conscious that, for the purposes of this part of the argument, the common law rules about jurisdiction where acts done in one place are intended to have their effect in another have no direct relevance, because this part of the argument assumes that the state of mind of the appellants is to be ignored. It is concerned only with their activities as observed by the police and the place where they occurred. But I think that it is helpful in this context to have regard to another passage in the judgment of Lord Griffiths in *Somchai Liangsiriprasert* at p.251C:

> 'Unfortunately in this century crime has ceased to be largely local in origin and effect. Crime is now established on an international scale and the common law must face this new reality. Their Lordships can find nothing in precedent, comity or good sense that should inhibit the common law from regarding as justiciable in England inchoate crimes committed abroad which are intended to result in the commission of criminal offences in England.'

Lord Griffiths was speaking there of a conspiracy entered into in Thailand with the intention of committing the criminal offence of trafficking in drugs in Hong Kong. The board held that the conspiracy was justiciable in Hong Kong even though no overt act pursuant to the conspiracy had yet occurred in Hong Kong. As I have said, that passage has no direct relevance to the situation in the present case where we are concerned with a statutory offence and where, it is to be assumed, there was no knowledge or intention as to the place to which the drugs were to be supplied. Nevertheless I think that it can also be said in the present case that there is nothing in precedent, comity or good sense to inhibit the Scottish court from treating as justiciable here acts in contravention of section 4(3)(*b*) of the 1971 Act committed in another part of the United Kingdom which formed [a] part in the chain of the supplying of controlled drugs to persons present in Scotland. The only argument to the contrary was that submitted by Mr Mackay which, as I have said, has no relevance to the present case since we are not concerned with the extraterritorial effect of the 1971 Act. No other authorities were cited to us to the effect that what I consider to be in accordance with common sense and the interests of justice could not be done in this case.

For these reasons I am of the opinion that the determinative factor, so far as jurisdiction over the appellants in this case is concerned, is the place where the drugs were to be supplied. This is consistent with the structure of section 4, because the purpose of subsection (3)(*b*) is to strike at all those whose activities may assist in the contravention of section 4(1)(*b*). The underlying mischief at which these provisions are directed is the supply or offer to supply of a controlled drug to another, and to look to the place of the mischief as the place where jurisdiction can be established against all those involved would be consistent with the idea that the courts of the place where the harmful acts occur may exercise jurisdiction over those whose acts elsewhere have these consequences: see Lord Diplock's discussion of this point in *R. v. Treacy* at p.562. This is not to say that the courts of other parts in the United Kingdom might not also have jurisdiction in an appropriate case. But, as Lord Diplock pointed out, the risk of double jeopardy is avoided by the common law doctrines in bar of trial, in England, of autrefois convict and, in Scotland, that the accused has tholed his assize.

That is sufficient for the disposal of these appeals. I should add that, had it been necessary to do so, I would have held that, there being sufficient evidence to infer that Clements knew that the drugs were to be taken to Scotland, he was undoubtedly subject to the jurisdiction of the Scottish courts in this matter. This is because in his case there was evidence of an intention that his actings should have harmful effects here. But, since I consider that proof of knowledge or intention as to the destination of the drugs is not necessary to establish jurisdiction in the case of this offence, I am of opinion that no relevant difference exists between the position of the two appellants. I would refuse their appeals against conviction."

LORD COULSFIELD: "The circumstances of these appeals and the material evidence are set out in the opinion of your Lordship and need not be repeated. On behalf of the appellant Clements it was submitted, first, that even if there was evidence from which it could be inferred that Clements was aware that the cannabis resin supplied to Dunn was destined for Scotland, the Scottish courts did not have jurisdiction to try him on charge (33) and, secondly, that, in any event, there was no evidence from which it could be inferred that Clements was aware that the cannabis resin was destined for Scotland. In my view, the second contention can be briefly dismissed. Looking to the whole evidence of the meetings and movements of Dunn, Clements and Gouner, a jury would clearly be entitled, in my opinion, to infer that Dunn went to London by arrangement to meet Clements and obtain the cannabis resin; and that Clements knew when and where to expect his arrival. There was evidence that the drugs were in fact taken to Edinburgh and that a number of persons, including the co-accused Wright, were involved in their further disposal. Against that background, the fact that Clements was in possession of Wright's telephone number is, in my view, very significant and would entitle the jury to infer that Clements was concerned in the arrangements for disposal of the drugs, including their destination. The fact that Clements had two Scottish £10 notes which, on his own admission, he received from Dunn, is a further piece of evidence pointing to knowledge of a Scottish dimension to the plan, although it is one of lesser significance. In my view, therefore, the jury were fully entitled to infer that Clements was aware that Dunn was collecting the resin to be taken to Scotland and distributed there. The quantity was, obviously, appropriate for a dealer, not a user.

Counsel for Clements submitted that, even on that basis, in the absence of evidence that Clements had ever been in Scotland or done anything in Scotland in any way related to the cannabis resin in question on the dates specified in charge (33), the High Court did not have jurisdiction to try him on that charge. He pointed out that there is no statutory provision, in the Misuse of Drugs Act 1971 or elsewhere, which confers on any court in the United Kingdom jurisdiction to try offences under the 1971 Act in circumstances other than those in which the courts normally have jurisdiction; and contrasted the position under section 148 of the Customs and Excise Management Act 1979, by which a very wide jurisdiction is created. It was clear that Clements could have been prosecuted in England on a charge under section 4(3)(b) of the 1971 Act, but there had been no offence other than the offence committed in England. In construing a criminal statute, there was a strong presumption that it was not intended that it should have extraterritorial effect: reference was made to *Somchai Liangsiriprasert* v. *Government of the United States of America*. In the case of a common law crime there might be jurisdiction in Scotland if an act done outside Scotland had a practical effect in Scotland (Macdonald's Criminal Law (5th edn), p.191); but that rule had no application in the case of a statutory offence. On the evidence, it could not be said that Clements had been concerned in the supply of cannabis resin anywhere else but in England.

In my view, on the evidence, the jury were entitled to hold that Clements was, knowingly, instrumental in the supply of the cannabis resin to persons in Scotland. The resin in fact reached Scotland, as it was intended to do. Clements was, therefore, in my view, concerned in the supply of drugs to persons in Scotland in a quite direct and straightforward sense. He took an active part in a plan for supplying drugs there and that plan was put into effect. He was, in my view, party to the carrying out of the plan in Scotland as well as in England. In the circumstances of Clements's case, therefore, I do not think it necessary to have recourse to the rule that there may be jurisdiction in Scotland when an act done entirely outside Scotland has a practical effect there. However, since it is relevant to the appeal at the instance of Gouner, I would add that I see nothing in principle or authority to prevent the application of the rule stated by Macdonald in the case of a statutory offence, subject, of course, to the particular terms of the statute. What matters is that the conduct of the accused had had an effect in Scotland which is contrary to the criminal law of Scotland. It is true that Clements might have been convicted of an offence in England, on the same facts, but I do not see that that makes any difference. The position would no doubt be different if he had actually been prosecuted in England.

The appeal at the instance of Gouner presents rather greater difficulty since, as the Solicitor-General conceded, there was insufficient evidence to entitle the jury to infer that Gouner knew that the cannabis resin was destined for Scotland. The argument for Gouner was, therefore, simply that it was not proved that he had done anything beyond being concerned in the supply of cannabis resin in England. On the other hand the Solicitor-General submitted, equally simply, that Gouner had been concerned in the supply of drugs which had ended up in Scotland and that that was sufficient, in the circumstances of this case, to entitle the Scottish courts to try him on charge (33).

The general rule undoubtedly is that 'In the absence of legislation to the contrary, the jurisdiction of the Scottish criminal courts is limited to crimes committed in Scotland' (Gordon, Criminal Law (2nd edn), paragraph 3–39). In the ordinary case, a crime may be held to have been committed in Scotland either if there has been conduct in Scotland which amounts to a crime there or there has been conduct abroad which has had as its result an actus reus in Scotland. In considering questions of jurisdiction, therefore, crimes may be classified as 'conduct crimes' and 'result crimes' although, as has been pointed out, it must not be forgotten that conduct on the part of the accused is an essential element in both types of crime (see Gordon, supra; R. v. Treacy, per Lord Diplock at p.560). I do not, however, think that it could be said that all offences under section 4(3)(b) of the 1971 Act must be either conduct crimes on the one hand or result crimes on the other. Section 4(3)(b) has a very wide scope and covers many difference types of conduct (see Kerr v. H.M. Advocate, per Lord Hunter at p.87). According to circumstances, section 4(3)(b) may apply where what is charged is conduct in Scotland or conduct which leads to a result in Scotland, or both. To decide whether the court has jurisdiction to try a particular accused on a charge under section 4(3)(b), therefore, it is necessary, in my view, to consider the precise conduct which is the subject of the charge in the particular case.

In the present case, it is clear, in my view, that a number of persons made and carried out a plan to obtain drugs and supply them in Scotland. Looked at as a whole, the plan included both conduct outside Scotland which was designed to have and did have a criminal result in Scotland, and conduct in Scotland which was, in itself, criminal there. On the facts proved, the appellant Gouner was one of those who participated in the plan. It is not proved that he knew, as other participants did, that the drugs were to be distributed in Scotland; but he must have known that he was engaged in an enterprise that was criminal both in the place where his own direct involvement had occurred and in the place to which the drugs were destined. There could be no other explanation for the elaborate and clandestine arrangements for obtaining the drugs and handing them over to Dunn. In these particular circumstances, I do not think that it is essential to prove that Gouner knew that the drugs were to be taken to

Scotland in order to render him liable to the jurisdiction of the Scottish courts. He freely participated in a plan which, as he must have known, would, inter alia, have a criminal result somewhere. That place was, in the event, Scotland, and, in my opinion, that is sufficient to give rise to jurisdiction to try him in Scotland. This is a result which, in my view, follows from the application of the accepted rules governing questions of jurisdiction and does not involve the assertion of any extraterritorial jurisdiction, in the sense described in *Somchai Liangsiriprasert*.

There are two points which should be added. First, at one stage in his argument the Solicitor-General submitted, as I understood him, that every person who had been involved in a chain of supply which ended in Scotland would, at least in theory, be subject to the jurisdiction of the Scottish courts in a charge under section 4(3)(*b*) without proof of knowledge of the destination of the drugs; and that that was so even if the transaction in which that person took part was lawful in the place where he was at the time. For the purposes of this case it is not necessary to decide how far that proposition may be correct, but, as at present advised, I am inclined to think that it goes too far. What degree of knowledge and participation in a plan to supply drugs in Scotland will render a person outside Scotland liable to the jurisdiction of the Scottish courts will, I think, require to be considered in particular circumstances as they arise. Secondly, the Solicitor-General made an alternative submission to the effect that if Gouner was not guilty of the offence under section 4(3)(*b*) in Scotland as actor, he could be held guilty art and part. It is not necessary to deal with that submission, but I would say that, as at present advised, in view of the wide variety of circumstances to which section 4(3)(*b*) may apply, as was pointed out in *Kerr* v. *H.M. Advocate*, I am not convinced that there is any conduct which could render a person guilty art and part under that subsection which would not also be a proper subject of a charge against him as actor."

Appeals refused.

NOTES

1. Lord Wylie delivered a concurring opinion.

2. Is it correct to say that the division of jurisdiction between Scotland and England is a matter simply of "constitutional practice?" That can hardly be the reason why causing death by dangerous driving in Jedburgh is not triable in the Crown court in Newcastle. The distinction between the two countries in jurisdictional terms is made clear by the Act of Union, Article XIX. It is true, of course, that Parliament may make laws which are applicable to the two jurisdictions (Article XVIID), but in the absence of legislation to the contrary, for the purposes of the criminal law the two countries are foreign to one another. The jurisdictional principles upon which the two countries operate may, of course, result in an offence being triable in either or both.

3. In the light of Lord Coulsfield's views, what would Gouner's position have been if (a) he had thought that the drugs were destined for delivery in England, or (b) if he had thought that they were destined for delivery in a country which, unknown to him, did not criminalise the conduct in question? In what way does the *mens rea* of an offence affect jurisdiction?

4. Although the court was careful to distinguish this case from *Liangsiriprasert*, it seems from some of the *dicta* that the court would not be hostile to a similar result should such a case arise in Scotland. If freely participating in a plan which the accused knows will have a criminal result

somewhere is sufficient to establish jurisdiction, then presumably taking part in a scheme which it is known will be criminal in a specific jurisdiction will also suffice.

5.   Gracie v. Stuart
(1884) 5 Couper 379

Gracie was charged in the sheriff court at Edinburgh with the reset of three silver watches "at some place in the city or county of Edinburgh to the complainer unknown." He was convicted and presented a bill of suspension to the High Court in which he stated that he had bought the watches in his own shop in Glasgow and brought them to Edinburgh and that consequently the sheriff at Edinburgh had no jurisdiction to try the offence.

> LORD JUSTICE-CLERK (MONCREIFF): "In the first place, it is contended that the Sheriff of Midlothian has no jurisdiction in this case, as it was not proved that the complainer got possession of the stolen property while within that jurisdiction. ... Now, upon the first objection I have no doubt whatever, and I am surprised that [counsel for the suspender] should have consumed so much time in arguing a proposition so self-evidently untenable. The crime of reset is committed wherever any person detains from its rightful owner any article which he knows has been stolen. ... It is beyond dispute that the resetter is committing a continuous crime during the whole time that the stolen article is in his possession, and although he may have passed through a great many places he is answerable to the Courts of each of these places if he went to them with the stolen articles in his possession."

The court refused to pass the bill.

NOTE

The principle applies to other offences of possession, such as possession of a controlled drug contrary to section 28 of the Misuse of Drugs Act 1971, and other continuing offences.

6.   Smith v. Inglis
1983 S.L.T. 160

OPINION OF THE COURT: "The respondents were charged with a contravention of s. 1(7) of the Companies Act 1976 in a complaint initiated in the sheriff court at Edinburgh. The complaint was in the following terms: 'you David Anderson Inglis, Margaret Inglis, Russell McKay and Nancy McKay being directors of Abercraggan Exports Limited, a company registered under the Companies Act 1948 to 1980, and having its registered office at 110 Coupar Angus Road, Birkhill, by Dundee, did fail to comply with a requirement of section 1(7) of the aftermentioned Act in that you did between 1 April 1978 and 1 February 1979 being the last day allowed for laying and delivering the documents aftermentioned computed in terms of section 6(1) and (2) of the aftermentioned Act, both dates inclusive, fail to deliver to the Registrar of Companies at 102 George Street, Edinburgh, a copy of every document required to be comprised in the accounts of the company in respect of the accounting reference period of said company ending 31 March 1978 whereby you David Anderson Inglis, Margaret Inglis, Russell McKay and Nancy McKay are guilty of an offence: Contrary to sections 1(7) and 4(1) of the Companies Act 1976.'

Under reference to s. 1(1) of the said Act which lays a duty on the directors of a company to prepare, lay and deliver accounts by reference to accounting reference periods which are specified in the succeeding subsections, s. 1(7)(*a*) provides 'Subject to subsection (8) below [which has no application here], in respect of each accounting reference period of a company the directors of the company—(*a*) shall deliver to the registrar of companies a copy of every document required to be comprised in the accounts of the company in respect of that period.'

It is a matter of agreement that the registered office of the company of which the respondents are directors is in Dundee, as are the residences of the respondents. It is further agreed that the office of the registrar of companies is in Edinburgh.

When the case called before the sheriff the respondents took a plea to the competency of the complaint on the ground that the alleged omission to comply with the requirements of s. 1(7) aforesaid must be deemed to have taken place in Dundee, and there was no jurisdiction in the Sheriff court in Edinburgh to entertain a complaint which libelled an offence committed in Dundee. The sheriff had previously decided this point in a manner favourable to the respondents in the case of *P.F. (Edinburgh)* v. *Jamieson* but as the Crown had failed to mark an appeal timeously in that case, he treated the instant case as a test case with a view to his decision in *Jamieson* being reviewed by this court. Towards that end he annexed to his report in the instant case his written judgment in the *Jamieson* case. He noted with understandable apprehension the volume of work which would accrue to the sheriff court in Edinburgh if all prosecutions under subsection 1(7) were to be funnelled into that court as a matter of Crown policy, as, he was informed, was the intention. Following his decision in *Jamieson* he sustained the plea to the competency in this case and dismissed the complaint.

In his judgment in *Jamieson* the sheriff made a detailed examination of the law in regard to the situation where an offence was committed partly in one jurisdiction and partly in another, and considered whether, in circumstances such as were there (and here) present, the offence was wholly committed at the point of time and place when the documents were dispatched. Coming to the conclusion that the latter point had be answered in the affirmative he found that the Edinburgh sheriff court had no jurisdiction to entertain such a complaint when it did not otherwise have the jurisdiction to do so.

We do not find it necessary to analyse and express any views upon the general law as canvassed by the sheriff, since the short answer here is to be found in the wording of s. 1(7) itself. The requirement therein is for the directors of the company to *deliver* to the registrar of companies a copy of every document. (The emphasis is ours.) Irrespective of where the documents are compiled, the omission which constitutes the offence is failure to deliver them to the registrar of companies whose office is in Edinburgh. The offence accordingly takes place in Edinburgh and the sheriff court there has jurisdiction to entertain a complaint libelling such an offence. Whatever further jurisdiction may have been introduced by statute, *e.g.* by s. 49(2) of the Companies Act 1976 or s. 287(2) of the Criminal Procedure (Scotland) Act 1975, that basic jurisdiction stands.

If it be suggested that this places an undue burden on company directors in that they might find it difficult to establish that the documents in question had in fact been delivered after they had been despatched, the answer is to be found in s. 4(2) of the Companies Act 1976 which makes it a defence for a director to prove that he took all reasonable steps for securing that the requirements of s. 1(7) would be complied with before the end of the prescribed periods for returns being made.

We are accordingly of the opinion that *Jamieson* was wrongly decided and that the sheriff's decision in the instant case was wrong. We allow the appeal, recall the decision of the sheriff sustaining the plea to the competency of the complaint and dismissing the complaint, and remit the case back to him to proceed as accords."

Appeal allowed.

NOTE

1. Previous cases in this section have been concerned with determining the place of criminal acts or conduct. *Smith* v. *Inglis* is concerned with the place of an omission. The view adopted by the court appears to have been that the place of the omission was the place where the duty to deliver should have been carried out: *cf.* Gordon, *op. cit.*, p.98; *H.M. Advocate* v. *McKay* (1866) 5 Irvine 329 and *Waugh* v. *Mentiplay*, 1938 J.C. 117. The duty in this case could only be performed in one place. Where the performance of a duty may be required in more than one place and is not performed in any of them presumably the courts in each of those places have jurisdiction.

2. *Cf. Aikman* v. *White* 1985 S.L.T. 636; 1985 J.C. 68; 1985 S.C.C.R. 176. In this case the respondent was acquitted on a charge of failing to furnish to the Controller of Customs and Excise a VAT return for a particular period, contrary to the Value Added Tax Act 1983 and the Value Added Tax Regulations 1980. The respondent carried on business in Edinburgh, and the Controller of Customs and Excise, VAT Central Unit, is in Southend-on-Sea, Essex. The respondent sent the required returns, by post, in a pre-paid envelope provided by the Controller of Customs and Excise but it never arrived at the VAT Central Unit. The court held that by his directions as to the manner in which the return was to be made, the Controller had adopted the Post Office as his agent for delivery of the return, and must therefore accept the possibility of loss in the post. The issue of jurisdiction as such was not discussed by the court which held that the duty to "furnish" did not impose an obligation to "deliver." The respondent's obligation was discharged by the sending of the return by the method indicated. There are good practical reasons for adopting this position:

> "If this were not so, the requisite act by the sender would be to all intents and purposes incapable of performance, as the Controller who is to receive the return is at Southend-on-Sea in Essex. It would be absurd to suggest that the senders of the form in all parts of the United Kingdom can only carry out effectively their duty under the regulation by travelling to Southend-on-Sea and handing it personally to the Controller." (*Per* Lord Robertson, 1985 S.L.T. 535 at p.538.)

On this basis, the obligation to furnish was to be discharged by the respondent in Edinburgh and the sheriff in Edinburgh had jurisdiction to try the case. If, however, the court had reached the conclusion that there was an obligation under the VAT rules to "deliver," then there would have been serious doubts about the jurisdiction of any Scottish court to deal with this case, since presumably the failure to discharge that obligation would have been located in Southend-on-Sea.

(iii)   Exceptions and Modifications to be Territoriality Rule

Certain exceptions and modifications to the territoriality rule are recognised, both at common law and under statute. These may be divided into three broad categories:

(A)   Cases where extra-territorial jurisdiction is conferred;

(B)   Cases where offences committed in Scotland are removed from the jurisdiction of the Scottish courts;

(C)   Special provisions permitting the sheriff and district courts to deal with matters not occurring within, or wholly within, their respective areas.

Only the more significant examples are included here. For further discussion see Renton and Brown, para. 1–08 *et seq.*

(A) Extra-territorial jurisdiction

Murder and culpable homicide

Criminal Procedure (Scotland) Act 1975

"**6.**—(1) Any British subject who in a country outside the United Kingdom does any act or makes any omission which if done or made in Scotland would constitute the crime of murder or of culpable homicide shall be guilty of the same crime and subject to the same punishment as if the act or omission had been done or made in Scotland. . . .

(3) A person may be proceeded against, indicted, tried and punished for an offence under this section in any sheriff court district in Scotland in which he is apprehended or is in custody as if the offence had been committed in that district, and the offence shall, for all purposes incidental to or consequential on the trial or punishment thereof, be deemed to have been committed in that district."

NOTE

For a discussion of the common law on this question see Hume, ii, 50–51. The crime of treason, being based on allegiance to the Crown, may be committed outwith the realm, and the Scottish courts have jurisdiction no matter where the offence is committed: Hume, iii, 49.

Theft and reset

Criminal Procedure (Scotland) Act 1975

"**7.**—Any person who has in his possession in Scotland property which he has stolen in any other part of the United Kingdom may be dealt with, indicted, tried and punished in Scotland in like manner as if he had stolen it in Scotland.

(2) Any person who in Scotland receives property stolen in any other part of the United Kingdom may be dealt with, indicted, tried and punished in Scotland in like manner as if it had been stolen in Scotland."

NOTE

Identical provisions may be found in section 292 of the 1975 Act with regard to summary proceedings. Section 7(1) may in fact reproduce a common law rule: *H.M. Advocate* v. *Taylor* (1767) Maclaurin's Criminal Cases No. 76, Hume, ii, 53. The Scottish courts may, therefore, have jurisdiction to try a person for a theft committed in, say, the Republic of Ireland, if he is found in possession of the stolen goods in Scotland. See Gordon, *op. cit.*, p.102, and the unsatisfactory cases of *Hay* (1877) 3 Couper 491 and *Stevenson* (1853) 1 Irvine 341.

Offences on ships

Merchant Shipping Act 1894

"**684**. For the purpose of giving jurisdiction under this Act, every offence shall be deemed to have been committed and every cause of complaint to have arisen either in the place in which the same actually was committed or arose, or in any place in which the offender or person complained against may be.

685.—(1) Where any district within which any court, justice of the peace, or other magistrate, has jurisdiction either under this Act or under any other Act or at common law for any purpose whatever is situate on the coast of any sea, or abutting on or projecting into any bay, channel, lake, river, or other navigable water, every such court, justice, or magistrate shall have jurisdiction over any vessel being on, or lying or passing off, that coast, or being in or near that bay, channel, lake, river, or navigable water, and over all persons on board that vessel or for the time being belonging thereto, in the same manner as if the vessel or persons were within the limits of the original jurisdiction of the court, justice, or magistrate.

(2) The jurisdiction under this section shall be in addition to and not in derogation of any jurisdiction or power of a court under the Summary Jurisdiction Acts.

686.—(1) Where any person, being a British citizen (within the meaning of the British Nationality Act 1981), is charged with having committed any offence on board any United Kingdom ship on the high seas or in any foreign port or harbour or on board any foreign ship to which he does not belong, or, not being a British citizen (within the meaning of the British Nationality Act 1981), is charged with having committed any offence on board any United Kingdom ship on the high seas, and that person is found within the jurisdiction of any court in Her Majesty's dominions, which would have had cognisance of the offence if it had been committed on board a United Kingdom ship within the limits of its ordinary jurisdiction, that court shall have jurisdiction to try the offence as if it had been so committed."

NOTE

The crime of piracy may at common law be tried by the Scottish courts irrespective of where the offence is committed or of the nationality of the offenders or the ship: *Cameron and Others* v. *H.M. Advocate*, 1971 S.L.T. 333. Section 4 of the Tokyo Convention Act 1967 confirms a similar jurisdiction in respect of piracy against an aircraft. Extra-territorial jurisdiction in respect of other offences committed on board British-controlled aircraft is conferred by section 1 of the same Act.

See also section 3(2) of the 1975 Act with regard to the sheriff's jurisdiction in offences committed at sea.

Offshore installations

Oil and Gas (Enterprise) Act 1982

"**22.**—(1) Her Majesty may by Order in Council provide that, in such cases and subject to such exceptions as may be prescribed by the Order, any act or omission which—

   (*a*) takes place on, under or above an installation in waters to which this section applies or any waters within five hundred metres of any such installation; and

   (*b*) would, if taking place in any part of the United Kingdom, constitute an offence under the law in force in that part,

shall be treated for the purposes of that law as taking place in that part.

(2) Her Majesty may by Order in Council provide that, in such cases and subject to such exceptions as may be prescribed by the Order, a constable shall on, under or above any installation in waters to which this section applies or any waters within five hundred metres of such an installation have all the powers, protection and privileges which he has in the area for which he acts as constable.

This subsection is without prejudice to any other enactment or rule of law affording any power, protection or privilege to constables.

(3) and (3A) [Liability of body corporate and responsible officers etc.]

(3B) Proceedings for anything that is an offence by virtue of an Order in Council under this section may be taken, and the offence may for all incidental purposes be treated as having been committed, in any place in the United Kingdom.

(4) The waters to which this section applies are—

   (*a*) territorial waters of the United Kingdom;

   (*b*) waters in any area designated under section 1(7) of the 1964 Act; and

   (*c*) waters in any area specified under subsection (5) below.

(5) Her Majesty may from time to time by Order in Council specify any area which—

   (*a*) is in a foreign sector of the continental shelf; and

   (*b*) comprises any part of a cross-boundary field,

as an area as respects which the powers conferred by this section and section 23 below are exercisable.

(6) In this section—

"cross-boundary field" means a field that extends across the boundary between waters falling within paragraph (*a*) or (*b*) of subsection (4) above and a foreign sector of the continental shelf;

"field" means a geological structure identified as such by Order in Council under subsection (5) above.

(7) This section ... shall apply to installations notwithstanding that they are for the time being in transit.

(8) Section 3 of the [Continental Shelf Act 1964] (which is superseded by this section ... below) shall cease to have effect.

NOTE

SEE ALSO THE CRIMINAL JURISDICTION (OFFSHORE ACTIVITIES) ORDER 1987 (S.I. 1987 No. 2198).

Torture

Criminal Justice Act 1988

"**134.**—(1) A public official or person acting in an official capacity, whatever his nationality, commits the offence of torture if in the United Kingdom or elsewhere he intentionally inflicts severe pain or suffering on another in the performance or purported performance of his official duties.

(2) A person not falling within subsection (1) above commits the offence of torture, whatever his nationality, if—

(a) in the United Kingdom or elsewhere he intentionally inflicts severe pain or suffering on another at the instigation or with the consent or acquiescence—
   (i) of a public official; or
   (ii) of a person acting in an official capacity; and
(b) the official or other person is performing or purporting to perform his official duties when he instigates the commission of the offence or consents to or acquiesces in it.

(3) It is immaterial whether the pain or suffering is physical or mental and whether it is caused by an act or an omission.

(4) It shall be a defence for a person charged with an offence under this section in respect of any conduct of his to prove that he had lawful authority, justification or excuse for that conduct.

(5) For the purposes of this section 'lawful authority, justification or excuse' means—

(a) in relation to pain or suffering inflicted in the United Kingdom, lawful authority, justification or excuse under the law of the part of the United Kingdom where it was inflicted;
(b) in relation to pain or suffering inflicted outside the United Kingdom—
   (i) if it was inflicted by a United Kingdom official acting under the law of the United Kingdom or by a person acting in an official capacity under that law, lawful authority, justification or excuse under that law;
   (ii) if it was inflicted by a United Kingdom official acting under the law of any part of the United Kingdom or by a person acting in an official capacity under such law, lawful authority, justification or excuse under the law of the part of the United Kingdom under whose law he was acting; and
   (iii) in any other case, lawful authority, justification or excuse under the law of the place where it was inflicted.

(6) A person who commits the offence of torture shall be liable on conviction on indictment to imprisonment for life."

NOTE
See also the War Crimes Act 1991.

(B)   Exclusion of local jurisdiction

Visiting Forces

Visiting Forces Act 1952

"**3.**—(1) Subject to the provisions of this section, a person charged with an offence against United Kingdom law shall not be liable to be tried for that offence by a United Kingdom court if at the time when the offence is alleged to have been committed he was a member of a visiting force or a member of a civilian component of such a force and—

(a) the alleged offence, if committed by him, arose out of and in the course of his duty as a member of that force or component, as the case may be; or

(b) the alleged offence is an offence against the person, and the person or, if more than one, each of the persons in relation to whom it is alleged to have been committed had at the time thereof a relevant association either with that force or with another visiting force of the same country; or

(c) the alleged offence is an offence against property, and the whole of the property in relation to which it is alleged to have been committed (or, in a case where different parts of that property were differently owned, each part of the property) was at the time thereof the property either of the sending country or of an authority of that country or of a person having such an association as aforesaid; or

(d) the alleged offence is the offence of hijacking on board a military aircraft in the service of that force or consists of inducing or assisting, in relation to such an aircraft, the commission of any such act as is mentioned in section 6(2)(a) of the Aviation Security Act 1982; or

(e) the alleged offence is an offence under section 2 or section 3 of that Act or consists of inducing or assisting the commission of any such act as is mentioned in section 6(2)(b) and (c) of that Act, where (in either case) one or more such aircraft was or were the only aircraft alleged to have been, or to have been likely to be, thereby destroyed or damaged or whose safety is alleged to have been, or to have been likely to be, thereby endangered; or

(f) the alleged offence is an offence under section 1(2)(a)(ii) of the Aviation and Maritime Security Act 1990, where one or more such aircraft was or were the only aircraft alleged to have been thereby destroyed or seriously damaged; or

(g) the alleged offence is the offence of hijacking a warship in the service of that force or any other ship used as a naval auxiliary in that service or consists of inducing or assisting, in relation to any such warship or other ship, the commission of any such act as is mentioned in section 14(4)(a) of the Aviation and Maritime Security Act 1990; or

(h) the alleged offence is an offence under section 11, 12, or 13 of that Act in relation to a ship, or consists of inducing or assisting the commission of any such act as is mentioned in section 14(4)(b), (c) or (d) of that Act in relation to a ship, where (in either case) one or more warships in the service of that force or other ships used as naval auxiliaries in that service were the only ships alleged to have been, or to have been likely to be, thereby destroyed or damaged or whose safe navigation is alleged to have been, or to have been likely to be, thereby endangered:

Provided that this subsection shall not apply if at the time when the offence is alleged to have been committed the alleged offender was a person not subject to the jurisdiction of the service courts of the country in question in accordance with the last foregoing section.

(2) In relation to the trial of a person who was a member of a civilian component of a visiting force at the time when the offence is alleged to have been committed, the last foregoing subsection shall not have effect unless it is shown that the case can be dealt with under the law of the sending country.

(3) Nothing in subsection (1) of this section—

(a) shall prevent a person from being tried by a United Kingdom court in a case where the Director of Public Prosecutions (in the case of a court in England or Wales), the Lord Advocate (in the case of a court in Scotland) or the Attorney-General for Northern Ireland (in the case of a court in Northern Ireland) certifies, either before or in the course of the trial, that the appropriate authority of the sending country has notified him that it is not proposed to deal with the case under the law of that country; or

(b) shall affect anything done or omitted in the course of a trial unless in the course thereof objection has already been made that by reason of that subsection the court is not competent to deal with the case; or

(c) shall, after the conclusion of a trial, be treated as having affected the validity thereof if no such objection was made in the proceedings at any stage before the conclusion of the trial ...

4.—(1) Without prejudice to the last foregoing section, where a person has been tried by a service court of a country to which this section applies in the exercise of the powers referred to in subsection (1) of section two of this Act, he shall not be tried for the same crime by a United Kingdom court.

(2) Where a person who has been convicted by a service court of such a country in the exercise of the said powers is convicted by a United Kingdom court for a different crime, but it appears to that court that the conviction by the service court was wholly or partly in respect of acts or omissions in respect of which he is convicted by the United Kingdom court, that court shall have regard to the sentence of the service court."

NOTE

The Act applies to the forces of the states listed in section 1 of the Act (as amended) and to those of any other country designated by Order in Council. The list of countries presently includes the Commonwealth countries, the United States, France, etc.

B. Jurisdictional Competence within Scotland

There are two elements to this question: territorial jurisdiction; and the division of competence with respect to the subject-matter of the offence.

(A) Territorial Jurisdiction

(i) The High Court

The jurisdiction of the High Court is general, extending to the whole of Scotland and the territorial waters round Scotland. The High Court's jurisdiction also embraces any extension of the territorial principle.

(ii) The sheriff and district courts

The jurisdiction of the sheriff and district courts is more limited. In general, the sheriff cannot take cognisance of any matter occurring outwith the limits of his sheriffdom. The jurisdiction of the district court is based on the "commission area" (i.e. a district or islands area within the meaning of the Local Government (Scotland) Act 1973) and the authority of that court is limited, subject to certain exceptions, to the relevant commission area.

Criminal Procedure (Scotland) Act 1975

"**3.**—(1) Subject to the provisions of this section, the jurisdiction of the sheriffs, within their respective sheriffdoms shall extend to and include all navigable rivers, ports, harbours, creeks, shores and anchoring grounds in or adjoining such sheriffdoms and shall include all criminal maritime causes and proceedings (including such as many apply to persons furth of Scotland) provided the accused shall upon any legal ground of jurisdiction be subject to the jurisdiction of the sheriff before whom such cause or proceedings may be raised.

(2) It shall not be competent to the sheriff to try any crime committed on the seas which it would not be competent for him to try if the crime had been committed on land.

(3) Where sheriffdoms are separated by a river, firth or estuary, the sheriffs on either side shall have concurrent jurisdiction over the intervening space occupied by water.

(4) Where an offence is alleged to have been committed in one district in a sheriffdom, it shall be competent to try that offence in a sheriff court in any other district in that sheriffdom.

4.—(1) Where an offence is committed in any harbour, river, arm of the sea or other water (tidal or otherwise) which runs between or forms the boundary of the jurisdiction of two or more courts, such offence may be tried by any one of such courts.

(2) Where an offence is committed on the boundary of the jurisdiction of two or more courts, or within the distance of 500 yards of any such boundary, or partly within the jurisdiction of one court and partly within the jurisdiction of another court or courts such offence may be tried by any one of such courts.

(3) Where an offence is committed on any person or in respect of any property on or upon any carriage, cart or vehicle employed in a journey by road or railway, or on board any vessel employed in a river, lake, canal or inland navigation, such offence may be tried by any court through whose jurisdiction such carriage, cart, vehicle or vessel passed in the course of the journey or voyage during which the offence was committed, and, where the side, bank, or centre or other part of the road, railway, river, lake, canal or inland navigation along which the carriage, cart, vehicle or vessel passed in the course of such journey or voyage is the boundary of the jurisdiction of two or more courts, such offence may be tried by any one of such courts.

(4) Where several offences, which if committed in one sheriff court district could be tried under one indictment, are alleged to have been committed by any person in different sheriff court districts, the accused may be tried for all or any of those offences under one indictment before the sheriff of any one of such sheriff court districts.

(5) Where an offence is authorised by this section to be tried by any court, it may be dealt with, heard, tried, determined, adjudged and punished as if the offence had been committed wholly within the jurisdiction of such court.

5.—(1) Where a person is alleged to have committed in more than one sheriff court district a crime or crimes to which subsection (2) of this section applies, he may be indicted to a court to be held in such one of such sheriff court districts as shall be determined by the Lord Advocate, whether that court is the High Court or the sheriff court.

(2) This subsection applies to—

(*a*) a crime committed partly in one sheriff court district and partly in another;

(b) crimes connected with each other but committed in different sheriff court districts;

(c) crimes committed in different sheriff court districts in succession which, if they had been committed in one such district, could have been tried under one indictment.

(3) Where, in accordance with the provisions of this section, a case is tried in the sheriff court of any sheriff court district, the procurator fiscal of that district shall have power to prosecute in that case and the sheriff of that district shall have power to try the case and to pronounce sentence on conviction even if the crime in question has in whole or in part been committed in a different district.

(4) The sheriff and procurator fiscal referred to in subsection (3) of this section shall have the like powers in relation to the case in question, whether before, during or after the trial, as they respectively have in relation to a case arising out of a crime or crimes committed wholly within their own district."

NOTE

For the purposes of summary proceedings, section 288 reproduces the provisions of section 3, with the addition of the following subsection:

"(4) The sheriff shall have a concurrent jurisdiction with every other court within his sheriffdom in relation to all offences competent for trial in such courts."

Section 4 is reproduced in section 287 in respect of summary proceedings.

Section 60 of the 1975 Act provides (*inter alia*) that under an indictment for theft the accused may be convicted of reset. Subsection (4) of that section provides that the power to convict a person of an offence other than that with which he is charged is exercisable by the sheriff before such person is tried notwithstanding that that other offence was committed outside the jurisdiction of that sheriff. In *Roy* v. *H.M. Advocate*, 1963 S.L.T. 369 the appellant was originally charged with theft of property in Scotland. It appeared that he had nothing to do with the theft, but that he had received the stolen goods from the thief in England. It was held that since all the elements alleged to constitute the crime of reset took place in England, the above provisions could not be relied upon to obtain a conviction for reset.

Section 3(4) of the District Courts (Scotland) Act 1975 contains, for the district court, provisions similar to those contained in section 4(4) (and section 287(4)) of the 1975 Act.

(B)   Subject-Matter Jurisdiction

(i)   The High Court

The jurisdiction of the High Court to try crimes committed within Scotland is almost universal. It may be excluded where jurisdiction is reserved by statute to some other court, but this must be done expressly or by necessary implication: *Rowet* (1843) 1 Broun 540, *Duncan* (1864) 4 Irvine 474.

The High Court exercises exclusive jurisdiction in cases of treason,

murder, rape, deforcement of messengers, breach of duty by magistrates
and in any case where exclusive jurisdiction is conferred by statute. The
crimes of robbery and wilful fire-raising which, along with rape and
murder, constituted the "pleas of the Crown" and thus fell within the
exclusive jurisdiction of the High Court, may now be tried summarily or
on indictment in the sheriff court (1975 Act, ss. 8 and 291, as amended by
s. 38 of the 1980 Act).

(ii)   The sheriff court

McPherson v. Boyd
1907 S.C. (J.) 42

McPherson was charged in the police court at Ayr on a summary
complaint with driving a motor car at a speed in excess of 20 m.p.h.,
contrary to section 9 of the Motor Car Act 1903. A preliminary objection
that the magistrate in a police court had no jurisdiction to try the complaint
was repelled. He was convicted, and presented a bill of suspension to the
High Court.

> LORD JUSTICE-GENERAL (DUNEDIN): "The question before your Lordships is a
> very plain one. It is whether under the Motor Car Act of 1903 jurisdiction is
> given to the Magistrates of burghs, and although it is not of course raised in
> this case, the determination will practically also decide whether it is given to
> Justices of the Peace. Now, the scheme of the Motor Car Act is first of all to
> declare that certain things shall not be done, and, next, to declare that, if they
> are done, the doers of them shall be guilty of offences under this Act. One of the
> things which is not to be done under the Act is to drive a motor car on the
> public highway at a speed exceeding twenty miles per hour. The section that
> deals with penalties says that a person guilty of an offence under this Act will
> be liable to summary prosecution and a fine not exceeding £20, and in the case
> of a second conviction to a fine not exceeding £50, or, in the discretion of the
> Court, to imprisonment not exceeding three months. There is also a set of
> provisions which I need not read, by which persons are not allowed to drive
> motor cars without licences, and provision is made for the Court which
> investigates the offence taking away the licence of the driver or suspending
> him from driving for a certain period.
>
> Now, the jurisdiction is admittedly not conferred *per expressum* upon either
> the Magistrates of the burgh or the Justices of Peace of the county. I confess
> that, as far as I am concerned, that is enough. It is the fact that in numerous
> statutes, too numerous to recite, which have created in modern times statutory
> offences, and imposed penalties for those offences, in all cases where it has
> been intended to confer jurisdiction upon the Magistrates' Courts or Justices of
> the Peace Courts, it is said in so many words that the offence shall be
> punishable before the Magistrates or the Justices of the Peace of the counties, or
> two Justices of the Peace, as the case may be; and the learned counsel who
> argued the case for the respondent, and who has said everything for the
> conviction that could be said, has not been able to point to any exception to that
> rule beyond citing the case of *M'Tavish* v. *Neilson* [(1903) 4 Adam 303], which I
> shall examine afterwards. That, to my mind, is sufficient. I have always
> understood it to be the law of Scotland that, in the case of statutory offences,
> which are not offences at all until they are created so by statute, the jurisdiction
> must be specially conferred on any Courts which have not universal
> jurisdiction, and the only Courts which have universal jurisdiction are the
> Sheriff Court and this Court. I am talking, of course, of criminal matters. When

I say universal jurisdiction I mean an inherent universal jurisdiction, which may, however, be curtailed in many ways. But there is an underlying universal jurisdiction in both the Sheriff Court and this Court, and it seems to me, therefore, to be quite settled by long practice that where Parliament is going to give jurisdiction to Courts other than the Sheriff Court or the Court of Justiciary it must say so."

The court passed the bill
and suspended the conviction.

NOTE

The court was also influenced by the fact that the Act gave a right of appeal, in certain circumstances, to the "sheriff-depute." This would have been a quite novel form of appeal from a police court:

"It is an attribute of the jurisdiction of County and Burgh magistrates that their judgments are only liable to be reviewed by this Court, and I should be slow to infer that this state of the constitutional law of the country regulating the co-ordination of the courts was intended to be taken away by Parliament by mere implication from a section dealing with other matters" (*per* Lord McLaren).

The police courts, along with other "inferior courts," were abolished by the District Courts (Scotland) Act 1975, s. 1. The jurisdiction and powers of those courts were, however, inherited by the district court (*ibid.*, s. 3). That jurisdiction has now been amplified by section 7 of the 1980 Act (as to which, see below). Subject to that modification, the High Court and sheriff court remain the only courts of universal jurisdiction.

The jurisdiction of the sheriff may, as the Lord Justice-General pointed out, be "curtailed" as, for example, in the case of offences reserved to the High Court. It may also be limited by the sheriff's powers of punishment. Where the minimum statutory penalty for an offence exceeded the sheriff's powers it was held that he had no jurisdiction to try the offence: *Gallagher* v. *H.M. Advocate*, 1937 J.C. 27.

(iii)   The district court

The district court was established by the District Courts (Scotland) Act 1975 and replaced the existing inferior courts (justice of the peace courts, burgh courts, police courts, etc.). The composition and jurisdiction of the district court is governed by the District Courts (Scotland) Act 1975 and the 1975 Act. Part II of the 1975 Act regulates procedures before the district court.

1.   Criminal Justice (Scotland) Act 1980

"**7.**—(1) Except in so far as any enactment (including this Act or an enactment passed after this Act) otherwise provides, the statutory offences which it shall be competent for a district court to try shall be those in respect of which the maximum penalty which may be imposed does not exceed 60 days imprisonment or a fine of level 4 on the standard scale or both.

NOTE

The offence in *McPherson* v. *Boyd* was punishable "on summary conviction" and this term was not sufficient to confer jurisdiction on an inferior court. In *Hall* v. *Macpherson* (1913) 7 Adam 173, however, it was held that where a statute imposed a penalty where a person was convicted before "a court of summary jurisdiction" the word "a" meant "any," and that inferior courts thus had jurisdiction. When the district court inherited the jurisdiction of the inferior courts it inherited this anomaly. The anomaly is now removed by section 7 above, so that the district court will have a general jurisdiction to try summary statutory offences, subject to the powers of sentence prescribed therein, and subject to any express exclusion, or extension of that jurisdiction.

2. Criminal Procedure (Scotland) Act 1975

"**285.** A court of summary jurisdiction other than the sheriff court shall not have jurisdiction to try or to pronounce sentence in, but shall, to the extent and in the manner mentioned in the next following section, be entitled to take cognizance of the case of any person—

(a) found within the jurisdiction of such court, and brought before it accused or suspected of having committed at any place beyond the jurisdiction of such court any offence, or

(b) brought before such court accused or suspected of having committed within the jurisdiction thereof any of the following offences:—

(i) murder, culpable homicide, robbery, rape, wilful fire-raising, or attempt at wilful fire-raising:

(ii) stouthrief, theft by housebreaking, or housebreaking with intent to steal:

(iii) theft or reset of theft, falsehood fraud or wilful imposition, breach of trust or embezzlement, all to an amount exceeding level 4 on the standard scale:

(v) assault whereby any limb has been fractured, or assault with intent to ravish, or assault to the danger of life, or assault by stabbing:

(vi) uttering forged documents or uttering forged bank or banker's notes, or offences under the Acts relating to coinage ...

286. If either in the preliminary investigation or in the course of the trial of any offence it shall appear that the offence is one which cannot competently be tried in the court before which an accused is brought, or is one which, in the opinion of the court in view of the circumstances of the case, should be dealt with by a higher court, it shall be lawful for the court to commit the accused to prison for examination for any period not exceeding four days, and the prosecutor shall forthwith give notice of such committal to the procurator fiscal of the district within which such offence was committed, or to such other official as may be entitled to take cognizance thereof, in order that the accused may be dealt with according to law."

NOTE

For the law on the "standard scale" of fines, see 1975 Act, s. 289G.

C.   Specification of the Locus of the Offence

The place of the alleged offence must be specified with precision in the complaint or indictment. This is necessary because the jurisdiction of the court depends on it and because of the rule that the accused is entitled to fair notice of where it is alleged that the crime was committed. As this problem is essentially one of relevancy and competency and arises at the point when the accused is served with a complaint or indictment, discussion of the cases is to be found, *infra*, in Chap. 9.

CHAPTER 4

ARREST AND DETENTION

A. GENERAL DISTINCTIONS

At common law there existed no power on the part of the police (or anyone else) to apprehend or detain a person short of arrest. "A person is either arrested or he is not; there is no half-way house" (*Swankie* v. *Milne*, 1973 J.C. 1 *per* Lord Cameron, *infra*, p.128). While certain statutes did confer on the police more or less limited powers of detention in particular circumstances, the Criminal Justice (Scotland) Act 1980 brought about a radical departure from the common law position by introducing certain general powers to detain suspected persons without arresting them. The justification for the introduction of these powers, and the conditions governing their use form the bulk of the discussion of detention in this chapter. It may be useful at this point to note certain general distinctions between power of arrest and powers of detention.

The power to arrest, with or without warrant, is recognised both at common law and under an increasing number of statutory provisions. Since, however, the common law does not recognise a power to detain, all powers of detention are statutory. One practical consequence of this is that the circumstances in which it is lawful to detain are, generally, more precisely defined than the circumstances in which arrest, or at least arrest without warrant, is lawful.

Warrants to arrest are granted, usually by a sheriff, on the application of the procurator-fiscal, and are executed by the police. The police may, however, arrest without warrant as (in theory at least) may judges, sheriffs and even private citizens in certain circumstances. Powers of detention, in contrast, are in general only exercisable by the police or by customs officers.

Arrest may be employed for a variety of purposes. As an initial step in criminal procedure it is used to secure the attendance of a suspect or accused person before a court. Similarly it may be used to ensure the attendance of persons required as witnesses. Post-trial arrest may be necessary to secure compliance with the order or judgment of the court. But so far as the police are concerned the power of arrest is not limited to such investigatory or administrative functions. The police have a responsibility for the preservation of order (see the Police (Scotland) Act 1967, s. 17) and in the discharge of this duty a constable may arrest without warrant any person committing or threatening to commit a breach of the peace. Detention powers, it is submitted, are in broad terms an addition to the investigatory powers of the police, and this should be borne in mind when considering the exercise of these powers. It would seem, for example, that an attempt to use the powers of detention contained in section 2 of the 1980 Act (*infra*, p.139) for non-investigatory purposes (such as the indiscriminate detention of a large group of persons for the purposes of preserving public order) would be unlawful. There are powers of arrest available in such cases and where they are not available detention should not be employed (*cf.* Thomson Committee, 2nd Report, para. 3.21).

Finally it should be noted that although this chapter is primarily concerned with powers of arrest and detention in the criminal process, a section has been included on arrest and detention in respect of matrimonial interdicts under the Matrimonial Homes (Family Protection) (Scotland) Act 1981. Given the quasi-criminal nature of the procedures involved it seems appropriate that they should be included here.

B.   ARREST

(i)   Under a Warrant

Any judge, sheriff or justice of the peace may issue a warrant for arrest, but in practice application is usually made by the fiscal to the sheriff. In solemn procedure this is done by way of petition, setting out the particulars of the accused (name, address, etc.) and the charge against him. A warrant to arrest may also be granted in summary procedure, though it is naturally less common and is usually granted because the whereabouts of the accused are unknown. The Thomson Committee (2nd Report, para. 4.10) recommended that in summary proceedings the fiscal should not ask for a warrant to arrest unless the whole circumstances of the case justified this.

Once granted, the warrant authorises officers of law to apprehend the accused. A warrant granted by a sheriff may be executed anywhere in Scotland (1975 Act, s. 15) and may be executed in England by an English constable (1975 Act, s. 17). A warrant to arrest is usually accompanied by a warrant to search the person, dwelling-place and repositories of the accused. (Powers of entry to effect a warrant are discussed below, p.125.)

According to Hume (ii, 79) a person arrested is entitled to see the warrant, at least where the officer executing it "is not generally known for such, or is acting out of his ordinary bounds." This issue arose, albeit obliquely, in *Stirton* v. *McPhail*, 1983 S.L.T. 34. Warrants were granted for the arrest of the appellant's husband for non-payment of fines. Two police officers were instructed by a superior officer to arrest him. The appellant, who had been informed of the existence of the warrants, tried to prevent the officers arresting her husband, and was convicted of obstructing and hindering the officers in the execution of their duty, contrary to section 41 of the Police (Scotland) Act 1967. At no time did the police officers have the warrants in their possession. The central issue was whether they were acting in the execution of their duty, and an argument was presented that in the absence of direct evidence of these warrants the court could not be satisfied that the officers were so engaged. The High Court held that the validity of the warrants, so far as the arrest of the appellant's husband was concerned, was not a relevant consideration. The officers were acting in the execution of their duty because they were carrying out the orders of a superior officer. The Lord Justice-Clerk did state, however, that:

> "The fact that it was not proved that such warrants were in existence, that they did not have these warrants in their possession at the time, and that their knowledge of them rested only on hearsay might be relevant when considering a complaint by the appellant's husband that he had been illegally arrested".

Lord Hunter expressly reserved his opinion as to whether it was in the circumstances necessary for the arresting officers to have the warrants in their possession at the time of arrest. While there may be administrative difficulties in ensuring such personal possession, and the production of a warrant cannot guarantee a trouble-free arrest, the added authority of a warrant may be of help in some cases. In any event, since an arrested person is entitled to be informed of the grounds of his arrest (*cf.* Hume, ii, 79) the availability of the warrant makes clear sense. For the legality of detention pending the production of the warrant, see *Farquharson* v. *Whyte* (1886) 1 White 26.

For a general discussion of arrest warrants, see C.N. Stoddart, *Criminal Warrants* (1991).

(ii)   Arrest Without Warrant

Here it is necessary to distinguish between common law and statutory powers of arrest.

(A)   Common law powers

Peggie v. Clark
(1868) 7 M. 89

LORD PRESIDENT INGLIS: "This is an action of damages against the superintendent of police of the county of Kinross, founded on the allegation that, on the 3d of February 1867, being Sunday, he entered the dwelling-house of the pursuer in search of him, and that he apprehended him on the following day, and detained him in custody for two hours, acting on both occasion without warrant, and therefore illegally and oppressively. The Sheriff-substitute found for the pursuer, assessing the damages at £6. The Sheriff altered that interlocutor, and assoilzied the defender. The Lord Ordinary returned to the Sheriff-substitute's interlocutor, and the question between these conflicting judgments is one of some nicety.

The pursuer is a carrier, and occupies, or did occupy, a dwelling-house in Kinross. He had also a horse and cart, and was employed by Gordon, a flesher in Milnathort, to deliver some meat in Burntisland, on Thursday, 31st January 1867, and to receive the price, which he engaged to pay over to Gordon on the following day. He failed to pay the money to Gordon in the course of Friday. He returned to Kinross on the Thursday evening, and was at home all next day till the afternoon in Kinross, which is only two miles from Milnathort. At 4 p.m. on Friday he went by train to the Bridge of Earn, where he remained till the following Monday. In the meantime Gordon, having heard nothing about his money, became alarmed, and, under the impression that the pursuer had absconded, he put himself in communication with the police. Being himself laid up, he sent his wife, who stated the circumstances to the superintendent, and thereafter the proceedings were adopted in respect of which the pursuer seeks reparation.

It appears to me that, if the superintendent had reasonable grounds for believing that the pursuer intended to appropriate the money, and for that purpose had absconded, it was right that he should take prompt measures for his apprehension; and the question therefore comes to be, whether he had reasonable grounds? Now, the event certainly goes far to justify him; for when the pursuer was apprehended on his return home, it appeared that he had spent a part of the money on his own account. Looking to all the circumstances, though it is a narrow case, I am inclined to agree with the Sheriff that the defender had a good ground for believing that the pursuer had committed a criminal breach of trust, and had thereupon absconded. What the defender did was first to go to the pursuer's own house and search for him. He could not get a warrant on Sunday, and I think he was justified in going without it. The pursuer's wife was at home and could give no account of him, except that he had gone to the Bridge of Earn to a marriage; and on the defender's expressing incredulity, she said, 'If you do not believe my word you can go yourself and look for him.' and he did so, without any harshness or rudeness, so far as I see. On the Monday the pursuer was apprehended, and he makes it part of his complaint that he was kept for two or three hours in custody. But that was a good deal owing to his own proceedings, for he wished Gordon to be sent for that he might satisfy him, and this appears to have caused delay. But Gordon came at his request to the police-office, and in the end he was liberated, Gordon having been satisfied about his money. Whether that was a strictly correct proceeding is not here the question ...

The ground on which the Sheriff puts his judgment is somewhat delicate and hazardous. He rests almost entirely on the 12th section of the County Police Act ... I am not satisfied that that enactment introduced any new law, or extended the powers of police officers to apprehend without warrant. But I am of opinion that, under special circumstances, a police-officer is entitled to apprehend without a warrant, and it will always be a question whether the circumstances justify the apprehension. There are somes cases about which there can be no doubt—thus, when a man is accused of murder, it would be a gross breach of duty on the part of a police-officer if, having an opportunity, he failed to apprehend the accused at once, and without a warrant. This is a different case, but, looking to the circumstances, I think they did justify the defender in proceeding without a warrant."

LORD DEAS: "It would be a strong thing to suppose that a discretionary power was meant to be given to inferior officers, under all circumstances, to apprehend any person they chose, and for offences of whatever kind, on their own suspicion, without a warrant. There are many exceptional cases in which police-officers or constables are entitled to apprehend without a written warrant, and for such cases no statute was required. If a policeman or constable sees a crime committed, it is his duty to apprehend the criminal at once; or if the criminal is pointed out to him running off from the spot, the same rule would apply. If, again, the criminal is in hiding, or the officer is credibly informed, or has good reason to believe, that he is about to abscond, the officer may de plano apprehend him, to prevent justice from being defeated. The same thing would hold if the crime believed to have been committed was murder or the like, the very nature of the punishment of which would render absconding the probable and natural result of the crime itself. Still further, if a suspected individual belongs to a class of persons reputed to live by crime, or who have no fixed residence or known means of honest livelihood, in all such cases a police-officer or constable has large powers of apprehending without a warrant. But I agree with your Lordship that the officer is not entitled to overstep the necessity or reasonable requirements of the particular case; and there ought, moreover, in no case, to be undue delay in the following out of such summary apprehension, by obtaining the appropriate formal warrant for the offender's detention. If an individual, even although expressly charged with crime by an aggrieved party, be a well-known householder—a person of respectability—what, in our justiciary practice, we call a 'law abiding party', and where there are no reasonable grounds for supposing that he means to abscond or flee from justice, I find nothing ... in the common law, to justify a police-officer or constable in apprehending him without a warrant."

The court assoilzied the defender.

NOTE

It is thus impossible to state with any precision either the offences in respect of which arrest without warrant is lawful or the circumstances in which such arrest may be made. The police may arrest without warrant in the case of common law offences and, though the limits of this power have never been authoritatively determined, in the case of statutory offences as well. But that does not take one very far, and it is clear that regard must be had to all the circumstances surrounding the arrest. Clearly the seriousness of the offence is a primary consideration: "arrest is more easily justified the more serious the offence" (Renton and Brown, para. 5–18), and in some cases the seriousness of the offence will of itself justify arrest. But in other cases regard must be had to the presence or absence of circumstances which would point to immediate arrest as opposed to some other procedure. Is the accused likely to abscond, or destroy evidence or tamper with witnesses? Is he or she likely to repeat the offence or commit further offences? And in weighing up these considerations it is relevant (though not conclusive of the matter) to have regard to the lapse of time between the commission of the offence and the arrest: *Leask* v. *Burt* (1893) 21 R. 32.

At common law it is unclear whether arrest without warrant on "mere suspicion" is permissible. Suppose, for example, a constable comes upon a broken shop window. Goods have been removed from the window, and there is blood on the broken glass. Nearby he apprehends X, who has a badly cut hand, but he is not in possession of the goods removed from the window. Is there a power of arrest here? The case does not fall into any of the categories expressly referred to in *Peggie* v. *Clark* or in earlier authorities (see, *e.g.*, Hume, ii, 75). The Thomson Committee were unsure (see paras. 3.06 and 3.30). In practical terms today this is not likely to present a problem for the constable who may rely upon his powers of detention in section 1 (and even section 2) of the 1980 Act.

The circumstances in which a private citizen may exercise a common law power of arrest were discussed in *Codona* v. *Cardle*, 1989 S.C.C.R. 287 and *Bryans* v. *Guild*, 1989 S.C.C.R. 569. In both cases the following passage from Renton and Brown was quoted with approval (para. 5–19):

"A private citizen is entitled to arrest without warrant for a serious crime he has witnessed, or perhaps where, being the victim of the crime, he has information equivalent to personal observation, as where the fleeing criminal was pointed out to him by an eye-witness."

In *Codona* v. *Cardle*, the appellant was convicted of assaulting the complainer by twisting his arm behind his back. The assault was carried out in an attempt to effect a "citizen's arrest." A window of an amusement arcade owned by the appellant had been broken, and the appellant had reason to believe that the complainer was the person responsible. He had not, however, seen the complainer break the window, nor had the complainer been identified as the culprit to the appellant by any eye-witness. In *Bryans* v. *Guild* the appellant was convicted of a similar assault on the complainer. In this case, the appellant believed, mistakenly as it turned out, that the complainer was one of a group of youths who had been throwing objects at the appellant's house and whom the appellant had been pursuing.

In neither case was the High Court prepared to hold that the appellants' actions were justified as amounting to a lawful arrest, and in *Bryans* v. *Guild* the court accepted the view expressed by the advocate-depute that the limited circumstances in which a citizen could exercise a power of arrest "should not be departed from lightly."

(B)   Statutory powers

One of the most significant developments in criminal law and procedure, especially in past 15 to 20 years, has been the proliferation of statutory powers of arrest without warrant. It would not be possible to include here anything other than a small sample of such powers, but certain broad groups of powers may be identified. The Royal Commission on Criminal Procedure (Vol. 2, Cmnd. 8092–1) identified three main groups (*ibid.*, App. 9): powers of arrest exercisable only where a person is found, or seen, committing the offence specified; powers exercisable where there is reasonable suspicion that a person has committed or is committing the offence specified; powers exercisable where the name and address of the person cannot be ascertained and/or he is likely to abscond, etc. The following extract contains an example of the first type of power.

1.   Civic Government (Scotland) Act 1982

"Powers of constables etc.

59.—(1) Subject to subsection (2) below, a constable may, where it is necessary in the interests of justice to do so, arrest without warrant a person whom he finds committing an offence to which this section applies or a person who is delivered into his custody in pursuance of subsection (3) below.

(2) A constable who is not in uniform shall produce his identification if required to do so by any person whom he is arresting under subsection (1) above.

(3) The owner, tenant or occupier of any property in, upon, or in respect of, which an offence to which this section applies is being committed or any person authorised by him may apprehend any person whom the owner or, as the case may be, the tenant, occupier or authorised person finds committing that offence and detain the apprehended person until he can be delivered into the custody of a constable.

In this subsection 'property' means heritable or moveable property.

(4) This section applies to offences under sections 50, 57 and 58 of this Act.

(5) This section shall not prejudice any power of arrest conferred by law apart from this section."

NOTE

The offences to which this section applies are: offences involving drunkenness in a public place (section 50), being in or on a building or other premises in circumstances inferring intent to steal (section 57), and being a convicted person found in possession or recent possession of equipment for theft (section 58).

Section 59(1) refers, in terms, to a person whom the constable finds *committing* an offence. In *Nicol* v. *Lowe*, 1989 S.C.C.R. 675 the High Court held that section 59 "must be construed as meaning that a constable is entitled to arrest without warrant a person whom *he has reasonable grounds to believe* is committing an offence" (p.679, emphasis added). Suppose that a constable, having such a belief, arrests someone who, it turns out, was not "committing an offence." The words of section 59(1) would seem to suggest that it ought strictly to be applied only where an offence is committed, but *Nicol* v. *Lowe* would be equally applicable here it seems.

In *Nicol* v. *Lowe* two police officers spotted the appellant coming out of the driveway of a private house just after midnight, and arrested him. He was searched, and found to be in possession of certain incriminating articles. However, an examination of the premises where he had been found revealed nothing untoward. In the circumstances, the court held that the police officers did not have reasonable grounds for suspecting that the appellant had committed an offence to which section 59(1) applied. In reaching that conclusion, the court offered the following guidance:

> "In cases under section 57(1) of the Act of 1982 it is not unusual to find other material being before the arresting officers. Thus it may be that they have observed individuals who have been acting in a suspicious manner, perhaps trying the door of lockfast premises, or perhaps they have seen individuals who have attempted to hide when they heard the police approaching, or, ... they have seen individuals who have taken one look at the police and have begun to run away. Where there is evidence of that kind one can well appreciate that police officers would have reasonable grounds for believing that an offence had been committed and therefore would be justified in arresting without a warrant. The present case, however, is not such a case. ...
>
> In our opinion, ... in the state of knowledge which they are found to have had in this case, they were not entitled to arrest the two youths there and then. ... they no doubt could have stopped the youths and asked them to wait while enquiries were made at the house to see if the householder could throw any light upon the question of whether the youths had any lawful authority to be there. Plainly, if the youths had declined to wait or had run away, then the police officers would no doubt have reasonable grounds for believing that an offence had been committed and thus would be entitled to detain or arrest the youths. In this case, ... we are driven to the conclusion that the two police constables acted too fast in arresting the youths when they did. As we say, it would have been a different matter if they had merely stopped them and questioned them or asked them to wait, but that was not the course which they followed. Instead, they proceeded straightaway to arrest them. In so doing we are of opinion that they exceeded the powers which were conferred upon them by section 59(1) ..."

2. McLeod v. Shaw
1981 S.L.T. (Notes) 93; 1981 S.C.C.R. 54

OPINION OF THE COURT: "[The respondent was charged with a contravention of s. 6(2) of the Road Traffic Act 1972]. It was established that the respondent was arrested while in charge of a motor vehicle and that the arrest had been made in purported exercise of the powers given to constables by s. 5(5) of the Act. It was established further that upon the faith of that arrest the procedure prescribed by s. 9(1) of that Act was carried out and that, in terms of an analyst's certificate to which s. 10(1) applied, the proportion of alcohol in his blood exceeded the prescribed limit. The submission made at the hearing on evidence at the end of the trial was that the arrest of the respondent had not been a lawful arrest under s. 5(5) with the result that the prosecutor could not rely on any of the subsequent procedure upon which the Crown case depended. The sheriff upheld that submission and acquitted the respondent. In this appeal the procurator fiscal has moved us to hold that the sheriff erred in so doing, and it is common ground that if this contention is well founded the case must be remitted to the sheriff with a direction to convict the respondent.

According to the stated case the circumstances in which the purported arrest of the respondent took place were these. An experienced woman police sergeant, accompanied by a male special constable, observed a motor car standing in the roadway about four feet out from the kerb. The time was 0040 hours on Saturday, 8 December 1979. They approached the car and found the respondent in the driving seat. There were two other persons in the car, both in the rear passenger seat. The sergeant went to the driver's door and had a brief conversation with the respondent who opened his window. Her evidence about this and what followed is recorded by the sheriff thus: 'Because of the position of the vehicle—my main thing—I decided to ask him to come out because we were standing right in the middle of the road. He came out and stood in front of the car. His eyes were glazed. As he came out I felt he put out his hand to steady himself. His speech was very precise. I felt there was slur in his speech. I didn't talk to him for long. I felt he shouldn't be driving. I formed the opinion he had been drinking and his ability was impaired. I told him he was under arrest and cautioned and charged him with s. 5(2) of the Road Traffic Act 1972. In 19 years' experience, I've dealt with drunks—not so many as others. I decided s. 5(2) as opposed to s. 6(5) because there had been no accident or anything.' Cross-examined: 'He was co-operative at all stages I conversed with him while he was seated—very little was said—for a moment or two. When he spoke to me in the car he spoke very precisely, but it was slurred. I decided I wasn't happy about the situation and asked him to come out of the car.'

It was in these circumstances that the sergeant formed the honest belief that the respondent was apparently committing an offence described in s. 5(2) of the Act, namely, the offence of being 'in charge of a motor vehicle which is on a road ... [while] unfit to drive through drink'. As the sheriff has found, she, the woman police sergeant, then arrested the respondent, taking the view that she was authorised to do so by s. 5(5) which is in these terms: 'A constable may arrest without warrant a person committing an offence under this section.' For the sake of completeness we should add that when the respondent was examined at the police station at 0120 hours, the examining doctor who noted the smell of drink and certain other matters certified that he was not then unfit to drive through drink.

It was not and could not be in dispute that under s. 5(5) a constable may arrest a person 'apparently' committing an offence under s. 5 and upon that understanding of the subsection the sheriff proceeded to consider the legality of the arrest of the respondent. After examining the authorities to which he refers in his note he decided that the question he must ask himself was this: 'whether on their own observations the police officers were justified in concluding that the respondent was probably guilty of s. 5(2)—being in charge of a motor vehicle when unfit to drive through drink and in arresting him without a warrant.'

He then proceeded to look not only at the evidence of the police sergeant, the arresting officer, but at the evidence of the special constable as well. Having done so he decided that it had not been proved that unsteadiness on the part of the respondent had been a factor in the decision to arrest him and that the only factors had been that there was 'some slurring in the respondent's speech which was precise and some glazing in his eyes'. He then reached his own conclusion that these two factors did not justify the belief that the respondent was probably unfit to drive through drink and the result was the respondent's acquittal.

We have no doubt that in reaching his decision to acquit the respondent the learned sheriff misdirected himself. He asked himself the wrong question and having done so made the mistake of attempting to reconcile the evidence of the two police officers present with the result that he excluded from his consideration one of the facts as they appeared to be to the arresting officer, the police sergeant—one of the several grounds upon which she formed the honest belief that the respondent was apparently committing the s. 5(2) offence. The question which the sheriff should have asked himself can, in this case, be put in this way: 'Am I satisfied that the experienced arresting officer, the police sergeant, had no reasonable grounds for her admittedly honest belief that the respondent was apparently committing the s. 5(2) offence which she had in mind?' That this was the proper question emerges from a consideration of the cases of *Wiltshire* v. *Barrett* [1966] 1 Q.B. 312; *Woodage* v. *Jones (No. 2)* [1975] R.T.R. 119; *Seaton* v. *Allan*, 1974 S.L.T. 234; 1973 J.C. 24; and *Breen* v. *Pirie*, 1976 S.L.T. 136; 1976 J.C. 60. It was the state of mind and knowledge of the arresting officer and of no other which is here in issue.

It is not surprising, therefore, that counsel for the respondent agreed that this was so. What the sheriff should have done, accordingly, was to ask himself that question with reference only to the facts as they appeared to the arresting officer, the police sergeant—the facts upon which her admittedly honest belief was founded. Had he done so he could not have held that she had no reasonable grounds for that honest belief. We are certainly not prepared so to hold.

In the result we conclude that the sheriff erred in law in acquitting the respondent for the reason which he gives, and that the prosecutor's appeal must be allowed."

Appeal allowed. Case remitted to the sheriff with a direction to convict.

NOTES

Although the decision is one on the construction of particular statutory provisions, the formulation of the issue in terms of whether the officer had reasonable grounds for believing an offence was being committed, means that the case is relevant to other statutory powers of arrest (and indeed detention) formulated in those terms. The decision effectively means that the arresting officer selects the "reasonable grounds" and provided that he reaches an honest conclusion on those grounds that an offence is being committed, the arrest is not open to challenge on the basis of other grounds which would render his honestly held belief unreasonable. (Such other grounds might, of course, affect the *honesty* of the officer's belief.) *Cf. Wills* v. *Bowley* [1982] 2 All E.R. 654 (H.L.).

Where does the onus lie in respect of the reasonable grounds? Must the prosecution show that the officer honestly believed that he was entitled to arrest, and that he had reasonable grounds (as defined above) for that belief? Or is it for the accused to demonstrate the absence of such reasonable grounds? General principle suggests the former, but in *Shields* v. *Shearer*, 1914 S.C. (H.L.) 33 the latter view was adopted. That was, however, a civil action for wrongful arrest where the onus would in any event have lain on the pursuer. See the commentary at 1981 S.C.C.R. 59.

3. **Binnie v. Donnelly**
1981 S.L.T. 294

The appellant was involved in a motor accident in Scotland. A short while later he drove into England, where he was involved in another accident. Two officers of Lothians and Borders police administered a breath test to him, in England. The proper procedures were followed, the test proved positive, and the appellant was arrested and taken back to Scotland. He was convicted before the sheriff court at Jedburgh of a contravention of section 6(1) of the Road Traffic Act 1972. On appeal by stated case:

LORD CAMERON: "...It was maintained for the appellant before the sheriff that the officers had no jurisdiction to require a breath test or make an arrest without warrant in England. After hearing submissions the sheriff applied his mind to the statutory provisions and, having concluded that the police officers were acting within their powers, proceeded to convict the appellant. Against that decision the appellant has appealed and maintains that the sheriff misdirected himself in law and that, as the police officers had no warrants granted in Scotland by a Scottish magistrate, they had no power to exercise any jurisdiction under their statutes on the English side of the border.

Counsel for the appellant submitted that a court had to be satisfied that the officer making the requirements and proceeding to arrest must be a 'constable' within the meaning of the Act at the material time. To say that at the material time the constables were given power for a particular purpose or purposes in terms of s. 17(8) of the Police (Scotland) Act 1967 was to beg the question. The question was whether the officers were 'constables' at that place and time: the Road Traffic Act required that the constable be not only a constable but a constable in uniform at the place and time where and when the requirement was or could be made. Counsel recalled the development of the jurisdiction of a constable in Scotland from his status and jurisdiction limited to his burgh to the nationwide jurisdiction exercisable by virtue of s. 17(4) of the 1967 Act. But this was a limited jurisdiction, its boundaries set at the border. Were it otherwise there would be no need for the very limited extension afforded to officers of border forces provided by s. 18 of the Act. The provisions of that section were a repetition of those which appeared in s. 11 of the Police (Scotland) Act of 1857, and the definition of a 'constable' contained in s. 51(1) of the 1967 Act showed that he was a constable of a Scottish police force not just a 'constable' which is the word used in s. 8 of the Road Traffic Act of 1972. The language of s. 17(8) was to be interpreted as referable to the power for particular purposes exercisable by a constable of a Scottish police force, but exercisable within the limits of his statutory jurisdiction, i.e. throughout Scotland.

For the respondent it was submitted that the sheriff's analysis of the statutory provisions led him to a correct conclusion. The Road Traffic Act applied throughout the United Kingdom and the powers of this Act were exercisable by a constable. There was nothing in the Act which suggested or supported the proposition that the power for the particular purpose of the enactment could not be exercised where, although the accident had happened in Scotland, the request by the constable seized of the event had been made in England. Such a construction could defeat the purpose of the Act, while there was nothing in the Act to suggest that any such incidental or accidental limit was to be placed upon the jurisdiction of constables in uniform engaged in operating the statutory procedure. Parliament must be assumed to have been aware of the existence of the border between England and Scotland, but no distinction was drawn between officers on either side of the border or any exception made as to the exercise of their powers in a trans-border situation as here. If the appellant's arguments were correct the object of the legislature and the intention of Parliament could in many cases be defeated, but such a result could be avoided by giving the words 'a constable' their ordinary and natural meaning—any constable whether Scottish or English. If that were correct then the officer possessed the necessary jurisdiction to carry out his duty in pursuance of this particular purpose, whether or not it involved his passage of the border to do so. The question should be answered accordingly.

In my opinion the solution to the problem of jurisdiction presented by this case is to be found in an examination of the language of the relevant statutory provisions which define and govern the powers and jurisdiction of police constables in Scotland and by reference to the precise wording of s. 8(2) of the Road Traffic Act 1972. The governing statute is the Police (Scotland) Act 1967 and in s. 17 it defines the general functions and jurisdiction of constables. By s. 51(1) of that Act 'functions' are defined to include 'powers and duties'. By s. 17(4) the geographical boundaries of a constable's jurisdiction are defined in these words: '(4) Any constable of a police force shall have all the powers and privileges of a constable throughout Scotland.' Subsection (5) provides: 'This section shall be without prejudice to s. 18 of this Act and to any other enactment conferring powers on a constable for particular purposes.' 'Enactment' also and necessarily includes Acts of Parliament, as is made clear by s. 82 of and Sched. 4 to the Act. Section 18, which repeats a provision of the earlier Act of 1857, provides a limited extension of the jurisdiction of constables of border counties of England or Scotland as respects the execution of warrants in such border counties. The language of s. 8(2) of the Road Traffic Act 1972 repeats precisely that of s. 2 of the Road Safety Act 1967 and provides: 'If an accident occurs owing to the presence of a motor vehicle on a road or other public place, a constable in uniform may require any person who he has a reasonable cause to believe was driving ... the vehicle at the time of the accident to provide a specimen of breath for a breath test' and goes on in subss. (4) and (5) to give the constable power to arrest without warrant if the result of the test is positive or there is a failure to provide the requisite specimen of breath. Now the provisions of the statute are applicable to the whole United Kingdom and there is no limitative definition of 'a constable'. All that the statute prescribes in order to clothe the constable with the requisite power to require a breath test or without warrant to arrest is that he be in uniform. The police officers in the present case were constables and were in uniform and they had reasonable cause to believe that the appellant was the driver of the vehicle concerned in an accident on a road, and on a road in Scotland. The statute makes no reference to the border between England and Scotland or distinction between a Scottish or an English constable, though it is to be assumed that Parliament was fully aware of this fact in enacting legislation to be effectual throughout the United Kingdom. Now the powers conferred on a constable in uniform are powers conferred on him for a particular purpose, to operate the scheme of control over drivers of motor vehicles contained in the provisions of the Road Traffic Act 1972. It is also the case that s. 8 of the Act of 1972 repeats precisely the language of s. 2 of the Road Safety Act 1967, which received the Royal Assent prior to the passage of the Police (Scotland) Act of that year, so that the enactment of this particular extension of jurisdiction was on the statute book at the time the police legislation was before Parliament. Clearly, therefore, it was such an enactment as is covered by the language of s. 17(8) of the Police Act. The concept of trans-border jurisdiction was familiar to the legislature, as the provisions of s. 18 of the 1967 Act were a re-enactment of a provision which had been on the statute book since 1857. In my opinion the natural meaning to be given to the language of s. 8(2) is that no distinction is made between a constable according to whether he belongs to a police force raised and administered on one side of the border or the other, and that this conclusion is reinforced by consideration of the express wording of s. 17(8) of the 1967 Police Act where it clearly refers to an enactment which may for a particular purpose or particular purposes extend the jurisdiction and powers of a police officer beyond those normally possessed and exercisable by him. In my opinion the jurisdiction and power claimed in this case by the police officer are just such as the statute contemplates and the Road Traffic Act confers. For these reasons the learned sheriff in my view reached the right conclusion and his decision should be affirmed and the question in the case answered in the affirmative."

Appeal dismissed.

NOTE

What are the limits of this decision? Clearly it refers only to powers conferred on a constable by legislation "effectual throughout the United Kingdom." It could be argued that the decision is limited to the taking of steps by the police in relation to offences committed in Scotland. But the dicta in the case are much wider. Does it mean that the police constable may exercise his statutory powers anywhere in the United Kingdom at any time? If a Scottish constable exercises in England a power of arrest conferred by a United Kingdom statute, is the lawfulness of the arrest determined by Scots or English law? Suppose, for example, that the officers had entered the appellant's land as trespassers and there administered the breath test and arrested him. Under English law they would have been acting unlawfully, so that neither the request for the breath test, nor the subsequent arrest would have been lawful: *Morris* v. *Beardmore* [1980] 2 All E.R. 753; *Finnigan* v. *Sandiford* [1981] 2 All E.R. 267.

In *Cairns* v. *Keane*, 1983 S.C.C.R. 277, *infra*, p.259, it was held that in a case of urgency a constable could lawfully require a breath test even though he was apparently at the time a trespasser. This implies a much broader power to enter onto private premises to administer a breath test than that which is enjoyed by a constable in England. It appears also that the courts in Scotland will allow the use of evidence obtained outside Scotland in exercise of the "urgency" power of search, even though that power is not recognised in the place where the search is conducted and the seizure of the evidence may otherwise have been unlawful: *MacNeil and Others* v. *H.M. Advocate*, 1986 S.C.C.R. 288, *infra*, p.265.

(iii)   Powers of Entry to Effect Arrest

(A)   Common law offences

Hume, Crimes, ii

"No officer shall in any case be justified for breaking open doors, to execute his warrant [to arrest] unless he have notified his errand to those within, and demand entrance. But, under that condition, he has a right by our law, though it may be otherwise in England, to break open the doors of a house, to take the person mentioned in his warrant; and this, whether he is certainly known to be the guilty person, or is charged only on probable suspicion; and equally in his own house, or at that of another person, where he is, or is on probable suspicion believed to be, at the time. For the officer is not obliged to trust the word of every one, perhaps the friend or associate of the felon, in that matter; and why should anyone refuse liberty to an officer of the law, to search his house, which is no injury to him, whether the person sought for be there at the time, or not? ... If the officer duly observe these several precautions, he certainly is not answerable, though in truth the person accused be innocent of the charge, or even though no such felony have been committed" (p.80).

"In cases of breach of the peace, or violent threats of immediate mischief as also in cases of felony which he has seen committed, or has information from others who are sure of the facts, the like power of arresting belongs to a constable, or other officer of the law, proper to the execution of criminal warrants ... As to the breaking open of doors on such occasions, I have not found any authority, to warrant a constable doing so, in his pursuit of one who flies after committing a breach of the peace; but rather a direction to him, in the act 1717, c. 8 to take notice of the master of the house, that he may be afterwards challenged for his contempt, in refusing admission. But it is not to be imagined, that a constable shall be subject to the like restraint in cases of murder, house-breaking, robbery or the like, committed in his presence, or known to him by complaints of others who were present, or have been the sufferers on such occasions ... It is always to be remembered, that to justify the officer in making a violent entry into any house, (and this is true, though he be the bearer even of a written warrant), he must first demand and be refused admission, and must notify who he is, and the purpose of his coming" (p.76).

NOTE

In summary procedure, section 321(1) of the 1975 Act provides that "any warrant of apprehension or search shall, where it is necessary for its execution, imply warrant to officers of law to break open shut and lockfast places."

(B) Statutory offences

Whether a statutory power of arrest without warrant infers a power of entry to effect the arrest is not clear. Some statutes confer both powers expressly, from which one might infer that the power to enter does not necessarily follow from the power to arrest. The majority of statutes are, however, silent on this point. While the question of a power of entry to effect an *arrest* has not been expressly discussed in recent Scottish authorities, it is suggested in *Turnbull* v. *Scott*, 1990 S.C.C.R. 614, *infra*, p.143 that in some circumstances a constable may enter private premises in order to *detain* a person under section 2 of the 1980 Act. In that case, it was stated by the High Court that "there is no absolute rule that police officers may only enter private premises if they have a warrant or statutory authority to do so" and whether in doing so they have acted illegally or exceeded their duty is a question of circumstance (1990 S.C.C.R. 614 at p.617). If that is so, then it should follow that the legality of an entry onto private premises to effect an *arrest* is likewise a question of circumstance.

It may be that among those circumstances which would justify an intrusion onto private property is the "urgency" of the situation. "Urgency" is a circumstance which has been held to justify conduct by the police in the gathering and securing of evidence which would otherwise have been unlawful (see *infra*, pp.255 to 266), and in *Turnbull* v. *Scott* (above) it was suggested (at least by the sheriff) that by analogy with the cases on search and seizure, "urgency" might justify actions taken to detain a person which would otherwise have been unlawful. It is difficult to deny the cogency of this argument, although it must be said that it begins from a suspect premise—the acceptability of the urgency doctrine—and for that reason should be carefully restricted to cases where other, regular, means for securing entry are not available. Clear examples would be where the offender is about to abscond or where he is about to commit further, serious, offences.

There are dicta in the case of *Shepherd* v. *Menzies* (1900) 2 F. 443 to the effect that a power of arrest without warrant conferred upon a constable by section 6 of the Cruelty to Animals (Scotland) Act 1850 entitled the constable to enter upon private premises for the purposes of making that arrest. (See Lord Kyllachy at p.446, affirmed by the Second Division at p.447.) However, it appears that their Lordships were relying on the special wording of the Act in question, coupled with common law powers of entry, rather than any general principle relating to statutory powers. In any event, these remarks must be considered *obiter*, since the constable did not in fact make an arrest in that case but proceeded by reporting the offence for prosecution by summary complaint.

(iv)   What Constitutes Arrest?

The Scottish courts have not been very successful in explaining the criteria by which one might determine whether or not a person has been arrested. This was inconvenient when the only distinction to be drawn was between arrest or liberty. But the introduction of powers of detention has made it necessary to draw the further distinction between these two forms of custody (see *Wither* v. *Reid, infra*). It is probably only a matter of time until the courts are called upon to determine whether, in a given case, a suspect was arrested, or merely detained under the 1980 Act. One cannot be wholly confident of the assistance they will receive from the following line of authorities.

1.   Muir v. Provost, Magistrates and Councillors of Hamilton
1910 1 S.L.T. 164

The pursuer raised an action against the provost, magistrates and councillors of the burgh of Hamilton, as being vicariously liable for an allegedly wrongful arrest carried out against him by a sergeant in the burgh police force. The Lord Ordinary (Salvesen) held that the defenders were not vicariously liable for the actions of the officer, but then went on to consider the merits of the action:

LORD SALVESEN: "... The only complaint against Sergeant Smith is that, having a suspicion that the pursuer had obtained exciseable liquor at the County Hotel, Hamilton, on the Sunday, by falsely representing himself to be a *bona fide* traveller, he 'insisted' that the pursuer should go with him to the hotel, in order to see whether the barmaid would identify him with a person of the same name who had written his name in the hotel book. The pursuer avers that, having protested his innocence, and having offered to meet the police at the hotel in the evening, Sergeant Smith refused to acquiesce in his proposal; and that the pursuer was thereupon marched off through the crowded streets, to Glenlee Street, where he and a constable took a tramway car. There is no suggestion that any force was used, or that anything happened but that the pursuer went in the company of the police to the hotel. It is not said that the sergeant acted maliciously; and, on the pursuer's own statement, he appears to have had probable cause. The only possible ground for action is that Sergeant Smith had no warrant for the alleged apprehension.

In my opinion these facts do not disclose a case of apprehension at all. Had the pursuer refused to comply with Sergeant Smith's request, and had then been handcuffed and forcibly taken to the hotel for purposes of identification, the pursuer's case would have been stronger. All that happened, however, was that the sergeant asked the pursuer to accompany him to the County Hotel, and that the pursuer—fearing that if he did not comply with the request worse might happen—agreed to go. The pursuer being, in fact, innocent, I should have thought it in his interest to get himself cleared of suspicion by at once going down to the hotel. This makes it unnecessary to consider whether the bare fact that the sergeant had no warrant would have been a good ground of action, whether with or without an averment of malice and want of probable cause."

The court assoilzied
the defenders.

NOTE

To use an overworked media expression, Muir was merely "Helping the police with their inquiries." Lord Salvesen's opinion suggests that the pursuer's agreement to accompany the police officer was the key factor in determining whether or not he had been arrested, but how does that "agreement" stand up in the face of the officer's "insistence"? In what sense does a person agree to do X when he has no choice, or believes he has none? In any case, is it not possible to be arrested even though one is quite willing to comply with the police officer's directions? "It's a fair cop, guv?"

2.   **Swankie v. Milne**
1973 J.C. 1

While driving his car on a public road the appellant was stopped by two plain-clothes police officers whose car he had overtaken in a dangerous manner. They formed the view that he had been drinking, but since they were not in uniform they could not administer a breath test. They summoned uniformed officers who arrived within five or 10 minutes. The sheriff found as a fact that if the appellant had attempted to leave during this time he would have been prevented, and indeed one of the officers took possession of the appellant's car keys. He gave a sample of breath which was positive and was then formally arrested, and taken to a police station where the remainder of the statutory procedure was carried out. He was convicted of driving with more than the permitted level of alcohol in his blood, and appealed. On appeal it was argued that since he had been arrested by the plain-clothes police officers, the breath test was not lawfully administered to a person driving or attempting to drive as required by section 2(1) of the Road Safety Act 1967.

LORD CAMERON: "... If there was no arrest then Mr Macaulay's first contention necessarily falls to the ground. Had the plain clothes officers in fact arrested or purported to arrest the appellant, then I can appreciate that a very difficult situation might arise with very difficult legal arguments. In such a situation it could be argued with force that once arrested a person is in the custody of the police and it would or might be difficult to maintain that he could at the same time be in the category of a person 'driving or attempting to drive a motor vehicle.' An arrest is something which in law differs from a detention by the police at their invitation or suggestion. In the latter case a person detained or invited to accompany police officers is, at that stage, under no legal compulsion to accept the detention or invitation. It may well be that in a particular case refusal to comply could lead to formal arrest, but until that stage is reached there is theoretical freedom to exercise a right to refuse to accept detention at the hands of police officers who are not armed with a warrant. I think it is important always to keep clear the distinction between arrest, which is a legal act taken by officers of the law duly authorised to do so and while acting in the course of their duty, carrying with it certain important legal consequences, and the mere detention of a person by a police officer such as is referred to in findings 3 and 4. Once arrested not only is the freedom of action of the person arrested circumscribed but he is also placed in the protection of the law in respect, *e.g.* of questioning by a police officer. None of these consequences flows from a mere 'detention' for inquiry or to enable the officers or their colleagues to pursue investigation or put forward (as in this case) certain statutory requests. And a person is either arrested or he is not; there is no half-way house. In my opinion it is plain that there was no arrest of the appellant by the plain clothes officers who stopped his van. No charge was preferred by them against the appellant nor is there any finding to establish or even suggest that at the stage when the officers stopped the van they had any intention of preferring the charge ultimately made or a charge under any other statute concerned with the driving of vehicles. If there was no arrest of the appellant by these constables then Mr Macaulay's first contention necessarily fails."

Appeal dismissed.

NOTE

The Lord Justice-General's opinion was that "the appellant was a man who, when driving, had merely been stopped by the police and who, under no lawful restraint, was awaiting the arrival of the uniformed officers." If this was a case of "detention" and the appellant was under no lawful restraint, then presumably any attempt physically to prevent him leaving would have been a criminal assault.

Lord Cameron comes close to putting the cart before the horse by enlisting the *consequences* of arrest as a means for distinguishing it from detention. Surely these consequences only become relevant once one has effected a lawful arrest. They cannot be employed to define what constitutes that procedure.

The following propositions are all consistent with the decision in *Swankie* v. *Milne*. Are they consistent with one another: the appellant was not arrested; the appellant was free to leave; the appellant would have been stopped if he had tried to leave; there is no half-way house between arrest and freedom?

The court did not consider whether the officers in question had a lawful power to stop the appellant's vehicle. Section 159 of the Transport Act 1972 (formerly section 43 of the Road Traffic Act 1962) confers such a power, but only on a constable in uniform. Nor did the application of section 228 of the Road Traffic Act 1960 (now section 164 of the 1972 Act) receive any attention. It has been held (*Squires* v. *Botwright* [1972] R.T.R. 462) that the power to demand identification of a person alleged to have committed any of the offences referred to in that section infers a power to detain.

3. Wither v. Reid
1979 S.L.T. 192

Section 24 of the Misuse of Drugs Act 1971 authorises a constable, in certain circumstances, to arrest without warrant a person suspected of committing an offence under the 1971 Act. Under section 23 of the Act a constable may, if he has reasonable grounds to suspect that a person is in unlawful possession of a controlled drug, search that person and detain him for the purpose of that search.

The respondent and a companion were suspected by the police of being in possession of drugs. They were approached by police officers who told them that they were arresting them on suspicion of being in possession of a controlled drug, and that they would be searched. They were taken to a police station where the search was carried out. The respondent violently resisted this search and was subsequently charged with assaulting a police officer in the execution of her duty. The sheriff acquitted her and the prosecutor appealed to the High Court:

> LORD JUSTICE-CLERK (WHEATLEY) (dissenting): "... The sheriff succinctly stated the issue which is the kernel of this appeal when he said in his note: 'If the search carried out by the two female police officers was lawful, there is in my view no question but that the accused is guilty of the offence charged; if, on the other hand, the search was unlawful, the accused in my view was entitled to use all necessary force—short of cruel excess—to resist the removal of her clothing and the indignity and humiliation of a body search.' ... The Crown case was that on the findings-in-fact the police officers were lawfully acting under the authority of s. 23(2)(*a*) (subject to the question of reasonable ground for suspicion), despite the fact that Detective Sergeant Souden undoubtedly informed the respondent that he was arresting her and not just detaining her, because it was clear from the findings as a whole that he was purporting to act under s. 23(2)(*a*) procedure. Counsel for the respondent submitted that the fact that Detective Sergeant Souden unequivocally and undisputedly informed the respondent that he was arresting her established that she was in fact arrested at the railway station without any legal authority and that accordingly anything which followed thereafter at the hands of the police was illegal, and that this included the search of the respondent at the police station. This latter view was the one which commended itself to the sheriff and was the basis of his acquittal of the respondent.
>
> Before turning to consider the competing arguments it is perhaps convenient to note a number of points. Counsel for the respondent accepted that if in the circumstances narrated the police were entitled to search the respondent the nature of the search was such as to justify the removal of the respondent to the police station for that purpose, since the railway station was manifestly unsuitable for it. Counsel for the appellant did not suggest that esto the search of the respondent was illegal the actions taken by the respondent amounted to cruel excess. And to crown this unfortunate incident the very thorough search of the respondent's clothing and person disclosed no presence of any drug whatsoever. In these circumstances it is easy to understand the respondent's annoyance, in the light of her personal

knowledge that she was not in possession of any drugs, at being subjected to what she considered was humiliation and indignity, but if the police had reasonable grounds for suspecting that she was in possession of a controlled drug, then assuming that the police acted legally in taking her to the police station for the purpose of conducting a search, and it was explained to her that it was, it was her legal duty to submit to and not resist such search even although she knew in her own mind that there was no justification for it. . . . There is, in my opinion, no doubt that Detective Sergeant Souden thought that he was acting under the s. 23(2)(a) procedure which provides the only statutory authority for a personal search. This, in my view, is borne out by the following facts. Detective Sergeant Souden informed the respondent (and her companion) at the railway station that they were being apprehended under the Misuse of Drugs Act 1971 on suspicion of being in possession of a controlled drug. Although he made it clear to the two suspects that they were under arrest, he informed them that they would be taken to Elgin police office and there searched for drugs, but that they would not be kept there any longer than necessary. In further explanation he informed the respondent that when the police had received information of a suspected drug offence they were bound to take suspects to a police station and search them for drugs and that she would be liberated as soon as possible. This explanation was repeated on at least two occasions in the police office. There was nothing in the evidence which would justify the invocation of s. 24(1) which authorises arrest. On the other hand the whole procedure followed the pattern of s. 23(2)(a) apart from the fact that Detective Sergeant Souden told the respondent that she was under arrest and not just being detained. Looking to the explanations referred to above, they seem to me to be much more consistent with being given to a person who is being detained for the purpose of a search than to a person who was being arrested. It would be passing strange if a person who had been arrested was informed that he or she would be liberated as soon as possible. But such an explanation is perfectly intelligible in relation to a person who is detained for the purpose of search. Does the fact that Detective Sergeant Souden used the word 'arrest' when he should have used the word 'detention' vitiate the Crown case, albeit he and his colleagues followed the procedure relevant to detention under s. 23(2)(a)? No definition of 'detention' in terms of that subsection was cited to us and it was said that there was none. Reference was made to what was said by Lord Cameron in *Swankie* v. *Milne*, 1973 S.L.T. (Notes) at p.29, but what his Lordship was there considering was 'detention' when there was no legal authorisation for it. Here, however, there is statutory authority for detention under s. 23(2)(a), and the citation has no relevance to this case. The issue may be put this way. Is the criterion what was said or what was done? Each case will have to be considered on its own facts, and in this case I have come to the conclusion that what was done had full statutory authority and was not vitiated by the fact that Detective Sergeant Souden informed the respondent that she was being arrested and taken to the police station to be searched for drugs when she should have been told that she was being detained and taken to the police station for that purpose. As she could have been detained and taken to the police station for that purpose under statutory authority I do not consider that the fact that Detective Sergeant Souden used the wrong word vitiates the procedure which was otherwise unimpeachable. I accept that a penal statute must be construed in favour of the subject when a doubt arises, but I do not consider this error in terminology should vitiate a conviction. The power of detention given under s. 23(2)(a) connotes that the subject can in the given circumstances be taken to the police station even against his or her will, just as a power of arrest does. If the conditions of s. 23(2)(a) are satisfied and the procedure thereunder is followed, and the error in the use of the word did not result in the respondent being taken, even against her will, to the police station when if the correct word had been used she would have been, I regard it as overstraining logic to say that such an error vitiated all that followed in this case. I have accordingly reached the conclusion that the sheriff erred in holding that it did."

LORD KISSEN: "... Whatever may have been in the mind of the detective sergeant, he did tell the respondent that she was under arrest. He purported to arrest her. I cannot see how the later explanation to the respondent, apparently based on s. 23(2)(a), can alter what he specifically said he was doing. His apparent confusion about his powers cannot, in my opinion, mean that he was not putting her under 'arrest', as he himself clearly thought he was doing despite the explanation. The actions which followed the 'arrest' and the events which occurred at Elgin police station are as consistent with a purported arrest as they are with search and detention under said s. 23(2)(a). If one looks at the actions which followed the events at the Elgin railway station, as counsel for the appellant suggested should be done in order to ascertain whether there was an 'arrest', these actions did not show that she was not 'under arrest'. What the detective sergeant did was to arrest the respondent unlawfully prior to the search despite an explanation by him which indicated a limited statutory detention. The search which followed was referable to the purported arrest and was, therefore, in my opinion, unlawful. It follows accordingly that the sheriff was correct in the view which he reached."

LORD ROBERTSON: "... According to the sheriff, the police officers gave clear and unequivocal evidence that the respondent was arrested at the railway station under the Misuse of Drugs Act 1971.
If this is so, then the arrest in my opinion was unlawful. It was not an arrest under s. 24, but was a purported action under s. 23(2)(a). But that section does not give authority to arrest, only to 'detain' for a limited purpose. There is a vital distinction between 'arrest' and 'detention' (*Swankie* v. *Milne*, 1973 S.L.T. (Notes), Lord Cameron at p.29). It is true that under s. 23(2)(a) of the 1971 Act the police are entitled to detain the person suspected for the purpose of searching him, and for this purpose may be entitled to take him to a place where the search may take place. This place might conveniently be the nearest police station. But a penal statute must be construed strictly. In my opinion, in deference to the rights of the citizen, it must be made perfectly clear to the person against whom action is being taken under s. 23(2)(a) that that is what is being done and that he is not being arrested. If, as apparently happened in this case, the respondent was arrested and told, that she was to be taken to the police station under arrest, then in my opinion that was an unlawful arrest. It will not do, in my opinion, to say that she was bound to know the law and so was bound to realise that, although the police officers used the word 'arrest', they really meant 'detain', and were proceeding under s. 23(2)(a). The police also should know the law and if they were proceeding under s. 23 they should have done so explicitly."

Appeal dismissed.

NOTE

It is submitted that the correct decision was reached in this case. If the issue had simply been one of "arrest or no arrest" then reliance on the use of that term could be considered highly technical, even artificial. In such a case what is crucial is that the constable brings home to the suspect the fact that he or she is no longer a free person (*cf. Alderson* v. *Booth* [1969] 2 Q.B. 216; *R.* v. *Inwood* [1973] 2 All E.R. 645; Thomson Committee, 2nd Report, para. 3.12, But this case is concerned with a rather different question from that considered in *Muir* and *Swankie*. There was no doubt in *Wither* v. *Reid* that the respondent was under compulsion. The question was whether that compulsion was arrest or detention. Given that the consequences of arrest and detention differ, it seems right in principle that the police should be put on their mettle to distinguish the two forms of compulsion, and explain unequivocally to the person apprehended which procedure is being adopted.

Compare the approach taken in this case to the following case.

4.   Forbes v. H.M. Advocate
1990 S.C.C.R. 69

The appellant was convicted on charges of conspiracy, contravention of section 10(1)(*b*) of the Prevention of Terrorism (Temporary Provisions) Act 1984, section 3(*b*) of the Explosive Substances Act 1883 and sections 1 and 16 of the Firearms Act 1968. He appealed to the High Court on the grounds, *inter alia*, that when he was taken into custody by the police he was not told, in terms, that he had been arrested nor was he informed of the reason for his arrest.

> LORD JUSTICE-GENERAL: "The first argument which was presented on behalf of the appellant relates to the fact that the appellant was not told in terms, when he was being taken into custody or at any time thereafter, that he had been arrested. Nor, it was said, was he given any specification of the reason why he had been detained. It was submitted that the police proceeded under a misapprehension of their powers because all that they had done was to detain him, whereas what section 12 of the 1984 Act requires is that there should be an arrest before the suspect can be said to be in a lawful state of detention under that section. Reference was made to section 321(3) of the Criminal Procedure (Scotland) Act 1975 which provides that a person apprehended under a warrant of apprehension or by virtue of the powers possessed at common law or conferred by statute shall whenever possible be brought before a court competent to deal with the case not later than in the course of the next lawful court day. Section 12 innovates on these provisions in respect that a person arrested under that section may be detained in right of the arrest for an extended period before being brought before the court, but this can only be done if there has been in the first instance a lawful and proper arrest. It was submitted that all that had happened in this case was a detention without warrant, so everything which followed from that initial unlawful detention must be regarded as vitiated. Furthermore, any questioning following upon that detention was unfair and any responses elicited by it were inadmissible because the appellant was not told even in general terms why he had been detained or of the nature of the offence or offences of which he was suspected of being guilty. He had been, it was said, left in total ignorance of the suspicions against him.
>
> In our opinion these submissions are not well founded and they must be rejected. It is clear that the power which has been given to the police by section 12(1) of the 1984 Act is a power of arrest without warrant, and that when the word 'detained' is used elsewhere in the section it is only with reference to a person 'detained in right of the arrest'. The word 'detained' is used to describe the state in which the person is being held following the arrest, so there must first be an arrest and the arrest itself must be lawful. The nature and character of an arrest and the distinction between an arrest and a detention have been described by Lord Cameron in *Swankie* v. *Milne* at p.6:
>
> > 'An arrest is something which in law differs from a detention by the

police at their invitation or suggestion. In the latter case a person detained or invited to accompany police officers is, at that stage, under no legal compulsion to accept the detention or invitation. It may well be that in a particular case refusal to comply could lead to formal arrest, but until that stage is reached there is theoretical freedom to exercise a right to refuse to accept detention at the hands of police officers who are not armed with a warrant. I think it is important always to keep clear the distinction between arrest, which is a legal act taken by officers of the law duly authorised to do so and while acting in the course of their duty, carrying with it certain important legal consequences, and the mere detention of a person by a police officer. ... Once arrested not only is the freedom of action of the person arrested circumscribed but he is also placed in the protection of the law in respect, *e.g.* of questioning by a police officer. None of these consequences flows from a mere "detention" for inquiry or to enable the officers or their colleagues to pursue investigation or put forward (as in this case) certain statutory requests. And a person is either arrested or he is not; there is no half-way house.'

But in our opinion it does not follow that the police officer who effects the arrest must in every case use the word 'arrest' when he explains to the person what is happening when he is being taken into custody. It is desirable that he should do so, because it is necessary that it should be made clear to the person concerned that he is under legal compulsion and that his freedom of action is being curtailed. The clearer and more simple the words used in this regard the better, and the word 'arrest' satisfies this test since it is a word with a clear meaning which is widely known and well understood. On the other hand any form of words will suffice to inform the person that he is being arrested if they bring to his notice the fact that he is under compulsion and the person thereafter submits to that compulsion: *Alderson* v. *Booth*, per Lord Parker C.J. at p.221. And the nature of what the police officer is doing may be conveyed by actions as well as words.

In the present case, although the appellant was told that he was being detained, he was taken from his house at an early hour to the police office in handcuffs. On his arrival there he was invited to sign the custody record which stated inter alia that he had been made aware of the reason for his arrest. Leaving aside for the moment the question whether that reason had been made known to him, the use of the word 'arrest' on this form together with the manner which he was taken into custody would, in our opinion, have left no reasonable doubt in his mind that he was under legal compulsion and that he was being detained in consequence of an arrest. We were referred to *Wither* v. *Reid* in which it was held that the accused had been arrested unlawfully because the police were proceeding under section 23(2)(*a*) of the Misuse of Drugs Act 1971 which gave them authority only to detain the person for the purpose of searching him. The police officers told the accused that she was being apprehended under the Act and that she was under arrest, prior to the search being carried out. If they had told her that she was being detained for the purpose of searching her, their actions would have been perfectly lawful, but Lord Kissen and Lord Robertson rejected the argument that the words used did not signify that she was being arrested but that she was being detained only for the purposes of the search. We do not doubt the soundness of that decision or of Lord Robertson's point at p.15 that in deference to the rights of the citizen it must be made perfectly clear to the person against whom action is being taken under section 23(2)(*a*) of the 1971 Act that that is what is being done and that he is not being arrested. But the present case does not present the same difficulty. The police officers' conduct together with the words used point clearly to this being in fact an arrest, and there has been no suggestion in this case that this was not what the police officers at that stage were empowered to do.

The other issue as to the lawfulness of the arrest relates to what the appellant was told about the reason for his arrest. In approaching this matter it is important to bear in mind the nature and circumstances of the power of arrest which is being exercised. Where the arrest is one which proceeds upon a warrant of arrest the police officer who executes it should state the substance of the warrant: Macdonald on the Criminal Law of Scotland (5th edn), p.199. As Hume on Crimes, vol ii, p.79 puts it, 'the officer, when proceeding to arrest, should briefly acquaint the party with the substance of his warrant'. Where, as in this case, the arrest is without warrant the requirements of the law are in effect the same. The person must be told immediately upon his arrest of the reason why he is being arrested. Where the power of arrest is being exercised in consequence of a statutory power of arrest because the police officer has reasonable grounds for suspecting that the person has been guilty of a specific offence such as that referred to in section 12(1)(a) of the 1984 Act, the person arrested must be told of the general nature of the offence of which he is suspected. Special considerations will apply where the arrest proceeds upon a provision such as that which is to be found in section 12(1)(b) of the 1984 Act which empowers a police officer to arrest without warrant a person whom he has reasonable grounds for suspecting to be a person who is or has been concerned in the commission, preparation or instigation of acts of terrorism to which Part IV of that Act applies—that is to say, acts of terrorism connected with the affairs of Northern Ireland and acts of terrorism of any other description except acts connected solely with the affairs of the United Kingdom other than Northern Ireland: see section 12(3). In such a case the suspicion is related to something which has not yet reached the stage of being capable of being described in terms of a specific offence, and it will not be possible to go further than state the general nature of the suspicion. The distinction between section 12(1)(a) and (b) for these purposes was explained in Ex parte *Lynch* by Lord Lowry L.C.J. at pp.130–131. He began his examination of the matter by referring to *Christie* v. *Leachinsky* in which Viscount Simon at p.587 and Lord Simmonds at p.593 both made the point that the policeman is not entitled to keep the reason for the arrest to himself since the principle is that the arrested man is entitled to know on what charge or on suspicion of what crime he is being arrested. He went on to say this, under reference to section 12(1) of the Prevention of Terrorism (Temporary Provisions) Act 1976 which was in substantially the same terms as those to be found in section 12 of the 1984 Act [at pp.130F–131C]:

'These observations seem to us to lay down that what must be communicated to the suspected person at the time of his arrest is the true ground of arrest, which, in the context in which the observations were made, means informing the suspect of the felony or arrestable offence of which he is suspected. Such crimes can be described and communicated to the suspect in reasonably precise terms, if a police officer is making an arrest either under section 2 of the Criminal Law Act 1967 in respect of the alleged commission of an arrestable offence (usually an offence or an attempted offence carrying a penalty of imprisonment of 5 years or more) or under the former position at common law before the 1967 Act when the commission of felony was suspected. The power of arrest under section 12(1) of the 1976 Act exists when there is a reasonable suspicion of the suspect's guilt of specific offences, as in section 12(1)(a) or where a person is suspected of being subject to an exclusion order, as in section 12(1)(c). But the power conferred by section 12(1)(b) is wider and more general, being derived from a suspicion of the suspect's being concerned in the commission, preparation or instigation of acts of "terrorism". This word is defined in wide terms in section 14(1) as meaning "the use of violence for political ends", and includes "any use of violence for the purpose of putting the public or any section of the public in fear". The scope of this language is such that no specific crime need be suspected in order to ground a proper arrest under section 12(1)(b). And it is further to be noted that an arrest under section 12(1) leads under section 12(2) to a permitted period of detention without preferring a charge. No charge may follow at all: thus an arrest is not necessarily (to use Scott L.J.'s phrase in the Court of Appeal in *Christie* v. *Leachinsky* [1946] K.B. 124, 130) "the first step in a criminal proceeding against a suspected person on a charge which was intended to be judicially investigated". Rather it is usually the first step in the investigation of the suspected person's involvement in terrorism.'

The learned advocate-depute submitted that this passage provided a complete answer to the point which had been raised by the appellant. We note, however, that in that case the arrest was made expressly with reference to the provisions of section 12(1)(*b*) which is the wider and more general power of arrest which is derived from a suspicion of being concerned in the commission, preparation or instigation of acts of terrorism. The constable who effected the arrest in that case told the appellant that he was being arrested as he was suspected of being involved in terrorist activities. That was not what was done in the present case. The appellant was told that he was being detained under section 12 of the 1984 Act and he was shown a search warrant which narrated that there were reasonable grounds to believe that he had committed an offence contrary to section 10 of the 1984 Act. The position in this case therefore is that the arrest was made under section 12(1)(*a*), because the appellant was suspected of being a person guilty of an offence under section 10. That suspicion had already been taken to the point of formulating an offence with sufficient precision for the search warrant to be obtained. So this case must, in our opinion, be approached on the basis that the appellant was suspected of being guilty of an offence which was, as Lord Lowry puts it, capable of being described and communicated in reasonably precise terms. Had the only information which was given to the appellant been that he was being detained under section 12 of the Act we should have had little difficulty in holding that insufficient information was given to him to make this a valid arrest. But that is not all that he was told, because he was shown and given to read for himself the search warrant which narrated in the petition the grounds on which it had been sought and granted and made express reference to section 10 of the Act. In our opinion the information which was afforded to him by this means was sufficient, when taken together with the words used by the police officers, to provide the appellant with the information which he was entitled to have as to the general nature and true ground of his arrest."

Appeal refused.

NOTES

1.   The difficulty with the approach adopted by the court in this case is that even if there is no "half-way house" between being arrested and not being arrested, there is another procedure by which a person may lawfully be deprived of their liberty, and that is detention. Depending upon the provisions under which the power to detain is exercised, the consequences of detention vary, and will often be quite different from the consequences of arrest. That being so, is it adequate to suggest that "any form of words will suffice to inform the person that he is being arrested if they bring to his notice the fact that he is under compulsion and the person thereafter

submits to that compulsion"? What form of words would suffice, and would not confuse arrest and detention in the mind of the person arrested? It is also clear from the opinion of the Lord Justice-General that in this case the words used by the police officers were not by themselves sufficient to indicate what had taken place. What took place afterwards clearly formed part of the process of informing the suspect of his status. But surely a person is entitled to know, at the point when he is deprived of his liberty, precisely what his situation is? Surely such information should be given so that he can, at as early a stage as possible, challenge the legality of his custody?

2.   In *Christie* v. *Leachinsky* [1947] A.C. 573, Leachinsky was arrested at a warehouse in which he ran a rag-merchant's business. The police officers who arrested him told him that he was being arrested for "unlawful possession" of certain bales of cloth. The power of arrest which the constables purported to exercise was contained in the Liverpool Corporation Act 1921, but under that Act it could only be exercised if the name and address of the suspect were unknown—circumstances which did not apply in this case. Leachinsky was tried for larceny of the bales, and acquitted. He raised an action for false arrest and imprisonment against the police. In defence to this action it was argued that since the officers suspected him of having stolen or feloniously received the cloth, the arrest was lawful by virtue of the officers' common law power to arrest for felony. Viscount Simon summed up the English law as follows:

> "(1.) If a policeman arrests without warrant ... he must in ordinary circumstances inform the person arrested of the true ground of arrest. He is not entitled to keep the reason to himself or to give a reason which is not the true reason. In other words a citizen is entitled to know on what charge or on suspicion of what crime he is seized. (2.) If the citizen is not so informed but is nevertheless seized, the policeman, apart from certain exceptions, is liable for false imprisonment. (3.) The requirement that the person arrested should be informed of the reason why he is seized naturally does not exist if the circumstances are such that he must know the general nature of the alleged offence for which he is detained. (4.) The requirement that he should be so informed does not mean that technical or precise language need be used. The matter is a matter of substance, and turns on the elementary proposition that in this country a person is, prima facie, entitled to his freedom and is only required to submit to restraints on his freedom if he knows in substance the reason why it is claimed that this restraint should be imposed. (5.) The person arrested cannot complain that he has not been supplied with the above information as and when he should be, if he himself produces the situation which makes it practically impossible to inform him, *e.g.*, by immediate counter-attack or by running away. There may well be other exceptions to the general rule in addition to those I have indicated, and the above propositions are not intended to constitute a formal or complete code, but to indicate the general principles of our law on a very important matter. These principles equally apply to a private person who arrests on suspicion. If a policeman who entertained a reasonable suspicion that X. has committed a felony were at liberty to arrest him and march him off to a police station without giving any explanation of why he was doing this, the prima facie right of personal liberty would be gravely infringed."

3.   In *Pedro* v. *Diss* [1981] 2 All E.R. 59, Lord Lane C.J. applied the principles set out in *Christie* v. *Leachinsky* and *R.* v. *Inwood* [1973] 2 All E.R.

645 to powers of detention as follows: "... a police constable ... must in one way or another make it known to the person detained that he is no longer a free man and the grounds on which he is being detained" ([1981] 2 All E.R. at p.63).

C. DETENTION

The simple distinction between arrest and detention tends to suggest that there is only one form of detention. In fact, statute has conferred upon the police, and other agencies such as H.M. Customs and Excise, a variety of powers of detention. There are, first of all, what might be termed "street detentions" which confer the power to detain for questioning, search, production of documents, etc., but which do not confer any power to take the person detained into custody. For an example of such a power see section 1 of the 1980 Act, *infra*. It appears to be accepted that the power to detain for search may, in some cases, extend to taking a suspect into custody to carry out the search—see the Misuse of Drugs Act 1971, s. 23 and *Wither* v. *Reid, supra*. Secondly, there is the power to detain analogous to the power of arrest, as contained in section 2 of the 1980 Act. Finally, there is the power to detain without charge, but subsequent to arrest, as, for example, in section 14 of the Prevention of Terrorism (Temporary Provisions) Act 1989. The first two types of detention depart from the common law rules by permitting interference with the liberty of the subject short of arrest. The third form derogates from the common law rule that arrest must be accompanied by a charge.

1. Criminal Justice (Scotland) Act 1980
"POLICE POWERS
Suspect or potential witness may be required by constable to identify himself
1.—(1) Where a constable has reasonable grounds for suspecting that a person has committed or is committing an offence at any place, he may require—

(*a*) that person, if the constable finds him at that place or at any place where the constable is entitled to be, to give his name and address and may ask him for an explanation of the circumstances which have given rise to the constable's suspicion;

(*b*) any other person whom the constable finds at that place or at any place where the constable is entitled to be and who the constable believes has information relating to the offence, to give his name and address.

(2) The constable may require the person mentioned in paragraph (*a*) of subsection (1) above to remain with him while he (either or both)—

(*a*) verifies any name and address given by the person:
Provided that the constable shall exercise his power under this paragraph only where it appears to him that such verification can be obtained quickly;

(*b*) notes any explanation proffered by the person.

(3) A constable may use reasonable force to ensure that the person mentioned in paragraph (*a*) of subsection (1) above remains with him.

(4) A constable shall inform a person, when making a requirement of that person under—

(*a*) paragraph (*a*) of subsection (1) above, of his suspicion and of the general nature of the offence which he suspects that the person has committed or is committing;

(b) paragraph (b) of subsection (1) above, of his suspicion, of the general nature of the offence which he suspects has been or is being committed and that the reason for the requirement is that he believes the person has information relating to the offence;

(c) subsection (2) above, of why the person is being required to remain with him;

(d) either of the said subsections, that failure to comply with the requirement may constitute an offence.

(5) A person mentioned in—

(a) paragraph (a) of subsection (1) above who having been required—

    (i) under that subsection to give his name and address; or

    (ii) under subsection (2) above to remain with a constable,

fails, without reasonable excuse, to do so, shall be guilty of an offence and liable on summary conviction to a fine not exceeding £200;

(b) paragraph (b) of the said subsection (1) who having been required under that subsection to give his name and address fails, without reasonable excuse, to do so shall be guilty of an offence and liable on summary conviction to a fine not exceeding £50.

(6) A constable may arrest without warrant any person who he has reasonable grounds for suspecting has committed an offence under subsection (5) above.

Detention and questioning at police station

2.—(1) Where a constable has reasonable grounds for suspecting that a person has committed or is committing an offence punishable by imprisonment, the constable may, for the purpose of facilitating the carrying out of investigations—

(a) into the offence; and

(b) as to whether criminal proceedings should be instigated against the person,

detain that person and take him as quickly as is reasonably practicable to a police station or other premises and, subject to the following provisions of this section, the detention may continue there.

(2) Detention under subsection (1) above shall be terminated not more than six hours after it begins or (if earlier)—

(a) when the person is arrested; or

(b) where there are no longer such grounds as are mentioned in the said subsection (1);

and when a person has been detained under subsection (1) above for a period of six hours, he shall be informed immediately upon expiry of this period that his detention has been terminated.

(3) Where a person has been released at the termination of a period of detention under subsection (1) above he shall not thereafter be detained, under that subsection, on the same grounds or on any grounds arising out of the same circumstances.

(4) At the time when a constable detains a person under subsection (1) above, he shall inform the person of his suspicion, of the general nature of the offence which he suspects has been or is being committed and of the reason for the detention; and there shall be recorded—

(a) The place where detention begins and the police station or other premises to which the person is taken;

(b) the general nature of the suspected offence;

(c) the time when detention under subsection (1) above begins and the time of the person's arrival at the police station or other premises;

(d) the time when the person is informed of his rights in terms of subsection (7) below and of subsection (1)(b) of section 3 of this Act and the identity of the constable so informing him;

(e) where the person requests such intimation to be sent as is specified in section 3(1)(b) of this Act, the time when such request is—
  (i) made;
  (ii) complied with; and
(f) the time of the person's departure from the police station or other premises or, where instead of being released he is arrested in respect of the alleged offence, the time of such arrest."

NOTES

1. Section 2 of the 1980 Act broadly follows the recommendations set out in paragraphs 3.07 to 3.26 of the Thomson Committee (2nd Report).

2. *Section 1.* The requirement under section 1(1)(a) and (b), and the requirement to remain with a constable under section 1(2) are backed up by criminal sanctions, which are in their turn enforceable by arrest without warrant under section 1(5). Is it really in the interests of police-community relations that a potential witness should be subject to this sort of procedure?

A suspect may only be "asked" to give an explanation of the circumstances which have given rise to the constable's suspicion. He cannot be required to do so. Section 1 makes no mention of cautions or warning before such questions are asked. A suspect might well make a self-incriminating statement, and presumably the admissibility of that statement depends on the common law test of "fairness." Given the approach adopted by the High Court in relation to questioning while under section 2 detention (see *Tonge* v. *H.M. Advocate, infra,* p.205) the proper approach, it is submitted, is for the constable to administer a caution. This view is reinforced by section 1(4) which requires a constable, when making a requirement under section 1(1) or 1(2) to inform the person in question "that failure to comply with the requirement may constitute an offence." Although this only relates to a "requirement" (which is limited to identification or remaining with the constable) this sort of distinction may well be lost on a suspect, and the general presence of such a threat might well suggest that failure to answer *any* question could be visited with criminal sanctions.

3. *Section 2.* This section follows the Thomson Committee in limiting detention to six hours. How is this period to be determined when the Act contains no indication of when detention commences? Section 2(4) makes provision for the recording of the time at which it begins, but that is only the police version. What happens when there is a dispute? Surely the point at which the police state that a person was detained cannot be conclusive of the matter.

What happens when the period of detention comes to an end? The detainee is informed of this fact: section 2(2). Is he told that he is free to go (if not arrested or otherwise detained)? Should he be asked to remain, is he to be told that he is free to go?

Section 2(3) prevents re-detention under subsection 2(1). It does not, apparently, prevent re-detention on the same grounds or grounds arising out of the same circumstances under any other power of detention. Note also, that the whole section appears to be premised on a detention which begins at a place other than the police station. Can detention begin when a person is already at the police station, whether voluntarily or while detained under some other power (such as that conferred by section 23 of the Misuse of Drugs Act 1971)?

4. The detention power contained in section 2 of the 1980 Act can only be exercised by a "constable" (which includes a constable of the transport police: *Smith* v. *Dudgeon*, 1982 S.C.C.R. 451). However, section 48 of the Criminal Justice (Scotland) Act 1987 confers an equivalent power of detention on customs officers.

Section 48(1) provides that where a customs officer has reasonable grounds for suspecting that a person has committed or is committing an offence punishable by imprisonment relating to an "assigned matter" the officer may, for the purpose of facilitating the carrying out of investigation into the offence and as to whether criminal proceedings should be instigated against the person, detain that person and take him as quickly as is reasonably practicable to a customs office or other premises where the detention may be continued. The maximum period of detention under section 48(1) is six hours: section 48(2).

An "assigned matter" for these purposes is any matter in relation to which the Commissioners of Customs and Excise are for the time being required in pursuance of any enactment to perform any duties: 1987 Act, s. 48(9) and Customs and Excise Management Act 1979, s. 1. For a discussion of the meaning of "an officer" in the context of section 48, see *Montes and Others* v. *H.M. Advocate*, 1990 S.C.C.R. 645.

Section 48 contains provisions relating to the procedures surrounding detention, including information which is to be given to the person detained, recording of time and place of detention, the general nature of the suspected offence, which are directly modelled on section 2 of the 1980 Act. The rights of persons detained under section 48 correspond to those of persons detained under section 2 of the 1980 Act (as to which, see *infra*, p.149).

5. One question that does arise out of the coexistence of two sets of detention powers (under the provisions of section 48 and those contained in the 1980 Act) is whether or not detention under one set of provisions precludes subsequent detention under the others. Subsection (4) above goes some way to restricting repeated detention, as does section 2(3) of the 1980 Act, but it appears that it does not completely exclude the possibility of repeated detention.

Suppose, for example, that A has been detained by a constable under section 2 of the 1980 Act. At the end of the period of detention he is released, and cannot be re-detained *under subsection 2(1)* of that Act. But can he then be detained under the provisions of the 1987 Act? The answer would seem to be that he cannot, because of section 48(4). However, suppose that he is detained first under section 48. He is then released, but then detained under section 2 of the 1980 Act. Is this possible? Section 48(4) does not apply because that limits the power of detention under section 48. Section 48(3) which limits the power to re-detain under section 48(1) does not apply either. Section 2(3) of the 1980 Act does not apply either, since it operates only when a person has already been detained under section 2.

It would appear, therefore, that detention by a customs officer under section 48 which is followed by release may be followed by immediate re-detention by a constable acting under section 2.

2. **Cummings v. H.M. Advocate**
1982 S.L.T. 487

The appellant was detained under section 2 of the 1980 Act. During that detention he made a number of statements to the police which later became central to the Crown's case against him. When he was detained he was given a full "common law" caution, and on his arrival at the police station he was warned, in terms of section 2(7) of the 1980 Act that he was under no obligation to answer any question other than to give his name and address. At his trial he objected, unsuccessfully, that the statements made in detention were inadmissible because there was no official record of the detention procedures, and in particular there was no such record that the requirements of section 2(4) had been complied with. The police notebooks contained such a record, and these were referred to at the trial. On appeal from conviction:

LORD JUSTICE-CLERK (WHEATLEY): "... It is stated in the written grounds of appeal that: 'no record in terms of section 2(4) was on the list of Crown labels or productions and it was not produced at the trial. The sheriff erred in law in allowing the case to go to the jury and in particular in allowing evidence of what the applicant was alleged to have said during his detention when the provisions of section 2 had not been fully complied with, in particular section 2(4)'. This was further developed by the appellant's counsel in argument. It was said that the statement was necessary to provide sufficient evidence in law to warrant a conviction. The procedure under s. 2 constituted an encroachment on personal liberty and accordingly it should be strictly construed and complied with. There should have been an official form in which the details called for by subs. (4) were recorded and this should have been spoken to by appropriate evidence. The failure to observe this requirement vitiated the police powers under the section which had thereby ceased to be operable, and accordingly the statement made by the appellant in purported pursuance of the powers conferred by the section was inadmissible in evidence. It was accepted that at the trial two police officers gave evidence that the requirements of subs. (4) were recorded in their notebooks and the notebooks were there and then produced and the entries therein spoken to. It was argued that as the notebooks had not been listed as productions, which meant that the defence had not had any prior opportunity to examine the entries therein, that evidence should not be regarded as satisfying the requirements of s. 2(4). Counsel took his argument to the extreme by submitting that even if there was failure to record one of the required entries that would be sufficient to vitiate the procedure under s. 2, including most particularly any statement purported to have been taken under the provisions thereof.

There are two matters to be considered arising out of the appellant's submissions, namely (1) the broad general question of the effect of non-compliance with the provisions of subs. (4) in whole or in part, and (2) the question whether there has been any failure to comply with these requirements in the instant case.

We propose to deal with the second of these matters first since in our view the reply to it provides a complete answer to the appellant's complaint. Subsection (4) calls for certain facts to be recorded. It does not specify in what manner or in what form they should be recorded. Therefore, even on the basis that it was necessary in order to sustain the conviction in this case to prove that the required facts were recorded, there was the evidence that they were recorded in the respective notebooks of the police officers, and the relative entries therein were given in evidence. These were presumably the original records from which any 'official' form would in due course be compiled. While these notebooks had not been lodged as productions, the police officers were allowed to refer to their notebooks without objection, and accordingly the requirements in relation to proof of recorded facts in an appropriate manner in terms of subs. (4) were satisfied. On that short ground alone we refuse the appeal.

Lest it be thought that in taking this short approach to the decision we were accepting that there was substance in the submission of the appellant's counsel in regard to the general effect of non-compliance with the provisions of subs. (4) in whole or in part, we wish to make it clear that no such subsumption should be made. We consider that any views which we have on it should be reserved for an occasion when the answer is necessary for the proper determination of the case."

Appeal dismissed.

NOTE

The general principle governing the use of notebooks used in this way is that unless they are lodged as productions, the notes contained therein are not of themselves evidence, but become part of the witness's oral testimony (Walker and Walker, *Law of Evidence in Scotland*, para. 341(b); Macphail, *Law of Evidence in Scotland* (Scottish Law Commission Research Paper), para. 8.47). If, therefore, police notebooks are to be relied upon as a "record" for the purposes of section 2(4) (which in itself would seem to be less than desirable) they should, it is submitted, be lodged as productions.

So far as concerns the question left open by the court, the question would presumably be whether non-compliance with the provisions of subsection (4) so prejudiced the suspect as to amount to unfairness.

3. Turnbull v. Scott
1990 S.C.C.R. 614

The appellant was convicted of obstructing two police officers in the course of their duty, and assaulting one of them in the course of his duty, contrary to section 41(1) of the Police (Scotland) Act 1967. The circumstances of the offences and the legal submissions of the parties are set out in the stated case and the sheriff's note.

The sheriff (Wilkinson) made the following findings in fact:

"1. About 7 a.m. on 9th May 1989, Gary Turner and Gary Smith, both constables of Central Scotland Police, attended at the appellant's house at 10 Castlehill Crescent, Banknock, in relation to alleged road traffic offences which had taken place several days previously. Their purpose in attending there was to detain the appellant under section 2 of the Criminal Justice (Scotland) Act 1980. The constables were in uniform.

2. Constable Turner knocked on the front door of the appellant's house. The appellant appeared at a window above the front door, but no one came to open the door in response to Constable Turner's knocking. Constable Turner continued knocking and did so for some four or five minutes, but there was no response.

3. In view of the lack of response at the front door, Constable Smith, followed by Constable Turner, went to the back door of the house. Constable Smith found that door ajar at an angle of about forty-five degrees.

4. Constable Turner and Constable Smith then entered the house through

the open door. They did so because they were unsure whether the appellant was still in the house or had gone away. They went into the back kitchen and shouted, 'Mr Turnbull, are you there?' They proceeded from there into the hallway and shouted again. They looked into the living-room and again shouted. Dogs were heard barking, but there was no other response to their calls. They then proceeded upstairs, calling out for the appellant as they went. There was still no response.

5. When they reached the upper landing, Constable Turner and Constable Smith found that two doors giving off the landing were ajar and a third door was shut. The door which was shut was the door of the room at the window of which the appellant had been seen. They called out again for the appellant and proceeded towards the shut door.

6. Before Constable Turner or Constable Smith could knock on or open the shut door, it was opened from the inside and two Alsatian dogs sprang out towards them. The appellant ran out of the room behind the dogs shouting and swearing and asking in obscene language why the constables were there. They attempted to explain, but, before they could do so, the appellant set upon them, kicking and punching. Constable Turner and Constable Smith endeavoured to restrain him but he struggled violently, with the result that Constable Turner fell backwards into one of the rooms and Constable Smith, after having been punched repeatedly by the appellant about the head and body, fell over one of the dogs. The appellant himself fell over the side of the banister and down the stairs and got away."

In his note the sheriff stated, *inter alia*:

"Police officers acting under section 2 of the Criminal Justice (Scotland) Act 1980 had, Mr McIntyre [solicitor for the accused] said, no greater powers than police officers acting without warrant in other circumstances. To enter domestic premises without a warrant or permission of the occupier was an illegality and so outwith the scope of the police power and duty. Mr McIntyre referred to *Great Central Railway Co.* v. *Bates* [1921] 3 K.B. 578. In reply, the procurator fiscal depute for the respondent said that the police were in uniform and were seeking to detain the appellant under section 2 of the Act. That, he said, was all that needed to be said about the matter. I repelled the submission of no case to answer for reasons similar to those which I give below in connection with the conviction of the appellant.

After the appellant had given evidence on his own behalf in which he claimed that he had been the victim of an assault by the police, had done nothing other than what was necessary to resist that assault and then had run away because he was frightened, Mr McIntyre renewed his argument that the police constables had been acting outwith their duty and so there could be no conviction under charges (2) and (3). In addition to *Great Central Railway Co.* v. *Bates*, Mr McIntyre referred to *Davis* v. *Lisle* [1936] 2 K.B. 434; [1936] 2 All E.R. 213; 30 Cox 412, and *Cairns* v. *Keane*, 1983 S.C.C.R. 277.

In *Cairns* v. *Keane* reference was made by the sheriff (at p.283) to the possibility that the specialities of the English law of trespass led to a different view of police powers of entry into premises from those which obtained in Scotland. I do not doubt that Scots law, no less than English law, protects the subject against unwarranted intrusions on his property and, particularly, on his domestic property, but the rigid character of the English rules may give rise to technical considerations which have no place in a Scottish case. With that caveat I found some assistance in the English cases which were cited to me. Mr McIntyre laid much stress on the fact that in *Great Central Railway Co.* v. *Bates* it was said that the policeman had no right to be on the premises. However, there is a certain ambiguity in the use of the word 'right'. The case was one of occupier's liability and the constable was held not to be in the premises as of right in a sense giving rise to the duties which, under the law as it then stood, he claimed were owed to him by the occupier. It is, however, another matter to say that the constable's presence on the premises was wrongful or unlawful and it is noticeable that both Lord Sterndale M.R. and Atkin L.J. stop short of saying that the constable was a trespasser. It is also noticeable that although the case does not decide that the constable was acting in the execution of his duty (*Davis* v. *Lisle*, per Du Parcq J. at pp.439 and 440), Lord Sterndale M.R. was of the view that he was so acting. In *Davis* v. *Lisle*, a case closer in its subject-matter to the present, the wrong committed by the police officers, which took them outwith the execution of their duty, was in remaining on the premises after they had been asked to leave. It was from that moment that they became trespassers (per Lord Hewart C.J. at p.438, Du Parcq J. at p.439 and Goddard J. at p.440). I did not have an opportunity of considering *Morris* v. *Beardmore* [1981] A.C. 446; [1980] 3 W.L.R. 283; [1980] 2 All E.R. 753; [1980] R.T.R. 321; 71 Cr.App.R. 256, as a report was not available to me, but it appears from the account given in *Cairns* v. *Keane* that there too the wrong may have consisted in remaining after being asked to leave. That, in my opinion, reflects the correct approach to matters of this kind. A person who goes through a doorway when the door has not been secured—and, particularly, if the door has been left ajar—enjoys an implied permission from the occupier to enter if he does so in pursuit of some legitimate purpose concerning the occupier. That permission may, of course, be withdrawn or countermanded, and the person who has entered is then obliged to leave. Since, in Scotland, no action for damages lies in respect of trespass unless damage has been caused, it may be that the matter can be put more strongly and without considering the question of implied permission—there is no wrong in going on to another's property unless or until one causes damage or refuses to leave when required to do so. In the present case, the appellant, if he had applied his mind to it, would no doubt have wished to countermand any permission he may be taken to have given and to require the constables to leave. Whether he did so, by asking in obscene language why they were there and assaulting them, is questionable, but it may be that, at that stage, Constables Turner and Smith came under an obligation to leave. They were, however, on the premises for the legitimate purpose of detaining the appellant under section 2 of the Criminal Justice (Scotland) Act 1980 and, in leaving, they were entitled to take the appellant with them and, if necessary, to use reasonable force to achieve that end (Criminal Justice (Scotland) Act 1980, section 2(6)). I accepted the account of events given by Constable Turner and Constable Smith and rejected the appellant's version. I concluded, therefore, that Constable Turner and Constable Smith were acting in the execution of their duty when the events libelled in the complaint took place.

There is a series of Scottish cases in which urgency has been held to justify actions by the police which would otherwise have been unlawful (*H.M. Advocate* v. *McGuigan*, 1936 J.C. 16; 1936 S.L.T. 161; *Laverie* v. *Murray*, 1964 S.L.T. (Notes) 3; *Bell* v. *Hogg*, 1967 J.C. 49; 1967 S.L.T. 290; and *McPherson* v. *H.M. Advocate*, 1972 S.L.T. (Notes) 71). These authorities are reviewed in *Cairns* v. *Keane* and *Cairns* v. *Keane* itself, in which the decision of the sheriff was upheld without comment, must now be added to that series. There were circumstances of some urgency in the present case. It was important for the constables to know there and then whether or not the appellant had gone away. If he had gone away, his detention might have been considerably postponed and the objects of the enquiry frustrated unless immediate steps were taken. It is, in my opinion, in the public interest and in accordance with the purposes which Parliament must have contemplated in enacting section 2 of the Criminal Justice (Scotland) Act 1980, that those purposes should not be defeated by denying to police officers, in circumstances of urgency, the right to enter premises. If, therefore, I have been of the opinion that the entry of

Constable Turner and Constable Smith into the appellant's house was otherwise unlawful, I should have held it to have been justified by the urgency of the situation with which they were faced."

LORD COWIE: "The appellant in this stated case is David Turnbull. On 11th December 1989 he was convicted at Falkirk Sheriff Court of three charges. The first charge was breach of the peace and the second and third charges were contraventions of the Police (Scotland) Act 1967, section 41(1). The appeal is only directed to the conviction of a contravention of the section 41(1) offences and the questions for the court are set out [in the stated case]. The [questions are]:

'(1) On the evidence as narrated, was I entitled to repel the submission of no case to answer made by the appellant in respect of charges (2) and (3)?

(2) Was I entitled to hold that police officers were entitled to enter the appellant's house without a warrant for the purpose of detaining him under section 2 of the Criminal Justice (Scotland) Act 1980?

(3) On the facts stated, was I entitled to hold that the constables referred to in the complaint were, in the circumstances, acting in the execution of their duty?

(4) On the facts stated, was I entitled to convict the appellant in respect of charge (2)?

(5) On the facts stated, was I entitled to convict the appellant in respect of charge (3)?'

Notwithstanding the number of questions which have been posed for our opinion the real issue in this case as the appeal was presented to us by Mr McBride was whether the police in the particular circumstances of this case were entitled to cross the threshold of the appellant's house in order to detain him. Now it is clear that the officers in the present case entered the appellant's house uninvited, but there is no absolute rule that police officers may only enter private premises if they have a warrant or statutory authority to do so. However, if they so enter, the question whether what they have done was unlawful and went beyond the execution of their duties must in our view be dependent on the particular circumstances of each case. For these reasons very properly Mr McBride did not refer us to a number of authorities to which the sheriff referred because in this case we do not consider that these authorities are really of very much assistance. In the present case, standing the findings of the sheriff, and in particular findings 1 to 4, it is clear that these officers went to the appellant's house in order to try and detain him under section 2 of the Criminal Justice (Scotland) Act 1980. They knocked on the door of the appellant's house and the appellant appeared at the window above the front door. They continued knocking but nobody came to open the door in response thereto. Constable Turner, it is said, continued knocking and did so for some four to five minutes but there was no response. Finding 3 says, in view of the lack of response at the front door, Constable Smith followed by Constable Turner went to the back door of the house and Constable Smith found that door ajar at an angle of about forty-five degrees. Finding 4 is that Constable Turner and Constable Smith then entered the house through the open door and, this is important, they did so because they were unsure whether the appellant was still in the house or had gone away. They went into the back kitchen and shouted, 'Mr Turnbull, are you there?' They proceeded from there into the hallway and shouted again. They looked into the living-room and again shouted. Dogs were heard barking but there was no other response to their calls. They then proceeded upstairs calling out to the appellant as they went. There was still no response.

It is clear therefore in the light of the findings of fact in this case that what the officers were doing in execution of their duty to detain the appellant was that, having seen him in the house, having seen the fact that the back door was ajar and therefore that he might have left the house, they were going [through] the appellant's house to see if he was still there with a view to carrying out their duty of detaining him. With those findings we are of the view that there is really no difficulty in this case. Obviously the position might have been different if the appellant had shouted from the window that the police officers were to go away and that he did not want them on his property or, indeed, if the back door had been shut, but we are not in that position in this case and therefore we express no view about what might have been the legal position in that situation. What we have here is police officers attempting to detain somebody and, after making all possible efforts to get the appellant to respond to their knocking and finding that he may well have left the house, entering it in order to see whether he was still there. In those circumstances we have no hesitation in saying that they were acting in the execution of their duty when they crossed the threshold. Indeed, we might go so far as to say that they would have been failing in their duty had they not done so. In these circumstances all the questions which have been posed by the sheriff fall to be answered in the affirmative."

Appeal refused.

NOTES

1.   There is clearly a difference of approach between the sheriff and the High Court in respect of the question of urgency, and the case cannot therefore be treated as an authority on the extension of the urgency doctrine to powers of detention, but both are agreed that in the circumstances, the police officers were entitled to enter the appellant's house without his express consent.

2.   At one point the sheriff adopts an "implied consent" approach. The High Court is less explicit. So far as concerns "implied consent" the following questions may be asked:
(a) What are the limits of "implied consent"? The sheriff refers to entry in pursuit of "some legitimate purpose concerning the occupier." But what if the purpose is one for which the occupier, had he been aware of it, would not have given actual consent?
(b) Does implied consent really extend to entering into a person's house, even if the door is open? One can see the practical value of an implied consent to enter onto the more "public" areas of a person's property—such as the path to the front door. But is there an implied consent to everyone to search through your home until they find you? Suppose, for example, that instead of police officers the persons seeking the appellant had been postmen with a recorded delivery letter. Delivering such a letter is clearly a "legitimate purpose concerning the occupier" but surely it would not permit them to enter the property in the way the police officers did. The leading English authority, Robson v. Hallett [1967] 2 Q.B. 939 limits the implied consent of the occupier to persons coming on lawful business to come through the front gate and to knock on the front door. There is no licence to enter the premises.

3.   The sheriff suggests an even broader justification for what took place here than "implied consent." It is suggested that there is no wrong done in entering into private property (even, it would seem, a person's home)

unless (a) damage is done, or (b) the trespasser refuses to leave when asked to do so. It would appear that this formulation ignores the presence or absence of a "legitimate purpose." So, it would appear, it would not be unlawful for the police simply to wander into any house, provided at least that it was not "secured" and there exercise any power that they might otherwise lawfully exercise. It is submitted that this is far too broad a proposition and should not be followed in any future case.

4.   The High Court accepts that the police were entitled (indeed obliged?) to enter the appellant's house in order to find out if he was still there to be detained. But this seems to be dependent on their having the power to enter the house actually to detain him. It would be odd to suggest that they could enter the property to see if he was there, but not have the power to detain him if he was.

5.   Both the sheriff and the High Court are agreed that matters might have been different if the appellant had expressly required the officers to go away, or if the house had been securely closed up. Certainly any notion of implied consent must bow to an express withdrawal of that consent. What would be necessary in order to expressly withdraw consent? It seems likely from dicta in the sheriff's note that mere obscenities or abuse would not suffice. It has been held in England that to say to the police "Fuck off" is not an effective withdrawal of implied consent: *Snook* v. *Mannion*, [1982] Crim.L.R. 601. But presumably nothing much more than "Go away. You're not wanted here" would do. Could any implied consent be withdrawn in advance? Suppose that the appellant had placed outside his gate a notice stating: "No Hawkers, No Circulars and No Policemen"?

It seems fair to suggest, also, that if a police officer is asked to leave then he or she should be given a reasonable amount of time to leave. Withdrawal of consent should not immediately take the officer outside the scope of his duty. *Cf. R.* v. *Thornley* (1980) 72 Cr.App.R. 302.

D.   THE INCIDENTS OF ARREST AND DETENTION

This section deals with that which follows upon, or which may be expected to follow upon, arrest and/or detention. Some of these matters, such as the appearance of the arrestee before a court, are required by law for the protection of the individual. Others, such as search and fingerprinting, arise from the exercise by the police of their investigatory powers. Two matters which are in this sense incidents of arrest or detention—interrogation and bail—are dealt with in separate chapters. (See *post*, Chaps. 5 and 6 respectively.)

(i)   Appearance Before a Court

It is the duty of every constable, in discharging his duty to bring offenders to justice, "to take every precaution to ensure that any person charged with an offence is not unreasonably and unnecessarily detained in custody" (Police (Scotland) Act 1967, s. 17(1)).

In solemn proceedings, an arrested person must be brought before a court as soon as possible, for the purpose of judicial examination (as to which, see *infra*, p.288). Section 19(3) permits the sheriff to delay such examination for a period not exceeding 48 hours from and after the time of arrest, but only in order to allow for attendance by the accused's solicitor. Where the accused is brought before the court for further examination, that examination may be delayed for 24 hours to allow time for the attendance of the accused's solicitor.

In summary proceedings, section 321(3) of the 1975 Act provides:

> "A person apprehended under any such warrant as aforesaid or by virtue of the powers possessed at common law, or conferred by statute, shall wherever practicable be brought before a court competent to deal with the case either by way of trial or by way of remit to another court not later than in the course of the first lawful day after such person shall be taken into custody, such day not being a public or local holiday."

It should be remembered that the right to be brought before a court without delay is only granted to persons arrested. It is for this reason that the safeguards surrounding detention procedures should be scrupulously adhered to.

(ii)   Intimation of Arrest or Detention and Access to Legal Advice

1.   Criminal Procedure (Scotland) Act 1975

"**19.**—(1) Where any person has been arrested on any criminal charge, such person shall be entitled immediately upon arrest:
  (a) to have intimation sent to a solicitor that his professional assistance is required by such person, and informing him of the place to which such person is to be taken for examination;
  (b) to be told what rights there are under paragraph (a) above and subsections (2) and (3) below.
(2) Such solicitor shall be entitled to have a private interview with the person accused before he is examined on declaration, and to be present at such examination.
(3) [Noted *supra*.]"

NOTE
Section 305 of the 1975 Act provides that in summary proceedings the accused is entitled, immediately upon apprehension, to have intimation sent to a solicitor and to have a private interview with such solicitor prior to being brought before the court. There is no obligation under section 305 to inform an arrested person of his rights.

2.   Criminal Justice (Scotland) Act 1980

"**3.**—(1) Without prejudice to section 19 or 305 of the 1975 Act (intimation to solicitor following arrest), a person who, not being a person in respect of whose custody or detention subsection (3) below applies—
  (a) has been arrested and is in custody in a police station or other premises, shall be entitled to have intimation of his custody and of the place where he is being held sent, to a person reasonably named by him;
  (b) is being detained under section 2 of this Act in a police station or other premises, shall be entitled to have intimation of his detention and of the place where he is being detained sent, to a solicitor and to one other

person reasonably named by him,

without delay or, where some delay is necessary in the interest of the investigation or the prevention of crime or the apprehension of offenders, with no more delay than is so necessary; and the person shall be informed of such entitlement—

   (i) on arrival at the police station or other premises; or

   (ii) where he is not arrested, or as the case may be detained, until after such arrival, on such arrest or detention.

(2) Where the person mentioned in paragraph (*a*) of subsection (1) above requests such intimation to be sent as is specified in that paragraph there shall be recorded the time when such request is—

   (i) made;

   (ii) complied with.

(3) Without prejudice to the said section 19 or 305, a constable shall, where a person who has been arrested and is in such custody as is mentioned in paragraph (*a*) of subsection (1) above or who is being detained as is mentioned in paragraph (*b*) of that subsection appears to him to be a child, send without delay such intimation as is mentioned in the said paragraph (*a*), or as the case may be paragraph (*b*), to that person's parent if known; and the parent—

   (*a*) in a case where there is reasonable cause to suspect that he has been involved in the alleged offence in respect of which the person has been arrested or detained, may; and

   (*b*) in any other case shall,

be permitted access to the person.

(4) The nature and extent of any excess permitted under subsection (3) above shall be subject to any restriction essential for the furtherance of the investigation or the well-being of the person.

(5) In subsection (3) above—

   (*a*) 'child' means a person under 16 years of age; and

   (*b*) 'parent' includes guardian."

NOTES

1.   A person detained by a customs officer under section 48 of the 1987 Act, is entitled to the same rights as are enjoyed under section 3(1) of the 1980 Act by a person detained by a constable under section 2 of that Act: Criminal Justice (Scotland) Act 1987, s. 49(1). Where the person detained appears to be under 16, he or she enjoys the same rights as a child enjoys under section 3(3) of the 1980 Act: 1987 Act, s. 49(2).

2.   None of the above provisions guarantees immediate access to a solicitor. The fact of arrest may be immediately intimated, but access is only guaranteed prior to appearance before a court. In the case of detention, intimation may be delayed, as may intimation to a "person reasonably named" whether the suspect is arrested or detained.

3.   No indication is given as to who might be a "person reasonably named." This should comprise any person who may reasonably be expected to take an interest in the suspect's welfare such as a parent, spouse, social worker, etc. A legal adviser would also be such a person and section 3 makes it clear that naming a solicitor does not exhaust this right. *Cf.* Home Office Circular No. 74/1978.

4.   No sanction is attached to failure to grant these rights of intimation (either under the 1975 Act or the 1980 Act). Presumably this would be a factor affecting the fairness issue if a question arose respecting the admissibility of statements made while under arrest or detention: *cf. Cheyne* v. *McGregor*, 1941 J.C. 17 and the following case.

3.   **Forbes v. H.M. Advocate**
1990 S.C.C.R. 69

The appellant was convicted on charges of conspiracy, contravention of section 10(1)(*b*) of the Prevention of Terrorism (Temporary Provisions) Act 1984, section 3(*b*) of the Explosive Substances Act 1883 and sections 1 and 16 of the Firearms Act 1968. He appealed to the High Court on the ground, *inter alia*, that, having been detained under section 12 of the 1984 Act, and having been denied access to a solicitor for more than 48 hours from the start of his period of detention, there was no evidence that the procedures required by section 3A(1) and 3C(4) had been complied with.

(For other issues raised by this case, see *supra*, p.133.)

LORD JUSTICE-GENERAL: "The appellant's remaining grounds of appeal relate to the fact that for more than forty-eight hours from the start of his detention under section 12 he was not allowed access to a solicitor. His rights in this regard were set out in section 3A(1) and (3) of the Criminal Justice (Scotland) Act 1980, which provides as follows:

'(1) A person who has been arrested or detained under the terrorism provisions and who is in detention in a police station or other premises shall be entitled to have intimation of his detention and of the place where he is being detained sent without delay to a solicitor and to another person reasonably named by him:
'Provided that a police officer not below the rank of superintendent may authorise a delay (not extending longer than the period of 48 hours from the start of the detention) where, in his view, such delay is necessary on one of the grounds mentioned in section 3C(3) of this Act. . . .
(3) A person arrested or detained under the terrorism provisions shall be entitled to consult a solicitor at any time without delay:
'Provided that a police officer not below the rank of superintendent may authorise a delay (not extending longer than the period of 48 hours from the start of the detention) where, in his view, such delay is necessary on one of the grounds mentioned in section 3C(3) of this Act.'

These provisions must be read together with those of section 3C(3) and (4) of the 1980 Act which are in the following terms:

'(3) The grounds mentioned in section 3A(1), 3A(3) and 3B(4) of this Act and in subsection (1) above are that it is in the interests of the investigation or prevention of crime, or of the apprehension, prosecution or conviction of offenders.
(4) Where delay or non-compliance is authorised in the exercising of any of the rights or, as the case may be, the carrying out of any of the duties, mentioned in sections 3A(1), 3A(3), and 3B(3) of this Act, there shall be recorded the reason for such delay or non-compliance.'

The evidence on this matter was to the following effect. Detective Inspector R. Watson stated that he attended a briefing at 4 a.m. on 21st February 1989 which was conducted by among others the Assistant Chief Constable, Detective Chief Inspector Hamilton and Detective Chief Superintendent Fisken. He was put in charge of the officers looking after the detained men. He was instructed that the detained men including the appellant were not to be allowed access to a solicitor until forty-eight hours had expired after the detention. The decision on this matter had been taken at an earlier meeting which he did not attend and he was not told the reason for this order. He was instructed that any requests made by a detained person were to be noted in the detention records. He stated that there was no note in the record of the appellant of any request to notify a solicitor prior to the expiry of forty-nine and three-quarter hours, at which point he was told of his rights. Detective Chief Superintendent Fisken, who had attended the earlier meeting, was not questioned on this matter by counsel for the appellant. He was asked about it in cross-examination on behalf of another accused, when he stated, as is narrated in the report by the trial judge, that the purpose of withholding access to a solicitor was because this was in the interests of solving crimes and investigating the offences. No question was asked of him or of Detective Inspector Watson or of Detective Chief Inspector Hamilton, who also gave evidence, as to whether the reason for the decision to delay informing the detained men of their right to inform and to see a solicitor was recorded, where it was recorded and if recorded what was recorded as the reason for this. Counsel for the appellant took an objection at a later stage in the trial when evidence was being led from the police officers who interviewed the appellant while he was being detained under section 12. His submission was that the appellant had been unfairly deprived of the services of a solicitor, but the objection was repelled by the trial judge.

There is no doubt that the provisions of subsections (1) and (3) of section 3A and of subsection (3) of section 3C are of an exceptional character. The general rule is that any person arrested on any criminal charge is entitled immediately upon his arrest to have intimation sent to a solicitor that his professional assistance is required and that he is entitled to have a private interview with such a solicitor before he is examined on declaration: see Criminal Procedure (Scotland) Act 1975, section 19. The importance of the rights of intimation to and consultation with a solicitor has been recognised by section 3A(1) and (3) of the 1980 Act where it is stated that they are to be afforded without delay to the arrested person. That person is only to be deprived of these rights on certain conditions, which are plainly designed to safeguard those rights so far as this can be done consistently with the wider public interest in the suppression and detection of crime. The decision to delay may be taken and authorised only by a senior police officer not below the rank of superintendent, and his view must be that such delay is necessary on one of the grounds mentioned in section 3C(3). Furthermore, the reason for the delay 'shall be recorded'. It is of the greatest importance that these conditions should in each case be scrupulously observed and that the senior police officer who authorises the delay should have applied his mind precisely to the question whether it is necessary on one of the grounds which section 3C(3) sets out. The accurate recording of the reason is also a matter of importance, as is indicated by the use of the word 'shall' in the relevant subsection.

The point which is raised in the present case, however, is not that the senior police officer did not apply his mind to the matter or that the grounds on which the delay was authorised were misconceived. Nor can it be asserted that the reason was not recorded, although counsel for the appellant put the matter in this way at one stage in his submissions. The point is simply that there was no evidence on this particular matter at all. The record, if any, was not produced and no questions were asked of the witnesses who were able to speak to the matter as to whether or not there was such a record and if so where it was and what were its terms. On the other hand two police officers who were present when the decision was taken to authorise the delay were led in evidence by the Crown, and they were thus available to give evidence in cross-examination, if required, as to the reasons for that decision. One of them, Detective Chief Superintendent Fisken, was of sufficient rank to have authorised the delay himself, and since he was present at the time when the decision was taken he can be said to have been directly concerned with the taking of it.

It was submitted that there was an onus on the Crown to prove that the decision had been recorded and that in order to satisfy this onus the record itself had to be produced. In the absence of the production of the record the delay must be taken to have been unfair to the appellant, and this together with the alleged unfairness about the circumstances of his arrest had the result of making the appellant's statements inadmissible. In our opinion, however, the primary question in regard to fairness to the appellant is whether the delay itself was properly authorised. On this matter there is no room for argument. The point was not taken on the appellant's behalf, but in his evidence under cross-examination Detective Chief Superintendent Fisken said all that was necessary to show that the decision had been taken under reference to the grounds set out in section 3C(3). Against this background the question is reduced, in the circumstances of this case, to this point as to whether it is essential to the lawful nature of the procedure that the record, if it exists, should be produced. It is to be noted that section 3C(4) does not go so far as to say that this must be done, so we are not concerned in this case with a failure to observe a rule of procedure which is expressed by the use of the word 'shall': see, *e.g.*, *H.M. Advocate* v. *Graham*. Nor is the answer to the point raised in this appeal to be found in *Cummings* v. *H.M. Advocate*, where a question was raised under reference to the provisions of section 2(4) of the 1980 Act which requires certain matters to be recorded when a person is detained under that section for questioning at a police station. The record was not produced, but the police officers referred to their notebooks which were produced and which contained a record of the warnings which had been given to the appellant of his rights. It was held that if it was necessary to prove that section 2(4) had been complied with the evidence of the officers and their notebooks constituted sufficient proof of such compliance. It was pointed out that the subsection did not say how or in what form the matter should be recorded and that the notebooks were presumably the original records from which any official form would in due course be compiled. The Lord Justice-Clerk made it clear at p.114 that the court reserved its opinion on the question whether there was substance in the submission that a failure to observe the requirement about recording vitiated the police powers under the section whereby they ceased to be operable.

The point which is raised directly in the present case is whether it is sufficient for the matter to be the subject of oral evidence given by one of the senior police officers who was concerned in the taking of the decision. Now it is plain that the purpose of the requirement that the reason should be recorded is to enable that reason to be examined at a later stage should the question arise, for any purpose, as to whether the decision has been made on proper grounds. The proof of making of the record and its production will be of the greatest importance where the evidence of the senior police officer who took the decision is not available to be heard and considered by the jury. In such cases a failure to produce the written record might well be fatal to the admissibility of any statements made by the accused person during the period of the delay. But in the present case the evidence of Detective Chief Superintendent Fisken was available for consideration by the jury because his evidence was led by the Crown and he was open to cross-examination on this matter on the appellant's behalf. The issue was presented to us as being one of fairness in the end of the day, and we cannot leave out of account the fact that the point about the grounds on which the delay was authorised was not put to Detective Chief Superintendent Fisken on the appellant's behalf, and in particular that the question as to the reliability or otherwise of his evidence on this matter in the absence of the production of the record, if a record was made, was not raised at the trial. In these circumstances we are not persuaded that the absence of any such record from the productions resulted in such unfairness to the appellant as to amount to a miscarriage of justice in this case.

What we have just said should not be taken as diminishing in any way the importance of the accurate recording of all matters required to be recorded under sections 2, 3A and 3C of the Criminal Justice (Scotland) Act 1980 and any analogous provisions. Nor should this be taken as an acceptance that the leading of oral evidence of matters which are to be recorded in terms of the sections is in all cases either admissible or sufficient to show that this requirement has been satisfied. There may well be matters, such as certain of the details to which section 2(4) refers, which can only be reliably spoken to if an accurate record of those matters has been timeously made. Each case must be considered on its own facts, but in the end of the day the proper course may well be, as was done in this case, to leave the overall question of fairness for the jury to consider since it is not a requirement of the statute that the record itself must always be produced.

For the reasons which we have given we have refused this appeal."

Appeal refused.

(iii)   Search

Jackson v. Stevenson
(1897) 2 Adam 255

While he was fishing, Jackson was seen by two water bailiffs who suspected that he was fishing illegally. They searched him to discover if he was in possession of implements for illegal fishing. He resisted this search and was convicted of resisting the bailiffs in the execution of their duties, contrary to section 39 of the Tweed Fisheries Act 1857. It was not clearly established whether the search took place before or after Jackson was apprehended. His appeal against conviction was upheld on the ground that the complaint was defective in form, but the court also considered the legality of the search.

LORD JUSTICE-GENERAL (ROBERTSON): "... The Sheriff's statement of the facts does not make it quite clear whether the appellant had been apprehended before the bailiffs searched his person, or only after. As I read the case, they did not apprehend him, and had not resolved to apprehend him, until the result of their search confirmed their previous suspicions. If this were so, then I do not think that they were within their powers, and therefore I could not hold them to have been in the execution of the Acts when the appellant resisted them.

The right of the bailiffs, be it observed, is to exercise the powers and authorities of constables in the same manner as if the statutory offences were breaches of the peace. Now, a constable is entitled to arrest, without a warrant, any person seen by him committing a breach of the peace, and he may arrest on the direct information of eye witnesses. Having arrested him, I make no doubt that the constable could search him. But it is a totally different matter to search a man in order to find evidence to determine whether you will apprehend him or not. If the search succeeds (such is the condition of the argument), you will apprehend him; but if the search does not succeed, you will not apprehend him. Now, I have only to say that I know no authority for ascribing to constables the right to make such tentative searches, and they seem contrary to constitutional principle. If the constable requires to make such a search, it can only be because without it he is not justified in apprehending; and, without a warrant, to search a person not liable to apprehension seems palpably illegal. A constable or bailiff must make up his mind on what he sees (or hears on credible information) whether to arrest or not; and, if he does arrest in good faith, the law will protect him, whether his opinion at the time of the guilt of the person arrested prove accurate or not."

Appeal allowed.

NOTE

Section 2(5) of the 1980 Act provides that where a person is detained under section 2(1) of that Act a constable may "exercise the same powers of search as are available following an arrest." He may use reasonable force in exercising these powers (section 2(6)).

It should be remembered that statute may permit search in order to justify arrest. See, for example, the breath test provisions of the Road Traffic Act 1972. It should also be noted that a warrant may be granted to search the person of a suspect who has not been arrested (*Hay* v. *H.M. Advocate*, 1968 J.C. 40, *infra*, p.243) and that in cases of urgency such a search may be carried out without warrant (*Bell* v. *Hogg*, 1967 J.C. 49, *infra*, p.255). Powers to search premises are discussed *infra*, Chap. 6.

(iv)   Fingerprinting and Analogous Procedures

1.   **Adair v. McGarry**
1933 S.L.T. 482

McGarry was arrested and charged with theft by housebreaking. His fingerprints were taken without a warrant and without his consent having been obtained. His fingerprints were found to correspond with prints found on one of the items of stolen property. Objection was taken at his trial to the admissibility of the evidence relating to the fingerprints, on the ground that it had been illegally obtained. The sheriff upheld his objection and acquitted McGarry. The prosecutor appealed. (Another case, *Byrne* v. *H.M. Advocate*, which raised the same issue, was heard at the same time.)

LORD JUSTICE-CLERK (ALNESS): "The question for decision in this case is whether the police are entitled to take finger-prints of persons who are detained by them as suspects though these persons have not yet been committed to prison. To that question the Crown answers—yea; The respondent replies—nay.

Manifestly the question before us is of importance, not only to the individual, but also to the public. On the one hand, the individual must be protected against any undue invasion of his rights; on the other hand, it is evident that the affirmation of the right claimed by the Crown may facilitate the investigation and detection of crime, and that the denial of that right may impede, if not frustrate, that process.

At the outset it is essential to bear in mind the distinction between the position of a person detained on suspicion of having committed a crime and the position of a person who has been committed to prison on a charge of crime. The rights of the police are wider in the former case than they are in the latter case. The police may arrest a suspect and may interrogate him; but that person may only be committed if a *prima facie* case against him is made out, and no interrogation is, after committal, permitted. Accordingly, the suggestion that finger-prints may be taken, once committal takes place, is far from meeting the demands of the situation.

I propose, first, to survey the problem apart from authority, and then to enquire whether the conclusion at which I arrive, on that survey, is rendered inadmissible by the state of the authorities.

Viewed apart from authority, then, the problem presents itself to my mind thus—the police must be armed with all adequate and reasonable powers for the investigation and detection of crime. Is finger-printing a reasonable incident in that process, not forbidden by the common law, and not unduly invading the rights of the accused?

I say 'not forbidden by the common law' because I think that phrase more correctly expounds the situation than the phrase 'authorised by the common law.' Let me explain what I mean by this. The system of detection of crime by means of finger-prints is a modern scientific discovery, later in date than any of the statutes to which reference was made in the course of the debate, and it would not therefore be reasonable to look for or to expect to find institutional or common law authority for its practice.

As regards undue invasion of the personal rights of the accused, one must have a sense of proportion. Certain it is that in practice, hitherto unchallenged, a person who is suspected of crime may be brought—with reasonable violence in the event of his resistance—to the police station, that he may be paraded for purposes of identification, that he may be stripped, and that he may be searched for any incriminating natural or artificial mark upon his person. That mark may include a birth mark or natural deformity, a tattoo mark, or bloodstain, or the like. All these things are done with a view to establishing the identity of the suspect. And yet it is argued that the comparatively innocuous process of taking a mould of the suspect's thumb is excluded from the rights of the police. I enquire—Why? To that question I have heard no adequate answer. The analogy of straining at a gnat and swallowing a camel suggests itself as apposite to the argument in question.

The suggestion seems to be that the existence of a warrant ... removes all objection to finger-printing. If I could see that any substantial protection is afforded to the accused by the existence of such a warrant I could understand that view. But nothing is more certain than that such a warrant is a pure formality, is granted for the asking, is, so I am informed, never refused, and, moreover, is granted by a person who may know less about the matter than the police know. The suggested protection by way of warrant is quite illusory.

If the accused is innocent, no harm is done by finger-printing. He has not been subjected to so great 'humiliation'—to use counsel's words—as he may admittedly be subjected to in accordance with time-honoured and unchallengeable practice. If, on the other hand, he is guilty, the process renders it more likely that his guilt may be established. That is, I apprehend, desirable.

Bearing all these considerations in mind, I should have no difficulty in reaching the conclusion, authority apart, that the Crown possess the right which is claimed by them.

[His Lordship then examined the authorities, and concluded:]

I reach the conclusion that I am unimpeded by authority from giving effect to the view which, apart from it, I should, as already stated, have entertained. To sum up then, I consider that the power claimed by the police is a reasonable and proper power, necessary for the investigation of crime and for the detection of the criminal and that it involves no undue invasion of the rights of the individual. To balance the claims of public interest on the one hand and the claims of private interest on the other is often not an easy task; but in this case I do not think it is difficult. There is, as the Lord Advocate said, no suggestion that the police, who have in the past claimed and exercised the powers which in this case are challenged, have abused these powers; there is no public outcry against the system; and, as the right claimed by the Crown is not withheld by the common law, and would in my opinion, if denied, hamper the police in the investigation and detection of crime, I am for sanctioning the right which the Crown claims, and I am for rejecting the argument which would negative its existence."

Appeal allowed.

NOTES

1.   Lord Hunter entered a vigorous dissent: "It was suggested that the taking of fingerprint impressions was useful in enabling the police to detect crimes which might otherwise go undetected. That may explain why the police are anxious to possess the right; it affords no excuse for their doing what is not warranted at common law. It was no doubt upon similar grounds that physical torture was in the Middle Ages employed to extract confessions from persons suspected of crimes. At the present time third degree methods adopted by the police in some countries in questioning suspected persons might equally well be justified, but the common law of Scotland has never sanctioned such procedure" (p.490).

2.   The taking of fingerprints, and analogous evidence, from a person who has been arrested or detained under section 2 of the 1980 Act (but not section 48 of the 1987 Act) is now governed by statute. Section 28(1) of the Prisoners and Criminal Proceedings (Scotland) Act 1993 provides that where a person has been so arrested or detained, a constable may (using reasonable force if necessary) take from that person, "fingerprints, palmprints and such other prints and impressions of an external part of the body as the constable may, having regard to the circumstances of the suspected offence in respect of which the person has been arrested or detained, reasonably consider it appropriate to take."

Section 28(3) provides that all record of such prints or impressions shall be destroyed immediately following a decision not to institute criminal proceedings against the person, or on the conclusion of such proceedings otherwise than with a conviction, an order for absolute discharge or a probation order.

3.   In Adamson v. Martin, 1916 S.C. 319 the police photographed and took the fingerprints of a suspect (a 17-year-old boy) whom they had not arrested (although a warrant to apprehend him had been granted). He later raised an action for the delivery or destruction of the photographs, negatives, fingerprint impressions, etc. The court held that the police action had been "unwarrantable and illegal" and ordered the fingerprints and photographs to be destroyed. The result would have been otherwise had the police arrested the boy before taking the action they did. This case was distinguished by the majority in Adair v. McGarry.

It is clear that in cases such as these much will depend upon the nature of the invasion of the suspect's person. Minor invasions are likely to be permitted, especially when the evidence obtained is of a reliable nature (as in Adair v. McGarry, and see also Forrester v. H.M. Advocate, 1952 J.C. 28—examination of a wound on the suspect's hand for comparison with a damaged glove found near the scene of the crime). Where, however, the invasion of the suspect's person is likely to be substantial, or the evidence inconclusive, the court should be reluctant to sanction examination without warrant: cf. H.M. Advocate v. Milford, 1973 S.L.T. 12.

(v)   Blood Tests, Samples and Intimate Searches

The court in Adair v. McGarry was prepared to accept fingerprinting because it did not involve a significant interference with the person of the suspect, and it has generally been accepted that, at common law, more intrusive types of evidence gathering should normally be carried out under warrant (see *infra*, Chap. 6). But there have been significant statutory departures from this approach in recent years:

A.   General powers to take body samples

Section 28(4) of the Prisoners and Criminal Proceedings (Scotland) Act 1993 provides that a constable may, with the authority of an officer of a rank no lower than inspector, take from the person (using reasonable force if necessary):

(a)   from the hair of an external part of the body, by means of cutting or combing, a sample of hair or other material;

(b)   from a fingernail or toe-nail or from under any such nail, a sample of nail or other material;

(c)   from an external part of the body, by means of swabbing or rubbing, a sample of blood or other body fluid, of body tissue or of other material.

Curiously, there is no provision for the destruction of such samples, or the information obtained from them (such as blood groupings or DNA profiling) comparable to that contained in section 28(3).

Section 28(6) provides that nothing in section 28 shall prejudice any power of search, any power to take possession of evidence where there is imminent danger of its being lost or destroyed (as to which, see Chap. 6) or any power to take prints, impression or samples under the authority of a warrant (as to which, see Chap. 4).

B.   Search in connection with drug smuggling

Section 50(1) of the Criminal Justice (Scotland) Act 1987 makes provision for the detention of persons by a customs officer where the latter has reasonable grounds for suspecting that the person is involved in drug smuggling offences and that a controlled drug is secreted in the person's body. Where these conditions are satisfied, then that person may be detained (even though he or she is already under detention under some other provision) for up to 24 hours and be required (section 50(2)):

(a)   to provide specimens of blood or urine for analysis;

(b)   to submit to intimate searches (*i.e.* the physical examination of body orifices) by a medical practitioner;

(c)   to submit to such other tests or examinations as may be prescribed by the Secretary of State under regulations.

Where a person detained under section 50(1) has failed or refused to provide specimens as required, or to submit to any search, test or examination as required, or where the customs officer continues to suspect on reasonable grounds that the person has committed or is committing a drug smuggling offence, and that a controlled drug is secreted in his or her body, the procurator-fiscal may apply to the sheriff for a warrant for further detention for a period not exceeding seven days.

(vi)   Participation in Identification Parade

A person arrested may be placed on an identification parade (*Adair* v. *McGarry, supra*). Although he is not entitled to do so, a suspect may refuse to take part. Since the use of force in such a case would defeat the object of the procedure he may thus effectively thwart the use of an identification parade. By doing so, however, he runs the risk of being viewed in circumstances less favourable than a full parade.

The Thomson Committee (2nd Report, para. 3.24, recommended that one of the purposes of detention should be identification of the detainee. The 1980 Act does not expressly confer a power to place a detainee on a parade. However, section 2(5)(*b*) of the 1980 Act authorises a constable to "exercise the same powers of search" with regard to a detainee "as are available following an arrest." The right to parade a suspect is sometimes treated as an extension of the right to search (*cf.* Renton and Brown, para. 5–30 and *Adair* v. *McGarry*). It is submitted, however, that this would be too great an extension of the statutory provision. The taking of fingerprints, for which express provision is made with respect to detainees, is likewise regarded as an extension of the power of search on arrest. It may be inferred, therefore, that "search" is not intended to include the parading of a detainee. It is further submitted that the considerations which apply to an arrestee who refuses to be paraded do not apply in the case of a detainee, so that the police would not be justified in allowing witnesses to view a detainee outwith a parade.

A suspect, whether detained or at liberty may, of course, volunteer to take part in an identification parade. In what circumstances can a suspect *demand* a parade?

1.   Criminal Justice (Scotland) Act 1980

"**10.**—(1) Subject to subsection (2) below, the sheriff may, on an application by an accused at any time after the accused has been charged with an offence, order that, in relation to the alleged offence, the prosecutor shall hold an identification parade in which the accused shall be one of those constituting the parade.

(2) The sheriff shall make an order in accordance with subsection (1) above only after giving the prosecutor an opportunity to be heard and only if—

(*a*) an identification parade, such as is mentioned in subsection (1) above, has not been held at the instance of the prosecutor;

(*b*) after a request by the accused, the prosecutor has refused to hold, or has unreasonably delayed holding, such an identification parade; and

(*c*) the sheriff considers the application under subsection (1) above to be reasonable."

NOTE

For a discussion of identification procedures, and identification parades, see, generally, *Report of the Working Group on Identification Procedure under Scottish Criminal Law* (Bryden Committee), Cmnd. 7096, (1978), Thomson Committee, 2nd Report, Chap. 12, and *Report to the Secretary of State for the Home Department of the Departmental Committee on Evidence of Identification in Criminal Cases* (Devlin Committee), House of Commons, (1976).

2. Scottish Home and Health Department Identification Parade Rules

"1. ...

2.   Every precaution should be taken to see that identification parades are fairly conducted and, in particular, to exclude any suspicion of unfairness or risk of erroneous identification through the attention of the witness being directed specially to the suspected person instead of equally to all the persons paraded. It is desirable in the interests both of the police and of the person on parade that he be legally represented.

Decision to hold an Identification Parade
3.   Subject to the requirements of the Procurator Fiscal, the decision to hold an identification parade would normally rest with the officer in charge of a case or his superior officer. In all cases where identification may be an issue the police should normally hold an identification parade. If a suspect or an accused or his solicitor requests an identification parade, and the police are in doubt about granting it, the request should be referred to the Procurator Fiscal for his instructions. ...

Rights of Suspect or Arrested Person
7.   When a suspect is not in custody and evidence is not sufficient to justify an apprehension, the suspect should be asked if he is willing to take part in an identification parade, the purpose of which should be clearly explained to him. Such a person's attendance is entirely voluntary, and there should be no question of pressure being exercised on him, or of any inducement to encourage his participation.

8.   An arrested person is not entitled to refuse to take part in an identification parade but any compulsion which results in his becoming particularly conspicuous is obviously undesirable. Where an arrested person declines to be paraded it may be possible for the police to let the witness see the accused, preferably along with others but in the last resort on his own, in the place where he is detained.

9.   A suspect or arrested person should be informed by a police officer reading the appropriate part of the parade form that an identification parade is to take place, the purpose of the parade, that he has the right to object to the composition of the parade, and that he may have his solicitor and/or solicitor's assistant present if he so desires. ...
   Any reasonable request which the suspect or arrested person or his solicitor or his assistant may make beforehand should be granted. He should also be informed that he may take up any position in the parade and that he can change position after each witness has viewed the parade and before the next witness enters. The arrested person/suspect or legal representative must not interfere with the conduct of the parade.

Composition of the Parade
10.   The suspect or arrested person should be placed beside persons of similar age, height, dress and general appearance. It is more important that the stand-ins should resemble the suspect or arrested person than that they should be like any descriptions given by witnesses. Similarly it is important that an identification should not be influenced by clothing—for example, if the witness has said that the suspect was wearing a red pullover it would be wrong if the suspect were the only person on the parade wearing a red pullover although the fact that he possesses such a pullover or that he was wearing one when invited to attend the parade would constitute a separate piece of evidence which should be recorded.

11.   ... The minimum number in any parade should be five (in addition to the suspect or arrested person) but where more persons, up to a maximum of eight (in addition to the suspect or arrested person) are available the larger number is to be preferred.

12.   It is undesirable that witnesses called to attend a parade should discuss either the case in question or the person whom they are being asked to identify. While it is recognised that the police have no power to prevent such a discussion, it is considered that the witnesses should be segregated before the parade if practicable and having regard to the needs of the case (*i.e.* where the witnesses are thought to be unknown to each other or not to have had an opportunity to communicate with each other about the case prior to coming to view the parade). Alternatively a police officer should be present in the assembly room with a view to inhibiting any discussion of this nature. ...

19.   The suspect or arrested person or his legal representative, if present, should be asked if he has any objection to make regarding the other persons forming the parade or the arrangements made for the parade. If the objection is to an individual he should be replaced. If the objection is to the arrangement and is reasonable, it should be met. Any objection made should be noted.

20.   The persons forming the parade should be lined up, preferably with their backs to a wall, and should be numbered consecutively, the position of each person being denoted by a number clearly displayed.

21.   The suspect or arrested person should be invited to choose his own position in the line, prior to the first witness being asked to view the parade. After each witness and before the next witness enters, the suspect or arrested person should be given the opportunity to change position. The position taken up on each occasion should be noted.

22.   One-way vision screens should generally be used in the conduct of parades. ... While it is highly desirable that a suspect or arrested person be legally represented when a one-way vision screen is used the fact that a suspect or arrested person has elected not to be legally represented at the parade in the knowledge that it is intended to use such a screen, shall not preclude the use of the screen. Where a one-way vision screen is employed it is essential that the suspect or arrested person, who will be unable to observe what is happening beyond the screen, should be able to hear all that is said on the other side by the officer conducting the parade. Where a legal representative and/or his assistant is present it is important that he should be able to observe the whole proceedings on both sides of the screen and hear all that is said.

23.   It is essential that the witnesses who are to view the parade should have no opportunity of seeing the suspect or arrested person, or the other members of the parade within the precincts of the place where the parade is to be held. It is equally essential that witnesses who have viewed the parade should have no opportunity of contact with those still to be called.

24.   Only one witness should be admitted at a time ...
When a witness identifies a person on the parade by number, the officer conducting the parade should ask that person his name and note the name that is given. The officer conducting the parade should repeat that name to the witness within the hearing of the person identified. If the witness is unable to make a positive identification, he should be asked a second question: 'Is there anyone on the parade who resembles the person?' [His response, if any, should be noted.] Additional questions designed to clarify the witness's evidence as to identification may be put to the witness and these and any answers given should be noted. The witness should then be conducted to the dismissal room

and should have no opportunity of communicating in any way with any witness still to view the parade. A witness should not be allowed to view the parade again after he has left the parade room."

NOTE
These rules have no statutory status and are purely administrative guidelines. A failure to observe these procedures will not of itself render inadmissible any evidence obtained, even where the reliability of the evidence is called into question through departure from the procedure. Such departure is, however, something which may properly be left to the jury in assessing the reliability of the evidence: *Morley* v. *H.M. Advocate*, 1981 S.C.C.R. 250.

E.   ARREST AND DETENTION IN CONNECTION WITH TERRORIST OFFENCES

The Prevention of Terrorism (Temporary Provisions) Act 1989 contains special provisions for the arrest and detention of persons in connection with terrorism. These have now been supplemented by the provisions of sections 3A *et seq.* of the Criminal Justice (Scotland) Act 1980, relating to the rights of persons arrested or detained in connection with terrorism.

Prevention of Terrorism (Temporary Provisions) Act 1989
"Arrest and detention of suspected persons
14.—(1) Subject to subsection (2) below, a constable may arrest without warrant a person whom he has reasonable grounds for suspecting to be—
  (*a*) a person guilty of an offence under section 2, 8, 9, 10 or 11 above;
  (*b*) a person who is or has been concerned in the commission, preparation or instigation of acts of terrorism to which this section applies; or
  (*c*) a person subject to an exclusion order.
(2) The acts of terrorism to which this section applies are—
  (*a*) acts of terrorism connected with the affairs of Northern Ireland; and
  (*b*) acts of terrorism of any other description except acts connected solely with the affairs of the United Kingdom or any part of the United Kingdom other than Northern Ireland.
(3) The power of arrest conferred by subsection (1)(*c*) above is exercisable only—
  (*a*) in Great Britain if the exclusion order was made under section 5 above; and
  (*b*) in Northern Ireland if it was made under section 6 above.
(4) Subject to subsection (5) below, a person arrested under this section shall not be detained in right of the arrest for more than forty-eight hours after his arrest.
(5) The Secretary of State may, in any particular case, extend the period of forty-eight hours mentioned in subsection (4) above by a period or periods specified by him, but any such further period or periods shall not exceed five days in all and if an application for such an extension is made the person detained shall as soon as practicable be given written notice of that fact and of the time when the application was made.
(6) The exercise of the detention powers conferred by this section shall be subject to supervision in accordance with Schedule 3 to this Act.
(7) The provisions of this section are without prejudice to any power of arrest exercisable apart from this section."

NOTES

1.   Section 15 of the 1989 Act provides that if a sheriff or justice of the peace is satisfied that there are reasonable grounds for suspecting that a person liable to arrest under section 14(1)(*b*) is to be found on any premises he may grant a search warrant authorising a constable to enter those premises for the purpose of searching for and arresting that person.

2.   The offences mentioned in section 14(1)(*a*) are: section 2 (belonging to, supporting or organising support for proscribed organisations); section 8 (offences in respect of exclusion orders); section 9 (contributions towards acts of terrorism); section 10 (contributions to resources of proscribed organisations); section 11 (assisting in the retention or control of terrorist funds).

3.   Section 3A of the Criminal Justice (Scotland) Act 1980 provides that a person who has been arrested or detained under the provisions of the 1989 Act and who is in detention in a police station or other premises shall be entitled to have intimation of his detention and of the place where he is being detained sent without delay to a solicitor and to another person reasonably named by him. A police officer of at least the rank of superintendent may authorise the delay of such intimation for up to 48 hours from the start of the period of detention where, in his or her view, such delay is necessary in the interests of the investigation or prevention of crime, or of the apprehension, prosecution or conviction of offenders.

4.   The provisions of section 3A of the 1980 Act apply in the case of children as they apply to adults: section 3B(1). However, a person arrested or detained who appears to be a child shall not be entitled to have intimation of his arrest or detention or the place of his detention sent to any other person named by him: section 3B(2). Such intimation should, however, be sent to the child's parent (if known) and the parent should be allowed access to the child, unless such access is denied on the authority of a police officer of at least the rank of superintendent: section 3B(3) and (4). The grounds for denying access by the parent to the child are the same as for delaying intimation of arrest and detention and the place of detention: section 3B(4).

5.   A police officer not below the rank of assistant chief constable may direct that consultation or access mentioned above may be in the presence of a uniformed officer not below the rank of inspector, if it appears to the officer giving the direction that this is necessary in the interests of the investigation or prevention of crime, or of the apprehension, prosecution or conviction of offenders: section 3C.

6.   Part II of the 1989 Act provides for the making of "exclusion orders" by the Secretary of State by which a person may be excluded from the United Kingdom, Great Britain or Northern Ireland. Schedule 2 makes further provision in connection with exclusion orders. Under paragraph 6 of that Schedule, the Secretary of State may give directions for the removal of any person subject to an exclusion order from the relevant territory. Under paragraphs 7 and 8 a person may be arrested and detained pending a decision to remove him, and pending his removal.

7.   Section 16 and Schedule 5 to the 1989 Act make provision for port and border controls. Under paragraph 2 of Schedule 5, an "examining officer" may examine any person who has arrived in, or is seeking to leave, Great Britain or Northern Ireland by ship or aircraft. The purpose of such examination is to determine whether (a) that person appears to be someone

who is or who has been involved in acts of terrorism, or (b) that person is subject to an exclusion order, or (c) that person has committed an offence under section 8 of the 1989 Act in connection with exclusion orders. Paragraph 6 of Schedule 5 provides for the arrest and detention of such person under the authority of an examining officer, pending conclusion of his examination, pending consideration by the Secretary of State whether to make an exclusion order against him or pending a decision by the Lord Advocate whether proceedings for an offence should be instituted against him. Detention under this paragraph shall not exceed 48 hours unless the period is extended by the Secretary of State, for a further period which cannot exceed five days: para. 6(3).

8.   Schedule 3 to the 1989 Act sets out a scheme for the supervision of detention and examination powers under section 14 or under paragraph 6 of Schedule 5.

9.   In *Brogan and Others* v. *United Kingdom*, European Court of Human Rights, Series A No. 145–B, 11 E.H.R.R. 117 four applicants, Brogan, Coyle, McFadden and Tracey, were arrested and detained under section 12 of the Prevention of Terrorism (Temporary Provisions) Act 1984 (now section 14 of the 1989 Act). Brogan was released after five days and 11 hours, Coyle after six days and 16½ hours, McFadden after four days and six hours, and Tracey after four days and 11 hours. None of them was charged with any offence and none of them was brought before a magistrate. All four complained to the European Commission on Human Rights of violations of Article 5 of the European Convention on Human Rights. The Commission held, *inter alia*, that in the cases of Brogan and Coyle there had been a breach of Article 5(3) (the right, following arrest or detention to be brought promptly before a judge or other officer authorised by law to exercise judicial power). The case was referred to the European Court of Human Rights for its opinion.

The court held, by a majority, that there had been a breach of Article 5(3) in respect of all four applicants. While the requirement that a person be brought "promptly" before a judicial authority following arrest or detention could not require immediate presentation before the court, and while a certain leeway had to be allowed in terrorist cases, nevertheless the periods of detention in all cases were excessive.

Rather than abide by the court's decision, the United Kingdom Government decided to invoke Article 15 of the Convention (which permits states to derogate from their obligations "in time of war or other national emergency threatening the life of the nation." The government also invoked Article 4 of the International Covenant on Civil and Political Rights which similarly provides for the right to derogate). In this way the government was able to ignore the judgment of the court while at the same time claiming that the United Kingdom was not in violation of the Convention.

F.   ARREST AND DETENTION IN CONNECTION WITH MATRIMONIAL INTERDICTS

The Matrimonial Homes (Family Protection) (Scotland) Act 1981 creates a form of matrimonial order known as an "exclusion order." By means of such an order one spouse (which term includes persons living together as husband and wife) may obtain an order suspending the occupancy rights of the other spouse in the matrimonial home (1981 Act, s. 4(1)). The object of such orders is the protection of the applicant or any child of the family from injury at the hand of the party excluded (section 4(2)).

In making an exclusion order the court has the power to grant interdict prohibiting the excluded spouse from entering the matrimonial home, removing furnishings and plenishings, etc., or approaching the matrimonial home (section 4(3)). Interdict may also be granted independently of an exclusion order under section 14, restraining conduct of one spouse towards the other or towards a child of the family, or prohibiting a spouse from approaching the matrimonial home.

A power of arrest may be attached to either form of matrimonial interdict. The procedures governing the granting and exercise of this power, and procedures following on such arrest are set out in the following materials.

Matrimonial Homes (Family Protection) (Scotland) Act 1981
"Attachment of powers of arrest to matrimonial interdicts

15.—(1) The court shall, on the application of the applicant spouse, attach a power of arrest—

(a) to any matrimonial interdict which is ancillary to an exclusion order, including an interim order under section 4(6) of this Act;

(b) to any other matrimonial interdict where the non-applicant spouse has had the opportunity of being heard or represented before the court, unless it appears to the court that in all the circumstances of the case such a power is unnecessary.

(2) A power of arrest attached to an interdict by virtue of subsection (1) above shall not have effect until such interdict [together with the attached power of arrest] is served on the non-applicant spouse, and such a power of arrest shall, unless previously recalled, cease to have effect upon the termination of the marriage.

(3) If, by virtue of subsection (1) above, a power of arrest is attached to an interdict, a constable may arrest without warrant the non-applicant spouse if he has reasonable cause for suspecting that spouse of being in breach of the interdict.

(4) If, by virtue of subsection (1) above, a power of arrest is attached to an interdict, the applicant spouse shall, as soon as possible after service of the interdict [together with the attached power of arrest] on the non-applicant spouse, ensure that there is delivered—

(a) to the chief constable of the police area in which the matrimonial home is situated; and

(b) if the applicant spouse resides in another police area, to the chief constable of that other police area,

a copy of the application for the interdict and of the interlocutor granting the interdict together with a certificate of service of the interdict and, where the application to attach the power of arrest to the interdict was made after the interdict was granted, a copy of that application and of the interlocutor granting it and a certificate of service of the interdict together with the attached power of arrest.

(5) Where any matrimonial interdict to which, by virtue of subsection (1) above is attached a power of arrest, is varied or recalled, the spouse who applied for the variation or recall shall ensure that there is delivered—

(a) to the chief constable of the police area in which the matrimonial home is situated; and

(b) if the applicant spouse (within the meaning of subsection (6) below) resides in another police area, to the chief constable of that other police area,

a copy of the application for variation or recall and of the interlocutor granting the variation or recall.

(6) In this section and in sections 16 and 17 of this Act—

'applicant spouse' means the spouse who has applied for the interdict; and

'non-applicant spouse' shall be construed accordingly.

Police powers after arrest

16.—(1) Where a person has been arrested under section 15(3) of this Act, the officer in charge of a police station may—

(a) if satisfied that there is no likelihood of violence to the applicant spouse or any child of the family, liberate that person unconditionally; or

(b) refuse to liberate that person; and such refusal and the detention of that person until his or her appearance in court by virtue of—

(i) section 17(2) of this Act; or

(ii) any provision of the Criminal Procedure (Scotland) Act 1975,

shall not subject the officer to any claim whatsoever.

(2) Where a person arrested under section 15(3) of this Act is liberated under subsection (1) above, the facts and circumstances which gave rise to the arrest shall be reported forthwith to the procurator fiscal who, if he decides to take no criminal proceedings in respect of those facts and circumstances, shall at the earliest opportunity take all reasonable steps to intimate his decision to the persons mentioned in paragraphs (a) and (b) of section 17(4) of this Act.

Procedure after arrest

17.—(1) The provisions of this section shall apply only where—

(a) the non-applicant spouse has not been liberated under section 16(1) of this Act; and

(b) the procurator fiscal decides that no criminal proceedings are to be taken in respect of the facts and circumstances which gave rise to the arrest.

(2) The non-applicant spouse who has been arrested under section 15(3) of this Act shall wherever practicable be brought before the sheriff sitting as a court of summary criminal jurisdiction for the district in which he or she was arrested not later than in the course of the first day after arrest, such day not being a Saturday, a Sunday or a court holiday prescribed for that court under section 10 of the Bail etc. (Scotland) Act 1980:

Provided that nothing in this subsection shall prevent the non-applicant spouse from being brought before the sheriff on a Saturday, a Sunday or such a court holiday where the sheriff is in pursuance of the said section 10 sitting on such a day for the disposal of criminal business.

(3) Subsections (1) and (2) of section 3 of the Criminal Justice (Scotland) Act 1980 (intimation to a named person) shall apply to a non-applicant spouse who has been arrested under section 15(3) of this Act as they apply to a person who has been arrested in respect of any offence.

(4) The procurator fiscal shall at the earliest opportunity, and in any event prior to the non-applicant spouse being brought before the sheriff under subsection (2) above, take all reasonable steps to intimate—

(a) to the applicant spouse; and

(b) to the solicitor who acted for that spouse when the interdict was granted or to any other solicitor who the procurator fiscal has reason to believe acts for the time being for that spouse,

that the criminal proceedings referred to in subsection (1) above will not be taken.

(5) On the non-applicant spouse being brought before the sheriff under subsection (2) above, the following procedure shall apply—

    (a) the procurator fiscal shall present to the court a petition containing—

        (i) a statement of the particulars of the non-applicant spouse;

        (ii) a statement of the facts and circumstances which gave rise to the arrest;

and

        (iii) a request that the non-applicant spouse be detained for a further period not exceeding 2 days;

    (b) if it appears to the sheriff that—

        (i) the statement referred to in paragraph (a)(ii) above discloses a *prima facie* breach of interdict by the non-applicant spouse;

        (ii) proceedings for breach of interdict will be taken; and

        (iii) there is a substantial risk of violence by the non-applicant spouse against the applicant spouse or any child of the family,

he may order the non-applicant spouse to be detained for a further period not exceeding 2 days;

    (c) in any case to which paragraph (b) above does not apply, the non-applicant spouse shall, unless in custody in respect of any other matter, be released from custody;

and in computing the period of two days referred to in paragraphs (a) and (b) above, no account shall be taken of a Saturday or Sunday or of any holiday in the court in which the proceedings for breach of interdict will require to be raised."

NOTE

Section 15 also makes provision for service of notice of the granting of a matrimonial interdict to which a power of arrest has been attached, or of its recall, to the chief constable of the area in which the matrimonial home is situated, and where the applicant spouse resides in a different police area, to the chief constable of that area.

These elaborate provisions are necessary to safeguard the position both of the spouse threatened with, or indeed suffering, violence, and also the position of the spouse who is the subject of the matrimonial interdict. As regards the former the effectiveness of the procedures depend largely on the willingness of the police to exercise their powers of arrest.

As regards the position of the arrested spouse it is worth noting that in some cases a considerable period of time may be spent in custody without any criminal charge being brought. Suppose, for example, the case of a spouse arrested on a Friday evening. He (since these procedures are generally directed towards the problem of battering men) is not released under section 16(1). The fiscal decides to take no criminal proceedings (section 17(1)(b)) (and there is evidence of reluctance on the part of some fiscals to take criminal proceedings in matrimonial cases: see Moodie and Tombs, *Prosecution in the Public Interest*, pp.67 et seq.). No court is available until the following Monday. On appearance before the sheriff the conditions specified in section 17(5)(b) are found to be satisfied, and detention for 48 hours is ordered. Thus over 96 hours' detention are possible under these provisions.

This should be contrasted with the situation where the arrested spouse is charged with an offence. The provisions of section 17 do not apply, and the normal procedures governing an arrested person come into force. The effect of this may well be that the arrestee charged with an offence is liberated more swiftly than the arrestee against whom no proceedings are to be taken.

CHAPTER 5

QUESTIONING OF SUSPECTS

It will be seen from the materials in Chap. 4 that the practical responsibility for the investigation of crime is devolved upon the police (subject to any instructions or guidance issued to them by the public prosecutor). In conducting their investigations the police are frequently required to question suspects and to search for and seize items of real evidence. In consequence, this chapter is effectively concerned with the powers of the police to question. Judicial examination of suspects is dealt with in Chap. 8.

The questioning of suspects, and the search for real evidence raise similar issues. Both procedures may be essential for the detection and investigation of crime. But at the same time, if not contained within proper limits, they may constitute a serious infringement of the liberty of the individual. This much is recognised by most democratic systems, which by and large adopt similar devices to control potential abuses. Such devices may be direct, or indirect.

Direct controls may consist in the taking of proceedings (civil, criminal or disciplinary as appropriate) against those who have acted unlawfully or irregularly in the questioning of suspects or the gathering of evidence. But such direct measures of control are rarely seen as being sufficient in themselves. A person aggrieved by the conduct of the police may be unable or unwilling to institute civil proceedings, and may encounter official antipathy to criminal proceedings (where the institution of such proceedings is an available option at all). Similarly, internal disciplinary procedures may not command sufficient public confidence to commend them as an appropriate check on the abuse of powers.

Consequently, recourse has been made to the indirect regulation of questioning and search by means of what is commonly called the "exclusionary rule." By means of this device a court may rule that evidence "illegally" or "irregularly" or "unfairly" (depending on local terminology) obtained is inadmissible against the accused. Legal systems do, however, vary widely in their attitude to this device, some applying it more or less strictly than others. In England, the view has been expressed (*R. v. Sang* [1979] 2 All E.R. 1222, *per* Lord Diplock at p.1230) that:

> "It is no part of a judge's function to exercise disciplinary powers over the police or prosecution as respects the way in which evidence to be used at the trial is obtained by them. If it was obtained illegally there will be a remedy in civil law; if it was obtained legally but in breach of the rules of conduct for the police, this is a matter for the appropriate disciplinary authority to deal with."

Even within a system which operates an exclusionary rule the conditions for invoking that rule may vary from time to time, even to the extent that it may decline to residual status, to be invoked only in "extreme" cases. (Compare, for example, the approach of the High Court in *Chalmers v. H.M. Advocate*, 1954 J.C. 66 with the approach of the court in *Lord Advocate's Reference (No. 1 of 1983)*, 1984 S.C.C.R. 62, *infra*, p.177.) Similarly, the exclusionary rule may be applied more rigorously in some areas than others. Generally speaking, one might expect the exclusionary rule to be more strictly applied to evidence of extra-judicial statements or confessions than it is to real evidence. This can be justified on the ground that while a confession extracted by unlawful or unfair means suffers from the additional drawback that it may be unreliable, the probative value of real evidence—such as a murder weapon with the accused's fingerprints on it—is not diminished by the fact that it was obtained without a warrant or otherwise irregularly obtained.

A. The "Right to Silence"

The starting point for a consideration of the police powers of interrogation is the so-called "right to silence." This is a convenient, if misleading shorthand for a number of well-established propositions.

At common law there is no duty on any person to answer questions put to them by the police: cf. *Twycross* v. *Farrell*, 1973 S.L.T. (Notes) 85. Although giving false information in response to police questions does not constitute obstruction of a police officer in the execution of his duty (*Curlett* v. *McKechnie*, 1938 J.C. 176) it may amount to an attempt to pervert the course of justice: *Dean* v. *Stewart*, 1980 S.L.T. (Notes) 85. (Deliberately and maliciously to set in motion an investigation by means of an invented story is an offence: *Kerr* v. *Hill*, 1936 J.C. 71.) The right to silence also encompasses the rule that no one is under a duty to answer questions which might incriminate that person.

1. H.M. Advocate v. Von
1979 S.L.T. (Notes) 62

Von was charged, along with 10 others, with conspiracy to further the aims of the Ulster Volunteer Force by criminal means, including contraventions of section 10 of the Prevention of Terrorism (Temporary Provisions) Act 1976 which prohibits, *inter alia*, soliciting or receiving money or property for use in acts of terrorism. During the trial objection was taken by the defence to the admissibility of a statement made by Von to the police while detailed under section 12 of the 1987 Act.

> LORD ROSS: "... The objection which has been taken is as far as I am aware novel since it turns upon the provisions of s. 11 of the Prevention of Terrorism (Temporary Provisions) Act 1976....
>
> Evidence shows that the accused was interviewed by the police on Saturday, 24 February, and again on the following day. On the Saturday the interviewing officers advised him that it was an offence to withhold information about acts of terrorism under s. 11 of the Act of 1976. That section provides as follows: 'If a person who has information which he knows or believes might be of material assistance—(*a*) in preventing an act of terrorism to which this section applies, or (*b*) in securing the apprehension, prosecution or conviction of any person for an offence involving the commission, preparation or instigation of an act of terrorism to which this section applies, fails without reasonable excuse to disclose that information as soon as reasonably practicable—(1) in England and Wales, to a constable, or (2) in Scotland, to a constable or the procurator fiscal, or, (3) in Northern Ireland, to a constable or a member of Her Majesty's forces, he shall be guilty of an offence'.

On the Saturday the accused apparently made a statement which did not incriminate himself or anyone else. On the Sunday he was seen by police officers on two occasions. On the first occasion he was apparently upset and asked to have some time to himself and added that he would then see the officers again.

After an interval of time the officers saw him for the second occasion when he stated that he wished to make a statement and to tell of his own involvement but that he would not name anyone. At this stage police officers, realising that he was about to make a statement implicating himself, advised him that what he said could be used in evidence.

Counsel for the accused objected to the admissibility of the statement which followed that warning on the ground that the accused in the circumstances had been forced to incriminate himself, being compelled after the provisions of the Act had been drawn to his attention, to make a statement against himself. He contended that the officers ought when they advised the accused of the terms of the section, to have drawn his attention to the fact that the offence was committed if there was failure without reasonable excuse to disclose the information, and he submitted that one could reasonably be excused from not disclosing information if the information would be self-incriminating.

In the circumstances here, if the statement which is now being objected to had been made on the Saturday then it would in my opinion be clear that the statement had been made in response to his being told of his obligations under s. 11 of the Act. As the Crown point out, however, there was an interval of time in this case and the statement objected to was not apparently made until the Sunday around 12.50 p.m., and the question which arises is whether that statement on the Sunday could be said to have been the result of his being told on the Saturday that he had an obligation to disclose the information. ...

The accused in the present case was apparently detained under the provisions of s. 12 of the Act of 1976, and he was undoubtedly a suspect, as the search warrant which was issued to search his premises indicates. That being so, it seems to me that the question which really arises regarding the admissibility of the statement is the familiar one of fairness.

If on the Sunday the accused had been given the usual full caution or had been informed that he was not obliged to give information which would incriminate himself and he had then made a statement, I would have thought that that statement would have been admissible as being a statement which had been fairly obtained and was not a statement made in response to pressure or inducement or as a result of other unfair means. In the event, however, the statement on Sunday was made by the accused after he had been told on the previous day of his obligations under s. 11 and without his ever having been told that he need not incriminate himself. That being so, I am satisfied that the statement here is not admissible.

So far as the evidence goes, the accused was left in total ignorance of the fact that he was not obliged to incriminate himself. Almost 150 years ago in the case of *Livingstone* v. *Murray* (1830) 9 Shaw 161, Lord Gillies said: 'It is a sacred and inviolable principle that no man is bound to incriminate himself'. I do not consider that a statement can be regarded as being fairly obtained if the accused was never advised of the fact that under our law no person is required to incriminate himself.

In enacting the provisions of the Act of 1976, if Parliament had intended to make statements of suspects admissible against them in the event of their being subsequently charged I would have expected Parliament to have made that clear. I cannot believe that Parliament intended to alter the well-established principle of our law that no man can be compelled to incriminate himself. If Parliament had intended so to do I would have expected it to be made clear.

As I have indicated, if a full caution had been given or clear advice given to the suspect that he need not incriminate himself, the statement might well have been admissible: but the only warning here given was that what he said could be used in evidence, and I do not regard that as a sufficient warning to the accused that he was not obliged to incriminate himself."

The court sustained
the objection.

NOTES

1.   *Cf.* the Thomson Committee (2nd Report, para. 7.02):

"Scots law on this matter has proceeded not so much on any fundamental constitutional or philosophic basis, such as the privilege against self-incrimination, as on a conception of fairness and a determination by the courts to control police activity in the interests of fairness."

2.   The equivalent provisions to section 11 of the 1976 Act are now contained in section 18(1) of the Prevention of Terrorism (Temporary Provisions) Act 1989. This section makes it clear that it is only an offence for an individual to withhold information which might be of assistance in preventing the commission of an act of terrorism *by another person* or in securing the apprehension or conviction *of another person.*

The provisions of the old section 11 of the 1976 Act were ambiguous in that they did not expressly make it an offence for a person to withhold information about their own involvement in terrorist activities. But what is the status of the right to silence where Parliament has expressly made it an offence for a person to refuse to answer questions about their own suspected offending? As to this, see the provisions of the Criminal Justice (Scotland) Act 1987, and especially sections 52(1), (2) and 53(4), *infra,* p.270.

2.   Criminal Justice (Scotland) Act 1980

"2.—(7) A person detained under subsection (1) above shall be under no obligation to answer any question other than to give his name and address, and a constable shall so inform him both on so detaining him and on arrival at the police station or other premises."

NOTES

1.   The warning contained in subsection (7) is, by comparison with a "common law caution," only a partial warning. It does not, for example, make it clear that any answers given may be taken down and used in evidence. For the effect of such a partial caution on the admissibility of any such answer, see *Tonge* v. *H.M. Advocate, infra.*

2.   The "right to silence" is not limited to the stage of pre-trial investigations by the police. It exists at the trial stage also, in the sense that the accused cannot be compelled to give evidence at his own trial: 1975 Act, s. 141(*a*) and s. 346(*a*). This is reinforced by the rule that the prosecutor may not comment upon the failure of the accused to give evidence: 1975 Act, s. 141(*b*) and 346(*b*). The judge may, however, comment upon such failure: *Knowles* v. *H.M. Advocate*, 1975 J.C. 6. The Thomson Committee (2nd Report, Chap. 50) considered this aspect of the right to silence and concluded:

"It should in our view be appropriate for the prosecutor, as well as the judge, to comment on the fact that the accused has failed to give evidence to counter the *prima facie* case against him. We accordingly recommend that in every case in which the Crown has established a *prima facie* case against the accused, it should be competent for the prosecution to comment on the failure of the accused to attempt to refute the case against him by giving evidence, and further that, in cases where the judge or jury may have some doubt as to whether or not they should accept the evidence for the Crown, they may draw an inference adverse to the accused from his failure to attempt to refute the evidence for the Crown." (Para. 50.16.)

The Committee rejected the suggestion made by the Criminal Law Revision Committee (11th Report, para. 111) that failure to testify could be taken as corroboration of the prosecution case. Nevertheless, it is worth noting that the Thomson Committee recommended placing some kind of onus upon the accused to refute the prosecution case. The suggestion appears to have the support of the Scottish Law Commission: Memorandum No. 46 (Law of Evidence), para. E.08.

3.   For the impact of the revived procedure of judicial examination on the right to silence, see *infra*, Chap. 8.

B.   POLICE QUESTIONING AND THE FAIRNESS RULE

(i)   Questioning before charge

This is an area of the law which has undergone significant changes over the years. In the years following *Chalmers* v. *H.M. Advocate*, 1954 J.C. 66 the Scottish rules governing the questioning of suspects, and the admissibility of extra-judicial statements by a suspect, moved from a relatively strict exclusionary rule to a generous inclusionary rule. The modern law has now been authoritatively summarised in *Lord Advocate's Reference (No. 1 of 1983)*, 1984 S.C.C.R. 62, *infra*, but this chapter begins, by way of historical introduction, with the case of *Chalmers*.

1.   Chalmers v. H.M. Advocate
1954 J.C. 66

The appellant, a youth of 16, was convicted of murder and robbery. During their investigations the police interviewed the appellant on several occasions. On the third occasion he was taken to a police station where he was cautioned and "cross-examined" for about five minutes until he burst into tears and made a "highly incriminating" statement. (This statement was not tendered in evidence by the Crown.) He then took the police to a field where, under his guidance, they obtained certain real evidence relating to the crimes. Over two hours later the appellant's father arrived. The appellant broke down again, and at this point was cautioned and formally charged. He is alleged to have stated: "I did it. He struck me." At the trial, objection was taken, unsuccessfully, to the admissibility of the evidence relating to the visit to the field and the final statement attributed to the appellant.

LORD JUSTICE-GENERAL (COOPER): "... I have sympathy with the police in the difficult position in which they are often placed. We have no power to give instructions to the police, but we have the power and the duty to exclude from the cognisance of a jury evidence which, according to our practice and decisions, is inadmissible; and the police have an interest to know why such decisions are taken. Were it possible to do so, I should like to be able to lay down comprehensive rules for the guidance of the police in all the situations which may arise in practice, but I am satisfied that this is impossible because in the border-line case so much turns upon the exact circumstances.

This, however, it is possible to say with regard to Scots law. It is not the function of the police when investigating a crime to direct their endeavours to obtaining a confession from the suspect to be used as evidence against him at the trial. In some legal systems the inquisitorial method of investigation is allowed in different degrees and subject to various safeguards; but by our law self-incriminating statements, when tendered in evidence at a criminal trial, are always jealously examined from the standpoint of being assured as to their spontaneity; and if, on a review of all the proved circumstances, that test is not satisfied, evidence of such statements will usually be excluded altogether. The theory of our law is that at the stage of initial investigation the police may question anyone with a view to acquiring information which may lead to the detection of the criminal; but that, when the stage has been reached at which suspicion, or more than suspicion, has in their view centred upon some person as the likely perpetrator of the crime, further interrogation of that person becomes very dangerous, and, if carried too far, *e.g.* to the point of extracting a confession by what amounts to cross-examination, the evidence of that confession will almost certainly be excluded. Once the accused has been apprehended and charged he has the statutory right to a private interview with a solicitor and to be brought before a magistrate with all convenient speed so that he may, if so advised, emit a declaration in presence of his solicitor under conditions which safeguard him against prejudice. The practice of emitting declarations has very largely fallen into disuse since the Evidence Act of 1898, but the underlying principle survives, and it may be applicable to situations which arise before apprehension and charge. Much reference was made to a person 'detained under suspicion,' an expression which has been used ambiguously in many of our decisions, but the emphasis is on the suspicion and not on the detention. Putting aside the case of proper apprehension without a warrant of persons caught more or less redhanded, no person can be lawfully detained except after a charge has been made against him, and it is for this reason that I view with some uneasiness the situation disclosed in this case, and illustrated by the recent cases of *Rigg* [1946 J.C. 1] and *Short* [May 30, 1950 unreported] in which a suspect is neither apprehended nor charged but is simply 'asked' to accompany two police officers to a police office to be there questioned. In former times such questioning, if undertaken, would be conducted by police officers visiting the house or place of business of the suspect and there questioning him, probably in the presence of a relation or friend. However convenient the modern practice may be, it must normally create a situation very unfavourable to the suspect. In the eyes of every ordinary citizen the venue is a sinister one. When he stands alone in such a place confronted by several police officers, usually some of high rank, the dice are loaded against him, especially as he knows that there is no one to corroborate him as to what exactly occurred during the interrogation, how it was conducted, and how long it lasted. If under such circumstances cross-examination is pursued with the result, though perhaps not with the deliberate object, of causing him to break down and to condemn himself out of his own mouth, the impropriety of the proceedings cannot be cured by the giving of any number of formal cautions or by the introduction of some officer other than the questioner to record the ultimate statement. In the ordinary case, as many decisions now demonstrate, that statement, if tendered in evidence at the trial, will not be treated as possessing that quality of spontaneity on which our law insists, and its rejection, when tendered in evidence, may, and sometimes does, wreck the prosecution. The practice exemplified by this and other recent cases in substance puts the suspect in much the same position as if he had been arrested, while depriving him of the privileges and safeguards which are extended by the statute and the decisions to an accused person who has been apprehended. The police have, of course, the right and the duty to produce all the incriminating evidence they can lay their hands on, from whatever source they legitimately derive the clue which leads to its discovery, so long as any admission or confession by the accused is not elicited before the jury as an element in proof of guilt. The matter may be put in another way. The accused cannot be compelled to give evidence at his trial and to submit to cross-examination. If it were competent for the police at their own hand to subject the accused to interrogation and cross-examination and to adduce evidence of what he said, the prosecution would in effect be making the accused a compellable witness, and laying before the jury, at *second hand*, evidence which could not be adduced at first hand, even subject to all the precautions which are available for the protection of the accused at a criminal trial."

LORD JUSTICE-CLERK (THOMSON): "... On the first of these topics the difficulty arises from the necessity of reconciling two principles:—(1) that no accused person is bound to incriminate himself, and (2) that what an accused says—apart from what properly falls within the doctrine of *res gestae*—provided he says it freely and voluntarily, is admissible evidence against him. It is when the police, in the course of their duty as investigators of crime, interview someone in relation to some specific crime that the problem arises for decision whether something which has been said by an accused is admissible as evidence against him. Extreme cases are easy. At the one extreme, once the investigation has gone to the extent that somebody is specifically cautioned and charged, thereafter nothing short of a voluntary statement is admissible against him. At the other extreme is the ordinary routine investigation of the police into the circumstances of the crime. In the course of such an investigation the man ultimately accused may be interviewed. It would unduly hamper the investigation of crime if the threat of inadmissibility were to tie the hands of the police in asking questions. It would help to defeat the ends of justice if what the person so questioned said in answer to ordinary and legitimate questions were not admissible in evidence against him. I am assuming throughout that the questioning is not tainted by bullying, pressure, third degree methods and so forth. Evidence obtained by such methods can never be admissible in our Courts, whatever stage the investigation has reached. But there comes a point of time in ordinary police investigation when the law intervenes to render inadmissible as evidence answers even to questions which are not tainted by such methods. After the point is reached, further interrogation is incompatible with the answers being regarded as a voluntary statement, and the law intervenes to safeguard the party questioned from possible self-incrimination. Just when that point of time is reached is in any particular case extremely difficult to define—or even for an experienced police official to realise its arrival. There does come a time, however, when a police officer, carrying out his duty honestly and conscientiously, ought to be in a position to appreciate that the man whom he is in process of questioning is under serious consideration as the perpetrator of the crime. Once that stage of suspicion is reached, the suspect is in the position that thereafter the only evidence admissible against him is his own voluntary statement. A voluntary statement is one which is given freely, not in response to pressure and inducement, and not elicited by cross-examination. This does not mean that, if a person elects to give a statement, it becomes inadmissible because he is asked some questions to clear up his account of the matter, but such questions as he is asked must not go beyond elucidation. It is important to keep in mind also that the point of time at which the axe falls is not necessarily related to the person being in custody or detention of some sort. The fact that he is detained may point to his being under suspicion but he may come under suspicion without having been detained."

The court allowed
the appeal.

NOTES

1. As indicated above, this "hardy perennial" (to use the words of Lord Avonside in *Hartley* v. *H.M. Advocate*, 1979 S.L.T. 26) is included here by way of historical background to what follows.

In so far as this case states that admissibility of statements depends upon the *stage* of the investigation at which they were elicited it probably no longer represents the law. However, there are indications even today that the stage at which the questioning takes place may still be relevant to the question of admissibility. In *Johnston* v. *H.M. Advocate*, 1993 S.C.C.R. 694 the appellant was convicted of murder. During the investigation of the offence he was questioned by the police, and three stages to this questioning could be identified: The appellant was at first questioned as a prospective witness to the murder. During this phase the police began to suspect that he might have been involved in the murder and he was then given a common law caution. Under further questioning he made an incriminating statement, and was then arrested. Following his arrest he was further questioned, without having been charged. During this third phase he made further incriminating statements, including one to the effect that he had struck the victim with a brick, but that he had not meant to kill him but only to "batter" him.

At his trial, objections were raised to the admissibility of the products of the police questioning. It was accepted that the test for the admissibility of the statements up to the point at which he was arrested would simply be one of "fairness," but that the evidence elicited during the third stage should not have been admitted because they had been elicited by police questioning after arrest. These objections were repelled by the trial judge.

On appeal it was argued that once the accused had been arrested it was not open to the police to question him, an argument which the appeal court has interpreted as meaning that questioning after arrest was necessarily unfair. Having reviewed the authorities (including *Stark and Smith* v. *H.M. Advocate*, 1938 J.C. 170; *Wade* v. *Robertson*, 1948 J.C. 117; *Forbes* v. *H.M. Advocate*, 1990 J.C. 215; *Morrison* v. *Burrell*, 1947 J.C. 43 and *Swankie* v. *Milne*, 1973 J.C. 1) the court concluded that there was no authority for the proposition that questioning must cease once an accused has been arrested. Once a person has been arrested *and charged* he is under the protection of the court and accordingly questioning should cease. But in the view of the court, it does not follow from this that the same protection is to be accorded to a person who has been arrested and not charged. The test, therefore, remains one of fairness.

But is it fair to arrest a person, and refrain from charging him in order to prolong the period during which questioning can take place? Surely the power of detention under section 2 of the 1980 Act is meant to cover the situation where a person is under strong suspicion but the police require a further opportunity to question him? But, of course, that would then trigger the operation of the rights of detained persons under that Act.

2. *Chalmers* occupies an odd position in the jurisprudence of confessions. It has never formally been overruled, "But if it cannot yet be declared dead, it has become so senile that it can be safely said to have faded away." (Gordon, "The Admissibility of Answers to Police Questioning in Scotland," in *Reshaping the Criminal Law*, ed. Glazebrook, at p.332.) And yet, even today, it is still cited to the courts—an example of legal rhetoric defying legal experience. Indeed, the following case (which re-affirms the replacement of the "stage" theory by the test of fairness) appears to have arisen in part because of the trial judge's adherence to a test of admissibility which owes more to *Chalmers* than to the line of authority which "explains" it.

2. Lord Advocate's Reference (No. 1 of 1983)
1984 S.C.C.R. 62

Eight accused were tried on indictment with contraventions of the Misuse of Drugs Act 1971. During the course of their investigations the police interviewed the suspects, and these interviews were recorded on tape. At the trial, the Crown sought to lead evidence of the transcripts of four of these interviews. Having considered these transcripts, and following submissions by the Crown and the defence, the trial judge (Lord Brand) ruled that this evidence was inadmissible. During the debate, the following exchange took place between the advocate-depute and Lord Brand:

"LORD BRAND: What does Lord Avonside mean then when he says [in *Hartley* v. *H.M. Advocate*, 1979 S.L.T. 26], 'Firstly, police officers may question a suspect so long as they do not stray into the field of interrogation?'

THE ADVOCATE-DEPUTE: I think the sort of interrogation.... What is happening is Lord Avonside is having his own little shot at explaining yet again the case of *Chalmers*, and there is no doubt that those who practised at the time of *Chalmers* would not recognise the law as it has since been explained. I understand that, but it has been so explained, and Lord Avonside is having his own little shot at explaining the word 'interrogation' as used in *Chalmers*. Now, my understanding of what he means there is the sort of interrogation which goes on in a gangster movie on the television set, or possible sort of interrogation which went on during the war years, but any questioning, whatever else goes, he says that people may question, so that is what, in my submission, he means. He is not using interrogation as synonymous with asking questions, and, in that case....

LORD BRAND: Mr Depute.

THE ADVOCATE-DEPUTE: Yes.

LORD BRAND: If interrogation does not embrace what we have heard in the transcript, Production No. 14, I don't know what interrogation means.

THE ADVOCATE-DEPUTE: My Lord, interrogation involves some element of third degree.

LORD BRAND: Oh no....

THE ADVOCATE-DEPUTE: My Lord, granted, you say the police are not entitled to question and lead in evidence the answers if that be granted.

LORD BRAND: I am just looking at Walkers on Evidence, Mr Depute.

THE ADVOCATE-DEPUTE: I know, I notice that.

LORD BRAND: Page 38 to 39, what we are dealing with, paragraph 44. 'Statements to Police—After Suspicion Focused On Accused.... Definition Of

Voluntary Statement.... The general rule regarding the admissibility of all statements made to the police after their suspicions have focused upon the accused can be stated both positively and negatively. A statement is admissible if it was truly spontaneous and voluntary, whether it was made before or after the accused was charged. It has been said that a voluntary statement is one which is given freely, not in response to pressure or inducement, and not elicited by cross-examination, apart from such questions as are necessary to elucidate the meaning of what has been said' [p.40, para. 46].

THE ADVOCATE-DEPUTE: Walker is wrong there, he is wrong on those authorities, quite clearly so if that is what he said. The other thing is I cannot recall when Walker was written, I think it is some time ago.

LORD BRAND: Not very old.

THE ADVOCATE-DEPUTE: 1975 or so. My learned friend says it was as long ago as 1969.

LORD BRAND: What was said by Lord Justice-General Cooper, was it in *Chalmers*?

THE ADVOCATE-DEPUTE: Yes.

LORD BRAND: Statements freely given and so forth.

THE ADVOCATE-DEPUTE: If your Lordship won't accept that *Chalmers* had been explained in the way I have suggested, then I am entirely, with great respect, at one with your Lordship, but *Chalmers* has been explained and I venture to submit respectfully whatever my Lord's own view, my Lord's unaided view, in a case like this your Lordship has now to be aided, in quotation marks, by what has been said by the court of appeal in these four recent cases [*Miln* v. *Cullen*; *Jones* v. *Milne*; *Murphy* v. *H.M. Advocate*, 1975 S.L.T. (Notes) 17; *Hartley* v. *H.M. Advocate*, 1979 S.L.T. 26]. On that authority I do take my stance pretty firmly and I have to say to my Lord that, granted that it is admissible to ask questions, the only remaining question for your Lordship is, are the questions, so unfair that your Lordship can take the matter away from the jury and say 'I decide it is unfair', rather than, as was indicated to be the correct course in *Tonge*, leave it to the jury to decide whether value is to be attached to these answers or not? Now, my learned friends in due course may make submissions on behalf of their clients, it was a leading question, it really is a matter for the jury and, my submission, and, on authority, and bearing in mind this is a case of some importance, I have to invite your Lordship to allow this evidence to be led. ..."

Following the decision to exclude the evidence contained in the transcripts, one of the accused was acquitted by Lord Brand on a submission of no case to answer. The Lord Advocate presented a petition to the High Court in terms of section 263A of the Criminal Procedure (Scotland) Act 1975.

LORD JUSTICE-GENERAL: "This is the first occasion on which the Lord Advocate has taken advantage of the right conferred upon him by the provisions of section 263A of the Criminal Procedure (Scotland) Act 1975 which derive from section 37 of the Criminal Justice (Scotland) Act 1980. As section 263A tells us: 'Where a person tried on indictment is acquitted of a charge the Lord Advocate may refer a point of law which has arisen in relation to that charge to the High Court for their opinion. ...'

The circumstances which form the background to the reference which is now before us are that a person, A, was one of eight persons tried on indictment in the High Court at Aberdeen upon a charge (charge 1) that between 27th February and 1st March 1983, both dates inclusive, within ... the City District of Aberdeen, the eight named persons were concerned in the supplying of controlled drugs to others, namely diamorphine and cocaine hydrochloride, both class A drugs specified in Part I of Schedule 2 to the Misuse of Drugs Act 1971, and amphetamine sulphate, a class B drug specified in Part II of that Schedule, in contravention of section 4(1)(b) of the Act. At the conclusion of the evidence for the Crown at the trial, the trial judge, on the motion of counsel for A, acquitted him of that charge upon the ground that he had no case to answer within the meaning of section 140A of the Criminal Procedure (Scotland) Act 1975.

Evidence was led at the trial that after the seizure of certain drugs by the police, on the evening of 1st March 1983, from a motor-car in the car park of [a] public house, A was suspected of having been a party to the offence libelled in charge 1, was detained under the provisions of section 2 of the Criminal Justice (Scotland) Act 1980, and was interviewed at a police station by two detective constables, Struthers and Duncan. The entire interview was recorded on tape and it effectively began when Detective Constable Struthers informed A that he was going to be asked questions about the drugs which had been seized, that he was not bound to answer but that if he did his answers would be tape recorded and might be noted and used in evidence. A, it seems, chose to answer all the questions which were put to him, and when Detective Constable Struthers was in the witness box the learned advocate-depute proposed to examine him about the interview with A and about similar interviews which took place with co-accused under reference to an accurate transcript of each recorded interview. Upon objection taken by counsel for A and for the other co-accused concerned an issue arose as to whether the answers of A and the others to the questions put to them at interview, which questions and answers had been tape recorded and were evidenced by accurate transcripts, were admissible in evidence. The trial judge held that all such evidence, including the transcripts of the interviews, was inadmissible, and it appears that he did so because he took the view that what was said by the suspects, including A, could not be regarded as having been voluntary and spontaneous because it had been in answer to questions, some of which were leading questions. In other words, the judge, without giving the transcripts any close examination, excluded the information given by A (and others) at interview from consideration by the jury, merely because it was contained in answers to questions some of which had been or might have been leading questions. Objection was taken to the admissibility in evidence of some of these transcripts upon another ground with which we are not concerned, for the objection so taken was repelled.

In the events which happened which have just been summarised the points of law which the Lord Advocate has referred to this court for our opinion are presented in the following two questions:

'(1) Were the answers given by A as evidenced by the transcript of his tape-recorded interview by the police admissible in evidence?
(2) Alternatively, and in any event, did said transcript of itself disclose unfairness such as entitled the trial judge to rule all evidence thereanent inadmissible and to withhold it from the jury?'

At the hearing the learned Lord Advocate submitted to us that question 1 must be answered in the affirmative but that, if we were not prepared to do so, we should at least answer question 2 in the negative. A did not appear personally nor was he represented by counsel, and in the circumstances we enjoyed the benefit of the assistance offered to the court by Mr Weir, Q.C., whom we had appointed under section 263A of the Act of 1975 to act as amicus curiae.

In approaching the first question it must be emphasised that we must answer it upon a consideration of the transcript of the tape-recorded interview of A by itself. We must assume that there are no other circumstances which might have a relevant bearing upon the admissibility of the answers of A as disclosed in the transcript, and that there is no suggestion that consideration of the text of the transcript may give a misleading impression of the atmosphere in which the interview took place, or of the tone of that interview.

Upon a consideration of the contents of the transcript, accordingly, are we required to conclude that the answers of A, some of which were self-incriminating, were inadmissible in evidence? I have no hesitation in saying that we are not required to do so and, putting the matter positively, I have no doubt whatever that the answers given were clearly admissible in evidence.

The law governing the admissibility of statements made or information of a self-incriminating character given by an accused person to police officers, while he was in the position of a suspect under caution, is well settled. It is to be found without difficulty in the line of authority beginning with *Chalmers* v. *H.M. Advocate*, 1954 J.C. 66 down to *Tonge* v. *H.M. Advocate*, 1982 S.L.T. 506. In particular it is well settled that it is not our law that the answers of a suspect, given under caution, to police questioning, will never be admissible in evidence. I do not wish to add to the length of this opinion by quoting what has been said by so many judges, each in his own way, upon this matter, and it will I think be quite sufficient to record as a sound statement of our law the following passage from the opinion of Lord Wheatley in the case of *Miln* v. *Cullen*, 1967 J.C. 21 at p.30:

> 'If the "suspect" is cautioned (but not charged), he is being warned that he is going to be asked questions but that he is not under any obligation to answer them. On the basis that such a caution is properly given and properly understood, it is unrealistic to proceed on the basis that questions which might elicit answers which might tend to incriminate him should automatically be disallowed. To adopt such a rule would so to circumscribe police investigation that the public interest, the protection of the public and the administration of justice might be completely ignored. In each case the issue is—was the question in the circumstances a fair one?'

A suspect's self-incriminating answers to police questioning will indeed be admissible in evidence unless it can be affirmed that they have been extracted from him by unfair means. The simple and intelligible test which has worked well in practice is whether what has taken place has been fair or not (see the opinion of the Lord Justice-General (Clyde) in *Brown* v. *H.M. Advocate*, 1966 S.L.T. 105 at p.107). In each case where the admissibility of answers by a suspect to police questioning becomes an issue it will be necessary to consider the whole relevant circumstances in order to discover whether or not there has been unfairness on the part of the police resulting in the extraction from the suspect of the answers in question. Unfairness may take many forms but 'if answers are to be excluded they must be seen to have been extracted by unfair means which place cross-examination, pressure, and deception in close company' (see my own own opinion in *Jones* v. *Milne*, 1975 J.C. 16). For the avoidance of doubt I should add that where in the opinions in the decided cases the word 'interrogation' or the expression 'cross-examination' are used in discussing unfair tactics on the part of the police they are to be understood to refer only to improper forms of questioning tainted with an element of bullying or pressure designed to break the will of the suspect or to force from him a confession against his will.

Applying the well-settled law to the transcript of the tape-recorded interview of A in a situation in which if unfairness there was, it was only to be found in the questioning of A by the two police officers, I find no basis for the suggestion that the answers of A were unfairly obtained. The picture presented by the transcript is of apparently relaxed exchanges between the parties to the interview. The questioning by the police officers was polite and was not in any sense pressed too far and, indeed, it is evident that A himself quite freely contributed to the flow of the conversation. In these circumstances it is nothing to the point that some of the questions put might be thought to have been leading questions. Although in certain circumstances leading questions may affect the weight to be given to the answers which they have elicited such questions are not necessarily unfair and in this case I am quite unable to detect the slightest hint of unfairness in any of the questions put to A, all of which he answered freely, and without having had any pressure put upon him to do so. For these reasons I would, without the slightest hesitation, answer question 1 in the reference in the affirmative and find it unnecessary to answer question 2.

What I have said so far is sufficient to dispose of the reference which is before us but I feel that it might be helpful to go a little further. In the first place it may be of assistance to all trial judges to be reminded that a judge who has heard all the relevant undisputed evidence bearing upon the admissibility of answers by a suspect, under caution, to police questioning, will normally only be justified in withholding the evidence of the alleged answers from the jury if he is satisfied that no reasonable jury could hold upon that evidence, that the answers had not been extracted from the suspect by unfair or improper means. Lord Cameron in *H.M. Advocate* v. *Whitelaw*, 1980 S.L.T. (Notes) 25, in a passage quoted with approval in *Tonge*, put the matter in this way:

> 'Evidence as to statements of a possibly incriminating character alleged to have been made by an accused person is prima facie of the highest relevance and the jury's function should not be in fact usurped and unless it is abundantly clear that the rules of fairness and fair dealing have been flagrantly transgressed it would be better for a jury seized of the whole evidence in the case and of all the circumstances, under such guidance as they should receive from the presiding judge, themselves to take that decision as to the extent to which, if at all, they will take into account evidence of statements ... given by a suspect after due caution.'

In the second place I wish to say that upon a consideration of an accurate transcript of an interview of a suspect under caution, whether or not it has been tape recorded, it may appear, for one of a number of reasons, that certain answers must be excluded from consideration by a jury. One such reason might be that the answers disclosed that the suspect had previously been convicted. Another such reason might be, for example, that certain particular answers had been extracted from the suspect by particular questions which were plainly improper questions of the kind which has been discussed earlier in this opinion. The point to be made is that the presence in a transcript of an interview with a suspect under caution of certain answers which, for a sound reason, must be withheld from a jury will not by itself normally justify a trial judge in excluding from the jury's consideration the remainder of the transcript."

NOTES

1.   This case can be seen as a formal re-affirmation of the development of the law since *Chalmers* and as such it does not change the law as it has developed in recent years. It is interesting to note that the Lord Justice-General refers to "the line of authority beginning with *Chalmers* v. *H.M. Advocate* ... down to *Tonge* v. *H.M. Advocate*." To suggest that there has

been a single "line of authority" in this area is, with respect, not wholly correct and serves to minimise the very great changes which have taken place since *Chalmers*. These are two-fold. In the first place the courts today apply a quite different *test* of admissibility from that which was suggested in *Chalmers* (at least by the Lord Justice-Clark). Secondly, it is clear that the courts today operate a quite different *standard* of admissibility. If there can be any doubt about this, compare the circumstances and the outcome of *Hartley* v. *H.M. Advocate*, 1979 S.L.T. 26 (*infra*) with those of *Chalmers*.

The case raises, once again, the issue not only of what are the proper standards for pre-trial inquiry, but also how these standards are to be determined. The current judicial policy is to leave this to the jury in the vast majority of cases. But is this an acceptable approach? Suppose, for example, that the jury are faced with a crime which has outraged public opinion, and one in which they are left to determine the fairness of the police questioning of the accused. It would be understandable, but regrettable, if the jury's judgment concerning the latter were to be influenced by former.

2.   This case also confirms the test for allowing evidence of a statement to go to the jury, or to be withheld from the jury by the judge:

> "...a judge who has heard all the undisputed evidence bearing upon the admissibility of answers by a suspect, under caution, to police questioning, will normally only be satisfied in withholding the evidence of the alleged answers from the jury if he is satisfied that no reasonable jury could hold, upon that evidence, that the answers had not been extracted by unfair or improper means."

It is clear that a decision to withhold evidence of this kind from the jury will be fairly exceptional.

3.   The court does not expressly discuss the onus of proof in questions of fairness. Is it for the accused to show that the statements were unfairly obtained, or for the Crown to show that they were fairly obtained? The tendency in earlier cases was to suggest the former (see, for example, *Boyne* v. *H.M. Advocate*, 1980 S.L.T. 56). The "no reasonable jury" test is confusingly formulated with its double negatives, and could be read either way. However, at an earlier stage in his opinion the Lord Justice-General states: "A suspect's self-incriminating answers to police questioning will indeed be admissible in evidence unless it can be affirmed that they have been extracted from him by unfair means." This clearly suggests that the onus rests on the accused to show unfairness.

It is most unfortunate that the court did not take the opportunity to state clearly, and in accordance with principle, that the onus of proving "fairness" lies on the prosecutor. If a party wishes to rely on evidence the onus is on that party to establish, in case of dispute, that it is admissible evidence. See, in this respect, *Thompson* v. *H.M. Advocate*, 1968 J.C. 61, *per* the Lord Justice-General at p.66.

3.   Boyne v. H.M. Advocate
1980 S.L.T. 56

Boyne was found art and part guilty of murder. The principal evidence against him consisted of certain statements allegedly made by him to the police. At the trial it was argued that in the circumstances of the case the statements had been unfairly obtained. The trial judge, however, directed the jury that there was no evidence from which they could infer that the statements were unfairly obtained. Boyne appealed on the ground, *inter alia*, of misdirection.

LORD JUSTICE-CLERK (WHEATLEY): "... In considering the submissions made in support of the various grounds of appeal we consider it appropriate to deal in the first place with the argument that the trial judge misdirected the jury in the case of Boyne in that he excluded from their consideration the question whether the statements made by Boyne to the police had been unfairly obtained. No argument was advanced in the case of Brown that any unfairness was attached to the taking of statements from him, so the point did not arise in his case. The importance of this point in Boyne's case is that the advocate-depute frankly admitted that without these statements no convictions would be warranted against Boyne on charges 4, 6 and 10.

The passage in the judge's charge to the jury which was the basis of this complaint was in these terms: 'There is accordingly, ladies and gentlemen, in this case against Boyne no evidence before you from which you could hold that these statements had been extracted unfairly in the legal sense from Boyne, and I so direct you.'

This passage was interpreted by counsel for Boyne as meaning that the judge was directing the jury as a matter of law that they were not entitled to consider the question of unfairness in the manner in which the statements were obtained or made in determining what evidential value if any, should be attached to them. This, said counsel for Boyne, was a clear misdirection in law. He prayed in aid the final passage in the judgment of Lord Justice-Clerk Thomson in *Chalmers* v. *H.M. Advocate*, 1954 S.L.T. p.186, where his Lordship said: 'It is impossible to ask a jury to accept as an item of evidence a statement made by an accused while preventing it from considering the circumstances under which it was made ... The jury's problem is to find out the truth; in their search for the truth a statement made freely by the accused may be of immense signification, but the degree of the significance must depend for the jury on their view of its spontaneity.' We in no way differ from what the Lord Justice-Clerk there said, but we cannot accept the wide interpretation which counsel for Boyne put on it. He submitted that once the judge had admitted the evidence about the taking of a statement it had to be left to the jury, under proper direction, in every case to decide on their view of the spontaneity of the statement whether the statement had been fairly obtained. In our opinion that passage should be regarded against the background of dispute as to the circumstances in which the statement was made or had been obtained. It should not be read as depriving the judge of the power to direct the jury as a matter of law that there was no evidence on which they could find that the rules of fairness had been infringed. Counsel for Boyne argued that it was not competent for a judge to make this decision where there was evidence of unfairness. Where there is evidence on which a jury, properly directed, could hold that there was unfairness, this is so. Where, however, there is no such evidence, the judge is entitled to direct the jury accordingly as a matter of law. That will turn on the circumstances of the particular case.

We now turn to consider the circumstances in which the judge's words which are the subject of complaint were uttered. The judge clearly was of the view that counsel for Boyne had represented to the jury that it was sufficient to establish unfairness that there was evidence to show that the statements made by Boyne resulted from questioning by the police and that this in itself rendered the statements inadmissible in evidence. Counsel's recollection was that this was not the submission which he made. We do not have the extended notes of what counsel said to the jury, but we are always prepared to take into consideration what responsible counsel who conducted the case at the trial recollects was said. We accordingly deal with the matter on the basis that the judge may have misunderstood what counsel's submission to the jury was. What the judge did, however, was to give the jury the law on the subject of when questioning of a suspect (as Boyne then was) is permissible and when it is not, in conformity with a line of recent decisions...

Having given these general directions in law, which were in no way criticised as being wrong in any respect, he went on to consider the facts of the instant case. He told the jury: 'in the case of Boyne in this case no objection was taken to any line of questioning by the police of Boyne, no evidence was led which showed that the police officers had strayed into the realm of cross-examination or interrogation or illegal methods.

It would have been perfectly possible for the accused to give evidence on this matter, but he did not do so, and he did not say that there was anything unfair about the giving of these statements or that anything unfair had been done'. It was at that point that he said: 'There is accordingly in this case against Boyne no evidence before you from which you could hold that these statements had been extracted unfairly in the legal sense from Boyne, and I so direct you'. He followed this up immediately with the following direction: 'The advocate-depute was quite right in referring to these statements which in his case are simply part of the evidence in the case, and are to be treated by you as any other piece of evidence. You would of course be quite entitled to consider all the circumstances in which they were taken, his youth and the length of time and all that sort of thing, but these criticisms in the circumstances would go to the quality of the evidence in the statements and not to their competence'.

The points taken by counsel for the appellant to support his claim of unfairness were founded not on any direct evidence but on inferences to be drawn from the youth of the appellant (he was 16 years old at the time), the length of the questioning and the hours at which the questioning took place. There was, however, no evidence, least of all from the appellant, that these factors had any effect on him in giving the statements or influenced him in any way. As we have already said, each case turns on its own special circumstances, and in the instant case we are of the opinion that, having regard to the factors alluded to by him above and the points taken by counsel and our observations thereon, the judge was entitled to hold that there was no evidence on which a reasonable jury could find that the statements had been extracted unfairly from Boyne in the legal sense."

> The court refused this ground of
> appeal. Appeal allowed on other
> grounds.

NOTES

1.   This case is authority for a number of important propositions:

(a) In general, "unfairness" is not simply a question of the circumstances in which the questioning took place or under which the statements were made, but also one of the effect of such circumstances on the suspect. It might be possible to envisage a case in which the questioning was unfair, but the accused withstood it and yet also made incriminating statements. It seems from this case that the court would not exclude the statements. In other words, there must be a causal link between the unfairness and the self-incrimination before the unfairness becomes relevant. However, there may be cases where the circumstances in which a statement is made are, in themselves, sufficient to lead to a conclusion of "unfairness" even though there is no "link" between those circumstances and the making of the statement. See *H.M. Advocate* v. *Gilgannon, infra*, p.188.

(b)   In some cases the judge will be entitled to withdraw the question of fairness from the jury entirely by telling them that there is no evidence on which they could find that the statements were unfairly obtained.

(c)   The court appears to favour placing the onus of proof in relation to fairness on the accused.

2.   In the above cases it is said that where the admissibility of answers by a suspect to police questioning becomes an issue, it is "necessary to consider the whole relevant circumstances in order to discover whether or not there has been unfairness on the part of the police resulting in the extraction from the suspect of the answers in question." (*Lord Advocate's Reference, supra, per* the Lord Justice-General.) But what are the "relevant circumstances"? The following cases raise a number of considerations which may be relevant to the question of fairness.

4.   Lord Advocate's Reference (No. 1 of 1983)
1984 S.C.C.R.

For the facts of this case and the full judgment of the court, see *supra*, p.177. The following passage is noted at this point as an indication of the court's views regarding the relationship between the way in which the questioning is conducted and the admissibility of evidence of statements made in response to police questioning.

> LORD JUSTICE-GENERAL: "Unfairness may take many forms but 'if answers are to be excluded they must be seen to have been extracted by unfair means which place cross-examination, pressure, and deception in close company' (see my own opinion in *Jones* v. *Milne*, 1975 J.C. 16). For the avoidance of doubt I should add that where in the opinions in the decided cases the word 'interrogation' or the expression 'cross-examination' are used in discussing unfair tactics on the part of the police they are to be understood to refer only to improper forms of questioning tainted with an element of bullying or pressure designed to break the will of the suspect or to force from him a confession against his will.'"

NOTES

1.   It is worth contrasting this statement with what was said by Lord Avonside in *Hartley* v. *H.M. Advocate*, 1979 S.L.T. 26:

> "cross-examination is just what it means. It consists in questioning an adverse witness in an effort to break down his evidence, to weaken or prejudice his evidence, or to elicit statements damaging to him and aiding the case of the cross-examiner."

In his commentary on *Lord Advocate's Reference (No. 1) of 1983)* (1984 S.C.C.R., at p.70) Sheriff Gordon suggests that "The police officer has perhaps not quite as much leeway as cross-examining counsel, but considerably more than an examining fiscal at judicial examination." But Lord Avonside's formulation of cross-examination seems to be based largely on a judicial perception of what is appropriate forensic conduct for counsel and, with respect, the *Lord Advocate's Reference* test would seem to leave much greater leeway to the investigating police officer.

2.   The length of time over which the questioning is conducted may also be relevant. A suspected person should not be subjected to prolonged questioning. In *H.M. Advocate* v. *Friel*, 1978 S.L.T. (Notes) 21 the accused was questioned for a period which "commenced around 7.55 a.m. and had continued off and on until the accused was charged about a quarter to one the following morning; that is over 16 hours." (*Ibid.*, *per* Lord Ross.) His Lordship held that the duration of the questioning, along with the manner in which it was conducted and the stage of the investigation at which it was conducted rendered it unfair.

5.   H.M. Advocate v. G.B. and D.J.M.
1991 S.C.C.R. 533

The accused were charged on indictment with assault. During the trial, objection was taken to the admission in evidence of statements allegedly made, voluntarily, by the first accused (who was 15) following his arrest.

SHERIFF GOW: "During the course of P.C. Alistair Fulton's evidence, Mr Logan for the first accused took objection to the line of evidence. The witness said that he and another police officer had visited several houses in Ayr looking for the two accused, and at 1.40 a.m. had found the two accused, and in particular [B] (aged fourteen [sic]) at 63 Whitletts Road. He had been admitted to the house by the occupant ... who was the mother of the accused. He had asked and obtained permission from [her] to search the house for the weapon used in the alleged assault. He had aroused the accused [B] from his bed, and had searched under the bed and mattress. He also administered a common law caution to the accused [B]. At a later stage he said he had apprehended both the accused, that is to say, he had placed them under arrest and taken them to King Street Police Station. Production No. 2 is a document relating to police procedure at King Street. In answer to a question from the fiscal, the witness said that [B] had volunteered certain information to the police. At this point Mr Logan intervened to object.

In the absence of the jury, he submitted that there were three possible ways under which a suspected person could be taken to a police station for interview. First, there could be detention under section 2 [of the Criminal Justice (Scotland) Act 1980]; secondly, the witness could be asked to make a 'voluntary' attendance; thirdly, a suspected person could be charged and then arrested and taken to the police station. In the present case, he pointed out that although there was a common law caution given to the accused, he had been arrested and taken to the police station without any formal charge having been administered. Mr Logan submitted that no detention was lawful unless a person had first been charged with an offence: Renton and Brown, paragraph 5–18, and *Chalmers* v. *H.M. Advocate* [1954 J.C. 66]. He further submitted that if a person was not lawfully charged or detained, then any answers given to police questioning are inadmissible: *H.M. Advocate* v. *McGrade and Stirton* [1982 S.L.T. (Sh.Ct.) 13]. He suggested that the proper procedure would have been to detain the suspect under section 2 procedure, in which case the accused, being under sixteen and therefore a child, would have the various statutory protections of section 3(3). In the present case, neither parent nor child had been advised of their rights under section 3(3) and the parent had not been given the opportunity to seek access to the child at the police station. In the present case the accused's mother was aware of the police interest in her son, and was aware that he was being taken away from home to the police station. It would have been quite practical and simple to offer to take her along with her son to the police station where she could have access to him as required. Mr Logan also referred to *Tonge and Ors* v. *H.M. Advocate* [1982

S.C.C.R. 313] which was a case under section 2 procedure where full common law cautions were not given. The subsequent statements were held inadmissible. Reference was also made to Renton and Brown, paragraph 18–32.

Mr. Logan further submitted that arrest could only proceed on a previous charge having been made, and referred to *Stark and Smith* v. *H.M. Advocate* [1938 S.L.T. 516] and *Wade* v. *Robertson* [1948 S.L.T. 491].

On a more general point, Mr Logan submitted that the circumstances in which the accused had elected to make a voluntary statement were unfair, within the criteria of admissibility as referred to in Renton and Brown at paragraph 18–26. He pointed out, in particular, that the accused was a fourteen [sic]-year-old child, and was entitled to special statutory protections when treated as a suspected person. The child had been in bed asleep when the police arrived to question him, and he had been roused from his slumbers at about 2 a.m. Although he was given a common law caution, he was arrested and taken to the police station without being charged. Although his mother was present at the time, it was not suggested to her that she had a right to come with the boy to the police station and to have access to him there.

In reply, the procurator fiscal depute referred to Renton and Brown, paragraph 18–33, and pointed out that the police were not obliged to charge anyone as soon as they had suspicions about him or full information concerning the case. The normal practice nowadays was to use the common law caution, as advised by the High Court in *Tonge*, and that was the course followed here. The court had to balance fairness to the accused against the public interest: *Miln* v. *Cullen* [1967 S.L.T. 35]. He submitted that the law did not support the view that an arrest must be followed immediately by a charge, and referred to *Murphy* v. *H.M. Advocate* [1975 S.L.T. (Notes) 17]. In that case the suspected person had been apprehended, cautioned and detained in a police station in London, but not charged. The Scottish police officer in charge of the London investigation did not charge the accused at that stage because he was awaiting a petition warrant from Scotland which would have enabled him to take the accused to Scotland where he was eventually charged. At some stage of the enquiry (which is not clear from the report), the accused made incriminating statements to the police, which were later put before the jury. The [appeal court] later confirmed that such statements were admissible and there was no criticism that the accused had been detained without a charge.

Mr Andrew also submitted that the whole question of fairness and admissibility was one rather for the jury than the judge, and referred to Renton and Brown, paragraph 18–42. The question whether the evidence was unfairly obtained in the circumstances was essentially one for the jury. He submitted that a judge could only withhold challenged evidence from the jury in normal circumstances if he was satisfied on the undisputed relevant evidence that no reasonable jury could hold the statement had been made voluntarily and had not been extracted by unfair and improper means: *Balloch* v. *H.M. Advocate* [1977 S.L.T. (Notes) 29].

I am not satisfied that there is a hard and fast rule that a person cannot be detained by the police without being charged (apart from section 2 detention). Circumstances may arise, as is shown by *Murphy*'s case, where this course is not immediately feasible or practical. The hands of the police cannot be tied in this way by a hard and fast rule. Mr Logan's submission does not therefore succeed in this point exclusively.

However, in my opinion, there is a degree of unfairness in the police approach in this case. I am particularly concerned that a fourteen [sic]-year-old boy should have been taken from his bed in the middle of the night and escorted to a police station without being formally charged with any offence, and without his parent being given the opportunity to accompany him to the police station and have access to him there. If the police had adopted what I consider would have been the appropriate procedure in the circumstances, namely, detention of a suspected person under section 2, then as a child the accused would have had the additional statutory protection provided by section 3(3).

I have considered whether the question of unfairness should be left to the jury or not. I appreciate that is the normal judicial approach, but in the present case there are questions of mixed fact and law, in particular the fact that the accused was possibly deprived of his statutory rights under section 3(3). In this case the relevant evidence is undisputed and there is no issue of credibility for the jury to determine. I think that no reasonable jury could hold that the alleged voluntary statement was made in circumstances which were not unfair to the accused; I hold that the test as laid down in *Balloch*'s case is met, and it is proper for myself as the trial judge to determine the matter. The whole surrounding circumstances, as I have already enumerated them, suggest to me that the procedures were tainted with unfairness, and that the purported voluntary statement from the accused should therefore be inadmissible.

Mr Logan further argued that all further police procedures following upon the voluntary statement, which I was told included an excursion on which the accused accompanied the police touring the district looking for certain objects, and also a reply to a later caution and charge, should also be inadmissible. That very point was taken in *Murphy*'s case, but Lord Justice-Clerk Wheatley said, 'I cannot accept that as a general proposition. Again it will be a question of the circumstances in each case.' I would respectfully agree, and follow Lord Wheatley's view. While it may be that statements or actings by the accused immediately following the alleged giving of the voluntary statement would also be tainted and inadmissible for the reasons given, it does not follow that matters occurring later in time should automatically be excluded. I shall reserve my opinion on the admissibility of these later matters until such time as the questions of their admissibility or otherwise specifically arise."

NOTE

It seems that the fact that the suspect was a young person would not of itself have rendered the police questioning unfair. But clearly the law should pay particular attention to safeguarding the interests of young persons in the process of investigation. It may be, for example, that a mode of questioning adopted by the police which would not fall foul of the fairness test in the case of an adult suspect would be unfair in the case of a young person. See for example, *H.M. Advocate* v. *Rigg*, 1946 J.C. 1. However, it does seem that the courts have on occasion given less weight to the youthfulness of a suspect than might have been expected. In *Hartley* v. *H.M. Advocate*, 1979 S.L.T. 26, statements made by a 17-year-old youth in connection with a murder investigation were held to be admissible notwithstanding the fact that he had been in police custody for 12 hours, had had no contact with a legal adviser or an adult and was, moreover, described as having a "disordered personality."

6. **H.M. Advocate v. Gilgannon**
1983 S.C.C.R. 10

The accused was charged with attempted rape. During the trial evidence was led to the effect that the accused had been examined while in custody by a police surgeon who had concluded that he was mentally subnormal and that he was unable to give a coherent account of the incident in connection with which he was in custody. Nearly five hours after this examination the accused had made a voluntary statement to police officers unconnected with the case, and the Crown sought to lead evidence of this statement at the trial. Counsel for the accused objected to the admission of the statement in evidence.

LORD CAMERON: "Counsel for the panel has taken objection to the admissibility of the voluntary statement alleged to have been made by the accused on the morning of 3rd July 1982 at 10.30 a.m. in the police station at Baird Street. The panel had already been arrested and charged with the offence of assault with intent to ravish.

By the time the voluntary statement was made the panel had been medically examined by an experienced police surgeon round about 6 a.m. on the day in question at Baird Street. The opinion of the surgeon was that Gilgannon was mentally subnormal. In the witness box Dr Banerjee explained in cross-examination that in describing an incident the panel could not describe it fully and that he would not be able to give a clear account of what happened at the bus shelter, which was the locus of the crime with which he was charged and indicted. In addition, the doctor noted a history of epilepsy and cautioned that he be kept under observation.

It was in these circumstances that the Crown sought to lead evidence of the contents of the statement taken on the forenoon of the same day. The statement is recorded as having begun at 10.30 and as having been completed at 11.00.

Mr Hamilton for the panel maintained this evidence of the contents of the statement was incompetent because it was unfairly taken and manifestly unfair to the accused. He founded strongly on the opinions of the court in *Tonge* v. *Her Majesty's Advocate*, 1982 S.L.T. 506. He pointed out that the unchallenged medical evidence was that the accused could not give a coherent account of an incident which led to the charge being preferred against him because of his state of mind and therefore that his objection should be sustained. In the alternative, he urged that a 'trial within a trial' should be conducted at which the evidence of 'everyone concerned' including the accused should be heard. The test of fairness to the accused is one that is purely objective. If at a later stage in the trial it should emerge that the evidence would show that the accused could not recollect the facts and had to be questioned then it would be unfair to him, as a matter of law, to allow anything he said to go to the jury.

In reply the advocate-depute submitted that the evidence should be allowed. It was not the police who acted unfairly; on the contrary, they acted with manifest fairness in taking a voluntary statement from one already charged. The real question was whether the police had followed a proper and fair course. Leaving aside any question of the accused's mental capacity the actings of the police were plainly fair; there was nothing indicative of improper threats or questioning and no such suggestion had been made. The test of fairness was related solely to the circumstances in which the statement was obtained and not related to the question whether the accused was capable of emitting a coherent and meaningful statement [with] a meaningful content. In any event, the matter should not be disposed of by a trial within a trial.

I agree with the advocate-depute that there is no question here of allegations of improper threats or questioning but to that extent the case does not fall within the category or ratio of such cases as *Tonge* or the earlier cases of *Balloch* or *Whitelaw*. I am not, however, prepared to accept the rigid proposition that the matter of fairness is confined to the detailed circumstances in which the voluntary statement is obtained; that is the questioning itself or the pressures put on the maker of the statement. The mental or physical state of the maker may well be an important and relevant circumstance in determining the issue of admissibility. Once, as here, a suspect is under arrest even before he has been formally charged he is under and is entitled to the protection of the court and therefore it is proper that the circumstances in which the statement is taken should be regarded as well as the manner itself in which the statement is obtained and elicited.

The physical or mental state of an accused at the time of making a statement may be such as to make it unfair on him though, particularly in the absence of his solicitor, a voluntary statement even if obtained without questions at all can be made admissible evidence against him. See such cases as *H.M. Advocate* v. *Aitken*, 1926, *H.M. Advocate* v. *Rigg*, 1946, cited in Walkers on Evidence, page 41.

In the present case, information was available to the police from Dr Banerjee's examination and report that this man was mentally subnormal with a history of epilepsy and had to be kept under observation. Although it was recorded that when detained originally the accused made an observation at 2.15, 'I'll say it to my lawyer in the morning', yet at 3.45 when asked if he wished intimation to be sent to a solicitor he replied 'No' as appears from the relevant unchallenged production compiled and completed by the police, no apparent explanation was given for this sudden change of attitude. No action was recorded as taken by the police officers concerned to ascertain whether the accused was in a fit state to give a proper statement having regard to his mental state.

I am far from saying, however, that the officers directly concerned were in any way deliberately acting unfairly towards the accused, but if the unchallenged evidence of Dr Banerjee is accepted then unless he were questioned a coherent and complete and therefore accurate account of an incident in which the accused was concerned could not be obtained.

In the particular circumstances of this case, however, I have come to the conclusion that such a statement as that to which objection has been taken, however carefully elicited in accordance with the rules of fair and proper practice, suffers from a vital and fatal flaw; it comes as an at least possibly if not probably incomplete narrative from one who is not only mentally subnormal but unable to give a coherent and complete and therefore accurate account of an incident in which he himself played a principal part.

In these particularly unusual circumstances, without any reflection on the police officers concerned, I shall sustain the objection which counsel for the panel has taken."

The court sustained the
objection.

NOTE

This is an example of "unfairness" being inferred from the circumstances in which a statement is made, rather than from the manner in which the investigation was conducted and its effect on the suspect. In general, it seems that "unfairness" results from the combination of the manner in which the investigation is carried out and its effect on the suspect. But here there was no suggestion of unfair conduct on the part of the police. If there was "unfairness" it arose from the condition of the suspect.

What this case may suggest is that there is, within the notion of fairness, some concern for the reliability of the statement where it is made in circumstances which suggest that the person making it is not competent to do so.

This is important, because reliability is, in principle, distinguishable from fairness, but is, of course, equally important. A statement should be both fairly obtained and obtained in circumstances which do not impugn its reliability. If a statement is obtained in circumstances under which the reliability of any such statement would be open to question, then, it is submitted, it should not be allowed in evidence, even if, in the circumstances there is no "unfairness."

7.   Montes and Others v. H.M. Advocate
1990 S.C.C.R. 671

The appellants were convicted on charges, *inter alia*, of being knowingly concerned in the fraudulent evasion of a prohibition on the importation of cocaine by importing cocaine at Greenock, contrary to section 170(2)(*b*) of the Customs and Excise Management Act 1979 and section 3 of the Misuse of Drugs Act 1971. One of the appellants, Veenstra, appealed against his conviction on the ground, *inter alia*, that statements which he made to officers of Customs and Excise should not have been admitted in evidence.

LORD WEIR: "The appellant Sjirk Veenstra was convicted or charges (1), (3) and (5) on the indictment. ... This appellant has a ground of appeal concerning the evidence of statements made by him to officers of Customs and Excise following upon his detention and this statement affects his conviction on all three charges. It was submitted that these statements were wholly inadmissible inasmuch as they were obtained at a time when he was said to have been detained unlawfully. The appellant was in the same situation as Jensen and counsel adopted the arguments advanced by Jensen's counsel to the effect that their detention was unlawful. This argument has been disposed of in the opinion of your Lordship and there is nothing in the case of Veenstra to distinguish his position from that of Jensen. However, a further and distinct argument was advanced by counsel for Veenstra and this requires separate consideration. It is set out in the grounds of appeal as follows:

'In respect of all the charges of which the appellant was convicted, the trial judge erred in admitting as evidence against the appellant evidence of statements allegedly made by him to Customs and Excise officers.
'In particular the circumstances in which these statements were allegedly made were clearly unfair to the appellant where he had a poor command of English and did not have the benefit of the services of an interpreter or solicitor. Had evidence of these alleged statements been excluded from consideration by the jury the Crown case against the appellant would have been substantially weakened and would have been insufficient to entitle the charges to go before the jury in respect of the appellant.'

The statement which was spoken to in evidence for the Crown is contained in Production No. 69. There is no need to narrate its terms in any detail, but in it Veenstra allegedly admitted to travelling from Amsterdam to Glasgow via Harwich and London and meeting two Colombian tourists at Greenock. He was asked to collect certain articles from a ship in the harbour there. He also made an admission to the effect that he inferred that what he was collecting from the ship was drugs. It is evident that this statement was highly incriminating. Objection to the admissibility of evidence as to this statement was made at the trial and this objection was repelled by the judge.

The appellant gave evidence at the trial through an interpreter and claimed that he neither spoke nor understood English. There was some support for this contention in the evidence of one of his co-accused and by a member of staff of a car-hire company in Greenock with whom Veenstra had dealings. On the other hand there was evidence to the opposite effect by a police officer and by customs officers. There was therefore a conflict of evidence regarding the ability of Veenstra to understand or speak the English language. His alleged language handicap was said to have a bearing on his ability to appreciate his rights during his interview as well as his ability to understand and respond to the questions which were put to him. The trial judge invited the jury to consider whether the statement in question was obtained in circumstances which were fair to him and left it to the jury to decide this question and to resolve the conflict of evidence regarding his proficiency in the English language. The issue raised in this appeal is whether that was the proper course to have taken.

The initial submission of counsel for Veenstra was that where it is sought to question a person detained under statutory powers who is known to be foreign and whose first language is not English, there was a duty on the interviewing officer to make arrangements to provide an interpreter. If that step was not taken any statement made by the individual is to be regarded as having been taken in circumstances which were unfair to him. In the development of his argument counsel modified this submission and the court was invited to accept the argument that if there existed a doubt as to whether a detained person who was to be interviewed could understand or speak English with perfect distinctness, an interpreter should be provided. Without such an interpreter any statement made in this situation should not be admitted as evidence.

Language problems have arisen in the past in connection with court proceedings or in events prior to court proceedings. The problem has been considered in cases where declarations before trial were made by prisoners. Such authority as exists has been concerned largely with prisoners whose native language was Gaelic and it is established that a declaration must be translated by a sworn interpreter if the prisoner does not understand English. Furthermore, it is a requirement that the interpreter explains to him the terms of the declaration both when taken and after completion (Bell's Notes, pp.242–243; Alison's Practice, p.569; Dickson on Evidence, para. 328). It is to be noted that these authorities deal with situations where the person in question was totally ignorant of the English language. They do not deal with the situation which arises here where the appellant was not totally deficient in understanding or speaking English and the question arose as to the extent of his understanding.

In *H.M. Advocate* v. *Olsson* [1941 J.C. 63 (*infra*, p.397)] the question was whether a statement made under caution by a Swedish sailor charged with murder was admissible. No interpreter was present when the statement was made. In disallowing the evidence the trial judge, Lord Jamieson, said at p.66:

> 'Now, the accused is a Swede. It is perfectly clear that he has an extremely limited knowledge of the English language, so much so that the evidence has been translated to him throughout the trial. The question I have to consider is, whether it would be fair to him, in the position in which he was placed, to allow this evidence to be received. The test laid down by Lord Anderson in the case of *H.M. Advocate* v. *Aitken* [1926 J.C. 83] was: Would it be fair to the accused person to allow the evidence of his statement to be admitted? I accept that as the proper test, and I have come to the conclusion that in the present case to admit the evidence would not be fair to the accused, and for three reasons. Firstly, I cannot see how either I or the jury can be satisfied that the accused fully appreciated the warning which was given to him in the English language. Secondly, while no doubt there was no intention on the part of the detectives to act

unfairly, the proper course would have been for them to send for an interpreter again, because I think it was only through an interpreter that the true import of what he desired to say could have been properly conveyed to the officials and understood by them. Without the services of an interpreter there might easily have been a misunderstanding. Thirdly, at that time the accused had not, I am told, been informed of his right to consult a law agent, and I have no doubt that, had he been given an opportunity of so consulting, he would have been advised that he should not make any statement at that stage. For these reasons I shall sustain the objection and disallow the evidence.'

I agree that the test to be applied in the case where a possible language problem exists is one of fairness to an accused person. However, it is not appropriate to lay down rules which can be applied to every situation. So much depends on the circumstances of each case. In particular I am not prepared to affirm that either of the propositions advanced by counsel which I have already referred to are necessarily applicable. It will be for the officer responsible for the taking of any statement made under caution to assess an individual's ability to understand and speak English before deciding on whether or not to send for an interpreter. If the decision is made that an interpreter is not needed, it may be for consideration in due course in court whether the accused on account of language difficulties failed to understand his rights upon being questioned, whether he understood the questions which were being put to him, or whether what he wished to say could have been properly conveyed to the officer and understood by him. These are all factors for consideration in judging of the fairness of the circumstances in which a statement was made.

In the case of *Olsson* Lord Jamieson felt able to make his own ruling on whether it would be fair to allow the evidence of the statement to be led, and his conclusion was that it was perfectly clear that the accused in that case had an extremely limited knowledge of the English language so that he could not be satisfied that the accused appreciated the position he was in. In our modern practice an assessment of this kind can only properly be done if the judge is able to conclude on the undisputed relevant evidence that no reasonable jury could hold that the statement in question had not been obtained unfairly (*Balloch* v. *H.M. Advocate*, per Lord Justice-Clerk Wheatley at p.28) In the absence of such circumstances, in my view, the correct approach to such a problem is for the judge to leave it to the jury with appropriate directions to decide whether it was or was not unfair to take into account evidence of a statement made by someone detained or in custody if a question of his ability to understand or speak English arises.

Counsel also referred the court to articles 5 and 6 of the European Convention of Human Rights and two cases in the European Court of Human Rights [*Luedicke, Belkacem and Koç* v. *Federal Republic of Germany*; and *Appeal No. 10210/82* v. *France*] but in my opinion it is unnecessary, even if it is competent to do so, to resort to this jurisprudence for assistance.

The trial judge gave full directions to the jury on the approach which they had to make to this evidence. He said:

'If you think what occurred when Mr Veenstra was interviewed by Customs and Excise officers was unfair because he did not understand his rights or what was being said to him, you must ignore the answers that he gave to these questions. On the other hand, the Customs and Excise officers said that they considered that Mr Veenstra understood what they were saying to him and they cautioned him and asked him if he wanted a solicitor and that they had noted his replies in confirmation of these questions. If having considered the evidence about this matter you are of the view that Mr Veenstra did understand what was being said to him, that he was told he could have a solicitor if he wanted, that he was cautioned and that what happened was fair, then you can have regard to this document in considering the evidence against Mr Veenstra. On the other hand, if you come to the conclusion that because he did not understand English and therefore did not understand his rights or if you have a reasonable doubt about that matter then you must put the evidence relating to the contents of the interview out of your mind and proceed only on the other evidence in the case relating to Mr Veenstra, namely his association with Mr Montes and Mr Lopez and at a later stage with Mr Jensen.'

In my opinion these directions were entirely to the point and cannot be faulted. The trial judge then examined the evidence as to Veenstra's ability in the English language in some detail and again reminded them of his view as to the proper approach to the problem. The jury had ample evidence before them to decide the issue of whether the statement was elicited in circumstances of fairness and it was a matter for them to reach a conclusion on the matter. It was not suggested that, assuming it was proper to leave it to them, no reasonable jury could have concluded that the statement was not elicited in circumstances of fairness. For these reasons this ground of appeal fails.

The attention of the court was drawn to the passage in the judge's charge ... where he begins to deal with the evidence concerning this particular appellant. He starts by referring to Veenstra's own evidence and asks the jury to ask themselves whether his story rang true. It was submitted that this amounted to a misdirection inasmuch as it implied that there was some kind of onus on the accused to exculpate himself by his own evidence. If this passage was read in isolation, such an inference might possibly be drawn, but this argument will not stand up if the charge is read as a whole. Upon a reading of the charge as a whole, the jury could not have failed to understand from the accurate directions which were given that the burden of proof remained on the Crown throughout and that an accused person, even if he gave evidence, had no onus resting upon him. In my view the trial judge summarised the evidence of the Crown and for the accused in a balanced way and no misdirection occurred.

For all these reasons I am of opinion that this appeal should be dismissed."

Appeal refused.

NOTES

1.   *H.M. Advocate* v. *Olsson* is noted *infra* on the question of the accused's ability to follow the proceedings in court where he or she does not speak English.

2.   The earlier authorities referred to by Lord Weir are not strictly in point. With the exception of *Olsson*, they relate to declarations made before magistrates, as opposed to statements allegedly made to the police, and the issue appears to have been whether the declarations as recorded accurately reflected the panel's declaration, not whether the panel understood questions put to him. It is very unsatisfactory to suggest that the police officer taking the statement can properly assess the interviewee's linguistic abilities in all but the most obvious cases. If a person clearly does not speak English then there will be no problem. The real difficulties arise where the interviewee may have a partial command of the English language. Such partial command may be insufficient to understand properly the nuances of questions (and the answers given) but may suggest to the interviewing

officer that it is safe to question the suspect. Surely any person whose first language is not English should always be offered the services of an interpreter during questioning, and there may be circumstances where the investigating officer should not proceed to question a suspect even if the latter declines the offer.

8.   Young v. Friel
1992 S.C.C.R. 567

The appellant was convicted on a charge of theft and appealed on the ground, *inter alia*, that evidence of statements made by him in the course of an interview with the police, and recorded by the police should not have been admitted because they had been obtained in response to an improper inducement held out by the police.

> LORD JUSTICE-GENERAL: "It had not been disputed that what was said by the appellant at the interview, if admissible, was sufficient to convict him of the crime. The issue which was taken at the trial, and which has been renewed in submissions today by Mr Nicol, relates to the fairness of the interview and the question whether the admissions which were critical to the conviction were obtained by improper means or undue pressure and ought not to have been allowed to be spoken to in evidence. The sheriff has made a finding, which is finding 8 in the case, that no pressure was placed upon the appellant or inducement offered to him to make any admissions. But Mr Nicol challenged that finding as being inconsistent with what appears from the finding about what was said at the interview.
>
> There are two points which he developed in argument. The first relates to an exchange at the beginning of the interview when, having been told that information had been received to link him with the theft of cigarettes from another motor vehicle, the appellant asked: 'What will happen if I tell you? Will I get kept in?' The answer was 'I can't offer you any deals at present. Just tell me if you were there.' Mr Nicol submitted that the addition of the words 'at present' in the response by the police officer had only one possible meaning. This was that an inducement was being offered to the appellant to give information to the police. That was the only proper construction to be placed upon these words, and if that construction was taken from them, that covered the rest of the interview. The result was that everything which followed was inadmissible, and the sheriff ought not to have made the finding which is set out in finding 8. . . .
>
> Dealing first with the inducement point, we consider that the submission which Mr Nicol made as to the meaning of the phrase 'at present' went too far. These words were in our opinion open to interpretation by the sheriff. It is questionable whether the officer, when making that response, was contemplating any particular stage in the future when circumstances might change, if indeed the future was being contemplated by him at all. Furthermore the statement which included these words was made in response to a question by the appellant which the police officer appears to have answered in good faith. The matter was one for the sheriff to consider, and the question is whether no reasonable sheriff properly directing himself could properly make finding 8 in the light of what was said during this passage in the interview. In our opinion the sheriff was entitled to take the view that the response which the police officer made to the appellant's question did not amount to pressure or to an inducement, and accordingly to make finding 8 in the terms recorded in the stated case."

Appeal refused.

NOTE

The court dealt with this aspect of the appeal on the basis that the sheriff was entitled to hold that the words used by the police officer did not amount to an inducement. It would have been different, perhaps, if the officer had gone on to say something which would have suggested that the accused would have benefited from making a statement. It would also require something more than simply saying "It would be better if you told us if you were there." Before there can be an inducement there must presumably be something offered to the accused which would suggest to him that the advantages in making a statement outweighed the benefits of remaining silent.

On the other hand, it should not be conclusive that the "inducement" should take the form of a response to a question from the suspect. If the suspect says "What will happen if . . ." and the response is one which offers him an advantage which he will not enjoy if he remains silent then, it is submitted, there is an inducement.

9. H.M. Advocate v. Graham
1991 S.C.C.R. 56

During the accused's trial in the High Court at Glasgow, objection was taken by defence counsel to evidence of statements allegedly made by the accused. The police obtained the evidence regarding the statements by secretly recording a conversation between the accused and a Crown witness on whose person they had concealed a radio transmitter for this purpose.

LORD CAMERON OF LOCHBROOM: "I am indebted to counsel for their helpful submissions and for the agreement on facts for the purpose of the debate before me. This arose from objection taken to the evidence of a police officer regarding Crown Production No. 8, a transcript of a conversation between the panel and a Crown witness, Aziz Rahman, recorded upon tape through the medium of a radio transmitter provided by police officers and concealed on the person of Rahman, prior to a meeting arranged by Rahman with the panel, in a car in a street in Glasgow on 9th June 1989. Before that date, police officers had been investigating a serious assault upon a man, Victor Browne, which assault forms a part of the libel of a charge of conspiracy, charge (6) of the indictment. They suspected that the panel had been involved and had a motive for doing so. They had interviewed the panel under full common law caution in relation to the assault on 31st May 1989. The panel had denied any involvement. However, although the police officers had no evidence against the panel in relation to the assault, they continued to suspect that he had been involved. In those circumstances, when informed by the witness Rahman that he was to have a business meeting with the panel on 5th June 1989 in which it was accepted by the advocate-depute it was anticipated that the subject-matter might involve matters relevant to their continuing enquiries into the assault, arrangements were made for police officers to overhear any conversation at the meeting since they hoped to receive information relevant to the enquiry. The meeting did not take place on that date, but subsequently the witness Rahman arranged a meeting for 9th June 1989.

The submission for the panel, shortly put, was that the incriminating statements made by the panel, so recorded and transcribed in Crown Production No. 8, were obtained unfairly. The panel being a suspect, the police were bound by the usual rules regarding admissibility of incriminating statements in evidence, and in particular the giving of a caution, and could not seek to elide them by the use of a third party to secure material evidence by means which, if they themselves had employed them, would have been objectionable. He reminded me of the principles adopted by the courts in judging of these matters, developed since *Chalmers* v. *H.M. Advocate* [1954 J.C. 66, *supra* p.173] in cases such as *Miln* v. *Cullen* [1967 J.C. 21] and *Lord Advocate's Reference (No. 1 of 1983)* [1984 S.C.C.R. 62, *supra* p.177] This was not an accidental overhearing of a spontaneous conversation voluntarily entered into with others who are unconnected with the criminal enquiry. Reference was made to *Jamieson* v. *Annan* [1988 S.C.C.R. 278] and *H.M. Advocate* v. *O'Donnell* [1975 S.L.T. (Sh.Ct.) 22].

The general approach adopted by the court in cases such as *H.M. Advocate* v. *Whitelaw* [1980 S.L.T. (Notes) 25] and *Tonge* v. *H.M. Advocate* [1982 S.L.T. 506, *infra* p.205] while concerned with interrogation by police officers, supported the view that what was done in this case was to use the meeting with the panel, then a suspect, to elicit incriminating material, while transgressing the rules protecting his right to silence as a suspect. The fact that the incriminating statements were made to a private person and not an official in the circumstances of this case, did not save it: reference was made to Walkers on evidence, paragraph 40, *Morrison* v. *Burrell* [1947 S.L.T. 190], *Waddell* v. *Kinnaird* [1922 S.L.T. 34], and *H.M. Advocate* v. *Campbell* [1964 S.L.T. (Notes) 78].

Here the enquiry in the transcript was made at least with the connivance of the police, of a suspect who at the time had no means of knowing he was still under suspicion, who received no warning by way of caution, and who was unaware that police officers were listening to the course of the conversation. Looking to the terms of the transcript, which Mr Scott examined in detail, the incriminating statements could not be said to be fairly obtained.

For the Crown, the advocate-depute accepted that the matter had to be judged by the test of fairness. He said that at this stage it could only be said that the statements were inadmissible if the evidence measured up to the standard required in *H.M. Advocate* v. *Whitelaw*. There was no police interrogation here. The conversation had been voluntarily entered into by the panel, the statements were spontaneous and uninduced by police officers engaged in the enquiry. It could not be said that Rahman was acting as an agent of the police, or acting in support of a police trick or subterfuge. These were statements made to a private person, and the transcript was competent evidence of the statements. Reference was made to Renton and Brown on Criminal Procedure, paragraphs 18–38 to 18–41, and *Hope & Lavery* v. *H.M. Advocate* [1960 S.L.T. 264]. There was no question of entrapment, albeit the police hoped to receive information helpful to their enquiry. Reference was made to *Jamieson* v. *Annan* and *H.M. Advocate* v. *Harper* [1989 S.C.C.R. 472 (Sh.Ct.)]

The facts in *H.M. Advocate* v. *Campbell* were materially different, and the decision there was no guide to the present case. Looking to the whole transcript, it could not be said that Rahman was in the category of a person acting as an arm of the police, albeit the police officers had taken advantage of the opportunity presented to them by Rahman to overhear the conservation between him and the panel at the meeting set up by Rahman. The police officers had not sought out Rahman in order to persuade him to set up the meeting; the statements were not unfairly obtained, and evidence regarding the conversation in the transcript and hence the incriminating statements was admissible.

It is important to note at the outset that in this case the police were enquiring into a crime already committed, therefore the present case does not fall within that category of cases of which *Hopes & Lavery* v. *H.M. Advocate* is an example, where eavesdropping is taking place on the commission of a crime, albeit by arrangement between the intended victim and the police beforehand. At p.107 Lord Justice-Clerk Thomson made clear the difference when he said this:

'Now, there can be no doubt at all that in the investigation of certain kinds of crime, especially those involving blackmail or fraud in its various aspects, it is quite a common practice, especially when the intended victim has gone to the police, for the police to suggest an apparent yielding to the criminal demands in circumstances where police officers can observe or can overhear what is going on. The taking of such a course is not an irregularity in the sense in which that word is used in the authorities with whose citation I have been so bountifully favoured. It does not contravene any principle or infringe any right. Indeed, it is often the only practical way in which such crimes as I have mentioned can be brought home to the persons who committed them. My view of the matter is that evidence given by the person who overhears a conversation in those circumstances is competent evidence, and can be properly admitted.'

The test which is applied in our courts in determining such matters is that set out by Lord Justice-General Clyde in *Brown* v. *H.M. Advocate* [1966 S.L.T. 105] at p.107. There he said this:

'The test, which time and again has been applied in Scotland to determine a matter of this nature, occurring prior to a suspect being charged with the crime, is whether or not the proceedings which led up to his statement were fair to him or not. As Lord Justice-General Cooper said in *Chalmers* v. *H.M. Advocate*:

' "It is not the function of the police when investigating a crime to direct their endeavours to obtaining a confession from a suspect to be used as evidence against him at the trial. In some legal systems the inquisitorial method of investigation is allowed in different degrees and subject to various safeguards."

'But our Scottish standards of fairness have always rendered inadmissible as evidence at the trial answers or admissions or statements obtained by methods of that sort.'

No doubt, as has been said in other cases in looking at the test, fairness will not only comprehend fairness from the point of view of the accused, but fairness also from the point of view of the public, who have an interest in the police being able to investigate crimes and bring to justice those who commit them. Furthermore, I bear in mind that it is only in an exceptional case that a judge should withhold evidence of a statement made by an accused from a jury, and that only upon the grounds set out in *Balloch* v. *H.M. Advocate* [1977 S.L.T. (Notes) 2] and *H.M. Advocate* v. *Whitelaw.*

Upon the agreed facts, the panel had already been interrogated by police officers under full common law caution; he was then a suspect. He continued to be a suspect, and thus one in whose favour the law may intervene to safeguard him when questioned, from possible self-incrimination. Against this background, the police officers, with no evidence available to them against the panel, but proceeding upon wholly unsupported suspicion, then promoted the eavesdropping upon the conversation between the panel and Rahman, who was aware of the purpose for which the equipment was provided. Having read and reread the transcript, it is clear that the most incriminating material in the transcript was obtained after the business between the panel and the witness Rahman appears to have been concluded, and after new topics were specifically introduced by the latter. I instance questions on pages ... of the transcript, and information offered by him elsewhere relating to incidents libelled and individuals named in charge (6). If such questions had been put at that time by police officers in the course of interrogation of the panel without due caution, statements made in response to them would have been inadmissible. I can see no reason why such statements should be rendered admissible by the fact that they were secured by a third party, not a police officer, where the third party asks them in the knowledge that he is being overheard by police officers concerned in an enquiry into the matters about which he is asking questions, and who has been provided by the police with equipment to enable them to overhear what passes. While it may be that the witness was not directly primed with questions, he was well aware of the subject-matter of the enquiry by the police officers, and looking to the form and manner of the conversation in the transcript, it is impossible in my opinion to suggest that it was simply the kind of disinterested questioning by a third party, statements made in reply to which are competent: see for instance Renton and Brown, paragraph 18–39. Rather, such statements in my view fall into the class of statements which have been extracted. In principle I see no distinction between a case such as the present and one where the third party is provided by the police officers investigating the crime with a list of questions to ask the suspect in the hope of securing admissions of guilt, or the example of inadmissible evidence cited in Macdonald on the Criminal Law of Scotland (5th edn), p.314, where an official procures a fellow prisoner to inveigle the accused into conversation to be overheard by the official, which last could only be regarded as entrapment.

I am accordingly of the opinion that this is just such a special case where it can be asserted at this stage upon agreed facts that the rules of fairness and fair dealing were flagrantly transgressed, and that any reasonable jury would have been bound to hold that the statements had been induced by unfair or improper means, and they had been thereby deprived of any voluntary character. In reaching this conclusion I am fortified by the approach adopted in *H.M. Advocate* v. *Campbell* by Lord Justice-Clerk Grant, who was subsequently party to the decision in *Miln* v. *Cullen*, where, as here, the accused was under suspicion at the time when the statement objected to was made. I shall therefore in the circumstances sustain the objection to the evidence."

THE ADVOCATE-DEPUTE: "I wonder if I could perhaps have slight clarification. Does that also cover the leading of any evidence of Mr Rahman in connection with that interview with the accused?"

LORD CAMERON: "Obviously I have only been asked to rule on the objection which was made, but I think it must be clear from what I have said that my view relates to the statements made, not simply to the transcript itself. The transcript is merely evidential; the objection is taken to the admissibility of the statements contained within it."

THE ADVOCATE-DEPUTE: "I am obliged."

The advocate-depute then withdrew the indictment and the accused was found not guilty of all charges.

NOTES

1. What is it, exactly, about this evidence which renders it inadmissible? It cannot be the fact that it was "overheard" by the police, since, as the following case (*Jamieson* v. *Annan*, 1988 S.C.C.R. 278) indicates, the fact that the police have deliberately listened in to a conversation in which the accused makes incriminating statements without warning the accused does not necessarily render evidence of the conversation inadmissible. What appears to be objectionable is the deliberate use of subterfuge in order to obtain information in circumstances where it would

not otherwise have been forthcoming and in circumstances under which whatever rights the suspect might enjoy (such as the benefit of the caution) were bound to be denied him.

2.   Suppose, however, that the Crown witness has not been acting, as it were, as an agent of the police. Would the position have been different? Or suppose that the "agent" had not led the suspect on to make incriminating statements, but that these had emerged quite spontaneously in the course of general conversation between the parties?

10.   Jamieson and Another v. Annan
1988 S.C.C.R. 278

The appellants were convicted on charges of theft. At their trial, evidence was led of a conversation between the appellants while they were detained in police cells after they had been cautioned and charged. The evidence relating to the conversation was provided by police officers who had overheard the conversation. The appellants appealed by stated case to the High Court on the ground that the sheriff should not have admitted this evidence.

The sheriff's findings-in-fact included the following:

"6.   At about 12.35 a.m. on 6th July 1986, Sergeant Hayton and Detective Constable Anderson went to the home of the first accused ... Sergeant Hayton explained the circumstances of the alleged theft. He took possession of Labels 4 and 5, being shoes belonging to the first accused, as he had noted grass seeds sticking to them of a similar type to those which stuck to his own shoes at or near said wood [where the stolen money was found]. The first accused was then detained in terms of section 2 of the Criminal Justice (Scotland) Act 1980, was conveyed to Livingston Police Station where he was cautioned and charged as libelled, made no reply, and was placed in a cell.

7.   At about 3.10 a.m. on 6th July 1986, Police Constable Pirie went to the home of the second accused, explained the circumstances of the alleged theft on the previous night and that the second accused was suspected of having committed it. He then arrested the second accused and conveyed him to Livingston Police Station. There he was cautioned and charged as libelled, made no reply and was placed in a cell which was close to and across the corridor from the cell where the first accused was.

8.   Shortly thereafter, the witness, Police Constable Wood was going along said corridor, when he heard each accused shouting to the other. There were no apertures or windows in the doors of their cells through which either accused could see if there was anyone in the corridor. Constable Wood returned to the charge bar and informed Sergeant Hayton about said conversation between the accused. Sergeant Hayton, Constables Wood, Pirie and Anderson then went to the corridor and overheard part of a shouted conversation between the two accused.

9.   At the time of said conversation, Constables Pirie and Anderson noted it in their police notebooks, and immediately thereafter, Sergeant Hayton and Constable Wood, who did not have their notebooks while the conversation was going on, noted their recent recollections of it in their notebooks at the charge bar. The following represents the gist and meaning of said conversation accurately, although its actual terms may have been slightly but insignificantly different.

'SECOND ACCUSED: How did they find the money?
FIRST ACCUSED: They got a dog out.
SECOND ACCUSED: How did they know to come to my house?

FIRST ACCUSED: We were seen.

SECOND ACCUSED: Were we, fuck: remember we know nothing about it; remember we've no seen each other for a fortnight.

FIRST ACCUSED: Let's keep it that way.'

10. Immediately thereafter, Sergeant Hayton opened the apertures in each cell door and warned each accused that conversation between them had been and could be overheard.

11. The first accused had learned from one or more of said police witnesses about the recovery of said sum of £420 as a result of tracking by a police dog, and that an eyewitness had seen each accused entering the manager's office in the circumstances narrated in finding 2."

LORD JUSTICE-CLERK: "The appellants are Stewart Francis Jamieson and Colin Heggie. They went to trial in the sheriff court at Linlithgow on a complaint libelling two charges of theft. After trial the sheriff found each accused guilty as libelled of charge (1) and guilty of charge (2) but substituting the sum of £420 for the sum of £1,686.72 which appeared in the charge. They have now appealed against conviction and on their behalf Miss McMenamin has presented three arguments to us. The first argument was to the effect that the sheriff had erred in convicting the appellants because there was no corroborating evidence that the offences libelled in charges (1) and (2) have been committed. [His Lordship dealt with and rejected that argument with which this report is not concerned, and continued:]

The next matter which Miss McMenamin raised related to the admissibility of evidence regarding a conversation which had been overheard by police officers while the appellants were in their cells in the police station. Details of and the gist of the conversation were set out in finding 9. Miss McMenamin maintained that the evidence regarding what the police say they heard at this time was not admissible. There is no doubt that the sheriff regarded the evidence of the conversation as critical. In his note he says that if he had had any reasonable doubt about whether such a conversation had taken place or if he had held that evidence to be inadmissible, he would have acquitted each of the accused. Miss McMenamin drew attention to a number of authorities on this matter. These are summarised in a very helpful judgment by Sheriff Macphail in *H.M. Advocate* v. *O'Donnell*. In that judgment the sheriff goes through the authorities on this branch of the law and expresses the view that evidence of an overheard remark made by an accused person while in custody and relating to a matter relative to the charge on which he is being tried is admissible provided that the remark is made voluntarily and not as the result of an inducement or trap. In our opinion the sheriff is well founded when he reaches that conclusion. Miss McMenamin drew attention to the fact that in some of these cases it appears to have been regarded as significant by the court that it was purely by accident that police officers heard the conversation in question. No doubt that is so, but it is plain from the cases that the test is one of fairness and that, of course, is not a unilateral matter, but it is fairness from the point of the accused and fairness also from the point of view of the public who have an interest in the police being able to investigate crimes and bring to justice those who have committed them. In the present case it is plain from the findings that the first police officer, Police Constable Wood, heard the beginning of the conversation by accident and Miss McMenamin accepted that if his testimony alone had been led regarding the conversation objection could not have been taken. Her objection was to the fact that Police Constable Wood had heard the conversation beginning and had gone off and brought other officers along to listen with him to what was being said by the two men in their cells. In our opinion there was nothing wrong with what Police Constable Wood did at all. He heard the conversation begin by accident and he then took steps to bring some of his colleagues to join him in listening to what was being said. It is plain from the findings that what these two men said to one another on the occasion in question was entirely voluntary; it was spontaneous, there had been no question of any inducement, no question of any trap and there was also, in our view, no question in the circumstances of any unfairness. Accordingly, the objection to the admissibility of evidence of this conversation is not well founded."

Appeal refused.

NOTE

In the light of this case, and the case of *H.M. Advocate* v. *Graham* (*supra*, p.196), would it be unfair to obtain evidence by deliberately placing a "bug" in a police cell? Would it be unfair to post a police officer outside a police cell in the hope that he or she might overhear some useful information? Would it be unfair to place someone in the cell with the suspect with instructions to engage him in conversation about the matter in connection with which the suspect had been taken into custody? See also *Fraser* v. *H.M. Advocate, infra,* and *Bailey* [1993] 3 All E.R. 513.

(ii)   Statements Made After Charge

Until recently it was fairly well understood that once a person had been cautioned and charged the police should not question him about the offence with which he had been charged. If they did so, then any answers to such questioning would not be admissible in evidence. The position was summed up in the following terms by Lord Weir in *Alton* v. *H.M. Advocate*, 1987 S.C.C.R. 252 at p.253:

"As a matter of law the police are not entitled to question an accused person about a particular charge once the investigation relating to that charge has been completed at the stage of his having been taken into custody and cautioned and charged. Statements made by an accused person after that stage, made in such circumstances, are inadmissible in evidence. The police may not question him or act in such a way as to give a plain invitation or otherwise to induce him to answer questions."

His Lordship referred to *Stark and Smith* v. *H.M. Advocate* 1938 J.C. 170 and *Wade* v. *Robertson*, 1948 J.C. 117. See also *MacDonald* v. *H.M. Advocate*, 1987 S.C.C.R. 581.

Fraser and Another v. H.M. Advocate
1989 S.C.C.R.

LORD JUSTICE-GENERAL: "The appellants are Kevin John Fraser and Angus McDonald Freer who were found guilty, after trial in the sheriff court on indictment, of charge (1) of that indictment. We say nothing about the second charge which is of no relevance for the purposes of the appeal proceedings before the court today. That charge, charge (1), was a charge that on a particular date in Inverness, the two appellants assaulted Leslie James Williamson, seizing hold of him, pulling him to the ground, repeatedly punching and kicking him in the face and body, to his severe injury and permanent impairment.

As the sheriff has told us, the Crown case against the appellants depended essentially upon statements emitted by each of the appellants which are described in the evidence of Detective Constable Wylie.

In this appeal it is not suggested that the sheriff misdirected the jury in any way. What the sheriff did was to leave it to the jury to decide whether they should accept that the statement emitted by each of the appellants was a spontaneous one, or putting it in another way, it was left to the jury to decide whether in light of certain evidence which had been given, they were satisfied that there had been no inducement put upon the appellants to make the statements which were critical to their conviction. ...

There is no doubt that when the statements which were put in evidence were taken from the appellant, the police followed perfectly regular procedure and the statements were made by each appellant after due caution and after each had declared his willingness and desire to make such a statement.

It is on certain antecedent events that the appellants rely in submitting that the statements emitted by each were in some way induced by Detective Constable Wylie. According to the evidence, and neither of the appellants gave evidence at the trial, what happened was this. Each appellant was arrested, cautioned and charged and they were placed in adjoining cells in the cell area of the police station. Both were apparently footballers. Detective Constable Wylie was a football referee. He was a friend of both. He happened to be in the cell area on other business, knowing generally of the circumstances which had led to Fraser and Freer being in custody and he engaged in conversation first of all with Fraser. An account of what happened is given by Constable Wylie and we refer to what is recorded in the notes of the evidence of Detective Constable Wylie which we ordered to be produced. As the matter is described by Wylie, he spoke to Fraser as a friend and in the course of so doing, Fraser gave him what is described as his side of the story. Very properly of course, no attempt was made to lead in evidence what Fraser had said at that stage and what he had had to say at that stage might have been entirely exculpatory.

In any event, Wylie allowed Fraser to tell his side of the story without cautioning him and at the end of this conversation, which on Wylie's account was entirely friendly, he asked Fraser if he'd told the police what he had just said to Wylie. Fraser said no, and Wylie then asked him if he wanted to make a statement about the matter and Fraser declared that he did.

It is possible that Freer, in the adjoining cell, could have heard what had passed between Wylie and Fraser; but what happened thereafter was that Wylie had an equally friendly conversation with Freer, in which the conversation followed along the same lines as the one that had taken place between Wylie and Fraser. One thing which emerges from the evidence of Constable Wylie is his resistance to the suggestion that he applied any pressure upon either of the appellants to make the statement, or that he had made any suggestion to them that it would be to their advantage if a statement were made.

What we have said so far provides the necessary background for consideration of the submission which we have heard. Mr Douglas is perfectly correct in saying that, after a person has been cautioned and charged, any statement admissible in evidence thereafter must be a voluntary one. The question of whether the statements of each appellant ought to be so regarded was left to the jury and it is not suggested that the sheriff erred in leaving that question to the jury or that in leaving that question to the jury he did not give to the jury proper directions as to how they should approach the question that was left to them.

Mr Douglas contends that the jury were not entitled, having regard to the evidence given by Detective Constable Wylie about the antecedent events, to hold that the statements were voluntary statements and, in particular, that the jury properly directed ought to have held that the statements were unfairly obtained in the sense that each had been invited or induced, as the grounds of appeal state. We have come to be of opinion that since it is conceded that the issue before us was properly left for decision by the jury, under proper directions, it is impossible to say that the jury were not entitled to have regard to the statements of each appellant for the purposes of the verdict which they returned. In our judgment, the jury were entitled to hold that the contact between Detective Constable Wylie and each appellant was not an unfair contract and they were clearly entitled, on the evidence of Constable Wylie which we have read, to hold that neither statement was procured by inducement or unfair invitation on the part of Detective Constable Wylie.

It is not the law that after a man has been cautioned and charged, there must be no contact whatever between him and police officers. What the law seeks to do is to protect the arrested person against unfair pressure and against the inducement to emit statements against his interest. In this case we have no hesitation in saying that under reference to the evidence of Constable Wylie, the jury were entitled to reach the verdict which they did, taking into account the statements taken after the personal conversations which had taken place between Detective Constable Wylie and each of the appellants.

The appeal will accordingly be refused."

Appeal refused.

NOTES

1. What happened in this case was that the police officer invited persons who had already been charged to make a statement about the events which formed the basis of the charge. It is difficult to see how there was not here a "plain invitation" to the suspects to make a statement. In the circumstances the concession made to the appeal court was surprising and unfortunate.

2. Where a person who has been charged wishes to make a statement on a voluntary basis, it is the normal and proper practice for this to be taken by a police officer who is not connected with the investigation of the case: *Tonge* v. *H.M. Advocate*, 1982 S.C.C.R. 313, *per* Lord Cameron at p.350. However, it appears that this is no more than good police practice. It is not a legal requirement:

"In my opinion, all that Lord Cameron is referring to in connection with the taking of statements is the practice of police officers. He is not to be taken as stating that if that practice is not followed, a statement taken from an accused person will be inadmissible. In my opinion, if a statement has not been taken by police officers unconnected with the investigation, that may be a circumstance bearing upon the question of whether the statement is to be regarded by the jury as a voluntary statement fairly obtained. The test is one of fairness and that is for the jury to determine." (*Cordiner* v. *H.M. Advocate*, 1991 S.C.C.R. 652, *per* the Lord Justice-Clerk at p.665.)

C. The Caution and the Question of Fairness

It is all too easy to regard the caution as a rather empty formula which it is better to administer, but whose omission does not fundamentally affect the admissibility of any statement or confession made by a suspect. This attitude, which appears to be increasingly reflected in some judicial opinions, conceals a more profound question.

The function of the caution in our system of criminal justice is, or ought to be, clear. In general, no one is legally obliged to answer questions put to her by the police. The caution serves as a reminder of that. The weight attached to the caution by the police and, more importantly, by the courts may, therefore, be seen as a reflection of the significance which these elements of the criminal justice system attach to the right of a suspected person to remain silent.

1.   Tonge and Others v. H.M. Advocate
1982 S.L.T. 506; 1982 S.C.C.R. 313

During the investigation of an alleged rape the appellants were interviewed by the police. Tonge and Gray were interviewed while detained under section 2 of the 1980 Act, and Jack when he attended voluntarily at a police office. During the course of these interviews all three appellants made self-incriminating statements. Immediately prior to making these statements Tonge and Gray had received warnings in terms of section 2(7) of the 1980 Act (*supra*, p.172), but neither received a full common law caution at that time. It was disputed whether Jack had received a caution at all, and if he received one, whether it was a common law caution or a warning under section 2(7). Consequent upon these statements the appellants were cautioned and charged with rape.

At the trial, objections to these statements were taken on behalf of all three appellants, but all were repelled. Tonge and Jack denied making the statements. Gray did not deny his statement but disputed the police version of how it was made. In his charge to the jury the presiding judge (Lord Ross) directed them that if they were satisfied that the statements were made, and were freely made, and that they had been accurately recorded, they would be entitled to accept them. He also stated that there was "no hard and fast rule about giving a caution" before a suspect was charged and that whether a caution should be given depends upon whether, in all circumstances, fairness required that a caution should be given, either at the outset or after the individual had begun to incriminate himself. So far as Jack was concerned, Lord Ross referred to a conflict between the police evidence that a caution was given and Jack's statement that no caution was given. He did not, however, refer to the confusion as to whether a full caution was given or only a section 2(7) warning. On appeal against conviction:

> LORD JUSTICE-GENERAL (EMSLIE): "... For the appellants Tonge and Gray their appeal against conviction is presented upon the ground that the trial judge erred in repelling the objections to the admissibility of their alleged voluntary statements. In light of the evidence before him as to the circumstances in which these alleged statements were made it was plain that they had been unfairly obtained, and the trial judge should have held them to be inadmissible on that account.

[His Lordship outlined the evidence relating to the offences and continued:]

> As it turned out the only persons who found themselves in the dock charged with the alleged rape of the complainer with others unknown were those who, it was said, had made voluntary statements to the police. It is perfectly clear in

the case of all three appellants that their alleged voluntary statements were of critical importance. Without these statements there was insufficient evidence against each to support conviction.

I come now to the circumstances in which the statements allegedly made by Tonge and Gray were obtained. It will be remembered that objection was taken on behalf of each to the admissibility of the alleged statements, the contents of which were self-incriminating, and that after a trial within a trial in each case the trial judge repelled the objection and allowed evidence of the alleged statements to go to the jury, leaving it to the jury to decide whether or not they had been fairly obtained.

The first chapter in the circumstances leading up to the emission of the alleged incriminating statement by Gray began when he was detained by two police officers who called at his home. According to these officers the first thing they did was to caution him at common law—a caution which not only advised him of his right to silence but warned him that anything he chose to say would be taken down and might be used in evidence. The detention was, however, in purported exercise of the entirely new powers of detention and inquiry conferred upon the police by s. 2 of the Criminal Justice (Scotland) Act 1980, and the evidence was that the requirements of that section were then fulfilled by the detaining officers. For the purpose of this appeal the provisions of s. 2(7) are of particular importance: 'A person detained under subsection (1) above shall be under no obligation to answer any question other than to give his name and address, and a constable shall so inform him both on so detaining him and on arrival at the police station or other premises.' It will be observed at once that while this subsection requires the giving of a warning to the detainee at each of the two separate stages of detention it does not in terms direct the constable to inform the detainee that anything he may choose to say in answer to questions or otherwise may be taken down and used in evidence. It is to be observed also that while subs. (5) authorises the constable to question a person who has been detained in relation to the suspected offence and, by necessary implication, to his own part in it, that subsection contains this very important proviso: 'Provided that this paragraph shall be without prejudice to any existing rule of law as regards the admissibility in evidence of any answer given.' The position is, accordingly, that the admissibility in evidence of anything said by a detainee falls to be determined by the common law and where the common law and proper practice would require, in the interests of fairness and fair dealing, that a full common law caution be given, the omission to give it before questioning a suspect who has received no more than the limited warning prescribed by s. 2(7), will, at the very least, on that account alone, place the admissibility of any evidence elicited from the suspect in peril. The giving of the statutory warning does not, accordingly, relieve any constable who intends to exercise the power to question, either at the time of detention or at any time while it is in force, from the obligation to observe the ordinary rules of law and proper practice which are designed to secure fairness to the suspect. In this case, as I have said, it appears that at the time Gray was detained he was at that stage given a caution in common law terms.

The second chapter began when Gray reached the police station at about 6.20 p.m. He was then given the statutory warning required by s. 2(7) and the s. 2 procedure was again carried out. He was searched and placed in a cell.

I now come to the third and crucial chapter of events relating to Gray. At about 6.40 p.m. two police officers, Detective Sergeant McMorran, accompanied by Constable Jenkins, the investigating officer, entered the cell. Until that moment they had not seen Gray at all. Their purpose was to question him. Detective Sergeant McMorran did not think that there was enough evidence against him to charge him and frankly admitted that it was in his interest to get some more evidence from Gray himself in order to be able to do so. What happened was this. They introduced themselves, explained that they were making inquiries into the alleged offence for which he had been detained, and asked him for his name and address. Gray was then, according to Constable Jenkins, 'fairly nervous'. Constable Jenkins then accused him of complicity in the crime. What he actually said was that they 'had reason to believe he was responsible, along with others, for the crime'. Gray then started to speak, beginning with the words: 'I'd like to get it all cleared up.' He then went on to make a fairly long statement of a self-incriminating character without, it was said, any interruptions by either officer and, according to their evidence, he was asked no questions. There were, however, they admitted, pauses from time to time while Gray gathered his thoughts. The important feature in the whole transaction was that although the police officers freely conceded that in dealing with a suspect in Gray's position before s. 2 of the Act of 1980 came into force, they would first have administered a full common law caution and would certainly have administered such a caution to a suspect as soon as he indicated that he wished to make a statement, they did not caution Gray at all before accusing him of the crime, immediately after he declared that he would like to get it all cleared up, or at any stage during the making of the relatively long statement when it was evident that he was almost certainly going to incriminate himself. Their reason for not cautioning Gray was that they assumed that he had received a full common law caution when he was detained in terms of s. 2.

The events leading up to the taking of the alleged voluntary statement by Tonge began when he was detained under the powers conferred by s. 2 of the Act of 1980 and taken to the police station where he remained in statutory detention. By this time the police had obtained the alleged statement by Gray. In Tonge's case there is no question of his having received a common law caution at any time in connection with his detention. All that he received at the two separate stages of detention was the limited information provided for in s. 2(7). He was, in short, merely informed that he was under no obligation to answer any questions other than to give his name and address.

In due course Detective Sergeant McMorran and Constable Jenkins went to see Tonge. Their only purpose, they said, was to charge him with the alleged crime of rape. They identified themselves as officers investigating the crime for which he was being detained and asked him for his name and address. They then asked him if he understood that he was being detained in connection with an alleged rape of a 22-year-old female in a field which they described. Instead of proceeding there and then to caution him and to charge him in formal terms—for that was their only purpose, they said,—what they did instead, without cautioning him at all, was to accuse him of the crime which had been described to him. The formula used by Constable Jenkins was: 'I believe you are responsible along with others for doing this', and he agreed that he would not normally say anything of the kind to a person he was about to caution and charge. The evidence of the two police officers was that this provoked an immediate response, for Tonge at once said, 'Aye, wait a minute, boys. You've got it all wrong', and proceeded, without interruption or questioning, to make a relatively long explanation which was self-incriminating. Tonge's first sentence which I have quoted indicated to the officers that Tonge was about to make a statement. They agreed that if this had happened in the case of a suspect in Tonge's position the practice would have been to have the statement which he obviously intended to make taken by officers unconnected with the investigation. Whether or not that practice was followed, a full caution would always be given and Detective Sergeant McMorran agreed that in such circumstances a full caution was essential. In the case of Tonge, however, they did not caution him after he had uttered his first sentence and they did not caution him at any stage thereafter even when it appeared that he was likely to incriminate himself. There was ample opportunity for the giving of a full caution at any of these stages. Why was no caution given? It was not given, they say, at any time while the officers were with Tonge because they assumed, wrongly as it turned out, that he had been fully cautioned in common law terms when he was detained under s. 2 of the Act. All that I need add is that when Detective Sergeant McMorran was asked why, after introducing themselves to Tonge, they did not immediately do what they had come to do—charge Tonge—his answer was that they were not given a chance.

For the appellants Gray and Tonge the short, sharp submission was that upon the undisputed relevant evidence which I have just set out the trial judge should have sustained the objections to the admissibility of the alleged statements. In the particular circumstances the failure of Detective Sergeant McMorran and Constable Jenkins to give to Gray and Tonge a full common law caution was fatal to the admissibility of their alleged statements in evidence. The long list of cases beginning with *Chalmers* v. *H.M. Advocate* shows that in questions of admissibility of such statements each case will depend upon its own facts and circumstances and that the decision must turn upon whether or not there has been unfairness on the part of the police. Self-incriminating statements which are induced from prime suspects by unfair actions on the part of police officers can be regarded as neither spontaneous nor voluntary and are thus inadmissible. In most cases it will be necessary for a trial judge to allow the alleged statements, and the evidence as to the circumstances in which they were made to go before the jury, so that they may, under proper directions, resolve the issue of fairness or unfairness. There are circumstances, however, in which the trial judge himself ought to withhold such evidence from a jury.

[His Lordship referred to the opinion of the Lord Justice-Clerk in *Balloch* v. *H.M. Advocate* 1977 S.L.T. (Notes) 29 and the opinion of Lord Cameron in *H.M. Advocate* v. *Whitelaw* 1980 S.L.T. 25 and continued:]

In the present case it is plain that on the relevant undisputed evidence no reasonable jury could have held the alleged statements of Gray and Tonge had been voluntary and had not been extracted by unfair or improper means. It was, ... abundantly clear that the rules of fairness and fair dealing had been transgressed. A wholly new chapter began when Detective Sergeant McMorran and Constable Jenkins approached these two appellants in detention. They had little or no evidence that the alleged crime had been committed or that either Gray or Tonge had been among its perpetrators. They hoped to get such evidence from Gray himself and it is an inescapable inference from the evidence that they hoped for the same response from Tonge. What they did was to accuse Gray and Tonge of participation in the alleged crime without first cautioning either. This was clearly calculated to provoke a response and the opening words of the response which the accusation elicited from each demonstrated that each was about to make a statement, possibly self-incriminating. Even then they did not caution either man and they did not caution either thereafter when it clearly began to appear that he was, in fact, about to incriminate himself. In these circumstances the unfairness of the police officers was manifest and it is clear from their own evidence that proper practice, prior to 1980, demanded the giving of a caution at least once to persons in the position of Gray and Tonge. Without their alleged statements there was not sufficient evidence to warrant their conviction and since the verdicts proceeded upon evidence which was inadmissible there has been a miscarriage of justice.

For the Crown the learned advocate-depute reminded us of the common law caution and the s. 2 warning given to Gray at the separate stages of his detention and of the s. 2 warning which had been given to Tonge. The existence or absence of a caution at common law when each was interviewed later by the Detective Sergeant and Constable Jenkins was, he argued, merely one of the circumstances which it would be proper to take into account in judging the question of fairness. The trial judge was perfectly correct when he decided that it should be left to the jury to judge that question and to determine under his directions whether each statement was truly spontaneous and voluntary. This in short was not one of the exceptional cases of the kind mentioned in *Balloch* and in *Whitelaw*.

The problem faced by the trial judge was an extremely difficult one. The circumstances which he had to consider were complicated, if not actively bedevilled, by what was done to these two appellants in purported exercise of the powers newly conferred by s. 2—a section which, inexplicably, does not require the detainee to be warned not only that he is not obliged to say anything, in answer to questions or otherwise, but that if he does so, what he chooses to say will be taken down and may be used in evidence. In the case of one of them a full caution appears to have been given when he was first detained and yet when he reached the police station he was merely given the limited information prescribed by s. 2(7). In the case of the other, he was told only what s. 2(7) says he must be told. It is, I think, easy to understand why the trial judge, in the urgency of the trial, considered that it might be going too far, too fast, to give effect to the defence submission that he should take the bold and irreversible course of ruling that the alleged statements were inadmissible in evidence. We, however, have had the advantage, which he could not enjoy, of reading closely, and rereading, in the extended notes precisely what was the course of events before the alleged statements were made, and of examining the questions of admissibility in light of a very full and excellent argument on both sides of the bar. Making full use of that special advantage, I have come to be of the opinion that the alleged statements of Gray and Tonge were clearly inadmissible and should have been withheld from the jury. This was, in my opinion, one of those exceptional cases in which, upon the undisputed relevant evidence, it can be said that no reasonable jury could have held that the statements had been voluntary and had not been induced by unfair or improper means (vide *Balloch* v. *H.M. Advocate*). In my judgment upon a close scrutiny of the notes of evidence it is abundantly clear that the rules of fairness and fair dealing were flagrantly transgressed (vide *H.M. Advocate* v. *Whitelaw*). I do not say that in no circumstances will a statement by a detainee (a suspect within the meaning of s. 2(1) be inadmissible merely because, when it was made, he had not received a full caution. What I do say is that the failure of the investigating officers to caution Gray and Tonge in the special circumstances of this case is fatal to the contention that the rules of fair dealing and fairness were properly observed.

In Gray's case the hope of the two officers was that when they saw him he would provide what was conspicuously lacking, namely, self-incriminating evidence. He was already impressed with the character of a suspect within the meaning of s. 2(1) and they undoubtedly approached him with that hope in their hearts, and with the intention of questioning him if necessary. It is of critical importance to notice what they did. They accused him of participation in the crime. Now, as is pointed out in Walkers' *Law of Evidence in Scotland*, p.39, para. 45: 'It is proper practice that, when a person is charged with a crime, the caution should be given, since, without it, the reading of the charge may be interpreted by the accused as a question, or as an invitation to reply, in which case any statement then made is not spontaneous and voluntary.' I go further and say that the proper practice is now so long and so well entrenched that it may be taken that a full caution before a charge is made is a requirement of the law itself. The reading of a charge is calculated to provoke a response from the accused and it is quite essential that he should know, in advance, of his right of silence, and of the use which may be made of any response which he chooses to make. To charge an accused person without cautioning him is to put pressure upon him which may induce a response and I have no doubt that by accusing

Gray, although not in the formal language of a charge, the accusation was clearly calculated, as a formal charge is calculated, to induce a response from the person accused. The accusation placed pressure upon Gray and I am persuaded that since no caution was administered before it was made, it is impossible to regard the statement made in response to it as spontaneous and voluntary. It was plainly induced by the accusation and in the circumstances was induced by unfair means. It cannot be left out of account either that no caution was administered when the first sentence uttered by Gray made it plain that he intended to make a statement, and that no caution was administered when it became obvious that he was about to incriminate himself. As the evidence of the police officers demonstrated, it would have been proper practice to caution a suspect in Gray's position before he was allowed to proceed with a statement and, in my opinion, nothing in s. 2 of the Act of 1980 excuses compliance with that practice.

In Tonge's case I reach the same conclusion. Tonge, who had not received at any stage of the detention procedure a full caution in common law terms, was seen by the investigating officers with the single purpose of charging him. Had they carried out that purpose, they would have required to caution him. They did not do so. What they did, without cautioning him, was to accuse him of the crime, just as they had accused Gray of the crime. This, as Constable Jenkins agreed, was not a usual thing to do where the sole purpose of the encounter was to charge the suspect. Be that as it may the accusation was made without caution, no caution was administered when the first sentence of Tonge's response demonstrated that he was about to make a statement, and no caution was administered at any point while the alleged statement was being made. It is impossible to accept that the officers did not 'get a chance' to charge Tonge and the excuse for not cautioning him was the unfounded assumption that he had already received a full caution when he was detained under s. 2. For all the reasons which led me to hold that the alleged statement by Gray was inadmissible I also hold that the alleged statement by Tonge was inadmissible and should not have been left for consideration by the jury.

In light of what I have said I would allow the appeals of Gray and Tonge and quash their conviction. . . .

. . . Before leaving this case, which has illustrated the problems and confusion created by the provisions of s. 2 of the Act of 1980, I would strongly urge police officers throughout Scotland who proceed to accuse a detainee or to question him or to take from him a voluntary statement, to rely not at all upon the efficacy of the warning described in s. 2(7), and to appreciate that if any use is to be made in evidence of anything said by a detainee in these circumstances the ordinary rules of fairness and fair dealing which have been developed by the common law should be strictly observed. The wise course will be, inter alia, to administer to the detainee in the events which I have mentioned a full caution in common law terms. The omission to give such a caution will, by itself, at the very least place the admissibility of anything said by the detainee in peril and the appeals by Gray and Tonge demonstrate circumstances in which the omission of the interviewing officer to caution these men in such terms was fatal."

LORD CAMERON: ". . . In expressing my concurrence with your Lordship in the chair I would only venture to add certain observations of my own on the provisions and operation of s. 2 of the Act of 1980. It is not a happily drafted section, and in particular it is not easy to understand the reasons which induced the legislature to enact subs. (7). The section, by subs. (1), confers new powers on the police of detention for a limited period of a person suspected on reasonable grounds of having committed or of committing an offence punishable by imprisonment and, during that period, to interrogate a suspect, search, and take fingerprints and other impressions, 'for the purpose of facilitating the carrying out of investigations—(a) into the offence; and (b) as to whether criminal proceedings should be instigated against the person'. The right to interrogate a suspect is contained in subs. (5) which provides that a constable 'may—(a) put questions to him in relation to the suspected offence'. The exercise of this power however is conditioned by the provisions of subs. (7) which provides that a person detained under subs. (1): 'shall be under no obligation to answer any questions other than to give his name and address, and a constable shall so inform him both on so detaining him and on arrival at the police station or other premises'—to which he is to be taken 'as quickly as is reasonably practicable'. Now whatever else subs. (7) may mean what it provides is neither an alternative to nor a substitute for the giving of a caution in the well-recognised and regular form in circumstances where the law and proper practice demands or requires. It is not indeed immediately apparent what useful purpose this innovative and possibly confusing provision is designed to serve, as the proviso to s. 5(a) states that 'this paragraph [sic] shall be without prejudice to any existing rule of law as regards the admissibility in evidence of any answer given'. This, in my opinion, means and can only mean that nothing in s. 2 alters the pre-existing rules of law or of safe and proper practice in the matters of cautioning persons who may be questioned in the course of police investigations of crimes or suspected crimes or at the time when a person is being charged with a crime or offence. It is of course well established that police officers are entitled to question a suspect as to his possible complicity in a crime which they are investigating, and that his replies will be admissible in evidence if they have not been extracted or compelled by unfair or improper means including threats, intimidations, offers of inducements, or cross-examination designed or intended to extract incriminating replies, but it is equally well recognised that in the case of one on whom suspicion of responsibility or complicity has centred, in order that his replies should be admissible in evidence, it is proper practice that any further questioning should be preceded by a caution in the common form. The proviso to subs. (5) is of such wide generality that it leaves no doubt in my opinion that the warning specified in such limited terms which is required to be given in compliance with the provisions of subs. (7), is not and cannot be in substitution for the cautions which the law and practice require to be given as a condition precedent to the admissibility of evidence obtained from questioning of a suspect or the replies to a charge made by an accused, but is of an entirely independent character which does not in any way determine the admissibility of evidence obtained by the questioning which the provisions of s. 2 permits.

It would appear to me to follow from this that in the case of a suspect of the kind figured in subs. (1) it would be wise and proper practice that he should receive a caution in recognised form before questions are put to him, in order that no conflict may arise as to the admissibility in evidence of any replies given by him in the course of such questioning. This conclusion appears to me all the more necessary when it is kept in view that the whole basis on which the right to detain or to question rests on the very definite character of the police officers' suspicion as set out in subs. (1).

Apart however from the question as to what is required to make admissible in evidence any replies made by a suspect detained under the powers given by s. 2 to questions by a police officer in course of his authorised investigation, there are two other matters to which I would refer in relation to the actions of the police officers concerned in the investigations in this case. The first is as to the regular and well-known practice of police officers in taking a voluntary statement from one either suspected or actually charged with a crime, and the second is the rule of law which requires a caution to be given to an accused when a formal charge is made if his reply to the charge is to be admissible in evidence—either for or against him. The regular and proper practice when an accused or suspect indicates or intimates he wishes to make a voluntary statement is that the statement should be taken by officers unconnected with the particular investigation, and authenticated by the signatures of the officers concerned and the maker of the statement himself. In the case of the appellants, although the detailed and incriminating statements ascribed to them are recorded in police notebooks, no attempt was made to have them given to or taken by independent officers or even to have what is recorded in the officers' notebooks signed by the appellants themselves. The investigating officers in this case were fully aware of this proper practice and of the reasons for it, so that it cannot be argued that what is recorded in their notebooks and testified to in evidence were at the time regarded as 'voluntary statements' of the kind I have referred to.

As to the second, in my opinion it is a requirement, which goes beyond one of proper practice and is now a requirement of law, that when preferring a charge against an accused, police officers should caution him as to the possible use to be made of any reply made to that charge. Now the circumstances and manner in which the investigating officers proceeded in the case of all the appellants have already been fully set out by your Lordship, and I have no doubt that not only had the officers determined to prefer charges of rape even before they proceeded to interview the appellants, but also that their immediate intimation of their purpose and intention was in a form which, while lacking the precise formality of a charge, was no more and no less than the levelling, in words which were indistinguishable from those of the formal charge which immediately followed the 'voluntary statement', of a detailed accusation of rape—but one which in the case of the detainees Gray and Tonge was admittedly not preceded by a caution. At that stage of the inquiry there were at the least serious grounds for doubt as to whether the police had sufficient evidence on which to justify making a charge, and it was thus a matter of the highest importance that the appellants should be induced to make some statements of an incriminatory character. In offering the explanation for their presence and the subject and purpose of their investigations the police officers concerned did so in a manner which was accusatorial in form and substance and, whether by design or inadvertence it matters not, would be likely to evoke from the person addressed some form of immediate response, explanatory or exculpatory or incriminating. That being so I am clearly of opinion that in the case of Gray and Tonge their statements, in the absence of a precedent caution, were inadmissible in evidence."

Appeals allowed.

2.   Pennycuick v. Lees
1992 S.C.C.R. 160

LORD JUSTICE-GENERAL: "The appellant is James Pennycuick who was found guilty in the sheriff court at Edinburgh on summary complaint of an offence under section 55 of the Social Security Act 1986. The offence consisted of making false statements on various occasions between 31st January and 19th April 1989 to the Social Security office that he had not worked during the period since his last claim for benefit because of incapacity, when the truth was that between these dates he was employed as a boardmarker by a firm of bookmakers and had net weekly earnings in excess of the statutory earnings limit. The point raised in this appeal was the subject of objections to the evidence in the course of the trial and of a submission that there was no case to answer, which was repelled. It relates to the admissibility of evidence given by two officers of the Department of Social Security of admissions which were made to them by the appellant when he was interviewed by them on two occasions in the course of their investigations. On neither occasion was he cautioned by the officers before these admissions were made, and the argument is that the sheriff erred in allowing these admissions to be spoken to in evidence.

The first of these interviews took place on 28th April 1989. The sheriff tells us in his findings of fact that on that date the appellant was under investigation, having been followed for the third time by two officials of the department and seen to be working. The purpose of the interview was to satisfy the officers that the man they had been following was the James Pennycuick who was in receipt of sickness benefit and to find out whether or not he would be entitled to benefit for the week in question. The appellant, who was not cautioned, confirmed to the officers that he was James Pennycuick and gave his address and date of birth. He then signed a statement which was in these terms:

> 'I, James Pennycuick of 46/1 Muirhouse Avenue, declare that I am employed by Longchamps Racing at their office in Nicolson Street for more than 24 hours per week.
> 'I wish to withdraw my claims for sickness benefit and income support.'

The second interview was on 30th August 1989 when the appellant was seen at his house by the same two officers of the department. He was advised that he was being interviewed in relation to an overpayment of supplementary benefit and income support, and was then shown and admitted signing four forms claiming benefit during the period referred to in the charge. It was only after these admissions had been obtained that he was cautioned and invited to sign the record of the interview below the written acknowledgement of the caution, which he declined to do. It is not disputed that the admissions which were obtained in the course of these interviews were essential to the Crown case as it was presented in evidence, and that if evidence about these admissions had been disallowed the appellant would have been entitled to an acquittal.

Mr McBride opened his argument by an examination of the question whether the appellant was a suspect at the time when he was first interviewed. It is plain from the sheriff's findings and from his note that the officers suspected that the appellant had committed an offence when they interviewed him for the second time. But Mr McBride submitted that that stage had already been reached by the time of the first interview, because by that date he was not only under investigation but had been followed and seen to be working on the bookmakers' premises for the third time. His point was that as soon as the appellant became a suspect a caution ought to have been administered to him before he was interviewed at all, and that the sheriff erred because he did not address himself to the question whether the appellant was a suspect at the relevant time.

As the argument proceeded, however, it appeared that the test which Mr McBride was inviting us to apply was that of fairness in all the circumstances of the case, the question whether the appellant was or was not a suspected person being one of the circumstances to be taken into account. It was to this test that the learned Solicitor-General addressed his argument in reply, and in our opinion he was well founded in this approach. We are dealing with interviews conducted by officers of the Department of Social Security, not by police officers. But in all these cases where enquiries are being conducted into activities which may be criminal the question is whether, looking at all the circumstances of the case, there has been unfairness to the accused in what took place. This was the test which was applied in *Miln* v. *Cullen* in which it was conceded by the Crown that, when the accused was asked by the police officers whether he was the driver of the car, he was a suspected person. As Lord Strachan put it at p.27:

> 'The whole circumstances must be taken into account, and the test in

every case is whether in the particular circumstances there has been unfairness on the part of the police.'

In *Irving* v. *Tudhope* evidence was given by Post Office enquiry officers that when they visited the appellant and asked her if she had a television licence she admitted she had not. It was submitted that her reply to these officers was inadmissible because it had been unfairly obtained. The argument was that since she was a suspect she should have been warned that she might be prosecuted and that any reply which she made might be used in evidence. This argument was rejected on the ground that there was no unfairness on the part of the enquiry officers in their asking, in the course of their enquiries, whether someone with a television set had a television licence. Here again once [*sic*] can see the same test being applied. There is, therefore, no rule of law which requires that a suspect must always be cautioned before any question can be put to him by the police or by anyone else by whom the enquiries are being conducted. The question in each case is whether what was done was unfair to the accused.

The sheriff was satisfied that at the time of the interview on 28th April 1989 the officers of the department were investigating the possibility of an offence. But they still had to discover whether the person to whom they were speaking was the same James Pennycuick as the man whom they understood to be claiming benefit. The purpose of the interview was to find out whether the appellant was that man and whether or not he was entitled to the benefit which he was claiming from the Social Security office. The answer to the latter question depended on whether he was working and, if so, whether his earnings were in excess of the statutory earnings limit. It was only when they had all this information that they were able to determine whether the appellant had committed an offence. There is no suggestion in the findings that the officials were trying to trap the appellant into an admission or to provoke an incriminating reply from him which would provide them with evidence which they could not otherwise obtain. Their questions were designed merely to obtain information from him on matters relevant to their enquiries, at a stage when they were still unable to say whether or not he had committed an offence. This line of questioning was fair and proper in the circumstances, and we are in no doubt that the sheriff was entitled to hold that evidence as to what was said was admissible. The appellant was then asked to sign a written record of the interview and he agreed to do so. But here again there was no unfairness in what was done. He had already answered the questions which had been put to him, and the purpose was to enable him to say whether or not the written record was correct.

The sheriff tells us in his note that it was only after this interview had been completed that the officials were aware that a crime had been committed. This provides the background to the second interview, because it is clear that by that stage they knew that the man whom they proposed to interview was the James Pennycuick who had been claiming benefit and, in the light of information which they had already obtained, that he had committed an offence because he was not entitled to the benefits which he had received. On this occasion they advised the appellant at the outset of the purpose of their visit, which the sheriff said was sufficient to put him on his guard. Nevertheless no caution was administered to him until after he had been shown and admitted signing the four forms claiming benefit, which became essential Crown productions in the case because they established that the appellant had been obtaining benefit from the Social Security office libelled in the charge. The officers said that the purpose of asking him whether he had signed these forms was to confirm his identity. That would have been a legitimate purpose and would have involved no unfairness if it was necessary for them to do this before the interview could proceed. But these officers, who were the same two officers as those who had conducted the previous interview, were already aware of the appellant's identity and they were also aware he had committed an offence. In these circumstances for them to show him the form merely to confirm his identity might seem to have been unnecessary, and the effect of the admissions was to provide them with evidence that the forms which were in their possession had been signed by the appellant.

Mr McBride submitted that it was not sufficient for the appellant in these circumstances merely to have been told the purpose of their visit before he was asked whether he had signed the forms. His argument was that in all the circumstances a caution was required, and that in its absence the evidence of the admissions should have been held to be inadmissible. At first sight there is some force in this submission, because the stage was no longer that of initial investigation. The officers were already in possession of the information which they needed to say whether or not the appellant had committed an offence. The question remains, however, whether, even at this stage, it was unfair for him to be asked whether he had signed the forms. This question has to be answered by taking into account the whole circumstances, and it is important to note that there is no suggestion in the case that any undue pressure, deception or other device was used to obtain the admissions. Nor can it be said that the appellant did not appreciate what was going on, because he was told at the outset by the officials what the purpose was of their visit. He was told that he was being interviewed in relation to an overpayment of supplementary benefit and income support. Taking all these factors into account, we consider that the sheriff was entitled to conclude that on this occasion also there was no unfairness to the appellant in what was done and to hold that the evidence of what he said was admissible."

Appeal refused.

NOTES

1.   A proper caution should inform the suspect that he or she is not obliged to say anything (*cf. Von* v. *H.M. Advocate, supra*, p.170) but that anything that he or she says will be taken down and may be given in evidence (*Tonge, supra*). In England it has been held that it is improper to tell the suspect that anything taken down may be given in evidence *against* him, since this might discourage a suspect from making any statement, including one consistent with innocence. The modern form of the caution in England is simply that the suspect is not obliged to say anything but that anything he or she does say may be given in evidence.

2.   When it was first handed down, *Tonge* appeared to mark a more strict approach by the courts to the question of admissibility where the police had failed to caution. It is not clear precisely what effect *Pennycuick* v. *Lees* has on *Tonge*. The following is an attempt to summarise the combined effect of these two cases:

(a)   To the extent that the police are expected to caution a suspect, there is no difference between a person detained under section 2 of the 1980 Act and other suspects. A full "common law" caution should be administered in all cases. A *detainee* should be warned that he or she is required to give a (genuine) name and address.

(b)   *Tonge* appears to support the view that different rules regarding the requirement of a caution apply:

(i)   at the stage of suspicion;

(ii)   at the stage of charge;

(iii) where the police questioning takes the form of an accusation, analogous to making a charge against the suspect.

In the case of (i), the court did not say that a failure to caution would render any statement inadmissible, but merely that such statement will normally be imperilled. Prior to *Tonge* the view had been taken that the absence of a caution was merely a factor to be taken into account in determining the question of fairness. The difference between *Tonge* and earlier cases such as *Miln* v. *Cullen*, 1967 J.C. 21 was, therefore, one of degree. The High Court's reliance on *Miln* v. *Cullen* in *Pennycuick* v. *Lees* suggests that this is the currently accepted view. See also, *McClory* v. *MacInnes*, 1992 S.C.C.R. 319.

So far as the "charge stage" is concerned, Lord Cameron is unequivocal. It is a "rule of law," a "requirement of the law itself" that a caution must be given to a person when a formal charge is made if his reply to the charge is to be admissible in evidence. The Lord Justice-General uses virtually identical language. These propositions have not subsequently been challenged or disapproved, and it is particularly unfortunate that *Tonge* is not even mentioned in *Pennycuick* v. *Lees* since it appears to call into question these propositions. In *Pennycuick* the court appears to suggest that there is no such rule, even at the stage of charging, and that the question is always one of fairness. The only way in which this unfortunate conclusion can be avoided is by reading *Pennycuick* as holding that this stage had not yet been reached. That would, at least, reconcile *Pennycuick* with *Tonge*.

Where the police pursue their inquiries by means of levelling an accusation at the suspect, then, according to *Tonge*, such accusation should be preceded by a caution if the prosecutor wishes to introduce the suspect's response in evidence. (Indeed, there are suggestions in *Tonge* that it is improper for the police to proceed in this manner at all.) The court appears to adopt this approach because such an accusation, like a charge, may, if not accompanied by a caution, put pressure upon the suspect to respond. (See, in particular, the language used by the Lord Justice-General in relation to the accusation levelled at the suspect Gray.)

There are problems with this approach. In the first place the distinction between an accusation and other forms of questioning is not easy to make and may unnecessarily inhibit the conduct of the investigation. Indeed, in *Pennycuick* the language used by the D.H.S.S. officers at the second interview is treated not so much as an accusation as more a form of words which could have put the accused on his guard. It is probably better to focus on the likely *effect* of the questioning rather than its *form* and to hold that where a police officer (or other person charged with investigating an offence) adopts an approach to questioning which is likely put the suspect under pressure to respond, such as directly accusing him or her of an offence, he or she should, before adopting such tactics, caution the suspect. *Cf. Custerson* v. *Westwater*, 1987 S.C.C.R. 389 and *Irving* v. *Tudhope*, 1987 S.C.C.R. 505 where the court appears to adopt the view that if the questioning is designed to provoke an incriminating reply and it is not preceded by a caution then any response should be treated as unfairly obtained.

One final point which appears to have been influential in *Tonge*, and which appears to have been overlooked in later cases, is that at a certain point it became apparent to the investigating officers that the suspects Gray and Tonge were about to make a statement and yet no caution was administered. Again, this should be an important consideration operating in favour of requiring a caution. If a caution has not already been administered, and it appears that a suspect is about to make a statement, then at that point a caution should be administered.

3.   In *Wilson* v. *Heywood*, 1989 S.C.C.R. 19 the appellant was charged with assaulting a young woman and indecently assaulting the same woman on two separate occasions. He was interviewed by the police about the second of these incidents. A caution was administered in respect of that incident, but during the interview he was also told that allegations had been made against him in respect of the first incident. The appellant eventually made a statement in which he admitted both incidents. At the trial an objection was taken to evidence of the statement in relation to the first incident. The objection was repelled and the appellant was convicted on both charges. On appeal the court held that although he had not been specifically cautioned in respect of the first incident, his statement was made under caution and that he was therefore aware that he was not required to make any statement. In the circumstances there was no unfairness. The case was distinguished from *Tonge* on the ground that in that case no caution at all had been given to Gray. (In fact, Gray was cautioned when he was first taken from his house and detained under section 2 of the 1980 Act, but this appears to have been disregarded by the court.)

Presumably, the fact that the two offences were closely related in character, and against the same victim, is a relevant consideration. It would hardly be fair, for example, to caution a person prior to questioning him about an offence and then seek to rely on that caution in relation to statements made about a quite different offence. But since this is all a question of "fairness" this is presumably a matter of degree.

D.   Statements While in Detention Under the 1980 Act

Criminal Justice (Scotland) Act 1980

"2.—... (5) Where a person is detained under subsection (1) above, a constable may—

(*a*) put questions to him in relation to the suspected offence:

   Provided that this paragraph shall be without prejudice to any existing rule of law as regards the admissibility in evidence of any answer given."

NOTE

The relationship between section 2(5), the warning under section 2(7) and the common law rules regarding admissibility of statements is discussed in *Tonge* v. *H.M. Advocate, supra.*

E.   The Trial-Within-a-Trial

The "trial-within-a-trial" procedure was adopted into Scots law by the High Court in *Chalmers (supra)*. The Lord Justice-General outlined the procedure as follows:

"When objection is taken to a line of evidence upon the alleged unfairness of the methods used in eliciting it, the jury ought to be excluded, and the evidence bearing upon the attendant circumstances should be heard by the Judge in the absence of the jury, including, if so advised, the evidence of the accused himself. If, in the light of such evidence and argument, the Judge sustains the objection, the jury should be told nothing about the matter. If on the other hand the Judge repels the objection, the case will proceed in the presence and hearing of the jury, and, if either prosecution or defence chose to do so, the evidence bearing upon the attendant circumstances can be made the subject of examination and cross-examination a second time. In the end of the day it will be for the Judge to direct the jury that, in considering the weight and value of the evidence to which objection has been taken and repelled, it is for the jury to have regard to the attendant circumstances as proved before them, and, in so far as they may consider that the evidence objected to is not to be relied upon by reason of the circumstances in which it arose, to discount it or exclude it from their deliberations."

The procedure has, however, met with increasing hostility. In *Thompson* v. *H.M. Advocate*, 1968 J.C. 61 the Lord Justice-General suggested that the procedure laid down in *Chalmers* might have to be reconsidered. This has not happened, but a series of recent decisions suggests that it will only exceptionally be employed. In *H.M. Advocate* v. *Mair*, 1982 S.L.T. 471 Lord Hunter stated (at p.473):

"In my view the procedure of a trial within a trial has a number of unsatisfactory and rather dangerous features and may conflict with the normal practice in our criminal procedure that the whole evidence should be led in the presence of the jury. Making the assumption for this purpose that the procedure may in appropriate circumstances survive as a competent procedure, I am disposed to think that the procedure ... is one which at best should only be used sparingly and in very special circumstances."

Lord Cameron in *H.M. Advocate* v. *Whitelaw*, 1980 S.L.T. (Notes) 25 suggested a rather more precise formula for determining the appropriateness of the trial within a trial procedure (at p.26):

"I have never been in favour of any extension of the practice of a trial within a trial unless ... the circumstances already established or admitted are such as to be prima facie indicative of unfairness towards an accused who is in the hands of the police and of transgression of the fundamental rules of fairness which lie at the root of our criminal procedure."

In that case the grounds of objection to the alleged confession were

"(1) the age of the accused [16]; (2) the presence of more than one senior police officer; (3) having indicated that he did not wish the presence of his father the accused was not at that stage informed he was entitled to the presence of a solicitor; and (4) he was not given a second caution after the police officer had informed him that he had reason to believe he was responsible for the offence."

His Lordship held that these circumstances did not warrant the use of a trial within a trial (*i.e.* that they did not amount to a prima facie case of unfairness).

F. TAPE RECORDING POLICE QUESTIONING

The tape recording of interviews between police officers and suspects, in police stations, was recommended by the Thomson Committee in their Second Report:

Thomson Committee (Second Report)

"**7.13** We *recommend* that it should be competent for the Crown to lead evidence of statements made by a suspect before arrest in answer to police questioning. We further *recommend* that the admissibility of such evidence should be subject to the following qualifications:

c. Interrogation of suspects in police stations must be recorded on tape. Tapes cannot easily be provided for questioning which occurs outside a police station. Our object is to provide a safeguard for persons being interrogated in the privacy of a police station and also to protect the police against unjustified allegations. We therefore do not suggest that interrogations conducted elsewhere need be recorded on tape."

H.M. Advocate v. Swift
1983 S.C.C.R. 204

The accused was interviewed by police officers and during that interview made certain statements which were recorded on tape. At the trial the tape was held inadmissible, and the procurator-fiscal called the officers who had taken the statement to give evidence as to its contents. An objection was taken to this evidence on the ground that it was not the best evidence.

SHERIFF YOUNGER: "Mr Oatway stated an objection to the question to Detective Constable Alexander Dowell which sought to elicit any reply made by the accused when he was cautioned and charged in similar terms to those now comprising charge four on the indictment. The basis of this objection, as I understood it, was two-fold. *In the first place*, there had already been some evidence to show that there was in existence a tape recording of the accused being cautioned and charged; standing that tape recording any reply which the constable may have noted in his notebook is not the best evidence; the tape recording is the best evidence. *In the second place*, the number of the tape recording referred to in evidence and confirmed by Miss Thom in the course of argument as 1302/82 does not coincide with any of the labelled productions; further, as again confirmed by Miss Thom, there is no transcript lodged relating to a tape 1302/82 although the defence were provided informally with one; the tapes produced are not identical copies of 1302/82; in addition, the error relating to the appropriate tape has been further confused by the serving of a notice in reliance on section 81 of the Criminal Procedure (Scotland) Act 1975 which has not been insisted upon but which would have altered the number of the tape relating to label 18 incorrectly; the result of this is that the defence have technically had no notice of the tape 1302/82 although Mr Oatway did not attempt to allege any prejudice occasioned thereby.

Miss Thom, in reply, contended that the answer which the constable was being asked to give from his notebook was primary evidence being evidence of what he heard at the time when the accused was cautioned and charged. The existence of the tape recording did not alter the character of the answer which the constable was being asked to give as primary evidence and the tape recording was not better evidence than that which the constable could give. The tape recording was an independent check as to what was said which was available in the event of there being a dispute as to what was said. As regards the difference in the numbers of the tapes, it was conceded that there was no prejudice thereby occasioned to the accused and there was no obligation on the Crown to state any number as regards the tape; if the label number 18 in the list of productions attached to the indictment had merely said 'tape' there would have been no possible objection. Miss Thom also offered to amend the label number 18 entry if that was thought to be necessary.

I have come to the view that there is no substance in Mr Oatway's submission insofar as based on the best evidence rule, a submission which I am afraid I may have encouraged at the time. Very frequently there are two sources of evidence which tend to prove the same fact and of course if the fact involved is a crucial fact, there must be two such sources. I consider that a reply to caution and charge may firstly be spoken to by the man who heard it and, secondly, be evidenced by a tape recording (always assuming that that tape recording is properly proved about which I make some observation later); the fact that such a reply is spoken to twice does not necessarily mean that one of those sources of evidence must be excluded as not being the best evidence. Each source, if properly proved, would be primary evidence of the same fact and each such source ranks in my opinion equally in standard as evidence; if there is a contradiction between the two sources, it would be up to the jury to decide which source was preferable. Even if (as here possibly) the same constable is to be used to speak to the reply heard and the accuracy of the tape recording, there are not thereby two independent sources of evidence admittedly, but there are simply two ways of proving the same fact which is again in my opinion not objectionable. There was some discussion to the effect that Lord Jauncey may have reached a different conclusion on this point in a High Court case in Dundee; if that is so, I can only apologise but I have been unable in the time available to me to trace any report of such a decision. I was not referred to any other authority and I know of none which would apply. Mr Oatway's submission insofar as based on the best evidence rule accordingly fails.

I consider, however, that there is some partial force in Mr Oatway's submission in relation to the tape recording apparently numbered 1302/82. Section 78(1) of the Criminal Procedure (Scotland) Act 1975 provides that a copy of the list of productions shall be lodged with the clerk of court ten clear days before the trial diet. Section 81 of the same Act provides with leave of the court for later production and putting in evidence if notice is given two clear days before the trial diet. It is beyond argument that the production of tape number 1302/82 does not specifically fall within section 78 or 81 and the notice issued in terms of section 81 was admittedly misleading which is still a fact despite that part of the section 81 notice not being relied upon. The fact that section 81 makes it competent with leave of the court for the prosecutor to put in evidence any production not lodged by him in the event of two clear days' notice being given by him seems to me to mean that the putting in evidence by the prosecution of any production not covered by the terms of section 78 or 81 is incompetent at least when there is objection. The admitted absence of prejudice does not seem to me to affect this legal position. Further, I consider that an alteration in the list of productions cannot be made by virtue of section 123 of the same Act which relates to amendment of the indictment; section 78 of the same Act seems to me to make a clear distinction between the indictment and such a list of productions and to allow amendment of the list would seem to me to be to circumvent the clear provisions of sections 78 and 81 of the same

Act. Finally, the submission that the prosecution could allegedly have merely put 'tape' on the list does not assist in my opinion; in this case they have specified the number which has proved to be incorrect. In the result, however, in view of my decision as regards the submission relating to the best evidence rule, I do not consider that the difficulties as regards the tape number 1302/82 affect the admissibility of the evidence which the question at present objected to is designed to elicit; the partial effect of this submission is therefore that it is my present opinion that no further reference should be made in this case to the tape 1302/82 although if it is so mentioned, objection should be taken afresh. This submission according likewise fails for present purposes.

I accordingly repel Mr Oatway's objection.

It may be helpful if I make some observations which are not essential for this case as to these tape recordings of interviews by the police. As I understand it, there are no statutory provisions relating to their admissibility or mode of proof as there are as regards judicial examinations, the Scottish Home and Health Department having instituted local trials of such tape recordings without additional statutory provisions. The admissibility and proof of such tape recordings are accordingly subject to the normal rules of evidence and procedure. As already indicated, I do not consider that such tape recordings, if properly proved, are inadmissible on the basis that they do not amount to the best evidence. However, if such tape recordings are to be put in evidence in a solemn trial, some further problems require consideration.

Firstly, it is worth remembering that it is often necessary to have a photographer speak to the taking of photographs although another witness who was present when the photographs were taken, or who is familiar with the subject, may be sufficient. Unfortunately, with these tape recordings there is at least normally no independent operator as there is for example in judicial examinations; the person operating the tape recorder and having control of the tapes is at least normally the person whose evidence as to what was said is supposed to be confirmed or denied or even made unnecessary by the tape recording. If there were to be any suggestion of tampering with the tapes, the jury would have to rely on their evaluation of the credibility of the same witness as to both the accuracy of what was said and as to the absence of tampering with the tapes.

Secondly, to use the photograph analogy again, there is never in my experience evidence that the camera has been working correctly, presumably because the existence of the photograph proves that; can the same be said as regards tapes? Does the existence of the tape or of three identical tapes produced by the same machine, prove that the machine was operating correctly, or is some proof of the accuracy of the machine required of a similar nature to that led as regards accurate equipment when a speeding charge goes to trial? The whole world knows as a result of ex-President Nixon's disaster that tapes can be most unreliable and I leave these questions open.

Thirdly, while I appreciate the laudable motives behind the practice, to have a sealed tape as a production which is not available to be listened to until the trial is underway seems to me to fly in the face of the requirements of section 83 of the Criminal Procedure (Scotland) Act 1975 which entitles the accused to see (and in this case presumably to hear?) a production. There should not be such an element of surprise in a solemn criminal trial in my opinion. To provide a transcript of an allegedly identical tape as another production is a doubtful practice; there is no statutory authority for it as with judicial examinations; it is pointless as a production unless the persons who transcribed it is available on the list of witnesses to speak to it, or unless possibly copies of it are available for everyone in the court so that each person can follow it as the tape is played. It seems to me that section 83 might be satisfied if an allegedly identical copy tape to the sealed tape was on the list of production and stated as such and was available to be listened to by the accused and his advisers.

Fourthly, in a previous trial when no objections were stated, it came to my notice that the shorthand writer was not taking down the contents of the tape while it was played; it was explained that she had instructions from someone not to do so, these instructions being justified on the basis that it was very difficult, if not impossible, for such a shorthand writer to take down what was being said on a tape, and on the basis that as a production the contents of the tape remained available; even if such failure to write down part of the evidence is not a breach of section 274 of the Criminal Procedure (Scotland) Act 1975 as amended [which requires shorthand notes to be taken of the whole proceedings at a trial] (about which I have doubts), the fact that shorthand writers cannot record the contents of such a tape must raise doubts as to the ability of those in the court to hear such tapes or at least to hear them correctly.

Fifthly, it is clear to me, again as a result of a previous trial in which no objections were stated, that the tape recording of a final interview in a police station with the accused after many other conversations/interviews have understandably taken place earlier is of very doubtful assistance for any purpose, since such a tape-recorded interview at least on the previous occasion in which I was involved seemed to involve the police in attempting to get the accused to renew on tape apparent admissions made previously; each such case would depend on its own facts but if objection is taken, the test of fairness might well result in the recording being ruled out as inadmissible in such circumstances.

Lastly, it could be thought or said that these observations reveal merely that I am acting in the way that a typically narrow-minded lawyer is expected to act in the face of brave technological innovations, but as I stated recently in the case of *Tudhope* v. *Lee*, 1982 S.C.C.R. 409 at page 414, 'I consider ... that we have not yet reached the stage when courts rely on the alleged workings of machines without evidence to show that their results are accurate or without statutory provisions rendering such evidence unnecessary.' In view of the lack of time available to me in preparing this ruling, I must stress that each of the foregoing views is a provisional one.

As I have said, the present objection is repelled with the proviso that any future attempt to mention tape number 1302/82 would be ruled inadmissible by me, if objected to, unless a fresh argument with which I have not already dealt is advanced so as to convince me to change my mind.

NOTES

1. One is tempted to ask, in the light of this decision, why one should bother with tape recording at all? Since the tape is not, according to Sheriff Younger, the best evidence of the terms of the interview (*i.e.* the contents of the tape) presumably there is no need to rely on the tape at all. The recollections of the interviewer can be used in preference. But, as the Thomson Committee recognised several years ago, a tape will give a far better indication, not only of *what* was said by the police (and the suspect) but also of *how* it was said.

In *H.M. Advocate* v. *McFadden*, Dundee High Court, August 1980, *unreported* (but see 1983 S.C.C.R. 208–209 and (1981) 56 SCOLAG Bul. 260) Lord Jauncey took a different view on the question of the best evidence rule:

LORD JAUNCEY: "While I am satisfied that a great deal of the interview which took place here was entirely fair to the accused, unfortunately, there were sufficient occasions upon which the questioning seemed to me to go beyond that which would normally be appropriate for police officers in questioning a suspect, and to reach the point at which it could be properly described as cross-examination. It is trite law that cross-examination of a suspect in an endeavour either to obtain an admission of his guilt or to break down his evidence on particular matters, is inadmissible as being unfair to him. I, therefore, conclude in this case that it would not be fair to the accused that this evidence of the interview should be admitted. I shall, therefore, sustain the objection by counsel for the defence."

MR MACFADYEN [advocate-depute]: "I wonder if I might ask my Lord as to the extent of my Lord's ruling on that. As I understand it, the objection was with reference to the tape recording. I am not certain whether my Lord's ruling covers my asking the officer questions as to his recollection of parts of the interview, or whether my Lord is ruling that I cannot ask any questions about the content of the interview at all. The tape recording cannot be regarded as unum quid. It might be possible to ask such questions of the interview as my Lord regarded as fair, and ask the officer about what was said in certain respects, without embarking upon the path that my Lord has ruled."

LORD JAUNCEY: "I haven't had an objection to that as yet."

MR MACFADYEN: "Indeed, but if my Lord could perhaps indicate that the ruling does not cover that. ..."

LORD JAUNCEY: "I would prefer not to rule upon a matter upon which I haven't had the assistance of counsel on both sides of the Bar. At the moment my ruling relates to the evidence of the transcript, of the transcript made from the tape recording."

MR MORTON [counsel for the accused]: "The difficulty about my Lord's proposal is that there is an obvious objection, because both to what is said at the interview or taking bits out of it, is that it is not the best evidence. The best evidence is the tape; this is the point. The tape has to be taken as a whole, and in my submission there is no way that your Lordship, having ruled that the interview is inadmissible, that one can then ask the person who took part in the interview, 'During the interview, did he say something about such and such?' In my submission, that is just improper."

LORD JAUNCEY: "Simply on the best evidence rule?"

MR MORTON: "Yes."

LORD JAUNCEY: "Thank you, Mr. Morton. Well, I will hear the advocate-depute on that."

MR MACFADYEN: "My Lord, in my submission the recollection of someone who was present when something was said as to what was said, is if not the best evidence, is certainly primary evidence of what was said and, therefore, I think there is other primary evidence in the form of a tape recording, and is not excluded by the best evidence rule. It is not secondary in the sense that it is the officer speaking to what is on the recording. It is primary in the sense that it is the officer speaking to his recollections on what was said, just as the tape recording is primary as being a direct record of what was said. In my submission, they are two primary sources of evidence on what was said at the interview and, therefore, it is not objectionable on that ground to ask the officer about what was said."

LORD JAUNCEY: "I think the difficulties would be great. Having heard Mr Morton, I think there is a good deal to be said for the view that where you have a tape recording, that must be better evidence. In the event of mechanical equipment being in good order, as we understand it was, there must be better evidence than a recollection of events some months ago. I think that the difficulties would be too great, Mr Advocate-Depute, and accordingly, I shall extend, as I understand Mr Morton has now made a further objection, and I shall sustain that objection. So, the effect of that will be that both the transcript, and the oral evidence as to what took place at the interview, will be inadmissible."

2. In recommending the introduction of tape recordings, the Thomson Committee made the following observations:

> "**7.21** ...
> *b. Answers made to police questions by a suspect*
> In paragraph 7.13c. we recommend that interrogation of suspects in police stations must be recorded on tape. ... we confidently expect that the availability of more sophisticated equipment will improve the standard of reproduction and that with training the technique of interrogation by police officers will also improve, so that vague or ill-expressed statements are not allowed to go unexplained. The cost of tape recording is not prohibitive ...
>
> The presence of a tape recorder may upset some persons, but on balance we consider that the vast majority of persons will be reassured by knowing that anything that is said will be accurately recorded. The fact that the police know that the interview is being recorded on tape will tend to reduce the chances of interrogation being conducted with any impropriety. We think that tampering is unlikely but to reduce that possibility we *recommend* that the tape be sealed and placed in the custody of the procurator fiscal as soon as possible after the conclusion of the interrogation. If the interrogation does not take place within a police station, and a tape recorder is not used, a police officer will require to rely on his notebook.
>
> **7.23** It is appreciated that our proposals rely to a large extent on the effectiveness of tape recorders. We realise that all or part of a police interrogation may not be recorded through failure of a tape recorder. The question arises whether or not an account of any unrecorded interrogation given by a police officer from memory and notes made at the time or immediately afterwards, should be admissible in evidence. We consider that it should not be admissible, as we feel strongly that particularly accurate recording of interrogation in a police station is essential as a safeguard to all the persons concerned. The same considerations do not apply to a voluntary statement which, although recorded on tape, will also be recorded in a written document authenticated by the accused. Such a statement should be admissible in evidence, even though the tape recorder has failed. We accordingly so *recommend*."

The comments in para. 7.23 were made in relation to reliance on other forms of evidence where, because of technical failure, no tape was available. The fact that the tape has been ruled inadmissible would seem to be an even better reason for excluding any attempt to get round the non-availability of the tape for use in evidence.

3. A tape may contain evidence of statements, some of which is admissible, and some of which is not. *Lord Advocate's Reference (No. 1 of 1983)*, 1984 S.C.C.R. 62 (*supra*, p.177) and the following case indicates how this problem should be dealt with:

Tunnicliffe v. H.M. Advocate
1991 S.C.C.R. 623

The appellant was convicted, *inter alia*, of possession of cannabis resin with intent to supply it to another, contrary to section 5(3) of the Misuse of Drugs Act 1971. On appeal against conviction, the Lord Advocate indicated that he did not seek to maintain the conviction on this charge.

Lord Justice-General: "The learned Lord Advocate intimated at the outset of the hearing in this appeal that he did not seek to maintain the conviction on charge (3), and we shall of course give effect to the position which he has very properly adopted in this case by quashing the conviction on that charge. In view of certain things which were said by the sheriff in his helpful report and also points which were drawn to our attention by both the Lord Advocate and Mr MacGibbon, who appeared on the appellant's behalf, we should, however, say one or two things about the circumstances, and in particular about the particular problem which has led the Lord Advocate to take the position which he has in this case.

The evidence which was led on charge (3) so far as it affected the position of the appellant was very substantially based upon an interview carried out at Colchester by police officers. There was also some other evidence of articles found in the appellant's house in Galashiels which supported the charge of possession of drugs with intent to supply, but these articles in themselves would not have been sufficient to justify a conviction on that charge had it not been for certain things which he was alleged to have said in the course of this interview. There were present in court two items which were available by way of evidence of what took place. There was Production No. 11, which was a transcript of the interview, and there was also Label No. 7, which was a tape recording of the interview. The transcript had been edited to remove from it some passages which referred to crimes not charged in this indictment because they had been committed in England. But there was a further problem because the transcript had been compiled in a form which is not familiar to the Scottish practice. We understand that among other difficulties it was presented partly in verbatim form and partly in narrative form. There is no doubt that the transcript contained certain features which created difficulty both for those representing the appellant and also for the Crown. When it came to be referred to in evidence the agent who was acting on the appellant's behalf objected to this being done. As Mr MacGibbon pointed out, had this been an interview conducted in Scotland according to Scottish practice it is very unlikely that an objection of that kind would have been taken or that it would have been sustained. This was made clear by Lord Justice-General Emslie in *Lord Advocate's Reference (No. 1 of 1983)*, at p.70:

> 'The point to be made is that the presence in a transcript of an interview with a suspect under caution of certain answers which, for a sound reason, must be withheld from a jury will not by itself normally justify a trial judge in excluding from the jury's consideration the remainder of the transcript.'

So in principle there is nothing objectionable in editing a transcript if it is capable of being so edited, so as to remove from it these passages which could be prejudicial to the accused. The problem in this case, however, which led to the sheriff's decision to sustain the objection is that the transcript was put together in a manner which made that process of editing very difficult, if not impossible, to achieve with fairness to the accused. The only criticism which we would wish to make of the way in which the sheriff dealt with the objection is that in his report in connection with this appeal he says that he sustained it on the basis that *any* interview must be looked at as a whole, and that it would be prejudicial to the appellant were certain parts of an interview to be highlighted and thereby unfairly crystallised in the mind of the jury. That approach, which is entirely general in its terms, goes too far since in the ordinary case it will be sufficient to follow the guidance which was given by the court in the case to which we have referred.

The problem which has led to the presentation of this appeal and the position which the Crown have adopted in response to it arises out of what happened next when the procurator fiscal sought to have the tape recording of the interview played in response to a point taken by the appellant that the entire interview had been conducted in a manner which was unfair to him. The appellant's agent submitted that this also was objectionable, no doubt for the same reason which had led him to object to the transcript, that is to say that the interview had in it material which was prejudicial to the appellant and that it would be wrong and inconsistent with the sustaining of the objection about the transcript for the tape to be played. The sheriff decided that it was appropriate for the tape to be played and he did so for the following reason which he has stated in his report. He tells us that it was suggested to him that if the jury were to hear the tape, it should be in some way edited in order that they might only hear evidence relative to the drugs in Scotland. But it seemed to him to be obvious from a practical point of view that this would be impossible, so he decided that the entire tape should be heard by the jury without any process of editing to remove the passages which were objectionable. He then left the matter on the basis that he would give directions to the jury in his charge so as to avoid any possible prejudice to the appellant. The Lord Advocate wished to reserve his position on the question whether it might be sufficient, in other cases where the tape of an interview which contains objectionable passages has been played in its entirety, for the question of prejudice to be dealt with by means of a direction by the trial judge. But the position which he adopted in this case was that the whole matter was so complicated by the fact that this interview had been conducted in England in accordance with English practice that it would be impossible for the point to be properly tested in this case. He accepted that in the circumstances of this case the decision which was taken by the sheriff was one which inevitably resulted in prejudice to the appellant, and that the conviction on charge (3) could not stand.

We have to say that we do not entirely understand the point which the sheriff has made that from a practical point of view it would have been impossible to edit the tape. Here again the particular circumstances of this case mask the normal situation which would have arisen if the interview had been conducted in Scotland according to Scottish practice. It is not impossible, we should have thought, for a tape to be edited in such a way that all those passages which could result in prejudice to the accused are excluded when the tape is played, in precisely the same way as passages are excluded from the verbatim written record which is lodged as a production. If that course is taken, there can normally be no objection on the ground of unfairness and the position will be the same as that which was described in *Lord Advocate's Reference (No. 1 of 1983)*.

That is sufficient for the purposes of this case. There may be cases where the difficulties created by interviews conducted in England will need to be explored more fully, but for the reasons given by the Lord Advocate that need not be done here. In the particular circumstances of this case what the sheriff should have done, if he was satisfied that the tape recording could only be played either as whole or not at all, was to sustain the objection to its being played. So if the Crown is intending to lodge and may have to rely upon the tape recording of an interview which contains material which may have to be excluded on the ground of unfairness it should provide the machinery and make all the necessary preparations so that an edited version of the recording can be played."

NOTE

Cf. the case of *McGee* v. *H.M. Advocate*, 1990 S.C.C.R. 710.

CHAPTER 6

SEARCH AND SEIZURE

The powers of the police to search the person of an arrestee or detainee were discussed in Chap. 4. This chapter discusses the remaining powers of the police to search persons and premises with, or without, a warrant.

Once again we are faced with potentially conflicting claims: the right of the individual to be free from interference with his person and his privacy as opposed to the need to search for a secure evidence of crime. Before considering the manner in which these interests are "balanced" it is worth asking what is meant by a "search" for these purposes:

Davidson v. Brown
1990 S.C.C.R. 304

The appellant was convicted of reset. The circumstances under which the stolen property was discovered by the police were as follows. The police stopped a car which they suspected might have been stolen. The appellant was sitting in the back seat of the car, holding a plastic swing-bin on her knee. Two of the other occupants of the car were known to the police as shoplifters. Having ascertained that the car was not stolen, the police asked the appellant if there was anything in the swing-bin. She replied "No." The police officers asked to look inside the bin and the appellant handed it to them. It was found to contain recently stolen property. At the trial an objection to the evidence relating to the discovery of the stolen goods was repelled and the appellant convicted. She appealed to the High Court.

LORD JUSTICE-GENERAL: "It should be noted that objection was taken at the trial to the leading of evidence about the contents of the bin. It was contended that there had been an illegal search and that the detention of the occupants of the car which followed thereafter was also illegal. The sheriff repelled these objections because he considered that the request to see inside the bin and the handing of it for inspection to the police did not amount to a search and because he did not think that a caution was necessary in the circumstances. Mr Ogg, for the appellant, submitted that the sheriff was wrong to take the view that this was not a search. Moreover, the appellant had not been told of her right to refuse to let the police see inside the bin. He referred to the following passage in the opinion of Lord Justice-General Cooper in *McGovern* v. *H.M. Advocate* at p.36 in which he said, with reference to the taking of scrapings from the fingernails of the appellant without his consent:

'Some point was made to the effect that it is nowhere stated in evidence that force was used against the applicant, or that his consent was expressly withheld; but my reading of the evidence is that his consent was never asked—at least in such circumstances as satisfy the requirements of the law—because no consent would avail in the situation here presented unless it was given after a fair intimation that the consent could be withheld.'

The only basis upon which it could be contended that the police officers were entitled to search the appellant was under section 60(1) of the [Civic Government (Scotland) Act 1982], namely that they had reasonable grounds to suspect the appellant of being in possession of stolen property. But on the findings in fact in the case they did not have reasonable grounds for such a suspicion at the time when Police Constable Farmer asked to see inside the bin. Mr Ogg conceded that the police had reasonable grounds to suspect that a theft had been committed at the stage when the road block was set up because two of the occupants of the car were known to be shoplifters and a check had shown that the car was not registered to the driver. He submitted, however, that the latter point flew off when, on being stopped, the driver produced his documents and these were checked and found to be in order. All that was then left was the presence in the car of two known shoplifters, neither of whom was the appellant. The mere fact that the appellant was with them was not enough to give reasonable grounds for a suspicion that she was in possession of stolen property. The appellant had the swing-bin on her knees, but it was not stolen nor even suspected of being such and there were no findings to suggest that there was anything about her demeanour to excite suspicion. Furthermore, no crime was being investigated because the shopkeepers were unaware that anything had been stolen. In the result the evidence about the contents of the bin were irregularly obtained, and he submitted that all that followed ... was illegal.

In our opinion the critical question in this case is whether the appellant's action in handing the bin to Police Constable Farmer for inspection was a voluntary act on her part, so that the search which revealed its contents was with her consent. We were referred by the learned advocate-depute to *Lucas* v. *Lockhart* [(1980) S.C.C.R. Supp. 256] in which at p.258 Lord Justice-General Emslie said that if the appellant had been a volunteer in the matter of search, it was not necessary to consider the statutory warrant under which the search purported to be carried out. The argument that he was a volunteer was rejected in that case because the findings indicated no more than that the appellant had at a certain stage ceased to resist the demands of the police officers that he come out and be searched. When we examine the findings in this case, however, we find that there was no such demand. The police officer merely asked whether there was anything in the bin and, having received a negative reply, he then asked to see inside it, to which the appellant agreed. There was no caution but in the circumstances of this case that does not mean that there was no consent. In *McGovern* v. *H.M. Advocate* the appellant whose fingernails were scraped was already under suspicion of having committed a crime of housebreaking and safe-blowing which the police were in the course of investigating. A search warrant had been obtained to search his house, and since it had not revealed sufficient evidence to take the matter beyond suspicion it was decided as a further precaution that the contents of his fingernails should be obtained. This was done without telling him that his consent to this could be withheld. In the present case, however, as Mr Ogg in his careful address was at pains to point out, the police were not investigating any crime. His contention was that they did not have reasonable grounds to suspect that a crime had taken place, let alone that the appellant was in possession of stolen property. We agree with the sheriff that a caution was unnecessary in the circumstances and that what took place was not a search for which a warrant or statutory authority was required. The position is simply that the appellant agreed that the police officer could look inside the bin, because she handed it to him at his request. The evidence about its contents was admissible because there was no irregularity in the obtaining of this evidence."

Appeal refused.

NOTES
1.   There are two ways of looking at this case. The first is that what took place was not a "search." the appellant simply co-operated with the police officer's request to see inside the bin. Alternatively, there was a search and this required some authority. There was no need to rely on a warrant or statutory authority because the appellant's consent was given.
2.   There are other problems with the instant case. Consider the following:
(a)   In response to the police officer's request the person holding the bin does not hand it over, but simply says "go ahead" or "suit yourself." If the police officer then looks inside the bin, is there a search? Has it been authorised?
(b)   Instead of telling the police officer to go ahead, the person holding the bin says "Well, you're going to look in it anyway, aren't you?" If the police officer then looks inside the bin, is there a search? If so, has it been authorised?
3.   Suppose that the appellant in the instant case had refused to co-operate. Would that have given the police reasonable grounds for suspecting that the appellant was in possession of stolen goods (for the purposes of section 60(1) of the 1982 Act)? As Sheriff Gordon suggests in his commentary to *Davidson* v. *Brown*, 1990 S.C.C.R., at p.309, "Heads I win, tails you lose."

A.   SEARCH UNDER WARRANT

(A)   The Scope of the Warrant

General and unspecific warrants are said to be illegal. But this must be read subject to (1) the qualification that they are illegal only if there is no safeguard against oppression in their execution, and (2) the tendency of the courts to allow specific warrants to be used as general warrants.

1.   **Bell v. Black and Morrison**
(1865) 5 Irv. 57
During the investigation of an alleged criminal conspiracy involving a man called Pringle the respondents, joint procurators-fiscal for the county of Fife, obtained information suggesting that other persons, including Bell, were involved in the conspiracy. The respondents presented a petition for a search warrant in which they stated: "That the petitioners are informed, and have reason to believe, that written documents and other articles referring to, and connected with, said conspiracy and threatening letters are in the possession of the said John Bell, ... and as it is necessary, for the purpose of said precognition, to recover and take possession of the same, the present application for warrant to search becomes necessary."
The prayer of the petition was "to grant warrant to officers of Court ... to search the dwelling-house, repositories, and premises ... occupied by the said John Bell ... for the said written documents, and all other articles tending to establish guilt, or participation in said crimes, and to take possession thereof."

The warrant having been granted and executed, Bell brought a bill for its suspension.

LORD JUSTICE-CLERK (INGLIS): "There are some marked and important peculiarities in this petition and warrant (for the warrant, as we read it, is granted simply in terms of the prayer of the petition). In the first place, the warrant is granted against five different persons, none of whom is under a charge for any crime. It is stated in the petition that the persons against whom the warrant is asked are shown, by documents recovered in the course of the precognition against Pringle, to have been engaged in the same conspiracy, and in writing and sending threatening letters. But as no charge has yet been made against any of these five persons, this amounts to no more than a statement of suspicion or belief of the Procurators-fiscal that they are implicated in the same crimes as Pringle. In the second place, the leading object of the warrant is to obtain possession of the papers of the parties against whom it is directed, without any limitation as to the kind of papers, for by the term 'written documents' nothing else can be meant than all writings of every description. The only limitation is to be found in the words which follow—'tending to establish guilt or participation in said crimes,' and in the words in the body of the petition—'referring to and connected with said conspiracy and threatening letters.' But these words, while they may be supposed in one sense to have a limiting effect, are in another view capable of a very elastic interpretation: for it is not proposed to limit the seizure of papers in each person's house to those which inculpate himself; but, on the contrary, the words of the warrant would justify the seizure of papers tending to inculpate anybody in the crimes charged against Pringle, or at least, and in the most favourable sense, would justify the seizure of all papers in the possession of the complainer Bell which would tend to inculpate any of the other four parties against whom the warrant is directed, in addition, of course, to Pringle, and so in regard to the papers of each of the four other persons against whom the warrant is issued. In the third place, the execution of the warrant is entrusted absolutely and without control to ordinary sheriff-officers and their assistants, who are thereby commanded, whether in the presence or absence of the parties, who are under no criminal charge, and who have no notice of the application for or granting of the warrant, to seize their whole papers *per aversionem*, and themselves to read and examine all these papers for the purpose of finding traces or proofs of guilt either against the owners and possessors of the papers, or against some other person or persons.

The question which is thus raised for our decision has been represented to us by the learned counsel as one of great importance, and no one can doubt that it is so. It involves considerations of such high constitutional principle, that if we had felt any hesitation as to the judgment we should pronounce, we should have asked the assistance and advice of the other Judges of this Court. But entertaining no doubt at all, we consider it our duty at once to pronounce this warrant to be illegal. The seizure of papers, as distinguished from their recovery as articles of evidence, and also as distinguished from the seizure of other articles which are invested with no character of confidentiality or secrecy, is, under all circumstance, a matter of extreme delicacy. But the seizure of papers made in the circumstances with which we have to deal, is a proceeding quite unknown to the law of Scotland. Something was said of practice, though no example of such a seizure as this was mentioned. We think it right to say that no mere official practice would, in our eyes, justify such a warrant. Nothing short of an Act of Parliament, or a rule of the common law founded on usage known to and recognised by the Court, would at all affect our judgment on this question. If any such practice really exists, which we do not believe, the sooner it is put an end to the better. The Court are therefore of opinion that the warrant must be suspended. They attach no importance to the objection stated for the respondents, that the warrant has been executed, and therefore the suspension is too late. The warrant, according to its letter, is not exhausted, and might be enforced again. But further, we hold that even if it were exhausted, the complainer would have a good title to apply to this Court to suspend the warrant, on the ground of illegality."

Warrant suspended.

2.   Nelson v. Black and Morrison
(1866) 4 M. 328

For the background to this case see *Bell* v. *Black and Morrison, supra*. Nelson was amongst those suspected by the respondents and a warrant, similar in terms to that granted in the above case, was granted for the search of his home, repositories, etc. The warrant was not executed in view of the successful suspension in the above case. Nelson brought an action for slander in respect of the allegations contained in the petition for the warrant. The respondents argued, *inter alia*, that without an averment of malice and want of probable cause the pursuer's action was irrelevant. The pursuer argued that since the warrant was illegal such averment was not necessary.

LORD PRESIDENT (McNEILL): "... That may lead to a question of great nicety, viz., how far a procurator-fiscal puts himself outwith that protection that he would otherwise have, by asking something which he is not entitled to have; and that again may depend upon the nature of the illegality involved. If it is out of all law and reason that a man's repositories should be searched, that is one form of illegality. If, on the other hand, the objection is merely that the premises ought not to have been searched in this particular form, that is another matter. The one relates to the substance of the proceedings; the other to the want of formality, or the want of caution in carrying them out. In regard to illegality of the first kind, I think the pursuer would be entitled to have an issue without malice and want of probable cause. In regard to the other, I am of a different opinion.

It appears to me that this case falls under the latter class. I think it was competent for the Sheriff, under this application, to grant a perfectly legal warrant. For example if he had limited the search to particular documents, or appointed it to be carried out at the sight of the Sheriff himself, I cannot say that there would have been any illegality in such a warrant. That has not been done. But it does not follow that the defenders' application was out and out, and in substance, contrary to law."

LORD ARDMILLAN: "... I ... am of opinion that the warrant as taken and executed in the case of Bell was illegal. It was a wide and indefinite warrant to search for written documents tending to establish guilt, or participation in guilt, of a serious crime. ... a general warrant for a sweeping and indefinite search in the dwelling-house of a person not put under a charge, for written documents, in regard to which there is this pecularity that they must be read before it can be seen what they instruct, is a very strong and startling procedure; and if granted at all, such a warrant should have been accompanied by some security against oppression, and against the violation of private confidence. The most secret and sacred writings were, or might be, exposed to the perusal of a Sheriff-officer and his concurrents; and the personal attendance of the Sheriff, or some person of discretion and authority, to superintend the search, and to inspect and select the documents, was, in my opinion, necessary to secure the fair execution of the warrant, and to prevent its having oppressive consequencess. The illegality of the warrant lay in the absence of such securities.

I am not prepared to say that a general search warrant for articles of evidence, and, among other articles, for written documents tending to instruct an occult conspiracy, could not, in any case, be granted to the public prosecutor against parties named in the petition, if accompanied by proper securities against oppressive execution. I agree with your Lordship that such a warrant might have been legally granted."

NOTE

The responsibility of the sheriff for the investigation of offences has passed to the fiscal, and from thence in practice to the police. Does the presence of a police officer at the execution of a search warrant secure the attendance of a person "of discretion and authority?" This may well depend upon the rank of the officer concerned. Presumably the attendance of the fiscal at such a search would provide a sufficient safeguard.

3. H.M. Advocate v. Turnbull
1951 J.C. 96

The accused, an accountant, was suspected of making fraudulent income tax returns on behalf of certain of his clients. A search warrant was obtained in relation to returns made on behalf of one client. During the execution of that warrant the police seized and removed a large number of documents relating to the affairs of other clients. All of these papers were contained in files clearly marked with the client's name. The information contained in these papers subsequently provided a foundation for further charges against the accused. Six months after the search a warrant was obtained retrospectively authorising the seizure of these documents. At the trial, objection was taken to the admissibility in evidence of these documents, on the ground that they had been unlawfully obtained:

LORD GUTHRIE: "... On these admitted facts counsel for the defence submitted, first, that possession of the documents other than those relating to charges 1(a) and 1(b) had been illegally obtained, and, second, that in the circumstances they were not admissible in evidence. ...

The basis of the first submission was that the warrant granted on the first petition did not include the other documents, so that their retention and examination was without authority. They were the private papers of the accused and their unwarranted use for the purpose of obtaining evidence to enable further charges to be made against him was an infringement of the rights of the citizen. The files and the documents contained therein showed *ex facie* that they did not refer to the affairs of the client named in the first petition. When this was ascertained they should have been returned to the accused. Their continued retention and examination of their contents were deliberate and inexcusable. The irregularity of their seizure and use could not be validated *ex post facto* by the warrant granted on the second petition. In these circumstances the documents so irregularly obtained should not be admitted in evidence.

The Advocate-depute argued in reply that, as the documents had been obtained under the first warrant, the police were entitled, when examination of them showed that other charges might lie, to retain and use them to assist inquiry into these charges. The objection was purely technical, he maintained, since a warrant was ultimately obtained under which these documents could have been secured. The evidence had not been obtained by an unfair trick and in these circumstances it was admissible. ...

The first matter argued, as to whether the retention and use of the documents was illegal, can be disposed of briefly. The general rule is that the search of private repositories by police officers is illegal unless a warrant has been obtained from a magistrate. Further, "a wide and indefinite warrant to search for written documents" is illegal—*Nelson* v. *Black and Morrison (supra)*, referred to in *Stewart* v. *Roach* (1950 S.C. 318). Accordingly, as is shown by the form of warrant ordinarily craved and granted, a warrant must be specific as to the purpose and limitations of the search. The warrant used in practice authorises the securing "for the purpose of precognition and evidence, all writs tending to establish guilt or participation in the crime (or crimes) foresaid." In the present case the warrant of 20th May 1949 was specifically limited to the recovery of writs relating to the crime specified in that petition. It contained no authorisation of a search for or seizure and retention of any other writs. Consequently the retention of files and their contents which obviously did not bear upon the affairs of the person mentioned in the first charge was not authorised by the warrant and was illegal. The initial illegality was not cured by the granting of the second warrant six months later after the contents of the writs had been examined and used to enable the subsequent charges to be brought. Possession and use of the documents was not obtained under that second warrant. It was not retroactive. It authorised future and not past actions of officers of law. The argument of the Advocate-depute that the objection taken by the defence is technical is without substance. To hold that the second warrant nullified the complaint of misuse of the first would be to utilise the results achieved by an illegal act to wipe out the illegality. Accordingly I am of opinion that the warrant of 20th May 1949 only authorised the police officers to examine the documents in order to ascertain whether they fell within the scope of that warrant, and that the retention and examination of them in order to obtain evidence of other crimes was unauthorised and illegal. To reach the opposite conclusion would largely destroy the protection which the law affords to the citizen against invasion of his liberties by its requirement of the specific warrant of a magistrate for interference with these liberties.

I have found the second submission for the defence as to the admissibility of evidence so obtained a matter of greater difficulty.

[His Lordship then considered the principles governing the admissibility of evidence unlawfully seized, referring to *Lawrie* v. *Muir, infra*, p.266; *H.M. Advocate* v. *McGuigan, infra*, p.255; *McGovern* v. *H.M. Advocate*, 1950 J.C. 33 and *Fairley* v. *Fishmongers of London*, 1951 J.C. 14, and continued:]

In the present case there were, firstly, no circumstances of urgency. Secondly, the retention and use over a period of six months of the documents bearing to relate to other matters than that mentioned in the petition show that the actions complained of were deliberate. The police officers did not accidentally stumble upon evidence of a plainly incriminating character in the course of a search for a different purpose. If the documents are incriminating, their incriminating character is only exposed by careful consideration of their contents. Thirdly, if information was in the hands of the criminal authorities implicating the accused in other crimes, these could have been mentioned in the petition containing the warrant under which the search was authorised. If they had no such information, the examination of private papers in the hope of finding incriminating material was interference with the rights of a citizen. Therefore to hold that evidence so obtained was admissible would, as I have said, tend to nullify the protection afforded to a citizen by the requirement of a magistrate's warrant, and would offer a positive inducement to the authorities to proceed by irregular methods. Fourthly, when I consider the matter in the light of the principle of fairness to the accused, it appears to me that the evidence so irregularly and deliberately obtained is intended to be the basis of a comparison between the figures actually submitted to the inspector of taxes and the information in the possession of the accused. If such important evidence upon a number of charges is tainted by the method by which it was deliberately secured, I am of opinion that a fair trial upon these charges is rendered impossible.

Accordingly, when I apply the principles to be derived from the authorities to the facts of this case, I am driven to the conclusion that the objection taken to the admissibility of the documents is well founded. I shall therefore sustain the objection."

The court sustained
the objection.

4. H.M. Advocate v. Hepper
1958 J.C. 39

The accused was charged with the theft of a quantity of whisky and an attaché case. At the trial objection was taken to the admissibility in evidence of the discovery of the attaché case in the accused's possession. The circumstances are set out in the opinion of Lord Guthrie:

LORD GUTHRIE: "On 19th November 1957 police officers called at the residence of the accused on business not connected with the present charge. The accused was at home and consented to the police searching his house. In the course of his examination in the witness-box, the detective superintendent who called at the accused's house was asked whether he had taken possession of anything, and objection was taken to the line of evidence. Counsel for the panel stated that the consent to search was restricted to the business upon which the police had called at the accused's residence, and that, if the police in the course of that search discovered and removed an article which it was proposed to prove in evidence as relating to the present charge, such evidence should be excluded on the ground that it had been improperly obtained. Reference was made to *H.M. Advocate* v. *Turnbull* [*supra*, p.232] and *Jackson* v. *Stevenson* [*supra*, p.154]. In such cases, as the Lord Justice-Clerk, Lord Thomson, has repeatedly pointed out in recent years, the problem is always to reconcile the interest of society in the detection of crime with the requirement of fairness to an accused person. In the present case I am of opinion that the evidence is admissible. The police, in the course of their duty, when searching the accused's house with his consent in connexion with another matter, came upon the article which they removed. In *Turnbull* I distinguished that case, in which I excluded evidence as to documents taken possession of by police officers searching the accused's premises under a search warrant which clearly did not cover these documents, from a case in which police officers accidentally stumbled upon evidence of a plainly incriminating character in the course of a search for a different purpose. That distinction was based upon earlier authorities in which I was referred in *Turnbull's* case. It may be that the article which the police officers stumbled upon in their search of the accused's house was not an article of a plainly incriminating character, but it was at least an article of a very suspicious character, since it was an attaché case which contained within it the name and address of another person. In the circumstances, I do not think that the police officers acted in any way improperly in taking away that article in order to make further inquiries about it. If they had not done so, it might have disappeared. It appears to me that in the circumstances it was their duty, being officers charged with the protection of the public, to have acted as they did. But even if it cannot be put so highly, and if it be thought that their action was irregular, I am still of opinion that the evidence, even if irregularly obtained, is admissible in view of the interest of society in the detection of crime. I do not think that this is a case in which the evidence ought to be excluded because of a breach of the principle of fairness to the accused. I therefore hold that the evidence is admissible."

The court repelled
the objection.

NOTES

1.   The police in this case were not acting in the execution of a warrant, but with the consent of the accused. The situations are, however, analogous in that consent and a warrant both authorise the search. They differ, however, in that while the authority conferred by a warrant is determined by its terms, the authority conferred by consent depends not only on the limits of the consent, but on the power of the person granting it to do so. Could, for example, the 16-year-old daughter of a suspect grant authority to the police to search her parent's house? And see *Leckie* v. *Miln*, *infra*.

2.   The effect of *Turnbull* and *Hepper* is that the police, while searching under a warrant or with consent, cannot actively search for evidence beyond the limits of the warrant or consent. If, however, they happen upon evidence of a suspicious character, they may seize that evidence. There need be no connection between the "extra" items seized and the offence originally under investigation, nor need the police even suspect such a connection.

3.   Note the element of "urgency" in this case. The court was concerned that if the police had not seized the evidence "it might have disappeared."

5.   **Leckie v. Miln**

1982 S.L.T. 177; 1981 S.C.C.R. 261

The appellant was arrested on petition on a charge of theft from a dentist's surgery. The petition craved warrants in the usual terms, including warrant to search "the person repositories and domicile" of the accused for articles related to the charge. Warrant for search was granted as craved. Two police officers were informed that the accused had been arrested and were instructed to search the house occupied by Leckie and a Miss D. At no time did these officers have in their possession, or see, the petition, nor did they know the nature of the charge on which the accused had been arrested. On arrival at the house they informed Miss D that the appellant had been arrested on a petition warrant, and received her permission to search the house. During this search certain items were found which were later alleged to have been stolen from an office and a school. He was subsequently convicted of these thefts and appealed by stated case on the ground that the evidence of these thefts was wrongly admitted by the sheriff.

OPINION OF THE COURT: "... The findings-in-fact which describe the search are findings 8, 9 and 10. According to finding 8 two police officers learned from their inspector that the appellant had been arrested on petition at Perth on a charge of sneak theft. That was all they were told. They were then instructed by the inspector to go to the appellant's house and search it. This they proceeded to do. But finding 8 tells us that the officers in question never saw the petition upon which the appellant had been arrested; that they were completely unaware of the nature of any charge in that petition except to the extent that it was a charge of theft of the sneak theft variety; that they did not know at all what articles had been stolen during that theft and did not, of course, in the circumstances, have the petition in their possession, containing the warrant to search, when they went to the appellant's house. On arrival at the house they met a lady called Miss Dailly (known as Mrs Leckie) and they informed her that they were police officers and that the appellant had been arrested by the police at Perth on a petition warrant. Having said that they informed Miss Dailly that they wished to search the house. No objection to the proposed search was made. Finding 10 then describes the search which took place and the discovery, in the course of that search, of the business cards to which we have referred in the top drawer of a chest of drawers in the only bedroom of the house, a top drawer which contained the clothing of Miss Dailly, and the discovery of the library ticket and the receipt which we have already mentioned inside a jacket hanging in the wardrobe of that bedroom. For the appellant the submission was that the search which was carried out in all the circumstances disclosed in findings 8, 9 and 10 was quite unlawful in respect that it was neither authorised by the warrant to search in the petition on which the appellant had been arrested in Perth nor was it authorised by any implied consent given by Miss Dailly. If that submission is sound, as counsel for the appellant urged us to accept, then it followed, according to counsel, that the evidence given by the police officers about their findings was inadmissible. This is not a case in which officers carrying out an active search within the scope of a lawful warrant came across articles unrelated to the particular crime with which they were concerned. In such a case the finding of other articles indicating guilt of other crimes may be perfectly admissible in evidence. The fundamental proposition here was that neither upon the warrant nor upon any implied consent was the active unlimited search carried out by the officers justified in law. The Crown position was simply this. There existed, no doubt, authority for a search of the appellant's premises and that authority was the warrant granted upon the petition on which the appellant had appeared in Perth. It is the case that the officers admittedly did not carry out an active search within the limitations of that warrant to search for they were wholly ignorant of the contents of the petition and the scope of the warrant to search granted upon its presentation. But given the authority for a lawful search of the premises, the search which was carried out was carried out by the officers in the manner in which they carried it out with the full consent given by Miss Dailly by plain implication. The question in the case therefore comes to be whether Miss Dailly did give consent for the unlimited search carried out by the officers. . . . We are of opinion that by no stretch of the imagination can it be said that the consent given by Miss Dailly was consent for an active unlimited search regardless of the limitations in the warrant which admittedly existed. Finding 9 tells us that before Miss Dailly was informed that the officers wished to search the premises they told Miss Dailly that they were police officers and that the appellant had been arrested by the police at Perth on a petition warrant. It follows from that that any consent given by Miss Dailly must be assumed to have been given upon the footing that the officers intended to carry out a search within the authority contained in the warrant to which they referred, and that authority was, it is perfectly plain, an authority of a limited character. The search was nothing of the kind for, as we have already pointed out, the officers had no knowledge of the contents of the petition and what they did was to carry out a random search of the appellant's house in the hope of finding something which might conceivably have been the proceeds of a sneak theft anywhere. In these circumstances we are satisfied that the evidence of the finding of labels 2 and 4 should not have been admitted and if that is right then it follows that the conviction cannot stand for the evidence aliunde was insufficient to warrant the conviction of the appellant."

Convictions quashed.

NOTES

1.   Objectively speaking, the warrant authorised a fairly extensive search, and had the police officers known of the terms of that warrant the seizure of items relating to different thefts would have been justified under the *Hepper* principle. But where the police are ignorant of the terms of a warrant any search carried out must be random and therefore unlawful.

2.   The court held that since the police referred to the warrant when obtaining Miss D's consent, her consent was limited to a search of the nature authorised by the warrant. Would this follow if (a) it was shown that Miss D had no idea of the limited authority conferred by the warrant, or mistakenly thought it conferred a much wider authority; (b) the police had not mentioned the warrant at all but merely asked to search the house?

3.   For a full discussion of this case see Finnie, "Police Powers of Search in the light of *Leckie* v. *Miln*," 1982 S.L.T. 289.

4.   In *Tierney* v. *Allan*, 1989 S.C.C.R. 334 the police were in possession of a warrant to search the appellant's house for stolen gas cylinders. During the search one officer came across a typewriter under a cot. Another officer identified the typewriter as of a type similar to some which he knew had been reported stolen. The appellant was charged with reset of the typewriter. At his trial the sheriff held that evidence of the finding of the typewriter was admissible. The sheriff's decision on this point was upheld on appeal:

LORD JUSTICE-GENERAL: "Now the submission was, in the first place, that on the evidence of [P.C.] Byrne, he was deliberately searching for material which was not identified in the warrant. The second submission was that he did search in a place where he did not expect to find gas cylinders and the third submission was that in finding the typewriter, there was nothing plainly incriminating about it and Byrne had accordingly no business in retrieving it and enquiring about it further. The typewriter was, as we have said, beneath the cot. The answer to the submission depends upon how we interpret the circumstances of the discovery. A lawful search was undoubtedly going on on the faith of the warrant. As we see it, P.C. Byrne came across a typewriter which, on the face of it, was in a place where typewriters would not normally be expected to be found. That is probably why it aroused his suspicion and that is probably why, when P.C. Russell saw it, he confirmed the suspicion by finding that it looked very like one stolen from Gracemount High School. Having regard to the nature of the place where the typewriter was, it does not appear to us that there was a deliberate search beneath the cot. A typewriter beneath a cot is something which would be seen upon a glance in that direction and what the case really comes to is that there was a lawful search during which one officer came across a typewriter in a strange place unexpectedly. It aroused suspicion with the consequences that we know. In all the circumstances this was not a case of random search as was dealt with in the case of *Leckie* v. *Miln* [1982 S.L.T. 177, *supra*, p.235.] It was the unexpected

discovery of an article which aroused suspicion during the course of a lawful
search for the material listed in the warrant. What we shall accordingly do is to
answer question 1 in the case in the negative and answer question 5 in the case
in the affirmative, and refuse the appeal."

5.   *Tierney* v. *Allan* should be contrasted with *Innes* v. *Jessop*, 1989
S.C.C.R. 441. In that case the appellant was charged with reset of a driving
licence and a tax exemption certificate. These items were found by the
police while searching the appellant's house for firearms and ammunition
under a warrant issued under the Firearms Acts 1968 and 1982. Several
other items were seized at the same time. No firearms or ammunition were
found. On appeal it was held that the search had been random and
therefore unlawful:

> LORD WYLIE: "In the course of the search of the house a detective sergeant
> found the driving licence and the subcontractor's tax certificate on the
> windowsill of the appellant's bedroom lying among other documents. These
> items were seized as productions and identified in court as being the items
> found in the appellant's house and they were likewise of course identified by
> the persons whose name they bore. Finding 8 makes reference to a whole
> variety of other items which were seized in the course of this search and
> included two coach-builder's slide hammers, a container with tablets, a pair of
> gloves, a balaclava-style face mask, a crossbow bolt and a knife. The one thing
> which was not found in the search was either a firearm or any firearm
> ammunition.
>
> A submission was made at the close of the Crown case, ... that there was no
> case to answer and the presiding judge repelled that submission. What has
> concerned us is that while the police were legitimately carrying out a search of
> premises in the context of a warrant entitling them to do so but which related
> to firearms and ammunition, they produced and recovered the two items with
> which this charge is concerned as well as the numerous other items to which
> we have referred as set out in finding 8. ... It is our feeling that particularly the
> findings set out in finding 8 carry with them an implication that the search
> which was carried out in this instance was more in the nature of a random
> search and in these circumstances we have come to the view that it would be
> unsafe to sustain this conviction. Accordingly we shall answer the three
> questions put in the negative and allow the appeal."

(B)   Search Without Prior Arrest

It is no objection to the competency of a search warrant that the person
whose premises are named therein has not been arrested or charged with
an offence.

1.   Stewart v. Roach
1950 S.C. 318

The pursuers brought an action of damages in the sheriff court against a
police officer on the ground that he had wrongly carried out a search
(under a warrant) of their house at a time when they had been neither
arrested nor charged. The sheriff found for the pursuers, and awarded
them £30 damages each. The defender appealed to the Court of Session,
where the case was heard by the First Division and three consulted judges
of the Second Division.

LORD PRESIDENT (COOPER) (delivering the opinion of the consulted judges, with whom the members of the First Division concurred): "This case was sent to seven Judges on the question 'whether it is illegal to grant and execute a warrant to search for stolen goods the premises of a person who has not been apprehended nor charged with an offence.'

The sole point taken is that the searches were wrongous because the pursuers were neither charged nor apprehended before the warrants were applied for and obtained. Prior charge or apprehension is said to be an essential prerequisite. Otherwise, the warrants are admitted to be sufficiently specific and the procedure regular.

It is difficult to see on principle why the lesser invasion of the pursuers' rights involved in a search of their houses for stolen goods should be objectionable simply because the more extreme step of charging or apprehending them had not been taken. However that may be, it was argued to us that the matter was concluded by authority, and particularly by a decision of the High Court of Justiciary—M'Lauchlan v. Renton [(1910) 6 Adam 378].

[The circumstances of that case were outlined, and the following observations of Lord Salvesen quoted:

'There can be no doubt, at common law, it is illegal to grant a warrant to search the premises of any citizen who has not been charged with an offence, however much the Crown authorities may have reason for suspicion against him.']

Lord Salvesen gives no authority for this pronouncement, but it is clear from the argument presented that the supposed basis of the doctrine is Bell v. Black and Morrison ...

The opinion of the Court [in that case] was delivered by the Lord Justice-Clerk. Three grounds for the decision are stated:—'In the first place, the warrant is granted against five different persons, none of whom is under a charge for any crime. It is stated in the petition that the persons against whom the warrant is asked are shown, by documents recovered in the course of the precognition against Pringle, to have been engaged in the same conspiracy, and in writing and sending threatening letters. But as no charge has yet been made against any of these five persons, this amounts to no more than a statement of the suspicion or belief of the Procurators-fiscal that they are implicated in the same crimes as Pringle.'

[The remaining grounds were here outlined.]

It will be observed that the first of these grounds is relevant to the present topic and indeed, as it turns out, is the only basis on which the argument for the pursuers rests. Had the Court regarded a charge as an essential prerequisite, we think that the opinion would have said so in terms and, indeed, that would have been decisive without further elaboration. It seems to us clear not only from the way in which the first ground is worded but also from the incidental reference to the absence of a criminal charge in the course of the formulation of the third ground, that they regarded the absence of charge as only one element for consideration in conjunction with the other circumstances of the case. The substance of the opinion is that, in the whole circumstances disclosed, what was sought was far too wide and not fenced with sufficient safeguards, especially having in view that no charge had been preferred. That this is the true emphasis of the opinion appears from this later passage:—'The seizure of papers, as distinguished from their recovery as articles of evidence, and also as distinguished from the seizure of other articles which are invested with no character of confidentiality or secrecy, is, under all circumstances, a matter of extreme delicacy. But the seizure of papers made in the circumstances with which we have to deal, is a proceeding quite unknown to the law of Scotland.'

That this is the true view of this case is borne out by what was said by the

Judges who took part in two subsequent cases in the Court of Session arising out of the same matter.

[The court referred to the opinions in *Bell* v. *Black and Morrison* (1865) 5 Irvine 57 and *Nelson* v. *Black and Morrison* (1866) 4 M. 328, *supra*, and continued:]

It is apparent that the First Division with both the previous cases before them give no countenance to the view that charge or apprehension is a prerequisite. Indeed, the opinion of Lord Deas goes far to negative it, while the opinion of Lord Ardmillan shows that he did not understand the opinion of the Court in the suspension as turning on that point.

In these circumstances we come without hesitation to the conclusion that charge or apprehension is not an essential prerequisite to the granting of a search warrant and that the proposition in *M'Lauchlan* v. *Renton* is too broadly stated. Special circumstances productive of exceptional hardship may make the granting of a search warrant illegal, and in such cases the absence of charge or apprehension may be a relevant consideration but will not *per se* render the warrant illegal. That is a very different thing from stating as a proposition of general application that 'it is illegal to grant a warrant to search the premises of any citizen who has not been charged with an offence, however much the Crown authorities may have reason for suspicion against him.'"

The court allowed the appeal and assoilzied the defender.

NOTE

The ratio of this case is not confined to searches of premises. The decision was followed in *Hay* v. *H.M. Advocate*, 1968 S.L.T. 334 (*infra*) which concerned a warrant to search the person of a suspect.

2. MacNeill, Complainer
1983 S.C.C.R. 450

The complainer was procurator-fiscal of Aberdeen. He had presented a petition to the sheriff craving warrant to search certain premises for obscene books, magazines and other articles which the complainer believed were being held at those premises with a view to their sale in contravention of section 51(2) of the Civic Government (Scotland) Act 1982. The sheriff refused the crave of the petition on the ground that the 1982 Act did not empower him to grant such a warrant. The complainer presented a Bill of Advocation to the High Court.

LORD CAMERON: "The learned sheriff has helpfully explained his decision in a note which he wrote on the petition which sets out his reasons. I do not think I do injustice to the sheriff's reasoning if I say that his ground of judgment is set out in [the] sentence: 'In the absence of statutory provision authorising search of premises to see if such a statutory offence [i.e., an offence under section 51(2) of the Act in question] was being committed (as for instance in drugs cases) I did not consider there was power in the court to grant warrant to search the premises.'

Section 51(2) of the Civic Government (Scotland) Act 1982 provides:

'Subject to subsection (4) below, any person who publishes, sells or distributes or, with a view to its eventual sale or distribution, makes, prints, has or keeps any obscene material shall be guilty of an offence under this section.'

It is to be noted that there is no specific provision in the statute for a power of search in cases of suspicion of breaches of section 51(2). The powers of search or seizure without warrant which by section 60 are conferred on constables relate to a limited category of offences and circumstances and have no application to an offence in breach of section 51.

For the Crown it was submitted by the advocate-depute that the power of the procurator fiscal to apply for and obtain a search warrant derived from the common law and was not inhibited by the silence of the 1982 Act as to authority to search. The power of the procurator fiscal arose out of the common law and in the matter of incidental warrant prior to the service of a complaint, was made subject of express statutory reference in section 310 of the Criminal Procedure (Scotland) Act 1975.

Contraventions of section 51(2) of the 1982 Act could be prosecuted on summary complaint. In section 310 of the Act of 1975 no distinction is made between proceedings initiated by complaint or by petition. The fact that there may or may not be in certain statutes specific provisions relative to the obtaining of warrants to search does not affect or diminish the common law powers of the procurator fiscal. The advocate-depute referred to the case of *Watson* v. *Muir*, 1938 J.C. 181, especially Lord Justice-General Normand and Lord Fleming at p.185, a case in which all the procedure under consideration took place before the service of a complaint, in support of his submission. In the Civic Government Act itself, the sections dealing with powers of arrest and search were directed towards the powers of a constable in relation to certain specified offences. These provisions could not be interpreted to limit or extinguish pro tanto the common law powers of the procurator fiscal. These powers could not be affected unless made the subject of specific statutory provisions. There was none such here. The statutory provisions referred to by the sheriff were not concerned with nor did they mention the common law powers of the procurator fiscal with the single exception of the Public Order Act 1936 where the statutory provision governing applications for a search warrant contained in section 2(5) was specifically applied to Scotland and the procurator fiscal named, by section 8(3). This related solely to the material or evidence upon which a warrant to search could be granted in a petition at the instance of the fiscal. In these circumstances the basis of the sheriff's reasoning was fatally undermined. Where, as here, there was no mention of the procurator fiscal's common law powers, these remained entire; they could only be limited or extinguished by specific reference and express wording. The learned sheriff had misdirected himself and his decision should be recalled and the case remitted to him to grant the crave of the petition.

In my opinion the submission for the Crown is correct and in accordance with the principles of our criminal law. In the case of *McMillan* v. *Grant; Rippie* v. *Grant*, 1924 J.C. 13, Lord Sands in considering whether a procurator fiscal has power at common law to prosecute a statutory offence, said:

'The Sheriff Court is the King's Court in the Sheriffdom, and the King's Court has jurisdiction in common law to take cognisance of any offence against the King's peace within the Sheriffdom, unless its jurisdiction to do so is expressly excluded by statute. An offence against a statutory enactment is an offence against the King's peace, and accordingly the Sheriff court has, at common law, jurisdiction to take cognisance of it. This consideration, as it appears to me, involves that the Procurator-fiscal, as the representative of the Crown in the Sheriff Court, may prosecute any offence cognisable by that Court, unless his title to do so has, either expressly or by necessary implication, been withdrawn by statute' (at 22–23).

To enable him properly to discharge his functions the procurator fiscal has at common law certain powers which include the power to search under warrant, and as Lord Justice-General Normand put it in *Watson v. Muir*, 1938 J.C. 181 at 184:

> '[I]t must be remembered that, from ancient times, the procurator-fiscal as the public prosecutor in Scotland has had powers to search in the course of his duties when he is investigating crime. It is doubtless true that that power of search depends upon obtaining a legal warrant for search. But it has never been doubted that it is unnecessary for the procurator-fiscal to obtain a legal warrant to search if the party in possession of, or having the custody of, any article of which the procurator-fiscal desires to obtain possession is willing to yield possession.'

This common law power to search extends to a power to search premises under warrant in a case where no person has as yet been arrested or charged (c.f., *Stewart v. Roach*, 1950 S.C. 318), the form of the requisite warrant being prescribed in section 310 of the Criminal Procedure (Scotland) Act 1975.

If then the procurator fiscal in virtue of his common law powers as representing the Crown in the sheriff court has jurisdiction to prosecute all offences cognisable there, whether statutory or common law, it must necessarily follow that, unless his common law power of search is expressly and specifically abridged or excluded by the provisions of the statute or regulation creating the offence, his common law powers remain intact. It is significant that in none of the statutes referred to by the sheriff in his note, citing examples quoted in Renton and Brown, 4th edn, para. 5–29, with the single exception of the Public Order Act 1936, is the common law power of search exercisable by the procurator fiscal specifically and directly referred to. Thus the powers of arrest and search referred to in the Salmon and Freshwater Fisheries (Protection) Scotland Act 1951, and set out in section 11(1), relate specifically to water bailiffs, constables and persons authorised by the Secretary of State to exercise the powers of a water bailiff. No mention of or reference to the procurator fiscal or his powers is contained in the Act. In the Firearms Act 1968, which is a United Kingdom statute, there is no mention of the powers of a procurator fiscal, and section 58(4) of the Act provides inter alia: 'The powers of arrest and entry conferred by Part III of this Act shall be without prejudice to any power of arrest or entry which may exist apart from this Act . . .', and Part III of the Act, headed 'Law Enforcement and Punishment of Offences', provides for the exercise by a constable of a power of search on a warrant obtained 'by information on oath'—but contains no reference to the common law power of the procurator fiscal. Clearly, where no specific reference is made to the power of the procurator fiscal eo nomine, no foundation can exist for the proposition that his common law jurisdiction or ancillary powers are limited or extinguished. In the Public Order Act 1936 the necessity for supporting an application for a search warrant by evidence on oath is specifically enacted by section 2(5) and this provision is made applicable in Scotland by section 8(3) which enacts that 'any application for a search warrant under the said subsection shall be made by the procurator fiscal instead of such officer as is therein mentioned'. This is a restrictive provision, restrictive in respect of the nature of the material upon which an application for a search warrant may be made but not of the power.

Parliament has given no reason for this restriction, though one may speculate that the politically sensitive subject-matter with which the statute deals could have led to such restriction on the manner of the exercise of the undoubted power of the procurator fiscal. Having regard to the position of the procurator fiscal in our Scottish scheme of criminal administration as representative of the Crown in the sheriff court charged with the duty of prosecuting offences cognisable in that court and with a consequent and necessary power of search in respect of all such offences be they common law or statutory, I am clearly of opinion that the power can only be taken away by express statutory provision or by necessary and inevitable implication. There is no such provision in the Civic Government (Scotland) Act 1982; it is of course true that in sections 59 and 60 of this Act specific powers to arrest and search persons and certain specified premises are given to be exercised without warrant, but as already noted these provisions and powers relate to constables: nowhere are the powers of the procurator fiscal in any way affected (except insofar as the provisions of section 8(3) of the Public Order Act 1936 are imported into the operation of the fasciculus of provisions in sections 62–65, a matter which does not arise in this case).

In my opinion therefore the learned sheriff misdirected himself in thinking that where a statute creating an offence did not specifically provide for a right and power to search on suspicion and for the manner in which that power was to be exercised in Scotland, whether the statute was of United Kingdom generality or applicable to Scotland alone, the common law power of the procurator fiscal was thereby extinguished in respect of such offence. In my opinion, having regard to the basic principles of this matter, the common law jurisdiction and powers of the procurator fiscal remain entire unless abridged or extinguished by specific and clear enactment. There being no such provision in the statute here the sheriff should have entertained the application for warrant to search. I would therefore pass the bill and remit to the sheriff to proceed as accords."

The court passed the Bill.

NOTE

This case confirms that the common law power of the procurator-fiscal to search premises under warrant, prior to arrest or charge, extends to search in connection with statutory offences as well as common law offences. The case also confirms that the fiscals powers in this respect cannot be excluded by implication. If they are to be "abridged or excluded" this must be done "expressly and specifically" by the statute or regulation creating the offence. The common law powers, therefore, will not only operate in the absence of statutory provision for a search warrant (as in this case) but will co-exist with statutory powers unless expressly excluded. See, in this connection, *Normand, Complainer*, 1992 S.C.C.R. 426.

(C) Personal Search Under Warrant

It is competent to obtain a warrant to search the person of a suspect who has not been arrested.

Hay v. H.M. Advocate
1968 S.L.T. 334

OPINION OF THE COURT (Five judges): "The appellant ... was found guilty ... on a charge of murdering L.P. When her body was found there were marks on her right breast of a human bite which had been inflicted at or about the time of her death. The precise shape and configurations of this bite formed an important element in the identification at the trial of the appellant as the murderer. Evidence was led from witnesses called on behalf of the Crown to show that the peculiarities of the tooth structure in the appellant's mouth exactly fitted the marks of the bite on the girl's breast. It was not in dispute that if that evidence was properly admitted there was ample evidence, if the jury accepted it, of identification of the appellant as the person who caused them.

At the trial a question arose as to the competency of the course adopted on behalf of the Crown to secure evidence of the configuration of the appellant's teeth. In view of the importance of the matter the presiding judge heard argument upon it along with two other judges. The presiding judge held that the course adopted on behalf of the Crown was competent and intimated that the two other judges concurred in this view. He therefore allowed the evidence. After the appellant had been convicted he appealed and a special sitting of five judges has therefore been convened to hear the appeal.

The appellant at the time of the offence was an inmate of Loaningdale Approved School which is situated not far from the scene of the crime. In an endeavour to identify the person who made the marks, and to eliminate the innocent, impressions of the teeth of some 29 inmates of the school (including the appellant) and of the staff there were obtained with their consent. As a result all 29 were eliminated with the exception of the appellant. The Crown's advisers then expressed a desire for a more elaborate and scientific examination of the appellant's teeth in order to enable them to express a confident opinion one way or the other. An application was accordingly presented by the procurator-fiscal to a sheriff-substitute for a warrant to the police to convey the appellant to the Glasgow Dental Hospital, and to grant warrant to two named medical men there to take such further dental impressions, photographs and measurements of the teeth of the appellant as they might consider reasonably necessary for and furtherance of the comparisons of his teeth with the marks on the murdered girl. The sheriff-substitute considered the petition and granted the warrant as craved. The appellant was not present nor represented at the hearing before the sheriff-substitute. When the warrant was obtained the appellant had not yet been apprehended, although he was obviously under considerable suspicion...

As regards the first and main issue in the appeal—namely the legality of the warrant—it has been observed in more than one of the cases (e.g., *Adair* v. *McGarry*, 1933 J.C. 72) that two conflicting considerations arise. On the one hand, there is the need from the point of view of public interest for promptitude and facility in the identification of accused persons and the discovery on their persons or on their premises of indicia either of guilt or innocence. On the other hand, the liberty of the subject must be protected against any undue or unnecessary invasion of it.

In an endeavour as fairly as possible to hold the balance between these two considerations three general principles have been recognised and established by the Court. In the first place, once an accused has been apprehended, and therefore deprived of his liberty, the police have the right to search and examine him. In the second place, before the police have reached a stage in their investigation when they feel warranted in apprehending him they have in general no right by the common law of Scotland to search or examine him or his premises without his consent. There may be circumstances, such as urgency or risk of evidence being lost, which would justify an immediate search or examination, but in the general case they cannot take this step at their own hand. But in the third place, even before the apprehension of the accused they may be entitled to carry out a search of his premises or an examination of his person without his consent if they apply to a magistrate for a warrant for this purpose. Although the accused is not present nor legally represented at the hearing where the magistrate grants the warrant to examine or to search, the interposition of an independent judicial officer holds the basis for a fair reconciliation of the interests of the public in the suppression of crime and of the individual who is entitled not to have the liberty of his person or his premises unduly jeopardised. A warrant of this limited kind will only, however, be granted in special circumstances. The hearing before the magistrate is by no means a formality, and he must be satisfied that the circumstances justify the taking of this unusual course, and that the warrant asked for is not too wide or oppressive. For he is the safeguard against the grant of too general a warrant.

We were referred to a series of cases which appear to us to confirm the propositions above set forth. In *Jackson* v. *Stevenson* (1897) 24 R.(J.) 38, (4 S.L.T. 277), the Lord Justice-Clerk, at p.41, said: 'I know of no authority for ascribing to constables the right to make such tentative searches (i.e., before apprehension) and they seem contrary to constitutional principle. If a constable requires to make such a search it can only be because without it he is not justified in apprehending: and without a warrant, to search a person not liable to apprehension seems palpably illegal.' (Compare Lord Kinnear, at p.42). In *Adamson* v. *Martin*, 1916, 1 S.L.T. 53, 1916 S.C. 319, it was held that the taking of photographs and fingerprint impressions by the police of an accused who had not been apprehended was illegal at common law and under the statute. As Lord Guthrie said at p.331: 'The pursuer not having been in custody, and the police not having obtained a warrant, the photographs and fingerprints were unwarrantably obtained.'

This case was distinguished in *Adair* v. *McGarry* (*supra*), where fingerprints were held to have been lawfully taken. But the reason was that in this latter case the accused had been apprehended. In the opinions of the judges there are references to a magistrates' warrant which, in the view of the Court, would legalise the taking of fingerprints from a man who has not yet been apprehended (see Lord Justice-General, at p.78). It was argued to us that as this was a fingerprint case the warrant in question was a warrant obtained under the regulations made in virtue of the Penal Servitude Act 1891. But this contention is unsound. The Court was dealing with common law warrants and the statute and regulations were held not to affect the issue. The observations of the judges are therefore inconsistent with the present appellant's contention.

The case of *Stewart* v. *Roach*, 1950 S.C. 318, 1950 S.L.T. 245, decided that it was competent to grant and execute warrants to search the houses of suspected persons prior to apprehension: If the safeguard of obtaining a warrant for this purpose makes it lawful in the case of a man not yet apprehended it seems difficult to appreciate why a similar safeguard in the case of such an accused should not equally legalise an examination of his person after a warrant for that purpose has been obtained.

Lastly, we were referred to *McGovern* v. *H.M. Advocate*, 1950 J.C. 33, 1950 S.L.T. 133. In that case scrapings from the finger nails of an accused person were taken without his consent and before his apprehension. The evidence so obtained was held to be incompetent. The distinction between that case and the present is that in that case the evidence was obtained without any warrant from a magistrate.

In the circumstances of the present case the obtaining of the warrant prior to the examination in question in our opinion rendered the examination quite legal, and the evidence which resulted from it was therefore competent."

The court refused
the appeal.

    1.   The court went on to hold that even if it had found that the warrant was illegal they would nonetheless have upheld the admissibility of the evidence, either on the ground of "urgency" (as to which, see *infra*, p.254) or in the exercise of the court's discretion to overlook irregularities in the obtaining of evidence (as to which, see *infra*, p.266).
    2.   Although the court refers to the need to maintain a balance between the interests of the public in the detection of crime and the need to protect the liberty of the subject it gives very little indication of the criteria to be applied in striking that balance. The court does say that a warrant of this kind will only be granted in "special circumstances," but again there is no indication of what those circumstances might be.
    Some guidance on these matters can be obtained from *Morris* v. *MacNeill*, 1991 S.C.C.R. 722. In that case the prosecutor sought a warrant to take a blood sample from the complainer who was suspected of breaking into a house and stealing £5,000 of jewellery therefrom. Blood had been found on a window in the house which belonged to the same group as blood found on clothing belonging to the complainer (who had been arrested in relation to a quite separate matter). In granting the warrant the sheriff held, relying, *inter alia*, on *Hay*, that it was competent for him to grant a warrant, before arrest, to search a person or to take blood or other sample from him. His Lordship then continued (1991 S.C.C.R. 722 at p.723):

> "Turning now to the question of whether I should grant or refuse the warrant. I must weigh the interests of the public in the suppression of crime and the interests of the individual, who is entitled not to have the liberty of his person unduly jeopardised (*H.M. Advocate* v. *Milford*, 1973 S.L.T. 12). I must only grant the warrant if I am persuaded that the circumstances are special. I am not prepared to accept ... [the] contention that the crime of housebreaking involving the theft of property worth a considerable sum is not a very serious crime. I can see no distinction in principle between a housebreaking and assault. Both are serious crimes. The analysis of blood will ... greatly assist in the clearing up of the ... housebreaking by either eliminating or implicating [the complainer]. The invasion of [the complainer's] body in obtaining a blood sample is minimal. The blood sample is to be taken by a highly qualified doctor. I am, therefore, persuaded that I should grant the warrant."

    The High Court held that the sheriff had adopted the proper approach to the granting of the warrant. The first step is to determine whether or not the circumstances are "special." The second involves the weighing of the public interest against that of the accused.
    3.   For the position of twins see *Smith* v. *Cardle*, 1993 S.C.C.R. 609.

(i) Special circumstances

The court held that the sheriff was entitled to hold that the circumstances were "special": (a) because the crime was a serious one; and (b) because the analysis of the blood would assist in clearing up the crime, either by implicating or eliminating the complainer.
    As to the first of these considerations it appears that the question is whether the alleged offence is a serious example of that type of offence ("Is this a serious case of theft, robbery, assault, etc?") rather than whether the

alleged offence is of a type which would always be considered serious, such as murder or rape. It remains to be seen what the courts will consider to be "serious" for these purposes. Warrants for personal search after committal have been granted in cases of assault and robbery (*Frame* v. *Houston*, 1991 S.C.C.R. 436), offences against the Misuse of Drugs Act 1971 involving drugs with a street value of £100,000 (*Lees* v. *Weston*, 1989 S.C.C.R. 177), rape (*H.M. Advocate* v. *Milford*, 1973 S.L.T. 12; *McGlennan* v. *Kelly*, 1989 S.C.C.R. 352; *G.* v. *Lees*, 1992 S.C.C.R. 252), murder (*Hay, supra., Currie* v. *McGlennan*, 1989 S.C.C.R. 466) and robbery and attempted murder (*Begley* v. *Normand*, 1992 S.C.C.R. 230). In *Hughes* v. *Normand*, 1992 S.C.C.R. 908, a case of assault and stabbing to severe injury, a warrant to take a blood sample from the complainer was granted but subsequently suspended as premature; after the case had been indicted for trial, a fresh warrant was sought and granted: see *Hughes* v. *Normand*, 1993 S.C.C.R. 69.

It is rather curious to see the second consideration—the value of the blood test in the process of investigation—being treated as an element of the "special circumstances" of the case. Either it suggests that the outcome of the analysis was especially significant in this case, or there is something almost tautological in the argument. Presumably, the prosecutor would not in any case seek a warrant to conduct tests which were wholly speculative or which were not expected to be of assistance in clearing up the matter under investigation. But in the event of such a request being made, it is probably as well that the courts have taken the view that a warrant should not be granted unless the procedure to be undertaken "would" assist in clearing up the matter.

(ii)   The balancing of interests

The supposed balance to be struck is between the public interest in clearing up the offence and the interest of the suspect. As has already been pointed out this simple distinction is questionable (*supra*, p.5). The public interest is not only in having the offence cleared up. The public also have an interest in ensuring that the rights of persons in the position of the complainer are protected. It is interesting to note that in *Lees* v. *Weston*, 1989 S.C.C.R. 177 the High Court appears to recognise that there is more to this issue than a simple dichotomy between public and individual interest:

> "The applicant for the warrant must show good cause; and the public interest in the proper prosecution of crime has to be balanced against the liberty of the citizen and the interests of the accused." (1989 S.C.R.R. 177, *per* Lord Murray at p.185.)

One factor which weighed heavily with the sheriff and the High Court in the case of *Morris* v. *MacNeill* was the extent of the personal invasion involved in the search, which was thought to be "minimal" and one which was not likely to cause the complainer any danger. The same considerations could be said to apply to other procedures, such as the taking of hair samples (*Frame* v. *Houston, supra*), and even pubic hair samples (*McGlennan* v. *Kelly, supra*).

If, on the other hand, the procedures cannot be carried out without risk to the subject then clearly no warrant should be granted. The possibility that the procedures might cause distress to the subject was raised as an objection in *G.* v. *Lees, supra.* In this case, warrant was granted to take blood samples from the complainer who had been fully committed on charges of rape and assault and released on bail. The complainer presented a Bill of Suspension to the High Court in which it was averred that the complainer suffered from a severe fear of needles and that in view of the amount of blood which would be required for the tests contemplated in the application for the warrant (DNA profiling) the warrant should be set aside. In response to these submissions the High Court modified the warrant so as to limit the taking of blood by finger pricks.

Where, however, the intended search involves a substantial violation of the person of the suspect, or where it cannot be carried out without risk to the health of the subject, or without distress to the subject then, it is submitted, the warrant should not be granted.

A further factor which has carried some weight with the court in determining this issue of "balance" is that in cases of search, as opposed to questioning, the accused is not required to take an "active" part in the proceedings. In *Lees* v. *Weston, supra,* an application for a warrant to take fingerprints after full committal, the Lord Justice-Clerk observed (at pp.183–184):

> "As Lord Sands observed in *Adair* v. *McGarry* [1933 J.C. 72, *supra*, p.155], a person whose fingerprints are forcibly taken
>
> > 'is entirely passive, and he is not compelled to do anything requiring any exercise of his own will or control of his body' [at p.89].
>
> Accordingly, in my opinion, to require an accused person to provide finger impressions is materially different from interrogating an accused person and requiring him to answer questions. No positive action is required of a person whose fingerprints are being taken."

Is this a strong argument? Unlike the case of interrogation, where a person has the right to remain silent, and where the suspect ultimately can control the investigator's access to information, fingerprinting, and other searches such as the taking of blood samples, effectively compel the suspect to provide evidence. And it should be recalled that once a warrant is granted, officers executing the warrant may use reasonable force to do so, so that any "passivity" which is non-co-operative may result in a measure of physical coercion.

Without a warrant the police may not search the person of a suspect (or any other person) prior to arrest unless this is permitted by statute or justified on grounds of urgency, and, in the latter case, it is submitted that a search excused on the ground of urgency is subject to conditions which are at least as stringent as a search authorised by a warrant, at least in respect of the form of the search.

In a sequence of recent cases the courts have been called upon to determine the legality and the appropriateness of granting warrants authorising personal search of, or other procedures involving, accused persons at a much later stage in the criminal process (in particular after the accused has been fully committed). Two questions arise from these cases: (i) What circumstances justify granting warrant at this stage? (ii) How late in the day may such a warrant be granted? The following cases discuss these two issues:

1. **Lees v. Weston**
1989 S.C.C.R. 177

The respondent had been fully committed on seven charges involving drugs, ranging from being concerned in the supply of a Class A drug (cocaine) to possession of cannabis resin, all contrary to relevant sections of the Misuse of Drugs Act 1971. Nearly two months after full committal the procurator-fiscal presented a petition to the sheriff for a warrant to take the respondent's fingerprints. It appeared that because of a misunderstanding between the two police offices which had been involved in his initial arrest and custody his fingerprints had not been taken. The failure to take fingerprints came to light more than a month after the arrest when a report was being prepared on a fingerprint impression found on a paper fold of a type usually used for the illicit distribution of controlled drugs which had been seized by the police as a production.

In refusing to grant the warrant the sheriff noted the general rule that an accused person cannot be obliged to provide evidence against himself after he has been fully committed, and held that there were no special features in this case which warranted departure form that rule. In his view the court should not lend itself to curing an administrative error by the police.

LORD JUSTICE-CLERK: "There was no dispute as to the right of the police to take fingerprints before full committal. It was not disputed that at common law the police are entitled to take the fingerprints of an arrested person without his consent and without any warrant up to the stage of full committal (*Adair* v. *McGarry*). Further, in terms of section 2(5)(*c*) of the Criminal Justice (Scotland) Act 1980, where a person has been detained under section 2(1), a constable may take fingerprints, palm prints and such other prints and impressions as he may, having regard to the circumstances of the suspected offence, reasonably consider appropriate. Section 2(6) provides that in exercising such a power a constable may use reasonable force.

Counsel, however, recognised that a distinction falls to be drawn between the position before committal and the position after an accused has been fully committed. In *Adair* v. *McGarry* the Lord Justice-Clerk stressed this distinction, and pointed out that the rights of the police are wider where a person is detained on suspicion than they are once he has been fully committed. He pointed out that the police may arrest a suspect and interrogate him, but that no interrogation is permitted after committal.

The advocate-depute founded on two cases where warrant was granted to take a sample of the blood of an accused person who had been fully committed. Such a warrant was granted by a sheriff in *H.M. Advocate* v. *Milford*. The sheriff stressed that it was necessary to reach a fair reconciliation of the interests of the public in the suppression of crime and the interests of the individual who is entitled not to have the liberty of his person unduly jeopardised. He expressed the view that a warrant of this kind would only be granted in special circumstances. The soundness of that decision was challenged in *Wilson* v. *Milne*. The court, however, rejected the criticism made of *H.M. Advocate* v. *Milford* and indeed approved of the approach of the sheriff in that case. The Lord Justice-General, after referring to *H.M. Advocate* v. *Milford*, stated [at p.27]:

'From these cases it is clear that it is not incompetent to grant warrant to take a blood sample from an accused person. It is equally clear, however, that such a warrant ought not to be lightly granted and it may safely be said ought only to be granted where the circumstances are special and where the granting of the warrant will not disturb the delicate balance which must be maintained between the public interest and the interest of the accused.'

The advocate-depute also referred to *Smith* v. *Innes*, but that case was truly a unique case and was different from the present case.

It is plain from the report provided by the sheriff that he based his decision upon the general rule that an accused person cannot be obliged to provide evidence against himself after he has been fully committed. Although that is no doubt a sound general rule, it must be borne in mind that an accused person is not required to take any positive action when providing finger impressions, but has a purely passive role. As Lord Sands observed in *Adair* v. *McGarry*, a person whose fingerprints are forcibly taken

'is entirely passive, and he is not compelled to do anything requiring any exercise of his own will or control of his body' [at p.89].

Accordingly, in my opinion, to require an accused person to provide finger impressions is materially different from interrogating an accused person and requiring him to answer questions. No positive action is required of a person whose fingerprints are being taken.

The advocate-depute maintained that the reasoning of the sheriff was seriously flawed. He drew attention to the fact that in his report the sheriff when referring to the fact that the police had omitted to take finger impressions used emotive language such as 'neglected', 'failure', 'error', 'mistake' and 'blunder'. The sheriff expressed the view that the court should be extremely slow to cure by judicial dispensation the errors of public servants in the investigation of crime, and he also stated that to grant warrant in this case would be to encourage slack practice. The advocate-depute accepted that the normal procedure was for finger impressions to be taken before committal, but he said there was no legal requirement upon the police to take fingerprints at that time. Accordingly, he stated that if for some reason finger impressions had not been taken before committal it was perfectly competent for the police to apply to the sheriff for a warrant to take finger impressions after committal. He submitted that when such an application was made all that the sheriff required to do was to carry out the balancing exercise referred to by the Lord Justice-General in *Wilson* v. *Milne*. He submitted that the sheriff had allowed himself to be blinded by reference to blunders and the like and that he did not therefore properly consider the application made to him and did not properly weigh up the conflicting interests.

So far as these submissions of the advocate-depute are concerned, I have some sympathy with the sheriff. There is no doubt that the petition to the sheriff to take finger impressions was based upon an allegation that the failure to take these impressions earlier was due to an administrative error. It is plain from the sheriff's report that it was the procurator fiscal depute who used many of these emotive expressions when he addressed the sheriff in support of the submission that warrant should be granted. However, I agree with the advocate-depute that these references may well have misled the sheriff as to the proper approach to be adopted in an application of this kind.

In my opinion, although it is no doubt competent to grant a warrant to take finger impressions from an accused after he has been fully committed, it is clear that such a warrant will only be granted where the circumstances are special. Accordingly, when considering an application of this kind, the sheriff must have regard to the whole circumstances, and he must weigh the public interest in the investigation and suppression of crime against the interest of an accused who has been fully committed.

In this case the sheriff has purported to have regard to the balancing exercise which required to be carried out, but I am satisfied that the approach which he adopted was seriously flawed. It is plain that the sheriff's view was that an error had taken place which could not be excused. In my opinion, having regard to the whole circumstances, that was a wholly unreasonable view for the sheriff to have entertained. The mistake which took place was entirely understandable. We were informed that a senior officer in K Division had stated that in a period of over ten years something like this had never occurred before. That being so, I am satisfied that the sheriff was not justified in describing the situation as amounting to 'slack practice'. To the contrary, what occurred appears to us to have been an isolated instance of a mistake being made because of the way in which different divisions of Strathclyde Police are organised and the fact that G Division encompasses areas which include parts of the sheriffdoms of both Glasgow and Paisley.

As well as placing too much emphasis upon the mistake or error, the sheriff also failed to recognise that the taking of finger impressions would involve the respondent in a purely passive procedure. He also failed to give sufficient weight to the fact that the taking of finger impressions would involve a relatively minor invasion of the bodily integrity of the respondent. Moreover, when he came to weigh these considerations against the public interest, I am of opinion that he attaches insufficient weight to the fact that this was a serious case involving a substantial quantity of drugs of a Class A type said to have a street value of around £100,000. In my opinion if the sheriff had approached this matter in the correct way and had had regard to the considerations to which I have referred he would undoubtedly have exercised his discretion in favour of granting the warrant sought.

Mr Thomson for the respondent contended that the sheriff had reached the correct conclusion, but I cannot agree. In my opinion, this was clearly a special case where there was a perfectly intelligible explanation for the fact that finger impressions had not been taken from the respondent sooner. In addition, the public interest was such that it outweighed the interest of the respondent whose bodily integrity, it was conceded, would suffer a minor invasion only.

For these reasons I move your Lordships to pass the bill, recall the decision of the sheriff and remit to him with instructions to grant warrant to take fingerprint imnpressions of the respondent."

The court passed the Bill.

NOTE

For further discussions of "special circumstances" see, *McGlennan* v. *Kelly*, 1989 S.C.C.R. 352; *Currie* v. *McGlennan*, 1989 S.C.C.R. 466; *Frame* v. *Houston*, 1991 S.C.C.R. 436, *infra*, and *K.J.G.* v. *Lees*, 1992 S.C.C.R. 252.

2. Frame v. Houston
1991 S.C.C.R. 436

The complainer was fully committed and remanded in custody in August 1990 on a charge of assault and robbery. In September 1990 he agreed to provide samples of his hair for comparison with hair found on masks worn by the robbers. The samples taken from the respondent were insufficient for the purposes of a meaningful comparison with the hair recovered from the masks. The complainer was indicted for trial in November 1990, but this was deserted *pro loco et tempore* because of an error in its drafting. The complainer was asked to provide further hair samples, which he declined to do. He was re-indicted in December 1990 for trial in January 1991, and shortly thereafter the procurator-fiscal presented a petition for a warrant to take further hair samples from the complainer.

LORD JUSTICE-CLERK: "This bill of suspension has been presented for the purpose of making such a challenge and it is contended on the complainer's behalf that since the complainer had already been indicted at the stage when the warrant was sought, it was not competent for the court to grant the warrant. A second contention was put forward to the effect that esto it was competent to grant such a warrant, the sheriff had erred in holding that there were any special circumstances to justify his exercising his discretion so as to grant the warrant. In moving us today to pass the bill Miss McGuire has presented arguments in support of these two contentions. As we have observed, the first contention is to the effect that having already been indicted it was not competent for the court to grant this warrant at this stage. The sheriff has provided a very full and helpful report in this case and under reference to what he says in his report, Miss McGuire accepted that it was competent in special cases at common law for the Crown to come to the court after full committal seeking a warrant of this nature. Her submission, however, was that a different situation arose once an indictment had been served. She drew attention to the case of *Beattie* v. *Scott*, but the observations in that case were made with regard to the situation once a case had come to trial. Miss McGuire drew attention in particular to a passage from the opinion of the Lord Justice-General at p.301C–D where he said this:

'But the stage of investigation is completed when the case comes to trial and at that stage the interests of the accused person demand that the Crown should prove its case against him without any assistance whatever on his part.'

That was a case under summary procedure and Miss McGuire accepted that the attention of the court was not directed towards the situation which arises in the present case. She submitted, however, that it was helpful to consider the situation of the case of an accused after full committal. She referred to a passage in Macdonald's Criminal Law of Scotland (3rd ed.) at p.269 where the following is stated:

'A prisoner may be re-examined on declaration after commitment for trial but not after service of a libel.'

She stated that that case was of some significance as it indicated that service of the indictment was a step which had certain consequences, such as the one mentioned by the learned author. That passage in Macdonald is said to be vouched by passages in Hume on Crimes, vol. ii, pp.331 and 332, but it appears to us when one looks at what is stated in the passage referred to that a different situation entirely was being considered because it is there stated:

'It has been held, that so long as not served with his indictment (for it cannot continue longer) the prisoner has a right to demand a re-examination, that he may rectify inaccuracies or retract, if he pleases, his acknowledgment of guilt.'

It will thus be seen that that passage is dealing with the right which a prisoner has under the procedure then in being to demand a re-examination so long as that demand was made before service of the indictment. Miss McGuire also referred to the case of *Smith* v. *Innes*. That was a case where observations were made by the sheriff as to the situation under summary procedure and the point appears to have been raised at the trial stage. That being so, we do not find this case of particular assistance and since the case proceeded under summary procedure we do not think it appropriate for us in the present proceedings to comment upon what the learned sheriff in that case said in particular at p.121 of the report.

Miss McGuire submitted that the matter ought to be approached in this way. That an accused person should not be put in a position of having to give evidence against himself once an indictment had been served. There must be protection for an accused person and his position should be protected from some appropriate cut-off point which she suggested was service of the indictment. The Solicitor-General on the issue of competency accepted that there appeared to be no authority directly in point. He suggested that this might be because in earlier days scientific procedures had not been as developed and sophisticated as they now are and there may well not have been occasions to make the type of application which has given rise to the present proceedings. No doubt when an indictment has been served that gives an accused person notice of the case which he has to meet and it provides him, among other things, with the list of witnesses and the list of the productions upon which the Crown propose to rely. But of course even after an indictment has been served there can be no assurance that the case will proceed to trial upon that indictment. A motion may be made to desert pro loco et tempore and that of course requires the leave of the court. But quite apart from that the Lord Advocate is master of the instance and the Crown may choose not to call the indictment, in which event the indictment will fall and an accused person may then be reindicted, subject always to the provisions conceived in favour of accused persons regarding time-limits. Accordingly, although the indictment is no doubt intended to give the accused notice of what he will have to meet at his trial, that is subject to the foregoing qualification. It is also subject to another qualification because of the provisions of section 81 of the Criminal Procedure (Scotland) Act 1975. That section provides for the situation where the prosecutor seeks to examine witnesses or to put in evidence productions which have not been included in the lists lodged. It is provided in that section that it is competent with the leave of the court for the prosecutor to examine any witness or to put in evidence any production not included in the lists lodged, provided that written notice containing the name and address of the witnesses has been given to the accused not less than two clear days before the day on which the jury is sworn to try the case. Accordingly, in a case such as the present case Miss McGuire was driven to concede that instead of having the case adjourned on 7th January until 4th March the Crown might not have the indictment called on 7th January or might have moved for the diet to be deserted pro loco et tempore and in that event it would have been possible for the warrant to be applied for, as was done in the present case, in which event such a step would not have been open to the objection that the application was being made after the indictment had been served. The situation in our opinion is that since service of the indictment does not irrevocably commit the Crown to go to trial, service of the indictment does not constitute a cut-off point of the kind contended for by Miss McGuire. In our view there is no bar to the competency of the granting of a warrant of this kind until the case comes to trial. That is the situation which appears to us to be in accord with principle and with such authorities as there are. Accordingly, there is no cut-off point until the indictment calls for trial, and it follows that it was competent for the sheriff to grant this warrant at the stage at which he was invited to do so, that is before the indictment was called for trial.

Of course it is recognised that although it was competent to grant such a warrant the sheriff was not obliged to grant the warrant but had a discretion and Miss McGuire contended that the sheriff here had not exercised his discretion properly because he had omitted to consider at least one material factor, namely that two indictments had been served upon the complainer. The sheriff in his report refers to a number of cases dealing with the way in which a sheriff ought to exercise discretion when faced with an application of this kind and particular reference is made by him to such cases as *McGlennan* v. *Kelly*; *Currie* v. *McGlennan*, and the case of *H.M. Advocate* v. *Milford* and also *Wilson* v. *Milne*. Having considered all these cases and having, as we see it, set out all the material factors, the sheriff reached the conclusion that he ought in the exercise of his discretion to grant the warrant. The sheriff was obviously well aware of all the facts of this case, including the fact that two indictments had been served and he obviously took considerable care in considering whether the warrant ought to be granted. He describes his approach to that question in his report as follows:

> 'Accordingly, in the delicate balancing act which I was required to carry out, I consider that the police interest outweighs the interest of the complainer whose bodily integrity in addition would suffer a minor invasion only.'

It was in these circumstances that the sheriff decided to grant the warrant and we are quite satisfied that, on the information before us, he was entitled to exercise his discretion in that way. For the foregoing reasons we therefore refuse to pass the bill."

B. Search Without Warrant

(A) Under Statute

A variety of statutes permit search without warrant, as they do arrest without warrant. The following is simply one example:

Civic Government (Scotland) Act 1980

"**60.**—(1) Subject to subsections (2) and (3) below, if a constable has reasonable grounds to suspect that a person is in possession of any stolen property, the constable may without warrant—
(*a*) search that person or anything in his possession, and detain him for as long as it necessary for the purpose of that search;
(*b*) enter and search any vehicle or vessel in which the constable suspects that that thing may be found, and for that purpose require the person in control of the vehicle to stop it and keep it stopped."

NOTE
For other commonly encountered examples of a statutory power of search, see the Criminal Justice (Scotland) Act 1980, s.4(1) (search for offensive weapons) and the Misuse of Drugs Act 1971 (search for controlled drugs). The powers of the police to search detainees under section 2 of the 1980 Act have already been noted (*supra*, p.155). Special powers in relation to the investigation of serious or complex fraud and terrorism are noted below (pp.268 and 270).

(B) At Common Law

It has already been noted (Chap. 4) that the police may search arrested persons (and that power is extended by section 2 of the 1980 Act to the case of detained persons). The following cases discuss the powers of the police to search without warrant in cases of "urgency." It will be seen that these powers may be employed whether or not the suspect has been arrested.

1.   H.M. Advocate v. McGuigan
1936 J.C. 16

The accused was charged with murder, rape and theft. At the trial, counsel for McGuigan objected to the admissibility of certain evidence taken without warrant by the police from the tent in which the accused lived. The circumstances in which the evidence was seized are outlined in the Lord Justice-Clerk's opinion:

> LORD JUSTICE-CLERK (AITCHISON): "... The ground of the objection is that this search was carried out, and I take it certain articles seized, without the warrant of a magistrate; and it is said, accordingly, that the search and the seizure of the articles were both illegal. Now, the facts are these: On the evening of 28th August the accused had been identified—or was alleged to have been identified—by Marjory Fenwick, and immediately thereafter he was apprehended and charged. The charges made against him were three in number. First, murder; second, rape; third theft of a pocket book; the apprehension and charge took place about eight o'clock at night. Thereafter the accused was searched. Both the apprehension and the search of the accused were carried out without warrant. I have no doubt that, in the circumstances, this was quite regular. The police were amply justified in acting at their own hand. Between 9 and 10 o'clock the same night Inspector Davidson went to the accused's tent. He found the tent occupied by the accused's mother and the accused's stepfather. He disclosed who he was, and what his purpose was. No objection was raised, as was natural enough. On the other hand, no consent was asked for, and the search proceeded. Now it must be obvious that, the accused having been arrested on so grave a charge as murder, it might be of the first importance to the ends of public justice that a search of the tent in which the accused had been living should be made forthwith. The police acted at their own hand, just as they acted at their own hand in apprehending and searching the person of the accused. In the circumstances, the matter being in the view of Inspector Davidson one of urgency, the police were entitled, in my view, to act without delay and without having obtained a warrant from a magistrate."

> The court repelled
> the objection.

NOTES
1.   The Lord Justice-Clerk went on to hold that even if he had concluded that the search was unlawful, the evidence would not necessarily have been inadmissible.
2.   *Cf. McLorie* v. *Oxford* [1982] 3 All E.R. 480; *Jeffrey* v. *Black* [1978] Q.B. 490 and the much more restrictive view of police powers in such a situation adopted by the English courts.

2.   Bell v. Hogg
1967 J.C. 4

While investigating the disappearance of a quantity of copper telegraph wire from a railway line, the police intercepted the appellants in a van.

They informed them of the nature of their inquiries, cautioned them, and asked to see their hands. The police observed on the hands of the appellants a substance which could have been verdigris. The appellants were then taken to a police station (not under arrest) where, in response to an invitation from a police officer, each gave a rubbing from his hands. They were not expressly told that they were entitled to refuse. The substance proved to be verdigris, and this evidence was crucial to their subsequent conviction for theft of the wire. They appealed against conviction on the ground that this evidence had been wrongly admitted, it having been unlawfully obtained.

LORD JUSTICE-GENERAL (CLYDE): "... In these circumstances, in my opinion, the sergeant took a perfectly proper and legitimate step in securing a record of what was on the appellants' hands before it was eliminated by washing or otherwise. The urgency of the matter is its justification, as was held by Lord Justice-Clerk Aitchison in *H.M. Advocate* v. *M'Guigan* [*supra*] where he held that in a case of urgency, in order to preserve evidence which might otherwise be lost, the police were entitled to search an accused person's tent without a warrant. This decision was quoted with approval in the Whole Court case of *Lawrie* v. *Muir* [*infra*]. In the course of the argument in the present case the decision in *M'Govern* v. *H.M. Advocate* [1950 J.C. 33] was also referred to. In that case, which the Lord Justice-General described as 'distinctly unusual', the accused had not yet been charged nor apprehended in connection with a safe-blowing, but had been kept in the police station for some six hours, when 'as a further precaution' the police obtained the contents of his finger nails by scraping them with a view to subsequent chemical analysis of the scrapings. After carrying out this operation the police then 'deemed it advisable' to charge him. This incident was treated by the Court on the concessions of the Crown as an irregular proceeding on the part of the police. There was no question of urgency and no knowledge by the police as to whether the scrapings would yield any evidence of the suspect's connection with the offence. This all makes it a highly special decision. In the present case there was on the contrary obvious urgency involved in the obtaining of the impressions; and the analysis of these impressions was necessary, not in the hope of connecting the appellants with the offences but in order to secure a reliable analysis of the gray-green marks on their hands which had been seen by the light of the torch at the railway station shortly beforehand, in order to confirm whether they were made by verdigris or not.

The test of the admissibility of the evidence of the analysis is whether what was done was done fairly. In this case there was no compulsion about what the police did. There is no trace or any suggestion of bullying or trickery on the part of the police, still less any element of third-degree treatment. I do not regard it as unfair that the accused were not specifically told that they need not consent to the impressions being taken. It might have been better if this had been said, but the absence of such a warning is not in the circumstances fatal, particularly as the appellants had already been cautioned. After all, the analysis might well have been favourable to the appellants and, if they had not been parties to the offences, it could have done them no harm. In these circumstances the actings of the police are not shown to be any way unfair, and, if so, the evidence arising out of these steps was properly admitted by the Sheriff-substitute."

LORD MIGDALE: "... In my opinion the Sheriff-substitute was right in accepting this evidence. I think, however, he could have held that Sergeant Muirhead acted within his rights as a police officer who acted in an emergency. The Sheriff-substitute has held that the taking of the rubbings was a justifiable infringement of the rights enjoyed by the appellants as citizens. I find authority for this view in the case of *H.M. Advocate* v. *M'Guigan*.

If the evidence could be recovered at a later stage after apprehension, as in the case of *M'Govern* v. *H.M. Advocate*, the balance would be in favour of the suspect, but if, as in the present case, the evidence is likely to be lost if not recorded immediately, I think the police are entitled to act at once. Urgency itself justifies the action and this falls under the first part of the ruling given by the Lord Justice-Clerk. It is part of the function of the police to preserve evidence which is likely to be useful in proving the guilt of a suspected criminal just as it is part of their function to prevent a crime being committed. For these reasons I think that the police acted properly.

Even if this is wrong, then in this case the action of Sergeant Muirhead was justified under the second part of the Lord Justice-Clerk's ruling and the principle laid down by Lord Cooper in *Lawrie* v. *Muir*. The balance of interest in the present case is clearly in favour of the action taken by the police."

LORD CAMERON: "... In the present case I have no doubt that the police officers were entitled to question the appellants and that any answers obtained by them were admissible in evidence. In these circumstances I should have thought that the use in evidence of a material substance handed over to the police at their request—a request related to the transaction which the police were investigating—would be equally admissible. But there was an additional circumstance which in my opinion justified the action of the police and made the use in evidence of the substance obtained competent and admissible. The problem which faced the police was whether they were to lose permanently evidence which was evanescent and once gone could not be recovered. It was thus from a practical point of view urgent that this evidence should be recovered for examination and identification. It is also to be noted that at the time it could not be determined whether the substance was wholly innocent—a factor in the appellants' favour—or whether its presence and nature might point towards their guilt. This could not appear until expert examination had taken place. To wait might have meant the loss of possibly vital evidence and, as it turned out, evidence which in this case was in fact of critical importance. The ultimate determination of whether the situation is truly one of urgency is, I think, for the Court to decide upon the whole facts and not for subjective decision. In my opinion the situation which was presented to the police at the time in question was one of urgency. If the material was to be of value, either criminative or exculpatory, its instant recovery and preservation in the hands of the authorities was imperative. It would obviously not have been practicable to obtain a search warrant there and then to permit a search of the appellants or a checking of their finger-prints; the use of force would have involved an assault and would certainly have led to the rejection of evidence so obtained. In these circumstances I should not have thought that there was any impropriety or unfairness to the appellants in asking them, particularly after they had already been cautioned and put on guard as to their rights at least in the matter of questioning, to make available for examination what was on their hands ... the principle of urgency as a justification for acts which would in less compelling circumstances require the authority of a warrant is settled beyond doubt. It is only where there has been irregularity, that is, lack of legal justification, in obtaining evidence that its admissibility may depend on whether the irregularity can be excused ... There is nothing in the present case to suggest that the appellants were unfairly induced or tricked into providing the material or that they were subjected to any kind of pressure. I therefore think that, apart from any other considerations to which I have referred and upon the single issue of urgency in the circumstances, as I think there was, the evidence which was obtained is admissible in law and that consequently the questions should be answered as proposed by your Lordship in the chair."

The court refused
the appeal.

NOTES

1. The police action in this case seems to have been entirely reasonable. The appellants were found in suspicious circumstances with what appeared to be prima facie evidence of connection with the offence on their hands. The public as a whole would have been entitled to be highly critical of police officers who stood idly by and allowed the destruction of such evidence. But the limits of the power under discussion should be closely confined to cases of genuine emergency, where no other lawful means of preserving evidence is available. *Cf. McHugh* v. *H.M. Advocate, infra.*

2. The use of the caution in such cases raises a difficult issue. It is submitted that a standard caution, directed towards the making of statements, is not appropriate where the police are seeking to obtain real evidence. The caution should be so phrased as to direct the suspect's attention towards what is being asked of him and his right to refuse that request.

It is interesting to note that in the case of *Hay, supra,* p.243, all of the individuals from whom dental impressions were taken gave their consent in the following terms: "I have been told that this [the taking of dental impressions] is in relation to the investigation into the death of [L.P.] ... It has been made clear to me that I can refuse ... It has also been made clear to me that should my dental impressions be linked with other evidence in the case they may be produced as evidence" (See, Keith Simpson, *Forty Years of Murder* (Granada Publishing, 1980), p.332).

3. See also *Walsh* v. *McPhail,* 1978 S.L.T. (Notes) 29.

3. McHugh v. H.M. Advocate
1978 J.C. 12

McHugh and another man were suspected of an assault and robbery in which a sum of money consisting of identifiable banknotes was stolen from a shop. In the early hours of the morning following the robbery the police went, without a search warrant or a warrant for arrest, to the house of McHugh's suspected accomplice. According to the police evidence (which was disputed by the accused), McHugh was then cautioned, charged and arrested. He was then searched, and some of the stolen notes were found in his possession. McHugh was convicted of assault and robbery and appealed on the ground, *inter alia,* that evidence relating to the finding of the banknotes in his possession should not have been admitted at the trial, as it had been illegally obtained.

LORD JUSTICE-GENERAL (EMSLIE): "... The second submission was that the trial judge misdirected the jury by admitting for their consideration the evidence of police officers of finding stolen notes, which were productions in the case, on the person of the appellant. As we understood the argument, counsel began by saying that this was a case in which the search was conducted without warrant. Although police who have lawfully arrested a person may quite properly search the arrested man without a warrant, it was not certain that an arrest had taken place in this case, or that if it had taken place, it had taken place legally. The only other circumstance in which a search of a citizen may be justified is where, although there is no warrant and no lawful arrest, the need to search is demanded as a matter of urgency to prevent the possible loss or destruction of important evidence. In this case, said Mr Taylor, it was by no means clear that the police were telling the truth when they said they arrested M'Hugh before they searched him. In any event, said Mr Taylor, it is by no means clear either that they had reasonable grounds for arresting M'Hugh, or that there were any considerations of urgency which could have justified the search which revealed the stolen property. In short the submission for the appellant seemed to be this:—Where the admission in evidence of the fruits of a search is challenged on the ground that they have been improperly obtained and the question of the credibility of the searchers on the matter of the propriety of the search is raised by the defence, the trial Judge should leave that question to the jury to resolve and direct the jury to consider the evidence as to the fruits of search only if the question of credibility is resolved in the searcher's favour. To this somewhat curious submission there is a short answer. It was for the Judge to dispose of the objection to the admissibility of the disputed evidence for that is a question of law. He has disposed of that objection and in our opinion his decision cannot be faulted. The evidence bearing upon the circumstances of the search was all one way and remained unshaken in cross-examination. It was to the effect that the officers had set out with the primary purpose of arresting M'Hugh, for that was their alloted task. They carried out that task and the search was a sequel to the arrest. They did not arrest without reasonable cause, and in particular merely to provide an excuse for a search. In any event it is perfectly clear that the search of M'Hugh, a prime suspect, was, according to the evidence, essential as a matter of urgency, to avoid any risk that any of the numbered notes which he might have in his possession would be lost, hidden or destroyed. In this state of matters and particularly having regard to the sufficient evidence of the urgent need to search, the criticism of the direction given by the trial Judge is without real substance."

The court refused
the appeal.

NOTES

1.   Strictly speaking the remarks about urgency in this case are *obiter* since the court found that the accused had been arrested prior to search, and the search can thus be justified on ordinary principles (see *supra*, Chap. 4).

2.   The court's reliance on urgency is unfortunate. It comes very close to permitting search without warrant to justify arrest, in conflict with the principle laid down in *Jackson* v. *Stevenson* (*supra*, Chap. 4). In any case, was there really a matter of urgency in the search of McHugh? What could he have done to dispose of the evidence with the police standing there?

3.   Compare the approach of the court in McHugh with *Leckie* v. *Miln*, *supra*. Why did the court not rely upon the notion of urgency in that case?

4.   Cairns v. Keane
1983 S.C.C.R. 277

Two police officers observed the appellant's vehicle being driven in an erratic manner and formed the suspicion that he was under the influence of alcohol. They followed him to his home where the appellant jumped out of the vehicle and ran towards his house. Both officers followed him. As he opened the door the officers took hold of the appellant who forced his way into the house. One officer entered the house with the appellant, the other entered immediately behind them. The officers smelt alcohol on the appellant's breath and, having informed him that they suspected him of driving while under the influence of alcohol, required him to take a breath test which he did. The test proved positive. The appellant was subsequently convicted of a contravention of section 6(1) of the Road Traffic Act 1972 (driving with a blood alcohol level above the permitted maximum). During argument it was submitted to the sheriff that the evidence obtained from the breath test analysis should not be admitted because the police officers, when they administered the test in the appellant's home, were trespassers and were not, therefore, acting in the lawful execution of their duty.

THE SHERIFF (MACMILLAN): "There was ... only one remaining ground upon which the appellant sought to avoid conviction, and that was that the certificate of analysis was inadmissible because the police officers, when they required the first breath test, were not acting in the lawful execution of their duty, in respect that they were trespassing on private property, namely the appellant's dwellinghouse, and that this vitiated all the rest of the procedure and the evidence obtained as a result of it.

So far as the facts are concerned, I was satisfied that, although the appellant did not expressly object to the presence of the police officers within his dwellinghouse, neither did he consent to it; and that on the face of it the police officers were therefore on private property without the consent of the owner.

Having given the appellant's solicitor and the procurator fiscal depute an opportunity to refer me to the authorities, I received detailed submissions on 12th August 1982. For the appellant, Mr Adair submitted that the matter was ruled by the decision of the House of Lords in *Morris* v. *Beardmore* [1981] A.C. 446 where it was held that a constable who is at the time acting unlawfully towards the person whom he requires to take a breath test under section 8(2) of the Road Traffic Act 1972, in that he is a trespasser in his house, is acting outside his authority; since, in enacting legislation, Parliament is presumed, in the absence of express provision, not to intend to authorise tortious conduct. The following year in *Lambert* v. *Roberts* [1981] R.T.R. 113 the Queen's Bench applied this decision to a charge under section 8(1). Mr Adair submitted that the police were entitled to go on to private property only in the pursuit of a person suspected of committing a serious crime, such as murder, rape, theft by housebreaking, etc.; where the offence charged was a breach of a statutory provision there could be an invasion of the right of private property only where there was statutory authority to do that.

For the prosecution, it was submitted that *Morris* v. *Beardmore*, although a case involving the construction of a United Kingdom statute, was primarily concerned with the doctrine of trespass in its peculiarly English connotation, and that this decision was therefore not only not binding upon me, but was not even to be regarded as persuasive. It was not disputed that there were limits to the extent to which police officers in Scotland were entitled to enter private property in the detection of crime and in the pursuit of offenders. One of the circumstances which justified this was that the evidence would otherwise be irretrievably lost (*McPherson* v. *H.M. Advocate*, 1972 S.L.T. (Notes) 71). That was the situation in this case. It was not conceded that the police were acting unlawfully, and reference was made to the decision in *Smith* v. *Hawkes*, Cr. Off.

Circular A32/80; but even if they were, the evidence should be admitted because of the special circumstances, namely the urgency of the situation.

The procurator fiscal depute also referred me to Schedule 8 to the Transport Act 1981 (not yet in force). This introduces a new section 7 to replace the existing section 8 of the Road Traffic Act 1972. The substituted subsection 7(6) appears to be designed to modify the effect of the decision in *Morris* v. *Beardmore*, by giving a constable power, in certain circumstances, to enter (if need be by force) any place where the suspected person is. The power is not however to be extended to Scotland (see subsection (7) which provides that nothing in subsection (6) shall affect 'any rule of law in Scotland concerning the right of a constable to enter any premises for any purpose'). The procurator fiscal depute claimed that this confirmed her submission that different principles applied in Scotland regarding the right of a police constable to enter private premises in a case such as this. It seemed to me desirable, therefore, to begin by considering what the rule of law in Scotland was on this matter.

In *McPherson* v. *H.M. Advocate* the police searched an accused person's house without a warrant and before he had been charged with the offences for which he was ultimately convicted, namely assault and robbery and various less serious offences. In the course of his opinion Lord Wheatley said: 'The law is careful to protect the individual from illegal or irregular invasion of his liberties by the authorities, and this includes the invasion of his house.' In *Smith* v. *Hawkes* it was said: 'On these findings, the fact that the constables were at any time within the house is quite irrelevant. What is relevant is that they had proper enquiries to make and reasonable grounds for making them.' These dicta did not appear to me to be inconsistent, because the findings referred to in the latter case were that the police had been summoned to the accused's house by a 999 call that a disturbance was taking place in the accused's home; that when they arrived they could hear raised voices from within; that they entered the house, and when they were told to leave they did so; and that as the accused was trying to shut the door in their faces one of the constables put his foot across the doorway and was then threatened with an axe, for which offence the accused was charged with assault, and ultimately convicted, following on the Crown's appeal to the High Court. This case did not therefore seem to me to contradict what was said in *McPherson* v. *H.M. Advocate* or to be an authority for the broad proposition that the police are in all and any circumstances entitled to go on to private property in order to investigate or prevent the commission of crime. On the contrary, it was noticeable that as soon as the police officers were told to leave, they did so. The case of *Shepherd* v. *Menzies* (1900) 2 F. 443, which was also referred to by the procurator fiscal depute, has been quoted in support of the view that property may be entered by a constable for the purpose of ascertaining whether a crime or offence is being committed; but that seemed to me to be a special case, depending on the construction of section 6 of the Cruelty to Animals (Scotland) Act 1850. In *H.M. Advocate* v. *McGuigan*, 1936 J.C. 16 it was held that police officers, after arresting the accused, were justified in searching his tent without a warrant, but Lord Justice-Clerk Aitchison seemed to imply that but for the fact that they were investigating a case of murder the search without the consent of the owner would otherwise have been unlawful. Macdonald on the Criminal Law of Scotland (5th ed.), p.197, states: 'In cases of serious crime officers may without a warrant break open doors and enter premises incidentally to the apprehension of an offender. But in mere breaches of the peace they may not break in, except to quell a disturbance actually proceeding.'

The effect of all these authorities seemed to me to show that the 'rule of law in Scotland concerning the right of a constable to enter any premises for any purpose' was that, except when investigating serious crime, police officers are no more entitled than any other member of the public to enter upon private property without a warrant and without the consent of the owner; and that if they do so they must be prepared to justify their conduct by reason of special circumstances before any evidence so obtained can be rendered admissible.

In considering such special circumstances I referred first to the principle enunciated by Lord Cooper in the Full Bench division, *Lawrie* v. *Muir*, 1950 J.C. 19 at 26, where he said:

> 'From the standpoint of principle it seems to me that the law must strive to reconcile two highly important interests which are liable to come into conflict—(*a*) the interest of the citizen to be protected from illegal or irregular invasion of his liberties by the authorities, and (*b*) the interest of the State to secure that evidence bearing upon the commission of crime and necessary to enable justice to be done shall not be withheld from Courts of law on any merely formal or technical ground. Neither of these objects can be insisted upon to the uttermost. The protection of the citizen is primarily protection for the innocent citizen against unwarranted, wrongful and perhaps high-handed interference, and the common sanction is an action of damages. The protection is not intended as a protection for the guilty citizen against the efforts of the public prosecutor to vindicate the law. On the other hand, the interest of the State cannot be magnified to the point of causing all the safeguards for the protection of the citizen to vanish, and of offering a positive inducement to the authorities to proceed by irregular methods.'

Lord Cooper went on to say: 'Irregularities require to be excused, and infringements of the formalities of the law in relation to these matters are not lightly to be condoned. Whether any given irregularity ought to be excused depends upon the nature of the irregularity and the circumstances under which it was committed.'

In *H.M. Advocate* v. *McGuigan* Lord Justice-Clerk Aitchison had stated as one of these circumstances the fact that the police urgently required to obtain evidence which would otherwise disappear if it were not obtained immediately, and this was the consideration which was principally urged upon me by the procurator fiscal in the instant case. I was referred to a number of authorities in which the plea of urgency had been raised as justifying actions by the police which would otherwise have been unlawful, namely *Laverie* v. *Murray*, 1964 S.L.T. (Notes) 3, a civil action for damages against a trespassing police officer; *Bell* v. *Hogg*, 1967 J.C. 49, in which rubbings were taken from the accuseds' hands before they were charged or warned that they might refuse; and *McPherson* v. *H.M. Advocate* in which it was held that the urgency of the situation justified a search without warrant of the accused's dwellinghouse. Other circumstances which might be taken into account were the gravity of the crime, the seriousness or triviality of the breach, the authority and good faith of those who obtained the evidence, and of course the general principle of fairness to the accused (see Walker & Walker on Evidence, p.3). In this case the evidence did not admit of any doubt but that the officers, in entering upon the appellant's premises, were solely concerned to obtain a breath specimen and thereby, ultimately, a specimen of blood or urine from a man they suspected (and with reason) of having alcohol in his body. This evidence being evanescent, the circumstances clearly were urgent. Moreover, although the offence could not perhaps be categorised as in the first rank of serious crime, it was nevertheless one of the most serious of the road traffic offences. Since the appellant was clearly trying to avoid detection (I refer to his drinking from the bottle in the kitchen) I could not believe that there was any breach of the general principle of fairness when the police officers followed him into the house. I would therefore have been inclined immediately to regard the irregularity as justified, particularly on the grounds of urgency, but for one other consideration.

The statutory offence for which the evidence was so urgently sought was subject to precise rules of procedure, and the question in issue in this case, it seemed to me, was whether the principles of law referred to above could still operate in such a case. In *Morris* v. *Beardmore* the House of Lords held that in such a case quite different considerations arise. Notwithstanding that this decision was not binding upon me, I found it impossible to accept the procurator fiscal depute's invitation wholly to ignore the considered judgments of their Lordships in construing a United Kingdom statute, merely because the issue involved the English law of trespass. In any event, my hesitation arose not solely because of the views expressed in *Morris* v. *Beardmore*, but also because of certain dicta in some of the Scottish cases.

I first considered the basis for the decision in *Morris* v. *Beardmore*. After a road traffic accident police officers had gone to Beardmore's house. They were asked to leave but three of them went into his bedroom where one of them, a superintendent, required him under section 8(2) to undergo a breath test. This he refused on the grounds that the police had no right to be there, whereupon he was arrested and ultimately prosecuted for failing to provide a specimen of breath and for failing to provide a specimen of blood or urine. After observing that sections 8 and 9 provide for considerable inroads by the police upon rights and liberties of private citizens that are recognised and protected by the common law, Lord Diplock, in the leading judgment, went on to consider the prosecution's argument that section 8(2) contains no express provision *prohibiting* a constable from requiring a person to undergo a breath test when the constable is only able to communicate the requirement to that person as a result of his violation of that person's property. Lord Diplock dismissed that argument, commenting that the 'boot is on the other leg; if Parliament intends to authorise the doing of an act which would constitute a tort ... this requires express provision in the statute' (at 455E). Lord Diplock reserved his position regarding a request for a breath test under section 8(1) but Lord Scarman expressly applied it to both sections 8(1) and (2). He went on: 'When one compares, as one must, the silence of Parliament in this section with the elborate provisions and safeguards enacted for the search of private premises and the seizure of evidence in two cases which have recently troubled your Lordships' House, it becomes inconceivable that Parliament in its breathalyser legislation could have authorised, by implication, the entry into a suspect's private house, against his will' (at 463–464), and he referred to the power conferred upon the Inland Revenue by section 20C of the Taxes Management Act 1970 and to the power conferred upon chief officers of police and others by section 441(1) of the Companies Act 1948. Section 2(6) of the Criminal Law Act 1967 was also cited as an example of the legislative practice of conferring an express power of entry.

I noted that in *Lawrie* v. *Muir*, Lord Cooper, in discussing the circumstances that might or might not excuse an irregularity, said: 'Again, there are many statutory offences in relation to which Parliament has prescribed in detail in the interests of fairness a special procedure to be followed in obtaining evidence; and in such cases (of which the Sale of Food and Drugs Acts provide one example) it is very easy to see why a departure from the strict rules has often been held to be fatal to the prosecution's case' (at 27).

The same approach seemed to be foreshadowed in *Harvey* v. *Sturgeon*, 1912 S.C. 974 (a civil action) where Lord Justice-Clerk Macdonald at 977 said: 'In recent times, when there is so much publicity, very large discretionary powers have been given to police-officers which would not have been tolerated in former times. That makes it all the more necessary that, while such officers are allowed a certain margin as regards dealing with persons upon suspicion, their powers should not be stretched beyond what is reasonable, and that, when these powers are conferred by statute, they should not be stretched beyond what the statute provides or what may be reasonably inferred from its terms.'

In a footnote to the report of *Smith* v. *McLean*, 1982 S.C.C.R. 39 the commentator (Sheriff Gordon) referring to *Morris* v. *Beardmore*, observed that 'The position of trespassing constables has not been raised in Scotland' (he meant, of course, in relation to the breathalyser legislation). *Smith* v. *McLean* was a case in which the accused, having driven into the grounds of his house, and whilst still in his car, was required to take a breath test. The case was however decided on other grounds, and the 'position of trespassing constables' does not seem to have arisen, possibly because the accused had not yet entered his dwellinghouse.

I came to the conclusion that so far as procedure in Scotland was concerned, if the actions of the police could be justified upon the basis of principles of law established over a long series of decided cases, because of the urgency of obtaining the evidence, or the gravity of the offence, or because of the overriding public interest or whatever, then the evidence so obtained could not be ruled inadmissible merely because Parliament did not see fit to make provision for the contingency that the breath test requirement might have to be made on private property. I could not, in any event, see any need for such legislative provision, so far as Scotland was concerned. If the procedure could be justified on the principles referred to above, I could see no need for legislation to 'authorise tortious conduct', because there was no tort if the conduct of the police was justified by the circumstances. The appellant's house was immediately adjacent to the road on which he had been driving, and was therefore 'nearby' in terms of section 8(1)(*a*). If the constables would otherwise have been justified by the urgency of the situation in going into his house to require him to take a breath test, I could see that such a procedure, so obviously desirable in the public interest, must be avoided or nullified merely because the Act did not expressly say that this was permissible. I considered that, so far as Scotland was concerned at any rate, this might be 'reasonably inferred from its terms' (to borrow the phrase employed in *Harvey* v. *Sturgeon*). It may be, as the procurator fiscal depute originally submitted, that it was the specialties of the English law of trespass that led their Lordships in *Morris* v. *Beardmore* to take the view that special legislative power was needed to enable a constable to enter an Englishman's home—his castle. It seemed to me that in Scotland the public interest provided the constable with a convenient drawbridge.

For the reasons stated, I repelled the objection and held the evidence of the blood analysis admissible. I therefore proceeded to find the appellant guilty as libelled."

Objection repelled.

NOTES

1.   A case was stated for the opinion of the High Court. The High Court dismissed the appeal without delivering any opinions.

2.   In his findings-in-fact, the sheriff stated: "(15) The appellant did not state any objection to the presence of the police officers in his dwellinghouse; nor did he consent to it." But what would have been the position if the appellant had asked the officers to leave? It may be inferred from certain *dicta* in *Turnbull* v. *Scott*, 1990 S.C.C.R. 614, *supra*, p.143, that where a trespassing officer is asked to leave he ceases to have lawful authority to act (provided he is given a reasonable opportunity to leave). That case concerned the exercise of powers of detention under section 2 of the 1980 Act and while the sheriff clearly thought that the case-law on

urgency was relevant the High Court did not think that those authorities were relevant. The issue would seem, therefore, to be an open one. The officers in the instant case were probably not relying on any doctrine of implied consent but, it would seem, on some notion of "hot pursuit" which is independent of the doctrine of implied consent. That being the case, then, it might be argued, that the express withdrawal of consent by the appellant would have been irrelevant. If, however, the appellant could instruct the officers to leave so as to deprive them of lawful powers to require the test then, it seems, that this would have to be done before the request is made. If the request is lawfully made then it cannot be rendered unlawful by a subsequent instruction to the officers to leave.

5.   MacNeil and Others v. H.M. Advocate
1986 S.C.C.R. 288

The appellants were convicted of various offences relating to unlawful importation of cannabis. During the investigation of these offences, customs officers, proceeding under a writ of assistance under section 16(1) of the Customs and Excise Management Act 1979, seized goods from the Liverpool home of one of the appellants, Noon. Section 16 allows only for the seizure of "anything liable to forfeiture under the customs and excise Act" and it transpired that the items seized were not so liable. On appeal, Noon, argued that the trial judge had erred in holding that this evidence was admissible since there was no statutory power to seize them, and no element of urgency in the case.

> LORD JUSTICE-GENERAL: "It is common ground that when customs officers accompanied by police arrived at Noon's house to search it under the writ of assistance they seized a number of articles not liable to forfeiture under the customs and excise Acts. The proposition was that these articles ought not to have been admitted in evidence because they had been irregularly obtained and because there was no evidence of any circumstances which might excuse the irregularity. Let us assume, without deciding, that these articles (and we do not require to identify them individually) were irregularly obtained. The articles were manifestly of evidential value in relation to the suspected importation of a large cargo of prohibited drugs at Seil in which Noon was believed to be implicated. From the evidence it is plain that the officers of the customs and excise in various parts of Great Britain, including Liverpool, were dealing with a fluid and developing situation which had in the early hours of 4th February 1985 become one of considerable urgency and which was liable to result in the disappearance or loss of evidence unless proper and rapid steps were taken to prevent it. By that time Noon had been detained as a suspect under section 138 of the Act of 1979, but leaving that consideration and its implications aside, the sheer urgency of the situation excuses any irregularity there may have been. The necessity of seizure of these articles can fairly be described as clamant. In any event we are persuaded that in the whole circumstances of this important investigation and of the prosecution of those charged in this indictment upon very serious charges, the interests of the public in the due administration of justice heavily outweighed those of the appellant Noon as an individual. In our opinion the trial judge was well founded, for the reasons given in his opinion, in repelling Noon's objection, in holding that the articles in question should be admitted in evidence. Noon's appeal on his fourth and final surviving ground of appeal will accordingly be refused."

Appeal refused.

NOTE

The interesting and important question which arises in this case, and which appears to have escaped the notice of all concerned, is whether the court applied the correct rules about the means whereby the evidence was obtained, and its admissibility. If the articles in question were irregularly obtained they were irregularly obtained outside Scotland. That being so, the question of the admissibility of the evidence requires consideration of the law of more than one jurisdiction. It is probably the case that the legality of the means whereby the evidence was obtained should be determined by the law of the place where the evidence was seized (*i.e.* English law) whereas their admissibility is to be determined by the law of the court before which the evidence is adduced—Scots law. This in turn requires a consideration of the theoretical basis of the "urgency" doctrine. Is "urgency" something which makes lawful the seizure of evidence, or is it a circumstance which excuses an irregular act and relates simply to admissibility? *Dicta* can be found in *McGuigan, Bell* v. *Hogg, McHugh* and *Cairns* v. *Keane* which suggest that the former is the correct approach. On the other hand, there are suggestions in *McGuigan* and *MacNeil* that what is in issue is the excusing of an "irregularity" in the seizure of the evidence.

Now, if "urgency" goes to the legality of the search (as opposed to admissibility) it is not a doctrine which can be invoked in respect of evidence seized in England, since there is no such general doctrine in English law which would permit the seizure of evidence. Of course, if urgency simply goes to the admissibility of the evidence, then the Scottish courts can apply the doctrine to allow the evidence to be admitted.

C. ILLEGALITY AND ADMISSIBILITY

The rules governing the legality of search and seizure are in principle distinguishable from the rules governing the admissibility of evidence obtained by these means. Thus, it is quite possible for a court to hold that the evidence was obtained by unlawful means (which may give rise to civil or other sanctions) and yet simultaneously hold that the evidence is admissible. (Compare this with the position with regard to statements and confessions where both these aspects are effectively merged in the fairness rule.)

Lawrie v. Muir
1950 J.C. 19

The appellant was convicted of an offence contrary to the Milk (Council and Maximum Prices) (Great Britain) Order 1947 in that she used for the sale of milk bottles belonging to other milk suppliers without their consent or other lawful authority. The evidence relating to the use of these bottles was obtained by two inspectors who had unlawfully, but in good faith, conducted a search of her premises. On appeal by stated case:

LORD JUSTICE-GENERAL (COOPER) (delivering the opinion of the Full Bench):

"From the standpoint of principle it seems to me that the law must strive to reconcile two highly important interests which are liable to come into conflict—(*a*) the interest of the citizen to be protected from illegal or irregular invasions of his liberties by the authorities, and (*b*) the interest of the State to secure that evidence bearing upon the commission of crime and necessary to enable justice to be done shall not be withheld from Courts of law on any merely formal or technical ground. Neither of these objects can be insisted upon to the uttermost. The protection of the citizen is primarily protection for the innocent citizen against unwarranted, wrongful and perhaps high-handed interference, and the common sanction is an action of damages. The protection is not intended as a protection for the guilty citizen against the efforts of the public prosecutor to vindicate the law. On the other hand, the interest of the State cannot be magnified to the point of causing all the safeguards for the protection of the citizen to vanish, and of offering a positive inducement to the authorities to proceed by irregular methods. It is obvious that excessively rigid rules as to the exclusion of evidence bearing upon the commission of a crime might conceivably operate to the detriment and not the advantage of the accused, and might even lead to the conviction of the innocent; and extreme cases can easily be figured in which the exclusion of a vital piece of evidence from the knowledge of a jury because of some technical flaw in the conduct of the police would be an outrage upon common sense and a defiance of elementary justice. For these reasons, and in view of the expressions of judicial opinion to which I have referred, I find it quite impossible to affirm the appellant's extreme proposition. On the contrary, I adopt as a first approximation to the true rule the statement of Lord Justice-Clerk Aitchison [*H.M. Adv.* v. *McGuigan, supra*] that 'an irregularity in the obtaining of evidence does not *necessarily* make that evidence inadmissible.'

It remains to consider the implications of the word 'necessarily' which I have italicised. By using this word and by proceeding to the sentence which follows, Lord Aitchison seems to me to have indicated that there was, in his view, no absolute rule and that the question was one of circumstances. I respectfully agree. It would greatly facilitate the task of Judges were it possible to imprison the principle within the framework of a simple and unqualified maxim, but I do not think that it is feasible to do so.

Irregularities require to be excused, and infringements of the formalities of the law in relation to these matters are not lightly to be condoned. Whether any given irregularity ought to be excused depends upon the nature of the irregularity and the circumstances under which it was committed. In particular, the case may bring into play the discretionary principle of fairness to the accused which had been developed so fully in our law in relation to the admission in evidence of confessions or admissions by a person suspected or charged with crime. That principle would obviously require consideration in any case in which the departure from the strict procedure had been adopted deliberately with a view to securing the admission of evidence obtained by an unfair trick. Again, there are many statutory offences in relation to which Parliament has prescribed in detail in the interests of fairness a special procedure to be followed in obtaining evidence; and in such cases (of which the Sale of Food and Drugs Acts provide one example) it is very easy to see why a departure from the strict rules has often been held to be fatal to the prosecution's case. On the other hand, to take an extreme instance figured in argument, it would usually be wrong to exclude some highly incriminating production in a murder trial merely because it was found by a police officer in the course of a search authorised for a different purpose or before a proper warrant had been obtained."

The court quashed
the conviction.

NOTE

The Lord Justice-General went on to hold that, in the circumstances of the case, and in particular the fact that the inspectors were not police officers enjoying "a large residuum of common law powers" but persons who "ought to know the precise limits of their authority," the balance ought to be held in favour of the appellant.

D.   SPECIAL POWERS OF INVESTIGATION

In addition to the already extensive powers of search and seizure, the authorities responsible for the investigation and prosecution of crime may call upon special powers of investigation to deal with two classes of offence which are regarded as particularly serious, and which pose special difficulties in investigation—terrorist offences and cases of serious or complex fraud. At the same time, one particular investigative method—the interception of telephone and other communications—presents particular threats to individual liberty and personal privacy, and for that reason Parliament has introduced a scheme to regulate its use. These special powers and the regulation of telephone tapping are noted in this section.

A.   Investigation of Terrorist Activities

Section 17 of, and Schedule 7 (Part II) to, the Prevention of Terrorism (Temporary Provisions) Act 1989 confer various powers to obtain information for the purposes of "terrorist investigations." "Terrorist investigations" will generally involve investigations into the commission, preparation or instigation of acts of terrorism to which section 14 of the Act applies (*i.e.* acts of terrorism connected with the affairs of Northern Ireland and acts of terrorism of any other description, except acts connected solely with the affairs of the United Kingdom or any part of the United Kingdom other than Northern Ireland). But they also include investigations into "any other act" which appears to have been done in furtherance of or in connection with such acts of terrorism, including any act which appears to constitute an offence under sections 2, 9, 10 or 11 of the 1989 Act (1989 Act, s. 17(1)).

The powers conferred under Schedule 7 for the purpose of terrorist investigations are grouped under the following heads:

— Orders for the production of material
— Warrants for search of premises
— Explanation of seized or produced material
— Urgent cases

Orders for the production of material

Under paragraphs 12 and 13 of Schedule 7, the procurator-fiscal may apply to the sheriff for an order requiring a person in possession of particular material, or material of a particular description to produce that material to a constable for him to take away or to give the constable access to the material. If the material is not in the possession of the person to whom the order is directed then that person may be required to state to the best of his knowledge and belief where it is.

The making of such an order is subject to the following conditions:

(a)   that a terrorist investigation is being carried out and there are reasonable grounds for believing that the material is likely to be of substantial value to the investigation; and

(b)   that there are reasonable grounds for believing that it is in the public interest that the material should be produced or access given to it, having regard—
   (i) to the benefit likely to accrue to the investigation if the material is obtained; and
   (ii) to the circumstances under which the person in possession of the material holds it.

Warrant for search of premises

Under paragraph 14 the sheriff may, on application by the procurator-fiscal, grant a warrant authorising a constable to enter and search premises if the sheriff is satisfied either that an order under paragraph 12 has not been complied with or if certain other conditions are satisfied. These conditions are that

(a)   there are reasonable grounds for believing that there is material on the premises which would be of substantial value to the investigation; and

(b)   it would not be appropriate to make an order under paragraph 12 because—
   (i) it is not practicable to communicate with any person entitled to produce the material, entitled to grant access to the material or entitled to grant entry to the premises on which the material is situated; or
   (ii) to avoid prejudice to the investigation, immediate access to the material is required.

A warrant under this paragraph "shall" authorise a constable to enter the premises specified in the warrant and to search those premises and any person found there, and seize and retain any material found there or on any such person, if he has reasonable grounds for believing that it is likely to be of substantial value to the investigation.

Explanation of seized or produced material

Under paragraph 15 a sheriff may, on application by the procurator-fiscal, order any person specified in the order to provide an explanation of any material produced or made available to a constable under paragraph 12 or seized in pursuance of a warrant under paragraph 14 above.

A person cannot be required under this paragraph to disclose any information which he would be entitled to refuse to disclose on grounds of confidentiality in legal proceedings as being (a) communications between a professional legal adviser and his client or (b) communications made in connection with or in contemplation of legal proceedings and for the purpose of those proceedings. However, a lawyer may be required to provide the name and address of a client.

Urgent cases

Paragraph 16 allows a police officer of at least the rank of superintendent to make a written order granting to a constable such authority as may be given by a search warrant under paragraph 14. This power may only be exercised if the senior officer "has reasonable grounds for believing that the case is one of great emergency and that in the interests of the State immediate action is necessary." Where an authority is granted under paragraph 16, particulars of the case must be notified to the Secretary of State as soon as possible.

All of the powers of investigation provided for in Schedule 7 are without prejudice to:

(a)   any power of entry or search or any power to seize or retain property which is otherwise exercisable by a constable; and

(b)   any rule of law whereby communications between a professional legal adviser and his client or communications made in connection with or in contemplation of legal proceedings and for the purposes of those proceedings are in legal proceedings protected from disclosure on the ground of confidentiality (Sched. 7, para. 17).

The powers of investigation conferred under Schedule 7 are backed up by criminal sanctions under section 17(2) of the 1989 Act which makes various acts of interference with, or disclosures likely to prejudice, the investigation punishable with up to five years' imprisonment.

B. Investigation of Serious or Complex Fraud

Sections 51 to 54 of the Criminal Justice (Scotland) Act 1987 make provision for the investigation of cases of serious or complex fraud.

Section 51 provides that where it appears to the Lord Advocate that a suspected offence may involve serious or complex fraud (which terms are not defined in the Act) and that for the purpose of investigating the affairs or any aspect of the affairs of any person it appears that there is good reason to do so, he may give a direction under that section. Where a section 51 direction has been given, sections 52 to 54 of the Act shall apply as regards the investigation of the offence. Any person (other than a constable) nominated by the Lord Advocate (a "nominated officer") may exercise the powers and functions conferred by those sections.

Criminal Justice (Scotland) Act 1987
"Powers of investigation

    52.—(1) A nominated officer may by notice in writing require the person whose affairs are to be investigated ('the person under investigation') or any other person who he has reason to believe has relevant information to attend before a nominated officer at a specified time and place and answer questions or otherwise furnish information with respect to any matter relevant to the investigation.

(2) A nominated officer may by notice in writing require the person under investigation or any other person to produce at a specified time and place any specified documents which appear to a nominated officer to relate to any matter relevant to the investigation or any documents of a specified class which appear to him so to relate; and—

    (*a*) if any such documents are produced, a nominated officer may—

        (i) take copies or extracts of them;

        (ii) require the person producing them to provide an explanation of any of them;

    (*b*) if any such documents are not produced, a nominated officer may require the person who was required to produce them to state, to the best of his knowledge and belief, where they are.

(3) Where, on a petition presented by the procurator fiscal, the sheriff is satisfied, in relation to any documents, that there are reasonable grounds for believing—

    (*a*) that—

        (i) a person has failed to comply with an obligation under his section to produce them;

        (ii) it is not practicable to serve notice under subsection (2) above in relation to them; or

        (iii) the service of such a notice in relation to them might seriously prejudice the investigation; and

    (*b*) that they are on premises specified in the petition,

he may issue such a warrant as is mentioned in subsection (4) below.

(4) The warrant referred to in subsection (3) above is a warrant authorising a constable together with any other persons named in the warrant—

    (*a*) to enter (using such force as is reasonably necessary for the purpose) and search the premises; and

    (*b*) to take possession of any documents appearing to be documents of the description specified in the petition or to take in relation to any documents so appearing any other steps which may appear to be necessary for preserving them and preventing interference with them.

(5) A statement by a person in response to a requirement imposed by virtue of this section may only be used in evidence against him in a prosecution for an offence under section 2 of the False Oaths (Scotland) Act 1933.

(6) A person shall not under this section be required to disclose any information or produce any document which is an item subject to legal privilege within the meaning of section 40 of this Act; except that a lawyer may be required to furnish the name and address of his client.

(7) No person shall be bound to comply with any requirement imposed by a person exercising power by virtue of a nomination under section 51(2) of this Act unless he has, if required to do so, produced evidence of his authority.

(8) In this section—

    'documents' includes information recorded in any form and, in relation to information recorded otherwise than in legible form, references to its production include references to producing a copy of the information in legible form; and

    'premises' has the same meaning as in section 40 of this Act.

(9) This section and sections 51 and 53 of this Act shall apply to England and Wales and Northern Ireland; and for the purposes of such application any reference—

    (*a*) to the sheriff shall be construed as a reference to a justice of the peace; and

    (*b*) to a petition presented by the procurator fiscal shall be construed—

(i) in England and Wales as a reference to an information laid by a nominated officer;

(ii) in Northern Ireland as a reference to a complaint laid by a nominated officer.

Offences in relation to investigations under section 52

53.—(1) Where any person—

(a) knows or suspects that an investigation under section 52 of this Act is being carried out or is likely to be carried out; and

(b) falsifies, conceals, destroys or otherwise disposes of, or causes or permits the falsification, concealment, destruction or disposal of documents which he knows or suspects or has reasonable grounds to suspect are or would be relevant to such an investigation,

he shall be guilty of an offence.

(2) In proceedings against a person for an offence under subsection (1) above, it shall be a defence to prove—

(a) that he did not know or suspect that by acting as he did he was likely to prejudice the investigation; or

(b) that he had lawful authority or reasonable excuse for acting as he did.

(3) A person guilty of an offence under subsection (1) above shall be liable—

(a) on conviction on indictment, to imprisonment for a term not exceeding seven years or to a fine or to both; and

(b) on summary conviction, to imprisonment for a term not exceeding six months or to a fine not exceeding the statutory maximum or to both.

(4) Any person who fails to comply with a requirement imposed on him under the said section 52 shall be guilty of an offence and liable on summary conviction to imprisonment for a term not exceeding six months or to a fine not exceeding level 5 on the standard scale or to both.

(5) In proceedings against a person for an offence under subsection (4) above, it shall be a defence to prove that he had a reasonable excuse for acting as he did."

NOTE

Smith v. *Director of the Serious Fraud Office* [1992] 3 All E.R. 456 raises an important question concerning the right to silence in the face of the powers of investigation of the Serious Fraud Office in England, which are virtually identical to the powers conferred by sections 52 to 54 of the Criminal Justice (Scotland)) Act 1987.

In that case the appellant was under investigation by the police and the Serious Fraud Office in respect of matters arising out of the collapse of a company of which he was a director. He had already been cautioned and charged with knowingly being a party to the carrying on of the business of a company with intent to defraud its creditors when a notice was served on him under section 2 of the Criminal Justice Act 1987 requiring him to attend for interview with the Serious Fraud Office.

The question which arises in this situation is whether the person under investigation is entitled to rely on the fact that he has been cautioned and charged as a bar to further questioning in respect of the same matters under section 2 of the 1987 Act. In an application for judicial review of the section 2 order the Divisional Court held that he was, but this decision was reversed by the House of Lords who held that the director's powers under section 2 did not come to an end when the person under investigation had been charged and that in view of the clear provisions of section 2 the appellant was not entitled to invoke the right to silence or rely on the caution which had previously been administered to him by the police. Indeed, their Lordships recognised that there was at least a theoretical possibility of the accused being questioned under section 2 even after he had been put on trial in respect of the matter under investigation!

It is not clear how this issue would be resolved should it arise in Scotland. The right to silence has been held to prevail against an apparent obligation to provide information reinforced by criminal penalties (*H.M. Advocate* v. *Von, supra*, p.170) but it could be argued that the statutory provisions under consideration in that case were ambiguous as regards their application to the accused. While the Scottish courts have treated with caution the taking of evidence from persons who have been charged it is clear that there is no absolute rule against this. It may, therefore, be the case that the powers contained in section 52 could be exercised even after a person has been charged. However, even if the statute permitted this, it is submitted, that there must be a "cut-off" point beyond which the powers contained in section 52 cannot be exercised. It is submitted that the appropriate point here is that of full committal. It is true that the courts will issue warrants to take evidence from an accused even after full committal, but it has always been made clear that this will not be permitted where the active participation of the accused is required. In other words, the courts will not grant a warrant authorising the interrogation of the accused after full committal and, in the absence of clear authority to the contrary in section 52, it is submitted that the section should similarly be limited in its effect.

C. Interception of Communications

The Interception of Communications Act 1985 regulates the interception of postal and telephone communications. Section 1 of the 1985 Act makes it an offence for a person to intentionally intercept a communication in the course of its transmission by post or by means of a public communication system. No offence is committed under this section if the communication is intercepted in obedience to a warrant issued by the Secretary of State under section 2 of the Act. Section 2 provides that the Secretary of State may issue a warrant for the interception of communications by post or by telephone, but a warrant cannot be issued unless the Secretary of State considers that it is necessary (a) in the interests of national security, (b) for the purpose of preventing or detecting serious crime, or (c) for the purpose of safeguarding the economic well-being of the United Kingdom. Matters to be taken into account in determining whether it is "necessary" to issue such a warrant shall include whether the information which it is considered necessary to acquire could reasonably be acquired by other means. Section 6 of the Act sets out various safeguards regarding access to, copying of and distribution of information acquired under a warrant issued by the Secretary of State.

In *R.* v. *Preston* [1992] Crim.L.R. 803 it was held that "preventing or detecting serious crime" did not include obtaining evidence to be used for prosecuting offenders. This phrase, as it appears in section 2 of the 1985 Act, was read by the court as referring to the less immediate one of gathering criminal intelligence in relation to serious crime. This conclusion was reached in the light of the past use of telephone tapping and also having regard to the safeguards set out in section 6 of the 1985 Act which, in the view of the court, did not accord with the purpose of gathering evidence for the prosecution of offenders.

Section 9 of the Act is headed "Exclusion of Evidence," and subsection (1) of that section provides that "in any proceedings before any court or tribunal no evidence shall be adduced and no question in cross-examination shall be asked" which (in either case) tends to suggest that an offence of unauthorised interception under section 1 has been committed or that a warrant for interception has been issued. In *R. v. Effick* [1992] Crim.L.R. 580 it was held that section 9 did not provide a statutory bar to the admission of *what* was obtained by the interception of a telephone communication, but excluded evidence which tended to show *how* it had been obtained. This was explained on the ground that public interest required that the means used to obtain evidence in certain types of proceedings (for example, espionage cases) should not be revealed.

In both *Effick* and *Preston* it was recognised that a court could exclude evidence obtained by an interception under section 78 of the Police and Criminal Evidence Act 1984, which allows evidence to be excluded if, having regard, *inter alia*, to the way in which it was obtained, its admission would affect the fairness of the trial. In *Preston* it was pointed out that while section 9 placed serious obstacles in the way of the defence finding out if an interception had taken place, the court could rely on section 78 to exclude evidence obtained in this way if, having regard to the difficulties placed in the way of the defence it would not be fair to admit the evidence.

CHAPTER 7

BAIL

The law on bail in Scotland was radically altered by the Bail etc. (Scotland) Act 1980, a statute which incorporated most of the reforms suggested in Chapter 11 of the Second Report of the Thomson Committee (1975 Cmnd. 6218). Formerly, the deposit of money was an essential precondition of release if a bail application was to be granted. But under the 1980 Act, the general position is that if bail is granted, the accused is liberated on a bail order under section 1(1). This order contains a number of conditions which are set out in section 1(2), such as are necessary to secure that the accused
  (a)   appears at the appointed time at every diet relating to the offence with which he is charged of which he is given due notice;
  (b)   does not commit an offence while on bail;
  (c)   does not interfere with witnesses or otherwise obstruct the course of justice whether in relation to himself or any other person; and
  (d)   makes himself available for the purpose of enabling inquiries or a report to be made to assist the court in dealing with him for the offence with which he is charged.
Under section 2 of the 1980 Act it is prescribed that a bail order must specify the conditions imposed and the address which will be regarded as the domicile of citation for the accused, where he can be cited to appear at court.

The above conditions are referred to as "the standard conditions" of bail, but section 1(2) does not preclude the court from adding further conditions, such as that the accused will not approach a particular individual who may be a witness in the case. Breach of bail conditions is an offence: s. 3(1) and see *Aitchison* v. *Tudhope*, 1981 S.L.T. 231 *infra*, p.335.

The court or the Lord Advocate may only impose a condition as to the deposit of money bail where such a condition is appropriate to the special circumstances of the case: s. 1(3). This is rare in practice.

But the Act did not alter the fundamental principles which must be considered by a court when confronted with a bail application by an accused person in custody. For this reason, the body of pre-1980 case law in which those principles were developed is still of relevance today.

A.   SHOULD BAIL BE GRANTED?

1.   Mackintosh v. McGlinchy
1921 J.C. 75
An accused person was charged with firearms offences and was granted bail by the sheriff. The procurator-fiscal appealed to the High Court.

LORD JUSTICE-GENERAL (CLYDE): "In one form or another bail was always, or at any rate from very remote antiquity, a part of our criminal law. Prior to the statute of 1701 the practice of exacting sureties from persons accused of even the gravest capital offences for their appearance to answer the charge was known and observed according to Baron Hume (Crimes, vol. ii., p. 87). But the advantages of this practice were not available to accused persons as matter of right. On the contrary, bail was allowed or refused according to the discretion of the Court. 'Though such an indulgence may have been given in particular cases,' says Baron Hume (p. 88), 'yet still it is difficult to believe that any police could ever be maintained under a system, which uniformly allowed so great a latitude of dismissing the highest and most notorious offenders, on so insecure a footing. And in truth, on the whole, the just construction of the foregoing statutes rather seems to be, that they marked out a course of proceeding to the magistrate, and bestowed a discretion on him, which he might use if he saw cause, or could not easily attach the criminal's person; than that they intended to create an absolute privilege of bail in favour of the delinquent, which he might insist on after imprisonment, as a matter of right.' There is little ground for thinking that, as the law was administered prior to the Act of 1701, the Court was in the habit of exercising this discretion with any excess of leniency.

The main defect in the criminal law and practice which led to the passage of the Act of 1701 was that persons who were under accusation of crime, and had been apprehended accordingly, had no efficient protection against prolonged incarceration before their case was brought to trial. The problem of bail and the problem of protecting accused persons against lengthy imprisonment without trial are closely related, and the statute of 1701 dealt with both. First with regard to bail, the statute divided offences into what it called bailable and non-bailable offences. With regard to the latter class, namely, non-bailable offences, the law and practice as existing prior to the Act was left unchanged. That is to say, the Court could be asked to exercise the discretion naturally belonging to it, after the Act of 1701 just as before, in the case of a non-bailable offence. But in the case of bailable offences, the statute provided certain hard-and-fast maximum measures of caution (applicable to persons of various degrees), which, if tendered to the Court, entitled those persons as a matter of right to bail. The value of this right must be measured in light of the fact that non-bailable offences included the whole range of offences to which at that time a capital sentence was applicable in accordance with the letter of the law—almost the whole field of crime, petty offences excluded. In Hume, vol. ii., page 89, and in Sheriff Alison's Criminal Law, vol. ii., page 162, there are included among non-bailable offences cases of deforcements of the officers of the revenue; assaults with loaded firearms, or sharp instruments; thefts by one habit and repute, or repeatedly convicted—or of articles of considerable value, as above £100—or of any thing, however small, by housebreaking, or of a horse, or ox, or more than one sheep; all cases of robbery or stouthrief, how small soever the value of the article taken; and all cases of forging notes, or uttering forged notes, or forging bills or instruments for payment of money. Further the Act of 1701 provided means by which a person who was not admitted to bail but remained in prison could take steps to hasten the trial of his cause. The machinery was cumbrous, and, judged by more modern standards, not over-effective.

The law with regard to these matters—subject to a variety of minor modifications—continued to rest upon the principles of the Act of 1701 until the passing of the Criminal Procedure Act, 1887, and the Bail Act of 1888. Both these Acts deal with the allowance of bail in words which admit of no doubt or ambiguity. Both of them say that, except in cases of murder and treason, bail can be granted in the discretion of the Court before whom the accused person is brought. The argument which has been presented to-day—in its major proposition—challenged the existence and reality of that discretion, and—in its minor proposition—sought to establish some limitation or restriction (it was not clear what) upon its exercise. So far as it related to bail, the Act of 1701 was completely repealed by the Act of 1888, and it follows that, if any ground exists for importing any particular limitation or qualification of the discretion expressly given to the Court by the Acts of 1887 and 1888, that ground must be found, not in the repealed provisions of 1701, but in the substituted enactments of 1887 and 1888. We have had our attention fully directed to the terms of those statutes. There is nothing whatever, either direct or indirect, express or implied, in the provisions of either of those statutes which would justify giving to the word 'discretion' any other meaning than that which it naturally bears. That answers the major proposition, and it really disposes of the minor proposition also. In considering generally what is the nature of that discretion of which the statutes of 1887 and 1888 speak, one cannot do better than have regard to the judicial description of the discretion which the Court undoubtedly possessed—prior to the passage of those Acts—in the case of the non-bailable offences under the Act of 1701. In 1878, in connexion with the trial of the Directors of the City of Glasgow Bank (who were indicted for an offence which was non-bailable, at least in one view of the *species facti*), Lord President Inglis said this 'The petitioners further appeal to the discretion of the Court to liberate them on such bail as may be sufficient to ensure their appearance hereafter to answer the charges made against them. That we possess such discretionary power cannot be disputed. But in prosecutions conducted by the public prosecutor the discretion is vested, in the first instance at least, in the Lord Advocate; and unless it can be alleged that the Lord Advocate has refused bail, not for the purpose of securing the ends of justice, but for some other and therefore illegitimate purpose, I think the Court ought not to interfere, because such interference would be nothing less than relieving the Lord Advocate of the responsibility attaching to his high office. He is subject to this responsibility, and vested with the corresponding discretion, because he has means and appliances for obtaining information and forming a judgment which are not within the reach of any other official, and are not possessed by this Court. But it has not been suggested that the Lord Advocate is not discharging his important and responsible duties with fairness and impartiality, and with a sole view to the public interest, and to secure the ends of justice.' In this passage the weight which the Court is entitled to attach to the view of the Lord Advocate in such matters—one of the incidental advantages of the system of public prosecution—is emphasised. But the principle laid down applies to the exercise of its discretion by the Court as much as to the discharge by the Lord Advocate of his duties. The discretion must be used with a sole view to the public interest and to secure the ends of justice. The Acts of 1887 and 1888 took away nothing from the discretion which was thus exercised prior to their coming into force. Accordingly, my opinion on the statutes is that the Court has in this matter of bail a discretion, and that the broad consideration which rules its exercise is a single regard to the public interest and the ends of justice, and that, in considering any appeal to that discretion, a statement made to the Court on the high responsibility of the Lord Advocate is entitled to great weight.

The particular ground on which the public prosecutor most commonly opposes bail, and on which the Court most frequently exercises its discretion by refusal of it, is that it is apprehended that bail will be ineffectual to secure that the accused will appear to answer the charge. That was the particular ground alleged by the Lord Advocate in the City of Glasgow Bank case, in which the general principles applying to the matter were expounded by the judgment just quoted. But it was said on behalf of the appellants here that this was the only consideration with reference to which the Court can exercise its discretion. In support of this contention reference was made to a passage in the judgment of Lord Dunedin in the case of *A B* v. *Dickson* [1907 S.C. (J.) 111]; and we were told that this passage had been thought in some quarters to imply a restriction of the breadth previously attributed to the discretion of the Court in this matter. The report of the case negatives the idea that any general question with regard to the discretion of the Court was raised or debated. The case was one of rape, and followed on a previous case for the same offence in which some expressions had been used which might be read as implying that bail ought to be refused in all rape cases. The propriety of any such general rule was the subject of discussion, but (as I have said) no general question with regard to the conditions under which bail should be allowed was raised or argued. In giving judgment Lord Dunedin said (at p.112), 'That the Court has power to grant liberation on bail I do not think can be doubted. If the Lord Advocate assures the Court that in his view the effect of that will in all likelihood be to defeat the ends of justice by the prisoner absconding, as the Lord Advocate's only object must be to secure his presence at the trial, the Court will no doubt give weight to that statement. If it is thought that that is not likely to happen, there is no reason why liberation should not be granted.' In this passage Lord Dunedin cites, as an example of the grounds on which the Court refuses bail, the particular ground which most frequently recurs. It was the only ground with which the discussion was concerned, as against the supposed rule excluding bail altogether in rape cases. But I cannot read the passage as one intended to contain an exhaustive exposition of the whole law on the subject, or as restricting the discretion of the Court as theretofore practised. Lord McLaren makes the true meaning of the judgment clear when he says (at p.112): 'I think it is in accordance with good sense and justice that great weight should be given to the representations of the procurator-fiscal on this question, if, for example, he states that he has good reason to fear that the accused will go away and forfeit his bail.' In short the probability that the accused will abuse his liberation by absconding is one, but only one, of a number of ways in which the ends of justice may be defeated by the indiscriminate allowance of bail, and which the refusal of bail can and ought to be used to prevent. The practice of the Court since 1888—at any rate as I have known it—has not conformed to the narrow view of the discretionary power of the Court which is contended for by the accused; and, if I thought that the passage from Lord Dunedin's judgment to which I have referred really supported that narrow view, I should be compelled respectfully but emphatically to dissent from it.

A good deal was said in the argument before us about the classes of case in which the discretion of the Court is appropriately exercised by refusing bail. It is neither possible nor expedient to categorise them; for, when appeal is made to a discretionary power, the only safe rule is that each case must be considered on its own merits, with the sole view to the public interest and to securing the ends of justice. As illustrations, cases have been mentioned in which the Lord Advocate has reason to apprehend that an accused person intends to defeat the ends of justice, if liberated, by tampering with the evidence. Again, there are cases such as incest or brutal domestic assault, where the gravest consequences will ensue from the return of the accused to his home pending trial. An important class of case also was referred to, where the person accused is not acting alone, but in association with others who may not themselves be the objects of criminal proceedings, and where liberation would leave the accused free to continue in association and co-operation with these people for the very same criminal objects participation in which has brought him to justice. Many other examples can be cited in which it might be proper to submit the facts to the Court, and to ask the Court to exercise its discretion with a sole view to the public interest, and to secure the ends of justice.

It is perhaps right to make in conclusion, the self-evident observation that, when an accused person asks for bail or appeals for bail, bail he must get, unless a sufficient ground is brought forward requiring the Court to exercise its discretion by refusing it. A good deal was said about the presumption of innocence. I prefer not to treat the matter as a question of presumption. The accused person has the right to ask for bail; he has the right to have his application considered; and, unless the Court has before it some good reason why bail should not be granted, bail ought to be allowed."

> The court refused bail after hearing that the Crown believed that the accused was likely to abscond.

NOTE

The stress placed by the Lord Justice-General on the discretionary function of the court considering a bail application is equally apt today. As in this case, the Crown's attitude to bail is very important. If the Crown do not oppose bail it should be granted: *Maxwell* v. *McGlennan*, 1989 S.C.C.R. 117. Other important factors are the gravity of the offence and the record of the accused.

2. McLaren v. H.M. Advocate
1967 S.L.T. (Notes) 43

An accused person was charged with murder. Under section 2 of the Bail (Scotland) Act 1888 it was provided that all crimes and offences, except murder and treason, were bailable, although section 8 of the Act specifically reserved the right of the Lord Advocate or the High Court to admit to bail any person charged with any crime or offence. The accused applied for bail by petition to the High Court.

LORD JUSTICE-GENERAL (CLYDE): "As the crime charged here is murder the bail provisions in the 1888 Act are consequently not available, hence the present application is made direct to the High Court of Justiciary not under the Act but at common law, in an appeal to the discretionary powers of this Court which lie behind any statutory provision in an Act of Parliament. Indeed, the existence of these discretionary powers is expressly preserved in s. 8 of the 1888 Act. The fact that there are these discretionary powers in the Court is recognised by our standard writers on Criminal Law (see Hume on *Crimes*, II, p.90), and they are only exercised when the Court sees reasons for such an indulgence in the whole circumstances of the case. The ambit of this discretionary power is similar to that exercisable under the statutes and is described in these terms by the Lord Justice-General in the full Bench case of *Mackintosh* v. *McGlinchy* 1921 J.C. 75 at p.80:—'The Court has in this matter of bail a discretion and the broad consideration which rules its exercise is a single regard to the public interest and the ends of justice and, in considering any appeal to that discretion, a statement made to the Court on the high responsibility of the Lord Advocate is entitled to great weight'.

In the present case the charge is one of murder. Moreover, the Lord Advocate in the exercise of a discretion which is vested in him is opposing the granting of bail in the light of the circumstances as known to him. This is a factor of very great importance in any consideration of the matter by this Court, for he has means of obtaining information and forming a judgment on the matter which are not possessed by us. It was suggested that the abolition of the death penalty has changed the situation and made murder a less important crime than it was in the past. But although Parliament has seen fit to abolish the death penalty for murder and to substitute a period of imprisonment, in the eyes of a court of law murder is still murder whatever the punishment for it may be and we cannot disregard the fact that the charge in the present case is murder.

In the light of these facts, a very strong argument would be necessary to entitle us in the exercise of our discretion to differ from the conclusion to which the Lord Advocate came. Notwithstanding the careful and clear argument presented to us by counsel for the petitioner, we see no reason for reaching any different conclusion from that at which the Lord Advocate himself arrived.

In these circumstances the prayer of the present petition will not be granted."

Bail refused.

NOTE

Sections 2 and 8 of the Bail (Scotland) Act 1888 are now sections 26(1) and 35 of the 1975 Act. In *H.M. Advocate* v. *McTavish*, 1974 S.L.T. 246 an accused charged with murder was released pending trial. The Crown had failed in an application to have extended the statutory time-limit for proceeding to trial; no bail was fixed and the accused was simply ordained to appear. Bail was granted in *Welsh, Petitioner*, 1990 S.C.C.R. 763, but refused in *McLeod, Petitioner*, 1993 S.C.C.R. 601, in both of which cases there were specialities about time-limits for proceeding to trial. On time-limits in solemn proceedings, see, *infra*, pp.306–319. See also *Schiavone, Petitioner*, 1992 S.C.C.R. 95 in which the fact that the Crown accepted a plea of guilty to culpable homicide where the original charge was murder was enough to render bail competent pending sentence; and *Boyle, Petitioner*, 1993 S.C.C.R. 251, where bail was granted to an accused pending retrial on a murder charge.

3. Young v. H.M. Advocate
1946 J.C. 5

A convicted prisoner appealed against conviction and applied for interim liberation pending his appeal. A single judge refused this application, and the accused then appealed to a Bench of the High Court.

LORD JUSTICE-CLERK (COOPER): "... Under section 9 of the Criminal Appeal (Scotland) Act, 1926, it is provided that the Court may, if it seems fit, on the application of an appellant, admit the appellant to bail pending the determination of his appeal. In such a case it appears to me that the considerations by reference to which bail should be granted or refused are not those which are properly applicable to the case of an application for bail by an untried prisoner. In the case of the untried prisoner the presumption of innocence involves, as the well-known case of *Mackintosh* v. *M'Glinchy* indicated, that, unless good reasons can be shown to the contrary, the applicant has a right to be released on bail, if the crime with which he is charged is a bailable crime. But once the prisoner has been convicted, the presumption of innocence is displaced, and the *onus demonstrandi* is on the applicant thereafter to show cause why, pending any appeal which he may take, he should be released from the prison confinement to which he was sentenced following upon the conviction. I note that, in applying a provision in identical terms, the English Court of Criminal Appeal have consistently taken the line that bail pending determination of the appeal is to be granted only in exceptional and unusual circumstances (cases cited in Archbold, Criminal Practice, (31st ed.) p. 285); and while we are not bound by decisions of the Court of Criminal Appeal, still I must state my own view that that rule impresses me as salutary and appropriate.

But in this case the facts are distinctly unusual. The applicant was convicted on 25th April and sentenced to three years' penal servitude on various charges of large scale theft and housebreaking. This is the 9th of October, nearly six months after the imposition of the sentence. The applicant has been granted an extension of the time within which to appeal, and an appeal has been lodged, and will be disposed of by other Judges of this Court within the next two weeks. The case thus comes before us in the extraordinary situation that the applicant, having remained in prison serving his sentence for the greater part of six months, now desires to be released for the final two weeks or thereby which remain before his appeal will be finally determined.

The only ground Mr Taylor put forward in support of this unusual plea is that a co-accused charged under the same indictment, against whom the evidence may or may not have been the same, has in the interval appealed to the High Court of Justiciary and the conviction against him has been quashed. On that ground Mr Taylor maintained that there was, as he put it, 'at least a possibility' of success in the present appellant's appeal. I should hope that the same could be said in the case of every appellant who appeals to the High Court, but such a circumstance seems to me to fall very far short of the exceptional ground which, in my judgment, ought to be advanced in a special case like this for releasing the prisoner and granting bail for the short period which has still to expire before his case is disposed of. I may add that it is to my mind a material consideration that the present applicant has nine previous convictions, and has served quite a number of long terms of imprisonment, the dates of which sufficiently indicate that on more than one occasion he cannot have long been released from prison on one offence before he had committed another. In these circumstances I have no hesitation in advising your Lordships that this application, which is in substance an appeal to us against a decision by the Lord Justice-General refusing bail, should be dismissed."

Bail refused.

NOTE

While it is no doubt true that the presumption of innocence is displaced by the conviction of the accused, Lord Cooper's view that bail pending an appeal should only be granted in exceptional and unusual circumstances is not of such force today.

Under the 1980 Act, the sanctions for non-compliance with the bail conditions may prove to be more onerous than the forfeiture of any money bail which was required prior to the Act, and in practice, since then, interim liberation on the standard conditions pending appeal against conviction has not been at all uncommon. But any grant of bail must be such as will achieve the immediate release of the applicant; where he is in custody for some other reason a bail application in a different case cannot be granted.

4. Currie v. H.M. Advocate
(1980) S.C.C.R. Supp. 248

The accused was serving a sentence of imprisonment. He was charged with another offence and applied to the sheriff for bail. This was refused and he appealed to the High Court against that refusal.

LORD JUSTICE-CLERK (WHEATLEY): "The appellant made an application for bail to the sheriff and this was refused. He then appealed against this decision to the High Court and the appeal came before me in chambers. His counsel made certain representations in support of the appeal, but when the advocate-depute came to address me he informed me, inter alia, that the appellant was presently serving a sentence of imprisonment for another offence. I asked counsel whether he or his Edinburgh agents were aware of this fact and was told that they were not. I refused the appeal but ordered enquiry to be made to ascertain whether the local solicitor who had appeared before the sheriff was aware of it. I have now been informed in a letter from the Edinburgh solicitors that the local solicitor was aware of the fact but had overlooked it when sending instructions to the Edinburgh solicitors for the appeal. I accept his explanation and apologies thereanent. That, however, is not the point with which I wish to deal. Sitting regularly on bail appeals I find that it is not uncommon for applications for bail being made when the applicant is in prison in respect of another offence. When submitting the report to me in the instant case the Edinburgh solicitors said this:

> 'We would point out that it is a not uncommon situation in the sheriff court for bail to be asked for when an accused is serving a sentence. That prevents the matter having to be brought back before the court when he would otherwise be due for release. In the writer's personal experience it is granted in these circumstances.'

This statement rather surprised me and I caused enquiries to be made in the two busiest sheriff courts to ascertain whether, and if so to what extent, such a practice prevailed. The answers provided were as follows. In the busiest court such applications are not uncommon but there were so many bail applications that the number of such applications could not be quantified. In the other court it was said that such applications are uncommon. In both it was said that such applications were normally only granted when the sentence being served is about to expire and the diet of trial, if known, is beyond the expiry of that sentence. It was pointed out that the court officials in the sheriff court are obliged to accept applications for bail and place them before the sheriff.

I accept this latter point, but I am concerned about the practice of allowing bail in such circumstances. I wish to make it clear that an application for bail (either in the first instance or on the appeal) should be decided on the circumstances which prevail at the time when the application is made. The phrase 'where a sentence is about to expire' is an elastic one, but it does not affect the principle which I have just enunciated. What may transpire in the interval, however short, between the application and the expiry of the sentence being served is imponderable, but in any event granting bail in anticipation is something which offends against the principle which I have enunciated, and where it exists it must stop. I appreciate that this may result in a further application being made after the sentence has expired with consequential additional work being placed on the court, but, however unfortunate, that is no reason for allowing a relaxation of the principle."

Appeal refused.

NOTE

Here, Lord Justice-Clerk Wheatley is setting a guideline which requires to be borne in mind when a bail application is being considered. An accused may have a number of cases pending, both solemn and summary, and may also be in custody at the same time for various different reasons, such as being on remand pending another case, serving a custodial sentence or awaiting an appearance where sentence has been deferred. All these matters must be explored before putting a bail application before a court. The Lord Justice-Clerk set out further guidelines in the following case.

5. Smith v. M.

1982 S.L.T. 421; 1982 S.C.C.R. 115

An accused person was granted bail by the sheriff, even although he had a number of previous convictions, was on probation and had three other cases pending, for one of which he was already on bail. The procurator-fiscal appealed to the High Court against the grant of bail.

LORD JUSTICE-CLERK (WHEATLEY): "The reasons for the Crown's opposition to bail were these. At the time when the alleged offence was committed the respondent was in the following position. (1) He was undergoing a probation order for one year which had been imposed on 2nd November 1981 on conviction of a charge of theft. (2) He had three cases outstanding against him in respect of two charges of theft on 28th April 1981 and 6th May 1981 and one charge of fraud on 20th June 1981. For the last of these he was made the subject of a bail order on 2nd February 1982. (3) He had a long list of previous convictions from 1970 onwards showing a regularity of offending. This record consisted of 31 court appearances involving 38 offences. In 1981 alone he had five convictions for theft, including one on indictment. In these circumstances I find it difficult to understand how the sheriff found it appropriate to grant bail to this man. Of course, no report is available from the sheriff under this procedure to explain the reasons for his decision and there might be a perfectly good one. None, however, is apparent to me, and the only one which counsel for the respondent could think of was that the respondent was undergoing outpatient treatment at the Andrew Duncan Clinic for a drink problem which, it was said, should not be interrupted. That certainly does not appear to me to be a legitimate reason for granting bail in view of the circumstances to which I have alluded. I accordingly grant the appeal.

In the light of a fairly extensive experience of the Bail, etc. (Scotland) Act 1980 I consider it desirable to set down certain guidelines in relation to the allowance or refusal of bail in the present state of the law. This is a field in which no absolute classifications can be made, as each case has to be dealt with on its own facts. But it seems to me that there are certain considerations which should generally regulate the decision on allowance of bail, and adherence to such general considerations while having regard to the facts of the individual case could, I am sure, save a lot of needless appeals, thus saving a great deal of judicial time and public expense.

Regard should be given not only to the letter but to the spirit of the Bail, etc. (Scotland) Act 1980. There is, however, the consideration of the public interest. An accused should be granted a bail order unless it can be shown that there are good grounds for not granting it. A complete catalogue of such grounds cannot be compiled. Generally, however, they can fall into two broad categories: (1) the protection of the public and (2) the administration of justice. Previous convictions per se should not be regarded as an automatic reason for refusal of bail, but if there is a significance in the record and the nature of the charge(s) then being preferred against an accused, the consideration of the protection of the public arises. Thus, to take an extreme case, if an accused who has had a persistent record of crime over the years, particularly in relation to one form of crime such as theft by house-breaking, had just recently been discharged from prison for such an offence or offences, it would be reasonable to infer that it was in the public interest that he should not be at large pending his trial. In such cases bail can appropriately be refused. Before turning to consider other considerations, I shall deal with the submission that the presumption of innocence should in logic and equity result in a person charged being released on bail. If this was a good argument in the sense that it should automatically apply, then no bail would be refused except in those cases where no bail is allowed. The presumption of innocence is no doubt a factor, but it does not exclude competing factors which may be more formidable in the circumstances of the case.

One of the factors which in my view is of importance is the allegation that at the time when the alleged offence (or offences) was (or were) committed the accused was in a position of trust to behave as a good citizen and not to breach the law. That can arise in a number of ways and the list which follows is merely illustrative of the more common examples and not exhaustive. I tabulate them as follows: (1) When the accused was already on bail in respect of another offence or offences. (2) When though not on bail he was in an equivalent position, namely, had been ordained to appear at a subsequent court diet for trial on another offence. (3) When he was on probation or undergoing a community service order. (4) When he was on licence or parole. (5) When he was on deferred sentence. In such circumstances I take the view that unless there are cogent reasons for deciding otherwise bail should be refused. Other circumstances which warrant refusal of bail are the nature of the offence in very special circumstances, alleged intimidation of witnesses by assaults or threats, absence of a fixed abode, or reasonable grounds for suspecting that the accused will not turn up for his trial. On the other side of the coin, I do not regard it as good ground for refusing bail that after full committal bail is opposed by the Crown on a vague or unspecified ground that the police are making further enquiries. If the Crown can show it is in the public interest or in the interest of the administration of justice that an accused should be further detained while further enquiries are being made, that is a different matter.

There is another situation with which I am called upon to deal on appeal, namely when after conviction an accused is remanded in custody for reports. As a result of enquiries made I have been informed that the tests which are made to determine the accused's fitness for borstal or a detention centre require his continued detention in a appropriate institution for a period of time. Refusal of bail in such circumstances is understandable. On the other hand, detention in custody is not normally required for a social enquiry report, and there seems no reason why an accused should not be released on bail pending the obtaining of such a report unless there are good reasons for keeping him in detention.

Finally, I am regularly asked to grant interim liberation pending appeals. If the appeal is against sentence alone, no technical problem arises. If the appeal is against conviction the appellant has first of all to lodge a note of intention to appeal and later on a note of appeal which contains the grounds of appeal. An application for interim liberation can only be properly considered when the grounds of appeal have been lodged, and it is at that point that such an application should be made. As I have already indicated, there may be other considerations one way or another in these various situations, but I have felt constrained to set out these guidelines in view of the divergent attitudes to bail in the lower courts which appeals have disclosed."

Crown appeal allowed; bail refused.

NOTE

These guidelines, although prescribed over 10 years ago, are still applicable today, although in relation to bail pending the preparation of reports the reference to the necessity of a remand in custody for a report on the accused's suitability for borstal or detention centre training is no longer apt, such sentences having been abolished. Very good reasons are required in order to justify a refusal of bail pending receipt of a social inquiry report: *McGoldrick* v. *Normand*, 1988 S.C.C.R. 83. It must be stressed that no bail "guidelines" have the force of law and each case must be considered on its own facts. In solemn cases, a bail application to a sheriff must be disposed of within 24 hours of its presentation: 1975 Act, s. 28(2); and see *Lau, Petitioner*, 1986 S.C.C.R. 140; *Gibbons, Petitioner*, 1988 S.C.C.R. 270. A bail order relates to offences, not proceedings, and so continues in force even if the proceedings are originally solemn but later become summary: *McGinn* v. *H.M. Advocate*, 1990 S.C.C.R. 170. See also *Walker* v. *Lockhart*, 1994 S.L.T. 209.

B. RIGHTS OF APPEAL AND REVIEW

Detailed provisions are to be found in sections 30 to 33, 299 and 300 of the 1975 Act, but there has been some case law on the circumstances in which review of a decision on bail is competent.

1. **H.M. Advocate v. Jones**
1964 S.L.T. (Sh.Ct.) 50

An accused person was refused bail by the sheriff, appealed against that decision and had his appeal refused by the High Court. Subsequently he applied to the sheriff to have the earlier decision reviewed.

SHERIFF C.H. JOHNSTON, Q.C.: "This is an application made today for review of the decision of this court purporting to be made under section 37 of the Criminal Justice (Scotland) Act, 1963. It is contended by the Crown that the application is incompetent. The material facts are these. The applicant originally applied in this court for bail in respect of the charges at present laid against him on 29th April 1964. The Crown opposed the granting of bail upon two grounds: (a) that the offences of which the applicant is now accused were said to have been committed while he was on bail in respect of other matters, and (b) that the applicant has a substantial record of convictions. This court refused the application for bail and this decision was appealed to the High Court of Justiciary and was upheld by that court. Yesterday, 9th June 1964, the applicant was acquitted by a jury of the charges in respect of which bail had earlier been granted. The applicant is now simply an untried prisoner awaiting trial. In that situation, his solicitor maintains that this court has power in terms of section 37(2) of the 1963 Act to review its earlier decision of 29th April 1964, albeit that decision has been upheld by the High Court on appeal. The Crown contends that the determination of the High Court of an appeal from a decision of this court is in itself a 'decision' within the meaning of section 37, and that all applications for review made thereafter must be made direct to the High Court of Justiciary, whether of the present type or as to the amount of bail fixed, if bail is fixed. I was informed by both parties that section 37 has not been the subject of any authoritative decision binding on me, and also that section 37 contains the whole of the provisions relating to review as distinct from appeal. In my view, the Crown's contention is well founded. There can be no doubt that the determination of the High Court on an appeal from a decision of this court is a decision in the general sense. The question is whether it is a decision within the meaning of this section. Such applications can be made only at the instance of an accused person. It is open to such a person to make repeated applications for review either of a decision to admit to bail or of a decision as to the bail fixed, and in fact many applications of the latter type come before this court. If the Crown's contention is sound, in every case in which the High Court on an appeal from an inferior court grants bail, or upholds the decision of the judge of first instance to grant bail, these repeated applications for review would require to be made to the High Court.

The result may be to encumber the High Court with an ever-increasing number of applications for review, but I do not find warrant in this section for the view that a judge in an inferior court has power to review either the amount of bail fixed by the Supreme Court, or, as in this case where a material change of circumstances has taken place, the ultimate determination as to the allowance or refusal of bail. Such a course would offend against all established practice, and could be pursued only upon the clearest legislative warrant. This is absent. This application is incompetent, and ought to have been made to the High Court of Justiciary. I think it right to add that I have been greatly assisted in my consideration of this technical but not unimportant point of procedure by the clear arguments of the procurator-fiscal depute and the solicitor for the applicant."

Application refused.

NOTE

Section 37 of the Criminal Justice (Scotland) Act 1963 is now sections 30 and 299 of the 1975 Act. Both of these sections apply only where a court has refused to admit a person to bail or, where a court has so admitted a person, the bail fixed has not been found, but the references to "bail," "amounts of bail" and "finding bail" found in those sections and other pre-1980 enactments have now to be construed in the light of section 1(4) of the Bail etc. (Scotland) Act 1980. So if an accused accepts bail conditions, but subsequently seeks to have one of them removed, he can apply for a review to the court which granted bail: *Gilchrist, Petitioner*, 1991 S.C.C.R. 699.

In practice, *H.M. Advocate* v. *Jones* is often thought of as authority for the proposition that once the matter of bail has been considered in the High Court, any reconsideration of the matter must also take place there. But this is not quite accurate, as the next case shows.

2.   **Ward v. H.M. Advocate**
1972 S.L.T. (Notes) 22

An accused person was allowed bail by the sheriff. The Crown appealed against the grant of bail, but the High Court refused the Crown appeal. The accused then presented a note to the High Court craving review of the amount of bail fixed by the sheriff.

LORD CAMERON: "When an appeal is taken by the prosecutor against allowance of bail and the appeal is refused, then further procedure depends upon the terms of the relevant statute, which in this case is the Criminal Justice (Scotland) Act 1963. Section 37(2) of that Act gives a court the power to review its decision as to granting or refusing bail, or, in particular, as to the amount of bail, if bail is allowed. In my opinion the court referred to in s. 37(2) is the same court as is referred to in s. 37(1) and therefore, when the question is one of reduction of the amount of bail already fixed, it is prima facie for the court which has in the first instance fixed the amount of bail to deal with that issue on a review. In the present case, as it is now admitted (contrary to what was said in the note of appeal) (1) the only appeal to the High Court was by the prosecutor against the allowance of bail and (2) the amount of bail to be found if the prosecutor's appeal failed, as it did, was not in issue; in these circumstances the question of the amount of bail to be found is still within the purview of the court which initially fixed the amount of the bail and whose decision in that respect has not so far been subjected to review. As the High Court dealt only with one particular point then, the case stands thus: The appellant was admitted to bail by the competent court: its decision in so doing was upheld on appeal and the initial statutory power of review of the amount of bail fixed by that court was not affected, as no determination on that point was made by the High Court. It therefore appears to me that it is still open to the court which originally fixed the amount of bail to exercise the power of review in that regard which is specifically provided for by s. 37(2) of the Act of 1963 and consequently that this appeal is incompetent as being premature.

My attention has been drawn to the case of *H.M. Advocate* v. *Jones*, 1964 S.L.T. (Sh.Ct.) 50. That was a somewhat unusual case and differed substantially in its circumstances from the present. In that case, far from the sheriff being invited to review his own decision in terms of the statute, he was being invited to review a decision of the High Court. All that s. 37 says is this—'A court shall . . . have power to review its decision.' The Act does not say a court which has allowed, refused or fixed the amount of bail shall have power to review the decision of another and a superior court in any of these matters. The issue in the case of *Jones* (*supra*) was in effect whether the sheriff-substitute had power to reverse a decision of the High Court on an appeal from the sheriff-substitute. In holding that such a review was incompetent, I think the sheriff-substitute was correct, but that is not this case. Where a High Court decision has been given on an appeal on whether or not bail should be allowed, but the issue of amount of bail, if allowed, is not raised, then I am of the opinion that review of the amount of bail is still within the competence of the court which originally allowed bail and fixed the amount of it. In these circumstances the present appeal will be refused."

Note refused.

NOTE

So if the High Court refuse an appeal by the Crown against the grant of bail, but the accused seeks to have the conditions of bail reviewed, then an application for review can be made to the original court even although the question of bail (in principle) has been considered in the High Court. Alteration of a bail address can be achieved by simple application in writing: 1980 Act, s. 2(2). Section 30 of the 1975 Act has no application to the situation where an accused is convicted and his case is continued for reports to be prepared. If bail pending those reports is refused, an appeal lies under section 179(2) of the 1975 Act and section 30 cannot be used: *Long* v. *H.M. Advocate*, 1984 S.C.C.R. 161.

CHAPTER 8

FIRST STEPS IN SOLEMN PROCEDURE

A. JUDICIAL EXAMINATION AND COMMITTAL

Once an accused person has been charged by the police and the procurator-fiscal decides to proceed by petition rather than summary complaint, the accused will normally be brought before the sheriff the next day for judicial examination. The sheriff court is not required to sit on Saturdays, Sundays or court holidays, but may sit on any day for the disposal of criminal business: Bail etc. (Scotland) Act 1980, s. 10(1). Prior to the first appearance of the accused in court the accused has a statutory right under section 19 of the 1975 Act to have intimation sent to a solicitor that legal assistance is sought, and to a private interview with the solicitor. No practical difficulties usually arise, as accused persons who have not availed themselves of this right are automatically offered the services of the duty solicitor acting under the provisions of the Legal Aid (Scotland) Act 1986.

Judicial examination as reconstituted under section 6 of the 1980 Act is encountered quite often in practice. For an excellent description of the procedure to be followed, see Sheriff I. D. Macphail, "Judicial Examination" (1982) 27 J.L.S. (Workshop) 296.

The following examples illustrate some of the problems which have come before the High Court wherein the procedures followed under sections 20A and 20B of the 1975 Act have been made the subject of challenge.

1. Carmichael v. Armitage
1983 S.L.T. 216

An accused person emitted a declaration at judicial examination. At a preliminary diet the fiscal objected to the declaration being read to the jury. The sheriff overruled the Crown objection and the fiscal appealed to the High Court.

OPINION OF THE COURT: "This appeal raises for the first time an important point in relation to the manner in which a declaration can be emitted by an accused during a judicial examination in terms of the Criminal Procedure (Scotland) Act 1975 as amended. The declaration was made on 15 March 1982 and at a preliminary diet on 20 September 1982 the appellant moved the sheriff not to allow the declaration to be read to the jury at the trial on 18 October 1982. The ground for the motion was that the declaration by the respondent was not an account by the respondent himself of the events described in his statement, since the statement had been written out by his solicitor, Mr Devlin. There was another ground submitted by the appellant to the sheriff, namely that the declaration was not spontaneous, being read by the respondent from a previously prepared statement, but this ground was not argued in this court, it being accepted that a previously prepared statement could be used by an accused provided it was truly his own, and prepared and written out by himself. The sheriff refused the appellant's motion, and against that decision this appeal has been taken.

288

The ground of appeal stated by the appellant in his note of appeal is in these terms: 'The said statement was written and edited by Gerald A. Devlin, solicitor, on behalf of his client said Andrew Armitage, and accordingly when said statement was read out by said Andrew Armitage at his judicial examination he was not giving an account in his own words of what happened but reading from a statement prepared by his solicitor. Said statement is accordingly not a true declaration by said Andrew Armitage and should not be allowed to be read to the jury'. In his report to this court the sheriff draws our attention to the fact that the appellant did not imply any question of impropriety on the part of the solicitor Mr Devlin, and this we unreservedly accept. The report goes on to provide the following facts. Mr Devlin agreed that the declaration at the judicial examination was read from a prepared script which was in his handwriting. He said, however, that what was written was prepared on the respondent's instructions, and that while the whole tenor, sense and meaning of the declaration were those of the respondent, there were some words in the declaration imported by himself to give cohesion to the declaration. He was unable to state from recollection which particular words fell into that category. At a later stage in the hearing Mr Devlin clarified his concession regarding the composition of the declaration by saying that it was virtually verbatim of the respondent but was *structured* to make it reasonable. (The emphasis is ours.) He pointed out to the sheriff that an accused is fully entitled to be advised before emitting a declaration and that such advice must include advice as to how best to express the meaning of his account of the matter. Without such advice, many inarticulate, weak and flustered accused could be deprived of the benefit of a declaration which is, and always has been, for the ascertainment of the truth of the matter and not for the benefit of one side or the other.

The sheriff in refusing the appellant's motion stated that he could find nothing in the agreed facts of the case which indicated that the declaration was not what the respondent deliberately said himself freely and voluntarily, when in his sound mind and sober sense, or that his solicitor did other than advise before the examination. Having so expressed himself, he gave leave to appeal.

The current statutory provisions regarding the judicial examination of an accused are in ss. 19, 20, 20A and 20B of the 1975 Act aforesaid. Subsection (2) of s. 19 provides: 'Such solicitor shall be entitled to have a private interview with the person accused before he is examined on declaration, and to be present at such examination.' Section 19 is in almost similar terms to s. 17 of the Criminal Procedure (Scotland) Act 1887. The only differences are: (1) the lay-out of the provisions, and (2) subs. (2) of s. 19 of the 1975 Act does not contain the suffix 'which shall be conducted according to the existing practice' which appeared in s. 17 of the 1887 Act. The only additional provisions which affect the position of the solicitor for the accused at the examination given by the 1975 Act are to be found in subss. (3) and (4) of s. 20A. The former provides that if the accused is represented by a solicitor at the examination the sheriff has to tell the accused that he may consult that solicitor before answering any question. The latter provides that, with the permission of the sheriff, the solicitor may ask the accused any question the purpose of which is to clear up any ambiguity in an answer given by the accused to the procurator fiscal at the examination, or to give the accused an opportunity to answer any question which he has previously refused to answer.

The learned advocate-depute submitted that the reason for the omission of the words 'which shall be conducted according to the existing practice' from s. 19(2) was that the existing practice was being innovated upon by the introduction of the rights to the accused and his solicitor conferred by subss. (3) and (4) of s. 20A. In this he was right in our opinion. The advocate-depute then submitted that the existing procedure provided no authority for the respondent's argument and the sheriff's decision, and that subss. (3) and (4) aforesaid in no way altered that submission. The basis of his argument was this. The procedure envisages that at the examination the accused will be asked certain questions. If he elects to answer these questions the answers must be his own. To allow him to read out a statement prepared by his solicitor, even if it purported to be what he himself said to his solicitor, was not the equivalent of his own answers. The advocate-depute accepted that if an accused prepared and wrote out a statement himself it would be admissible, treating it as an aide-memoire, because it was entirely his own composition, but once everything beyond that was allowed it could give rise to all kinds of questions of authorship of and responsibility for the contents. While it was not suggested that the statement here had been in any way affected other than as frankly admitted by Mr Devlin, once the principle that only the accused's own and unassisted statement was admissible was breached the door was being opened to innumerable problems. Neither statute nor authorities lent countenance to the sheriff's view, which seemed to run contrary to the whole concept of the procedure. In support of his contention the advocate-depute referred us to certain authorities which dealt with the earlier procedure, and counsel for the respondent accepted that these fully and properly represented the law on the purposes for which they were cited. Hume on *Crimes*, vol. 2 at p.328 says: 'Fully to establish the credit of a declaration, the witnesses must have been present while it was emitted, and be able to swear, that it was the pannel's own free and advised act, done by him in his sound mind, and sober senses'. This, in effect, is repeated in Alison's *Criminal Law*, vol. 2 at p.557. In Anderson's *Criminal Law of Scotland* (2nd ed.) it is stated that the agent is not allowed to interfere during the examination of the prisoner. It is further stated that 'strictly speaking a prisoner's declaration is not evidence, and it may be used by either party merely as an explanation of actual evidence'. In the article on Crime—Solemn Procedure by Mr J. Robertson Christie, Q.C., then Clerk of Justiciary, in vol. 5 of the *Encyclopaedia of the Laws of Scotland* (1928) at p.210, para. 518, the author states: 'But where, failing declinature, the examination proceeds, the function of the law agent becomes merely advisory, and it would seem that he is not entitled to intervene in the examination, as the Act of 1887 provides that this is to be conducted according to the practice previously existing.' These authorities, it was maintained, neither sanctioned nor envisaged the procedure which the sheriff had accepted as permissible. On the contrary, they ran contrary to it, and there was nothing in the statutory provisions which either authorised or countenanced it.

Counsel for the respondent argued that each case involving this procedure has to be decided on its own facts. The passage in Hume supra talks of the pannel's own free and advised act. This clearly indicates that an accused is entitled to have full advice from his solicitor concerning his declaration and this must include advice on how it should be stated. There was no practical difference between the solicitor discussing with the accused beforehand what he would say in his declaration and writing down what his client says in that regard to enable the client to use the written statement properly to facilitate the presentation of his declaration. The fact that in the instant case the solicitor had 'structured' the statement to make it reasonable did not invalidate it, since it was accepted that the solicitor had done nothing more than he had frankly admitted doing. The basic question is—was the statement the respondent's own declaration or did the solicitor's help change the character of the document? That question should be answered in the respondent's favour and the sheriff's decision should be upheld.

In our opinion the Crown's contention is well founded and the appeal must be granted. The whole concept of the procedure is that it is the accused and the accused alone who must make the declaration, whatever prior advice he may have had from his solicitor. While the declaration may not be strictly evidence the basic rules of evidence must attach to it. What the respondent and his advisers seem to regard as permissible procedure in the taking of the statement from the accused which the solicitor reduces to writing seems not to differ from the taking of a precognition, and a precognition cannot be used in evidence. The dangers envisaged by the Crown in the procedure sought to be sanctioned are very real indeed. Even in cases like the present one when no impropriety of any kind is imputed to the solicitor, well-intentioned solicitors in 'structuring' the statement may, even unconsciously, affect its nature. Terminology different from that used by the accused may be used and that can affect the content of the statement. A reason why a precognition cannot be used in evidence is that it is not the document of the witness but the document of the person taking the precognition. By parity of reasoning the statement is not that of the accused when reduced to writing by his solicitor. We agree with the Crown that such a substitution for the oral evidence of an accused can play no part in the procedure, and that the sheriff here came to the wrong decision. We shall accordingly sustain the appeal and order that the record of the declaration made by the respondent at the judicial examination should not be read to the jury,"

Crown appeal allowed.

NOTE

This case is a perfect example of eighteenth and nineteenth century institutional authority still influencing the development of modern law. None of the statutory provisions dealt with the unique problem thrown up, so the High Court went back two centuries to try to find an answer by reference to first principles. So well-intentioned solicitors must not "structure" a declaration, any more than well-intentioned policemen may "structure" a statement by a suspect or accused.

2. MacKenzie v. H.M. Advocate
1983 S.L.T. 304

An accused person allegedly made a "confession" to the police. This was put to him at judicial examination, where the prosecutor asked him whether he made the statement alleged. The accused accepted he may have done so, but his solicitor asked the sheriff to disallow any questions on the alleged statement on the ground that it was not a confession. The sheriff refused to do so. At a preliminary diet this decision was upheld and the accused appealed to the High Court.

LORD ROBERTSON: "This is a note of appeal in a case from the sheriff court in Glasgow where a preliminary diet was held in the case of Her Majesty's Advocate against Lewis Wylie MacKenzie. The diet for trial is fixed for 29 November 1982. The question posed in the note of appeal is the competency of a question put by the procurator fiscal at the judicial examination of the said Lewis Wylie MacKenzie on 25 February 1982 in the sheriff court. The matter arose in the course of the questioning of the panel by the procurator fiscal. The matter arose in this way. The procurator fiscal, in the course of his examination posed the following question: 'Can I direct your attention to the sheet of paper which was attached to the copy petition which contains an alleged confession made by you? The sheet of paper contains a written record of an extra-judicial confession allegedly made by you at Rutherglen Police Office on 24 February 1982 or in the hearing of Detective Constable Philip MacDonald and Douglas Brown and reads "just my luck, I knew I'd be picked out" '. "The question then was: 'Did you make that statement to the police officers?" Apparently at this point the solicitor for the panel took exception to the question on the basis that the purported extra-judicial confession was not a confession as such and asked the learned sheriff to rule on the matter. It was submitted to the learned sheriff that the words did not constitute a confession and in particular they were not of an incriminating character and relevant to the charge and in the circumstances the question should not have been allowed and as a consequence thereof the further remarks appearing in the transcript of the proceeding should be struck out because they were incompetently received in the course of the judicial examination. The sheriff rejected the submission and allowed the question. On appeal it was submitted by counsel for the appellant that the sheriff had not taken the proper course in terms of the procedure laid down in the statute. Section 20A of the 1975 Act as amended lays down that an accused on being brought before the sheriff for examination on a charge may be questioned by the prosecutor in so far as such questioning is directed towards eliciting any denial, explanation, justification or comment which the accused may have as regards (a) matters referred to in the charge or rather matters averred in the charge and (b) the alleged making by the accused to or in the hearing of an officer of police of an extra-judicial confession whether or not a full admission, relevant to the charge, provided that questions under this paragraph may only be put if the accused has, before the examination received from the prosecutor, or from an officer of police, a written record of the confession allegedly made.' The argument put was that the statement allegedly made by the panel was not or did not come within the clear category of an extra-judicial confession and accordingly that questioning under s. 20A(1)(b) was not legitimate. The wording of this particular section does not appear to be as clear as it might have been. There is no definition of 'confession' in the statute and it is accordingly doubtful as to exactly what is intended. The wording 'extra-judicial confession (whether or not a full admission) relevant to the charge' suggests that the confession referred to is something less than a full admission and must be susceptible of interpretation provided the statement is relevant to the charge. In the context it seems to me that the definition of 'confession' must be that the statement is clearly susceptible of being regarded as an incriminating statement. I did not understand counsel for the appellant to differ from that. In the present case the statement allegedly made is perhaps not a full admission but in my view it cannot be said that the statement was not or cannot be susceptible of being regarded as an incriminating statement. In my view the margins of what can be properly regarded as coming under the definition of 'confession' in the section may not be entirely clear but in the present case (and that is all that we are considering here) I do not think it can be properly said that this statement is not susceptible of being so interpreted. Taking that view I do not think that the sheriff has been shown to have been wrong in making the decision he made with regard to the statement. The matter remains for fuller consideration at the trial. It, as I understand, was accepted, that it will be open to the panel to challenge the admission of this statement at a later stage. This court at the present moment is only considering the matter in terms of s. 76 of the Act, 76(1)(c) of which in setting out the court's jurisdiction, says that there must be some point which could be resolved with advantage before the trial. It is upon that section that the appeal is based. I am not able at present to see how it can be said that the matter can be resolved with advantage before the trial. On the narrow basis that each case must be decided upon its own facts I consider that this matter would be better left for future consideration. I do not accept that the panel will suffer any prejudice if that course is taken. I accordingly move your Lordships to reject the note of appeal."

Appeal refused.

NOTE

This seems a very narrow decision and Lord Robertson appears to concede as much. Was the court right in its view that the phrase "Just my luck, I knew I'd be picked out" was susceptible of being interpreted as a confession of crime as opposed to an admission of ill-fortune? Such matters must be left for consideration at trial in the light of other evidence, when a decision is made whether the proceedings at the judicial examination are to be founded upon and read to the jury. The trial judge may have to decide whether any part of the record of the examination can be withheld from the jury under the provisions of section 151(2) of the 1975 Act. See also *Moran* v. *H.M. Advocate*, 1990 S.C.C.R. 40 where this course of action was approved.

The right of the defence solicitor to intervene at judicial examination is very limited: see 1975 Act, s. 20A(4).

Once the examination is complete, the next step is committal, either for further examination or "until liberated in due course of law," known as "full committal." Where the committal is in custody, the period thereof is restricted.

3. Herron v. A, B, C and D
1977 S.L.T. (Sh.Ct.) 24

Four accused persons appeared on petition on April 14, 1976. They were committed for further examination. On April 23, 1976 warrants for full committal were placed before the sheriff. He refused to grant the warrants.

SHERIFF MACPHAIL: "At 2 p.m. this afternoon [April 23, 1976], before the commencement of the business of the summary court, the procurator fiscal depute appeared before me in chambers and moved me to commit accused persons for trial in a number of cases. In each case the pro forma warrant of committal was, as usual, printed on the same sheet as the petition, warrant for apprehension and search, and warrant of committal for further examination. When looking over these documents I observed that in three of the cases—the cases of A, who is charged with housebreaking with intent to steal, B, who is charged with assault, and C and D, who are charged with housebreaking—the warrant of committal for further examination had been signed by Sheriff Stone on 14 April 1976. I am informed that these accused persons had appeared before Sheriff Stone at 2 p.m. on that date, and it is recorded in each warrant that no declaration was emitted and the sheriff committed the accused for further examination. In each of these cases the pro forma warrant of committal for trial which was laid before me today had been date-stamped '22 April 1976'. But today's date is 23 April 1976. I was informed that the warrants should have been placed before me yesterday, but that had not been done, through some administrative oversight, the details of which I shall consider later in this judgment. In view of the fact that eight clear days had elapsed between the signature of the warrants for committal for further examination on 14 April and the placing of the warrants of full committal before me today, I was in some doubt as to the competency of granting warrants of full committal in these cases, and asked the procurator fiscal depute to address me on the matter after the disposal of the business of the summary court. That hearing took place in chambers at 4.30 p.m. Neither the accused persons nor their solicitors were present at any part of these proceedings today: that is another matter about which I will have something to say later. At the conclusion of the hearing I announced my decision, which was to refuse to grant the warrants for full committal. Since it is highly unusual, if not unique, in modern practice for a sheriff to refuse to commit an accused person for trial, I have decided to issue a written statement of the reasons for my decision.

It appears that in modern times two different views are entertained as to the present law relating to the length of time which may elapse between committal for further examination and committal for trial. The first is that the length of time is not absolutely fixed, but as a general rule does not exceed eight days. The second is that the length of time is absolutely fixed at no longer than eight days by the Criminal Procedure Act 1701. If the first view of the law is correct, I must consider whether any good reason has been stated for departing from the general rule. If the second view is correct, it is impossible for me to grant a warrant because the limit of time fixed by the Act of 1701 has been exceeded.

Because of the pressure of other judicial duties as summary sheriff and the desirability of issuing as soon as possible a written explanation of my decision for the consideration of the Crown authorities and the legal advisers of the accused, it is impossible to examine the law as fully as the importance of the subject deserves. From a cursory review of the sources available to me, it appears that the first view is derived from Hume, ii, 81–82, and the authorities there cited: *Andrew* v. *Murdoch* (1806) 13 F.C. 569, *Mor. App.* s.v. 'Wrongous Imprisonment' No. 3, and (1814) 2 Dow's App. 401; and *Arbuckle* v. *Taylor* (1815) 3 Dow's App. 160. Hume, having explained that a prisoner who has been committed for further examination is not entitled to bail, continues: 'Yet certainly, on the other hand, in this as in all other things, the magistrate must observe good faith and fair dealing with the prisoner: For if he unreasonably delays to proceed with his precognition, or make use of false and affected pretences of further inquiries, on purpose to lengthen the man's confinement; this, without a doubt, is a malversation, and an act of oppression, for which the magistrate shall be answerable at common law'. Hume's footnote to that passage is in the following terms: 'In this opinion, the author has been confirmed by that of the Lord Chancellor, given on occasion of remitting the case of *Arbuckle and Taylor*: "At the same time, what I said in the case of *Andrew* v. *Murdoch*, I repeat in this: A commitment for further examination must not be made use of, as a commitment for custody in order to trial, and, therefore, the law has properly limited it: the law has said that it shall be a commitment for further examination, to take place within a reasonable time. What is a reasonable time, may be difficult to say; whether one, two, three, four or five days; for what may be a reasonable time in one case, may not be so in another; but a Magistrate is bound to terminate his commitment for further examination within a reasonable time. And I cannot entertain a doubt, that an action might be maintained against a Magistrate for committing for further examination, if his view and purpose in so doing were, to put the party under the same hardship and oppression as would belong to a commitment for custody in order to trial." See Dow's Reports of Appeal Cases, vol. iii, p.184.'

The second view is based on the Criminal Procedure Act 1701, which was originally entitled, 'Act for preventing wrongous Imprisonments and against undue delayes in Tryals.' In its original form, the Act provided: 'And his Majestie with advice and consent forsaid Extends this Act for preventing of wrongous imprisonment to the case of all confinements not either consented to by the party or inflicted after tryal by sentence And farder Discharges all closs imprisonments beyond the space of Eight dayes from the commitment under the pains of wrongous imprisonment above set down' (A.P.S., x, 272 at pp.274–275). Much of that passage was repealed by the Statute Law Revision (Scotland) Act 1964, Sched. 1, so that the only remaining clause is, 'And farder Discharges all closs imprisonments beyond the space of Eight dayes from the commitment.' The Act of 1701, so far as unrepealed by the Statute Law Revision (Scotland) Acts of 1908 and 1964, is conveniently set out in the volume of the *Acts of the Parliaments of Scotland, 1424–1707,* second revised edition, printed by authority in 1966, at pp.162–163. The first part of the Act, from 'Our Sovereign Lord' to 'shall be void and null' was repealed by the Criminal Procedure (Scotland) Act 1975, Sched. 10, Pt. I, but it would appear that otherwise the Act of 1701, to the extent printed by authority in 1966, remains in force.

As to the passage which I have quoted, Hume observes in ch. IV of his second volume, 'The statute concludes with forbidding, under the same pains, all *close* imprisonment, or, as I understand it, solitary and inaccessible imprisonment, for more than eight days from the time of commitment' (Hume, ii, 117). He does not, however, suggest in ch. II that the statute limits to eight days the period for which the prisoner may be imprisoned between the two diets of committal.

Alison, in his chapter on 'Arrest and Precognition', stated that the Act of 1701 has no application to committal for further examination. He writes: 'A prisoner committed under a warrant for farther examination, is entitled to have that temporary state of confinement brought to a conclusion within a reasonable time, as applied to the circumstances and nature of the case; but he is not entitled, as a matter of right, to bail, nor does his incarceration fall under the Act of 1701' (Alison, ii, 135). He goes on to say that the provisions of the Act apply only to a 'custody in order to trial' and not 'that temporary detention, while as yet it is undetermined whether there shall be any custody in order to trial or not.' It is true that the earlier provisions of the Act are concerned with 'custody in order to trial', but the latter part of the Act, in which the clause discharging 'closs imprisonment' occurs, begins, in its original form, with a statement that the Act 'for preventing of wrongous imprisonment' is extended to the case of *all* confinements not either consented to by the party or inflicted after trial by sentence. The authorities cited by Alison (*Fife* v. *Ogilvie* (1762) Mor. 11750; *Andrew, supra; Arbuckle, supra*) are primarily concerned with the question whether a prisoner committed for further examination is entitled to apply for bail, and it may be that any opinions therein to the effect that the Act does not apply to commitments for further examination are to be understood secundum materiam subjectam. Indeed, elsewhere, when discussing the clause of the Act which discharges 'closs imprisonment', Alison writes: 'By close confinement, here mentioned, is to be understood solitary and inaccessible confinement; and, therefore, it is worthy of consideration, whether it is safe to prolong the solitary confinement, in which prisoners are usually kept in the interval between their being committed for further examination, and committed till liberated in due course of law, beyond that period. Indeed, in the general case, it is not expedient to continue the confinement on this hazardous warrant for a longer time than eight days, and it will require special circumstances to render any longer continuance not a matter of risk at common law' (Alison, ii, 209–210).

Alison's work was published in 1833. In the first edition of Macdonald's *Criminal Law* (1867), the law was stated thus: 'When the prisoner has been examined, he may then be committed, either for trial or for further examination—if the latter, he is not entitled to bail, and therefore such confinement must only be for a reasonable time. No exact time can be fixed, as the reasonableness of a delay may depend very much on circumstances. But whatever be the time during which the accused is detained under commitment for examination, it is not lawful to keep him in close confinement for more than eight days from the first commitment' (p.297). The authorities cited are Hume, ii, 81–82; Alison, ii, 134–135; *Fife, supra; Andrew, supra; Arbuckle, supra*; and the Act of 1701. That passage was preserved, substantially unaltered, in the second edition (1877), p.263. By the time of the succeeding edition, s. 18 of the Criminal Procedure (Scotland) Act 1887 had been passed, enabling the accused to apply for bail at any time after being brought before a magistrate for examination. The last sentence of the passage quoted was dropped, and the third edition (1894) read: 'When the accused has been examined, he may be committed to prison until liberation "in due course of law", or for further examination—if the latter, it must be for a reasonable time. ... What may be a reasonable time depends on circumstances. But as the accused can now apply for bail after he has been brought before a magistrate, for examination, the duration of commitment for further examination is of little consequence' (p.272). The same sentences appeared in the fourth edition (1929), pp.303–304, and a passage to the same effect appears in Green's *Encyclopaedia of the Laws of Scotland*, vol. 5 (1928 ed.), para. 523. But in the current (5th) edition of Macdonald (1948), the paragraph is entirely rewritten, and includes the following passage: 'The object of a commitment for further examination is to enable the prosecutor to complete his enquiry, *e.g.* by precognition of persons who may be cited to attend for that purpose under the warrant granted on the petition to apprehend. This commitment ought not to exceed a reasonable time (Hume, ii, 81–82; Alison, ii, 134–135), which in practice means eight days' (pp.203–204). No reference is there made to the Act of 1701.

In Anderson's *Criminal Law of Scotland* (2nd ed., 1904), p.240, the law is stated thus: 'In the case of commitment for further examination the commitment must be for a reasonable time (*Fife; Andrew; Arbuckle*). In no case can close confinement be ordered for more than eight days from the first commitment (Act 1701, cap. 6).'

Successive editions of Renton and Brown's *Criminal Procedure* have included the following passage (at p.46 in the current edition): 'The length of time which may intervene between committal for further examination and committal for trial is not absolutely fixed, but as a general rule does not exceed eight days. This must be particularly observed in those cases where bail cannot be insisted upon till after committal until liberation in due course of law.' The learned editor of the current (4th) edition (1972) has added at the end of the first sentence a footnote reference to the speech of Lord Eldon, L.C., in *Arbuckle* supra at p.184; but no reference is made to the Act of 1701.

The most recent statement of the law is contained in the Second Report of the Departmental Committee on *Criminal Procedure in Scotland* (Chairman: The Hon. Lord Thomson) (1975, Cmnd. 6218). In ch. 10, on committal procedure, the committee state: 'Eight days is laid down by the Criminal Procedure Act 1701 as being the limit of the time which an accused may spend in prison between the two diets of committal' (para. 10.05; see also para. 10.01). Against that view must be set the statement by Professor J. D. B. Mitchell that the Act of 1701 'does not of itself deal with the period between arrest and committal for trial' (*Constitutional Law* (2nd ed.), p.339). Professor T. B. Smith appears to share that view because he suggests 'that express provision by statute should be made limiting the lawful period of detention for "further examination" without commitment for trial' ('Bail before Trial: Reflections of a Scottish Lawyer' (1960) 108 Univ. of Pennsylvania L.R. 305, reprinted in *Studies Critical and Comparative*, p.252, at p.264).

It is clear from the foregoing survey of the sources and literature which are available to me that two views are held in modern times. On the one hand, according to the current editions of Macdonald and of Renton and Brown, the length of time which may intervene between the two diets of committal is not absolutely fixed, but 'ought not to exceed a reasonable time, which in practice means eight days' (Macdonald), or 'as a general rule does not exceed eight days' (Renton and Brown). According to the Thomson Committee, on the other hand, the Act of 1701 has absolutely fixed eight days as the limit. It is obviously difficult to make a quick decision on this matter, but I have formed the opinion that the latter view is to be preferred. The clause of the Act which discharges 'all closs imprisonments beyond the space of Eight dayes from the commitment' appears in a different part of the Act from that which is concerned with persons 'imprisoned for custody in order to tryal.' The clause was understood by Alison, Macdonald (who was himself responsible for the first and second editions of his work) and Anderson to refer to persons who had been committed for further examination. Parliament must be assumed to have been aware of the law and practice as enunciated by these writers when it took care to preserve that clause, while repealing other clauses of the Act, by the Statute Law Revision (Scotland) Acts of 1906 and 1964 and the Criminal Procedure (Scotland) Act 1975. I have already noted that the Act of 1964 repealed the surrounding clauses while leaving the clause under discussion standing. It must therefore still have an effective meaning today. In my opinion its only possible application is to imprisonment upon a warrant of commitment for further examination. The rights of those who are imprisoned upon a warrant of commitment for trial are fully dealt with elsewhere in the Act of 1701 and in the modern rules in s. 101 of the 1975 Act (formerly s. 43 of the Criminal Procedure (Scotland) Act 1887). If the expression 'closs imprisonment' means no more than solitary confinement, it would have been unnecessary to preserve the clause in 1964, because by that date it was not competent for a judge to order imprisonment with solitary confinement. The expression must therefore mean no more than the condition of detention appropriate to a person committed for further examination.

If the clause is so understood, it follows that in the cases presently before me it is now impossible to commit the accused for trial. The warrants of committal for further examination are now spent, and all procedure on the present petitions has come to an end."

Warrants refused.

NOTE

The peculiar Glasgow practice which gave rise to this case has now ceased. Full committal now takes place in the presence of the accused and his solicitor. It is, of course, very unusual for a sheriff to refuse to commit an accused who has been brought before the court on petition. For another example, see *Normand* v. *McQuillan*, 1987 S.C.C.R. 440. On the assumption that the 1701 Act prescribes a fixed period of eight days for further examination, that period is to be seen as one of eight days between the two committal dates: *Dunbar, Petitioner*, 1986 S.C.C.R. 602. It should be noted that neither committal for further examination nor full commitment bear any similarities whatever to English committal proceedings. The primary importance of full committal in Scotland is in relation to bail (see, *infra*, Chap. 7) and in relation to time limits for trial, on which see, *infra*, pp.306 *et seq*.

B.   PRECOGNITION

Following full committal, the Crown moves to the stage of precognition, so that the case may be reported to the Crown Office for directions on how to proceed. Crown precognitions are confidential to the Crown, although where the defence have difficulty in obtaining their own precognition from a Crown witness, the Crown will sometimes disclose the contents of its precognition to the defence.

1.   **Arthur v. Lindsay**
(1894) 1 Adam 582

In a civil action for slander, the pursuer claimed that the defender, a procurator-fiscal, had inserted false and calumnious statements about the pursuer in various Crown precognitions, and had shown these precognitions to persons not entitled to see them. The pursuer sought diligence to recover the precognitions and certain communications between the fiscal and the Crown Office.

LORD PRESIDENT (ROBERTSON): "The Lord Advocate has appeared by Counsel to object to the diligence asked by the pursuer being granted, and we have to attend to the responsible statement made by his representative. His Lordship objects to allow the precognitions to be produced, on the ground that to do so would be an infringement of that confidentiality which enables the effectual prosecution of crime in this country. I readily grant that, in the present case, the precognitions are relevant to the issues to be tried. They are even of a high materiality, and it may be that the want of them will be prejudicial or even fatal to the pursuer's claim. But it is undoubted that private rights must sometimes yield to the requirements of general public policy, and it seems to me that the essential confidentiality of communications passing between a Procurator-Fiscal and the head of the Criminal Department in Scotland is a paramount consideration. I do not say that there would be anything illegal in the production of such documents, because the Lord Advocate, as head of the department, might, in the exercise of his discretion, conceive that the general administration of public justice might, in some highly exceptional circumstances, not be prejudiced by the production. The Lord Advocate is the judge of that. But, in the present case, the Lord Advocate comes forward to object on the ground of this general rule and principle founded on the public interest, and I see nothing to shew that in the present case that rule should give way. It has been said that in a statement made for the Crown in the case of *Donald* v. *Hart*, 6 D. 1255, it was admitted that the general rule might yield to some 'great and overwhelming necessity.' These are very large and general words, and I do not think that an ordinary action of damages for defamation of character in which a Procurator-Fiscal is defender is such a case as is there described. I have shewn, I hope, that I realise the evil which is done to the pursuer's case by the enforcement of the general rule and the consequent loss to him of the precognitions; but, at the same time, I think that this is just one of those instances in which private rights have to yield to the general rule upon which the successful prosecution of crime so largely depends. I am for sustaining the objection made by the Lord Advocate and refusing the diligence."

LORD MCLAREN: "Two points in this case seem to me to be settled beyond dispute. The first is, that according to the present law and practice in the official investigations of crime, precognitions taken under the authority of the Lord Advocate, and reported to him or his depute, are confidential, and, unless under very exceptional circumstances, cannot be obtained for the purposes of evidence in a cause. The second point is that the confidentiality is personal to the head of the Criminal Department; his consent would remove any difficulty, and therefore it cannot be said that in such cases there would be a wrong without a remedy. It may be presumed that the Lord Advocate has obtained all the necessary information to enable him to judge whether this is a case in which it is proper for him to give up these precognitions to a pursuer in a civil action. He has before him information which the Court cannot get, for we have only the statements made by Counsel at the bar in accordance with their instructions. No doubt the Court has always maintained its right to make such an order in case of emergency, some of which duly figured in the judicial opinions referred to at the debate, but this is qualified by the fact that no authority has been found where the jurisdiction was in fact exercised, and it is most unlikely that, while criminal administration remains as at present, the Court ever will exercise this supplemental power.

In the circumstances there is no reason for doubting that the objection of the Crown Office is well founded, and if it were to be got over by the mere averment of malice against a procurator-fiscal, any one wishing to harass the Crown officials might get access to these confidential documents simply by averring malice, and this would certainly be prejudicial to the public interest."

Diligence refused.

NOTE

Normally, witnesses are simply summoned to attend at the offices of the procurator-fiscal for precognition and in the vast majority of cases will do so. As a matter of civic duty, a citizen is under an obligation to give such information to the Crown or to the defence as he may be asked to give: *H.M. Advocate* v. *Monson* (1893) 1 Adam 114 at p.135. If, however, the Crown has reason to fear that the witness might subsequently go back on his precognition later by giving different evidence in court, the fiscal may precognosce that witness on oath.

2. Coll, Petitioner
1977 J.C. 29

A witness was precognosced on oath before the sheriff. He read over and signed his precognition. He was then cited to give evidence in a trial, but presented a petition to the *nobile officium* of the High Court craving the production and destruction of his precognition.

LORD JUSTICE-CLERK (WHEATLEY): "Counsel for the petitioner submitted that, before giving evidence at the trial of a case in respect of which he had been precognosced, a witness is entitled to have destroyed a precognition which was taken on oath. Support for that submission was sought from Hume's Commentaries (1844 edition), vol. 2, pp.81, 82 and 381; Alison's Criminal Law, vol. 2, pp.504 and 534; Dickson's Law of Evidence, vol. 2, para. 1591; Macdonald's Criminal Law, 5th edition, p.298; Renton and Brown's Criminal Procedure, 4th edition, pp.55 and 398; and the *obiter dictum* (for which no authority was given) of Lord Justice-Clerk Macdonald, with whom his brethren concurred, in *Cook* v. *McNeill*, 5 Adam 47: 'And it is also competent for a witness to ask that his precognition be delivered up to him to be destroyed before he can be called upon to give evidence.'

Prima facie this would appear to be a formidable body of support for the petitioner's claim. An examination of the texts of these writers discloses that Alison based his proposition on Hume and the later writers based their views on Hume and Alison. It is accordingly necessary to consider whether the circumstances which prevailed in the days of Hume and Alison, which no doubt had a bearing on the opinions expressed by them, are those which exist at the present time, or whether there have been changes in the interval which affect the applicability of their *dicta* to modern requirements. In particular, consideration has to be given to whether the different forms which a 'precognition' can take has a bearing on the issue in the instant case. In those earlier days there were many more private prosecutions than there are today, when virtually all prosecutions are public prosecutions and private prosecutions are so circumscribed that (statutory exception apart) they are now an extreme rarity. The procedure initiating prosecutions in those days was much different from our present-day procedure. None the less, what was said by those earlier writers was applicable to a 'precognition,' whether it was a statement made on oath on judicial examination or a statement taken *ex parte* and not on oath by a person preparing the case for one side or the other. The reason given by Hume and Alison why a witness should be given the right to have his precognition delivered up to him and destroyed before he could be called upon to give evidence was that unless this was done a witness might feel trammelled by his previous statement and would try to make his evidence agree with it instead of speaking freely from his recollection at the trial. The view was taken that a person could not be tried for perjury because at the trial he had given evidence on oath which contradicted the evidence he had given in his declaration—cf. the case of *Patrick Maccurly* in 1777, referred to in Hume *supra*, vol. 2 at p.381 Note 4 and also in Vol. 1 at p.369 (Note). All this, however, was before the passing of the Evidence (Scotland) Act 1852. Section 3 of that Act provides: 'It shall be competent to examine any witness who may be adduced in any action or any proceeding as to whether he has on any specified occasion made a statement on any matter pertinent to the issue different from the evidence given by him in such action or proceeding; and it shall be competent in the course of such action or proceeding to adduce evidence to prove that such witness has made such different statement on the occasion specified.'

This was undoubtedly enacted to secure in the interests of the administration of justice that a person who was giving evidence on oath in an action or proceeding could have the veracity or reliability of that evidence tested by what he had said thereanent on a previous occasion. That statutory enactment supersedes any previous common law rule of law that conflicts with it. The Hume and Alison concept of the law that a person should not be constrained by his previous statement from giving his evidence freely when on oath in an action or proceeding is obviously affected by it. How then is a precognition affected? Is it a statement within the meaning of section 3? There are several ways in which a statement can be made. One is by a person engaged in preparing the case for one of the parties in an action or proceeding taking a statement from a potential witness. This is what is now commonly called a precognition. Another is, for example, a statement taken from a potential witness by a police officer who is investigating a crime. A third is a judicial declaration taken on oath *ex parte* from a potential witness in an action or proceeding.

Whatever latitude may have been given to allow a precognition in the first of these categories to be used for the purposes of section 3 aforesaid in the period following the passing of the 1852 Act, it is quite clear from the cases of *McNeilie* v. *H.M. Advocate* 1929 J.C. 50 and *Kerr* v. *H.M. Advocate* 1958 J.C. 14 that it cannot be so used. The reason for this was succinctly given by Lord Justice-Clerk Thomson in *Kerr* when he said: 'In a precognition you cannot be sure you are getting what the potential witness has to say in a pure and undefiled form. It is filtered through the mind of another, whose job it is to put what he thinks the witness means into a form suitable for use in judicial proceedings. This process tends to colour the result. Precognoscers as a rule appear to be gifted with a measure of optimism which no amount of disillusionment can damp.'

It will always be a question of circumstances whether a statement is a precognition or not. Even a statement made to a police officer may fall into the category of a precognition if it is taken at a time when the stage of preliminary investigation has passed and the police officer is in fact taking a 'precognition'—see *McNeilie* and *Kerr, supra.*

What then is the position of a statement made in the form of a judicial declaration on oath? While it is a statement obtained *ex parte* it is obtained subject to safeguards which are calculated to avoid the possible defects and unfairness which Lord Justice-Clerk Thomson had in contemplation. The presence of the judge who has control of the proceedings should ensure that words are not being put into the witness's mouth. The official record should ensure that what is recorded is what the witness has said, not what a precognoscer wishfully thought he had said. The statement when recorded is read over and signed by the witness. Added to all this is the fact that the statement was made on oath. It is difficult to conceive a situation more apposite for the invocation of the section 3 procedure. While, therefore, each case has to be determined on its own facts, in our opinion such a declaration would normally be competent as a basis for challenging under that section the evidence of a witness. It would only be when it is alleged that the safeguards of the procedure had not been observed that a challenge to its use for that purpose could be made.

If, then, the statement which a witness has made under that procedure may competently be used to challenge the accuracy of the evidence he has given in the action or proceeding, what justification is there for a rule of law which entitles him to have the written record of his statement, which he has signed, destroyed? In our opinion there is none. That signed statement might be the best evidence on the point. On his averments as to how the statement was obtained we are of the opinion that the petitioner is not entitled to recover it and have it destroyed before he is called upon to give evidence. We shall accordingly refuse the petition.

In arriving at this decision we find comfort in the thought that the clarification of the legal position on this point gives legal sanction to a procedure which can be invoked to counter one of the deadly blows which is being struck at the administration of justice at the present time, namely, witnesses going back on their earlier statements when giving evidence in criminal trials."

Petition refused.

NOTE

Precognition on oath is becoming increasingly necessary. The procedure is conducted in private in the presence only of the sheriff, his clerk, the fiscal, the witness and a shorthand writer to record the precognition. A solicitor for the witness is not normally allowed to be present: *Carmichael* v. *J.B.*, 1991 S.C.C.R. 715. From the viewpoint of the Crown, precognition on oath strengthens its position should there be subsequent proceedings for perjury, where the problem often arises of proving exactly what was said on the previous occasion. But since section 9 of the Criminal Justice (Scotland) Act 1980 came into force, precognition on oath by the defence has become possible, simply as a means to overcome the reluctance of some Crown witnesses to speak to the defence. However, it may be that section 9 can only be invoked in exceptional circumstances.

3.   Low v. MacNeill
1981 S.C.C.R. 243

A defence solicitor tried to obtain a precognition from a crucial Crown witness, who refused to co-operate. The procurator-fiscal gave the solicitor some general information about what the witness might be expected to say, but the solicitor petitioned the court under section 9 seeking a precognition on oath. The fiscal indicated he would make the Crown precognition available to the defence.

SHERIFF SCOTT: "... Section 9(1) of the 1980 Act provides: 'The sheriff may, on the application of an accused, grant warrant to cite any person (other than the co-accused), who is alleged to be a witness in relation to any offence of which the accused has been charged, to appear before the sheriff in chambers at such time or place as shall be specified in the citation, for precognition on oath by the accused or his solicitor in relation to that offence, if the court is satisfied that it is reasonable to require such precognition on oath in the circumstances.' The cardinal points of the provision are (1) that the precognition is to be *on oath*, and (2) that the procedure is only to be permitted if the court is satisfied that it is reasonable in the circumstances to require it.

Provision is made for the procedure to be followed under section 9 in the Act of Adjournal (Procedures under Criminal Justice (Scotland) Act 1980 No. 1) 1981 (S.I. 1981/22). The procedure envisaged by section 9 and by paragraph 2 of the Act of Adjournal is to my mind likely to prove cumbersome and expensive. The petition has to be prepared in the form set out in the Schedule to the Act of Adjournal. The sheriff has to order intimation and fix a diet. If the prayer of the petition is granted he must order the precognition to be taken, fix a diet and grant warrant to cite the witness or witnesses. There has to be personal service. Where the witness appears the proceedings have to be recorded by an official shorthand writer. The notes have to be extended and lodged. Yet another diet has to be fixed for the witness to sign the precognition. The shorthand writer has to be paid and the witness is entitled, if he wishes, to have his expenses paid in advance.

It is the legal aid fund, for the most part, which defrays the cost of persons tried on indictment. If the procedure made possible by section 9 is frequently used the cost to the public purse, through criminal legal aid, may be considerable.

If this application proves typical of others under section 9, such applications will almost inevitably be made at a late stage, when the trial is imminent. Solicitors often say that they cannot set about precognoscing Crown witnesses until they have had the list of witnesses annexed to the indictment and are unlikely, if this is so, to find that a witness will not make himself available for precognition until the date for trial is almost upon them. The pressure on sheriff court diaries is well known. In this court, certainly, it is extremely difficult to find space in the diary at short notice for any kind of urgent business. When such space has to be found it frequently means that other business has to be put off.

It is well known that it is by no means rare for the defence to be unable to obtain precognition from *Crown* witnesses. There are many reasons for this. One of them, and it may be the reason in this case, is that letters from the accused's solicitor never reach the witnesses. If all Crown witnesses who do not respond to a defence request for precognition had to be precognosced on oath the work of the sheriff courts would be thrown into confusion.

It is more than likely that there will be cases where a reluctant witness, having been cited for precognition on oath, will fail to attend. Although a warrant may then be issued for his arrest the chances of his being arrested and brought before the sheriff for precognition before the trial diet may be small. If he cannot be found in time, the question may well arise whether the trial should be adjourned. If a sheriff has decided that it is reasonable for the accused to be allowed to precognosce a witness on oath it may be difficult for the court to insist on the trial proceeding when the witness has not been precognosced.

There is no inexhaustible supply of official shorthand writers and the difficulty of arranging diets for proof or jury trial in the confidence that a shorthand writer will be available is also well known.

All of these considerations lead me to the conclusion that, on practical grounds, the power conferred on the sheriff by section 9 is one to be exercised with caution. Nevertheless, I recognise that each application must be examined on its own merits and the overriding consideration must be to ensure so far as possible that the accused person is in the end of the day fairly tried.

The practice of precognoscing witnesses on oath dates back to the days when precognitions in criminal cases were compiled by the examining judge or magistrate before whom a person arrested was brought. After taking the prisoner's declaration the judge or magistrate had to satisfy himself that there were grounds for detaining the prisoner and, if there were, the particulars thereof, in order that they might be transmitted to the prosecutor. The prisoner would ordinarily be committed to prison for further examination and, when the precognition was completed, until liberated in due course of law. The examining judge or magistrate then submitted the precognition to Crown counsel who would decide whether to raise an indictment.

It was a matter for the examining judge or magistrate to decide which witnesses to precognosce. Witnesses could be cited for precognition on his own motion or that of the prosecutor. The prisoner had no right to cite witnesses for precognition but in practice the examining judge or magistrate would examine witnesses, of his own authority, where it was suggested by the prisoner that their evidence might be material to the defence.

It appears that sometimes, but by no means always, the examining judge or magistrate might precognosce a witness on oath. If he chose to do so it was in order that by means thereof he might extract the truth from witnesses (Alison's Criminal Practice, 138); or if the truth could not be otherwise ascertained (Hume on Crimes, ii, 82). In other words, the purpose in putting witnesses on oath was to obtain evidence thereby which could not otherwise be ascertained.

It was only the examining judge or magistrate who could put witnesses on oath. The prosecutor was not permitted to precognosce on oath privately (Alison's Criminal Practice, 504).

In time the role of the examining judge or magistrate in ascertaining whether or not there was evidence to justify a prisoner's committal became vestigial. Subject to provisions for prevention of delay in trials, and the right of a prisoner to ask for bail, prisoners came to be committed to prison, either for further examination or until liberated in due course of law, on the ex parte statement of the prosecutor that he had credible information that a crime had been committed. The procurator fiscal took over the function of preparing the precognition and submitting it to Crown counsel. Precognition on oath became a rarity (Renton and Brown's Criminal Procedure, 4th ed., para. 5–69). The procurator fiscal as a matter of course obtains warrant to cite witnesses for precognition and exceptionally he may request the court to supervise the taking of a precognition on oath. The modern practice, so far as it goes, is for certain 'suspect or reluctant' witnesses to be precognosced on oath, not so much with the object of eliciting evidence which cannot otherwise be obtained as with a view to ensuring that evidence given on precognition is not departed from at a trial: see *Coll, Petnr*, 1977 J.C. 29.

It is against this background that section 9 was enacted. The defence never had the right to precognosce witnesses on oath. Now they have, subject to the court being satisfied that it is reasonable in particular circumstances to allow it. Prima facie, Parliament's intention in enacting section 9 was to give the defence the same facility as the Crown to take precognitions *on oath*. If so, it is my opinion that the circumstances in which it should be allowed must be circumstances which are analogous to circumstances in which, in modern practice, the Crown precognosces *on oath*.

Section 9 does not give the defence the right to seek a warrant to cite witnesses for precognition privately. This is puzzling at first glance, because one would imagine that in many cases the granting of such a warrant would be enough to serve the purpose of enabling the defence to obtain a precognition. Only if a citation to attend for private precognition was ignored might it become necessary to have a witness cited to appear before the sheriff. Perhaps it was feared that there would be a danger of a power of compulsion granted to defence solicitors being overworked, although it is difficult to see how this could happen if the court was given a discretion to grant or refuse warrant to cite witnesses for private precognition. In my view, the reason for the omission to give the defence a right to seek warrant to cite witnesses for private precognition must be that such a right is in general unnecessary. There is a duty on Crown witnesses to give information to the defence and the Crown if need be reminds its witnesses of this duty. Often, as in this case, the Crown will oblige defence solicitors by making information available to them. The court may adjourn a diet of trial in order that witnesses who have refused to be precognosced may be seen by the defence. If witnesses are in custody, say, the Crown will make arrangements for them to be seen in prison by the defence. It may still be competent, in exceptional cases, for an accused to present to the court a petition stating that a witness is in custody or otherwise inaccessible, whereupon the court will give such remedy as the justice of the case requires (Alison's Criminal Practice, 535).

Accordingly, in my opinion, the situation where it is a case simply of finding out what a Crown witness is going to say is adequately catered for by existing law and practice. Section 9 is not, in my opinion, designed to deal with the everyday situation where the defence has difficulty in getting hold of some Crown witnesses in order to obtain an indication of the evidence they are to give. Rather it is intended to deal with unusual and exceptional circumstances, analogous to those in which the Crown seeks to precognosce *on oath*. The circumstances must be such that it is reasonable that a precognition should be given *on oath*, not merely such that it is reasonable that a witness should be required to give a precognition.

In my opinion, the kind of circumstances referred to in section 9 must in general be those where evidence cannot be obtained other than by putting a potential witness on oath or where it is necessary to put a potential witness on oath lest he depart from his precognition at a trial. There may be other categories of circumstances where a petition under section 9 should be granted, but they cannot, in my opinion, extend to circumstances where it is immaterial whether the desired precognition be on oath or not.

I can appreciate Mr Monro's desire to take all proper steps on his client's behalf. He has shown responsibility in confining his application to the cases of the crucial Crown witnesses and not those whose evidence is to be uncontroversial. Clearly Mr Monro has to take all steps reasonably open to him to ascertain the line of the Crown evidence. In this case, though, I am satisfied that he has done so. Once he has in his hands the Crown precognitions of the witnesses named in the petition he will be in as good a position as the Crown to know what the evidence of these witnesses is likely to be. The situation would be quite different if, say, he was seeking to have precognosced witnesses whom he had reason to believe had information favourable to the defence which they had declared they were unwilling to give in court. I do not think that it is a proper consideration to take into account that if Mr Monro saw these witnesses a plea of guilty would be more likely to be forthcoming. If he knows as much as the Crown does about the likely evidence of these witnesses he should already be in a position to give appropriate advice to his clients.

For these reasons I refused the prayer of each petition."

Petition refused.

NOTE

While the reasoning of Sheriff Scott in this case seems clear enough, the defence in a criminal case are perhaps less likely than the Crown to know if a witness is likely to perjure himself at the trial. Information can always be obtained relatively easily about potential witnesses by the procurator-fiscal from the police, but the defence do not have quite the same resources at ready disposal.

While *Low* v. *MacNeill* was followed in *Cirignaco* v. *Lockhart*, 1987

S.C.C.R. 157, a different view of section 9 was taken by Sheriff Lunny in the next case.

4.   Brady v. Lockhart
1985 S.C.C.R. 349

The only two witnesses to an assault refused to give precognitions to the defence, even after a joint approach by the defence solicitor and the fiscal after the original trial had been adjourned to allow such precognition. The accused presented a petition under section 9(1).

SHERIFF LUNNY: "... The procurator fiscal ... indicated that he wished to assist the court in this matter and pointed out the decision in the case of *Low* v. *MacNeill*, 1981 S.C.C.R. 243 (Sh.Ct.) in which the sheriff refused similar petitions. The point at issue according to the procurator fiscal's argument, was the interpretation of the intention of Parliament when it allowed precognition 'on oath'. The procurator fiscal adopted the meaning in the above case and referred me to *Cirignaco* v. *Lockhart* in which a sheriff (Macmillan), although the facts were quite different, appeared to approve Sheriff Scott's reasoning in *Low* v. *MacNeill*.

Further, the procurator fiscal indicated that he was prepared to make police statements of the reluctant witnesses available to the defence. I understand that these witnesses had been precognosced for the Crown. The procurator fiscal made no offer to make the precognition available.

With all due respect to Sheriff Macmillan, I must disagree with their interpretation of section 9. While I concur in Sheriff Scott's outline of the history of precognition on oath, it appears to me that the purpose of section 9 is to allow the defence to prepare on equal terms with the Crown. To suggest that the words 'on oath' in that section indicate that the purpose is to have it as a preliminary to suspected or anticipated perjury is really to give the defence no assistance at all. The defence benefits nothing from a witness later being charged with perjury. I asked myself, is there any other way in which the defence could compel a reasonable precognition from a reluctant hostile Crown witness if it was not taken on oath? In my view no existing law or practice prior to the inception of the 1980 Act answered that problem. For Parliament to introduce a form of precognition not on oath would in my view be of little assistance. If the power given to the defence were merely to compel a witness to give a precognition, such witness in precognition could clearly refuse to give information within his knowledge, prevaricate or simply avoid telling the truth without necessarily telling lies. This would be of no assistance whatever to the defence. In my view the fact that the precognition is to be taken on oath is merely for administrative purposes so that the exercise can be a meaningful one, and of some value to the defence.

Having come to this conclusion, in this particular case I am of the view that it is reasonable in all the circumstances to require such precognition, and accordingly I granted the petitions.

However, it should be noted that each case requires to be looked at on its merits and the question at issue is really whether in the circumstances it is reasonable to compel a witness to be brought before the court to be precognosced on oath. This may not arise in many cases but I am quite satisfied that this is one of the cases where it does."

NOTE

Which of these differing judicial approaches is correct, if either, has never been finally decided, for no specific provision is made for an appeal against the refusal by a sheriff to grant a warrant for such precognition and the matter has not come before the High Court. But it may be that the approach of Sheriff Lunny is preferable, at least from the standpoint of fairness to an accused, who ought to have equal access as the Crown to what witnesses are likely to say. "Balance" in the criminal justice system is an important consideration.

C.   Time-Limits for Trial

The date of full committal is vitally important from the viewpoint of the time-limit for proceeding to trial. Before the 1980 Act, there was no outside time-limit beyond which an accused on bail could not be tried, and many such trials took place many months after the initial appearance of the accused on petition. The 110-day rule (as then constituted) provided protection only for accused in custody whose trials normally had to be concluded within 110 days of full committal. Now, under section 101(1) of the 1975 Act (as amended by section 14 of the 1980 Act) bail cases must normally be commenced within 12 months of the first appearance of the accused on petition in respect of that offence, on which see Renton and Brown, paras. 7–41 to 7–41c and the cases there discussed. Custody cases are governed by section 101(2), which provides that an accused who is fully committed in custody cannot be detained "by virtue of that committal for a total period of more than ... 110 days, unless the trial of the case is *commenced* within that period." So periods of custody not referable to *that* committal are left out of account. The following case was decided before section 101 was re-written in 1980, but shows that the re-written section has not changed the law in this regard.

1. **Wallace v. H.M. Advocate**
1959 J.C. 71

An accused appeared on petition in August 1958 and was allowed bail. Subsequently he was charged with a further offence on which he was fully committed in custody on October 31, 1958. In November 1958 he was sentenced to two years' imprisonment on the charge relating to August of that year. He appeared for sentence on the subsequent offence on March 3, 1959, when he objected to the competency of proceeding further on the ground that more than 110 days had elapsed since his committal. This objection was repelled and the accused appealed against the sentence then imposed. At the appeal hearing it was argued that the proviso to section 43 of the 1887 Act (the forerunner of section 101, *supra*) applied to him.

> Lord Justice-General (Clyde): "... The section makes provision for the service of an indictment not being unduly delayed where a prisoner 'is in prison on a commitment until liberated in due course of law.' No question arises in the present case in regard to that aspect of the matter. The section then goes on to provide—and this is the provision which falls to be construed by us in the present appeal—'Provided always, that where a person accused has been incarcerated for eighty days, and an indictment is served upon him, and he is detained in custody after the expiry of such eighty days, then, unless he is brought to trial and the trial concluded within one hundred and ten days of the date of his being committed till liberated in due course of law, he shall be

forthwith set at liberty, and declared for ever free from all question or process for the crime with which he is charged.' The appellant's contention is that this proviso applies to him, and that, as the one hundred and ten days from the date of his committal until liberated in due course of law (namely 31st October 1958) expired before the conclusion of his trial on 2nd March 1959, the sentence pronounced on him on 3rd March 1959 is incompetent.

But, in my opinion, this proviso cannot be invoked by the present appellant, for it does not apply to him.The proviso applies to an accused who is incarcerated and held because of a committal warrant or warrants. The present appellant was not such an accused. Since 19th November 1958 he was held in prison in virtue of a sentence pronounced on 19th November of two years' imprisonment in respect of the first charge of which he had been found guilty. On 19th November 1958 that sentence superseded, at any rate during its currency, the committal on the other charge. He cannot therefore, in my view, invoke the proviso, since it does not relate to his case at all.

I have reached this conclusion in view of the language of the proviso itself. It relates to a person accused, not to a person convicted and held in prison because of that conviction. Moreover, my conclusion seems to be put beyond doubt by the consequences enacted in the section in the event of the proviso being applicable. These consequences include that 'he shall be forthwith set at liberty,' a consequence quite inappropriate and inapplicable to the situation of a convicted person already in course of serving a sentence for another crime, who can obviously not be set at liberty forthwith.

The ostensible purpose of the section is to prevent delay in bringing accused persons to trial, but the real underlying object is to prevent the lieges being deprived of the liberty to which they are entitled if they are not guilty of the pending charge. But this has no bearing upon the person who has during the currency of the one hundred and ten days been convicted on a different charge, and who at the end of the one hundred and ten days is in course of serving a sentence of imprisonment in respect of it, for such person cannot be set at liberty unless the sentence on which he has been convicted has expired. That is the appellant's position."

Appeal refused.

NOTE

In this case the sentence imposed in November 1958 interrupted the 110 days which started to run on the other committal warrant of October 31, 1958. In *H.M. Advocate* v. *Park*, 1967 J.C. 70, the case of *Wallace* was applied to cover the situation where an accused who was serving imprisonment committed a further offence while in jail. It was held that in his case the 110 days commenced on the expiry of his sentence. See also *H.M. Advocate* v. *Boyle*, 1972 S.L.T. (Notes) 16. "Commencement" of a trial is the point when the oath is administered to the jury: 1975 Act, s. 101(6).

As will be seen from sections 101(1) and (2)(*b*), if a trial is not commenced within the relative time-limit, whether the accused is on bail or not, he cannot be tried at all for the offence. However, specific provisions are made whereby the time-limits can be extended, both in bail and custody cases. In bail cases, the period of 12 months may be extended "on cause shown."

2. H.M. Advocate v. Swift
1985 S.L.T. 26

Three accused persons, Swift, Allen and Young, were charged with fraud and embezzlement. Swift, who was on bail, was not properly served with his indictment. By the time this was discovered his trial date was imminent, as was the expiry of the 12-month period. The Crown applied to the sheriff for an extension, which was refused. The Crown appealed to the High Court.

OPINION OF THE COURT: "At the hearing before us the relevant facts and circumstances in which the application to the sheriff came to be made, and in light of which the sheriff's decision falls to be considered, were not in dispute.

(i) The offences charged cover the period 19 January 1980 to 15 September 1980.

(ii) In October 1980 the practising certificate of the respondent, who was a solicitor, was suspended after an investigation by the Law Society of Scotland. At some later date, after a hearing before the discipline tribunal, the respondent was 'struck off'.

(iii) Shortly after October 1980 a police investigation began and on 21 November 1980 Detective Inspector McBean had a long and full interview with the accountant of the Law Society.

(iv) The police investigation was continued over a long period. Interviews took place with various persons including the respondent, Allen and Young, and it was not until 22 June 1983 that the Crown was in a position to present a petition for a warrant to arrest the three men.

(v) The petition, which correctly recorded the addresses of Allen and Young, gave as the address of the respondent '31 Inchmarnock, East Kilbride'. The respondent had ceased to live there in the summer of 1982 and the house had become owned and occupied by a Mrs Small.

(vi) On 1 July 1983 police officers who went to the East Kilbride address to arrest the respondent, found that he no longer lived there. They then approached the respondent's father and were informed that the respondent's new address was 8 Fowlis Drive, Newton Mearns. To that address they went at once and arrested the respondent upon the petition warrant.

(vii) On the same day the respondent appeared before the sheriff on that petition and his solicitor informed the court of his change of address which was already known to the police officer in charge of the investigation. The respondent was then released on bail and the bail order specified as his 'proper domicile of citation' for the purposes of s. 2 of the Bail etc. (Scotland Act 1980, the respondent's new address: '8 Fowlis Drive, Newton Mearns'.

(viii) In due course the Crown prepared an indictment for service upon the respondent and his two co-accused with a view to a trial diet for 23 January 1984. It began as follows: 'James Aloysius Swift, whose domicile of citation has been specified as 31 Inchmarnock, East Kilbride'. This was, of course, an error.

(ix) On 23 December 1983 this indictment was served upon the respondent's two co-accused along with a notice calling upon them to appear and answer to the indictment in the High Court at Glasgow on 23 January 1984.

(x) On the same date P.C. Robert Main and P.C. Alexander McLeod were instructed to serve the indictment and the relevant notice upon the respondent at the address shown in the indictment which was not his proper domicile of citation. He had not lived there since the summer of 1982. On arrival at this address they were informed by the owner-occupier, Mrs Small, that the respondent did not live there and that she knew nothing whatever about him. The police officers then sought further instructions from the responsible department of the procurator fiscal. In spite of the information which they gave to the official who answered their telephone call they were instructed to go back to the house and leave the service copy of the indictment and the relevant notice of citation with Mrs Small. This they duly did, and in the execution of citation it was explained by P.C. Main that he had done this 'as he failed to find [the respondent] personally'. We have only to add that the service copy of the indictment and the notice of citation did not reach the respondent. They remain in East Kilbride and may yet still be there.

We interrupt the narrative to observe that even if the indictment had been served upon the respondent on 23 December such service would not have satisfied the requirements of s. 75 of the Criminal Procedure (Scotland) Act 1975 which is in these terms: 'Except where the indictment is served under section 102(1) of this Act, the notice served on the accused with the indictment shall call upon him to appear and answer to such indictment at a trial diet (either in the High Court or in the sheriff court) not less than 29 clear days after the service of such indictment and notice.' The 29th day before the diet of trial fell upon Saturday, 21 January 1984 and in terms of s. 111A of the Act the period prescribed by s. 75 was extended until Monday, 23 January 1984, the diet of the trial itself. In the events which happened, however, the failure to serve the indictment upon the respondent at all, and the question which might have arisen if it had been served on 23 December 1983, did not attract any consideration because, early in January 1984, in consequence of the illness of a vital Crown witness, the Crown intimated to the respondent's solicitor, and to those acting for his co-accused, that the indictment would not be called on 23 January 1984.

(xi) By the beginning of May 1984 the sick witness had recovered and on 11 May 1984 a fresh indictment in the same terms as the indictment of December 1983 was served upon the respondent's co-accused for trial on Monday, 11 June 1984. It repeated the error as to the respondent's 'proper domicile of citation'. On 11 May 1984 two police officers were instructed to serve this indictment and the relevant notice of citation upon the respondent. One of them was P.C. Main who had been involved in the events of 23 December 1983, and once again these officers were directed to effect service by leaving the relevant documents in the hands of Mrs Small at the respondent's former address in East Kilbride. The two officers did precisely what they were instructed to do and, so far as anyone is aware, Mrs Small simply added them to her collection. They certainly did not reach the hands of the respondent.

Once again we interrupt the narrative to observe that even if this indictment had been served upon the respondent on 11 May 1984 such service would not have satisfied the requirements of s. 75 of the Act in respect that the relevant period of notice after 11 May 1984 was, because of the provisions of s. 111A, extended to include the day of the trial diet itself.

(xii) It is the practice of the Crown acting through the relevant department of the procurator fiscal in Glasgow to send to the solicitor for a person on whom an indictment is served a courtesy copy thereof, normally on the date of service itself. This practice was followed in December 1983 in the case of the respondent. It was also followed in May 1984 in his case with this difference: the courtesy copy was not despatched to the respondent's solicitor on 21 May 1984 and he did not receive it until 23 May 1984.

(xiii) After 23 May 1984, although it was known to the respondent's solicitor that the respondent had not received service of the indictment (a copy of which was in the respondent's solicitor's hands) it was not known whether it had been 'sent' to his proper domicile of citation within the meaning of s. 2 of the Bail etc. (Scotland) Act 1980, but, for some reason, had not been delivered. In these circumstances the respondent's legal advisers were faced with a problem. They had to assume, leaving aside the question which might arise under s. 75, that there might have been, technically, sufficient service upon the respondent, and since they wished to argue for separation of charges 7 and 8 from the other charges in the indictment, and to take advantage of s. 76 of the Act to that end within 'the appropriate period', defined in s. 76(7)(b) thereof, senior counsel for the respondent, who had been unable to get instructions from the respondent's solicitor because of the Glasgow public holiday, decided, after various communings with the advocate-depute, the Justiciary

Office, and the Edinburgh correspondents of the respondent's solicitors, that it was essential to move the court on 28 May 1984 to hold a preliminary diet on 31 May 1984. The appropriate notice was given. A preliminary diet was held on 31 May 1984 and of consent of the Crown, the co-accused not objecting, charges 7 and 8 were dropped from the indictment. As the respondent was required to do by s. 76(6) he then tendered a plea of not guilty to the remaining six charges therein.

(xiv) No intimation was made to the court or to the Crown on or before 31 May 1984 that the respondent had not received service of the indictment. Senior counsel learned of this matter for the first time on the afternoon of 30 May but thought it necessary to cause further inquiries to be made before drawing the possible absence of service to the attention of the Crown. Following certain inquiries which were then made the procurator fiscal was informed on 4 June 1984 that a notice under s. 76 was to be lodged with a view to the holding of a preliminary diet to entertain a motion based upon the absence of service upon the respondent. It was on this date that the Crown learned that they had failed to serve the indictment upon the respondent and that it would no longer be possible to bring him to trial before the expiry of the 12-month period mentioned in s. 101(1). It was in these circumstances that the application was made to the sheriff to extend that period.

For the Crown the learned advocate-depute submitted that in reaching his decision the sheriff had misdirected himself in law in two respects. Further, it was said, he had failed to give sufficient weight to (i) the gravity of the charges against the respondent, which the advocate-depute described as 'the most serious charges', and to the public interest in bringing him to trial, and (ii) to the absence of any material prejudice to the respondent if the extension were to be allowed. No suggestion was made that the preparation of his defence had been in any way affected by the absence of service of the indictment. In all the circumstances disclosed, and balancing the interests of the respondent and the public interest, the extension sought was justifiable. The sheriff's decision to refuse it was so inherently unreasonable that the appeal should be allowed and the extension sought should be granted.

We have reached the conclusion with little hesitation that the appeal should be refused. Let us begin by making a few general observations on s. 101(1). The right conferred upon accused persons by the general rule laid down in that subsection is clearly a very important right and the general rule is only to be departed from if the appropriate judge is prepared, on cause being shown, to exercise his discretion in favour of granting an extension of the time-limit prescribed by the general rule. This was the approach of the Court in *H.M. Advocate* v. *McTavish*, 1974 S.L.T. 246 which was concerned with the right, for the protection of the lieges, conferred by s. 43 of the Criminal Procedure (Scotland) Act 1887. If an extension is to be granted under proviso (ii) to s. 101(1) the first question for the judge concerned is, accordingly: 'Has a sufficient reason been shown which might justify the grant of an extension?'; and the second question is: 'Ought I, in the exercise of my discretion in all the relevant circumstances of the case, to grant the extension for that reason?' We have only to add that the provisions of proviso (ii) to s. 101(1) are to be contrasted with the provisions of s. 101(3) and (4) (governing the power of the court to extend the time-limits prescribed by s. 101(2)). In the case of proviso (ii) an extension may be granted even if there has been some fault on the part of the prosecutor. In the case of that proviso any particular fault on the part of the prosecutor and its nature and degree will, however, be relevant considerations in deciding whether sufficient reason has been shown for allowing an exception to the general rule, and in deciding whether to exercise the discretion in favour of the Crown.

The first question for us is to decide whether we are entitled to interfere with the decision of the sheriff in the exercise of his discretion. We are certainly entitled to do so if he misdirected himself in law.

According to the Crown the learned sheriff misdirected himself by taking the view (i) that the errors on the part of the Crown which resulted in the Crown being unable to bring the respondent to trial before the expiry of the relevant period of 12 months precluded him from allowing the extension sought and (ii) when he said this: 'so far as the contentions that the extension sought is as short as possible and that little prejudice would be suffered by the respondent, in my opinion both of these points are answered by Parliament's own insistence on the fact that except in exceptional circumstances proceedings must be begun within 12 months'.

Upon a fair reading of the sheriff's report we are not persuaded that the sheriff misdirected himself in his approach to the decision which he had to take. He did not, as we read his report, take the view that he was disabled from granting an extension under proviso (ii) if, but for some fault on the part of the prosecutor, the accused could have been brought to trial in compliance with the general rule. What he did was to reject the Crown contentions that the errors in this case were fairly minor human errors, and that the charges against the respondent were of exceptional gravity. He held in our opinion, quite correctly, although he was not aware that even if service had been effected on 11 May 1984 it would not have satisfied the requirements of ss. 75 and 111A, that there had been disclosed to him a history of repeated and wholly unexplained inexcusable and wholly unexplained major errors on the part of the Crown culminating in inability to bring the respondent to trial within the prescribed time-limit, and that the charges against the respondent could not properly be described as being of unusual or exceptional gravity. His view was that in these circumstances the Crown's 'reason' for seeking an exception to the general rule was not a sufficient reason for granting the extension sought. As his report shows he appreciated that the general rule in s. 101(1) was intended to apply to all trials on indictment save in the exceptional circumstances defined in proviso (ii) and that it cannot be a sufficient reason for the grant of an extension of the general limit merely to show that the charges are serious charges. Section 101(1) after all, applies to trials on indictment 'for any offence' and accordingly applies to those offences which in our criminal law are commonly regarded as being the most serious of all. Having rejected the contention that the charges against the respondent in this case were unusually or exceptionally serious charges, the sheriff decided that if all the Crown could really say in support of the grant of an extension was that an extension was necessary only because of major errors on the Crown's part, that could hardly be held by itself to be a sufficient reason, within the contemplation of proviso (ii), for permitting an exception to the important general rule which exists for the benefit of the public generally. In our opinion, no material fault is to be found with the sheriff's process of reasoning and it appears to us that he did not, as was contended on behalf of the Crown, shut his mind to the propositions that the extension sought was as short as possible and that little prejudice would be suffered by the respondent if the extension were granted. When his report is properly understood it is plain that his view—in our opinion a correct view—was that these propositions are irrelevant in considering whether there is a sufficient reason for holding that an extension is justifiable. The length of an extension sought and the possible absence of prejudice to an accused if an extension were to be granted may, of course, have a proper part to play when the judge concerned has been satisfied that a sufficient reason has been shown for the possible grant of an extension, and proceeds to ask whether in all the circumstances he ought to exercise his discretion in the Crown's favour.

As to the remainder of the Crown submission we do not accept that the sheriff gave insufficient weight to the serious nature of the charges against the respondent and to the public interest in bringing him to trial. As we have already indicated he gave to these factors the weight which they deserved. We do not accept either, for the reasons which we have already given, that he failed to give sufficient attention to the absence of material prejudice to the respondent if the extension sought were to be granted. Finally we have only to say that we see no merit whatever in the proposition that in all the circumstances the sheriff's decision was so unreasonable that it ought to be recalled. If it had been open to this court to reach its own decision in all the circumstances which are now before us we, too, would have refused to grant the application.

For all these reasons the appeal will be refused."

Appeal refused.

NOTE

This case makes it clear that an extension can only be granted if two hurdles are overcome: there must be a sufficient reason for the extension, but the court retains a discretion to refuse the extension if, in all the circumstances, it is not satisfied by the reason. Pressure of business is not, in itself, a ground for extension: *McGinty* v. *H.M. Advocate*, 1985 S.L.T. 26. In *Lyle* v. *H.M. Advocate*, 1992 S.L.T. 467 where it was held that it was fundamental to the operation of the 12-month rule that those responsible should identify with care and accuracy the date when the period was due to expire; in that case, where no calculation had been done until too late, an extension was refused. See also *Mejka* v. *H.M. Advocate*, 1993 S.C.C.R. 978; *Stewart* v. *H.M. Advocate*, 1993 S.C.C.R. 1010.

In cases where the accused is fully committed in custody and the 110-day period is running, the Crown have a more restricted power to seek from the court an extension of the 110 days, now contained in section 101(4) of the Act (formerly embodied in section 43 of the Criminal Procedure (Scotland) Act 1887 and then as section 101 of the 1975 Act before its amendment in 1980). Where the delay in proceeding is due to, *inter alia*, "any other sufficient cause which is not attributable to any fault on the part of the prosecutor" the High Court may extend the 110 days.

3. H.M. Advocate v. Bickerstaff
1926 J.C. 65

An accused person was detained in custody after full committal. At the trial diet he was found insane and unfit to plead and was thereupon detained in an asylum. He recovered, was discharged and then re-arrested and re-indicted. At the trial diet a motion was made for his immediate release. This was referred to a Full Bench of the High Court. At the hearing, the Lord Advocate moved the court to extend the 110 days, if the court held that the 110 days had been exceeded.

LORD JUSTICE-GENERAL (CLYDE): "... It is true in a very broad sense that any question which concerns the right of an accused person to be set at liberty, either after trial or (as in the present case) without ever having been tried, raises what may be called a constitutional question. The subject of delay between commitment and a completed trial was the matter of reference in the Claim of Right, and has been the subject of legislation at least twice since. But the area of constitutional right in this department is now so fully covered by the definite statutory provisions that such a point as that which we now have to determine rises hardly, if at all, above the position of a question of statutory construction. Even so, I think Mr Aitchison, whose advocacy of the accused's case lost nothing by the moderation and restraint with which it was presented, was right in saying that the flavour of constitutional right which still adheres to the topic should influence the Court to construe the statutory provisions to which I have referred benignly, and in favour of liberty rather than against it. But whether either the necessity or the opportunity of applying a general consideration of that kind does or does not occur must, of course, depend upon the particular circumstances and character of the question raised.

In the first place, I think it is made out in the present case that the accused had been detained in prison for more than 110 days prior to the date when he was brought up for trial at Stirling. The circumstances are no doubt special; but leaving out of account the period of the accused's temporary unsoundness of mind (while he was under the care of the authorities in lunacy), and adding together the period of detention in prison prior to his being found insane and the period of subsequent to his re-arrest upon recovery, the total period of detention prior to his appearance the other day at Stirling appears to have amounted to 140 days or thereby. Some argument was presented to us on behalf of the prosecution with regard to the effect of section 52 of the 1887 Act (which keeps the original commitment in force notwithstanding a desertion of the diet *pro loco et tempore*) on the provisions of section 43. But I do not think that argument touches the present question, and I do not find it necessary to discuss it further. I think we must take it that—within the meaning of section 43—the 110 days had been exceeded in the present case.

The crux of the matter depends upon whether counsel for the accused is well founded in contending that the provisions of the section (to the effect that when the 110 days have expired without a completed trial the prisoner is entitled to be released and declared immune from further question) are absolute, peremptory, and unqualified, or whether, on the contrary, the section does not itself contain a qualification of them. I say that question lies at the root of the case, because, if the contention for the accused is sound, there is an end of the matter. The earlier part of the section is directed to prevent any undue delay in serving a prisoner with the indictment on which he is to be tried, and is not in question here. But the later part is directed to secure that there shall be no undue delay in bringing the entire proceedings against a prisoner to the final conclusion of a completed trial, and enacts that—whether an accused person has been continuously detained in prison, or whether the period of his imprisonment has been interrupted by a liberation—he shall not be detained in prison more than 110 days in all, and that, unless his trial is concluded within such 110 days, 'he shall be forthwith set at liberty and declared for ever free from all question or process for the crime with which he was charged,' or 'for which he was committed' (both of these expressions are used in the later part of the section). The case for the accused is founded entirely on this enactment; and, if the section ended there, his right to go free would be abundantly clear. But the section does not end there. On the contrary, it immediately thereafter proceeds as follows: 'But it shall be competent for the High Court of Justiciary in any case brought before it under this section, upon its being shown to the satisfaction of the Court, that the trial of a person accused ought to be suffered to proceed after the lapse of 110 days as aforesaid, when the delay in prosecuting to verdict is owing to the illness of the accused, or the absence or illness of any necessary witness, or the illness of a judge or juror, or any other sufficient cause for which the prosecutor is not responsible, to order the person accused, notwithstanding the expiry of the said period of 110 days, to be kept in custody, with a view to trial, for such further period or periods as to the said Court may seem just.' Now, it appears to me plain that this clause contains a very material qualification of the provisions which immediately precede it. If the contention of counsel for the accused were to be accepted to its full extent, it seems to me that this clause would have to be read out of the statute altogether. But this would be obviously inadmissible. There is no method of expression more familiar in draftsmanship, and in the draftsmanship of statutes in particular, than that of beginning with a general proposition stated in absolute terms, and then proceeding to expound it by means of qualifications or exceptions; and in all such cases the meaning of the Legislature can only be arrived at by reading the qualifications or exceptions along with the general proposition (however absolutely stated) which they explain and control.

The Lord Advocate has submitted that, in the circumstances of this case, the Court should use the discretion conferred upon it by the clause to which I have just drawn attention. But before we can determine upon our duty in that matter, it is necessary to consider a second line of defence relied on by counsel for the accused. Assuming—contrary to their primary contention—that the right of the accused to be liberated after confinement in prison for 110 days in all is not absolute, but, on the contrary, is subject, in a proper case, to possible qualification in the discretion of the Court, counsel for the accused contended that, on a sound construction of the clause, appeal to such discretion could only be made *before* expiry of the 110 days, and not (as in the present case) *after* it. Now, the clause applies, in terms, to '*any* case brought before the Court under this section'; and there is certainly no express limitation of the Court's power to cases brought before it prior to the expiry of the 110 days. The present is none the less a 'case brought before the Court under the section,' although it is so brought after the 110 days have elapsed. Again, the power given to the Court is 'to order the person accused, *notwithstanding* the expiry of the said period of 110 days, to be kept in custody with a view to trial.' A natural reading of these words leads to the result that the order can be made although the prisoner has already been in confinement for 110 days; and I have not been able to find anything in the section as a whole, or in that part of it which is the immediate subject of discussion, pointing to an intention to exclude the exercise of the power in such a case. The conclusion indicated by these considerations seems to me to be reinforced by the *species facti* on which the Court's discretion is to be exercised. The first ground mentioned in the clause is 'the illness of the accused'—say, a physical ailment which overtakes him during his confinement in prison. The duration of such an ailment may be impossible to foretell, and so also may be the after effects it will have in making it impossible—consistently with the dictates of justice and humanity—to put the prisoner in the dock and complete his trial within the 110 days. I think it would be unreasonable, in the absence of any positive provision to that effect, to construe the section to mean that, in such a case as I have just figured, the discretion given to the Court must be exercised (if at all) before the expiry of the 110 days. How, in such a case, could the Court fix (in advance) a period during which the accused should be kept in custody with a view to trial? It may be that your Lordships would be less disposed to exercise the discretion conferred by the statute, the longer the delay (from whatsoever cause arising) in appealing to it. But I do not think it is possible to affirm the contention of counsel for the accused that the appeal cannot competently be made after the 110 days have expired.

The question thus comes to be whether the circumstances of the present case require the exercise of the discretion conferred by the section. The fact that the accused's temporary unsoundness of mind is the origin of the difficulty in prosecuting the case to a verdict cannot be left out of account. That temporary unsoundness was established on the ninety-eighth day of the accused's confinement in prison, and he was then (on being brought up for trial) handed over to the authorities in lunacy, the trial diet being deserted *pro loco et tempore*. The authorities in lunacy dismissed him, as recovered, after some six or seven months' treatment, on 22nd October 1925. It was not maintained on behalf of the accused—I do not suggest that it could have been—that this period of treatment should be imputed to the 110 days of confinement in prison. He was re-arrested on the day on which the authorities in lunacy dismissed him, and was re-committed five days thereafter, and re-indicted without avoidable delay on 19th November 1925. But, before service of the re-indictment, the total period of his confinement in prison had exceeded 110 days, that period having expired on 7th November 1925. The statutory time-table was thereafter strictly observed, and he was brought up for trial at the second diet at Stirling on 7th December 1925, when the questions we are now considering were raised by his counsel. It is impossible in these circumstances to say that the delay which has occurred in prosecuting the case to a verdict is due to any cause for which the prosecutor is responsible. On the contrary, the case is one which appears to me to call for the exercise of the discretion which the statute confers upon us. My opinion, therefore, is that—notwithstanding that the 110 days have expired—the case is one in which the accused should be kept in custody with a view to his trial, but only for such period as to the Court may seem just, and we will hear what the parties have to say with regard to that matter."

The court extended the 110 days for just over a month.

NOTE

Although this case was decided at a time when the 110 days ran to the end of the trial, there is no reason to suppose that the reasoning today would be any different. In 1979 and 1981 when industrial action by civil servants disrupted the Scottish courts, the High Court frequently granted extensions of 40 days to the Crown, holding that court strikes fell within the exceptions listed in section 101(4). This was in spite of arguments that the Lord Advocate (as public prosecutor) was through his Ministerial role as a Law Officer of the government somehow responsible for the situation which had arisen. Considerable disquiet was felt on all sides that the constitutional protections to accused persons in custody were being insidiously eroded.

4. H.M. Advocate v. McTavish
1974 S.L.T. 246

An accused person was charged with murder and detained in custody. The Crown discovered that due to complexities in the preparation of their case, it would not be possible to conclude the trial within the 110 days. The Crown sought an extension.

LORD JUSTICE-CLERK (WHEATLEY): "... The primary ground on which the petition is founded is that certain tests are being carried out at the present time and that some time of necessity must elapse before the results of these tests are known. These tests might disclose that there would be evidence to justify a more serious charge being brought against Miss McTavish than the charge on which she has been committed. Various arguments of a preliminary nature were debated before us, but I think it is unnecessary to deal with these in this case. Assuming in favour of the Crown that what has been referred to as the ejusdem generis rule does not apply to the circumstances under which such a petition can be brought by the Crown authorities, and assuming in the Crown's favour that, in any event, such a petition is not confined to delays occasioned by procedural matters but can be founded on any ground reasonably stated for which the prosecutor is not responsible, I am of the opinion that the Crown has failed to satisfy the court that there are good reasons in this case to justify the court exercising the power conferred on it by s. 43 of the 1887 Act. That section was designed to give protection to the lieges, to ensure that they were not held in custody for an undue period of time before the case was finally disposed of. That is a very important right, and it can only be departed from when sufficient cause is shown to the court to justify that departure. Whatever the other conditions may be, it is certainly a positive condition that the delay in respect of which the case is said not to be able to go on within 110 days is not a delay for which the prosecutor is himself responsible. We are told, however, that in the present case it would be possible to bring to trial within 110 days the charge on which Miss McTavish has been committed, and that the purpose of the extension so far as the Crown is concerned is to see whether these further tests might disclose the possibility of a more serious charge being preferred against Miss McTavish. On the face of it, that seems to me to be a wholly unjustifiable ground for the court granting the extension. In any event, I am not satisfied that the Crown has shown that despite all due expedition it has not been possible to get the results of these tests to enable the prosecution to proceed to its conclusion within the requisite 110 days period. In these circumstances I am of the opinion that the petition should be refused.

I wish, however, to make reference to another argument which was advanced by the learned advocate-depute. It was that the mental health of Miss McTavish was such that it would be desirable in her own interests to have her detained in custody for this extended period, rather than have her liberated if the petition were not granted. In his view, rightly or wrongly, proceedings could not be taken under the Mental Health (Scotland) Act of 1960 to have Miss McTavish detained for what might be deemed to be the requisite treatment in an appropriate place, and it was argued that if the extension was granted and bail was refused then she would be detained in prison, but that would be in her own interests. In my view this is not a reason in itself for depriving the accused of her statutory rights in terms of s. 43 of the 1887 Act. We have been assured by her counsel that appropriate safeguards would be taken if she was released from prison.

I would only add in conclusion that the learned advocate-depute explained that this petition was brought because it was thought desirable in the interest of justice that it should be brought, and that the point relating to accused's mental health had been taken, so that it should not be thought that the Crown had been unaware of the possibilities flowing from the possible release of the accused and wanted it to be made public that the Crown were alive to these possibilities and were taking all steps in their power to see that they had discharged their duty not only to the accused but to the public. I appreciate this, but it is not a reason for granting the prayer of the petition. I would accordingly move your Lordships to refuse the petition."

Petition refused.

NOTE

Following Lord Wheatley's decision the accused was released without bail and simply ordained to appear for trial. She was eventually indicted many months later and duly appeared.

5. **Gildea v. H.M. Advocate**
1983 S.L.T. 458

An accused person appealed to the High Court against an order by Lord Murray extending the 110-day period by 30 days. The extension had been sought and granted on the basis that administrative difficulties, time-tabling and pressure had rendered it impossible for the Crown to proceed timeously.

OPINION OF THE COURT: "The appellant was, on 29 November 1982, committed until liberated in due course of law upon serious charges of contravention of ss. 1(1) and 4(1) of the Firearms Act 1968, and of assault. He was thereafter detained in custody and the period of 110 days provided for in s. 101(2)(b) of the Criminal Procedure (Scotland) Act 1975 was due to expire on 18 March 1983. An indictment was served upon him on or about 4 February 1983 for trial at the circuit in Glasgow commencing on 7 March 1983. The trial of the appellant and the co-accused was the fourth in the list of trials set down to be held in the south court and it was contemplated that it would be begun on or about 15 March 1983. By that date it had become clear that for various reasons it was unlikely that the trial could be commenced on or before 18 March 1983, and on 15 March 1983 the Crown applied to the judge of the High Court, sitting in the south court in Glasgow, to extend the period of 110 days, and the judge, acting under s. 101(4) of the Act granted the application by extending the period by a further 30 days. It was and is contemplated that the trial of the appellant will commence on 25 March 1983. This appeal is brought under s. 101(5) to challenge the grant of the extension sought by the Crown.

It is accepted that the extension was granted because the judge was satisfied that the inability of the Crown to commence the trial of the appellant on or before 18 March 1983 was, under reference to the words of s. 101(4), due to a sufficient cause which was not attributable to the fault of the prosecutor. The submission for the appellant was that the judge erred in being so satisfied.

In approaching the question for our decision which is, we think, whether the judge was entitled to be so satisfied, it must be remembered that it was for the Crown to demonstrate that there was a sufficient cause for the difficulty in which they found themselves which was not attributable to any fault on the part of the Crown. As the Lord Justice-Clerk (Wheatley) pointed out in *H.M. Advocate* v. *McTavish*, 1974 S.L.T. 246; 1974 J.C. 19 (a case concerned with s. 43 of the Criminal Procedure (Scotland) Act 1887): 'That section was designed to give protection to the lieges, to ensure that they were not held in custody for an undue period of time before the case was finally disposed of. That is a very important right, and it can only be departed from when sufficient cause is shown to the court to justify that departure.'

These observations apply with full force to the provisions of s. 101 of the Act of 1975 which in its present form, was introduced by the Criminal Justice (Scotland) Act 1980. Equally apt are the words of the Lord Justice-Clerk (Macdonald), speaking again of s. 43 of the Act of 1887, in *H.M. Advocate* v. *Macaulay* (1892) 3 White 131 at p.135: 'I remark first that this exception is framed to meet such difficulties as might happen without any failure in diligence upon the part of anyone at all. viz:—the illness or absence of a necessary witness or of a judge or juror. The words "or any other sufficient cause" must, therefore, relate to some other cause of a similar nature to those mentioned. But in addition to that, it must also be the fact that the prosecutor shall not be responsible for the failure.'

In this case the Crown sought to justify the grant of their application for extension in the following submission. It cannot be contended that in serving the indictment upon the appellant on 4 February 1983 there was any failure of due diligence, for it was then within reasonable contemplation that having regard to the business set down for disposal in Glasgow on the March circuit, the trial of the appellant would commence before 18 March 1983. The probabilities fall to be tested by consideration of the business set down for disposal in the south court for it was known that the first trial for disposal on that circuit in the north court was quite unlikely to end before 18 March 1983.

The first case for trial in the south court involved charges of injury and the danger of life, murder and contravention of s. 3(1)(b) of the Bail (Scotland) Act 1980. The accused was in custody and the 110-day period in his case was due to elapse on 20 March 1983. The wholly reasonable expectation that this trial would be concluded within two days was borne out in the result because it ended on 9 March. The second trial for south court disposal also involved an accused in custody and in his case the 110-day period was due to expire on 18 March 1983. This trial was reasonably estimated to require no more than two days to complete. In the event no trial took place because when the diet was called the accused pled guilty. The third trial was of a single accused charged with rape and there were only 23 witnesses on the Crown list. The entirely reasonable expectation was that this trial would be completed within two days and at worst on the third day. The fourth trial, that of the appellant, was accordingly expected to begin not later than 15 March and since it could not reasonably be expected to last more than two days it was confidently expected that the fifth trial of five accused, in the case of three of whom the 110-day period was due to expire on 18 March 1983, was likely to begin before that date. What in fact happened was unforeseen and was not reasonably foreseeable. The third trial on the south court list, contrary to all reasonable expectation, and for reasons difficult to understand, consumed not two days, not three days but five days of the time of the court. It was not suggested that this expenditure of time was due to any cause for which the Crown was or could be held responsible. In this situation the Crown had a difficult decision to make. The decision was to proceed at once with the fifth case on the list involving the five accused and to apply in the case of the appellant for the extension of time granted by the judge on 15 March 1983.

For the appellant the submission was that this explanation by the Crown did not satisfy the test which was prescribed by s. 101(4)(c). By delaying service of the indictment until 4 February 1983 the Crown failed to exercise due diligence and it was evident upon the explanation given by the advocate-depute that from that moment on they were at grave risk. Even if it be accepted that the forecasts of the time likely to be consumed by the first three south court trials were those mentioned by the advocate-depute the Crown was allowing to itself a safety margin of only two days, at the most, if it were to be able to commence both the trial of the appellant and the fifth trial in the list before 18 March 1983. It is, it was said, notoriously difficult to predict the length of a trial on a charge of rape and it cannot be said that because the third trial in the list took five days to complete instead of two or three days this was not reasonably to be foreseen. The risk courted by the Crown was quite unacceptable, and by neglecting to requisition a special sitting for the disposal of the indictment against the appellant, or to release him from custody, the Crown cannot be held to have demonstrated that there was sufficient cause for which the Crown was not responsible, for their failure to be in a position to commence the trial of the appellant before 18 March 1983.

We do not pretend that the problem presented by this appeal is easy to resolve. With some hesitation, however, we have decided that the appeal should be refused. The Crown undoubtedly took a calculated risk in relation to the commencement of 110-day cases for disposal on the March circuit in the south court. The question is whether the decision to take that risk was unreasonable and whether the judge who heard the application and was himself the presiding judge in the south court was entitled to decide it was not. In our opinion he was so entitled and his decision was correct. The critical factor was the expected duration of the single accused rape trial, number three in the list. In our judgment it was wholly reasonable to predict, for that trial, a disposal time of one-and-a-half days to two days, and at the very worst three days. That it should take five days to complete, is, we think, almost impossible to understand, and it was not from what we know of the case reasonably to be anticipated. In the foregoing circumstances we are persuaded that the Crown was suddenly faced with such a difficulty as might happen without want of due diligence on the Crown's part, and that the judge who granted the extension sought, who, incidentally was the trial judge in the disposal of the single accused rape case which grossly overran its reasonably anticipated span, was well entitled to be satisfied that the Crown had established what required to be established in support of their application in terms of s. 101(4)(c) of the Act of 1975."

Appeal refused.

NOTE

In the decade since this case was decided, it appears that the Crown have not required to advance again such unconvincing arguments for extending the 110 days, nor has the High Court required to rule on their cogency or otherwise. *Gildea* was the subject of much adverse comment at the time it was decided, but the kind of situation which presented itself there has not since been founded on in support of an application for an extension. Perhaps this is because the Crown recognise that the case has a number of flaws, namely:

(1) The *ratio* of the decision appears to be that where delay in proceedings is not reasonably to be foreseen by the Crown, then an extension can be justified. But the 110-day rule is not, and never has been, about what is, or may be foreseeable, either subjectively or objectively assessed. The rule is couched in peremptory terms, with no room for considerations of this sort.

(2) It appears that the appeal would have been allowed if the court had been convinced that the Crown's decision to take its calculated risk about the 110-day cases was unreasonable. But it has always been thought that extensions are only justified, *inter alia*, where the prosecutor is not at fault,which presupposes a situation *outwith his control*. But "calculating risks" is within a prosecutor's control, and if he miscalculates the risk he pays the penalty. In *McTavish*, the Crown sought an extension so that further tests might be carried out. They *calculated* that they could not proceed in time. The extension was refused, the clear implication being that calculations, whether correct or not, do not enter into the problem.

(3) It may be true that no one could foresee that an apparently short rape trial would overrun. But who is responsible for precognoscing cases, serving indictments, requisitioning a High Court sitting and deciding the running order of cases?

(4) What protection does an accused have against other Crown miscalculations? Here they miscalculated the running time of the previous case, an admittedly patent miscalculation. But what about all the miscalculations which may be latent, such as the time taken to interview witnesses, or draft the indictment? The accused cannot know what goes on in the Crown Office, only what he can observe or what his advisers can find out. It was primarily to *protect* the accused against such latent happenings that the 110-day rule was enacted in 1701.

A final ironic twist to the case. The accused's trial duly proceeded on March 25, 1983. He was acquitted of all charges.

CHAPTER 9

THE PROBLEMS OF RELEVANCY AND COMPETENCY

A. FRAMING THE INDICTMENT—RELEVANCY

Following the completion of the Crown precognition, the procurator-fiscal sends all the papers to the Crown Office for directions on further procedure. The next step is usually the drafting of the indictment in the Crown Office, its revisal by the fiscal and service on the accused. Styles of indictment are to be found in Schedule A to the 1887 Act as amended by the Criminal Justice (Scotland) Act 1949, s. 39(1) and Sched. 12. Indictments run in the name of the Lord Advocate, or the Solicitor-General if there is no Lord Advocate in office. A defect in the instance may lead to a fundamental nullity.

H.M. Advocate v. Hanna
1975 S.L.T. (Sh.Ct.) 24

"Archie Murray Hanna was charged on indictment with offences under the Firearms Act 1968 and the Prevention of Crime Act 1953. The indictment was 'at the instance of The Right Honourable William Ian Stewart, Her Majesty's Advocate,' and was signed 'By Authority of Her Majesty's Advocate "J. L. MacLeod" Procurator Fiscal ...' Before the jury was balloted it was argued for the panel that there was no effective indictment. Mr Stewart had held the office of Solicitor General for Scotland and in the period following the former Lord Advocate's appointment as a Senator of the College of Justice he continued in office as Solicitor General for Scotland but was never Lord Advocate. Reference was made to Renton and Brown, *Criminal Procedure According to the Law of Scotland*, 4th edition, at pp.23–24 (paras. 4–02 and 4–03). The Criminal Procedure (Scotland) Act 1887, s. 3, and the Law Officers Act 1944, s. 2, detailed the provision for public prosecution in Scotland where the office of Lord Advocate was vacant. The general rule was that the Lord Advocate did not demit office until his successor was appointed, albeit that he had resigned. In circumstances where the Lord Advocate died in office or was removed from office there was provision that indictments should be brought in the name of the Solicitor General for Scotland until a new Lord Advocate was appointed. Following the decision in *The Solicitor General for Scotland* v. *Lavelle*, 1914 J.C. 15, 1913 2 S.L.T. 427, it was the case that when a Lord Advocate was appointed to judicial office he was deemed to be removed from the office of Lord Advocate. In such circumstances public prosecutions should be brought in the name of and by the authority of the Solicitor General. In the circumstances the present indictment was fundamentally null and any trial would be a nullity. Faced with this argument the procurator fiscal moved to desert the diet of trial pro loco et tempore and the sheriff granted the motion."

Diet deserted.

NOTE

It has been argued that the indictment was not, in fact, fundamentally null, since all that was wrong was a misdescription of the designation of Mr Stewart, the Solicitor-General, who had actually authority to raise indictments: see G. H. Gordon, "Fundamental Nullity and the Power of Amendment," 1974 S.L.T. (News) 154. If the sheriff had allowed the fiscal to amend the indictment, the accused would not have suffered any prejudice. It is this question of prejudice which looms large when challenges are made to the terms of indictments. To avoid such a challenge, the Crown must frame a *relevant* indictment; relevancy has three aspects in that the indictment must set forth with sufficient specification: (1) the time of the alleged crime; (2) the place where it occurred; and (3) the *modus* by which it was committed.

(i)   Specification of Time

At common law the general rule was that a latitude of three months was allowed in stating the time of the offence. By sections 50 and 312(f) of the 1975 Act this is now implied in all charges, except where an exact time is of the essence of the charge. But in some cases an exceptional latitude as to time is allowed.

1.   H.M. Advocate v. MacKenzies
(1913) 7 Adam 189

An accused person was charged that "between 3rd July 1907 and 2nd April 1913 ... you ... did steal a book." A preliminary plea to the relevancy of the charge was stated on the ground that too great a latitude of time had been taken.

> LORD JUSTICE-CLERK (MACDONALD): "The first charge in this indictment is a charge of theft against the male prisoner. It sets forth a very great latitude in respect of time, ranging over nearly six years. The justification of the latitude taken, which is unprecedented so far as I am aware, is made in argument on the ground that the book said to have been stolen was a book of recipes, and that it was taken in order to obtain copies of these recipes, and that the prosecutor does not know when the actual taking occurred. I should myself have expected that a prosecutor proposing to take such a latitude would have set forth facts to indicate his difficulty in being more precise, as, for example, that the accused was in the employment of the owners of the book during the period given, and thus had the opportunities of taking possession of it without his having done so becoming known to the owners. And certainly if the case were allowed to go to trial, the prosecutor would have to show by his evidence that the latitude taken was not unfairly taken; and if he failed to do so, his failure might lead to his not being able to obtain a verdict. While I refrain from expressing an opinion as to whether the extreme latitude of time taken should not be fatal to the charge, for lack of justifying statement, I may say that as I understand no trial is to proceed on the present indictment without a new service, the advisers of the Crown may well consider whether, if they are to proceed further with the case, they will not frame an indictment which may be more satisfactory in this respect. I am not prepared to cast the indictment on this point, but it certainly would be more satisfactory in a case so peculiar for the prosecutor to express in the indictment the cause justifying a latitude so extreme."

Objection repelled.

NOTE

Under sections 50(3) and 312(*f*) of the 1975 Act, there is no obligation on a prosecutor who takes an exceptional latitude as to time to set out in the charge the facts and circumstances which he alleges justify the exception. But in *Mackenzies* it was clear that the court felt great unease about the Crown's position in the absence of such statements.

2.   H.M. Advocate v. A.E.
1937 J.C. 96

An accused was charged with incest on various occasions with his two daughters. The first charge spanned the periods between April 1, 1927 and July 5, 1933, and November 28, 1933 and January 14, 1937. The second charge covered the periods 1 February, 1931 and July 5, 1933, and November 28, 1933 and June 3, 1936. He objected to the relevancy of the indictment.

> LORD JUSTICE-CLERK (AITCHISON): "I have some doubt as to the relevancy of this indictment owing to the very exceptional latitude taken by the Crown. The panel is called upon to meet two separate charges, the first extending over a period of five years. I am not aware of any case in which so great a latitude has been taken by the Crown, but, having regard to the nature of the charges, and to the statement of the learned Advocate-Deputy that what he is going to seek to prove is not an isolated instance or isolated instances but a course of criminal conduct over a period of time, I think it would be wrong to exclude inquiry. I am influenced in this by the fact that in the case of the first of the two girls named in the indictment, the alleged improper conduct began when she was only about eight years of age. In the case of the second of the two girls named, the alleged improper conduct began when she was only ten years of age. That being the position, it may not be possible for the Crown to give very much in the way of specification, at any rate as regards the earlier periods, but I wish to point out that there will rest a heavy onus on the Crown owing to the latitude of time they have thought right to take, and it may be necessary to give a direction to the jury that they must be satisfied that the panel has suffered no prejudice owing to the latitude taken. That, however, is a matter that does not arise now. I repel the objection to the relevancy, and the case must proceed to trial."

Objection repelled.

NOTE

Thus, an exceptional latitude will be allowed where the Crown seeks to prove a course of conduct by the accused, but not where the offences have merely taken place on various unspecified occasions between particular dates.

3.   Ogg v. H.M. Advocate
1938 J.C. 152

An accused was charged with committing acts of gross indecency "on various occasions between 1st January 1930 and 1st June 1937, the particular dates being to the prosecutor unknown." An objection to the relevancy of the charge was taken.

LORD RUSSELL: "Objection is taken by counsel for the panel to the relevancy of charge (1) in respect that the latitude in the time over which the offences charged are alleged to have taken place is so unusual and exceptional that it renders the charge irrelevant from lack of specification. In this charge the accused is charged with committing on various occasions between 1st January 1930 and 1st June 1937 certain acts, at a locus described, with another male person described. The particular dates are said to be unknown to the prosecutor. Now, on the face of this charge it is clear that the intention of the Crown is not to prove a continuous course of conduct during which the offences charged were committed by the accused with the person named. The indictment clearly specifies various occasions, the particular dates of which are unknown. I think that the principle by which the time latitude—which in the normal case extends to three months and which in exceptional cases may be extended—is usually regulated is well given in one of the passages cited from Alison, where the learned author says this: 'In general, however, it is true of all those cases where an extraordinary latitude in point of time is allowed, that the law allows it unwillingly, and from necessity only; and therefore, that it will not sustain such a latitude where, by due diligence, a more accurate and specific detail could have been given, or where there is nothing appears, either from what is set forth on the face of the libel, or from the nature of the facts charged, to warrant such a departure from the ordinary rule.' Now, I am prepared to assume that in this case by due diligence a more accurate and specific detail could not have been given, but even on that assumption, apart from the fact that the offence charged is one of an occult nature, there is nothing set forth *in gremio* of the charge itself which seems to me to warrant such a departure from the ordinary rule as to justify a period of seven years and five months as a tract of time during which various offences on various occasions in that time are said to have occurred. I am impressed by what was said by Lord Justice-Clerk Macdonald in the case of *H.M. Advocate* v. *Mackenzie*, where, with reference to a latitude of time taken in an indictment charging the accused with stealing a book by making copies of various recipes contained in the book, and where the latitude in time extended over nearly six years, the learned judge said this: 'I should myself have expected that a prosecutor proposing to take such a latitude would have set forth facts to indicate his difficulty in being more precise, as, for example, that the accused was in the employment of the owners of the book during the period given, and thus had opportunities of taking possession of it without his having done so becoming known to the owners. And certainly if the case were allowed to go to trial, the prosecutor would have to show by his evidence that the latitude taken was not unfairly taken; and if he failed to do so, his failure might lead to his not being able to obtain a verdict. While I refrain from expressing an opinion as to whether the extreme latitude of time taken should not be fatal to the charge for lack of a justifying statement, I may say that, as I understood no trial is to proceed on the present indictment without a new service, the advisers of the Crown may well consider whether, if they are to proceed further with the case, they will not frame an indictment which may be more satisfactory in this respect.' Now, it is true that that was an *obiter dictum*, but it was an *obiter dictum* of a judge whose pronouncements are entitled to the greatest weight in the criminal courts. I keep in view that the offences here charged are of an occult nature. I also keep in view that the conduct libelled is not libelled as a continuous course of conduct, but is one of conduct which is said to have taken place on various unspecified occasions, the particular dates being unknown. In that situation I am satisfied that no precedent has been quoted which would justify me in holding that exceptional latitude is justified by the circumstances in this case. The case cited of *H.M. Advocate* v. *A.E.*, a case of incest, was obviously a case where the circumstances were very special, and very peculiar, and I am satisfied that the course that was taken by the Lord Justice-Clerk in that case was right and proper. In the present case, however, the situation is quite different, and I am of opinion that the wide latitude in time taken here, without any justification therefor appearing *ex facie* of the indictment, is unreasonable; and that, if it were to remain unaltered, the charge to which it relates could not be allowed to go to trial."

Objection sustained.

NOTE

Exceptional latitudes are, thus, in the main confined to exceptional cases. Nor will the statutory implied latitude which replaced the common law in section 10 of the Criminal Procedure (Scotland) Act 1887 (now sections 50 and 312(f) of the 1975 Act) necessarily avail a prosecutor who perils his case on stating a specific date or dates between which the crime is alleged to have been committed.

4.   Creighton v. H.M. Advocate
(1904) 4 Adam 356

A man was charged with having unlawful carnal knowledge of a 15-year-old girl "between 14th January and 6th February 1904 (the particular date being to the prosecutor unknown)." The evidence disclosed that the offence definitely did not occur between these dates, but pointed to a date sometime in December 1903. The sheriff charged the jury that they could convict, provided they found that the crime occurred subsequent to 11 December 1903, that being within three months of service of the indictment. The accused was convicted and sought to have the conviction suspended by the High Court.

LORD STORMONTH-DARLING: "This indictment charged the complainer with having committed an offence under the Criminal Law Amendment Act, 1885, 'between 14th January and 6th February 1904 (the particular date being to the prosecutor unknown)'; and the leading question is, whether under such an indictment the prosecutor was entitled to avail himself of the provision in section 10 of the Criminal Procedure (Scotland) Act, 1887, to the effect that 'the latitude now in use to be taken in stating time in indictments at the instance of Her Majesty's Advocate shall be implied in all statements of time where an exact time is not of the essence of the charge,' so as to warrant a conviction for an act done in December 1903. It is admitted by the prosecutor that at the trial he failed to prove the commission of the offence within the period expressly libelled, and therefore that, in order to obtain a conviction, it was necessary for him to resort to the latitude implied by the statute, if he could competently do so.

Now, what the statute declares to be implied is 'the latitude now in use to be taken in indictments'; and this refers us to the practice in existence before 15th October 1887. The first thing to be noted with reference to that practice is that the latitude was always express. Sometimes in crimes of an occult or continuing character it extended to a period of months or even years. In the ordinary case where the information in possession of the prosecutor enabled him to condescend on the actual day of the month it was usual to guard against any slip of memory on the part of his witnesses by stating, as an alternative, one or other of the days of that month or of the month immediately preceding or of the month immediately following. Sometimes this common mode of libelling time was varied by the prosecutor confining himself to the month of the crime and the month immediately preceding, as, for example, where the accused had been taken into custody shortly after its commission, and the succeeding month was therefore impossible. This limitation to two months frequently occurred when the crime was said to have been committed in the night beginning with the last day of one month and ending with the first day of another. But it would, I think, be correct to say that the most common latitude was three months, and that this was never exceeded unless in special cases and for the reasons of which the Court was judge, and which were expressed in the libel, unless it was obvious that the nature of the crime made specification difficult, as, for example, in the case of reset. In any event, the latitude being always carefully expressed, the accused person could have no difficulty in knowing the precise length of time over which the evidence for the prosecution might extend, and he could take objection before the case went to trial, if so advised.

Under the existing law it is still quite competent for the prosecutor to express the latitude which he intends to take. The 10th section of the Act of 1887 nowhere forbids that. It merely abolishes the necessity of setting out at length words which had come to be words of style, where to imply them could raise no ambiguity and cause no prejudice to the accused. It is in conformity with the whole scope and tenor of the Act of 1887 that criminal writs shall be shortened by leaving out mere alternatives, which, under the old practice, were set forth always in the same manner. But the Act is equally careful to provide that indictments shall tell accused persons everything which is material for them to know in order to meet the case against them. While, therefore, the framer of an indictment is quite right to avail himself of the latitude implied by section 10 wherever it is quite simple to ascertain the limits of time by implication, it is in my judgment a misuse of the section to trust to the implied latitude in any case where to do so may create an ambiguity. In all such cases the proper course is to express the latitude which the prosecutor desires to take.

The present case is a fair illustration of the ambiguity resulting from this mode of libelling. Crown counsel were unable to define the latitude for which they contended. Was it the whole months of January and February 1904, with the addition of December 1903, or of March 1904, or of both these months, or was it a period of three months, calculated from the middle of the express period, and so beginning 25th December 1903 and ending 25th March 1904? As it happens, the section of the Criminal Law Amendment Act requiring that no prosecution shall be commenced for the offence more than three months after its commission made it specially material for the accused person to know what the prosecutor's case was to be, for as he was apprehended and charged on 11th March 1904, he could not lawfully be prosecuted for any offences committed prior to 11th December 1903. We are told that the Sheriff so directed the jury (in my opinion rightly), and we must assume that the jury obeyed the direction. But if one of the definitions which I have suggested as a possible definition of the latitude claimed by the Crown had been expressed the indictment would have been seen to be incompetent on the face of it. I mention this as an illustration of the practical inconvenience of the mode of libelling here adopted; but I desire to rest my judgment on the broad ground that the latitude implied by section 10 of the Act of 1887 ought never to be resorted to except in cases where no ambiguity can arise as to its commencing and concluding dates, and where, therefore, it is impossible for the accused to be misled."

Conviction quashed.

NOTE
  As will have been observed from all the foregoing cases, the undercurrent running through each is that the accused is entitled to fair notice of the case which he has to meet. For example, he might be able to plead a defence of alibi in relation to particular dates. Fair notice is at the heart of all disputes as to relevancy. In *R.L.* v. *H.M. Advocate*, 1969 J.C. 40, where there were three charges each alleging that on one occasion between August 1, 1966 and June 17, 1968 the accused used indecent practices towards a child, an appeal against conviction was successful on the ground that too great a latitude had been taken by the Crown. Another practical difficulty arises now since judicial examination under section 6 of the 1980 Act has been introduced. At this stage a petition is the only notice which the accused has of the charge against him. While hitherto it has been quite common for the terms and dates specifying the crime contained in any subsequent indictment to be somewhat different from those in the petition, due to the fact that the case has by then been precognosced properly by the Crown, there would now seem to be a greater necessity for the petition to be as accurate as possible if the Crown is going to examine the accused immediately. This may even require the Crown to state the actual time of day at which it alleges the commission of the crime, if it wishes to preclude the accused from concocting an alibi at a later stage. In any event, it may be impossible for an accused to give notice of an alibi where an excessive latitude is taken. On this problem, see *Murray* v. *H.M. Advocate*, 1987 S.C.C.R. 249.

(ii)   Specification of Place

  This is important from the viewpoint of jurisdiction, on which generally see Chap. 3, *supra*. It is essential also that the accused is given fair notice of where it is that the crime is said to have been committed.

1.   Stevenson v. McLevy and Others
(1879) 6 R. 33

The respondents were charged on a summary complaint with an offence contrary to section 21 of the Salmon Fisheries Act 1868. They objected to the competency of the proceedings on the ground that the complaint did not specify the *locus* at which the offence was allegedly committed. After the evidence had been led, but before judgment, the sheriff on the motion of the prosecutor allowed the complaint to be amended so as to specify the *locus*. The respondents having been acquitted, the procurator-fiscal appealed by stated case. The first question for the High Court was: "Whether the amendment ... was competently made after the proof had been led but before judgment?"

  LORD YOUNG: "There are two questions submitted to us here.
  The first raises an important point, and certainly a novel one, under the Summary Procedure Act of 1864, an Act which is of vast importance in all summary prosecutions. The question is, whether a complaint under the Act charging an accused with an offence is competent without a *locus*; or whether, if there be no *locus*, one may be added during or at the end of the trial, to suit the facts which have come out in evidence. It was admitted for the appellant that

the omission of the *locus* was a blunder. Such things do happen occasionally, but the prosecutor must take the consequences, though the ends of justice may sometimes be defeated by such an oversight. It is one of the fundamental rules of our law that any complaint charging an offence shall state the *locus* where the offence was committed. I know of no exception to this rule, even where the complaint is a statutory complaint. In a complaint before an inferior Judge, such as a Sheriff, the *locus* is more necessary to shew that the Judge has jurisdiction, and he cannot proceed at all unless the fact that he has jurisdiction appears on the face of the complaint. I think that may be fairly stated as a universal proposition. It is a rule of our law, and it is also a rule of the law of England, and the reason and good sense of it must commend itself to every one.

In addition to this, it is necessary to give this information that the accused may have an opportunity of defending himself. The accused must have reasonable information of the charge against him, of which the *locus* is first and foremost, for the purposes of his defence. I know, as I have said, of no authority for the proposition that a prosecutor may omit the *locus* and then fill it in at his convenience to suit the evidence led. There would be the greatest possible danger in sanctioning or countenancing such a course, and it would be giving a most unfair advantage to the prosecution. I think, therefore, that the Sheriff went wrong in allowing this amendment, and this is sufficient to dispose of the case; and I understood the counsel for the appellant to assent to this, for it would be an idle proceeding in us to send the case back to the Sheriff when no conviction could, in our opinion, follow upon it."

Appeal dismissed.

2. McMillan v. Grant
1924 J.C. 13

McMillan, the manager of a firm in Rothesay, was charged with fraudulently altering the registration of a motor vehicle, contrary to section 13(4) of the Roads Act 1920. The *locus* of the alleged offence was not specified and objection was taken to the competency of the complaint. That objection was repelled. McMillan was convicted and presented with a bill of suspension to the High Court.

LORD JUSTICE-GENERAL (CLYDE): "... A separate point was taken with reference to the second of the three bills, namely, that no specification of *locus*, even of the widest kind, is given in the complaint. The charge is against the managing director of a firm (whose address is given), as the person who was in charge of the firm's business at the date of the offence, and the offence is stated as having been committed 'between Saturday, 31st March, and Monday, 2nd April'; but, so far as the statement in the complaint is concerned, the alleged alteration of the identification mark may have been made at any place to which the motor carriage could have gone between these dates. Specification of *locus* is essential not merely for the reasons given in Hume, but because the jurisdiction of the Court before which the complaint is brought depends upon it. It might have been enough, if the place of the offence was unknown to the prosecutor, to avail himself of the latitude of the sheriffdom. It was suggested that as Rothesay is in Bute, and as Bute is an island, it was unnecessary to give any further specification of *locus* than is implied in the address of the managing director's firm. But so important a matter as the *locus delicti* cannot be left to inference in that way; and, in any case, we cannot know anything of the possibilities of transit to the mainland. I think the entire absence of any specification of *locus*, such at least as to determine the jurisdiction of the

Sheriff, amounts to a case of incompetency within the meaning of section 75 of the Summary Jurisdiction (Scotland) Act, 1908, and that—however little the accused may have been actually misled or prejudiced—the conviction which followed on a complaint so deficient as this is ought to be quashed."

The court passed
the bill.

NOTES
1.   See also *Macintosh* v. *Metcalfe and Others* (*infra*, p.462) and *Herron* v. *Gemmell*, 1975 S.L.T. (Notes) 93. In *Craig* v. *Keane*, 1981 S.C.C.R. 166 the prosecutor successfully sought leave to amend a complaint to add an additional *locus*. The case was distinguished from *Stevenson* v. *McLevy* on the ground that that case was concerned with the situation where the original complaint specified no *locus* whatsoever. The jurisdictional problems were not considered by the High Court.
2.   See also *Tudhope* v. *Fulton*, 1986 S.C.C.R. 567, where it was observed that it was now clearly established that it is competent to allow an amendment of a complaint which alters the *locus* of an alleged offence. But see section 335 of the 1975 Act on the general power of amendment of a summary complaint.
3.   In cases of embezzlement, theft and reset, considerable latitude will be allowed in stating the *locus* of the offence.

3.   Gold v. Neilson
(1907) 5 Adam 423

An accused person was convicted of reset at four separate places "all in Glasgow, or at one or other of said places, or elsewhere in Glasgow." He objected to the relevancy of the change, both before the magistrate and, subsequently, after conviction, to the High Court.

LORD JUSTICE-CLERK (MACDONALD): "... But it is said here that the prosecutor took too great a latitude. The place of the crime is stated as, *inter alia*, 'or elsewhere in Glasgow to the prosecutor unknown.' I should like to say that prosecutors ought always to avail themselves of the simpler forms of stating place and time which are authorised by the statute, which makes a great deal that is often found in complaints like this, such as this statement of 'elsewhere to proscutor unknown,' quite superfluous. But as regards the latitude here taken, such latitude has been long ago decided to be legitimate in cases of reset. There are two cases in Bell's 'Notes' which clearly show this. In the first of these cases, *M'Intosh*, 4th January 1831, Bell's 'Notes to Hume on Crimes,' p.213, the place libelled was 'within your house in King Street, Leith, or in some other part within the town or in the vicinity of Leith to the prosecutor unknown.' In the second case, *Wilkinson*, 30th September 1835, Bell's 'Notes to Hume on Crimes,' p.213, the place libelled was 'some place in the county of Perth to the prosecutor unknown.' Such latitude is necessary in cases of reset. It is a continuing crime. The person accused may originally have got the goods honestly, but if he afterwards finds that he got them from a thief, the moment he knows this he is guilty of reset, unless he takes steps at once by informing the police to show that he has no guilty intention with regard to the goods."

Appeal refused.

NOTE
Such a latitude is often necessary because of the circumstances of the crime of reset itself. But where the *locus* of the crime is capable of precise description, it should always be specified, from the viewpoint of fairness to the accused. Mere misdescription, as opposed to non-description, will be capable of amendment: see *Herron* v. *Gemmell*, 1975 S.L.T. (Notes) 93.

(iii)   Specification of Mode

The essential element here is that the indictment or complaint must set forth facts and circumstances such as to constitute a crime known to the law of Scotland. No *nomen juris* is necessary.

1.   **H.M. Advocate v. Anderson**
1928 J.C. 1
An accused woman was charged with attempted abortion. The defence objected to the relevancy of the indictment.

LORD ANDERSON: "The charge against the panel is that she 'did insert pieces of slippery elm bark or other substances into the private parts of Agnes M'Kain in the belief that she was then pregnant, and for the purpose of causing her to abort and did attempt to cause her to abort.' An objection to the relevancy of this charge has been stated in the following terms: 'That the indictment does not set forth that Agnes M'Kain was in fact pregnant at the time of the alleged crime, and that no facts are set forth from which facts, if proved, the crime of attempting to procure abortion could be inferred.'

The question for decision is whether or not this objection to the relevancy is well founded. If I had any serious doubts as to how this question ought to be decided, or if the point taken raised any matter of general importance, I should have thought it my duty, in order that an authoritative judgment should be pronounced, to report the case for consideration of the High Court in Edinburgh. But I have formed a clear impression that the objection to the relevancy is well founded, and it does not appear to me that any point of general importance is involved in the decision. The objection is concerned with the particular facts of this case, facts which are so special, and indeed unique, that it is barely conceivable that they will ever recur. I therefore propose to decide the question here and now.

The Crown, according to the libel, offers to prove three things, (1) that the accused inserted pieces of bark or other substances into the private parts of Agnes M'Kain, and I assume, as I am bound to do, that this part of the libel can be proved; (2) that the accused was in the belief that Agnes M'Kain was then pregnant, and I again assume, although this assumption is more difficult to make, that the Crown is able to prove what was in the mind of the accused; and (3) that the purpose of the accused was to cause Agnes M'Kain to abort. On these allegations being established by evidence, the view of the Crown is that the jury would be bound to hold that the crime libelled had been proved, and that the accused had thereby attempted to cause Agnes M'Kain to abort.

There is, however, a noteworthy omission from the libel, which, in my judgment, is fatal to its relevancy. It is not alleged that Agnes M'Kain was, in point of fact, pregnant. I am bound to assume that she was not pregnant, for if she had been, this fact, which I hold to be essential to the relevancy of the charge, would have been libelled by the prosecutor. An allegation of pregnancy is, in my opinion, an essential part of a charge of procuring or attempting to procure abortion. To insert deleterious substances into the private parts of a non-pregnant female, with her consent, may or may not give rise to a criminal charge. If death results, the charge of culpable homicide would probably lie. If injury short of death were the consequence, it is doubtful whether any criminal offence has been committed. At all events, I am satisfied that this present charge would not lie. Again, it does not appear to me to be material that the accused believed there was pregnancy, if in point of fact there was none, or that the purpose of the act was to cause abortion, if there was nothing to abort. In short, in the absence of an allegation of pregnancy, I consider that I am bound to treat this charge as if the libel had been that the accused had inserted injurious substances into the private parts of a virgin in order to effect an abortion. Had the indictment been so framed, it would manifestly have postulated a contradiction in terms, and have charged the accused with the commission of what was a physical impossibility. To attempt to do what is physically impossible can never, in my opinion, be a crime.

The ground of my judgment is that, in a charge of procuring or attempting to procure abortion, which is a charge of an attempt to commit a well-known crime, the prosecutor must libel, and, to secure a conviction, must prove, that the patient was pregnant. This proposition seems to be made good by consideration of what is involved in the crime, and by having regard to the presumptive reasons whereby the acts resulting in abortion are regarded as criminal. Abortion, in the sense of the criminal law, is held to be criminal because its successful accomplishment results in the destruction of a potential human life. That is the main consideration. I agree with the Advocate-depute that, incidentally, but only incidentally, regard is also had to the possible injury to the prospective mother. If, however, there is no pregnancy, none of these considerations are applicable.

All that I have said seems to be warranted by what is found in the text books and in the statements of institutional writers. At the time when Hume wrote, the crime was not recognised under its now well-known *nomen juris*, because Hume only refers incidentally to the matter in his first volume at page 187, and he alludes to the case, commented upon in Alison, of Catherine Robertson and George Bachelor. Hume points out that the libel in that case was found relevant to infer an arbitrary punishment, the crime being 'wilful causing or procuring a pregnant woman to abort, or to part in an untimely manner with the *fœtus* or child in her womb'; and Alison refers to the same case in a chapter in which he is dealing with innominate offences. He states in section 4: 'Administering drugs to procure abortion is an offence at common law, punishable with an arbitrary pain, and that equally whether the desired effects be produced or not,' and then he goes on to refer to the case of Catherine Robertson and George Bachelor alluded to in Hume. When the late Lord Justice-Clerk Macdonald came to write, the crime had been fully recognised and had been described by the well-known *nomen juris* of 'procuring abortion,' and the learned author deals with it at page 382 of his Treatise on Criminal Law, where he suggests the appropriate charge to make in a case when this particular offence is meant to be libelled. He puts the matter in this way:—'A charge of procuring the abortion of a pregnant woman, after a narrative of a certain woman having become pregnant, states—"You did" (a certain act described) "for the purpose of causing her to abort, and did cause her to abort." ' The Act of 1887 does not, if I remember aright, contain in its Schedule a form applicable to abortion, but what I have quoted is the suggestion of Lord Justice-Clerk Macdonald as to the proper form of indictment, and, according to him, an essential part must be a narrative that the woman operated upon had become pregnant.

It may, at first sight, appear to be a narrow construction to which I am subjecting this indictment. The accused, according to the charge, acted just as she would have done had M'Kain been pregnant, and she owes her escape from trial to the fortuitous circumstance that there was no pregnancy. But, in the realm of criminal law, an accused person is entitled to have the charge construed with the utmost strictness, and to take advantage of any chance which enables a conviction to be avoided. The Advocate-depute submitted two points in support of the libel. He said, and I have already dealt with this point, that it is an element in the crime of abortion that the woman operated upon may be injured, and he submitted that, as that element was present in this case, whether there was pregnancy or not, the crime might be committed. I doubt whether any crime, in such circumstances, would have been committed; but it is enough to destroy his first contention that the crime of attempting to procure abortion could not have been committed. His other point is based upon a well-known doctrine in criminal law, which is referred to in Hume, vol. i, p.12, and by Macdonald at p.252, to the effect that the High Court of Justiciary is entitled to stamp with the mark of criminality any new offence which presents criminal features. There is no doubt about that, but this is not a libel of a new offence. This is a libel of an old and well-known offence, and in my opinion, it is a bad libel. The same answer falls to be made to the argument of the Advocate-depute which was based upon the terms of section 5 of the Criminal Procedure (Scotland) Act, 1887. That section provides that 'It shall not be necessary in any indictment to specify by any *nomen juris* the crime which is charged, but it shall be sufficient that the indictment sets forth the facts relevant and sufficient to constitute an indictable crime.' Now, this indictment does specify the crime charged by a *nomen juris*. The *nomen juris* is 'attempt to cause abortion.' Accordingly, this is not a novel form of crime, but a recognised form of crime; and, it being such, and having a known *nomen juris*, I reach the conclusion, without difficulty, that the objection to the relevancy is well founded and falls to be sustained. I accordingly sustain the objection to relevancy."

Objection sustained.

NOTE

For a discussion of the declaratory power of the High Court referred to by the Crown in argument in this case, see Gordon, *The Criminal Law of Scotland* (2nd ed., 1978), paras. 1–15 *et seq.*

2. H.M. Advocate v. Grainger and Rae
1932 J.C. 40

Two accused were charged that they had carnal knowledge of and did ravish a named woman, "while she was in a state of insensibility or unconsciousness from the effects of intoxicating liquor." They claimed the indictment was irrelevant in respect that it did not disclose the crime of rape according to the law of Scotland.

LORD ANDERSON: "... Rape (save in the exceptional cases of pupils and idiots) is the carnal knowledge of a woman forcibly and against her will— Macdonald's Criminal Law, (4th ed.) p.175; Hume on Crimes, vol. i., pp.301–302; Alison's Criminal Law, vol. i., p.209. Accordingly, it was urged by the accused, the crime cannot be committed unless a woman is in a condition physically and mentally, to exercise her will power and offer resistance. In the present case the libel sets forth that the woman was in a condition when she was incapacitated, by reason of intoxication, from offering any resistance to her assailants or from exercising her will power in the way of giving or refusing consent. The offence charged, accordingly, it was said, does not amount to rape. This contention seems to me to be well founded. It is not alleged that the accused supplied the woman with the liquor with which she became intoxicated. Had this allegation been made, the charge of rape might have been sustained, as it has been decided that it is rape to have connexion with a woman whose resistance has been overcome by drugging her—Macdonald's Criminal Law, (4th ed.) p.176; Hume on Crimes, vol. i., p.303; Alison's Criminal Law, vol. i., p.212; *Fraser* [(1847) Ark. 280]; *Sweenie* [(1858) 3 Irv. 109]. It might be suggested that the present case falls to be assimilated to that of an idiot female; but this does not seem to me to be a true analogy. The idiot has, in law and in fact, no will; in the present case the woman assaulted had a will, the activity of which was but temporarily suspended by her intoxication. The true analogy seems to me to be the case of the woman who is taken advantage of while asleep. Such an offence is not rape—Macdonald's Criminal Law, p.175; *Sweenie*. Just as a sleeping woman is temporarily in a state of unconsciousness wherein she is incapable of exercising her will power, so here it seems to me that the woman was in the same temporary condition of unconsciousness by reason of intoxication.

The objection to relevancy must therefore be sustained."

Objection sustained.

NOTE

Lord Anderson went on to indicate that in his view the actings of the accused amounted to another separate criminal offence: that of inflicting clandestine injury on a woman, which goes to show the flexibility of the law, provided the prosecutor libels conduct which *is* criminal.

3.   **H.M. Advocate v. Smith**

1934 J.C. 66

An accused person was charged with perjury during the trial of two persons, Turner and Ord. He stated two objections to the relevancy of the indictment, the second of which is dealt with in the following extract:

LORD JUSTICE-CLERK (AITCHISON): "... The second objection to the relevancy of this indictment is much more formidable. It is maintained by Mr Duffes that the evidence of the accused Smith, which is alleged by the Crown to have been knowingly false, was incompetent evidence, and accordingly that perjury cannot attach to it. Now, the first question, accordingly, that arises is whether the evidence of the accused Smith in relation to the matters to which I have referred was or was not competent evidence. I have no doubt at all that that evidence was incompetent. Statements made by Mr Graham, Mr Wilson, and Mr M'Lellan to the accused Smith outwith the presence of Turner and Ord could not be evidence against Turner and Ord. Similarly, the evidence that Graham, Wilson, and M'Lellan had called at the accused Smith's house and reported that Turner and Ord had solicited bribes could not be evidence against Turner and Ord. It appears to me to be equally clear that any statement by the accused Smith, whether by way of admission or denial, when he was a witness in the previous trial, that Graham, Wilson, and McLellan had called and had made statements to him could not be evidence against Turner and Ord, and similarly any statement made by Smith at the alleged interview, or his admission or denial of any statement, could not competently be received in evidence.

It must be kept in view that Mr Wilson and Mr Graham were really in the position of complainers in the former trial. It is so well settled that no authority is required to vouch it, that statements made by complainers outwith the presence of the party accused are never evidence against that party, except in certain very exceptional cases. *A fortiori*, statements made to complainers outwith the presence of the party accused can never be evidence. In cases of assault committed on women or on children, where complaint is made *de recenti*, the Court will allow such complaint to be received in evidence, but that is the exception to the rule. So also if the statements made by Graham, Wilson, and M'Lellan had been made at the time of the alleged offence, so as to form part of the *res gestae* of the crime alleged, it may be that they would have been admissible in evidence, and any statement made by the accused Smith at the time of the alleged offence might, if part of the *res gestae*, have been admissible in evidence. But the statements here upon which the indictment for perjury is based are statements alleged to have been made on the 11th of April 1933, whereas the crime libelled in the former trial occurred, as I have pointed out, on the 9th of April 1933.

It was maintained on behalf of the Crown that the questions put to the accused Smith and the answers given by him were competent as bearing upon the credibility of Smith as a witness. I am quite unable to assent to this view. Great latitude is allowed in cross-examination of a witness in order to test the credibility of the witness, but the latitude can never be extended so far as to admit evidence that is incompetent evidence, and that may be prejudicial evidence against the prisoner who is being tried. I therefore have no doubt that, if objection had been taken at the trial of Turner and Ord to the admissibility of the evidence of the accused Smith upon the matters set forth in this indictment, the learned judge at the trial would have had no alternative but to disallow the evidence, upon the ground that it was incompetent and could not be regarded as either relevant or pertinent to the issue. No objection was in fact taken to the admission of the evidence, but that circumstance will not make incompetent evidence competent.

If, accordingly, the evidence was incompetent, the only remaining question is whether perjury can attach to it. Now, that matter appears to me to be concluded beyond all doubt against the Crown upon authority which I am bound to follow. The most authoritative statement of the law is the statement contained in Hume in his Commentaries on the Criminal Law. Baron Hume says this: 'The oath, in that part of it which is challenged as false, must be pertinent to the point at issue: It must relate to some of those substantial facts, which may have an influence in the decision of the interest that is at stake, in the proceeding where the oath is made.' It is not possible to get a more authoritative statement of the law than that. Exactly the same doctrine is laid down by Burnett in his Criminal Law, by Alison, and by Lord Justice-Clerk Macdonald, than whom there is no greater authority. I will not occupy time in reading what they say, because what they say is simply what Hume said in the passage I have read.

I accordingly in this case, without difficulty, reach the conclusion that the second objection to the relevancy of the indictment is well founded and must be sustained. I desire to add this observation. The rule that perjury cannot attach to incompetent evidence is not a technical rule; it is a rule of substance. The foundation of the rule is that incompetent evidence is so prejudicial to the administration of justice that the Courts will not assign to it the character of perjury and will treat it as if it had not been given. That rule has been laid down by lawyers of great distinction with a proper appreciation of what justice requires, and in my view it is a rule that should be rigidly adhered to. The result is that I sustain the second objection to the relevancy of this indictment, and direct that the accused be liberated."

Objection sustained.

NOTE

This is an unusual case, but perjury is of its essence a crime which involves the libelling of the alleged false statement previously given in a judicial proceeding. Presumably the perjury indictment would never have been raised if the original evidence had been rejected as inadmissible. See also *Lord Advocate's Reference (No. 1 of 1985)*, 1986 S.C.C.R. 329; 1987 S.L.T. 187.

4.   Campbell v. McLennan
(1888) 1 White 604

An accused person was charged that "having on 14th November 1887, within the inn of Dunvegan, found in money one pound, you did deny having found the same and did appropriate and thus steal same." He challenged the relevancy of the indictment.

> LORD McLAREN: "... Now, in my opinion, that is not a relevant charge of theft, because everything set out might be true, and yet the accused might not be guilty of theft. I am not prepared to affirm that the mere finding of a £1 note, coupled with a denial of having found it, is tantamount to felonious appropriation. One would like to know who the owner of the note was, and whether the person to whom the accused is said to have denied having found it, had a right to ask the question. The circumstances set out are only these two: that the accused found a £1 note, and that he denied having found it. Now it may be morally wrong to deny having found a £1 note; on the other hand, such a denial, if addressed to a person who had no business to put the question, does not raise a presumption of theft.
>
> In the result, my opinion is that the Procurator-Fiscal having undertaken, by the form of the charge, to set out such particulars as would amount to charge of theft, has failed to do so. He has in the terms of the charge given an argumentative statement of circumstances which he considers amount to theft, but which are also consistent with a possible case of innocence."

Charge irrelevant.

NOTE

Nowadays charges of theft by finding simply proceed on a narrative that on a particular date at a particular place the accused "did find [article], dishonestly appropriate the same to his own use and did thus steal the same."

5.   Strathern v. Seaforth
1926 J.C. 100

An accused person was charged with clandestinely taking possession of a motor car belonging to another, well knowing that he had not received permission from the owner and that he would not have obtained permission to his so doing, and with driving and using the car. He challenged the relevancy of the charge on the ground that the *species facti* did not infer any crime known to the law of Scotland. The sheriff sustained the objection and the Crown appealed to the High Court.

> LORD JUSTICE-CLERK (ALNESS): "... Counsel for the Crown say that that

complaint discloses a crime which the Court was bound to investigate, and that that crime consists in taking and using something clandestinely, without the permission of the owner having been given. It appears to me that the proposition for which the Crown contends is supported by the authorities which were cited. But, speaking for myself, I should not have required any authority to convince me that the circumstances set out in this complaint are sufficient, if proved and unexplained, to constitute an offence against the law of Scotland.

The matter may be tested by considering what the contention for the respondent involves. It plainly involves that a motor car, or for that matter any other article, may be taken from its owner, and may be retained for an indefinite time by the person who abstracts it and who may make profit out of the adventure, but that, if he intends ultimately to return it, no offence against the law of Scotland has been committed. I venture to think that, if that were so, in these days when one is familiar with the circumstances in which motor cars are openly parked in the public street, the result would be not only lamentable but absurd. I am satisfied that our common law is not so powerless as to be unable to afford a remedy in circumstances such as these."

Objection repelled.

NOTE

Nowadays, such an accused would be charged under section 178 of the Road Traffic Act 1988. But the case clearly confirms that the test of relevancy is met if the charge sets forth sufficient facts from which criminal liability can be inferred, even if the crime is not named: see 1975 Act, s. 44; *Grant* v. *Allan*, 1988 S.L.T. 11. On the problem which can arise where an indictment is not clearly framed, see *Cordiner* v. *H.M. Advocate*, 1991 S.C.C.R. 652, particularly the remarks of Lord McCluskey at pp.670 *et seq.*

B.   ARE THE PROCEEDINGS COMPETENT?

Preliminary pleas to the competency should not have anything to do with the adequacy or otherwise of the facts laid out in the indictment. Such a plea is directed to the essential validity of the proceedings themselves, for example lack of jurisdiction, want of proper citation and the like. The following cases illustrate the nature of the plea.

1.   Aitchison v. Tudhope
1981 S.L.T. 231

An accused person was charged with driving while disqualified and, on the same complaint, a contravention of the Bail etc. (Scotland) Act 1980. He was convicted and appealed by stated case.

LORD JUSTICE-CLERK (WHEATLEY): "The appellant was charged on a summary complaint at the instance of the respondent which set forth that: 'You did on 12 June 1980, at the premises at 41 Netherton Road, Wishaw, District of Motherwell, having been liberated from Hamilton Sheriff Court on 14 May 1980 on a Bail Order issued under the Criminal Procedure (Scotland) Act 1975 and the Bail (Scotland) Act 1980, and being subject to the conditions therein, break the said conditions of the Bail Order by contravening the Vagrancy Act 1824, section 4: Contrary to the Bail (Scotland) Act 1980, section 3(1).'

Section 3(1) aforesaid is in the following terms: 'Subject to subsection (3) below, an accused who having been granted bail fails without reasonable excuse—(b) to comply with any other condition imposed on bail, shall be guilty of an offence'. One of the conditions in the bail order was: 'That the accused does not commit an offence while on bail'. There is express warrant for such a condition being imposed in s. 1(2)(b) of the Bail etc. (Scotland) Act.

The major issue in the appeal raised a question of general importance. To obtain a conviction on the charge libelled in the complaint the Crown had to establish that the appellant had committed an offence while on bail. The question is—can the Crown prove that fact within the ambit of the trial of the alleged contravention of s. 3(1) or must the Crown establish it in a prosecution on a separate complaint libelling the offence?

In the instant case the former procedure was followed without objection. There is no mention of any such objection having been taken either in the minutes of procedure or in the sheriff's note appended to his findings-in-fact. The Crown adduced two police witnesses to establish that the appellant had contravened s. 4 of the Vagrancy Act 1824. The relevant part of that very long section is in these terms: 'Every person being found in or upon any dwelling house, warehouse, coach-house, stable, or outhouse, or in any inclosed yard, garden, or area, for any unlawful purpose' shall be guilty of an offence. No evidence was led for the defence, and the sheriff held that the offence had been proved. His finding on this matter was not challenged in the appeal.

The submission by the appellant's counsel was that even if no objection was taken to this procedure, it was funditus null and the conviction should accordingly be quashed. There could not be a conviction under s. 3(1) unless the appellant had been convicted of a contravention of s. 4 of the Vagrancy Act. He had not been convicted and was entitled to the presumption of innocence until he was convicted. There were two separate offences involved here. One was a contravention of s. 3(1) and the other a contravention of s. 4 of the Vagrancy Act. Each could be charged separately, but it was wrong to libel the latter within the framework of the former, and in effect get a finding of guilt in respect of the latter when it could not be recorded as a conviction in the complaint before the court. It was necessary for the Crown to obtain a conviction of the offence alleged to be a breach of a condition of the bail order before a contravention of s. 3(1) could be established, and such a conviction could only be obtained on a separate complaint. The advocate-depute on the other hand maintained that the procedure followed was quite competent. It was not the policy of the Crown in cases of this nature to charge a person both with a contravention of s. 3(1) and with the offence which was a breach of the bail order. It was a matter for the Crown to decide which of the two offences would be charged. It was accordingly competent for the Crown to prove within a s. 3(1) complaint the manner in which the condition of the bail order had been breached in order to constitute the offence libelled.

What has to be decided is the competency of the procedure followed here, not whether another procedure would be more desirable. We are not concerned with Crown policy about not charging an accused with two separate offences. The charging of offences in our criminal law (with very limited exceptions) is entirely a matter for the Crown. That does not necessarily mean that because of that policy it would be competent here to libel two separate charges. In my opinion, however, the contention of the Crown that the procedure followed here was competent is well founded. The condition of the bail order said to have been breached was that the appellant should not commit another offence. It does not say that the appellant has been convicted of another offence. What the Crown has to prove is that the accused has committed an offence during the currency of the bail order. The manner in which that is done may vary according to circumstances. If, leaving aside the current Crown policy, an accused had already been convicted of another offence, an extract conviction of that offence could suffice. If the accused had not been already convicted of that offence I see no reason why the Crown should not prove that the accused was guilty of a contravention of s. 3(1) by leading evidence to establish that he had committed the libelled offence which was of the essence of the complaint. The fact that this would not result in a conviction on that offence is not in my view material. A person charged with fraud may be face with a libel that in pursuance of that fraud he uttered forged documents to enable the fraud to be perpetrated. It is not necessary to charge him with a separate charge of uttering, and if found guilty, he would only be guilty of fraud, not of uttering and fraud. If the other offence was the modus whereby the charge libelled was committed, then, provided fair notice of the nature of that other offence is given in the libel, it must surely be competent to lead evidence about the modus. And I reiterate, what had to be established here was that the applicant had committed the specified offence in breach of the condition of the bail order, not that he had been convicted of that offence, and that was the modus whereby the contravention of s. 3(1) took place.

Two other points were taken by counsel for the appellant. The first, which was also taken before the sheriff but rejected by him, was that the Crown had failed to prove that at the time of the libelled contravention of s. 4 of the Vagrancy Act the bail order was still in operation. There is certainly no finding-in-fact that it was. The advocate-depute, however, submitted that it was not necessary to do so because of the provisions of s. 312(x) of the Criminal Procedure (Scotland) Act 1975 which is in the following terms: 'where an offence is alleged to be committed in any special capacity, as by the holder of a licence, master of a vessel, occupier of a house or the like, the fact that the accused possesses the qualification necessary to the commission of the offence shall, unless challenged by preliminary objection before his plea is recorded, be held as admitted'. The libel here narrates that 'having been liberated—on a Bail Order—and being subject to the conditions therein [you did] break the said conditions of the Bail Order by contravening the Vagrancy Act 1824, section 4: contrary to the Bail (Scotland) Act 1980, section 3(1).' In my opinion that libel brought the appellant within the provisions of s. 312(x) aforesaid and no preliminary objection was taken. He had been granted what in effect was a licence to be at liberty pending his trial, but that was on certain conditions, and it was only such a person who had the qualification necessary for the commission of the offence libelled under s. 3(1). I accordingly reject the submission by the appellant's counsel.

The second point taken was that the alleged contravention of s. 4 of the Vagrancy Act was lacking in specification. As I have already indicated, if the Crown seeks within the trial of the charge under s. 3(1) to establish that another offence has been committed in violation of a condition of the bail order fair notice should be given of what the Crown seeks to prove. Normally that involves notice of when, where and how that offence took place. In the present complaint notice is given of where and when but not how. Even if this was a material deficiency it was one which could have been rectified by amendment. However, no objection was taken to the relevancy of the complaint for lack of specification either at the pleading diet or the trial diet. Having regard to the provisions of s. 454(1) of the Criminal Procedure (Scotland) Act 1975 that point is not now open to the appellant."

Appeal dismissed.

NOTE

It appears that in this case the defence were confusing the question of specifying the *modus* (a problem of relevancy) with that arising from the revelation in the charge that a previous crime had been committed, (a problem of competency). It is quite competent (and quite common) to charge an accused with committing an offence in breach of all the bail orders to which he is subject: see *H.M. Advocate v. Kerr*, 1987 S.C.C.R. 283. Where an accused is charged with driving while disqualified and other road traffic offences, those other offences are usually embodied in a separate complaint. Both complaints will be prima facie relevant and no problem of competency should arise. As to the timing of a plea to the competency (or relevancy) in solemn proceedings, the accused should apply for a preliminary diet under section 76 of the 1975 Act (as inserted by the 1980 Act, Sched. 4, para. 5). In summary procedure the matter is regulated by section 334(1) of the 1975 Act.

2.   **Sugden v. H.M. Advocate**
1934 J.C. 103

An accused person was in 1934 charged with bigamy, allegedly committed in 1909. He presented a preliminary plea to the competency of the proceedings, claiming that the crime had prescribed and the prosecutor had no title to proceed. This plea was repelled and the accused was convicted after trial. He appealed to the High Court.

LORD JUSTICE-CLERK (AITCHISON): "... If this question can be regarded as an open one, for myself I have little difficulty in reaching the conclusion that there is no prescription of crime by the law of Scotland. I would agree in that matter with the view of Lord Justice-Clerk Macdonald in his Criminal Law (4th ed., at p.312), that 'there is no rule of law establishing a prescription of crime.' But the real difficulty arises upon the case of *H.M. Advocate v. Macgregor* [(1773) Mor. 11146]. In that case, in the year 1773, a full bench of the High Court of Justiciary, consisting of five Lords Commissioners, was invited by the Crown, on a plea stated by the panel *in limine*, to decide this very question. Whether the Court did so is, I confess, left in some obscurity. It is accordingly necessary to examine the case carefully in order to see what it did decide, and, if it did lay down a rule, what the rule was, and whether it was absolute or subject to limitation.

The panel Malcolm or Callum Macgregor, *alias* John Grant, was charged on indictment that, on the evening of Christmas Day, 1747, he did attack and barbarously murder one John Stewart, tenant in Abergairn, in the Parish of Glengairn and Shire of Aberdeen, and the libel proceeds that the panel did immediately abscond and flee from that part of the country, and was never again seen there, except to some few persons by stealth and in the night time, and further that a justiciary warrant was thereupon issued for apprehending and incarcerating him, which warrant bears date 21st January 1748. The Books of Adjournal record that the indictment was read over in open Court and thereafter 'Mr Alexander Lockhart, as counsel for the pannell, represented that no proceedings could be had upon this indictment exhibited against the pannell in respect the crime therein charged is said to have been committed so far back as the year 1747, and therefore is prescribed by the elapse of more than twenty years.' The record proceeds: 'Partys procurators were then heard at great length thereupon,' and informations were ordered. The informations are set out at length, and then under date 9th August 1773, there is this interlocutor: 'The Lords Justice-Clerk and Commissioners of Justiciary having considered the Information given in for His Majesty's Advocate, for His Majesty's interest, and the said Malcolm or Callum Macgregor, *alias* John Grant pannell, and before recorded, and in respect it does not appear, that any sentence of fugitation passed against the pannell, they therefore sustain the defence and dismiss the Indictment and the pannell from the barr.'

Prima facie there can, I think, be no doubt that this judgment did sustain a prescription of twenty years as a competent defence to an indictment for crime by the law of Scotland. Such a decision may seem surprising and indeed anomalous. Each of the civil prescriptions in the law of Scotland is statutory; here there is no statute. Nor is there uniform and unvarying usage. According to Baron Hume (Commentaries respecting Crimes, vol. ii., p.136), the equitable rule of the Roman law 'which gives the accused his *quietus* at the end of twenty years,' although sustained in this case, was not established in our older practice. Sir George Mackenzie, who published his Laws and Customs in matters Criminal in the year 1678, 'inclined' to the opinion, based on some analogy drawn from the law of Saxony, that there was a vicennial prescription of crime. But, notwithstanding, he writes, 'It may be doubted with us, if prescription has place at all.' And again, 'There being *jus quaesitum* to the King, by the committing of the crime, both *quoad vindictam et bona fisco applicanda*, that right cannot be taken away from him, but by a publick law, or his own privat remission'; and he adds, 'There is no instance in all our practicks, where prescription hath been sustained, but on the contrary, crimes of an old date, even after forty years, have been punished.' Instances of the contrary practice to which Sir George Mackenzie refers are to be found in the case of *James Wilson*, tried on 20th December 1649 for incest and adultery committed by him thirty-five years before, and also the cases of *Jean Weir, William Dodds*, and *George Turnbull* referred to by Hume and the older authorities. The case of *William Dodds* was a trial on 2nd October 1663 for the murder of one Andrew Hardie, committed in November 1640. Thus there was not only no statute and no unvarying custom, but there were instances of a contrary custom. And also, prior to 1773, the Roman law in this matter had not been received into the law of Scotland. The Lord Justice-Clerk (Sir Thomas Miller of Barskimming) referred to the question as 'quite entire.'

When the matter is examined in the light of these considerations, and when regard is had to the recorded opinions of the judges, to which I shall afterwards refer, I think the sounder view is that the rule of a twenty years' limitation of the Advocate's title was really laid down as a rule of practice based on justice and expediency, and not as a prescription in the absolute sense. The judgment in the case of *Macgregor* is explained as a striking illustration of the exercise by the High Court of Justiciary of the inherent right the Justiciary had always claimed to formulate and declare rules in all matters criminal. This inherent power, so far as the declaring of new crimes is concerned, is stated by Hume (Com., vol. i, p.12) in these words: 'Our Supreme Criminal Court have an inherent power as such competently to punish (with the exception of life and limb) every act which is obviously of a criminal nature; though it be such which in time past has never been the subject of prosecution.' This fundamental assertion of right was judicially affirmed by a Full Bench in 1838 in the case of *Greenhuff* [(1838) 2 Swin. 236]. A modern example of its exercise is to be found in the case of *Strathern* v. *Seaforth* [1926 J.C. 100]. The power so claimed and asserted is not a usurpation of the powers of the Legislature, it is a prerogative of the Justiciary derived from its history, and coming down from the days of the Justiciar, to do what it deems to be just in all matters criminal, and affecting on the one hand the rights of the Crown, and on the other hand the liberties of the subject. The exercise of this power was seen not only in the declaring of new crimes—that is, crimes not before known to the law of Scotland—but also in the abrogation of old defences, and an illustration of this is furnished in the very matter of prescription itself.

Under the old law of Scotland there existed certain customary limitations of the prosecutor's title or prescriptions of crime. They are referred to by Hume. There was, for instance, a customary prescription of rape. The title of the complainer to proceed with a libel was extinguished under the older law if she delayed to make a complaint to the magistrates of the vicinity of the crime beyond a single night. This at one time was admitted as a plea *in limine* as a bar to prosecution. A relic of this old rule survives in our modern rule that the complaint of the assaulted woman must be made *de recenti*, but under the older law the objection went to the title of the prosecutor and not merely to the weight of the complaint. Again, in the case of hamesucken, no man could be heard to accuse another if he delayed to make his accusation 'by the space of ane nicht and wha maks nae fresh and recent pursuit.' According to Hume (Com., vol. i., p.322), 'The prosecution for hamesucken, like that for robbery or murder, is said to have been subject of old to a very strict limitation in respect of time (Reg. Maj., C. 4. c. 10). But this rule, if observed of old, has now, for more than a century, been so entirely laid aside, that in the case of Keith of Lentush, action was sustained at the distance of more than three years. In the case of Richard Hamilton, in July 1807, the lapse of ten years even was found to be no bar to the prosecution.' A similar limitation at one time applied in the case of assault or real injury.

The point to be noticed is, that these customary prescriptions (there may be dispute as to whether they were not all statutory), which went to the title of the prosecutor, and were not pleadable merely to set up a defence of prejudice before the assize, were all abrogated by decision of the Court of Justiciary. They were treated as rules of practice, and as matters within the competency of the Court to discard. This abrogation I regard as of great importance as pointing to the inherent power of the Justiciary to modify the practice of the Courts where circumstances no longer require the imposition of restraints. If the rule of *Macgregor* is to be read as truly a rule of practice, then it is within the authority of this Court, in the exercise of its inherent power, as a Court to admit such exceptions to the rule as considerations of justice may require, or to abrogate the rule itself. And this is specially to be insisted in when the rule was laid down in times that are far removed from our own, as regards both the instance of prosecutions and the motives by which they are inspired.

I read the decision in Macgregor as having introduced into our practice and laid down that in the ordinary case the expiry of twenty years from the date of the crime will extinguish the right of the prosecutor to proceed with a libel. But the rule was not absolute. I reach this conclusion upon the following grounds. In the first place, the judgment itself introduced a limitation. It was not put on the lapse of time *simpliciter*; it was put *per expressum* in respect that it did not appear that any sentence of fugitation had passed against the panel. No warrant had been executed against the panel although one had been taken out, a precognition had not been taken, nor had any libel been raised although the panel was all the while within the kingdom and not absconding. The libel, indeed, sets forth that the panel had absconded and fled from justice, but it appears from the information for the panel that he had had his constant residence in Scotland, and for a great part of that time in the county of Aberdeen not far distant from the place where the supposed crime was alleged to have been commited, and that he had carried on business as a dealer in different parts of the country and at various fairs and markets. I think the interlocutor proceeds upon the view that the prosecutor had been in a position to proceed with a libel and had refrained from doing so. In the second place, it is, I think, quite impossible to read the opinions of the judges—we have not the full text, but I see no reason to think the record inaccurate—without seeing that the judges treated the matter as one rather of bar than of prescription in the absolute legal sense. This construction of the judgment is strongly supported by these passages which I quote from Maclaurin (Decisions, p.603)—

Auchinleck: 'Do not consider this as a prescription, but as a rule of justice . . . clear that prosecutions ought not to last for ever: the question—How long?' Kames: 'Do not say that a prescription is here fixed, but take this case as it stands.' Pitfour: 'I am now reconciled to this prescription, though at first had some difficulty . . . prosecution extinguished no matter whether the word *prescription* can be used or not.' Coalston: 'Had the panel absconded or been fugitated'—showing very clearly that the Court did not accept the allegation in the libel that the panel had absconded—'he could not have pleaded this defence. But the question is, Whether can a man that has appeared publicly for fifteen years be prosecuted . . . taciturnity a strong plea in law . . . independent of statute and listened to in questions as to bills. Claim for the *jus relictae* at the instance of the widow's executors, repelled at the distance of twenty years.' These passages all confirm that what the judges had in mind was bar based upon *mora*, and not prescription. Again Kennet: 'Highly expedient there should be a limitation . . . Prosecutor may always stop the prescription.' This I think clearly implies that the prosecutor is aware of the crime and of the person who committed it. Finally, the Lord Justice-Clerk said this: 'Law pays great attention to the just defence of pannels. If such prosecution competent to the public, it must be equally so to the nearest-in-kin of the deceased. The private prosecutor may be supposed to have watched his opportunity.' This latest observation is significant, because it must not be forgotten that, in 1773, the right of prosecution was not vested, as now, solely in the public prosecutor, with certain limited exceptions, but the right of the private individual to prosecute for an injury done to himself or his kin still existed alongside the title of the Advocate for the public interest. There were obviously strong and compelling reasons for a limitation. Political rancour, clan antagonisms, and civil tumult, with their legacy of hatred, and bigotry, and the lust for vengeance, all enforced the argument from expediency. The Lord Justice-Clerk goes on, after referring to the Roman law, 'Why then not sustain a defence for the prisoner founded on that law or on expediency?' Coalston added: 'Interlocutor ought to be guarded. Fugitation—effect of it would have lasted till the party accused surrendered himself to justice.'

I think it is a fair and reasonable reading of these recorded opinions that what the Court did in the case of *Macgregor* was to introduce a rule of practice that the title of the prosecutor is subject to a limitation of twenty years to be reckoned from the date of the crime. The rule, however, was qualified by exception in any case in which the panel had absconded and sentence of fugitation had been passed upon him. I am unable to read the decision as laying down that the rule would not have been subject to exception in any case in which twenty years had expired without discovery of the crime or of the person by whom the crime was committed. The decision did not, in my view, introduce into the law of Scotland, or declare as our law, the vicennial prescription of the Roman law. If the contrary view were to be affirmed, the result would be to introduce into our law what would be essentially a one-sided prescription. In the civil prescriptions the right of the person against whom the prescription runs is a right that continues throughout the whole prescriptive period. But I think cases can be figured in which the Court might sustain a plea of bar on a lapse of time far short of twenty years, where it appeared to the Court *in limine*, on facts admitted by the Crown, that gave prejudice to the accused might result if the trial were allowed to proceed. The correct doctrine in this matter is, I think, stated by Mr Burnett in his Criminal Law (at p.309) in this passage: 'As His Majesty's Advocate . . . cannot be compelled to give his *instance*, so this officer cannot be controlled as to the way and manner in which he is to give it, or as to the *time* when he is to exercise his right, except in as far as he has been restrained by express enactment as to the form of trial and the period within which it must be brought, or by the interference of the Court of Law upon any case of hardship or oppression towards the party accused, by undue delay or otherwise, in conducting the trial.'

As I have already pointed out, the rule laid down in *Macgregor's* case was laid down in times that are far distant from our own, and under social and political conditions affecting the purity of prosecutions, that have long since passed away. I cannot regard a rule so laid down 160 years ago as fixed and unalterable, and so sacrosanct that it is beyond the power of this Court to declare that the rule no longer exists. I think it should be so declared.

This appears to me to be in accordance with justice and expediency. Twenty years may be a long time when men look forward, but it is a short time when men look back. It requires no effort of the imagination to figure a notorious crime committed twenty years ago, in which, were the criminal allowed to walk abroad with impunity merely because twenty years had run, such a liberty would be against the public conscience, and contrary to the community sense of what is just, upon which the law and respect for the law must ultimately be based. I am glad that we are not compelled to acquiesce in any such situation. I accordingly think that the learned Sheriff was right in repelling the plea of prescription, and that the appeal should be refused."

Appeal dismissed.

NOTE

This case was in fact decided by a majority of a Full Bench of 12 judges. The Lord Justice-General was apparently the only absent judge. The case also illustrates the power of one Full Bench to overrule another Full Bench comprising a lesser number of judges.

Sugden does not, however, mean that delay in prosecuting a crime cannot act as a bar to the proceedings. On this problem see, *infra*, pp.351 *et seq*. For cases on jurisdiction, see Chap. 3, *supra*; and on time-limits for trial, see Chap. 7, *supra*.

CHAPTER 10

PRE-TRIAL PROCEDURE

Once the indictment has been framed under reference to the problems discussed in the last chapter, it is served on the accused, either at his domicile of citation or on him at any prison or other institution in which he may have been detained. Until the 1980 Act, accused persons were cited to attend both a pleading diet and a trial diet, but under section 12 of the 1980 Act the mandatory first diet has been abolished. If, however, some preliminary point needs to be raised prior to trial, any party may apply for a preliminary diet to deal with such a matter, all in accordance with section 76 of the 1975 Act, as inserted by the 1980 Act, Sched. 4, para. 5 and as amended by s. 39 of the Prisoners and Criminal Proceedings (Scotland) Act 1993. In particular, if the accused wishes to take a plea to the competency or relevancy of the indictment, this procedure must be used. This chapter deals with other pre-trial problems which may arise.

A. SEPARATION OF CHARGES

An accused who is charged with more than one offence on the same indictment may seek that the charges be separated. If the accused wishes to move for separation, he should seek a preliminary diet, as explained above.

1. H.M. Advocate v. Bickerstaff
1926 J.C. 65

An accused person was charged with (1) indecent assault on one complainer, and (2) indecent assault, including a charge of murder, involving another complainer. The offences were alleged to have happened on the same day. He moved for separation of charges.

> LORD JUSTICE-GENERAL (CLYDE): "... There was, as I have explained above, a further question raised, viz., whether there should be a separation of the charges. The question is not one of the separation of trials (a question not so uncommon), but as to the separation of charges (a point which is less common). The two charges here are (*first*) an indecent assault on one little girl, and (*second*) an indecent assault amounting to murder on another little girl, occurring on the same day and in the same place, by which is meant the town of Stirling. It is familiar that more offences than one should be charged under the same indictment. The submission made on behalf of the prisoner is that some prejudice may be suffered by him if the two charges are taken and tried together. I think it would be extremely difficult—and I have no intention of attempting the task—to define the circumstances in which the combination of more charges than one in the same indictment is legitimate and fair to the accused. But it is familiar that there are many instances of criminal conduct which are divisible into successive stages, and in which each stage is distinguished by the commission of some particular act which (regarded in isolation) would in itself be a crime. It has never been the practice of the Court to insist, in such a case as that, that there should be a separation of charges. On

343

the contrary, there exists in such a case a connexion of time, of circumstances, of character (one, or more, or all) between the acts charged which makes it both fair and legitimate to put them all in one indictment and to lead evidence in respect of all of them together. It was suggested that this principle has no application to a case in which (as in the present case) the persons assaulted or attacked were different persons. I am unable to follow the grounds upon which that suggestion can be made good. A man may assault more than one person in turn against whom he is moved by a common and equal sentiment of anger or revenge; so, a man may commit a continuous series of crimes of the class to which the present indictment relates against one little girl after another, moved by the same criminal impulses or desires. Without attempting to dogmatise upon the matter, it seems to me that the present case presents an illustration of offences, in themselves capable of being treated as separate crimes, which are so closely connected in time, circumstances, and character as to make it fair and legitimate to try them together. I realise that in all such cases—I mean in all cases where more than one charge is tried under one indictment—there may arise in the course of the trial questions of more or less difficulty with regard to what shall be regarded as competent and relevant evidence, depending on the closeness of the relation—in time, circumstances, and character—between the charges included in the same indictment. Questions of that class inevitably arise, and it is the function of the Judge to allow or disallow evidence, and to guide and direct the jury with regard to what evidence they are entitled to consider in relation to the various parts of the case they have to decide. But that is an incident common, more or less, to all criminal trials. What we are asked to do is *ab ante* to decide that the two charges in the indictment against the accused should be tried separately. I do not think there are any good grounds for so deciding in the present case."

Motion for separation refused.

NOTE

It is thus apparent that no fixed rule exists on this question: whether to separate charges is purely discretionary. The onus is clearly on the accused to demonstrate prejudice.

2. H.M. Advocate v. McGuinness
1937 J.C. 37

An accused was charged with two charges of assault allegedly committed on October 3, 1936, a charge of murder allegedly committed on October 24 or 25, 1936, and a further charge of assault allegedly committed on the latter day or days. He moved for separation of charges.

LORD JUSTICE-CLERK (AITCHISON): "Counsel for the panel Richard M'Guinness has moved for a separation of charges in this indictment to the effect that charges 1 and 2, which affect his client only, should be tried separately from charges 3 and 4, which affect four and five persons respectively, including the panel M'Guinness. Charge 3 in the indictment is a charge of murder. Now, the law as to separation of charges was laid down by a Court of five judges in the case of *Bickerstaff*, and I do not think there is any doubt as to what that law is. Separation of charges is a matter in the discretion of the Court, and the test to be applied in every case is whether it is fair to the person or persons accused to put a particular accumulation of charges in one indictment. The crimes charged may be separated by an interval of time, and yet may be so inter-related by circumstances, or by similarity of character, or by the relevancy of one to proof of another, that the charges cannot reasonably be separated. Now, in the present case the learned Advocate-Depute has very fairly and properly admitted that he is unable to say that the evidence to be led in charges 1 and 2, which are charges of assault, is relevant to charge 3, which is a charge of murder, and to charge 4, which is a charge of assault. The date libelled in charges 1 and 2 is the 3rd of Ocober 1936. The date libelled in charges 3 and 4 is 24th or 25th October 1936, and charge 3, as I have already said, is a charge of murder. Wherever murder is charged I am quite clear that it is the duty of the Court to prevent any risk of prejudice which might arise to the panel if the whole of the charges in the indictment were tried together. If there is any risk of prejudice, it is the clear duty of the Court to separate the charges. I propose, therefore, to give effect to the motion which Mr Thomson has made on behalf of his client, and to direct that charges 1 and 2 be tried separately, which means by a different jury from charges 3 and 4."

Motion granted.

NOTE

With the abolition of the death penalty, the reasoning of the Lord Justice-Clerk may have slightly less force. It has become not unusual to find indictments against one accused containing other charges additional to the murder charge. The only link in such cases is that it is the same accused who is charged: see Hume, ii, 172.

3. **Reid v. H.M. Advocate**
1984 S.L.T. 391

An accused person was charged with (1) rape, committed in Stevenston on October 28, 1983; (2) and (3) theft by housebreaking and wilful fire-raising, respectively having occurred in Saltcoats on February 6 or 7, 1984; and (4) a contravention of the Bail etc. (Scotland) Act 1980 by committing the crimes libelled in charges (2) and (3) while on bail for charge (1). His motion for separation of charges was refused. He appealed to the High Court.

OPINION OF THE COURT: "At a preliminary diet the counsel for the appellant moved the trial judge to separate charge 1 in the indictment from the other three charges. The submission was that there was a clear risk of prejudice to the appellant if he were to be tried on charge 1 and on charges 2 and 3 at the same time. Charge 1 was a charge of a very different kind from charges 2 and 3 and, it was said, if the jury formed an adverse view of the appellant's credibility in relation to charge 1 and decided to find him guilty of that charge, the jury could hardly fail to be prejudiced against the appellant in their consideration thereafter of the question of the appellant's guilt or innocence in respect of the crimes libelled in charges 2 and 3. In light of this risk of prejudice there is no good reason why charge 1 should be tried together with charges 2 and 3 for there is no connection between them in time, place or circumstances and it is not suggested by the Crown that any evidence led in relation to charge 1 will be relevant in relation to charges 2 and 3.

"The trial judge refused the motion and granted leave to appeal to this court. Before us counsel for the appellant renewed the submission which he had presented to the trial judge and, recognising that he had to persuade us that the trial judge erred in some material respect in exercising his discretion, contended only that the risk of prejudice which the appellant would suffer if he is tried on charge 1 at the same time as on charges 2 and 3 is so obvious and so grave that a refusal to grant the motion was a palpable failure of justice. In other words no reasonable trial judge, properly exercising the discretion conferred upon him, would have refused the appellant's motion.

"We have no hesitation in refusing this appeal. The risk of prejudice to the appellant is neither so obvious nor so grave that the trial judge's refusal to grant the motion was a palpable failure of justice. In our opinion the trial judge erred in not the slightest respect in refusing to exercise his discretion in favour of the appellant and we are fully persuaded that his reasons for his decision were perfectly sound reasons which commend themselves to us. For centuries it has been the practice to try all outstanding charges against an accused on a single indictment at the same time. It is pointed out in Hume, ii, 172: 'This is allowed, not only for the sake of doing justice as expeditiously, and with as little expense and trouble as may be to the public, but also (provided it is kept within certain bounds) for the advantage of the pannel; that he may be relieved of a long confinement, and of the anxiety and distress, which would attend a series of successive trials.' It is only where a material risk of real prejudice to the accused can be demonstrated that a trial judge will normally be justified in granting a motion for separation of charges and, let it be said at once, it simply will not do for an accused to contend, as was done in this case, that such a material risk of real prejudice arises merely because the charges in an indictment are of different kinds of crime committed at different times in different places and circumstances. If that proposition were to be accepted it would have to be accepted also that several charges of crimes of the same kind, e.g. theft by housebreaking committed at different times and places and in different circumstances must carry an even greater risk of prejudice and should never be tried together. Experience however shows that under proper directions juries are well able to consider each charge in an indictment separately and to demonstrate by their verdicts that they have done so. We have only to add that if in any case it appears prima facie that it might be prejudicial to an accused to stand trial on a number of charges at the same time it will be open to a trial judge to refuse a motion for separation of charges if it should also appear that the charges are connected in time, place and circumstances or that the evidence in relation to one charge, for example, may be relevant in relation to other charges."

Appeal refused

NOTE

In this case the High Court also expressed surprise that leave to appeal had been granted at all. Where there are multiple charges it will normally be very difficult for an accused to show that he will suffer a material risk of real prejudice if the charges are tried together. For recent applications of the *Reid*, principle, see *H.M. Advocate* v. *Johnstone*, 1991 S.C.C.R. 96; *Jackson* v. *H.M. Advocate*, 1991 S.C.C.R. 206 and *Styr* v. *H.M. Advocate*, 1993 S.C.C.R. 278.

B. SEPARATION OF TRIALS

Where several accused are indicted together, they may apply to be tried separately, and such an application should again be made at a preliminary diet convened for this purpose.

Sangster and Others v. H.M. Advocate
(1896) 2 Adam 182

Five persons were indicted before sheriff and jury on a total of eight charges, each charge being against two or three accused. Each accused applied for separate trials, so that the evidence of each on a charge in which he was not implicated should be available to the others, but only one such motion was granted. After three others had been convicted they appealed to the High Court.

LORD MONCRIEFF: "This bill of suspension is presented by three parties, Andrew Sangster, Thomas Henderson, and John Roger. In the indictment two other parties, John Craib and William Roger, were charged, but we have nothing to do with them. At the first diet a motion was made for separation of the trials of the various prisoners, and the Sheriff-Substitute, after consideration, sustained the motion with regard to John Craib, whose name appears only in the fifth charge, and the diet against him was deserted *pro loco et tempore*. The result of the trial of the other parties was that William Roger was acquitted, and therefore we have only to deal with the cases of Andrew Sangster, Thomas Henderson, and John Roger, who were convicted.

Now the first ground of suspension, which has been very fully argued, is that the conduct of the Sheriff in refusing to allow a separation of the trials was oppressive. A motion for separation of trial is very frequently made, but very seldom granted. Still more seldom does this Court quash a conviction on the ground that it has been refused. There may be other cases, but at present I know of no other except *Kerr* v. *Phyn* (21st March 1893, 3 White 480, 20 R. (J.C.) 60). The reason is that the question is one for the discretion of the presiding Judge, and unless it can be made out conclusively that he was wrong in the exercise of that discretion, we will not interfere. Now in the present case it would seem that the Sheriff has carefully applied his mind to the question, with the result that he has allowed a separate trial in the case of John Craib, and refused it in the case of the other prisoners. All the accused were represented by competent procurators. There is therefore *primâ facie* no sign of oppressive conduct, but we are bound to look at the indictment to see whether the case is one in which any real injustice would be done by refusal to separate the trials. The case is undoubtedly a peculiar one. There are three bankruptcies, those of William Henderson, John Roger, and William Roger, and there are five prisoners; but then we find that all the acts charged are of the same kind, and amount to a charge of fraudulent bankruptcy by putting away and concealing the bankrupt's effects from the creditors. We find also that all the offences were committed about the same time. What is still more peculiar is that Andrew Sangster, Thomas Henderson and John Roger were all more or less involved in all the acts alleged. Thus in the first two charges relating to the bankruptcy of William Henderson, Andrew Sangster and Thomas Henderson are charged. Turning to the bankruptcy of John Roger, we find that Andrew Sangster, Thomas Henderson, and John Roger are all implicated in the charges connected therewith; and in the bankruptcy of William Roger we find Thomas Henderson and Andrew Sangster again involved. That being the case as appearing on the face of the indictment, it indicates a close connection and contingency between the various charges. That in itself is a reason for a single trial stronger than we find in most cases where prisoners are charged together. The passage quoted from Hume seems to me to apply directly to the present case. He says (vol. ii., p.177), 'For although, as I have said, our practice does disown this sort of cumulation in ordinary cases, and in respect to crimes and persons nowise connected with each other; yet in numerous instances the prosecutor has been allowed to accumulate his charges on account of an affinity among the panels or their crimes, much less intimate than in the case of these two riots. And indeed wherever there was any natural contingency of the matters charged, as when the several crimes arose out of each other, or were directed towards the same object, or when the several panels appeared to be in a society for committing crimes of a certain sort—nay, in some instances where the offences were only of the same class and were not the result of any such confederacy; or where all the panels were charged with some of the articles in the libel though not with others—in any of these cases it seems to have been nowise unusual to allow the cumulated action.' It seems to me that on the face of this indictment there is disclosed a confederacy among the prisoners to assist in concealing the effects of those of them who were or pretended to be bankrupt from their creditors. We have not the evidence before us, neither had the Sheriff, but I think that, looking to the indictment, the Sheriff acted quite properly in refusing separation of the trials."

Appeal on this ground refused.

NOTE

Once again, it is oppressive conduct only on the part of the trial judge which will give rise to an appeal against his decision not to separate the trials. But on the particular point thrown up in this case, of one accused wishing to call another, the law has been re-written: see section 28 of the 1980 Act, which re-casts sections 141 and 346 of the 1975 Act. However, it is highly doubtful whether the change in the law makes separation of trials easier to obtain. That one accused desired the evidence of another was held in *Morrison* v. *Adair*, 1943 J.C. 25 *per se* not to be a sufficient reason for separation of trials; see also *Gemmell and McFadyen* v. *H.M. Advocate*, 1928 J.C. 5 *per* the Lord Justice-General at p.8. For the converse situation in which conjunction of trials may be appropriate, see *H.M. Advocate* v. *Clark and Others*, 1935 J.C. 51.

C.   PLEAS IN BAR OF TRIAL

The accepted pleas in bar of trial are: non-age; insanity in bar of trial; *res judicata*; where the accused has immunity from prosecution; personal bar against the Crown; oppression; and prejudicial publicity: see Renton and Brown, paras. 9–23 to 9–36a. If the accused seeks to raise such an issue in solem proceedings, he should ask for a preliminary diet under section 76 of the 1975 Act. The question of immunity is more evidential than procedural: see *O'Neill* v. *Wilson*, 1983 S.L.T. 573. On personal bar against the Crown, see Chap. 2 *supra*. The following cases deal with *res judicata*, otherwise known as the plea of "tholed assize," oppression and pre-trial publicity.

(i)   Tholed Assize

1.   **Hilson v. Easson**
(1914) 7 Adam 390

An accused person was charged on summary complaint and pleaded in bar of trial that he had tholed his assize. The sheriff upheld the plea and the Crown appealed to the High Court.

LORD JUSTICE-GENERAL (STRATHCLYDE): "The procedure in this case appears to me to be hopelessly deranged, and can only be put in gear again by the commencement being made *de novo*.

The accused was charged in the Sheriff Court at Jedburgh, at the instance of the procurator-fiscal of Roxburghshire, with the crime of obtaining goods of the value of some £31 by false pretences from a certain firm of wood merchants in Jedburgh. It is not disputed that the complaint is relevant and that the Sheriff Court at Jedburgh was a Court of competent jurisdiction; but, when the complaint was called in Court on 5th January 1914, as the minutes of procedure bear, the accused objected to the relevancy of the complaint in respect that he had already tholed an assize, and the Sheriff-substitute adjourned the case to the 8th of January for the production of evidence thereupon. That plea was palpable nonsense; but nevertheless, the Sheriff-substitute heard evidence in support of it on 8th January. The sister of the accused and his solicitor from England were examined, and certain productions were given in. The evidence discloses that, on 13th October 1913, the accused had been charged before a Court of Quarter Sessions, at Wakefield, with the crime of obtaining goods under false pretences from English people on 5th April 1913. After trial, he was found guilty by the jury, and was sentenced to three months' imprisonment with hard labour by the Court of Quarter Sessions. But a note appended to the extract conviction bears that, before sentence, the prisoner admitted committing an offence at Jedburgh for which a warrant had been issued, and the Court took this further offence into consideration in fixing his punishment. How all that came about is very clearly disclosed in a conversation which is set out in the appendix to the case, and of which I will read a portion: [His Lordship read the extract from the shorthand-writer's report].

It is difficult to take this procedure seriously. A more complete travesty of justice and orderly procedure I have never seen. But upon the evidence of what transpired at Wakefield, the learned Sheriff-substitute expresses the opinion that the course taken was equivalent to a formal trial for the Jedburgh offence, and that it must consequently be held that the accused had been duly tried for the offence, even although the warrant proceeded from a Court in Scotland instead of from an English Court. I am exactly of the contrary opinion. How it could be said that what took place before the Court of Quarter Sessions at Wakefield is equivalent to a formal trial at Jedburgh of the offence charged in the complaint in the Sheriff Court at Jedburgh at the instance of the procurator-fiscal it is very difficult to see. There was no trial at Wakefield, and there could be no trial at Wakefield, for there was no prosecutor at Wakefield, there was no accused at Wakefield, and there was no Court of competent jurisdiction at Wakefield. There could, therefore, be no plea either of guilty or of not guilty. The procedure might just as well have taken place before the Town Council or the Chamber of Commerce for that matter. And, therefore, to speak of this man having 'tholed an assize' was nothing more or less, in my opinion, than downright nonsense.

Accordingly, I am very clearly of opinion that all the interlocutors which have been pronounced in the Sheriff Court must be recalled, for it is nothing to the purpose to say that no objections could have been taken if this man had been properly charged with this offence, as he might have been, at Newcastle upon Tyne, and if the complaint preferred against him at Newcastle upon Tyne had been before the Court at Wakefield, and if the prosecutor at Newcastle upon Tyne had given his consent to the prisoner's offence at Newcastle upon Tyne being considered at Wakefield in pronouncing sentence there; for none of these things happened. Accordingly, this case must go back to the Sheriff Court and be commenced anew. When the prisoner is brought before the Sheriff Court and, for the first time, pleads guilty to the complaint preferred against him, it will be for the Sheriff-substitute to hear both the accused and the procurator-fiscal upon the question of the appropriate punishment to be pronounced, and the Sheriff-substitute will then give such weight as he thinks proper to what happened before the Court of Quarter Sessions at Wakefield and modify the punishment or, possibly, inflict no punishment at all, according as he in his discretion thinks proper, for he is master, and he alone, of all procedure in his own Court.

I am of opinion, therefore, that we ought to answer the question put to us in the negative, and remit the case to the Sheriff Court."

Crown appeal upheld.

NOTE

This judgment makes the true nature of the plea very clear indeed, but in spite of the outrage expressed by the High Court and the almost intemperate language used, misconceptions did not completely vanish, as the next case shows.

2. H.M. Advocate v. Cairns
1967 J.C. 37

An accused person gave exculpatory evidence at his own trial for murder and was acquitted. He subsequently confessed his guilt to *The Daily Express*. He was charged with having committed perjury at the murder trial and pleaded that he had tholed his assize.

LORD JUSTICE-CLERK (GRANT): "The plea in bar of trial and the objections to competency and relevancy are three different facets of what is basically the same point. The question raised in each case is whether, if an accused person is acquitted at his trial, having given evidence on oath denying the crime charged, the Crown is entitled thereafter to charge him with perjury in respect of that evidence. In seeking to persuade us to answer that question in the negative Mr Bennett based his argument on the maxim that no man can be made to thole an assize twice for the same matter (Hume, vol. ii, pp.465–467) and on considerations of practice and natural justice.

As Hume points out (at p.466), the prosecutor cannot evade the maxim by altering the shape of the former charge and laying the second libel 'for the same facts, under a new denomination of the crime,' *e.g.* by charging fraud instead of theft or falsehood instead of forgery. On the other hand, for the maxim to apply, the previous trial 'must have been for the same crime, depending upon the same evidence, and not for what is truly another crime.' [Macdonald on the *Criminal Law of Scotland* (5th ed.), p.272.] Thus it is well settled that a person who has been tried and acquitted, or tried and convicted, on a charge of assault may subsequently be tried on a charge of murder if, after the first trial, the victim dies (*Cobb or Fairweather* [(1836) 1 Swin. 354]; *Stewart* [(1866) 5 Irv. 310]). That is so notwithstanding the fact that the Crown will seek to establish at the second trial the assault which was the sole *de quo* at the first. The supervening event changes the character of the offence and the second charge is one which could not possibly have been made at the earlier trial.

In the present case the Crown are, in my opinion, in an even stronger position than in the cases to which I have just referred. The perjury charged in the present indictment is alleged to have occurred in the course of the earlier trial. Not only could it not have been the subject of a charge at that trial, but it is a crime wholly different in nature from that of which the panel was acquitted and it is libelled as having taken place at a different place and on a different date. In *Fraser* [(1852) 1 Irv. 66] Lord Justice-General M'Neill points out (at p.73) that a person may be tried if he has never been in jeopardy *for the offence with which he is charged*; and in *Dorward* v. *Mackay* [(1870) 1 Coup. 392] Lord Neaves refers (at p.397) to the 'plain identity' of charges which is needed if the maxim is to apply. The panel here has never been in jeopardy for any offence libelled as having been committed in the High Court at Glasgow on 1st March 1966 and I can find no identity between the present charge and the charge of murder of which he was acquitted. Evidence will no doubt be led tending to show that, as is set out in the indictment, he did in fact assault and stab Malcolmson, but that seems to me to be of no more avail to the panel than it was in *Cobb or Fairweather* and *Stewart*. It is identity of the charges and not of the evidence that is the crucial factor. In my opinion, the plea that the panel has tholed his assize clearly fails.

Nor do I think that the panel can succeed on the basis of practice or natural justice. Practice is a matter for the Lord Advocate of the day and the decision whether to prosecute or not must in each case rest with him as master of the instance. He is not bound by any practice which may have been followed by his predecessors nor is it for us to lay down what practice should or should not be adopted by him. Furthermore, in order to succeed on the 'natural justice' argument the panel would have to show that, even though he does not come under the rule in regard to tholing an assize, there is something so inherently inequitable in prosecuting a person for giving false evidence at his trial denying his guilt that the giving of such evidence does not amount to perjury under the law of Scotland. Mr Bennett founded on a passage in Sir George Mackenzie's Criminal Law (1678 ed., at p.298) as giving some support to this view, although the question could not, as I understand it, have become a live one until the panel became a competent witness on his own behalf under the Criminal Evidence Act, 1898. In my opinion, the right given to the panel by that Act to give evidence on his own behalf does not carry with it a licence to tell falsehoods upon oath. In principle and in logic I can see no good reason for making any distinction, so far as the law of perjury is concerned, between an accused person who falsely denies his guilt on oath and a witness who equally falsely supports him. The exception to the normal law of perjury which the panel seeks to establish here is not, in my opinion, justified by authority and is indeed contrary to principle.

For these reasons the plea in bar and objections must, in my view, be repelled."

Plea repelled.

NOTE

Cairns was never tried on the perjury indictment: he committed suicide before the trial.

(ii)   Oppression

As has already been observed, the court does retain an inherent power to prevent a case proceeding to trial where it would be oppressive and unfair to the accused: see *H.M. Advocate* v. *Stewart*, 1980 J.C. 4, discussed *supra*, Chap. 2. While common law crimes do not prescribe (*Sugden* v. *H.M. Advocate*, 1934 J.C. 103) delay in proceeding may result in oppression. Until very recently, whenever this point was raised, the defence had to pass the two-fold test laid down in a summary case: *Tudhope* v. *McCarthy*, 1985 J.C. 48. Before a plea based on delay could succeed it had to be shown that the delay was "undue" and that it had caused grave prejudice to the accused. *Tudhope* v. *McCarthy* was the foundation of a line of authority on this point. However, that case (and the ensuing line of cases) was overruled by a Full Bench in the following case.

McFadyen v. Annan
1992 S.C.C.R. 186

A police officer was served with a summary complaint in May 1991 alleging that he had assaulted a man in August 1990. That man had been acquitted in September 1990 of several charges, including resisting arrest. Those charges had been the subject of a trial at which the officer was a witness. He pleaded that the case against him was incompetent on the ground of "undue delay giving rise to gross prejudice." His plea was repelled; he appealed to the High Court, where the case was sent for hearing before a Full Bench.

LORD JUSTICE-CLERK: "In opening this appeal before the enlarged bench, Mr Findlay for the appellant gave a short history of events leading up to the plea to the competency being taken. On 5th August 1990 police officers attended at an incident in Bathgate, and a number of persons were arrested. One of those arrested was the complainer in the complaint, and he was arrested by the appellant and another police officer. On 6th September 1990 a complaint was made on behalf of the complainer to the effect that he had been assaulted by a police officer. No officer was named at the time, but it was a blanket complaint against police officers. On 10th September 1990 a man named Irvine, who had been arrested along with the complainer, also complained of having been assaulted when he was arrested by police officers on 5th August 1990. Again it was a blanket complaint. No specific complaint was ever made by Irvine against the appellant. The complainer and Irvine went to trial on 10th and 19th September 1990 on charges of breach of the peace, assault and resisting arrest. On the second day of this trial the appellant, who was waiting to give evidence, was brought into court and shown to a female witness. The appellant is unaware whether she purported to identify him. At the end of the day both the complainer and Irvine were acquitted. Thereafter police investigations commenced into the blanket complaint. It appeared that suspicion had focused upon the appellant by 1st November 1990 because on that date he was interviewed by senior police officers under caution.

On the basis of Mr Findley's information, supplemented by information provided by the Solicitor-General, it appears that the case was reported to the procurator fiscal in January 1991, and that the case was passed to the regional prosecutor fiscal in March 1991. The regional procurator fiscal reported the case to the Crown Office on 5th April 1991, and on 9th April 1991 the Crown Office issued instructions for a prosecution of the appellant. The appellant was charged on 17th April 1991 and the summary complaint already referred to was served on 14th May 1991. After sundry procedure a plea to the competency of the complaint was taken and, as already noted, the sheriff in due course repelled the plea.

Mr Findlay explained that although three grounds had been stated in support of the plea to the competency he was not now seeking to support the second ground based upon pre-trial publicity. His principal ground was that there had been undue delay in this case, and this was covered by the first ground stated in support of the plea to competency, and to a lesser extent by the third ground. Mr Findlay explained that the appellant's contention was that in the circumstances, having regard to the delay which had occurred, it would be oppressive for the Crown to continue proceedings against the appellant. At the beginning of his submissions he maintained that the delay had resulted in grave prejudice to the appellant. Subsequently, however, he maintained that whether or not prejudice could be described as grave, there had been undue delay with the result that there was a risk of such a level of prejudice that the appellant would not be able to be fairly tried. His ultimate position also was that it did not matter whether the delay had been due to fault on the part of the Crown.

Mr Findlay stated that in the present case the Crown had proceeded to a conclusion against the complainer and Irvine before embarking upon any investigation against the police officers. He maintained there was no reason for doing so, and in particular no reason for delaying the investigation against the police officers. He went on to explain that there had been some doubt as to precisely what the complaint of the complainer and Irvine was; originally there had been a general complaint, then a complaint of an assault in the police cells, and subsequently a complaint made against the police officers in a wider context. He maintained that it was more appropriate to investigate the police complaints, and that if necessary the Crown should have sought an adjournment of the trial against the complainer and Irvine as soon as a complaint of the police conduct was made. I am bound to say that I am not impressed by this submission of Mr Findlay. A complaint at the instance of the complainer Robb was first made on 6th September 1990. Police investigations appear to have commenced shortly after the conclusion of the trial of the complainer and Irvine on 19th September, that is somewhere about the beginning of October. Accordingly if steps had been taken to adjourn the trial of the complainer and Irvine as soon as the complaint against the police was made, at best this would have expedited the commencement of the investigation by approximately four weeks. The sheriff tells us that the complainer Robb had been held in custody pending his trial and, that being so, that there would have been great difficulty in adjourning his trial pending police investigations into the complaint of police conduct which had been made at his instance.

The real issue raised in this appeal, however, is as to the proper approach to be made when a plea of this nature is put forward. Under reference to Renton and Brown's Criminal Procedure (5th ed.), paragraph 9–35; *Sugden* v. *H.M. Advocate*; *H.M. Advocate* v. *Stewart*; and *Stuurman* v. *H.M. Advocate* Mr Findlay pointed out that it was well recognised that this court had an inherent power to dismiss a prosecution where the Crown had acted oppressively, although he recognised that the power was one which was rarely exercised where oppression was said to result from the delay in bringing an accused person to trial. Since 1984 it had been recognised that the test was whether there had been undue delay which had resulted in grave prejudice to the accused. In *Tudhope* v. *McCarthy* the court had approved the approach adopted by Lord Hunter in *H.M. Advocate* v. *Leslie* (31st January 1984). The test was said to be '(1) Was there undue delay? and (2) Did it result in gross or grave prejudice?' Mr Findlay maintained that it did not matter whether the delay was due or undue; if there was delay which caused prejudice then it would be oppressive for the Crown to proceed further against the accused. As his submission proceeded, he suggested under reference to the second question that the test should be whether there was real prejudice rather than grave prejudice. At the end of the day his principal submission was that although the plea was founded upon oppression, the court should take a wider approach than had been laid down in *Tudhope* v. *McCarthy*.

In the present case the complaint about police conduct had first been made on 6th September 1990, and the complaint had been served upon the appellant on 14th May 1991. Under reference to *Connachan* v. *Douglas* Mr Findlay maintained that the length of time necessary to constitute undue delay had been coming down and that the delay here was sufficiently long to be prejudicial. He also reminded the court under reference to *Newell* v. *Jessop* that the proper test in such cases was not whether a case was rare and exceptional, but whether the delay had caused gross prejudice.

For the Crown the Solicitor-General accepted that the basis of any plea of this kind was oppression, and he drew particular attention to what the Lord Justice-General had stated in *Stuurman* v. *H.M. Advocate*. In cases such as the present, where the complaint is based upon the delay in bringing an accused to trial, the Solicitor-General submitted that the proper approach was found by adapting what had been laid down in *Stuurman*. At the same time he stressed that the Lord Advocate is in all senses of the word master of the instance, and that the court cannot control his decision as to whether or not a criminal prosecution should proceed. Adapting the language used in *Stuurman* the Solicitor-General contended that the general principle could be stated as follows—where there is no statutory time-limit, the Crown can raise proceedings at any time; the court can interfere to stop proceedings only where the court is satisfied that, having regard to the principles of substantial justice and of fair trial, to require an accused to face trial would be oppressive.

The Solicitor-General then proceeded to suggest the following test which would apply to a case such as the present where oppression was said to have resulted from delay in bringing an accused to trial—where alleged oppression is said to arise from events or from the effects of lapse of time, which are alleged to be prejudicial to the prospects of fair trial, the question for the court is whether the risk of prejudice is so grave that no direction by the trial judge, however careful, could be expected to remove it. The Solicitor-General recognised that a different formulation would be required for a case under summary procedure. In such cases he suggested that the prejudice would have to be so grave that the sheriff or justice could not be expected to put that prejudice out of his mind and reach a fair verdict. The Solicitor-General accepted that this was a high test but he stressed that this was consistent with such cases being rare and exceptional.

It was a corollary of the foregoing propositions that the reason for delay before proceedings had been raised was irrelevant. It was after all difficult for the court to determine whether delay at that stage was due or undue. The Crown has to decide what cases are to be brought to trial, and the Crown has to decide upon priorities; a period of apparent inactivity in one case may be because another case is being dealt with. He submitted that the court should not be involved in deciding such priorities; the question for the court was whether it was appropriate for a particular case to go to trial.

The Solicitor-General recognised that the approach which he was suggesting was different to that which had been approved by the court in *H.M. Advocate* v. *Leslie* and *Tudhope* v. *McCarthy*.

In my opinion the general approach for which the Solicitor-General contended is the correct one although there may be instances where the reason for delay before proceedings were raised should properly be considered. In cases where the court has been invited to dismiss a prosecution, the plea has been stated in different ways. Thus in *H.M. Advocate* v. *Stewart* and *Stuurman* v. *H.M. Advocate* the accused stated pleas in bar of trial; in *H.M. Advocate* v. *Leslie* the accused stated pleas of mora and moved the court to desert the diet simpliciter; in *Tudhope* v. *McCarthy* the accused took a plea to the competency. In the present case the appellant has stated a plea to the competency, but, in my opinion, the appropriate plea to raise this issue would be a plea in bar of trial. In *H.M. Advocate* v. *Stewart* Lord Kincraig said at pp.88–89:

> 'I am, however, of the opinion that the delay by itself is sufficient to constitute prejudice to the accused, and that it would be unfair to him to go to trial on this charge. While it may not be possible to assess the degree of prejudice caused by the dimming of the recollection of witnesses after

such a long delay between events and the giving of evidence in relation to them, it is possible in my judgment to affirm that some prejudice will be caused to the accused through these circumstances. In my judgment it is unfair to the accused, if not oppressive, to compel him to answer allegations of corruptly receiving bribes between 1960 and 1964 some 14 or so years later.'

In *Stuurman* v. *H.M. Advocate*, which was a case where there had been prejudicial pre-trial publicity, at p.122 the Lord Justice-General said:

'The test which fell to be applied and which was applied in disposing of the plea in bar is not in doubt. As the authorities show, the High Court of Justiciary has power to intervene to prevent the Lord Advocate from proceeding upon a particular indictment but this power will be exercised only in special circumstances which are likely to be rare. The special circumstances must indeed be such as to satisfy the Court that, having regard to the principles of substantial justice and of fair trial, to require an accused to face trial would be oppressive. Each case will depend on its own merits, and where the alleged oppression is said to arise from events alleged to be prejudicial to the prospects of fair trial the question for the Court is whether the risk of prejudice is so grave that no direction of the trial Judge, however careful, could reasonably be expected to remove it. [See the opinion of the Court delivered in the case of *Stewart* v. *H.M. Advocate* 1980 J.C. 103.]'

This line of authority has been followed in cases such as *H.M. Advocate* v. *Leslie*, the 'Whitehall Properties Case' (25th March 1983), where Lord McDonald said:

'From the authorities I am satisfied that the court can only intervene to prevent the discretion of the Crown to insist in an indictment where, if they were allowed to do so, it would cause prejudice to the accused of such gravity as to amount to oppression, and that this result was due to excessive unexplained delay on the part of the Crown.'

In *H.M. Advocate* v. *Leslie* Lord Hunter relied principally upon observations made by Lord Justice-Clerk Aitchison in the Full bench case of *Sugden* v. *H.M. Advocate*. In that case, after holding that there was no vicennial prescription for crime under the law of Scotland, the Lord Justice-Clerk said [at pp.111–112]:

'But I think cases can be figured in which the Court might sustain a plea of bar on a lapse of time far short of twenty years, where it appeared to the Court *in limine*, on facts admitted by the Crown, that grave prejudice to the accused might result if the trial were allowed to proceed. The correct doctrine in this matter is, I think, stated by Mr Burnett in his Criminal Law (at pp.309–310) in this passage:

'"As his Majesty's Advocate ... cannot be compelled to give his *instance*, so this officer cannot be controlled as to the way and manner in which he is to give it, or as to the *time* when he is to exercise his right, except in as far as he has been restrained by express enactment as to the form of trial and the period within which it must be brought, or by the interference of the Court of Law upon any case of hardship or oppression towards the party accused, by undue delay or otherwise, in conducting the trial."'

The Lord Justice-Clerk referred to 'grave prejudice' and the passage from

Burnett refers to 'undue delay'. These words were adopted by Lord Hunter in *H.M. Advocate* v. *Leslie* and were subsequently employed by Lord Justice-Clerk Wheatley in *Tudhope* v. *McCarthy* in formulating the test to be applied in cases of this kind. With all respect to Lord Hunter and Lord Justice-Clerk Wheatley, it appears to me that they erred in failing to appreciate the context in which Burnett was using the words 'undue delay', and in treating cases where oppression is alleged to have resulted from delay as forming a special category different to other cases where oppression is alleged to be due to other causes.

In my opinion, in the context in which they appear, it is clear that Burnett is using these words in relation to undue delay by the prosecutor after proceedings have been raised and that he is not dealing with the raising of proceedings. The words 'in conducting the trial' make it clear that he is at that stage referring to a time after proceedings have been raised. That this is so is clear from the words in Burnett which follow the passage quoted by Lord Justice-Clerk Aitchison:

> 'Thus, though the public prosecutor has the uncontrolled right of passing from his *instance* at any period, and of moving the Court to desert the diet, either *simpliciter* or *pro loco et tempore*, which motion they must give effect to, yet he possesses not the uncontrolled right of insisting on the diet's being *continued*. The party accused may object to this demand, as creating undue and vexatious delay, and may call on the prosecutor to assign his reasons for not going on with the trial; and the Court will, upon sufficient cause shewn, sustain the objection, and ordain the trial to proceed' [Burnett, p.310].

In that passage, Burnett mentions desertion and continuation, which of course arise only after proceedings have been raised. These comments were made in a paragraph where Burnett stressed the freedom of the Lord Advocate to 'give his *instance*,' that is to raise proceedings. I am accordingly satisfied that when Burnett in the passage quoted by Lord Justice-Clerk Aitchison was referring to 'undue delay' he was referring to delay which occurred after the raising of proceedings and not to delay at any earlier stage. This does not appear to have been appreciated by the court in *H.M. Advocate* v. *Leslie* and *Tudhope* v. *McCarthy*.

In *H.M. Advocate* v. *Leslie* and *Tudhope* v. *McCarthy* the court appears to have asked itself whether there was undue delay during the whole period from the date of the alleged assault by the accused. In *Tudhope* v. *McCarthy* counsel for the accused appeared to accept that the only period which could be considered as constituting undue delay was the period following upon the trial of the complainer's mother, but the court appears to have thought that in determining whether delay was due or undue it was necessary to consider the whole period from the date of the alleged assault by the accused. It also appears clear from *McFarlane* v. *Jessop* that when a plea of this kind is taken the whole period from the date of the alleged assault requires to be considered. On the other hand, in *H.M. Advocate* v. *McKenzie* the court appears to have regarded the only relevant period as being the period not from the period of the date of the alleged offence but the date when notice of the existence and possible participation of the accused first came to the attention of the Crown. In *Hamilton* v. *W* the court regarded it as significant that there was no question of any delay in bringing the charges being attributable to the police or the procurator fiscal. In *McGeown* v. *H.M. Advocate* the court rejected an allegation of undue delay which had been due to complex investigations undertaken by the police and the procurator fiscal. In *Buchan* v. *H.M. Advocate* the sheriff appears to have approached the matter from the point of view of determining whether the case was one of those rare and exceptional cases where delay could be held to be of an order sufficient to constitute oppression. In *Newell* v.

Jessop the court held that the proper test was not whether a case was rare and exceptional, but whether the delay had caused gross prejudice. In *H.M. Advocate* v. *Mechan* the court held that the delay had not been undue and that in all the circumstances the prejudice involved could not properly be regarded as grave.

As is clear from a number of the foregoing cases, in which the tests laid down in *Tudhope* v. *McCarthy* were applied, the main emphasis has been laid upon the period of time after the Crown became involved but, in considering that, it has sometimes been necessary to take account of the period of time before the Crown became involved as being the background against which the subsequent delays have to be considered. The critical question raised in the present case is whether the approach adopted in these cases is the correct one and in particular whether it is correct to apply in every case the bipartite test: Was there undue delay? and Did it result in gross or grave prejudice? I have come to the conclusion that the bipartite test is not a sound one. I do not, however, agree with the Solicitor-General that the reason for any delay is always irrelevant. What the court has to ask itself is if the delay, whether caused by the Crown or not, has been such as to prejudice the prospects of fair trial. The court is not really in a position to determine whether delay which took place before the Crown raised proceedings was justified or not. The Crown has to determine its priorities and it is, for example, for the Crown and not the court to determine whether, in cases like the present, proceedings should be taken first against the accused civilian or the accused policeman. On the other hand, if the Crown concede that delay before raising proceedings was due to some failure on the part of the Crown, that would appear to me to be relevant; it would also be a relevant consideration that delay at that stage was due to fault on the part of the accused. Further, irrespective of fault, the court is certainly entitled to consider any delay before the Crown raised proceedings as part of the overall delay which is allegedly prejudicial. Moreover, where there has been delay after the Crown has raised proceedings, the court can determine whether such delay has been due or undue, and that is a circumstance to which the court is entitled to have regard. However, the real question which the court has to consider in all cases where delay is alleged is whether the delay has prejudiced the prospects of a fair trial. This involves the court asking itself whether the risk of prejudice from the delay is so grave that no direction by the trial judge could be expected to remove it. In the case of summary procedure the question must be whether the risk of prejudice from the delay is so grave that the sheriff or justice could not be expected to put that prejudice out of his mind and reach a fair verdict. I would again stress that cases where such a plea in bar of trial will be upheld will be rare and exceptional cases. The test to be applied where oppression is alleged to have been the result of delay is the same as that which falls to be applied in cases where oppression is alleged to be the result of pre-trial publicity or any other cause. In my opinion, the court in *Tudhope* v. *McCarthy* was wrong where it laid down a different test in cases where the alleged oppression is based on delay. There is no justification in principle for any different test in such cases. An unfortunate consequence of adopting a different test has been that pleas in bar of trial or competency have been put forward in many cases where such pleas have not been justified.

In the present case I am quite clear that the appellant's plea to competency, even if it be regarded as truly a plea in bar of trial, could not be sustained. Applying the tests which I have just formulated, the court is being asked to take the view that the lapse of ten and a half months between the alleged offence and the service of the complaint has prejudiced the prospects of a fair trial, and that the risk of prejudice is so grave that the sheriff could not be expected to put such prejudice out of his mind and to reach a fair verdict. I am satisfied that the court cannot affirm such a view. I have already observed that if the police investigation had not been postponed until the conclusion of the trial of the complainer, at best the investigation would have begun approximately four weeks earlier. Although Mr Findlay also founded on the delay after the commencement of the police investigations, he appeared to recognise that the procedures would inevitably take some time, and he did not suggest there had been any excessive delay at any particular stage during that period.

The approach of the sheriff here was based on *Tudhope* v. *McCarthy*. For the reasons set forth above, I am of opinion that that case was wrongly decided, and that it and the cases following upon it should be overruled. Although these cases do constitute an established (though relatively recent) line of authority, they have been shown to be based on a misconception, and they should no longer be followed. The absence of a contradictor to which Lord Morison has referred should not inhibit the court from giving effect to submissions in law which appear to be well founded.

Once the matter is approached in accordance with the tests which I have formulated, I am of opinion that the proper conclusion is that there is no question of any delay being so grave as to prejudice the prospects of a fair trial. It follows that the sheriff was well founded in rejecting the preliminary plea stated before him.

For the foregoing reasons I would move your Lordships to refuse the appeal."

Appeal refused.

NOTES

Lords Cowie, Cullen and Milligan delivered separate reasoned opinions concurring with that of the Lord Justice-Clerk, although there were some differences on the extent to which, if any, the court is entitled to inquire into actings of the parties. Lord Morison, however, dissented from the majority view; he disagreed with the interpretation of the authorities adopted by his colleagues and affirmed the correctness of the two-fold test in *Tudhope* v. *McCarthy*.

The case confirms in the most explicit terms that a plea in bar of trial based on oppression will be very difficult to sustain. In every case proceeding under solemn procedure the judge will only do so if nothing he could say to the jury about the delay could be expected to remove the risk of prejudice to the accused. The judge has a duty to ensure that the accused receives a fair trial; this case reinforces his duty to intervene to stop a case proceeding, but only where delay has resulted in such *grave* prejudice as to make the matter unsuitable for a direction to the jury on the effect of the delay. See also *H.M. Advocate* v. *Reekie*, 1993 S.C.C.R. 460; *Campbell* v. *H.M. Advocate*, 1993 S.C.C.R. 1034.

So far as concerns summary cases, *McFadyen* v. *Annan* has been further explained: see *Normand* v. *Rooney*, 1992 S.C.C.R. 336, discussed, *infra*, p.430.

(iii) Pre-Trial Publicity

The landmark decision in *Hall* v. *Associated Newspapers Ltd.*, 1979 J.C. 1 and the Contempt of Court Act 1981 (as to which, see *supra*, Chap. 1) have had the combined effect of giving the press and media relatively clear indications as to the point at which pre-trial publicity may become contemptuous. The other side of this problem is, of course, whether court proceedings may become fatally tainted by publicity.

1. Stuurman v. H.M. Advocate
1980 J.C. 111

Four accused persons were arrested on drugs charges. The following day a radio station broadcast a detailed account of the circumstances and the next day further similar publicity was given to the case by a Scottish national newspaper. The material published was highly prejudicial to the accused and was made the subject of contempt proceedings. Several months later each accused tabled pleas in bar of trial, alleging that, in consequence of the publicity, they could not expect to receive a fair trial. These pleas were repelled by the trial judge, after argument before him and two other consulted judges, and the accused were convicted. They appealed on the ground that their pleas in bar of trial should not have been rejected.

LORD JUSTICE-GENERAL (EMSLIE): "... The only question for us is whether, as the applicants contend, the Court of three Judges erred in allowing the trial to proceed in the circumstances which we have already mentioned.

The test which fell to be applied and which was applied in disposing of the plea in bar is not in doubt. As the authorities show, the High Court of Justiciary has power to intervene to prevent the Lord Advocate from proceeding upon a particular indictment but this power will be exercised only in special circumstances which are likely to be rare. The special circumstances must indeed be such as to satisfy the Court that, having regard to the principles of substantial justice and of fair trial, to require an accused to face trial would be oppressive. Each case will depend on its own merits, and where the alleged oppression is said to arise from events alleged to be prejudicial to the prospects of fair trial the question for the Court is whether the risk of prejudice is so grave that no direction of the trial Judge, however careful, could reasonably be expected to remove it. [See the opinion of the Court delivered in the case of *Stewart* v. *H.M. Advocate*, 1980 J.C. 103.]

In presenting his submissions the single proposition advanced by counsel for Stuurman was that the Court which repelled the pleas in bar of trial erred in their application of the correct test to the special circumstances of this case. The contents of the publications which were the subject of contempt proceedings were highly prejudicial. In the case of the radio broadcasts in particular the offending news item was repeatedly transmitted on 1st October 1979 in the very area from which the jurors for the trial of the applicants were drawn. Other newspapers of varying kinds and quality, circulating throughout Scotland, contained articles of the same character as the one published in the Glasgow Herald on 2nd October 1979. All of this prejudicial material was, accordingly, the subject of the widest dissemination in Scotland, and the Edinburgh area in particular, in the period 1st to 3rd October 1979. In these particular and special circumstances the risk of prejudice to the fair trial of the applicants was so grave that no direction by the trial Judge, however careful, could reasonably be expected to remove it. The Court which repelled the pleas in bar erred in failing to recognise this. The trial should not have been allowed to take place, and, having taken place, a miscarriage of justice has occurred, and the convictions of the applicants should be quashed.

The submissions of counsel for Ruiter and Merks were upon similar lines. In the case of the applicant Ruiter, counsel conceded that his client's position was virtually indistinguishable from that of Stuurman. He therefore contended himself by adopting the argument presented by Mr Daiches for Stuurman, and by inviting us to take into account, in addition, the possiblity that the minds of the witnesses at the trial might also have been prejudiced by reading or hearing the offending news items. The point, it was said, was important, for the defence of Ruiter and Merks was that they were unaware of what others might have been doing. The contents of these publications may have encouraged witnesses to associated Ruiter and Stuurman in their minds. Counsel for Merks urged us to accept that the publication of the offending material was even more gravely prejudicial to his client than it was in the case of Stuurman and Ruiter. He was present in the place or places in which Stuurman was said to be producing drugs only for relatively short periods, and his defence was that he came merely to deliver some equipment which had been ordered and once to buy a car. The case against him entirely depended upon the inference to be drawn from his proved presence from time to time. In these circumstances there was a grave risk that in considering what inference to draw the jury might take into account something that had been said in one of the prejudicial news items. These news items contained many statements damaging to Merks which were wholly untrue. These mis-statments of 'fact,' it was contended, made it quite impossible for the trial Judge to give any direction which would be adequate to secure for Merks at least a fair trial at the hands of the jury.

Upon considering all the submissions for the applicants and the reply by the Lord Advocate, we have reached the conclusion that the Court did not err on 25th January 1980 in repelling the pleas in bar of trial. We are not impressed by the supposed risk that the evidence of witnesses would or might be tainted by anything they had read or heard in the period 1st to 3rd October 1979 for the basis upon which any witness's evidence or opinion was given or expressed was open to the test of cross-examination. We are not impressed either by the contention that a distinction falls to be made between representations in the offending publications which were unfounded in fact and those which were true. What matters is that the contents of these publications, true or false, were such as might prejudice the prospects of fair trial of the persons described therein and the question for us is whether on 25th January 1980 the risk of prejudice as the result of these publications was then so grave that even the careful directions of the trial Judge could not reasonably be expected to remove it. In our opinion that question falls to be answered in the negative. The publications occurred almost four months before the trial diet was called. In considering the effect of these publications at the date of trial the Court was well entitled to bear in mind that the public memory of newspaper articles and news broadcasts and of their detailed contents is notoriously short and, that being so, that the residual risk of prejudice to the prospects of fair trial for the applicants could reasonably be expected to be removed by careful directions such as those which were in the event given by the trial Judge.

Upon the whole matter we are satisfied that the pleas in bar of trial were correctly repelled for the right reasons and that all three applications for leave to appeal against conviction must be refused."

Appeal refused.

NOTE

So, such a plea in bar of trial will only succeed if it would be oppressive to proceed. This is a very high test indeed, although it was very nearly passed in the "Glasgow Rape case," reported *sub nom* X. v. *Sweeney*, 1982 J.C. 70 and *H.* v. *Sweeney*, 1983 S.L.T. 48. That case is discussed, on the question of whether criminal letters should have been issued, *supra*, at p.71. One of the principal arguments advanced in *Sweeney* was that a fair trial was impossible and, under reference to *Stuurman*, that it would be oppressive to proceed. This argument was rejected only "with considerable hesitation": see 1982 J.C. 70 at p.85.

After the issue of criminal letters, pleas in bar were in fact tabled and rejected, and the trial proceeded. It seems therefore that only in the clearest case, such as pre-trial publicity immediately preceding the trial diet, could the test of oppression be met: see *Atkins* v. *London Weekend Television Ltd.*, 1978 J.C. 48, a shocking case of contempt of court. However, in *Stuurman*, Lord Avonside, one of the judges consulted by the trial judge, cast doubt on whether a plea in bar, had it been tabled in *Atkins*, would have succeeded: see 1978 J.C. 111 at p.117. See also *H.M. Advocate* v. *Mitchell*, 1993 S.C.C.R. 793.

At the end of the day, the plea will only be sustained if the prejudice is so grave that *no* direction by the trial judge, however careful, could be expected to remove it. Lapse of time is an important factor, along with the nature of the publicity. The following case shows how *Stuurman* is applied in current practice.

2. Spink v. H.M. Advocate
1989 S.C.C.R. 413

An accused person was indicted on charges of assault and breach of the peace. His plea in bar of trial based on pre-trial publicity was dismissed by the sheriff. He appealed to the High Court.

LORD JUSTICE-GENERAL: "The appellant is John Spink, who was indicted for trial in the sheriff court at Arbroath upon three charges. The first was a charge of assault upon Laura Matthews on 6th April 1988. The second was a charge of a more serious assault upon Beverley Jeffries, to severe injury, permanent disfigurement and permanent disability. There was a third charge of breach of the peace. The appellant had been indicted for trial on these charges on an earlier occasion. He went to trial on a similar indictment on 30th January 1989. Evidence was led and concluded on that day and the trial was adjourned for speeches and charge until 31st January 1989. On that date, for reasons into which we need not go because we are unaware of them, the presiding sheriff deserted the trial pro loco et tempore, and what we are concerned with today is the new indictment which the Crown has served upon the appellant, which we understand is to go to trial on 11th July 1989.

As one might expect, there were press reports of the evidence led at the trial on 30th January 1989 and, because there had been these press reports, a preliminary diet was sought and was held on 6th June 1989. The proposition at that preliminary diet was that in light of the publicity which took place on Tuesday, 31st January, and on successive days in the same week, it was oppressive to have reindicted the appellant for trial in the town of Arbroath. The decision of the sheriff at the preliminary diet was that he saw no reason why the trial should not proceed in Arbroath, taking the view that he was not convinced that public memory is such that it was likely to recall in June or July 1989 articles which had been published at the end of January 1989 or the beginning of February 1989. It was his view, and we see this in his report, that under proper directions from the trial judge there was no reason to think that a fair trial for the appellant cannot be assured.

In this appeal, with leave of the sheriff, Mrs Cowan has renewed the submission which the sheriff rejected. Her proposition was that the publicity about the earlier trial and the events of 30th January 1989 was such as to constitute grave prejudice to the appellant if he is to face trial in Arbroath. First of all, the nature of the offence was such, and Mrs Cowan was talking about the offence libelled in charge (2), that it was quite likely to stick in the public memory in a small area such as the Arbroath Sheriff Court District for a considerable time. A further consideration which would lead to the matter remaining in the recollection of readers of newspapers circulated in that district was the youth of the victim in charge (2), a girl of sixteen, who lost her sight as the result of being struck by a stone. The headline, indeed, in *The Courier and Advertiser* of Tuesday, 31st January, is in itself memorable because it says 'Weeping girl witness tells of being blinded.' Now no criticism whatever is levelled at the reports which were published in the newspapers which have been submitted to us. They were properly published as contemporary reports of evidence led in court and although jurors at the original trial might well have read *The Courier* on January 31st before returning to court that morning, it cannot be suggested that the contents of these newspapers, fully and fairly reporting what had passed the day before, were likely to cause prejudice to the appellant at his trial then. But these events having happened, the submission was that the prejudice to the appellant created by the publication of the various newspaper reports was likely to be so grave at his trial in July that no direction of the trial judge, however careful, could reasonably be expected to remove it.

We are not persuaded that that submission should receive effect. The lapse of time between 3rd February 1989 and 11th July 1989 is considerable and, as has been said before, public memory of newspaper articles and of their detailed contents is notoriously short. The further consideration is this. The articles themselves contained no material which is inherently prejudicial towards the appellant. Unlike some articles which have come before the court, in earlier cases, these articles do not purport to inform the public that the appellant was guilty of the charges which have been levelled against him. They do not, as some articles have done in the past, contain any material about the appellant's history which might be thought to be prejudicial to his interests if he were to go to trial now. They contain nothing more nor less than a fair and accurate summary of the evidence for the Crown and the evidence for the defence, including the evidence of the appellant himself, led before the court on 30th January 1989. For these two reasons—the lapse of time and the absence of directly prejudicial material in the articles—we are satisfied that, if necessary under proper directions from the trial judge, any hint of prejudice can be removed if the appellant goes to trial on 11th July this year."

Appeal refused.

D. SPECIAL DEFENCES

The four accepted special defences in Scotland are alibi, self-defence, incrimination (sometimes called impeachment) and insanity: but see Renton and Brown, paras. 7–20, 7–21, where the possibilities of the existence of other special defences are canvassed. For time-limits for lodging a special defence, see section 82(1) of the 1975 Act. With the exception of the special defence of insanity, a special defence does not have to be proved to any particular standard and therefore the only purpose in lodging a special defence is to give the Crown fair notice.

Lambie v. H.M. Advocate
1973 S.L.T. 219

An accused person was convicted of theft. He appealed against conviction on the ground that the sheriff had misdirected the jury to the effect that there was an onus on the accused to establish the defence of incrimination, which he pled. The appeal was heard by a Full Bench.

OPINION OF THE COURT: "... The relevant passage in the sheriff's charge is in the following terms: 'Reverting now, ladies and gentlemen, to the accused Lambie, and the charge upon which he faces you, he has given evidence himself. Now, if you believe what he says and if what he says is consistent with innocence, then, of course, you will acquit him. He has put forward a special defence of impeachment—this means that he is saying it was not he who committed the crime, but that it was some others. In order that he may succeed in this he must produce evidence and corroborated evidence. Now, it seems to me that he certainly has not done the second thing, and it is doubtful if he has done the first thing. There is no corroborated evidence which would entitle you to come to a decision on the special defence of impeachment put in by the first accused. Therefore you will not consider that special defence. Now, in saying that I am not in any way saying that you have to consider the allegations—because that is really what his evidence amounted to—with regard to other people being involved. All I am saying is that there is insufficient evidence to entitle you to find the accused not guilty on the basis that he has made out a special defence of impeachment. The other evidence, and the inference which Mr McSherry invited you to draw from the evidence relating to some other people having been involved, is still before you, and if that evidence produced in your minds a reasonable doubt then, of course, you will acquit the accused because, as I say, it is for the Crown to prove beyond reasonable doubt that the accused person is guilty.'

As will be seen from the quoted passage the direction plainly asserts (i) that there is an onus on the accused to prove his special defence; (ii) that the onus can only be discharged by corroborated evidence; and (iii) that there is no corroboration of the accused's evidence incriminating any of the persons named in the special defence. For the applicant it was conceded that the third of these propositions was accurate. It was conceded further, for the purposes of the argument, that in presenting the first two of these propositions to the jury the sheriff was merely following a widespread practice among trial judges which appears to have developed since the cases of *H.M. Advocate* v. *Lennie*, 1946 J.C. 79, 1946 S.L.T. 212 and *H.M. Advocate v. Owens*, 1946 J.C. 119, 1946 S.L.T. 227. Against the background of these concessions the submission was that a proper charge required the sheriff to proceed to tell the jury that although they could not hold the special defence to have been affirmatively proved, they must still consider the appellant's uncorroborated evidence on incrimination and if they believed him or if, while not wholly believing him, found that his evidence created a reasonable doubt as to his guilt of the crime charged, they must acquit him. In this case, however, the sheriff followed up his first three directions by saying: 'Therefore you will not consider that special defence.' Now, it was not disputed by the Crown that, had the charge stopped there, there would have been a plain and grave misdirection by the sheriff, and the question at the end of the day came to be whether the sufficiency of the charge was saved by reading the quoted sentence in the context of the whole passage dealing with the special defence and, in particular, in conjunction with the sentences which immediately follow it. Upon this question we have come to be of opinion, albeit with some hesitation, that, standing the practice to which we have referred, the charge on the special defence read as a whole would sufficiently inform an intelligent lay jury, in spite of the quoted sentence which might otherwise have misled them, that they *were* to consider the applicant's evidence of incrimination and to acquit if it produced in their minds a reasonable doubt of his guilt. In these circumstances we would not have been disposed to sustain the appeal on the second ground.

The matter cannot, however, be allowed to rest there since in course of the argument the soundness of the practice to which we have referred, and the soundness of the observations in *Lennie* (supra) and *Owens* (supra) on which it was based, were seriously questioned. Suffice it to say that the criticisms made were such that it is desirable to look afresh at the whole matter of the proper charge which should be given where there has been lodged by an accused person a special defence of alibi, self-defence or incrimination.

It must be accepted that it has been the practice of many judges since the cases of *Lennie* and *Owens* to direct juries, where any of these special defences is in issue, (i) that there is an onus upon the accused to prove it by evidence sufficient in law on a balance of the probabilities, but (ii) that even if the special defence is not established, the jury must, nevertheless, consider even the evidence of a single witness speaking to alibi, self-defence or incrimination, and if they believe that witness, or find that his evidence creates in their minds a reasonable doubt of the guilt of the accused, they must acquit him, since the burden of proof of guilt is on the Crown throughout. The critical question is whether it is at all appropriate to introduce into a criminal trial, where such a special defence has been lodged, any suggestion that there is at any time any onus on an accused person.

In searching for the answer to this question we begin by noticing what was said in *Lennie* and *Owens*. In *Lennie*, which was a case involving alibi, the Lord Justice-General (Normand) in delivering the opinion of the court said this:

> 'As regards the question of onus, there is no doubt that the onus is throughout on the Crown to prove its case. But it is also true that the onus of proving the alibi was on the appellant. That that has been from the earliest times our law is made clear by the passages in Hume on *Crimes* upon the proving of alibi in olden days. I refer particularly to Vol. II, pp.298 *et seq.*, and pp.410 *et seq.*, and these passages also show that it was not uncommon in olden times to take the proof of alibi separately and before remitting the libel to assize. To lay on the Crown the onus of disproving the alibi of which the defence has given notice would be a complete inversion of the rules for the conduct of proofs or trials of which one of the most fundamental and most rational is sempter praesumitur pro negante. But, if the jury deals first with the defence of alibi and decides not to sustain it, so that they must then address themselves to the Crown evidence, they must not treat the onus as transferred or affected by the failure of the defence of alibi. The question whether the jury are entitled to reconsider the evidence for the alibi in connection with the evidence for the Crown and in rebuttal of it does not admit of a simple answer yea or nay.'

In *Owens* where self-defence was in issue the same Lord Justice-General in giving the opinion of the court said this:

> 'When we speak of the onus being on the panel to set up self-defence we merely mean that the accused must take the sting out of his own admission that he delivered the fatal blow. If he does this by proving that he was attacked and put in danger of his life (or had reasonable apprehension of danger to his life), he has set up his defence so that he must be acquitted. But, although he may choose to undertake complete legal proof as the best line of defence in the circumstances of his case, he is not bound to lead such evidence as would amount to a discharge of proof.

He can rely on his own sworn statement that he was acting in self-defence and rely on his own credibility to outweigh any colourable case the Crown has laid before the jury; and the jury, if satisfied on a review of the whole evidence in the case of his credibility, is entitled to accept the panel's single sworn explanation and to reject evidence which would probably, without the explanation, have been sufficient for a conviction ... It may therefore be necessary for the presiding judge, not only to ask the jury to consider whether the special defence has been made out but to ask them also to consider whether it has not had the effect of so shaking reliance on the Crown evidence as to warrant an acquittal from the charge.'

In our opinion there can be no doubt that in *Lennie* and less explicitly in *Owens* the court did subscribe to the proposition that the onus of proving not only alibi but self-defence affirmatively rests on the accused although the judgments at the same time emphasise that the onus of proof of guilt remains on the Crown throughout and that even if proof of the special defence fails for want of corroboration the jury must still consider, in the context of the evidence as a whole, the evidence of even a single witness speaking to alibi or self-defence; and if the evidence of that witness creates in their minds a reasonable doubt of guilt, must acquit. We must accordingly consider whether there was, in law, any warrant for these references to an onus upon the defence, since it is from these references that the charging practice to which we have referred has been derived. What, then, was the state of the law with regard to special defences before 1946? In posing this question we ignore the special defence of insanity at the time since it is quite clear that there is in such a case an onus upon the defence to establish it, since proof of insanity is required before presumption of sanity can be displaced.

Special defences in our law derive from the requirements of the law in earlier centuries for written defences in answer to a criminal libel when accused persons were limited in their defence to evidence in support of these defences, the relevancy of which had to be affirmed by a court before the matter was remitted to an assize. The 'special defence' of today is the vestigial survivor in modern criminal practice of the written defences of our earlier criminal procedures.

An examination of the earlier authorities discloses no trace of a rule that couples putting forward of a 'special defence' with the necessary acceptance by an accused of an onus of proof of that defence by sufficient, *i.e.* corroborated evidence, far less of any statement that, should he fail to discharge that onus, the defence as such must fail. It is not to be found in Hume in the passages dealing with 'special defences' (see Hume, Vol. II, pp.283 and 301) nor in Burnett's *Criminal Law* (published 1811) p.596, Alison, Vol. II, pp.369 and 624 nor Macdonald's *Criminal Law* in any edition, nor is it to be found in Anderson's *Criminal Law of Scotland*, p.274. It is to be observed also that in summary proceedings no notice of such special defences as self-defence or incrimination is required of an accused. In the most recent editions of Renton and Brown, *Criminal Procedure*, the matter is put thus—'The burden of proof that the accused committed the crime libelled against him rests upon the prosecutor throughout the trial. The standard required is proof beyond reasonable doubt. This onus is not transferred or affected by any common law defence pleas other than insanity or diminished responsibility.' The only current statutory requirement relative to the presentation of a special defence in solemn procedure is contained in s.36 of the Criminal Procedure Act 1887.

By the time Hume was writing, the function of a special defence was limited to giving fair notice to the prosecutor of the line which an accused's defence might take and the requirement of the law was that due notice should be given to the prosecution of such an intention. As put by Hume (Vol. II, p.301) it was (and is) because 'to let him maintain silence in that respect, till the proof in support of the libel has been closed, would be downright injustice to the prosecutor, who might thus lose the fair means of meeting the defences and strengthening his own case with evidence, in the relative and proper parts'.

It is of course true, as is pointed out in the judgment of the court in *Lennie*, that in earlier times, for reasons which are set out in the passages from Hume cited in that judgment, when in his written defences an accused pleaded alibi, a preliminary proof on the separate issue of alibi was frequently held and if the plea succeeded the libel fell and was not proceeded with. This practice, however, had, at least by the time Hume was writing, fallen into desuetude.

In the case of *H.M. Advocate* v. *Hillan*, 1937 J.C. 53, 1937 S.L.T. 396 one of the grounds of appeal was that the presiding sheriff in a charge of assault had misdirected the jury in respect that he directed the jury on a plea of self-defence to this effect—'that defence (self-defence) is entirely shouldered and must be discharged by the panel ... He must have corroborative evidence before you can accept it as established that he did this in self-defence'. The appeal on this point succeeded and Lord Justice-Clerk Aitchison said this at p.398: 'I think that this direction was unsound. Many cases occur in which from their very circumstances a plea of self-defence must depend upon the evidence of the panel himself. ... It is no doubt true that a plea of self-defence cannot be affirmatively established upon the evidence of the panel himself, but great injustice might arise if the jury were left with a direction that the plea must fail from want of corroboration. Wherever a plea of self-defence is put forward and supported by evidence, the jury should be explicitly directed that the special defence must be weighed by them in light of the whole proved facts in the case.'

This option was before the court in the subsequent cases of *Lennie* and *Owens* and no doubt was cast upon the accuracy of Lord Justice-Clerk Aitchison's statement of the law or of the decision at which the court arrived.

In light of this review of the law and practice before 1946 we have come to be of opinion that the references in *Lennie* and *Owens* to there being an onus upon the defence were unsound. It follows that the passage in Walkers' *Law of Evidence*, §83(b) to the effect that 'when a special defence is stated by the accused, the onus of proving it is upon him' can now be regarded as an accurate statement of the law only in the case of the plea of insanity at the time. Apart from the unsoundness of its source the practice of referring at all to an onus being upon the defence inevitably complicated the directions of the presiding judge to such an extent as to be calculated to confuse most juries.

The only purpose of the special defence is to give fair notice to the Crown and once such notice has been given the only issue for a jury is to decide, upon the whole evidence before them, whether the Crown has established the accused's guilt beyond reasonable doubt. When a special defence is pleaded, whether it be of alibi, self-defence or of incrimination, the jury should be so charged in the appropriate language, and all that requires to be said of the special defence, where any evidence in support of it has been given, either in course of the Crown case or by the accused himself or by any witness led for the defence, is that if that evidence, whether from one or more witnesses, is believed, or creates in the minds of the jury reasonable doubt as to the guilt of the accused in the matters libelled, the Crown case must fail and that they must acquit.

Thus, for example, evidence given of acting in self-defence, as this is defined by law, is in no different position from any other evidence consistent with the innocence of the accused and ought to be considered by the jury in precisely the same way."

Conviction quashed.

NOTE
The comments of the High Court thus relate only to the special defences of self-defence, alibi and incrimination. The special defence of insanity is in a different position: the onus is on the accused to prove on a balance of probabilities that he was insane at the time of the offence: see, *e.g.*, *Brennan v. H.M. Advocate*, 1977 S.L.T. 151. For a general discussion of the burden of proof in criminal cases, see Chap. 1, *supra*.

E. EXAMINATION OF PRODUCTIONS

Statutory rules govern the lodging of productions for both Crown and defence: see the 1975 Act, ss. 82–84. So far as examination of the productions by each side is concerned, there is usually no difficulty, but occasionally it may be necessary to crave a specific warrant.

1. **William Turner Davies, Petitioner**
1973 S.L.T. (Notes) 36

An accused was charged on indictment before sheriff and jury. Before the indictment was served, the Crown refused to allow the defence to examine a pair of gloves which were to be a Crown production. The accused applied to the *nobile officium* of the High Court.

OPINION OF THE COURT: "This is a petition to the nobile officium of the court seeking a warrant for the scientific examination by a named scientist of gloves which are labelled as a production in the indictment against the petitioner at the instance of Her Majesty's Advocate, under such conditions as to their delivery and care as the court may direct.

The petitioner avers that for the proper preparation and presentation of the defence it is necessary for the gloves to be subjected to scientific examination under laboratory conditions for specified reasons. On the instructions of the Crown the gloves have been subject to a scientific examination by two forensic scientists who are listed as Crown witnesses in the indictment.

The history of events is as follows. Before the indictment was served, the solicitor for the petitioner made a request to the procurator-fiscal to make the gloves forthcoming for examination by a named expert. The procurator-fiscal, who already had in his possession a joint report by the two Crown forensic scientists which had disclosed a negative result, did not accede to the request but simply sent the gloves back to the Crown's forensic scientists for a further examination and so informed the petitioner's solicitors. Some nine days later the procurator-fiscal informed the solicitor that he had received the gloves back. By this time the indictment had been served, and at the pleading diet on 12th February 1973 the petitioner's solicitor made a motion to the sheriff in terms similar to those of the prayer of this petition. The sheriff refused the motion, basically on the ground that there was no precedent or authority for it. At the hearing before this court the learned advocate-depute said that the Crown was anxious to get an authoritative ruling on the point, and that if the motion was competent he had no objection to it being granted in the circumstances of this case.

Counsel for the petitioner submitted that the motion was competent. He referred to s. 37 of the Criminal Procedure (Scotland) Act 1887, which is in the following terms: 'A person accused shall be entitled to see the productions according to the existing law and practice in the office of the sheriff clerk of the district in which the court of the second diet is situated, or where the second diet is to be in the High Court of Justiciary in Edinburgh in the Justiciary Office.'

In relation to the then existing law and practice he referred to Hume's *Commentaries* II, p.388 and, in particular, to the case of *William Muir* in the footnote at pp.389 and 390, and to *H.M. Advocate* v. *Alexander Humphreys* or *Alexander* (1839) 2 Swin. 356.

I am satisfied from the authority of Hume (supra) and the case of *William Muir*, that an application for a warrant to inspect is competent. It will then be a matter for the court to decide whether in the particular circumstances it should be granted. In the normal case I am of the opinion that provided sufficient safeguards can be attached it should be granted. I see no reason why, generally speaking, the defence should not have the same facilities as the prosecution to make an inspection and examination of a production in a case. In saying this, I realise that there may be special circumstances which make the granting of such a warrant impossible, impracticable or undesirable.

The question of procedure was raised before us, and it is desirable that the procedure should be made clear. Where an indictment is served, the productions referred to therein are lodged with the sheriff clerk who has a duty to retain them in his custody and make them available at the trial. At that stage, the only body with the authority to allow the productions to be inspected and examined is the court, and the proper procedure is to make application to the court thereanent. It is then for the court to decide whether the application should be granted or refused. Before the indictment is served, the productions, which at this stage are only potential productions, are in the possession and control of the procurator-fiscal. He has a responsibility to safeguard such productions so that they can be lodged with the sheriff clerk at the appropriate time. In any given case it would be a matter for this discretion in the first instance whether at that earlier stage productions should be handed over to the defence for inspection and examination. Whether he could be compelled at that stage by an order of court to hand over to the defence productions for inspection and examination is another matter, and is not a point on which I would like to express an opinion until the issue is specifically raised. This is not the issue, however, in this petition, and for the reasons which I have given I am of the opinion that the application was competent and that in the circumstances it should have been granted. I would accordingly grant the prayer of the petition.

I would add, for the benefit of practitioners, that in my opinion an application for a warrant to inspect and examine a production listed in an indictment is competent in the court where the trial is to take place without recourse to the *nobile officium* of the High Court of Justiciary."

Warrant granted.

NOTE

Section 37 of the 1887 Act is now section 82 of the 1975 Act. Only the High Court has a *nobile officium* to deal with unforeseen matters—see Chap. 18, *infra*. There are a number of rules of evidence regarding the production at the trial of articles which are relevant to the case. An examination of these rules, which relate to the distinction between primary and secondary evidence, is outwith the scope of this work, but the matter is summarised in Renton and Brown, at para. 18–04.

F. RECOVERY OF DOCUMENTS

Normally all documents which the defence require and which are in the hands of the Crown will be made available to the defence. Sometimes, however, a commission and diligence for their recovery is necessary, especially where the documents are in the hands of third parties.

1. **Downie v. H.M. Advocate**
1952 J.C. 37

An accused person was charged before sheriff and jury with embezzlement. She petitioned the High Court for recovery of certain documents.

LORD JUSTICE-GENERAL (COOPER): "We have had presented to us this morning a petition by a person who has been indicted on a charge of embezzlement before a Sheriff of Lanarkshire and a jury at Hamilton. The first diet is to-day, and the trial is fixed for Monday week, the 28th January. There is to be lodged at the first diet to-day a special defence to the effect that 'the panel pleads not guilty and specially and without prejudice to said plea that the sums set out in the indictment' (except one item), 'if embezzled, were embezzled' not by the panel but by another person named, who was at the material times the servant of the panel at the post office at which the alleged embezzlement took place. The purpose of the petition is to obtain recovery of a number of documents set out in an annexed specification.

We were informed that during the present century there have been two precedents in the High Court for an application of this kind, and that its competence is supported by a statement in Hume and a case of a distinctly exceptional character referred to in the note of the passage in Hume. So far as I am aware there is no reported case dealing with such an application, and no record of an application to the High Court in relation to a case appointed to be tried before a Sheriff and jury. The point of practice is obviously of importance in every case and especially in a case such as this in which this rare type of special defence is presented; and, had it been necessary, I should have been in favour either of convening a larger Court to lay down the appropriate practice, or of dealing with the matter by the enactment of an Act of Adjournal. It seems to me, however, that it is possible for us to solve the immediate difficulty upon the following basis.

The second and third items of the specification relate to documents *ex facie* innocuous, the objection to the production of which rests upon the Crown's submission that they have no conceivable relevance either to the prosecution or to the special defence. As we do not have before us the closed record, which is the guide to the Court in dealing with similar applications in a civil case, we have of course no means of knowing whether the documents are required or not. It is well known that, in accordance with the traditions which have prevailed for generations, the Crown is always ready in every prosecution to make available to the defence, and if necessary to make a Crown production in the case, any documents which could reasonably be regarded as likely to be of assistance to the defence and to further the interests of justice; and the Solicitor-General has indicated that, if the petitioner is able to show to him—what so far she has made no endeavour to do so far as this Court is concerned or so far as the Crown Office is concerned—for what purpose and to what end production of the second and third documents is required, he will be prepared to consider that application on its merits and to deal with it in the generous and fair spirit in which such matters have always been dealt with in the Crown Office.

As regards the first item, however, which relates to statements made by the third party to Post Office investigators and put in writing either at the time they were made or subsequently, relative to the affairs of the post office in question, I do not think that it is going beyond our present function to say that I find it very difficult to figure circumstances in which any Court would order the production of such a document. The absolute privilege attaching to Crown precognitions (or to documents such as those in question which are *prima facie* indistinguishable from Crown precognitions in the case of a Post Office embezzlement charge) is undoubted, and its preservation is vital to the system of criminal administration which prevails in this country.

Having said as much I meantime propose to say no more as regards the competency or the form or the merits of this application as addressed to this Court, but simply to continue the petition, upon the footing that, if, in order to investigate the propriety of production of the documents in 2 and 3, it is necessary for some time to be absorbed, the Solicitor-General will, should the necessity arise, desert the diet for the trial on the 28th of this month."

Petition continued.

NOTE

It will be observed that although the trial was to be taken before sheriff and jury, the petition was presented to the High Court. The case illustrates the general attitude of the Crown in dealing with such requests: this attitude still persists today.

2.   Hasson v. H.M. Advocate
1971 S.L.T. 199

An accused person was charged with, *inter alia*, fraud and embezzlement. He sought a commission and diligence to recover certain documents.

LORD CAMERON: "... The real difficulty in dealing with such an application as the present lies not in deciding as to its competency, but as to the relevance and width of the calls which are made and as to the accused's right to recover the particular documents covered by the calls in the specification. As the Lord Justice-General pointed out in *Downie* there is the obvious initial difficulty in considering such a specification that it is not—as in civil procedure—related to adjusted pleadings. Beyond the indictment and (where tendered) the terms of a special defence, there are no written pleadings. Further, in the presentation of a defence, very considerable latitude is necessarily allowed to an accused person and, in practice, it is often difficult, if not impossible, to discern ab ante the relevance of a particular document or piece of evidence. This means that the familiar tests of the legitimacy of a call for production of a document cannot be applied nor, in particular, is it in consequence easy to recognise and reject a particular call as being of the character of a 'fishing' diligence.

The case of *Downie* is subjected to criticism of an adverse nature in Renton and Brown on *Criminal Procedure*, 3rd edition, p.77, as though it laid down certain principles of universal or at least general application. But consideration of the judgment and arguments in the report of this case show that the observations of the Lord Justice-General to which particular reference is made in Renton and Brown were directed to particular circumstances of a somewhat unusual character in that case, and did not touch the wider issues of the tests to be applied in determining whether to grant or refuse a specification for the recovery of documents. I certainly demur to the suggestion (which appears implicit in the criticism of the particular passage in his judgment referred to in

Renton and Brown) that Lord Cooper was in effect taking the decision as to the
relevancy of a call in a specification out of the hands of the court and placing it
in the hands of the Crown. But there is a further observation I would make on
the case of *Downie*. At the date when *Downie* was decided there was no system
of legal aid in criminal cases such as obtains today and, therefore, the advisers
of accused persons were more under the necessity and the habit of seeking the
aid of the Crown to recover documentary productions and even to obtain the
evidence of skilled or lay witnesses. It was obviously in light of, and with
reference to, this well established and valuable practice that Lord Cooper
made the observations which are adversely criticised in Renton and Brown on
Criminal Procedure, 3rd edition, p.77. Although the situation has been
materially changed by the introduction of criminal legal aid, the problem
remains for solution of deciding which documents are or are not recoverable
and the limits of such recovery. On this point the late learned editor of the
edition expresses the opinion 'That in general a statement by the accused's
responsible adviser that the document in question is required for the conduct
of the defence should be regarded by the court as sufficient'. As at present
advised, I would regard this as too broad and bald a statement of the law and
am not prepared to accept it as an adequate or sufficient test of the relevancy of
a call for production of documents in the hands of third parties, especially
when themselves not on the list of witnesses for the Crown or defence. In light
of modern conditions I think this is an issue of very considerable difficulty
and one which will at some time require authoritative definition and
determination. I think something more than the mere ipse dixit of a
responsible adviser is required, even if it be only an indication in general terms
of the relation of the call to the charge or charges and the proposed defence of
them. There are, as I have briefly indicated, very obvious difficulties in
defining the limits within which such specifications may be granted. I do not
think that it can be safely assumed that the well-known rules which are
applicable to specifications in civil proceedings are necessarily applicable in
criminal practice. Thus, for example, the rule which protects a witness against
self-incrimination may place certain difficulties in the way of forcing a
particular haver to produce incriminating documents, and there are other
matters of substance and procedure which will require consideration.
Fortunately, however, in this case it is not necessary to enter upon them.
Counsel for the accused was able to link his calls to what is contained in the
indictment. He was in a position to point to the terms of charges three and four
in the indictment as justifying the first call (as amended). The second call (as
now amended) was justified by reference to the special defence of
incrimination which has been tendered; in addition to which, the person
named in that special defence is himself on the Crown list of witnesses and
presumably will be called by the Crown. In any event, being placed on the
Crown list, he is absolved from the risk of prosecution for any part he may
have played in the transactions libelled. These two calls as now amended make
plain first, the purpose for which the calls are made in relation to the charges
contained in the indictment and to which they specifically refer and also
provide sufficiently clear guidance to the Commissioner as to the documents
for which recovery is sought and authorised. The right of a haver, however, to
take any objections competent to him at the diet (if any) of course reserves
itself. No question arose on call three, as I understand that the process in the
civil action referred to has already been made available to the defence. No
objection in the form or substance of the calls as amended was made by the
Crown. In these circumstances I shall, therefore, grant a commission in terms
of calls one and two of the specification as amended and refuse call three as
unnecessary."

                              Commission and diligence granted.

NOTE

This case indicates that the responsibility lies with the defence advisers to indicate in general terms the relationship between the call and the charge, with the defence thereto. One can see the court in a sense straining not to import the rigours of the rules in civil proceedings into criminal cases. In practice, applications for recovery of documents in the latter are relatively rare. In *P. Cannon (Garages) Ltd., Appellants*, 1983 S.L.T. (Sh.Ct.) 50, Sheriff Principal Dick refused an appeal by a company against refusal by a sheriff to make an order against the Crown in terms of section 1 of the Administration of Justice (Scotland) Act 1972 requiring the police and the fiscal to release to the company a blood sample and the certificates by the doctor and the analyst under section 10 of the Road Traffic Act 1972. The sample and the certificates had been prepared in connection with potential criminal proceedings but, due to a strike of court officials, the prosecution did not proceed. It was held that the company could not recover the sample and the certificates for use in a civil litigation pursued by them, as the totality of all reports by the police of procurators-fiscal were confidential and that recovery by the appellants would not be in the public interest. See also *H.M. Advocate* v. *Ward*, 1993 S.C.C.R. 595.

CHAPTER 11

THE TRIAL DIET

When the indictment is served on the accused person, he is cited to attend his trial, which will take place either in the High Court of Justiciary at a convenient location, or before sheriff and jury, usually in the court where the accused made his first appearance. High Court trials are held nowadays at many Scottish towns outwith the four cities of Edinburgh, Glasgow, Aberdeen and Dundee, the precise venue depending on a number of factors, such as the availability of a court house, the convenience of witnesses and the need to obtain a jury whose members may not have been privy to local knowledge of the crime or the accused. Cases of great importance are often held in the High Court in Edinburgh, wherever in Scotland the crime is alleged to have been committed.

But whether the case is taken in the High Court or before sheriff and jury, the solemn procedure followed at the trial is basically the same.

A. DIET PEREMPTORY

The case always starts with a formal calling by the clerk of court using the hallowed words "Call the diet: Her Majesty's Advocate against A.B." The case must be called on the date set down, or at the sitting of the court to which the accused has been cited, otherwise the instance falls.

1. Hull v. H.M. Advocate
1945 J.C. 83

An accused was charged before sheriff and jury. At the pleading diet objections to relevancy were stated, and that diet was twice adjourned to later dates, due to the length of the debate. On September 14, 1944 the court further adjourned until September 21 so that judgment on the objections might be given. Nothing at all happened on September 19, which was the date set down for trial. A trial was, however, held in October, at which the accused was convicted. She appealed against conviction.

> LORD JUSTICE-CLERK (COOPER): "... It is a cardinal rule of our criminal procedure that a criminal diet is, and must be made, peremptory, and that, if the diet is not called or duly adjourned or continued on the date in the citation, the instance falls (Hume, vol. ii, 263, 264; Alison, vol. ii, 343, 344; Macdonald, (4th ed.) 471). The rule has again and again been rigorously enforced, its non-observance being treated as involving a fundamental nullity requiring that any conviction which has followed should be quashed. It was applied to a High Court case in *H.M. Advocate* v. *Fraser* [(1852) 1 Irv. 1], and it was extended to summary procedure even before the Act of 1908, and declared to be equally applicable to 'all cases truly criminal, whether the proceedings are summary or not, or whether in the Sheriff Court or in the High Court' (*M'Lean* v. *Falconer* [(1895) 22 R. (J.) 39, Lord Adam at p.41]). It was again applied with the result of quashing convictions in *MacArthur* [(1896) 23 R. (J.) 81], *Craig* [(1897) 24 R. (J.) 88], *Jamieson* [(1901) 3 F. (J.) 90], *Taylor* [(1906) 8 F. (J.) 74], *Corstorphine* [(1910 S. C. (J.) 21], and *Coubrough* v. *Howman*, 6th July 1939 (unreported). In most, if not

all, of these cases, the acquiescence of the accused was treated as irrelevant. In face of this impressive array of precedents, it would be impossible for us, even if we were disposed to do so, to treat the rule as a mere technicality. But it is not a mere technicality. As Lord M'Laren said in *M'Lean* (at p.41), 'although in the particular case the error may have resulted in no tangible injustice to the accused, it is of essential importance that we should enforce the strict observance of rules which are intended as securities for the liberty of the subject. One can easily see that if a dispensing power were permitted to be exercised by the Judge, or if deviations from this proper and regular form of procedure were allowed in one case, it might be that in other cases injustice or oppression might result.' I respectfully accept that statement, believing that the vigilance advocated in 1895 is no less necessary at the present time.

It has further to be kept in view that the trial of criminal causes before the Sheriff and jury is no novelty in our law, and that, except in so far as expressly modified by later statutes, the procedure in the Sheriff Court (as in the High Court) is based on long-established practice. That practice was partially codified in the Act of Adjournal of 17th March 1827 (Alison, vol. ii, 39 *et seq.*), which, as Alison observes, was practically a replica of the then practice in the Court of Justiciary, and which in terms directs that in trials by Sheriff and jury the forms of the Court of Justiciary shall be observed. By the Sheriff Courts (Scotland) Act, 1853 [16 & 17 Vict., c. 80], section 35, the expedient of two diets of compearance, with the requisite procedural machinery, was applied compulsorily to the Sheriff Court. That expedient was only applied optionally to the High Court fifteen years later, but the statute of 1868 [31 & 32 Vict., c. 95] became a dead letter (*Muir* v. *Hart* [1912 S.C. (J.) 41], at p.47), and the High Court was only brought into line with the Sheriff Court in this respect by the Act of 1887 [50 & 51 Vict., c. 35]. In the Act of 1887 the direction as regards both first and second diets is that the procedure shall be according to the existing law and practice, except in so far as varied by the Act (sections 28 and 40). It follows that the basic principles of procedure enunciated by Hume and Alison and applied in decisions are just as applicable to trial by Sheriff and jury as to trial before the High Court, and indeed that the Sheriff Court has had considerably longer experience of the two diet system than the High Court.

With these considerations in mind I return to this case, putting first the question—What was the effect of the order of 14th September adjourning the Court until 21st September for judgment? This order cannot be read as an adjournment by implication of the second diet fixed for 19th September, for it was not within the power of the Sheriff on 14th September to adjourn by anticipation the peremptory second diet for 19th September. That could only be done on 19th September. The order can therefore be read as an adjournment of the first diet; and as this adjournment carried the first diet to a date two days after the second diet, the statutory procedure was reduced to confusion, for there were then outstanding two contradictory orders against the appellant, one citing her to the second diet on 19th September and the other citing her to the adjourned first diet on 21st September. The next question is—Was anything done on 19th September to rectify the position? I do not consider that anything could be done; but, in any event, nothing was in fact done, for the general continuation of 'the whole remaining cases' to 20th September cannot be read as a continuation of the second diet in a case the first diet of which had already been made the subject of an express continuation to 21st September. For these reasons, and as the peremptory diet of 19th September was neither called nor otherwise disposed of on that day, it follows that the instance fell at latest at midnight on 19th September, and the position became irretrievable so far as the original indictment was concerned, except possibly by resort to section 42 of the Act, which was never invoked. The Crown's attempt to defend the propriety of the procedure therefore fails."

Conviction quashed.

NOTE

The rule that a criminal diet is peremptory is thus inviolable. It cannot be overcome by the argument that no prejudice has been suffered. At page 88 of the report, the Lord Justice-Clerk commented further: "Were it once admitted that it was a question of facts and circumstances in each case whether a serious deviation from regular procedure should be ignored, the anchor of the entire system would drag." On the calling of the case, therefore, something must happen, whether it be, for example, an order for an adjournment to another specific day, or a plea of guilty, or a trial itself. But the falling of the instance does not bar the prosecutor from further proceedings *in the case*, only from further procedure on that indictment. See also section 127 of the 1975 Act (as amended by the 1980 Act, Sched. 4, para. 27) which provides, *inter alia*, by subsection (1):

> "Where at the trial diet
> (*a*) the diet has been deserted *pro loco et tempore* for any cause, or
> (*b*) an indictment is for any cause not brought to trial and no order has been given by the court postponing such trial or appointing it to be held at a subsequent date at some other sitting of the court,
> it shall be lawful at any time within nine clear days after the date of such trial diet to give notice to the accused on another copy of the indictment to appear to answer such indictment at a further diet."

It is, however, competent on conviction of an accused in solemn proceedings to interrupt those proceedings by (a) considering a conviction against that person in other proceedings pending before the court for which he has not been sentenced, (b) passing sentence on that person in respect of the conviction in those other proceedings: Act of Adjournal (Consolidation) 1988, r. 74(1). By r. 74(3) of that Act of Adjournal no such interruption has the effect of causing the instance to fall, a provision effectively overruling the decision in *Law and Nicol* v. *H.M. Advocate*, 1973 S.L.T. (Notes) 14. But r. 74 must be interpreted strictly.

2. **Watters** v. **H.M. Advocate**
1992 S.L.T. 149

Watters appeared with three others in the sheriff court. They pleaded guilty to parts of an indictment. Without the case being adjourned, another indictment against Watters alone was called, to which he pleaded guilty. The Crown then narrated the circumstances of all the offences. Watters appealed against his conviction on the first indictment, claiming that the interruption of the proceedings thereon by the calling of the second indictment (upon which no conviction had previously been recorded) had given rise to a fundamental nullity.

OPINION OF THE COURT: "The question which arises in these present appeals is whether when the interruption took place the sheriff was considering the conviction against the appellant Watters in other proceedings which were pending before this court for which that appellant had not been sentenced. Counsel who appeared for the appellant Watters next drew attention to the case of *Law and Nicol* v. *H.M. Advocate*. That case is a case which gave rise to the provision which is now to be found in rule 74 of the 1988 Act of Adjournal. The situation in that case was that two accused were tried together on indictment in the sheriff court; the jury returned a verdict of guilty against both and the procurator fiscal then moved for a sentence. He then mentioned to the sheriff that there was outstanding against one of the accused a separate finding of guilt in a summary complaint. The sheriff then heard speeches and mitigation on behalf of both accused and sentenced the one accused to imprisonment in respect of his conviction on indictment and then considered the conviction on the summary complaint and imposed a concurrent sentence of imprisonment on that accused. He also dealt with the second accused.

An appeal was taken on the ground that the conduct of the proceedings had rendered them a nullity. The appeal was not opposed by the Crown and the court proceeded to allow the appeal. The Lord Justice-General in delivering the opinion of the court stated that what we have just described disclosed an irregularity of procedure. He went on to describe what the nature of the irregularity was.

The irregularity was that the diet had been interrupted unlawfully before the indictment had been disposed of. He then said this: 'The question which arises is as to the effect of this failure to continue the diet, without interruption, until disposal of the indictment. In our opinion the result of the interruption permitted by the sheriff is clear. At the moment of interruption the instance fell, and there occurred an event amounting to a fundamental nullity requiring that the conviction of both applicants should be quashed.' He then proceeded to refer to *Hull* v. *H.M. Advocate* and to what Lord Justice-Clerk Cooper said in that case regarding the peremptory nature of criminal diets.

As is correctly observed in Renton and Brown's *Criminal Procedure* (5th ed.), para. 10–76, rule 74 of the 1988 Act of Adjournal originated in the Act of Adjournal (Sentencing Powers etc.) 1978, which was passed in order to alter the law as laid down in *Law and Nicol* v. *H.M. Advocate*. The case of *Law and Nicol* differs from the present case in that when the interruption took place there was a finding of guilt in existence on the summary complaint against one of the two accused. In the report in *Law and Nicol*, it is recorded that after the sheriff heard speeches in mitigation 'he then considered the conviction on the summary complaint against Law and sentenced him to a concurrent sentence of six months' imprisonment'. It may well be that it was the words from that report which were repeated in what now appears as rule 74 of the 1988 Act of Adjournal.

It is plain that in *Law and Nicol* v. *H.M. Advocate* there was a conviction in existence at the time when the interruption had taken place. Under the law which existed at the time when the case was decided that interruption was not permitted and it is clear that the purpose of what is now rule 74 was to allow an interruption in such circumstances. The question which sharply arises here is whether rule 74 is expressed in such wide terms as to cover not merely the situation where there is an existing finding of guilt in other proceedings but where the intention is to take a plea of guilty in these other proceedings.

What occurred in the present case would not fall under rule 74 unless the words 'considering a conviction' could be held to cover the situation where there was no conviction but where a plea of guilty had still to be tendered. We have come to the conclusion that the language used in rule 74 is not wide enough to cover such a situation. All that rule 74 is dealing with is the *Law and Nicol* situation where there is an already existing finding of guilt. The language does not extend to the situation where there are in the other proceedings no conviction and no finding of guilt but where a plea of guilty has still to be tendered. We observe that this is the view which is expressed by Sheriff Gordon in the paragraph to which we have already referred in Renton and Brown where he says this: 'The rule speaks of "considering a conviction ... in other proceedings", so that it would seem to be incompetent to interrupt the proceedings to take a plea of guilty on another charge and then sentence on both.' We agree with Sheriff Gordon that it would indeed be incompetent to interrupt proceedings in such circumstances. When rule 74 refers to 'considering a conviction' that must mean that there is a conviction in existence, and in the present case where there was in the other proceedings no conviction in existence, rule 74 did not permit interruption.

It follows that these appeals must succeed and we shall therefore uphold the appeals and quash the convictions."

Conviction quashed.

NOTE

A trial on indictment must proceed from day to day until concluded, unless the court sees cause to adjourn over a day or days: 1975 Act, s. 136. It can only be interrupted where statute provides: see 1975 Act, ss. 156, 157; or in the circumstances set out in r. 74. Adjournments should always be formally pronounced and overnight adjournments are minuted by the clerk of court. While the jury are retired to consider their verdict, the judge may sit in any other proceedings; and the jury trial does not fail by reason only of his so doing: 1975 Act, s. 155A, inserted by s. 37 of the Prisoners and Criminal Proceedings (Scotland) Act 1993. See also *Boyle* v. *H.M. Advocate*, 1990 S.C.C.R. 480.

B.   ADJOURNMENT OF THE TRIAL DIET

In certain circumstances it may appear to either Crown or defence that an adjournment of the trial is appropriate. Often the matter can be disposed of by agreement between the parties; but where there is objection by one side to the other's motion, the court will be asked to adjudicate. The following cases illustrate the principles to be applied.

1.   **Vetters v. H.M. Advocate**
1943 J.C. 138

An accused person was served with an indictment. He sought a postponement of his trial on the ground that an essential witness would be unavailable for the trial.

> LORD JUSTICE-GENERAL (NORMAND): "This is a petition to the Court praying it to discharge the diet of trial of the petitioner on 22nd June 1943 on the ground of the absence of a witness essential to the defence. The charge against the petitioner is one of culpable homicide, in respect that, while under the influence of intoxicating liquor, he drove a motor omnibus in a culpable and reckless manner and at an excessive speed and failed to keep a sufficient and proper look-out, and that he did cause the said omnibus to mount the grass verge on the side of the road, that he permitted the witness (whose absence is the occasion of this petition), who was then under the influence of drink, to enter and remain in the driver's cabin of the motor omnibus although the cabin was not constructed to hold more than one person, that he did cause the said motor omnibus to collide with a motor car then being driven in the opposite direction, whereby its three occupants were so severely injured that they died there almost immediately thereafter, and that he did kill these three persons.

The witness is a seaman. He is at present absent from this country on a voyage, and it is uncertain whether, or when, he will return to it. He is also a foreigner, and it may be impossible to compel his attendance, if he does not voluntarily return to this country. As the indictment stands, it is obvious that part of the charge could not fairly proceed in his absence, because it is of the essence of that part of the charge that this man himself, while in a state of intoxication, was allowed to enter and remain in the cabin. The Advocate-Depute, however, gave an undertaking that he would delete from the indictment at the appropriate time that part of the indictment which founds upon the alleged permission by the petitioner to the witness to remain in the cabin. Nevertheless, the counsel for the petitioner was not satisfied with that concession, and maintained that, upon the charge as a whole, even with the omission of the particular part of it which refers specifically to the witness, the witness's evidence is essential. I would find it difficult to decline to accept a statement that a witness is essential from a counsel of experience, especially when he states that, after consideration, he puts it forward with all the responsibility which rests upon him. But it is obvious that, as this witness was alongside the driver who was charged with reckless conduct in the driving of the motor omnibus, he must be a witness of the very greatest importance.

The Crown had in its list certain witnesses who are in the armed forces of the Crown, and it succeeded in making arrangements with the naval and military authorities for their attendance at the second diet. These witnesses were certainly no more essential than this seaman who has now gone abroad on a merchant ship, and I think the Crown might have made equal endeavours to retain him. It would be deplorable if the petitioner were to be put on his trial, and possibly convicted, in the absence of a witness who might have given him the most material, and even conclusive, assistance. I think, therefore, that the justice of the case requires that the diet should be discharged, and I say so though fully recognising that the Crown may find considerable difficulty in obtaining the attendance at one time of all the witnesses."

Adjournment granted.

NOTE

This case was distinguished in *Wilson, Petitioner*, 1991 S.C.C.R. 957, in which it was indicated that a refusal to adjourn cannot be challenged prior to trial, but only after trial and conviction.

The prime question is thus: "Is it in the interests of justice that an adjournment be granted?" The discretionary element in the court's decision cannot be stressed too highly. Many of the authorities turn on their own facts. If the court misuses its discretion on a motion to adjourn, such misuse can be attacked on appeal. Both the following cases deal with summary trials, but illustrate the general principle.

2. Skeen v. McLaren
1976 S.L.T. (Notes) 14

A sheriff refused a Crown motion to adjourn a trial. A Crown witness was on holiday and would not be available, but the sheriff held that this was an insufficient reason. The prosecutor appealed to the High Court by bill of advocation.

OPINION OF THE COURT: "... The motion of the prosecutor was made upon the ground that an essential witness was not available. When a motion is made by

one party or the other to adjourn a diet of this kind on this ground and no question arises as to whether it is well founded in fact, there are two questions to which the sheriff must address his mind if he is to arrive at a proper decision upon the motion. The first question is whether the granting or refusal of the motion will be prejudicial to the accused and if so what is the probable extent of that prejudice. The second question is whether prejudice to the prosecutor would result from the granting or refusal of the motion and once again the degree of probable prejudice must be estimated. These two questions are the cardinal questions and this can be discovered in the judgments delivered by the court in the case of *Mackellar* v. *Dickson* (1898) 2 Adam 504. To these two questions we would add a possible third, namely, prejudice to the public interest which may arise independently of prejudice to the accused or to the prosecution in the particular case in which the motion is made. It is plain from the reasons which he has given that the sheriff did not address himself either to the two cardinal questions or even to the third which we have suggested. In the result, he has arrived at his decision upon a wrong principle and a decision arrived at upon a wrong principle is per se oppressive. We do not in this case reach the stage of having to consider whether the degree of prejudice to the complainer can itself be called oppressive. That stage would only be reached in a case in which the sheriff has proceeded to his decision upon a balancing of prejudice and where it is sought to show that his decision on that balance is erroneous. In the whole matter, as we have indicated, we shall pass the bill and remit to the sheriff to proceed as accords."

Appeal allowed.

NOTE

The third of the court's possible questions to be considered in dealing with a motion to adjourn is one which has come to assume equal importance with the two traditional questions of prejudice to Crown or defence. The next case brings this out clearly.

3. **Tudhope v. Lawrie**

1979 S.L.T. (Notes) 13

The procurator-fiscal at Hamilton moved the sheriff to adjourn a trial diet, due to pressure of business in the court that day. The sheriff refused the motion, but when the fiscal indicated he would lead evidence, the sheriff refused to hear the evidence and left the bench. The fiscal appealed by bill of advocation against the sheriff's refusal of the Crown motion.

OPINION OF THE COURT: "There can of course be no doubt that it lies within the power of a sheriff to refuse to grant an adjournment of a diet with the consequence (as in this case) that an instance may fall and a prosecution be brought to an end. But at the same time this is a power which, in view of the possible consequences of its exercise to parties and to the public interest, must be exercised only after the most careful consideration on weighty grounds and with due and accurate regard to the interests which will be affected or prejudiced by that exercise. And when it appears that the sheriff has either failed to have proper regard to the interests which will suffer or may suffer prejudice by a refusal of an adjournment, whether sought by the prosecutor or on behalf of an accused, has misdirected himself as to the extent or consequences of the prejudice to be suffered or has erred in his balancing of relative prejudice which will or is likely to arise from such a refusal, then his

decision is open to attack and may be set aside. Nor will it suffice that a sheriff has paid lip service to the principles which should guide his decision should it appear that in substance he has failed to pay due and proper regard to them.

The matter came under review in this court in the recent case of *Skeen* v. *McLaren*. There the court laid it clearly down that in considering whether or not to refuse a motion for adjournment the sheriff must have regard to three questions: prejudice to the prosecutor; prejudice to the accused; and prejudice to the public interests in general. In that case it appears from the report that the sheriff had not applied his mind to the issue of actual or possible prejudice and this failure was of course fatal to his decision. In the course of his judgment however the Lord Justice-General said: 'We do not in this case reach the stage of having to consider whether the degree of prejudice to the complainer can itself be called oppressive. That stage would only be reached in a case in which the sheriff has proceeded to his decision on a balancing of prejudice and where it is sought to show that his decision on that balance is erroneous.'

It is the issue of balance which arises in this case and in our opinion when the sheriff's report is examined it is clear that he has failed to give proper weight to the prejudicial consequences which would follow if his decision were sustained. The sheriff 'realised that the Crown was bound to be prejudiced'—as indeed was the fact. The instance fell at midnight and further proceedings on the complaint were brought to an end. The sheriff however added that the 'situations would never have arisen had the trials been organised so as to give this trial precedence'. This can only imply that the Crown had only itself to blame—for which there is not a shred of evidence in the bill or the answers. Indeed it would appear that the Crown, for reasons that do not appear but which are not suggested as the responsibility of the prosecutor, was overtaken by events in respect that the first trial to be taken exceeded its estimated duration causing the prosecutor to seek a 2 o'clock adjournment of four cases including that in question here. In any event, it is the court which fixes diets and puts cases out for trial and not the prosecutor—though doubtless there is some measure of communication between the sheriff clerk and the prosecutor when the roll of cases for trial is prepared and intimated—but the responsibility for the roll is that of the court. On the information contained in the statements in the bill and in the answers and in the sheriff's report there appears no foundation for this implied criticism of the Crown. So far as the respondent was concerned no doubt there would be prejudice if an adjournment were granted, but principally of a pecuniary character, but here the sheriff erred in fact. The respondent was not self-employed: it was his witness, according to the accused, who was in that category. It is not possible to assess what weight the sheriff attached to this point, but obviously it was of some materiality in his balancing of relative prejudices. Further, the sheriff gives no reason for his assertion that an adjourned diet of trial 'would probably have been in July 1978 or later', although he was aware that the case had been set down for trial in March as a 'priority' trial. This question of further delay is obviously one of importance or at least appeared so to the sheriff, yet he deals with it in a manner which verges on the perfunctory.

When the sheriff came to consider the prejudice to the public interest he indicates that no *serious* prejudice was likely to result—on the ground that the charge was 'not a very serious one'. The offence was one which could attract a fine of £100 plus a further £5 for every day the offence continues. The complaint which was served on the respondent on 1 October 1977 libels a contravention between 7 May 1976 and 27 July 1977 and that the contravention continued to the date of the complaint. The offence itself was not one which in light of its circumstances and prolonged duration could, in our opinion, be lightly regarded having regard to the continuing and prolonged risk of injury and damage consequent upon the offence libelled. Here the sheriff failed to give due weight to the circumstances libelled in the complaint and in our opinion plainly misdirected himself as to the true quality of the prejudice to the public interest with his refusal to grant the adjournment sought by the Crown.

Having considered the sheriff's report we are of opinion, for the reasons we have given, that he has materially miscalculated the relative weights to be given to the prejudicial consequences to which his decision would give rise and that this material miscalculation fatally vitiates his decision. In our opinion to refuse the adjournment which the Crown sought was oppressive and the sheriff's interlocutor must be recalled and the case remitted to the sheriff at Hamilton to proceed as accords."

Crown appeal allowed.

NOTE

The problem facing the sheriff had been that the Crown had set down too many summary trials for that day, but the High Court indicated that his method of solving the problem was inappropriate. Overcrowding of the court's calendar has been an increasing problem, particularly in summary cases, but the issue being the decided here is whether adjournment in the particular circumstances was justified. On the mechanics of seeking an adjournment in solemn cases, see section 77A of the 1975 Act, inserted by the 1980 Act, Sched. 4, para. 7. See also Renton and Brown, paras. 10–12 to 10–14; 14–55 to 14–60a; and *Carruthers* v. *H.M. Advocate*, 1993 S.C.C.R. 825.

C.   DESERTION *SIMPLICITER* AND *PRO LOCO ET TEMPORE*

Where a prosecutor deserts the diet *simpliciter*, he cannot raise a fresh libel; that position also now represents the law where a *court* deserts *simpliciter* either *ex proprio motu* or, perhaps, on the motion of the accused: see section 127(1A) of the 1975 Act, as inserted by section 18 of the 1980 Act.

If there is a serious difficulty in proceeding to trial, the diet may be deserted *pro loco et tempore*, that is, put off for the time being. The Crown must then serve a fresh indictment or avail itself of section 127 of the 1975 Act if it wishes to proceed. A motion to desert may be made either by the prosecutor, or the court may take this step at its own hand. If the motion is made by the prosecutor, its grant or refusal is entirely discretionary. It may be opposed and, indeed, refused if there would be injustice to the accused.

1.   H.M. Advocate v. Hannah McAtamney or Henry
(1867) 5 Irv. 363

Two accused persons were served with an indictment. One accused objected successfully to its relevancy, and the diet against him was deserted *pro loco et tempore*. So far as the second accused was concerned, the indictment was held relevant, but the prosecutor sought to desert *pro loco* against her. She objected to this.

LORD DEAS: "It would be contrary to the ends of justice to give effect to this motion. The female prisoner though she may have been assisted, was the sole party implicated in the commission of the alleged offence. She has been in prison since December last; and is now present with counsel, agent, and witnesses in attendance. It would therefore be a great hardship for her if this motion was granted. I cannot see how the ends of justice will suffer by the case going to trial now. The public prosecutor has all the witnesses present and he can afterwards, if he thinks proper, bring the other panel to trial. If the counsel for the prisoner had not objected, the motion would have been granted."

Crown motion refused.

NOTE

It is somewhat unusual for the defence to object to a Crown motion to desert *pro loco* except, as here, where an accused is in custody. The question of whether the accused would suffer any prejudice is the core issue.

2.   H.M. Advocate v. Brown and Foss
1966 S.L.T. 341

During a trial on indictment of two accused, one became medically unfit to give evidence or to instruct his defence. The defence were given leave to lead evidence to this effect. The High Court pronounced the following interlocutor:

"The Court being satisfied on the evidence adduced that the panel, Andrew Galloway Brown, was unfit by reason of his medical condition to continue to give evidence or to give instructions for his defence in the foreseeable future, *discharged* the jury as regards the trial of both panels, and *deserted* the diet *pro loco et tempore, reserving* to Her Majesty's Advocate the right to raise a new libel against either or both panels."

Diet deserted.

NOTE

In such cases there is clearly a duty on the defence to bring to the attention of the court the difficulty which has arisen. Whether it is at the instance of the prosecutor or the court itself, the essence of desertion *pro loco et tempore* is that the Crown may serve a fresh indictment, if so advised. On the whole subject of desertion, see Renton and Brown, paras. 10–15 to 10–16.

D.   JURY SELECTION AND MANAGEMENT

The selection of the members of the jury proceeds by ballot. By section 180(1) of the 1975 Act each accused may challenge three jurors, as may the prosecutor, without giving any reason. Beyond these peremptory challenges, further challenges may be allowed on cause shown. There is very little authority on what constitutes sufficient cause. In *McKie* v. *H.M. Advocate*, 1992 G.W.D. 31–1805 it was held that the fact that there had been a greater number of one gender on the jury did not justify the assertion that there had been a miscarriage of justice.

1.   H.M. Advocate v. Devine and Another
(1962) 78 Sh.Ct. Rep. 173

In a sheriff and jury trial, the solicitor for two accused used all his peremptory challenges for each, and then sought to challenge a further juror "on cause shown."

> SHERIFF-SUBSTITUTE C. H. JOHNSTON, QC: "Objection to a member of the public balloted for service on a jury other than an objection which constitutes a peremptory challenge must be an objection personal to that member of the public. In this case the solicitor for the accused has, on behalf of one of his clients, objected to a jurywoman upon a ground which he states to be a personal one, that by reason of her service on a jury in a case concerned with an incident at or about the same time, at the same locus and on the same date as that with which she is now called upon to serve she may have a view antagonistic to the present accused.
>
> I have heard careful debate upon this matter, both from Mr Reilly for the accused and from Mr Smith, who although not holding any particular view on behalf of the Crown was good enough to give me such assistance as he had available. Neither of the procurators before me was able to give me any direct authority, and accordingly I have to consider this matter as it affects this particular case upon first principles.
>
> I am in no doubt that it is within the capacity of a member of the public acting as a juror and properly directed to set aside from her mind the evidence which she may have heard in one case when considering the evidence in another case, which, if perhaps similar, is not identical either in the terms of the indictment or in the particular nature of the case. I accordingly repel the objection."

Objection to juror repelled.

2.   M. v. H.M. Advocate
1974 S.L.T. (Notes) 25

An accused person was charged on indictment with contraventions of the Explosive Substances Act 1883. The *locus* of one alleged offence was the Derry Apprentice Boys Club in a district in Glasgow. He was convicted and successfully appealed to the High Court. In the course of his opinion allowing the appeal on other grounds, the Lord Justice-General (Emslie) commented on the method of jury selection adopted at the trial.

> LORD JUSTICE-GENERAL (EMSLIE): "Before the jury were balloted, an invitation was made to the judge by counsel for one of the accused to put a question to the persons who had been cited for possible jury service. That question was eventually put, of consent, and the matter arose in this way. Counsel suggested that the case involved matters possibly associated with the current religious and political disturbances in Ulster, and that there might, therefore, be potential jurors who had, for example, lost near relatives in these disturbances, who, as a result, would not be able to give unbiased consideration to the issues involved. As it turned out, no juror declared himself in any difficulty or in any fear of bias and the ballot proceeded in the ordinary way.

We do not approve of the course which was followed, for two reasons. Firstly, there should be no general questioning, either by the judge or on behalf of the prosecutor or the accused, of persons cited for possible jury service to ascertain whether any of them could or should be excused from jury service in a particular trial. Secondly, apart from peremptory challenges, special cause must be shown before a juror can be excused. It is not a sufficient cause for a juror to be excused that he is of a particular race, religion or political belief or occupation, or indeed that the juror might or might not feel prejudice one way or the other towards the crime itself or to the background against which the crime has been committed. A juror can, of course, be excused on limited personal grounds. If he is personally concerned in the facts of the particular case, or closely connected with a party to the proceedings or with a witness, or if he suffers from some physical disability such as deafness or blindness or dumbness, there would be special cause for excluding him. Personal hardship or conscientious objection to jury service by itself may also be a ground for excusing a juror, at the discretion of the trial judge. The essence of the system of trial by jury is that it consists of 15 individuals chosen at random from amongst those who are cited for possible service."

NOTE

It is thus apparent that there is little room in Scots procedure for challenging jurors. Anything even approaching an American-style *voir-dire* is out of the question. But at the stage when the unempannelled jurors present themselves at court for jury service, some steps must be taken to ensure that they do not sit on a case where they know the accused or persons named in the charge.

3.   **Pullar v. H.M. Advocate**
1993 S.C.C.R. 514

A number of persons were cited for jury service. Before the sheriff came on the bench, they were asked by the clerk of court if any of them knew the accused or the circumstances of the case. There was a negative reply. The ballot proceeded.

The sheriff did not ask if any of the jurors had any knowledge of the case or of any of the persons named in the indictment. During the trial the clerk was told by a Crown witness, McLaren, that a man, Forsyth, an employee of one of the accused, was serving on the jury; without consulting the sheriff, the clerk decided no action was necessary. The accused were convicted; one of the grounds of appeal was that the employee's presence on the jury constituted a miscarriage of justice. In the course of its opinion, the High Court gave the following guidance as to the practice which ought to be followed before and after the ballot:

LORD JUSTICE-GENERAL: "The first point relates to what should be said to the unempannelled jurors by the clerk of court at the preliminary stage before the presiding judge arrives on the bench. All those cited for jury service will, under the current practice, have received a leaflet giving information for potential jurors in which they are told that if they think that they know the accused they should inform the clerk of court immediately. It follows that when they arrive in court they should be told the name or names of the accused whose case is to be tried. They should be reminded at that stage that if they know the accused they should make this known to the clerk. But it would be advisable for them also to be told the name of the complainer or of anyone else who is sufficiently important to the case to have been named in the charge or charges in the indictment. This simple step should ensure that, so far as reasonably practicable, the potential jurors are made aware of the names of all those persons knowledge of whom might give rise to the suspicion of prejudice. We understand that practice varies as to how much information is given to the potential jurors at this stage, but since the aim is to eliminate the risk of prejudice to the accused so far as possible, it is appropriate that they should be given the information which we have described so that if they know any of these persons the clerk may be made aware of this fact.

The next point relates to the stage when the jury has been empanelled and the jurors are ready to try the case. There is an opportunity at this stage for them to be reminded that if they feel that there is any reason why they should not serve on the jury they should inform the court of this fact immediately. It is in the discretion of the trial judge whether he should issue a direction to this effect. In *Spink* v *H.M. Advocate* [1989 S.C.C.R. 413 at p.416] Lord Justice-General Emslie said that it would be appropriate to ask jurors if there are any reasons known to them which would make it desirable that they should not take part in the particular trial. There should, however, be no questioning of the jury in order to find out whether or not any of them should be excused: *M* v *H.M. Advocate* [1974 S.L.T. (Notes) 25, *supra*]. If the trial judge thinks it desirable to do so, therefore, he should simply ask them, or tell them, to let the court know if they think that there is any particular reason why they should be excused. It would be appropriate also to remind them at this stage that they should take this step if they know the accused or any person named in the charge or charges in the indictment. If this further precaution is taken, and an opportunity is given to the jurors by means of a brief adjournment to act on the direction before any evidence is led, steps can then be taken for another juror to be balloted to replace a juror who has to be excused. As can be seen from *Hughes* [1989 S.C.C.R. 490], it is competent for jurors to be excused at this stage under section 133 and for a fresh juror to be balloted for and sworn under section 129 of the Act. That was an unusual case where it was necessary for the whole jury to be discharged and another jury to be empanelled but, as the Lord Justice-Clerk indicated at p.495D, what was held to be competent in that case for the whole jury applies also where only one member of the jury requires to be excused and, provided that evidence has not been led, is to be replaced by another juror.

The sheriff in the present case has asked for guidance as to the stage at which unempanelled jurors may be released. In a Practice Note which was issued on 22nd January 1988, Lord Justice-General Emslie said that the practice which all judges should follow is to discharge unempanelled jurors only when the first witness for the Crown has entered the witness box and taken the oath. That note was issued following the amendment to section 129 which was made by paragraph 7 of Schedule 1 to the Criminal Justice (Scotland) Act 1987, by which the words 'or shall before any evidence is led be excused' were introduced. This amendment was designed to secure that when a trial judge begins there shall be fifteen jurors in the jury box, even if after fifteen jurors have been balloted and sworn one or more jurors has had to be excused. The sheriff tells us that his practice is not to release the unempanelled jurors until the oath has been administered to the first witness, so it is clear that his practice conforms to that which was described in the Practice Note. He describes the practice as clumsy, but we consider it to be essential that the unempanelled jurors should not be released while there is still an opportunity for one or more of the empanelled jurors to intimate a reason why he or she should be excused.

As for the question whether it is essential that the first witness should have entered the witness box and taken the oath, we can understand that in some cases this may indeed be clumsy and may even be undesirable. On the other hand, the trial judge should be careful not to release the unempanelled jurors so long as it remains possible that, before any evidence is led, an empanelled juror may have to be excused. Accordingly, the stage at which the unempanelled jurors should be released depends on whether there is to be an adjournment before any evidence is led. If there is to be an adjournment, the unempanelled jurors must not be released until the jury has returned to the jury box and the court is in a position to start the trial. This is necessary in order to provide an opportunity for any juror who has to be excused to be replaced by another juror before any evidence is led in terms of section 129 of the Act. If there is to be no adjournment and it is clear that the court is in a position to start the trial immediately, the unempanelled jurors can be released then. It will not always be necessary for the further step to be taken of requiring the first witness to enter the witness box and take the oath, but it is in the discretion of the trial judge not to release the unempanelled jurors until this further step has been taken, if he thinks this is appropriate.

The next point related to two particular events which occurred in the course of this trial. When McLaren told the clerk of court that one of his employees was on the jury, the clerk took no steps to draw this fact to the attention of the sheriff, the procurator fiscal depute or the defence. This was an error on his part, because there was at least a question on this information whether Forsyth ought to continue to serve on the jury in the circumstances. It is the duty of all those in attendance on the court who become aware during the trial of circumstances which might suggest that a juror has personal knowledge of the case or might be suspected of being prejudiced, to draw this at once to the attention of the presiding judge, so that such steps can then be taken as may be appropriate. On the other hand, it is not appropriate for counsel to take the step which Mr Turnbull took in this case, when he was addressing the jury, of asking them to disclose at that stage whether they had any interest in the case. These are matters for the presiding judge and the proper time to put the point to the jury is after they have been empanelled but before any evidence is led. If there is a particular reason at a later stage for suggesting that a juror should be excused, this should be made known to the presiding judge so that the necessary steps may be taken by the court under section 133 of the Act."

Appeal refused.

NOTES

1. The appeal was refused on the basis that it was not to be assumed that a juror's prejudice or knowledge would have led him to ignore the evidence and the trial judge's directions and to vote only on the basis of personal prejudice in defiance of his oath, since nothing had occurred in open court in the presence of the sheriff, or was drawn to his attention, to suggest that Forsyth's presence on the jury might be objectionable.

2. The emphasis in the court's opinion on the duty of those in attendance at court to reveal personal knowledge or grounds for a suspicion of prejudice is, of course, to be welcomed. But in busy jury sittings in many courts where a number of cases are set down for trial, it may be difficult for those involved to discharge their duties. Cases are often called at short notice, with little or no time for those involved to reflect on their positions.

3. In notorious cases, it may also be difficult to find a jury whose members have not heard something of the circumstances. What happens where there has been widespread publicity?

4. H. v. Sweeney and Others
1983 S.L.T. 48; 1982 S.C.C.R. 161

Miss H. brought a bill for criminal letters to the High Court seeking authority to raise a private prosecution for rape against three youths. The Crown had previously decided not to prosecute, a decision which caused widespread media comment. One of the objections stated by the respondents to the granting of the bill was that the pre-trial publicity would fatally taint the minds of prospective jurors, and that it would be oppressive to proceed. In repelling this objection the High Court made the following observations:

LORD JUSTICE-GENERAL (EMSLIE): "... The remaining question of importance is focused in statement 5 in the answers for each of the respondents. Shortly stated, the submission was that the widespread publicity about this case in the period 13 January to 13 February 1982, in the press, on television, on radio, and in Parliament itself, has made it impossible for the respondents at any time to obtain fair and impartial trial anywhere in Scotland. To put the respondents on trial would, in short, constitute oppression. In presenting this submission on behalf of all three respondents, counsel for the second respondent recognised, under reference to the recent cases of *Stewart* v. *H.M. Advocate* and *Stuurman* v. *H.M. Advocate*, that the question for this court to answer is whether the risk of prejudice to the prospects of fair and impartial trial is so grave that no direction of a trial judge, however careful, could reasonably be expected to remove it. In this case he contended that the answer is emphatically in the affirmative, when the nature and contents of the publicity are considered. The publicity began when there was a public outcry about an apparently inappropriate sentence imposed upon a convicted rapist by a circuit judge in England. The subject of rape and the handling of this crime by the courts became then of immediate concern to the media and to Parliament. In this situation it became known to a reporter of the *Daily Record* newspaper that proceedings against the three respondents on the two charges in the two fallen indictments had been dropped by the Crown on or about 15 September 1981. Having regard to the serious nature of the two alleged crimes and upon the assumption—an erroneous one as it has now been demonstrated—that those who had been accused of these crimes could never be brought to trial, there was sparked off a welter of publicity, informed and ill-informed, designed to find out why the decision to abandon public prosecution of the respondents had been taken. This legitimate public discussion, however, said the second respondent's counsel, got out of hand because it began to focus attention upon the three respondents as a group, without differentiating among them, and upon their alleged guilt of the crimes which had been libelled against them. In no time at all the case became notorious. It acquired the label of 'the Glasgow rape case' and the general effect of the whole saturation coverage which it received was to encourage a wave of public sympathy for the alleged victim, and public animosity against those alleged to be responsible. For almost a month (before and after the Lord Advocate made his now well-known statement in Parliament on 21 January 1982—a statement repeated by the then Solicitor-General in the House of Commons) the complainer, 'her case', and the three respondents, who were not, of course, named, were kept constantly in the public eye. The implication of all that was said and printed was that a mistake may have been made by the Crown Office, and the average reader, it was said, could not fail to draw the inference that the three respondents should have been prosecuted and that the probable result would have been conviction. In the period in question no fewer than 160 articles about the case appeared in daily newspapers circulating in Scotland, 46 of them before the Lord Advocate's statement in the House of Lords on 21 January 1982. The case received similar massive coverage in television and radio programmes in course of some of which there were interviews with the complainer herself and with the solicitor who came to act for her after she was apparently spirited away to the Highlands by a newspaper and her former solicitor had been prevented from getting in touch with her. Further, the publicity included remarks attributed to sources in the police and in the procurator fiscal service expressing disquiet that the proceedings had been abandoned and the idea that a grave mistake had been made was fostered by linking the resignation of the Solicitor-General, quite wrongly, with the decision to abandon proceedings itself. The worst feature of the publicity, however, was in the *Daily Record* of 19 January 1982 (before the possibility of private prosecution was indicated in the Lord Advocate's statement in the House of Lords). In that newspaper, on that day, there were published, inter alia, some of the dramatic contents of an alleged 'confession' by one of the three respondents (who were not identified) and of alleged 'statements' by two of the respondents (also unidentified) and by a fourth youth who was to have been a Crown witness.

Publication of such material and of references to other so-called 'evidence', much of which was picked up and repeated in the media generally, was by itself so damaging to the prospects of the presentation of a defence by any of the three respondents that it destroyed the slightest chance that they could ever be tried fairly by an unprejudiced jury. No matter where and when any trial might take place in Scotland the whole public outcry will be recalled to the minds of those balloted for jury service in a trial of a unique character, and it cannot be said, as was said in *Stuurman*, that the only problem will be a residual risk of prejudice. The risk is large and substantial and will still be large and substantial even if the respondents were to face trial at the earliest practicable date, namely the end of May 1982.

I have considered closely the contents of the selected publicity material placed before us by counsel for the second respondent and, as the learned Dean of Faculty very properly conceded, his proposition is a formidable one which I have examined with more than usually anxious care. It cannot be disputed that the massive publicity, and in particular the matters referred to first in the *Daily Record* of 19 January 1982, have created a risk of injustice in that the respondents might not receive a fair trial from an uninstructed jury. As the cases of *Stewart* and *Stuurman* show the question for us is whether, in a few months' time, the risk of prejudice as the result of the publicity, true or false, the most damaging of which occurred before 21 January 1982, will still be so grave that even careful directions by a trial judge could not reasonably be expected to remove it. In this case this question is of the greatest difficulty and it is only after considerable hesitation that I have been persuaded to answer it in the negative. In considering what the answer should be I have not forgotten that while the public interest in securing fair trial of accused persons is of the highest importance, so too is the public interest in the fair administration of justice and the detection and trial of alleged perpetrators of crime. Great weight must be given to this latter aspect of the public interest in this case, for the crimes alleged are of a particularly serious and horrible nature. In light of this consideration, and my assessment of the probable course which presentation of available evidence at a trial would follow, can I confidently affirm now that fair and impartial trial of the three respondents cannot reasonably be secured? I have come to be of the opinion that I cannot so affirm. Trials in cases which have become notorious are not uncommon, and that this case should be remembered as the notorious 'Glasgow rape case' does not move me to think that fair and impartial trial of those accused by the complainer will be, on that account, impossible. As to the particular allegations made first in the *Daily Record* newspaper on 19 January 1982, it must be borne in mind that public memory of the detailed content of newspaper articles and of broadcasts is notoriously short. Having read all the relevant material for myself I have formed the distinct impression that the burden of its message is that the alleged perpetrators of the alleged crimes ought to have been put on trial, and that what will remain in the minds of potential jurors in a few months' time will be a recollection that the massive publicity between 13 and 21 January 1982 had been directed to express public anxiety that this might not happen. There was then sufficient evidence to justify prosecution of the three respondents, always on the assumption that the complainer herself was fit to testify. The fact that the three respondents were twice indicted so demonstrates. That is still the position today and while, for obvious reasons, I wish to say nothing whatever about the apparent strength or otherwise of possible evidence apparently available against any one of the respondents in relation to one or other or both of the alleged crimes, I am prepared to accept that the particular references to alleged 'evidence' in the *Daily Record* of 19 January 1982 are unlikely to be remembered in any detail by potential jurors, and to have any material influence upon their ability to remain true to their oath, and to accept faithfully and to apply the directions of the trial judge who will, no doubt, in this case, find it necessary to identify precisely for the jury the only evidential material upon which they are entitled to consider whether the guilt of any accused has been established beyond reasonable doubt. The *risk* of prejudice will undoubtedly be present. I find myself unable to hold, however, that a trial judge will be unable, when all the admissible evidence has been led, to secure, by careful directions, that the members of the jury will reach their verdicts upon an unprejudiced consideration of that evidence, and that evidence alone. The risk of prejudice arising in various ways is present inevitably in the course of many trials and our system essentially depends upon the assumption that jurors will behave with propriety and exclude from their deliberations all considerations which have not been presented to them in evidence in court in the course of the trial. In this case I have concluded, although not without some hesitation, that this necessary assumption can still be made."

NOTE

For further discussion of the case, see *supra*, Chap. 2. The factual basis for the assumption made by the court can never be established one way or the other, given the fact that jury deliberations are secret. One is tempted to think this is just as well; the reasons for the decisions of some juries might not stand too close scrutiny.

In Scotland there has been none of the controversy which arose in England in relation to "jury vetting." No statutory provisions exist nor are any guidelines laid down by the Lord Advocate on the matter. In England, the Attorney-General issued guidelines in 1975 permitting jury vetting in very rare cases, such as those involving serious offences where strong political motives were involved. Lord Denning M.R. was highly critical of the practice in *R. v. Crown Court at Sheffield, ex p. Brownlow* [1980] 2 All E.R. 444, describing it as "unconstitutional." However, the practice of supplying prosecuting counsel with information about potential jurors' convictions was held in *R. v. Mason* [1980] 3 All E.R. 777 not to be unlawful. Following that case, the Attorney-General issued revised guidelines: see [1980] 3 All E.R. 785. These were in turn revised in 1986 and the full text may now be found at (1989) 88 Cr.App.R. 124. Essentially, the guidelines recognise that juries should be selected at random and that exclusion from jury service should be based on the provisions of the Juries Act 1974 and the Juries Disqualification Act 1984. In exceptional cases, however, "extra precautions" may be taken (a) in cases in which national security is involved and part of the evidence is likely to be heard *in camera,* and (b) terrorist cases.

In view of the remarks of the High Court in *M.* v. *H.M. Advocate (supra),* such a practice in Scotland would appear to be utterly inappropriate. Nor have we yet encountered here the problem which faced Nottingham Crown Court in *R.* v. *Danvers* [1982] Crim. L. R. 680, where a West Indian accused challenged the entire jury panel on the ground that not a single member was non-white. He claimed that, as such, the jury panel could not reflect the ethnic composition of the jury, that an all-white jury could not comprehend the mental and emotional atmosphere in which black families live, and that a black accused could not have unreserved confidence in an all-white jury. The recorder repelled the objection, holding that there existed in English law no requirement that there should be a black member of a jury or a jury panel.

5.   Stewart and Others v. H.M. Advocate
1980 J.C. 103

Mrs Gallo, one of the jurors in a long trial at Edinburgh High Court, was approached by a person claiming to be the brother of one of the accused, who attempted to bribe her. She indicated to the presiding judge that she had important information for him, but he told her to discuss the matter with the other jurors before doing anything further. Subsequently the juror made the nature of the information known to the judge, who discharged her. The judge refused a defence motion to desert the diet *pro loco et tempore* and the accused was convicted. They appealed on the ground that the judge should have discharged the whole jury and that what he had done had created a substantial risk of grave prejudice to the accused.

LORD JUSTICE-GENERAL (EMSLIE): "We are here concerned to examine (i) an irregularity consisting of the alleged approach to the juror Mrs Gallo which was brought to the notice of the trial Judge and the other jurors in course of the trial before the jury had retired to consider its verdicts; and (ii) the soundness of the action taken by the trial Judge thereafter. There is no doubt that the question for our decision must be considered in light of two general principles—those of substantial justice and of the requirements of a fair trial (Hume on Crimes, ii, p.418). The problem facing the trial Judge fell to be resolved in light of these very same principles, and since the submission for the appellants was to the effect that the action taken by the Judge was the wrong one leading to a miscarriage of justice, we propose to begin by considering the probable effect of the report of the alleged approach upon the minds of the jury, in the absence of any instruction from the trial Judge. That the events which happened created a risk of injustice, in that the appellants might not receive a fair trial from an uninstructed jury, may be accepted at once. The learned trial Judge obviously thought so and this was conceded by the Advocate-Depute. The first question therefore comes to be whether the risk of prejudice was so grave that no direction of the trial Judge, however careful, could reasonably be expected to remove it. In posing this question we have to record that counsel for the appellants very properly did not contend that the mere disclosure of an irregular approach to a juror carrying some risk of prejudice to the fair trial of the accused must result in the discharge of the diet. It was recognised, and correctly recognised, that when an irregularity of this kind is disclosed in course of a trial, the question whether it is one which introduces a degree of prejudice incapable of being removed by proper direction must be a question of circumstances in every case. This being so it is, we think, impossible and undesirable to attempt to lay down any rigid criteria against which the quality and effect of such an irregularity are to be judged. In each case, however, the actual facts of the particular irregularity and the context in which its disclosure occurred will obviously be matters for consideration. In so saying it must not be forgotten that while the public interest in the accused receiving a fair trial is of the highest importance so, too, is the public interest in the fair administration of justice and the detection and punishment of criminals. To seek to apply any rigid rule that any interference or intercourse with a juror in course of a trial must automatically result in bringing a trial to an abortive conclusion would invite mischievous and ultroneous interventions designed solely to have this effect. Equally to permit the same result to follow where the intervention is deliberate on the part of the accused, his associates or friends, would place a weapon ready to the hand of guilty persons. This was noted by Hume in writing of interference with juries or jurors after their inclosure (Hume, ii, 427) and in our judgment the observation applies with equal force to similar activities prior to the jury's inclosure.

In the light of these considerations we return to the particular disclosed irregularity with which this submission is concerned. The trial Judge did not, it seems, doubt the veracity of the juror who reported it. It may be accepted, too, that he recognised that the disclosure of Mrs Gallo's report to the other jurors gave rise to a risk of prejudice to the appellants. In some cases it may be desirable for a Judge faced with disclosed intercourse with a juror to go a stage further and attempt to investigate the merits of the reported incident. This was the course followed by Lord Ross in the case of *H. M. Advocate* v. *Dingwall* on 14th July 1977, and there may be other cases in which a similar investigation, or even a Crown investigation during an adjournment, would be appropriate and desirable. In this case, however, the trial Judge cannot be criticised for declining to institute an investigation of the events reported by Mrs Gallo in order to discover, if possible, the identity of the person responsible. Such an investigation in this case was, we think, neither necessary nor likely to be fruitful, and if one had been ordered by the trial Judge it might have led him into very deep waters. The form of the alleged attempt to interfere with Mrs Gallo was itself so bizarre as to suggest very strongly the likelihood that it was a hoax or a piece of singularly reprehensible mischief. The self-identification of Mrs Gallo's visitor was in the highest degree reckless and self-defeating, and the absence of any suggestion as to how the bribe offered was to be paid over in the event of Maxwell's acquittal is again suggestive of mischief or folly rather than of criminal intent in the interests of Maxwell. In these circumstances the trial Judge was entitled to examine the possible effect upon the trial of Mrs Gallo's report, in light of the reasonable assumption that the members of the jury were not unintelligent, and in the knowledge that if the trial proceeded they would receive careful directions and warnings that they must proceed solely upon the evidence which had been led before them and, in particular, must consider the evidence against each accused separately and avoid all speculation. He was entitled to have regard, also, to the fact that the jury had taken the appropriate oath and would be directed specifically as to the matters to which they were entitled to have regard in reaching their verdicts. Finally the trial Judge was entitled to have in mind the presumption upon which our system of trial by jury depends, namely, that jurors will accept and obey implicitly every direction in law given to them by the presiding Judge, including directions such as are given in many trials to put out of their minds certain matters which have been disclosed to them which do not constitute admissible evidence against particular accused. In all these circumstances the trial Judge was, in our judgment, well entitled to conclude that any possible prejudice or risk of injustice which might have been created by the report of the bizarre event by Mrs Gallo could readily be corrected by clear and specific direction on the matter to a reasonably intelligent and sworn jury. He was not, in the circumstances of this case, bound to desert the diet *pro loco et tempore*, and we go further and say that while cases will occur in which such a course will be dictated as the only proper course open to a trial Judge, such cases are likely to be rare. The primary submission for the appellants accordingly fails.

All that remains for consideration on this branch of the appeal is the subordinate contention that the specific directions in fact given by the trial Judge were not adequate in the circumstances of this case to eliminate the risk of a miscarriage of justice. The specific directions, although brief and succinct, were clear and to the point. We cannot and do not agree that they were inadequate. More might have been said, but what was said was quite enough to remove the risk that a miscarriage of justice might otherwise occur.

Before leaving this chapter of the case we wish to say only this. Where alleged interference or other intercourse with a juror is brought to the notice of a Judge in course of a trial it will usually be of assistance to him in deciding on his course of action to inform the prosecutor and those appearing for the defence of the report which has been made to him (if they do not know of it already) and invite discussion of the problem in court in the absence of the jury."

Appeal dismissed.

NOTE

The circumstances of this case are obviously special, but guidance has now been given as to dealing with this sort of problem when it recurs. For a discussion of the earlier proceedings in this case, see *supra*, Chap. 2. See also *Russell* v. *H.M. Advocate*, 1992 S.L.T. 25. The final case in this section deals with the situation where it is alleged that during a trial a jury member has made prejudicial statements against the accused.

6.   McCadden v. H.M. Advocate
1985 J.C. 98

An accused appealed against his conviction on the basis of malpractice by a juror.

LORD JUSTICE-CLERK (WHEATLEY): "The appellant was convicted by a majority verdict of the jury of a contravention of section 4(1) coupled with section 4(3)(*b*) of the Misuse of Drugs Act 1971 and sentenced to 10 years' imprisonment. He has appealed against that conviction and has tabled three grounds of appeal, two of which relate to 'the insufficiency of evidence' and the third to an alleged wrongful admission of evidence by the trial judge.

When counsel for the appellant, Mr Jackson, who had not been counsel at the trial, opened the appeal he stated that there was a further ground of appeal which he wished to lodge and argue. This had become necessary, he said, because of information that had come to light after the trial, which established that there had been a miscarriage of justice. This was to the effect that one of the jury had made a statement publicly during the course of the trial, and before the Crown case had closed, showing prejudice against the accused and a fixed intention to find him guilty. When asked to explain why this matter was being raised at this late date, Mr Jackson made a statement to the following effect. The trial started on 5th February 1985 and ended on 15th February 1985. About mid-March certain persons called at the office of the appellant's solicitor and gave certain information to the solicitor about remarks alleged to have been made by a juror during the currency of the trial. The solicitor consulted counsel who had acted at the trial and he advised that statements should be taken from the persons who had provided the information. This was done and precognitions from Joseph Elder, aged 21, and Steven Hall, aged 20, were produced to this court. These two, along with the appellant's brother John McCadden, were the people who had called at the solicitor's office in March. Elder's precognition is in these terms: 'On Saturday evening, 9th February 1985, at around 7.30 p.m., I went into the "12 Club" Orange Hall in English Street, Glasgow, along with two friends of mine, a Mr Steven Hall of 91 Crozon Street, Haghill, and a Mr Malcolm Nichol, presently c/o Barlinnie Prison. We were sitting having a drink when I overheard a man at the next table making sectarian remarks. I myself am a Catholic and was annoyed by the remarks he was making, although at that stage I thought it better to keep my mouth shut. I turned round and noticed the person making the remarks was a Mr Alan Scott who is a well-known member of the club. I do not know his present address. Mr Scott was openly stating that he was on the jury in the case of that guy McCadden and that he (McCadden) had made all his money from drugs and that he (Scott) was going to find that "tarry bastard guilty". Alan Scott also made a reference to the fact that McCadden had obtained his Rolls Royce from the money he made from drugs. Mr Scott referred to Mr McCadden as a "fenian bastard". Sometime at the beginning of March this year, I was in Barlinnie Prison visiting Mr Malcolm Nichol who is presently serving a sentence for Road Traffic offences. Nichol's release date is 18th June. Whilst I was speaking to Nichol, he asked me if I remembered the events in the "12 Club" about a month earlier, because he had met the man to whom Alan Scott was referring and he was inside doing 10 years. Malcolm Nichol told me that he had told Pat McCadden of the conversation we had overheard and that he had given McCadden my name and address together with that of Steven Hall and that we might get a visit from McCadden's brother shortly. In due course I was approached by Mr James McCadden who I assume got my address from Pat McCadden and I attended with James McCadden and my friend, Steven Hall at Mr Bannigan's office in Renfield Street on 15th March 1985.' Hall's precognition states 'I have read Mr Joseph Elder's statement and can corroborate the events in the "12 Club" Orange Hall in English Street, Glasgow, on the evening of 9th February 1985. I know that Mr Elder, who is a Catholic, was upset by the remarks made about the people of that persuasion by Mr Scott. I had to restrain him from saying anything at that time. I also attended at the office of T. G. Bannigan and Co., along with James McCadden and Joseph Elder on 15th March and gave a statement.'

The solicitor for the appellant thought that it would be at least indiscreet for him to approach the juror for a statement, and the motion which Mr Jackson ultimately made rested on these two precognitions. Mr Jackson informed the court that the former counsel for the appellant had approached the advocate-depute concerned about the matter, following which, on counsel's advice, a letter was sent to the procurator fiscal by the appellant's solicitor on 11th June 1985. The latter was informed that the circumstances were being placed before the prosecutor fiscal and was advised that no ground of appeal thereanent should be lodged until the matter was cleared up. A reply to the said letter was sent by the procurator fiscal on 27th June 1985 stating that the solicitor's letter of 11th June had been received and had been sent to the Crown Office to be considered by Crown counsel. According to Mr Jackson, no further reply had been received from the procurator fiscal, and enquiries from Crown counsel had elicited that the Crown would take no further steps in the matter unless the court ordered them to do so. This was Mr Jackson's explanation for the lateness in bringing the question of a further ground of appeal before the court.

Mr Jackson submitted that if the facts contained in the two precognitions were substantiated the verdict of the jury, which was a majority one, was vitiated and a substantial miscarriage of justice had resulted. Appreciating the particular difficulties involved in establishing the allegation counsel suggested that an inquiry into the whole matter should take place under a remit by this court to a judge in terms of section 252(d) of the Criminal Procedure (Scotland) Act 1975.

It is only fair to Mr Jackson to say that he appreciated some of the practical disadvantages in, and the basic objections to any inquiry, but he maintained that these were outweighed by the consideration that a miscarriage of justice might have taken place, and if an inquiry was necessary to establish whether it had taken place, then an inquiry there should be.

The advocate-depute began his reply by drawing to the attention of the court that on four occasions during the last year certain judges had seen fit to desert trials where it had been brought to the attention of the court that a juror had said something to the prejudice of an accused. He said that if these judges were right, and a similar situation came to light after the trial (as had occurred here) it might be difficult to distinguish between the two. He submitted that the ramifications of the proposal were extensive, and if it became settled practice it would be open to abuse and indeed great abuse. The possibility of jurors being influenced by external considerations and prejudices had caused general concern for many years. This was countered by the fact that juries are selected on a random basis and comprise a cross-section of the community. On a broad basis this tends to even out matters, even assuming that jurors ignore their oath as jurors and the directions of the trial judge. On the practical side there are grave difficulties in carrying out such an inquiry. At the end of the day, nothing other than the juror's own admission would suffice.

In approaching a solution to the matter we are very conscious of the ramifications to which the advocate-depute referred and the deep waters into which the court might be plunged in such a type of inquiry. Nevertheless we have no doubt that an inquiry under section 252(d) of the Criminal Procedure (Scotland) Act 1975 would be competent in a situation such as we have here. The question is—in what circumstances should it be resorted to? In our opinion this involves not only looking at the matter complained of and the evidence or information placed before the court in substantiation of the complaint, but taking into consideration the safeguards built into our system of trial by jury to prevent the sort of thing complained of here taking place with the desired effect. It also calls for consideration of the possible dangers to which the allowance of such an inquiry might expose the administration of justice. It is only after all these matters have been considered that an answer can be given in the individual case.

Before coming to consider these matters in detail, there is one matter with which we wish to deal arising out of a point raised in the debate. We do not consider that it is necessarily difficult to distinguish between the case where the improper conduct of the juror comes to light during the trial and when it comes to light after the trial has been concluded. In the former case the matter can be investigated by the trial judge on the spot, including *inter alia* an interview with the juror, and an instant decision can be reached with a view to preventing a damaging result, either by dismissing the juror from service on the jury, or, if the damage extends beyond the offending juror, discharging *pro loco et tempore*, or allowing the juror to continue with his service if the allegation is not established. In particular, in an inquiry during the trial, it would appear that the juror and his co-jurors could be questioned by the trial judge under the provisions of section 8(2) of the Contempt of Court Act 1981 not only about the matters complained of, but about the extent, if any, to which the allegedly offending juror had influenced or sought to influence the other members of the jury on the issues in the case. These advantages would appear to make it much easier to deal with the problem during the trial than it is to deal with it after the trial proceedings have terminated, when the same advantages are not available. For instance, the provisions of section 8(2) *supra* would not be available, and the provisions of section 8(1) of that Act might be prayed in aid by a juror who was unwilling to be questioned.

We shall deal now with the built-in safeguards in our jury system. The whole concept of a trial by jury has inherent in it the possibility that conflicting personal views and prejudices will exist among the jurors. When political or religious feelings run high the danger may be at its greatest, but it can exist in other circumstances when the social conscience is being outraged. It was the former situation which caused Lord Advocate Sir George Mackenzie to alter the system of trial by jury in Scotland and incidentally introduce the not-proven verdict. There may never be a process which eliminates the possibility of personal prejudices existing among jurors, the nearest practical one (and it is not foolproof) being possibly the 'vetting' of jurors, a system against which the law of Scotland has steadfastly closed the doors. Evidence of how it is used and abused in countries in which it is operated only tends to confirm the wisdom of that decision. The existing system of empannelling a jury from a list of assize is so broadly based that it provides a wide opportunity of a mix which is liable to level itself out. The limited right of peremptory challenge enables the defence to exclude jurors who have been ballotted without giving any reason, but presumably because they are considered to be a disadvantage, if not a liability, to the defence case. Then there is an unlimited right of challenge to jurors on cause shown. Without a vetting system this is as near as one can get to securing a jury which can be trusted to provide as a body the correct result under proper direction from the trial judge. This latter point is of great importance. It is not to be assumed that persons with prejudices would automatically put their prejudices aside when ballotted for membership of a jury, but neither is it to be assumed that they would not. It has to be realistically accepted however that, left to themselves, some jurors might fall into the latter category. But when they are properly directed on how they should approach and carry out their duties, as they were in the instant case, it is not to be lightly assumed that jurors will ignore the directions and pursue their prejudices in defiance of the oath which they had taken. What Lord Allanbridge said was this: 'Finally, on the matter of judging the facts you must not allow yourselves to be swayed by any preconceived notions or prejudices or on your own personal reactions to the kind of offences which are the subject of this indictment. You must view, as I am sure you will, the evidence dispassionately and judicially. ... Your duty is to discharge without fear or favour your responsibility as citizens serving on a jury and in accordance with your oath, and you must judge the case solely on the evidence that has been laid before you in this Court'. Generally speaking it is difficult to accept that reasonable jurors would ignore such a direction and deliberately flout it, but human nature being what it is the possibility of such a thing happening cannot be ruled out. There is of course, the further safeguard of the majority verdict system in Scotland which is fortified by the fact that the jury empannelled consists of an uneven number of 15 jurors. In most cases this would prevent an individual juror using his prejudiced vote to affect the outcome, but there are two qualifications to that. The extent to which he might use his prejudice to affect other jurors in their decision is perhaps incalculable, but it presupposes that the other jurors would also act in defiance of their oath and the judge's directions. On the other hand there is always the possibility when the verdict is by a majority that the one prejudiced vote could tip the balance. The uncertainty of this flows from the system of not taking the figures of the jury's voting decision. There is no statutory provision preventing the jury's voting figures from being disclosed. It is simply a custom which has been preserved. There may be fears that the giving of the actual figures with three possible verdicts might give rise to contradictions and confusions, resulting in long arguments, appeals and possibly the setting aside of verdicts, but that does not seem to us to be a deterrent to what would seem to be a reasonable way of returning verdicts. In any event, we see a possible compromise which would be sufficient for purposes such as we are discussing in this appeal. It is now obligatory for a judge to inform a jury that before they can return a verdict of guilty there must be eight of the jury in favour of a guilty verdict. It would seem a logical step from that, even simply as a check, to require the jury to answer the question after a majority verdict of guilty has been returned: 'How many of you were in favour of guilty?' The final point is indeed a vital one. A juror may say or do some stupid things which would indicate that he was prejudiced against the accused in some way or another and is prepared to carry that prejudice into the jury room and to his vote. That in itself does not result in any prejudice to the accused until it is established that he in fact carried his threat into action or in all the circumstances it is a reasonable assumption that he did so. Whether such an assumption can be properly made will depend on the circumstances of the case.

It is clear from the foregoing that there are many practical obstacles in the present system against an ill-intentioned juror effecting a miscarriage of justice. Nevertheless despite these safeguards there is no absolute guarantee that a miscarriage of justice cannot occur in circumstances where a juror has acted contrary to his oath and allowed his prejudice to affect his vote and the decision of the jury. Since such an allegation might only be effectively countered by an inquiry of some sort or another to establish whether the allegation is well-founded and has produced an objectionable result, it is necessary to consider the problems that such a procedure might give rise to. Having examined the strengths and possible weaknesses of our present system in a general way, it seems logical to examine in general the strengths and weaknesses of the proposal for an inquiry which Mr Jackson has proposed.

If it is deemed sufficient to produce statements from two people to warrant an inquiry into malpractice by a juror, the door might be opened wide to abuse. Particularly in cases where a great deal of money is involved or is available, the dangers of manufactured evidence or bribery cannot be ignored. We pause to make it clear that this is only a generalisation. If a genuine case of malpractice on the part of a juror resulting in a miscarriage of justice can be made out, no amount of judicial time is too much to secure that justice is done. However, experience of 'new evidence' cases has shown that few of such cases are well-founded, and we are of the opinion that this experience should be carried into our deliberations as indicating the need for great care in scrutinising the evidence and information presented. In general we have reached the conclusion that the administration of justice is more likely to be affected in the present climate by the abuses that could be caused by easily obtained inquiries, than by abuse of the present system.

We have accordingly decided that it cannot be held that an appeal based on alleged malpractice by a juror resulting in a miscarriage of justice can never be entertained whatever the circumstances. However, before an inquiry into the facts to ascertain whether the allegation is well-founded is ordered the appeal court must be satisfied that the evidence placed before it to substantiate the claim is *prima facie* sufficiently substantial, convincing and trustworthy to warrant an inquiry. Having regard to the built-in safeguards in the present system to prevent such a miscarriage of justice, and the dangers to the administration of justice which could result from a too facile resort to such a form of inquiry, we regard such an exacting test to be fully justified.

Applying these considerations to the instant case we find the precognitions of Joseph Elder and Steven Hall far from convincing. Elder's precognition contains two coincidences which are passing strange and Hall's precognition is substantially a stated corroboration of Elder's precognition, which is always a most unsatisfactory method of presenting *prima facie* evidence in a case where clear and convincing evidence is called for. But most particularly, no evidence is presented to establish that the juror's statements were translated into effective action in the jury room, and we do not consider that the inadequate precognitions entitle us to assume that they were.

We shall accordingly refuse Mr Jackson's motion to allow an extra ground of appeal to be tabled with a view to the court allowing the inquiry desiderated."

Motion refused.

NOTE
See also *Pike* v. *H.M. Advocate*, 1986 S.C.C.R. 633.

E. SPECIALITIES OF THE TRIAL ITSELF

(i) Does the Accused Understand English?

The trial is conducted in the English language: if the accused (or a witness) does not understand English, an interpreter must be provided.

1. H.M. Advocate v. Olsson
1941 J.C. 63

A Swedish sailor was charged with murder. The following direction was given prior to the trial by the judge:

LORD JAMIESON: "The panel is a foreigner and does not understand the English language. It is inherent in the proper administration of justice that a person tried on indictment must be present during the proceedings, in order that he may hear the case against him, and it is obvious that the mere physical presence of the accused in this case will not satisfy the requirements of justice, and that provision must be made for having the evidence led communicated to him through an interpreter. I am informed that such a course was adopted by Lord Mackenzie in the trial of Alexander Kindereso, otherwise Gilbert, for murder in 1913, and that he expressed the hope that it would be followed in similar cases.

The question was fully considered by the Court of Criminal Appeal in England, and the English authorities and practice reviewed, in the case of *Rex* v. *Lee Kun* [[1916] 1 K.B. 337]. The Court there laid it down that, where a foreigner who is ignorant of the English language is on trial on an indictment for a criminal offence and is not defended by counsel, the evidence given at the trial must be translated to him, and the compliance with this rule cannot be waived by the prisoner. The Lord Chief Justice (Reading), who delivered the opinion of the Court, after pointing out that, where such an accused was defended by counsel, the practice had varied, said (at p.343):—'We have come to the conclusion that the safer, and therefore the wiser, course, when the foreigner accused is defended by counsel, is that the evidence should be interpreted to him, except when he or counsel on his behalf expresses a wish to dispense with the translation and the judge thinks fit to permit the omission.' I propose to follow that course, and the evidence must be translated to the accused, except where his counsel asks that translation be dispensed with; but subject to this comment, that the evidence, the translation of which the Chief Justice appears to have thought might fairly be omitted, was evidence repeating what had been said at the preliminary proceedings before the magistrates under the English procedure. That does not apply to our procedure, and the only evidence which I think counsel for the defence will probably be justified in asking not to be translated will be evidence of a purely formal nature, such as proof of productions and the like. But, even where a request is made to omit translation, if there is any point which in my view it is material that the accused should be informed of, I will see that this is done."

Proceedings translated.

NOTE

A further feature of this case was the refusal by the trial judge to admit evidence of a statement said to have been made by the accused, on the ground that no interpreter was present when the statement was made.

2. Liszewski and Others v. Thomson
1942 J.C. 55

Three Polish soldiers were convicted of breach of the peace. They appealed against conviction.

LORD JUSTICE-GENERAL (NORMAND): "Three Polish soldiers complain in this case of a miscarriage of justice. They were convicted by the magistrate on a charge of breach of the peace. Two of them had no knowledge of the English language. The third knew a little English. A sworn interpreter was not employed at the trial, and in place of such an interpreter the soldier who had some knowledge of the language was allowed to act as an interpreter for the others. ...

That appears to me to be entirely inconsistent with the due administration of justice. It is clear that the magistrate neglected his judicial duty and failed to take the proper steps to make sure that each one of these men had the fullest opportunity of understanding the charge that had been made against him and the proceedings which were taking place in Court. Two of them were wholly unable to follow the proceedings, and the third man was, so far as I can judge, not competent to follow them accurately and confidently. It was manifestly unfair and improper that he should have been put in the position of acting as interpreter for his two fellow-soldiers, who were accused along with him, and at the same time attending to those aspects of the case which concerned him personally. In my opinion, an interpreter should have been got for these three men, and the failure to get one was inconsistent with the traditional methods of administering justice in this country. The conviction must be quashed."

Conviction quashed.

NOTE

Either Crown or defence should bring any translating difficulties to the notice of the court without delay, so that an interpreter can be engaged as an official of the court. See also *Mikhailitchenko v. Normand*, 1993 S.C.C.R. 56. Similar considerations apply where the accused or a witness is deaf and/or dumb. However, a Gaelic speaker whose first language is English is not entitled to have the trial conducted in Gaelic: see *Taylor v. Haughney*, 1982 S.C.C.R. 360. See also the European Convention on Human Rights, Art. 6(3).

(ii)   The Leading of Evidence

The rules of evidence in criminal cases are outwith the scope of this book, although it is sometimes difficult to ascertain whether any particular rule is truly evidential or procedural. The reader is referred to the standard work on evidence.

The order in which the evidence is taken in a criminal trial emphasises the accusatorial nature of the system: the Crown accuses and must prove its case: the accused is presumed innocent until proven guilty. The Thomson Committee on Criminal Procedure commented in 1975 (Cmnd. 6218, para. 1.10):

> "It became apparant to us early in our deliberations and from the evidence we received from our witnesses that our existing system of criminal procedure was fundamentally sound and that improvement was all that was needed and not radical change. We are of the view that there is no *prima facie* case for abandoning the present accusatorial system in favour of an inquisitorial system of the kind adopted in certain European countries."

Thus, the procedural reforms of 1980 have left intact the basic system, although individual rules, such as those on "six hour" detention have been criticised from a libertarian viewpoint.

Since the onus of proof is on the Crown to establish the guilt of the accused beyond reasonable doubt, the Crown leads its evidence first. That evidence must be sufficient in law to support the charge. If the defence feel that at the end of the Crown case there is no case to answer, a submission to this effect may be made to the judge, in the absence of the jury: section 140A of the 1975 Act (as inserted by section 19 of the 1980 Act). By subsection (1) thereof, such a submission may be made both on an offence charged in the indictment and on any other offence of which he could be convicted under the indictment, were the offence charged the only offence so charged. By subsection (3), the effect of a successful submission of no case to answer is the acquittal of the accused for that offence. By subsection (4), if the submission is rejected, the accused may still give evidence and call witnesses.

Even if no submission is made, the accused has the right to lead evidence in exculpation, although there is generally no onus on him at all. By section 142 of the 1975 Act: "Where the only witness to the facts of the case called by the defence is the accused, he shall be called as a witness immediately after the close of the evidence for the prosecution."

Once all the evidence is in, both sides address the jury and thereafter the judge delivers his charge.

(iii)   The Judge's Charge

Following speeches, the judge charges the jury. Unlike the position in England, where the judge frequently reviews the whole evidence in some detail, in Scotland a judge often does so in far less exhaustive terms. The position was summed up in the following case.

1. Hamilton and Others v. H.M. Advocate
1938 J.C. 134

A number of accused were convicted of fraud. They appealed to the High Court. Various objections were made at the hearing to aspects of the judge's charge.

LORD JUSTICE-GENERAL (NORMAND): "... As your Lordship has pointed out, a number of objections were taken to the charge of the learned Sheriff-substitute. Upon these it is not necessary to pass judgment. I feel, nevertheless, impelled to say that I was far from convinced that any one of these objections was well founded. Some of them appeared to be based on a misconception of the duty of the presiding judge. For example, it was said that he ought to have rehearsed certain evidence and to have pointed out that it might be held to exculpate the panels from one of the less important charges, although it was admitted that counsel for the panels had not put this view of it before the jury in their addresses. I say this not as reflecting on counsel, for I think that there were excellent reasons from the point of view of the defence for concentrating on the main charges. But it is altogether unreasonable to complain, after that course had been taken, that the presiding judge did not make the point for the defence in his charge. The primary duty of the presiding judge is to direct the jury upon the law applicable to the case. In doing so it is usually necessary for him to refer to the facts on which questions of law depend. He may also have to refer to evidence in order to correct any mistakes that may have occurred in the addresses to the jury, and he may have occasion to refer to the evidence where controversy has arisen as to its bearing on a question of fact which the jury has to decide. But it is a matter very much in his discretion whether he can help the jury by resuming the evidence on any particular aspect of the case. I am confident that the anxious willingness of judges to give every help that they can to the jury may be relied on to guide them aright on the extent to which they ought to review the evidence in the case, and I am little disposed to attend with patience to the criticism that more should have been said about the evidence by way of exposition or explanation than the judge thought proper at the time. A Court of appeal is not in a position to review this discretion of the presiding judge on matters which concern the best way of conducting the case before him."

Appeals allowed.

NOTE

These remarks have been reiterated frequently in recent years. Appellants often try by diligent dissection of a judge's charge to find factual errors, misquotes or apparent unfairness to the defence. But the appeal court will look at a charge broadly, not as if it were a conveyancing document. Provided the proper issues have been identified and fairly put in the living context of the trial, then the appeal court will not interfere.

There have been a host of cases on what a judge is required to say in his charge. The authorities are reviewed in Renton and Brown, para. 10–54, where there is a discussion of topics such as the need to warn a jury to take care where identification is in issue (see *McAvoy* v. *H.M. Advocate*, 1991 S.C.C.R. 123); the desirability of specific information on the existence of three verdicts (*MacDermid* v. *H.M. Advocate*, 1948 J.C. 12); and the withdrawal of a possible verdict (*Parr* v. *H.M. Advocate*, 1991 S.C.C.R. 180).

Considerations of space preclude the inclusion of all these authorities here, but the following case is included since it makes the point that the judge should never usurp the function of the jury.

2.   Sinclair v. H.M. Advocate
1990 S.C.C.R. 412

An accused person appealed against his conviction on the ground that the jury had been misdirected on the *Moorov* doctrine.

LORD JUSTICE-CLERK: "The appellant is George Denholm Sinclair who went to trial in the sheriff court at Glasgow on an indictment containing a number of charges. As the sheriff tells us in his report, the charges which ultimately went to the jury in this trial so far as the appellant was concerned was three in number, namely charges (1), (5) and (9). These were each charges of attempted fraud. The sheriff tells us that charges (1) and (9) were in the same format, namely that the appellant while acting along with a named person carried out a number of different acts with the intention of defrauding the Industry Department for Scotland of certain sums of money. Charge (5) was a slightly different charge in that the appellant was apparently charged along with his brother as his co-accused. It should be recorded that his brother was ultimately acquitted on a submission of no case to answer at the end of the Crown case. The appellant was found guilty of these three charges and was sentenced to twelve months' imprisonment. He has now appealed against conviction. A note of appeal was initially lodged containing two grounds of appeal, and subsequently amended grounds of appeal were lodged. Today on behalf of the appellant Mr Henderson has presented this appeal. He started by reminding us that the indictment had been amended so as to include in the case of charge (1), an allegation that the appellant had been acting along with a man Kolasinski, and as regards charge (9) that he had been acting along with a man called Rough. Mr Henderson informed us that both these individuals were called as witnesses for the Crown. They gave evidence regarding their own activities but Mr Henderson maintained that the evidence which they had given was exculpatory of the appellant. This is confirmed by what the sheriff says in his report because he tells us that in their evidence these two witnesses, Kolasinski and Rough, had, as he put it, tried to be exculpatory of the appellant. Mr Henderson also informed us that this had been a lengthy trial extending to some twenty-three days. Detailed evidence had been given by a number of witnesses including accountants.

When we turn to the grounds of appeal, these are several in number and Mr Henderson addressed us on a number of these grounds. The first ground of appeal upon which he addressed us is ground (*a*). This ground of appeal refers to directions which the sheriff gave on the so-called *Moorov* doctrine. The complaint made is that in his charge the sheriff failed to leave it to the jury to decide whether the connection which the application of the rule required was proved to their satisfaction. Mr Henderson referred to the case of *H.M. Advocate* v. *Stewart* which is unreported, but a report of which appears in Crown Office Circular A7/81. The sheriff in his charge ... referred to the *Moorov* doctrine. He told the jury that the case of *Moorov* established the principle that where evidence in relation to separate charges is so linked in time, character and circumstance the credible evidence of one witness to each charge can provide the necessary corroboration of each of the charges. So far so good, but the sheriff then went on to say this:

'[I]n the present case, the charges are linked in time, character and circumstance in that they are all claims for a regional development grant. They all took place between October 1986, as I recall, and March 1987.

They all involved claiming for workers who were never actually employed and for assets which were never ultimately purchased.'

Mr Henderson maintained that that was an erroneous direction because it ought to be left for the jury to determine whether the charges were linked in time, character and circumstance. In our opinion Mr Henderson is well founded in making that submission. It is plain from the case of *Moorov* and from other cases such as *Ogg* v. *H.M. Advocate* [1938 J.C. 152] that the proper course is for the presiding sheriff or judge to direct the jury that it is open to them on the evidence to find that there is such an interrelation but it is for the jury and not the judge to decide whether that necessary link has been established in the evidence. In our opinion the sheriff in this passage of his charge was incorrect in giving the jury the direction to the effect that the link in time, character and circumstance existed. He was usurping one of the jury's functions. What he ought to have done was to tell the jury that there was evidence before them which would have entitled them to draw that conclusion. We would only add that it is not at all clear to us in any event what the doctrine of *Moorov* had to do with this case, and it may well be that the reference to *Moorov* in fact served to confuse the jury."

Appeal allowed.

NOTE

For a discussion of the topic of misdirection, and the extent to which misdirections may give rise to a successful appeal, see Chap. 15, *infra*.

(iv)   Essential Qualities of a Verdict

For a verdict of a jury to be appropriate in law, it must be express, it must be consistent with the indictment and it must be unambiguous: see Renton and Brown, para. 10–60.

1.   MacMillan v. H.M. Advocate
(1888) 1 White 572

An accused person was charged with embezzlement. The jury found that he had "misappropriated" certain funds and the sheriff sentenced him to three months' imprisonment. He appealed by bill of suspension. The bill stated:

"The complainer was, on 23rd December 1887, tried on the said indictment at Cupar before the Sheriff-Substitute and a Jury.

The Jury returned a verdict in the following terms:—'The Jury unanimously find the prisoner guilty to the extent of £276, 10s, 9d. of misappropriation of the Burgh Assessment Fund of Pittenweem; and owing to the loose manner in which the accounts of that burgh were looked after, strongly recommend him to the leniency of the Court.'

The Sheriff-Substitute requested the Jury to substitute the word 'embezzlement' for the word 'misappropriation' but the Jury, after a short consultation among themselves declined to accede to his request. The Sheriff-Substitute then expressly put it to the Jury, 'The charge, gentlemen, is embezzlement; is it your feeling that you don't want to return a verdict of embezzlement?' The Jury, through their Chancellor, replied, 'Yes.' Thereupon the verdict was recorded in the terms above written, as it had been drafted by the Jury.

It was contended for the complainer that this was a verdict of not guilty, and the motion of the Procurator-Fiscal for sentence was opposed. The Sheriff-Substitute, however, in respect of the above verdict, sentenced the complainer to three months' imprisonment. The complainer was removed to the prison of Cupar, where he is undergoing the said sentence of imprisonment.

The complainer is innocent of the said charge, and the said verdict was a verdict of not guilty. He was wrongly sentenced in respect of said verdict, and the conviction should be set aside, and the sentence suspended."

These arguments were supported in the bill by the appropriate pleas-in-law to the effect that the conviction and sentence were inept. When the bill was called in the High Court, the Crown offered no opposition to it being passed and the conviction and sentence were quashed.

NOTE

Embezzlement is, of course, a notoriously difficult crime to define, let alone establish to the satisfaction of a jury: see Gane and Stoddart, *Casebook on Scottish Criminal Law*, (2nd ed.), Chap. 12, pp.578 *et seq.*

2.   **Young v. H.M. Advocate**
1932 J.C., 63

A number of accused were charged on indictment with issuing a company prospectus which they knew to be false in pursuance of a common fraudulent purpose to deceive the public and thus defrauding members of the public of a sum of money. The indictment set forth by certain subheads the particulars in respect of which it was alleged that the scheme was false. Young and another accused Todd were convicted of this charge as libelled, except as regarded a common fraudulent purpose. The verdict made no mention of the various subheads. Both appealed against conviction.

LORD JUSTICE-GENERAL (CLYDE):
"*Reasonableness of verdict in point of form (Charge* (1)).

The appellants' first contention was that the verdict was an unreasonable one in relation (as they put it in their notes of appeal) to the law and to the directions given by the trial Court to the jury. This point refers only to charge (1) of the indictment, which is a charge against a number of persons (including the appellants) of concealing material particulars in the prospectus of a new company (to be called Scottish Amalgamated Silks), for the purpose of deceiving those who were invited to apply for shares, in pursuance of a common fraudulent design. The material particulars in respect of which the crime is said to have been committed are separately libelled under six distinct heads (*a*) to (*f*). The verdict on charge (1)—so this Court is informed—was announced by the foreman as a general one of guilty of the charge. But head (*d*) of charge (1) had been withdrawn at some time during the trial; and further, the trial Court, in its summing up to the jury, had directed that there was no evidence of common fraudulent purpose on the part of any of the accused. Accordingly the verdict—as actually recorded with the assent of the jury—excepted head (*d*), and also excepted 'the aggravation of acting in pursuance of a common fraudulent purpose.' Apart from these two exceptions, the verdict remained a general one of guilty of charge (1).

The appellants' contention is that, where—as in the present case, a number of distinct sets of particulars are separately libelled under one general charge, the verdict must disclose which set of particulars the verdict proceeds upon; and that it is an unreasonable verdict if it does not do so. They relate this contention to the Criminal Appeal (Scotland) Act, 1926, on the one hand, and to the directions given to the jury with regard to their verdict on the other hand. They say, *in the first place*, that, now that a convicted person has the right of appeal, it is only reasonable that the verdict should clearly disclose (by way of exception or otherwise) which of the sets of separately libelled particulars it proceeds upon, because it is inconsistent with the right of appeal that a convicted person should be left in any doubt as to the matters in respect of which he has been convicted. In the present case, the particulars separately libelled in heads (*a*) to (*f*) vary greatly from the point of view both of criminality and of facility of attack upon appeal; and it is (they say) unfair to require an appellant to assail the verdict on each and all of the separately libelled particulars, when (for aught he knows) the verdict may really have proceeded only on one or two of the sets of particulars, which may be comparatively trivial, and which (by themselves) might be comparatively easy for him to displace on appeal. *In the second place*, the appellants say that the only direction relevant to his matter which was given by the trial Court to the jury was one to the effect that a verdict under charge (1) could be returned if the jury thought the charge proved with respect to any one or more of the separately libelled sets of particulars; and they contend that this direction should have been accompanied by a further direction to the effect that, if the jury thought the charge was proved with respect only to one or more of the separately libelled sets of particulars, they must disclose in their verdict (by way of exception or otherwise) on which of those sets the verdict truly did proceed. The trial Court gave no such direction; and the appellants contend that the verdict is vitiated accordingly.

At first sight, the point appears a formidable one. So far as mere form goes, it might be formally answered that—as the verdict was recorded with the assent of the jury—the natural, and indeed the necessary, meaning to be attributed to it is that the jury found the appellants guilty under all the heads of charge (1), except (*d*), and subject to the qualification that the appellants had not acted in pursuance of a common fraudulent purpose; but, in the administration of criminal justice, points of form must not be pressed against the person charged. As, however, the argument on the appeal proceeded, it became evident that the appellants' complaint against the inadequacy of the direction (and against the general form of the verdict which they attributed to that inadequacy) lost the materiality which at first sight it seemed to possess. They attacked the verdict on charge (1) on the merits—with what result will appear in the sequel; but the attack was based on grounds substantially common to all the heads, and, accordingly, the dimensions of their complaint—even on the assumption that the jury did not truly mean to convict on all the heads of charge (1) other than (*d*)—was reduced to such hardship as was involved in having to attack the verdict on each and every one of the heads; for the jury must (even on the assumption made by the appellants) have convicted on one or more of them. In these circumstances it is in vain to complain that the Court's direction was inadequate; and this ground of appeal must therefore fail.

Nothing that has been said is intended to throw doubt on the need for care on the part of the Court to see that, in any case where separately libelled particulars are comprehended under a general charge, the verdict is returned and recorded in a shape which excludes doubt as to which of the separate particulars forms (or form) the basis of it. The proper way of exercising this care is no doubt by way of direction given to the jury by the Court. Before the Criminal Appeal Act, the only importance of disclosing these particulars was for the purpose of enabling the Court to impose an appropriate sentence; but, since the Act, it is right that the convicted person should have them plainly disclosed to him."

Appeal on this ground refused.

NOTE

The problem for a jury in sorting out verdicts on a general charge with subheads must be enormous. This arises today particularly in relation to charges of conspiracy, where the convoluted forms of indictments now encountered make charging the jury, reaching a verdict and recording it a major problem. See generally, Gordon, *Criminal Law* (2nd ed.), paras. 6–57 to 6–62 and the cases there discussed. See also Gane & Stoddart, *Casebook on Criminal Law*, pp.202 *et seq.*, and *Clements* v. *H.M. Advocate*, 1991 S.C.C.R. 266, *supra*, p.91.

3.   Hamilton and Others v. H.M. Advocate
1938 J.C. 134

Three accused where charged, *inter alia*, with fraud. Certain convictions were recorded and the accused appealed.

LORD MONCRIEFF: "The three appellants were tried by jury in the Sheriff Court in Glasgow on charges of having, while acting in concert, formed a fraudulent scheme to defraud the Scottish Milk Marketing Board by means of pretences and with consequences specified; and in pursuance of that scheme, while acting in concert, having by various specified detailed pretences defrauded or attempted to defraud the Board of various sums more particularly set forth in the indictment. There are three separate charges, set forth in detail in the indictment, of fraud or attempted fraud. The indictment contains a fourth charge of having, by exhibiting them to a representative of the Board as part of the machinery of the execution of these acts or attempts, uttered as genuine false and fabricated books. All three of the appellants are indicted upon each of these four charges, and it is a principal feature of each of the offences charged that they were carried through and completed by the three appellants acting in concert in the execution of the single fraudulent scheme previously described in detail.

The fraudulent scheme which is charged as having underlain the particular acts or attempts complained of is set forth in much detail in the indictment, but may be summarised as follows. The three appellants were directors of limited companies each of them dealing in bulk with milk; the milk required for the operation of these companies had to be obtained by them from the Scottish Milk Marketing Board; that Board gives its licensees supplies of milk at different prices according as the licensees are to distribute the milk for liquid consumption or are to use the milk as raw material for the manufacture of butter, cheese or cream; the price of milk fixed by the Board is higher when the milk is supplied for liquid consumption than in cases of supply for purposes of further manufacture. The appellant John Hamilton was a director of Ideal Dairies, Limited, a company which had a large business as distributors of milk for liquid consumption. Had that limited company applied to the Board direct for a supply of milk, it would have required to pay the higher prices charged by the Board for such milk. The appellant William Barr Haddow was a director of the Cardowan Creameries, Limited, and the appellant Walter Brown Kyle was a director of that company and was also a director of the West of Scotland Buttermakers, Limited. These two latter companies did an extensive business in the manufacture of margarine and butter from liquid milk, and held manufacturers' licences from the Board. These licences overlapped, but covered a composite period extending from February 1935 to June 1936. As licensees these limited companies applied for and got deliveries of milk for manufacture. This milk was then transferred to Ideal Dairies, Limited, and distributed by that company for liquid consumption. The appellants are charged with having, in the execution of the fraudulent scheme to defraud the Board which they carried out while acting in concert, and by means of false and fraudulent returns and false and fraudulent books and records, pretended to the Board that the whole milk supplied on the application of the Cardowan Creamies and the West of Scotland Buttermakers for milk at manufacturing prices had been used for the purpose of manufacture; whereas large quantities of the milk so supplied had not been so used, but had been transferred or sold by these companies to Ideal Dairies for liquid consumption. A consequence of the operation of such a scheme would be, of course, as set forth in the indictment, that Ideal Dairies would obtain milk for liquid consumption at the manufacturing rate; and that those responsible for the scheme (as the appellants are charged with having been responsible) would thereby succeed in defrauding the Board of the difference between the manufacturing price which in fact was paid for the milk and the liquid price which ought to have been paid. It is in execution of this scheme, and as acting in concert, that the three appellants are charged in the indictment with having done the acts and made the attempt which are the subject of the first three particular charges. The first of these acts is specified as having been executed by the three appellants in concert by using, as the machinery of the fraud, applications for milk made by the Cardowan Creameries, Limited. The second act and the attempted act which are the subjects of the second and third particular charges, are in like manner said to have been executed by the three appellants in concert by using, as the machinery of the fraud, applications for milk made by the West of Scotland Buttermakers, Limited. The books which are said to have been fabricated in concert by the three appellants are books which record the operations of both these limited companies.

At the conclusion of the trial all the appellants were convicted by the jury, but each of them was not found guilty in similar terms. The appellant John Hamilton alone was found guilty as libelled of all four charges; the appellant William Barr Haddow was found guilty as libelled of the first and fourth charges only; while the appellant Walter Brown Kyle was found guilty as libelled of all four charges except the first. As regards charges 2 and 3, the jury found these charges not proven against Haddow, and in like manner found the first charge not proven against Kyle. Numerous reasons of appeal were intimated on behalf of each of the appellants, and various grounds of appeal were relied on by the counsel who represented them at the hearing of the appeal. As a principal ground of appeal it was maintained on behalf of each of the appellants that the verdict returned by the jury contained findings which were irreconcilable one with the other, that the verdict was self-contradictory as evidenced by its terms, and that such a verdict could not be allowed to stand.

I propose to deal in the first instance and at this stage with this objection. Analysing the verdict, and reading the requisite passages together, it results, as regards the first charge, in a finding of guilty as libelled against Hamilton and Haddow, with a finding of not proven in favour of Kyle. It was maintained that such a verdict was in itself irreconcilable with the terms of the indictment, seeing that the act had been charged against each of the appellants as having been executed by all three of them in concert. It was suggested that a finding of guilty as libelled implied a finding that each of the parties so found guilty had acted in concert with both the other two, and that, therefore, the acquittal of one of the three was inconsistent with the terms of the charge. In my opinion, this suggestion is not well founded. I see no reason why, when concert of three parties is charged in an indictment, such an indictment should not be read as charging concert among these parties or between two of them, and as available to support a verdict against any two of them with acquittal of the third. This view appears, moreover, to receive support from the terms of section 6 of the Criminal Procedure (Scotland) Act 1887. I find little assistance, however, from the cases of *Myers* [1936 J.C. 1] and *Hamilton* [(1844) 2 Broun 313], which were cited as authorities. Seeing that concert was a principal and conditioning element of the charge, a different question would have arisen if two of the three parties to the concert had been acquitted; but it is not necessary in this case to entertain that question.

In like manner the jury, in returning their verdict as regards the second charge, convicted two only of the appellants and acquitted the third. In this case, however, they made a different selection among the three, having acquitted Kyle under charge 1, while in this case acquitting Haddow under charge 2. It was argued that, whereas it might be competent to make a selection of any particular group from among the parties charged with having acted in concert, once such a group had been selected as had been done in this case in the verdict returned on the first charge, that group must be regarded as having been crystallised for all effects in the reading of the indictment, so that a verdict of 'guilty as libelled,' (which was the verdict returned in answer to both charges in this case) could only be supported by proof of concert between the members of that one particular group. Although this argument when first stated appeared to be logical and attractive, on further consideration I do not see my way to sustain it. The flexibility which is introduced by the Act of 1887 seems to make such an indictment open to be read as regards concert in all its possible permutations, and with every such occasional shifting of these permutations as may at any stage be required. Under an indictment which charges A, B and C as having acted in concert, unless indeed a single indivisible concert of three be quite determinately charged, a verdict is, in my opinion, within the indictment and may properly find 'guilty as libelled' any duality of persons selected from the group of three; may so find whether A and B or A and C or B and C be selected; and may affirm 'guilty as libelled' against one or other or more than one of these groups, whether in repetition or in succession. Nevertheless, I am clearly of opinion that, in all such cases of variation, and more especially of repeated dissimilar variation between indictment and verdict, special verdicts, and not verdicts of 'guilty as libelled,' should be adjusted and returned. While I desire to draw attention to this as a point of practice, I am, however, of the opinion that neither of these two arguments can be sustained.

A more formidable challenge against the consistency of the verdict was, however, based upon a contrast between the findings of the jury in answer to the first and second of the charges as above narrated, and the answer given by them to the fourth charge. This argument was stated as follows. In answer to the first and second charges, as already noted, the jury had not only found various selected groups of two among the accused guilty, but had in each case acquitted one of the accused. In so acquitting in succession these two of the accused, the jury had necessarily negatived that there was proof against them of having had part in the fraudulent scheme so far as concerted with reference to these charges. Notwithstanding these verdicts of acquittal, the jury had nevertheless proceeded in answer to the fourth charge to find each of the three appellants guilty as libelled; and so to affirm an active share in the conspiracy from start to finish as against *inter alios* the two appellants who had already been acquitted of participation in the scheme at least in part. It was argued for the appellants, and was eventually not disputed by the learned Solicitor-General, that the answers so given by the jury to the various elements of charge were inconsistent and irreconcilable, and that the verdict as a whole could not stand as so returned. In my opinion, such a concession could not have been withheld. Unless some solution of the difficulty can be found, it is clear, accordingly, that the verdict must be set aside.

Alternative solutions of the difficulty were suggested by counsel for the Crown. In the first of these the Court was invited somewhat half-heartedly to remodel the verdict returned by the jury in answer to the fourth charge, and edit and reconstruct that element of the verdict in the light of the verdicts given in answer to charges 1 and 2. Once remodelled as so suggested the verdict would read as a verdict finding Hamilton and Haddow guilty under the fourth charge during the earlier period detailed in the charge (being the period of the active operations of the Cardowan Creameries, Limited), and finding Hamilton and Kyle guilty during the subsequent period throughout which the West of Scotland Buttermakers, Limited, was the agent of the fraud. It may be conceded that, if this reconstruction should be made, all inconsistency appearing on the face of the verdict would disappear. It would so disappear, however, by the intervention of the Court for the exercise of the functions, and for the redirection of a completed self-misdirection, of the jury. Such an intervention by the Court does not appear to be authorised either by practice or in principle. I have no hesitation in rejecting this first alternative solution. A verdict must be left to reflect the mind of the jury, but may not be made a medium of introducing illumination to it.

The second alternative solution suggested for the Crown, which was that the verdict of the jury in answer to the fourth charge should be deleted as being inconsistent with the earlier part of the verdict, appears to me to invite action by the Court which should be regarded as even less permissible. If a jury have given evidence, in the verdict which they have returned in a criminal case, of complete inconsistency of outlook in their treatment of the questions submitted to them for adjudication, and if this be made apparent by an *ex facie* irreconcilability one with another of the separate elements of that verdict, the right of persons convicted by that verdict is not merely a right to insist on the inconsistencies being eliminated from it, but is a right to challenge *ab initio* the competency of the jury to deal with the question of liberty which had been referred to them for adjudication. It is an inevitable consequence of the answer of the jury to the fourth charge that they must be regarded as having found Kyle and Haddow as having acted in concert in the execution of the single fraudulent scheme. *Per contra* it is a consequence of their answers to the first and second charges in the indictment that they failed to find evidence of any such concert between Kyle and Haddow. The conviction of all three in answer to the fourth charge must, in my opinion, be contrasted, not with the partial conviction of selected groups under charges 1 and 2, but with the acquittal of two among the three conspirators in successive answers to the first and second charges. As so contrasted, one or other branch of the verdict, and it is impossible to tell which branch, is contradictory of the single determination of the jury on the question of concerted guilt, and cannot be reconciled with any single determination of that question as consequential on it. Seeing that, in my opinion, the answer of the jury to the fourth charge can neither be reconstructed nor deleted from the verdict, I am, accordingly, of opinion that a verdict, of which the answer to that charge forms part and falls to be taken along with the answers previously given by the jury to the first and second charges, is one which is vitiated *ex facie* by a vice and a defect which is insusceptible of cure and is fatal to the verdict.

It is, accordingly, not necessary to deal with the particular reasons of appeal which were maintained against the charge of attempting to commit a fraud which follows the first and second charges. These reasons would have deserved particular examination had it not been that, as the verdict must stand or fall together, and as in my opinion for the reasons I have given the verdict cannot stand, no purpose would be served by examining any further reasons of appeal. For the same reason I find it unnecessary to refer to the various other reasons of appeal which were maintained.

I desire to add that I entirely agree with the views to be stated by your Lordship, in an opinion which I already have had the advantage of reading, as to the limits of the duty of a judge, when charging a jury in criminal cases, to make particular reference to matters dealt with in the evidence, yet not made prominent on behalf of the prosecution or of the defence; or by formal repetition to deal afresh with matters which in the opinion of the judge are not controversial and which have been already made entirely clear in the speeches of counsel. It may be that certain judicial observations, or even certain recent decisions, will require to be reconsidered by the Court.

I further desire to add that I have arrived at the conclusion that this verdict cannot stand with quite unusual regret. It was directly admitted by learned counsel who represented the appellants that their clients did not come before this Court of appeal with clean hands; nor did counsel dispute that, had the indictment been more wisely framed or the verdict more intelligently returned, the circumstances surrounding these transactions were such as would have made it salutary that penalties should have been imposed. I regard it as unfortunate in this case that the indictment was so heavily charged in its framework and in its detail. The substance of the complaint is contained in what I have referred to as the first and second charges. Had these two serious charges stood alone, the difficulties which have resulted in the shipwreck of this verdict would not have been introduced into the proceedings, while the accused would have been rendered answerable, in substance if not in logic, for all the criminal conduct which in such cumbrous form has been charged against them."

Convictions quashed.

NOTE
The lessons for the Crown are clear. An indictment should not resemble a closed record: it might be intelligible to a jury.

(v)   What Happens if the Jury is Split?

A majority of eight votes of the jury is necessary before a conviction can be recorded. The following case is reproduced as an example of what can happen where there are a number of votes for each possible verdict.

Kerr v. H.M. Advocate
1992 S.C.C.R. 281

An accused was convicted and appealed on the ground that there had been a miscarriage of justice.

LORD JUSTICE-GENERAL: "The appellants are Robert Kerr and Sean Thomas Fulton who were both found guilty at the High Court in Glasgow on a charge of attempted murder and sentenced to nine years' imprisonment. Robert Kerr was also found guilty on a related charge of committing an offence while on bail. The appellants have appealed against their conviction on grounds which allege a misdirection by the trial judge about the verdicts which it was open to the jury to return. No point arises as to the sufficiency of the evidence or any of the directions by the trial judge on other matters in the course of his charge.

The trial judge gave the usual directions to the jury about the verdicts which were open to them before he invited them to retire. These directions appear [in] his charge, and Mr Henderson for the [first] appellant accepted that they were clear and accurate and he did not suggest that they were in any way open to criticism. At 1.10 p.m. the jury retired for lunch and thereafter to consider their verdicts. It was what happened upon their return at 3 p.m. which has given rise to these appeals.

The trial judge tells us in his report that at about 3 p.m. the jury summoned his clerk, and that shortly thereafter he was informed by the clerk that, although the jury were still in the course of their deliberations, they required directions as to what would be the position if they were inclined to acquit but were evenly divided between verdicts of not proven and not guilty. He requested that the jury be brought back into court in order that he could give them any necessary additional directions. It appears that he was not expecting a verdict at that stage but merely a request for further directions. That, however, was not the impression given to counsel when the clerk of court explained to them why the jury were being brought back into court. Mr Henderson told us that their recollection is that the clerk used words to this effect: 'We will have to have the jury brought back into court. They are split on their vote. There are seven for guilty, four for not guilty and four for not proven.' So far as counsel were concerned, the jury were being brought back into court to receive directions as to how their verdicts should be expressed in these circumstances. Nothing was said to counsel to indicate that the jury were still in the course of their deliberations, or that they had not yet reached a decision as to what their verdicts were to be. The learned advocate-depute confirmed that the advocate-depute who conducted the trial also understood that it was being suggested that the jury were split 4–4 on the verdicts for acquittal. It is perhaps unfortunate that no indication was given to the trial judge that that was the position, although it must be said that there is a clear difference of recollection on this point. According to the judge's recollection, no specific figures were mentioned to him by his clerk and his clerk also, with whom he has discussed the matter, does not recall receiving any indication that the jury were ready to return a verdict. Nevertheless it seems clear that when the jury returned to the court the trial judge was under the impression that they were still in the course of their deliberations. This may explain why he responded to their request in the way he did.

What then happened was this. On their return to court the following exchange took place between the clerk of court, the foreman of the jury and the trial judge:

'THE CLERK OF COURT: Ladies and gentlemen of the jury, would your foreman or forewoman please stand? I understand you wish further directions from his Lordship.

THE FOREMAN OF THE JURY: Yes, your Lordship. We have a split jury here.

LORD CAPLAN: Yes, well, if you have a split jury you will remember what I told you. You cannot bring in any guilty verdict unless there is an absolute majority for it: at least eight. If the position is that there are not eight of you for a guilty verdict then you must acquit. In respect of the verdict for acquittal you don't need an absolutely [sic] majority, it can just be a majority. If your position was such as to result in an acquittal, then you have to consider what the proper acquittal verdict would be.

If there was a majority for not proven, albeit it fell short of an absolute majority, your verdict would be not proven. If there was not such a majority you would have to bring in a not guilty verdict. In other words, if you could not decide by a majority that it should be one way or the other, then I think the appropriate verdict would be not guilty. But the thing I must emphasise, if there are less than eight for guilty then you certainly could not bring in a guilty verdict. Now, would that meet your problem? There seems to be a certain affirmatory nodding of heads.'

The trial judge seems to have thought that he had given the jury the directions which they required, especially since he was receiving some indications by the nodding of heads to that effect. But the foreman then said something which indicated that he at least was not satisfied by what he had heard. There then followed this exchange between him and the trial judge:

'THE FOREMAN OF THE JURY: Can I show you this bit of paper, your honour?

LORD CAPLAN: Well, we have got the bit of paper. Well, I don't know if that represents your final verdict but if the position is there is no majority for not proven, the appropriate [verdict] would be not guilty on the assumption that it is your intention to acquit, if there is a lack of a clear majority of eight for a conviction. Now, does that require you to go away and reconsider? I see that you would like an opportunity to reconsider what your final verdict is. Very well, when you arrive at a final verdict would you please indicate what it is.'

The jury retired at 3.05 pm, and at 3.25 pm they returned to the court to pronounce verdicts of guilty by a majority in respect of each appellant.

Mr Henderson accepted that it was possible that the clerk had said different things to different people and he made no criticism of the clerk in that respect. His point, however, was that, as soon as the foreman said to the judge in open court that there was a split vote, the trial judge should have asked him to explain the position so that he could identify the point on which the direction was required. He emphasised that this was a matter which had to be clarified in open court, because otherwise the accused would have no conception of what was going on. The matter was not to be dealt with by private communication between the jury and the judge through the clerk of court. Having then seen what was written on the paper, the trial judge should at least have made its contents known to the defence so that they could make representations about it which were relevant to his consideration of the case. As it was, the defence were deprived of that opportunity and the trial judge proceeded on an assumption as to what was in the jury's mind which might well have been false and in any event was untested by questions in open court. He submitted that this was contrary to section 145(1) of the Criminal Procedure (Scotland) Act 1975, which provides that no part of a trial shall take place outwith the presence of the accused. He also criticised the directions given by the trial judge as being confusing. Reference was made to *Affleck* v. *H.M. Advocate* [1987 S.C.C.R. 150]. They were not directed to the point which the jury wanted to know about. The jury might have been misled by the direction that in respect of the verdict for acquittal they did not need an absolute majority but that it could be just a majority. In the result, after directions which were unhelpful and confusing, the jury were invited to reconsider their verdict and they plainly did so with the result that a miscarriage of justice had occurred.

The learned advocate-depute accepted that it was undesirable for the jury to communicate with the trial judge by written messages, the contents of which were not revealed in open court. But, in contrast to what happened in *Cunningham* v. *H.M. Advocate* [1984 S.C.C.R. 40], where the communications took place in chambers in the presence of counsel for both sides but in the absence of the accused, everything took place here in open court in the accused's presence. It was not a breach of section 145(1) for the judge to read what was on the paper which had been passed to him by the jury without announcing its contents in open court. The directions which he then gave to the jury were appropriate in the circumstances in which he found himself, which were of some difficulty in view of the limited information which he had been given. It would have been wrong for him to have directed the jury there and then to state what their verdict was without any further opportunity for deliberation. He was right to leave it to the jury to say whether or not they wanted to reconsider their verdicts in the light of his directions. The situation was, he said, similar to that which had arisen in *Jones* v. *H.M. Advocate* [1991 S.C.C.R. 290] where the clear impression from what the foreman was saying was that the jury had not reached a final conclusion on the issue on which they were seeking directions.

But the situation in this case is clearly quite different from that which arose in *Jones*, where the jury, who had been reduced to fourteen, sought a direction as to what to do when they were equally divided about the deletion of a word from the charge. It should be noted that at no stage in the course of the exchanges in the present case did the trial judge ask the foreman to explain more fully the point on which directions were being sought. The first thing he was told by the foreman was that 'We have a split jury here'. That statement was a clear indication that the jury had at least taken the matter to a vote. It raised the question whether they were still in course of their deliberations or whether they had taken their decision and were in doubt only as to its effect. The fact that the trial judge did not seek to clarify the position at the outset is consistent with his understanding that the jury were still in the course of their deliberations and that they wished directions as to what the position would be if they were equally divided between verdicts of not proven and not guilty. But it would have been better if he had paused at this point prior to giving his directions in order to discover more precisely what was the matter on which the directions were required. Then he was shown the bit of paper on which, as he tells us in his report, was written 'G–7, NP–4, NG–4'. His response to seeing this information was to say, 'Well, I don't know if that represents your final verdict. . . .' He makes the same point in his report, when he tells us that there was no indication on the paper as to what these figures represented and in particular as to whether, if they reflected a vote of the jury, they represented final figures or merely the state of mind of the jury at that point in their deliberations. These comments suggest that the trial judge did not fully appreciate the significance of what he had been shown. It will be remembered that the foreman had already told him that 'We have a split jury here'. The paper had on it figures which clearly indicated that a vote had been taken and what the result was of that vote. Moreover the number for guilty fell short of that which was required for a verdict of guilty to be returned. In these circumstances what he should have done was to ask the jury whether the figures on the paper represented their final verdict in respect of both accused. A negative answer would have confirmed that the jury were still in the course of their deliberations and that it was appropriate for them to retire after receiving the further directions in order to reach a verdict. But an affirmative answer would have shown that there was no need for the jury to retire, since the only question was how their verdicts for acquittal should be expressed.

We have some sympathy for the trial judge who seems to have been under a misapprehension as to the stage which the jury had arrived at in their deliberations. He assumed that they were still incomplete and that it was in order to assist them in their deliberations that further directions were required. Everything which he said and did can be explained on that assumption, including his reaction to the piece of paper when it was shown to him at the foreman's request. It was not a breach of section 145(1) for him to look at the paper, since it was handed to him in open court in the presence of the accused. Whether the contents of such a piece of paper must be read out by the trial judge, or at least must be shown to the defence, is a question of circumstances and no absolute rule can be laid down. It may be clear that the information is confidential to the jury, in which case it ought not to be disclosed. But it may contain information which, in fairness to the defence, should be disclosed either by reading out the contents or by showing the paper to those representing the accused. Disclosure is likely to be appropriate where what is on paper is relevant to directions which are being sought from the trial judge. But, although the trial judge was right to look at the paper before deciding what he should do about it, he ought not to have proceeded to make any comment about its contents without first being told what they were intended to represent. All he said on receipt of the bit of paper was, 'Well, I don't know if that represents your final verdict. ...' What he should have done was to put that question to the foreman. He could have done this by asking him simply whether what was on the paper was the verdict of the jury. If it was not, the judge would have been right not to disclose the contents of the paper to anyone since the figures on it would have been of no significance. But if he had been told that this was their verdict, it would have been clear that all that required to be done was to discover whether it applied to both accused and to decide how it should be expressed. These matters could and should have been cleared up without inviting the jury to retire to reconsider their verdicts. And it would have been proper for the trial judge to disclose the contents of the paper so that counsel were aware of them before he took any further steps to clarify what had been written down.

As it is, what happened in this case seems likely to have resulted in an injustice to the appellants. In the first place, the foreman's statement that 'We have a split jury here' and the contents of the piece of paper suggest that in all probability the jury had reached their verdict. There was no indication as to whether the figures on the papers related to both accused, but there was no material difference in the evidence against either of them. As the trial judge pointed out [in] his charge, the crucial evidence was that of two witnesses who said that the accused both admitted that they had stabbed the complainer, and the evidence of a single witness who had seen them both rushing into the night in pursuit of him. There is no reason to think that the jury would be likely to have returned different verdicts against them in these circumstances, and in the end of the day the verdicts which they returned were the same, both being verdicts of guilty by a majority. In the second place, the trial judge gave directions to the jury about the verdicts open to them which were in part confusing and which, when taken as a whole, might well have been thought to be an indication that they should reconsider what their verdicts ought to be. In these circumstances any further consideration of the matter was likely to be prejudicial to the accused.

It is not our practice to give directions to the jury as to the difference between a verdict of not guilty and one of not proven. Nor is it our practice to give directions as to what a jury should do if those for acquittal are equally divided between these verdicts. The matter is left to the good sense of the jury to resolve, and in practice it very rarely gives rise to difficulty. But if, as in this case, the jury have been unable to resolve the matter for themselves and have returned to the judge for directions about a split vote, the proper course is for the judge to take the verdict from them as it stands and not to invite them to reconsider it with a view to arriving at a majority view as to which verdict of acquittal they should return. This is because directions of this issue may be difficult for them to understand and because the risk is that a further discussion on this issue may lead to a redistribution of votes as between those for guilty and those for an acquittal. The only way to prevent that risk of injustice to the accused, since the verdict is not final until it has been recorded, is to accept the verdict as it stands. The proper course also is for an acquittal verdict which is split equally to be recorded as one of not proven. This is the only position which can logically be adopted where the necessary majority for a verdict of guilty does not exist, and where there is no majority for a positive finding of not guilty among those who have voted for an acquittal.

The trial judge told the jury that if there was no majority for not proven the appropriate verdict would be not guilty on the assumption that it was the jury's intention to acquit. Mr Henderson said that there was some sense in this direction, but it illustrates the point that for the jury to be allowed to reconsider their verdict at this stage in the light of a direction to this effect could result in an injustice to the accused. It is not inconceivable that a member of the jury who is in favour of a not proven verdict but against a verdict of not guilty could change his vote to guilty in order to prevent that result. There is more than a suspicion that that indeed is what occurred in this case. The result of the vote disclosed by the piece of paper was an acquittal verdict, yet this became a verdict of guilty by a majority some [twenty] minutes later after the jury had reconsidered their verdict following the directions by the trial judge. It is hard to believe that this was due to a further consideration of the evidence. The more likely explanations are that the jury were misled into thinking that it was necessary for them to arrive at a majority view as to which verdict of acquittal they should return or that they thought that there were in effect only two verdicts open to them, these being guilty or not guilty. Whatever the explanation, it is clear that a miscarriage of justice has occurred, and we are in no doubt that we must allow the appeals.

The learned advocate-depute invited us to set aside the verdicts and to grant authority to the Crown to bring a new prosecution in accordance with section 255 of the [Criminal Procedure (Scotland)] Act [1975]. But that seems to us to be inconsistent with what was disclosed by the piece of paper, which revealed a split in the jury only as to the acquittal verdicts, there being insufficient votes for a conviction. It would be unjust in these circumstances to expose the appellants to a further trial on charges on which, on these figures, they were entitled to be acquitted. We have decided therefore to set aside the verdicts of the trial court and to quash the convictions."

Connections quashed.

(vi)   Motion for Sentence

For cases on this topic, see Chap. 2, *supra*.

(vii)   Remit for Sentence

The provision covering this matter is section 104 of the 1975 Act (as amended by the 1980 Act, Sched. 4, para. 15). The amended provision enjoins the sheriff to remit an accused where he "holds that any competent sentence which he can impose is inadequate so that the question of sentence is appropriate for the High Court."

(A)   What happens if there are multiple accused?

H.M. Advocate v. Duffy
1974 S.L.T. (Notes) 46

Two accused pleaded guilty before the sheriff to various offences. The sheriff remitted one and dealt with the other himself. When the remitted accused appeared in the High Court, the following comments were made:

LORD JUSTICE-CLERK (WHEATLEY): "I have repeatedly said that where two or more accused appear on the same indictment in the sheriff court, and are convicted, then the sheriff, if he decided that one of them should be remitted to the High Court for sentence, should remit both or all of them.

The purpose of this procedure is to allow the same judge to determine the appropriate sentences for all accused, having regard to such relative matters as the number of offences on which each accused has been convicted, previous records, personal circumstances and backgrounds. When accused in such circumstances are dealt with in different courts, disparities which sometimes create embarrassment are liable to creep in.

It is only in exceptional circumstances that the procedure should not be followed. If, for instance, there are two accused, and each is convicted of offences not involving the other, the sheriff would be entitled to deal with one of them himself while remitting the other to the High Court for sentence. But where both are convicted of the same offence or offences, whether or not they are also convicted of other offences not involving the co-accused, then both should be remitted to the High Court.

If the sheriff is of the opinion that in the case of one of the accused there are circumstances present which would justify him imposing a sentence within his competence, he can refer to these circumstances in his report to the High Court.

Since even an experienced and conscientious sheriff like the one involved in this case seems to have misunderstood the directions previously given on this matter, I deem it expedient to repeat and emphasise the procedure which should be followed."

NOTE

The effect of this procedure is, of course, that the High Court often finds itself passing sentence well within the competence of a sheriff on accused persons who perhaps have relatively short records, compared to a more experienced co-accused who is the real reason for the remit. However, uniformity of sentencing practice is doubtless enhanced thereby.

(B) What happens if there are multiple indictments?

H.M. Advocate v. Stern
1974 S.L.T. 2

LORD JUSTICE-CLERK (WHEATLEY): "The accused in this case was charged on two separate indictments. The first was a common law charge of the reset of a motor car. The second was a contravention of s. 99(b) of the Road Traffic Act 1972 (driving while disqualified). The circumstances of the two offences were inter-connected, and the reason why the charges were in separate indictments and not in a single indictment was apparently the current practice of the Crown not to include in the same indictment two charges, one of which would indicate to a jury that the accused had been previously convicted of an offence. This is an understandable practice, since it is designed to prevent prejudice to an accused, but, as in the present case, it can lead to complications if proper regard is not had to the procedure. Each indictment has to be called and dealt with separately. The accused in the present case pled guilty to both indictments. In view of his long list of previous convictions the sheriff remitted him to the High Court for sentence in terms of s. 2 of the Criminal Procedure (Scotland) Act 1921. This was quite a competent course in relation to the first indictment (the common law charge of reset). Presumably to allow the inter-connected events to be dealt with at the same time by the same court, he also remitted the accused to the High Court for sentence on the second indictment (contravention of s. 99(b) of the Road Traffic Act 1972). This was quite incompetent. The statutory authority for such a remit is s. 2 aforesaid. It only operates when the sheriff holds that any sentence which he can competently pronounce is inadequate. The maximum sentence on indictment for a contravention of s. 99(b) is 12 months or a fine of £100 or both. Any sentence which the sheriff could impose for this charge was completely within his competence, and he had accordingly no authority to remit this single charge on that separate indictment to the High Court. That remit is therefore incompetent, and I shall accede to the advocate-depute's motion to desert the diet pro loco et tempore.

This situation has arisen more than once, and despite directions from the High Court about the proper procedure to be followed the practice continues of remitting cases incompetently in circumstances such as were present here. I accordingly deem it desirable to restate the proper procedure in the hope that it will be regularly followed in the future.

If an accused is charged on two or more indictments, each has to be dealt with separately. If the indictments are being dealt with in the sheriff court, the sheriff has to consider what should be done in each separate case. If the circumstances in a case are such that any appropriate sentence which he could competently pronounce would, in his view, be inadequate, he can remit the case to the High Court for sentence. If more than one case falls into that category he can remit all such cases so that they can be disposed of together in the High Court. Where the charges in such indictments are inter-connected that is an obviously desirable course, even although separate sentences have to be passed on the individual indictments. The ability of the court to pass concurrent or consecutive sentences provides the latitude necessary to meet differing conditions. Where, however, the maximum sentence which he can impose is within his competence, then he must dispose of the case himself and not remit it to the High Court. If the offence is inter-connected with another offence which has been remitted to the High Court for disposal, the sentence for that offence can be taken into account by the judge in the High Court when considering the other offence.

It will be appreciated that what I have said only relates to the situation where there are separate indictments. Where a number of charges are contained in the one indictment then if, in relation to one or more charges, the s. 2 procedure is competent and appropriate, there can be a remit of the whole indictment even if it contains a charge (or charges) which, if it stood by itself in an indictment, could not be competently remitted."

NOTE

The situation in this case is really only likely to be encountered where charges of driving while disqualified are involved. Most other offences can be libelled on the same indictment. The "sheriff" who remits need not be the "sheriff" who took the trial: Borland v. H.M. Advocate, 1976 S.L.T. (Notes) 12.

CHAPTER 12

THE INITIATION OF SUMMARY PROCEEDINGS

Summary criminal procedure is applied in the sheriff court and district courts only: see Chap. 3, *supra*. The issues which arise at the stage of initiating a summary case are similar to those which relate to cases which proceed by petition under solemn procedure.

A. ARE THE PROCEEDINGS TIMEOUS?

As has been observed, common law offences never prescribe: see *Sugden* v. *H.M. Advocate*, 1934 J.C. 103, *supra*, p.338. Statutory offences prescribe according to any terms of the relative statutes: *e.g., Robertson* v. *Page*, 1943 J.C. 32. Where no time-bar is stated, then section 331 of the 1975 Act applies. By section 331(1) it is provided, *inter alia*, that in such cases proceedings must be commenced within six months (that is, calendar months) after the contravention occurred; by section 331(3) proceedings are deemed to commence on the date on which a warrant to apprehend or to cite the accused is granted, if such warrant is executed without undue delay. On warrants and citation generally, see sections 314 and 315 of the 1975 Act.

1. Smith v. Peter Walker & Son (Edinburgh) Ltd.
1978 J.C. 44
A building firm was charged on summary complaint. This complaint was dismissed as incompetent by the sheriff. The Crown appealed by stated case.

LORD JUSTICE-GENERAL (EMSLIE): "The respondents in this Crown appeal were charged with four contraventions of the Construction (Working Places) Regulations 1966. They were, it seems, undertaking the rebuilding of a chimney head at 30 Woodburn Terrace, Edinburgh, and the charges related to the state of a ladder used by their men on 14th December 1976, and to a working platform and suspended gin wheel used on the site on 16th December 1976. The alleged contraventions, accordingly, related to a certain transient state of matters on two separate days only, and were contraventions within the scope of section 331(1) of the Criminal Procedure (Scotland) Act 1975. In terms of that subsection as it applied in the circumstances of this case, proceedings in respect of these contraventions required to be commenced within six months of 16th December 1976, *i.e.*, not later than 15th June 1977.

The complaint in this case was not served until 30th June 1977. At the first diet on 21st July 1977 an objection that the complaint was out of time was intimated and, after debate on 25th August 1977, the Sheriff upheld the objection and sustained a plea to the competency of the proceedings. His decision involved consideration of section 331(3) of the Act which is in these terms: 'For the purposes of this section proceedings shall be deemed to be commenced on the date on which a warrant to apprehend or to cite the accused is granted, if such warrant is executed without undue delay.' It was common ground (i) that warrant to cite the respondents was granted on 10th June 1977 (when the diet of 21st July 1977 was assigned by the Court) and, as we have said, (ii) that that warrant was not executed until 30th June 1977. The dispute between the appellant and the respondents involved the single question viz., whether in all the circumstances of this case the warrant to cite had been executed 'without undue delay.' The decision of the Sheriff was that it had not and the question which both parties invited us to answer is this: 'Having regard to the whole circumstances stated, including particularly the dates of raising the complaint, assignation of a diet and postal service of the complaint, was the Sheriff entitled to hold that there had been undue delay in execution of the warrant to cite the respondents within the meaning of section 331(3) of the Criminal Procedure (Scotland) Act 1975?'

For the Crown the submission was that although there is little guidance to be found in authority on the meaning of 'undue delay' in section 331(3) it is clear enough that it means 'excessive' delay. If the delay which occurred in this case between the granting of the warrant to cite on 10th June 1977 and the execution thereof on 30th June was not excessive it would follow that the proceedings had been commenced within the time limit prescribed by section 331. Whether a delay is or is not 'excessive' in any case will be a question of degree in the particular circumstances. In this case the interval between the date of the warrant and its execution was only 20 days. Execution was only 15 days later than the expiry of the six-month period. The assigned diet was 21st July 1977 and ample notice of that diet was given to the respondents. Had the warrant been executed before 15th June 1977 the citation would have told the respondents precisely the same as the citation of 30th June, namely, that they were required to appear to answer the complaint at the assigned diet on 21st July. The Sheriff, it was said, had given no good reason for holding the delay which occurred in this case to be excessive, and since the respondents were not prejudiced thereby the appeal should be allowed.

In reply the respondents submitted that the question of whether delay in execution of a warrant to cite an accused person is or is not undue is one of fact, circumstance and degree. In this case the Sheriff adopted the correct approach and in the circumstances of this case was entitled to reach the conclusion that execution of the warrant had been unduly delayed.

In our judgment the submission for the respondent must receive effect. It can no doubt be said that undue delay in the context in which these words appear in section 331(3) connotes delay which is excessive in the circumstances, but this does not take us very far. The provisions of section 331(1) are designed for the protection of those accused of statutory contraventions and the clear intention is that no one shall be exposed to prosecution for any such contravention if proceedings have not been commenced before the expiry of the statutory time limit of six months. Where no complaint has been served upon a person accused of a statutory offence until after that time limit has expired, proceedings by the prosecutor will only be saved in the special circumstances set out in section 331(3). These special circumstances are: (1) that a warrant to cite the accused has been granted before the expiry of the time limit, and (2) that citation of the accused on the authority of that warrant after the expiry of the time limit has been effected without undue delay. It appears to us, accordingly, that if a prosecutor seeks to avail himself of the very limited latitude allowed to him by section 331(3) it is for him to demonstrate that execution of a warrant to cite after the expiry of the time limit can, in the circumstances of the case, be regarded as justifiable. To delay service of a complaint charging a statutory contravention until after the expiry of the time limit is a circumstance which will always call for explanation and we are clearly of opinion that the expression 'undue delay' in section 331(3) carries the implication that any delay in service of such a complaint may be regarded as excessive if, in the circumstances of the case, no justification for it can be seen. In the case of *Farquharson* v. *Whyte* 1 White 26, the Court in holding that an admittedly long delay in service of the complaint was fatal to the conviction attached importance to the fact that the delay was entirely unexplained and we see no reason to quarrel with the treatment of 'undue delay' in Renton and Brown's Criminal Procedure, 4th Edn., at p.187 in a passage in these terms: 'What constitutes undue delay must be a question of fact in each case. It must not be due to any act for which the prosecutor is responsible. The expression "without undue delay" implies that there has been no slackness on his part and that any delay in execution is due to some circumstance for which he is not responsible, e.g., the conduct of the accused.'

When the expression 'without undue delay' is understood as we have explained it, it cannot be affirmed that the Sheriff was not entitled to reach the conclusion which he did. No explanation for the delay which occurred in this case was offered by the prosecutor. The six-month time limit was almost at an end before warrant to cite the respondents was sought and granted. There is nothing in the stated case to suggest that the respondents in any way contributed to the delay which occurred thereafter before the warrant was executed. The charges contained in the complaint relate to states of fact said to have existed on only two separate days in December 1976 in course of the operation of rebuilding a chimney head. The passage of time is bound to prejudice investigation of charges such as these and, if the prosecutor delays in seeking a warrant to cite an accused to answer such charges as these until almost the eve of the expiry of the statutory time limit, the need to act on the warrant with all speed is clamant. As we read the stated case it cannot be said that the Sheriff reached his conclusion without considering all the relevant circumstances or that he took into account any irrelevant considerations. It follows, accordingly, that his decision on a question which is one of fact, circumstances and degree cannot be disturbed and we shall answer the question in the case, as we have restated it of consent of parties, in the affirmative, and refuse the appeal."

Appeal refused.

NOTE

So it all depends on the circumstances. There is no doubt that pressure of business in many fiscals' offices often leads to several months' delay before non-custody cases are processed, and the lesson for the defence must always be: scrutinise the complaint carefully to ensure (1) that section 331 of the 1975 Act applies; and (2) that it has been complied with. A court strike is not a good excuse for not executing a warrant: see *Tudhope* v. *Mathieson*, 1981 S.C.C.R. 231.

Lord Emslie's comment that the proceedings required to be commenced no later than June 15, 1977 has been held to be *obiter*; the prescriptive period is computed *de die in diem*: see *Lees* v. *Lovell*,1992 S.C.C.R. 557.

2.   Young v. Smith
1981 S.L.T. (Notes) 101

An accused person challenged the competency of summary proceedings in respect of a complaint served on him. His plea was repelled and, after conviction, he appealed by stated case.

OPINION OF THE COURT: "The circumstances which led to the appearance of the appellant before the sheriff to challenge the competency of the proceedings were these: (i) The alleged contraventions of the statute were said to have occurred on 22 October 1979; (ii) On Friday, 18 April 1980—four days before the expiry of the period of six months after 22 October 1979—the procurator fiscal applied for and was granted a warrant to apprehend the appellant. He received it in the afternoon just as his office was about to close, and when the clerical staff were leaving; (iii) Monday, 21 April 1980 was a public holiday; (iv) On Wednesday, 23 April the procurator fiscal posted a letter to the appellant informing him of the grant of the warrant to apprehend him 'in respect of the driving incident on 22 October 1979 when you were charged with contraventions of sections 2, 6, 25 and 143 of the Road Traffic Act 1972.' The letter went on to say: 'I write to give you an opportunity of attending the Court voluntarily in respect of those matters and you should therefore attend on Thursday, 1 May at 10 a.m. in Court 1, when the complaint will be served on you. Please note that failure to attend on that date will result in the Warrant being passed to the Police for enforcement.' This letter was probably dictated on Tuesday, 22 April. It was received by the appellant on Thursday, 24 April; (v) On 1 May 1980 the appellant accompanied by his solicitor duly presented himself at court in response to the invitation in the procurator fiscal's letter. The complaint with which this stated case is concerned was then served upon him, and the court adjourned the diet without plea until 15 May 1980 when the plea to competency was tabled. ...

In this case it is common ground that no complaint was served upon the appellant before the expiry of the statutory time limit of six months. If these proceedings against the appellant are to be saved, accordingly, it must be because, in the particular circumstances of this case, they are saved by s. 331(3), properly understood.

For the appellant the submission was that in the events which happened there was no 'execution' of the warrant at all within the meaning, and for the purposes, of s. 331(3), and, in any event, there was no 'execution' thereof without undue delay. Subsection (3) is in effect an escape clause for a prosecutor who has, for one reason or another, failed to satisfy the primary intention of Parliament, namely, to serve a complaint upon statutory charges within the six months' time limit laid down. If, therefore, the prosecutor is to pray it in aid to permit prosecution for alleged statutory offences, otherwise out of time, he must comply strictly with the terms of the escape clause, strictly construed. The language of subs. (3) is clear and unambiguous. If the prosecutor chooses to obtain a warrant to apprehend in the hope of beating the time bar nothing short of execution of that warrant (without undue delay) will satisfy the requirements. Execution means just what it says. In the case of a warrant to apprehend there is and can be no execution unless and until apprehension on the faith of the warrant has been effected. Nothing less will do and the writing of the letter of 23 April and the appellant's appearance in court on 1 May in response to it, do not and cannot demonstrate that the only conditions upon which out of time prosecution may be saved have been satisfied. In any event in respect that the prosecutor could have written and posted his letter to the appellant on 18 April, or at the latest on 23 April, and that there was no sound explanation tendered for his failure to do so, it cannot be said that there was execution of the warrant without undue delay.

The response of the learned advocate-depute was that it cannot be supposed that it was the intention of Parliament that where a prosecutor has obtained the grant of a warrant to apprehend an accused within the six months' period, he must, whatever the circumstances, proceed to the physical arrest of the accused in order to be able to rely upon s. 331(3). To construe s. 331(3) in this way offends against common sense and considerations of humanity. The object of obtaining such a warrant is to secure the early attendance at court to receive service of a complaint and there can be no good reason why, if an accused who learns of the existence of the warrant wishes to attend voluntarily, and so achieve the object of the warrant, he should nevertheless be denied that opportunity and be subjected to the humiliation and indignity of arrest and, perhaps, search of his house, merely to enable the prosecutor to satisfy the supposed demands of the subsection. It has for long been the practice for prosecutors, in possession of a warrant to apprehend, in cases such as this, to adopt the procedure followed by the procurator fiscal here. Until this case it has never been contended, far less held, that where an accused has appeared voluntarily in court in response to a letter like the letter of 23 April 1980, the prosecutor may not rely on s. 331(3) because the warrant to apprehend, which it was not necessary to enforce, was not followed by the arrest of the accused. Upon a proper construction of the subsection in accordance with the demands of common sense steps such as were successfully taken here on the faith of the existence of the warrant to apprehend, constitute sufficient 'execution' of the warrant. Alternatively the question of execution of such a warrant without delay should be seen to arise for the purposes of s. 331(3) only where, in order to secure the objective of the warrant, it has been necessary to proceed to its execution.

The first question for consideration is whether what happened in this case can possibly be said to amount to 'execution' of the warrant to apprehend. The answer to that question is, emphatically, no. There cannot, in law, be 'execution' of such a warrant until what is authorised is carried out in accordance with its terms. The next question—and the real question in the case—is whether a prosecutor who has obtained, timeously, a warrant to apprehend, and who seeks to rely upon s. 331(3) must, in order to do so, proceed to the physical arrest of the accused in all circumstances, and even where it is quite unnecessary to do so. We do not consider that it is permissible to presume that Parliament had any such intention. Section 331 of the Act of 1975 repeats and re-enacts the provisions of s. 23 of the Summary Jurisdiction Act of 1954 which, in turn, echo the terms of s. 26 of the corresponding Act of 1908. Section 331(3) provides that, for the purposes of the section, 'proceedings shall be deemed to be commenced on the date on which a warrant to apprehend ... is granted, if such warrant is executed without undue delay.' It does not provide that it is an essential prérequisite of the competency of such proceedings that the warrant to apprehend therein mentioned be enforced according to its terms in all circumstances, including the circumstances that enforcement, without undue delay, is rendered quite unnecessary by the voluntary action of the accused concerned. Execution of such a warrant without undue delay on the prosecutor's part may be forestalled by an accused's voluntary surrender of his person to the court when, for example, he has learned of its issue before effective action upon it has been possible. Is it to be supposed that Parliament contemplated that such an act by an accused should have the result of denying to the prosecutor any right to rely on s. 331(3)? We think not. Such a situation is not covered by the language of the subsection. We are certainly not prepared to accept that an accused who learns of the existence of a warrant to arrest him on statutory charges, and who makes his arrest unnecessary by voluntarily submitting himself to the jurisdiction of the court before it has been enforced without undue delay should be able thereby to nullify subsequent proceedings merely by asserting that he had not been subjected to an unnecessary arrest. Nothing in the language of s. 331(3) compels us to hold that unnecessary arrest on the faith of a competent and timeously obtained warrant to apprehend is a condition precedent to the prosecutor's right to rely upon it. The reference in the subsection to execution without undue delay must, we think, be understood to deal only with the situation in which a warrant to apprehend for the purposes of s. 331(3) requires to be enforced and is enforced. It has no application whatever to the situation in which, there having been no undue delay on the prosecutor's part, the necessity for its execution is elided by the voluntary act of the accused concerned which achieves the entire objective of the warrant. That is the situation disclosed by the facts of this case and for this reason, and upon our construction of s. 31(3), the appeal fails.

We are fortified in the conclusion which we have reached upon a consideration of the practice referred to by the learned advocate-depute and by the sheriff in his note. Counsel for the appellant did not attempt to deny the existence of this practice over many years. As we have said s. 331(3) is not new. It is, to say the least, surprising if the competence of this practice had been in doubt—a practice which is consistent with good sense—that it should not have been the subject of decision on appeal long since. It has not, as we understand it, hitherto been challenged in the context of s. 331 and its statutory precursors, and it is perhaps instructive to observe that in the recent but unreported case of *Aird* v. *Macnab* [noted at [1971] J.C.L. 114] the appellant was a seafarer whose frequent absences defeated the efforts of the police to arrest him on the faith of a warrant granted within the six months' time limit. In the result he came before the court after a substantial lapse of time and the warrant was never, in fact, executed. The only challenge to the competency of the proceedings was on the ground of alleged 'undue delay' and in affirming the competency of the proceedings the sheriff and this court on appeal were well aware that the arrest of the accused, for long impossible, had in the event proved to be unnecessary.

Upon the whole matter and upon grounds which differ from those on which the sheriff's decision was based we affirm that decision and refuse the appeal by answering the question in the case in the affirmative. In so doing we have not overlooked the question of 'undue delay.' The sheriff held that there was none and we see no ground upon which his decision on that matter—a question of fact, circumstances and degree—could possibly be disturbed (see *Smith* v. *Peter Walker & Son (Edinburgh) Ltd.*, 1978 J.C. 44)."

Appeal refused.

3.   Young v. MacPhail
1991 S.C.C.R. 630

An accused was charged on summary complaint, but pleaded undue delay in the execution of the warrant to apprehend. The sheriff repelled the plea and the accused appealed to the High Court.

LORD COWIE: "The case first called at Perth Sheriff Court on 24th September 1990 and, since there was no appearance, it was continued without plea until 2nd October 1990. Again on that date there was no appearance by the appellant and a warrant was therefore granted for his arrest.

It should be noted that had that warrant not been obtained on 2nd October 1990 the complaint would have become time-barred on 4th October 1990 by virtue of the provisions of section 331(1) of the Criminal Procedure (Scotland) Act 1975, but by obtaining the warrant to apprehend the appellant the proceedings were deemed to have been commenced on 2nd October 1990 by virtue of section 331(3) of the said Act *always provided* that the warrant was executed 'without undue delay'.

Accordingly the sole question in this appeal is whether the warrant for apprehension of the appellant was executed 'without undue delay'.

The facts are that at the time when the warrant to apprehend was obtained the appellant was in prison in Hull and this was known to the procurator fiscal at Perth.

Notwithstanding that knowledge the warrant was not executed until 9th November 1990, being the day on which the appellant was released from prison. It is clear that the warrant could have been executed earlier but it was accepted by counsel for the appellant that that would have entailed transferring the appellant from Hull Prison to the prison at Perth. It is well known that there are difficulties in obtaining the transfer of prisoners from England to Scotland and although there is a recognised procedure for doing so we were informed that it takes about twenty-eight days to complete. Accordingly on that timetable this warrant could not have been executed effectively until 30th October 1990 or ten days earlier than it was in fact executed.

In these circumstances the procurator fiscal had to decide whether to proceed by way of having the appellant transferred to Perth Prison before executing the warrant or waiting a further ten days until the appellant was released from Hull Prison.

He chose the latter course and it was submitted to the sheriff that that amounted to undue delay in executing the warrant, and that accordingly the complaint was incompetent. The sheriff repelled that plea and granted leave to appeal to this court.

Before us in support of the appeal counsel for the appellant put forward two propositions which he extracted from the case of *Smith* v. *Peter Walker & Son (Edinburgh) Ltd.* They were to be found in the opinion of the court delivered by Lord Justice-General Emslie and could be summarised as follows: (1) the question whether there had been undue delay was one of fact, circumstances and degree; and (2) that in order to avail himself of the very limited latitude allowed to him by section 331(3) of the Criminal Procedure (Scotland) Act 1975 the procurator fiscal had to demonstrate that execution of the warrant after the statutory time-limit had expired could, in the circumstances of the case, be regarded as justifiable.

In putting forward these propositions counsel for the appellant recognised that in order to succeed in this appeal he would, in the first place, have to demonstrate that the sheriff had erred in law or in some other material way in reaching his decision on the question of whether there had been undue delay since this question was one of fact, circumstances and degree. He accepted that the decision involved the exercise of the sheriff's discretion but he maintained that it had been exercised wrongly in three respects and that accordingly the question was open for us to decide.

He submitted, first of all, that the sheriff had inverted the onus by stating in his report that the appellant had not demonstrated that the procurator fiscal had exercised undue delay. If that could be said to be a proper reading of what the sheriff says in his report then that would be a sound basis for saying that the sheriff had erred in his approach to this question because it is well recognised that on a question of undue delay it is for the procurator fiscal to demonstrate that there had been none. However, in our opinion the passage referred to by counsel does not fall to be interpreted in that way since it must be read in its context. That context demonstrates that the sheriff was in fact applying the criteria of undue delay and as we have indicated that includes the requirement that it is for the procurator fiscal to demonstrate that no undue delay has occurred.

Secondly, counsel for the appellant submitted that the sheriff had erred in his decision by giving undue weight to the factor of the trouble and expense which would have been caused by transferring the appellant to Perth Prison rather than waiting until he was released from Hull. We do not consider that that is a fair criticism of the sheriff, who clearly had regard to the interests of the appellant as well as the public interest in arriving at his decision.

Finally, counsel submitted that the sheriff had erred because on any view a delay of ten days in executing the warrant between 30th October 1990 and 9th November 1990 was excessive. We are not prepared to give effect to that submission either. The precise period of delay is always a question of circumstances and degree and in our opinion such a period in the context of this case cannot be said to have been undue.

For all these reasons we are not prepared to hold that the sheriff has erred in any of the respects put forward by counsel for the appellant and since the question of whether undue delay has occurred is, in the words of the Lord Justice-General in *Smith* v. *Peter Walker & Son (Edinburgh) Ltd*, one of fact, circumstances and degree, we are not prepared to interfere with the sheriff's decision on this matter.

Even if we had been of a different view and had felt justified in setting aside the sheriff's decision for any of the reasons put forward by counsel for the appellant and had then applied our own minds to the question we would not have differed from the sheriff.

Having regard to the second of the general principles relied on by counsel for the appellant, we are satisfied that the execution of the warrant after the time-limit had expired was in the circumstances of this case 'justifiable'.

As we have indicated, on a fair assessment of the facts in this case the relevant delay was only of ten days' duration and the procurator fiscal was perfectly justified in taking the view that, all things considered, he should delay executing the warrant until the release of the appellant rather than adopting the procedure for having him transferred from Hull to Perth. Certainly that was in the public interest and there was no suggestion by counsel for the appellant that such a course was in any way adverse to the interests of the appellant or prejudicial to his defence.

In all these circumstances we are satisfied that the sheriff reached the correct decision on the plea to the competency of this complaint and we shall refuse the appeal."

Appeal refused.

NOTE

This case is merely one of a number of cases on the question of "undue delay." See, for example, *Lockhart* v. *Bradley*, 1977 S.L.T. 5; *McNeillie* v. *Walkingshaw*, 1990 S.C.C.R. 428; *Kennedy* v. *Carmichael*, 1991 S.C.C.R. 458; *McGlennan* v. *Johnston*, 1991 S.C.C.R. 895.

B.   FRAMING THE COMPLAINT: RELEVANCY AGAIN

The initiating document in summary procedure is a complaint drawn up by the procurator-fiscal. The general principles of relevancy discussed at pp.320 *et seq.* apply equally to summary cases as to those taken in indictment. Forms of complaint, including samples of charges, are to be found in Schedule 2 to the Summary Jurisdiction (Scotland) Act 1954.

(i)   Common Law Charges

Renton and Brown (para. 13–38) say that the safe rule in framing complaints for common law offences is strictly to adhere to the statutory forms. But this can have some odd results.

McLeod v. Mason
1981 S.L.T. (Notes) 109

Three accused were charged that they did "force open a lockfast motor car
... with intent to steal and did attempt to steal." They were acquitted. The
procurator-fiscal appealed by stated case.

OPINION OF THE COURT: "The first charge was a charge of opening a lockfast
motor car in a particular location with intent to steal and the charge libels that
they did attempt to steal. The second charge was a charge that at another locus
the three respondents attempted to force open a lockfast motor car with intent
to steal and that they did attempt to steal. No objection to the relevancy or
specification of the complaint in these terms was tabled at any stage of the
proceedings. Evidence was led and concluded and the sheriff ex proprio motu
decided to question the specification of the two charges. He appeared to think
that because the lockfast places were motor cars it was necessary for the Crown
to libel and prove that the intention to steal was directed at the contents of the
car or directed at the car itself or both. In the absence of such specification he
took the view that it would be wrong to convict the respondents who had had
no notice that the Crown might at the end of the day contend that it did not
matter that they were unable to show that the intention was to steal the car or
the contents or both. In effect, therefore, the sheriff held that the two charges
were irrelevant for want of essential specification. In so holding he misdirected
himself. As many decided cases show the charges as framed in this complaint
were relevant in all essential respects. There was no need for the Crown in
order to establish the commission of a completed crime to show that it was the
intention of the respondents to steal the car or its contents or both. It is quite
sufficient to libel the opening of a lockfast motor car with the criminal intent of
theft and in many cases it will be impossible to prove more. Contrary to the
sheriff's view we do not consider that a verdict of guilt upon a charge thus
libelled presents any real difficulty in the matter of sentencing.

We now turn to the sheriff's second reason for holding the charges not
proven. It was not established, he said, whether the illegitimate object of the
respondents was theft or merely the statutory offence of contravention of
s. 175 of the Road Traffic Act 1972. That is no doubt a perfectly accurate
observation, so far as it goes, but in the circumstances of this case it ought to
have been presumed, in the absence of evidence that the illegitimate intention
was merely contravention of a statute, that the intention was theft.

Upon the whole matter we are satisfied that the sheriff's reasons for holding
the charges not proven cannot be supported. Upon the facts found he ought to
have convicted as libelled and we shall answer the question in the case in the
negative and remit to the sheriff with a direction to convict and to proceed to
sentence."

Appeal allowed.

NOTE

Attempted theft and forcing open a lockfast place with intent to steal are
individual crimes. In charges of attempted theft, the item which the
accused is trying to steal is always specified, while the criminality of
opening a lockfast place with intent to steal is clear from the unauthorised
effraction of the lockfast article. But coupling the two together, without
specifying what is to be stolen, makes this form of charge difficult to
defend logically, hence the sheriff's decision. The accused might have had
a perfectly adequate defence if the charges had specified the article they

were allegedly attempting to steal. The rejection by the High Court of this appeal leads to the conclusion that this peculiar crime consists in "doing something which displays wickedness," which of course is consistent with Humean notions of dole, but inconsistent with modern views of *men rea*. In England, the difficulties highlighted in this case would not have occurred, for the three accused would have been charged with the statutory offence of vehicle interference: see Criminal Attempts Act 1981, s. 9 whereby:

"(1) A person is guilty of the offence of vehicle interference if he interferes with a motor vehicle or trailer or anything carried in or on a motor vehicle or trailer with the intention that an offence specified in subsection (2) below shall be committed by himself or some other person.

(2) The offences mentioned in subsection (1) above are

(a) theft of the motor vehicle or trailer or part of it;

(b) theft of anything carried in or on the motor vehicle or trailer; and

(c) an offence under section 12(1) of the Theft Act 1968 (taking and driving away without consent); and,

if it is shown that a person accused of an offence under this section intended that one of those offences should be committed, it is immaterial that it cannot be shown which it was."

(ii) Contravention of statutes

A complaint (or indeed an indictment) including a charge of contravening a statute must aver facts sufficient to constitute the offence and give the accused fair notice. See also the 1975 Act, s. 312 (*p*)–(*r*).

1. Yeudall v. William Baird & Co.
1925 J.C. 62

An accused company was charged with a contravention of section 29(1) of the Coal Mines Act 1911. The sheriff dismissed the complaint as irrelevant and the procurator-fiscal appealed by stated case.

LORD JUSTICE-GENERAL (CLYDE): "By subsection (1) of section 19 of the Summary Jurisdiction Act, 1908, it is enacted that 'the description of an offence in the words of the statute contravened shall be sufficient.' It follows that, since this alteration of the law, there are many complaints which must be regarded as relevant and sufficient, although they may not have passed muster prior to the Act of 1908. It is therefore in vain to quote cases decided before the 1908 Act, when the requirements of the law in the matter of specification of *modus* were applied rigorously—it may be too rigorously—to summary complaints.

I do not, however, mean to cast any doubt upon the opinions which have been expressed in cases since the Act of 1908, to the effect that, if in the case of a statutory offence some further specification is necessary as a condition of fair notice, the Court has the right to insist on such further specification as a condition of relevancy. But it must be recognised that, since the Act of 1908 became law, the necessity of specifying *modus* has suffered, in the case of summary complaints founded upon statutory enactments, a material modification.

In the present case the accused are charged with having failed to produce an adequate amount of ventilation to dilute and render harmless noxious gases in a particular part of a mine belonging to them. They complain that there is not fair notice of what they are called to meet. I think—having due regard to the nature of the offence—it is fair notice. It is notice that, at the time and place in question, the ventilating system of the pit was defective for its purposes. It is true that the prosecutor does not attempt to trace the defect to its sources, and that the true source may be more or less recondite. But the respondents presumably know their own system—they work it and are responsible for it: the prosecutor is not. A system of ventilation is by its own nature an integral whole, and depends for its efficiency on the co-operative relations of all its parts. The complaint gives the respondents fair notice that, time and place mentioned, their system of ventilation was inadequate to perform its statutory function; and, that being so, I do not think they have any good ground for grievance. In my opinion the complaint complies with the Act of 1908, and is not so defective in respect of want of fair notice as to justify the learned Sheriff-substitute in holding it irrelevant."

Appeal allowed.

NOTE

Section 19(1) of the 1908 Act referred to by Lord Clyde is now section 312(*p*) of the 1975 Act.

2. Macrorie v. Bird
(1911) 6 Adam 527

An accused person was charged on a summary complaint with a revenue offence, in that he did not give full particulars in a statutory declaration required of him under the Revenue Act 1869. The magistrate repelled a preliminary objection to the relevancy of the complaint. The accused was convicted and appealed by stated case.

LORD DUNDAS: "The first question, and indeed in the view I take of it, the only question for consideration here, is whether or not the complaint is relevant and sufficiently charged. I have come to the conclusion that it is not. The appellant is charged with a contravention of the Revenue Act, 1869, section 22, in respect that, on a certain day he did 'deliver a declaration such as is mentioned in the Revenue Act, 1869, section 22, relating to a motor-car numbered S.D. 148, wherein the particulars required by said Act to be therein set forth were not fully and truly stated,' in certain respect which is set forth, 'contrary to said section, whereby you are liable to the penalty of twenty pounds.' With regard to that complaint I would make several observations. In the first place, it is libelled wholly and solely upon one Act, and upon one section of that Act, namely, the Revenue Act of 1869, and section 22 thereof. Next, that Act and that section of the Act cannot and do not apply to a motor-car at all. They apply to carriages; and 'carriage,' as defined by the Act of 1869, excludes the idea of motor-car altogether. Accordingly it seems to follow that no 'declaration such as is mentioned in' section 22, and no 'particulars required by said Act,' could or do refer to a motor-car at all. And, lastly, I would point out that the sole section libelled, namely, section 22 of the Revenue Act of 1869, neither creates an offence nor imposes any penalty therefor. At first sight it is rather difficult to see the connection between the section under which the complaint was libelled and this declaration referring to a motor-car, but the Solicitor-General has bridged the gap by making reference to (I think) section 4, sub-section 3, of the Act of 1888 (Customs and Inland Revenue Act), and section 86 of the Finance Act (1909–10), 1910, and the Treasury regulations as to motor-cars. But he admitted, and in my opinion he was quite right to admit, that to maintain the relevancy and sufficiency of this complaint would have been a hopeless task if it had not been for the provision of the Summary Jurisdiction Act, 1908, section

19(2); and the question comes to be narrowed to this, whether that provision is such as to make proper and relevant this complaint which otherwise would not have been in proper and relevant form. It is enacted by section 19(2) of the Act of 1908, that 'where the offence is created by more than one section of one or more statutes or orders, it shall only be necessary to specify the leading section or one of the leading sections.' I confess that I am not clear as to the precise scope and intention of that enactment, and I should be sorry to attempt to lay down any definition or pronounce any general opinion on the subject. I think that its scope and application will require to be defined by experience, and I further think that the Court will have to go step by step, and that it will be for the Court in every case to say whether the enactment does or does not apply to the particular case before it. It must always be for the Court to decide whether the sections libelled are or are not 'leading sections' within the meaning of the enactment. If one tries to apply the Act in this spirit I cannot think that this section can be said to be the leading section in the matter. It is difficult to see how a section which admittedly has no reference and could have no reference to a motor-car, could be the 'leading section' in a complaint founded on the failure to give particulars in regard to a motor-car. In my opinion the test in each case for the Court to apply must be whether the complaint on the face of it gives to the person charged fair and reasonable notice of what he is charged with, and what offence he is said to have committed; and I do not think it can be said to be fair notice to select as the sole ground libelled one section of an Act, and to reserve the future introduction and application any number of unlibelled sections, some of which may bear directly on the charge. I have already pointed out that the sole section libelled neither creates an offence nor imposes a penalty; and I think it must be at least a minimum of what is required of the prosecutor, that he should give a definite notice in the complaint of the offence which is said to have been committed and the penalty said to be incurred. For the reasons I have stated it seems to me that this particular case does not come within the scope and application of section 19(2) of the Act of 1908; and I do not intend to go into the region of what may require to be laid down in future cases.

I therefore suggest that we should answer the first question in the negative; and, so far as we are concerned in the matter, that disposes of the present case."

Appeal allowed.

NOTE

Section 19(2) of the 1908 Act is now section 312(r) of the 1975 Act. Such mistakes as that made by the prosecution in this case may be curable by amendment, on which see the 1975 Act, s. 335.

3.   Marshall v. Clark
1957 J.C. 68

A bus conductress was charged under statutory regulations with failing to take all reasonable precautions to ensure the safety of passengers in, or on, or entering or alighting from her vehicle. Her solicitor objected to the relevancy of the complaint on the ground that the particular regulations did not specify what were reasonable precautions. He also claimed that the regulations were too vague to infer criminal liability. The objection was repelled, the accused was convicted and an appeal by stated case was presented to the High Court.

LORD JUSTICE-CLERK (THOMSON): "By virtue of section 85 of the Road Traffic

Act, 1930, the Minister of Transport may make regulations as to the conduct of, *inter alios*, conductors of public service vehicles when acting as such. Subsection (2) of that section provides that, if any person to whom any such regulations apply contravenes or fails to comply with any of the provisions of the regulations, he shall be liable to a fine.

The Public Service Vehicles (Conduct of Drivers, Conductors and Passengers) Regulations, 1936, which were made by the Minister of Transport in virtue of that section and which therefore have the force of an Act of Parliament, provide, *inter alia*, that a conductor, when acting as such, shall take all reasonable precautions to ensure the safety of passengers in or on or entering or alighting from his vehicle. The appellant, a conductress, was charged with failing to comply with this regulation. The objection which she took to the relevancy of the complaint was that it is not possible for a Scots prosecutor to frame a relevant complaint based on that regulation. In other words Parliament has stultified itself and, while appearing to create an offence, has failed to do so, as the offence cannot be translated into a relevant charge.

This proposition is on the face of it somewhat startling and would appear to accuse an omnipotent parliament of legislative ineptitude. The ineptitude lies, according to the argument, in the failure of Parliament to point out a standard against which the negligence of the conductress can be measured. As there is no touchstone, there can be no offence. The foundation of this attack on the relevancy is *Allan* v. *Howman* [1918 J.C. 50] which has been followed, not always with great enthusiasm, in a number of cases. I am entirely in agreement with your Lordship's review of this trend of authority and with your conclusion that it should be overruled. I shall confine myself to a few observations on *Allan* v. *Howman* as being the *fons et origo malorum*.

The attitude of the Court is succinctly put by Lord Johnston (at p.53): 'It is for the Order which creates the offence to leave no dubiety as to what the offence is and not to leave it to the Judge who tries the case to determine on evidence, and to a large extent according to his opinion, in what the offence consists.' The Lord Justice-General said (at p.53): 'I seek to throw no blame upon the prosecutor for having laid before the Court an irrelevant complaint. In the circumstances it would have been impossible for him to have done otherwise.' Lord Mackenzie also said (at p.54): 'There are not, at present, materials from which the Procurator-fiscal could construct a relevant complaint ... I cannot assent to the proposition that a man can be charged in a criminal Court on a complaint which merely tells him that he did something unreasonable.'

No doubt in 1918 regulations of this kind were something of a novelty but since then a good deal of water—some of it pretty muddy—has flowed under Parliamentary bridges and we are now habituated not only to regulations but to legislative enactments of all sorts couched in similar general terms. For myself—quite apart from the duty which rests on both prosecutors and Courts to do what Parliament tells them—I feel no particular anxiety that the liberty of the subject will be imperilled or fair trial impeded because an enactment made by Parliament or on Parliamentary authority says that a man must take adequate care or reasonable steps and so forth and leaves it to the Judge to determine on evidence in what the offence consists. The theory of *Allan* v. *Howman* is that no measuring rod has been provided in advance. I see no reason why the measuring rod should not emerge at the trial. This is the only practical way to look at the matter. When a man is accused of doing something unreasonable or of failing to take adequate precautions or reasonable steps or the like, the accusation is made in regard to some particular sphere of human activity in which he is engaged and of the ordinary incidents of which he must be well aware. It may be in regard to his family, his factory, his farm, his driving of his motor car or similar activities. In some of these activities the reasonableness or adequacy of his conduct may be easily enough ascertained by the Judge. In others, the situation may be complicated and a good deal of investigation may be necessary. Where there is a complicated background, if the prosecutor does not provide material sufficient to enable the Judge to reach a proper conclusion, the case against the accused will fail. It is all a question of circumstances. But in neither class of case is there any impropriety or injustice in leaving the measuring rod to be sought at the trial. In the varied activities of modern life it would be impracticable to provide it in advance.

Once it is established that the *ratio decidendi* of *Allan* v. *Howman* is unsound and that a statutory enactment does not necessarily lose its force by its failure to provide in advance a standard by which the conduct of the accused is to be measured, this stated case is plain sailing. As your Lordship has observed, there may be enactments so defectively worded that it is impossible to spell a relevant charge out of them. This particular regulation presents no such problem. There is, moreover, very full specification of the *modus* and indeed no question of relevancy in its secondary sense of lack of specification was raised. I wish, however, to reserve my opinion as to whether a complaint following literally the terms of a widely drawn and unspecific enactment might be successfully attacked on the ground of absence of fair notice, either as irrelevant in the strict sense of the word or as lacking in specification. On this aspect issues of some nicety might arise, the solution of which would turn on the precise terms of the enactment and the relative complaint."

Appeal dismissed.

NOTE

On specification in statutory offences, see generally Renton and Brown, paras. 13–43 to 13–47, and also paras. 13–52 to 13–57 for a discussion of the law on exceptions and qualifications in describing statutory offences and the situation where an offence is said to have been committed in a special capacity.

C.   Are the Proceedings Competent?

Just as in solemn proceedings, in a summary case it may be necessary to take a preliminary plea to the competency. This should be done at the first calling of the complaint: see 1975 Act, s. 334(1). The same competency points may be taken as in a solemn case (on which, see, *supra*, pp.335 to 342); a plea in bar of trial is also a plea to the competency of the proceedings, as the following case on delay shows.

Normand v. Rooney
1992 S.C.C.R. 336

An accused person was charged on summary complaint with an offence which had allegedly been committed in December 1989. The complaint was dated May 13, 1991. The accused pleaded that there had been undue delay in proceeding. The sheriff dismissed the complaint, applying the tests laid down in *Tudhope* v. *McCarthy*, 1985 S.C.C.R. 76. The Crown appealed; while the appeal was pending, the High Court in *McFadyen* v. *Annan*, 1992 S.C.C.R. 186 overruled *Tudhope* v. *McCarthy*.

LORD JUSTICE-GENERAL: "As the learned advocate-depute remarked in the course of his address in this appeal, an unfortunate consequence of the tests which were applied in *Tudhope* v. *McCarthy* is that they have tended to focus too much attention on the question of undue delay and to divert attention from the true issue in these cases, which is that of gross prejudice. He submitted that the sheriff had erred in precisely this respect in the present case because, having satisfied himself that there was delay which could fairly be regarded as undue, he concluded that the result of the undue delay was that the respondent would suffer gross or grave prejudice, without embarking upon any discussion of this matter or providing any explanation of the respects in which the respondent would be likely to suffer prejudice which could properly be described as gross or grave. But the advocate-depute also submitted that the sheriff ought not to have entertained the argument at all at this stage, on the ground that the respondent's plea was one which could not competently be taken under section 334(1) of the Criminal Procedure (Scotland) Act 1975 since it was not truly a plea to the competency. The complaint itself, which alleged a simple common law assault, was perfectly competent and there was no doubt as to the right of the prosecutor to proceed with it, subject only to the question whether for him to do so would amount to oppression. The respondent's plea, being a plea in bar of trial, could only be stated at the trial diet, since no provision had been made in the statute in regard to summary proceedings for it to be taken at any other stage.

Mr Drummond accepted that the respondent's plea was essentially a plea in bar of trial rather than a plea to the competency of the complaint. But he submitted that it was nevertheless open to the respondent to state his objection at the preliminary stage in terms of section 334(1). Any other approach to the procedural issue would lead to unnecessary confusion and delay. On the merits of the argument he accepted that the sheriff did not appear to have addressed himself to the question of gross prejudice as a separate issue from that of undue delay. But he submitted that the question of gross prejudice was closely linked to the passage of time, which had been so extreme in this case that it was bound to have affected the recollection of witnesses. In the result, although the sheriff had applied the test which had now been held to be unsound, his decision could be regarded as soundly based on the essential question as to whether there was such prejudice as to amount to oppression.

The first point which must be decided in this case therefore is whether the respondent's plea on the ground of undue delay was one which the sheriff could competently entertain in terms of section 334(1) before the respondent was called upon to state how he pleaded to the charge. The argument which the advocate-depute submitted on this issue is one which has not, I think, been taken in any previous case where an objection on the ground of delay has been stated by the accused. It was prompted by the comment by several of the judges in *McFadyen* v. *Annan* that an objection on this ground is not, as was submitted to the sheriff in the present case, one as to the competency but was properly to be regarded as a plea in bar of trial. That being so, said the advocate-depute, it was not open to be stated as 'an objection to the competency or relevancy of the complaint or the proceedings' in terms of section 334(1). In my opinion, however, this argument is unsound, because it involves a misreading of the wording of the subsection. As I see it, the phrase which I have just quoted can be analysed into three parts. The objections which may be stated at this stage comprise objections (1) as to the competency of the complaint, (2) as to the relevancy of the complaint and (3) as to the proceedings. In the present case the respondent has not sought to challenge the competency of the complaint or its relevancy. But he has challenged the proceedings on the ground of undue delay, and this is an objection—in essence, one of oppression—which it was open to him to take, prior to pleading, in terms of section 334(1). In my opinion a failure to state his objection at that stage would have led to the consequence, in terms of the concluding part of the subsection, that he would have been allowed to state it at any future diet only with the leave of the court and then only on cause shown.

This brings me to the merits of the question which the sheriff had to decide. As the advocate-depute correctly pointed out, the respondent's approach was concerned too much with the issue of undue delay and it paid too little regard to the point of gross or grave prejudice, which is the essential matter on which an objection about oppression must depend. It is not altogether surprising therefore than when he came to examine the arguments the sheriff followed the same approach, but in my opinion in doing so he fell into error. The only argument which appears to have been put to him on the issue of prejudice was that the respondent found himself in the position, several months after the events alleged in the complaint, of having to prepare a defence in circumstances where he might still be called upon to give evidence as a Crown witness at the trial of the complainer. But, as Lord Justice-General Emslie pointed out in *McFarlane* v. *Jessop* [1988 S.C.C.R. 186] at p.191, prejudice as a result of lapse of time is a feature common to many prosecutions and cannot be avoided. So the real question is whether the prejudice for that reason can be regarded as gross or grave—either adjective will do, because the test in each case is the same.

It was said that in all probability it would be at least two years after the alleged events before the respondent's trial would call in court. As matters have turned out, because of inevitable delays in the disposal of this appeal, that prediction has now been exceeded. But I do not find in this argument a sound basis for concluding that any prejudice to the respondent which is due to delay is so gross or grave as to amount to oppression. There was no suggestion that the respondent suffers from difficulty in recollecting the events which gave rise to the charge against him in the complaint or that he has suffered any other material disadvantage in the preparation of his defence which is due to the delay. It was suggested by Mr Drummond that since he might be required first to give evidence at the trial of the complainer in his capacity as a police officer, he would be at a particular disadvantage which would not affect civilian witnesses, because he would be bound to give evidence which identified himself as the other man involved in the incident. That may be so, but it does not follow that the respondent will be grossly prejudiced in his defence to the charge which has been brought against him in this complaint. It seems unlikely that the question of identification will be an issue at his trial. The essential questions are likely to be whether he struck the complainer as he is alleged to have done and whether, if he did, this was an assault.

In *McFadyen* v. *Annan* the Solicitor-General suggested that the test which should be applied in cases under summary procedure where oppression was said to have resulted from delay in bringing an accused to trial is whether the prejudice was so grave that the sheriff or justice could not be expected to put the prejudice out of his mind and arrive at a fair verdict. His formulation of the test was accepted by the majority of the judges in that case as being entirely consistent with the principles set out by Lord Justice-General Emslie in *Stuurman* v. *H.M. Advocate* [1980 J.C. 111] at p.122, which was a case where the alleged oppression arose because of pre-trial publicity. But it became clear in the course of argument in the present case that in cases where the alleged oppression is due to delay in bringing the case to trial, the sheriff or justice may require to take account of the delay, rather than ignore it, in his assessment of the evidence if he is to arrive at a fair verdict. The Solicitor-General's suggestion that the test is whether he can be expected to put the prejudice out of his mind seems to me therefore to require some explanation when applied to cases of that type, of which the present is an example. The essential point which he was seeking to make, and which the decision in *McFadyen* v. *Annan* has accepted as accurate, is perfectly clear. What he was seeking to do was to translate the test which was described in *Stuurman* with regard to proceedings on indictment to cases which have been brought under summary procedure. In solemn proceedings the question is whether the risk of prejudice is so grave that no direction by the trial judge, however careful, could be expected to remove it. That formulation creates no difficulty, because it leaves open the question whether the appropriate direction is to ignore the events which are alleged to be prejudicial or to take them into account in the assessment of the evidence. In its application to summary proceedings the test has to recognise that the sheriff or justice is the judge of the facts at the trial, and it is from his mind that the prejudice has to be removed. He has to be able, if he is to arrive at a fair verdict, to remove from his mind the harm or injury which has resulted from the delay. If the harm or injury is so grave that no sheriff or justice could be expected to remove it from his mind, the test of oppression will be satisfied and the plea must be sustained. In effect the test is whether the prejudice is so grave that no sheriff or justice could be expected to reach a fair verdict in all the circumstances.

Applying that test to the circumstances of the present case as they have been described in the sheriff's report, I am of the opinion that any prejudice which the respondent may suffer due to the delay is not of that character. I see no reason to doubt on this information that the sheriff who hears the evidence at the trial will be able to arrive at a fair verdict, after making such allowances as may be appropriate for any disadvantage which the respondent may suffer due to the lapse of time which has occurred. Accordingly, I think that we should allow this appeal and quash the sheriff's decision to dismiss the complaint. It follows that we should remit the case to the sheriff to receive a plea from the respondent and therefore to proceed as accords."

Crown appeal allowed.

NOTE

Excerpts from *McFadyen* v. *Annan* are to be found, *supra*, at pp.352 to 358. Sheriff Gordon in his commentary to *Normand* v. *Rooney* at 1992 S.C.C.R. p.341 suggests that the real question in assessing questions of delay is whether the accused can receive a fair trial.

CHAPTER 13

CITATION AND RECORD

A. CITATION—FORMALITIES

Once the complaint is duly prepared, the next usual step is service. Various modes of service are competent, on which see generally the 1975 Act, ss. 315–319. It is essential that, where citation is necessary, the formalities thereof should be properly carried out, otherwise the proceedings may be imperilled. By section 334(6) of the 1975 Act, it is not competent for any person appearing to answer a complaint, or for a solicitor appearing for the accused in his absence, to plead want of due citation or informality therein or in the execution thereof.

1. Beattie v. McKinnon
1977 J.C. 64

An accused person was convicted of a statutory offence and appealed by stated case.

LORD JUSTICE-CLERK (WHEATLEY): "The appellant was charged with the statutory offence of a contravention of section 6(1) of the Road Traffic Act 1972 (cap. 20) on 4th March 1976, and by reason of the provisions of section 331(1) of the Criminal Procedure (Scotland) Act 1975 (cap. 21) proceedings had to be commenced within six months of that date. By subsection (3) of that section proceedings are deemed to be commenced on the date on which a warrant to apprehend or cite the accused is granted, if such warrant is executed without delay.

On 16th August 1976 a police officer served a copy of the complaint in the appropriate statutory form on the appellant personally. However, apart from the fact that the copy signature of the clerk of court assigning the diet had not been inserted in the copy complaint, the date when the appellant had to appear in court was also omitted. There was a date stamp '31 August 1976' on the front of the copy complaint, but it was not maintained, nor could it be, that this was due notice to or proper citation of the appellant to appear in court on 31st August 1976. On that date, however, the case was called in court and understandably neither the appellant nor anyone on his behalf appeared. The Procurator-fiscal produced an *ex facie* valid execution of citation by a police officer, and on the strength of that the Sheriff granted a warrant to apprehend the appellant under section 338 of the 1975 Act. This warrant was not executed, but in due course the appellant came to hear about it. He consulted his solicitor who contacted the Procurator-fiscal and the latter arranged for the appellant to appear in court in answer to the complaint on Monday 20th September 1976. On that day the appellant and his solicitor arrived at the court only to find the building shut, it being the Autumn holiday in Paisley. They turned up on the following day and the case was called, whereupon the appellant's solicitor submitted a plea to the competency of the proceedings basically on the ground that the citation was inept in respect that no date of a diet was contained therein. The Sheriff repelled this plea for reasons which will be stated later, whereupon a plea of not guilty was tendered on behalf of the appellant and a

434

diet of trial was fixed for 20th December 1976. When the case was called on this date, the plea of not guilty was withdrawn and a plea of guilty tendered. The Sheriff thereupon admonished the appellant and disqualified him from holding or obtaining a driving licence for one year and endorsed his licence. The question stated by the Sheriff for the opinion of the Court is: 'Was I right in repelling the objection to the competency of the proceedings?'

The Sheriff explains that he accepts that the appellant was not properly cited, but states that he can see no reason why that should invalidate the appearance of the appellant to answer the charge on 21st September 1976. He considers that the situation is covered by section 334(6) of the Act of 1975 which enacts that it shall not be competent for any person appearing to answer a complaint to plead want of due citation or informality therein or in the execution thereof. Moreover, he expresses the view that on the information provided to the Court the warrant to apprehend was properly granted and that the appellant's apprehension (he was never in fact apprehended) and subsequent appearance in Court were entirely lawful; and that any defects in the earlier citation were superseded by the granting of the warrant and the actual appearance in Court of the appellant who had been served with a copy of the complaint.

The alleged offence took place on 4th March 1976 and accordingly proceedings had to be commenced by midnight on 3rd September 1976 (section 331(1)). Proceedings could be deemed to have commenced on the date on which the warrant to apprehend or the warrant to cite was granted if executed without delay (section 331(3)). The learned Advocate-depute accepted that the citation was inept by reason of the failure to state a date therein, thereby echoing the view of the Sheriff, and also reflecting the view of this Court. He argued, however, that the defect in the citation could not be pleaded by the appellant because of his appearance in Court on 21st September 1976 and the provisions of section 334(6) of the Act. That being so proceedings in this case must be deemed to have commenced when the copy complaint and the imperfect citation were served on the appellant on 16th August 1976, which was within the statutory period of six months.

In order successfully to invoke the provisions of section 334(6) the Crown must establish that the omission to state a date in the citation was 'want of due citation or informality therein.' The absence of a date cannot be said to be an informality. It was crucial for the appellant to know when he had to appear in court and he could not possibly know this from the citation served on him. 'Want of due citation' may be a temporal matter—for instance, failure to observe the proper *induciae*, e.g., in relation to sections 315(2) and 319(1) of the Act. In our opinion, it cannot be held that failure to state the date on which an accused is to appear in court is simply want of 'due citation.' It is not citation at all. For these reasons we are of opinion that section 334(6) is not applicable in the circumstances of this case and, that being so, proceedings cannot be deemed to have commenced in this case on 16th August 1976. The Advocate-depute did not argue that even if this were so the proceedings could be deemed to be commenced on 31st August 1976 when the warrant to apprehend was granted, which was still within the six-month statutory period, but as the Sheriff seemed to think that they could, we shall deal with that point too. The warrant to apprehend must presumably have been granted by the Sheriff under section 338(1)(c) of the Act. That section reads: 'Where the accused on a summary prosecution fails to appear at a diet of which he has received intimation, or to which he has been cited, the following provisions shall apply—(c) the Court may grant warrant to apprehend the accused.' The appellant here neither received intimation of the diet nor was cited to attend on 31st August 1976. The prerequisite of the application of the section was accordingly not satisfied. While there was *ex facie* evidence that the appellant had been cited to attend on that date, *de facto* he had not. The section does not say that the Court may grant the warrant to apprehend if satisfied that the accused has received intimation or has been cited to attend at the diet. It says that non-appearance when the accused *has* received intimation or *has been* cited to the diet authorises the granting of a warrant to apprehend. A warrant granted when these conditions have not been fulfilled is not in our opinion a warrant which can be founded on to date the commencement of proceedings in terms of section 331(3).

We accordingly hold that the proceedings were not commenced within the statutory six-month period and that the objection to the competency was well founded. We therefore answer the question of law in the negative."

Appeal allowed.

NOTE

So the lack of proper citation was fatal to the Crown case. Forms of complaint and citation are now regulated by the Act of Adjournal (Consolidation) 1988, rr. 87 *et seq.* Furthermore, some statutes, such as the Road Traffic Act 1988, make special provision for service of particular documents, such as notices of intended prosecution.

2. McGlynn v. Stewart
1974 S.L.T. 230

An accused person was convicted of careless driving and appealed by stated case.

LORD JUSTICE-CLERK (WHEATLEY): "The answer to the questions raised in this stated case turns on the interpretation of s. 179(2) of the Road Traffic Act 1972 and its application to the circumstances of the case.

On 11th August 1972 the appellant was the driver of a motor car which was in collision with another motor car on a public road on the Island of Islay. After the accident the appellant was cautioned by the police that he need not make a statement, and that the facts would be reported to the Procurator-fiscal. He was given no other warning by the police. The appellant was at that time taking his annual holiday in Islay, something which he has done for the past nine years. He gave to the police both his home address in Pencaitland in East Lothian and his holiday address in Islay, informing them that he would be at the latter address until 2nd September 1972. He did not have his driving licence with him, and in view of the information that he would be in Islay until 2nd September 1972 a police constable marked the appropriate form H.O./ R.T.I. 'to be produced after 2/9/72.' This information was conveyed by the police to the respondent, who is the Procurator-fiscal for the area, with his office at Campbeltown. On 18th August 1972 the respondent sent a notice of intended prosecution addressed to the appellant at his Pencaitland address. The appellant did not receive this notice, which was returned to the respondent marked 'no answer.' As a matter of courtesy the respondent sent a second but out-of-time notice on 1st September 1972. This was the only notice received by the appellant.

When the trial took place it was argued by counsel for the appellant that there could not be a conviction of the charge under s. 3 of the Road Traffic Act 1972, which had been preferred against the appellant, since the provisions of s. 179(2) of that Act had not been obtempered. Section 179(2) provides that a person prosecuted for an offence under the section shall not be convicted unless ... '(c) within ... fourteen days a notice of the intended prosecution specifying the nature of the alleged offence and the time and place where it is alleged to have been committed, was (ii) . . . served on him or on the person, if any, registered as the keeper of the vehicle at the time of the commission of the offence; and the notice shall be deemed for the purposes of para. (c) above to have been served on any person if it was sent by registered post or recorded delivery service addressed to him at his last known address, notwithstanding that the notice was returned as undelivered or was for any other reason not received by him.'

Section 179(3) provides that 'the requirement of subs. (2) above shall in every case be deemed to have been complied with unless and until the contrary is proved.'

The sheriff rejected this argument, holding, under reference to the case of *Phipps* v. *McCormick* [1972] R.T.R. 21, that the appellant's address at Pencaitland was the place where the appellant would normally expect to receive correspondence, and that a notice of intended prosecution sent to that address was in the circumstances a fulfilment of the requirement imposed by s. 179(2). He then proceeded to convict the appellant of the charge under s. 3.

Two questions are submitted for the opinion of this court. The first is whether the notice of intended prosecution sent to the appellant on 18th August 1972 was addressed to him at his last known address in accordance with the provisions of s. 179(2). The second is whether the sheriff was entitled to find the appellant guilty of a contravention of s. 3 of the 1972 Act.

It was not argued that the sheriff was not entitled to convict under s. 3 on the evidence adduced on the merits, but it was strongly argued that the conviction was bad because the provisions of s. 179(2) had not been obtempered. Thus, the answer to the first question determines the answer to the second question. In *Phipps* v. *McCormick* (supra), Cook, J., giving the leading judgment, in which Lord Widgery, C.J. and Bean, J. concurred, said in relation to the corresponding provision of s. 241(2) of the Road Traffic Act 1960 as amended by the Road Traffic Act 1962: 'It seems to me, however, that the purpose of the service provision in the subsection requiring that the notice should be served at the last known address is that the notice should be served at a place where he would normally expect to receive correspondence, an address which, from his point of view, has some degree of permanence.'

The Crown in this appeal, like the sheriff in the court below, founded strongly on this opinion as justifying an effective service on the appellant in this case. In *Phipps* v. *McCormick* the defendant was involved in a motor accident on 20th September 1970, out of which the proceedings arose. Following the accident he was admitted to hospital, a fact of which the prosecutor was aware. On 23rd September 1970 a notice of intended prosecution was sent by recorded delivery addressed to the defendant at his home. At the time when the notice was sent the defendant was still in hospital, but he was in fact discharged therefrom on the following day, 24th September 1970. There is nothing in the report to indicate that the prosecutor knew for how long the defendant would be in hospital. Cooke, J., held that in the circumstances the hospital did not satisfy the requirements of his formula, whereas the defendant's home address did.

In my opinion, the proper approach to the issue is to look at the intendment of the subsection. It is manifestly to provide a prospective accused with notice within a reasonable time of the intention to prosecute. In the interest of fairness this is plainly desirable, because it not only prevents the person involved from being kept unduly long in a state of suspense without knowing whether or not he is going to be prosecuted, but it enables him, if need be, to collect evidence for his defence at a time when the recollection of potential witnesses is fresh. The 'deeming' provisions of s. 179(2)(c) were introduced originally in the 1962 Act to cover circumstances revealed by cases such as *McLeod* v. *Anderson*, 1961 J.C. 32, 1961 S.L.T. 297 in Scotland, and *R.* v. *London Quarter Sessions, ex p. Rossi*

[1956] 1 Q.B. 682 in England. In regard to the latter—cf. Lord Parker, C.J., in *Burt* v. *Kirkcaldy* [1965] 1 All E.R. 741, at p. 743.

It is quite clear from the reported cases that although the intention of the subsection is to certiorate the prospective accused of the proposal to institute appropriate proceedings, the requirements of intimation may be satisfied in certain circumstances even if he has not personally received the notice or has not personally been served with it, e.g., if it has been received on his behalf by an agent. Thus the non-receipt personally of the notice is not in itself any criterion, a fact which is underlined by the final words of the subsection. What then is the construction to be given to the phrase 'his last known address'? It is not necessarily the permanent residence, or for that matter the permanent business address. In my opinion it must also mean an address at which it is reasonably to be expected that the person on whom the notice is served will receive it. Hence the conditions desiderated by Cooke, J., namely (1) that it is a place where a person would normally expect to receive correspondence, and (2) that it is an address which, from the person's point of view, has some degree of permanence. Thus, if a person is absent from home for short periods on business or pleasure, posting of the notice to his home address would normally satisfy the requirements of the sub-section. Manifestly, since the prosecutor cannot be expected to know the person's movements, there ought to be a place where it is reasonable to expect that a posted notice will be received by him. But is the sending of a notice to a person's normal home address sufficient to qualify for the provisions of the subsection in every case, or has each case to be considered on its own facts to see whether some other address is the appropriate one? In my opinion it must be the latter.

If the prosecutor is informed that the person will not be at his home address (at which he would normally receive correspondence) for the currency of the statutory period during which the notice has to be served, but will be at another stated address during that period, then, unless the statute otherwise requires, common sense as well as fairness seems to demand that the notice should be sent to the latter and not the former address. I doubt if Parliament intended that a notice would be good if sent to an address where it was known that it would not be received by the addressee, although there was another address where it was known that it would be received.

In the present case the prosecutor was informed that the appellant would be at the address in Islay during the whole currency of the statutory period. When Cooke, J., referred to the address having some degree of permanence, he was presumably recognising that this was a relative term, depending on circumstances. So far as the prosecutor knew, the appellant was going to be in Islay during the whole of the effective period and beyond, and so during that period there was going to be permanence of address in Islay, relatively speaking. Accordingly, in my view, the address in Islay, (1) was the last address known to the prosecutor for the purpose of this statutory notice, (2) was the place where for the purpose of *this* correspondence (i.e., the notice) the appellant would normally expect to receive it, and (3) had a sufficient degree of permanence, relatively speaking, to make it the effective one for the receipt of the notice as part of his correspondence during this period. I am, therefore, of the opinion that in the circumstances here present the appellant has proved that his home address did not satisfy the provisions of s. 179(2), whereas the Islay address did. I would add that if, for any reason, the appellant had left Islay for home (or elsewhere) within the statutory period and before the notice was served, without informing the prosecutor, and the notice was thereafter timeously posted to the Islay address, the appellant could not have successfully challenged the validity of the service on the ground that it should have been served at his home address, in view of the provisions of s. 179(4). I would accordingly answer both questions of law in the negative."

Appeal allowed.

NOTE

This case, of course, relates only to the specific wording of section 179 of the Road Traffic Act 1972, which is now section 1 of the Road Traffic Offenders Act 1988. The phrase "last known address" is not used in section 316 of the 1975 Act. See also *Laird* v. *Anderson* (1895) 2 Adam 18, where it was held that where the mistake renders the proceedings fundamentally null, appearance by the accused does not cure the defect.

3.   Jessop v. Christie
1986 S.C.C.R. 7

An accused person was charged with road traffic offences and took a plea to the competency of the proceedings on the ground of defective citation.

SHERIFF RUSSELL: "The present summary prosecution relates to a number of Road Traffic Act offences alleged to have been committed on 14th December 1984. A copy of the complaint was served (by post) on the accused in the body of which it was stated that his case would be heard on 3rd May 1985 at 10.30 a.m. This document was signed by a procurator-fiscal depute and according to the wording of the citation form told the accused that he must answer the complaint on or before the date the case was to be heard. It then advised him to do one of three things: (1) attend personally, or (2) arrange for your lawyer or some other person to attend, or (3) write to the court. The document then states 'What will happen if I do nothing?'—the answer in red ink is given—'A warrant may be issued for your arrest.'

It now transpires that the case never did call in court on 3rd May 1985, the reason according to the depute fiscal being that there was a mistake between the date on the citation and the date on which the depute fiscal intended to call the case which was on 8th May 1985. This latter date apparently appears in small type on the top of the principal complaint along with some reference numbers and initials but without further explanation. It was submitted for the Crown that there was a mistake in the date in the citation of the accused and he should have been cited for 8th May not 3rd May. At least there was a clear inconsistency between the two dates and the case never called on 3rd May 1985.

On the day to which the accused was cited, he had in court a solicitor who waited all day in court, but the case never called. I am informed this solicitor even spoke at the end of the roll to the depute fiscal taking the court to enquire but was told that he knew nothing about that case.

The next stage in this unhappy drama occurred on 8th May 1985 when the depute fiscal called the case and, not surprisingly, there was no answer by anyone. The case was on the motion of the depute fiscal continued without plea to 29th May. On 10th May a letter was sent from the procurator-fiscal's office to the accused and purporting to be signed by a secretary in the fiscal's office. This letter referred to the previous citation for him to appear on 8th May and requir[ed] him to answer the complaint on 29th May at 10.30 a.m. No action resulted from this letter but it is not disputed that the accused received it. This procedure was repeated on 29th May when the case called again and there was no appearance for or on behalf of the accused. Again a letter dated 31st May was sent by the fiscal's office to the accused requiring him to appear in person on 12th June or to write indicating how he was pleading and that if he did neither of those things the court would be moved to grant a warrant for his arrest. This letter was signed by a depute fiscal on this occasion and was served personally on the accused.

On 12th June a solicitor for the accused appeared in court and stated that he was attending in response to the letter that had been received and that he took objection to the competency and relevancy of the prosecution. The accused through his solicitors was not called upon to plead to the complaint and a diet of debate on the competency was fixed for 10th July 1985 which took place before me on that date.

Mr Garden for the accused submitted that his client had been cited for 3rd May, that a solicitor had been in court that day and the case never called. The accused's obligation was to appear in answer to the citation; if as the Crown now said there had been a mistake in the citation date, the accused would be unaware of this. He never received any citation to appear on 8th May. When the solicitors for the accused appeared in court on 12th June this was specifically stated as being in response to the letter of 31st May 1985 from the fiscal's office; the solicitor had immediately tabled a plea to the competency. Therefore it was said the citation was either no citation at all as it had the 'wrong date' or if it was an effectual citation it was for the 3rd May and on that date the case never called whereupon the instance fell and there was no warrant or justification for calling the case on 8th May. Thereafter there was therefore no case to continue.

I was referred to *Beattie* v. *McKinnon* [1977 J.C. 64], to *Scott* v. *Annan* [1981 S.C.C.R. 172], and to section 334(6) of the Criminal Procedure (Scotland) Act 1975. In *Beattie* where the copy complaint served personally on the accused had no date for the accused to appear in court, it was held (on appeal) that the absence of a date resulted in it being no citation at all. Although the accused with solicitors came to court in *Beattie* after 'hearing' that a warrant had been issued, the court regarded the warrant as not capable of being founded upon where the condition that the accused had been cited to the diet had not been fulfilled (section 338(*c*) of the 1975 Act). Therefore the court held that section 334(6) was not applicable in the circumstances as there was no citation at all.

Conversely in *Scott* v. *Annan* it was assumed that no citation of the accused took place from the outset and when the case called in court in his absence it was continued without plea and the accused then received a letter requiring him to appear in person on 30th December. On that date the accused appeared in person by himself and on being called upon to plead, pled not guilty and a trial was fixed. When a solicitor appeared for him at the trial diet and took a plea to the competency, the sheriff held that the accused had appeared and answered the complaint and therefore under section 334(6) he was not allowed to plead want of due citation. This decision was upheld on appeal.

The depute fiscal in argument pointed out that the accused had received a service copy of the complaint with the appropriate forms as required by the Act of Adjournal 1984 (Schedule 3). All that had happened was that the wrong date was put by mistake on the citation. He said that the proper date was 8th May typed at the top of the principal complaint. I venture to wonder which one contains the mistake and whether it could not equally well be said that the wrong date was put on the principal complaint. Curiously enough the Crown apparently do not have a copy of the citation sent to the accused and it was only by Mr Garden producing the accused's copy to me that it becamed quite clear that the accused *had* been cited for 3rd May and not 8th May. The fiscal argued that the subsequent letters were enough to give the accused notice of the subsequent diets and that there was no distinction between the diets of 8th May and 12th June.

It appears to me that if an accused person is cited by the procurator fiscal for a certain day, and his case is not called on that day, then there is no warrant for the first calling taking place on any later date. Such a date would be unknown to the accused and it thereby could be any date at the whim of the prosecutor.

In my view, therefore, any continuation of the diet after 8th May would be equally tarnished with the same defect. I consider, however, this situation to be qualified by one matter which can cure the apparent defect—that qualification is where at any calling of the case an accused person or his solicitor appears 'to answer a complaint' within the meaning of section 334(6) of the 1975 Act; for in that event it is not then competent for him to plead 'want of due citation or informality therein or in the execution thereof.'

In the present case I am satisfied that neither the accused nor his solicitor has ever appeared to answer the complaint. I accept that it was in response to the letter of 31st May that Mr Garden appeared in court and tabled a plea to the competency. Herein lies the vital distinction between this case and *Scott* v *Annan* where the accused in person pled not guilty and a trial was fixed. He was then barred by section 334(6) from taking issue with the citation. In the present case that section has no application as the complaint has never been 'answered.' It is perhaps unfortunate that in *Scott* v. *Annan* the presiding sheriff had not asked the accused whether he had received a copy of the complaint and whether he understood it, before asking him how he plead. Sheriff Gordon's commentary at 1981 S.C.C.R. 176–178 also takes this point and is a most useful analysis of the situation.

It is also surprising to find that *Beattie* v. *McKinnon* was not cited in *Scott*. In the former no date on the service was held to be no citation at all and the warrant granted for non-appearance could not be founded on. In *Scott*, where there had been no citation at all the very fact of pleading guilty by the accused in person brought in section 334(6).

In the present case I do not consider that the proceedings could be deemed to have commenced on 8th May and certainly nothing called on the 3rd May. A wrong date on the citation is as crucial in effect as no date at all if the case never called on the 3rd May. Indeed if nothing called on 3rd May then there was no other date at all in the citation. Accordingly, I will sustain the plea to the competency and hold that no prosecution was ever validly commenced here. (See also Renton and Brown 5th ed., para. 13–79.)

A subsidiary argument was presented for the defence that the instance fell on 3rd May at midnight when the case never called. This might have applied to a continued diet or where there has been an assigned diet but neither of these will apply to 3rd May (see Renton and Brown, para. 14–02). It is only in assigned diets and continued diets that the instance falls in summary prosecutions. The situation is, however, by no means the same in solemn procedure.

In the whole circumstances I will dismiss the complaint. It is for the prosecution to consider their position in relation to time bar now. The events are said to have occurred on 14th December 1984. Accordingly six months after that date (by midnight on 13th June 1985 [sic]) any further prosecution became time-barred."

Complaint dismissed.

NOTE

It was held also in *Scott* v. *Annan* that section 334(6) does not apply to cure a failure to serve a notice of penalties under section 311(5) of the 1975 Act. The citation provisions of the 1975 Act do not clearly state how service of such a document must be proved, but see *Muir* v. *Carmichael*, 1988 S.C.C.R. 79; *Cowan* v. *Guild*, 1991 S.C.C.R. 424.

B. Is Citation Essential?

In normal practice, whether the offence is statutory or at common law, the accused is served with the complaint prior to his being called upon to plead. But this does not appear to be essential.

Kelly v. Rae
1917 J.C. 12

An accused person was convicted of a statutory offence and appealed by bill of suspension.

> LORD JUSTICE-CLERK (SCOTT DICKSON): "The complainer's senior counsel ultimately supported the bill of suspension on two only of the grounds set forth in his printed case. Of these grounds the two he has selected, although I do not think them good grounds, are undoubtedly the best.
>
> The first is that no complaint was served upon the complainer. I think the objection is a bad one. I can find no warrant in the Summary Jurisdiction Act of 1908 for the proposition that, until a complaint is formally served upon an accused person, the proceedings against him are not initiated, and that, consequently, everything which is done in the case, unless and until a complaint has been *served*, is null and void. In this case the complainer on Saturday 12th August 1916 was arrested by the police *in flagrante delicto*, and was charged with an offence under the Street Betting Act, 1906, section 1. On the following Monday he was brought before the magistrate, and a charge of committing the offence in question was made against him in his presence. He pled not guilty, and the Court adjourned the diet to the 21st and (as the minutes of procedure bear) ordained the accused to appear then. Upon that day he appeared in Court, represented by a law-agent, and the complaint was read over to him. In my opinion this complied sufficiently with the statutory requirements anent the initiation of summary criminal proceedings.
>
> Section 18 of the Summary Jurisdiction Act, 1908, provides that all proceedings shall be instituted by complaint in the form contained in Schedule C. That clearly is an imperative requirement, but no reference is there made to citation or service of the complaint. In section 29 it is provided that, where the accused is present at the first calling of the case, the complaint, or the substance thereof, shall be read to him. That seems to me to imply that service is not necessary, because, if service were an essential, there would be no reason for providing that the complaint should be read. What, however, is still more striking, is the provision in section 32(2), that, in the circumstances there dealt with, 'the prosecutor shall, if desired by the accused, furnish him with a copy of the complaint if he has not already got a copy.' It seems to me that that provision is consistent only with the view that in certain circumstances service of the complaint is not an essential to the institution of the proceedings. I think one of the cases—it may, indeed, be the only case—where such service can be dispensed with is, where the accused is, as in the present case, apprehended *in flagrante delicto*. This seems to be in accordance with what has been an ancient practice in summary proceedings of this kind. I think that practice is founded on good sense and on good law, and that no reason has been stated for our interfering with it. I am, therefore, of opinion that the suspension, so far as founded upon that ground, ought to be refused."

Appeal refused.

NOTE

To a certain extent, this case has been overtaken by section 311(5) of the 1975 Act which *requires* service of a complaint and notice of penalty in relation to a statutory offence, whether the accused is to be cited or in custody. But these statutory provisions apply only to statutory offences. The only other provision which seems to *require* service of a complaint is section 357(1)(*a*) of the 1975 Act, which relates to the situation where the prosecutor wishes to libel a previous conviction. So, where the accused is a first offender charged at common law, it appears that no service of a complaint is necessary. See also section 334(1) of the 1975 Act. Thankfully, for, *inter alios*, duty solicitors, this situation is never now encountered in practice. Proceedings without a complaint may constitute oppression—see *Carlin* v. *Malloch* (1896) 2 Adam 98.

C. THE RECORD OF PROCEEDINGS

In summary cases this is governed by section 359 of the 1975 Act which provides:

"Proceedings in a summary prosecution shall be conducted summarily *viva voce* and, except where otherwise provided, no record need be kept of the proceedings other than the complaint, the plea, a note of any documentary evidence produced, and the conviction and sentence or other finding of the court:

Provided that any objections to the competency or relevancy of the complaint or proceedings, or to the competency of admissibility of evidence, shall, if either party desires it, be entered in the record of the proceedings."

It is incompetent to proceed in the absence of the principal complaint, which must be produced at all diets, before and after conviction: see *McSeveney* v. *Annan*, 1990 S.C.C.R. 573; *Wilson* v. *Carmichael*, 1991 S.C.C.R. 587. The minutes of procedure are kept by the clerk of court.

1. Barr v. Ingram
1977 S.L.T. 173

An accused person appealed by bill of suspension against his conviction, on the ground that the proceedings were fundamentally null. His trial had proceeded in stages on the due date, with various interruptions throughout the day so that the court might deal with other business. None of these interruptions were treated as adjournments nor minuted by the sheriff clerk. When the bill came before the High Court, it was conceded that the interruptions were effectively adjournments.

OPINION OF THE COURT: "Despite the terms of the first plea-in-law for the complainer in the bill, and the averments in support of it, his counsel did not dispute that the sheriff had adjourned the trial on the various occasions referred to or that it was competent for him to do so. The gravamen of his complaint was that these adjournments were not minuted and authenticated on each occasion, as they ought to have been. His argument entailed an assertion from which he did not shrink, that when an adjournment to a later period on the same day, was granted during the course of the day on which an accused had been cited to attend for his trial, not only should the adjournment be minuted, but the time on that day to which the trial was adjourned should also be minuted. If, when that time arrived, the court was not in a position to re-start the trial, the case should nevertheless be called and further adjourned to a later specified time, again to be minuted and authenticated in the minute of proceedings. Incidentally, if at that point another case was in progress, the same procedure would have to be followed for that case.

The learned advocate-depute accepted that if a trial had to be continued from one day to another, the date and time of the adjourned diet should be recorded and authenticated in the minute of proceedings. He submitted, however, that this did not apply to adjournments during the course of the day on which the accused had been cited to attend for trial. An accused is required by his citation to attend court on the date specified therein in the knowledge that his case must be dealt with that day or continued formally to another day when the same considerations would apply. When he attends on the day of citation he can object to any continuation or adjournment proposed, it being for the court to decide whether it should be granted. A citation to attend court on a particular day extends to midnight on that day. The considerations underlying the fixing of a peremptory diet are threefold: (1) to secure fairness to the accused and not prejudice him by not having a fixed date for the hearing of his case; (2) convenience of the public—e.g. witnesses who are under citation to attend the trial; and (3) to avoid delays in the hearing of the case. Accordingly, if the court adjourns the trial at any time to a later hour on that day in order to dispose of other business, the accused is still under citation to be in attendance on that day, and there is no real risk of prejudice or unwarranted delay in the disposal of the case, since the basic underlying considerations referred to are observed. Another consideration, however, was the reasonable expedition of the court's whole business for the day. In the instant case what were described by counsel for the complainer as 'interruptions' but what were in fact unminuted adjournments by the court were for the general convenience, since other people had been brought to the court on the same day, as the history of events narrated by the sheriff principal disclosed. So far as the complainer was concerned there was no loss of certainty about when his case would be heard, namely on that day, and no real inconvenience had been suffered by him. In the circumstances the absence of a recorded entry of the adjournments in the minute of proceedings was not fatal to the convictions and sentences.

We are only concerned here with adjournments during the day on which the complainer was cited to attend the court. In that narrow context, the submission by complainer's counsel was based on the decision in *Corstorphine* [1910 1 S.L.T. 86] and the dicta of Lord Justice-Clerk Macdonald and Lord Low therein, to which reference will be made shortly. The advocate-depute conceded that if the particular passage in the Lord Justice-Clerk's judgment correctly represented the law, there was no answer to the submission made by complainer's counsel, since admittedly the adjournments here had not been minuted. He argued, however, that the passage in question did not properly represent the law and should not be followed.

We accordingly turn to examine the case of *Corstorphine*. In that case an accused was charged with different offences in two separate summary complaints. On the conclusion of the evidence in the first case the sheriff-substitute found the accused guilty but delayed sentence until the conclusion of the evidence in the second case on the same day, whereupon he proceeded to sentence the accused on the first charge. There was no written record of the adjournment in the first case, and the court suspended the conviction and sentence on the ground that this omission was fatal to the proceedings. The passage in the Lord Justice-Clerk's opinion on which counsel for the complainer founded is to be found in 1910 1 S.L.T. at p.87: 'In my opinion the proceedings in the first case fell, in respect that no means were taken to keep them in life by adjourning them either to a later period of the same day or to a new day. It is quite true that the first case was both tried and finally disposed of on the same day; but that does not seem to me to make any practical difference, because a case must be kept going, either by its being proceeded with or by its being formally adjourned. That was not done, and I am of opinion that the omission is fatal to the proceedings in the first case.'

Lord Ardwall agreed, saying that as far as he knew it was universal practice both in the sheriff court and in the High Court that all adjournments must be minuted. Lord Low accepted that if the adjournment was to a later date it had to be minuted but had obvious doubts on the applicability of that rule to an adjournment to a later time on the same day, regarding that as too technical a point. However, apparently in deference to the longer experience of his colleagues in such matters, he did not dissent from the judgment proposed.

If the decision in *Corstorphine* was correct, and the dictum of the Lord Justice-Clerk therein correctly states the law, then ex concessu the omission to record the adjournments in the minute of proceedings in the instant case was fatal to the proceedings.

Counsel for the complainer maintained that *Corstorphine* was merely illustrative of a cardinal rule which had been enunciated by Hume and endorsed as early as *H.M. Advocate* v. *Fraser*, and had been approved by Lord Justice-Clerk Cooper in *Hull* v. *H.M. Advocate*, 1945 S.L.T. at p.202. Moreover, *Corstorphine* had stood unchallenged in the 68 years since it was decided, and the Lord Justice-Clerk had stated in his opinion therein that the rule—which was a fixed rule—had always been one which our courts had observed (1910 1 S.L.T. at p.86). That was still the position in our courts both in principle and in practice. He sought recent support for his contention in the case of *Law* v. *H.M. Advocate*, but the facts in that case were different, and the irregularity which foundered the conviction was an interruption to deal with another case without adjourning the case that was being heard.

While it would appear from Lord Justice-Clerk Macdonald's opinion that he considered that all and every adjournment required to be minuted, counsel was ultimately constrained to admit that, standing the decision in *Tocher* v. *H.M. Advocate* the rule was not universally applicable. When that seemed to weaken his argument, he sought to make a distinction between what he called 'physical interruptions' and 'procedural interruptions.' Whether such a distinction is justified in principle only requires to be considered if the extension of the rule by Lord Justice-Clerk Macdonald was correct.

The question is not what is the rule but how far does it extend? If the adjournment is to another day, it has been clearly established by an anthology of decisions that the adjournment must be minuted. The rule applies whether the procedure is solemn or summary: *McLean* v. *Falconer* (1895) 1 Adam 564, per Lord Adam at p.567. Does the rule apply to adjournments within the day of citation?

The recording of adjournments is not one of the matters which successive statutes have required to be inserted into the record of proceedings—cf. s. 42 of the Summary Jurisdiction (Scotland) Act 1908; s. 38 of the Summary Jurisdiction (Scotland) Act 1954; and s. 359 of the Criminal Procedure (Scotland) Act 1975. The rule is founded on common law, and it was accepted by both parties here that its inclusion in the matters which had to be recorded fell within the phrase 'except where otherwise provided,' in all the forementioned sections. The Lord Justice-Clerk in *Corstorphine* so treated it. The genesis of the rule is said to be found in Hume's *Commentaries*, vol. ii at p. 263. What is said there is: 'the diet of a criminal process is a peremptory diet . . . Unless expressly continued by an act of Court on the day of compearance, the libel must be called therefore on that day, and in some way or other disposed of; otherwise the particular action, or *instance* as we call it, perishes, and can never afterwards be stirred or resumed ... unless the diet be continued to another day, by an act of Court. But so it may be, by an entry in the Book of Adjournal ... The reason is obvious why the diet is peremptory in a criminal process ... [it] requires the personal presence of the accused, whose anxiety and distress must be considered: Not to mention the witnesses and persons of assize, who cannot be kept waiting indefinitely, out of indulgence to the prosecutor, who ought to be finally resolved and fully prepared, before he stir in a matter of such importance.' The rule thus stated clearly relates only to a continuation to another day, and does not relate to a case which is 'disposed of in some way or another' on the day of the peremptory diet, as was the case here. This passage in Hume was the basis of the views expressed in Alison and Macdonald's *Criminal Law*, and in *Hull* itself and in the reported cases cited by Lord Justice-Clerk Cooper therein (1945 S.L.T. at p.202) (with the exception of *Corstorphine*) the adjournment in question was one to another day. When the rule was being considered, as for example by Lord Justice-General McNeill and Lord Justice-Clerk Hope in *Fraser*, it was in relation to an adjournment to a future date.

It was said by counsel for the complainer that Lord Justice-Clerk Cooper had endorsed the decision in *Corstorphine*, but Lord Cooper was referring to the passage in Hume cited supra and was dealing with the position where the diet is not called or duly adjourned or continued on the date of citation. The Lord Justice-Clerk in *Corstorphine* (with the approval of Lord Ardwall) stands alone in applying the rule to an adjournment or continuation to a later hour on the date of the preremptory diet. The decision in *Corstorphine* was in direct conflict with the decision in the earlier case of *McIntyre* v. *Linton*, where another trial had been interposed during the trial of the accused, but the court held that this in itself was no ground for a suspension. There were no opinions delivered in that case, and it was not referred to either in argument or in the opinions in *Corstorphine*. Nonetheless it was a case to which attention should have been paid, and reasons stated (and if need be expedients adopted) for giving a contradictory decision. Lord Justice-Clerk Macdonald, after examining the rule, simply extended it to adjournments during the date of citation without giving any reasons for doing so, and without examining the considerations which justify the application of the rule to an adjournment to a future date to see whether such considerations require the extension of the rule to adjournments to a later hour on the day of citation. Some of these considerations were examined by Hume and by Lord Justice-Clerk Hope in *Fraser* at p.16, and these and others were submitted to this court by the advocate-depute as noted supra. In our opinion the dangers and/or the prejudice which the rule was devised to avoid relate only to an adjournment to a later day and do not arise when an adjournment is simply to a later hour on the date of the citation. The reasons why it was thought necessary to have the adjournment minuted in the former type of case do not arise in the latter one. The fact that the case is either completed on the date of citation or is continued by an adjournment duly minuted to a later date is sufficient to give an accused adequate protection. We are accordingly of opinion that the extension of the rule by *Corstorphine* to adjournments during the date of citation was not justified and must be overruled. Thus the fact that an adjournment on the day of citation is not minuted is not per se a ground of suspension. If the practice of minuting such an adjournment had been one of long standing and universal application there might have been difficulties in altering it. It would seem from the case of *McIntyre*, however, that the practice was not universal in those earlier days, and it is clear from the sheriff principal's report that 'interruptions' or adjournments during the day of citation, such as those complained of, are not minuted in the sheriff court today—a practice which is not outwith our own experience. The operation of the *Corstorphine* rule would have made the work in some of the already over-burdened sheriff courts today an almost intolerable task, but if it had been a rule which the principles of the common law required to be observed only legislation could have altered it. It is with some satisfaction, therefore, that we have been able to find that the *Corstorphine* view of the law is not justified.

We accordingly refuse to pass the bill."

Appeal refused.

One can almost hear the sighs of relief from sheriff clerks up and down the country. Indeed, the next case again shows the High Court's unwillingness to overrule convictions on excessively technical grounds.

2.   Pettigrew v. Ingram
1982 S.L.T. 435; 1982 S.C.C.R. 259
An accused person appealed by bill of suspension against his conviction.

LORD JUSTICE-CLERK (WHEATLEY): "An accused person presented a bill of suspension to the High Court of Justiciary in which he craved suspension of a pretended conviction and sentence recorded against him at Forfar Sheriff Court, on the ground that the sheriff clerk had failed to minute until 18 September 1981 an adjournment of the proceedings ordered on 17 September 1981. The complainer argued that this failure rendered the whole proceedings fundamentally null. The facts are not in dispute. On 10 September 1981 the complainer appeared in court to answer the complaint and pled guilty. On that date the sheriff deferred sentence until 17 September and ordained the complainer to appear to produce his licence. When the case called on 17 September, the complainer was not present and the sheriff again deferred sentence until 24 September 1981 and ordained the complainer to appear on that date. On 24 September the complainer appeared with his solicitor, when the sheriff fined him £50 and disqualified him from driving for a period of three years. The sheriff clerk did not on 17 September 1981 record in the minute of proceedings the adjournment ordered by the sheriff on that date, and the explanation given by the respondent is that, due to pressure of business, the sheriff clerk was unable to minute this adjournment until the morning of 18 September 1981. It is not disputed that the adjournment was ordered by the sheriff on 17 September, but the submission by counsel for the complainer was as previously noted that that order was of no effect unless recorded in the minute of proceedings before midnight on 17 September.

There is no doubt that the minuting of the adjournment ordered by the sheriff on 17 September was essential to the validity of these proceedings—*Barr* v. *Ingram*, 1977 S.L.T. 173 at p.176; but the question is whether the failure to minute the adjournment eo die is a fundamental nullity or merely an irregularity which is not fatal to the validity of the proceedings.

Section 430(1) of the Criminal Procedure (Scotland) Act 1975 (hereinafter referred to as 'the 1975 Act') requires 'any order of a court of summary jurisdiction ... [to] be entered in the record of the proceedings in the form, as nearly as may be, of the appropriate form contained in Part V of Schedule 2 to the Summary Jurisdiction (Scotland) Act 1954 or in an Act of Adjournal under this Act, which shall be sufficient warrant for all execution thereon and for the clerk of court to issue extracts containing such executive clauses as may be necessary for implement thereof.' The section re-enacts verbatim s. 56 of the Summary Jurisdiction (Scotland) Act 1954, which itself was a re-enactment of s. 53 of the Summary Jurisdiction (Scotland) Act 1908. Any doubt whether the word 'order' in s. 430(1) of the 1975 Act includes an order adjourning the diet would seem to be removed by reference to Pt. V of Sched. 2 to the 1954 Act, which includes a form of entry in 'the minutes of procedure' for adjournment. So, on the basis that s. 430(1) of the 1975 Act requires adjournments of diets to be entered in the minutes of procedure, neither that subsection nor any other statutory provision requires that a record of an order of court adjourning a diet must be made and signed on the day when the order was made. This is undoubtedly the proper procedure, but it is not required expressly or impliedly by statute.

The answer to the question whether the adjournment requires to be minuted on the day on which the court made the order can be found in the case of *Furnheim* v. *Watson*, 1946 S.L.T. 297; 1946 J.C. 99. In that case there was a delay of 16 days in recording the conviction and sentence of an accused, owing to the absence of the clerk on holiday, yet the court refused to quash the conviction on the ground of fundamental nullity. The Lord Justice-Clerk (Cooper) said this (1946 S.L.T. at p.301): 'Now, I am extremely reluctant in this or in any other case to attempt to lay down rigid cast-iron rules to regulate the day-to-day practice of inferior criminal Courts; but, it does appear to me that the Act of 1908, though it nowhere in express terms prescribes after what interval the record or minute of the proceedings may be signed by the clerk or by the Judge, plainly implies that that shall be done as soon as reasonably possible, and, I should think, in almost every case on the day on which the sentence is pronounced or order made. I do not attempt by any generalisation to state the rule more strictly than that, if that is the rule—the rule of good statutory practice—and if in particular it is essential, as I think it is, that the authentication of the record should, in any event, be complete before extract or execution, then the delay which occurred in this case from 4 August until 20 August, a period of 16 days, attributable merely to the fact of the absence of the depute clerk on holiday, was quite unjustifiable, and I do not think that this Court can do otherwise than condemn laxity of the type which this case displays and which in some cases might be fatal to the proceedings. But while that is so, the question which remains for us as the serious question is—what is to be the effect upon the proceedings which have taken place in this case?' Later on his Lordship said: 'Finally, it is, I think, necessary to note that in this instance we are not concerned with a breach of an exact statutory requirement, for, as I have observed, there is no exact statutory requirement prescribing when the record must be authenticated.' He concluded: 'I suggest to your Lordships that this is a case where, while we can certainly hold that the proceedings were irregular and characterise them as such, nevertheless the interests of justice do not require that these proceedings should be set aside. On the contrary, on a fair view of the general obligation imposed on the Court by section 75 of the Act of 1908, it is, in my view, right that we should, while condemning the irregularity, decline to visit it with the extreme penalty.' The general obligation to which the Lord Justice-Clerk referred to in the context of *Furnheim* was the penultimate provision of s. 75 of the 1908 Act that no conviction should be quashed unless the High Court was of opinion that the accused had been prejudiced in his defence on the merits and that a miscarriage of justice had resulted thereby. This provision appeared in s. 454(2) of the 1975 Act but was repealed by para. 14 of Sched. 3 to the Criminal Justice (Scotland) Act 1980 and replaced in the context of this bill in more general terms by s. 453A(1), which relates to miscarriage of justice in criminal proceedings. There is, in our opinion, nothing in the summary procedure legislation since 1908 which affects the statement of the law by the Lord Justice-Clerk in *Furnheim*, a statement with which we respectfully agree. We consider that this was a statement of general applicability and was not confined to the circumstances of that particular case. On that view we regard it as apposite to the circumstances of the instant case.

The authorities primarily relied upon by counsel for the complainer related to the peremptory nature of criminal diets and the fact that if a diet is not called or duly adjourned or continued on the date in the citation the instance falls—Lord Justice-Clerk Cooper in *Hull* v. *H.M. Advocate*, 1945 S.L.T. 202; 1945. We do not require to follow counsel through that tract of authority, which is not in dispute. If counsel was right in his submission that the oral intimation in court on 17 September of the adjournment to 24 September was not sufficient to keep the instance alive after midnight on the 17 September because the adjournment had not been minuted by then, he would of course succeed. But in view of the decision which we have reached regarding the minuting of the adjournment, which was executed before the adjournment diet was reached, the diet was duly adjourned on 17 September. That kept the instance alive and the proceedings on 24 September were accordingly valid. On any view there was not, and could not be, any suggestion that this delay had prejudiced the complainer, who had pled guilty, nor could it be said that what was done here had resulted in a miscarriage of justice. We therefore refuse to pass the bill."

Appeal refused.

NOTE

As with many procedure niceties, the crucial question is thus whether the accused has suffered any prejudice. As a matter of good practice, minuting should be done at the time. Errors in the record may be corrected under section 439 of the 1975 Act. But if there is no minute at all, the case falls.

3. Heywood v. Stewart
1992 S.C.C.R. 42

An accused pled guilty to certain charges on summary complaint on May 22, 1991. The sheriff adjourned the diet until June 12, 1991 for reports. The clerk noted this on the side of the complaint, but no formal minute was prepared. On June 12, 1991 the sheriff noticed the absence of a minute and dismissed the complaint. The Crown appealed by Bill of Advocation.

LORD JUSTICE-GENERAL: "It is stated in the bill that the plea which was tendered by the respondent on 22nd May 1991 was noted on the principal complaint, as was the date of the adjourned diet of 12th June 1991. But it appears that these details had merely been noted by the clerk on the side of the principal complaint. As the sheriff points out in his report, this was merely an aide-mémoire in his own form of shorthand, from which an appropriate minute could be prepared in due course when he had time to do so. These annotations were no doubt in one sense a record of the proceedings which took place on 22nd May 1991. But they were not minutes of procedure in the form set out in Schedule 2 to the Summary Jurisdiction (Scotland) Act 1954 to which section 309 of the Criminal Procedure (Scotland) Act 1975 refers, and more importantly they were not signed by the clerk of court.

The sheriff was invited to take the view that the clerk's annotations were capable of amendment in terms of section 439(1) of the 1975 Act. That subsection provides that it shall be competent to correct an entry in the record of proceedings insofar as that entry constitutes an error of recording or is incomplete. It was submitted that there was no requirement in the Act that a minute had to be completed by any particular date and, since the respondent had suffered no prejudice, that the sheriff should, in the exercise of this power, order that a record of the proceedings on 22nd May 1991 be completed in the prescribed form. The sheriff was not convinced that his powers of correction enabled him to take this course, and although the bill contains averments that he was in error in taking this view, the Solicitor-General did not seek to support this argument. He recognised that the absence at the adjourned diet of a signed minute of the proceedings on 22nd May 1991 constituted a fundamental defect in the proceedings which was incapable of being cured.

There is ample authority to support this view. As Lord Justice-General Emslie pointed out in *Barr* v. *Ingram* [1977 S.L.T. 173] at p.176, it has been clearly established by an anthology of decisions that where a diet is adjourned to another day the adjournment must be minuted. Furthermore, since an adjournment can proceed only on an order of the court, the minute which records the adjournment must be signed if it is to take effect. In *McLean* v. *Falconer* [(1895) 22 R.(J.) 39; 1 Adam 564] the sheriff adjourned the diet but, since the interlocutor appointing a day for the next diet was not signed, it was held that the subsequent proceedings were incompetent. The objection was that the case must be treated as if there had been no interlocutor at all, since, as Lord McLaren said at p.568, an interlocutor which is unsigned is no interlocutor. There is no express requirement in the 1975 Act that an adjournment must be minuted or that the minute which records the adjournment must be signed. As was pointed out in *Barr* v. *Ingram* at p.176, the recording of adjournments is not one of the matters which successive statutes have required to be inserted into the record of proceedings, although the form of an appropriate minute to this effect is contained in Schedule 2 to the Summary Jurisdiction (Scotland) Act 1954. There is no doubt, however, that the common law requires that these things must be done if there is to be an effective adjournment to another date. The only relaxation which has been provided by the statutes is that an order of the court, other than a warrant of apprehension and search, may be signed either by the judge or by the clerk of court. So it is sufficient if the minute of proceedings which records the adjournment is signed by the clerk of court.

The Solicitor-General recognised that, in the absence of a signed minute, he could not properly argue that the sheriff's decision to dismiss the complaint was erroneous. It follows that, as he in effect invited us to do, we must refuse to pass the bill. But the Solicitor-General took the opportunity to draw to our attention a further difficulty which he said had been raised by the sheriff's helpful note in this case and to which no satisfactory answer was available in the authorities. It is, as he pointed out, a cardinal rule in our criminal procedure that a criminal diet is a peremptory diet, and unless it is expressly continued by an act of the court on the date in the citation the instance falls and cannot be resumed: Hume on Crimes, ii, 263; *Hull* v. *H.M. Advocate* [1945 J.C. 83], per Lord Justice-Clerk Cooper at p.86. What then is the position if no minute has been prepared and signed by midnight on the date when the adjournment to another day is ordered by the court? The rule as described by Hume is that the diet must be expressly continued by an act of the court on the day of compearance, and if that rule is applied according to its terms there would, it was suggested, seem to be no escape from the conclusion that if no signed minute was in existence by the end of that day the instance falls and all further proceedings in the case are incompetent. Yet in *Pettigrew* v. *Ingram* [1982 S.C.C.R. 259] it was held that, since there was no exact statutory requirement prescribing when the order must be recorded, the late recording of the adjournment in that case—and it was recorded on the very next day after the date when the adjournment was ordered by the sheriff—did not render the proceedings a nullity. A contrast was drawn between what was said at p.261 to be undoubtedly the proper procedure, which was for the record of the order to be made and signed on the day when the order was made, and the effect on the case if this was not done.

The decision in that case was based on a consideration of *Furnheim* v. *Watson* [1946 J.C. 99]. In that case there was a delay of sixteen days in the signing of the minute of proceedings, including the record of conviction and sentence by the clerk of court. It was held that, while the delay was unjustified and the proceedings were irregular, there was no fundamental nullity. It was observed that although there was no exact statutory requirement as to when the record or minute of the proceedings was to be signed by the clerk or by the judge, it was plainly implied by the Act that this should be done as soon as reasonably possible and that the authentication of the record should in any event be complete before extract or execution: see the opinion of Lord Justice-Clerk Cooper at p.106, with which the other judges concurred. No doubt this statement of the rule was the foundation for the comment in *Pettigrew* v. *Ingram* at p.262 that, since the minuting of the adjournment in that case was executed before the adjournment diet was reached, the diet was duly adjourned on 17th September. But the Solicitor-General submitted that that conclusion was illogical, given the peremptory nature of the original diet and the requirement that there should be an act of the court on that date if the diet was to be adjourned to another day. It seems also to be in conflict with the recognition in *Smith* v. *Bernard* [1980 S.L.T.(Notes) 81] at p.82 that a formal minute, duly signed, had to be in existence at the latest before midnight to keep the instance of the complaint alive.

We observe that the Solicitor-General's argument was the same argument as that which was advanced for the complainer in *Pettigrew* v. *Ingram* and was rejected in that case. The question for us is whether the decision in *Pettigrew* v. *Ingram* must now be regarded as unsound and open to review by a larger court. There is also a question whether the present case provides an appropriate opportunity for this to be done. We are not persuaded that the decision in *Pettigrew* v. *Ingram* requires to be reviewed. It is true, as the sheriff points out in his report, that *MacLean* v. *Falconer* was not cited in *Furnheim* v. *Watson* and that *Furnheim* v. *Watson* was concerned not with an unsigned interlocutor in a case where an adjournment had been ordered but with the late signing of a final interlocutor recording conviction and sentence after the diet of trial. But the decision in *Pettigrew* v. *Ingram* cannot be treated as having been reached without a full consideration of the authorities. It is quite clear from what Lord Justice-Clerk Wheatley said in the last paragraph of his opinion at p.262 that the court in that case were referred by the complainer's counsel to the authorities about the peremptory nature of criminal diets and to the fact that if a diet is not called or duly adjourned or continued on the date of citation the instance falls. Nevertheless it was held that the statement of the law about the effect of the irregularity which is to be found in *Furnheim* v. *Watson* was of general applicability and was not to be seen as confined to the circumstances of that particular case. We are not inclined to dissent from that decision at this stage, and in any event the present case does not provide a suitable occasion for it to be reviewed even if it was appropriate for this to be done. Both sides were agreed that, since there was no signed minute at the adjournment diet in this case, the essential requirements for the continuation of these proceedings had not been fulfilled and that the instance must be treated as having fallen as a result.

It follows that whatever view is taken of the decision in *Pettigrew* v. *Ingram* the long-established rules to which we referred earlier in this opinion show that the decision which the sheriff took in this case was the only one which was open to him in the circumstances. For these reasons we refuse to pass the bill."

Appeal refused.

Section 359 of 1975 Act requires also that a note be kept "of any documentary evidence produced." The following case, decided under previous equivalent legislation, deals with the point.

4. Jacobs and Another v. Hart
(1900) 3 Adam 131

An accused person was charged with stealing 600 Italian liras to the value of £24 sterling. Certain Italian and Scots banknotes were produced during the trial, but the record of proceedings did not record that fact. The accused appealed against his conviction.

LORD MCLAREN: "The Summary Jurisdiction Acts, while exempting the sheriff or magistrate trying the case from the duty of preserving a note of the evidence, directs him to note the documentary evidence put in at the trial, and that in the form set forth in a schedule annexed to the Act of 1864. Now, although the words used in the schedule are slightly different, I take it that we must interpret the words there used as being identical in meaning with the words used in the enacting section.

In this case the charge was the theft of 600 liras (Italian money), and the objection to the conviction is that certain bank-notes produced in evidence are of the nature of documentary evidence and ought to have been noted on the record. I suppose, although we are not directly informed, that the Italian notes produced were represented to be the money alleged to be stolen, and the question is whether notes alleged to be stolen and produced in proof of the theft, are on a fair construction of the statute, documentary evidence required to be noted.

While I am unable to agree with Lord Adam in the result of his opinion, I think we are at least in agreement on the question of principle, that there may be things stolen and referred to in evidence and yet not required to be noted as documentary evidence. The case of a printed book was referred to, and I may remark that the person whose pocket is picked may be able to identify the book by its binding, or other external marks, without the book being read or even opened. In such a case it would be absurd to say that the book was put in as documentary evidence. In the present case I do not think that the notes produced were documentary evidence any more than a book, or gold or silver coin, or a watch with an inscription on it, because in all those cases the inscription, if read at all, is only read for the purpose of identifying the thing and not for using its contents as evidence.

I venture to suggest as the true criterion for the determination of what is or is not documentary evidence requiring to be noted; the question, 'Is it necessary that the judge should read the contents of the writing produced, or is it only shewn to the witnesses for the purposes of identification?' I cannot see that there is any difference in legal effect between the production of the notes stolen in the case and the production of gold or silver coin in any other case where money is alleged to be stolen. The judge may look at the shilling or sovereign to satisfy himself that it is genuine, or that it corresponds with the description of the articles libelled as stolen. Part of the process of identification may be that he or the witness may have to read the inscription on the coin, not because that is documentary evidence, but because you identify the coin by means of the written and pictorial marks upon it.

A banker or money-changer is doubtless familiar with the external appearance of the notes of all the leading States, and he may be able to distinguish a real note from a counterfeit without being able to read the language in which the obligation is written. Many people who cannot read or write know a bank note and its denomination: to such persons the note is certainly not documentary evidence. It is not necessary that the judge should personally inspect the notes if he is satisfied with the statement of the expert witness that they are Italian notes. But if the notes are documentary evidence, it would be the duty of the judge to read the printed words which are said to be evidence.

What I have said applies equally to the Scotch notes which were given to the accused in exchange for the Italian notes. These, in my opinion, are not documents which the judge is required to note. I think the Note of Suspension should be refused."

Appeal refused.

NOTE

Lord Adam dissented from the view expressed by Lord McLaren and the Lord Justice-General. For a discussion of this case and the nature of the documentary evidence, see Renton and Brown, paras. 14–75, 14–76.

Under section 353(2) of the 1975 Act it is provided that:

"Any order by any of the departments of state or government or any local authority or public body made under powers conferred by any statute, or a print or copy of such order, shall when produced in a summary prosecution be received in evidence of the due making, confirmation and existence of such order without being sworn to by any witness and without any further or other proof, but without prejudice to any right competent to the accused to challenge any such order as being *ultra vires* of the authority making it or on any other competent ground, and where any such order is referred to in the complaint it shall not be necessary to enter it in the record of proceedings as a documentary production."

Production of the order is, however, vital.

5. **Herkes v. Dickie**
1958 J.C. 51

A licensee was convicted of an offence under a local bye-law. He appealed by stated case.

LORD PATRICK: "The appellant was tried and convicted in the Police Court of the Burgh of Dumfries. The charge against him was that he sold by the hands of his servants three bottles of ale after one P.M. on New Year's day, that being the hour appointed by the licensing authority for the Burgh of Dumfries for the closing of premises licensed to sell exciseable liquor within the burgh, contrary to the terms of his certificate and the Licensing Act, 1921, section 4(*a*).

Neither the Act nor the certificate prescribes the hour at which licensed premises shall cease to sell liquor on New Year's day. Section 4 forbids the sale of exciseable liquor except during the permitted hours. The certificate has the same effect. For specification of the permitted hours we must look elsewhere. Section 41 of the Licensing (Scotland) Act, 1903, empowers a Licensing Court to make bye-laws for, *inter alia*, closing licensed premises wholly or partially on New Year's day. It is said that the Licensing Court for the Burgh of Dumfries made bye-laws in 1931 and 1941 whereby all licensed premises within the burgh must be closed on New Year's day with the exception of such hours before one P.M. as are permitted hours, provided that exciseable liquor might be sold to any person lodging in the licence-holder's inn or hotel, or during such hours as are permitted on weekdays to travellers.

CITATION AND RECORD

At the trial of the complaint before the magistrates the prosecutor closed his case without putting in evidence a copy of these alleged bye-laws, but in his address to the magistrates he referred to them in order to establish that a sale of exciseable liquor after one P.M. on New Year's day was a sale outwith the permitted hours, and therefore an offence. Counsel for the accused contended that the bye-laws had not been proved and consequently that no offence had been proved. The magistrates thought there was no need to prove the terms of the bye-laws which were within the knowledge of the Court, the licensing court being the magistrates of the burgh.

We were referred to a number of cases in which the question has been discussed whether bye-laws and orders of bodies other than Parliament must be put in evidence in the course of a criminal prosecution. These were *Todd* v. *Anderson* [(1912) 6 Adam 7131], *Brander* v. *Mackenzie* [1915 J.C. 47], and *Macmillan* v. *McConnell* [1917 J.C. 43]. I need not consider these cases in detail, because it is conceded by counsel for the prosecutor that bye-laws made under the authority of the Licensing Acts must be proved by the prosecutor putting a copy of them in evidence before he closes his case, unless there is something in these Acts which can be construed as giving such bye-laws the status of an Act of Parliament, which of course does not require to be proved in any Court. Every one is presumed to know the statute law of the land.

Now, counsel for the prosecutor (Mr Johnston) was unable to point to any provision of the Licensing Act which had that effect. Apart from that fatal defect, subsection 41(5) of the Licensing (Scotland) Act, 1903, provides that a copy of any bye-laws made under the section signed and certified by the clerk to a Licensing Court to be a true copy and to have been duly confirmed shall be evidence, until the contrary is proved, in all legal proceedings of the due making, confirmation, and existence of such bye-laws, without further or other proof. That plainly implies that the bye-laws have not the status of an Act of Parliament. If they had that status, there would be no need for the subsection.

Mr Johnston then suggested that in this matter of the proof of bye-laws in criminal proceedings we should, as he put it, 'start afresh' by dividing bye-laws into two categories, those in which the penalty was prescribed in the bye-law, in which case the bye-law must be proved, and those in which the penalty was prescribed in the statute empowering the making of the bye-law, in which case there should be no necessity to prove the bye-law. I can see no reason for adopting the presence or absence of a penalty in a bye-law as the test whether the bye-law need be proved. I suspect that the only reason for choosing this test is that it is one which would suit Mr Johnston's case, since the Licensing Acts do in fact prescribe the penalties for breach of the bye-laws made in virtue of them. I should have thought that an accused person was as interested in having it proved that there was a bye-law which created an offence as he was in having it proved that a bye-law prescribed a penalty. In any event there is no warrant in our law for dividing bye-laws into categories by the application of the test suggested.

A further argument for the prosecutor was that if no challenge was made of the relevancy of the complaint there was no necessity to prove the bye-laws. The basis of this argument was section 16 of the Summary Jurisdiction (Scotland) Act, 1954. That section deals with the form of complaints, and subsection (*b*) provides that the statement that an act was done contrary to a statute or order shall imply a statement that the statute or order applied to the circumstances existing at the time and place of the offence, that the accused was a person bound to observe the same, that any necessary preliminary procedure had been duly gone through, and that all the circumstances necessary to a contravention existed. The argument is wholly misconceived. The subsection is dealing solely with the form of complaints and pruning them of matters it was thought unnecessary to include in them. It does not deal with the proof of matters, and does not render unnecessary the proof of any matter which it would otherwise be necessary to prove.

The last point made by Mr Johnston on this branch of the case was that the magistrates could take judicial notice of the bye-laws in as much as the magistrates made them. Now these bye-laws were made in 1931 and 1941. It does not in the least appear that the magistrate who tries a case of alleged contravention of the bye-laws in 1958 took part in the making of them and has an exact knowledge of their contents. In any event if any matter requires to be proved in a criminal prosecution the want of proof of the matter cannot be mended by the private knowledge of the Judge. In my opinion, the prosecutor should have put a copy of the bye-laws, duly authenticated, in evidence before he closed his case. He did not do so and there was not evidence to warrant a conviction. That is sufficient for the disposal of the stated case. I express no opinion on other grounds of challenge of the conviction which were argued before us.

I suggested to your Lordships that we answer the question in the case in the negative."

Conviction quashed.

NOTE

This case is confined to the situation where the order relied on did not have statutory status. Acts of Parliament and statutory instruments do not, of course, have to be proved. See also Schedule 3 of the Prisoners and Criminal Procedings (Scotland) Act 1993 for important changes to the law on documentary evidence in criminal proceedings and the discussion thereof at Crim. L.B. 2–2.

CHAPTER 14

PRELIMINARY OBJECTIONS, PLEADING AND TRIAL

A.   PRELIMINARY OBJECTIONS AND PLEADING

If there are any preliminary objections to competency or relevancy, these should be dealt with at the first calling of the complaint. Section 334(1) of the 1975 Act provides, *inter alia*, that no such objections shall be allowed to be stated at any further diet in the case, except with the leave of the court, which may be granted only on cause shown. The general principles of competency and relevancy discussed *supra* in Chap. 9 apply equally to summary as to solemn procedure.

However, an appeal court will take note of the situation where the complaint is fundamentally null, even if no preliminary objection has been stated, and this may lead to quashing of the conviction even although section 454 of the 1975 Act appears to exclude appeals based on alleged irrelevancy where the point has not been taken in the lower court.

1.   O'Malley v. Strathern
1920 J.C. 74

An accused person was charged on summary complaint with an offence under the Spirits (Prices and Description) Order 1919. He was convicted and appealed by stated case. In dealing with an argument by the appellant which related to the relevancy of the complaint, the Lord Justice-General (Clyde) made the following preliminary observations on the interpretation of section 75 of the Summary Jurisdiction (Scotland) Act 1908 (the forerunner of section 454 of the 1975 Act).

> LORD JUSTICE-GENERAL (CLYDE): "... Preliminary to the consideration of whether the Order itself was a lawful order or not, there comes the question of how far that point is open in the present case. For the respondent, reference was made to the Summary Jurisdiction Act of 1908, and particularly to section 75. Section 75 provides that no conviction shall be quashed for want of form; and that no conviction shall be quashed, where the accused was represented by a law-agent, in respect of any objection to the relevancy of the complaint unless such objection shall have been timeously stated. In this case the accused was represented by a law-agent. No objection to relevancy based on the alleged invalidity of the Order was tabled, and it was accordingly maintained that the objection with regard to the validity of the Order comes too late. There can be no doubt at all, I think, that section 75 did make some difference on the law as it was practised prior to 1908. I think that is shown by the fact that the exclusion of objections to relevancy which section 75 enacts is made applicable only to cases in which the accused was represented by a law-agent. And, although in practice, prior to 1908, there may have been some distinction made in cases where a law-agent was employed, so far as I am aware no such hard-and-fast line was drawn in that matter as is drawn by the Act of 1908. I should be very sorry to be compelled to read section 75 as excluding from this Court power to deal with cases, even though no objection to relevancy has

456

been taken, where *ex facie* of the proceedings themselves, and particularly *ex facie* of the complaint, there is what has been called in the course of the debate a fundamental nullity. Such cases do occur; and the justification for doing right in such cases as those, even although no objection has been taken to the relevancy, is that the objection is patent on the face of the complaint or of the proceedings, and the prosecutor is, therefore, not entitled to say that he had no notice of the objection. I do not read section 75 as excluding from the Court power to deal with such cases, and I found on the case of *Rogers* v. *Howman* [1918 J.C. 88], and particularly upon the first paragraph in the opinion of the Lord Justice-General in that case. I found upon that as authority for the proposition that this Court has recognised that, notwithstanding section 75, the power to which I have referred still remains to it. The appeal in *Rogers* was by stated case, and the only question submitted to the Court was similar to the only one submitted here. If the language used by the Lord Justice-General is examined, it will be found that the legitimacy of entertaining an objection to relevancy, not stated in the Court below and not raised by the stated case, but patent on the face of the complaint, is affirmed. His Lordship contrasted the case he was deciding with one in which an irrelevancy is disclosed on the face of the complaint. I think, accordingly, that the Court retains the power of dealing with cases in which, although no objection to the relevancy was taken in the Court below, there is patent, and disclosed on the face of proceedings, an irrelevancy which makes the proceedings fundamentally null."

NOTE

In this case, the High Court went on to uphold the conviction on the ground that the alleged irrelevancy did not, in fact, arise *ex facie* of the proceedings. But some comfort can be derived from Lord Clyde's remarks, which have in fact been followed in a number of cases. The most recent appears to be *Shaw* v. *Smith*, 1979 J.C. 51, in which three people were charged on summary complaint with boarding a train without paying or intending to pay. On appeal, the High Court held that this complaint was irrelevant since it disclosed no crime known to the law of Scotland. The court affirmed that it was competent even at the stage of an appeal to raise a matter constituting a fundamental nullity in the proceedings although it had not previously been raised.

Once any preliminary objections have been dealt with, the accused is called upon to plead guilty or not guilty. In certain cases he may do so in absence and, if he pleads not guilty, the case is usually adjourned to a later date for trial. If the accused pleads guilty, he will usually be dealt with there and then.

Normally, an accused person who has pleaded guilty on summary complaint, and whose plea has been accepted by the prosecutor, cannot change his mind. The plea must now be taken from the accused personally, if he is present in court: see Act of Adjournal (Consolidation) 1988, r. 119(1). See also *Donaldson* v. *Lees*, 1989 S.C.C.R. 484. But where there is genuine misapprehension the court may, in special circumstances, allow withdrawal of the plea.

For a discussion of section 454 of the 1975 Act see *infra*.

2. **Williams and Another v. Linton**
(1878) 6 R. (J.) 12

Two accused were charged with shebeening. They initially pleaded not guilty, but when their case was called for trial, both their counsel and agent were not present in court. They both pleaded guilty and were in the process of being sentenced when their counsel returned to the courtroom. He asked the magistrate to allow the plea to be withdrawn, but this was refused. The accused appealed to the High Court by bill of suspension.

LORD JUSTICE-CLERK (MONCRIEFF): "My first impression in reading the evidence in this case was, I am bound to say, that it was not a case for interference, because I thought that the magistrate had acted to the best of his judgment in a matter which was properly for his discretion. But, on maturer reflection, though I still think that the magistrate did act to the best of his judgment, I have come to be of opinion that the conviction ought not to stand.

I do not mean for one moment to say that in all cases a prisoner is entitled to have his trial postponed and postponed indefinitely till professional advice is forthcoming. But this is a very special case. In the first place, the charge is a serious charge, one of the most serious that can come before a police magistrate, and the penalty imposed is about the most severe that a police magistrate can inflict. But, besides this, the magistrate was informed that the prisoners were to be represented by a professional adviser, though he was not informed by whom. A member of the bar had also communicated with the magistrate, and informed him that he was engaged in one of the cases to be tried before him, but was obliged to leave the Court for a short period. In these circumstances, if it did not occur to the magistrate that the case in question was most likely the one to which the counsel referred, at least it would have been proper for him to inquire who the legal adviser of the accused was, before allowing them in his absence, and I may almost say because of his absence, to withdraw a plea of not guilty which they had at first given. When counsel returned to Court he was not at first aware of what had occurred, but, on hearing the magistrate proceed to give sentence he at once interposed to stop the proceedings. The magistrate refused to go back upon what had been done, thinking that it was not competent for him to do so. In this, I think, he was in error. I think, as the sentence had not been taken down and signed, even if it was formally pronounced, which is a matter of doubt, that the magistrate had power to go back upon the proceedings and try the case as requested.

On these grounds I think there has been a departure from substantial justice in this case, and that the conviction should be quashed."

Appeal allowed.

NOTE

So once a sentence has been recorded and signed, a plea of guilty cannot be withdrawn. This case was followed in *Tudhope* v. *Colbert*, 1978 S.L.T. (Notes) 57, where a solicitor who had been delayed by bad weather on the way to the court arrived there to find his client had pleaded guilty in person. But since the conviction and sentence had not been minuted, the court allowed the guilty plea to be withdrawn. The High Court dismissed as incompetent a Crown appeal against this decision. See also the saga of *MacNeill* v. *MacGregor*, 1975 J.C. 55; 1975 S.L.T. (Notes) 46 and *MacGregor* v. *MacNeill*, 1975 J.C. 57; 1975 S.L.T. (Notes) 54, *infra*, Chap. 16.

B. STATEMENTS IN MITIGATION INCONSISTENT WITH PLEA

If a plea of guilty is accepted by the prosecutor, he will narrate the facts to the court so that the appropriate sentence can be fixed. While the defence are always entitled to address the court in mitigation, care must be taken by both sides not to make factual assertions inconsistent with the plea accepted.

Galloway v. Adair
1947 J.C. 7

An accused person pleaded guilty to driving at a speed "which was dangerous to the public." He was sentenced to a term of imprisonment and appealed by bill of suspension. In disposing of the bill, Lord Moncrieff made the following observations:

LORD MONCRIEFF: "Before the appellant was sentenced the depute-fiscal had made a statement as to the circumstances attending the commission of the offence. This was in accordance with practice and was, in my opinion, entirely proper. Indeed, without such a statement it would not only be embarrassing, but might scarcely be possible, to pronounce an appropriate sentence in the case of a plea of guilty. If a prisoner pleads guilty to an offence under a charge of assault or a charge of homicide or any charge of an offence in committing which the culpability may vary within wide limits, it is proper and in accordance with practice that an explanation of the circumstances attending the offence should be given to the Court which has the duty of imposing the sentence. At the same time it must be kept in view that by pleading guilty an accused person becomes entitled to the advantage of excluding all sworn evidence as to the circumstances of the offence which he has committed, and therefore that, if the accused denies any of the statements made by the Crown, these are statements which cannot be taken into consideration by the Court; unless indeed it can be demonstrated that such a denial is inconsistent with his plea of guilty, or should be disregarded as being manifestly false when taken along with the circumstances admitted by him. The accused has, of course, a corresponding right, either by himself or by his solicitor or counsel, to make a statement in extenuation, and the same considerations apply to any statement which may be so made by him or on his behalf. If such a statement is not disputed by those representing the Crown, it may be accepted as introducing extenuating circumstances in considering what sentence should be imposed, but if, it be disputed, it also must be left out of consideration.

When the statement was made by the depute-fiscal in the present case, being a statement in considerable detail to which I shall have to refer hereafter, it was not suggested by or on behalf of the accused that that statement was not in accordance with the facts. Accordingly, had the circumstances adverted to in that statement been relevant to illustrate and support the charge, I do not think it would now be competent before this Court of appeal to deny either in whole or in part the truth or accuracy of the statement which was so made; and I therefore do not find myself able to take into consideration the partial denial of the truth of the statement which is made part of the replies of the complainer in this bill of suspension. At the same time it is always the right of the complainer to have any charges contained in such a statement strictly directed towards the supporting of the charge to which he has pleaded guilty and not towards the support of any other and different charge. It is clear that, if that right were not asserted in his favour, it would result in his being sentenced for an offence other than that which was covered by his plea, and accordingly it is necessary to consider first of all what were the limits of the charge in the complaint to which the appellant pleaded guilty, and secondly what was the substance of the statement which was made by the depute-fiscal.

Section 11 of the Road Traffic Act of 1930 deals in all its applications with driving to the danger of the public, but it deals with this under three heads. If a person drives a motor vehicle on a road recklessly to the danger of the public, he commits an offence under the section; secondly, if he drives a motor vehicle at a speed which is dangerous to the public, he commits the statutory offence; and thirdly, if he drives a vehicle in a manner which is dangerous, he again is guilty of an offence under the section. In this complaint the prosecutor ignores all heads of the statutory offence except the second, and charges the appellant only with driving a motor vehicle at a speed which was dangerous to the public. He makes no reference, as he might have done, to reckless driving to the danger of the public or driving in a manner which was dangerous; and accordingly the only offence to which the appellant pleaded guilty was an offence of driving at a speed which was dangerous to the public. Any circumstances illustrating the committing of an offence in respect of speed were thus properly included in the statement which the depute-fiscal thought proper to make; and there are certain details of conduct included in the statement so made by him which are strictly limited and related to this question of dangerous driving in respect of speed. But in the eight particular details referred to in the depute-fiscal's statement there are I think only two which are solely concerned with the offence of driving dangerously in respect of speed. Thus in the first detail where a rather high rate of speed is charged incidentally, the substance of the offence which was narrated by the depute-fiscal was that the appellant had started his car before the green light at a crossing had appeared. That was an act of reckless driving to the danger of the public, but was not an act of driving at a speed dangerous to the public. In the same way in the second detail the charge again is of starting while the yellow and red lights were showing. The third is a charge of starting before the green light permitted a start, and also of thrusting his vehicle between a stationary lorry and a north-bound tramway car with so little warning that the driver of the tramway car had to make a sudden emergency stop to avoid the risk of an accident. That again is not an offence which need have resulted from dangerous speed, but is a definite offence of reckless driving. In the next detail the appellant is said to have ignored a clear hand signal from a moving vehicle about to turn off its course, resulting in a sudden swerve on his own part and his narrowly missing striking a lamp standard. The other offences are again (without going into them in detail) associated only remotely, if at all, with speed, except the last detail which is of a speed of 40 miles per hour and of such speed only.

Now, although there was no denial of the truth of these details before the learned Sheriff, that judge had still a farther duty to consider whether or not he was entitled to take these details into his consideration as relevant to aid him in measuring the sentence to be imposed for an offence of driving only at a speed which was dangerous to the public. In my opinion, these circumstances should not have been taken into consideration in measuring the sentence for that single offence. The appellant had pled guilty to the offence of driving at a dangerous speed, but he did not plead guilty to the various disregards of traffic lights and to the various trespasses upon the rights over the road of other vehicles, which form the substance of the statement; and it is always open to an accused person to say, *esto* the facts stated be accepted as true, these facts are not relevant to support or to measure the only offence to which I have pleaded guilty. In the present case it is, however, only if such irrelevant facts be taken into consideration that the learned Sheriff would have been justified in remarking that the case was among the worst of its kind in his experience. Had the circumstances upon which the learned Sheriff proceeded been relevant, I think that the sentence pronounced by him might have been regarded as an appropriate sentence. If on the other hand the irrelevant circumstances disappear from the case, a wholly different question requires to be determined. It is accordingly necessary to consider in this Court, and to determine as of new, what would be an appropriate sentence for the only offence to which the appellant has pleaded guilty. That plea convicts him of having driven his vehicle at a speed which is dangerous to the public, and that is far from a negligible offence; but beyond the statement of the depute-fiscal that at certain stages he had been driving at a rather high rate of speed and the circumstances that for four-tenths of a mile he maintained a speed of 40 miles an hour until he was stopped by the constables, there appears to be nothing left in the statement which it was proper for the learned Sheriff when measuring the sentence to entertain or have in view.

That being so, the sentence of sixty days' imprisonment with the suspension of the licence for the period of a year may, I think, be properly regarded as oppressive, though, had the circumstances which the learned Sheriff thought he was entitled to take into consideration been properly before him, it would have been difficult to make or to entertain such a suggestion. It is clear therefore that the sentence must be revised, and I would suggest to your Lordships that in place of a sentence of imprisonment a fine should be imposed, and that the fine might be for a sum of £15 with the usual alternative of sixty days' imprisonment. I would farther suggest that we should allow a period of three weeks within which to make payment of the fine."

Appeal allowed.

NOTE

It is thus of paramount importance to keep the narration of facts within relevant bounds. The sheriff here had before him material which he was not entitled to consider, a situation which led to a revisal of the sentence.

C.   PROCEDURE ON A PLEA OF NOT GUILTY

Once a plea of not guilty has been taken and recorded, the diet is adjourned for trial to take place on a later day. On that day, the diet must be called, or the instance falls. Evidence will then be led.

Certain statutes require that certain steps be taken before the trial commences. For example, under section 26(1) and (2) of the 1980 Act, statutory certificates on which the Crown intend to rely must be served 14 days before the trial. This raises the question of when the trial commences, a question not really answered in *Handley* v. *Pirie*, 1977 S.L.T. 30. (For a discussion of this case, see C.N. Stoddart, "When does a summary trial commence?" (1976) 21 J.L.S. 393.) However, it is relatively clear from *English* v. *Smith*, 1981 S.L.T. (Notes) 113 that the trial commences on the day to which the diet has been adjourned for trial, although the court still failed to identify the point in the proceedings on that day at which it commenced. Nowhere in the 1980 Act is a general provision made, but section 18(2) thereof inserted a new section 338A in the 1975 Act to the effect that a prosecutor in a summary trial cannot move the court to desert the diet *pro loco et tempore* after the first witness is sworn. The clear implication is, therefore, that a summary trial commences at that point, and phrases such as "before the trial" must be construed accordingly.

Once the trial has commenced by the leading of evidence, various procedural specialities may arise.

(i)   Amendment of the Complaint

Section 335 of the 1975 Act provides:

"(1) It shall be competent at any time prior to the determination of a summary prosecution, unless the court sees just cause to the contrary, to amend the complaint or any notice of penalty or previous conviction relative thereto by deletion, alteration or addition so as to cure any error or defect therein, or to meet any objection thereto, or to cure any discrepancy or variance between the complaint or notice and the evidence.

(2) Nothing in this section shall authorise an amendment which changes the character of the offence charged, and if the court shall be of opinion that the accused may in any way be prejudiced in his defence on the merits of the case by any amendment made under this section, the court shall grant such remedy to the accused by adjournment or otherwise as it shall think just."

It will thus be observed that many defects can be cured by amendment under the above section, on which see, generally, Renton and Brown, para. 14–66. The following examples deal with problems of *locus* and date.

1.   Macintosh v. Metcalfe and Others
(1886) 1 White 218

An accused person was charged on summary complaint with a statutory offence. No *locus* of the offence was specified, but the sheriff allowed the complaint to be amended to specify the *locus*. The accused was convicted and appealed by stated case.

LORD MCLAREN: "Your Lordships have not thought it necessary to call for a reply except upon the want of specification of the *locus*. This is an important point, as it bears upon the jurisdiction of the Sheriff. It is now admitted and it appears *ex facie* of the proceedings, that the complaint did not specify the place or places where the alleged crimes were committed. It does not even say that they were committed within the county of Forfar. But the Sheriff-Substitute allowed an amendment to be made, supplying this defect, and the question is whether that amendment was rightly allowed. The *locus* is a very material point, especially in the case of crimes of the peculiar nature here charged, viz., the attempt to transfer the members of one friendly society to another without their written consent. One sees that very delicate questions of jurisdiction might be raised under a libel of this description, such as whether the crime was committed at the residence of the transference or at the office of the society's agent. Under the Summary Procedure Act, section 5, power is conferred upon the Judge or Magistrate to amend the complaint, and to rectify all mistakes in substance as well as in form. These are very wide words, for 'substance' and 'form' include really everything in the libel. The question here is, I think, partly solved by considering what is meant when an action is dismissed for want of jurisdiction. In that case 'want of jurisdiction' means that the Court has no jurisdiction. Now, to remedy a defect does not mean to transform into a libel what was never a libel. But before the Sheriff can consider the complaint at all he must have a complaint before him which contains the essentials of a criminal charge. In the Stornoway case [*Matheson* v. *Ross, infra*] there was a misdescription; a mistake was made as to the date of the offence charged, and the Court thought that that could be remedied. But I find that in giving the leading opinion, Lord Young said,—'I cannot think that this amendment is otherwise than competent. It differs from an amendment of the *locus*, because that may raise a question of jurisdiction.' It is my opinion that failure to specify the *locus* is the kind of defect which cannot be rectified by amendment."

Appeal allowed.

NOTE

So a complaint which is fundamentally null cannot be cured by amendment. Here there was nothing to amend, or indeed any indication that the sheriff had jurisdiction: *cf. Stevenson* v. *McLevy & Others* (1879) 6 R. (J.) 33; 4 Couper 196, *supra*, p.326.

2. Matheson and Others v. Ross
(1885) 5 Couper 582

An accused was tried on summary complaint. After the Crown case closed, the prosecutor sought to amend the date of the alleged offence. This was allowed and the accused appealed by bill of suspension.

LORD YOUNG: "The appellants here were brought to trial before the Sheriff-substitute of Ross-shire, at Stornoway, for the crime of deforcement and assault, and were convicted and sentenced by him to various periods of imprisonment. The conviction and sentence is complained of, first, upon the ground that the Sheriff allowed the complaint on which it proceeded to be amended in the date in the course of the trial, and, indeed, after the close of the prosecutor's evidence. The date originally stated in the complaint as the date of the offence was the 8th of November 1884. On that day, the prosecution alleged the appellants had deforced and assaulted an officer and his assistant in the exercise of his duty in serving summonses, dated the 29th November, or three weeks after the offence was said to have been committed. Although it was plain that the dates were incompatible, and one or both must be wrong, it did not appear on the face of the libel which was wrong, or whether both were wrong. But I assume, for that alone is consistent with the course the case took, that the real date was 8th December, and accordingly that was the date the Sheriff allowed in the course, or rather at a late period, of the trial to be substituted for the original one of 8th November. The question is whether he was lawfully entitled to allow that amendment at that stage. Now one thing is quite clear, assuming December to be right, and not November, that no injustice was done in making the charge, and it is not suggested that any injustice or disadvantage has been suffered. Of course that is subject to the observation that, if the amendment was illegal, the appellants were legally entitled to any unearned advantage out of the prosecutor's error, of which they were deprived by the amendment. But I take it that they suffered no disadvantage and were put to no inconvenience. I mean that they were in no way prejudiced in their defence or put to any greater peril by the amendment than they would have been if the date had been right at first.

Now, taking the case so, was the amendment legal? I think the prosecution would have been competent under the Act 9 George IV., c. 29, Sir Wm. Rae's Act; for I do not agree with Mr Kennedy's argument that a case of deforcement such as this—an assault upon an officer of the law in the execution of his duty—could not be competently tried under that Act. It might be more or less discreet to try it under that Act and there are certainly many cases of

deforcement and assault which might with perfect propriety be so tried. But as
to the competency of so trying such a case I cannot entertain a doubt for a
moment. If it had been so tried, the prayer of the complaint would have limited
the punishment on the very face of it. But then the Summary Procedure Act of
1864 applies expressly to all complaints before the Sheriff in the exercise of the
summary jurisdiction conferred upon him by the Act 9 George IV., c. 29; that is
to say, it applies to all complaints which, before the statute, might competently
have been brought under the older Act of Geo. IV. The complaint here bears on
the face of it that it is under the Summary Jurisdictions Acts of 1864 and 1881,
and the punishment which, under the Act of Geo. IV., is limited by the terms of
the complaint, does not require in this prosecution to be limited in the prayer
as under the Act of George IV., because in all prosecutions under the Summary
Procedure Act the punishment is limited by statute, and the Act of 1881, which
is one of the Acts mentioned in the title of the complaint, prohibits for the
future any prosecution under 9 Geo. IV., and *requires* that any which
previously would have been brought under it should thereafter be brought
under the Acts 1864 and 1881. The importance of these provisions is that clause
5 of the Act of 1864 provides that no objection shall be allowed by the Court to
any complaint under this Act, or for any alleged defect therein in substance or
in form, or for any variance between any such complaint and the evidence
adduced on the part of the prosecutor or complainer at the hearing thereof, not
changing the character of the offence charged; but if any such objection or
variance shall appear to the Court to be such that the respondent has been
thereby deceived or misled, it shall be lawful for the Court to adjourn the
hearing till some future day, and at the same time, or at any stage of the
proceedings, to direct such amendment to be made upon the complaint as may
appear to be requisite, not changing the character of the offence; and such
amendment shall be authenticated by the signature or initials of the Judge or
Clerk of Court. Now I think that in the Sheriff's place it would not have
occurred to me that the accused could take any prejudice from the amendment
being made upon the spot when the error was pointed out; nevertheless, I
think the Sheriff acted with becoming discretion when he offered to the
accused or their agent to adjourn the case if they desired it. No such desire was
expressed, and the amendment was ordered and authenticated as the statute
required. I cannot think that this amendment was other than competent. It
differs from an amendment of the *locus*, because that may raise a question of
jurisdiction. As it is not of that nature, we have not to determine any such
question as was raised in the case of *Stevenson* cited, Couper, vol. iv., p.495, in
which the Appeal Court declined to sanction the insertion of a *locus* for the first
time after the conclusion of the evidence, to fit the evidence that had been led.
The matter in the present case is one of time, and I assume that the evidence
upon which the appellants were convicted, of violent conduct upon the 8th
December, applied to that date. In one view, and I think the right view, of
clause 5 of the Summary Procedure Act, the Sheriff might have proceeded
upon that evidence, and made his conviction apply to the 8th December,
disregarding the discrepancy between that date and the 8th November. The
magistrate is required to proceed on the truth of the substance of the matter,
disregarding any such discrepancy owing to an error; but I think the Sheriff
acted properly in correcting the error, and, indeed, that was necessary if a
conviction was to be made by reference to the complaint."

Appeal refused.

NOTE

Section 335 of the 1975 Act is founded on the equivalent provision of the
1864 Act under discussion in the instant case. Once again, the question of

prejudice is paramount. For a discussion of this problem generally, see G.H. Gordon, "Fundamental Nullity and the Power of Amendment," 1974 S.L.T. (News) 154. In *Duffy* v. *Ingram*, 1987 S.C.C.R. 286 it was held that section 335 was wide enough to cover the curing of such a defect as the *absence* of a date for the commission of the offence; *cf.* the remarks of Lord Moncrieff in *Stevenson* v. *McLevy* (1879) 4 Couper 196 at pp.203, 204.

(ii) Abandonment of Proceedings

The common law relating to desertion of diets, whether *simpliciter* or *pro loco et tempore*, is, of course, the same in summary proceedings as it is in solemn cases—see, *supra*, pp.381, 382. See also section 338A of the 1975 Act (as inserted by section 18(2) of the 1980 Act) which provides as follows:

"(1) It shall be competent at the diet of trial, at any time before the first witness is sworn, for the court, on the application of the prosecutor, to desert the diet *pro loco et tempore*.
(2) If, at a diet of trial, the court refuses an application by the prosecutor to adjourn the trial or to desert the diet *pro loco et tempore*, and the prosecutor is unable or unwilling to proceed with the trial, the court shall desert the diet *simpliciter*.
(3) Where the court has deserted a diet *simpliciter* under subsection (2) above (and the court's decision in that regard has not been reversed on appeal), it shall not be competent for the prosecutor to raise a fresh libel."

In *Tudhope* v. *Gough*, 1982 S.C.C.R. 157, Sheriff Kearney held that it was competent to desert *pro loco et tempore* even after refusing an adjournment, but in the particular circumstances of that case, where the prosecutor had omitted (without explanation) to cite an essential witness, he refused a Crown motion to desert *pro loco* and instead deserted the diet *simpliciter*.

Proceedings may also be abandoned by not calling a complaint and, if appropriate, substituting another complaint.

Cochran v. Walker
(1900) 3 Adam 165

An accused was convicted after trial on summary complaint, the third which had been called. He appealed by bill of suspension.

LORD JUSTICE-CLERK (MACDONALD): "We have heard a very clear statement of the case from counsel for the suspender, and it is not necessary to call for a reply.

It is said that the suspender was brought up for trial on more than one complaint, and that no copy of any complaint was served on him. What happened was this. The suspender was apprehended on 3rd March on a charge of assault, and pleaded not guilty before the magistrate on 5th March. Some doubt arose as to whether the nature of the injuries inflicted on the person assaulted might not necessitate a graver charge being libelled, and the magistrate remitted the case to the Sheriff. The prosecutor, however, departing from the first complaint brought a second summary complaint, to which the suspender again pleaded not guilty, and the case was adjourned. In all this there was nothing irregular—nothing unfair.

At the adjourned diet on 13th March the prosecutor allowed the previous complaint to drop, and the suspender was asked to plead to a third complaint.

All this was quite competent. The same course is followed in all our criminal tribunals from the most summary up to the highest Court in the country. It is always in the power of the public prosecutor to depart from one libel and proceed to charge the accused upon a fresh libel. In the higher Court the *induciæ* must be allowed to run in each case, but in the case of a summary complaint there are no *induciæ*. But in neither case is any record made of the dropping of the old libel.

In the present case the suspender, having appeared in court on the 13th March, the diet to which the second complaint had been adjourned, was asked then and there to plead to a new complaint. He was informed by the reading over of the charge that it differed from the previous libel in that the prosecutor now added the aggravation of a previous conviction of assault. It is of importance to note that during all these proceedings the suspender was represented by a law-agent and no objection was taken to the legality of the proceedings, nor was any motion made on his behalf for any adjournment. I know of no case where in a Summary Court the accused has been represented by an agent and no objection has been stated at the time in which this Court has afterwards interfered to quash the proceedings on the ground of the alleged illegality by there being no adjournment. But, further, I do not think that it could be held that there was any irregularity in the proceedings here even if objection had been taken earlier. It is not said that an adjournment was asked for and refused. It is said that no copy of the complaint was handed to the accused, but it was not necessary to do so in the circumstances, and it is not said that a copy was asked and refused."

Appeal refused.

NOTE

On abandonment generally, see Renton and Brown, paras. 13–97, 13–98. On adjournment of diets, see *supra*, pp.377 *et seq*.

(iii)   Conduct of a Summary Trial

The rules of evidence relating to the testimony given at a summary trial are outwith the scope of this work, but various cases have arisen in which summary courts have made procedural mistakes. The following points have sometimes given rise to difficulty.

(A)   Declinature of jurisdiction

Bradford v. McLeod
1985 S.C.C.R. 379

Fourteen persons were charged on separate summary complaints with breach of the peace. Each sought that the sheriff presiding should decline jurisdiction. He refused: each accused was convicted and appealed by bill of suspension. The facts and arguments appear in the following opinion.

LORD JUSTICE-CLERK: "Each of the complainers was charged at the instance of the respondent that he did on 7th [or 8th] May 1984, at the entrance to British Steel Terminal, Hunterston, Cunninghame District, Strathclyde, conduct himself in a disorderly manner, form part of a disorderly crowd, shout and swear ... and commit a breach of the peace.

The background to the charges was that there was a miners' strike, and that each of the complainers was a striking miner who was said to have been involved in picketing at the British Steel Terminal at Hunterston.

In all fourteen bills the point raised is the same. However, the cases were not all heard by the sheriff on the same day, and there are some differences of detail between the cases and the allegations made therein. It was agreed, however, that the same result should follow in each case.

Put shortly, it is averred in each bill that at the trial diet the agent for the complainer moved the sheriff to disqualify himself from considering the case in the light of certain views which he had expressed when present at a function in Ayr on 22nd June 1984.

When the bills first came before this court on 11th June 1985, this court remitted to the sheriff principal to enquire and report on certain matters relating to the bills. The sheriff principal has now reported, and on 23rd October 1985 counsel for the complainers moved us in each instance to pass the bill and to suspend the conviction and sentence pronounced on each complainer.

In each bill it is averred that the sheriff had attended a social function organised by Ayr Curling Club at Ayr Ice Rink on 22nd June 1984. The sheriff was a member of the committee of the club, as was Mr J. R. B. Penny, solicitor, who acted for some of the complainers. A committee photograph was to be taken, and prior to that being done some discussion took place in the course of which the sheriff made certain remarks. It is not necessary to go into the matter in detail, since the sheriff principal has done that in his report. More than one statement regarding miners is attributed to the sheriff in the bills, and the sheriff principal has made it clear in his report that there were discrepancies between the witnesses whom he interviewed. However, the sheriff principal's conclusion on the matter is that at some point during the evening, either before or after the photographs, two gentlemen who were present expressed views hostile to certain miners arising from what they considered was happening on the picket lines. The sheriff and Mr Penny were present during this conversation although neither initiated it. At some point in the conversation the sheriff observed that he personally would not grant legal aid to miners. The sheriff principal states that it is not clear whether he meant miners in general or miners who had been engaged in particular activities; nor is it clear whether he specifically addressed this observation to Mr Penny or whether Mr Penny just happened to hear it. The sheriff principal adds: 'Beyond what may be inferred from anything he said about legal aid I cannot be satisfied that Sheriff Smith gave vent to any expression of prejudice towards miners or any group of them.'

At this stage I would only refer to two other observations of the sheriff principal. He interviewed the sheriff and states that the sheriff simply cannot remember any detail of the various social conversations he had at the function. It is thus clear that the sheriff did not deny that he made the observation quoted above regarding legal aid. The other point is this. According to the sheriff principal, both Mr Penny and one of the other two gentlemen who heard the remark understood the observation about legal aid to be seriously made.

The first trials of any of the complainers took place on 11th September 1984. At no time prior thereto had any hint been given by Mr Penny or anyone else that Sheriff Smith was unacceptable to Mr Penny's clients as a trial judge. The first case to call was one involving a client of Mr Penny, who is not one of the complainers. Before the trial began Mr Penny made a submission to the effect that Sheriff Smith should disqualify himself from hearing the miners' cases in the light of the views which he had expressed on 22nd June 1984. He stated that the views which the sheriff had expressed with regard to miners clearly indicated that he had made up his mind with regard to the miners and the accused who were appearing before him.

When this motion was made to him, the sheriff expressed himself as being flabbergasted that what had passed between two members of the committee of the curling club at a social gathering late in the evening should form the basis of such a submission in court. No doubt the sheriff considered on 22nd June 1984 that he was conversing with friends on a private occasion. It may be that he was confident that others present would treat his remarks on the same basis, but, if so, his confidence in Mr Penny appears to have been misplaced. However that may be, on 11th September 1984 Mr Penny referred to the conversation in open court, and the sheriff had then to rule upon the motion which had been made.

The sheriff adjourned the court for approximately twenty minutes. Apparently he regarded the allegation which had been made as reflecting on his judicial competence and integrity. He consulted the sheriff clerk. We are informed by the sheriff principal that the sheriff clerk was in no doubt that the sheriff gave the motion anxious and judicial consideration. In the event, when he returned to court, he stated that he did not propose to disregard the judicial oath which he had taken, and he refused to decline jurisdiction. Three trials took place that day, and on subsequent dates in September and October 1984 the trials took place of the remaining complainers. Before each trial the sheriff was moved to disqualify himself from hearing the case on grounds similar to those advanced before the first trial, and in each case he refused to decline jurisdiction. In the result each of the complainers was convicted and sentenced.

For the complainers, Mr Hope put at the forefront of his submissions the following proposition in the form of a question: whether there were circumstances affecting the sheriff which would create in the mind of a reasonable person a suspicion of his impartiality. If that question fell to be answered in the affirmative, Mr Hope submitted that that would disqualify the sheriff even though no bias in fact existed.

I am entirely satisfied that what are commonly referred to as the rules of natural justice apply to criminal trials in this country. In the unreported case of *Stewart* v. *Agnew* (18th June 1953), the Lord Justice-General said: 'But it is vital in every criminal prosecution not only that justice should be done but that justice should be visibly done.' In the same case, Lord Russell stated: 'By tradition and practice it is fundamental to the proper conduct and proceedings in our criminal courts that justice should not only be done but should also be seen to be done.'

This principle which applies to criminal trials also applies to persons performing judicial duties in a domestic forum. The rule was well expressed by Eve J. in *Law* v. *Chartered Institute of Patent Agents* [1919] 2 Ch. 276 at p.289 where he said:

'Each member of the council in adjudicating on a complaint thereunder is performing a judicial duty, and he must bring to the discharge of that duty an unbiassed and impartial mind. If he has a bias which renders him otherwise than an impartial judge he is disqualified from performing his duty. Nay, more (so jealous is the policy of our law of the purity of the administration of justice), if there are circumstances so affecting a person acting in a judicial capacity as to be calculated to create in the mind of a reasonable man a suspicion of that person's impartiality, those circumstances are themselves sufficient to disqualify although in fact no bias exists.'

That dictum, in my opinion, also represents the law in Scotland upon this matter.

Applying that dictum to the present case, I am clearly of opinion that the contentions of the complainers must prevail. When the solicitor for the complainers moved the sheriff to disqualify himself from considering the case, I am of opinion that the sheriff misdirected himself as to the test to be applied. The sheriff regarded the motion as reflecting on his judicial competence, and emphasised that he would observe his judicial oath. For myself, I am quite satisfied that the sheriff, in trying the various complainers, did not disregard his judicial oath. Investigations have been carried out by the sheriff principal, and there is nothing in his report to suggest that at the trials the sheriff acted unfairly. What the sheriff failed to note, however, when the motion was made that he should decline jurisdiction, was that the interests of justice required not merely that he should not display bias but that the circumstances should not be such as to create in the mind of a reasonable man a suspicion of the sheriff's impartiality.

It could hardly be suggested that a sheriff who had refused an applicant legal aid was thereby precluded from taking the trial of that applicant. But that was not the situation here. The effect of section 1(7)(a)(ii) of the Legal Aid (Scotland) Act 1967 (c.43) is that a person shall not be given legal aid in connection with summary criminal proceedings unless the court considers that in all the circumstances of the case it is in the interests of justice that legal aid should be available to the accused and grants a legal aid certificate. In his report, the sheriff principal explains that at Kilmarnock the sheriffs have a policy, under reference to the foregoing subsection, that legal aid should only be granted in summary criminal proceedings if the accused can satisfy the sheriff that he has a serious defence in advance. In that situation, the effect of the sheriff's observation on 22nd June 1984 to the effect that he personally would not grant legal aid to miners is that irrespective of the circumstances his view was that no miners should receive legal aid as they had no answer to the charges. He was indicating ab ante that without considering the merits of an application for legal aid at the instance of any miner, he would refuse it.

In my opinion, a reasonable person on hearing that the sheriff had made that observation would be likely to conclude that the sheriff was biased so far as cases involving miners were concerned. Indeed the generality of the observation is such as to create in the mind of a reasonable man a definite suspicion that the sheriff may have such a bias. As explained by Eve J. in the passage quoted above, that is sufficient to disqualify a judge from performing his duty even though as a matter of fact the judge is not biased. I appreciate that at the time when the sheriff made the observation about legal aid, he had no reason to suppose that he personally would be involved in the determination of legal aid applications by any miners as he was not the nominated legal aid sheriff at Kilmarnock for the year in question. In my opinion, that does not matter since the important question is the effect that hearing the observation would have on a reasonable person. I should add for the sake of completeness that, in the absence on leave of the nominated legal aid sheriff and the other permanent sheriff at Kilmarnock, Sheriff Smith did in fact deal with and refuse legal aid applications lodged by the seven complainers represented by Mr Penny. The seven complainers subsequently made second applications for legal aid which were refused by the nominated legal aid sheriff. The remaining seven complainers (not represented by Mr Penny) had their legal aid applications dealt with and refused by the nominated legal aid sheriff who also refused second applications at their instance. It is thus clear that as regards the seven complainers represented by Mr Penny, Sheriff Smith duly acted as he had said he would when he made the observation on 22nd June 1984.

In my opinion, in refusing the motion to decline jurisdiction, the sheriff acted in error. He mistakenly thought that the sole issue was whether he was prepared to act fairly and in accordance with his judicial oath; he failed to realise that it was not enough that justice should be done, but that justice must also be seen to be done. Regrettably, because of the observations which it is established that the sheriff made on 22nd June 1984, justice could not be seen to be done when he conducted the trials of the complainers.

I can readily appreciate, as the sheriff principal observes, that the sheriff was naturally concerned about the impact which this matter could have on the conduct of court business. There were many trials to be taken involving miners, and if the motion made to him was well founded, then he would be disabled from carrying out part of the business of the court. None the less, once Mr Penny had made public what the sheriff had said on 22nd June 1984, the inevitable consequence was that the sheriff was disabled from dealing with any case involving a miner.

As I have already indicated, having read the sheriff principal's report, I have no reason to think that the complainers did not in fact receive fair trials. Indeed we were informed by the advocate-depute that in three other instances Sheriff Smith had acquitted miners who had been charged with similar offences. That would certainly go some way towards negativing the suggestion that the sheriff was in fact biased against miners. However, as already explained, that was not the sole issue raised by the motion.

It follows that the convictions cannot stand. It is a tribute to the law in Scotland that there are so few recorded cases where it has been alleged that justice has not been seen to be done. This case may serve as a reminder that the law in Scotland is jealous of its reputation for doing justice and for ensuring that justice is seen to be done; it may also serve to remind judges that if justice is not merely to be done but is to be visibly done, they, like Caesar's wife, must be above suspicion.

In all the circumstances I move your Lordships to pass these bills, and to suspend the convictions and sentences passed."

Convictions quashed.

NOTE

Needless to say, the overall consideration is that the accused must receive, and be seen to receive, a fair trial, on which see generally, *supra*, Chap. 1. Nowadays, applications for legal aid for summary criminal trials are not dealt with by the court at all, but by the Scottish Legal Aid Board under section 24 of the Legal Aid (Scotland) Act 1986. On declinature, see also *Tennant* v. *Houston*, 1986 S.C.C.R. 556; *Anderson* v. *Hillary*, 1990 S.C.C.R. 684.

(B)   Whole case to be taken in presence of accused

Aitken v. Wood
1921 J.C. 84

An accused person was convicted in the police court of assault. He appealed by bill of suspension.

LORD JUSTICE-GENERAL (CLYDE): "This bill of suspension is brought against a conviction for assault. It is alleged that the assault was committed on the person of a Mrs M'Niddler, whose arm was seized and compressed by the accused. Mrs M'Niddler was herself a witness at the trial, and spoke to the assault and to the fact, as she alleged, that her arm still bore a mark which was the result of the violence used upon her. She was asked if she was willing to show the bruise on her arm, to which question she returned an affirmative answer, but the matter was not pursued further during the proof. After the evidence on both sides had been closed, however, and after hearing argument, the magistrates, having retired to consider their decision, asked Mrs M'Niddler to come into the room to which they had retired, and examined her arm there, without the presence of the accused and of parties' solicitors—one of the magistrates being a medical man. Whether they asked her any questions we do not know, but I assume they did not.

This procedure, however well intended, and however harmless it may have been in this particular case, strikes at the principle—deeply rooted in the criminal law of Scotland—that no proceedings in a criminal trial, and particularly no proceedings connected with the taking of evidence can go on outwith the presence of the accused. The examination of the arm was just a means of taking evidence additional to that which was presented at the proof. The taking of such evidence, in the absence of the accused, is plainly an irregularity which vitiates the proceedings; and there is therefore nothing for it but to quash the conviction."

Appeal allowed.

NOTE

Not only must a summary trial always take place in the presence of the accused (except where trial in absence is otherwise competent, for example under section 338(*b*) of the 1975 Act), the prosecutor must also be present: see *Skeen* v. *Summerhill and Another* (1975) 39 J.C.L. 59. It is improper for a judge who has been at or near the *locus* at which the crime was committed to preside over a subsequent trial of a person arrested there, but it may not be oppressive: see *McDevitt* v. *McLeod*, 1982 S.C.C.R. 282; *supra*, Chap. 1.

(C)   Unsworn statement from dock

Gilmour v. H.M. Advocate
1965 J.C. 45

An accused person was convicted after trial on indictment. The sheriff refused to allow the accused to make an unsworn statement from the dock. He appealed against conviction.

LORD JUSTICE-GENERAL (CLYDE): "In this case the applicant was found guilty by a jury in the Sheriff Court at Kilmarnock of assaulting his wife and striking her on the face with an axe or similar instrument to her injury.

At the close of the Crown evidence at the trial the solicitor appearing for the applicant informed the court that the accused 'wished to elect his right to make a statement from the dock.' The object of this motion was to enable the accused to avoid giving his evidence on oath and, in consequence, not to subject himself to cross-examination. This motion was refused by the Sheriff but thereafter the accused did not go into the witness-box to give evidence and the trial proceeded to a conviction.

The only ground argued to us in the present application is that the Sheriff erred in the course which he took in not permitting the accused to make a statement from the dock without giving evidence on oath. The basis put forward to justify this ground of appeal was section 1(*h*) of the Criminal Evidence Act, 1898.

The Act in question is an Act applicable to Scotland and to England. The principal object of section 1 of the Act was to enable accused persons to be competent witnesses for the defence in a criminal case. Prior to that Act an accused person could not give evidence on his own behalf in the witness-box and the object of the Act was to remove this disability, which, in many cases, proved a real hardship to the accused. Section 1(*h*) of the Act provides: 'Nothing in this Act shall affect the provisions of section eighteen of the Indictable Offences Act, 1848, or any right of the person charged to make a statement without being sworn.' The contention of the applicant in the present case is that the latter words in the subsection recognised his right to make a statement without going into the witness-box and taking an oath.

But it is to be observed in the first place that the subsection confers no new right of any kind on an accused. It merely preserves certain rights which he may have had when the 1898 Act came into operation. In the second place, the Indictable Offences Act, 1848, mentioned in section 1(*h*) is an English Act, which does not, and never did, apply to Scotland. The outlook of the subsection is English in character and not Scottish. But, in the third place, the subsection does not preserve the right of an accused person to make a statement without being sworn. It is much more tentatively phrased. It does not recognise that there is such a right. It only preserves any right which there may be. It is consequently crucial to the success of the applicant's ground of appeal that he should be able to establish that such a right on the part of an accused to make a statement without being sworn, prior to the verdict of a jury, did exist in the law of Scotland in 1898. It appears that there is some such right in English criminal law (see Archbold, Criminal Pleading, Evidence and Practice, paragraph 553).

On the crucial matter, however, the applicant has completely failed to produce any decision or text-book in Scotland in support of such a right. The Crown informed us that they had been unable to find any warrant for the existence of such a right in Scotland.

I am satisfied that before 1898 an accused could make a judicial declaration before a magistrate, but that otherwise he had no right to give evidence in his own defence, either on oath or otherwise. It is quite impossible, if he had a right before 1898 to make a statement at the trial not on oath, that such a vitally important right would not have been referred to in the authorities or in the decided cases. Indeed, had there been such a right, it would obviously have frequently been invoked and there would have been little, if any, advantage in the main provisions of the 1898 Act, which, for the first time, entitled an accused to give evidence in his own defence. In my opinion, therefore, section 1(*h*) of the 1898 Act applies only to England and has no application in Scottish criminal proceedings.

Since that Act came into operation an accused person who wishes to challenge any of the facts spoken to by the Crown witnesses has the opportunity, if he so wishes, of controverting these facts. But for that purpose he must go into the witness-box and, consequently, be liable to cross-examination. This is in accordance with our conception of fair play. If he does not take that course, he cannot give evidence at all. If he is represented by counsel or by a solicitor, he has, of course, the right, through them, to address the jury before they give their verdict. If he is not legally represented, he can himself address the jury. But these addresses can only be based on the evidence which has been led before the jury, and the judge is entitled to direct the jury to disregard facts alleged in these addresses which are not included in sworn testimony given at the trial. Any other rule can only lead to injustice.

We were informed that in recent years a practice has grown up in certain Sheriff Courts of allowing witnesses or accused persons to make statements without being put on oath or making a solemn affirmation before the statements were made. This practice is alleged to occur especially in summary cases. This court has had occasion to criticise such a practice in *Forbes* v. *H.M. Advocate*. If it does occur, it is quite an improper practice, whether in relation to witnesses or to accused parties. There is no warrant for it under our law either in summary or solemn proceedings and, indeed, *Forbes's* case is an illustration of how completely the court or the jury may be misled by slipshod procedure of this kind.

We were referred to the terms of an Act of Adjournal of 22nd March 1935, which deals with shorthand notes in criminal proceedings. Paragraph 1 of this Act of Adjournal does not recognise, nor imply, that any accused person has a right, prior to the verdict, to make a statement regarding the facts without going on oath. It merely includes within the expression 'proceedings at the trial' any statements made by or on behalf of the prisoner, whether before or after the verdict. It says nothing whatever as to the validity or competency of any such statement, but is merely intended to secure that the court has a clear record of all that has taken place in the court below them. This provision, therefore, is of no assistance to the applicant in the present case.

In my opinion the ground upon which this application for leave to appeal is made is unsound in law and the Sheriff was correct in rejecting it. The application must, therefore, in my opinion be refused."

Appeal refused.

NOTE

The law is thus clear, both in summary and solemn cases. Nevertheless, mistakes have still occurred since this decision; clerks to lay magistrates sitting in the district court sometimes encounter this problem, particularly where the accused is unrepresented. It should also be noted that the accused is entitled, after conviction, whether by trial or on a plea of guilty, to address the court in mitigation of sentence: *Falconer* v. *Jessop*, 1975 S.L.T. (Notes) 78.

In England the right of an accused to make an unsworn statement from the dock was abolished in 1982.

(D)   Is it necessary to identify the accused?

By section 26(5) of the Criminal Justice (Scotland) Act 1980 it is provided: "At any trial of an offence under summary procedure it shall be presumed that the person who appears in answer to the complaint is the person charged by the police with the offence unless the contrary is alleged."

Smith v. Paterson
1982 S.L.T. 437

An accused person was acquitted of breach of the peace. The fiscal appealed by stated case. In the case, the sheriff made the following findings-in-fact:

1.   On August 8, 1981 a football match took place in Edinburgh between Hibernian and St Johnstone.

2.   After the match, a crowd of about 150 young Hibernian supporters set off from Easter Road, and walked along London Road.

3.   There was unruly behaviour within this crowd; it split into various groups, of which one, numbering about 20 persons, walked on towards Princes Street.

4.   Two police officers followed this crowd, and thereafter followed this

group to Princes Street, where they observed its behaviour from a police vehicle.

5.   At Princes Street this group sang songs, and swore and gestured at buses and pedestrians.

6.   The police officers left their vehicle, moved forward and arrested a member of this group whom they had seen give a "V" sign at a passing vehicle.

7.   This man was taken by the police officers to Gayfield Square police station, where he was cautioned and charged with the offence libelled in the complaint.

Neither of the two police officers who gave evidence was asked to identify the respondent.

LORD CAMERON: "This appeal by way of stated case from the sheriff court in Edinburgh raises sharply a short point of statutory interpretation. By s. 26(5) of the Criminal Justice (Scotland) Act 1980 it is provided that 'at any trial of an offence under summary procedure it shall be presumed that the person who appears in answer to the complaint is the person charged by the police with the offence unless the contrary is alleged.' The procedure for challenging the presumption is laid down in s. 334(1) of the Criminal Procedure (Scotland) Act 1975 as amended by para. 54 of Sched. 7 to the Act of 1980. No question as to the proper construction or application of these procedures arises in the present case as no such challenge was made by the respondent who was the accused. The appeal is at the instance of the prosecutor. The circumstances out of which the appeal arises are set out in the case. The respondent, along with some others, was charged on summary complaint with breach of the peace in that 'on 8 August 1981 in the street in Princes Street, Edinburgh [he] did conduct [him]self in a disorderly manner, shout and swear and commit a breach of the peace.' When the case called on 2 October 1981 the respondent was represented by a solicitor who tendered a plea of not guilty; his co-accused all pleaded guilty.

Trial took place on 8 January 1982 and evidence was led for the prosecution from two police officers. Their evidence is summarised by the sheriff as follows: [his Lordship quoted the findings-in-fact and continued:] Neither police officer was asked to identify the respondent. At the conclusion of the evidence for the prosecution the solicitor for the respondent submitted that in terms of s. 345A of the Criminal Procedure (Scotland) Act 1975 as now amended there was 'no case to answer'. The ground of the submission for the respondent was that there was no evidence identifying the respondent with the commission of the crime charged against him. Having heard parties the sheriff gave effect to the respondent's motion and acquitted him of the charge in the complaint. It is against this decision that the Crown have taken this appeal.

In his opinion the learned sheriff records that 'he had no reason to disbelieve the police officers and that the evidence which they gave was sufficient from which to infer that a breach of the peace had taken place'. It may therefore be accepted that there was corroborated and credible evidence sufficient to establish: (1) the fact of a breach of the peace being committed, (2) that the police arrested a person concerned in the commission of the offence, and (3) that this person after arrest was taken to a police station and there cautioned and charged with the offence libelled. The basis of the sheriff's judgment appears to be that, while rightly concluding that the provisions of s. 26 are dealing with matters of formal or routine evidence: 'identification of an accused person is not normally a formal matter, however. It is normally of the first importance requiring the best evidence and in a case like the present case it can be crucial'. Because the police officers did not formally identify the respondent the sheriff concluded that there was no evidence which would entitle him in this case to hold that the respondent had been identified as acting as alleged in the complaint. He therefore sustained the respondent's motion and acquitted him. For the Crown it was submitted that the sheriff erred. It was clear from the sheriff's narrative of the evidence that there was sufficient evidence of a breach of the peace being committed and of the arrest of a man and that man being taken to Gayfield Square and there charged. When the statutory presumption provided for in s. 26(5) was taken into account the identity of the accused as the person charged with the offence was established. That person was the respondent. That person was (if the police were believed) the person who was seen committing a breach of the peace and was arrested. Therefore the position was this: there was sufficient evidence of a breach of the peace; there was sufficient evidence that a person was seen committing such a breach; there was sufficient evidence that this person was arrested and taken to Gayfield Square; and there was no suggestion that a different person was subsequently charged as libelled. At this stage the presumption created by s. 26(5) which was, as its language and context plainly show, a limited presumption, came into play, there being no denial or challenge timeously made. In these circumstances there was certainly a 'case to answer' and the sheriff wholly misconstrued both the evidence and effect of the presumption in linking the respondent with the offender observed in the act of committing the offence and thereupon taken into and retained in custody until cautioned and charged with the offence. The chain of evidence linking the respondent to the offence charged was complete. Counsel referred to the case of *Muldoon* v. *Herron*. It was merely a coincidence that the witnesses to the incident and the officers who charged the respondent were the same individuals. The chain of evidence here was completed by the two police witnesses in the circumstances of the particular case. The sheriff had confounded identification of an accused as perpetrator of an offence and proof of the identity of the person in the dock as the individual charged. The question should be answered in the negative and the case sent back to the sheriff to proceed as accords. For the respondent, counsel submitted that identification of the perpetrator of an offence as the accused was vital. Here no witness identified the respondent as such and it was not to be assumed that in a question of 'routine evidence' the vital element of identification of the accused with commission of the offence could be 'presumed'. There was here a misuse of the presumption because the police could and should have been asked to identify the accused. The appeal should be refused.

In my opinion the learned sheriff has plainly erred in his construction of s. 26(5) of the Act of 1980. The provisions of s. 26(5) of the Criminal Justice (Scotland) Act 1980 are concerned with a presumption of limited operation and directed to matters of what are described in the side-note of the section as 'routine evidence'. Not only so but the presumption only applies in the absence of challenge by the accused. The right to exercise this challenge and precise time and circumstances in which it is to be exercised are dealt with in s. 334(1) of the Criminal Procedure (Scotland) Act 1975 as amended by para. 54 of Sched. 7 to the Act of 1980. The presumption thus enacted is concerned solely with the identification of an accused on trial as the person whom the police have charged with the offence libelled against him in the complaint before the court. It does not therefore in terms or by any necessary implication create a presumption of identification of the person charged as the perpetrator of the offence libelled. In many cases the officers concerned in charging an accused can speak to no other relevant matter, far less be witnesses to identification of the accused as participants in the offence. It may happen, however, by coincidence that police witnesses give evidence which identifies or serves to identify the person charged by them as responsible for the criminal acts libelled. This however is a coincidence which may arise from the circumstances of the particular case. It is in no sense a necessary and conclusive consequence of the operation of this limited statutory presumption. Where the learned sheriff has fallen into error is in confusing the issue of identification of the culprit with that of identification of the accused as the person charged. The effect of the presumption in the circumstances of the present case however could have and did have no effect on the issue of the accuracy or credibility of the evidence of the police officers as to the actions of the culprit which led to his arrest and subsequent charge by them. It was therefore open to the defence to challenge the evidence of the police officers on the merits by cross-examination and, if felt such a course was possible or desirable, by leading evidence to controvert such evidence. In the present case the sheriff had before him unchallenged evidence—the credibility of which was for him to assess—which, if accepted, provided legal and sufficient proof of the commission of an offence and the arrest of the offender but in addition, and this is important, of the conveyance of the offender to a police station where that offender was charged with the particular offence libelled in the complaint. Now, subsequent to that charge a complaint was served on the respondent who answered to the complaint and was legally represented. He did not allege that he was not the person charged by the police and consequently the presumption applied. This, if the evidence, which the learned sheriff had no reason to disbelieve, was accepted completed an unbroken chain of proof linking the respondent with the commission of the offence charged. The presumption does no more and no less than provide one, but only one, step towards establishing the charges laid against an accused; the importance of that step in any particular case will depend on the circumstances of the case. Indeed it may have very little, depending again on the facts and nature of the particular case itself. Here the respondent by acceptance of the statutory presumption admitted that it was he who had been charged with the offence. The direct evidence of the police established, if accepted, that they had charged a person whom they had seen committing the offence charged on the date and in the place libelled. If then the accused not only makes no denial that he was the person charged but by his silence when appearing in answer to the complaint, admits that fact in the most formal way then in such circumstances the chain of evidence is complete. The sheriff's error here lay not so much in a misapprehension of the limited purpose of the new statutory presumption, but in his misapprehension of its effect as an element of proof in the identification of an accused with the commission of the offence libelled. In my opinion the sheriff fell into error in that he failed to note that if the respondent was by operation of the presumption held to be the person charged by the police there was evidence in law sufficient, if accepted, that this person was seen committing the offence libelled and arrested on the spot and thereafter taken to the police station and there charged with the offence. Therefore the person charged and the person who committed the offence libelled in the charge was one and the same—the respondent.

The respondent's motion should therefore have been refused by the sheriff. In these circumstances the questions in the case should be answered in the negative and the case remitted to the sheriff to proceed as accords."

Appeal allowed.

NOTE

It must be observed that section 26(5) of the 1980 Act applies only to summary cases. If any denial that the accused is the person charged by the police is to be made, it should be made at the first calling of the case: section 334(2) of the 1975 Act, as amended by the 1980 Act, Sched. 7, para. 54. It will no longer be open to the defence to sit back and hope that the Crown witnesses are not asked or fail to identify the accused.

(E) Can the accused be required to stand in order to assist in identification?

Beattie v. Scott
1990 S.C.C.R. 296
An accused was convicted of assault and appealed by stated case.

LORD JUSTICE-GENERAL: "The appellant is Jeffrey Beattie, who appeared in the sheriff court at Falkirk charged along with three other men on a summary complaint of assault. There were two charges, the allegation being that the accused had attacked two men, James Alexander Ellis and John McIver, on 17th December 1988 in Cadzow Avenue, Bo'ness. The accused all pled not guilty and the case went to trial on 1st September 1989. At the conclusion of the Crown case the charge relating to the assault on Mr Ellis was withdrawn. A submission on behalf of the appellant that there was no case to answer in respect of the charge of assaulting Mr McIver was repelled, and the appellant was then convicted on that charge. He has challenged his conviction by means of this stated case.

The incident took place while Mr Ellis and Mr McIver were walking together along a road in Bo'ness at about 1.30 a.m. on 17th December 1988. A group of youths came up behind them shouting abuse and a scuffle broke out, after which Mr Ellis and Mr McIver proceeded on their way. While they were walking along Cadzow Avenue they were confronted by a group of four youths who emerged from behind a hedge. They proceeded to attack Mr Ellis, who was on one side of Cadzow Avenue, and Mr McIver, who was separated from him when the confrontation occurred and was on the other side of Cadzow Avenue. The appellant did not dispute that he was one of the members of the group which emerged from behind the hedge. The point at issue was whether there was sufficient evidence to identify him as one of those who had assaulted Mr McIver.

The starting-point for an examination of this issue is a statement which the appellant made on 17th December 1988 when he was interviewed in Falkirk Police Office by two police officers. He was informed of allegations against him relating to the two assaults earlier that day. He was cautioned in common form and then made a statement in which he described how he had been in the company of three other youths and taken part in an assault on two men in a street called Clydesdale Street. That street adjoins Cadzow Avenue and it forms a junction with it not far from where the assault took place. There was no evidence to suggest that there had been any other incident in or near Clydesdale Street. The sheriff regarded this statement as amounting to a clear confession of guilty participation in the assault on Mr McIver. Mr McBride for the appellant accepted that the sheriff was entitled to take this view and, accordingly, that very little other evidence was required in order to enable the sheriff to proceed to convict him of the assault.

The submission for the appellant was that in these circumstances the evidence of Mr McIver was of particular significance. Two points were made in support of the appeal. The first was that there was insufficient evidence of identification because the only acceptable evidence given by Mr McIver was that the appellant resembled one of his attackers but it might not have been him. The second was that the sheriff erred in allowing a Crown motion for the appellant to stand up in the dock to assist Mr McIver in identifying him at the trial. This, it was said, was in effect obliging the appellant to give evidence against himself. If the identification which followed was left out of account there was insufficient evidence to corroborate the confession.

The sheriff's narrative of what occurred in the trial is as follows. In the course of his evidence Mr McIver identified the appellant and his three co-accused, all of whom were sitting in the dock, as the persons who had jumped out in front of him. He indicated the appellant and one of his co-accused as the persons who had been responsible for the attack on him, but said that he would be better able to say that with confidence if he could see the appellant standing up. The procurator fiscal depute then moved the sheriff to require the appellant to stand. Objection to that motion was taken on behalf of the appellant, but this was repelled by the sheriff and the appellant then stood up. The sheriff was satisfied that Mr McIver had identified the appellant as one of his assailants and he summed the matter up in these words:

'His evidence in chief, although given after some initial hesitation and, as it impressed me, careful consideration, was positive to that effect. In cross-examination he admitted the possibility that it might not have been the appellant who attacked him and spoke of a resemblance between one of his assailants and the appellant. His evidence that the group of four, two of whose members had assaulted him, consisted of the appellant and his co-accused remained unqualified.'

Two other pieces of evidence were relevant to the case against the appellant. One was a reply when he was cautioned and charged, which the sheriff held could properly be construed as a further admission of guilt on his part. There was also evidence from Mr Ellis who identified the appellant as one of the group of four which had been involved in the assault. There is no doubt, therefore, that there was corroboration from Mr Ellis of the appellant's admission that he was one of the group, which, as I have said, was not disputed by the appellant.

The learned advocate-depute submitted that there was no miscarriage of justice in this case because Mr McIver had already given sufficient evidence of identification to corroborate the admission before the appellant was asked to stand up. Very little was required of Mr McIver in the light of the admission of guilt and the evidence of Mr Ellis that the appellant was one of the group. According to the sheriff's description of events, Mr McIver had already identified the appellant before the procurator fiscal depute moved the sheriff that he be required to stand. That motion was made in response to his remark that he would be better able to say with confidence that the appellant was one of those who had attacked him if he could see him standing up. Even if, as the appellant has contended, Mr McIver could only say that the appellant resembled one of his attackers, this was enough to corroborate the admission, since it was accepted that the appellant was one of the group.

In my opinion there was sufficient evidence to convict the appellant even without the confirmation of Mr McIver's identification of him which he obtained when the appellant stood up. It is not necessary to examine the details of his admissions of guilt, since Mr McBride accepted that the sheriff was entitled to treat them as unequivocal with the result that very little other evidence was required. In *Ralston* v. *H.M. Advocate* there was an emphatic positive identification by one witness which required very little else by way of corroboration to establish guilt. As to what was required in these circumstances the Lord Justice-Clerk said this at p.472:

'That little else must of course be evidence which is consistent in all respects with the positive identification evidence which has been given. At the end of the day one must look at the whole evidence to ask whether the supporting evidence consistent with the positive identification evidence, taken together with the positive identification evidence, is sufficient to entitle the jury beyond reasonable doubt to conclude that the particular accused was the perpetrator of the particular crime.'

The evidence of Mr Ellis, who identified the appellant as one of the group two members of which had assaulted Mr McIver, when taken together with the evidence of Mr McIver that the appellant resembled one of his attackers, was consistent with the appellant's confession of participation in the assaults. In my opinion this evidence when taken together with that confession was sufficient to entitle the sheriff to hold that the appellant was one of those who had assaulted Mr McIver.

This makes it unnecessary to decide the question whether the sheriff erred in requiring the appellant to stand up in the dock to assist Mr McIver in his identification. But, since the point was fully argued, I think that it is proper to say something about it. The appellant's argument was that he should not have been required to stand because this was, in effect, requiring him to give evidence against himself. He was entitled to put the Crown to its proof and to do and say nothing in the course of the trial, so long as he did not conduct himself in a way calculated to defeat the ends of justice. The witness could, if he wished, have left the witness box to have a closer look at him, but he should not have been obliged to provide the witness with assistance in any way. The learned advocate-depute's reply was that the overriding requirement was fairness to the accused and that the question was one of circumstances and degree. There was an absence of authority on what could or could not be done at the trial, but so far as pre-trial procedure was concerned, it had been recognised that there was a balance to be struck between the importance of the criminal investigation with a view to the detection and suppression of crime on the one hand and the liberty of the subject on the other: *Adair* v. *McGarry*, per Lord Sands at p.88. He referred to the Lord Justice-Clerk's observations to the same effect in *Lees* v. *Weston* and *Currie* v. *McGlennan* at p.470.

Had the correct view of what was being asked of the appellant been that he was being asked to give evidence against himself, there would plainly have been no doubt whatever that what the sheriff did was oppressive and that it should not be allowed. In my opinion the advocate-depute was right when he said that the appellant was not in fact being asked to give evidence against himself. On the contrary, he was being asked to assist the witness who was giving the evidence. But that still begs the question whether an accused person should ever be required to assist the Crown in any way in the presentation of the evidence at his trial. In my opinion that question admits of only one answer and that is in the negative. No doubt a proper balance must be struck between the interests of the public on the one hand and the interests of the accused on the other, and questions of degree may arise both before and after full committal as to what may be done by way of investigation of the crime. But the stage of investigation is completed when the case comes to trial and at that stage the interests of the accused person demand that the Crown should prove its case against him without any assistance whatever on his part.

The sheriff has referred to the possibility that an accused person might seek to prevent an identification by covering his face with his hands or with a veil or a mask. In my opinion acts of this character which are taken with a view to defeating the ends of justice are in a different category from acts which are designed to assist the presentation of the case by the Crown. They can be dealt [with], if the need arises, by an order that the face be uncovered or the veil or mask be removed. But so long as the accused does nothing of that kind he is entitled to remain sitting in the dock. He is entitled to refuse to do anything by way of movement or adjustment of his appearance and of course to say anything which might assist in his identification. He is to be regarded purely as an object, as one whose role in the trial is an entirely passive one as it unfolds around him. It is on that basis that the Crown must present its case.

For these reasons I move your Lordships to answer the questions in the case in the affirmative, with the exception of question 3 which is in these terms:

> 'Was I entitled to grant the motion made by the procurator fiscal depute that the appellant be required to stand in order to facilitate identification?'

Had it been necessary to do so I would have answered that question in the negative."

Appeal refused.

NOTE

Dock identification thus remains primarily identification of facial features, which leaves all sorts of questions unanswered. What about profile identification? What about the situation where height is relied on? And is dock identification fair anyway, having regard to the isolation of the accused and the presence of police escorts?

(F)   Comments by trial judge: prejudging credibility?

Hogg v. Normand
1991 S.C.C.R. 26

An accused was convicted of lewd and libidinous practices. He appealed by stated case.

LORD MURRAY: "At the outset of this stated case Mr Duguid for the appellant explained that the point which he intended to argue was reflected in the first question posed in the case, namely whether certain remarks made by the sheriff during the course of evidence for the Crown were unfair to the appellant and constituted a miscarriage of justice. The appellant had been convicted of lewd and libidinous practices towards two young girls aged nine and seven in respect of whom the remarks had been made. This point could and should have been taken by bill of suspension but the matters to be brought under review were fully covered by the stated case and he was prepared to argue it as a suspension if the court permitted it. The advocate-depute agreed that a bill of suspension was the proper mode of review but consented to the course proposed by Mr Duguid.

The appellant was convicted by the sheriff of the lewd behaviour towards the two girls to which they had testified in evidence. Their mother had been present in court when they gave evidence. After the second girl had given evidence the sheriff advised the mother that she could leave the court with her two daughters. The sheriff then said to her, as he states in his note ... that she should be proud of her daughters who were a credit to her. The sheriff goes on to explain that he made this remark not because he had reached a view about the weight, quality or effect of their evidence (which he had not), but because he thought that a little courtesy and reassurance from the bench at the conclusion of their evidence was entirely appropriate. We accept that this was the sheriff's motivation and that he did not in fact reach a concluded view on the credibility and reliability of the girls' evidence before all the witnesses had testified. The issue, however, remains as to whether justice was seen to have been done to the appellant in light of the remark which the sheriff did in fact make.

Mr Duguid founded upon *Millar* v. *Lees* [1991 S.C.C.R. 799] where a procurator fiscal depute had asked a sheriff during the Crown case whether he accepted certain witnesses and the sheriff had replied that he did. He cited a passage at the foot of p.802 to the top of p.803 from the opinion of the court as follows:

> 'The advocate-depute did not seek to defend what the procurator fiscal depute had done in this case. He accepted that there was an irregularity and he accepted that it was improper for her to have asked the sheriff the question which he [sic] did. He also accepted that it was wrong of the sheriff to indicate the view which he had formed as to the credibility and reliability of the Crown witnesses before he had heard all the evidence.'

It was submitted that, on the principle that justice must not only be done but must manifestly be seen to be done, the ratio of *Millar* applied to a remark of the kind made by the sheriff in this case which could reasonably be understood to indicate that he had accepted the girls' evidence before he had heard all the witnesses. The first question posed for the court should be answered in the affirmative and the conviction quashed.

The advocate-depute did not dispute the application of the foregoing principle nor that the sheriff's remark had been unfortunate. He referred us to two cases indicating the test to be applied by the court to such circumstances. These were *Bradford* v. *McLeod* [1985 S.C.C.R. 379] at p.382 (top) and p.384, and *Harper of Oban (Engineering) Ltd* v. *Henderson* [1988 S.C.C.R. 351]. We are satisfied that the effect of these cases is that, even without any actual unfairness, if the circumstances complained of are such as to create in the mind of a reasonable man a suspicion that justice is not impartial, a conviction cannot stand. We are satisfied that the sheriff's remark in this case, though made in good faith with the best of intentions, was such as to raise a suspicion in the mind of a reasonable man that the appellant's case might not be properly considered so that he would not receive a fair trial. The Crown's case entirely depended on [the] acceptance of both girls as credible witnesses. Accordingly the appeal must be allowed and the first question answered in the affirmative. The Crown did not seek to argue that a new trial should be allowed. We therefore quash the conviction."

Conviction quashed.

NOTE

It is common for judges to make remarks on credibility when delivering judgment; indeed, credibility is often the only main issue in a summary trial. But here the remarks were made, albeit innocently, before the issue had to be decided. See also *Dott* v. *Cardle*, 1993 S.C.C.R. 834.

CHAPTER 15

APPEAL IN SOLEMN PROCEEDINGS

Prior to the Criminal Appeal (Scotland) Act 1926, the opportunities for review in solemn proceedings were very limited. A person convicted before the High Court had nothing in the nature of the general right of appeal against conviction or sentence. In solemn proceedings before the sheriff court, the accused enjoyed a limited right of appeal on points of law by way of bill of suspension. Similarly, the prosecutor could, by bill of advocation, bring under review decisions on the competency and relevancy of the indictment. But apart from these cases, the only method of review open to a convicted person was to petition the Secretary for Scotland for the exercise of the Royal Prerogative of Mercy.

In 1925, a committee on criminal appeals in Scotland recommended that a court of criminal appeal be established (along lines similar to the English Court of Criminal Appeal established in 1907) to review convictions on indictment in the High Court and sheriff court (Cmnd. 2456, 1925). Such a court was established by the Criminal Appeal (Scotland) Act 1926.

The provisions of the 1926 Act (as amended by the Criminal Appeal (Scotland) Act 1927) were re-enacted in sections 228 *et seq.* of the 1975 Act. These provisions have been very substantially amended, or replaced by Schedule 2 to the 1980 Act. Throughout this chapter, therefore, references to the 1975 Act incorporate these and other changes, unless otherwise indicated.

A. COMPOSITION AND STATUS OF THE APPEAL COURT

Criminal Procedure (Scotland) Act 1975
"245.—(1) For the purpose of hearing and determining any appeal under this Part of this Act or any proceeding connected therewith three of the Lords Commissioners of Justiciary shall be a quorum of the High Court, and the determination of any question under this Part of this Act by the court shall be according to the votes of the majority of the members of the court sitting, including the presiding judge, and each judge so sitting shall be entitled to pronounce a separate opinion.

262. Subject to the provisions of [section 263] of this Act, all interlocutors and sentences pronounced by the High Court under this Part of this Act shall be final and conclusive and not subject to review by any court whatsoever and it shall be incompetent to stay or suspend any execution or diligence issuing from the High Court under this Part of this Act."

NOTES
1. Section 263 confers on the Secretary of State the power to refer the case of a convicted person to the High Court for consideration. For a consideration of this power see *Leitch* v. *Secretary of State for Scotland, infra*, p.526. Section 263 also provides that nothing in the appeals provisions shall affect the prerogative of mercy, for a consideration of which see *infra*, Chap. 18.

2.   Section 262 extends to the High Court as a court of appeal the finality of judgment enjoyed by the High Court at common law. There is, in particular, no further appeal from the High Court to the House of Lords in criminal cases. *Cf. Mackintosh* v. *Lord Advocate* (1876) 3 R. (H.L.) 34. The Thomson Committee (3rd Report) concluded that there was no strong demand for any change in this respect (para. 21.03).

3.   The High Court does, however, exercise its *nobile officium* in certain cases to prevent injustice or oppression, where no right of appeal exists: see *infra*, Chap. 18.

B.   THE GROUND OF APPEAL AND ITS EFFECT ON CONVICTION

1.   Criminal Procedure (Scotland) Act 1975

"228.—(1) Any person convicted on indictment may appeal in accordance with the provisions of this Part of this Act, to the High Court—

(*a*) against such conviction;

(*b*) against the sentence passed on such conviction;

or

(*c*) against both such conviction and such sentence:

Provided that there shall be no appeal against any sentence fixed by law.

(2) By an appeal under subsection (1) of this section, a person may bring under review of the High Court any alleged miscarriage of justice in the proceedings in which he was convicted, including any alleged miscarriage of justice on the basis of the existence and significance of additional evidence which was not heard at the trial and which was not available and could not reasonably have been made available at the trial.

254.—(1) The High Court may ... dispose of an appeal against conviction by—

(*a*) affirming the verdict of the trial court;

(*b*) setting aside the verdict of the trial court and either quashing the conviction or substituting therefor an amended verdict of guilty:

Provided that an amended verdict of guilty must be one which could have been returned on the indictment before the trial court; or

(*c*) setting aside the verdict of the trial court and granting authority to bring a new prosecution in accordance with section 255 of this Act."

(2) In setting aside, under subsection (1) above, a verdict the High Court may quash any sentence imposed on the appellant as respects the indictment, and—

(*a*) in a case where it substitutes an amended verdict of guilty, whether or not the sentence related to the verdict set aside; or

(*b*) in any other case, where the sentence did not so relate,

may pass another (but not more severe) sentence in substitution for the sentence so quashed."

NOTE

The 1926 Act (whose provisions were reproduced in the 1975 Act) provided for three grounds of appeal against conviction, namely, that the verdict was unreasonable or could not be supported having regard to the evidence, that there had been a wrong decision of law by the trial court, or that on any ground there had been a miscarriage of justice: 1975 Act (unamended), s. 254(1). These grounds of appeal were subject to "the proviso" which permitted the court to dismiss the appeal "notwithstanding that they were of opinion that the point raised in the appeal might be decided in favour of the appellant ... if they considered that no substantial miscarriage of justice had actually occurred."

There is now only one ground of appeal—miscarriage of justice under section 228—and it applies both to appeal against conviction and appeal against sentence. The meaning of this term, and its effect upon conviction, are discussed in the following cases. Appeal against sentence is discussed *infra*, p.507.

2.   McCuaig v. H.M. Advocate
1982 S.L.T. 383

An accused person appealed against conviction on the ground of miscarriage of justice. The alleged miscarriage lay in the inadvertent disclosure by the sheriff to the jury of the appellant's previous convictions prior to the verdict.

LORD JUSTICE-CLERK (WHEATLEY): "On the basis that the disclosure in the instant case was a breach of s. 160(1) of the Criminal Procedure (Scotland) Act 1975 as amended, I am of the opinion that the matter has to be looked at in the light of the new terms of s. 254(1) of that Act as amended. The disclosure arose out of a question put to a police witness by the presiding judge in an endeavour on his part to clarify the contents of a charge preferred against the appellant to which he had given an answer. The police witness had spoken to a charge which was in the terms of the charge in the indictment, but on being asked by the judge to be more specific he referred to his note-book and substantially repeated the words of the charge with the addition of the words 'and to conceal your true name and to avoid production of a reference to previous convictions relative to you and you did by said means attempt to defeat the ends of justice'. In these circumstances the question is whether or not that breach of s. 160(1) is sufficient to warrant the conviction being quashed. The matter in my view is now entirely one for the discretion of the court. In terms of s. 254(1) as amended the provision is that the High Court *may* subject to subs. (4) dispose of an appeal against conviction either by: (a) affirming the verdict of the trial court; or (b) setting aside the verdict and either quashing it or substituting therefor an amended verdict of guilty; or (c) setting aside the verdict of the court and granting authority to bring a new prosecution. This is in marked distinction to the original terms of s. 254 which provided that the appeal court '*shall* allow the appeal if they think ... (c) that on any ground there was a miscarriage of justice' (my emphasis). There was a proviso, however, to the effect that the court 'may ... dismiss the appeal if they consider that no substantial miscarriage of justice has actually occurred'. Thus an imperative requirement to allow the appeal and quash the conviction, subject to a proviso giving a discretionary power to the court not to do so in stated circumstances has been replaced by a discretionary power to the court inter alia to quash the conviction or amend the verdict of guilty. This seems to me to give wider power to the court than the previous legislation.

Looking at the circumstances of this case through the eyes of that amended subsection, I am of the opinion that the circumstances here do not warrant a finding that a miscarriage of justice has been sustained sufficient to warrant the setting aside of the verdict. I am accordingly of the opinion that the verdict which was returned should be affirmed and the appeal refused."

Appeal refused.

NOTES

1.   Prior to the 1980 Act, the relationship between the grounds of appeal recognised by the old section 254 and the disposal of the appeal was as follows. Once the appellant had established the ground of appeal, the appeal court was obliged to quash the conviction unless the Crown persuaded the court that there had been no substantial miscarriage of justice. The new appeal provisions, as interpreted in *McCuaig*, require the appellant to establish that there has been a miscarriage of justice. So that even if the appellant shows, for example, that there has been a misdirection or some other error of law, this may not of itself result in the conviction being quashed. There must also be a miscarriage of justice. The onus relating to miscarriage has, therefore, switched from a "negative" onus on the Crown, to a "positive" onus on the appellant.

2.   But even where the court is satisfied that there has been a miscarriage of justice, it would now seem that this will not necessarily result in the conviction being quashed. It must be a miscarriage of justice "sufficient to warrant the setting aside of the verdict." The Lord Justice-Clerk further developed this point in *Burns* v. *H.M. Advocate*, 1983 S.L.T. 38, a case involving a clear misdirection of a jury by a sheriff:

> "In that situation have the appellants established a case for the quashing of the convictions? That the sheriff misdirected the jury is accepted on all hands. But did that misdirection create a miscarriage of justice, and, if so, was it so weighty as to warrant the quashing of the convictions? The phrase 'substantial miscarriage of justice' which found its place in previous legislation as a qualification of the otherwise mandatory direction to quash is no longer with us. But that mandatory direction to quash has been replaced by a permissive power to affirm, quash, or amend the verdict or authorise a new prosecution: s. 254(1) of the Criminal Procedure (Scotland) Act 1975, as amended. That permissive power has to be exercised having regard to all the circumstances of the case. Looking to all the circumstances of the instant case I do not consider that any miscarriage of justice resulted from the sheriff's unfortunate errors in law in directing the jury."

What has happened, in effect, is that the court has interpreted the new appeal provisions as meaning that the appellant is not entitled to succeed unless he shows that there has been, not simply a "miscarriage of justice" but a "substantial" or "material" or "weighty" miscarriage. That, indeed, was the formula adopted by the Lord Justice-Clerk in *Mackenzie* v. *H.M. Advocate*, 1983 S.L.T. 220 *infra*, p.518 where he stated:

> "Having regard to all these factors, I am of the opinion that the presiding judge erred in directing the jury ... These errors resulting in such prejudice to the appellant that I have no alternative to holding that a substantial miscarriage of justice resulted and that the verdict of the court ... must be set aside."

3.   It is submitted that this is a most unfortunate interpretation of the new provisions. It is, however, inevitable, once it is held that the court has a complete discretion under section 254, since it then becomes necessary to devise a formula to distinguish between those miscarriages which justify interfering with the verdict and those which do not. This interpretation is

particularly unfortunate when one has regard to the provisions for re-trial. As will be seen from the case of *Mackenzie*, even where the appellant shows that there has been a substantial miscarriage he may still be faced with the prospect of a fresh indictment.

4. Notwithstanding the very wide discretion apparently enjoyed by the court, it is submitted that there are some cases in which the quashing of a conviction is inevitable. In *McAvoy and Another* v. *H.M. Advocate*, 1982 S.C.C.R. 263; 1983 S.L.T. 16, Lord Dunpark expressed the view (at 1982 S.C.C.R. 274) that: "While the power to affirm a verdict is *ex facie* unfettered, it must, in my opinion, be qualified by certain implied limitations. Obviously a court would not affirm a verdict which seemed to the court to be perverse or not supported by the evidence." See also the wholly exceptional case of *Boyle* v. *H.M. Advocate*, 1976 J.C. 32.

5. More recent cases suggest that the court will place more emphasis on the seriousness and materiality of the flaw at first instance in deciding whether to allow an appeal. See, *e.g.*, McCluskey, *Criminal Appeals*, paras. 7–03 *et seq.* for a discussion of the current position. The following case is an example of a situation where no miscarriage of justice was held to have occurred, albeit the trial judge misdirected the jury.

3. **Surman v. H.M. Advocate**
1988 S.L.T. 371

An accused person was charged with murder and pleaded self-defence. He gave evidence that the fatal blow was delivered by him in the course of a struggle after he had been attacked by the deceased. The trial judge withdrew from the jury consideration of self-defence as it affected the fatal wound and the accused was convicted of murder. He appealed on the basis that his evidence supported his plea, which should not have been withdrawn.

> LORD JUSTICE-CLERK: "In my opinion it was for the jury to decide what they made of the appellant's evidence in this regard. Although the appellant's evidence differed greatly from the evidence upon which the Crown relied, what he was maintaining was that he was engaged in defending himself against an attack made upon him by the deceased. His evidence was that a struggle took place between the two men following the attack made upon him by the deceased, and that it was in the course of this struggle that the fatal wound must have been delivered. The struggle as described by the appellant was one continuous operation in the course of which both punches and stab wounds were delivered. Obviously a question would arise for the jury to determine as to whether the retaliation which the appellant used was excessive. There was no question of the deceased being armed but according to the appellant he was trying to throttle the appellant with his hands at the time. In my opinion it was for the jury to determine whether the appellant was acting in self defence or whether his evidence was sufficient to raise in their minds a reasonable doubt as to whether the Crown had established its case. In my opinion the trial judge was wrong in taking the defence of self defence from the jury in this case, and that constituted a misdirection on the judge's part.
>
> Although I am satisfied that there was a misdirection on the part of the trial judge, the question then arises as to whether the appellant has established a case for quashing the conviction. This raises the question of whether the misdirection on the part of the trial judge created a miscarriage of justice of such a nature as to warrant the quashing of the conviction. Section 254 of the

Criminal Procedure (Scotland) Act 1975 confers upon the court a permissive power to affirm, set aside, quash or amend the verdict of the jury. There is also power to authorise a new prosecution. It is plain that a misdirection is not always fatal to the conviction; there may be a misdirection and yet no miscarriage of justice (*Burns* v. *H.M. Advocate* [1983 S.L.T. 348]).

In the present case, I have come to be of opinion that no miscarriage of justice resulted from the trial judge's misdirection. Although the trial judge directed the jury that self defence did not arise in regard to the fatal wound, he reminded the jury of the appellant's evidence and informed them that if they believed his evidence they should acquit him, and that it would also be their duty to acquit him if they had any reasonable doubt as to whether the version of events described by him was correct. Admittedly this direction was given on the basis that it would be open to the jury to conclude from the evidence of the appellant that there had been no deliberate intent to kill on his part nor such wicked recklessness as would constitute the crime of murder. Nevertheless the trial judge directed the jury in regard to how they should treat the evidence which the appellant had given in much the same way as he would have required to have directed them about this evidence if the plea of self defence had been left open. What the trial judge said in this regard is as follows:

> 'What does the accused say? Well, in the first place there is no dispute that the accused was holding the knife which was responsible for the deceased's wounds, including that from which on the undisputed evidence he died. The accused's position, you may think, ladies and gentlemen, is perfectly clear. He was set on, according to him, by the deceased. He fell back, the knife fell out of his pocket, he picked it up, and in his attempting to fend off the deceased who was engaged in attacking him the knife, without any intention on the part of the accused, caused the wounds from which the deceased ultimately died. Now, if you believe that version of events, ladies and gentlemen, it is your duty to acquit the accused and it's your duty to acquit the accused if you have a reasonable doubt as to whether that version of events is correct, and the reason would be, and it's pretty plain, that you would have to acquit in these circumstances because there was no such wicked recklessness or deliberate intention such as is required to constitute the crime of murder.'

If the trial judge had been charging the jury upon self defence, what he would have said to the jury would have been very much along the lines of the passage quoted above except for the reference of the deliberate intention or the wicked recklessness required to constitute the crime of murder. Accordingly, since the jury received this direction, I am of opinion that no miscarriage of justice flowed from the fact that the trial judge informed them that there was no question of self defence in relation to the fatal wound.

There is a second reason for concluding that there was no miscarriage of justice in this case. The trial judge did leave the special defence of self defence open to the jury in relation to the assault by punching. The verdict of the jury makes it plain that they did not accept that the punching had occurred in the course of self defence, and if that is so, then in my opinion the jury clearly would not have concluded that the stabbing had taken place in the course of self defence. In other words since the jury had rejected the question of self defence in relation to the punching, it is plain that they would also have rejected the question of self defence in relation to the assault by stabbing.

The advocate-depute contended that there was a third reason for concluding that there had been no miscarriage of justice in this case. He pointed out that the trial judge had charged the jury to the effect that they could bring in a verdict of culpable homicide if they were satisfied that the appellant had been acting under provocation. The advocate-depute, treating provocation as a form of unjustifiable self defence, concluded that since the jury had clearly negatived provocation, there could have been no question of the jury holding that the appellant had been acting in self defence in relation to the fatal wound if such a verdict had been left open to them. The trial judge, however, made it plain to the jury that provocation was quite different from self defence, and he correctly directed the jury that provocation was quite different from self defence, and he correctly directed the jury that provocation would only arise if they were satisfied that the appellant had lost control. Accordingly in concluding that there was no miscarriage of justice here, I do not found upon the fact that the jury rejected any question of provocation.

The fact of the matter is that the jury were clearly reminded of what the appellant had said in his evidence and were directed that if they believed him or if his evidence raised any reasonable doubt in their minds, then they ought to acquit the appellant. In these circumstances, although there was a misdirection on the part of the trial judge in that he withdrew the issue of self defence from their consideration, I am of opinion that there was no miscarriage of justice in this case. I would therefore move your Lordships to refuse the appeal against conviction."

Appeal refused.

C. THE MEANING OF MISCARRIAGE OF JUSTICE

The extent to which the court is prepared to develop the notion of a miscarriage of justice independent of the pre-1980 Act cases is as yet unclear, although it would appear from *McCuaig* that they are unlikely to do so. The following cases are included as examples of the sort of issue which has in the past been presented to the court of appeal as amounting to a miscarriage of justice.

(i) Misdirection by the Judge

1. McPhelim v. H.M. Advocate
1960 J.C. 17

The appellant was convicted on charges of assault and robbery committed in concert with three other men. He appealed to the High Court on the ground that certain omissions from the presiding judge's charge to the jury amounted to misdirection.

LORD JUSTICE-CLERK (THOMSON): "[His Lordship outlined the circumstances of the offence, and continued:] In these circumstances, the evidence being so recent, the competing stories being so clear and the jury having been addressed by counsel in what the presiding Judge described as two excellent speeches, it would not be surprising if the Judge were to say to the jury:—'This is a simple, straightforward issue of fact for you; you have heard the evidence and the speeches; are you satisfied beyond reasonable doubt that it has been brought home to the accused that he was one of the group who carried this thing out?' That is pretty much what the Judge did. I cannot help feeling that any detached and disinterested observer, who had sat through that trial, who had absorbed its atmosphere, and who had appreciated what the real issue was, would have agreed readily that there was little call for much more, and that there could be little doubt that the jury fully appreciated that the true issue at the trial was, whether the appellant was in the affair as a participator, or was the innocent victim of circumstances and propinquity.

The atmosphere in a Court of Appeal is apt to be a little different, and that, no doubt, is why this appeal has been taken. The criticism of the charge is that it was too brief, and that it failed adequately to instruct the jury on the way in which they should approach their consideration of the case.

In reviewing the proceedings at a criminal trial, a Court of Appeal has certain obvious advantages. It has before it a complete record of what has happened, and it has the time and opportunity to consider it dispassionately. The tension is over; it knows the result. It can be wise after the event. But these advantages are counterbalanced by obvious disadvantages. No Court of Appeal can truly recapture the feel and atmosphere of a trial. The drab record of proceedings cannot reproduce the ebb and flow of the trial, or the variations of emphasis. A Court of Appeal must therefore be constantly on its guard against failing to appreciate what were the vital issues—the matters to which those actively engaged in the trial were directing their attention. The very drabness of the record may lead the Court of Appeal to dwell unduly on matters which were perhaps taken for granted at the trial, or to pay undue attention to omissions which, while they are obvious enough on the written record, may have had little or no significance in the living context of the trial. Paradoxically enough, a Court of Appeal is quite as much in danger of getting the case out of focus as is the Judge who conducted the trial. For that reason, it is our duty to view with confidence and charity the course taken by an experienced Judge in charging a jury. If a charge is to be a good charge, it ought to be one addressed to the fifteen people in the jury-box, and not to the Court of Appeal. A charge, which meticulously covers every theoretical aspect, may be so complicated that the jury's capacity to appreciate what it is being told may be blunted long before the real matters with which it has to deal are reached. On the other hand, a vital and effective charge which brings the relevant issue squarely before the jury may on subsequent analysis be found to have technical weaknesses. No hard and fast rule can be laid down. Sometimes the charge must of necessity be technical, and the various legal issues must be fully and accurately defined; at the other extreme, little or no legal instruction is required. There are certain things which must be said, but the way in which they are said or the emphasis which need be laid on them, varies with the particular case."

Appeal refused.

NOTE

See also *McKenzie* v. *H.M. Advocate*, 1959 J.C. 32, *supra*, Chap. 1; *Hamilton and Others* v. *H.M. Advocate*, 1938 J.C. 134, *supra*, Chap. 10, and *McIntyre* v. *H.M. Advocate*, 1981 S.C.C.R. 117. In the latter case, the court expressed the opinion that "if on vital issues a direction given is so inadequate as to amount to a misdirection any conviction must be quashed." The court further expressed the view that what were "vital issues" would depend upon the circumstances of the case, and that "a judge must at least focus the vital issues in the context of the evidence" (p.122). In *McAvoy and Another* v. *H.M. Advocate*, 1983 S.L.T. 16; 1982 S.C.C.R. 263, Lord Dunpark stated:

"... if the appeal is based, for example, upon a misdirection by the trial judge or the admission by the judge of inadmissible evidence and either of these grounds is established, then I am of opinion that the court is empowered to consider the materiality of that misdirection, or of the evidence which ought not to have been admitted, in relation to all the factors relevant to the verdict of guilty. If, having done that, the court is satisfied that neither the misdirection nor the admission of the inadmissible evidence, whatever it may be, was sufficiently material to cast doubt upon the guilty verdict, then the appeal should be dismissed."

A failure to focus the "vital issues" may, on the above views, necessarily constitute a material miscarriage of justice. Such a failure may arise when a vital direction to the jury is omitted by the trial judge, as the following case shows.

2. McTavish v. H.M. Advocate
1975 S.L.T. (Notes) 27

The appellant, a nurse, was convicted of the murder of one of her patients by injecting into the latter an overdose of insulin. She appealed on the ground, *inter alia*, of misdirection. The nature of the alleged misdirection is set out in the opinion of the court.

OPINION OF THE COURT: "... Counsel for the appellant's argument can be summarised as follows. It was common ground that the appellant had given Mrs Lyon an injection. In this highly important respect the issue was whether she injected insulin, as the Crown contended, or sterile water as she maintained. In reviewing the Crown evidence in his charge to the jury the presiding judge made specific reference in detail to the replies attributed to her by the police witnesses when she was cautioned and charged. The charge at that time was simply one of assault. The relevant portion of that charge was that on 30th June 1973 in Ward 5, Ruchill Hospital, she assaulted Mrs Lyon, a patient in the hospital, and administered to her a substance which was to the procurator-fiscal unknown to her injury. According to the police witnesses the appellant's first reply was: 'I gave a half c.c. of insulin soluble to Mrs Lyon only because she wanted to be put out of her pain and misery and had trouble with her bowels.' Her second reply was: 'I gave Mrs Lyon a half c.c. of soluble insulin. She was taking a cerebral and was wanting out of her misery.' The presiding judge had prefaced his recital of this evidence by saying that the crucial statements made by the accused were those made in answer to the caution and charge. These statements, if accepted by the jury, were conclusive against the appellant in this vital issue in the case, and whereas the presiding judge had given prominence to them in his review of the Crown evidence, he made no reference whatsoever to the appellant's denial of them and her counter-account of what she said either when reviewing the defence case and the evidence in support of it, or indeed at any point in his charge. In the circumstances if was a fault of commission and not just one of omission. It was so highly prejudicial to the appellant that it constituted a misdirection in law on a vital matter which called for the quashing of the conviction on this murder charge.

In support of his submission counsel for the appellant founded strongly on various passages in the opinion of Lord Justice-Clerk Aitchison in the case of *H.M. Advocate* v. *Mills*, 1935 J.C. 77, 1935 S.L.T. 532. The one passage which seems most apposite to the present case is at p. 534 where his Lordship said: 'The charge proceeded on the view that the accuracy of Warnock's statement was not in doubt.' [Warnock was the police officer to whom the statement was made]. 'But the appellant himself gave evidence, and he disputed the accuracy of Warnock's evidence and gave a vitally different account of the words which he used. According to the appellant, it was Warnock who said: "We know you did not mean to murder her" and not himself who said: "I did not mean to murder her." The attention of the jury, in my view, ought to have been directed specifically to the appellant's evidence, and they ought to have been told that they must consider it in making up their minds whether the appellant had in fact used the words attributed to him by Warnock. No such direction was given. On the contrary, the charge was calculated to convey to the jury the impression that the statement as alleged by Warnock was indisputably proved.' Counsel for the appellant submitted that the present case was in pari casu, and that if one substituted the competing versions of the statements in the present case for the competing versions in *Mills'* case (supra) Lord Aitchison's words were exactly apposite. As the evidence on the point had been presented by the presiding judge to the jury, without any attention, specific or indeed otherwise, having been directed to the appellant's contradictory evidence, the charge was calculated to convey to the jury the impression that the statements as alleged by the police witnesses were indisputably proved. The omission to give proper direction on such a vital matter was, as he had argued, fatal to the conviction.

In his reply the Solicitor-General pointed out correctly that each case had to be considered on its own particular facts. He, accordingly, sought to distinguish the facts in the present case from those in *Mills*. We need not go into this in detail. It suffices to say that, in our opinion, the passage in Lord Aitchison's judgment quoted above is apposite to the present case. In both cases there was ample evidence to warrant a conviction. But in both cases the statement or statements were, on the Crown evidence, admissions of guilt, whereas the accused's version was a declaration of innocence. Nothing could be more vital. Faced with that situation, the Solicitor-General maintained that the attention of the jury to the appellant's denial of the police version of her statements need not be contained in a specific reference to what she said if it could be found by necessary inference from the charge read as a whole and under specific reference to certain passages therein. Without accepting that this is a legitimate extension of Lord Aitchison's phrase 'directed specifically' we are prepared to examine the Solicitor-General's argument on the basis that it is.

In limine, he argued that while the contents of the appellant's statements were in issue, this was not a vital issue in the case. We cannot agree. In our opinion this was a most vital issue. It related to a matter which could have swung the case one way or another.

Turning to the contents of the judge's charge, he first of all drew attention to some general and normal directions given by the presiding judge. These were that in the last analysis it was for the jury to make the final decisions; that it would be impossible in a case of this length to go into all the evidence in detail; that the facts were for them; that while he might indicate lines of approach, anything he said could be ignored or discarded by them; and that it was their recollection of the evidence, not his, which counted. The Solicitor-General then pointed out that throughout her evidence the appellant had maintained that it was sterile water which she had injected into Mrs Lyon, and that the presiding judge in his charge had made reference to appropriate passages where she said this. We pause to observe that while this is so, he nowhere made reference to the fact that she said that in her replies to the charge she denied the injection of insulin but talked about sterile water. His next point was that in dealing with statements to the police the presiding judge said: 'We have heard a good deal of evidence about certain statements which the accused made, or is alleged to have made to the police after the investigation into the death of Mrs Lyon was being carried out.' He argued that the use of the phrase 'or is alleged to have been made to the police' was a clear indication to the jury that the question of what the appellant said in any of her statements was an issue to be resolved, and that in turn involved consideration of what the appellant said she had said on any such occasion. That of necessity included a direction to consider what she said that she said in her replies to the charge. This is perhaps the strongest point in the Solicitor-General's argument. But at this point the presiding judge was dealing with all the statements made by the appellant after the police investigation had begun, and these included statements made before the charge was preferred against her as well as the statements made in reply to the charge. Not without some hesitation we have come to the view that the Solicitor-General's point is too fine a one, and that it cannot be said that the use of the phrase 'or is alleged to have been made to the police' is so unambiguous that any reasonable jury would have known that this was a clear invitation to them to have regard to the appellant's denial of the replies said by the police to have been made by her in reply to the charge. Here again the passage quoted is within a section of the charge where the issues being canvassed were the credibility of witnesses and the fairness or otherwise of the obtaining of the statements and not the contents of the statements. The same observation falls to be made in regard to the final excerpt quoted by the Solicitor-General, where the presiding judge said: '... on the other hand, if you think what she says is correct or if you think that what she says puts any doubt on the matter, then I direct you that you should exclude that evidence and these statements from your consideration.' But there his Lordship was dealing with the question whether the statements as spoken to by the police were truly voluntary or whether there was any unfairness about them, and not about the conflicting versions of the contents of the statements made in reply to the charge.

Of course, it is not sufficient to look at passages in a judge's charge in isolation. In respect of any point at issue the charge has to be read as a whole. We have given careful and anxious consideration to the charge. At the end of 13 days of evidence and two long and detailed speeches by counsel in a highly complicated case it was a far from easy task for the presiding judge to give a comprehensive, but clearly defined charge to the jury. In our opinion, but for a single omission which a few words could have cured, this was a well-constructed, clear and accurate charge. It is not disputed that in the course of it he failed to direct the jury specifically to consider whether in fact the appellant in her replies to the charge had made the statements attributed to her by the police which, if accepted, were vital pieces of evidence of a highly incriminating nature. On the authority of *Mills* such a failure would be fatal to a conviction. Even the most experienced judge may fail to give a direction which ought to have been given, particularly at the end of a long and exhausting trial. The judge here failed to give such a direction, and failed to draw the attention of the jury to the appellant's versions of the replies she gave. We are unable to find in the charge as a whole or in any of the selected passages therein which were cited to us sufficient to repair that deficiency by necessary inference or implication. We have reached the conclusion that in these circumstances counsel for the appellant was well founded in his submission that the charge was calculated, in the sense of being liable, to convey to the jury that the statements as alleged by the police witnesses were indisputably proved, and that the presiding judge's failure to give an adequate direction thereanent constituted a misdirection in law. The question then as always, is whether this omission was sufficiently material to vitiate the verdict. The answer to that can only be that it was. In so finding we echo the concluding words of Lord Aitchison in *Mills*, words which might have been coined for this very case. He said: 'I reach this conclusion with regret. It can never be a light thing to interfere with the verdict of a jury on a charge of murder, and, as I have already said, there is, in my view, ample evidence to support the verdict; but, by the law of Scotland, an accused person is entitled to have his case tried with an adequate direction to the jury, and, if on any vital matter the direction is inadequate, so as to amount to misdirection, it is our plain duty to set the verdict aside. We are not entitled to depart in any way from that imperative rule.'"

Appeal allowed; conviction quashed.

NOTE

At the time this case was decided, there was no provision whereby the court could set aside the verdict and grant authority for a new prosecution. That power was added by the 1980 Act and has been used from time to time: see *infra*, p.517. In particular, it was used in the following case where there was a misdirection on the question of corroboration.

3. McGougan v. H.M. Advocate
1991 S.C.C.R. 49

An accused was convicted of lewd, indecent and libidinous practices. He appealed against conviction.

LORD JUSTICE-CLERK: "Various grounds of appeal were put forward and Mr Bell has addressed us upon these and has laid particular stress upon the third ground of appeal which is in these terms:

'The jury were not directed by the learned trial judge to any relevant elements of evidence which could be taken to corroborate the appellant's statement. This was a material misdirection which led to a miscarriage of justice.'

As his argument developed, however, it was plain that he was laying particular stress upon one direction which the trial judge gave to which we shall refer presently. As the trial judge made plain in his charge, the background to this case was that the appellant was a baby-sitter for the family of the girl referred to in charge (1), and on occasions he was left alone in the house with her. The Crown in this case relied upon certain admissions which the appellant had made to different people at different times. The trial judge in his charge to the jury reminded them of the terms of these admissions. He stressed to the jury that before they could convict in this case they would require to be satisfied that these admissions had been made and freely made and that they inferred guilt on the part of the accused. He correctly reminded the jury that there were a number of admissions made at different times but that the admissions could not corroborate each other as they came from the same source. He therefore reminded the jury that the starting-point was these admissions or statements and that the jury would also require to be satisfied that there was corroboration. What the trial judge said [in] his charge in that connection is as follows:

'Because they are made at different times they do not corroborate each other, so you have to look for evidence elsewhere. The Crown ask you, as I understand it, to consider certain factors and it is for you to decide what weight you put upon them. Well, ladies and gentlemen, the factors, as I understand it, which may be relevant—it is entirely a matter for you what consideration you give to them—are or may be as follows. You are entitled to consider the reaction of the accused on being confronted by the [complainer's parents] and at the police station.'

He then proceeded in his charge to describe the demeanour and behaviour of the accused at this time and . . . evidence that he had tried to throw himself out of a window. Mr Bell submitted that that direction by the trial judge constituted a misdirection inasmuch as the reaction and demeanour of an accused person while making an admission could not amount to corroboration of his admissions. The advocate-depute accepted that the jury could not find corroboration in that fact and it was therefore a matter of admission that in that portion of his charge there had been a material misdirection.

The trial judge then went on to refer to certain other matters which might afford corroboration. What is surprising, however, is that in his charge to the jury when dealing with the matter of corroboration the trial judge did not refer to certain evidence which he has referred to in his report to this court. In the course of his report to this court the trial judge tells us that the appellant, as we say, used to act as a baby-sitter and that there was evidence that on the last occasion before the police became involved, the child had been left with the appellant at the address referred to in the libel. The appellant apparently in his evidence recalled that specific occasion. The trial judge goes on to say this in his report:

'When the parents returned the child was found to be naked, whereas she was dressed when they left her; her underpants had disappeared and were found later by the father in a cabinet beside the appellant's bed; and on the evening of this occasion the child's vagina was seen to be red and the child was complaining that it was sore.'

It is clear that evidence of that kind would have been available as corroboration but the trial judge did not refer to that evidence in his charge to the jury. (We were informed that the advocate-depute had not referred to the evidence either when he addressed the jury.) The trial judge did refer to the fact that there had been medical evidence regarding the child's condition. That of course would support the view that the offence had taken place, but of course it would not be linked to the appellant unless it was read in the context to which we have just referred. The result in this case is that the jury were not reminded in the judge's charge of evidence which was undoubtedly capable of affording corroboration, and on the contrary they were directed in the charge that for corroboration they could rely on material which the Crown now concede was not capable of affording corroboration. The question then for us is as to whether that constituted such a miscarriage of justice as to make it necessary to set aside this verdict of the jury. It can hardly be denied that the direction was prejudicial to the appellant because the jury were being directed that they could treat as corroboration something which it is now conceded was not capable of affording corroboration. On the other hand, the advocate-depute argued strongly that having regard to all the evidence which was available, there was ample evidence to corroborate the admissions which the appellant had made. That being so he contended that there had been no miscarriage of justice.

Whether or not a misdirection produces a miscarriage of justice must depend upon the circumstances and we can readily accept that there may be cases where there is no miscarriage of justice despite the fact that there has been a misdirection by the trial judge. In this case, however, we regard the circumstances as somewhat special. In the first place, as we have observed, the trial judge did not in the course of his charge remind the jury of evidence which clearly was capable of affording corroboration. In the second place, this was a majority verdict. In the third place, we are influenced by the place where this direction occurred in the judge's charge. As we have explained, having reminded them that corroboration was necessary, the very first thing which the trial judge suggested could be taken into consideration by the jury as affording corroboration was the reaction or demeanour of the accused when he made his admissions and it is now, as we say, conceded that he was wrong so to direct the jury. In these circumstances it appears to us that there must be a real risk that some at least of the jury may have voted in favour of conviction under the erroneous impression that they were entitled to rely upon the demeanour and reaction of the accused as corroborating the admission which he made. In these circumstances we have come to be of opinion that the misdirection in this case has produced a miscarriage of justice. The advocate-depute contended as a last resort that if we were to take that view we should not quash the conviction but should set the conviction aside and grant authority to bring a new prosecution in accordance with section 255. We did not understand Mr Bell to suggest that that was something which we ought not to do in this case. In all the circumstances therefore we shall, for the reasons given, set aside the verdict of the jury and grant authority to the Crown to bring a new prosecution in accordance with section 255 of the Criminal Procedure (Scotland) Act 1975."

Verdict set aside.

NOTE

The Crown did not, in fact, bring a new prosecution. The case emphasises that the court considers itself able to look at the whole circumstances before deciding whether to allow an appeal. See also *Khan* v. *H.M. Advocate*, 1992 S.C.C.R. 146; *Greenhalghse* v. *H.M. Advocate*, 1992 S.C.C.R. 311.

(ii) Introduction of Previous Convictions

Section 160(1) of the 1975 Act provides that previous convictions against an accused shall not be laid before the jury, nor shall reference be made thereto in the presence of the jury, before the verdict is returned. Breach of this provision has frequently been the subject of appeal to the High Court, on the ground of miscarriage of justice.

Cordiner v. H.M. Advocate
1978 J.C. 64

The appellant was charged, *inter alia*, with attempted extortion. The offence was alleged to have been committed during the month of June 1976. During that month the appellant was in prison. He lodged a special defence of alibi, which was read to the jury at the commencement of the trial (in accordance with normal practice). That charge was withdrawn by the Crown, but the appellant was convicted on two other charges contained in the same indictment. He appealed on the ground of miscarriage of justice, on the basis of a breach of section 160(1) of the 1975 Act. A second accused, Newby, also appealed on the ground of miscarriage. It was his contention that he had been tainted by association with Cordiner, and that his right to a fair trial have been prejudiced.

LORD JUSTICE-CLERK (WHEATLEY): "... Although there is a superficial similarity in the grounds stated by the two appellants there are important differences and we consider each case separately. Before we discuss Cordiner's appeal, we should mention that it was not disputed that Cordiner had been sentenced to 60 days' imprisonment in Edinburgh Sheriff Court on

24th May 1976, being released from Saughton prison on 2nd July 1976, and that this conviction did appear on the schedule of previous convictions. In the course of his evidence Cordiner himself, despite advice from the Court, made it clear that he had a 'criminal record' although the full details were not stated. His insistence on stating this was, he explained, because he had been 'framed' by the police and because 'the Crown has already forced me to produce my criminal records.' This reference to 'criminal records' was a distortion of the necessary reference to the one conviction of imprisonment for 60 days. We add that the trial Judge, in his charge to the jury, stressed that they should put out of their minds any references to previous records and ignore the fact that the appellant had been 'serving a minor prison sentence for what must have been a very minor offence' in June 1976.

It was conceded on behalf of the Crown that in the particular circumstances of this case, so far as relating to Cordiner, there had been a breach of section 160(1) of the Criminal Procedure (Scotland) Act 1975 which provides: 'Previous convictions against the accused shall not be laid before the jury nor shall reference be made thereto in presence of the jury before the verdict is returned.' It was agreed that in lodging the special defence of alibi in answer to the second charge Cordiner was forced to disclose the fact that he was in prison in June 1976. This, it was conceded on behalf of the Crown, was equivalent to laying a previous conviction before the jury. In our opinion this concession could not have been withheld.

There was a difference of opinion on the effects of this breach of section 160(1). For Cordiner, it was argued that this breach constituted prejudice which amounted to a substantial miscarriage of justice which vitiated the entire proceedings and must result in the allowance of the appeal and the quashing of his convictions. Reliance was placed on the observations of Lord Jamieson in *Bryce* v. *Gardiner* 1951 J.C. 134 at p.142, where certain *dicta* in previous cases are considered, and on these *dicta* themselves. For the Crown, it was argued that although the breach amounted to a 'miscarriage of justice' it did not amount to a 'substantial miscarriage of justice,' and that accordingly the proviso to section 254(1) of the Act of 1975 should be applied and the appeal dismissed. ...

Reference was made to the opinions of various Judges in support of the contention that a breach of section 160(1) or its equivalent was in itself sufficient to warrant the quashing of a conviction. The genesis of these opinions was the opinion of Lord Kyllachy in *Cornwallis* v. *H.M. Advocate* 3 Adam 604 where he said, when referring to previous convictions being laid before a jury: 'But I am bound to say that if the Sheriff or prosecutor had during the trial conveyed this information to the jury the action would have been bad.' Lord Young expressed a contrary view. Lord Anderson, in his dissenting opinion in *Corcoran* v. *H.M. Advocate* 1932 J.C. 42, when referring to the similar proviso in the Act of 1926, treats Lord Kyllachy's views in *Cornwallis* as meaning that 'there is always a substantial miscarriage of justice when a previous conviction has been disclosed by the prosecutor during trial ...' The Lord Justice-Clerk (Alness) also supported Lord Kyllachy but made no reference to the Act of 1926. In *Kepple* v. *H.M. Advocate* 1936 J.C. 76 Lord Justice-General Normand reserved his opinion on the question whether a breach of section 67 of the Criminal Procedure (Scotland) Act 1887 (corresponding to section 160 of the Act of 1975) necessarily leads to the quashing of a conviction. In *Bryce* v. *Gardiner, supra,* Lord Jamieson supported the view of Lord Anderson in *Corcoran, supra.* What has not been noticed is that the case of *Cornwallis* was decided before the passing of the Criminal Appeal (Scotland) Act 1926, and the introduction of the proviso in section 2(1) thereof. Accordingly Lord Kyllachy could not be addressing his mind to the present question. *Bryce* v. *Gardiner* was a stated case on a summary complaint, to which section 2(1) and its proviso did not apply, and so the issue could not arise and accordingly could not be discussed. In *Corcoran*, which was a case under solemn procedure, no reference was made to the proviso. Accordingly the support given to Lord Kyllachy in these cases has no relation to the point here.

In our opinion a breach of section 160(1) of the Act amounts to a 'miscarriage of justice' but this does not necessarily lead to a quashing of the conviction. The proviso in section 254(1) allows the Court to dismiss the appeal if they are of the opinion that the miscarriage of justice has not been 'substantial.' Taking an extreme illustration of the contrary view, we do not consider it conceivable that the wrongful disclosure of a conviction for a trivial motoring offence could be regarded as a substantial miscarriage of justice so as to vitiate a conviction on a charge of murder.

It was accepted on behalf of the Crown that the test for the application of the proviso was 'high and exacting' to quote the words of the Lord Justice-Clerk (Thomson) in *M'Kenzie* v. *H.M. Advocate* 1959 J.C. 32 in adopting the test of Viscount Simon in *Stirland* v. *D.P.P.* [1944] A.C. 315. That test was in these terms, *viz*.:—'the provision that the Court of Criminal Appeal may dismiss the appeal if they consider that no substantial miscarriage of justice has actually occurred in convicting the accused assumes a situation where a reasonable jury, after being properly directed, would, on the evidence, properly admissible, without doubt convict.' The basis of the argument for the Crown for the application of the proviso was the appellant's own evidence about his previous criminal record, which went far beyond the limited reference in the special defence, and the appellant's allegations that he had been 'framed' as a line of defence. Any possible prejudice which could have arisen from the disclosure that the appellant had been in prison in June 1976 was, it was said, 'swamped' by his own evidence which was deliberately exploiting the fact that the Crown had erred in regard to the enforced disclosure of a previous conviction. It has to be noted that the Crown's original error in including the offensive date in the charge when his list of previous convictions *prima facie* disclosed that he could not have committed the offence on that date was compounded by the fact that after the special defence had been lodged at the pleading diet the Crown took no steps to seek to have the charge amended so as to exclude the date which occasioned the special defence in this respect to be lodged. This failure to take appropriate action in the face of their attention being specifically drawn to a fact which was almost instantly verifiable, in the knowledge that otherwise the disclosure that the appellant had been in prison would inevitably be drawn to the attention of the jury, was in our opinion quite unjustifiable. It may well be that the appellant deliberately exploited the situation which had arisen from the inexcusable conduct of the Crown which had led to disclosure of the previous conviction, but we cannot dissociate the appellant's admission and line of defence from the initial error made by the Crown and ignore the possible prejudicial effect on the jury. We cannot say that the jury would have convicted if the Crown had not erred at the outset in forcing the appellant to admit that he was in prison in June 1976. The fact that, save in charge 1(1) which was unanimous, the verdicts against the appellant were all by a majority reinforces that view. Accordingly we cannot apply the proviso here. For these reasons we have no alternative to quashing the conviction against Cordiner.

We turn to the appeal of Newby. We have earlier stated the first reason put forward in his application. The submission was that Newby was so closely associated with Cordiner that any prejudice sustained by Cordiner because of the breach of section 160 of the Act of 1975, involving Cordiner, must affect Newby. This association, it was said, related not only to the charges against them in the indictment, which were based on their acting in concert, but also to their private lives where there was evidence of a close association. It was furthermore argued that, even if Cordiner's appeal was refused because he had taken advantage of the Crown's initial error by expanding on his own criminal activities in support of his allegations of a 'frame up' by the police, Newby's appeal should succeed because of the resulting prejudice to Newby by Cordiner's actions. Reliance appeared to be placed on the fact that Newby did not have control of Cordiner's special defence and of any prejudicial evidence which Cordiner might give.

We cannot accept this submission for which no authority was produced. There was no breach of section 160 of the Act so far as Newby was concerned. The miscarriage of justice was in the breach of that section and only related to and affected Cordiner. The breach cannot, in our view, be founded on by a co-accused simply because they were charged together or were closely associated. An accused may suffer prejudice in the course of a trial in a number of ways but such prejudice may not amount to a 'miscarriage of justice.' An accused may prejudice a co-accused by giving evidence against the co-accused but that is not a miscarriage of justice. In a case like the present, an accused person might, voluntarily and for his own purposes, disclose a long list of previous convictions. A co-accused with whom that accused has a close association might say that he had no control of the accused and had been prejudiced thereby but he could not be heard to maintain that there was a miscarriage of justice as a result. We cannot see any basis for a transfer of prejudice against a co-accused amounting to a miscarriage of justice in this case."

Appeal by first appellant allowed.
Appeal by second appellant refused.

NOTES

1.   The view that a breach of section 160(1) amounts to a miscarriage of justice but not necessarily a *substantial* miscarriage was probably what lay behind the decision in *McCuaig*. The court accepted that there had been a breach, and may, therefore, have been of opinion that there was a miscarriage of justice. If the court had not insisted on the discretionary nature of section 254, it would have been faced with the prospect of holding that any breach of section 160(1) justified the quashing of a conviction on the ground of miscarriage. (The court could, of course, have held that the 1980 Act introduced completely new grounds of appeal, enabling it to develop a new line of authority on "miscarriage of justice" but it does not appear to have considered this possibility.)

2.   In *McAvoy and Another* v. *H.M. Advocate*, 1983 S.L.T. 16; 1982 S.C.C.R. 263, however, it was suggested (1983 S.L.T., at p.20) that the view expressed in *Cordiner* (that a breach of section 160(1) amounts to a miscarriage) might not be of universal application. If this is so, then the assumption behind *McCuaig* flies off, and with it a substantial part of the reason for the decision.

3.   The cases of section 160(1) are legion. For a general discussion of the authorities, see Renton and Brown, paras. 10–42 *et seq.*

(iii)   Oppression by the Trial Judge

Oppressive conduct on the part of the trial judge may well constitute a miscarriage of justice of sufficient materiality to justify interference with the verdict. A typical case of oppression may arise where the judge abandons his role of impartial "referee" and takes on the role of inquisitor or prosecutor.

Tallis v. H.M. Advocate
1982 S.C.C.R. 91

The appellant was charged, along with his partner, Wands, with the theft of a quantity of rails. His partner pleaded guilty, and after trial the appellant was convicted. He appealed against conviction and sentence on the ground that the conduct of the trial judge may have constituted a miscarriage of justice.

LORD JUSTICE-GENERAL (EMSLIE): "In this appeal the appellant challenges his conviction upon the following ground: 'The sheriff interrupted the cross-examination of the procurator fiscal and proceeded to cross-examine the panel, and thereafter the terms of this charge were such as to show a bias and may have constituted a miscarriage of justice resulting in the panel being convicted by a majority of the jurors.' The appeal on this ground was presented under reference to the cases of *Nisbet* v *H.M. Advocate*, 1979 SLT (Notes) 5 and *Dobbins* v *H.M. Advocate*, as yet unreported save in Crown Office circular A28/80. In the former case the critical issue was whether the accused's admitted possession of certain articles was innocent or guilty. In the second it was whether the accused, who had admittedly caused the death of the deceased, was guilty of murder, as the Crown contended, or of culpable homicide. In both cases the credibility of the accused was of prime importance and conviction was challenged upon the ground that the conduct of the trial judge, who had himself questioned the accused at some length, had resulted in oppression of such a nature as to constitute a miscarriage of justice. In *Nisbet* Lord Thomson, with whose opinion Lords Robertson and Allanbridge agreed, said this: 'The law on this matter is not in dispute and was canvassed by this court in the case of *Ernest Livingstone* v *H.M. Advocate*, 22 March 1974. In that case the Lord Justice-Clerk said: "I must deprecate the practice of such constant interruptions by a presiding judge. Basically his function is to clear up any ambiguities that are not being cleared up either by the examiner or the cross-examiner. He is also entitled to ask such questions as he might regard relevant and important for the proper determination of the case by the jury, but that right must be exercised with discretion, and only exercised when the occasion requires it. It should not result in a presiding judge taking over the role of examiner or cross-examiner." ' He [Lord Thomson] also pointed out that the question whether the conduct of a judge has so far strayed beyond the bounds of propriety as to result in oppression of such a nature as to constitute a miscarriage of justice, required to be resolved as a question of degree, and under reference to the particular issue before the court he said this: 'In our opinion, as it is was not disputed that the articles in question were found in the accused's possession, and the whole question for the jury to decide was whether his possession was honest or dishonest, it was particularly important for the sheriff to demonstrate and maintain his complete impartiality on that question. This in our view he failed to do.'

In this appeal the particular submission of counsel for the appellant came to be that the presiding sheriff took over the role of cross-examiner in the course of the evidence of the accused himself, that he conspicuously failed to demonstrate and maintain his complete impartiality upon the vital issue of the credibility of the accused and of Miss Veryan, and that he suggested to the jury that the Crown case might be such a strong one that they would be entitled to acquit the appellant only if they were satisfied with the explanation which he gave in the witness box.

In our opinion the submission of counsel for the appellant is well founded and must receive effect. In evidence certain police witnesses stated that before the appellant was charged he had explained his part in the removal of the rails and that he had believed that the work had been authorised by the order which Wands had shown him, which he had by that time discovered to be quite bogus. The appellant in evidence explained that he had then thought that both he and Wands had been the dupes of the author of the bogus order, and had only learned two months before the trial, that the 'order' had been prepared by Wands himself. During his cross-examination by the procurator fiscal the appellant stated: 'At the police station I was charged but before that they did tell you that I in fact explained my full position.' That was of course perfectly correct, and what the appellant was referring to was, clearly, 'his full position' as he had then understood it to be. The sheriff, alas, did not appreciate this, and intervened to cross-examine the appellant upon the basis that he was misleading the court, for he recalled that there had been no evidence from the police officers that the appellant had explained Wands' actings which had allegedly deceived him. There is, we think, little doubt that in the exchanges between the sheriff and the appellant they were at cross purposes, and that the sheriff's adverse view of the appellant's credibility was unfortunately made clear. The damage done by the sheriff's intervention could, of course, have been repaired by an impeccable charge. The sheriff's charge, however, cannot be so described, for he carried forward into his charge itself, in the short passage in which he introduced the question of the credibility of the appellant and Miss Veryan, the quite mistaken impression he had formed about the appellant's veracity. What he said was this: 'You have seen Mr Tallis giving evidence. It is a matter for you to assess whether you consider Mr Tallis to be a person who found it easy to shift his ground if he found a question a bit difficult or a bit tricky, ladies and gentlemen, and you will recall the point that I put to him, ladies and gentlemen—although it is a matter entirely for you whether you accept my version of the evidence—but you recall the point that he said he told the police all about it. Well, ladies and gentlemen, my recollection is that the police were not asked that and they certainly did not say that, but it is a matter entirely for you, ladies and gentlemen.' The only other thing he said was as follows: 'Then there is a girl Fiona Veryan, do you believe her, ladies and gentlemen? You may recall her dramatic exit line when asked why she had come to give evidence. She said that she had asked Wands, that is George Wands, what to say and that he had said, "Say that Tallis wrote the contract", and that she simply refused to do that because she wasn't prepared to let Tallis bear the brunt of something which she had in fact done. Well, ladies and gentlemen, as against that there is the alternative view that "Hell holds no fury like woman's scorn". You may take that view, ladies and gentlemen. You recall that she said she was annoyed and had split up with Mr Wands because he had not visited her in hospital. These are all factors which you have to take into account when you make up your minds where you think the truth lies.' The observation of the sheriff about Miss Veryan was not only inaccurate: it was, at the very least, gratuitously unfortunate. The clear impression conveyed to the jury in this passage in the charge was that, in the sheriff's view the credibility of the appellant and of Miss Veryan was suspect. That this is a fair interpretation of the passage we have so far considered is, we think, confirmed in a later and lengthier chapter of the charge in which, in the examination of the evidence led for the Crown, piece by piece, the sheriff repeatedly said to the jury, 'Why should he be involved at all if he wasn't in fact a party to the whole fiddle', or words to that effect. The matter does not, however, end there, because the sheriff severed the last link in the chain of impartiality required of him by giving to the jury what appears to us to be a serious misdirection in law. He said this: 'Though the situation may arise, ladies and gentlemen, that the Crown puts forward such a strong case that it is only if you are satisfied with the explanation given by the accused, that you would be entitled to acquit him and again that may very well be the situation here you feel, but again it is a matter for you to make up your minds about, ladies and gentlemen.' The gravity of this misdirection lies in the plain indication to the jury that in certain circumstances the onus of proof shifts to the accused and unless he can discharge it by an explanation which 'satisfies the jury', i.e., of his innocence, then conviction must follow. Upon a consideration of all these circumstances we are driven to the conclusion, without casting any doubt upon the accuracy of the guidance offered to judges in the cases of *Nisbet* and *Dobbins*, that in this case the sheriff's failure to demonstrate and maintain his complete impartiality upon the vital issue which was for the jury to resolve, may well have influenced the jury and resulted in oppression of such a nature as to constitute a miscarriage of justice. In the result we have no alternative but to allow the appeal and quash the conviction."

Appeal allowed; conviction quashed.

NOTES

1. Judicial interventions in the course of a trial may be objectionable, therefore, not only on the ground of their frequency, but also to the extent that they disclose bias or lack of impartiality. It is clear, also, from *Nisbet* (*supra*) that there are cases of interruption or intervention which cannot be cured by the judge's charge to the jury. The charge in *Nisbet*, for example, was said to be "quite adequate," and, indeed, no criticism was levelled at the judge's general conduct of the trial.

2. *McMillan* v. *H.M. Advocate*, 1979 S.L.T. (Notes) 68 should also be noted in this context. In that case the trial judge allowed his views on the appellant's guilt to become known by canvassing before the jury the appropriate method of disposal of the offender, before a verdict had been returned. It was held that, in the circumstances, his conduct constituted a miscarriage of justice, even although he had not intended to be unfair, and was probably acting in what he considered to be the best interests of the accused.

(iv) Unreasonable, Incompetent or Ambiguous Verdict

Section 254(1) of the 1975 Act formerly provided for an appeal on the ground that the verdict of the jury was unreasonable or could not be supported having regard to the evidence. The Thomson Committee (1st Report, Cmnd. 5038) recommended minor changes to these provisions, which would have removed the reference to the verdict being unsupportable having regard to the evidence (para. 12). The 1980 Act, of course, has removed all such references from the ground of appeal. The question remains as to whether the attitude of the courts has changed.

1. Webb and Others v. H.M. Advocate
1927 J.C. 92

The appellant was convicted, along with two other men, of assaulting a man with a razor. He appealed to the High Court on the ground, *inter alia*, that the verdict of the jury was unreasonable or could not be supported having regard to the evidence.

LORD JUSTICE-CLERK (ALNESS): "... Now, it is necessary, in the first place, to apprehend the principles in accordance with which such an appeal as this falls to be determined, and then, having ascertained these principles, to apply them to the case in hand.

As regards the principles involved, some points, I apprehend, are clear. This is not a Court of review. Review, in the ordinary sense of that word, lies outside our province. We have neither a duty nor a right, because we might not have reached the same conclusion as the jury, to upset their verdict. The ambit of the Court of Criminal Appeal is circumscribed by narrower limits. We cannot interfere unless we think the verdict is unreasonable. The duty of this Court, in short, is similar to, if indeed it is not the same as, the duty devolving on a civil Court of appeal when considering the verdict of a jury on a motion for a new trial on the ground that the verdict is contrary to the evidence. In a civil Court the verdict of the jury is invulnerable, unless the Court of appeal thinks that it is perverse. I know of no better statement of the law relating to that topic than that contained in the opinion of Lord Kinnear in the case of *Campbell*, where the Lordship says: 'The verdict is not to be set aside merely because we disagree with it. If all we think of it is that we should not have agreed with it, then to set it aside would be to take upon ourselves the function of a jury. On the other hand, if it is apparent that the jury have not duly performed their functions, and have given a verdict which no reasonable jury, properly instructed, would have given, or, as the late Lord President put it, which is flagrantly wrong, the Court will set it aside, and that whether it be a verdict on a question of slander, or on any other question of fact. The question then is, Is the verdict before us so flagrantly wrong that no reasonable jury discharging their duty honestly under proper direction would have given it? In my judgment our duty in the Court of Criminal Appeal is indistinguishable from the duty of a civil Court in dealing with the verdict of a civil jury."

The court refused the appeal.

NOTES

1. The tone of the court's opinion echoes the views expressed by the Committee on Criminal Appeals who were very much concerned to preserve jury responsibility. The fear was that if juries became aware that their decisions could easily be reversed on appeal they would approach their task that much less seriously, which might have an adverse effect on the position of the accused (Cmnd. 2456, *supra*). The sanctity of the jury verdict was further enhanced by the highly restrictive approach adopted by the court to the admission of fresh evidence on appeal, as to which, see *infra*, p.512.
2. Despite the changes in the law made by the 1980 Act, it seems very unlikely that the High Court will depart from the traditional view taken of the jury verdict where credibility and reliability of witnesses is concerned.

The following case makes it clear that the former law is still of great importance.

2. Rubin v. H.M. Advocate
1984 S.L.T. 369

Rubin was convicted of instigating a co-accused, Walsh, to set fire to a hotel; Walsh was convicted of the fire-raising itself. Walsh appealed, *inter alia*, on the ground that "the quality, character and strength of the evidence" against him when viewed as a whole was insufficient to justify conviction against him. One of Rubin's grounds of appeal made a similar point, specifically directed to the evidence of a Crown witness, Findlay, who had allegedly retracted his evidence after the trial.

LORD JUSTICE-GENERAL: "Even if the evidence of Findlay about the events which took place in the hotel in the early hours of 30 August 1982 was, in terms, sufficient to provide a foundation for the Crown case against Walsh by implicating him directly in setting fire to the hotel the argument was that no reasonable jury, properly directed, was entitled to treat him as a reliable and credible witness. Although the transcript of his evidence-in-chief, and of the early part of his cross-examination by counsel for Walsh, is, unfortunately, not available, it is clear from the notes that he was a quite extraordinary witness. He was a man who lived in a fantasy world, much given to recording his rambling 'thoughts' on tape. He was verbose, bombastic and discursive and found it difficult to give straight answers to simple questions. His use of the English language was bizarre, and his vocabulary included words which find no place in any dictionary. His capacity for self-deception was illustrated in many ways, all detailed in the note of counsel's speeches to the jury. Upon points of detail in his evidence, generally, he was contradicted by the weight of the other evidence led at the trial. There was much evidence to suggest that his story of Walsh's presence in the hotel was a figment of his imagination. In particular nobody even called Rubin 'Davie', yet this is the name which Walsh is reported to have used. He spoke, too, of Walsh having an Irish accent. Unchallenged evidence showed this to be quite untrue. He claimed to have found 'the pay-off cheques' which turned out to be cheques for staff wages during Rubin's absence. The evidence of Police Constable Ritchie cast the gravest doubt upon Findlay's account of the fire raisers' arrival in the hotel between 1 a.m. and 1.30 a.m. At 1.50 a.m. Ritchie, making his second patrol visit to the hotel by car, observed that there were no cars in the car park, and having driven round the hotel and having remained in the vicinity of the grounds until about 2 a.m., he observed nothing unusual. The fire, upon the evidence, must have taken hold and spread quickly and the probability is that it had been started after Ritchie's departure from the area at 2 a.m. There was weight in the defence contention that Findlay's critical evidence was a tissue of lies invented to cover his own dereliction of duty or in an attempt to injure Rubin who had refused to provide him with money. He was already bankrupt by 30 August 1982.

I find myself quite unable to accept these submissions either. The words 'quality, character and strength' in ground 6 are taken from the opinion of the court in the case of *Reilly* [v. *H.M. Advocate*, 1981 S.C.C.R. 201] but in that case the court was not concerned at all with any question as to the reliability or credibility of any of the witnesses. The answer to the question at issue turned upon a consideration of the content of the evidence of certain witnesses in whose testimony the Crown sought to find corroboration for the direct identification of the accused by a single witness as the perpetrators of the crime. That case, accordingly, affords no authoritative support for the particular proposition which has been presented to us by counsel for Walsh. Questions of the reliability and credibility of witnesses are essentially, in our law, questions for the jury and we know of no case in which this court has interfered with any conviction upon the ground that, in its opinion, a jury had been perverse in treating a key witness as both reliable and credible. I do not, however, bearing in mind Lord Keith's reservation of opinion in *Dow* v. *MacKnight*, require in this case to consider and decide whether there could ever be circumstances sufficiently exceptional in which an appellate court might properly quash a conviction upon that ground. All that I require to say is that in the circumstances of this case I am far from being persuaded that this jury was not well entitled to rely upon Findlay and to believe him when he described in evidence how he came to leave the hotel in the early hours of 30 August 1982. Findlay, in spite of a long, forceful, and skilful cross-examination, remained unshaken on this vital chapter of his evidence. He had, it will be remembered, given the same account to his wife and to Rubin shortly after the fire, and this took a great deal of force away from the attempts of the defence to show that Findlay had been induced by police pressure, on 10 March 1983, to agree to give evidence incriminatory of Walsh at the trial. There was, of course, for all the reasons given by counsel for Walsh in his submissions in support of ground 6, a real question about Findlay's worth as a witness for the jury to answer, but I am not prepared to say that in accepting Findlay's account of the events in the hotel shortly before it was set on fire the jury was in any way perverse. There were many serious criticisms of Findlay as a witness of reliability and credit for the jury's consideration. All these were before them. On the other side of the account there was material before the jury from which they might reasonably conclude, regardless of the view they might have formed in general of this extraordinary witness, that he was unlikely to be lying in giving the evidence which he did against the interests of Walsh and his brother-in-law [Rubin]. That evidence indeed, provides, perhaps, the only plausible reason for his totally unexpected abandonment of his post in the early hours of the morning. For my own part, upon a reading of the bulk of Findlay's evidence which has been recorded in the notes, I do not find it even surprising that the jury took the view which they evidently did."

Appeal refused.

NOTE

The court also refused to take any account of Findlay's alleged retraction of his evidence contained in a tape recording made after the trial, holding not only that Rubin's motion to do so under section 252(*c*) of the 1975 Act was incompetent, but also that no weight ought to be attached to the retraction.

Where the verdict of the jury is incompetent, it may be set aside and a competent verdict substituted.

3. Salmond v. H.M. Advocate
1991 S.C.C.R. 43

An accused person was convicted of attempted murder, "under extreme provocation." He appealed on the basis that the verdict was incompetent.

LORD JUSTICE-CLERK: "The indictment against the appellant libelled assault to severe injury, permanent disfigurement and danger of life and closed with the words 'and attempt to murder her'. A defence of self-defence was put forward and, in addition, in the course of his charge to the jury, the trial judge pointed out to the jury that one matter that they might wish to consider was whether the appellant had been acting under provocation. When the jury returned to court to give their verdict the clerk of court asked them what their verdict was and the foreman of the jury replied, 'The verdict is guilty by reason of reckless indifference with extreme provocation.' That was an unusual verdict for a jury to have returned and there is no doubt that the trial judge was faced with a difficult situation when the jury gave their verdict in that form. He tells us in his report that after consultation with his clerk he decided to let the verdict be recorded and read back to the jury. The verdict, however, was not recorded in the precise words which they jury had used. The clerk of court said to the jury as follows, 'is this a true record of your verdict: the jury, by a majority, find the accused guilty as libelled under extreme provocation? Is that your verdict correctly recorded?' and the foreman of the jury replied in the affirmative. As we say, the trial judge was in a difficult position and he apparently chose not to seek to clarify from the jury what they meant by that verdict nor to ask for submissions on the matter, but he allowed the verdict to be recorded in the form which we have mentioned.

Today, Mr Mackay has pointed out that the verdict which was recorded was an incompetent verdict. He maintains that it is incompetent because the jury had found the appellant guilty of attempted murder under extreme provocation. He drew attention to the case of *Brady* v. *H.M. Advocate* [1986 S.L.T. 686]. In that case the court held that a verdict of attempted murder with provocation was not a good verdict and that the appropriate verdict would have been one of guilty of assault under provocation. The court took the view that it was now well settled that the same mens rea is required for attempted murder as for muder; if the charge is murder and the accused is successful in a plea of provocation, the offence is reduced to culpable homicide. The court went on to express the view that when the charge is one of attempted murder, if the plea of provocation succeeds, there can be no question of a verdict being returned of guilty of attempted murder under provocation. That is what the jury did in this case and accordingly Mr Mackay maintained, as we say, that the verdict was incompetent.

The advocate-depute accepted that the verdict which the jury had returned was indeed incompetent. The question then arises as to what should now happen. Mr Mackay maintained that this was not a case where it would be appropriate for this court to substitute an amended verdict as was done in *Brady*. He maintained it would be unsafe to do so because of the language which the jury had used in returning their verdict, and he accordingly maintained that what should be done in this case would be to set aside the verdict in its entirety, leaving it to the Crown if so advised to seek leave to bring a fresh prosecution. He contended that since the jury had used the words 'reckless indifference' there was doubt as to what the jury meant and he submitted that one could not assume that the jury by using these words were referring to 'wicked recklessness', being the words which the trial judge, in accordance with custom, had used when defining to the jury the offences of murder and attempted murder. Mr Mackay maintained that there was evidence supporting the view that the complainer had struck the first blow and in the circumstances he maintained that it could not assumed that the jury by their verdict meant to affirm all parts of the libel, and for these reasons he submitted that it would be unsafe for this court to substitute an alternative verdict.

The advocate-depute, on the other hand, maintained that despite the language used by the jury, it was plain that the jury were affirming all parts of the libel and the only thing that was wrong with the verdict was that the jury had affirmed attempt to murder. There is no doubt that, as the trial judge himself recognises in his report, the jury should have been directed along the lines of *Brady* to the effect that, if they were holding that there had been provocation, there could be no question of a verdict of guilty of attempted murder under provocation, but that the effect of provocation would be to reduce the charge from one of attempted murder to one of assault with or without the necessary aggravations. The advocate-depute, however, maintained that the proper conclusion to draw was that the jury were affirming everything that was contained in the libel. We have come to the conclusion that that submission by the advocate-depute is well founded. When the foreman of the jury first conveyed the jury's verdict to the court, he stated that their verdict was guilty by reason of reckless indifference with extreme provocation. In our opinion that is a clear indication that the jury were affirming what was libelled against the appellant in the charge. The trial judge tells us that the reference to reckless indifference may well have been made because of some remarks made in his speech by the advocate-depute. It is not unusual when the definition of murder is being referred to for persons to pose the question as to whether an accused was so reckless as to be indifferent to the question of whether the victim lived or died. We can readily accept that that may be the explanation for the words which the jury used initially, but the matter does not rest there because the clerk of court, having ascertained that the jury's verdict was by a majority, went on to ask the following question, 'Is that subject to any amendment or deletion?' and the foreman of the jury replied, 'No, just as it stands.' That accordingly makes it absolutely plain that the jury were making no deletions from the charge but were satisfied that everything libelled had been made out. As we say, the jury's verdict was then recorded and, as has already been observed, when they were asked whether their verdict was truly recorded as being that the accused was guilty as libelled under extreme provocation they answered in the affirmative. Mr Mackay suggested that a jury might not understand what was meant by the words 'guilty as libelled' but we were reminded by the advocate-depute that in the course of his charge the trial judge said this to the jury, 'You may find the accused guilty as libelled or under any deletions you care to make.' Having regard to that direction, we are satisfied that the jury ought to have understood, and we have no reason to think that they did not understand, what was meant by the words 'as libelled'. In these circumstances it appears to us that the proper course to follow is a similar course to that which was followed in *Brady*, namely to set aside the verdict of the jury and to substitute an amended verdict, and the amended verdict will be a verdict of guilty under deletion of the words 'and attempt to murder her' and with the addition of the words 'under extreme provocation'."

Amended verdict substituted.

NOTE

Where there is a flaw in the verdict, the proper course is for the trial judge to draw the jury's attention to it and to provide them with an opportunity of reconsidering it: see *McGeary* v. *H.M. Advocate*, 1991 S.C.C.R. 203.

(v)   Other Cases

It would be impossible in a work of this kind to cover the whole range of potential miscarriage of justice. See generally, Renton and Brown, paras. 11–33 *et seq.*; McCluskey, *Criminal Appeals*, Chap. 7. In particular, one interesting question remains unresolved: suppose the trial judge wrongly repels a submission of no case to answer and the accused then gives evidence filling the gaps in the Crown case. Would the appeal court hold that a miscarriage of justice had occurred? This point is yet to arise: see the remarks of Lord Justice-General Emslie in *Little* v. *H.M. Advocate*, 1983 S.C.C.R. 56 at p.65.

D. APPEAL AGAINST SENTENCE

As was pointed out above (p.483) the only ground of appeal by an accused against sentence is that there has been a miscarriage of justice (section 228(2)). Whether or not there has been a miscarriage of justice in relation to a sentence depends upon the rules and principles governing sentencing, which are outwith the scope of this book.

So far as disposal of appeals against sentence is concerned, section 254(3) of the 1975 Act provides that the High Court may dispose of an appeal by:

"(*a*) affirming such sentence; or

(*b*) if the Court thinks that, having regard to all the circumstances, including any additional evidence such as is mentioned in section 228(2) of this Act, a different sentence should have been passed, quashing the sentence and passing another sentence whether more or less severe in substitution therefor."

The Lord Advocate may appeal against an unduly lenient sentence: see 1975 Act, s. 228A, as inserted and amended by s. 42 of the Prisoners and Criminal Proceedings (Scotland) Act 1993 and s. 68 of the Criminal Justice Act 1993.

E. MENTALLY ABNORMAL OFFENDERS

In relation to any appeal under section 228(1), where it appears to the High Court that the appellant committed the act charged against him but that he was insane when he did so, the High Court shall dispose of the appeal by (a) setting aside the verdict of the trial court and substituting therefor a verdict of acquittal on the ground of insanity, and (b) quashing any sentence imposed on the appellant and ordering that he be detained in a state hospital (or such other hospital as for special reasons the court may specify): 1975 Act, s. 254(4).

F. PROCEDURE FOR APPEALING

The 1975 Act, as amended, contains detailed provisions governing the procedure for appealing, and the Act should be referred to for the terms of these procedures.

(i) Grounds of Appeal

The grounds of appeal must be adequately specified, whether the appeal is against conviction or sentence. In relation to the former, the whole point of the procedure is to ensure that grounds of appeal are formulated on the basis of a print of the charge to the jury, at least where it is suggested that the charge is deficient in some particular. The practice of lodging deficient grounds has been strongly deprecated; in disposing of one case, such a practice prompted the following comment from the Lord Justice-Clerk (Wheatley) (*McAvoy and Another* v. *H.M. Advocate*, 1983 S.L.T. 16 at p.19):

> "I wish to add two post-scripts. Two of the five grounds of appeal, both of which alleged failure by the presiding judge properly to direct the jury, were not insisted upon. This sort of thing is happening far too often. Whatever difficulties existed previously in formulating grounds of appeal on inadequacies in the judge's charge because the charge was not available in time to be considered before the grounds of appeal had to be lodged, that cannot be said now. Since the judge's charge should now be available timeously, practitioners have a professional responsibility to see that criticisms of a judge's charge can be read out of the charge and do not stem from recollections which can be imperfect and unjustified. Whatever advantages unchecked and erroneous criticisms of a judge's charge may have for the defence, they constitute an unwarranted public criticism of the judge's professional competence and result in a waste of time and money."

The matter was re-emphasised in the following practice note issued by the High Court on March 29, 1985:

> "All too often the time of the appeal court is wasted, and proper disposal of appeal is hampered, where the grounds stated in notes of appeal are wholly unspecific. In appeals against conviction, for example, it is common to find grounds stated thus:
> (i) 'Misdirection' without any specification whatever;
> (ii) 'Insufficient evidence' without any specification of the particular point, if any, which is to be taken, e.g. the absence of corroboration of evidence identifying the appellant as the perpetrator of the crime, or an alleged insufficiency of evidence to establish that the crime libelled, or a crime within the scope of the libel, was committed;
> In appeals against sentence, for example, the ground of appeal is more often than not equally uninformative, e.g. 'sentence excessive in the circumstances' or merely 'severity of sentence'. No hint is given of the circumstances to be relied on and it often happens that at the hearing the court is told of allegedly relevant circumstances which, it is said, were not before the judge or sheriff or which, it is said, the judge or sheriff ignored.
> It will be appreciated that the consequence of the statement of unspecific grounds of appeal is that the trial judge or sheriff is unable to report upon them, and the appeal court is at a grave disadvantage in preparing for and hearing appeals without the benefit of the observations of the trial judge or sheriff upon the position which the appellant submits to the court without notice.
> This practice note is intended to remind practitioners that grounds of appeal must be stated with sufficient specification to identify the particular criticism of the conviction or sentence which the appellant hopes to present at the hearing. In the case of notes of appeal lodged after the issue of this practice note the appeal court may be expected, save in exceptional circumstances and on cause shown, to refuse to entertain any appeal upon any unspecific ground."

(ii) Abandonment of Appeal

1. Criminal Procedure (Scotland) Act 1975

"**244.**—(1) An appellant may abandon his appeal by lodging with the Clerk of Justiciary a notice of abandonment in as nearly as may be in the form prescribed by Act of Adjournal under this Act; and on such notice being lodged the appeal shall be deemed to have been dismissed by the court.

(2) A person who has appealed against both conviction and sentence may abandon the appeal in so far as it is against conviction and may proceed with it against sentence alone."

2. Ferguson v. H.M. Advocate
1980 J.C. 27

The petitioner was convicted of assault and attempted robbery and sentenced to 21 months' imprisonment. He presented a note of application for leave to appeal against sentence, and this application was set down for hearing in 10 weeks time. He applied for, but was refused, legal aid. Refusal was intimated to him six weeks before the hearing of his appeal. His solicitor informed him that he could see counsel at the court on the day of the hearing. Having spoken to counsel on the morning of the hearing, the petitioner instructed counsel to abandon his application for leave to appeal. But since his case was the first on the court's roll, there was no opportunity for him to lodge the appropriate notice of abandonment. When the case was called counsel moved the court for leave to abandon the application. This was refused, and counsel was invited to address the court on the question of sentence. Having heard counsel, the court quashed the sentence of 21 months and substituted a sentence of four years. He presented a petition to the *nobile officium* of the High Court for review of the decision of the appeal court.

Lord Justice-Clerk (Wheatley): "... The applicant now submits that the sentence of 4 years' imprisonment was incompetent in respect that he had intimated to the Appeal Court the requisite abandonment of his Application for Leave to Appeal immediately after his case was called and before the Court has begun to consider the Application. He further submitted there was no appeal against sentence properly before the Court in terms of section 233(5) of the Criminal Procedure (Scotland) Act 1975, and that in any event the procedure adopted by the Appeal Court and the increase in sentence were oppressive and unfair to him. He argues that if he had lodged a formal notice of abandonment timeously in terms of section 244 of the said Act the Application would not have been before the Appeal Court and would have been deemed to have been dismissed, and that by waiting to discuss the Application with counsel on 15th December 1977, he being in prison and not free to obtain advice earlier, he has been unnecessarily and unjustly punished by the Appeal Court.

Section 262 of the aforementioned Act is in the following terms: 'Subject to the provisions of the next following section of this Act, all interlocutors and sentences pronounced by the High Court under this Part of the Act shall be final and conclusive and not subject to review by any court whatsoever and it shall be incompetent to stay or suspend any execution or diligence issuing from the High Court under this Part of this Act.' Faced with this provision counsel for the petitioner submitted that this Court in the exercise of its inherent power under its *nobile officium* could overcome and over-ride the apparent finality of the Appeal Court's interlocutor and sentence of 15th

December 1977 and determine the competency of those proceedings. He founded on a passage in Alison's Criminal Law, Vol. 2, at p.23 where the learned author says: 'The Court of Justiciary has the exclusive power of providing a remedy for all extraordinary or unforeseen occurrences in the course of criminal business whether before themselves or any inferior Court.'

We do not need to consider the general effect of this statement of the law in relation to the finality of the provisions of section 262 aforesaid, since we are satisfied that the circumstances narrated by the petitioner do not fall within the category of extraordinary or unforeseen occurrences. The petitioner knew by early November 1977 that he was not getting legal aid for his appeal. On his *ex parte* statement he was told by his solicitor that by some private arrangement he could see a counsel on the morning of the day when his Application was due to be heard. Even if that be so, he and those advising him were taking the risk that this might make it difficult though not impossible to lodge a notice of abandonment under section 244. It cannot be said that this was an extraordinary or unforeseen occurrence. Counsel submitted that it was quite common practice for motions for leave to abandon an appeal to be made verbally to the Court after the case had been called and this was presumably in the mind of the petitioner's legal advisers. This may be so, but for the reasons which we give later there is a distinction between a notice under section 244 which by statute results in the Application being deemed to have been dismissed by the Court and a verbal request to the Court after the case has been called asking the Court for leave to withdraw the Application. Even if the petitioner and his legal advisers did not appreciate this in law they ought to have appreciated it, and again it cannot be said that this constituted an extraordinary or unforeseen occurrence. For these reasons alone the petition would fall to be dismissed, since the criteria for invoking the *nobile officium* have not been established.

In view of what may be a common misapprehension about the procedure in relation to the withdrawal of Applications for Leave to Appeal or Appeals themselves we consider it desirable to state a further reason why this petition falls to be dismissed. Counsel for the petitioner submitted that up until the point when the argument in support of the Application had been started it is competent to withdraw the Application, and if a withdrawal is intimated to the Court before that point the Court has no option but to accept it and hold the Application to have been refused. When asked why if that be so it was necessary to have section 244 he submitted that it was simply there for administrative convenience and really did not matter. That is a startling proposition and in our opinion it is an entirely ill-founded one. Section 244 lays down a procedure which, if followed, results in a 'deemed' dismissal of the Application or Appeal by the Court when the notice is lodged. A 'deemed' dismissal cannot be obtained otherwise. No time limit is laid down in the section as to when the notice of abandonment has to be lodged. No such notice was lodged here. Once the case has called, the Court becomes master of the procedure. If any motion is made to the Court thereafter it is a matter for the discretion of the Court whether it should be granted or refused, unless there is statutory authority governing the matter. There is no statutory authority governing the situation here. In our view our Scottish procedure does not give an absolute right to an applicant or an appellant to withdraw an Application or an Appeal after the case has been called and is before the Court provided the motion is made before the argument in support of the Application or Appeal has started. Support for the opposite view was sought from the English case of *Rex v. Gibbon* [1946] 31 Cr.App.R. 143 and certain *dicta* by Lord Justice-General Clyde in *West v H.M. Advocate* 1955 S.L.T. 425. In *Gibbon* the circumstances were identical with those in the instance case. Gibbon had appealed against sentence and the moment when the case called his counsel informed the Court that he wished to abandon his appeal. The Rule of Court regulating the abandonment of appeals was basically in the same terms as those in section 24. Lord Goddard L.C.J. said in that case: 'But if it be the fact that the appellant has the right to abandon his appeal at any time, the Court would not prevent him from exercising that right merely because, not having had the advantage of seeing counsel until the last moment, he has not had time to put that notice in writing. That would be taking too severe and too technical a view in a case of this sort. It seems to me clear under the statutory rule that the appellant can at any time abandon the appeal.' Lord Goddard, who was giving the opinion of the Court, went on to affirm that Counsel had a right to abandon the Appeal at the point when he did. The Appeal, which seemed basically to be one to canvas whether the sentence should be increased, was dismissed.

The opinion and judgment in *Gibbon ex facie* give full support for the argument advanced by counsel for the petitioner, but it is not an authority binding on this Court and we are not prepared to follow it. We prefer to consider this question in the light of our own procedure and our own statutory provisions. As previously indicated we consider that an abandonment which carries an automatic dismissal of an Application or an Appeal can only be achieved if the statutory procedure of section 244 is followed. If it is not, and the Application or Appeal is before the Court, as it is when the case is called, the applicant or appellant has no right under statute or at common law to abandon the Application or Appeal except with the leave of the Court.

In *West* v. *H.M. Advocate* the facts were quite different. The appellant had been given leave to appeal on the question of sentence. The appellant had been sentenced to 10 years' imprisonment, but in view of the nature of the offences the Court decided that consideration should be given to substituting a sentence of preventive detention. A report on the suitability of that form of disposal for the appellant was called for and when it was received it was adverse to the appellant and recommended that preventive detention should be imposed. On receiving a copy of this report the Appellant lodged a notice of abandonment of the appeal in terms of Rule 13(a) of the Act of Adjournal 1926, which was the equivalent of section 244. When the hearing of the appeal was subsequently resumed the Court refused to admit the notice of abandonment and substituted a sentence of 12 years of preventive detention for the one of the 10 years' imprisonment. In the course of his opinion Lord Justice-General Clyde, with whom the other judges agreed, said: 'What the Rule is contemplating is an abandonment by an accused before the Court has begun to consider the appeal or application in question. In those circumstances there is no Court to dismiss the appeal or application, and the appeal or application is consequently deemed to have been dismissed. The situation is quite different where the Court has begun to hear the appeal or application. At that stage it is too late to invoke Rule 13(a). If the appeal or application is to be dismissed then it is the Court which must do it, and the situation where the appeal or application can be deemed to be dismissed does not arise. The Rule applies only up to the stage at which the actual hearing of the appeal or application begins and the accused or his Counsel begins to address the Court. I am confirmed in this view by the decision in England in *Rex* v. *Gibbon* on the interpretation of the Rule in England corresponding to Rule 13(a). The appellant there was entitled to invoke the Rule and abandon his appeal because the moment the case was called the appeal was abandoned. That is not the situation here, for the appellant has presented in full to us the arguments in favour of his appeal against sentence.'

It has to be observed that in that case the Court was dealing with an entirely different situation. A full argument had been addressed to the Court before the attempt to abandon the appeal was made. The question whether the calling of the case and the invitation to counsel to address the Court or the start of the argument marked the point at which a statutory notice of abandonment was no longer competent did not arise and was not canvassed. It is true that, following *Gibbon*, Lord Justice-General Clyde said that the point of no return was the stage when the actual hearing of the appeal or application begins and the accused or his Counsel begins to address the Court. Since in the circumstances of that case this was not a point which was necessary for the decision of the case we do not consider that what was there said was a binding decision on the issue before the Court here. On the contrary we have reached the conclusion previously stated that the hearing of the Application or Appeal begins when the case is called and the applicant or appellant is called to address the Court on the Application or Appeal. From that point onwards the Court is the master of procedure and a written notice of abandonment and *a fortiori* a verbal intimation of abandonment comes too late to warrant an automatic dismissal of the Application or Appeal. It is then a matter for the discretion of the Court whether such a motion in either form should be granted.

It follows from this that in the instant case the Court of Appeal were entitled to refuse the request for leave to abandon the application, and for this further reason we shall dismiss the petition."

The court dismissed the petition.

NOTE

This case was decided before the 1980 Act abolished the concept of an application for leave to appeal, but the *ratio* of the decision is still valid today. The importance of an effective abandonment of an appeal against sentence lies, of course, in the fact that the court cannot increase a sentence on appeal unless it has before it an appeal against that sentence: see 1975 Act, s. 254(3).

For a discussion of the *nobile officium* of the High Court, see *infra*, Chap. 18.

(iii)   Powers of the Court in Relation to Appeals

1.   Criminal Procedure (Scotland) Act 1975

"**252.** Without prejudice to any existing power of the High Court, that court may for the purposes of an appeal under section 228(1) of this Act—

(a)   order the production of any document or other thing connected with the proceedings;

(b)   hear any additional evidence relevant to any alleged miscarriage of justice or order such evidence to be heard by a judge of the High Court or by such other person as it may appoint for that purpose;

(c)   take account of any circumstances relevant to the case which were not before the trial judge;

(d)   remit to any fit person to enquire and report in regard to any matter or circumstance affecting the appeal;

(e)   appoint a person with expert knowledge to act as assessor to the High Court in any case where it appears to the court that such expert knowledge is required for the proper determination of the case."

NOTE

This is a much-simplified re-working of the powers contained in the former section 252. The matters of greatest significance in section 252 are contained in paragraphs (*b*) and (*c*). In the past the court has shown great reluctance to admit fresh evidence. It will be remembered that, under section 228(2) of the 1975 Act, an alleged miscarriage of justice may be based on the existence and significance of additional evidence which was not heard at the trial *only* where the evidence was not available and could not reasonably have been made available at the trial; and that under section 254(1) the appeal court has power, on setting aside a verdict, to quash the convictions, substitute an amended verdict of guilty or grant authority for a new prosecution. For some time after these provisions were introduced, there was uncertainty as to the extent to which (if any) the former case law was of assistance in interpreting these provisions: see, *e.g.*, *Gallacher* v. *H.M. Advocate*, 1981 J.C. 38; *Green* v. *H.M. Advocate*, 1983 S.C.C.R. 42; *Moffat* v. *H.M. Advocate*, 1983 S.C.C.R. 121. But the law was clarified in the following case.

2.   Cameron v. H.M. Advocate
1987 S.C.C.R. 608

An accused was convicted of two separate murders. He appealed on the basis of fresh evidence which had allegedly come into the hands of the defence. The appeal court refused the appeal after hearing the evidence and made the following comments on the interpretation of sections 228(2) and 254(1) of the 1975 Act:

> LORD JUSTICE-GENERAL: "In our opinion, the approach which the court must take in an appeal such as this is to be discovered in light of a proper construction of the provisions of section 228(2) read together with section 254(1) of the Criminal Procedure (Scotland) Act 1975, as amended. In the first place, it is clear that the court may allow an appeal against conviction on any ground only if it is satisfied that there has been a miscarriage of justice. In the case of an appeal in which it is contended that there has been a miscarriage of justice on the basis of the existence and significance of certain additional evidence which was not heard at the trial, it is obvious that the court will be in a position to give effect to that contention if it is satisfied that, if the original jury had heard the new evidence, its significance was such that the jury would have been bound to acquit. In such a case the appeal court will quash the conviction. The problem arises, however, where in an appeal based upon additional evidence within the meaning of section 228(2) the court cannot be so satisfied. Bearing in mind the provisions of section 254(1)(*c*) there must nevertheless be circumstances in which a court which could not be satisfied that, had the jury heard the additional evidence, they would have been bound to acquit would be entitled to be satisfied that a miscarriage of justice had occurred. What then are these circumstances? In our opinion they must be such that the court is persuaded that a verdict returned in ignorance of that additional evidence must be regarded as a miscarriage of justice. Plainly, the court will require to be satisfied not merely that the additional evidence was relevant for consideration by the trial jury. Setting aside the verdict of a jury is no light matter, and before the court can hold that there has been a miscarriage of justice it will, under reference to the language of section 228(2), require to be satisfied that the additional evidence is not merely evidence which it would have been relevant to lead at the trial but that it is relevant evidence of such significance that it will be reasonable to conclude that the verdict of the jury, reached in ignorance of its existence, must be regarded as a miscarriage of justice. The decision on the issue of the significance of the additional evidence is for the appeal court, and before the court will be in a position to decide that

the verdict of the jury represents a miscarriage of justice, it will require to be satisfied that the additional evidence is important evidence, of such a kind and quality that it was likely to have been found by a reasonable jury under proper directions of material assistance in their consideration of a critical issue which emerged at the trial.

This, in our opinion, will require the appeal court to be persuaded in the first place that the witnesses who have given the additional evidence were credible and that the evidence given was plainly reliable or was at least capable of being so regarded by a reasonable jury. It will also, however, require the appeal court to be satisfied that the additional evidence would have been likely to have had a material bearing upon, or a material part to play in, a reasonable jury's determination of a critical issue at the trial. In the case of *Green* the court found that the additional evidence could be described as important evidence of quality which was highly relevant to the particular critical issue in that case, with the consequence that the verdict which had proceeded in ignorance of the existence of that evidence could properly be regarded as a miscarriage of justice. That case, however, did not require the court to attempt to define for all such cases the approach which the court must take.

To summarise what we have said so far, in our opinion, if the court is to find that a miscarriage of justice had occurred in an appeal such as this, it must be satisfied that the additional evidence is at least capable of being described as important and reliable evidence which would have been bound, or at least likely, to have had a material bearing upon, or a material part to play in, the jury's determination of a critical issue at the trial. If the court is so satisfied, it will be open to it to hold that a conviction returned in ignorance of the existence of that evidence represents a miscarriage of justice and it may exercise its power to authorise the bringing of a new prosecution."

Appeal refused.

NOTE

The difference between fresh evidence which is so overwhelming as to leave no doubt that, had it been before the jury, it *must* have affected the verdict, and that which falls into a lesser category if importance, in the key distinction made in this case. For a full discussion of these issues, see Renton and Brown, paras. 11–41 *et seq.*; McCluskey, *Criminal Appeals*, paras. 6–26 *et seq.* For an example of the *Cameron* test in operation, see *Mitchell* v. *H.M. Advocate*, 1989 S.C.C.R. 502 and *Brodie* v. *H.M. Advocate*, 1993 S.C.C.R. 371.

3. Maitland v. H.M. Advocate
1992 S.C.C.R. 759

An accused, Maitland, was tried along with two co-accused, Smith and Hay, for murdering a man, McGloine. Maitland was convicted, but Smith and Hay were acquitted. Maitland appealed on the basis that after the verdict five persons had sworn affidavits that each of them had, while in custody at the same time as Hay was awaiting trial for the murder, heard Hay admitting to the crime.

LORD JUSTICE-GENERAL: "The evidence contained in these affidavits is said to be the basis of the alleged miscarriage of justice. Each of these five witnesses has deponed that they heard Hay admitting to having carried out the stabbing of the deceased. These alleged admissions appear to have been made either before the trial of the three accused began or during the period when the trial was proceeding. At this stage the critical question to determine is whether the evidence contained in the affidavits is of such a nature that this court should hear the evidence in order to determine whether the evidence is of such a kind and quality that it was likely to have been found by a reasonable jury and on proper directions to be of material assistance to them in their consideration of a critical issue at the trial of these three accused, including the appellant (*Cameron* v. *H.M. Advocate*). After hearing the evidence, if it were found to be reliable, this court would require to be satisfied that its relevance and significance was such that it was reasonable to conclude that a verdict reached in ignorance of that evidence must be regarded as a miscarriage of justice.

At this stage what we have to determine is whether we should allow this additional evidence to be led before the court and we could only do that if we were satisfied that if the evidence appeared to us to be credible it was evidence of the nature described above.

At the end of his submissions, Mr Findlay moved the court to set aside the conviction of the appellant and to grant authority to the Crown to bring a new prosecution in accordance with sections 254 and 255 of the Criminal Procedure (Scotland) Act 1975. Such a motion was, in our opinion, clearly premature. Before the court could hold that there had been any miscarriage of justice on the basis of the existence and significance of additional evidence which had not been heard at the trial, it would be necessary for the court to hear such additional evidence in accordance with section 252(*b*) of the Criminal Procedure (Scotland) Act 1975. Where precognitions or affidavits have been lodged to support an appeal based on section 228(2) of the Act of 1975 and the court is invited to exercise its power under section 252(*b*) to hear additional evidence, what the court has to decide initially is whether the proposed additional evidence could be regarded as evidence which was not available and could not reasonably have been made available at the trial and, further, whether the alleged additional evidence contained in the affidavits is prima facie of materiality (*Cameron* v. *H.M. Advocate*). According to what the witnesses say in their affidavits, the admissions which they allege that Hay made were made either shortly before the trial or during the trial of the appellant and his co-accused. Having regard to the circumstances in which these alleged admissions were made, we are at present prepared to accept that they constitute evidence which was not available and could not reasonably have been made available at the trial. Accordingly the critical question at this stage is to determine whether the alleged additional evidence is prima facie of materiality and, accordingly, whether it is evidence which we ought to hear under the powers conferred upon us by section 252(*b*) of the Act of 1975.

Having given the matter consideration, we have come to be of opinion that the evidence is not of such a nature that we should hear it. In the first place, it is well established that this court will decline to hear additional evidence which merely adds to evidence already given (*Temple* v. *H.M. Advocate* [1971 J.C. 1]). We recognise that if the circumstances are special, the court may allow additional evidence even though its effect will be merely to add to evidence already given at the trial, but it is plain that it will not do so unless the circumstances are very special (*Morland* v. *H.M. Advocate* [1985 S.C.C.R. 316]).

We do not regard the present case as very special in this sense. At the trial, as we have already observed, there was evidence supporting the involvement of Hay in the crime. The appellant stated that he saw the deceased stabbed by Hay and the co-accused Smith said he heard Hay say, 'I got him.' The appellant also said that he took a knife away from Hay. Mrs Morag Smith also said that after the incident Hay passed a knife to the appellant.

All this evidence was before the jury. So far as Hay was concerned the trial judge reminded the jury that there was evidence to the effect that he had delivered the fatal blow and that, if they were satisfied beyond doubt that it was he who delivered the fatal blow, they would then require to consider whether that was done with murderous intent. Alternatively, they were instructed that it would be open to them to consider whether Hay was guilty on the basis of art and part.

The trial judge also tells us in his supplementary report that the co-accused Smith in the course of his evidence in chief spoke to a conversation in Barlinnie Prison shortly after he, the co-accused Hay and the appellant had been arrested and taken into custody. According to Smith the appellant suggested that it must have been Hay who had stabbed the deceased and Hay had then gone on to suggest that whoever saw him stab the deceased should turn Queen's evidence. When the appellant had said that he had seen Hay stabbing the deceased, Hay had responded to the effect, 'If you seen it, you tell them you seen it.' Smith apparently agreed that Hay had not admitted that he had stabbed the deceased, but rather had said that he could not remember what had happened. Smith also agreed that there had been discussions about the incident a couple of times when the accused were in Barlinnie. Hay in his evidence stated that there was a conversation in Barlinnie to the effect that he might have carried out the stabbing; the appellant's position was that he never did it and that it must have been Hay, and that Hay had then said that he himself did not know that he had done it; he knew nothing about the incident. He stated that he had had in mind the possibility that he had carried out the stabbing until his wife told him later what she had seen. The appellant also spoke to conversations to this effect in Barlinnie.

In thus seems plain that at the trial evidence was given regarding conversations involving Hay in Barlinnie Prison before the trial. It appeared to be generally agreed by all three accused at that time that Hay's position was that he did not remember what had happened. Evidence was also given at the trial to the effect that Hay had stabbed the deceased. It follows that what the appellant is now seeking to do inviting the court to hear evidence from the witnesses who have sworn affidavits, is merely to add to evidence which has already been given to the effect that it was Hay who stabbed the deceased, that he had admitted the stabbing, and regarding conversations to which Hay was a party in Barlinnie Prison. The proposed new evidence does not add significantly to what was already before the jury. This is one reason for concluding that it would not be appropriate to allow this additional evidence to be led.

There is a further reason for reaching that conclusion. As already observed, the case was presented to the jury upon the basis that they might conclude on the evidence that either the appellant or Hay had delivered the fatal blow. They were also directed upon the doctrine of concert and, so far as the appellant and Hay was concerned, they were given a direction to the effect that if they were satisfied that the fatal blow had been struck by one or other of the appellant or Hay and that both were throughout acting in concert with a common criminal purpose to attack persons in the house with knives, then the jury would be entitled to convict both of them. In the event, the jury acquitted both Smith and Hay and convicted only the appellant of the charge of murder. Accordingly, the jury cannot have been satisfied that Smith or Hay was guilty on the basis of concert, and they must have convicted the appellant upon the basis that it was he who had delivered the fatal blow.

The case against the appellant Maitland depended principally upon the evidence of James McGloine, Angela McGloine and Linda Hay, and that evidence supported the view that the appellant was guilty as actor. The question must be as to what effect, if any, the proposed new evidence would have had upon the evidence which implicated the appellant as actor. If there had been reliable evidence that Hay had carried out the stabbing, that might have led the jury to reject the evidence which they accepted that the appellant had struck the fatal blow. The evidence led at the trial supporting the involvement of Hay in the crime was clearly not accepted by the jury. The proposed new evidence is to the effect that the fatal blow was struck by Hay rather than the appellant, but the source of the evidence is Hay himself, and it is plain that the jury could not have proceeded upon the basis of the evidence given by Hay at the trial, and it is difficult to see how any reasonable jury now could place any reliance upon evidence of what he had previously said. According to the evidence led at the trial, shortly after his arrest, when he was in Barlinnie Prison, Hay was maintaining to the two co-accused that he could not remember what had happened. According to what is stated in the affidavits, shortly before and during the trial, Hay was telling all and sundry that he had stabbed the deceased. When Hay gave evidence at the trial, he testified that he had no recollection of events in the house where the killing took place. If the proposed new evidence were allowed to be led, it would clearly establish that Hay was not a person on whom any reliance could be placed.

The proposed new witnesses may be telling the truth, but we are satisfied that we could not properly hold their evidence to be reliable evidence regarding the alleged involvement of Hay in the crime. None of them claims to have seen Hay commit the crime; they merely say that he told them so after the event. Hay gave evidence at the trial and there is no suggestion that he should be called to give fresh evidence. In any event, since he has been acquitted, he no longer has any interest to deny what is now attributed to him. We are accordingly satisfied that this is a case where we are driven to the conclusion that no reasonable jury could have regarded the proposed new evidence as reliable evidence of Hay's involvement (*Stillie* v. *H.M. Advocate* [1990 S.C.C.R. 719]). There is accordingly no reason to think that the proposed new evidence throws any doubt on the evidence on which the jury must have relied in holding that the appellant was guilty as actor.

Appeal refused.

NOTE

The case of *Morland* was very special: there, the conviction was quashed. For a summary of the current approach of the appeal court (by a judge who regularly presides), see McCluskey, *op. cit.*, para. 6.32, where the author concludes that the term "significance" in section 228(2) is a synonym for "materiality," judged in the context of the whole evidence, both that which was before the jury and that which is tendered as additional, all against the test of what constitutes a miscarriage of justice. See also *McCormack* v. *H.M. Advocate*, 1993 S.C.C.R. 581 on the term "additional" where it is used in section 228(2).

G.   RE-TRIAL

The possibility of a re-trial was introduced by the new section 254(1)(c) of the 1975 Act. The procedures governing the re-trial are identical to those governing any other trial on indictment, although section 255 of the 1975 Act does contain certain supplementary provisions in respect of new prosecutions:

1. Criminal Procedure (Scotland) Act 1975

"**255.**—(1) Where authority is granted under section 254(1)(*c*) of this Act, a new prosecution may be brought charging the accused with the same or any similar offence arising out of the same facts; and the proceedings out of which the appeal arose shall not be a bar to such new prosecution:

Provided that no sentence may be passed on conviction under the new prosecution which could not have been passed on conviction under the earlier proceedings.

(2) A new prosecution may be brought under this section, notwithstanding that any time limit (other than the time limit mentioned in subsection (3) below), for the commencement of such proceedings has elapsed.

(3) Proceedings in a prosecution under this section shall be commenced within two months of the date on which authority to bring the prosecution was granted; and for the purposes of this subsection proceedings shall, in a case where such warrant is executed without unreasonable delay, be deemed to be commenced on the date on which a warrant to apprehend or to cite the accused is granted, and shall in any other case be deemed to be commenced on the date on which the warrant is executed.

(4) Where the two months mentioned in subsection (3) above elapse and no new prosecution has been brought under this section, the order under section 254(1)(*c*) of this Act setting aside the verdict shall have the effect, for all purposes, of an acquittal."

NOTE

Sections 254(1) and 255 are both silent on the question of whether the court may grant authority for a new prosecution *ex proprio motu*, or whether this can only be done on the application of the prosecutor. In the absence of any requirement it would seem that such application is not necessary, and this is the course adopted by the court. What criteria govern the authorisation of a new prosecution? See the following case:

2. Mackenzie v. H.M. Advocate
1983 S.L.T. 220

The appellant was charged with murder. He tabled a special defence of self-defence, although, in fact, the true defence was one of accident. The trial judge directed the jury that they could not acquit on the ground of accident, but left the issue of self-defence for their consideration. The appellant was found guilty of culpable homicide and appealed on the ground of misdirection. The court held that there had been a material miscarriage of justice and quashed the conviction. They then considered the question of whether to authorise a new prosecution:

LORD JUSTICE-CLERK (WHEATLEY): "... Having decided that the verdict of the trial court must be set aside, I have now to consider what action should be taken thereon. Under the provisions of s. 254(1)(*c*) of the Criminal Procedure (Scotland) Act 1975 (as amended), instead of quashing the conviction this court can grant authority to bring a new prosecution in accordance with s. 255 of the Act. The new provision of allowing the court of appeal to grant such authority leaves the matter to the discretion of the court without specifying any grounds on which that course is warranted. Each case will require to be dealt with on its own facts. Where it is not suggested that there was not sufficient evidence to warrant the conviction, or any fault on the part of the Crown, and the one thing which has led to the setting aside of the verdict is a material misdirection in law by the trial judge, that is something which, in the interests of justice and the public interest, must be seriously taken into account when deciding whether to grant authority to bring a new prosecution instead of simply quashing the conviction. In the instant case I consider that this consideration weighs heavily, and I am further influenced by the fact that the unnecessary introduction by the defence of the plea of self-defence in the terms tendered created a confusion which, although it should have been avoided, should not have been introduced. Accordingly I move your Lordships to set aside the verdict on charge 2 but to grant authority to bring a new prosecution in terms of s. 254(1)(c) aforesaid. This leaves to the Lord Advocate the decision whether such a new prosecution should be brought."

Conviction quashed; authority to
bring new prosecution granted.

NOTES

1.   *Cf. McTavish* v. *H.M. Advocate, supra,* p.490 in which the only ground for quashing the conviction was a material misdirection by the trial judge. It seems likely that in future such "technical" acquittals, even if they satisfy the miscarriage of justice test, will result in a new trial.

2.   Retrials are, in any event, a rather unsatisfactory proceeding. Evidence once rehearsed loses its impact, and witnesses are in a position to adjust their testimony as necessary.

3.   It is suggested that in determining whether or not to bring a fresh prosecution the Lord Advocate is governed by the rule that his discretion must not be exercised oppressively (*supra,* Chap. 2), but it is clear from the following case that the court has no *locus* to determine the charges in any fresh prosecution.

3.   **Boyle v. H.M. Advocate**
1992 S.C.C.R. 824

An accused was charged with breach of the peace, murder and three contraventions of the Bail Act. He was convicted of culpable homicide in respect of the murder charge and was also convicted of all the other charges. He appealed only against the conviction for culpable homicide, but the High Court set aside the whole verdict on the ground of misdirection by the trial judge. The court then dealt with the question of how the appeal should be disposed of.

LORD JUSTICE-CLERK: "Since the miscarriage of justice arose from misdirection on the part of the trial judge and in view of the serious nature of charge (2), we are satisfied that it is in the public interest that the Crown should be granted authority to bring a new prosecution in terms of sections 254 and 255 of the Criminal Procedure (Scotland) Act 1975. We are mindful too that some of the difficulty in the case appears to have arisen from the fact that counsel for the appellant conceded that he was guilty of breach of the peace and the appellant must therefore accept some responsibility for what has occurred. The fact that there is to be a new prosecution emphasises the desirability of setting aside the jury's verdict on all charges, so that the jury at the new prosecution can hear all the evidence which is relevant and material to the issues which were the subject of the first indictment.

Counsel for the appellant suggested that if authority was to be granted for a new prosecution, the court as regards charge (2) should only authorise a fresh prosecution on a charge of culpable homicide, that being the offence of which he was convicted by the jury. Counsel referred to *Mackenzie* v. *H.M. Advocate* [1982 S.C.C.R. 499]. That was a case where an accused was charged with murder and was found guilty of culpable homicide. The verdict was set aside on the grounds of a misdirection on the part of the trial judge and authority was granted to bring a new prosecution. As the report shows, the accused was retried on an indictment containing only a charge of culpable homicide. The advocate-depute, on the other hand, contended that it was not for the court to consider what charge might be brought in the new prosecution; it was for the Crown to decide what charge should be brought.

We agree with the advocate-depute. Section 254(1)(c) enables the court to dispose of an appeal by setting aside the verdict of the trial court and granting authority to bring a new prosecution in accordance with section 255 of the Act of 1975. Section 255(1) makes it plain that where such authority has been granted, a new prosecution may be brought charging the accused with the same or any similar offence arising out of the same facts. In our opinion, however, it is for the Crown and not the court to determine what charges should be levelled against the accused in the new prosecution. What the court does is to grant authority for the bringing of a new prosecution, leaving it to the Crown to decide whether to exercise that right and, if so, what charges to bring. In *Mackenzie* v. *H.M. Advocate* it was the Crown which decided that the new indictment should contain only a charge of culpable homicide.

In all the circumstances we shall set aside the verdict of the jury and grant authority to the Crown to bring a new prosecution in terms of section 255 of the Act of 1975."

Verdict set aside.

NOTE

This was not the end of the story. The Crown thereafter re-indicted the accused on all the original charges, including the charge of murder. At a preliminary diet held in respect of that indictment, the judge held the indictment was competent, but unfair. He dismissed it. The Crown appealed.

4. H.M. Advocate v. Boyle
1992 S.C.C.R. 939

LORD JUSTICE-GENERAL: "Although the basis for the decision at the preliminary diet was that it was oppressive for the respondent to be charged in these proceedings with murder rather than with culpable homicide, it is necessary first to examine the issue of competency. The two points are closely related to each other, since the learned advocate-depute sought to rely on the competency of the charge in his submission that the judge erred in law in holding that it would amount to oppression for the charge to proceed as one of murder. And Mr Bell for the respondent renewed the argument that it was incompetent for the respondent to be charged with murder at this stage as part of his submission that the decision at the preliminary diet should be affirmed.

Section 228(1) of the 1975 Act provides that any person convicted on indictment may appeal, in accordance with the provisions of that Part of the Act, to the High Court against such conviction. The provisions as to the disposal of an appeal against conviction are set out in section 254(1) of the Act, as substituted by Schedule 2 to the Criminal Justice (Scotland) Act 1980, which is in these terms:

'The High Court may, subject to subsection (4) below, dispose of an appeal against conviction by—

 (*a*) affirming the verdict of the trial court;

 (*b*) setting aside the verdict of the trial court and either quashing the conviction or substituting therefor an amended verdict of guilty:

Provided that an amended verdict of guilty must be one which could have been returned on the indictment before the trial court; or

 (*c*) setting aside the verdict of the trial court and granting authority to bring a new prosecution in accordance with section 255 of this Act.'

The power set out in paragraphs (*a*) and (*b*) of this subsection are a re-enactment in substantially the same terms of the powers which were available to the court under sections 254 and 255 of the 1975 Act as originally enacted. But the power to grant authority to bring a new prosecution was introduced for the first time by the 1980 Act, Schedule 2 to which substituted a new section 255, subsection (1) of which is in these terms:

'Where authority is granted under section 254(1)(*c*) of this Act, a new prosecution may be brought charging the accused with the same or any similar offence arising out of the same facts; and the proceedings out of which the appeal arose shall not be a bar to such new prosecution:

Provided that no sentence may be passed on conviction under the new prosecution which could not have been passed on conviction under the earlier proceedings.'

Reference was made in the course of the argument to the power of the Court of Appeal in England in terms of section 7 of the Criminal Appeal Act 1968, as amended by section 43 of the Criminal Justice Act 1988, to order a retrial. This power is available to be exercised where the Court of Appeal have decided to allow an appeal against conviction and it appears to them that the interests of justice so require. There are significant limitations on the order which may then be pronounced. Subsection (2) of section 7 provides that a person shall not under that section be ordered to be retried for any offence other than the offence of which he was convicted at the original trial and in respect of which his appeal has been allowed by reason of the fresh evidence, or an offence of which he could have been convicted at the original trial on an indictment for that offence, or an offence charged in any alternative count of the indictment in respect of which the jury were disabled from giving a verdict in consequence of convicting him of that offence. It is plain that if a restriction in these terms had been enacted as part of the substituted section 255(1) of the 1975 Act, the Crown would be unable to bring any charge in the new prosecution in this case other than one of culpable homicide. This is because that was the offence of which he was convicted and in respect of which his appeal was allowed. But Mr Bell accepted that no advantage was to be gained in seeking to draw a comparison between the Scottish and English legislation on this point, except perhaps to demonstrate that if Parliament had wished to do so it could have enacted a restriction to the same effect in express terms in the Scottish legislation. There are significant differences of approach, since the Court of Appeal in England is empowered by the statute to exercise a much closer control over the process of retrial than has been thought appropriate in Scotland. The Scottish approach is no doubt based on the principle which is fundamental to our system of criminal prosecution that the Crown is at all times the master of the instance, and it has due regard to the discretion which is vested in the public interest in the Lord Advocate.

In the course of the trial on the original indictment the trial judge explained to the jury that it was open to them to convict the respondent on charge (2) either of murder or of culpable homicide. What he said was this:

'If you convict him of murder it is quite simple. You simply say in
relation to charge (2), the clerk asks you what is your verdict, you reply
guilty. And that is guilty of murder. If you return a guilty verdict but not
of murder then you would simply say guilty of culpable homicide, and I
invite you, although you are not obliged to follow my invitation, if you do
return a verdict of culpable homicide to explain whether it is provocation,
cruel excess or the absence of murderous intent.'

In the event when the jury were asked what their verdict was on charge (2)
they found him guilty of culpable homicide, as can be seen from the following
exchange between the foreman and the clerk of court:

'THE CLERK: What is your verdict in respect of the accused Daniel Boyle
on charge (2)?
THE FOREMAN: Guilty of culpable homicide.
THE CLERK: Is that verdict unanimous or by a majority?
THE FOREMAN: By a majority.
THE CLERK: Is there anything further you wish to add in respect of
charge (2)?
THE FOREMAN: It is without murderous intent.'

It was to his conviction in consequence of that verdict that the respondent
directed his appeal, and in disposing of the appeal it was that verdict which
was set aside by the appeal court.

The critical issue, so far as the question of competency is concerned, is
whether the authority granted under section 254(1)(c) to bring a new
prosecution is subject to limitation because of the terms of the verdict or
whether the verdict, having been set aside, is now to be left entirely out of
account so that no such limitation is to be implied. Mr Bell accepted that no
such limitation was to be found in the express language either of section
254(1)(c) or section 255(1). But he contended that the effect of the jury's verdict
was, by the clearest implication, to acquit the respondent of murder. His
appeal had been directed to the conviction, not the acquittal. And if the verdict
was set aside in order to remove the conviction of culpable homicide, that left
the implied verdict of acquittal of murder undisturbed. It was contrary to the
whole spirit of the Act that the respondent should find himself worse off as a
result of a successful appeal against his conviction, as he would be if he were to
be exposed once more to the charge of murder of which he had been acquitted.
It was also illogical that that should be the result of granting authority under
section 254(1)(c) since the statute gave no right to the Crown to appeal against a
conviction. The furthest it went, as the result of another amendment
introduced by section 37 of the 1980 Act, was to enable the Lord Advocate to
refer a question of law to the High Court for their opinion under section 263A.
But it was expressly provided by subsection (5) of that section that the opinion
on the point referred was not to affect the acquittal in the trial.

Accepting as he did that no restriction similar to that in the English
legislation was expressed in either section 254(1)(c) or section 255(1) of the 1975
Act, Mr Bell submitted that if there was an ambiguity it should be resolved in
favour of the accused. This was, he said, in accordance with the presumption
of innocence and with the general proposition already mentioned that it was
unfair for the appellant to be exposed to the risk of being worse off as a result of
his appeal than he would be if the conviction appealed against were to be
allowed to stand and the verdict of the jury was affirmed.

The contrary view, which was contended for by the advocate-depute, is that
once the verdict of the jury has been set aside it cannot be founded on for any
purpose. Any rider attached to it, as was done in the present case, must also be
ignored. This meant that a verdict which had the effect of convicting the

accused of a lesser offence than that libelled in the charge was in precisely the same position as one by which part of the narrative had been deleted. The scope of the authority granted under section 254(1)(c) was to be determined by the provisions of section 255(1), which made no reference to the terms of the verdict. The only restriction on the authority which was granted to the Crown was that expressed in terms of that subsection, by which it was provided that the new prosecution might be brought charging the accused with the same or any similar offence arising out of the same facts. The appropriate point of reference for the purposes of this restriction was the original indictment, not the verdict of the jury at the trial. It was the facts on the basis of which the original prosecution had been brought, not the evidence led at the previous trial or the view formed by the jury in the light of that evidence, to which one should have regard.

We agree with Mr Bell that by convicting the respondent of culpable homicide the jury at the previous trial were by implication acquitting him of the charge of murder. And it is clear that the respondent's appeal against his conviction on charge (2) was directed against his conviction for culpable homicide in terms of the verdict of the jury on that charge. His acquittal on the charge of murder which was implied by that verdict could not have been, and was not, the subject of any appeal. In setting aside the verdict of the trial court in terms of section 254(1)(c), the appeal court were therefore setting aside the verdict by which the respondent was convicted of culpable homicide, just as they would have been doing if they had set aside the verdict under section 254(1)(b) as a preliminary to quashing his conviction on that charge.

But in our opinion the effect of setting aside the verdict is that that verdict is no longer available to be used for any purpose. It must be disregarded entirely and all its effects and implications have ceased to exist. There is no indication in the statute that, although it ceases to have effect for one purpose, it is to continue to have effect for another. Mr Bell accepted that, if a verdict of guilty which merely deleted part of the narrative of a charge was set aside, the deletion would fall to be disregarded if a new prosecution were then to be brought charging the accused with the same offence. His point was that a verdict which implied an acquittal of a more serious offence libelled in the same charge was different, because there could be no appeal against the acquittal and only the conviction on that charge was being set aside. We do not accept this distinction. In our view verdicts which include deletions from the narrative, verdicts which have riders attached to them and verdicts which reduce the crime libelled to a lesser crime are all in the same position. Once the verdict has been set aside under section 254(1)(c), all exculpatory elements which are expressed in or implied by it are struck out also, as a preliminary to the bringing of a new prosecution.

Much was made of the fact that it was unfair that an accused person who had been convicted of a lesser crime should be put at risk of facing the more serious charge once again following a successful appeal. But it is necessary to have regard also to the public interest in this matter, since this is an important factor to be taken into account when consideration is given to the question whether authority should be granted for the bringing of a new prosecution. That point was recognised in the present case in the following passage of the opinion delivered by the Lord Justice-Clerk [at p.837F, *supra*]:

'Since the miscarriage of justice arose from misdirection on the part of the trial judge and in view of the serious nature of charge (2), we are satisfied that it is in the public interest that the Crown should be granted authority to bring a new prosecution in terms of sections 254 and 255 of the Criminal Procedure (Scotland) Act 1975.'

It is not difficult to envisage cases—a miscarriage of justice due to the existence of significant new evidence which was not available at the trial is one example—where the appropriate course in the public interest would be to wipe the slate clean so that the prosecution may begin again. What Parliament has done is to provide the court with the power to set aside the verdict in all those cases where it is in the public interest that there should be a fresh prosecution rather than a quashing of the conviction. A single rule that once the verdict is set aside it ceases to have effect for all purposes is consistent with this approach.

The limitations on the new prosecution are to be found therefore in section 255, not in section 254(1)(c). It is provided here that the new prosecution may be brought charging the accused with the same or any similar offence arising out of the same facts. The use of the word 'similar' shows that a measure of discretion is available to the Crown as to the offence charged, although the facts out of which it arises must be the same. No mention is made at this stage of the verdict which has been set aside. The point of reference against which to test the sameness or similarity cannot reasonably be the precognition, nor can it be evidence which was led in the proceedings out of which the appeal arose. It must therefore be the terms of the indictment and, where more than one charge was contained in it, the charge or charges in respect of which the accused was previously convicted and to which he directed his appeal. Taking charge (2) on the original indictment as the point of reference in the present case, we find that in the new prosecution the respondent has been charged with precisely the same offence arising out of precisely the same facts as those set out in the original charge, so this requirement has clearly been satisfied.

There was a suggestion that to charge the respondent with murder at this stage was inconsistent with the proviso to section 255(1), by which it is declared that no sentence may be passed on conviction under the new prosecution which could not have been passed on conviction under the earlier proceedings. But we agree with the advocate-depute that the purpose of this provision is to deal with those cases where the sentence has been regulated by statute and the statutory penalty on conviction for the offence has been increased since the date of the original conviction. In the present case the crime libelled in charge (2) in the original indictment was a common law offence and there has been no change since the original conviction in the sentences available to the court.

For these reasons we are of the opinion that the bringing of the charge of murder on this indictment was competent. The remaining issue is whether for the Crown to charge the respondent with murder at this stage amounted to oppression. Now it is important to notice that it has not been suggested that the action of the Crown is oppressive in the sense that the respondent would be unable to receive a fair trial. Accordingly this is not one of those cases, such as H.M. Advocate v. Stewart [1980 J.C. 84] or Stuurman v. H.M. Advocate [1980 J.C. 111], where the issue was whether there was a risk of prejudice to the accused so grave that no direction by a trial judge could be expected to remove it. The alleged oppression in the present case consists solely in the bringing of the charge as one of murder [and] not [as] one of culpable homicide.

The judge reached the view at the preliminary diet that the circumstances of this case were very special, and indeed unique, because the jury had decided to assert in the rider to their verdict that the respondent had acted without murderous intent. Comparing this rider with the charge of murder in the present indictment he concluded that there was a fundamental unfairness in the decision taken by the Crown. Mr Bell sought to support this approach, submitting that there was here a fundamental unfairness in the action of the Crown which could not be cured by any direction from the trial judge. But this argument, which was submitted as one of principle and thus equally applicable to all cases where the accused had been convicted of a lesser crime on the first occasion, seems to us to be misconceived. The sole basis for the argument is a comparison between the charge in this indictment and the verdict at the previous trial. But, in order to clear the way for the bringing of a new prosecution, that verdict has been set aside. It has ceased to exist, and any attempt to compare the charge on this indictment with the conclusion reached by the jury on the evidence led in the earlier proceedings must be rejected as irrelevant.

Furthermore it is clear from their opinion that the appeal court were well aware that the respondent was liable to be tried again for murder if authority were to be given for the bringing of a new prosecution. Yet they held that it was in the public interest that authority to this effect should be granted. In bringing charge (2) against the respondent as one of murder therefore, the Crown were acting within the limits of the authority given to them by the court and in accordance with the provisions of the Act. We find it impossible in these circumstances to say that, having decided that this charge should be brought against the respondent as one of murder rather than one of culpable homicide, the Crown were acting oppressively. Furthermore no case was cited to us, and we are not aware of any, in which it has been held that the court is entitled to substitute its own view of what is fair or unfair as regards the charges to be included in an indictment for that formed by the Lord Advocate.

Accordingly we are of the opinion that the decision taken by the judge at the preliminary diet was unsound in law and must be reversed. We shall accordingly allow this appeal and remit the case to the trial judge to proceed as accords."

Crown appeal allowed.

NOTE

Again, the matter did not rest. The accused then brought a petition to the *nobile officium*: see *Boyle, Petitioner*, 1992 S.C.C.R. 949 (*infra*, p.615), where it was held, *inter alia*, that the course taken by the Crown in re-indicting on all the charges was in the public interest, since the jury ought to be able to hear all the evidence bearing on the principal charge (murder) to which it was clear that the subsidiary charge (breach of the peace) was related. This was so even although no appeal had been taken against the conviction for breach of the peace; nonetheless the whole verdict had been set aside.

Boyle's retrial finally took place in the spring of 1993. He was acquitted of all charges by the jury.

5. Farooq v. H.M. Advocate
1991 S.C.C.R. 889

An accused was convicted of lewd practices towards children. He was convicted and appealed on the ground that the trial judge had misdirected the jury. In allowing the appeal and quashing the conviction, the court refused to authorise a new prosecution.

LORD JUSTICE-CLERK: "The advocate-depute's final submission was that if the court should be of the view that there had been a miscarriage of justice, then instead of quashing the conviction the court should set aside the verdict of the jury and should grant authority to bring a new prosecution in accordance with section 254(1)(c) and section 255 of the Criminal Procedure (Scotland) Act 1975. He stressed that if there had been any fault in this case it was not fault on the part of the Crown, and since the miscarriage of justice had resulted from a failure on the part of the trial judge, the proper course would be to allow a fresh prosecution to be brought. Mr Totten on the other hand reminded us that this was a case which concerned young children. He pointed out that there had been difficulties at the trial because of the age of the children and because of the fact that much of the evidence had to be taken with the aid of an interpreter. He also reminded us that in his report to us the trial judge has emphasised that the evidence which was led at the trial was unsatisfactory and was full of apparent contradictions and inconsistencies. To such an extent was that so that the trial judge, when giving us his opinion on the case, expresses the view that there had been a miscarriage of justice. When all these matters are taken into account, it appears to us clear that this is not a case where the court should grant authority to bring a fresh prosecution. In *Kelly* v. *Docherty* [1991 S.C.C.R. 312] one of the circumstances which persuaded the court that authority should not be granted for a fresh prosecution was that a child would have to give evidence again and that doing so might well distress the child. That is undoubtedly a factor which we regard as of importance in this case and when we take into account the whole circumstances of this case, including the unsatisfactory nature of the evidence led at the first trial, we have come to the conclusion that this is clearly not a case where authority should be given to bring a fresh prosecution. Accordingly, being satisfied that there was a miscarriage of justice in this case, the convictions are now quashed."

Convictions quashed.

NOTE
So where the witnesses are young and the evidence given at the first trial is unsatisfactory, it is unlikely that authority will be given for a fresh prosecution.

H.   REFERENCE TO THE HIGH COURT BY THE SECRETARY OF STATE

Leitch v. Secretary of State for Scotland
1982 S.L.T. (Sh.Ct.) 76

Section 263(1) of the Criminal Procedure (Scotland) Act 1975, as amended, provides, *inter alia*, that the Secretary of State, on the consideration of any conviction of a person or the sentence (other than sentence of death) passed on a person who has been convicted, may, "if he thinks fit" refer the whole case to the High Court for consideration by that court, whether or not an appeal has been heard against that conviction. A prisoner convicted of armed robbery raised an action of damages against the Secretary of State alleging, *inter alia*, abuse of process and oppression on the latter's part. The pursuer founded, *inter alia*, on the defender's refusal to exercise his powers under section 263 to refer the pursuer's case to the High Court. The defender contended that his decision was not subject to review by the sheriff court, or indeed by any court. The sheriff dismissed the action as irrelevant. The pursuer appealed to the sheriff principal.

SHERIFF PRINCIPAL (GIMSON): "... I turn now to the pursuer's case of oppression contained in his averments regarding the Secretary of State's decision not to refer his case back to the High Court of Justiciary under s. 263 of the Criminal Procedure (Scotland) Act 1975. That case is indicated in the craves of the action by the references to oppression and abuse of legal process and in his second and fourth pleas-in-law.

The assumption of the pursuer's case is that the Secretary of State's decisions on the exercise of his powers under s. 263 are open to consideration by the courts. I share the sheriff's doubt whether such a question, if justiciable, could have been litigated in the sheriff court: but as I am satisfied that there can be no recourse to any court in respect of the powers conferred in s. 263, I need not consider that specialty.

There appears to be no reported decision in Scotland on this matter, and no authority was quoted to me on it. However, the statutory position in England is precisely the same as in Scotland, and I find that the courts there have held that they will not either act to require the Secretary of State to refer a case under the equivalent section (Criminal Appeal Act 1907, s. 19) or allow his decision to be questioned in the court (*Ex parte Kinally* [1958] Crim. L.R. 474 per Goddard L.C.J., Cassels and Diplock L.JJ.; *Hanratty* v. *Lord Butler of Saffron Walden* (1971) 115 S.J. 386 per Lord Denning M.R., Salmon and Stamp L.JJ.). The second of these cases were put on grounds similar to those averred here.

While these decisions may not be formally binding on the courts in Scotland, they are of strongly persuasive force on the question of the correct interpretation of the statutory words 'the Secretary of State ... *may, if he thinks fit*' (refer a case to the High Court). The English decisions support what I consider to be the primary and correct view: that these words confer an absolute discretion on the Secretary of State."

Appeal dismissed.

NOTES

1.   Section 263 also provides that the appeal provisions of the 1975 Act have no effect on the prerogative of mercy. The reference to the appeal court is quite distinct from the Secretary of State's functions with regard to the latter. The prerogative of mercy is discussed *post*, Chap. 18.

2.   Leitch subsequently appealed to the Court of Session against the decision of the sheriff principal, but this appeal was also refused.

I.   ADVOCATION

Advocation is a produce whereby a party may bring under review irregularities in the preliminary stages of a case. It cannot be employed to obtain a review of the merits. It is a competent method of review in solemn and summary proceedings, but since it is most frequently encountered today in the latter it is discussed in the following chapter on review and appeal in summary proceedings, *post*, pp.562 to 569.

J.   LORD ADVOCATE'S REFERENCE

Criminal Procedure (Scotland) Act 1975

"**263A.**—(1) Where a person tried on indictment is acquitted of a charge, the Lord Advocate may refer a point of law which has arisen in relation to that charge to the High Court for their opinion; and the Clerk of Justiciary shall send to the person and to any solicitor who acted for that person at the trial, a copy of the reference and intimation of the date fixed by the Court for a hearing.

(2) The person may, not later than seven days before the date so fixed, intimate in writing to the Clerk of Justiciary and to the Lord Advocate either—

(*a*) that he elects to appear at the hearing; or

(*b*) that he elects to be represented thereat by counsel;

but, except by leave of the Court on cause shown, (and without prejudice to his right to attend), he shall not appear or be represented at the hearing other than by and in conformity with an election under this subsection.

(3) Where there is no intimation under subsection (2)(*b*) above, the High Court shall appoint counsel to act at the hearing as *amicus curiae*.

(4) The costs of representation elected under subsection (2)(*b*) above or of an appointment under subsection (3) above shall, after being taxed by the Auditor of the Court of Session, be paid by the Lord Advocate.

(5) The opinion on the point referred under subsection (1) above shall not affect the acquittal in the trial."

NOTES

1.   This section was inserted in the 1975 Act by section 37 of the 1980 Act. So far, it has been used on only four occasions: see the references reported at 1984 S.L.T. 337; 1986 S.C.C.R. 329; 1992 S.C.C.R. 724 and 1992 S.C.C.R. 960.

2.   Notice that the procedure is not a procurator's appeal against acquittal. The opinion on the point referred to the court has no effect on that acquittal. It is also an interesting feature of this procedure that it will only be instituted on *acquittal*. No doubt the argument is that the accused will appeal if he wishes to challenge a point of law arising out of his conviction, or on a preliminary matter such as competency or relevancy.

3.   In *Attorney-General's Reference (No. 1 of 1975)* [1975] Q.B. 773 the court held that the procedure should be used for "short but important points which require a quick ruling ... before a potentially false decision of law has too wide a circulation in the courts."

K.   APPEAL IN CONNECTION WITH PRELIMINARY DIETS

Criminal Procedure (Scotland) Act 1975

"76A—(1) Without prejudice to any right of appeal under section 228 or 280A of this Act, a party may, with the leave of the court of first instance (granted either on the motion of that party or *ex proprio motu*) and in accordance with such procedure as may be prescribed by Act of Adjournal under this Act, appeal to the High Court against a decision at a preliminary diet; but any such appeal must be taken not later than 2 days after such decision.

(2) Where an appeal is taken under subsection (1) above, the High Court may postpone the trial diet for such period as appears to them to be appropriate and may, if they think fit, direct that such period (or some part of it) shall not count towards any time limit applying in respect of the case.

(3) In disposing of an appeal under subsection (1) above, the High Court may affirm the decision of the court of first instance or may remit the case to it with such directions in the matter as they think fit; and where the court of first instance has dismissed the indictment or any part of it, may reverse that decision and direct that the court of first instance fix a trial diet if it has not already fixed one as regards so much of the indictment as it has not dismissed."

NOTES

1.   Since the object of the preliminary diet is to enable matters of a preliminary nature to be disposed of prior to the actual trial, it is necessary to have an expedited form of pre-trial appeal to deal with disputed decisions at the preliminary diet. This is provided for by section 76A.

2.   The right of appeal provided for is without prejudice to the accused's right of appeal against conviction or sentence under section 228, or the prosecutor's right of appeal by way of advocation under section 280A. This presumably means that a matter which could have been appealed under section 76A but which was not so appealed may still be appealed after conviction. What it probably does not admit (but does not in terms exclude) is the possibility of two appeals—one pre-trial and the other post-conviction—on the same point.

3.   There is no absolute right of appeal. Appeal is only permitted with the leave of the court of first instance. There appears to be no provision for a party to challenge a refusal of leave to appeal.

4.   Procedures for appeal are governed by the Act of Adjournal (Consolidation) 1988, r. 34 et seq.

CHAPTER 16

APPEAL AND REVIEW IN SUMMARY PROCEEDINGS

The materials in this chapter discuss the following methods of appeal and review in summary proceedings: appeal by stated case; suspension; advocation; appeals from decisions on competency and relevancy; and appeal against sentence by note of appeal. Extraordinary methods of review, such as petitions to the *nobile officium* of the High Court, applications to the European Commission on Human Rights and references to the Court of Justice of the European Communities, are dealt with in Chap. 18, *infra*.

A. RIGHT OF APPEAL AND GROUND OF APPEAL IN SUMMARY PROCEEDINGS

Criminal Procedure (Scotland) Act 1975
"**442.**—(1) Without prejudice to any right of appeal under section 453A of this Act—

  (*a*) any person convicted in summary proceedings may appeal under this section to the High Court—
    (i) against such conviction;
    (ii) against the sentence passed on such conviction; or
    (iii) against both such conviction and such sentence;
  (*b*) the prosecutor in such proceedings may so appeal on a point of law—
    (i) against an acquittal in such proceedings; or
    (ii) against a sentence passed in such proceedings;
  (*c*) the prosecutor in such proceedings may, in any class of case specified by order by the Secretary of State under this paragraph, so appeal against the sentence passed on such conviction if it appears to the prosecutor that the sentence is unduly lenient.

(2) By an appeal under subsection (1)(*a*) of this section or, as the case may be, against acquittal under subsection (1)(*b*) of this section, an appellant may bring under review of the High Court any alleged miscarriage of justice in the proceedings, including, in the case of an appeal under the said subsection (1)(*a*), any alleged miscarriage of justice on the basis of the existence and significance of additional evidence which was not heard at the trial and which was not available and could not reasonably have been made available at the trial."

NOTES
1. An appeal under section 442(1)(*a*)(i) or (iii) (appeal against conviction or conviction and sentence) or under section 442(1)(*b*) (prosecutor's appeal on a point of law against acquittal or sentence) is made by way of application for a stated case, in accordance with the procedures set out in sections 444 to 453, 453D and 453E of the 1975 Act: *ibid.*, s. 442A(1).

An appeal by an accused against sentence alone under section 442(1)(*a*) (ii) is made by means of a "note of appeal" in accordance with the procedures set out in sections 453B to 453E of the 1975 Act: *ibid.*, s. 442B. "Provided that nothing in this section shall prevent a convicted person from proceeding by way of bill of suspension in respect of any alleged fundamental irregularity relating to the imposition of the sentence" (1975 Act, s. 442B). A prosecutor's appeal against a lenient sentence under section 442(1)(c) is likewise made by note of appeal under section 453B.

2. Section 453A, which provides for appeal by way of bill of suspension or advocation on the ground of miscarriage of justice where an appeal under section 442 would be incompetent or inappropriate, is set out *infra*, p.556.

B. APPEAL BY STATED CASE

This method of appeal was introduced by the Summary Prosecutions Appeals (Scotland) Act 1875. Amended by subsequent legislation, the law relating to the stated case was radically reformed by Schedule 3 to the 1980 Act. The nature of those changes is indicated, where appropriate, below.

(i) Competency

As was pointed out above, a stated case is a competent method of appeal against conviction, conviction and sentence or, at the instance of the prosecutor against acquittal or sentence. It is not a competent method of appeal against sentence alone by a convicted person. Where there has been neither an acquittal nor sentence pronounced, a stated case is not competent:

1. **Tudhope v. Mathieson**
1981 S.C.C.R. 231

An accused person was charged on summary complaint with various contraventions of the Road Traffic Act 1972. The sheriff dismissed the complaint as incompetent, on the ground that it was time-barred under section 331(1) of the 1975 Act. The prosecutor applied to the sheriff for a stated case:

SHERIFF KEARNEY: "In this cause under the Criminal Procedure (Scotland) Act 1975 I dismissed the complaint as time-barred by interlocutor dated 5th October 1981 to which interlocutor was appended a note which explained, as fully as I was able, my reasons for my decision. The prosecutor by note of appeal dated 9th October 1981 and lodged with the sheriff clerk's department on 12th October has craved the court to state a case for the opinion of the High Court of Justiciary under the said Act. So far as I am aware the only provision entitling the prosecutor to request a stated case under the said Act is to be found in sub-paragraph (b) of section 442(1) of the Act. The said sub-paragraph reads as follows:
'(b) The prosecutor in such proceedings may so appeal on a point of law—
(i) against an acquittal in such proceedings; or
(ii) against a sentence passed in such proceedings.'
The instant proceedings were terminated by dismissal. It clearly could not be contended that a dismissal was a form of sentence. As to the possible contention that dismissal is a form of acquittal I have always understood acquittal to imply the absolving of the accused from the charge in a manner

comparable to a jury's verdict of 'not guilty'. When I became seized of the difficulty I asked the sheriff clerk to ventilate the matter and the prosecutor, the agent for the defence not objecting, asked for a hearing, and, at very short notice, Mr Lowe, assistant procurator fiscal, and the accused's agent, Mr Gordon, were able to attend at my chambers at 4 p.m. on 21st October.

Mr Lowe submitted that it was reasonable in the whole context of section 442 of the said Act to treat dismissal as being a form of acquittal. He also pointed out that in the circumstances of the present case the accused was, if the dismissal were justified, as immune from prosecution as he would have been had a verdict of 'not guilty' been returned in respect that the Crown could no longer initiate a prosecution as the case was time-barred.

The accused's agent informed me that his client was not greatly concerned either way but he did draw my attention to the wording of section 447(1) of the 1975 Act as now amended which states, inter alia, 'Within three weeks of the final determination of proceedings in respect of which an application for a stated case is made under section 444 of this Act ... the judge who presided at the trial, shall prepare a draft stated case.' Mr Gordon suggested that the mandatory language of the statute perhaps carried the consequence that the judge of first instance had no option but to state a case when requested to do so even if he thought it was incompetently asked for. Mr Lowe indicated that he was not happy to adopt this line of reasoning and in any event I think it is fallacious. It seems reasonably clear to me that the mandatory obligation on the judge to state a case arises only in the event of the case being lawfully requested and accordingly that it always remains open to the judge of first instance to decline to state a case if he is of opinion that the case has not been lawfully requested.

Although the word 'acquittal' has never, according to my researches (or indeed according to Mr Lowe's researches), been formally defined in Scottish legal literature or case-law it has, in my experience, always been used as equivalent of a complete absolvitor which frees the accused forever of the pending charge and lays a firm foundation for a possible plea of tholed assize or res judicata in exactly the same way as a jury's verdict of 'not guilty' would. I have now ascertained that the word is so used in the marginal note at p.297 of the second volume of Benjamin Robert Bell's edition of *Hume's Commentaries on the Law of Scotland Respecting Crimes*, published in Edinburgh by Bell and Bradfute in 1844. This definition also derives support from the definition of 'acquittal' appearing at p.12 of *The Oxford Companion to Law* recently published by Professor D. M. Walker, Q.C. The word is also used in this sense in section 140A of the 1975 Act as now amended. I would also mention, quantum valeat, that the same usage is adopted at para. 15.07 of Criminal Appeals in Scotland (3rd report) Cmnd 7005/1977 (being the 3rd report of the Thomson Committee). The consideration that the accused in the present case cannot now be prosecuted seems to me to be irrelevant since the reason for a new action not being able to be raised against this accused flows not from the instant action having been dismissed but from the lapse of six months from the date of the initial offence in terms of section 331(1) of the said 1975 Act.

I have always understood that the correct method of bringing under review alleged procedural irregularities, including those arising in the preliminary stage of a case, was by bill of advocation (see Renton & Brown on Criminal Procedure, 4th edn, para. 16–128) and section 453A of the said 1975 Act, as now amended, would seem to preserve such method of appeal.

I have no wish unnecessarily to hold up this already delayed matter, but as I conceive that it would be incompetent for me to state a case I have concluded that I have no proper option but to decline to do so."

Application refused.

NOTES

1.   Prior to the 1980 Act amendments, section 442 of the 1975 Act provided that appeal by stated case could be taken "on the final determination of any summary prosecution." Under the present section 442(1)(*b*), the prosecutor's appeal is only competent on "acquittal" or against a "sentence."

2.   It would have been competent for the prosecutor to have appealed by way of advocation (as to which, see *infra*, p.562). The procedure for appeal from a decision on competency or relevancy provided for by section 334(2A) of the 1975 Act is also now available, although it had not been brought into force at the time of the case.

3.   For a discussion of the appropriateness (as opposed to the competency) of this method of appeal, see *infra*, pp.538 to 540.

2.   **MacNeill v. MacGregor**
1975 J.C. 55

A plea of guilty was entered by a solicitor on behalf of an accused person. The following day (July 26, 1974) the solicitor appeared before the sheriff and explained that that plea had been entered in error and should have been one of not guilty. The sheriff recalled the sentence and order of the court, allowed the plea of guilty to be withdrawn and, a plea of not guilty having been intimated, adjourned the diet until a later date. No objection was entered by the prosecutor. The accused duly appeared at the adjourned diet, and after trial was found not guilty. At the request of the procurator-fiscal, the sheriff stated a case for the opinion of the High Court.

LORD JUSTICE-CLERK (WHEATLEY): "... *In limine* this Court raised the question of the competency of the proceedings on 26th July 1974, since if these were *ultra vires* the present appeal which arose from, and was consequential upon, those proceedings would also be incompetent.

The Advocate-depute stated that he could not defend or justify the procedure which had taken place on 26th July 1974 and what had followed thereon, and that accordingly he could not insist on the present appeal. Since a finding that the order of the Court of 26th July was *ultra vires* and inept would restore the order of the Court of 25th July 1974 which found the respondent guilty and imposed the sentence above noted on him, we allowed Mr Younger, who appeared for the respondent, the opportunity of defending the *vires* of the proceedings on 26th July 1974. Mr Younger was unable to point to any precedent which authorised the procedure which the Sheriff followed here.

It has to be observed that what took place on 25th July 1974, as recorded in the Minutes of Procedure was that the Sheriff convicted the respondent of the charge and proceeded to sentence him. The Sheriff, in our view, thereby became *functus*, and had no authority thereafter to alter the finding *quoad* conviction. This he did, however, by recalling the order pronounced on 25th July 1974. There is statutory provision for a Sheriff to alter or modify a sentence under certain conditions—Summary Jurisdiction Act 1954, section 57. There is, incidentally, statutory power given to a Sheriff to review a previous decision on bail—Criminal Justice (Scotland) Act 1963, section 37. But there is no statutory provision for a Sheriff to review, amend or recall a conviction once it has been passed and recorded.

In view of the statutory provisions enabling him to amend or vary a sentence, this is significant. Since once he had convicted the respondent and this was recorded the Sheriff was *functus*, and his actions on 26th July 1974 were *ultra vires*, as was all that followed thereon. This in effect means that the only valid order standing is that of 25th July 1974.

It was in recognition of that situation that the Advocate-depute intimated that he could not ask the Court to answer the questions raised in the Stated Case. This is inevitably so, since the facts on which the questions are based arose from a trial which on the ground of our decision was *ultra vires* and inept.

We shall accordingly formally find that the order of 26th July 1974 was incompetent and must be quashed. That being so, and for the reasons stated we must dismiss the appeal which is an appeal against an order of the court which was itself incompetent.

We fully recognise the anomalous position in which the respondent may now find himself, but if he has a remedy it is not in this process.

While the view we have taken might appear to be a highly technical one, there seems to be justification for the technicality not only in the statutory provisions regulating the procedure but in the fact that if the course followed in this case was authorised as legitimate, it might well result in that course becoming commonplace and the subject of abuse by accused persons dissatisfied by the sentence imposed following a plea of guilty. If it is thought that provision should be made for exceptional cases, that would appear to be a matter for the legislature. As we have previously noted, the fact that the legislature has not made provision for this heretofore is not without its significance in the context of this case."

Appeal dismissed.

NOTE

For the final outcome of this case see *MacGregor* v. *MacNeill*, *infra*, p.554.

(ii)   Questions of Fact and Questions of Law

Prior to the 1980 Act, the decision of the trial judge on questions of fact was, in the ordinary run of cases, final. This meant that appeal by stated case was only competent on points of law, so that it was necessary in all cases to distinguish between questions of fact and questions of law. So far as appeal by a convicted person is concerned, it is no longer necessary to make this distinction since appeal under section 442 is competent at the instance of the convicted person on grounds of fact as well as law. This is not so, however, in the case of appeals by the prosecutor, where the fact/law distinction remains relevant. The following cases are examples of this problem:

1.   Fraser v. Anderson
(1899) 2 Adam 705

The appellant was convicted of theft and appealed by stated case. The question of law for the opinion of the High Court was "Whether, on the facts as stated, an act of theft was committed by the appellant."

LORD KINNEAR: "I have some difficulty in answering the question put to us in this case. The question really at issue is rather one of fact than of law. But when we read the Sheriff's statement of the case, it seems to me that his conception of the matter was that, having found certain facts as proved, they appeared to him to raise a question of law, viz., whether these facts amounted to the crime of theft. Taking these facts, we have to consider whether or not the necessary legal inference is that the appellant was guilty of theft.

As I read the facts stated by the Sheriff to have been proved, there was a completed sale of certain heifers to Mr Chisholm on 16th June, but the cattle were by arrangement left in the possession of the appellant until the price should be paid. I agree with the Solicitor-General that although the cattle were left in the appellant's possession they were the property of Mr Chisholm, and were in the appellant's possession on a qualified title and for a limited purpose. Upon 22nd June the appellant not having received the price of the cattle, which according to arrangement he ought to have received, goes to his bank and finds that the money has not been paid into his account. I am not sure whether the Sheriff means us to take that as a fact which he finds as proved, or whether he only means to state it as a fact alleged by the accused in defence. But, however that may be, he does not find that in fact the appellant knew or believed that the money had been remitted. In these circumstances it is found that the appellant removed the cattle from his field and handed them over to a relative of his own with instructions to sell them, and the cattle having been sold the price so obtained was entered to the credit of the appellant in his bank account at Beauly. In so acting the appellant was doing what he was plainly not entitled to do, and if I were satisfied that he had so acted with any felonious intent, I should have no difficulty in holding that he had been guilty of theft. But the real question is whether any felonious intention was in fact proved. Now, it is said for the appellant that he believed on reasonable grounds that the purchaser had broken his contract, and the Sheriff does not find in fact that he did not so believe. It may quite well be on the facts found to be proved that the appellant acted as he did in ignorance of his legal remedy in the circumstances, and that he thought that the money not having reached him, he had a right to proceed to sell the cattle at his own hand. Such a supposition would have been negatived if the Sheriff had found as matter of fact that the accused acted as he did with felonious intent. But he has not done so. The things he finds that the appellant did may or may not have been done with felonious intent; that is a matter of fact and not of law. Therefore, when he asks us whether on the facts as stated an act of theft has been committed, my answer is that that is not proved. The facts proved may or may not amount to theft according as the appellant's intention was theftuous or not; and the Sheriff does not find that it was theftuous. I cannot infer that he meant so to find from the mere fact that he convicted the appellant, for the one question he puts in the case is whether that conviction rested on valid grounds; and the specific grounds on which it in fact rested are set forth in the case, and not in the conviction itself. The question stated is in effect whether the judge required to be satisfied of anything more than the bare facts specified in order to justify a conviction, and if anything further is necessary to complete the crime of theft, it appears to me that the defect cannot be supplied by inference from the very conviction that is put in question.

LORD ADAM (diss): "In these cases stated on appeal we have only to deal with questions of law. We do not deal with questions of fact. We are here asked whether on the facts stated an act of theft was committed? When it is said that, looking to the facts proved, the crime may have been committed if a certain inference is drawn from those facts, then I say that that inference is a matter of fact, and is therefore a question for the Sheriff, and we will only interfere with his decision if it can be made out that on no possible view of the facts are they capable of bearing out the inference he has drawn ... Now, I can understand that one inference from these facts may be that the appellant, not knowing that the price had been already paid into his account on 22nd June, thought he might legitimately sell the cattle, but there is another inference, and that is that he acted as he did with felonious intent. Which of these inferences is correct is matter of fact and therefore for the Sheriff. Either inference may be drawn from the facts stated in the case."

The court answered the question in the negative and allowed the appeal.

2. **Waugh v. Campbell**
1920 J.C. 1

The respondent was charged with driving a vehicle recklessly and negligently contrary to section 1 of the Motor Car Act 1903. The sheriff found him not guilty and, at the request of the procurator-fiscal, stated a case for the opinion of the High Court. The question for the opinion of the court was "Ought the respondent to have been convicted?"

LORD DUNDAS: "I think there is no doubt that the question stated in this case will not do in the form in which it is stated. We are asked: 'Ought the respondent to have been convicted?' This is not a question that should be put to us. I think the proper form of the question would have been—Did the facts stated afford legal evidence on which the Sheriff-substitute was entitled to acquit? or something like that.

I have had some doubt and difficulty, but I have come to the conclusion that there was not such evidence. It is certain that we cannot review an inferior judge in a case of this sort upon facts, but we can, and, I think, ought to, interfere in any case in which we consider the evidence does not legally warrant the judgment at which he has arrived. I am bound to say that not only do I think the acquittal by the Sheriff-substitute was wrong, but I am really unable to see any evidence which could warrant it at all. The evidence seems to me to be all the other way.

The facts, to put them briefly, disclose that, as the respondent was going along this public road, with which he was well acquainted, and approaching Kirkdale Bridge, he was driving at about 14 miles an hour. Just at the end of the bridge there is a very sharp turn shown on the map—a blind turn, as it appears that, owing to the parapet wall and foliage, no one can see round it. Then when he got about halfway across this bridge he deliberately crossed to the wrong side of the road. He sounded no horn, but, proceeding on his way, although the road was admittedly broad enough easily to have allowed two cars to pass one another if each was on its proper side, he collided with a motor car coming in the other direction upon its own proper side of the road. These facts seem to me to involve a contravention of the section of the Act we are considering.

The learned Sheriff-substitute explains his ground of judgment in this way. He says that the respondent would probably be liable for the civil consequences of the collision. We have nothing to do with that, but probably the surmise is right. He goes on to say: 'There was nothing in the nature, condition, or use of the road, nor anything on account of the amount of traffic which was actually on it at the time or which might reasonably be expected to be on it at the time, which entitled me to hold that the respondent, in crossing from his left or proper side of the road to his right hand side under the circumstances and in the manner above described, was driving his motor car recklessly and negligently.' I cannot understand that. As regards the nature of the road, we have the facts I have summarised; this blind turn, and the other conditions. As regards the use of the road, we have this silent unheralded swerve at considerable speed round a right-angled turn. Then, as regards the traffic, I should have thought that the duty of the respondent was to anticipate that there might be traffic on this road coming in the other direction. We have it stated that the road is the public highway between Creetown and Gatehouse of Fleet, known as the Mail Coach Road, a comparatively quiet road, but one on which motor cars and other vehicular traffic pass along from time to time every day.

I do not hesitate to say that, upon this evidence, if I had been sitting as judge of first instance, I should have convicted. That is not enough by itself to warrant me in interfering in the matter; but I am constrained to go further and say that, viewing the evidence, it seems to me to be all one way, and that I am unable to see what facts can be laid hold of as affording any evidence at all to justify an acquittal. In other words, it seems to me not only that one differs—as I understand both your lordships differ—in opinion from the result arrived at by the learned Sheriff-substitute, but that really it amounts to this that he misdirected himself in law, and said to himself that the accumulated mass of evidence all in one direction warranted a verdict in the other. I do not see how we can avoid interfering in such a case; and, accordingly, in my opinion, we should find on the facts stated that the Sheriff-substitute was not entitled to acquit."

LORD SALVESEN: "... My greatest doubt in connexion with the case was whether after all it was not a question of fact, with regard to which we have no right to interfere. The Sheriff-substitute, I think, has not treated it as a question of fact, but has stated for us a question of law arising upon the facts; and on that question of law I am constrained to hold, though I confess I do it reluctantly in the case of an acquittal, that he misdirected himself, and that the statutory offence may be constituted merely by negligence, although the judge who tries the case thinks the negligence was not gross negligence and involved no moral blame. In that view of it I concur in the judgment, although I hope it will not lead to many appeals on what are primarily questions of fact, just because the prosecutor does not concur with the Sheriff in the verdict—for it is really a verdict—at which he arrives. I hope nothing we do in this case will encourage such a practice."

LORD GUTHRIE: "I agree on both points to which your Lordships have referred, first, that there are no facts here to support the verdict, and second, that the Sheriff-substitute has misdirected himself in law. On the first point Mr Jameson referred to the case of *Cromwell* v. *Renton* [(1911) 6 Adam 498], and to the Lord Justice-Clerk's opinion where he says:—'Whether, in these circumstances, the appellant was rightly convicted is a pure question of fact on which we cannot interfere with the Sheriff-substitute's decision.'"

> The court answered the question in the negative and allowed the appeal.

NOTE

The absence of an effective means of challenging the trial judge's findings-in-fact was one of the criticisms voiced to the Thomson Committee (3rd Report, para. 8.09). The committee did not, however, accept this criticism. In considering whether or not there should be a right to a re-hearing in summary proceedings, the committee expressed the view that, "on the evidence before us, we see no need for such a radical departure from the principle that in summary procedure the trial judge is the final arbiter on questions of fact" (*ibid.*, para. 7.06). For an example of an appeal by stated case on a question of fact, see *Wilson* v. *Carmichael*, 1982 S.C.C.R. 528 and the commentary thereon at p.532.

(iii)   Limitations on Appeal

1.   Criminal Procedure (Scotland) Act 1975

"**454.** No conviction, sentence, judgment, order of court or other proceeding whatsoever under Part II of this Act shall be quashed for want of form or, where the accused had legal assistance in his defence, shall be suspended or set aside in respect of any objections to the relevancy of the complaint, or to the want of specification therein, or to the competency or admission or rejection of evidence at the trial in the inferior court, unless such objections shall have been timeously stated at the trial by the solicitor of the accused."

NOTE

Section 454 must be read subject to the rule that the High Court may quash a conviction on the ground of fundamental nullity even though no preliminary objection has been stated. See *O'Malley* v. *Strathern*, 1920 J.C. 75, *supra*, p.456 and other authorities there cited, and *Robertson* v. *Aitchison*, 1981 S.L.T. (Notes) 127, *infra*, p.547.

Section 454 does not refer in terms to acquittals, but see the following case:

2.   Skeen v. Murphy
1978 S.L.T. (Notes) 2

The respondent was charged with a contravention of section 6(1) of the Road Traffic Act 1972. The appropriate analyst's and doctor's certificates were produced by the fiscal at the beginning of the trial. No objection was taken to these certificates by the respondent's solicitor at any time. During the trial the sheriff, *ex proprio motu*, raised the question of the competency of these certificates, and held that since it had not been proved that they had been served on the respondent in accordance with section 10(3) of the 1972 Act, their contents had not been properly proved in evidence. In the absence of the evidence provided by the certificates, the sheriff held the prosecution had not proved their case, and he acquitted the respondent. The prosecutor appealed by stated case.

LORD JUSTICE-CLERK (WHEATLEY): "It was argued by the advocate-depute that the tendering of these certificates by the procurator fiscal at the beginning of the trial was, by virtue of the statutory provisions relating thereto under s. 10(1) of the 1972 Act, the factual presenting of evidence to the court, and that if any objection was to be taken to the admission of that evidence it should have been taken at the time the evidence was presented or at least before the end of the Crown case. He relied on s. 354(1) of the Criminal Procedure (Scotland) Act 1975 in support of his argument. Counsel for the respondent submitted that in the absence of a prior agreement, which presumably would have to be recorded, s. 354(1) did not apply to documents such as those we are concerned with here. He submitted that in the circumstances the sheriff was right in holding that the contents of the certificates had not been properly admitted in evidence and that the facts therein had not been proved, and this whether or not an objection had been taken at the time, because such a consideration was not relevant. That being so, the Crown had not proved all the essential evidence for a conviction on the charge, and accordingly there was bound to be an acquittal. We are of the opinion that the question here falls to be answered by reference to general principles without any reference to

s. 354(1) of the 1975 Act. In terms of s. 454(1) of the Act of 1975 it is provided: 'No conviction, sentence, judgment, order of court or other proceeding whatsoever under this Part of this Act shall be quashed for want of form or, where the accused had legal assistance in his defence, shall be suspended or set aside in respect of any objections to the relevancy of the complaint, or to the want of specification therein, or to the competency or admission or rejection of evidence at the trial in the inferior court, unless such objections shall have been timeously stated at the trial by the solicitor of the accused.'

While that section relates to convictions etc., and not to acquittals, the underlying reasoning is that unless objection to the competency or admission of evidence is timeously taken, it cannot be subsequently taken, and, if not, such evidence becomes part of the evidence in causa. We do not see why such evidence should not be regarded as evidence in causa simply because an acquittal and not a conviction resulted. It is on the evidence in causa that the question of conviction or acquittal has to be determined. In any event it is a general rule that objections to the competency and admissibility of evidence should be taken when that evidence is tendered. That being so, what is the position here? The prosecutor tendered the reports as evidence in terms of the statute, together with the appropriate certificate of posting. No objection was taken at the time to the validity or competency of the evidence thus tendered. It was only during the hearing on evidence that the sheriff ex proprio motu raised the question whether the Crown had proved that these reports had been timeously served, and if not, whether the evidence contained therein should be excluded from the case. In our opinion, it was then too late for this point to be taken. The defence had not taken any objection to the competency or admissibility of that evidence when it was tendered, because the reports were not timeously served, and it was then properly before the court. On that short ground alone we can sustain the appeal."

Appeal allowed.

NOTE

On the effect of failure to take a point of law during a trial (other than a point mentioned in section 454), see *Hamilton v. Ross*, 1991 S.C.C.R. 165.

(iv) Miscarriage of Justice

As was pointed out above, the sole ground of appeal in a stated case is that there has been a miscarriage of justice. Prior to the 1980 Act's amendments, a stated case could be brought to review the relevancy of the complaint, any irregularity in procedure, any alleged error of the court in point of law and, generally, any matter which immediately prior to the 1975 Act could have been competently reviewed by suspension (see *infra*, p.551), advocation (see *infra*, p.562) or appeal under the Heritable Jurisdictions (Scotland) Act 1746 (which had been obsolete for many years) or otherwise. (See the former terms of section 442 of the 1975 Act.)

Section 454(2) of the 1975 Act (now repealed by the 1980 Act) provided that no conviction, sentence, judgment, order of court or other proceeding could be quashed except on the ground of incompetency, corruption, malice or oppression, or unless the High Court was of opinion that the accused had been misled as to the true nature of the charge against him or been prejudiced in his defence on the merits, and that a miscarriage of justice had resulted thereby.

The question arises as to the relevancy of the old law to the new ground of appeal. It is submitted that those matters which constituted a miscarriage of justice under the provisions of section 454(2) should continue to be so considered. It is further submitted that cases of incompetency ("an inability in the Court to deal with the matter in hand ... any case with which the Court, as a Court, had not power to deal," *per* Lord Justice-General Dunedin in *Robson* v. *Menzies* (1913) 7 Adam 156 at p.161), corruption, malice and oppression must necessarily amount to miscarriages of justice, and for a discussion of these matters see Renton and Brown, paras. 16–25 to 16–59.

It would appear, however, that not every irregularity in procedure or error of law on the part of the court will be fatal to a conviction or acquittal. In every case, the question is whether there has been a miscarriage of justice, and this must be established by the appellant, whether he be convicted person or prosecutor. On this point compare *Pettigrew* v. *Ingram*, 1982 S.L.T. 435; 1982 S.C.C.R. 259, and *McCuiag* v. *H.M. Advocate*, 1982 S.L.T. 383; 1982 S.C.C.R. 125, *supra*, Chap. 14.

Whether or not there has been a miscarriage of justice in relation to sentence (which is the test to be applied in the case of a convicted person's appeal) will depend upon the rules and principles governing sentencing. These matters are outwith the scope of this book.

(v)   Method and Time of Appeal

1.   Criminal Procedure (Scotland) Act 1975

"**444.** (1) An appeal under section 442(1)(*a*)(i) or (iii) or (*b*) of this Act shall be by application for a stated case, which application shall—

    (*a*) be made within one week of the final determination of the proceedings;

    (*b*) contain a full statement of all the matters which the appellant desires to bring under review and where the appeal is also against sentence, a statement of that fact; and

    (*c*) be signed by the appellant or his solicitor and lodged with the clerk of court;

and a copy of the application shall within the period mentioned in paragraph (*a*) above be sent by the appellant to the respondent or the respondent's solicitor."

NOTES

1.   Where an application is made under section 444(1) the court prepares, within three weeks of final determination of the proceedings in respect of which the application is made, a draft stated case which is issued to the appellant and a copy provided for the respondent (section 447(1)). During this three-week period the appellant may amend any matter stated in his application or add a new matter (section 444(1B)).

2.   Where the appellant is in custody, the court may grant bail, grant a sist of execution or make any other interim order (section 446(1)).

3.   It is essential that the application for a stated case be specific on the matters to be raised in an appeal. If it is not, the sheriff or justice may refuse to state a case.

2.   Durant v. Lockhart
1986 S.L.T. 312

An accused person was convicted after summary trial. He applied for a stated case. The sheriff refused and commented as follows:

SHERIFF MACMILLAN: "The requirements for an application for a stated case are set out in s. 444 of the Criminal Procedure (Scotland) Act 1975. The application must contain 'a full statement of all the matters which the appellant desires to bring under review'—see s. 444(1)(b). In this application the matters which the applicant desires to bring under review are expressed in the following terms: '(a) was there evidence sufficient to justify conviction? (b) was the sheriff correct in believing that the absence of sworn evidence from the accused required him to apply a presumption of guilt?'

In *Galloway* v. *Hillary*, 1983 S.C.C.R. 119, Sheriff Kermack refused to state a case where the ground of appeal was said to be: 'Insufficient evidence for conviction'. Sheriff Kermack expressed the view that this was not a statement of matters at all, certainly not a full statement of matters enabling him to focus them in a stated case; but was, as he put it, 'merely a brute assertion'. In this application the same words are used in para. (a) as appeared in *Galloway* v. *Hillary*, and I cannot see that as a ground of appeal they are at all improved by being posed in the interrogative rather than the assertive form. If the applicant believes that there were deficiencies in the prosecution evidence then he should be able to say what they were, thus allowing the issue to be focused in the stated case. That is what is meant by a statement of the matters which it is desired to bring under review. No doubt it is tempting to ask for a stated case in the hope that once it appears something will turn up; but such a Micawberish attitude receives no encouragement from the requirements of s. 444(1)(b).

As to the second ground of appeal, when I first read para. (b) I thought that the suggestion was being made that the applicant had been convicted because he chose not to give evidence, the court having on this basis presumed his guilt. Such a suggestion would of course have been quite unacceptable, but the applicant's agent is not such as would have been prepared to sign an application containing so improper an implication. I think on reflection that something else is meant. The applicant was charged under certain statutory provisions with interference with an electricity meter. One of those provisions which applied to his case was, oddly enough, para. 20(3) of Sched. 4 to the Gas Act 1972. In terms of this paragraph a presumption may be drawn in certain circumstances to the effect that interference with an electricity meter was the work of the registered consumer—the applicant in this case. What is required is evidence of the existence of artificial means for causing an alteration to the index when the meter is under the consumer's control. If that is proved then there is a presumption that the interference was caused by the consumer. The matter is discussed in detail in *Keane* v. *Bathgate*, 1983 S.L.T. 651; 1983 S.C.C.R. 251, to which case reference was made in the course of the trial. It appears to me that what the applicant may be attempting to suggest is that the statutory presumption did not apply in this case, presumably because the necessary circumstances had not been established by the prosecution evidence. But if that is what he means then he has certainly not said so, and his reference to 'the absence of sworn evidence from the accused' serves only to make his position even more obscure. Moreover he has failed to indicate what were the alleged deficiencies in the prosecution evidence. Once again this falls far short of a 'full statement of all the matters which the appellant desires to bring under review'.

This application does not enable me to formulate any question suitable for review by the High Court of Justiciary. The setting out of findings in fact would be pointless in the absence of any appropriate question of law for the opinion of the court. I have therefore refused the application."

The accused then appealed by bill of suspension, claiming that the decision to refuse to state a case was oppressive.

LORD JUSTICE-CLERK: "The third matter raised in the bill is a complaint that the sheriff had refused, at an earlier stage, to state a case for the opinion of the court. There has been produced a note by the sheriff explaining why he refused to state a case. One can readily understand why the complainer sought at that stage to have a case stated because the principal issue which he sought to raise in this bill, and which I have referred to as the first matter [concerning the onus on the Crown in view of the statutory presumption] was a matter which in our view should properly have been raised in stated case and we have been in some doubt as to whether it is really an issue which can properly be entertained in the course of proceedings by bill of suspension. However that may be, the sheriff in his note explaining his refusal to state a case refers to the provisions of s. 444 of the Criminal Procedure (Scotland) Act 1975 and points out that an application for a stated case must contain a full statement of all the matters which the appellant desires to bring under review. We have no doubt that this provision was introduced in order to require applicants for stated cases to explain in some detail what it was they were seeking to bring under review so that the sheriff when he stated the case could be in no doubt as to what particular issues it was that the applicant was seeking to bring under review, and so that he could state in his findings in fact the matters which were appropriate to that issue. The complainer, when applying for a stated case, indicated that he desired to bring under review (a) the question, was there evidence sufficient to justify the conviction. So far as that is concerned no specification was given as to what part of the evidence it was that was being attacked and which the sheriff was being asked to state so that the question could be answered. It appears now that what the complainer was seeking at that stage to bring under review in the case was the matter which I referred to earlier as the first matter. If indeed that was what he was seeking to bring under review, in our opinion, a better and fuller indication should have been given to the sheriff that that was the matter which he was seeking to bring under review. The application also stated, as well as the matters to be brought under review, the following: (b) 'Was the sheriff correct in believing that the absence of sworn evidence from the accused required him to apply a presumption of guilt?' It is not at all clear what that means. We were informed that it was a reference to what has been referred to earlier as the presumption but, however that may be, having regard to the terms in which the complainer made his application for a stated case, we are not at all surprised that the sheriff refused to state the case. It follows that the complaint which is now made to the effect that there was a miscarriage of justice in this respect is without foundation."

Suspension refused.

NOTES

1. This decision shows that in summary cases as in solemn cases, care has to be taken in framing the grounds of appeal: cf. the High Court Practice Note of March 29, 1985 on appeals in solemn procedure (supra, p.508). For a further discussion of the statement of matters for review, see McCluskey, Criminal Appeals, para. 3.19.

2. On suspension generally, see infra, p.551.

(vi) Adjustments

Criminal Procedure (Scotland) Act 1975

"**448.** (1) Subject to subsection (6) below, within three weeks of the issue of the draft stated case under section 447 of this Act, each party shall cause to be transmitted to the court and to the other parties or their solicitors a note of any adjustments he proposes be made to the draft case or shall intimate that he has no such proposal:

Provided that adjustments proposed shall relate to evidence heard (or purported to have been heard) at the trial and not to such additional evidence as is mentioned in section 442(2) of this Act.

(2) Subject to subsection (6) below, if the period mentioned in subsection (1) above has expired and the appellant has not lodged adjustments and has failed to intimate that he has no adjustments to propose, he shall be deemed to have abandoned his appeal; and subsection (4) of section 446 of this Act shall apply accordingly.

(2A) If adjustments are proposed under subsection (1) above or if the judge desires to make any alterations to the draft case there shall, within one week of the expiry of the period mentioned in that subsection or as the case may be of any further period afforded under subsection (6) below, be a hearing (unless the appellant has, or has been deemed to have, abandoned his appeal) for the purpose of considering such adjustments or alterations.

(2B) Where a party neither attends nor secures that he is represented at a hearing under subsection (2A) above, the hearing shall nevertheless proceed.

(2C) Where at a hearing under subsection (2A) above—

(a) any adjustment proposed under subsection (1) above by a party (and not withdrawn) is rejected by the judge; or

(b) any alteration to the draft case proposed by the judge is not accepted by all the parties,

that fact shall be recorded in the minute of the proceedings of the hearing.

(2D) Within two weeks of the date of the hearing under subsection (2A) above, or where there is no hearing, within two weeks of the expiry of the period mentioned in subsection (1) above, the judge shall (unless the appellant has been deemed to have abandoned the appeal) state and sign the case and shall append to the case—

(a) any adjustment, proposed under subsection (1) above, which is rejected by him, a note of any evidence rejected by him which is alleged to support that adjustment and the reasons for his rejection of that adjustment and evidence; and

(b) a note of the evidence upon which he bases any finding of fact challenged, on the basis that it is unsupported by the evidence, by a party at the hearing under subsection (2A) above."

NOTES

1.   There was an obligation under the former section 448(2) for the trial judge to consider proposed adjustments, but he was not obliged to hear parties on such proposals, nor was he obliged to incorporate them into the final stated case, or even give grounds for rejecting them. The Thomson Committee (3rd Report, para. 8.18), recognising the difficulties this presented for those advising appellants when the case as finally stated "was so completely within the discretion and control of the judge," recommended a hearing on adjustments, which should be compulsory, and which both parties should have the right to attend.

2.   It remains the case, in accordance with the views of the Thomson

Committee, that the court is not obliged to accept proposed adjustments, but is obliged to indicate any adjustments which it has rejected, and its grounds for doing so. For an example of the High Court taking account of a rejected adjustment under the current procedure, see *Wilson* v. *Carmichael*, 1982 S.C.C.R. 528.

3. Section 448(6) makes provision for the High Court to extend time-limits provided for in relation to adjustments.

(vii)   Form of the Case

The case must be stated in the form provided for by the Act of Adjournal (Consolidation) 1988, r. 127, and must "set forth the particulars of any matters competent for review which the appellant desires to bring under review of the High Court, and of the facts, if any, proved in the case, and any point of law decided, and the grounds of the decision. Findings-in-fact must be just that. Mere assertions that the guilt of the appellant is established will not suffice": *Mitchell and Others* v. *Smith*, High Court, January 21, 1981, unreported, C.O.C. A2/81.

Particular problems arise when one of the matters sought to be brought under review is the correctness of the decision on a submission of no case to answer under section 345A of the 1975 Act. The following cases set out the approach to be followed.

1.   Keane v. Bathgate
1983 S.C.C.R. 251

An accused person was acquitted following a successful submission of no case to answer. The procurator-fiscal appealed by stated case. The sheriff made certain findings-in-fact.

> LORD JUSTICE-CLERK: "In stating the case the sheriff has set out 'findings in fact' from which he reached his decision that there was no case to answer. In doing so he was following the long-established pattern of stated cases that on all the evidence which the parties have elected to adduce findings in fact can be made and held proved if not already admitted. An appeal against a decision of 'no case to answer' under the provisions of section 345A aforesaid calls for a different approach to the evidence. At the stage when that decision is made only evidence for the prosecution has been tendered. The motion made by the defence does not call for a decision by the court at that stage whether that evidence warrants the making of conclusive and final findings on which a verdict can be determined. All that the court has to decide at that point is whether or not there has been adduced by the prosecution sufficient evidence which, if accepted, would warrant a conviction. If there is not, there has to be an acquittal. If there is, that evidence has then to be considered against any evidence which the defence may thereafter adduce. It is only then that findings in fact can be made. Accordingly, in setting out the case for an appeal where the section 345A procedure has been successfully invoked, the proper thing for the court to do is simply to set out the evidence which has been adduced by the prosecution and any inferences drawn therefrom for arriving at the decision."

NOTE

The court subsequently upheld the Crown appeal on its merits. But other situations can arise where the decision on a submission under section 345A affects the form of any stated case.

2. **Wingate v. McGlennan**
1991 S.C.C.R. 133

Two accused were tried on summary complaint. At the end of the Crown case, their submissions of no case to answer were repelled. Neither gave evidence; both were convicted and appealed by stated case. At the hearing before the High Court, the Crown asked the court to give guidance as to the form of stated cases where a question was included asking whether the sheriff was justified in dealing with a submission of no case to answer as he did.

LORD JUSTICE-CLERK: "The sheriff has chosen an unusual way of stating these cases, and he has not made clear precisely what evidence was led by the prosecution. Counsel for the appellants maintained that what the sheriff had stated regarding the evidence showed that it was insufficient, and the advocate-depute accepted that on the basis of what the sheriff had said it was not possible to be satisfied that the evidence led by the prosecution had been sufficient in law to justify the appellants being convicted. He accordingly consented to the convictions being quashed.

What the sheriff did in this case was to record that submissions of no case to answer were made and then to say:

'at the stage of close of the Crown case there was no dispute that there was evidence sufficient to establish findings in fact as follows:'

and then to list eight numbered findings in fact.
Thereafter he added:

'The evidence relative to the submissions made can be briefly narrated as follows:'

and he then set out the evidence in the form of eight further findings in fact. After further rehearsing the submissions made to him, the sheriff explained that he repelled the submissions of no case to answer, and that no evidence was led for the appellants. The sheriff then proceeded to state the facts which he found admitted or proved at the end of the day.

It was quite inappropriate for the sheriff to indicate that at the close of the Crown case there was evidence sufficient to establish certain findings in fact.

'The motion made by the defence does not call for a decision by the court at that stage whether that evidence warrants the making of conclusive and final findings on which a verdict can be determined. All that the court has to decide at that point is whether or not there has been adduced by the prosecution sufficient evidence which, if accepted, would warrant a conviction. If there is not, there has to be an acquittal' (*Keane* v. *Bathgate* at p.255).

The advocate-depute invited the court to offer some guidance to inferior courts as to how cases should be stated where submissions have been made in terms of section 345A of the Act of 1975. In this connection we identify three different situations.

(1) Where a submission of no case to answer in terms of section 345A has been upheld, and the accused has been acquitted, the Crown may appeal against that decision of the sheriff. In that event the stated case should not contain any findings in fact, but should simply set out the evidence adduced by the prosecution and any inferences drawn therefrom by the sheriff (*Keane* v. *Bathgate*).

(2) Where a submission of no case to answer in terms of section 345A has been made and has been rejected, the accused may choose to lead no evidence. If the sheriff proceeds to convict the accused in such circumstances, and the accused then appeals against conviction, and the stated case includes a question asking whether the sheriff was justified in rejecting the submission of no case to answer, the stated case should contain findings in fact in the usual form. Normally there will be no need for the sheriff to set out separately the evidence adduced by the prosecution and the inferences drawn from it because, since no evidence was led by the defence, his findings in fact must necessarily be based solely upon the evidence adduced by the prosecution, and must accordingly represent what the evidence for the prosecution established. The sheriff should, however, in the note annexed to his findings in fact explain briefly upon what evidence his findings were based. There may, however, be exceptional cases where questions arise as to whether the evidence led justified the sheriff in drawing particular inferences, and in such cases the sheriff may require to set out in detail the evidence adduced by the prosecution. In making the findings in fact, the sheriff may not have accepted all the Crown evidence, but the court will usually be able to ascertain the evidence adduced by the prosecution from the findings in fact and from what the sheriff says about the evidence in the note annexed to the findings in fact. If the sheriff has not accepted certain evidence in making the findings in fact, the accused who is contending that there was no case to answer cannot be prejudiced if no reference is made in the case to such evidence. In a case where the accused had led no evidence, the issue which is raised by the question whether the sheriff was justified in rejecting the submission of no case to answer is virtually the same as that raised by the question whether the sheriff on the facts stated was entitled to convict.

(3) Where a submission of no case to answer in terms of section 345A has been made and has been rejected, and the accused has proceeded to lead evidence and has thereafter been convicted, he may appeal against his conviction. If the stated case contains a question as to whether the sheriff was justified in rejecting the submission of no case to answer, the stated case will require, first, to set out the evidence adduced by the prosecution and any inferences drawn therefrom and, secondly, to set out the findings in fact which, of course, must be made on the whole evidence that has been led before the sheriff (*Bowman* v. *Jessop* [1990 J.C. 72]). As was observed in *Keane* v. *Bathgate* if the defence have led evidence, findings in fact can only be made by considering the evidence led by the prosecution against any evidence which the defence have thereafter adduced. In a case where the accused has led evidence, the question whether the sheriff was justified in rejecting the submission of no case to answer raises a different issue from that raised by the question whether the sheriff on the facts stated was entitled to convict.

Categories (2) and (3) represent exceptions to the general rule that where a stated case contains findings in fact, it should not set forth the evidence upon which the findings are based unless there is a question asking whether there was sufficient evidence to entitle the sheriff or justice to make a specific finding."

Convictions quashed of consent.

NOTE

These cases make clear the distinction between evidence sufficient to establish facts necessary for convictions and findings-in-fact made upon the whole evidence in the case. See also McCluskey, *Criminal Appeals*, para. 3–23.

(viii)   Form and Statement of the Questions

1.   Prentice v. Skeen
1977 S.L.T. (Notes) 21

Two accused were found guilty of stealing a quantity of meat. A stated case was applied for and the sheriff duly stated the case which, in findings-in-fact 1 to 6, incorporated the evidence on which he based his finding that the appellants were guilty as libelled. In finding 7 he found as follows: "the meats in the possession of the appellants had been stolen by them from the deep freeze unit." The first question stated in the case for the opinion of the High Court was: "On the facts stated was I entitled to find the appellants guilty as libelled?" At the stage of adjustment the solicitor for the appellants asked the sheriff to incorporate a question to the following effect: "was there sufficient evidence to entitle me to make finding-in-fact No. 7 ?," but the sheriff refused.

> OPINION OF THE COURT: "It has been stated time and time again in this court that when the issue raised in a stated case is incorporated in a finding-of-fact conclusive or at least indicative of guilt and the point sought to be argued is that there was not sufficient evidence in law to warrant that finding, it is not appropriate merely to pose a question of law in general form such as 'On the facts stated was I entitled to find the appellants guilty as libelled?' The proper method of stating the question in such circumstances is in the form proposed by the appellants' solicitor to the sheriff above quoted. Legal advisers for appellants have been criticised in the past by the court for not seeking to have such a question in proper form incorporated in the stated case. There is no reason why the same salutary rule should not be applied to judges in the inferior courts.
>
> The court wishes to draw attention to the fact that when such an issue is the only issue in the case, or is a crucial issue in the case, it is imperative that the judge in the inferior court should incorporate a question in the appropriate form either ex proprio motu or on request. Failure to do so may well frustrate the whole method of this form of appeal. I cannot understand why the sheriff refused to incorporate such a question in the instant case."

NOTE

Cf. Waugh v. Campbell, supra.

2.   Robertson v. Aitchison
1981 S.L.T. (Notes) 127

The appellant was charged with driving while disqualified, and a co-accused was charged with aiding and abetting him, contrary to sections 99(*b*) and 176 of the Road Traffic Act 1972. They were convicted and appealed by stated case.

> OPINION OF THE COURT: "The sheriff in the very full and clear note appended

to his findings-in-fact and his conclusions, draws attention to the fact that an extract conviction referable to the first accused was produced and proved in the course of the trial, and that the extract conviction demonstrated not only that the appellant mentioned had previously been convicted of a contravention of s. 8(1) and (3) of the Road Traffic Act but also of a further contravention of s. 9(3). In so doing he was careful to add in a case which, as he said 'turned solely on the question of credibility' that his judgment had been in no way influenced by the production of a potentially prejudicial piece of evidence, the production of which was in plain contravention of s. 357 of the Criminal Procedure (Scotland) Act 1975.

It is in these circumstances that the present appeal comes before the court, but upon a series of questions which do not specifically raise the issue of fundamental nullity of a conviction where, in the course of proceedings, a previous conviction or convictions have been laid before the court in circumstances other than those covered by the precise terms of s. 357(5) of the Act of 1975.

The point which counsel for the appellant sought to raise is short, but it is not one to which any of the questions posed in the stated case appear to relate unless it be, as counsel maintained, that it is covered by the wording of the third question relating to Sinclair. We are not persuaded that it can be said that any of the questions do precisely relate to this issue, but the matter has been presented by counsel as one which, if the argument is well-founded, goes to the root of the conviction and reduces it to a nullity. For the Crown it was not disputed that, if a true issue of fundamental nullity was disclosed in the proceedings that could properly be submitted for decision, even though not expressed or implied in any of the questions in the stated case. This is clearly right. The sheriff in his note has brought it to our notice, and while he himself did not apparently regard the reference to a previous conviction of the appellant Robertson of contravention of s. 8(3) of the Road Traffic Act 1972, as nullifying the whole proceedings, the point has now been taken and we are in no doubt that where it appears on the face of the proceedings that a conviction is affected by a fundamental nullity it is for the court to take notice of it, however and in whatever form it comes to notice and, if that is found to be the case, to take the necessary action and quash the conviction so tainted."

Conviction quashed.

NOTES

1.   *Cf. O'Malley* v. *Strathern*, 1920 J.C. 74, *supra*, Chap. 13. For the terms of section 454 see *supra*, p.538.

2.   The court went on to hold that the conviction was fatally flawed by a fundamental nullity as a result of the introduction of the previous conviction. They also held that the conviction of the co-accused was similarly flawed:

"The appellants in this case were charged in one complaint, the charges arose out of one transaction in which both are alleged to have been simultaneously engaged. There is therefore no means or measure by which a different conclusion can be arrived at in their individual cases. The 'proceedings' are those in this complaint and, as the statute has been breached, the conviction obtained cannot stand."

See also McCluskey, *Criminal Appeals*, paras. 3–25 to 3–29.

(ix)   Hearing and Disposal of Appeals

Criminal Procedure (Scotland) Act 1975

"**452.**—(1) A stated case under this Part of this Act shall be heard by the High Court on such date as it may fix.

(2) For the avoidance of doubt, where an appellant, in his application under section 444(1) of this Act (or in a duly made amendment or addition to that application), refers to an alleged miscarriage of justice, but in stating a case under section 448(2D) of this Act the inferior court is unable to take the allegation into account, the High Court may nevertheless have regard to the allegation at a hearing under subsection (1) above.

(3) Except by leave of the High Court on cause shown, it shall not be competent for an appellant to found any aspect of his appeal on a matter not contained in his application under section 444(1) of this Act (or in a duly made amendment or addition to that application).

(4) Without prejudice to any existing power of the High Court, that court may in hearing a stated case—

(a) order the production of any document or other thing connected with the proceedings;

(b) hear any additional evidence relevant to any alleged miscarriage of justice or order such evidence to be heard by a judge of the High Court or by such other person as it may appoint for that purpose;

(c) take account of any circumstances relevant to the case which were not before the trial judge;

(d) remit to any fit person to enquire and report in regard to any matter or circumstance affecting the appeal;

(e) appoint a person with expert knowledge to act as assessor to the High Court in any case where it appears to the court that such expert knowledge is required for the proper determination of the case;

(f) take account of any matter proposed in any adjustment rejected by the trial judge and of the reasons for such rejection;

(g) take account of any evidence contained in a note of evidence such as is mentioned in section 448(2D) of this Act.

(5) The High Court may at the hearing remit the stated case back to the inferior court to be amended and returned.

452A.—(1) The High Court may, subject to subsection (2) below and section 453D(1) of this Act, dispose of a stated case by—

(a) remitting the cause to the inferior court with their opinion and any direction thereon;

(b) affirming the verdict of the inferior court;

(c) setting aside the verdict of the inferior court and either quashing the conviction or substituting therefor an amended verdict of guilty:

Provided that an amended verdict of guilty must be one which could have been returned on the complaint before the inferior court; or

(d) setting aside the verdict of the inferior court and granting authority to bring a new prosecution in accordance with section 452B of this Act.

(2) The High Court shall, in an appeal—

(a) against both conviction and sentence, subject to section 453D(1) of this Act dispose of the appeal against sentence; or

(b) by the prosecutor, against sentence, dispose of the appeal by exercise of the power mentioned in section 453C(1) of this Act.

(3) In setting aside, under subsection (1) above, a verdict the High Court may quash any sentence imposed on the appellant as respects the complaint, and—

(a) in a case where it substitutes an amended verdict of guilty, whether or not the sentence related to the verdict set aside; or

(b) in any other case, where the sentence did not so relate, may pass another (but not more severe) sentence in substitution for the sentence so quashed.

(4) Where an appeal against acquittal is sustained, the High Court may—

(a) convict and sentence the respondent;

(b) remit the case to the inferior court with instructions to convict and sentence the respondent, who shall be bound to attend any diet fixed by the inferior court for such purpose; or

(c) remit the case to the inferior court with their opinion thereon:

Provided that the High Court shall not in any case increase the sentence beyond the maximum sentence which could have been passed by the inferior court.

(5) The High Court shall have power in an appeal under this Part of this Act to award such expenses both in the High Court and in the inferior court as it may think fit."

NOTES

1.   Where authority is granted to bring a new prosecution, such prosecution may be brought charging the accused with the same or any similar offence arising out of the same facts: section 452B. For the analogous provisions with regard to solemn proceedings, see, *supra*, Chap. 14.

2.   Where an appeal has been taken against conviction or conviction and sentence, the prosecutor may, if he is not prepared to maintain the judgment appealed against, consent to the conviction and sentence being set aside, either in whole or in part. See section 453 of the 1975 Act, as amended by section 43 of the Prisoners and Criminal Proceedings (Scotland) Act 1993.

(x) Abandonment of Appeal

Criminal Procedure (Scotland) Act 1975

"**449.**—(1) An appellant in an appeal such as is mentioned in section 444(1) may at any time prior to lodging the case with the Clerk of Justiciary abandon his appeal by minute signed by himself or his solicitor, written on the complaint or lodged with the clerk of the inferior court, and intimated to the respondent or the respondent's solicitor, but such abandonment shall be without prejudice to any other competent mode of appeal, review, advocation or suspension.

(2) Subject to section 453A of this Act, on the case being lodged with the Clerk of Justiciary, the appellant shall be held to have abandoned any other mode of appeal which might otherwise have been open to him."

NOTES

1.   For alternative methods of appeal, etc., see *infra*. Under 448(2) an appellant may also be deemed to have abandoned his appeal if he fails to comply with the procedure therein: see *supra*. He may also abandon his stated case after lodging, or abandon an appeal against conviction (but proceed with an appeal against sentence), all in accordance with the procedures laid down in the Act of Adjournal (Consolidation) 1988, r. 129.

2.   Abandonment of an appeal may, in exceptional circumstances, be subject to recall by an application to the *nobile officium*: *Mathieson, Petitioner*,

1980 S.L.T. 74, *infra*, p.613 (but *cf. Ferguson* v. *H.M. Advocate*, 1980 J.C. 27, *supra*, p.509).

C. SUSPENSION

"Suspension is the appropriate mode of bringing under review of the High Court an illegal or irregular warrant, conviction, or judgment of an inferior Court" (Moncreiff on *Review in Criminal Cases*, pp.169–170). As a form of review it is not open to the prosecutor, whose corresponding remedy is advocation (*infra*, p.562).

(i) Competency

High Court proceedings cannot be made the subject of a suspension (see Moncreiff, *loc. cit.*). Section 230 of the 1975 Act states that it shall not be competent to appeal to the High Court by bill of suspension against any conviction, sentence, judgment or order pronounced in any proceedings on indictment in the sheriff court.

But a finding of contempt of court in solemn proceedings either before the High Court or the sheriff court can competently be appealed only by petition to the *nobile officium*: *George Outram & Co. Ltd.* v. *Lees*, 1992 S.C.C.R. 181.

Before a suspension can be brought, however, there must be something in the way of an unlawful warrant, judgment, etc., to suspend:

1. Jupp v. Dunbar
(1863) 4 Irv. 355

The suspender appeared in court, charged with a contravention of the Day Poaching Act. He pleaded not guilty to the charge. The minute of proceedings was as follows: "Thereafter, the following witnesses were examined on oath in support of the complaint:—1. Andrew Cleugh, junior, residing at Ochclate, on the estate of Thrumpster.

The Justices having considered the complaint, with the evidence adduced, finds the"—(No more of the sentence was written out.)

The suspender presented a bill of suspension in which he stated that, notwithstanding the omission of any finding of guilt or note of sentence, the magistrates imposed a fine of £2 and informed him that unless he paid the fine instantly he would be sent to prison. He paid the fine.

> LORD JUSTICE-CLERK (INGLIS): "... There is nothing to suspend. The suspender complains that the fine has been extorted from him on the representation that he had been sentenced, while in fact no sentence had been pronounced. On that ground he may or may not have a remedy in another form; but it cannot enable the Court to quash a sentence which never existed. The suspension must be refused as incompetent."

Suspension refused
as incompetent.

As was pointed out above, suspension may be employed to bring under review matters other than the judgment of a court, such as a warrant. For modern examples of this see *Wilson* v. *Milne*, 1975 S.L.T. (Notes) 26; *Currie* v. *McGlennan*, 1989 S.C.C.R. 466.

2.   Morton v. McLeod
1982 S.L.T. 187

An accused person was charged on summary complaint with a contravention of section 2(1) of the Food and Drugs (Scotland) Act 1956. A plea to the competency of the complaint was presented on his behalf and repelled by the sheriff. The accused then presented a bill of suspension to the High Court seeking review of the sheriff's decision on competency.

LORD CAMERON: "... It is in respect of the sheriff's decision that the present bill of suspension has been presented. The ground on which the competency of the complaint was challenged before the sheriff is set out in his note which is also appended to this bill. It was submitted on behalf of the accused that: 'As the bottle of milk was a sample and had been procured under the provisions of the Food and Drugs Act, proceedings in respect of the contents of the bottle should have been commenced before the expiry of two months from the date on which the sample was procured in compliance with the provisions of s. 41(3) of the Act.' This plea was not accepted by the sheriff [ante, 1981 S.L.T. (Sh. Ct.) 107] and trial has been fixed for 7 September.

Prima facie the complaint, which makes no reference to the procurement of any sample or to the consequences of the analysis of any sample, would appear to be both competent and relevant.

The question which now sharply arises is whether this bill should be permitted to proceed further and a first order granted.

In the course of the debate before the sheriff certain statements of fact were made by the prosecutor as to the actual course of events on the date libelled in the complaint and as the sheriff records: 'a consignment of milk was delivered to Springside Primary School at 7.30 a.m. on 10 February 1981. The consignment was distributed round the classes and some surplus was left in the office. The janitor took one of the surplus bottles from the office to the kitchen staff. He noticed a drinking straw inside the bottle. He showed it to the school secretary who informed the local environmental health department at Irvine. At about 2.45 p.m. an assistant environmental health officer and a senior assistant environmental health officer called at the school. They saw the bottle still unopened with the straw inside. They took possession of the bottle and sent a letter concerning the matter to the defender on 11 February asking for his comments. The public analyst was not asked to analyse the contents of this bottle. The argument submitted to me was on the basis of these facts.'

This narrative however does not and could not constitute a minute of admissions of all the facts relevant to this complaint.

For the suspender, counsel maintained that he was entitled to a first order and to an interim suspension of proceedings as the issue between the parties was one of competency alone and the argument would be solely one on matters of law. He agreed that the complaint as libelled was both relevant and competent ex facie, but maintained that on the facts agreed, as set out in the passage in the sheriff's note which I have quoted, the bottle of milk itself forming the subject of the complaint—the corpus delicti—was to be held to be a 'sample' within the meaning of the statutory provisions in that when the officers of the local authority obtained possession of the offending bottle they were 'procuring a sample' within the meaning of s. 28(1) of the Act of 1956, and that consequently as the proceedings had not been initiated within the period prescribed by s. 41(3) the complaint was incompetent. This, he said, was placing a legal interpretation on the admitted actions of the officers of the local authority and therefore the issue of competency could and should be determined at this stage. The observations of the Lord Justice-General in *Fairley* v. *Muir*, 1951 S.L.T. 237 were in point in his favour. The issue was 'crisp' in the words of Lord Cooper, was purely one of law, and the first order should be granted.

For the Crown it was submitted that the bill was premature and the first order should be refused. Admittedly there was a depending process and the remedy of suspension was not available at this stage—only after trial and conviction, if conviction followed. In support of his general proposition the advocate-depute referred to Hume on *Crimes*, ii, 513 and 515, which made it clear that this remedy was only available after the conclusion of the trial and opened up all the proceedings. Alison, ii, 27–30 was to the same effect, as was Moncreiff at p.170 who made it clear also that incidental warrants, i.e. those which do not form part of the main proceedings could be subject of suspension pendente processu (see Moncreiff, p.186). The same views were expressed in Trotter at p.62 and Renton and Brown, paras. 16.95 and 98. These principles do not admit of exceptions. In *Fairley* v. *Muir* the court was not dealing with a suspension in the course of proceedings, but after conviction and the judgment of Lord Cooper must be read in that context. The order sought should be refused and the bill dismissed. In any event, the suspender would still have his remedy if at the end of the day he were convicted on the present charge which admittedly was ex facie both relevant and competent.

In my opinion the argument presented for the suspender fails. The general rule is not in doubt; suspension as a mode of review is competent only after the conclusion of the trial. Nothing which was said in *Fairley* v. *Muir* casts any doubts on the general principle which was enunciated by Hume, ii, 513 in the simple phrase: 'The remedy of suspension applies after conclusion of a trial in the inferior court.' To this general rule it is recognised that an exception exists in respect of 'incidental warrants which do not form part of the case' (cf. Renton and Brown (4th ed.), para. 16.99).

In the present case the suspender seeks to review a decision of the sheriff on the competency of the complaint itself, a decision on which could dispose once and for all of the whole subject-matter of the charge. In my opinion there is no warrant or authority for such a procedure at this stage. The suspender will not lose his remedy if a conviction is recorded against him, while if he is acquitted the issue will not arise.

In any event, and apart from any question of general principle it was clear enough from the submissions of counsel for the suspender that the interpretation which he would seek to place on the facts of the case would necessarily depend on the findings which the sheriff would have to make as to the actions of various individuals and officers of the local authority—so that in no sense could it be said that 'the relevant circumstances are instantly, or almost instantly, verifiable, and the point sought to be raised is ... a crisp issue of ... competency' (*Fairley* v. *Muir*, 1951 S.L.T. at p.238, per Lord Cooper). Indeed, while I appreciate the clarity and ingenuity with which counsel for the suspender presented his argument, I find it difficult to understand how a bottle of milk which is alone said to form the offending article of food can in any sense of the word be held in fact or in law to be a 'sample' of something which does not itself figure anywhere in the complaint. However, it is not necessary to pursue this because for reasons which I have already given I am of opinion that this is an incompetent application and the motions for a first order and for interim suspension of the proceedings in the lower court will be refused."

> First order on bill and interim
> suspension refused as incompetent.

NOTE

The appropriate procedure for challenging decisions on competency (and relevancy) before the final determination of the cause is provided by section 334(2A) of the 1975 Act (*infra*, p.570).

3.   MacGregor v. MacNeill
1975 J.C. 57

For earlier proceedings related to this case see *MacNeill* v. *MacGregor, supra*, p.533.

The complainer brought a bill of suspension for review of the sentence imposed by the sheriff, that sentence having been imposed as a result of a guilty plea tendered in error.

LORD JUSTICE-CLERK (WHEATLEY): "... The first question to be decided is whether in the circumstances the bill of suspension is competent. Mr Younger submitted that it was and the learned Advocate-depute conceded that it was. Suspension is a competent method of review when some step in the procedure has gone wrong, or some factor has emerged which satisfies the court that a miscarriage of justice has taken place, resulting in a failure to do justice to an accused. In the case of *Spowart* v. *Burr* (1895) 1 Adam 539 Lord Adam at 545–6 made it clear that a bill of suspension would not be entertained in the ordinary case where the panel has pleaded guilty, and after sentence wishes to go back on his plea. I endorse that view. If it were otherwise the doors would be opened wide to people seeking review because the sentence imposed following a plea of guilty was more than they had bargained for. In the same case Lord M'Laren said this at p.546: 'But in the present case the statement for the complainer really amounts to nothing more than this, that the record of his plea is untrue. He says that he never gave such a plea. If enquiry were allowed on a mere circumstantial statement of this kind, I do not see how it could be refused in any case where the accused came forward and said that he had not in fact tendered the plea which the record bears that he had tendered. Where relief is asked on the ground that there has been an error in the proceedings, or some mistake on the part of the judge, there must be clear averments as to how the error or mistake originated, and unless upon such averments, enquiry cannot be allowed.' Again I would endorse what was there said. In that case the accused appeared on his own behalf at the trial and tendered the plea of guilty according to the record of the proceedings, but what Lord M'Laren said is, in my opinion, equally applicable where the accused is legally represented.

The present case has to be considered on the basis of the case as it stood when the conviction and sentence were passed and recorded on 25th July 1974. The submission on behalf of the complainer is that these proceeded on the vital mistake of a plea of guilty being tendered when the instructions given were to tender a plea of not guilty. This is accepted by the Crown. The complainer further submits that the miscarriage of justice here is underlined by the fact that in the inept trial which followed upon the inept proceedings on 26th July 1974 he was found not guilty. The learned Advocate-depute again frankly and fairly conceded that in the circumstances here present, prejudice had been suffered by the complainer.

I am of the opinion that in all the circumstances placed before the court, this bill of suspension is competent and there has been disclosed such prejudice to the complainer as to have resulted in justice not having been done to him. It is true that the error or mistake which caused this was not due to anything done by the judge or prosecutor, but in my view the court is entitled to look at all the circumstances in deciding whether an injustice has resulted to an accused person.

I would like to point out, however, that there were very special circumstances here present, that a very full explanation has been given to the court, and that the explanation has been fully accepted by the Crown. I would not like it to be thought that this decision can be regarded as a precedent which would allow any claim that a wrong plea had been tendered automatically to result in proceedings being quashed. Each case will depend on its own circumstances, and very special circumstances will be required to justify the remedy which the complainer seeks in this case. In the very special circumstances of this case I am prepared to grant the complainer the remedy he seeks. I would accordingly move your Lordships to pass the bill, to quash the proceedings of 25th July 1974, and to remit the case back to the Sheriff to proceed as accords, if the Crown are so minded to proceed with the complaint."

The court passed
the bill.

4. O'Hara v. Mill
1938 J.C. 4

The complainer was convicted on summary complaint of an offence under the Prevention of Crimes Act 1871. He brought a bill of suspension in which he alleged, *inter alia*, that there was no evidence sufficient in law to support the conviction.

LORD JUSTICE-CLERK (AITCHISON): "... The question which the suspender now seeks to raise in this bill of suspension is whether the magistrate had evidence before him which was sufficient in law to entitle him to convict the suspender. I think it is obvious that, whenever a question of that kind is sought to be raised, the appropriate process in which to raise it is a stated case ... If the suspender had proceeded by way of stated case, we should have had before us in the stated case the facts as found by the magistrate, and we should then have been able to say whether, on the facts found by the magistrate, there was sufficient evidence in law to entitle the magistrate to find the suspender guilty. It has always been recognised that this Court will not review the magistrate, either in a suspension, or in a stated case, so far as the facts found are concerned. 'To settle the fact is the peculiar province of every assize in what Court soever the trial be.' (Hume, ii, 514.) Accordingly, it is not open to us, even if we desired to do so, to review the magistrate upon the facts. But then, there are cases in which the Court has in a suspension entertained the question whether the evidence was sufficient in law to warrant a conviction. When one looks at these cases, of which *M'Shane* is an example, it appears that they were cases in which there was no dispute between the parties as to what the facts were, and the cases could be taken upon that footing. In the present case there is some agreement between the suspender and the respondent as to the facts, but in some material respects there is disagreement. That being the position, Mr Guthrie for the suspender conceded that he must take the case upon the statement of the respondent, as set out in the respondent's answers. [His Lordship then examined the averments contained in the respondent's answers, and stated his reasons for holding that they established that the evidence was sufficient to warrant the magistrate in finding the suspender guilty of the offence charged.]

The bill of suspension will, accordingly, be refused; but I desire to repeat that, when it is desired to raise a question of this kind, the appropriate form of appeal is a stated case, so that the Court may have before it the facts found by the magistrate. Although the Court has allowed in this case the question to be argued in a suspension, it must not be assumed that a similar indulgence will be granted in the future."

The court refused to pass the bill.

NOTES

1.   Lords Pitman and Wark agreed. The latter stated that "Nothing is better settled in our criminal law than that the merits of a conviction cannot be reviewed in a process of suspension." See also *Moffat* v. *Skeen*, 1963 J.C. 84; *James Y. Keanie* v. *Laird*, 1943 J.C. 73 and *Fairley* v. *Muir*, 1951 J.C. 56, *infra*, p.557.

2.   Notwithstanding the above, the High Court has power under section 452(4)(*b*) of the 1975 Act to remit to any fit person to inquire and report in regard to any matter or circumstance affecting the appeal: section 453A(2). In *Neilands* v. *Leslie*, 1973 S.L.T. (Notes) 32 there was a dispute on matters of fact between the bill and the answers lodged thereto. The High Court gave the following general indication of its approach in such cases:

"Where there is conflict between the bill and answers the court will usually accept the latter and although there may be cases where a remit to a reporter would be justified when there is a degree of doubt as to the accuracy of a respondent's answers the instant bill did not reveal such a case."

5.   Criminal Procedure (Scotland) Act 1975

"**453A.**—(1) Notwithstanding section 449(2) of this Act, a party to a summary prosecution may, where an appeal under section 442 of this Act would be incompetent or would in the circumstances be inappropriate, appeal to the High Court, by bill of suspension against a conviction, or as the case may be by advocation against an acquittal, on the ground of an alleged miscarriage of justice in the proceedings:

Provided that where the alleged miscarriage of justice is referred to in an application, under section 444(1) of this Act, for a stated case as regards the proceedings (or in a duly made amendment or addition to that application) an appeal under subsection (1) above shall not proceed without the leave of the High Court until the appeal to which the application relates has been finally disposed of or abandoned ...

(3) The foregoing provisions of this section shall be without prejudice to any rule of law relating to bills of suspension or advocation in so far as such rule of law is not inconsistent with those provisions."

NOTES ·

1.   The competency of appeals by stated case is discussed above, p.531. The appropriateness of that method of appeal has generally been discussed in the context of proceedings by way of bill of suspension.

2. Section 444(2) of the 1975 Act provides that it shall be competent for an appellant to proceed by way of bill of suspension where an application for a stated case cannot proceed because the judge by whom he was convicted cannot sign the case owing to death or illness. In such a case, "it shall be competent for the convicted person ... to bring under review ... any matter which might have been brought under review by stated case."

(ii) Appropriateness

Even where review by bill of suspension is competent, it may not necessarily be the appropriate method of review. It should be noted also that in many cases the issues of competency and appropriateness cannot always be kept clearly apart.

1. Fairley v. Muir
1951 J.C. 56

LORD JUSTICE-GENERAL (COOPER): "This bill of suspension relates to a conviction for alleged contravention of the Food Rationing Regulations obtained in Edinburgh Sheriff Court on 30th November 1950. The statement of facts contains three or four pages of type devoted to a description of the evidence oral and documentary which was adduced, and the point sought to be raised by the bill is whether the proceedings at the trial were vitiated by the illegal admission of incompetent evidence. In the course of the statement of facts it is disclosed that the complainer applied for a stated case, and evidently got it, but that in the course of the adjustment of the stated case he was advised that the question involved would be more appropriately dealt with in a bill of suspension. The present bill of suspension was presented to this Court on 20th January, when I declined in chambers to take the responsibility for pronouncing a first order, and directed that the case should be heard by this Court.

Within the last thirteen years there have been, I think, no fewer than nine cases before this Court in which pointed attention has been drawn to the requirements of our law and practice as regards the review of summary convictions, and the two considerations by reference to which the competency or propriety of a bill of suspension should be judged, (first) the delay in presentation of the bill, and (second) the nature of the question sought to be raised.

In the case of *O'Hara* v. *Mill* [*supra*] the matter was the subject of comment by a Court presided over by Lord Justice-Clerk Aitchison, and the views there expressed were subsequently reinforced by the Court as differently constituted in the case of *Dawson* v. *Adair* [16 Sept. 1941, unreported]. Two years later in the case of *James Y. Keanie, Limited* v. *Laird* [1943 J.C. 73] this Court, again differently constituted, took occasion for the third time to stress the different types of review which were appropriate to a stated case and to a bill of suspension respectively. I need not read from my own judgment in that case, in which I pointed out that a bill of suspension and a stated case are not alternative and equivalent methods of submitting to this Court questions determined in Courts of summary jurisdiction; but I would draw attention to the observation of Lord Wark who said (at p. 77): 'I think it is high time that it should be quite clearly understood by the profession that the rule laid down in *O'Hara* and *Dawson* is one which will be enforced, and that the indulgence which was given in some of the cases prior to *O'Hara* will not be allowed in future cases.' There have been a number of other cases which are not reported, but I need not deal further with the general question except to say this, that, from the point of view of the due administration of justice, there are certain types of question capable of being brought for review from a summary Court which are essentially appropriate only to a stated case, in which we are given the benefit of the considered views of the Court of first instance formed at a time when the evidence is fresh in the memory of the Sheriff or magistrate, and that (while I do not say that the function of a bill of suspension is strictly confined to cases of this kind) the type of cases to which a bill of suspension is truly appropriate is the case where the relevant circumstances are instantly, or almost instantly, verifiable, and the point sought to be raised is raised promptly, a crisp issue of, say, jurisdiction, competency, oppression, or departure from the canons of natural justice.

Returning to this case, the issue which the complainer desires to raise is the competency of the admission by the Sheriff-substitute of certain items of documentary evidence. That raises an issue in law peculiarly appropriate to a stated case, and one which, broadly speaking, could never be determined satisfactorily, so far as I can see, without a narrative of the conclusions on the evidence on which the Sheriff-substitute proceeded, so that we might discover, amongst other things, how far the documents challenged were indispensable to the conviction, and whether in the words of section 75 their admission if incompetent inferred a miscarriage of justice. The complainer evidently recognised that by applying for a stated case. Why he was advised that the question involved would be more appropriately dealt with in a bill of suspension I am still, I regret to say, unable to understand. The Dean of Faculty has informed us that the case as drafted raised a number of other issues which he could not have maintained with success. If so, it would be no new thing in this Court for counsel to have so stated, and to have confined his attention to the matters upon which he did desire to present argument. It has been suggested that a difficulty, the nature of which I cannot appreciate, would have been encountered, or was encountered, in obtaining from the Sheriff-substitute a stated case properly directed to the question which it is desired to raise. If such a difficulty arose, or may yet arise, it is a difficulty of a type by no means unfamiliar in this Court, and for which we are always ready, if necessary, to afford a remedy in a remit to the Sheriff-substitute with instructions as to the nature of the findings and information which we require.

In the result I find myself unable to discover either within the four corners of the bill or in the candid explanation offered by the Dean of Faculty any sufficient explanation for a delay of roughly two months in presentation of the bill, still less for the substitution of a bill of suspension as a means of reviewing this issue in place of the stated case which is to my mind manifestly the more appropriate, if not the only appropriate, method of raising the issues sought to be determined. In view of the repeated judgments which have been directed to questions of this type I do not feel any hesitation in suggesting to your Lordships that our proper course in this case is to decline to pronounce the first order."

The court refused
to let the bill proceed.

NOTE

There is no statutory time-limit for bringing a suspension, but delay may be fatal as indicating acquiescence in the judgment or order complained of. See e.g. *Storie* v. *Friel*, 1993 S.C.C.R. 955. Whether or not a delay will be considered undue, and thus operate as a bar, will depend upon the facts and circumstances of each case. See, for examples, Renton and Brown, para. 16–152 and the following case.

2. Handley v. Pirie
1977 S.L.T. 30

An accused person was charged with a contravention of section 6(1) of the Road Traffic Act 1972. He was convicted on the sheriff's acceptance of an analyst's certificate tendered under section 10 of the 1972 Act. The accused had pled not guilty at the first diet and was ordained to appear for trial on November 3. On that date he again appeared and pleaded not guilty. The prosecutor, however, moved the court to adjourn the diet, the reason being that he had omitted to serve upon the accused the analyst's certificate or to cite the analyst as a witness. Despite objections by the accused the diet was adjourned to November 28, 1975, by which time the prosecutor served upon the accused a copy of the analyst's certificate in accordance with section 10(3) of the 1972 Act. The accused presented a bill of suspension to the High Court.

LORD JUSTICE-GENERAL (EMSLIE): "... The single question with which this bill is concerned is whether in the particular circumstances disclosed therein the certificate relied on by the sheriff was by itself competent evidence of the matters which it purported to certify. ...

Although the bill appears to raise a separate question relating to the allowance of the adjournment this question was not insisted in and in the result the short sharp issue is whether the certificate was served upon the complainer not less than seven days before his trial began. The complainer contends that it was not upon the submission that the trial began on 3 November 1975 before the diet was adjourned. The respondent contends that it had not begun and that it did not begin until 28 November. There is no dispute or doubt about the facts and it is clear that this issue falls to be resolved upon a consideration of the events which happened and the terms of s. 10(3).

At the hearing on the bill the Crown argued in limine under reference to the case of *Fairley* v. *Muir*, 1951 S.L.T. 237, 1951 J.C. 56, that we should refuse the bill as incompetent, upon the ground that a challenge of the merits of a conviction is essentially appropriate only to a stated case and, in any event, upon the view that the complainer had delayed too long in presenting the bill. We reject this submission in the peculiar circumstances of this case, and in so doing we wish to cast no doubt upon the general rule which will be enforced, that a challenge of a conviction on its merits will, save in exceptional circumstances, only be entertained when the matter is brought before the court by a stated case in which the considered views of the trial judge will be expressed. In this case, however, to quote what was said by the Lord Justice-General in *Fairley*: 'the relevant circumstances are instantly ... verifiable and the point sought to be raised is ... a crisp issue of ... competency' of the certificate as evidence of its contents. For this reason the bill is an appropriate and competent method of raising the issue and since we have been satisfied that there was no undue delay in presenting it the grounds of objection relied on by the Crown have not been made out."

The court passed the bill and quashed
the conviction.

3. Galloway v. Smith
1974 S.L.T. (Notes) 63

The complainer pled guilty to a contravention of section 143(1) of the Road Traffic Act 1972 and was fined £10 and disqualified from holding or obtaining a driving licence for a period of six months. He presented a bill of suspension to have the sentence of disqualification quashed. It was argued on his behalf that the sheriff had proceeded on misleading information given to the court on behalf of a co-accused, but denied by the complainer's solicitor at the trial. There was nothing in the bill to indicate that the sheriff had proceeded on such a basis.

LORD JUSTICE-CLERK (WHEATLEY): "All that counsel for the complainer said was that it was a matter of inference that the sheriff had so proceeded. I cannot see how this court can be expected to accept that as a matter of inference. I wish to reiterate something which I have said from time to time in this court, which is that if an appeal is taken against a sentence, and allegations are going to be made that the presiding judge proceeded on a certain basis and had misdirected himself on that basis, then the proper method of appeal is by way of stated case, which would enable the judge in the court below to present to this court a full statement of the reasons why he disposed of the case in a certain manner. I trust that this will be noted by people who are wishing to proceed by way of appeal on such a basis. When it proceeds by way of bill of suspension we are then presented with an ex parte statement that is not capable of being checked by the best authority possible, namely, the presiding judge himself.

Accordingly, I am unable to proceed on the basis that the sheriff in reaching his decision to disqualify relied on the misleading information given on behalf of the co-accused, but denied by the complainer's agent. On the merits of the appeal I am of the opinion that in all the circumstances it cannot be said that the sentence of disqualification imposed was harsh and oppressive."

The court refused to
pass the bill.

NOTE

Since a stated case is no longer a competent method of appeal against sentence alone, it might be thought that this case was no longer of authority. But the court's concern that the judge at first instance should have an opportunity to state his reasons for selecting a particular sentence is still valid and is met under present procedure by the provision of a report on a note of appeal against sentence under section 453B of the 1975 Act.

(iii) Grounds of Appeal

It will be apparent from the foregoing that suspension may be brought on a variety of grounds, including miscarriage of justice (under section 453A). It would be impracticable to give examples of all of the grounds so far recognised in this book: see, generally, Renton and Brown, para. 16–149. The following case is merely one instance of the kind of situation where a bill of suspension is the correct mode of appeal.

Stewart v. Lowe
1991 S.C.C.R. 317

An accused person was convicted after summary trial and appealed by bill of suspension.

LORD JUSTICE-GENERAL: "The complainer is Jack Richard Stewart, also known as Stevens, who went to trial in the sheriff court at Edinburgh with a co-accused on summary complaint. The principal charge which he faced was one which was expressed in these terms: that he did on 3rd June 1989 with his co-accused, by means of attempting to remove a window grill, attempt to break into the shop premises at 16 Bank Street, Edinburgh, occupied by Castle Photographic, with intent to steal. There were certain related charges alleging contraventions of conditions of bail. The only charge on which evidence was led against the appellant was charge (1), and at the conclusion of the evidence there was a motion made by each accused who were represented by the same solicitor that there was no case to answer. The sheriff did not call on the procurator fiscal depute to respond to the submissions which [were] made to him and without further ado he rejected both of these submissions. At the conclusion of the evidence the procurator fiscal depute intimated that she was no longer insisting on the charge against the co-accused. Thereupon the sheriff, without calling on the complainer's solicitor to address him, proceeded to convict the complainer and to give his reasons for doing so. Having realised his error he then attempted to retrieve the situation by adjourning the matter overnight and, next morning, when the case had called again, he formally convicted the appellant.

The bill which we have before us today directs attention to two matters which had previously been mentioned in an application for a stated case which was abandoned for the reasons described in statement 2 of the bill. So we have had the benefit of considering the note which the sheriff appended to the stated case.

The first point which is raised relates to an alleged persistent and partial manner of questioning which the sheriff embarked [on] in the course of the trial. We have not been addressed on that point and, since there is a more significant and more fundamental issue which arises on the second point, nothing more need be said about it, except to note the sheriff's comment that nothing which he did by way of questioning was oppressive or improper in this particular case.

The point which we come to now, however, is the central issue, and we have had the benefit of submissions on it from the learned advocate-depute. First of all there is the fact that the sheriff did not call upon the procurator fiscal depute to address him on the defence submission that there was no case to answer. As the advocate-depute points out, that was a breach of the provisions of section 345A(2) and (3) which make it clear that the sheriff must hear both parties before sustaining or rejecting a submission on this ground. That error would not, however, of itself, persuade us that the trial had been conducted in a manner which was oppressive to the complainer.

The more serious error lies in the sheriff's conduct in proceeding to convict the complainer without having heard any submissions at all for the defence. In this case because of the sheriff's attitude to the only defence witness, Marie Cummings, whose evidence might be thought to have cast doubt on the reliability of the one witness who corroborated the evidence of a police officer in support of the principal charge, the sheriff dismissed her evidence as totally irrelevant. It is averred in the bill that he did so peremptorily, and we have confirmation of this by the sheriff's own note that the evidence of Miss Cummings was totally irrelevant to the guilt or innocence of either accused. In our opinion that is not self-evident and there was a point of substance to be made in the submissions on behalf of the defence. The advocate-depute points out that there may also have been a question as to whether the essential matter alleged in the complaint had been proved at all.

In our opinion this is a case where it can be said without hesitation that the sheriff's conduct was such that the complainer was not seen to have received a fair trial and that the conduct which is narrated in the bill is sufficiently serious to justify the remedy which is sought. For these reasons the course which we must take is to pass the bill and quash the conviction."

Appeal allowed;
Conviction quashed.

(iv)   Limitations on Appeal

The limitations on appeal imposed by section 454 apply in the case of suspension (see *supra*, p.538).

(v)   Disposal of Appeals

In disposing of an appeal by way of suspension, the High Court may pass the bill and suspend the sentence, order, etc., reject the grounds of suspension and refuse the bill, or amend any conviction or sentence. The court may also remit the case to the inferior court, with instructions to proceed if necessary.

In the case of an appeal against conviction under section 453A, the powers of hearing and disposal provided for by sections 452(4)(*a*) to (*e*), 452A(1)(*d*), 452A(3) and 452B apply in the same way as in the case of appeals under section 444(1): section 453A(2). These powers, which apply only to appeals under section 453A, are without prejudice to any rule of law relating to bills of suspension in so far as such rule of law is not inconsistent with those powers.

The provisions of section 453, as amended, relating to the prosecutor's consent to the setting aside of a conviction apply to appeals by way of suspension.

D.   ADVOCATION

Advocation originally denoted the removal of a case from an inferior court (of summary or solemn jurisdiction) to the High Court. Section 280A of the 1975 Act now provides that the prosecutor's right to bring a decision under review of the High Court by way of bill of advocation "in accordance with existing law and practice" shall extend to the review of a decision of any court of solemn jurisdiction. Decisions of the High Court itself as a court of first instance are now subject to review by advocation.

Section 280A refers in terms to the "prosecutor's right" to bring a bill of advocation. Apart from this provision, advocation is, in theory, a procedure available to accused persons as well as the prosecutor. In practice, however, it is only available to the accused in exceptional circumstances and is generally regarded as a prosecutor's remedy, equivalent to the accused's right to bring a suspension.

1. **Muir v. Hart**
1912 S.C. (J.) 41

An accused person was charged on indictment with fraud. At the first diet the sheriff repelled objections to the relevancy of the indictment, lodged on behalf of the accused. The accused then brought an advocation of that interlocutor before the trial diet.

LORD JUSTICE-CLERK (MACDONALD): "... Had this question arisen for the first time, my view therefore would have been that as regards what the complainer proposes to do in this case there is no law, as there is no practice, to support it. But I am supported in this view by the case of *Jameson* v. *Lothian* [(1855) 2 Irv. 273], when this very question was brought before a bench of five Judges, and was decided on the competency, as I think this case ought to be decided. From that day to this no similar case has been brought before the Court. Neither has any such attempt been made under the Act of 1887, to which I shall refer presently. Thus no advocation such as this has been attempted for more than fifty years. I say nothing as to what might be done in any special case, such as was suggested in *Jameson's* advocation, where action might be taken at an early stage of procedure, if, as Lord Justice-Clerk Hope said, something was done 'which outraged all the principles of the liberty of the subject,' or if, as Lord Ivory said, there was 'an objection to the jurisdiction *funditus*.' Such a case, if it ever occurs, must be dealt with as it presents itself. ... Here we are asked to intervene, not because by any action of the Judge there has been a stoppage of proceedings before him, not because there has been any fundamental nullity by which the course of justice has been stopped. Nothing has been done which can be impugned as not being according to practice, or that in itself stopped procedure under the indictment. All has been regular and according to statute. All that is said is that the Sheriff has formed a wrong opinion on a point of relevancy. In my opinion we have no duty or right to interfere at such a stage."

LORD JOHNSTON (*diss.*): "... To refuse advocation at the stage in question would, as appears to me, be to obliterate the process of advocation from our criminal procedure, and to make suspension the sole mode of review of proceedings in an inferior Court. Advocation can only be resorted to *pendente processu*, and was introduced for the very purpose of correcting errors in procedure of the inferior Court Judge at a stage prior to final sentence. Suspension, with or without liberation according to the form of the sentence, can only be brought of a sentence, and is the only process by which such can be reviewed, though on the ground of error in law or procedure only, and not of fact. The one is the advocation of a process for correction of procedure before sentence—the other is the suspension of a sentence after the process is concluded.

It is for these reasons that I have ventured to maintain that the judgment in *Jameson's* case ought not to be regarded as binding in the somewhat altered circumstances. The considerations which these circumstances present have led me to the conclusion that to refuse this advocation as incompetent would be to reject the opportunity, which the passing of the Acts of 1853 and 1887 has afforded, of facilitating procedure, and instead to perpetuate inconvenience and expense."

LORD SALVESEN (*diss.*): "... We were not referred to any authority, apart from the decision in the case of *Jameson*, which supports the view that advocation of an interlocutor pronounced by a Sheriff finding the libel relevant is incompetent. The institutional writers seem to take it for granted that such a process is competent. Thus Hume says (p.509) that there are three forms of process in which decrees of the inferior Courts may be submitted to the revisal of the Lords of Justiciary, namely, advocation, suspension, and appeal, and he goes on to point out that advocation is the proper remedy before a trial has taken place, just as suspension is that which applies after conclusion of the trial in the inferior Court to hinder execution of the sentence. With regard to advocation he says,—'This form of redress seems to be universally applicable with the exception only of the sentences of the Court of Admiralty, with respect to which all advocation is absolutely forbidden by the statute of 1681, cap. 16.' It is true he does not expressly mention that advocation is competent in order to review a finding upon relevancy, but he says that 'the manner of the process seems to have been thus. That on a bill offered to the Lords of Privy Council, or Council and Session, an order was made and intimated enjoining the inferior Judge not to proceed.' This was before the Court of Justiciary was established; and shortly after that Court came into existence Hume says,—'The Lords of Justiciary attained to the quiet and exclusive possession of the right of passing bills of advocation for themselves in all cases which fall properly within their charter.' Further, there are two recent decisions which seem not entirely consistent with the case of *Jameson*. In *Craig* v. *Galt* [4 Coup. 541] the Sheriff had dismissed a criminal libel at the instance of a private prosecutor with concurrence of the public prosecutor, because of the non-production, the day before the first diet at which the case was called, of an article libelled as to be produced at the trial. The complainer thereupon brought a bill of advocation and contended that 'in criminal cases before the Sheriff productions did not require to be lodged till the day before the trial, and that the trial was now regarded in practice as being at the second diet.' The Court were of opinion that the Sheriff had erred; and they sustained the advocation, recalled the interlocutor complained of, and remitted to the Sheriff to proceed according to law. Now, under the old practice, as there was only one diet, it is plain that the objection would have been a good one; but it was held to be bad, not because of any new act of adjournal regulating the time for production of documents, but because of the introduction of two diets, and the practice which had followed upon that introduction. In the subsequent case of *Macrae* v. *Cooper* [4 Coup. 561] the Sheriff had deserted the diet *simpliciter* in a criminal trial, because at the first diet the prosecutor was not personally present, although a person holding a commission from him was in attendance. On a bill of advocation being presented, the Court advocated the cause, reversed the judgment of the Sheriff, and remitted to him to proceed according to law.

It would thus appear that where at the first diet an interlocutor is pronounced adverse to the prosecutor, it is competent for him to bring a bill of advocation, and for the Court to remit to the Sheriff who has finally decided the cause to proceed with the trial. If that be so, I can see no reason in principle why the same privilege should not be accorded to the accused; and there is nothing, so far as I know, either enacted by statute or in our mode of administering justice in criminal causes which requires that we should discriminate thus unfairly between the remedies open to the prosecutor and those open to the accused.

On the question of the expediency of advocating a deliverance sustaining the relevancy of a libel I have already pointed out the advantage to the accused of not having to undergo a trial on an irrelevant indictment. From the public point of view the expediency is even more obvious. If a mistake has been made in framing an indictment on which the accused has been tried and convicted, the conviction may be quashed by the High Court. The mistake may have been a formal one, and the conviction just on the facts proved at the trial, but the accused person having tholed an assize cannot again be indicted. If, however, the same decision had been pronounced in an advocation on relevancy the prosecutor would have an opportunity of serving a new and relevant indictment which would obviate the risk of a guilty person escaping all punishment because of a formal and technical defect in the original indictment.

On the whole matter, therefore, I am of opinion that this advocation is not merely competent, but that it is expedient in the interests of both of the accused and of the administration of justice, and that we should entertain it."

The court held the advocation
to be incompetent.

NOTES

1. So far as appeal against a decision on relevancy (or competency) prior to final determination is concerned, the appropriate procedure now is that provided by sections 76 and 334(2) of the 1975 Act. In so far as *Muir* v. *Hart* (and *Jameson*) prevent recourse to advocation prior to final determination, they remain unaffected by section 334(2).

2. The majority of the court (four judges) thought that the advocation was incompetent. Of the remaining three judges, two (Lord Salvesen and Johnston) thought it both competent and expedient in the circumstances. The Lord Justice-General thought it was competent but inexpedient.

2. MacLeod v. Levitt
1969 J.C. 16

The respondent was disqualified for holding or obtaining a driving licence for a total of seven years and six months. He applied under section 106(1) of the Road Traffic Act 1960 for removal of that disqualification. His application was granted by the sheriff, and the procurator-fiscal presented a bill of advocation for recall of the sheriff's interlocutor.

LORD JUSTICE-GENERAL (CLYDE): "...A preliminary matter arises first of all as to the competency of our entertaining the present bill of advocation at all, as a means of reviewing the Sheriff-substitute's order in Mr Levitt's petition.

It is important in the first instance to see what section 106 envisages. It contemplates not a continuation of the original complaint process, but the start of a totally new and independent application to the Court which ordered the disqualification. That application is made by way of a petition, and the petition is at the instance not of the procurator-fiscal, but of the disqualified person. Service is not required on the procurator-fiscal, although in practice this is done, so that he can place before the Court any information in the possession of the Crown relative to the matters mentioned in section 106(1). Thus he is not a party to the process, although in practice he usually attends as a purveyor of information if the Sheriff-substitute requires it. The process is of a discretionary and administrative character, and no provision is made for an appeal from the decision of the Sheriff-substitute in such process. Section 105 of the 1960 Act provides for an appeal against an order of disqualification, but in marked contrast to this section 106 says nothing about any appeal from an order removing a disqualification. We are here in the realm of statutory provisions and not common law, and in the absence of a statutory provision for appeal in such an application I am of opinion that an appeal by stated case ... would not be competent.

It is in this situation that the question of the competency of a bill of advocation arises. In modern times this procedure has become very rare, and for practical purposes is really out of date. It was invoked more frequently before appeals by stated case were competent. In my view the very limited sphere in which it could be invoked is accurately summed up in Trotter on Summary Jurisdiction, p.68, where a bill of advocation is described as a process by which review is sought of a decision pronounced in a preliminary part of a prosecution and prior to final judgment. (Compare Renton and Brown's Criminal Procedure (3rd ed.), p.324). The order removing the disqualification from driving in the present case was not pronounced in a preliminary part of a prosecution: it was not pronounced in a part of a prosecution at all, but in a separate petition to which the prosecutor was not a party and indeed in which there was no prosecutor: and in any event it was not pronounced prior to final judgment, and it was in fact itself the final end of the matter. In these circumstances, in my opinion, the bill of advocation is incompetent."

LORD CAMERON: "... The process of advocation, though not wholly obsolete ... has been almost entirely superseded in practice as a method of appeal by the introduction of appeal by way of stated case in summary procedure and by the forms of appeal applicable to procedure on indictment provided by the Act of 1926. The limited sphere of competence of the process of advocation lies in the correction of irregularities in the preliminary stages of a case, though recourse to the process is incompetent until the cause is finally determined, unless in very special circumstances—see Muir v. Hart [supra], Strathern v. Benson [1925 J.C. 40], and Renton and Brown's Criminal Procedure (3rd ed.), p.324. It cannot be used to obtain review on the merits—see List v. Pirie [(1867) 5 Irv. 559]."

> The court dismissed
> the bill.

NOTES

1. The court's views on the obsolescence of advocation were premature. There have been a string of cases since 1969. It has been competently (but unsuccessfully) used before the final determination of the cause by accused persons: see, e.g., Grugen v. Jessop, 1988 S.C.C.R. 182; Platt v. Lockhart, 1988 S.C.C.R. 308. But advocation cannot be used by the Crown during a trial for the purpose of obtaining a review of decisions taken on objections to evidence: H.M. Advocate v. Thomson, 1994 S.C.C.R. 40.

2. The rule that advocation cannot be employed to obtain a review on the merits may be qualified by section 453A of the 1975 Act, which allows an appeal by advocation on the ground of miscarriage of justice in limited circumstances.

3. For a review of decisions on the appropriateness of advocation as a remedy, see Renton and Brown, para. 16–177. One interesting situation where advocation was used by the Crown in a solemn case prior to final disposal is illustrated by the following case.

3. H.M. Advocate v. McKenzie
1989 S.C.C.R. 587

An accused person pleaded guilty to assault with intent to rape and attempted murder. Before sentence, the judge continued the case so that the Crown could seek the victim's views on disposal. The Crown appealed by bill of advocation.

LORD JUSTICE-GENERAL: "In moving for sentence the advocate-depute for the assistance of the presiding judge provided a narrative of the events which had given rise to these charges. He also intimated that the respondent had no previous convictions. In mitigation the respondent's counsel made reference to a pre-trial report dated 25th September 1989 which had been obtained by the court in implement of section 42(1) of the Criminal Justice (Scotland) Act 1980. This report had been prepared on the basis that the accused was maintaining his pleas of not guilty to the offences libelled against him. It is unnecessary to rehearse the contents of this report in detail, but it stated that the respondent came from a good family, that he had presented no disciplinary problems to his parents and performed well both at school and in his apprenticeship and had been in regular employment. His conduct prior to his being charged with the offences in the indictment was described as exemplary and it was stated that these offences were completely alien to the respondent's previous good character. We understand that the respondent's counsel could offer no explanation for the crimes, which he described as inexplicable. After having listened to these submissions, the presiding judge adjourned the diet until 13th October 1989 in order to obtain a psychiatric report. In doing so he was adopting a suggestion which was made at the conclusion of the pre-trial report that it might be in the interests of justice if a psychiatric report was obtained from the Sexual Problems Clinic at the Royal Infirmary in Edinburgh prior to sentencing. A psychiatric report was duly obtained and it was placed before the presiding judge prior to the adjourned diet. It repeated the respondent's inability to explain his actions in committing the offences. He was said to be ashamed and bewildered by his behaviour, but there was no evidence of any disordered thinking, confusion or impairment of intellect. The consultant psychiatrist found no features of psychotic mental illness or mental abnormality and he made no psychiatric recommendation.

On 13th October 1989 the presiding judge decided to adjourn the diet for a further fourteen days until 27th October. The power which he was exercising in that regard is to be found in section 179(1) of the Criminal Procedure (Scotland) Act 1975. His reasons for doing so have been narrated in article 2 of the statement of facts which have been placed before us in this bill of advocation. The presiding judge has provided us with a report, some parts of which must remain confidential at this stage since sentence has not yet been passed upon the respondent, but we think it proper to quote his version of what he believes he said in court, which is as follows:

'The reason I am doing this is that I am unable today, in light of what I have been told about this case and what is in the psychiatric report, to determine the proper disposal for this accused. One matter I am anxious to be informed on—and I think the Crown must undertake this on behalf of the court—I am very anxious indeed to discover, if she is prepared to assist the court on this matter, what the feelings of the victim are in relation to the disposal of the case. I appreciate this is a highly unusual circumstance, but the case itself is highly unusual and I should certainly feel in a better position to settle on the appropriate form of punishment if I had that information. Of course, it is entirely up to the lady herself whether she chooses to assist, and there could be no hint of criticism on the part of the court if she felt she wanted nothing more to do with it.'

The presiding judge has agreed in his report that the Crown was right to treat his request to undertake this task on behalf of the court as a requirement. The learned Solicitor-General has approached the matter on this basis and he has invited us to pass the bill and to set that requirement aside.

In fairness to the presiding judge we should say that he made it clear in his report that he did not and does not seek to challenge or impair the fundamental rule that the trial judge must decide upon the appropriate sentence in the light of all the information put before him in court. As he put it, he sought only to obtain the fullest information which might be relevant before determining what the appropriate sentence would be. In our opinion he was right to describe the rule that the trial judge must decide upon the appropriate sentence as fundamental. It is a rule which we would not wish to see impaired in any way whatsoever. Prosecutions in this country are brought in the public interest in the name of Her Majesty's Advocate so that there may be due and equal distribution of criminal justice to all her subjects. That fundamental principle is to be found in Hume on Crimes (4th edn), volume ii, p.125. The Lord Advocate has the right to prosecute whether or not the complainer is disposed to do so. He is the master of the instance at all times, right up to the moment when he has moved the court to pronounce sentence after the jury's verdict has been returned, and at that stage in the interests of justice our law has already entrusted the matter of sentencing entirely to the judge. As Hume, volume ii, p.463, points out, this is an act of the court pronounced in pursuance of the verdict. No doubt the judge must decide upon the appropriate sentence in the light of the information which may be placed before him in court. There exist various rules of practice and procedure whereby information is placed before him so that he may take it into account. But in the end of the day the responsibility for what the sentence should be is his and his alone.

It is right at this stage to emphasise the position of the Crown in this matter. As we have said, the Crown is the master of the instance at all times up to the moment when the prosecutor has moved the court to pronounce sentence. But at that stage the matter moves entirely from the Crown to the court, and it is desirable for good reasons of public policy that the Crown should not be involved in the process of sentencing in any way whatever. It is known to all who practise in the criminal system of this country that the Crown has absolutely no role or interest in this process. The learned Solicitor-General today has quite rightly emphasised the importance of this principle and he has stressed that nothing should be done to weaken it in any way by putting the burden of a requirement such as placed on the Crown in this case to participate in the process.

We now consider the question briefly whether the bill which is brought before us is competent. Mr Henderson, for the respondent, has not challenged the competency of the bill. It is sufficient to say simply that we are quite satisfied, having considered the references which we were given to Alison's Practice, p.26, and passages in Renton and Brown (5th edn), paragraphs 16–169 and 16–173, that the bill is competent in this case. We are satisfied that there are present here such special and peculiar circumstances, and that the stage which the matter has reached is such, that it is right for us to entertain this bill.

The point at issue therefore, in this case, is whether there is any basis in law or principle for the requirement which the presiding judge has imposed on the Crown. We should say, since the matter arose initially out of the pre-trial report, that there is no support whatever in the legislation relating to that matter, or indeed any other legislation, that the court has power to require that such matters be investigated by the Crown. Section 42 of the 1980 Act relates to persons of or over the age of twenty-one years who have not previously been sentenced to imprisonment or detention by a court in any part of the United Kingdom. For the purpose of determining whether any method of dealing with such an offender other than imprisonment is appropriate, the court is required to obtain such information as it can about the circumstances of the offender and it is required also to take into account any information before it concerning the offender's character and his physical and mental condition. But there is no reference in this section or indeed anywhere else in the relevant legislation to the views or feelings of the complainer in the indictment as being either a matter about which the court is obliged to obtain information or indeed as a matter which it is required to take into account. This is hardly surprising because this is a factor which in many cases will be of no significance whatever to the judge's assessment of what is appropriate in the interests of punishment and general deterrence in respect of the offence. This is not to say that it may not be legitimate to enquire into certain objective matters of fact which might indicate the attitude of the complainer subsequent to an offence where, for example, there has been previously a close relationship, such as that of husband and wife. But it is sufficient to say that the relationship does not exist here, and it must at the least be highly doubtful whether the victim of such an ordeal as the complainer was subjected to in this particular case would be able at this stage to bring a balanced judgment to bear on matters relating to punishment of the offender, as a pointer either to greater leniency or greater severity in the sentence.

In these circumstances we consider that it is entirely wrong that the complainer should be asked for her views on the basis that what she may say might affect the ultimate disposal of the case. As the learned Solicitor-General has pointed out, the complainer would be asked to do something in which she has no expertise. She could not know the range of possible disposals or indeed the principles upon which the court would need to proceed in considering the appropriate sentence. It would be invidious in these circumstances to expose the complainer to the risk of public pressure by passing any comment on matters which lie outside her expertise and which in the circumstances could be of no relevance to the decision which the court and the court alone must take.

The learned Solicitor-General went on to address us further on the position of the Crown's participation in the matter. Once again we would stress that it is desirable for sound reasons of principle that the prosecution should not be involved in the process of sentencing. It is clear that if the requirement which was imposed on the Crown in this case were to be followed, it would be necessary for processes to take place to obtain by precognition information from the complainer. In fairness to the respondent, that information would require to be tested in some way or another, and it is not surprising that in his helpful address to the court Mr Henderson has made it clear that he would take the view that the requirement would give rise to the risk of prejudice to the respondent. As he put it, in this case it is neither necessary nor desirable that such difficult territory should be entered into.

Before we leave the case, we should say this. We do not wish in any way to usurp the functions of the presiding judge whose responsibility it is to pronounce sentence in this case. But in our opinion no judge, when faced with the facts of this case and the information about the offender's background which is now available, could responsibly do otherwise than impose a sentence of imprisonment for a substantial period of years. The interests of punishment and general deterrence which are paramount in dealing with a crime of this nature require that this should be so. For these reasons we shall pass the bill and the presiding judge will proceed as accords."

Bill refused.

E. APPEALS AGAINST SENTENCE BY NOTE OF APPEAL

Criminal Procedure (Scotland) Act 1975

"**453B.**—(1) An appeal under section 442(1)(a)(ii) or by virtue of section 442(1)(c) of this Act shall be by note of appeal, which shall state the ground of appeal.

453C.—(1) An appeal against sentence by note of appeal shall be heard by the High Court on such date as it may fix, and the High Court may, subject to section 453D(1) of this Act, dispose of such appeal by—

(a) affirming the sentence; or

(b) if the Court thinks that, having regard to all the circumstances, including any additional evidence such as is mentioned in section 442(2) of this Act, a different sentence should have been passed, quashing the sentence and passing another sentence, whether more or less severe, in substitution therefor:

Provided that the Court shall not in any case increase the sentence beyond the maximum sentence which could have been passed by the inferior court."

NOTES

1.   The note of appeal must be lodged with the clerk of the court from which the appeal is taken within one week of the passing of sentence. On receipt of the note of appeal, the clerk sends a copy to the respondent or his solicitor and obtains a report from the sentencing judge: section 453B(3) and (3).

2.   See *Galloway* v. *Smith*, 1974 S.L.T. (Notes) 63, *supra*, p.560. For further details of the procedures governing this form of appeal see sections 453B and 453C of the 1975 Act and Renton and Brown, Chap. 16.

F.   APPEALS AGAINST DECISIONS ON COMPETENCY AND RELEVANCY

The Thomson Committee (3rd Report, para. 13.15) recommended that both the prosecutor and the accused should have rights of appeal on issues of competency and relevancy in summary proceedings as soon as the issue was determined. They were influenced in this view by the fact that where an issue of competency or relevancy was decided against an accused who maintained a plea of not guilty, the issue of competency or relevancy might yet be decided in his favour after the time and expense of a trial. The following provision goes some way to meeting that objection:

Criminal Procedure (Scotland) Act 1975

"334.—(2A) Without prejudice to any right of appeal under section 442 or 453A of this Act, a party may, with the leave of the court (granted either on the motion of that party or *ex proprio motu*) and in accordance with such procedure as may be prescribed by Act of Adjournal under this Act, appeal to the High Court against a decision of the court of first instance (other than a decision not to grant leave under this subsection) which relates to such objection or denial as is mentioned in subsection (1) above; but such appeal must be taken not later than two days after such decision.

(2B) Where an appeal is taken under subsection (2A) above, the High Court may postpone the trial diet (if one has been fixed) for such period as appears to them to be appropriate and may, if they think fit, direct that such period (or some part of it) shall not count towards any time limit applying in respect of the case.

(2C) If leave to appeal under subsection (2A) above is granted by the court it shall not proceed to trial at once under paragraph (*a*) of section 337 of this Act; and paragraph (*b*) of that section shall be construed as requiring sufficient time to be allowed for the appeal to be taken.

(2D) In disposing of an appeal under subsection (2A) above the High Court may affirm the decision of the court of first instance or may remit the case to it with such directions in the matter as they think fit; and where the court of first instance had dismissed the complaint, or any part of it, may reverse that decision and direct that the court of first instance fix a trial diet (if it has not already fixed one as regards so much of the complaint as it has not dismissed)."

NOTE

A party seeking review of a decision on competency and relevancy does not have the right to appeal to the High Court, but must obtain the leave of the court.

CHAPTER 17

PROCEDURES INVOLVING CHILDREN

The matters discussed in this chapter are principally—but not exclusively—concerned with children as offenders. The involvement of children in criminal offences is rightly a matter of great concern, whether that involvement be as offender, victim, or even in a less central role as witness. This concern is reflected not only in the existence of special procedures for young offenders but also in the existence of rules protecting young persons who have become involved in the criminal process from publicity and, in some cases, from being subjected to potentially harmful or distressing court appearances.

As offenders, children may be dealt with, broadly, in one of two ways: by prosecution under the Criminal Procedure (Scotland) Act 1975, as modified or adapted by special provisions and administrative practice, or by the non-criminal procedure of reference to a children's hearing provided for by Part III of the Social Work (Scotland) Act 1968, as amended.

A.   ARREST, DETENTION, QUESTIONING

The general rules regarding arrest, detention and questioning of suspected persons apply in the case of children, although there are some specialities. Thus, the provisions of sections 19 and 305 of the 1975 Act (intimation of arrest and access to a solicitor) and section 3 of the 1980 Act (intimation of arrest to a third party and intimation of detention to a solicitor and a third party) apply in the case of a child for these purposes. Section 3(3) of the 1980 Act also provides that where the person arrested or detained appears to be a child, intimation of arrest or detention should be notified to the child's parent who should, normally, be granted access to the child. See also, section 49(2) of the Criminal Justice (Scotland) Act 1987 (detention of child by customs officers) and section 3B of the 1980 Act (detention of child in connection with terrorism). For a full discussion of these rules, see Chaps. 4 and 5 above.

Where someone, who is, apparently, a child, is arrested or detained he or she should be brought forthwith before a sheriff sitting summarily. Where this is not possible, a police officer of the rank of inspector or above or the officer in charge of the police station to which the child is brought must inquire into the case, and may release the child on a written undertaking by the child or its parent that the child will attend at the hearing of the charge. The police officer is obliged to release the child unless the charge is one of homicide or other "grave crime" or it is necessary in the child's interest to remove him from association with any reputed criminal or prostitute or the police officer has reason to believe that the child's liberation would defeat the ends of justice. See, generally, the 1975 Act, section 296(1).

Where a child is not so released, he should be detained in a "place of safety," other than a police station, until he can be brought before a sheriff sitting summarily, unless the police officer certifies that it is impracticable to do so, or that he is of so unruly a character that he cannot safely be so detained or that by reason of his state of health or of his bodily or mental condition it is inadvisable for him to be so detained: 1975 Act, section 296(2). For these purposes, a "place of safety" is a place of safety within the meaning of section 94(1) of the Social Work (Scotland) Act 1968, *i.e.* "any residential or other establishment provided by a local authority, a police station, or any hospital, surgery or other suitable place, the occupier of which is willing temporarily to receive a child."

B.   PROSECUTION

(i)   General Provisions

1.   Criminal Procedure (Scotland) Act 1975, ss. 170 and 369
"It shall be conclusively presumed that no child under the age of eight years can be guilty of any offence."

2.   Social Work (Scotland) Act 1968
"**31.**—(1) No child under the age of sixteen years shall be prosecuted for any offence except on the instructions of the Lord Advocate, or at his instance; and no court, other than the High Court of Justiciary and the sheriff court, shall have jurisdiction over a child under the age of sixteen years for an offence. . . .

30.—(1) Except where otherwise expressly provided, a child for the purposes of this Part of this Act means—
  (*a*) a child who has not attained the age of sixteen years;
  (*b*) a child over the age of sixteen years who has not attained the age of eighteen years and in respect of whom a supervision requirement of a children's hearing is in force under this Part of this Act;
  (*c*) a child whose case has been referred to a children's hearing in pursuance of Part V of this Act.

(2) For the said purposes the expression 'parent' includes a guardian.

(3) Where a child attains the age of sixteen years after the date on which a children's hearing first sit to consider his case, but before the date of the conclusion of the proceedings on his case, the provisions of this part of this Act and of any statutory instruments made thereunder shall continue to apply to him in relation to that case as if he had not attained that age."

NOTE

The definition of "child" contained in section 30 applies, broadly speaking, for the purposes of the 1975 Act: 1975 Act, s. 462(1).

3.   M. v. Dean
1973 J.C. 20

The appellant, a 14-year-old boy, was charged on a summary complaint, along with three other persons, with assault. He pleaded not guilty. An objection to the competency of the proceedings was lodged on his behalf on the ground that there was no evidence of instructions having been given for the prosecution by the Lord Advocate. That objection was repelled and the appellant was convicted. At the appellant's request the sheriff stated a case for the opinion of the High Court.

LORD JUSTICE-CLERK (WHEATLEY): "... The essence of the argument advanced on behalf of the appellant is this. Since the appellant is aged 14 he is a child within the meaning of the Social Work (Scotland) Act, 1968. [His Lordship quoted the terms of section 31(1) of the Act and paragraph 3 of the Act of Adjournal (Summary Proceedings) (Children), 1971 and continued—] There is no provision that the complaint against a child should bear to be on the instructions of the Lord Advocate. On the contrary, paragraph 4 of the Act of Adjournal provides that the forms used in such proceedings (which would include the complaint) shall be, *mutatis mutandis*, those applicable to proceedings under the Summary Jurisdiction (Scotland) Act, 1954, with such variations as circumstances may require. In other words, the complaint in the present case should be, as in fact it was, in accordance with the common form set out in Part 2 of the Second Schedule to the Summary Jurisdiction (Scotland) Act, 1954. If in summary proceedings in the Sheriff Court the complaint did not bear *ex facie* to be on the instructions of the Lord Advocate, the Court should be satisfied by some means or other that it was proceeding on the instructions of the Lord Advocate before the Court could entertain it as competent. In the present case no such information was laid before the Court, and the proceedings were accordingly incompetent. Counsel for the appellant maintained that there was a marked distinction between cases proceeding on indictment and cases proceeding by way of summary complaint so far as a 'child' is concerned. In indictable cases the indictment is at the instance of the Lord Advocate, and accordingly there is *ex facie* of the indictment in a 'child' case sufficient to satisfy the requirement that the proceedings have been initiated on the instructions of the Lord Advocate. When the indictment is in the Sheriff Court, and is signed by the Procurator-fiscal, the words 'By authority of Her Majesty's Advocate' must be prefixed to his signature.

But summary prosecutions are in a different position. They are conducted by the Procurator-fiscal and in his own name—Lord Justice-General Clyde in *Hester* v. *MacDonald* [1961 S.C. 370 at p.378, *supra*, Chap. 2]. As this complaint did not bear to be authorised by or to proceed on the instructions of the Lord Advocate, and there was no information before the Court regarding the Lord Advocate's instructions, as could have been produced by an appropriate statement by the Procurator-fiscal depute, the complaint is incompetent.

The point raised is one of general application and importance. The position is quite clear in indictable cases, since the indictment itself produces *ex facie* evidence of the Lord Advocate's instructions. In summary cases the complaint could bear on the face of it that it was proceeding on the instructions of the Lord Advocate and that would suffice to meet the requirements. That, however, might be a cumbersome procedure in some cases, such as the present one where there are several accused some of whom are and some of whom are not 'children,' and I do not consider this style of complaint to be necessary. In my opinion the presumption *omnia rite acta* applies to a complaint at the instance of a Procurator-fiscal where the instructions of the Lord Advocate are required by statute. This is only a presumption and it can be rebutted. If an accused challenges the competency of the proceedings on the ground that such instructions do not appear *ex facie* of the complaint, the presumption will fly off and the Procurator-fiscal will have to satisfy the Court on the point *aliunde*. If no challenge is made, then the presumption is sufficient to regularise the proceedings. But if such a challenge is to be made, at what point in the proceedings should it be taken? Normally it would be at the first diet as a challenge to the competency of the proceedings—section 26 of the Summary Jurisdiction (Scotland) Act, 1954. How can the Procurator-fiscal satisfy the Court *aliunde*? He could, of course, produce written authority. This might be a communication under the hand of the Lord Advocate himself, or of an accredited representative—*Stevenson* v. *Roger* [(1914) 7 Adam 571]. But in my opinion it is not necessary for the Procurator-fiscal to produce written authority. It would be sufficient if he simply made an oral statement. In fact the instructions of the Lord Advocate could be given orally and there would be no written evidence of them. The next question is whether there requires to be individual instructions in each case. In my opinion this is not necessary. General instructions given by the Lord Advocate to cover groups of cases would be sufficient authority for any case within any of the groups. There is nothing in section 31 of the 1968 Act to indicate that the instructions require to be individual and not general.

The learned Advocate-depute informed the Court that at the material time when this prosecution was initiated there were in existence general instructions by the Lord Advocate authorising proceedings in various groups of offences, and the charge was comprehended within one of the groups. This statement was not made by the Procurator-fiscal depute when the challenge was made at the conclusion of the evidence, but then the challenge came too late. That in itself would be sufficient to dispose of this appeal, and I have less hesitation in relying on such a technical solution when it is clear that the requisite instructions had in fact been given by the Lord Advocate. The learned Advocate-depute stated that while such a situation was unlikely to arise, he would like to reserve the Crown's position as to what was required in a case which was not covered by general instructions.

I, too, would prefer to reserve my views on such a situation until it rose as a practical question in relation to actual circumstances. It does not arise here, and on the facts of the present case, viewed in the light of the procedure which I envisage should apply in these circumstances, I am of opinion that the appeal fails."

The court refused
the appeal.

NOTES

1. The Lord Advocate's instructions contain general guidance as to the considerations governing the prosecution of children. Thus, no child under the age of 13 can be prosecuted except on the specific instructions of the Lord Advocate, and all very serious offences, which would normally be tried in the High Court (murder, rape, etc., see *supra*, Chap. 2) will be brought to the attention of the fiscal.

Where the powers of the children's hearing may not be adequate, it may be appropriate to take criminal proceedings. So, for example, it may be appropriate to prosecute in a case involving offensive weapons, since the court has the power to order forfeiture of the weapon, whereas the children's hearing does not.

2. Where a child is to be brought before a court on a criminal charge, notification of the time of the appearance and the nature of the charge must be made by the chief constable of the area in which the offence is alleged to have been committed to the local authority for the area in which the court will sit. On receipt of such notification, the local authority makes certain investigations into the background of the child (home surroundings, school record, health and character of the child). These matters are reported to the court to the extent that the local authority considers that they will assist the court in the disposal of the case: 1975 Act, ss. 40 and 308.

(ii)   Prosecution on Indictment

Since there are no juvenile criminal courts in the Scottish system, prosecution of a child on indictment follows the same pattern as for an adult.

(iii)   Summary Prosecution

As with solemn proceedings, summary prosecution of a child broadly follows the same pattern as for an adult, in the sense that there is no special juvenile court. However, there are special provisions governing procedure in the case of summary prosecution of a child, which are to be found in Part V of the Act of Adjournal (Consolidation) 1988. It should further be noted that the words "conviction" and "sentence" are not used in relation to children dealt with summarily, and any reference in any enactment to a person convicted, a conviction, or a sentence, is, in the case of a child, to be construed as including a reference to a person found guilty of an offence, a finding of guilt or an order made upon a finding of guilt: 1975 Act, s. 429.

The 1975 Act contains a number of provisions designed to protect the interests and welfare of children brought before the criminal courts, both in solemn and summary proceedings. The most important of these is to be found in sections 172 and 371: "Every court in dealing with a child who is brought before it as an offender shall have regard to the welfare of the child and shall in a proper case take steps for removing him from undesirable surroundings." Sections 38 and 306 of the 1975 Act contain provisions intended to ensure the separation of children from adult offenders while detained in a police station or while being conveyed to or from any criminal court.

Where a child is charged with an offence, his parent or guardian may, and, if he can be found and resides within a reasonable distance, shall, be required to attend all stages of the court proceedings against the child, unless the court is satisfied that it would be unreasonable to require such attendance: 1975 Act, ss. 39(1) and 307(1). Where a child has been charged with an offence, the court may order his parent or guardian to give security for his co-operation in securing the child's good behaviour: 1975 Act, ss. 37(1) and 304(1).

C.   Disposal of Child Offenders

(i)   Custodial Measures

Three provisions of the 1975 Act should be noted here: section 205, which concerns the punishment for murder; section 206, which makes general provision for the detention of children convicted on indictment; and section 413, which makes provision for children in respect of whom a finding of guilt has been made in summary proceedings: 1975 Act, s. 429.

A. Detention following conviction in solemn proceedings

Criminal Procedure (Scotland) Act 1975
"Punishment for murder
   205.—(1) ...
   (2) Where a person convicted of murder is under the age of 18 years he shall
not be sentenced to imprisonment for life but to be detained without limit of
time and shall be liable to be detained in such place, and under such
conditions, as the Secretary of State may direct.

Detention of children convicted on indictment
   206. Subject to section 205 of this Act, where a child is convicted and the
court is of the opinion that no other method of dealing with him is appropriate,
it may sentence him to be detained for a period which it shall specify in the
sentence; and the child shall during that period be liable to be detained in such
place and on such conditions as the Secretary of State may direct."

NOTES
   1.   The sentence referred to in section 205(2) is mandatory, and is the
equivalent of life imprisonment in the case of a person aged 18 or over:
R.J.K. v. *H.M. Advocate*, 1991 S.C.C.R. 703.
   2.   In *R.J.K.* v. *H.M. Advocate* (*supra*) the appellant, a 12-year-old boy,
was convicted of the culpable homicide of a three-year-old child.
Psychiatric reports indicated that he had suffered a considerable degree of
disturbance in the past, that this was likely to continue, and that
assessment over a prolonged period would be necessary in order to
determine whether his behaviour pattern would change. The appellant
was sentenced to be detained "without limit of time." He appealed on the
ground, *inter alia*, that the sentence was incompetent. Section 206 provided
that the court should specify the period of detention it was imposing, and
"without limit of time" did not satisfy this requirement. The High Court
held that the order which the trial judge made was competent. In ordering
that the appellant should be detained "without limit of time," he was
specifying a period for the detention. It was true that it was an unlimited
period, but it was still a period which was specified.

B. Detention following a finding of guilt in summary proceedings

Criminal Procedure (Scotland) Act 1975
"Detention of children
   413.—(1) Where a child appears before the sheriff in summary proceedings
and pleads guilty to, or is found guilty of, an offence to which this section
applies, the sheriff may order that he be detained in residential care by the
appropriate local authority for such period, not exceeding one year, as the
sheriff may determine in such place (in any part of the United Kingdom) as
the local authority may, from time to time, consider appropriate.
   (2) This section applies to any offence in respect of which it is competent to
impose imprisonment on a person of the age of 21 years or more."

NOTES

1. For the purposes of section 413, the "appropriate local authority" means, where the child usually resides in Scotland, the regional or islands authority for the area in which he usually resides, and, in any other case, the regional or islands authority for the area in which the offence was committed: 1975 Act, s. 413(3).

2. Where a child is detained in residential care under section 413(1), he shall be released not later than the date by which half of the period specified in the order has elapsed. However, such child may be required by the local authority to submit to supervision until the entire period specified has elapsed: 1975 Act, s. 413(6)(*a*).

The local authority may at any time review the child's case and may, as a result of such review and having regard to the best interests of the child and the need to protect members of the public, release the child unconditionally or for such period and on such conditions as the local authority consider appropriate: 1975 Act, s. 413(6)(*b*).

(ii)   Non-Custodial Measures

The main non-custodial measures available to the court when dealing with adult offenders are:

> absolute discharge (1975 Act, ss. 182 and 383);
> admonition (*ibid.*, ss. 181 and 382);
> community service (Community Service by Offenders (Scotland) Act 1978);
> fines;
> supervised attendance orders in default of payment of a fine (Law Reform (Miscellaneous Provisions) (Scotland) Act 1990);
> compensation orders (1980 Act, Pt. IV);
> forfeiture;
> disqualification; and
> probation (1975 Act, ss. 183 and 384).

For the most part, these measures are available to the court when dealing with child offenders. Certain exceptions and modifications should, however, be noted:

(A)   Community service orders

These may only be employed in respect of offenders aged 16 or over. This will exclude most, but not all, of those offenders falling within the definition of a "child."

(B)   Fines

Generally, the provisions of the 1975 Act governing fines apply in respect of children. However, section 406 of the 1975 Act makes special provision for the detention of a child in default of paying a fine, and a supervised attendance order in default of a fine cannot be imposed on a person under 16.

(C) Probation

The making of probation orders in respect of children is subject to the same rules as adult probation. Rule 145 of the Act of Adjournal (Consolidation) 1988 sets out the procedure to be followed where a child has failed to comply with any of the requirements of a probation order.

(D) Compensation orders

A compensation order may be made against a child, but the limited means of most children are likely to inhibit the making of such orders.

(iii) Remits to Hearings

The 1975 Act contains provision for the involvement of the children's hearings in the disposal of children and certain young offenders brought before the ordinary courts. These provisions do not apply where the offence in question is one for which the sentence is fixed by law: 1975 Act, ss. 173(5) and 372(5).

(A) Children already subject to supervision requirement

Where a child who is subject to a supervision requirement (within the meaning of section 44(1) of the Social Work (Scotland) Act 1968) is found guilty of an offence, the sheriff court shall (whether in summary or solemn proceedings), and the High Court may, request the reporter of the local authority to arrange a children's hearing for the purposes of obtaining their advice as to the treatment of the child. On consideration of that advice the court may, as it thinks proper, dispose of the case itself, or remit the case to the reporter to arrange for the disposal of the case by a children's hearing: 1975 Act, ss. 173(3) and 372(3).

(B) Children not already subject to a supervision requirement

Where a child who is not subject to a supervision requirement is found guilty of an offence, the court may, instead of dealing with the case itself, remit the case to the reporter to arrange for its disposal by a children's hearing, or to arrange a hearing for the purposes of obtaining advice as to the treatment of the child. Where such advice is obtained, the court may, as it thinks fit, dispose of the case itself or remit it to the reporter for disposal by a hearing: 1975 Act, ss. 173(1), (2) and 372(1) and (2).

(C) Persons over 16 but under 18 years of age

Where a person over the age of 16 who is not within six months of being 18, and who is not subject to a supervision requirement, is found guilty before a summary court, that court may request the reporter to arrange a hearing to obtain advice as to the treatment of that person. On consideration of that advice, the court may dispose of the case itself or, where the hearing so advises, remit the case to the reporter to arrange for its disposal by a hearing: 1975 Act, s. 373.

D.   PROTECTION OF CHILDREN IN CRIMINAL PROCEEDINGS

Various measures exist to protect children who are involved in criminal proceedings, whether as the subject of those proceedings, or as a witness in those proceedings. This section considers (i) restrictions on reporting proceedings; and (ii) special procedures for taking evidence from children.

(i)   Restrictions on Reporting

Criminal Procedure (Scotland) Act 1975

"**169.**—(1) No newspaper report of any proceedings in a court shall reveal the name, address or school, or include any particulars calculated to lead to the identification, of any person under the age of 16 years concerned in the proceedings, either—

(a) as being a person against or in respect of whom the proceedings are taken; or

(b) as being a witness therein;

nor shall any picture which is, or includes, a picture of a person under the age of 16 years so concerned in the proceedings be published in any newspaper in a context relevant to the proceedings:

Provided that, in any case—

(i) where the person is concerned in the proceedings as a witness only and no one against whom the proceedings are taken is under the age of 16 years, the foregoing provisions of this subsection shall not apply unless the court so directs;

(ii) the court may at any stage of the proceedings if satisfied that it is in the public interest so to do, direct that the requirements of this section (including such requirements as applied by a direction under paragraph (i) above) shall be dispensed with to such extent as the court may specify;

(iii) the Secretary of State may, after completion of the proceedings, if so satisfied by order dispense with the said requirements to such extent as may be specified in the order.

(2) This section shall, with the necessary modifications, apply in relation to sound and television programmes included in a programme service (within the meaning of the Broadcasting Act 1990)."

NOTES

1. This section applies to solemn proceedings. An identically worded section 374 applies to summary proceedings. Any person who publishes matter in contravention of these provisions is guilty of an offence.

2. Note that the restrictions in section 169 (and section 374) are mandatory. No publicity of the kind referred to is permitted unless covered by proviso (i), (ii) or (iii).

3. Although section 169 does not apply to reports of proceedings before courts in England and Wales or Northern Ireland (s. 169(4)), it does

apply to reports of Scottish proceedings published in those parts of the United Kingdom: 1980 Act, s. 84(5) and (6).

(ii)   Taking Evidence from Children

Giving evidence in court is likely to be a rather bewildering experience for many children, and for some it may be distressing. This is particularly true where the child gives evidence as the victim of an alleged offence. Quite apart from the anxiety associated with recounting, in public, events which may have been bewildering, frightening or even traumatic for the child, the child may suffer additional stress from being confronted with the alleged offender. This is especially the case in sexual offence cases.

At the same time, however, measures taken to reduce the difficulties faced by the child should not, further than strictly necessary, diminish the rights of the accused to confront and challenge the prosecutor's witnesses.

The difficulties facing children in cases of sexual offences were considered, briefly, by the Thomson Committee in their Second Report (paras. 43.31–43.32) and while they noted that some children would face considerable problems in giving evidence, they were unable to find satisfactory alternatives to the traditional methods of giving evidence in court. They therefore proposed (para. 43.32) that the existing procedures should be retained, while emphasising the obligation which rested on all concerned with court proceedings "to create an atmosphere of reassurance when children are being examined."

Problems associated with children, and other vulnerable witnesses, were considered by the Scottish Law Commission in a discussion paper and a report on *The Evidence of Children and Other Potentially Vulnerable Witnesses* (Scottish Law Commission No. 125, H.C.P. 161, 1990). The report proposed a number of ways of reducing stress and anxiety, both in relation to the taking of evidence by conventional means and by alternative ways of adducing the evidence of children. The former included minimising the "strangeness" of court proceedings by the removal of wigs and gowns by the judge, counsel and solicitors while a child is giving evidence, positioning a child witness at a table in the well of the court along with the judge, counsel and solicitors rather than in the witness box, and permitting a relative or other supporting adult to sit alongside the child while he or she gives evidence (report, para. 2.22). The Commission also recommended more formal changes to the manner in which evidence could be taken from a child witness. The following provisions give effect to these recommendations, which are also reinforced by a Memorandum to judges by the Lord Justice-General, dated July 26, 1990.

1.   Law Reform (Miscellaneous Provisions) (Scotland) Act 1990

"Evidence of children through television link in criminal proceedings

56.—(1) Subject to subsections (2) and (3) below, where a child has been cited to give evidence in a trial, the court may, on an application being made to it, authorise the giving of evidence by the child by means of a live television link.

(2) The court may grant an application under subsection (1) above only on cause shown having regard in particular to—

(a) the possible effect on the child if required to give evidence, no such application having been granted; and (*b*) whether it is likely that the child would be better able to give evidence if such application were granted.

(3) In considering whether to grant an application under subsection (1) above, the court may take into account, where appropriate, any of the following—

(*a*) the age and maturity of the child;

(*b*) the nature of the alleged offence;

(*c*) the nature of the evidence which the child is likely to be called on to give; and

(*d*) the relationship, if any, between the child and the accused.

Identification of accused by child

58. Where a court has, or is deemed to have, granted an application made under section 56 of this Act in relation to a child cited to give evidence in a trial, and the child gives evidence that he recalls having identified, prior to the trial, a person alleged to have committed an offence, the evidence of a third party as to the identification of that person by the child prior to the trial shall be admissible as evidence as to such identification."

2. Prisoners and Criminal Proceedings (Scotland) Act 1993

"**34.** Subject to section 35 of this Act, where a child has been cited to give evidence in a trial, the court may, on application being made to it authorise the use of a screen to conceal the accused from the sight of the child while the child is present to give evidence; but arrangements shall be made to ensure that the accused is able to watch and hear as the evidence is given by the child.

35. Subsections (2) and (3) of section 56 (restrictions on power of court to grant application for child's evidence to be given by means of live television link) and sections 57 (transfer of case where accommodation or equipment is lacking) and 58 (identification of accused by child whose evidence is given by such link) of the Law Reform (Miscellaneous Provisions) (Scotland) Act 1990 shall apply in respect of an application under section 33(1) or 34 of this Act as those provisions of that Act apply in respect of an application under subsection (1) of the said section 56; and in sections 33 and 34 of this Act 'child', 'court' and 'trial' have the same meanings as in the said sections 56 to 58."

3. Memorandum by the Lord Justice-General on Child Witnesses

"**1.** The following memorandum of guidance has been prepared at the suggestion of the Scottish Law Commission: see Report on the Evidence of Children and Other Potentially Vulnerable Witnesses (Scot. Law Com. No. 125). Its purpose is to provide assistance to judges in the exercise of their discretionary powers, where a child is to give evidence by conventional means in open court, to put the child at ease while giving evidence and to clear the court of persons not having a direct involvement in the proceedings.

2. The general objective is to ensure, so far as is reasonably practicable, that the experience of giving evidence by all children under the age of 16 causes as little anxiety and distress to the child as possible in the circumstances.

3. The following are examples of the measures which may be taken, at the discretion of the presiding judge, with a view to achieving that objective—

(*a*) the removal of wigs and gowns by the judge, counsel and solicitors;

(*b*) The positioning of the child at a table in the well of the court along with the judge, counsel and solicitors, rather than requiring the child to give evidence from the witness box;

(*c*) Permitting a relative or other supporting person to sit alongside the child while he or she is giving evidence;

(*d*) The clearing from the court room of all persons not having a direct involvement in the proceedings.

4. In deciding whether or not to take these or similar measures, or any of them, the presiding judge should have regard to the following factors—

(a) The age and maturity of the child.

In general the younger the child the more desirable it is that steps should be taken to reduce formality and to put the child at ease while giving evidence.

(b) The nature of the charge or charges, and the nature of the evidence which the child is likely to be called upon to give.

Particular care should be taken in cases with a sexual element or involving allegations of child abuse especially where the child is the complainer or an eye witness. Children directly involved in such cases are likely to be especially vulnerable to trauma when called upon to give evidence in the presence of the accused. The giving of evidence of a relatively formal nature, especially in the case of an older child, is unlikely to cause anxiety or distress and in such cases it will rarely be necessary to take special measures in the interests of the child.

(c) The relationship, if any, between the child and the accused.

A child who is giving evidence at the trial of a close relative may be especially exposed to apprehension or embarrassment, irrespective of the nature of the charge. The positioning of the child and the support of a person sitting alongside the child while giving evidence are likely to be of particular importance in these cases.

(d) Whether the trial is summary or on indictment—

While informality may be easier to achieve in summary cases, the presence of a jury in cases taken on indictment is likely to present an anxious or distressed child with an additional cause for anxiety or distress. This makes it all the more necessary under solemn procedure that steps should be taken to put the child at ease.

(e) Any special factors placed before the court concerning the disposition, health or physique of the child.

All children are different, and judges should take each child's particular circumstances into account before deciding what steps, if any, should be taken to minimise anxiety or distress.

(f) The practicability of departing from normal procedure, including the size and layout of the court and the availability of amplification equipment.

Whatever steps are taken, a child witness who gives evidence by conventional means must remain visible and audible to all those who have to hear and assess the evidence, including the jury and the accused.

5. In all cases before a witness under 16 years is led in evidence an opportunity should be given to those representing the Crown and the defence to address the judge as to what special arrangements, if any, are appropriate. Under solemn procedure such representations should be made outwith the presence of the jury and preferably before the jury is empannelled or at least before the commencement of the evidence.

6. If a relative or other supporting person is to sit alongside the child, that person should not be a witness in the case and he or she should be warned by the judge at the outset not to prompt or seek to influence the child in any way in the course of the evidence.

7. The clearing of the court while a child is giving evidence will normally be appropriate in all cases which involve an offence against, or conduct contrary to, decency or morality: see section 166 and section 362 of the Criminal Procedure (Scotland) Act 1975. In other cases this should only be done if the judge is satisfied that this is necessary in order to avoid undue anxiety or distress to the child. The statutory provisions that bona fide representatives of a newspaper or news agency should not be excluded should be applied in all cases.

8. When taking any of the measures described above the judge should have regard to the court's general duty to ensure that the accused receives a fair trial and is given a proper opportunity to present his defence.

J. A. D. HOPE
LORD JUSTICE-GENERAL

26 July 1990"

NOTES

1.   Generally, no child under 14-years-of-age (other than an infant in arms) is permitted to be present in court during the trial of any other person, or during any proceedings preliminary thereto, except during such time as his presence is required as a witness or otherwise for the purposes of justice: sections 165 and 361, 1975 Act.

2.   Where a child is called as a witness in proceedings relating to an offence against decency or morality, the court may direct that persons not directly concerned in the case shall be excluded during the taking of the evidence: 1975 Act, ss. 166 and 362, provided that nothing in these sections authorises the exclusion from court of bona fide representatives of a newspaper or news agency: *ibid.*

3.   In the case of certain proceedings (such as cases of offences against the Sexual Offences (Scotland) Act 1976) in which the alleged victim is under 17, the case may be proceeded with and determined in the absence of that person if the court is satisfied that his or her attendance is not essential to the just hearing of the case: 1975 Act, s. 167.

4.   There is no age below which a child is not a competent witness in a criminal trial. In *Rees* v. *Lowe*, 1989 S.C.C.R. 664 (a case involving a three-year-old witness), the High Court approved the following passage from Dickson on *Evidence* (vol. ii, para. 1548):

"the competency of a young witness has to be determined by the judge, after a preliminary examination of the child, and other evidence (if necessary) as to his intelligence."

The court stressed the importance, in cases involving child witnesses, of the judge determining at the outset whether the witness "knows the difference between telling the truth and telling lies" and of admonishing the witness as to the importance of telling the truth. It was held in *Anderson* v. *McFarlene* (1899) 1 F. (J.) 36 that whether a child or young person called as a witness should be required to take the oath before giving evidence is a matter for the discretion of the trial judge, but it appears to be accepted in *Rees* v. *Lowe* that where the child is under 12-years-of-age, the child may not be sworn but should be admonished to tell the truth. In *M.* v. *Kennedy*, 1993 S.C.L.R. 69, which was an appeal to the Inner House against a decision of a sheriff on a referral under section 42 of the Social Work (Scotland) Act 1968, it was held that in order to decide whether a child was admissible, it was not necessary for a court to establish *ab ante* that the child was able to give a spontaneous account of events, this being something which related to the quality of the evidence and not to its admissibility. The test of admissibility was whether the child was likely to give truthful evidence.

E.   CHILDREN'S HEARINGS

In line with the recommendations of the interdepartmental Committee on Children and Young Persons (Scotland) (Cmnd. 2306, 1964), Part III of the Social Work (Scotland) Act 1968 established a framework for the treatment and disposal of young persons in need of compulsory measures of care. These procedures are not restricted to disposal of young offenders, although such cases necessarily represent a substantial proportion of the work of those involved in operating the system. The provisions governing the operation of the children's hearings system are lengthy, complex, and not always satisfactory. Any account of criminal procedure in Scotland would, however, be incomplete without at least an outline of the system. The materials in this section attempt to do no more than that, and for a full account of the system the reader is referred to the accounts contained in Renton and Brown, Chap. 19, Kearney, *Children's Hearings and the Sheriff Court*, Martin and Murray, *The Scottish Juvenile Justice System*, Moore and Wood, *op. cit.*, Martin, Fox and Murray, *Children out of Court*, the articles by J. P. Grant at 1971 J.R. 149, 1973 S.L.T. (News) 190, 1974 S.L.T. (News) 213, 1975 J.R. 209, 1978 S.L.T. (News) 301, and by J. Thomson at 1991 S.L.T. (News) 421.

1.   Social Work (Scotland) Act 1968
"Children in need of compulsory measures of care
32.—(1) A child may be in need of compulsory measures of care within the meaning of this Part of this Act if any of the conditions mentioned in the next following subsection is satisfied with respect to him.
(2) The conditions referred to in subsection (1) of this section are that ...
    (g) he has committed an offence...
(3) For the purposes of this Part of this Act 'care' includes protection, control, guidance and treatment.

Formation of children's panels
33.—(1) A panel (to be called 'the children's panel') shall be formed for every local authority area for the purposes of this Part of this Act ...

Children's hearings
34.—(1) Sittings of members of the children's panel, hereinafter referred to as children's hearings, shall be constituted from the panel in accordance with the provisions of this section to perform, in respect of children who may require compulsory measures of care, the functions assigned to those hearings by this Part of this Act.
(2) A children's hearing shall consist of a chairman and two other members and shall have both a man and a woman among the members.

The reporter and deputies
36.—(1) For the purpose of arranging children's hearings and for the performance of such other functions in relation to the children's panel or to children's hearings as may be assigned to him by this Part of this Act, a local authority shall, appoint an officer, whole-time or part-time, to be known as the reporter, and such other officers as deputies of the reporter as may be required."

NOTES

1.   The reporter need not be legally qualified. In the past, this created problems since he or she had no right of audience *qua* reporter before the sheriff on an application under section 42(2)(*c*): *Kennedy* v. *O'Donnell*, 1975 S.L.T. 235. The matter is now governed by section 36A of the 1968 Act (inserted by section 82 of the Children Act 1975) and regulations made thereunder. The Reporters (Conduct of Proceedings before the Sheriff) (Scotland) Regulations 1975 (S.I. 1975 No. 2251) provide that any officer appointed under section 36, and having held an appointment under that section for any period or periods amounting to not less than one year may conduct before the sheriff any proceedings under Part III of the Act which are heard by the sheriff in chambers, or any application under sections 37 to 40 in relation to a warrant.

2.   The reporter may receive information from any person or source that a child may be in need of compulsory measures of care: sections 37 and 38. On receiving such information the reporter conducts an initial investigation. The duty imposed on the police of reporting offences to the appropriate prosecutor has effect so as to include a duty to make reports to the appropriate reporter: section 38(2).

3.   Sections 170 and 369 of the 1975 Act provide that "it shall be conclusively presumed that no child under the age of eight years can be guilty of any offence." In the light of those sections, does a children's hearing have any jurisdiction to deal with a child whose case is referred to it under section 32(2)(*g*)? See the following case:

2.   Merrin v. S.
1987 S.L.T. 193

Lord Justice-Clerk (Ross): "This appeal relates to an application by the area reporter of Tayside under s. 42 of the Social Work (Scotland) Act 1968 craving the sheriff to find whether or not the grounds of referral, not understood by the child, were established. The grounds of referral were that in terms of s. 32 of the said Act the respondent had committed the offences specified, namely, wilful fire raising and giving false information to the police with intent to pervert the course of justice.

Before any evidence was led, the sheriff was informed that the respondent was under the age of eight years. The sheriff accordingly invited submissions on the competency of the application. Having heard the appellant and the solicitor for the respondent, and without hearing evidence, the sheriff dismissed the application on the ground that the respondent was under the age of eight years. The appellant has now appealed against that decision by way of stated case. . . .

The question which arises here is whether it would be competent for a sheriff to find established a ground of referral which alleged that a child under the age of eight had committed an offence.

Counsel for the appellant contended that the sheriff had erred in his conclusion; he contended that ss. 170 and 369 of the Act of 1975 dealt with criminal procedure, whereas the Act of 1968 was concerned with measures of care for the welfare of children; 'child' was defined in s. 30 of the Act of 1968 without reference to any lower age limit, and accordingly he submitted that the various subsections of s. 32 dealt with all children. If the sheriff were correct, he submitted that this meant that subs. (2)(*g*) alone related to children of eight or over instead of all children as in the case of the other subsections. He contended that there was no warrant for holding that subs. (2)(*g*) was concerned only with children of eight or over. He further submitted that the case law regarding responsibility of children was concerned with punishment. He also submitted that the sheriff had erred in dismissing the application without hearing evidence; he was bound to hear evidence as to the facts.

For the respondent, counsel contended that 'offence' in s. 32(2)(g) could only mean a criminal offence; and a criminal offence could not be committed without the necessary mental element being present. A child below a certain age could not have the necessary means rea, and this was much more than a procedural rule. It must be presumed that the legislature in 1968 understood what the age of criminal responsibility was. As regards counsel for the appellant's final submission, counsel for the respondent contended that where it was agreed that a child was under the age of eight, it would be pointless for the sheriff to hear evidence.

It is plain from the terms of the long title of the Criminal Procedure (Scotland) Act 1975, that the purpose of that Act was to consolidate certain enactments relating to criminal procedure in Scotland; this would tend to support the proposition that ss. 170 and 369 are dealing with procedure. However, although Pt. IV of the Children and Young Persons (Scotland) Act 1937 is headed, 'Protection of Children and Young Persons in relation to Criminal Proceedings', the sidenote to s. 55 reads, 'Age of criminal responsibility'. Although a sidenote probably cannot be used as an aid to construction, in the present case, I am of opinion that s. 55 did indeed deal with the age of criminal responsibility, and that that was more than merely procedural. As already pointed out, the provisions now to be found in ss. 170 and 369 of the Act of 1975 are derived from s. 55 of the Act of 1937, and in turn from s. 14(1) of the Act of 1932. The long title of the Act of 1932 is in the following terms: 'An Act to make further and better provision in Scotland for the protection and welfare of the Young and the treatment of Young Offenders; to amend in their application to Scotland the Children Act, 1908, and other enactments relating to the Young; and for objects connected with the purposes aforesaid.' Section 14 appears in Pt. II which is headed, 'Juveniles in need of care or protection and juvenile offenders'. In all the circumstances I am satisfied that what is now enacted in ss. 170 and 369 of the Act of 1975 deals with a matter of substance and not merely of procedure. Irrebuttable presumptions of this kind—presumptions juris et de jure—are normally rules of substantive law (Walker and Walker on *Evidence*, pp.50–51). In Macdonald on *The Criminal Law of Scotland* (5th ed.), at p.271, the view is expressed that the fact that an accused was under eight years of age at the time of the alleged crime and so was incapable in law of committing it, might be treated as a good plea in bar of trial. The authority for that proposition is stated to be s. 55 of the Act of 1937, and in my opinion this supports the view that the statutory provision is substantive and not merely procedural.

I accept that 'child' is defined in the Act of 1968 without reference to a lower age limit, but, when considering the various subsections of s. 32, it is necessary to consider whether the context requires 'child' to be given any lower age limit. Section 32(2)(g) defines one condition which may be applicable to a child—'he has committed an offence'. I agree with counsel for the respondent that 'offence' must mean a criminal offence. The two offences alleged here are common law offences. In my opinion, such common law offences would require mens rea; actus non facit reum nisi mens sit rea. The question thus arises as to whether a child or under eight could have mens rea. In my opinion, that question falls to be answered in the negative. I appreciate that it may be possible to distinguish between 'has committed an offence' and 'been guilty of an offence'. For example, a person may commit an offence, but not be found guilty but granted an absolute discharge (s. 383 of the Act of 1975). But I am quite clear that an offence at common law can only be committed if the accused has mens rea. A child under the age of eight years cannot have mens rea. When considering the earlier common law, when the age of criminal responsibility was seven, Baron Hume said of the law of England: 'In the case of mere infants, or persons under seven years of age, the presumption of freedom from dole is absolute, and does not allow a conviction to be obtained' (*Crimes*, i, 30). On the law of Scotland he said: 'No authority has ever maintained, that a mere infant, one who is under seven years old, is in any case liable to any sort of punishment' (i, 35). Similar views are expressed by Alison: 'Children under *seven* years of age are held to be incapable of crime, and not the object of any punishment' (*Criminal Law*, i, 666). Although both Baron Hume and Alison refer to immunity from punishment, the rules which they propound are much more than rules of procedure; they are rules of substantive law.

In these circumstances, having regard to the terms of ss. 170 and 369 of the Act of 1975, which are also not merely procedural but deal with a matter of substantive law, I am of opinion that a child such as the respondent who was under the age of eight years at the material time could not be guilty of an offence. It follows that the sheriff in the present case was well founded in holding that the ground of referral could not be established.

I would add that even if ss. 170 and 369 of the Act of 1975 were regarded as solely procedural, I am of opinion that they would still be applicable where the sheriff was determining whether or not this particular ground of referral had been established. In terms of s. 42(6) of the Act of 1968, where the applicant is relying on s. 32(2)(*g*), the sheriff in hearing the application shall apply to the evidence relating to that ground the standard of proof required in criminal procedure. In my opinion, in such proceedings he would be bound to apply the irrebuttable presumption that a child under the age of eight years is incapable of committing a crime.

Counsel for the appellant contended that in any event the sheriff was not entitled to dismiss the application without hearing evidence. In support of this submission, he drew attention to the terms of s. 42(5) and (5) of the Act of 1968, and contended that these provisions clearly envisaged that the sheriff would hear evidence. He also founded upon the terms of the Act of Sederunt (Social Work) (Sheriff Court Procedure Rules) 1971, rule 8(1) which is in the following terms: [his Lordship quoted the rule and continued:] He also founded on *McGregor* v. *D.*

I entirely accept that in the normal case where an application has been made under s. 32, evidence will be led. The present case, however, is a somewhat special one. The age of the respondent was not in dispute, and it was agreed that he was under the age of eight at the material time. In these circumstances, if the respondent's argument was well founded and the submissions for the appellant were not well founded, there would be no point whatsoever in the sheriff hearing evidence.

In all the circumstances I am of opinion that the sheriff reached the correct conclusion in this case. I would accordingly move your Lordships to answer the question in the case in the affirmative and to refuse the appeal.

It may well be thought unfortunate that s. 32(2)(*g*) does not apply to a child under the age of eight, but that is a consequence of what Parliament enacted in 1968. Only Parliament can alter the law applicable to children of this age."

LORD DUNPARK (*Diss.*) "The issue in this case stated under s. 50(1) of the Social Work (Scotland) Act 1968 (hereinafter referred to as 'the Act') is whether the word 'offence', where it occurs in s. 32(2)(*g*) of the Act, falls to be read as one would read it in a statute relating to crime, that is to say, as an act which constitutes a criminal offence of which the prerequisite is criminal intent or dole. I know of no legal use of the word 'offence' in any other sense, but I am not convinced by the sheriff's reasoning that it must properly be construed in that sense in s. 32(2)(*g*).

Here we have a child aged seven years referred by the area reporter to a children's hearing under s. 39(3) of the Act for their decision whether the child was in need of compulsory measures of care. The grounds of referral were that the child had committed two offences within the meaning of s. 32(2)(g), namely, those of wilful fire raising and of giving false information to the police with intent to pervert the course of justice. The hearing were not satisfied that the child understood the chairman's explanation of both grounds of referral and directed the reporter in terms of s. 42(7) to apply to the sheriff for a finding as to whether either of the grounds were established. Having heard the reporter and a solicitor for the child, but without hearing evidence, the sheriff dismissed the application on the ground that the child was under eight years of age. His reasons were that, as ss. 170 and 369 of the Criminal Procedure (Scotland) Act 1975 stated: 'It shall be conclusively presumed that no child under the age of eight years can be guilty of any offence', this child must be presumed to have been incapable of formulating the criminal intent necessary for the commission of an offence within the meaning of s. 32(2)(g). The sheriff said that 'committing an offence' meant exactly the same thing as 'being guilty of an offence', carrying the same implication of ascription of responsibility.

At first sight this may seem to be a logical proposition but, in my opinion, it ignores the radical distinction between our criminal law and procedure in relation to children and the philosophy of Pt. III of the Act which replaced the concept that children who committed criminal offences should be prosecuted and punished with a totally different concept that children in need of compulsory measures of care should receive 'protection, control, guidance and treatment' (see s. 32(3) of the Act).

Prior to the 1968 Act, children from the age of eight upwards could be prosecuted for crimes and offences in the High Court, the sheriff courts or in the juvenile courts, introduced by the Children and Young Persons (Scotland) Act 1932, which was re-enacted in 1937. Sections 14 and 55 of these Acts were in the same terms as ss. 170 and 369 of the Criminal Procedure (Scotland) Act 1975. Section 14 of the 1932 Act innovated upon the common law which presumed that children under seven years of age were incapable of crime and that they should not therefore be prosecuted in criminal courts (see Alison, i, 666 and Hume on *Crimes*, i, 35). The 1932 and 1937 Acts empowered juvenile courts to make orders in relation to children and young persons who were in need of care or protection, and s. 6(1) of the 1932 Act seemed to have supplied the basis for s. 32(2) of the 1968 Act except that the commission of an offence was not included in s. 6(1). The reason for that omission was, of course, that, if a child or young person aged eight or over committed an offence, the child was prosecuted. The 1968 Act, however, converted the prosecution rule into the exception in respect that s. 31 provides inter alia that: 'No child shall be prosecuted for any offence except on the instructions of the Lord Advocate, or at his instance.' The subsequent sections makes it clear that, with the exception of s. 31, every child who commits an offence is not to be prosecuted but is to be referred to a children's hearing, who may, if that ground of referral is accepted or proved, make supervision requirements in terms of s. 44. So, apart from s. 31, the emphasis is upon 'control, guidance and treatment'.

It is plain that in ss. 31(1) and 32(2)(d) and (e) the word 'offence' means an offence for which the offender may be prosecuted and convicted in criminal proceedings, so the conclusive presumption that no child under eight may be convicted of any offence applies. The question is whether that conclusive presumption must also be applied to s. 32(2)(g).

'Offence' is not defined in the Act, and the prima facie inference is that, wherever the word 'offence' is used in this Act, it bears the same meaning. The result of that would be that every child under eight, who committed an act which would be an offence if committed by a child of eight or over, would be outwith the jurisdiction of a children's hearing and would therefore be deprived of the compulsory measures of care which he might require. In his note the sheriff says: 'If a young child is in need of compulsory measures of care I would have thought some other paragraph of s. 32(2) would be available and much more appropriate.' He does not, however, suggest which other paragraphs could be applied in this case. The child has not yet been found to have committed the offence alleged, but what he is alleged to have done is to set fire to a quantity of baled straw stored in a shed and to have subsequently told lies to the police that he saw two other persons running away from the locus. In my opinion, none of the other conditions specified in s. 32(2) could have been applied on these narrow grounds. The fact that the child may have committed the two acts specified does not, in my opinion, necessarily demonstrate that he is beyond the control of his parent. A well behaved child under eight years of age, who has always been amenable to his parents' discipline, is capable of committing an isolated act of vandalism. It may be said that in such a case the reporter would decide in terms of s. 39(1) that referral was unnecessary, but that is not the inevitable result. It would be clearer, simpler and without any imputation against the parents' ability to control such a child for the reporter to refer a child under eight years of age on the ground that he had committed an offence. That would enable the hearing to inquire into the true ground of referral and to consider whether or not the child was in need of compulsory measures of care. Unless the Act permits a child under eight to be referred to a hearing for the commission of an offence, the reporter may be forced to refer on the spurious ground that the child is beyond the control of his parent.

I am of opinion that I am entitled to have regard to the purpose of this Act and to construe s. 32(2)(g) in accordance with that purpose. The purpose is obvious. It is to take all children out of the scope of criminal procedure, unless the Lord Advocate decides otherwise, and to subject them instead to the caring jurisdiction of children's hearings composed of lay members. As Lord Reid said in *Gartside* v. *I.R.C.* at p.612: 'It is always proper to construe an ambiguous word or phrase in light of the mischief which the provision is obviously designed to prevent, and in light of the reasonableness of the consequences which follow from giving it a particular construction.' I regard the phrase 'has committed an offence' in s. 32(2)(g) as ambiguous, because in criminal parlance it excludes a child under the age of eight but in the context of this Act it may include children under that age.

'Child' is defined in s. 30(1)(a) of the Act as 'a child who has not attained the age of sixteen years'. All the conditions in s. 32(2) which, if satisfied, suggests that a child may be in need of compulsory measures of care, with the possible exception of condition (g) (the commission of an offence), are unqualified quoad the age of the child and comprehend every child under the age of 16, whether or not below the age of eight. There is therefore no indication in this Act that the legislature intended children under eight years of age to be exempt from reference under condition (g). It has been stressed more than once than once that the hearing procedure is civil, not criminal. In *McGregor* v. *D.*, 1977 S.L.T. at p.185, the Lord President (Emslie) said this: 'The Social Work (Scotland) Act 1968 was conceded to provide compulsory measures of care for children in need of such care and, in particular, for any child who 'has committed an offence'. Such a child is no longer, save in an exceptional case, to be subject to prosecution or conviction, or the jurisdiction of the ordinary criminal courts. The scheme of the Act is the search for a solution which will be in the best interests of the delinquent child and other children in need of care. It is not surprising, therefore, to find that the body responsible for considering and disposing of a child's case is a lay body, that the reporters need not be lawyers, that the procedure, without pleadings or pleas on behalf of the child in question, may be conducted without the intervention of lawyers, and is intended to be quite informal (see *Kennedy* v. *B*). In no sense are proceedings under Pt. III of the Act criminal proceedings. They are, on the contrary, civil proceedings sui generis (*McGregor* v. *T.*, and *Kennedy* v. *O.*). To such proceedings accordingly, although the basic rules of evidence must be observed in applications before the sheriff, the ordinary codes of civil and criminal procedure do not apply.' At p.187 Lord Cameron said this: 'The procedure introduced by the statute [the 1968 Act] is novel and without parallel in the familiar course of civil or criminal process. The proceedings are in no sense criminal nor are they governed by the rules of procedure which for long have regulated procedure in the sheriff court. Indeed, the plain intention of the legislation is to introduce a simplicity of procedure avoiding, as far as possible, technicalities of legal process which will, on the one hand, enable the requisite action in the interest and for the benefit of the child to be taken by panels of laymen while, at the same time, providing an effective and simple structure within which the purpose of the legislation can be secured. This being so, I do not think it is appropriate or even competent to look outside the statute or the relevant rules to interpolate into this very simple procedural scheme the more elaborate and technical rules of formal process in the courts, be they civil or criminal.' I therefore feel free to regard the conclusive presumption stated in ss. 170 and 369 of the 1975 Act as applicable only to criminal proceedings, confined, as these sections are, to solemn and summary proceedings respectively.

I appreciate that my construction involves adding to 'has committed an offence' the words 'and, in respect of a child under eight years of age, has committed an act which would have been an offence but for the age of the child', or other words to the same effect; but I am convinced that this addition is essential if the Act is to achieve its purpose. I would therefore answer the question posed in the negative, namely, that the sheriff was not entitled to dismiss the application on the ground that the child was under the age of eight years."

3. Social Work (Scotland) Act 1968
"**Action on initial investigation by reporter**

39.—(1) Where the reporter decides that no further action on the case is required, he shall, where he considers this to be the proper course, so inform the child and his parent and the person who brought the case to his notice, or any of those persons.

(2) Where the reporter considers it to be the proper course, he shall refer the case to the local authority with a view to their making arrangements for the advice, guidance and assistance of the child and his family in accordance with Part II of this Act.

(3) Where it appears to the reporter that the child is in need of compulsory measures of care, he shall arrange a children's hearing to whom the case shall stand referred for consideration and determination.

(4) Where the reporter has arranged a children's hearing in pursuance of the last foregoing subsection, he shall request from the local authority a report on the child and his social background and it shall be the duty of the authority to supply the report which may contain information from any such person as the reporter or the local authority may think fit.

(5) Where the reporter has decided that no further action on the case is required, or has taken action in pursuance of subsection (2) of this section, he shall not thereafter take action under subsection (3) of this section in relation to the same facts."

NOTES

1.   There is no obligation on the part of the reporter to notify the child or its parents that the reporter has received information concerning the child,

nor is there any obligation, where he decides that no further action is required, to inform the child or its parents that he has conducted an initial investigation.

2. Children's hearings are conducted in private, in accommodation which must be dissociated from criminal courts and police stations: 1968 Act, ss. 35(1) and 34(3).

3. Where a child is notified that his case has been referred to a children's hearing he is obliged to attend that hearing, unless the hearing is satisfied that it would be detrimental to the interests of the child to be present at the hearing of his case, and in that event the case, in whole or in part, may be considered in the absence of the child: 1968 Act, s. 40(1) and (2).

4. The parent of a child has a right to attend a hearing, and is required to attend unless the hearing are satisfied that it would be unreasonable to require such attendance, or that such attendance would be unnecessary to the consideration of the case: 1968 Act, s. 41.

4. Social Work (Scotland) Act 1968
"Conduct of children's hearing and application to sheriff for findings

42.—(1) Subject to the provisions of subsection (7) and (8) of this section, at the commencement of a children's hearing, and before proceeding to the consideration of the case, it shall be the duty of the chairman to explain to the child and his parent the grounds stated by the reporter for the referral of the case for the purpose of ascertaining whether these grounds are accepted in whole or in part by the child and his parent.

(2) Thereafter—
(a) where the child and his parent accept that grounds stated by the reporter for the referral the hearing shall proceed;
(b) where the child and his parent accept those grounds in part and where the children's hearing consider it proper so to do the hearing may proceed in respect of the grounds so accepted; and
(c) in any other case, unless they decide to discharge the referral, the children's hearing shall direct the reporter to make application to the sheriff for a finding as to whether such grounds for the referral, as are not accepted by the child or his parent, are established having regard to the provisions of section 32 of this Act.

(3) It shall be the duty of the chairman of a children's hearing who have made a direction under the last foregoing subsection to explain to the child and his parent the purpose for which the application to the sheriff is being made, and to inform the child that he is under an obligation to attend at the hearing of the application, and where a child fails to attend the hearing of the application the sheriff may issue a warrant for the apprehension of the child; and any warrant so issued shall be authority for bringing him before the sheriff and for his detention in a place of safety until the sheriff can hear the application, but a child shall not be detained under this subsection for a period exceeding seven days or after the sheriff has disposed of the application.

(4) An application under subsection (2) of this section shall be heard by the sheriff in chambers within twenty-eight days of the lodging of the application and, without prejudice to their right to legal representation, a child or his parent may be represented at any diet fixed by the sheriff for the hearing of the application.

(5) Where a sheriff decides that none of the grounds in respect of which the application has been made has been established for the referral of a case to a

children's hearing, he shall dismiss the application and discharge the referral in respect of those grounds.

(6) Subject to subsection (6A) of this section, where the sheriff is satisfied on the evidence before him that any of the grounds in respect of which the application has been made has been established he shall remit the case to the reporter to make arrangements for a children's hearing for consideration and determination of the case, and where a ground for the referral of the case is the condition referred to in section 32(2)(g) of this Act, the sheriff in hearing the application shall apply to the evidence relating to that ground the standard of proof required in criminal procedure.

(6A) Notwithstanding the provisions of subsection (2)(c) of this section, where, in the course of the proceedings before the sheriff, the child and his parent accept any of the grounds in respect of which the application has been made, the sheriff may dispense with the hearing of evidence relating to that ground unless he is satisfied that in all the circumstances such evidence should be heard, and deem that ground to have been established for the purposes of this section.

(7) Where a children's hearing are satisfied that the child for any reason is not capable of understanding the explanation of the grounds of referral required by subsection (1) of this section, or in the course of, or at the conclusion of that explanation, it appears not to be understood by the child, the hearing shall, unless they decide to discharge the referral, direct the reporter to make application to the sheriff for a finding as to whether any of the grounds for the referral have been established, and the provisions of this section relating to an application to the sheriff under subsection (2)(c) thereof shall apply as they apply to an application under that subsection except that where any of the grounds for the referral are accepted by the child's parent, whether or not accepted by the child, then, notwithstanding subsection (6A) of this section, the sheriff may dispense with the hearing of evidence relating to that ground if he is satisfied that in all the circumstances it would be reasonable to do so.

(8) The acceptance by a parent of the grounds of referral shall not be a requirement to proceeding with a case under this section where the parent is not present."

NOTES

1. In *Sloan* v. *B.*, 1991 S.L.T. 530 a reporter referred the cases of several children to a hearing. At two preliminary meetings, the hearing decided to dispense with the presence of the children at the initial hearing of their case. At the hearing, the parents of the children refused to accept the grounds of referral (which were not that the children had committed offences, but that offences mentioned in Sched. 1 to the 1975 Act were believed to have been committed against them or against children who were members of the same households, and that they were falling into bad associations or were exposed to moral danger). An application was then made to the sheriff for proof of the grounds of referral in the case of each child. The sheriff dismissed the applications on the ground, *inter alia*, that since, under section 42(1), the chair of the hearing was obliged to explain to the children the grounds of referral at the start of the hearing, the children had been entitled to attend the hearing and it should not have dispensed with their presence. On appeal, the Court of Session held that while section 40(2) (which allows the hearing to dispense with the presence of the child) of the 1968 Act was expressed as being "without prejudice to the provisions of section 42(1)," its purpose, which was to protect children

against harm or distress, would be defeated if section 42(1) were to be interpreted as always requiring the attendance of the child. In delivering the opinion of the court, the Lord President (Hope) made the following observations (1991 S.L.T. 530 at p.549):

> "We wish it to be understood, before we leave this topic, that what we have just said is not intended to minimise the rights of the children in any way. On the contrary, what we have been doing is to analyse where the balance lies between the two important provisions for their protection which Parliament has laid down in the Act. The protection against harm or distress, which is what s. 40(2) is all about, is as important as the protection against a determination of the case until the grounds for referral have been accepted or established, which is what s. 42(1) is designed to achieve. ... The discretion which is given to the children's hearing in s. 40(2) may seem at first sight to involve a denial of rights to the children. But properly understood its true purpose is that of protection where the children's hearing are satisfied that this is required, and it is important that the opportunity to provide that protection where it is most needed should not be denied to them."

In the circumstances of this case, it seems that the court's approach is the correct one and the balance between the interests of the child was correctly struck. But it should be remembered that this was not a case in which the children were alleged to have committed offences, but rather that they were the victims of offences. It would surely be an exceptional case in which it was thought to be in the child's interests that he or she should be excluded from a hearing which was considering an allegation under section 32(2)(*g*) of the 1968 Act.

2. Where there is a risk of conflict between the child's interests and those of the parent, it is the duty of the chairman to ensure that the interests of the child are safeguarded. This may be done by the appointment of a person to safeguard the child's interests: section 34A.

3. Proceedings before the sheriff are not criminal proceedings, but civil proceedings, to which the ordinary civil rules of evidence apply:

5. McGregor v. T. and P.
1975 S.C. 14.

LORD PRESIDENT (EMSLIE): "These are two appeals by stated case under section 50 of the Social Work (Scotland) Act 1968. The appellant is the Reporter for the County of Dunbarton. The respondents in the first appeal are T., a child within the meaning of Part III of the statute, and his father. In the second the respondents are a child, P., and his mother.

As the stated case in the first appeal discloses, the reporter referred the child to a children's hearing. The grounds of referral, to use the jargon of the statute, were that the child had committed 19 separate offences. These grounds of referral were not accepted by the child or his father. In short they did not accept that the child had committed any of the alleged offences. The reporter was thereupon directed by the children's hearing, acting under section 42(2)(*c*) of the statute, to apply to the Sheriff for a finding as to whether the grounds of referral or any of them were established.

At the hearing of the application before the Sheriff, the child and his mother appeared and were represented by the same solicitor. The reporter then intimated that he did not intend to proceed with 13 of the alleged offences. The child and his mother did not accept the remaining six grounds of referral which are set out in the stated case. In five of these alleged offences the child T.

was said to have acted together with two other boys. One of these was P. He also had been referred to the children's hearing and there was before the Sheriff a similar application for a finding as to whether certain grounds of referral in the case of P. were established. These grounds included the five alleged offences in which he is said to have acted together with T. At the hearing before the Sheriff, P. also appeared with his mother and they were represented by the same solicitor who appeared for the T.s. On the motion of all parties the two applications were heard together and evidence was led by the reporter. At the conclusion of the evidence led by the reporter the Sheriff found that none of the grounds of referral in the case of T. had been established. He accordingly dismissed the application and discharged the referral. He also found that the five grounds of referral common to the two applications had not been established in the case of P.

The short point in these appeals arises from what happened during the proof for the reporter. He had duly cited the mothers of T. and P. and tendered them as witnesses. An objection was taken by the solicitor representing the T.s and the P.s. The Sheriff sustained the objection, holding that neither mother was a competent and compellable witness against her own child. It is the reporter's contention that the Sheriff erred in law in so holding. The first question of law in the cases is accordingly in these terms—'Was I entitled to hold that said Mrs T. and Mrs P., the mothers of said children, were not competent and compellable witnesses at the instance of the appellant?'

Shortly stated the Sheriff's decision proceeded upon the view that although the mother of a child is by the general law of evidence of Scotland both a competent and compellable witness against her child in all criminal proceedings, and is also competent and compellable as a witness at the instance of the opposing party against the interest of her child who is a party to civil proceedings, the provisions of Part III of the Social Work (Scotland) Act 1968, and the terms of the Act of Sederunt (Social Work) (Sheriff Court Procedure Rules) 1971 clearly imply that in hearings of applications by a Sheriff under section 42 of the statute, the mother of a child is neither a competent nor a compellable witness for the reporter.

There is no doubt that before the Sheriff it was not disputed that the hearing before him was a judicial proceeding and that, by the law of Scotland, subject to the alleged innovation introduced by the Social Work (Scotland) Act 1968, the competency and compellability of a mother against the interest of her child in all judicial proceedings is clear. It is, however, necessary at the outset, in view of certain arguments canvassed in the appeals before us, that we should examine briefly these two assumptions on which the hearing before the Sheriff proceeded.

The first question accordingly is as to the nature of the hearing by the Sheriff of an application under section 42 of the Social Work (Scotland) Act 1968. For the respondents, T., Mr Craik at one point appeared to contend that it did not qualify for the description 'judicial proceeding' because of its special nature. In my opinion this contention is quite without substance. The hearing is conducted by the Sheriff *qua* Sheriff under the direction that it must take place in chambers. It is governed by Rules of Court. If he takes a certain view of the facts the Sheriff is empowered to dismiss the application and to discharge the referral in whole or in part. Although he must give his decision orally at the conclusion of a hearing, that decision is then to be embodied in an interlocutor which must be transmitted by the Sheriff Clerk to the parties involved.

In these combined circumstances, the hearing of an application by a Sheriff, notwithstanding its lack of formality, can be regarded as nothing but a 'judicial proceeding.'

The next question is whether the judicial proceeding ought to be regarded as a criminal proceeding. It arises because in an alternative submission, Mr Philip for the respondents in the P. case, sought to persuade us that it ought so to be regarded and, if it were so regarded, that we should accept that by the Law of Scotland, a mother is at least not a compellable witness against her accused child in criminal proceedings in respect that she has an option to decline to give evidence against her child if she is called as a witness by the prosecutor.

In my opinion whatever else this judicial proceeding is it is not a criminal proceeding. Hearings may take place in relation to all or any of the grounds set out in section 32(2) of the Act, many of which have or may have nothing to do with offences of a criminal character. Although the ground set out in section 32(2)(g) is that the child referred has committed an offence, and the standard of proof to be applied by the Sheriff in a hearing directed to that ground is that required in criminal procedure (see section 42(6)), a hearing of an application involving ground 32(2)(g) is not a criminal proceeding, since it is not concerned with a prosecution and it can lead to no conviction. In any event, even if contrary to my opinion, such a hearing were to be regarded as a criminal proceeding it is not now the Law of Scotland, and for over 130 years at least has not been the Law of Scotland, that a parent may decline, if called as a witness against his or her accused child, to give evidence against him. By the early years of the nineteenth century it was clear that a parent was a competent witness against his or her child. I recognise, however, that at that time there was some basis in authority for the proposition that a parent called by the prosecutor was entitled to decline to give evidence against his child. Whatever the scope of the proposition, however, and whether or not it rested upon any sound foundation, the law since 1840 has recognised no such entitlement in such a parent. By section 1 of the Evidence (Scotland) Act 1840 3 and 4 Victoria cap. 59 it was enacted as follows—

'That from and after the passing of this Act it shall by the Law of Scotland be no objection to the admissibility of any witness that he or she is the father or mother, or son or daughter, or brother or sister, by consanguinity or affinity, or uncle or aunt, or nephew or niece, by consanguinity, of any party adducing such witness in any action, cause, prosecution, or other judicial proceeding, civil or criminal; nor shall it be competent to any witness to decline to be examined and give evidence on the ground of any such relationship.'

The important words are these—'nor shall it be competent to any witness to decline to be examined and give evidence on the ground of any such relationship.' By one reading the expression 'such relationship' might, as Mr Philip contended, be restricted to relationship to the 'party adducing' the witness. This, however, is not the only reading which the expression will bear, nor is it the reading which was approved in the case of HMA v. Cairns 2 Swin. 531 decided in 1841. In that case the Court plainly regarded the important words of the section which I have quoted as taking away any option which may formerly have been available to, inter alios, parents, to decline to be examined on the ground of parental relationship to the accused. This construction found contemporary support in Bell's Notes to Hume's Commentaries, Vol. 2, p.249 and has never been questioned since. Further in Dickson on Evidence, as edited by Grierson in 1887, Vol. 2, p.866, the following categorical statement is made. 'By the Act 3 and 4 Vict. c. 59, the privilege enjoyed by the parents and children of accused persons of declining to give evidence against them was abolished; and, in consequence, the pupil children are competent witnesses against the prisoner.' I have only to add that not only has the interpretation placed upon section 1 of the Act of 1840 by the Court in Cairns stood unchallenged for over 130 years, but it is, in my opinion, the only reasonable interpretation which it can bear.

In light of the opinion which I have to this point expressed, the remaining question to be resolved is whether, as the Sheriff has held, Part III of the Social Work (Scotland) Act 1968 and the Rules made in the relevant Act of Sederunt, innovate upon the otherwise universal rule applicable to all judicial proceedings with the result that neither parent of any child may be called as a witness by the reporter in the hearing of any application to secure a finding as to whether any grounds of referral are established.

As I understand them the Sheriff's reasons are these. His first is that the Act of 1968 makes the parent a party to the various proceedings contemplated by Part III. In support of this proposition, he refers to the parent's right under section 41 to attend at all stages of a hearing and, indeed, a parent must attend unless in certain circumstances the hearing rules to the contrary. He also notices that not only must the child accept the grounds of referral if the hearing is to proceed without an application to the Sheriff under section 42 but the parent must accept them as well. In addition he draws attention to the right given to a parent to be represented either separately or jointly with his child and the rights of appeal available to a parent under sections 49 and 50. In my opinion the Sheriff is probably right in saying that a parent is, or in some instances may be, a party in proceedings for the purposes of Part III of the Act. Having said that, however, the fact that a person is a party to judicial proceedings which are not criminal proceedings does not make it incompetent for another party to call him as a compellable witness and by itself, accordingly, this reason does not advance the matter in the respondent's interest. To be fair to the Sheriff I do not understand him to say that it does and he contents himself by saying that because of the special position of the parent prescribed by Part III the 'competency of calling the parent of an accused child as a witness for the prosecution in ordinary criminal procedure is not necessarily applicable.'

The Sheriff's second reason is that the main object of Part III of the Act is the welfare of the child; that the compellability of the parent as a witness for the reporter might often be contrary to the interests of the child; that the interest of the child in having the advice and guidance of his parent in the statutory proceedings, even where a solicitor is employed, and the confidentiality of communications between them, might suffer; and that to allow the parent to be a compellable witness for the reporter before the Sheriff would put a strain upon the parent–child relationship. In my opinion this reason is unsound.

It is no doubt the case that Part III of the Act is designed to secure the welfare of children in the sense that, subject to the provisions of section 31, they are not to be prosecuted for offences and that those children in need of compulsory measures of care should have the appropriate measures applied in their interests. To say, however, that these laudable objects may be frustrated if the parent of a child who has not been prosecuted may be called as a compellable witness by a reporter at a Sheriff's hearing is, with respect to the learned Sheriff, absurd. The better view is that, if the parents were neither competent nor compellable the attainment of the objects of Part III of the Act would in many cases be seriously impeded and children who, *ex hypothesi*, may require compulsory measures of care under direction of a children's hearing may be deprived of them when they are most needed. One has only to look at the various grounds of referral listed in section 32(2) to see that the evidence of a parent may be essential to the establishment of some of them, and if a parent is not to be a competent and compellable witness where the ground is the alleged commission of an offence, that ground would be incapable of being established in many cases, including, in particular, cases where the parent was the victim of the alleged offence. In such situations if the law is as the Sheriff declares it to be, the result might well be that the Lord Advocate would be forced in the public interest and in the interest of the child concerned to prosecute in circumstances in which the aim of the Act is to avoid prosecution.

It is no doubt also the case that Part III of the Act and the relevant Rules recognise that it is in the interests of a child to have the advice and guidance of his parents in course of the statutory proceedings, but there is nothing new in this. These interests of a child may be supposed to have existed as matter of fact before 1937 and although they received statutory recognition in the Children and Young Persons (Scotland) Act 1937, section 42, and in the Act of Adjournal (Summary Proceedings) (Children) 1971, it has never been suggested that these interests afforded any ground of objection to the competency and compellability of a parent as a prosecution witness. I am therefore quite unable to see that they should constitute such a ground of objection in a hearing before the Sheriff under section 42 of the Social Work (Scotland) Act which can in no circumstances result in findings of guilt within the meaning of the criminal law or in conviction of the child of any crime. If, because of the position of the parent as guide and counsellor of the child in connection with any proceedings under Part III of the Act, it could be shown that certain communications made to the parent actually representing a child would, if made to a solicitor in the same situation, be protected by confidentiality, then no doubt objection could be taken to disclosure of the alleged confidential communication, but this in no way goes to the competence or compellability of such a parent as a witness and there is no good reason in law or fairness why it should. As to the strain which might be put upon the parent–child relationship if the parent were to be a competent and compellable witness at the instance of a reporter, I have only to say that such a strain could be expected in even greater measure in many cases whenever a parent is required to give evidence for the prosecution in a criminal trial.

In so far, therefore, as the Sheriff's decision depends upon the provisions of the Social Work (Scotland) Act 1968, I am unable to find in these provisions any colourable justification for it.

The Sheriff's third reason is derived from the Act of Sederunt (Social Work) (Sheriff Court Procedure Rules) 1971 and in particular rule 8 therefore. It can be briefly disposed of. I do not in the first instance understand that an Act of Sederunt made under the powers conferred on the Court by section 34 of the Administration of Justice (Scotland) Act 1933 could competently alter the general law governing the competency and compellability of witnesses in any judicial proceedings in the Sheriff Court for which Rules of Court are required. In any event the Rules in question are plainly procedural only. If an intention to change the law so to the competency and compellability of a parent as a reporter's witness in proceedings under section 42 of the Act of 1968 cannot be discovered in that Act, it certainly cannot be derived from a consideration of the terms of these Rules. In particular, I see nothing difficult in reconciling the right of a parent provided by rule 8(2) to confine himself to making an unsworn statement, with the right of a reporter to call him as a witness if his evidence is required in proof of a ground of referral.

In the whole matter I am of opinion that as was said by the Lord Justice Clerk (Grant) in *Kennedy* v. *B. and Another* 1973 S.L.T. 38 at 41—'the basic rules of evidence must be observed.' I am therefore for answering question 1 in the negative. It follows that the appeals should be allowed and the cases should be remitted back to the Sheriff to enable the reporter to lead the evidence which was wrongly excluded. I regret the necessity for the remit back but it is inevitable. It might have been avoided with obvious advantages in time and expense had the Sheriff taken the course of hearing the evidence to the admission of which objection was successfully taken. This is plainly the course which ought properly to be followed in future in similar circumstances."

NOTE

The sheriff has no power to amend the grounds of referral which are brought before him by the reporter: *McGregor* v. *D.*, 1977 S.L.T. 183.

6.   **Social Work (Scotland) Act 1968**

"**44.**—(1) Subject to the provisions of this Part of this Act a children's hearing, where, after the consideration of his case, they decide that a child is in need of compulsory measures of care, may make a requirement, in this Act referred to as a supervision requirement, requiring him—

(a)   to submit to supervision in accordance with such conditions as they may impose; or

(b)   to reside in a residential establishment named in the requirement and be subject to such conditions as they may impose;

and a condition imposed by virtue of head (a) of this subsection may be a condition as to the place where the child is to reside, being a place other than a residential establishment, and the place may be a place in England or Wales where arrangements have been made in that behalf."

NOTES

1.   No child may continue to be subject to a supervision requirement for any time longer than is necessary in his interest, and where the local authority think that in the interests of the child a requirement should be varied or brought to an end, they shall refer the case to their reporter for review of that requirement by a children's hearing. The hearing may continue the requirement, vary it, or terminate it: 1968 Act, s. 47.

2.   In any event, the supervision requirement is subject to review under section 48 of the 1968 Act by the children's hearing, and no supervision requirement shall remain in force for a period extending beyond one year. Where a requirement is not reviewed within the period of one year from the making or continuing of the requirement it ceases to have effect at the expiration of that period: s. 48(3).

3.   Within the time-table provided for by section 48(4), a child or its parent may require a review of the requirement. If a supervision requirement has not been reviewed during the nine months following its making or its last review, the reporter may arrange for it to be reviewed: s. 48(4A).

4.   A child or parent or both may, within three weeks of the date of any decision of a children's hearing, appeal to the sheriff in chambers against that decision, provided that is a decision as to the final disposal of the hearing: s. 49(1); H. v. McGregor, 1973 S.C. 95.

5.   Appeal lies to the Court of Session by way of stated case on a point of law or in respect of any irregularity in the conduct of the case, at the instance of a child or its parent or both or a reporter acting on behalf of a children's hearing, from any decision of the sheriff under Part III of the 1968 Act: 1968 Act, s. 50.

6.   Section 50 cannot be employed to bring under review the decision of the hearing to impose a supervision requirement where the sole ground of the objection to that requirement is that the treatment prescribed thereby is inappropriate for the child: 1968 Act, s. 50(4).

CHAPTER 18

EXTRAORDINARY REMEDIES

A.   THE *NOBILE OFFICIUM* OF THE HIGH COURT

"In addition to its powers of review, the High Court of Justiciary, as the supreme Court in criminal matters, has, in respect of its *nobile officium*, the power of interfering in extraordinary circumstances, for the purpose of preventing injustice or oppression, although there may not be any judgment, conviction, or warrant brought under review." (Moncreiff on *Review in Criminal Cases*, p.264.)

Procedure is by way of petition to the *nobile officium* of the High Court, and such petitions may be taken by an accused or convicted person, the Crown (see, *e.g.*, *H.M. Advocate* v. *Greene*, 1976 S.L.T. 120) or other aggrieved party (see, *e.g.*, *Wan Ping Nam* v. *Federal German Republic Minister of Justice and Others, post*, and *Lloyds and Scottish Finance Ltd.* v. *H.M. Advocate*, 1974 S.L.T. 3). A single judge of the High Court cannot entertain an application to the *nobile officium*. It must be presented to a quorum of the High Court (three judges): *H.M. Advocate* v. *Lowson*, (1909) 2 S.L.T. 329.

In recent years attempts have been made to invoke the *nobile officium* in a wide variety of situations, but certain guiding principles have fairly clearly emerged:

(i)   The *Casus Improvisus*

Where there is a lacuna, or *casus improvisus*, in a statute, the *nobile officium* may be invoked to remedy the oversight:

Wan Ping Nam v. Federal German Republic Minister of Justice and Others
1972 S.L.T. 220

OPINION OF THE COURT: "This is a petition presented under the nobile officium to the High Court by one Wan Ping Nam, who has been committed as a fugitive offender to the prison of Barlinnie by the sheriff at Greenock. The order so committing him was made under s. 10 of the Extradition Act 1870. The prayer of the petition in effect seeks relief, by way of suspension of the committal order, it being alleged in the petition that it was unlawful, in respect that the petitioner is a British subject. It should be explained that by the Federal Republic of Germany (Extradition) Order (S.I. 1375), which gave effect to the subsisting agreement between Her Majesty's Government and the Federal German Republic for the extradition of fugitive criminals, it is provided inter alia by art. 4 of the First Schedule thereof, that no British subject shall be delivered up by the Government of the United Kingdom to the Government of the Federal Republic of Germany. It follows from these terms of the statutory instrument, under reference to s. 6 of the Extradition Act 1870, that where the alleged criminal is a British subject the Act does not apply in the case of the Federal Republic of Germany; and that no British subject is a person 'liable to be apprehended and surrendered in manner provided by' the Act.

The background against which the petition falls to be considered is briefly as follows. In February 1972 the petitioner was a member of the crew of the motor vessel *Taiping* registered in Bremen in the Federal Republic of Germany. This ship, which may be owned by the Island Navigation Company, Hong Kong, was then on charter to a West German company. While the ship was at sea the chief steward, one Ho On Hing, was the victim of an incident, as the result of which he later died. On 11th February 1972, when the ship called at Campbeltown, the petitioner, who was suspected of the murder of Ho On Hing, was removed from the ship by the police. On 12th February 1972, he appeared on petition before the sheriff at Campbeltown upon a charge of murder, and was committed to prison for further examination. On 18th February 1972, the petitioner was committed to prison until liberated in due course of law. Subsequently, when it was ascertained that the crime with which the petitioner had been charged had been committed on the high seas, he was formally liberated by administrative action. He was, however, at once rearrested and the proceedings with which this petition is concerned were begun. These were proceedings under the Extradition Act 1870.

Essentially what happened was that a warrant for the apprehension of the petitioner as a fugitive criminal was issued by the sheriff at Greenock acting under s. 8 of the Extradition Act 1870. An order from the Secretary of State was then presented to the sheriff signifying that a requisition for the surrender of the petitioner under the Extradition Act 1870 had been made by the Federal German Republic. Thereupon, the sheriff, after a hearing on 3rd May 1972, committed the petitioner to the prison at Barlinnie pending his possible surrender to the Federal German Republic. It is against the order so committing him, which purported to be made under s. 10 of the Act, that this petition is directed.

This petition was served upon the Minister of Justice of the Federal Republic of Germany, the Secretary of State for Scotland and Her Majesty's Advocate. At the hearing before us all three respondents were represented and the primary question for our decision was whether the relief sought by the petitioner was available at the hands of this court.

It is clear from an examination of the Extradition Act 1870 (and the problem before us is not affected by any of the subsequent amendments to that Act) that it was contemplated that proceedings with a view to the extradition of a fugitive criminal would normally be before a police magistrate in England. Indeed the statute is couched in language which plainly has the jurisdiction and the procedure of the English courts primarily in mind. In particular, s. 10, which deals with the stage of committal of the alleged fugitive criminal to prison, is in the following terms:—'10. In the case of a fugitive criminal accused of an extradition crime, if the foreign warrant authorising the arrest of such criminal is duly authenticated, and such evidence is produced as (subject to the provisions of this Act) would, according to the law of England, justify the committal for trial of the prisoner if the crime of which he is accused had been committed in England, the police magistrate shall commit him to prison, but otherwise shall order him to be discharged.

'In the case of a fugitive criminal alleged to have been convicted of an extradition crime, if such evidence is produced as (subject to the provisions of this Act) would, according to the law of England, prove that the prisoner was convicted of such crime, the police magistrate shall commit him to prison, but otherwise shall order him to be discharged.

'If he commits such criminal to prison, he shall commit him to the Middlesex House of Detention, or to some other prison in Middlesex, there to await the warrant of a Secretary of State for his surrender, and shall forthwith send to a Secretary of State a certificate of the committal, and such report upon the case as he may think fit.'

Where a person has been committed under s. 10 the procedure under s. 11 then comes into play. This section, which deals with the surrender of the fugitive criminal upon a warrant granted by the Secretary of State, opens thus:—'If the police magistrate commits a fugitive criminal to prison, he shall inform such criminal that he will not be surrendered until after the expiration of 15 days, and that he has a right to apply for a writ of habeas corpus.'

From what we have said so far it is plain that had the petitioner been committed to prison by a police magistrate in England, relief by way of application to the court for a writ of habeas corpus would have been available to him. As we understand it, this prerogative writ provides, in England, the means by which unlawful detention can be brought to an end by the High Court. It need hardly be said that it does not run in Scotland and is wholly unknown to our law.

We come now to s. 16 of the Act which deals with extraditable crimes committed on the high seas. So far as is relevant to the problem before us it is in the following terms:—

'16. Where the crime in respect of which the surrender of a fugitive criminal is sought was committed on board any vessel on the high seas which comes into any port of the United Kingdom, the following provisions shall have effect:

1. This Act shall be construed as if any stipendary magistrate in England or Ireland, and any sheriff or sheriff-substitute in Scotland, were substituted for the police magistrate throughout this Act, except the part relating to the execution of the warrant of the police magistrate:

2. The criminal may be committed to any prison to which the person committing him has power to commit persons accused of the like crime'. It is as the result of these provisions of s. 16 that the sheriff at Greenock came to commit the petitioner to prison under s. 10 of the Act.

When, however, s. 11 is construed as provided by s. 16, paras. 1 and 2, it will be seen at once that the only form of relief expressly mentioned as being available to a person who has been committed by a sheriff under s. 10, is one which is unknown to the law of Scotland. In this situation, and since the statute, read as a whole, provides no means whereby a person committed by a sheriff in Scotland can seek his release from detention under an unlawful order purporting to be made under s. 10, the question is whether this court can and should under its inherent power to prevent injustice, supply the apparent omission in the Act by affording a remedy to the petitioner. It is to be noted in passing that this is not the only point at which, in the statute, there is an omission to deal with the consequences of a committal order pronounced in Scotland. There appears, indeed, to be a similar omission as regards Scotland in the procedure provided by s. 12 for the discharge of persons committed but not surrendered within two months. By s. 17(4) Parliament expressly recognised the need to secure that his power of discharging a criminal should be available to a judge of any court exercising, in a British possession, the like powers as the court of Queen's Bench exercises in England. As in the case of s. 11, however, the Act gives no recognition to the contingency that a fugitive criminal may have been committed under s. 10 within the jurisdiction of the courts in Scotland.

The answer to this question depends essentially upon the intention of the Act. In our opinion the intention that relief shall be available to all persons committed under s. 10 is plain. This we discover from the express reference to habeas corpus procedure in s. 11. In any event, we cannot decern in the statute any indication of an intention that persons committed by a sheriff in Scotland should be in any less advantageous position than those committed by a police magistrate in England. In these circumstances we are in no doubt that, the statute having disclosed the intention, this court has ample power to provide what the statute has omitted to provide, namely, the means of giving effect to that intention. As we were reminded recently in the case of *Wylie and Another* v. *H.M. Advocate*, 1966 S.L.T. 149, at p.151—'This court, of course, is not a mere creation of recent statutes; it has as Alison, *Criminal Law of Scotland*, Vol. II, p.23, states: "The exclusive power of providing a remedy for all extraordinary or unforeseen occurrences in the course of criminal business whether before themselves or any inferior court. Akin to the well-known nobile officium of the Court of Session is a similar power enjoyed by Justiciary Court". Moncreiff on *Review in Criminal Cases*, p.264, states: "In addition to its power of reviewing, the High Court of Justiciary as the Supreme Court in criminal matters has in respect of its nobile officium the power of interfering in extraordinary circumstances for the purpose of preventing injustice or oppression although there may not be any judgment, conviction or warrant brought under review". The same proposition is to be found in Macdonald on *Criminal Law*, at p.193'. In our opinion, the circumstances of this case to which we have drawn attention are, on any view, extraordinary and we are satisfied that in the exercise of the nobile officium this court may properly examine the allegation of injustice made by the petitioner, and suspend the order under which the petitioner is committed if it should be established that it is unlawful in the respect set out in the petition. In the whole matter, we shall order the respondents to lodge answers to this petition, if so advised, within seven days, when the case will be put out by order for further procedure. This procedure may involve inquiry into the petitioner's claim to be a British subject. Any necessary inquiry will take place before one of our number. In so saying we observe that a similar claim was investigated, de novo, in England, by the court itself, in the case of *Re Guerin* (1889) 58 L.J. 42."

> Answers were lodged. After inquiry
> it was held that the petitioner had
> failed to prove that he was a British
> subject. The court then refused the
> prayer of the petition.

NOTE

The *nobile officium* was invoked by a person in custody where no other remedy existed. The problem arose because the remedy envisaged by the Extradition Act 1870 (*habeas corpus*) is not available in Scotland—a classic *casus improvisus* attributable to the draftsman omitting to bear in mind Scottish procedure when drafting United Kingdom legislation. A similar problem arose in *Lloyds and Scottish Finance Ltd.* v. *H.M. Advocate* (*supra*). The petitioners hired a vehicle to P. under a contract of hire purchase. P. was subsequently convicted of reset, the stolen goods being found in the car. The sheriff made a forfeiture order in respect of the car, under section 23 of the Criminal Justice Act 1972. As the 1972 Act applied to England, section 23(3) afforded the true owners of property forfeited an opportunity to vindicate their rights to the property. That subsection did not apply in Scotland. The court held since Parliament had clearly expressed the intention that the rights of third parties should be protected, but had merely omitted to provide the appropriate machinery for Scotland, the *nobile officium* could be invoked to protect the rights of the petitioners.

(ii) Conflict with Statutory Intention

It is accepted that the *nobile officium* cannot be invoked when to do so would conflict with a statutory intent, express or implied. So, where

Parliament has intentionally conferred a non-reviewable discretion on a judge or court, the *nobile officium* cannot be invoked to circumvent that intention or to review the exercise of that discretion. Conversely, where Parliament has provided a method of appeal or review, it is not competent to refer to the *nobile officium* matters which should be raised under the statutory scheme.

(A) Exclusion of review

1. Bernard Heslin, Petitioner
1973 S.L.T. (Notes) 56

"The Act of Adjournal (Criminal Legal Aid Fees) 1964 (as amended by the Act of Adjournal of 29th November 1968) provided by s. 13(2):—

'It shall be competent immediately on conclusion of the trial for the counsel or solicitor who appeared for the accused to make oral application to the court for a certificate that the case has necessarily been one of exceptional length, complexity or difficulty.

If such a certificate shall be granted, then any limitation contained in the foregoing paragraphs, or such of them as are referred to in such certificate, on the amount of any fee payable shall not apply and such fees shall be allowed, after taking into account all the relevant circumstances of the case, in respect of the work done, as appears to represent fair remuneration according to the work actually and reasonably done, due regard being had to economy.'

The petitioner had acted as a solicitor for a man accused of murder, who pleaded not guilty and tendered a special defence of self-defence. In preparing the case the petitioner precognosced 42 Crown witnesses and 16 defence witnesses, in addition to carrying out a great deal of other work. As questions of forensic medicine arose, he instructed a pathologist to attend the post-mortem. The trial occupied three days, and the accused was eventually convicted of culpable homicide. At the conclusion of the trial counsel, who had been instructed by the petitioner, applied for a certificate under s. 13(2). The trial judge stated that in his opinion the case was no more difficult, complex or longer than the usual murder trial, and refused the application. He also refused to adjourn the hearing of the application to chambers.

There being no provision for appeal, the petitioner presented a petition to the High Court of Justiciary craving the court to exercise its nobile officium by reviewing the trial judge's decision.

The court (Lord Justice-Clerk (Wheatley), Lords Milligan and Kissen) heard the petition on 24th May 1973.

In arguing that the petition was competent and that the decision of the trial judge should be reviewed in respect that he had wrongly exercised his discretion in refusing to adjourn to chambers and in refusing to grant the application, counsel for the petitioner referred to *H.M. Advocate* v. *Gray*, 1969 J.C. 35; *J. P. Hartley* [1968] J.C.L. 191; and *H.M. Advocate* v. *Wylie*, 1966 S.L.T. 149. Counsel for the Crown argued that while the court might exercise its nobile officium where there was a casus improvisus or a lacuna in a statute, as in *Wan Ping Nam*, 1972 S.L.T. 220, in the instant case it could not do so, as there was no casus improvisus but merely an intention in the Act of Adjournal that the trial judge alone should decide. The petition was therefore incompetent.

Eo die the court held that the Act of Adjournal intended that the decision on applications under s. 13(2) should be entirely in the discretion of the trial judge and *refused* the petition as incompetent."

Petition refused.

2. Rae, Petitioner
1982 S.L.T. 233

OPINION OF THE COURT: "This petition invites the court to exercise its nobile officium by reviewing the refusal of the trial judge to grant to the petitioner a certificate under para. 13(2) of the Act of Adjournal (Criminal Legal Aid Fees) 1964 as amended.

The petitioner acted as solicitor for a youth named William Albert Speirs, who, with five co-accused, stood trial on indictment in the High Court upon a charge of murder and a charge of attempted murder. All were in receipt of legal aid. At the conclusion of the trial which lasted for eight days, Speirs and four of his co-accused were convicted as libelled.

According to the petition the petitioner carried out a great deal of work in preparation for this trial, in which Speirs lodged a special defence of alibi, and claims, no doubt correctly, that the maximum fees available to her under para. 6 of the act of adjournal represent wholly inadequate remuneration for her professional services. In these circumstances junior counsel on her instructions moved the trial judge, when the trial had ended, to grant a para. 13(2) certificate on the grounds of the exceptional length, complexity and difficulty of the case, or, alternatively, on the grounds of exceptional length alone. Similar motions were made on behalf of the solicitors acting for all Speirs' co-accused on the single ground that the case had necessarily been one of exceptional length. The motions on behalf of these solicitors were granted at once. The motion on behalf of the petitioner was not.

In the petition it is averred that the senior counsel who was instructed by the petitioner to represent Speirs was a Member of Parliament and was absent on Parliamentary business for some days during the trial. According to the petition it appears that at the hearing of the application on the petitioner's behalf, and thereafter, what happened was as follows:

[His Lordship then narrated the following facts as set out in the petition:]

"In respect of the application made on behalf of the petitioner his Lordship made an observation to the effect that the agents themselves could not have considered the case to be one of exceptional complexity if they had instructed as senior counsel someone who was to be absent for such a significant proportion of the trial. Junior counsel explained to his Lordship that he understood from the agents that senior counsel had confirmed his availability to them for the trial, and that at no time prior to the commencement of the trial were the agents given to understand that senior counsel would be absent for such a proportion of the trial. It was further submitted to his Lordship that notwithstanding his observations regarding complexity, the case was one of exceptional length and at least merited certification on that ground alone. His Lordship indicated that he was not prepared to grant said application to any extent and junior counsel then requested him to adjourn the application for a further hearing in chambers in terms of said paragraph. This request was granted. His Lordship indicated that in his view the petitioner was making very serious allegations against senior counsel whereupon junior counsel indicated that he wished to lodge written submissions in support of the application. In the interim junior counsel would himself speak to the partner in the petitioner's firm who had personally checked in advance on senior counsel's availability and would include in said written submissions a full account of the circumstances in which senior counsel had come to be instructed. A written submission was accordingly prepared and submitted to his Lordship. Said submission dealt with inter alia the circumstances in which senior counsel was instructed and his Lordship indicated that he was willing to hear junior counsel in further amplification thereof. Junior counsel explained that he had thoroughly investigated the matter. He had spoken to

Mr Ross Harper, the senior partner of the petitioner's firm and had ascertained that Mr Harper had spoken to senior counsel on 24 November 1978 regarding his availability for the case, on which occasion senior counsel had confirmed his availability apart from the possibility that he might require to leave the court around mid-afternoon on one day of the trial to attend an evening engagement in Oxford. It was explained that Mr Harper was prepared to give evidence on oath to that effect, and that junior counsel was now specifically instructed to seek certification only on the ground of exceptional length. His Lordship indicated that it would not be necessary for Mr Harper to give evidence on oath, but that he considered the matter as very serious and wished further amplification in writing of the circumstances in which senior counsel came to be instructed as spoken to by junior counsel in support of the written submissions. He specifically indicated that if further specification were forthcoming, he would be prepared to grant the restricted application which was now being made. It was agreed that further written submissions would be prepared, and that a date would be arranged between junior counsel, the petitioner's firm and his Lordship's clerk for a hearing in respect of the further written submissions. Further written submissions were prepared and were duly lodged and junior counsel appeared by arrangement with his Lordship's clerk on 21 December 1978 in chambers to review the earlier application. On said occasion his Lordship again refused said application."

Against the background of this narrative the petitioner avers that the whole written submissions submitted to the trial judge in support of the application dealt with the matters which had been raised by the trial judge as fully as could reasonably have been expected. She further avers that, in any event, the case in respect of Speirs was, in the matter of its length, indistinguishable from that of his co-accused. Her complaint is that, in refusing her application 'His Lordship exercised his discretion unreasonably and oppressively; and that he misdirected himself as to the elements in the case to which it was appropriate to have regard when considering an application for certification'.

At the hearing of the petition the petitioner's submissions were presented by the learned Dean of Faculty and were supported by counsel on behalf of the Law Society of Scotland. To the learned advocate-depute we are indebted for a brief submission made for our assistance.

In presenting his argument the learned Dean of Faculty recognised that it was expressly held in *Heslin, Petr.* that this court will not, in the exercise of its nobile officium, entertain an application seeking review of the refusal by a trial judge to grant a certificate under para. 13(2) of the act of adjournal. The reasons for that decision are to be found in the full text of the opinion of the court in *Heslin* to which we have had access and we do not rehearse them here. Suffice it to say that it has not been suggested to us that the judgment in *Heslin* was not perfectly well founded. The submission was, however, that that judgment does not preclude us from interfering in the extraordinary circumstances of this case. Under reference to the discussion of the scope of the nobile officium of this court in the opinion of the court in the case of *Wan Ping Nam* v. *Federal German Republic Minister of Justice* it is clear that the power will be exercised to interfere in extraordinary circumstances for the purpose of preventing injustice or oppression. This petition is not to be regarded as an attempt to defeat the intention of the act of adjournal that there should be no right of appeal against a trial judge's discretionary decision in a para. 13(2) application. The complaint which it makes is of an extreme nature and the petition, properly understood, discloses a decision taken in quite extraordinary circumstances, a decision which amounted to an abuse of the discretion confided to the trial judge, and which constituted an act of oppression leading to injustice.

We have no difficulty in accepting that the High Court of Justiciary as the supreme court in criminal matters has, in respect of its nobile officium, the power of interfering in extraordinary circumstances for the purpose of preventing injustice or oppression. We bear in mind, however, that this power may never be invoked when to do so would conflict with statutory intention clear or implied. These propositions which formed the background against which the decision in *Heslin, Petr.* was taken emerge clearly in the opinions of the court in the case of *Wan Ping Nam* and in the later case of *Anderson v. H.M. Advocate* and require no amplification here.

The real primary question to be decided in this case is however not as to the scope of the nobile officium of this court but whether we are precluded by the judgment of this court in *Heslin, Petr.* from entertaining the petitioner's complaint against the decision of the trial judge when it is properly understood. Upon consideration of the history disclosed in the petition and a report by the trial judge which he provided for us on our invitation, we have come to be of opinion, not without hesitation, that we should give effect to the learned Dean's submission. On consideration of all the circumstances in so far as they can be ascertained from these sources we conclude that this case is to be regarded essentially as one in which the trial judge did not, in the event, exercise his discretionary judgment at all upon the application, which in its final form, sought the grant of a certificate upon the ground of exceptional length alone. He refused the application but, when one considers the circumstances, it is reasonably clear that he did so, simply because he had formed a certain view of the behaviour of senior counsel for the accused Speirs. Initially, when he was moved to grant the application on all three grounds specified in para. 13, the conduct of that senior counsel might properly have been taken into account as a relevant consideration in relation to the issue of complexity. In its final form, however, the issues of complexity and difficulty disappeared and if, as seems likely, the trial judge proceeded to reject it only because of the absence of senior counsel for Speirs during part of the course of the trial, it may be said with justification that he did not apply his mind at all to the only issue before him, namely, whether to grant or refuse the application on the ground that the case had necessarily been one of exceptional length. It will be recalled that applications upon the same ground, made by solicitors for the co-accused of Speirs, were granted by him without hesitation at the conclusion of the trial.

The circumstances of this case are exceptional and we are prepared to take the view that to neglect to consider the petitioner's application on its merits (for this is in effect and substance what the trial judge appears to have done) constituted oppression resulting in injustice. Notwithstanding the decision in *Heslin* that this court will not in the exercise of the nobile officium embark upon any review of a trial judge's decision of the issue before him in the exercise of his discretion, we are persuaded that our exceptional power should be exercised in this case to secure that the trial judge will address his mind to, and dispose of, the petitioner's application for a para. 13 certificate on the ground of exceptional length alone. We shall accordingly remit the petitioner's application with a direction to the trial judge to dispose of it on its merits. There can be no question of its disposal by this court because disposal is for the trial judge alone and because a certificate of a trial judge is the only certificate which may be recognised for the purpose of para. 13."

Application remitted to trial
judge who, after considering the
application on its merits, granted
the application.

NOTES

1. *Heslin* and *Rae* should be read along with *Harper, Petitioner*, 1982 S.L.T. 232 and *Lloyds and Scottish Finance Ltd.* v. *H.M. Advocate (supra)*. These cases make it clear that a distinction should be drawn between the case of the true lucana or *casus omissus*, in legislation and the case where it is the intention of the legislator not to provide for a method of review or other remedy. Thus, in the case of para. 13(2), the absence of a method of review was not due to an oversight, but rather it was the intention of the legislation that the court's discretion should not be subject to review. This may be contrasted with the situation in *Lloyds and Scottish Finance Ltd.* v. *H.M. Advocate* where the lack of protection for third party rights arose not from the intention of Parliament but from an oversight on its part. Where the intention of the legislator is clearly expressed it cannot be avoided by an application to the *nobile officium*. (For a further discussion of this point, see *Anderson* v. *H.M. Advocate, infra*.)

For further discussion of this point, see *Anderson* v. *H.M. Advocate, infra*; *Macpherson, Petitioners*, 1989 S.C.C.R. 518, *City of Edinburgh District Council, Petitioner*, 1990 S.C.C.R. 511, *Berry, Petitioner*, 1985 S.C.C.R. 106.

2. The *nobile officium* cannot be invoked to review the merits of a decision taken on a matter which falls within the sole discretion of a judge or court: *Heslin* and *Rae, supra*. This is so even where the High Court is of the view that the decision taken in exercise of that discretion is "misguided" or even "wholly unreasonable": *McLachlan, Petitioner*, 1987 S.C.C.R. 195.

3. Where, however, the court fails to address its mind to the real issues (as in *Rae*) or refuses to exercise the discretion at all (as in *Harper*, and see also *City of Edinburgh District Council, Petitioner, supra*) such failure or refusal may be reviewed by the High Court in the exercise of the *nobile officium* so as to ensure a proper exercise of the discretion. Where the High Court is prepared to intervene on these grounds, it is clear that it will not substitute its own decision on the merits (*Rae* and *Heslin, supra*).

4. Criminal legal aid fees are no longer fixed by Act of Adjournal, but by regulation under the Legal Aid (Scotland) Act 1986.

(B) The existence of a statutory remedy

1. Anderson v. H.M. Advocate
1974 S.L.T. 239

The petitioner was charged on summary complaint with breach of the peace. He tendered a plea of not guilty and lodged a special defence of alibi. He was convicted after trial and thereafter required the sheriff to state a case for the opinion of the High Court of Justiciary. The stated case was pursued to its conclusion when the court answered the only question of law in the affirmative and dismissed the appeal. The sole question raised by the appellant concerned the evaluation of evidence and the credibility of witnesses in the summary trial before the sheriff. Thereafter the appellant presented a petition to the *nobile officium* of the High Court craving that his conviction be quashed on the ground that there had been a miscarriage of justice in that the sheriff had failed in his appreciation of the evidence adduced before him and in his preparation of the stated case.

LORD JUSTICE-GENERAL (EMSLIE): "The petitioner was charged on summary complaint under the Summary Jurisdiction (Scotland) Act 1954 with breach of the peace during the hours of darkness on 18th December 1972. The complainers were two 14-year-old girls. To this charge the petitioner tendered a plea of not guilty and lodged a special defence of alibi. He was convicted after trial, and thereafter required the sheriff to state a case for the opinion of the High Court. The petitioner, being dissatisfied with the draft stated case, proposed extensive adjustments which the sheriff, to all but an insignificant extent, refused to incorporate in the case in its final form. The stated case was duly lodged and was pursued by the petitioner to its conclusion when the High Court, having refused to remit the case back to the sheriff to amplify the findings-in-fact as they had been moved by counsel for the petitioner to do, answered the only question in the case in the affirmative and dismissed the appeal.

At the trial the only point at issue was the identification of the petitioner as the person involved in the offence and the sheriff convicted, as the stated case shows, because he believed and accepted as reliable the evidence of the two complainers, and because he must be disbelieved the evidence given by the petitioner. Notwithstanding the straightforward nature of the sole question for decision at the trial—a question essentially of credibility and reliability well within the competence of an experienced sheriff to resolve upon the evidence—the petitioner in this petition of quite remarkable length avers that a substantial miscarriage of justice has occurred and prays that the High Court in the exercise of its nobile officium should quash the conviction. The alleged substantial miscarriage of justice is said to be the result of (i) alleged failures in duty on the part of the sheriff in his appreciation and evaluation of the evidence led before him; (ii) alleged failures in duty on the part of the sheriff in the preparation of the stated case, in the course of which he declined to adjust the case on the lines desiderated by the petitioner; and (iii) alleged prejudice suffered by the petitioner in the conduct of his defence on the merits by reason of the method used by the police to identify him before he was charged, and by reason of the failure of the sheriff to find as proved facts certain evidence given by certain defence witnesses which, it is said, was not subject to express challenge in cross-examination on behalf of the Crown.

For the moment we shall say of these allegations only this: it is obvious that essentially they amount to no more than assertions that no reasonable sheriff should have held the identification of the petitioner by the two credible complainers as reliable in light of the whole evidence led at the trial, and that it was the duty of the sheriff not only to state his findings upon the sole question of disputed fact at issue in the trial but to incorporate in the stated case other facts which emerged in evidence which were relevant only to the assessment of the credibility of the petitioner and of the reliability of the complainer's evidence of the identification of the petitioner upon which the critical findings-in-fact depends. In short, it is plain from this petition that the petitioner is seeking once more to have the merits of his conviction reviewed.

With this introduction we now turn to the question of the competency of this petition which has been challenged by the Crown.

At the outset it is as well to remind ourselves of the true scope and purpose of the valuable but exceptional jurisdiction which the petitioner has invited us to exercise. As is stated by Alison, *Criminal Law of Scotland*, Vol. II, in the well-known passage beginning on p.23: 'Akin to the well-known nobile officium of the Court of Session, is a similar power enjoyed by the Justiciary Court, of providing a remedy for any extraordinary or unforeseen occurrence in the course of criminal business in any part of the country. This is an unusual remedy, not to be called into operation when any of the ordinary courts are adequate to the matter; but still abundantly established wherever no other means of extricating it appears. ... In short, the principle is, that wherever the interposition of some authority is necessary to the administration of justice, and there exists no other judicature by whom it can competently be exercised; or which has been in use to exercise it, the Court of Justiciary is empowered and bound to exert its powers, on the application of a proper party, for the furtherance of justice.' To the same effect is Moncreiff in *Review in Criminal Cases*, p.264, who says 'In addition to its power of reviewing, the High Court of Justiciary as the Supreme Court in criminal matters has in respect of its nobile officium the power of interfering in extraordinary circumstances for the purpose of preventing injustice or oppression although there may not be any judgment, conviction or warrant brought under review.' These classical descriptions of the power have been accepted by this court as authoritative in all cases in which the scope of its power under the nobile officium has been called in question, and as the cases show, have been interpreted to mean that the power will only be exercised where the circumstances are extraordinary or unforeseen, and where no other remedy or procedure is provided by the law. Examples of these cases which clearly show the approach which this court will follow in considering the competency of exercising this very special power are *Wylie and Another* v. *H.M. Advocate*, 1966 S.L.T. 149 and *Wan Ping Nam* v. *Minister of Justice of the Federal German Republic*, 1972 S.L.T 220. In both of these cases the power was exercised because no procedure or remedy of any kind was available to the petitioners. To complete this review of the nature, scope and limits of the power we have only to add that the nobile officium of this court, and for that matter of the Court of Session, may never be invoked when to do so would conflict with statutory intention, express or clearly implied (see *Adair and Others* v. *Colville*, 1922 S.C. 672, 1922 S.L.T. 532).

In light of this discussion of the law, what is the position of this application by this petitioner?

In the first place it cannot be said that the petition discloses any extraordinary or unforeseen circumstances and it is clear that the primary justification for the exercise of the nobile officium cannot be said to exist. Summary prosecution and appeals have for long been governed by statute, and the relevant statute now in force is the Summary Jurisdiction (Scotland) Act 1954 as amended. Examination of that statute shows that for review of the merits of any summary conviction and adequate procedure was provided, and that is appeal by stated case. It is not in doubt that the intendment of the provisions of this Act is that although certain common law procedures were preserved to enable convictions to be challenged on grounds extraneous to the merits, the only mode of appeal competent where review of the merits of conviction is sought is appeal by stated case; and that in summary prosecutions the trial judge is to be final on all questions of fact. If authority were needed for the soundness of this interpretation of the statute it is to be found in *Rush* v. *Herron*, 1969 S.L.T. 211, in which the Lord Justice-General, in his opinion, stated the position thus: 'It is well settled in Scotland that, to quote the passage always referred to in this connection in Renton and Brown's *Criminal Procedure*, p.316:—"The merits of a conviction cannot be reviewed in a suspension." There has been a long series of cases in which this principle has been laid down. The latest reported case is the decision in *Moffat* v. *Skeen*, 1963 J.C. 84, in which at p.89, the following passage from Lord Wark is quoted from the case of *O'Hara* v. *Mill*, 1938 J.C. 4, at p.7, 1938 S.L.T. 184, at p.185: "Nothing", says Lord Wark, "is better settled in our criminal procedure than that the merits of a conviction cannot be reviewed in a process of suspension. Where it is the desire of a complainer against a conviction to evaluate the evidence his proper course is to apply for a stated case to the judge who has tried it, in order that the court may have before it an authoritative statement of what the evidence was and with the grounds upon which the judge proceeded." In the present case it is impossible to avoid the conclusion that the issue between the complainer and the respondent turns directly on a question of evaluation of evidence and the credibility of witnesses.

In the case of this petition it is just as impossible as it was in *Rush* (supra) to avoid the conclusion that the real issue between the petitioner and respondent turns directly on a question of the evaluation of evidence and the credibility of witnesses. For the ventilation of such a question Parliament has prescribed the sole remedy—a remedy, indeed, which the petitioner has resorted to and which has now been exhausted. On this ground alone we have no doubt that this petition is incompetent. Lest it be thought, however, that in so saying we have overlooked the petitioner's criticisms of the sheriff in relation to the preparation of the stated case we have to add that all these circumstances were advanced and rejected by the High Court of Justiciary which heard the petitioner's appeal. In delivering the opinion of the court the Lord Justice-Clerk said this:—

'It was forcibly submitted by appellant's counsel however, that the facts stated indicated that the sheriff had obviously accepted the evidence of identification given by the two girl complainers without due regard having been given to all the other evidence in the case which conflicted with the reliability of the identification. And that, in any event there were elements in the stated facts relating to their evidence which indicated that their identification was not reliable. On this latter point I confine myself to saying that the criticisms of the girls' evidence as stated were not well founded. These criticisms were valid matters of comment before the sheriff, and were admittedly made to him, but he did not regard them as affecting the reliability of their identification and that was a matter for him and not for this court. The stronger argument was that the sheriff had made no reference to the evidence adduced which reflected on, if not wholly contradicted, the accuracy of the girls' identification. This is perfectly true, and the question is whether his failure to do so vitiated the stated case as it stands, either to the extent of necessitating a quashing of the conviction, or at least remitting the case back to him, asking him to expand his note to explain why he had omitted to deal with this evidence in his note, and to make appropriate findings-in-fact relating to this evidence. When a case is being stated it is not necessary for every fact adduced in evidence to be incorporated. All that require to be included are the facts admitted or proved relevant to the charge under consideration. It is not necessary to state facts which are not relevant thereto. The judge stating the case has to provide a note explaining why he has reached his decision, but that does not require him to rehearse the whole of the evidence. He is not in the same position as a judge of first instance in a civil proof. The gravamen of the criticism by appellant's counsel was that the sheriff had believed the girls and had not taken into account the evidence adduced by the defence. This evidence was fully rehearsed before us, but we were informed that it has also been submitted to the sheriff. When submitting his alternative proposal that the case should be remitted back to the sheriff, for an explanation as to whether he took this evidence into account when he decided to accept the girls' evidence, appellant's counsel seemed to proceed on the assumption that the sheriff had not done so. I do not consider that the court is entitled to make this assumption. On the contrary, I think that there is a presumption that a sheriff, and indeed a very experienced sheriff, would take this elementary step in the administration of justice.'

With this opinion of the sheriff's duty in the circumstances of this case we entirely concur.

In the second place, however, the petition is clearly incompetent for quite a different reason. Section 68 of the Summary Jurisdiction (Scotland) Act 1954 is in the following terms:—

'(1) An appellant under s. 62 of this Act may at any time prior to lodging the case with the clerk of justiciary abandon his appeal by minute signed by himself or his solicitor, written on the complaint, or lodged with the clerk of court, and intimated to the respondent, but such abandonment shall be without prejudice to any other mode of appeal, review, advocation, or suspension competent. (2) On the case being lodged with the clerk of justiciary, the appellant shall be held to have abandoned any other mode of appeal which might otherwise have been open to him.'

By this section Parliament has provided expressly, in the interests of securing finality in summary criminal proceedings, that the right to follow any common law mode of appeal whatsoever should cease to be available the moment an appellant has elected to pursue the statutory mode of appeal, and election is of course, complete the moment a stated case has been lodged. In this case the petitioner not only lodged a stated case but pursued his chosen mode of appeal to an unsuccessful conclusion. In these circumstances, in the face of the clear and express statement of the intention of Parliament to which we have referred, it would be quite improper for this court to exercise its power under the nobile officium at the invitation of this petitioner. It is, no doubt, the fact, as the petitioner pointed out to us in argument, that this court has on one occasion exercised its power under the nobile officium to quash a conviction after a stated case had been lodged. The case was the case of *Patrick McCloy, Petitioner*, 1971 S.L.T. (Notes) 32. This case, however, does not assist the present petitioner since the question of competency was not considered at all, and all that can be said of the case of *McCloy* (supra) is that it disclosed a manifest, admitted, and quite exceptional miscarriage of justice before a magistrate who invented a witness to justify his alleged findings-in-fact. It did not, be it noted, involve in any way any question of review of the merits of conviction.

What we have said so far is sufficient for the disposal of the petition, but in the present interest there are certain observations we feel bound to make. We have already dealt with the ill-founded allegations of breach of duty on the part of the sheriff in connection with the preparation of the stated case. As to the remaining averment in the petition we are satisfied that they disclose no proper basis for the assertion that the sheriff failed in duty in any other respect. In this connection it is important to remember what was said by the Lord Justice-Clerk, in the passage which we have already quoted, in delivering the opinion of the court in this petitioner's appeal. It must not be forgotten that the credibility of the complainers is not disputed, and that the critical questions for the sheriff to resolve were as to the reliability of their evidence of identification of the petitioner which they undoubtedly gave in the witness box, and as to the credibility of the petitioner who denied having been the man involved. Both questions were essentially for decision by the sheriff who had the advantage, which no appellate court could have, of seeing and hearing the witnesses concerned. All the other evidence in the case, including the evidence of the way in which the police conducted their initial investigation, was relevant only to the solution of these two questions, and even if we were to assume that the petitioner's whole averments about this other evidence are true, it would be quite impossible for any appellate court to say that the sheriff was not entitled to reach the conclusion which he did. It is inconceivable that the experienced sheriff concerned in the case did not have regard to all this other evidence and to the arguments thereanent submitted to him by counsel for the petitioner, and there is accordingly no reason to suppose that, had this petition gone further, any 'oppression' or 'miscarriage of justice' would have been demonstrated."

The court held the petition incompetent.

NOTES

1.   This application was doomed from the start in that it was a virtually undisguised attempt to have the trial judge's decision on the facts reviewed by the High Court. This is not to say that the criticisms of the stated case procedure which lay behind this application were not well founded (although the Thomson Committee did not discover widespread demand for change in stated case procedure). Many of the defects highlighted by the *Anderson* case (the limitation to questions of law, the trial judge's absolute control over adjustments, etc.) were met by the changes to stated case procedure brought about by the 1980 Act; as to which, see *supra*, Chap. 16 and Renton and Brown, Chap. 16.

2.   The *Anderson* case illustrates the point that the *nobile officium* cannot be invoked to supplement an established procedure, even where the defects in that procedure are recognised. The existence of a process of review was fatal. (See also *Berry, Petitioner*, 1985 S.C.C.R. 106.)

3.   It would have been otherwise if there had been no such process. Thus, in *Wylie and Another* v. *H.M. Advocate*, 1966 S.L.T. 149 it was held that the *nobile officium* could competently be invoked to appeal against the imposition of a three-year sentence for contempt of court where no other form of appeal was available. Notice, also, the court's insistence that the matter to be brought under review must be "extraordinary and unforeseen." As to this, see *Mathieson, infra*.

4.   For an examination of this case and its wider implications, see *The Case of David Anderson*, a Report for Justice prepared by a Scottish Working Party, 1978.

2.   Mathieson, Petitioner
1980 S.L.T. 74

An accused person appealed against a sentence of five years' detention in a young offender's institution and then abandoned his appeal. He subsequently presented a petition to the *nobile officium* craving the High Court to review his sentence. On February 21, 1980 the High Court granted the prayer of the petition and allowed the petitioner to be heard on the question of sentence.

OPINION OF THE COURT: "This is a petition presented to the nobile officium of this court by James Mathieson, presently a prisoner in H.M. Remand Unit at Longriggend. Mathieson is a young man, just 18 now, who pled guilty when charged on indictment with the crime of wilful fire-raising. After sundry procedure including the obtaining of a series of psychiatric reports Mathieson was remitted for sentence to the High Court. In the High Court, when further psychiatric reports had been considered and when the evidence of two psychiatrists had been led before the judge concerned with sentencing, the sentence imposed on Mathieson was one of five years' detention in a young offender's institution. Thereafter it was desired by Mathieson, with legal advice, to challenge that sentence as excessive. To that end an application for legal aid was made and granted and a note of application for leave to appeal against sentence was duly lodged. What happened thereafter was that without consulting his legal advisers, and it seems on the advice of his mother, this young man signed on his own behalf and lodged a note of abandonment of his proposed appeal against sentence. By statute the effect of the lodging of that note was of course that his appeal is deemed to have been dismissed and there is now no statutory means by which the sentence can be examined by this court. It is for this reason that the petitioner invites the court, in the exercise of its nobile officium, to take the extraordinary step, in spite of the lodging of the note of abandonment of his appeal, of allowing him to be heard on the question of his sentence. The law as to the scope and purpose of the valuable by exceptional jurisdiction which the court possesses is fully set out in the case of *Anderson* v. *H.M. Advocate*, 1974 S.L.T. 239. For that reason it is unnecessary to rehearse it here. From that case it is plain, we think, that the power which this court undoubtedly possesses will be excised to avoid possible miscarriages of justice or to cure a miscarriage of justice in circumstances which are both extraordinary and unforeseen provided that to exercise the power would not defeat the intention of Parliament as that intention may appear in public general statutes. The question for us in this petition is whether the circumstances which have been disclosed, and these circumstances not only include what is contained in the petition itself but in the various reports to which our attention has been drawn, can be described as sufficiently extraordinary and unforeseen to justify us in granting the prayer of the petition. Without rehearsing the details of the matter we have come to be of opinion that the prayer should in this case be granted simply upon the very special ground that the circumstances are sufficiently extraordinary and unforeseen and unlikely to be repeated. For these reasons the petition succeeds and the opportunity to argue sentence will be permitted to the petitioner."

The court granted
the prayer of the petition.

NOTES

1. There is clearly a link between the *casus omissus* and the "extraordinary and unforeseen" situation, and indeed the latter is capable of encompassing the former. This case illustrates the point that "extraordinary and unforeseen" circumstances may arise above and beyond the case of the *casus omissus*. Compare, on this point, *Fenton, Petitioner*, 1982 S.L.T. 164. A convicted person lodged a note of appeal against sentence, and at the same time applied for interim liberation pending his appeal. This was refused. An appeal against this refusal was also lodged, but not within the 24-hour time-limit required by section 446(2) of the 1975 Act as amended. The appellant then presented a petition to the *nobile officium* seeking admission to bail. The High Court refused the petition:

"In our view it is not for the court to exercise its power under the nobile officium simply because an accused or his legal advisers have been mindless of a statutory time-table. If it were otherwise the court could be flooded with petitions to the nobile officium. If the legislature intended that failure to obtemper a strict time-table could be excused on cause shown, that could have been provided for in the statute, as is the case in other procedural matters. That was not done and there is no justification for considering that this was a casus omissus. A statutory procedure was enacted, and in the absence of any provision to excuse non-compliance, non-compliance is fatal. The exercise of the nobile officium should not be regarded as the kiss of life in such circumstances."

It could be said that if Parliament had intended that an abandonment of appeal could be withdrawn on cause shown that too could have been provided for. No doubt the flood-gates argument is as strong (or as weak) in relation to bail applications as anywhere else, but it seems difficult to justify the court's refusal of a remedy, whatever the circumstances. What would have been the situation if, for example, the applicant in *Fenton* had been incorrectly advised by his legal advisers?

2. *Fenton* was discussed, and distinguished, in *H.M. Advocate* v. *Wood and Cowie*, 1990 S.C.C.R. 195. In that case, the Crown failed to observe the time-limits laid down in rule 116(2) of the Act of Adjournal (Consolidation) 1988 for an appeal to the High Court against a reference to the Court of Justice of the European Communities for a preliminary ruling under Article 177 of the Treaty of Rome. It appeared that the order making the reference was not made in open court or otherwise announced, with the result that the Crown, who opposed the reference, were not aware, until after the expiry of the time-limit for an appeal, that the order had been made. The Crown presented a petition to the *nobile officium*. In granting the prayer of the petition, the Lord Justice-General observed (1990 S.C.C.R. 195 at p.199):

"In the present case the circumstances show that the orders against which the Crown wish to appeal were not made at the hearing in open court or in the presence of the parties. It appears from the information before us that no steps were taken by the sheriff, as perhaps they might have been, to alert the procurator fiscal to the fact that he did intend to and had in fact made the orders on 11th January. This is not, therefore, in our opinion, a case of a mindless disregard of the statutory time-table, and we consider that it is in the interests of the administration of justice that the time should be extended."

3. The petitioner in *Mathieson* appears to have been fortunate in his treatment by the court. There was a statutory remedy available to him, and, indeed, he had at one time initiated it. Is an ill-advised withdrawal of an appeal really an "extraordinary" circumstance?

4. It is important to determine the limits of the statutory remedy. What is the situation where the court, in the exercise of its appellate or review jurisdiction, does something which Parliament has not permitted it to do? See the following case:

3. Boyle, Petitioner
1992 S.C.C.R. 949

LORD JUSTICE-GENERAL: "This is a petition to the nobile officium, in which the petitioner seeks review of a decision of the High Court under section 254 of the Criminal Procedure (Scotland) Act 1975 when disposing of an appeal at his instance against his conviction.

He had been convicted in the High Court in Glasgow on an indictment which contained five charges. Charge (1) was a charge of breach of the peace, charge (2) was one of murder and charges (3), (4) and (5) were charges of contravening section 3(1)(b) of the Bail etc. (Scotland) Act 1980. He was found guilty as libelled on charges (1), (3), (4) and (5), and on charge (2) he was found guilty of culpable homicide. He then appealed against his conviction for culpable homicide on the ground of misdirection by the trial judge. His grounds of appeal were all related to the issue of self-defence which arose only in regard to charge (2). There was no suggestion either in the grounds of appeal or in the course of the argument that the alleged misdirections affected the petitioner's conviction on the other four charges, against which he had not appealed. On 10th July 1992 his appeal was allowed and it was disposed of by setting aside the verdict of the trial court and granting authority to bring a new prosecution in accordance with section 255 of the 1975 Act.

No mention was made in the course of the decision which was intimated on that date of the extent to which the verdict of the jury was being set aside. But in an opinion which was subsequently issued on 24th August 1992 it was made clear that the court considered it appropriate to set aside the whole verdict of the jury, including their verdict on charges (1), (3), (4) and (5). The petitioner now seeks to challenge that decision on the ground that his conviction on these charges was not before the High Court for their consideration in the appeal and, accordingly, that the court had no power to set aside the verdict of the trial court except in regard to his conviction of culpable homicide under charge (2). He claims that this decision was unlawful and incompetent as being outwith the powers of the High Court in terms of the 1975 Act. He claims also that it has resulted in an injustice, because he has now been served with an indictment in the new prosecution under section 255 which contains the same five charges as those which he faced in the original proceedings, four of which were the subject of convictions against him which he did not appeal.

It is well settled that the nobile officium of this court can be invoked only in exceptional circumstances. So the first question is whether the application is competent, having regard to the finality which attaches to all interlocutors and sentences of the High Court in terms of sections 262 and 281 of the Act. Mr Bell submitted that the provisions of these sections did not preclude a challenge to a decision of the High Court on the ground that it was unlawful and incompetent, and that since this was the only point which he sought to raise we should consider the application and review the decision to set aside the jury's verdict on these four charges. The learned advocate-depute informed us that he did not challenge the competency of the application in view of the nature of the argument which Mr Bell wished to present. We were invited to regard this as a case where, on the petitioner's argument, the High Court had done something in the exercise of its appellate jurisdiction which it was not permitted to do by Parliament. Reference was made to *Beattie*, Petitioner [1992, S.C.C.R. 812], in which it was recognised that in such a case there may be said to have been a circumstance which was unforeseen because the statutory provisions for the finality of appeals assume that the High Court will exercise its jurisdiction in accordance with the statutes and that the nobile officum may then be exercised to prevent such injustice or oppression as may result.

But in the present case the issue of competency is incapable of being separated from the merits of the application. This is not one of those cases suggested in argument where, due to a mistake or oversight, the court has acted contrary to the express terms of an enactment, such as by imposing a sentence on a statutory charge other than one provided for by Parliament. The argument here is directed to something which the appeal court did in the belief that what they were doing was competent. It was a decision which was deliberately taken, for reasons which were clearly set out in the following passages in the opinion of the court which was delivered by the Lord Justice-Clerk:

'Although the misdirection related to charge (2) on the indictment only, it was accepted that charges (1) and (2) were intimately connected and it is clear that charges (3), (4) and (5) were consequential charges. It therefore appears to us to be appropriate to set aside the whole verdict of the jury. ...

The fact that there is to be a new prosecution emphasises the desirability of setting aside the jury's verdict on all charges, so that the jury at the new prosecution can hear all the evidence which is relevant and material to the issues which were the subject of the first indictment.'

Two questions arise in these circumstances. The first is whether it is open to argument that the course taken by the appeal court was one which the High Court was entitled to take in the exercise of its jurisdiction under section 254(1) of the Act. The second is whether, if the point is open to argument, it is competent for the view which was taken by the appeal court to be reviewed by us in the exercise of the nobile officium, having regard to the final and conclusive nature of all interlocutors and sentences pronounced by the High Court which are declared by statute not to be subject to review. A third question which was raised in the course of argument by Mr Bell is whether it was competent for the appeal court to state in the opinion which was issued on 24th August 1992 that the whole verdict of the jury was to be set aside, since no mention of the setting aside of the verdicts on charges (1), (3), (4) and (5) was made in the decision which was announced on 10th July 1992.

We take first the third question, since it raises a short point on a matter of procedure. Both Mr Bell and the advocate-depute were agreed that there was some discussion about the relationship between charges (1) and (2) on the original indictment in the course of the appeal, but they were also agreed that no mention was made of charge (1) or of charges (3), (4) and (5) in the context of the discussion as to what charges might be brought in the new prosecution. As can be seen from the opinion delivered by the Lord Justice-Clerk, it was suggested by counsel for the petitioner that the court should only authorise a new prosecution on a charge of culpable homicide, since that was the offence of which the petitioner had been convicted by the jury on charge (2). The court's decision on that point was that section 254(1)(c) enabled the court to dispose of an appeal by setting aside the verdict of the trial court and granting authority to bring a new prosecution, leaving it to the Crown to decide whether to exercise that right and, if so, what charges to bring. Mr Bell maintained that the impression shared by all those who listened to the court's decision on this point was that it was only the conviction on charge (2) which was being set aside. He then pointed to the determination as recorded by the Depute Clerk of Justiciary, which was in these terms:

'The court, having heard counsel for the appellant and the advocate-depute, allowed the appeal; set aside the verdict of the High Court sitting at Glasgow on 18th November 1991 and granted authority to bring a new prosecution in accordance with section 255 of the Criminal Procedure (Scotland) Act 1975.'

Mr Bell submitted that this was consistent with what had been discussed and that it was a final interlocutor which was incapable of being altered by the terms of the opinion.

We have no hesitation in rejecting this argument. The suggestion that the appeal court were attempting in the opinion to alter the terms of their own interlocutor was based on a misconception of the function which was being performed by the Depute Clerk of Justiciary. As was pointed out in *Perrie, Petitioner* [1991 S.C.C.R. 475], at p.480D, it is not the practice of the High Court in appeals under solemn procedure to issue interlocutors signed by the presiding judge. But section 261 of the 1975 Act provides that, on the final determination of any appeal under that Part of the Act, the Clerk of Justiciary is to give notice of such determination to the appellant or applicant if he is in custody and was not present at such final determination, to the clerk of the court in which the conviction took place, and to the Secretary of State. The words which we have quoted above were written on a form of notice addressed to the clerk of the trial court, the Director of Prison Services, the Governor of H.M. Prison at Edinburgh and the officer in charge of the Criminal Records Office in Glasgow. They were introduced by these words on the printed form:

'THIS IS TO GIVE YOU NOTICE, That the Court of Criminal Appeal has finally determined the said Appeal, and on 10-7-92 pronounced the following Judgment.'

It is incorrect to describe the notice of determination given by the Clerk of Justiciary as an interlocutor or to suggest that its terms are incapable of alteration by the court. The function of the notice is to intimate the determination to those who require to be made aware of its terms. But it is not shown to the presiding judge and it is always open to him to correct it if it should appear later that it is not in accordance with the decision of the court. In the present case, however, no such correction is required. The notice records the determination of the appeal in terms which reflect precisely the language of section 254(1)(c) of the 1975 Act. It states that the court allowed the appeal, set aside the verdict of the trial court and granted authority to bring a new prosecution. No express reference is made here to any particular charge or charges on the indictment. It is open to the interpretation that the whole verdict of the trial court was being set aside. That interpretation is confirmed by the words which we quoted earlier from the opinion which was subsequently delivered by the Lord Justice-Clerk. The opinion is the best evidence of what was decided by the court and it is consistent with the terms of the notice signed by the Depute Clerk of Justiciary. We can find nothing in this part of Mr Bell's argument which would entitle us to say that the High Court did something here which it was not permitted to do by the 1975 Act.

We turn now to the question whether it was within the power of the High Court to set aside the verdict of the trial court on charges which were not the subject of the appeal. This is an issue of some general interest and importance, because the statute contains no express provision for the situation which has arisen in this case. No distinction is made in the statutory framework between cases where the indictment in the original proceedings contained only one charge and where it contained several. Section 228(1) provides that any person convicted on indictment may appeal to the High Court against such conviction, and section 254(1) sets out the powers which the High Court may exercise in disposing of such appeals. In cases where the appeal is to be determined by affirming the verdict of the trial court under section 254(1)(a) or by setting aside its verdict and quashing the conviction under section 254(1)(b) there is no difficulty. There is no need in these cases to look beyond the conviction which was the subject of the appeal. But the position is different when the disposal which has been selected is to set aside the verdict under section 254(1)(c) and to grant authority for the bringing of a new prosecution under section 255.

It is clear that the powers of the High Court under section 254(1) are limited to disposing of an appeal against conviction. No mention is made in this subsection of any other steps which may be taken in regard to verdicts which are not the subject of the appeal. There is no power to set aside the verdict of the trial court on other charges on which the appellant may have been convicted, or to set aside verdicts of acquittal on other charges against which no appeal could competently be taken since no right of appeal is given to the Crown. But the purpose of granting authority for a new prosecution is to enable a new prosecution to be brought for the same or any similar offence arising out of the same facts, and it is expressly provided in section 255(1) that the proceedings out of which the appeal arose shall not be a bar to such new prosecution.

The problem, to which no express reference has been made in the statute, arises where the original indictment contains charges other than the charge or charges which were the subject of appeal. These charges could include charges which were in the indictment purely for evidential reasons or as background to the principal charge. Charges of this character would need to be included in the fresh indictment if the new prosecution was to proceed with any reasonable prospect of success. The principle is that notice must be given in the indictment of the intention to lead evidence of anything done or omitted to be done by the accused which constitutes a crime. This is so even if the evidence is to be directed only to proof of the principal crime or crimes libelled against him. That principle applies equally to a new prosecution brought under authority granted under section 254(1)(c) as it does to the original proceedings. For this reason it is not difficult to see that the new prosecution would be at a material disadvantage if the Crown were to be unable to lead evidence relevant to the principal charge because the events had not been libelled in the indictment. But the petitioner's argument is that that is the effect of sections 254 and 255, since they do not permit the court to interfere with the verdict of the trial court finding the appellant guilty on ancillary charges against which he did not appeal, or with its verdict where, as not infrequently happens for technical reasons, the ancillary charges were disposed of by an acquittal.

In the opinion which we have just delivered in the Crown's appeal under section 76A of the 1975 Act against a decision taken at a preliminary diet in the new proceedings, we said that the point of reference to determine whether the accused has been charged under section 255 with the same or any similar offence arising out of the same facts must be the terms of the previous indictment. We also said that, where more than one charge was contained in that indictment, it must be the charge or charges in respect of which the accused was previously convicted and to which he directed his appeal. But Mr Bell accepted that it would be open to the Crown to expand the narrative in the charge or charges in the indictment in the new prosecution to include what had been libelled separately in the previous indictment in charges to which no appeal had been directed, if this narrative was relevant to the proof of the offence or offences which were now being prosecuted. He made it clear that his objection was to the taking of any step in the disposal of the appeal which would enable the Crown to libel these facts as separate charges, since it would then be open to the Crown to obtain a fresh conviction in respect of them for offences of which he had already been convicted.

The advocate-depute drew our attention to *Morrison v H.M. Advocate* [1990 S.C.C.R. 235] at p.249, where reference was made to what was seen in that case to be an insuperable difficulty. The appellant in that case had gone to trial on two charges of rape against the same complainer, which arose out of what was essentially one incident. He was convicted on the second charge and he appealed against that conviction. But the jury had acquitted him of the first charge, which had been amended to one of attempted rape, and it was accepted that the Crown could not lead evidence in relation to that charge at a retrial of the charge on which the appellant originally had been convicted. In view of the impossible situation which this would create the advocate-depute accepted that the court should simply set aside the verdict of the jury in terms of section 254(1)(b) and quash the conviction. So far as the present case was concerned, however, he submitted that it would be open to the Crown to narrate the events which in the previous indictment had been charged in charge (1) as a breach of the peace, as what he described as a hanging particle to the charge of murder, so that all the events relevant to that charge could be led.

Although both Mr Bell and the advocate-depute were agreed that the narrative in charge (2) of the original indictment could be expanded to include matters which were previously libelled as a breach of the peace, this course also is not without difficulty. Section 61(2) of the 1975 Act provides that any part of what is charged in an indictment, constituting in itself an indictable crime, shall be deemed separable to the effect of making it lawful to convict of such a crime. A narrative of the kind suggested would, therefore, leave it open to the jury to convict the petitioner of disorderly conduct amounting to a breach of the peace although they had decided to acquit him of the principal elements of the charge. There seems to us therefore to be no significant distinction for present purposes between narrating this conduct as part of the principal charge and presenting it as a separate charge in the indictment. Either course would leave it open to the Crown to seek a conviction on this narrative for breach of the peace. The only difference is that if the narrative were to be the subject of a separate charge, it would be open to the jury to return a separate verdict of guilty of breach of the peace in addition to a verdict of murder or culpable homicide on the principal charge. But the decision of the trial judge in the previous proceedings to take both charges together for the purposes of sentence and to treat them as being effectively part of the same event shows that the practical consequences of either course as regards sentence are likely to be the same.

It was suggested by the advocate-depute that a statutory basis for the use of the hanging particle was the provision in section 255(1) that the proceedings out of which the appeal arose are not to be a bar to the new prosecution. He seemed to be reluctant to take that proposition to its logical conclusion, which appears to us to be that nothing which took place in the previous proceedings is to be a bar to a new prosecution for the same or any similar offence arising out of the same facts which were narrated in the charge which gave rise to the appeal. Yet it is at this stage that the real difficulty for the petitioner in this application must be faced. In our opinion there are good reasons for regarding it as appropriate, in those cases where the verdicts not appealed against related to ancillary charges which were intimately connected with the principal charge which gave rise to the appeal, that the authority to bring a new prosecution should extend to these ancillary charges also. This is in the public interest, since the jury in the new prosecution ought to be able to hear all the evidence bearing on the principal charge so that they can arrive at a fair verdict. Furthermore, as the advocate-depute pointed out, it is in accordance with the intention of Parliament, as indicated by the declaration in section 255(1) that the previous proceedings are not to be a bar to the new prosecution. And there could not reasonably be said to be any unfairness in this course, since the only purpose of including the ancillary charges in the original indictment would be to enable the Crown to lead all the evidence which was relevant and material to the question whether the accused was guilty of the principal charge. What the appeal court did in this case seems to us therefore to be entirely in accordance with this approach. Unlike the charge of attempted rape in *Morrison*, the appellant's acquittal on which was seen to present an insuperable obstacle to a new prosecution on the other charge, the breach of the peace in the present case was of a minor character in comparison with the offence libelled in charge (2) and would not, taken on its own, have justified the taking of proceedings against the petitioner on indictment.

Accordingly, the question is whether it was open to argument that the course taken by the appeal court was one which the High Court was entitled to take in the exercise of its jurisdiction under section 254(1) of the Act. We have put the question in this way because, if it was open to argument, it was clearly a matter for the appeal court to decide and not for us. The High Court, in the exercise of its appellate jurisdiction under the Act, is entitled to do all such things as may be necessary to give effect to that jurisdiction in accordance with the intention of Parliament. Its decisions on these matters are as final and conclusive and beyond the power of review of any court as any other decision or determination in the disposal of an appeal. To a large extent therefore it is for the High Court to determine the limits of its own jurisdiction, so long as this does not conflict with what Parliament has provided, either expressly or by necessary implication, in any enactment.

So far as the limits of its jurisdiction under section 254(1)(c) are concerned, the provision that it may dispose of an appeal against conviction 'by setting aside the verdict of the trial court' is loosely phrased and open to construction.

As against the argument that, in its context, the words 'the verdict' must be taken to be the verdict which has been appealed against, there is the point that, in order to give effect to the granting of authority for a new prosecution, section 255(1) provides that the proceedings out of which the appeal arose shall not be a bar to such new proceedings. Section 254(1)(c) does not state in terms that only the verdict which has been expressly appealed against can be set aside, and it seems to us at least open to argument that it permits the setting aside of the verdict on all charges which are intimately connected with the charge which was the subject of the appeal. An argument in support of this approach would be that the appellant had, by necessary implication, submitted the verdict on all these charges also to review by the High Court, thus enabling the court, if this was appropriate in the public interest, to set aside the verdict on these other charges so that the jury in the new prosecution could hear all the relevant evidence. The argument has particular force in regard to the charges under the Bail etc. (Scotland) Act 1980, because it would make no sense for the convictions under section 3(1)(b) of that Act, which were entirely dependent on the petitioner's conviction for the offences libelled in charges (1) and (2), to remain standing along with the sentences attached to them when the verdict of the trial court on the other charges had been set aside.

For these reasons we are in no doubt that the issue as to whether this course was competent was one for the appeal court to decide when disposing of the appeal. It is an inevitable consequence of this opinion that the decision which they took is not open to us to review in these proceedings and that the petition must therefore be dismissed as incompetent. But we should add that, even if we had been persuaded that it was a decision which could be reviewed in the exercise of the nobile officium, we would have found it impossible to hold that what occurred in this case had resulted in such injustice or oppression to the petitioner as would entitle us to interfere to prevent it. Mr Bell confined his argument on this point to the submission that it was unjust and oppressive for the court to exercise a power which it did not possess. But, in the wider context of a decision which was taken for the express purpose of enabling a new prosecution to be brought in accordance with section 255 of the Act, that is not an approach which we can accept. It was not suggested that the petitioner had been prejudiced by the decision in any respect which was not necessary to serve the public interest. By setting aside the verdict on all charges, the appeal court relieved him from the consequences of his conviction on all of them, leaving it to the Crown to decide whether or not to bring a new prosecution. The decision would in terms of section 255(4), have had the effect, for all purposes, of an acquittal had fresh proceedings not now been brought. And it has not been suggested that the petitioner is in any different position as regards the new proceedings than he was when he went to trial under the previous indictment. For these reasons also we would have declined to interfere with the decision of the appeal court that the whole verdict of the jury should be set aside."

NOTES

1.   The critical question in this case was whether or not the decision of the appeal court was subject to review under the *nobile officium*. The approach adopted by the High Court appears to be as follows: If it was "open to argument" that the course adopted by the court of appeal was one which it was entitled to take, then it was for the court of appeal to decide whether it was entitled to take that course. The only proviso appears to be that the court would not be entitled to determine the limits of its own jurisdiction where to do so would conflict with what Parliament has provided, either expressly or by necessary implication in any enactment.

2. Having decided that the petition was not competent it was, of course, not necessary for the court to address the question of oppression and injustice (which, of course, it is the function of the *nobile officium* to prevent). They did, however, express the view that not only was it not oppressive in the circumstances for the court to exercise a power which had not clearly been conferred on it, but that there was no suggestion that the petitioner had been prejudiced by the decision "in any respect which was not necessary to serve the public interest." Leaving aside the point that the issue is one of "injustice or oppression" rather than "prejudice" (which is surely a weaker test), it is noteworthy that the court has raised the argument that prejudice may be excused in the public interest. Indeed, the court appears to suggest that the petitioner benefited from the decision of the court of appeal in that he was relieved of the consequences of conviction on all of the charges!

3. Finally, the court notes that the petitioner was in no different position as regards the new proceedings than he was when he went to trial under the previous indictment. But, of course, he would be if the Crown proceeded to re-indict on the murder charge since he would already have been acquitted on that charge.

B. THE ROYAL PREROGATIVE

H.M. Advocate v. Waddell
1976 S.L.T. (Notes) 61;
High Court, November 29, 1976, unreported
(For the background to this case see *H.M. Advocate* v. *Waddell, supra,* p.36.)

LORD ROBERTSON: "... A further matter of some importance appeared in the course of the argument. It seems that one of the witnesses elicited by the Crown in the present case, Patrick Connolly Meehan, has already been convicted of the robbery and murder which formed the basis of charge 2 against Waddell. On appeal the conviction was apparently upheld and has never been quashed by this court. The Crown however refer to the pardon granted to him 'in respect of the said conviction' under the Royal Prerogative. The terms of the pardon produced did not appear to go further than 'pardoning, remitting and releasing unto him all pains, penalties and punishments whatsoever', coming from the same conviction. It was argued by the Lord Advocate on behalf of the Crown that the effect of the pardon was to purge the offences and was equivalent to quashing the conviction. In reply it was submitted on behalf of Waddell that the pardon did not quash the conviction which remains standing and was extractable. Apparently there is no other case in which this point has been considered or has even arisen. It is to be noted that the Crown has not chosen in the Meehan case to proceed as it could have done to attempt to have the conviction quashed in the original appeal court. This procedure was carried out in the Oscar Slater case in 1928 (*Slater* v. *H.M. Advocate,* 1928 S.L.T. 602).

It seems to me that this matter may well be of critical importance at a later stage. The point has not formally been presented on behalf of Waddell as a plea in bar of trial and it is not prima facie clear at this stage that the Crown have proceeded incompetently in presentation of the indictment against Waddell. As the Lord Advocate said there is no rule of law which renders the procedure so far incompetent. It is therefore in my view premature to decide this point at this stage. I should add that it was expressly conceded by the Lord Advocate on behalf of the Crown, as I understood him, that he would be bound to withdraw charge 2 against Waddell if it were found that the conviction against Meehan stands.

In the result I shall repel the preliminary pleas on behalf of the panels."

The preliminary pleas having been repelled, the accused tendered a plea of not guilty. The legal effect of the free pardon granted to Meehan was further considered at the trial:

LORD ROBERTSON: "When the Crown led a police officer as a witness to speak to charge 2 of the indictment, counsel for the accused Waddell objected on the ground that it was incompetent for the Crown to lead evidence in relation to this charge as there is a conviction standing against Patrick Connolly Meehan, witness no. 94 on the Crown list. Extract conviction defence production no. 7 was referred to. It showed that Meehan was convicted of the crime libelled in charge 2 of the present indictment, no notice being made of any pardon in the margin of the record of conviction to which it applies.

The argument presented on behalf of Waddell elaborated upon the argument presented in the course of the diet on 5 October 1976 when I repelled it as not truly a plea in bar of trial. In view of the importance attached to the argument by the Lord Advocate, I adjourned the trial for consideration of the objection by a larger court.

It was argued that the conviction of Meehan for the murder still stands as extractable and has indeed been extracted. The pardon, defence production No. 8, has not had the effect of quashing the conviction. What it says is that the Sovereign, by virtue of the Royal Prerogative, was graciously pleased to extend Her Grace and Mercy to the said Patrick Connolly Meehan and to grant him a Free Pardon in respect of said conviction, thereby pardoning, remitting and releasing unto him all pains, penalties and punishments whatsoever that from the said conviction may come.

The effect of this pardon, according to counsel for Waddell was not to quash the conviction. It was conceded on behalf of the Crown that there was no question of Meehan and Waddell acting together. It was incompetent now for the Crown, standing Meehan's conviction, to prosecute another person for the same crime. In my opinion, this argument is unsound. No principle or law or authority was put forward in support of it. I see no reason why the previous conviction of an individual upon a particular charge should, of itself, render incompetent subsequent prosecution of another person for the same offence.

Circumstances may readily be envisaged under which such a prosecution might be required in the interests of justice. It must be for the Lord Advocate, in his discretion, to decide whether such circumstances exist in any particular case. It is not necessary, in my view, to consider the exact meaning and effect of the Free Pardon, which is not a live issue, the decision of which is necessary for the proper conduct of this trial. The existence of such a pardon would no doubt be one of the circumstances which the Lord Advocate would take into account when exercising his discretion. This is enough to decide the point of competency taken by counsel for Waddell in his objection to the evidence.

Counsel for Waddell, however, took a further point that the Crown was now barred from proceeding further against his client in view of certain remarks made by the Lord Advocate at the first diet on the 5 October 1976 and in the course of argument following upon the present objection. These remarks were

represented as amounting to a concession, that unless the effect of the Free
Pardon was equivalent to a quashing of Meehan's conviction, he would not
proceed further against Waddell on charge 2.

I have carefully considered the remarks in question and have studied the
transcript of certain passages in the debate of 5 October 1976. These remarks,
while they might be construed as conditional concessions, are couched in
imprecise terms. In my view, they are not properly to be regarded as duly
considered and accurately formulated concessions as to the circumstances in
which the Lord Advocate might decide not to proceed. I do not think that they
amount to such unequivocal statements as to justify the principle of *Thom* v.
H.M. Advocate, 1976 S.L.T. 232, being applied.

In any event, I do not consider that it is the proper function of the court to
giving rulings on questions of law which do not have to be decided to the
proper conduct of the trial, merely for the purpose of deciding whether
concessions expressed as conditional are to be given a practical effect.

I should add that Lord Keith and Lord Maxwell, who heard the arguments,
agree with what I have said. I shall repel the objection."

Objection repelled. The
jury returned a verdict of
not guilty.

NOTES

1.   For a full discussion of the issues raised by this case see Gane, "The
Effect of a Pardon in Scots Law," 1980 J.R. 18.

2.   Lord Robertson returned to the question of the effect of the pardon
during his charge to the jury (*supra*, p.23). There he expressed the opinion
that "in the ordinary use of language ... if you pardon someone, you
pardon them for something that they have done, and not for something
that they haven't done. This indeed is an interpretation supported by the
actual terms of the Free Pardon itself which appear to free Meehan from the
consequences of the conviction and not from the conviction itself. It
certainly doesn't quash the conviction by due process of law."

His Lordship may well be correct with regard to the "ordinary use of
language," but it is clear that in several instances the Royal Pardon has
been used to remedy clear miscarriages of justice, including wrongful
conviction, (as to which, see Gane, *loc. cit.* and C. H. Rolph, *The Queen's
Pardon*, Chap. 6). As regards the effect of the pardon, in *R.* v. *Foster* [1984] 2
All E.R. 679 the Court of Appeal held that, in English law, since the Crown
no longer had a prerogative of justice, but only a prerogative of mercy, a
pardon cannot remove a conviction but only pardon its effects. The only
body which has the power to quash a conviction is, therefore, the Court of
Appeal, Criminal Division. It is probably the case that, were the issue to
arise today in Scotland, the courts would be inclined to the same view,
although in the light of the history of the pardon, and the differences in the
extent of the prerogative in the United Kingdom, it may be that an
adequately worded pardon could, under Scots law, extend to the
conviction itself.

The opinion that the pardon cannot quash a conviction was shared by
the government (see the statement of the Solicitor-General during the
Scottish Grand Committee Debate on the Hunter Report on the murder of
Mrs Rachel Ross and its aftermath: (1983) 76 SCOLAG Bul. 7).

The obvious solution is a revision of the wording of the present "free pardon" so as to make it clear what its effect is intended to be. The view has been expressed, however, that this might raise certain difficult issues as to the extent of the Royal Prerogative: Hunter Report, Comment No. 4, p.1014.

3.   As noted in Chap. 15, the appeal procedures contained in the 1975 Act have no effect on the prerogative of mercy: 1975 Act, s. 263(1); and see the case of *Leitch* v. *Secretary of State for Scotland* (*supra*, p.526).

C.   THE EUROPEAN CONVENTION ON HUMAN RIGHTS

The provisions of the Convention guaranteeing minimum procedural standards in the criminal process are set out in Chap. 1. The Convention is not limited, of course, to the regulation of procedures, but is intended also to secure certain substantive rights and freedoms. A discussion of these matters would be out of place in a work such as this, but it is felt that an outline of the procedures established to ensure the observance of the Convention by its signatories might usefully be included here.

The Institutions

Article 19 of the Convention establishes two institutions whose function is "to ensure the observance of the engagements undertaken by the High Contracting Parties." The institutions are (1) the European Commission on Human Rights, and (2) The European Court of Human Rights. The Commission was set up immediately following upon the entry into force of the Convention. By Article 56, however, election of judges to the court was made conditional upon recognition of the court's compulsory jurisdiction by at least eight states. This condition was not satisfied until five years after the entry into force of the Convention.

The members of the Commission are elected by the Committee of Ministers of the Council of Europe for a period of six years. The Commission consists of a number of members equal to that of the high contracting parties (though there is no requirement that members be nationals of a high contracting party). No two members of the Commission may be nationals of the same state. Members of the Commission sit in their individual capacity, *i.e.* not as representatives of any state. No special qualifications are laid down in the Convention for membership of the Commission, although members of the Commission traditionally have held qualifications similar to those required of judges of the court.

Members of the court are elected for a period of nine years by the Consultative Committee of the Council of Europe from a list of persons nominated by the Members of the Council. Candidates for election "shall be of high moral character and must either possess the qualifications required for appointment to high judicial office or be jurisconsults of recognised competence" (Article 39(3)). The court consist of a number of judges equal to that of the members of the Council of Europe (*i.e.* it is not limited to the number of high contracting parties) and no two judges may be nationals of the same state.

In addition to these specially created bodies, the Committee of Ministers of the Council of Europe exercises certain judicial functions in accordance with Article 32 of the Convention.

European Convention on Human Rights

"Article 24
Any High Contracting Party may refer to the Commission, through the Secretary-General of the Council of Europe, any alleged breach of the provisions of the Convention by another High Contracting Party.

Article 25
1.   The Commission may receive petitions addressed to the Secretary-General of the Council of Europe from any person, non-governmental organisation or group of individuals claiming to be the victim of a violation by one of the High Contracting Parties of the rights set forth in this Convention, provided that the High Contracting Party against which the complaint has been lodged has declared that it recognises the competence of the Commission to receive such petitions. Those of the High Contracting Parties who have made such a declaration undertake not to hinder in any way the effective exercise of this right.
2.   Such declarations may be made for a specific period. ...

Article 26
The Commission may only deal with the matter after all domestic remedies have been exhausted, according to the generally recognised rules of international law, and within a period of six months from the date on which the final decision was taken.

Article 27
1.   The Commission shall not deal with any petition submitted under Article which
(*a*) is anonymous, or
(*b*) is substantially the same as a matter which has already been examined by the Commission or has already been submitted to another procedure of international investigation or settlement and if it contains no relevant new information.
2.   The Commission shall consider inadmissible any petition submitted under Article 25 which it considers incompatible with the provisions of the present Convention, manifestly ill-founded, or an abuse of the right of petition.
3.   The Commission shall reject any petition referred to it which it considers inadmissible under Article 26.

Article 28
In the event of the Commission accepting a petition referred to it:
(*a*) it shall, with a view to ascertaining the facts, undertake together with the representatives of the parties an examination of the petition and, if need be, an investigation, for the effective conduct of which the States concerned shall furnish all necessary facilities, after an exchange of views with the Commission;

(*b*) it shall place itself at the disposal of the parties concerned with a view to securing a friendly settlement of the matter on the basis of respect for Human Rights as defined in this Convention.

Article 30
If the Commission succeeds in effecting a friendly settlement in accordance with Article 28, it shall draw up a Report which shall be sent to the States concerned, to the Committee of Ministers and to the Secretary-General of the Council of Europe for publication. This Report shall be confined to a brief statement of the facts and of the solution reached.

Article 31
1.   If a solution is not reached, the Commission shall draw up a Report on the facts and state its opinion as to whether the facts found disclose a breach by the State concerned of its obligations under the Convention. The opinions of all the members of the Commission on this point may be stated in the Report.
2.   The Report shall be transmitted to the Committee of Ministers. It shall also be transmitted to the States concerned, who shall not be at liberty to publish it.
3.   In transmitting the Report to the Committee of Ministers the Commission may make such proposals as it thinks fit.

Article 32
1.   If the question is not referred to the Court in accordance with Article 48 of this Convention within a period of three months from the date of the transmission of the Report to the Committee of Minister, the Committee of Ministers shall decide by a majority of two-thirds of the members entitled to sit on the Committee whether there has been a violation of the Convention.
2.   In the affirmative case the Committee of Minister shall prescribe a period during which the High Contracting Party concerned must take the measures required by the decision of the Committee of Ministers.
3.   If the High Contracting Party concerned has not taken satisfactory measures within the prescribed period, the Committee of Ministers shall decide by the majority provided for in paragraph (1) above what effect shall be given to its original decision and shall publish the Report.
4.   The High Contracting Parties undertake to regard as binding on them any decision which the Committee of Ministers may take in application of the preceding paragraphs.

Article 44
Only the High Contracting Parties and Commission shall have the right to bring a case before the Court.

Article 45
The jurisdiction of the Court shall extend to all cases concerning the interpretation and application of the present Convention which the High Contracting Parties or the Commission shall refer to it in accordance with Article 48.

Article 46
1.   Any of the High Contracting Parties may at any time declare that it recognises as compulsory *ipso facto* and without special agreement the jurisdiction of the Court in all matters concerning the interpretation and application of the present Convention.
2.   The declarations referred to above may be made unconditionally or on condition of reciprocity on the part of several or certain other High Contracting Parties or for a specified period.

Article 47

The Court may only deal with a case after the Commission has acknowledged the failure of efforts for a friendly settlement and within the period of three months provided for in Article 32.

Article 48

The following may bring a case before the Court, provided that the High Contracting Party concerned, if there is only one, or the High Contracting Parties concerned, if there is more than one, are subject to the compulsory jurisdiction of the Court or, failing that, with the consent of the High Contracting Party concerned, if there is only one, or of the High Contracting Parties concerned if there is more than one:

(*a*) the Commission

(*b*) a High Contracting Party whose national is alleged to be a victim;

(*c*) a High Contracting Party which referred the case to the Commission;

(*d*) a High Contracting Party against which the complaint has been lodged."

NOTES

1. It might be concluded from the above provisions that the function of the Commission is to act as a "filter," ensuring that only appropriate cases reach the court. In a sense this is true, and indeed "the figures show ... that the Commission has functioned as a fine-meshed filter" (Mikaelsen, *European Protection of Human Rights*, p.15). Over 95 per cent. of cases registered with the Commission are held to be inadmissible by that body. But the Commission is also charged with a primary function under Article 28 of seeking a "friendly settlement" between the parties. Such settlements are, in practice, rare, and indeed the first was not achieved until 1962 (*Boeckmans* v. *Belgium*, 1727/62; 8 Yearbook 410).

2. Procedure is by way of a simple application stating details of the applicant, the country against which the application is made, the facts, the alleged violations of the Convention, the objects of the claim, and a statement of the remedies pursued before the appropriate domestic judicial and administrative bodies.

3. Although Article 24 of the Convention provides for inter-state enforcement of Convention obligations, the "cornerstone" of the Convention's enforcement system is the right of individual application under Article 25. The right of individual application is not limited to natural persons. Under Article 25 any person, non-governmental organisation, or group of individuals may complain to the Commission alleging a violation of their rights under the Convention. Applicants have thus included companies and other legal persons (see, for examples, *Times Newspapers Ltd.* v. *U.K.*, 18 Yearbook 202; 3 E.H.R.R. 615; *Lithgow Ltd.* v. *U.K.*, 7 E.H.R.R. 56), organisations such as trade unions (*Belgian National Police Union* v. *Belgium*, 15 Yearbook 288; *Swedish Engine Drivers Union* v. *Sweden*, 1 E.H.R.R. 617), churches (*Church of Scientology* v. *Sweden*, 16 D. & R. 68), political parties (*Liberal Party* v. *U.K.*, 21 D. & R. 211; *Communist Party* v. *F.R.G.*, 1 Yearbook 222) and *ad hoc* pressure groups (*Christians* v. *Racism and Fascism* v. *U.K.*, 15 D. & R. 138).

4. Although Article 25 states that only those claiming to be a "victim" of violation of their rights by a high contracting party can bring an action before the Commission, this does not mean that the Convention's remedies are limited to those who have actually suffered a violation of their rights.

The European Court of Human Rights has developed the notion of the "victim" in such a way as to include those who are at risk of a violation by a member state: *Klass and Others* v. *F.R.G.*, Series A, No. 28; 2 E.H.R.R. 214; *Dudgeon* v. *U.K.*, Series A, No. 45; 4 E.H.R.R. 149; *Norris* v. *Ireland*, Series A, No. 142.

In principle, however, it is not open to an individual to bring a complaint on behalf of the public at large (the so-called *"actio popularis"*) or to bring a complaint in the abstract about the non-compliance of a state's laws or practices with the standards set down in the Convention (see, *inter alia*, the authorities cited above).

5.   Substantial procedural hurdles are contained in Article 26. In particular the requirement of exhaustion of local remedies should be noted. In many cases, this would require an applicant to exhaust all local avenues of appeal, though an exception is recognised where the existing state of the local law offers no reasonable prospect of success. (See, further, Jacobs, *The European Convention on Human Rights*, pp.235 *et seq.*) The application may be required to resort to administrative remedies, such as, for example, remedies afforded to a prisoner under the Prison Rules (*Courcy* v. *U.K.*, 2749/66; 10 Yearbook 388).

6.   It has been stated (Jacobs, *op. cit.*, p.24) that "incompatibility" under Article 27(2) arises if a complaint is "altogether outside the scope of the Convention." On the other hand, a complaint is "manifestly-ill founded" within the same article if "while it falls *prima facie* within the scope of the Convention, a preliminary examination of the merits shows that there is no need for any further such examination. This may be because the applicant has made wholly unsubstantiated allegations, ... Or it may be because the allegations which he makes, even if substantiated, would not suffice to establish a violation" (*ibid.*).

7.   Only where the Commission has declared an application admissible and has acknowledged the failure of efforts for a friendly settlement may the court deal with a case. The high contracting parties undertake to abide by the decisions of the court in any case to which they are parties (Article 53) and the judgment of the court is final (Article 52). The court may, where it finds that there has been a violation of the Convention and where local remedies are inadequate, "afford just satisfaction to the injured party" (Article 50). However, the court has no power to enforce its judgments directly.

8.   For detailed discussions of the Convention and the procedures for enforcing the rights and freedoms secured by it, see Mikaelsen, *op. cit.*; Jacobs, *op. cit.*; Nedjati; *Human Rights under the European Convention*; Beddard, *Human Rights and Europe.*

D.   REFERENCE TO THE COURT OF JUSTICE OF THE EUROPEAN COMMUNITIES

The possibility of a reference to the Court of Justice of the European Communities may arise where a ruling is required on the interpretation of the EEC Treaty (the Treaty of Rome), the interpretation of the treaty establishing the European Atomic Energy Community, or interpretation of acts of the institutions of the Communities. By Article 177 of the EEC Treaty, and Article 150 of the EURATOM Treaty such questions of interpretation when arising before a court of a member state, may be referred to the Court of Justice. Where, however, that local court is one from which there is no appeal (as, for example, in the case of the High Court sitting on appeal in summary or solemn proceedings, or hearing an application to the *nobile officium*) the question must be referred to the Court of Justice for a ruling on interpretation.

The procedures are governed by Act of Adjournal (Consolidation) 1988. For a discussion of these procedures see Renton and Brown, Chap. 16.

INDEX

Absolute discharge. *See* Sentence
Advocation. *See* Bill of advocation
Appeal. *See* Appeal in solemn proceedings;
  Bill of advocation; Bill of suspension;
  Competency; Nobile officium; Note of
  appeal against sentence; Preliminary
  diet; Relevancy
Appeal in solemn proceedings,
  abandonment of, 509–512
  fresh evidence in, 513–517
  ground of, 483–488
    introduction of previous conviction as,
      495–498
    miscarriage of justice, 483–507
    misdirection of jury as, 498–501
    oppression by trial judge as, 498–501
    unreasonable, incompetent or
      ambiguous verdict, 501–506
  High Court as court of appeal in, 482–
    483
  powers of court in relation to, 512–517
  procedure for,
    grounds of appeal, 507, 508
Arrest, 114–138, 148–168
  access to legal advice following, 149–
    154
  admissibility of statements made under,
    169–226
  appearance before court, following,
    148–149
  citizen's power of, 118
  common law powers of, 116–119
  definition of, 127–138
  detention and, distinguished, 114, 115
  entry to effect,
    common law powers, 125, 126
    statutory powers, 126, 127
  fingerprinting of persons following,
    155–157
  intimation of fact of, 149–154
  magistrates' powers of, 115
  matrimonial interdict, 164–168
  police powers of, 114–127
  questioning of persons following, 169–
    226
  search following, 154, 155
  search prior to, 154, 155, 238–243
  statement of grounds for, 137–138
  with warrant, 114–116
  without warrant, 114–125
    common law offences, 116–119
    common law powers of, 116–119
    statutory offences, 119–125
    statutory powers,
      Civic Government (Scotland) Act
        1982, under, 119

Arrest—*cont.*
  without warrant—*cont.*
    statutory powers—*cont.*
      exercise outwith Scotland, 123–125
      types of, 119
    suspicion, on, 118, 120–122

Bail, 275–287
  breach of conditions of, 335–338
  commission of offence while on, 335–
    338
  discretion of court and, 275–279
  guidelines for granting, 283–285
  money deposit as precondition of, 275
  murder cases in, 279–280
  pending appeal, 280–281
  prosecutor's attitude to, 275–279
  rape cases, in, 277–278
  refusal of,
    appeal against, 285–287
    review of, 285–287
  standard conditions of, 278–279
  treason cases, in, 279
  "Wheatley guidelines" for, 283–285
Bill of advocation, 562–569
  availability of,
    prior to final determination, 565–566
    to accused, 563
    to prosecutor, 562–563
  High Court proceedings in, 562–563
  merits, review of, 565–569
  proceedings, review of, 565–569
  relevancy, review of, 563–565
Bill of suspension, 550–560
  appropriate, where, 557–560
    "crisp issue", 557–560
    review of merits, 555, 556
  availability of,
    prior to final determination, 552–554
    to prosecutor, 551
  competent, where, 551–557
  delay in bringing, 559
  disposal of, 559, 560
  facts, remit for ascertaiment of, 556
  grounds of, 556, 560–562
  High Court proceedings, 551
  limitations on appeal, 562
  merits, review of, by, 555–556
  miscarriage of justice, 556
  sheriff court solemn proceedings, 551
  warrant, review of, by, 551
Burden of proof, 8–17
  accused, on, 12–17
  Crown, on, 10, 11
  evidential, 11, 13, 14, 16
  legal, 11, 14

631